DISPUTE RESOLUTION AND LAWYERS

Third Edition

By

Leonard L. Riskin

C.A. Leedy Professor of Law and and Isidor Loeb Professor of Law
Director, Center for the Study of Dispute Resolution
University of Missouri–Columbia School of Law

James E. Westbrook

Earl F. Nelson and James S. Rollins Professor of Law, Emeritus
University of Missouri-Columbia School of Law

Chris Guthrie

Associate Dean for Academic Affairs and Professor of Law
Vanderbilt University Law School

Timothy J. Heinsz (deceased)

Earl F. Nelson Professor of Law
Dean, University of Missouri–Columbia School of Law (1988–2001)
Director, Center for the Study of Dispute Resolution (2003–2004)
University of Missouri–Columbia School of Law

Richard C. Reuben

Associate Professor of Law
University of Missouri–Columbia School of Law

Jennifer K. Robbennolt

Professor of Law and Psychology
University of Illinois College of Law

AMERICAN CASEBOOK SERIES®

THOMSON
™
WEST

Mat # 17861433

COPYRIGHT © 1987 WEST PUBLISHING

© West, a Thomson business, 1997

© 2005 Thomson/West

  610 Opperman Drive

  P.O. Box 64526

  St. Paul, MN 55164–0526

  1–800–328–9352

Printed in the United States of America

ISBN 0–314–25307–6

TEXT IS PRINTED ON 10% POST CONSUMER RECYCLED PAPER

Dedication

To Timothy J. Heinsz (1947–2004)

*Our friend, dean, and colleague, who embodied—in his life and work—
the highest aspirations of the conflict resolution field.*

*

Special Acknowledgments

To Casey, Andrew, Matilda & Barney with love. L.L.R.

To my wonderful grandchildren: Daniel, Jimmy, Collin and Laura. JEW

To my parents, who taught me most of what I know about dispute resolution. C.P.G.

To Robin, with gratitude, and to Patrick and Daniel, with hope for the future. R.C.R.

To Grant, Dale, and Jake, with love. J.K.R.

*

PREFACE

This book is premised upon the idea that the essential task of lawyering is to help clients and society solve problems well. To do this, the lawyer must be able not only to grasp and promote legal rights and positions; he or she also must be able to identify and articulate underlying interests and the motives or goals that impel people to act. In addition, the lawyer must know the nature and potential advantages and disadvantages of various methods of managing or resolving disputes.

Litigation, of course, is one way of resolving disputes, and many courses in law school are devoted to this approach. But there are other methods, commonly called ADR for "Alternative Dispute Resolution."

Working with the various methods of dispute resolution effectively takes knowledge and skill, and in this book we seek to provide law students, lawyers, and other readers an understanding of the theory, law, and practice of what we think of as appropriate dispute resolution. Such a grounding has become essential to law practice in the nearly two decades since the publication of the first edition of *Dispute Resolution and Lawyers* in 1987. Today, alternatives to traditional litigation, such as mediation and arbitration, affect the practices of the bulk of lawyers in most parts of the United States and have virtually transformed law practice in some areas (both substantive and geographic). In addition, many lawyers have found great satisfaction working as dispute resolution neutrals.

Yet ADR presents unique challenges for lawyers. The legal tradition historically has revolved around formal processes and adversarial practices and perspectives. But some alternative methods of dispute resolution tend to be informal and to require such interpersonal skills as understanding, consensus-building, and accommodation, which necessitate a very different mindset. This book seeks to help law students and lawyers meet these challenges by introducing them to the nature of conflict and disputes, the fundamental principles of dispute resolution, the wide array of dispute resolution options, the law that affects these processes, and the bases upon which one may discern which process is most appropriate for a particular dispute. In so doing, it recognizes that conflict can present opportunities for significant change and growth, and that the best lawyering will strive to achieve such benefits.

This Third Edition of the book represents its most significant revision, with important contributions by three new co-authors—Professors Chris Guthrie of the Vanderbilt University School of Law, Richard C. Reuben of the University of Missouri-Columbia School of Law, and

Jennifer K. Robbennolt of the University of Illinois College of Law; tragically, a fourth new co-author, former Dean Timothy J. Heinsz of the University of Missouri-Columbia School of Law, passed away during the drafting of the Third Edition and this edition of the book is dedicated to his memory. All of us have been colleagues at the University of Missouri-Columbia School of Law, which underscores the importance of the school's contribution to the field.

In the Third Edition, we have attempted to build upon the best qualities of prior editions. The Third Edition retains the same basic structure as the previous editions, as well as their balanced use of theory and practice, accessibility, and focus on dispute resolution from a variety of perspectives: those of the lawyer, the client, and society at large. Teachers and others who have worked with previous editions will recognize many familiar landmarks.

However, the field has evolved significantly since the Second Edition, and this new edition reflects that evolution, including major cases, theory, and practice developments through the Spring of 2005. Once something of a novelty, ADR has become institutionalized in most legal settings, and the Third Edition tracks that process. In addition, we recognize that deeper understanding of a conflict — e.g. its behavioral, cognitive, and emotional dimensions — better enables the lawyer to steer it toward an appropriate — and, hopefully, constructive — resolution. For that reason, we have incorporated more conflict theory into the book. This begins in Chapter I, Overview of Dispute Resolution and Conflict Management, and continues throughout. However, we have still maintained the central focus on the role and perspectives of lawyers. Thus, we have continued to emphasize client interviewing and counseling — in Chapter II and throughout the book. In Chapters III, IV, and V, we continue the book's tradition of addressing the nature, varieties, and advantages and disadvantages of the primary alternative dispute resolution processes — negotiation, mediation, and arbitration.

We have also emphasized the importance of innovation, adaptation, and creativity in the field, re-engineering Chapter VI to reflect these qualities in dispute resolution by and through courts and administrative agencies, as well as in the private sector. We have also acknowledged the important role that empirical research using social science methods has played in shaping our understanding of dispute resolution processes, as well as in the design and evaluation of dispute resolution methods and programs. The Negotiation chapter, Chapter III, particularly reflects these cutting edge insights, as does the wholly revamped Chapter VII, which addresses the choice, design, and evaluation of dispute resolution methods and programs.

Finally, we have added a new chapter, Chapter VIII, looking ahead, to connect the dispute resolution movement with other similar developments in the law, and to provide guidance on how readers may further their interest in dispute resolution. Chapter VIII also emphasizes the importance of a dispute resolution professional's emotional intelligence, and the use of mindfulness meditation as a means of cultivating that quality.

In incorporating these and other substantive changes, we have also strived to make the volume more user-friendly, both for students and other readers and for teachers. The main readings are shorter, and the Notes and Questions that follow highlight key points with questions and exercises that can be discussed in or out of class, and that can provide a basis for reflection or for research papers or other course assignments. We have also taken advantage of technology by launching a web site for the casebook on The West Education Network (TWEN). It includes many important documents in an Online Appendix that complements the book's main appendix, as well as role play instructions and new cases, policies, and other developments. To access the *Dispute Resolution and Lawyers, 3rd Ed.*, web site, follow these instructions:

1. Go to   and click the TWEN tab.

2. Enter either your West OnePass Username and Password or your Westlaw password in the appropriate field(s) and click GO.

3. Once you are signed on to TWEN click Drop/Add a Course.

4. Select the check box next to *Dispute Resolution and Lawyers, 3rd Ed.*

5. Click Submit at the bottom of the page to return to the TWEN home page. The site you added is now displayed on your TWEN home page.

6. Click *Dispute Resolution and Lawyers 3rd ed.* to view information related to the book.

We are again publishing both hardcover and abridged paperback editions of the Third Edition, each of which has a variety of potential uses. The **hardcover edition** is suitable for a dispute resolution survey course for three or four credits as well as for courses that include Interviewing, Counseling, Negotiation, and Mediation. The **abridged edition** is especially appropriate for integrating dispute resolution instruction into standard courses. The first abridged edition was the foundation for the program to integrate dispute resolution into all first-year courses at the University of Missouri-Columbia.[1] In addition, it is suitable for

---

1. The project to integrate dispute resolution into all standard first-year courses was developed under a grant from the National Institute for Dispute Resolution and a series of grants from the U.S. Department of Education's Fund for the Improvement of Post-Secondary Education (FIPSE) to the Center for the Study of Dispute Resolution at the University of Missouri-Columbia School of Law. In addition to the first two editions of this book, the project produced the Dispute Resolution and Lawyers Videotape Series (West 1991). An

early history and description of the project appears in Leonard L. Riskin and James E. Westbrook, *Integrating Dispute Resolution into Standard First-Year Courses: The Missouri Plan*, 39 J. LEGAL EDUC. 509 (1989).

In 1995, the Center received another grant from FIPSE to work with six other law schools that wished to develop adaptions of this program. Each of these schools—DePaul, Hamline, Inter-American, Ohio State, Tulane, and the University two- or three-credit courses that include Interviewing, Counseling, Negotiation, and Mediation.

The **Instructor's Manual** contains scores of exercises and problems prepared by professors at more than a dozen law schools, as well as suggestions for teaching dispute resolution as a separate course and for integrating such material into standard first-year law school courses. The Instructor's Manual is available in hard copy and through the book's web site.

In addition, the book contains general information for several role play exercises that employ facts on which available demonstration videotapes are based.

We have inserted three asterisks (***) to indicate omissions in reprinted material. However, we have omitted footnotes, parenthetical references to authorities, and some citations to cases and statutes without so indicating. In the few instances where we retained footnotes, we kept their original numbering. Footnotes prepared by the authors of this book are marked by asterisks.

To avoid awkward language, we generally use either masculine or feminine pronouns to include their opposites.

We are grateful to many people who helped produce this new edition. The deans, faculty, and library staff at the University of Missouri-Columbia have been endlessly supportive. John Lande and Nancy Welsh provided extraordinary helpful and detailed comments on an earlier draft of Chapter IV. Colleagues who used a manuscript for this book to teach a new first-year, second semester course called *Lawyering: Problem-Solving and Dispute Resolution* — Bob Bailey, Phil Harter, John Lande, and Huyen Pham — gave many constructive suggestions, which grew out of that experience. So did a number of the students in that course. Several current or former MU law students provided outstanding research assistance: Kathy Birkhofer, Daniel Cayou, Jonathan Eccer, Robert Fischer, Jessica Gunder, Jay Hastings, Cecily Helms, Shonda Ireland, Tammy Steinle, and Michelle St. Germain. We also thank the many students and professors, here and elsewhere, who informally have given us valuable suggestions for improving the book. Karen Neylon helped with graphics,

---

of Washington—began with unique circumstances and goals; as we anticipated, each produced a one-of-a-kind adaptation, some of which focus on integrating dispute resolution into the advanced, rather than the first-year curriculum. Some of the exercises prepared at these schools appear in the Instructor's Manual for this book. For an overview and analysis of the Missouri program to integrate dispute resolution into first-year courses as well as programs at the other six participating law schools, see *Symposium, Dispute Resolution in the Law School Curriculum: Opportunities and Challenges,* 50 FLA. L. REV. 583 (1998).

In 2004, for a variety of complex reasons, the University of Missouri School of Law shifted emphasis from the integrated approach to a a required, first-year second semester course called *Lawyering: Problem-Solving and Dispute Resolution*. We used the manuscript for this book to teach the course in 2005 and expect to experiment with using the abridged edition in 2006.

and Sandra Kubal and Laura Coleman provided crucial administrative support. We also appreciate the skillful handling of the book by our editors at West, Staci Herr and Jeff Becker, and Eagan Analytical Team 8.

Finally, Chris, Jen, Jim, and Len give special thanks to Richard, who assumed the essential role of executive editor, which he discharged with a wonderful blend of editorial skill, enthusiastic optimism, humor, and dogged persistence.

L.L.R.

J.E.W.

C.P.G.

R.C.R.

J.K.R.

August 2005

*

ACKNOWLEDGEMENTS

We gratefully acknowledge the permission extended to reprint the works listed below.

CH. I

BERNARD MAYER, THE DYNAMICS OF CONFLICT RESOLUTION: A PRACTITION-ER'S GUIDE. 2-4. Copyright © 2000 Jossey-Bass, Inc. Reprinted with permission of John Wiley & Sons, Inc.

CHRISTOPHER MOORE, THE MEDIATION PROCESS: PRACTICAL STRATEGIES FOR RESOLVING CONFLICT 60, 2d ed., 1996. Copyright © 1996, Jossey-Bass, Inc. Reprinted with permission of John Wiley & Sons, Inc.

Richard Miller & Austin Sarat, *Grievances, Claims and Disputes: Assessing the Adversary Culture*, 15 LAW & SOC'Y REV. 524, 544 (1980-81).

Owen Fiss, *Against Settlement*. Reprinted by permission of The Yale Law Journal Company and Fred B. Rothman & Company from THE YALE LAW JOURNAL, Vol. 93, pp. 1073, 1075, 1076-78, 1082-90 (1984).

Carrie Menkel-Meadow, *Whose Dispute is it Anyway? A Philosophical and Democratic Defense of Settlement (In Some Cases)*, 83 GEO. L.J. 2663, 2663-71, 2692 (1995). Reprinted with the permission of the publisher, Georgetown Law Journal. Copyright © 1995 Georgetown University.

Jethro K. Lieberman & James F. Henry, *Lessons from the Alternative Dispute Resolution Movement*, 53 U. CHI. L. REV. 424, 432, 433–35 (1986).

Warren E. Burger, ISN'T THERE A BETTER WAY? ANNUAL REPORT ON THE STATE OF THE JUDICIARY (January 24, 1982).

Frank E.A. Sander, *Varieties of Dispute Processing*, Address Delivered at the National Conference on the Causes of Popular Dissatisfaction with the Administration of Justice, 70 F.R.D. 111, 112, 130–133 (1976).

Judith Resnik, *Many Doors? Closing Doors? Alternative Dispute Resolution and Adjudication*, 10 OHIO ST. J. ON DISP. RESOL. 211, 212, 216–18, 241–58, 261–65 (1995).

Albert Alschuler, *Mediation with a Mugger: The Shortage of Adjudicative Services and the Need for a Two-Tier Trial System in Civil Cases*, 99 HARV. L. REV. 1808, 1818 (1986).

Thomas J. Stipanowich, *Contract and Conflict Management*, 2001 WIS. L. REV. 831, 831-838.

Richard C. Reuben, *Constitutional Gravity: A Unitary Theory of Alternative Dispute Resolution and Public Civil Justice*, 47 UCLA L. Rev. 949, 952-960 (2000).

BERNARD MAYER, THE DYNAMICS OF CONFLICT RESOLUTION: A PRACTITIONER'S GUIDE. 98-102, 106-08. Copyright © 2000 Jossey-Bass, Inc. Reprinted with permission of John Wiley & Sons, Inc.

ROBERT F. COCHRAN , JR., JOHN M.A. DiPIPPA, & MARTHA M. PETERS, THE COUNSELOR-AT-LAW: A COLLABORATIVE APPROACH TO CLIENT INTERVIEWING AND COUNSELING 198-202 (1999). Copyright © 1999 Matthew Bender & Company, Inc., a member of the LexisNexis Group. Reprinted with permission. All rights reserved.

WILLIAM L. URY, JEANNE M. BRETT, & STEPHEN B. GOLDBERG, GETTING DISPUTES RESOLVED: DESIGNING SYSTEMS TO CUT THE COSTS OF CONFLICT. Copyright © 2005 Jossey-Bass, Inc. Reprinted with permission of John Wiley & Sons, Inc.

Lon L. Fuller & John D. Randall, *Professional Responsibility: Report of the Joint Conference*, 44 A.B.A. J. 1159, 1160–61 (1958). Reprinted with permission of the ABA Journal.

MONROE FREEDMAN, LAWYERS' ETHICS IN AN ADVERSARY SYSTEM (1975). Professor Freedman has elaborated on his views in several subsequent articles, including *Personal Responsibility in a Professional System*, 27 CATH. U. L. REV. 191 (1978).

Leonard L. Riskin, *Mediation and Lawyers*, 43 OHIO ST. L.J. 29, 43–48, 57–59 (1982).

Derek Bok, *A Flawed System of Law Practice and Law Teaching*, 33 J. LEGAL EDUC. 570, 580, 582, 583 (1983).

Marguerite Millhauser, *The Unspoken Resistance to Alternative Dispute Resolution*, 3 NEGOTIATION J. 29, 31–32 (1987).

MARK TWAIN, *The War Prayer, in* THE COMPLETE SHORT STORIES AND FAMOUS ESSAYS OF MARK TWAIN 861–863 (Collier 1928) 202–205 (1981).

Gary J. Friedman, *Comment on the War Prayer*, in BECOMING A LAWYER: A HUMANISTIC PERSPECTIVE ON LEGAL EDUCATION AND PROFESSIONALISM 205-206 (Elizabeth Dvorkin, Jack Himmelstein & Howard Lesnick), Copyright © 1981 West Publishing Co. With permission of the West Group. Gary J. Friedman presently is the Director of the Center for Mediation in Law and is practicing as part of Mediation Law offices in Mill Valley, California.

Howard Lesnick, *Comment on the War Prayer*, in BECOMING A LAWYER: A HUMANISTIC PERSPECTIVE ON LEGAL EDUCATION AND PROFESSIONALISM 205-206 (Elizabeth Dvorkin, Jack Himmelstein, and Howard Lesnick 1981). Copyright © 1981 West Publishing Co. With permission of the West Group.

Carrie Menkel-Meadow, *Ethics in ADR: The Many "Cs" of Professional Responsibility and Dispute Resolution*, 28 FORDHAM URB. L.J. 979 (2001).

Leonard L. Riskin, *Mediation and Lawyers*, 43 OHIO ST. L.J. 29, 57–59 (1982).

Ch. II

Robert D. Dinerstein, *Client-Centered Counseling: Reappraisal & Refinement*, 32 ARIZ. L. REV. 501, 503-4, 506-9 (1991).

ROBERT F. COCHRAN , JR., JOHN M.A. DIPIPPA, & MARTHA M. PETERS, THE COUNSELOR-AT-LAW: A COLLABORATIVE APPROACH TO CLIENT INTERVIEWING AND COUNSELING 6-7 (1999). Copyright © 1999 Matthew Bender & Company, Inc., a member of the LexisNexis Group. Reprinted with permission. All rights reserved.

MODEL RULES OF PROFESSIONAL CONDUCT RULES 1.2, 1.4, 2.1 (2004). Copyright © 2004 American Bar Association. Reprinted by permission.

HERBERT M. KRITZER, THE JUSTICE BROKER: LAWYERS AND ORDINARY LITIGATION 60-65 (1990).

Gary Neustadter, *When Lawyer and Client Meet: Observations of Interviewing and Counseling Behavior in the Consumer Bankruptcy Law Office*, 35 BUFF. L. REV. 177, 177-78, 229 (1986).

Rodney J. Uphoff & Peter B. Wood, *The Allocation of Decisionmaking Between Counsel and Criminal Defendant: An Empirical Study of Attorney-Client Decisionmaking*, 47 U. KAN. L. REV. 1, 6, 30-35, 59-60 (1998).

Seven Zeidman, *To Plead or Not to Plead: Effective Assistance and Client-Centered Counseling*, 39 B.C. L. REV. 841, 847-48 (1998).

ROBERT H. MNOOKIN, SCOTT PEPPET & ANDREW S. TULUMELLO, BEYOND WINNING: NEGOTIATING TO CREATE VALUE IN DEALS AND DISPUTES 14-15, 64-65, 70-71, 83-86, 240-242 (The Belknap Press of Harvard University Press, 2000). Copyright © 2000 by the President and Fellows of Harvard College. Reprinted by permission of the publisher.

Chris Guthrie, *The Lawyer's Philosophical Map and the Disputant's Perceptual Map: Impediments to Facilitative Mediation and Lawyering*, 6 HARV. NEGOT. L. REV. 145, 156-57, 158-60 (2000).

Jeffrey Z. Rubin & Frank E.A. Sander, *When Should We Use Agents? Direct vs. Representative Negotiation*, 4 NEGOTIATION J. 395, 396, 397-98, 399-400 (1988).

LINDA LOPEZ, INTERVIEWING THE DOMESTIC VIOLENCE VICTIM, 345-48 (Practicing Law Institute, Practice Skills Course Handbook Series, New York 2000).

Roy M. Sobelson, *Interviewing Clients Ethically*, 37 PRAC. LAW. 13, 18-21 (1991). Copyright © 1991 The American Law Institute. Reprinted with the permission of THE PRACTICAL LAWYER. Subscription rates $49/year; $10.75/single issue. This article appeared in the January 1991 issue of THE PRACTICAL LAWYER.

ALEX F. OSBORN, APPLIED IMAGINATION: PRINCIPLES AND PROCEDURES OF CREATIVE PROBLEM-SOLVING (3rd ed. 1963). Reprinted by permission of Pearson Education, Inc.

Jennifer Gerarda Brown, *Creativity and Problem-Solving*, 87 MARQ. L. REV. 697, 699-702, 703-4, 705, 706 (2004).

ROBERT PIRSIG, ZEN AND THE ART OF MOTORCYCLE MAINTENANCE 278-79, 285-86 (Bantam Books 1975).

ATUL GAWANDE, COMPLICATIONS: A SURGEON'S NOTES ON AN IMPERFECT SCIENCE. 210-11, 211-12, 219-22. Copyright © 2002 by Atul Gawande. Reprinted by permission of Henry Holt and Company, LLC.

DAVID A. BINDER, PAUL BERGMAN & SUSAN C. PRICE, LAWYERS AS COUN-SELORS 348-50(2d Ed. 1991). With permission of the West Group.

Robert F. Cochran, *Introduction: Three Approaches to Morals Issues in Law Office Counseling*, 30 PEPP. L. REV. 591, 592, 593, 594-95, 595-97, 597-98, 598-99, 600 (2003). Reprinted from Pepperdine Law Review Volume 30, Number 4, 2003. Copyright © 2003 Pepperdine University School of Law.

Linda F. Smith, *Medical Paradigm for Counseling: Giving Clients Bad News*, 4 CLINICAL L. REV. 391, 391-92, 417-19, 421-22, 423-24 (1998).

Sana Loue, *A Guide to Better Client Interviews*, 89-07 IMMIGR. BRIEFINGS 1 (1989). With permission of Thomson West.

Robert Dinerstein, Stephen Ellman, Isabelle Gunning & Ann Shalleck, *Connection Capacity and Morality in Lawyer–Client Relationships*, 10 CLINICAL L. REV. 755, 758-62 (2004).

DAVID MAISTER, CHARLES GREEN & ROBERT GALFORD, THE TRUSTED ADVI-SOR 97-102 (2000). Reprinted with permission of Charles Green, Trusted Advisor Associates (cgreen@trustedadvisor.com) and The Free Press, a Division of Simon & Schuster Adult Publishing Group, from THE TRUSTED ADVISOR by David H. Maister, Charles H. Green, Robert M. Galford. Copyright © 2000 by David H. Maister, Charles H. Green, Robert M. Galford. All rights reserved.

Steven Keeva, Heart-Healthy Conversations, ABA Journal 73-74 (September 2003). Copyright © 2003 the American Bar Association and Steven Keeva. Reprinted by permission.

Leonard L. Riskin, *The Contemplative Lawyer: On The Potential Benefits of Mindfulness Meditation to Law Students, Lawyers and their Clients*, 7 HARV. NEGOT. L. REV. 1, 49-53 (2002).

Marshall J. Breger, *Should an Attorney be Required to Advise a Client of ADR Options?*, 13 GEO. J. LEGAL ETHICS 427, 430-31, 433-36, 439-41 (2000). Reprinted with permission of the publisher, Georgetown Journal of Legal Ethics. Copyright © 2000 Georgetown Journal of Legal Ethics and Marshall J. Breger.

CH. III

Stone, Bruce M. Patton & Sheila Heen. Used by permission of Viking Penguin, a division of Penguin Group (USA) Inc.

ROBERT H. MNOOKIN, SCOTT PEPPET & ANDREW S. TULUMELLO, BEYOND WINNING: NEGOTIATING TO CREATIVE VALUE IN DEALS AND DISPUTES (The Belknap Press of Harvard University Press) 14-15, 64-65, 70-71, 83-86, 240-242. Copyright © 2000 the President and Fellows of Harvard College. Reprinted by permission of the publisher.

Chris Guthrie & David Sally, *The Impact of the Impact Bias on Negotiation*, 87 MARQ.L. REV. 817, 817-22 (2004).

Carrie Menkel-Meadow, *Aha? Is Creativity Possible in Legal Problem Solving and Teachable in Legal Education?* 6 HARV. NEGOT. L. REV. 97, 105-6, 109-11 (2001).

Chris Guthrie, *Panacea or Pandora's Box? The Costs of Options in Negotiation*, 88 IOWA L. REV. 601, 607-08 (2003). Reprinted with permission.

James J. White, *The Pros and Cons of "Getting To Yes"*, 34 J. LEGAL EDUC. 115-16 (1984).

Roger Fisher, *Comment*, 34 J. LEGAL EDUC. 120, 121-23 (1984). Roger Fisher (with William Ury) is author of GETTING TO YES: NEGOTIATING AGREEMENT WITHOUT GIVING IN, (Houghton Mifflin, 1981).

James E. Westbrook, *How to Negotiate With a Jerk Without Being One*, 1992 J. DISP. RESOL. 443, 444–46. Permission granted by the Curators of the University of Missouri and the Journal of Dispute Resolution.

JONATHAN M. HYMAN, MILTON HEUMANN, KENNETH J. DAUTRICH & HAROLD L. RUBENSTEIN, CIVIL SETTLEMENT: STYLES OF NEGOTIATION, New Jersey Administrative Office of the Courts 165-68 (1995).

Marc Galanter & Mia Cahill, *"Most Cases Settle": Judicial Promotion and Regulation of Settlements*, 46 STAN. L. REV. 1339, 1339-40, 1341-42 (1999).

Jeffrey J. Rachlinski, *Gains, Losses, and the Psychology of Litigation*, 70 S. CAL. L. REV. 113-190 (1996). Reprint with the permission of the Southern California Law Review.

Russell Korobkin & Chris Guthrie, *Psychological Barriers to Litigation Settlement: An Experimental Approach*, originally published in 93 MICH. L. REV. 107, 108-9, 144-47 (1994). Reprinted from MICH. L. REV., May 1992, Vol. 90, No. 6. Copyright © 1992 the Michigan Law Review Association.

Jennifer K. Robbennolt, *Apology—Help or Hindrance? An Empirical Analysis of Apologies' Influence on Settlement Decision Making*, DISP. RESOL. MAG., Spring 2004. Copyright © 2004 by ABA. Reprinted by Permission.

David P. Hoffer, *Decision Analysis as a Mediator's Tool*, 1 HARV. NEGOT. L. REV. 113, 134-37 (1996).

William F. Coyne, Jr., *The Case for Settlement Counsel*, 14 OHIO ST. J. ON DISP. RESOL. 367, 369-70 (1999). Reprinted with the permission of William F. Coyne, Jr. & the Ohio State Journal on Dispute Resolution. Originally published at 14 OHIO ST. J. ON DISP. RESOL. 367 (1999).

Russell Korobkin, Michael Moffitt & Nancy Welsh, *The Law of Bargaining*, 87 MARQ. L. REV. 839, 839-44 (2004).

Lynne H. Rambo, *Impeaching Lying Parties with Their Statements During Negotiation: De-Mysticizing the Public Policy Rationale Behind Evidence Rule 408 and The Mediation-Privilege Statutes*, 75 WASH. L. REV. 1037, 1044-49, 1051-54, 1056-57, 1066-73, 1075-77 (2000).

MODEL RULES OF PROF'L CONDUCT R. 4.1 (2004). Copyright © 2004 American Bar Association. Reprinted by permission.

James J. White, *Machiavelli and the Bar: Ethical Limitations on Lying in Negotiation*, 1980 AM. B. FOUND. RES. J. 926, 927-29, 931-35.

Gerald Wetlaufer, *The Ethics of Lying in Negotiations*, 75 IOWA L. REV. 1219, 1223 (1990). Reprinted with permission.

Jonathan R. Cohen, *When People Are the Means: Negotiating with Respect*, 14 GEO. J. LEGAL ETHICS 739, 741-43, 749-51 (2001). Reprinted with permission of the publisher, Georgetown Journal of Legal Ethics. Copyright © 2001 Georgetown Journal of Legal Ethics & Jonathan R. Cohen.

Jayne Seminare Docherty, *Culture and Negotiation: Symmetrical Anthropology for Negotiators*, 87 MARQ. L. REV. 711, 712-13, 713-14, 714-17 (2004).

Iyla Davies & Gay Clarke, *The Art of War Between Friends: Successfully Negotiating With the Chinese*, L. & Soc'y J. (Australia), Mar. 1994, p. 38, at 38-40, 42.

Leonard L. Riskin, *Obey the Rule: Just Say "No, No, No"* CHICAGO TRIBUNE, June 25, 1992, at Sec. 1, p. 19.

LINDA C. BABCOCK & SARA LASCHEVER, WOMEN DON'T ASK: NEGOTIATION AND THE GENDER DIVIDE 1-3, 9-10, 165-66, 167-69, 170, 171-72. (2003). Princeton University Press. Reprinted by permission of Princeton University Press.

Andrea Schneider, *Effective Responses to Offensive Comments*, 10 NEGOTIATION J. 107, 111-13 (1994).

Ian Ayres, *Fair Driving: Gender and Race Discrimination in Retail Car Negotiations*, 104 HARV. L. REV. 817-19, 27-33 (1991).

Ch. IV

Leonard L. Riskin, *Understanding Mediators' Orientations, Strategies, & Techniques: A Grid For The Perplexed*, 1 HARV. NEGOT. L. REV. 7, 8-13, 17- 39, 41-48 (1996).

ROBERT A. BARUCH BUSH & JOSEPH P. FOLGER, THE PROMISE OF MEDIATION: THE TRANSFORMATIVE APPROACH TO CONFLICT 45-46, 49-56, 60,

62, 65-66, 68, 72, 75, 78-81 (Revised ed. 2005). Copyright © 2005 John Wiley & Sons, Inc. Reprinted with permission of John Wiley & Sons, Inc.

Gary J. Friedman & Jack Himmelstein, THE HEART OF MEDIATION: RESOLVING CONFLICT THROUGH UNDERSTANDING (forthcoming 2006).

Hank de Zutter, *Proponents Say ADR Spells Relief,* ILL. LEGAL TIMES, Jan 1988, at 1.

Frank Scardilli, *Sisters of the Precious Blood v. Bristol-Myers Co.,* Address at Harvard Faculty Seminar on Negotiation (Apr. 13, 1982).

Alana S. Knaster & Philip J. Harter, *The Clean Fuels Regulatory Negotiation,* INTERGOVERNMENTAL PERSPECTIVE 20-22 (1992).

MARK UMBREIT, BETTY VOS, ROBERT B. COATES & KATHERINE A. BROWN, FACING VIOLENCE: THE PATH OF RESTORATIVE JUSTICE AND DIALOGUE 45-52, 11-12 (2003).

LEONARD L. RISKIN, MEDIATION TRAINING GUIDE (2004).

Jennifer Gerarda Brown & Ian Ayres, *Economic Rationales for Mediation,* 80 VA. L. REV. 323, 327-29 (1994).

SOCIETY OF PROFESSIONALS IN DISPUTE RESOLUTION, REPORT OF THE SPIDR COMMISSION ON QUALIFICATIONS (1989). Association for Conflict Resolution, 1015 18th Street, NW, Suite 1150, Washington, D.C. 20036, (202) 464-9700.

Ellen Waldman, *Credentialing Approaches: The Slow Movement Toward Skills-Based Testing,* DISP. RESOL. MAG., Fall, 2001. Copyright © 2001 American Bar Association. Reprinted by permission.

MODEL STANDARDS OF CONDUCT FOR MEDIATORS Sec. 9 (1994). Copyright © 1994 American Bar Association. Reprinted by permission.

MODEL RULES OF PROF'L CONDUCT R. 1.12 (2004). Copyright © 2004 American Bar Association. Reprinted by permission.

MODEL RULES OF PROF'L CONDUCT R. 2.2 (2001). Copyright © 2001 American Bar Association. Reprinted by permission.

MODEL RULES OF PROF'L CONDUCT R. 2.4 (2004). Copyright © 2004 American Bar Association. Reprinted by permission.

MODEL STANDARDS OF CONDUCT FOR MEDIATORS (1994). Copyright © 1994 American Bar Association. Reprinted by permission.

UNIFORM MEDIATION ACT, Sections 4-6 (2003) Permission given by the National Conference of Commissioners on Uniform State Laws.

ABA SECTION OF DISPUTE RESOLUTION, RESOLUTION ON MEDIATION AND THE UNAUTHORIZED PRACTICE OF LAW (Feb. 2, 2002). Copyright © 2002 American Bar Association. Reprinted by permission.

Michael Moffitt, *Suing Mediators,* 83 B.U. L. REV. 147, 204, 206-7 (2003).

J.H. Wade, *Liability of Mediators for Pressure, Drafting and Advice: Tapoohi v Lewenberg,* BOND DISP. RESOL. NEWS (Jan. 2004), available at www.bond.edu.au/law/centres/drc/newsletter/Vol16Jan04.doc (last visited July 28, 2004).

J. Michael Keating, Jr., *Getting Reluctant Parties to Mediate: A Guide for Advocates,* 13 ALTERNATIVES TO THE HIGH COST OF LITIG. 9. CPR Institute for Dispute Resolution, 1995. Copyright © 1995 by CPR Institute for Dispute Resolution, 366 Madison Avenue, New York, NY 10017. Reprinted with permission. All rights reserved.

Leonard L. Riskin, *Decision-Making in Mediation: The New Old Grid and the New New Grid System,* 79 NOTRE DAME L. REV. 1, 2-30, 32-45 (2003). Reprinted with permission. Copyright © 2003 Leonard L. Riskin.

DANIEL BOWLING & DAVID HOFFMAN, BRINGING PEACE INTO THE ROOM: HOW THE PERSONAL QUALITIES OF THE MEDIATOR IMPACT THE PROCESS OF CONFLICT RESOLUTION, Copyright © 2004 John Wiley & Sons, Inc. Reprinted with permission of John Wiley & Sons, Inc.

Tom Arnold, 20 *Common Errors in Mediation Advocacy*, 13 ALTERNATIVES TO THE HIGH COST OF LITIG. 69. CPR Institute for Dispute Resolution, 1995. Copyright © 1995 by CPR Institute for Dispute Resolution, 366 Madison Avenue, New York, NY 10017. Reprinted with permission. All rights reserved.

Leonard L. Riskin, *The Represented Client in a Settlement Conference: The Lessons of G. Heileman Brewing Co. v. Joseph Oat Corp.,* 69 WASH.U.L.Q. 1059, 1098–99, 1100–02, 1103–06 (1991). (Reprinted with permission).

Jeff Kichaven, *Avoidable Sins: When a Mediator Steps Beyond the Boundaries,* 22 ALTERNATIVES TO HIGH COST LITIG. 77, 91-92 (2004). Copyright © 2004 the CPR Institute for Dispute Resolution. Reprinted with permission of John Wiley & Sons, Inc.

Gary Friedman & Jack Himmelstein, *Deal Killer or Deal Saver: the Consulting Lawyer's Dilemma,* DISP RESOL. MAG. Winter 1997, pp. 7-8. Copyright © 1997 by the American Bar Association, Gary Friedman and Jack Himmelstein. Reprinted with Permission.

UNIFORM MEDIATION ACT Prefatory Note & Sec. 4-6 (2001). Permission given by the National Conference of Commissioners on Uniform State Laws.

Nancy A. Welsh, *The Thinning Vision of Self-Determination in Court-Connected Mediation: The Inevitable Price of Institutionalization?,* 6 HARV. NEGOT. L. REV. 1, 3-8 (2001).

Richard Delgado, Chris Dunn, Pamela Brown, Helena Lee, & David Hubbert, *Fairness and Formality: Minimizing the Risk of Prejudice in Alternative Dispute Resolution* 1985 WIS. L. REV. 1359, 1387-91, 1400-04 (1985).

MICHELE HERMANN ET AL., METROCOURT PROJECT FINAL REPORT: A STUDY OF THE EFFECTS OF ETHNICITY AND GENDER IN MEDIATED AND ADJUDICATED CASES AT THE METROPOLITAN COURT MEDIATION CENTER viii-xii (1993).

Trina Grillo, *The Mediation Alternative: Process Dangers for Women* 100
YALE L.J. 1545, 1549–50, 1600–1610 (1991). Reprinted by permission
of The Yale Law Journal Company and Fred B. Rothman & Company from The Yale Law Journal, Vol. 100, pp. 1545-1610.

Joshua D. Rosenberg, *In Defense of Mediation*, 33 ARIZ.L.REV. 467,
468–69, 492–500, 503–05 (1991). Copyright © 1991 the Arizona
Board of Regents. Reprinted by Permission.

Nancy Ver Steegh, *Yes, No, and Maybe: Informed Decision Making about
Divorce Mediation in the Presence of Domestic Violence*, 9 WM &
MARY J. WOMEN & L. 145, 186-87 (2003). Originally published in
William & Mary Journal of Woman & The Law.

Joan B. Kelly, *Mediated and Adversarial Divorce: Respondents' Perceptions of Their Processes and Outcomes*, MEDIATION Q., 1989. Reprinted with permission of John Wiley & Sons, Inc.

Craig A. McEwen, Nancy H. Rogers & Richard J. Maiman, *Bring in the
Lawyers: Challenging the Dominant Approaches to Ensuring Fairness in Divorce Mediation*, 79 MINN.L.REV. 1317, 1319–23, 1347–50,
1373–78 (1995).

PROSANDO V. HIGH TECH (Roleplay) Instructions. This exercise was created for the CPR International Institute for Conflict Prevention and
Resolution (formerly CPR Institute for Dispute Resolution) by Cathy
Cronin-Harris, Vice President, and Professor Stephen Goldberg as a
basis for CPR's 36-minute videotape, Mediation in Action: Resolving
a Complex Business Dispute (1994). The videotape and accompanying Study Guide are available at an educational price of $50 from
CPR, 575 Lexington Ave., New York, N.Y. 10022. Copyright © 1994
by the CPR Institute for Dispute Resolution. Reprinted with permission of CPR.

DANCE INNOVATION Role Play Mediator's Instructions. Copyright © 2001,
Center for Mediaton in Law. Reprinted with Permission.

Ch. V

Stephen Hayford & Ralph Peeples, *Commercial Arbitration in Evolution:
An Assessment and Call for Dialogue*, 10 OHIO ST. J. ON DISP. RESOL.
343, 367, 368-70, 370-71, 375, 375-76, 381, 394, 396, 397-98, 399,
400, 401, 403, 405, 413-14 (1995).

Yves Dezalay & Bryant Garth, *Merchants of Law as Moral Entrepreneurs: Constructing International Justice from the Competition for
Transnational Business Disputes*, 29 L. & SOC'Y REV. 27, 30-31
(1995).

Stephen L. Hayford, *Federal Preemption and Vacatur: The Bookend Issues Under the Revised Uniform Arbitration Act*, 2001 J. DISP.
RESOL. 67-76, 79-80 (2001). Reprinted with permission of the author
and the Journal of Dispute Resolution, University of Missouri-Columbia, Center for the Study of Dispute Resolution.

Christopher Drahozal, *Federal Arbitration Act Preemption*, 79 IND. L.J.
393, 393-395, 407-408, 420, 423-424 (2004). Copyright © 2004 the

Trustees of Indiana University & Christopher Drahozal. Reproduced with permission from the Indiana Law Journal.

Richard C. Reuben, *First Options, Consent to Arbitration, and the Demise of Separability: Restoring Access to Justice for Contracts with Arbitration Provisions*, 56 SMU. L. REV. 819, 832-33 (2003).

REVISED UNIFORM ARBITRATION ACT, Sec. 6, Comment 7 (2000). Permission given by the National Conference of Commissioners on Uniform State Laws.

Theodore O. Rogers, Jr. & Judith P. Vladeck, Address at the Symposium on Arbitration in the Securities Industry, 63 FORDHAM L. REV. 1507 at 1617, 1618, 1619, 1620, 1621, 1622. (1995).

Edward Brunet, *Arbitration and Constitutional Rights*, 71 N.C. L. REV. 81, 119 (1992).

W. Laurence Craig, *Some Trends and Developments in the Laws and Practice of International Commercial Arbitration*, 30 TEX. INT'L L.J. 1, 3-4, 6-7, 8-9, 10, 11, 57 (1995).

Charles N. Brower, *The Global Court: The Internationalization of Commercial Adjudication and Arbitration*, 26 U. BALT. L. REV. 9, 11-12, 13 (1997).

Yves Delazay and Bryant Garth, *Fussing About the Forum: Categories and Definitions as Stakes in a Professional Competition*, 21 L. & SOC'Y REV. 285, 295–299 (1996).

Stephen B. Goldberg, *The Mediation of Grievances Under a Collective Bargaining Contract: An Alternative to Arbitration*, 77 NW.U.L.REV. 270, 272–278 (1982). Reprinted by special permission of Northwestern University School of Law, Northwestern University Law Review.

Lewis L. Maltby, *Private Justice: Employment Arbitration and Civil Rights*, 30 COLUM. HUM. RTS. L. REV. 29-34, 39-43, 45-48, 49-54-55, 56-58, 63-64 (1998).

Thomas J. Stipanowich, *Rethinking American Arbitration*, 63 IND. L.J. 425, 425, 455, 458, 460–62, 477 (1988).

DAVID B. LIPSKY & RONALD L. SEEBER, THE APPROPRIATE RESOLUTION OF CORPORATE DISPUTES: A REPORT ON THE GROWING USE OF ADR BY U.S. CORPORATIONS 17, 26 (1998).

Ch. VI

Dorothy Wright Nelson, *ADR in the Federal Courts — One Judge's Perspective: Issues and Challenges Facing Judges, Lawyers, Court Administrators, and the Public*, 17 OHIO ST. J. ON DISP. RESOL. 1, 3-14 (2001).

Christine N. Carlson, *ADR In The States: Great Progress Has Been Made, But There Is Still Much to Do*, DISP. RESOL. MAG., Summer 2001, at 4, 4-6. Copyright © 2001 American Bar Association. Reprinted by permission.

Charles Pou Jr., *"Wheel of Fortune": or "Singled Out?": How Rosters 'Matchmake' Mediators*, DISP. RESOL. MAG., Spring 1997, at 10, 12. Copyright © 1997 American Bar Association. Reprinted by permission.

ELIZABETH PLAPINGER & DONNA STEINSTRA, ADR AND SETTLEMENT IN THE FEDERAL DISTRICT COURTS: A SOURCEBOOK FOR JUDGES AND LAWYERS 7, 8 (1996), a joint publication of the Federal Judicial Center and the CPR Institute for Dispute Resolution.

Deborah R. Hensler, *A Glass Half Full, A Glass Half Empty: The Use of Alternative Dispute Resolution in Mass Personal Injury Litigation*, 73 TEX.L.REV. 1587, 1593–94, 1606-19, 1623-24 (1995). Published originally in 73 TEXAS LAW REVIEW 1587 (1995). Copyright © 1995 by the Texas Law Review Association. Reprinted by permission.

Bobbi Mcadoo, Nancy A. Welsh & Roselle L. Wissler, *Institutionalization: What Do Empirical Studies Tell Us About Court Mediation?* 9 DISP. RESOL. MAG. (Winter 2003). Copyright © 2003 American Bar Association. Reprinted by Permission.

Laurel Wheeler, *Mandatory Family Mediation and Domestic Violence*, 26 S. ILL. U. L. J. 559, 564-570 (2002).

John Lande, *Using Dispute System Design Methods to Promote Good-Faith Participation in Court-Connected Mediation Programs*, 50 UCLA L. REV. 69, 70, 86-89, 93-95, 98-99, 102-104, 106-08 (2002).

Thomas D. Lambros, *The Summary Jury Trial and Other Alternative Methods of Dispute Resolution*, 103 F.R.D. 461, 468–472 (1984). Reprinted with permission of the West Publishing Company.

Thomas B. Metzloff, *Improving the Summary Jury Trial*, 77 JUDICATURE 11–12 (1993).

Joshua D. Rosenberg & H. Jay Folberg, *Alternative Dispute Resolution: An Empirical Analysis*, 46 STAN. L. REV. 1487, 1488–1493 (1994). Copyright © 1994 the Board of Trustees of the Leland Stanford Junior University.

Philip J. Harter, *Negotiating Regulations: A Cure for the Malaise*, 71 GEO. L. J. 1, 28-31 (1982).

Lisa Bingham, *Mediation at Work: Transforming Workplace Conflict at the United States Postal Service*, IBM ENDOWMENT FOR THE BUSINESS OF GOVERNMENT (October) 5, 12-23 (2003).

Richard C. Reuben, *Democracy and Dispute Resolution: The Problem of Arbitration*, 67 L. & CONTEMP. PROBS. 279, 279-82, 285-295 (2004).

Eric D. Green, *Corporate Alternative Dispute Resolution,* 1 OHIO ST .J. ON DISP. RES. 203, 238–242 (1986).

Barlow F. Christensen, *Private Justice: California's General Reference Procedure*, AM. B. FOUND. RES. J. 79, 79-82 (1982). Publisher: University of Chicago. Copyright © 1982 University of Chicago Press.

Stephen B. Goldberg, *The Mediation of Grievances Under a Collective Bargaining Contract: An Alternative to Arbitration,* 77 NW. U. L.

REV. 270, 281–284 (1982). Reprinted by special permission of Northwestern University School of Law, Northwestern University Law Review.

Arnold Zack, *The Quest for Finality in Airline Disputes: A Case for Arb-Med*, DISP. RESOL. J., 34, 36-8 (January 2004).

Philip J. Harter, *Ombuds—A Voice for the People*, DISP. RES. MAG., Winter 2005, at 5, 5-6. Copyright © 2005 American Bar Association. Reprinted by Permission.

Mary B. Rowe, *The Corporate Ombudsman: An Overview and Analysis*, 3 NEGOTIATION J. 127, 135 135 (Apr. 1987).

John Lande, *Possibilities for Collaborative Law: Ethics and Practice of Lawyer Disqualification and Process Control in a New Model of Lawyering*, 64 OHIO ST. L. J. 1315, 1315-1330 (2003).

John G. Bickerman, *Partnering in the Construction Industry: Teaming Up To Prevent Disputes*, 9 PROB. & PROP. 61-64 (March/April 1995). Reprinted by permission.

Ethan Katsh, *Online Dispute Resolution*, in THE HANDBOOK OF DISPUTE RESOLUTION (Michael Moffitt, & Robert Bordone, eds. 2005). Copyright © 2005 Michael Moffitt and Robert Bordone. Reprinted with permission of John Wiley & Sons, Inc.

Ch. VII

NATIONAL INSTITUTE FOR DISPUTE RESOLUTION, PATHS TO JUSTICE: MAJOR PUBLIC POLICY ISSUES OF DISPUTE RESOLUTION 3-4, 8-18, 30, 34-35. (Report of the Ad Hoc Panel on Dispute Resolution and Public Policy, National Institute for Dispute Resolution, 1983). This project was supported in part by a grant (No 83-NI-AX-0002) from the Federal Justice Research Program, U.S. Department of Justice. Points of view or opinions stated in this document are those of the author and do not necessarily represent the official position or policies of the U.S. Department of Justice.

Nancy A. Welsh, *Making Deals in Court-Connected Mediation: What's Justice Got to do With It?* 79 WASH. U. L.Q. 787, 817-826, 826-27 (2001).

Jean R. Sternlight, *ADR is Here: Preliminary Reflections on Where it Fits in a System of Justice*, 3 NEV. L. J. 289, 297-300 (2002-2003).

Harry T. Edwards, *Alternative Dispute Resolution: Panacea or Anathema?* 99 HARV. L. REV. 668, 671–672, 675–682 (1986). Copyright © 1986 the Harvard Law Review Association.

Frank E. A. Sander & Stephen B. Goldberg, *Fitting the Forum to the Fuss: A User–Friendly Guide to Selecting an ADR Procedure*, 10 NEGOTIATION J. 49, 60–61 (1994).

Jeanne M. Brett, Stephen B. Goldberg, & William L. Ury, *Designing Systems for Resolving Disputes in Organizations*, 45 AM. PSYCHOLOGIST 162, 165-169 (1990). Copyright © 1990 the American Psychological Association. Adapted with permission.

Cathy Costantino, *Using Interest-Based Techniques to Design Conflict Management Systems*, 12 NEGOTIATION J. 207, 207-14 (1996).

Lisa B. Bingham, *Self-Determination in Dispute System Design and Employment Arbitration*, 56 U. MIAMI L. REV. 873, 878-880, 881-886 (2002). Originally published in the University of Miami Law Review.

Donna Stienstra, *Evaluating and Monitoring ADR Procedures*, 7 FJC DIRECTIONS (Dec. 1994).

David G. Meyers, *Intuition: Its Powers and Perils* 113-14 YALE U. PRESS (2002). Copyright © 2002 Yale University Press.

ROBERT J. MacCOUN ET AL., ALTERNATIVE ADJUDICATION: AN EVALUATION OF THE NEW JERSEY AUTOMOBILE ARBITRATION PROGRAM, (South Monica, CA: RAND Corporation, 1988). Copyright © 1988 RAND. Reprinted with permission.

Roselle L. Wissler, *Barriers to Attorneys' Discussion and Use of ADR*, 19 OHIO ST. J. ON DISP. RES. 459, 462-468, 470-472, 493-497, 500 (2004). Reprinted with the permission of Roselle L. Wissler and the Ohio State Journal on Dispute Resolution.

Frank E.A. Sander & Stephen B. Goldberg, *Making the Right Choice*, ABA J. 66, 66–68 (Nov. 1993). Reprinted by permission.

CPR INSTITUTE FOR DISPUTE RESOLUTION, ADR SUITABILITY GUIDE 22-25 (2001). CPR Mediation Screen Questions Worksheet. Copyright © 2001 CPR Institute for Dispute Resolution, 366 Madison Avenue, New York, NY 10017-3122; (212) 949-6490, www.cdr.org. This excerpt from CPR ADR Suitability Guide is reprinted with permission from CPR Institute for Dispute Resolution. All rights reserved.

David Berreby, *Thoughts on ADR: An Interview with a Veteran Neutral*, 4 ALTERNATIVES TO THE HIGH COST OF LITIGATION, May 1986, (Eric Green being interviewed) Copyright © 1986 the Center for Public Resources Inc.

Kathleen M. Scanlon & Harpreet K. Mann, *Inside Guide to Multi-Step Dispute Resolution Clauses*, ADR COUNSEL IN-BOX, No. 12, March 2003. Copyright © 2003 CPR Institute for Dispute Resolution. Reprinted with permission of John Wiley & Sons.

Ch. VIII

Susan Daicoff, *The Role of Therapeutic Jurisprudence Within the Comprehensive Law Movement*, in PRACTICING THERAPEUTIC JURISPRUDENCE: LAW AS A HELPING PROFESSION 471-482 (Dennis Stolle, David B. Wexler, & Bruce J. Winick, eds. 2000).

Leonard L. Riskin, *Mindfulness: Foundational Training for Dispute Resolution*, 54 J. LEGAL EDUC. 79, 79-80, 83-86, 88, 89-90 (2004).

JAMES J. ALFINI & ERIC GALTON, ADR PERSONALITIES AND PRACTICE TIPS 6-8, 13-14, 50-53, 104, 107, 136-39 (1998). Copyright © 1998 American Bar Association. Reprinted by permission.

Appendices

UNIFORM MEDIATION ACT (2003). Permission given by the National Conference of Commissioners on Uniform State Laws.

MODEL STANDARDS OF CONDUCT FOR MEDIATORS (1994). Copyright © 1994 American Bar Association. Reprinted by permission.

UNIFORM ARBITRATION ACT (1997). National Conference of Commissioners on Uniform State Laws.

AMERICAN ARBITRATION ASSOCIATION, COMMERCIAL ARBITRATION RULES AND MEDIATION PROCEDURES/COMMERCIAL ARBITRATION RULES, THE EXPEDITED PROCEDURES AND THE PROCEDURES FOR LARGE, COMPEX CASES (amended and effective as of July 1, 2003)

AMERICAN ARBITRATION ASSOCIATION, SAMPLE ADR CLAUSES, from DRAFTING DISPUTE RESOLUTION CLAUSES: A PRACTICAL GUIDE (amended and Effective July 1, 2004).

*

Summary of Contents

Table of Contents

DISPUTE RESOLUTION AND LAWYERS

Third Edition

*

Chapter I

OVERVIEW OF DISPUTE RESOLUTION & CONFLICT MANAGEMENT

Conflict and disputes are pervasive in society. They touch every individual, every family, every organization, and every relationship between and among these individuals and groups.

Most lawyers are intimately involved in conflict and disputes. Trial lawyers, for example, use the law and the courts to resolve specific disputes between specific parties. Public interest lawyers, too, whose work is devoted to individual rights, the environment, or other such causes, often use individual disputes to address more fundamental issues of social conflict.

Traditionally, law schools focused on only one method of dispute resolution — trial. However, in recent years they have come to recognize that other methods, such as negotiation, mediation, and arbitration, often may be more appropriate for resolving particular disputes. Collectively, these other methods are commonly called "Alternative Dispute Resolution," or simply ADR. In our view, all of these methods are legitimate in advancing the broader individual and societal need for dispute resolution. The task of the lawyer is to determine, ordinarily along with the client, which method is most appropriate for a given dispute, and to be able to work effectively within that process.

This book seeks to enhance this capacity by providing a better understanding of three sets of issues:

    A. The nature of conflict, and the disputes that conflict produce, as well as the various processes available for resolving them appropriately;

    B. The significant law and policy issues surrounding these processes; and

    C. The multiple and complementary roles of lawyers in managing and resolving disputes, as well as the unique challenges that lawyers face as participants in conflict and disputes.

In addressing these issues, we draw upon a wide range of resources. The field of dispute resolution is broad, and has been informed not only by the teachings of law, but also of psychology, anthropology, economics, and political science, among other disciplines.

A. THE NATURE OF CONFLICT AND DISPUTES

Consider the case of Bob and Mary. They were married in their late twenties, and settled into a fairly ordinary and happy life in the 1980s. Bob worked as a manager for a large company. Mary enjoyed her work as a secretary before the marriage, but quit to take care of the kids when they started raising a family a few years into the marriage.

After about ten years of marriage, the two began drifting apart. Bob became more involved in his career, taking frequent business trips, while Mary took primary care of their three children and other family matters. Five years later, each of them happened upon evidence indicating that the other may be having an affair, Bob with a secretary for a nearby company, and Mary with Bob's best friend, Jim. Both denied the allegations in heated arguments in which Mary accused Bob of abandoning his family, and Bob accused Mary of not supporting him or his career.

The arguments grew increasingly bitter as the two careened among friends, acquaintances, and workmates in search of proof of the affairs, and tried to win each of the three children and other family and friends to their side. At this point, the only thing that Bob and Mary can agree on is the need to divorce.

* * *

Such situations are tragic but not unusual. For lawyers and others involved in dispute resolution, the key question is whether such disputes will lead to more constructive or more destructive outcomes. Most conflict, of course, has the potential for both outcomes. Bob and Mary's divorce, for example, can be nasty or amicable, even healing; it may well be a little bit of all of these. For instance, they could come to dislike each other to such a degree that they could not bear to be in communication at all during or after the divorce. However, it is also possible for Bob and Mary to use the divorce process to come to better understand themselves, each other, and their situations. They may also be able to develop a working relationship based on a shared interest in the welfare of their children and perhaps even each other. As lawyers, the more aware we are of the sources, structure, and dynamics of the conflict that gives rise to legal and other disputes, the greater our capacity will be to steer conflict toward processes and outcomes that are more constructive, and away from conflict's more destructive consequences.

1. SOURCES OF CONFLICT

Conflict may be defined simply as a clash of interests or aspirations, actual or perceived. Disputes are immediate manifestations of conflict, and arise when people take actions based on this actual or perceived clash.

There are many perspectives and theories about why conflict arises. In our view, no single answer provides adequate explanation. Rather, there are different perspectives that help inform our understanding of the tensions that may lie beneath a particular dispute. The following materials provide a brief overview of the different theoretical perspectives on the sources of conflict and then offer a helpful way of analyzing different dimensions of any particular dispute.

a. Theoretical Underpinnings

There are many different ways of approaching the amorphous question of the source of conflict. Professor Schellenberg suggests they may be generally organized into three sets of theories: individual characteristics theories, social process theories, and social structure theories. JAMES A. SCHELLENBERG, CONFLICT RESOLUTION: THEORY, RESEARCH, AND PRACTICE 39–102 (1996). Significantly again, in our view none of these theories alone is likely to provide an exclusive explanation of a conflict; rather they are different lenses through which to understand conflict, some of which may be more dominant in a particular situation than others.

i. Individual Characteristics Theories

The first set of theories relate to individual characteristics of people, entities, and institutions, and suggests that a propensity toward conflict is just an innate characteristic of humankind. Needs theory is a prominent example, and suggests that conflict arises from any one of a number of unmet human needs, ranging from physical needs for food and shelter to psychological needs for love and self-actualization *See, e.g.*, ABRAHAM MASLOW, HIERARCHY OF NEEDS (1954). From this perspective, one might suggest that Bob and Mary's conflict rested in Mary's unfulfilled need for esteem or self-actualization as a person beyond what motherhood could provide, or Bob's unquenched need for professional achievement and respect, or both. Similarly, modern identity theory holds that conflict arises from threats to individual and social identity, or our senses of self and self-worth. *See generally* JAY ROTHMAN, RESOLVING IDENTITY-BASED CONFLICT IN NATIONS, ORGANIZATIONS, AND COMMUNITIES 1–20 (1997). From this perspective, one might interpret the conflict as grounded in Bob's failure to acknowledge Mary's worth as a mother, perhaps because doing so would threaten his own sense of identity as the head of the family, or in Mary's failure to demonstrate appreciation of Bob's economic support of the family.

ii. Social Process Theories

Social process theories build on the individual characteristics theories, but emphasize the relationship between the parties, particularly along distributional lines. For a social process theorist, conflict is the result of the competition for resources. This was essentially the view of economist Adam Smith, who argued that people seek to maximize their rational self-interest, and that conflict arises when these interests collide *see* WEALTH OF NATIONS (E. Cannon Ed., 1937) (1776). Today, rational choice and public choice theorists sound similar themes in explaining social phenomena ranging from economic markets to legislative behavior. For accessible accounts, see Chris Guthrie, *Prospect Theory, Risk Preference, and the Law,* 97 Nw. U. L. Rev. 1115, 1115–20 (2003); Russell B. Korobkin & Thomas S. Ulen, *Law and Behavioral Science: Removing the Rationality Assumption from Law and Economics,* 88 Cal. L. Rev. 1051, 1060–66 (2000). From this perspective, one might find that the conflict between Mary and Bob springs from a competition for resources, such as money, space in the home, or the affections of the children.

iii.   Social Structure Theories

Finally, social structure theories of conflict place their emphasis on the institutionalized structures organizing a given society. Karl Marx was an early and influential proponent of this school, which essentially holds that conflict arises from the nature of the social system itself, particularly as it relates to disparities of power and influence. Marx, for example, saw conflict as resulting from the competition between "haves" (or "bourgeois") and "have nots" (or "proletariat"), with the "haves" being the propertied elite seeking to preserve the status quo and the "have nots" being the subservient working class seeking greater wealth. KARL MARX & FREDERICK ENGELS, MANIFESTO OF THE COMMUNIST PARTY (Int'l Publishers, 1948 Ed.) (1848). Social structure theory often finds its expression today in critical theory, which looks to power and other disparities between genders, races, and other classes to explain social conflict. *See, e.g.,* DERRICK BELL, AND WE ARE NOT SAVED: THE ELUSIVE QUEST FOR RACIAL JUSTICE (1987); JUDITH SHKLAR, AMERICAN CITIZENSHIP: THE QUEST FOR INCLUSION 64 (1991). From this perspective, one might think, or argue, that Bob and Mary's conflict derives from the advantages — in terms of power and influence — that American culture can give to men over women.

Each of these sets of theories describe an understanding of conflict that may seem beyond the "real world" focus of many practicing lawyers. In some respects this is true. However, lawyers often deal with the disputes that are manifestations of these underlying conflicts. Such disputes may include landlord-tenant disputes over ill-repaired conditions and withheld rent, disputes over job hiring and promotion decisions, disputes between computer hardware and software manufacturers over the contours of fair competition, or disputes regarding the prosecution and punishment of criminal acts. All of these are the kinds of disputes that constitute the daily work of the majority of lawyers, disputes that are manifestations of underlying conflict.

Notes and Questions

1.   People tend to use the words "conflict" and "dispute" interchangeably. This is certainly adequate in lay conversation. However, for the lawyer and dispute resolution professional, a more precise understanding of these

phenomena is helpful. Conflict, as we use the term, is an actual or perceived clash of interests, which can develop from any or all of the sources addressed in this section (individual characteristics, social process, or social structure). Disputes arise out of those sources of conflict, and are the concrete manifestations of the underlying conflict. Put another way, a dispute is a conflict that has been acted upon, a product of the conflict. For example, two residents of an apartment complex may live in a state of conflict because one likes to play loud music at late at night and the other likes to go to sleep early. But they do not have a dispute until the early sleeper seeks to have his neighbor turn down the volume.

2.   Disputes are not the only manifestations of conflict. In an organization, for example, conflict can be manifest in a variety of other ways, including:

> • *Competition*: * * * Obviously, not all competition is a form of conflict. For example, healthy competition with other companies that produce and market the same product is normal and expected. More serious, however, may be the conflict generated by uncontrolled, aggressive competition between or among work units or colleagues within the company itself.* * *

> • *Inefficiency/lack of productivity*: Slow work, deliberate delay, or decreased output can be evidence of conflict. Hidden conflict can lead a disgruntled yet vital employee to refuse to participate efficiently and meaningfully as part of a team effort.

> • *Low morale*: Similar to inefficiency or lack of productivity, low morale is often a reaction to hidden conflict. Often, it is the result of attempting to avoid or deny conflict or of frustration with attempts to protest organizational action or inaction.

> • *Withholding knowledge*: Within many corporate cultures, knowledge is power, and withholding knowledge (information) is practiced as a form of control.

CATHY A. COSTANTINO & CHRISTINA SICKLES MERCHANT, DESIGNING CONFLICT MANAGEMENT SYSTEMS: A GUIDE TO CREATING PRODUCTIVE AND HEALTHY ORGANIZATIONS 5–6 (1996).

What other indicia of unresolved conflict might be added to this list?

3.   People often view conflict as undesirable. But clearly that is not always the case. For example, many would say that the desegregation of public schools ordered by the U.S. Supreme Court in *Brown v. Board of Education*, 349 U.S. 294, 75 S.Ct. 753, 99 L.Ed. 1083 (1955), elevated American society with respect to race relations. Similarly, effective management of Bob and Mary's situation through communications and counseling could reunite their marriage in a deeper, more fulfilling way. What are some beneficial attributes of conflict? Consider this quote from Mary Parker Follett:

> As conflict — difference — is here in the world, as we cannot avoid it, we should, I think, use it. Instead of condemning it, we should try to set it to work for us. Why not? What does the mechanical engineer do with friction? Of course his chief job is to eliminate friction, but it is true that he also capitalizes on friction. The transmission of power by belts

depends on friction between the belt and the pulley. The friction between the driving wheel of the locomotive and the track is necessary to haul the train. All polishing is done by friction. The music of the violin we get by friction. We left the savage state when we discovered fire by friction. So in business, too, we have to know when to try to capitalize it, when to see what work we can make it do.

Mary Parker Follett, *Constructive Conflict, in* Dynamic Administration: The Collected Papers of Mary Parker Follett 30–31 (Henry C. Metcalf & L. Urwick eds.) (1940).

4. Conflict theorists, such as Morton Deutsch and Lewis Coser, often distinguish between constructive and destructive conflict. *See generally* Lewis Coser, Functions of Social Conflict (1954); Morton Deutsch, The Resolution of Conflict: Constructive and Destructive Processes (1973). In your view, what are some of the differences between constructive and destructive conflict? Can you think of a situation in your life in which conflict has produced a constructive or positive outcome for you? Would this result have been possible without the conflict? Why did the surfacing of the conflict make a difference?

5. For Bob and Mary, what might constructive and destructive outcomes look like?

b. An Analytical Approach

The foregoing discussion articulates different ways of understanding the deep conflict dynamics that lead to particular disputes. In the following passage, Bernard Mayer, a well-known mediator and scholar, suggests that people experience conflict in different ways, all of which are important to the ultimate resolution of conflict.

BERNARD MAYER, THE DYNAMICS OF CONFLICT RESOLUTION: A PRACTITIONER'S GUIDE
4–5 (2000).

Conflict may be viewed as occurring along cognitive (perception), emotional (feeling), and behavioral (action) dimensions. This three-dimensional perspective can help us understand the complexities of conflict and why a conflict sometimes seems to proceed in contrary directions.

Conflict as Perception

As a set of perceptions, conflict is a belief or understanding that one's own needs, interests, wants, or values are incompatible with someone else's. There are both objective and subjective elements to this cognitive dimension. If I want to develop a tract of land into a shopping center, and you want to preserve it as open space, then there is an objective incompatibility in our wants. If I believe that the way you desire to guide our son's educational development is incompatible with my philosophy of parenting, then there is at least a significant subjective component. What if only one of us believes an incompatibility to exist, are we still in conflict? As a practical matter, I think it useful to think of conflict as existing if at least one person believes it to exist. If I believe us to have incompatible interests, and act accordingly, then I am engaging you in a conflict process whether you share this perception or not.

Conflict as Feeling

Conflict also involves an emotional reaction to a situation or interaction that signals a disagreement or some kind. The emotions felt might be fear, sadness, bitterness, anger, or hopelessness, or some amalgam of these. If we experience these feelings in regard to another person or situation, we feel that we are in conflict — and therefore we are. As a mediator, I have sometimes seen people behave as if they were in great disagreement over profound issues, yet I have not been able to ascertain exactly what they disagreed about. Nonetheless, they were in conflict because they felt they were. And in conflicts, it does not take two to tango. Often a conflict exists because one person feels in conflict with another, even though those feelings are not reciprocated by or even known to the other person. The behavioral component may be minimal, but the conflict is still very real to the person experiencing the feelings.

Conflict as Action

Conflict also consists of the actions that we take to express our feelings, articulate our perceptions, and get his or her needs met in a way that has the potential for interfering with someone else's ability to get our needs met. This conflict behavior may involve a direct attempt to make something happen at someone else's expense. It may be an exercise of power. It may be violent. It may be destructive. Conversely, this behavior may be conciliatory, constructive, and friendly. But, whatever its tone, the purpose of the conflict behavior is either to express the conflict or to get one's needs met. Again, the question of reciprocity exists. If you write letters to the editor, sign petitions, and consult lawyers to stop my shopping center, and I do not even know you exist, are we in conflict? Can you be in conflict with me if I am not in conflict with you? Theory aside, I think the practical answer to both of these questions is yes.

Notes and Questions

1.   Think of a dispute in which you have been involved — with a friend, relative, teacher, or anyone else. Using Mayer's framework, see whether you can discern behavioral, cognitive, and emotional dimensions. In other words, what behaviors, thoughts, and emotions affected the development and evolution of the conflict? Did all parties experience the three dimensions equally?

2.   Mediator Gary Harper says that we often conceptualize our conflicts in terms of a "drama triangle" that appears in fairy tales, movies and television programs. This drama typically includes a victim (usually us), a villain (the person we think caused the conflict), and a hero (the person we think should rescue us). GARY HARPER, THE JOY OF CONFLICT: TRANSFORMING

VICTIMS, VILLAINS AND HEROES IN THE WORKPLACE AND AT HOME (2004). Does this describe any of the stories of conflicts in which you are or have been involved?

3. Christopher Moore offers an alternative way of thinking about the "amorphous" question of the source of conflict in the following chart. CHRISTOPHER W. MOORE, THE MEDIATION PROCESS 58–62 (2d ed. 1996). Significantly, Moore suggests that individual conflicts and disputes will implicate each of these dimensions, although some perhaps more than others. Try applying the dispute you worked with in Question 1 to the model Moore proposes.

The Circle of Conflict

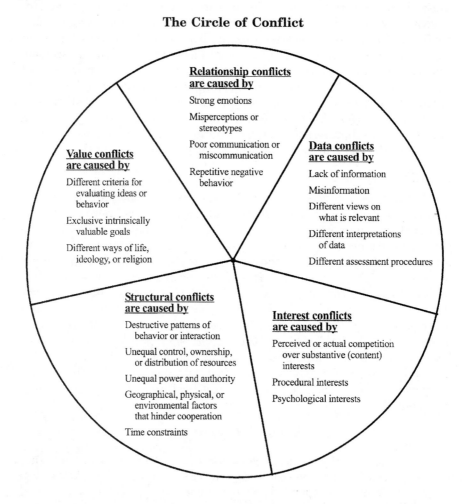

CHRISTOPHER W. MOORE, THE MEDIATION PROCESS 60 (2ND ED. 1996).

4. The Mayer and Moore models provide helpful ways for achieving a broader and more nuanced understanding of conflict and disputes. Other models are certainly possible. *See, e.g.,* KENNETH CLOKE & JOAN GOLDSMITH, RESOLVING CONFLICT AT WORK: A COMPLETE GUIDE FOR EVERYONE ON THE JOB 114

(2000). As you learn about various dispute resolution processes in this book, try to notice their capacities to affect the dimensions of these conflict models.

2. THE LIFE CYCLE OF A DISPUTE

Students of dispute resolution have identified what may be described as a life cycle for most disputes, one with a beginning, a middle, and an end. It begins with what William Felstiner, Richard Abel, and Austin Sarat call a "perceived injurious event" — some divergence between the interests, aspirations, preferences, and desires between two or more parties. More often than not, perceived injurious events are minor and simply brushed aside as part of the normal wear and tear of social life. Some, however, are deemed by a party or parties to be more significant, worthy of recognizing (naming), assigning fault (blaming), and sometimes even seeking recompense (claiming). William L. F. Felstiner, Richard L. Abel & Austin Sarat, *The Emergence and Transformation of Disputes: Naming, Blaming, Claiming . . .* , 15 Law & Soc'y Rev. 631 (1981). Depending upon the response, some of these perceived injurious events may be resolved informally, through avoidance, discussion, or negotiation. Others, however, may lead to a more formalized dispute resolution process, such as the assertion of a grievance to a supervisor or a complaint to a superior. The research is clear that the formalization of conflict tends to be structured as a pyramid, indicating there are far more perceived injurious events than formalized disputes, and that fewer and fewer disputes become more and more formalized.

A Dispute Pyramid: The General Pattern
No. per 1000 Grievances

Court Filings	50
Lawyers	103
Disputes	449
Claims	718
Grievances	1000

Richard Miller & Austin Sarat, *Grievances, Claims and Disputes: Assessing the Adversary Culture*, 15 Law & Soc'y Rev. 524, 544 (1980–81).

Once a dispute has begun a formalization process, it will likely either escalate or stabilize, in whole or in part, depending upon a wide array of conditions, such as the parties' tactics and responses during the dispute, the level of trust between the parties, and group and social

A Dispute Pyramid: Tort Patterns
No. per 1000 Grievances

Court Filings	38
Lawyers	116
Disputes	201
Claims	857
Grievances	1000

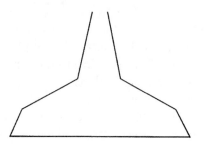

Id.

norms that may affect the conflict. DEAN G. PRUITT & SUNG HEE KIM, SOCIAL CONFLICT: ESCALATION, STALEMATE, AND SETTLEMENT 121–151 (3d ed. 2004). When a dispute escalates, it expands along several different dimensions. One dimension is the amount of resources that are committed to the dispute (in terms of time, money, etc.). Another is the nature of the tactics used by the parties, with tactics tending to become heavier and more confrontational as a dispute escalates. A third dimension of expansion is in the size of the dispute, as the number of issues and participants in a dispute tend to increase and generalize during escalation. For example, one may readily imagine that the tactics in the dispute between Bob and Mary may have started with questions during a discussion, turning to accusations and threats, and, ultimately, the commitment to divorce. The parties' investment of time, money, emotional energy, and other resources likely also increased during this expansion, along with the number of issues presented by the dispute, including the need to deal with the many issues involving the children and property, as well as the impact of the divorce on other areas of their personal and professional lives.

Skillful lawyers can manage both conflict and disputes effectively by working with each of these dimensions of expansion to prevent the inappropriate escalation or persistence of conflict, either in individual disputes or in the design of systems to manage conflict in organizations and institutions. For example, lawyers for Bob and/or Mary may wish to advise their clients to limit their conversations about the divorce to avoid raising new issues, or complicating ones already in play. An international example also illustrates the point vividly. In October 1963, American intelligence discovered that the Soviet Union had begun to develop offensive nuclear weapons in Cuba. President John F. Kennedy is widely credited with keeping the so-called Cuban Missile Crisis contained by preventing the release of unsettling information about it until after he and his most trusted advisors had agreed upon a plan for addressing the problem. He also prevented the dispute from unnecessary expansion in terms of the number of issues to be addressed by remaining focused on the narrow issue of the Cuban missile build-up, rather than expanding the size of the dispute to include American military bases in Berlin and Turkey. The crisis brought the U.S. and the Soviet Union to the brink of nuclear war for several days, and one can readily imagine how its resolution could have become much more difficult had it escalated to involve more countries, more issues, and more global resources. *See* IRVING L. JANIS, CRUCIAL DECISIONS: LEADERSHIP IN POLICYMAKING AND CRISIS MANAGEMENT 132–158 (1989); ROBERT F. KENNEDY, THIRTEEN DAYS: A MEMOIR OF THE CUBAN MISSILE CRISIS (1969).

Lawyers can apply these same principles as they represent clients. For example, a client in a medical malpractice case may be tempted to take matters into his own hands, and confront the doctor, perhaps even physically. A good lawyer will, of course, advise the client not to engage in this conduct — and the reasons include its potential to expand, or escalate, the dispute by adding new people (such as medical staff who might be present during the confrontation), by expanding the number of issues (such as civil and/or criminal assault or battery charges), and by requiring more resources in terms of time, energy, and perhaps money. Similarly, an attorney working for an organization who is aware of the sources and dimensions of conflict can take steps to minimize the likelihood of predictable disputes arising, and to provide appropriate processes, such as a mediation procedure, in which grievances can be aired and addressed.

This is not to suggest that such conflict containment strategies are always appropriate. For example, as we discuss in Chapter III, sometimes increasing the number of issues in a dispute may help facilitate settlement by "expanding the pie." Transactional attorneys struggling with the price term of a commercial lease, for example, may wish to add a provision for maintenance and repair in order to take the pressure off the price term by considering the overall value of the contract for the parties. Similarly, raising the profile of a dispute can aid in its resolution by bringing third party pressures to bear on the problem. A public interest attorney representing tenants in a slum, for example, may seek media coverage of the dispute to encourage a reluctant landlord to make necessary improvements to the property.

This kind of conflict management is often most helpful before a dispute has formalized. However, lawyers often get involved in disputes well after a dispute has formalized and escalated. While escalation can and should still be managed, the emphasis at the point of attorney intervention often shifts to how the dispute may be resolved. In this regard, there are a number of methods by which these more formalized disputes may be resolved, primarily negotiation, mediation, arbitration, and trial. These methods may be seen as falling on a continuum that is based on who will determine the outcome of the dispute. At one end of the continuum are adjudicatory methods (trial and arbitration), in which a third party decides the dispute. At the other end of the continuum are consensual methods of dispute resolution (negotiation and mediation), in which the parties resolve the disputes themselves. Such a continuum might look like this:

The Conflict Resolution Continuum

Consensual Processes   *Adjudicatory Processes*

negotiation   mediation   arbitration   trial

Trial as a dispute resolution method is the focus of much of our law school experience. This book emphasizes the other alternative processes for resolving disputes.

B. AN INTRODUCTION TO THE ALTERNATIVE PROCESSES FOR RESOLVING DISPUTES

The expansion of legal problem solving beyond trial is one of the primary contributions of the ADR movement, and is one of the most significant developments in American law during the last quarter of a century.* Much of the initial energy and innovation came from non-lawyers, who created a variety of dispute-resolution vehicles in which lawyers play a minor role, or none at all. Some of these served local communities through informal processes. As the movement took root, the legal community became active, too, with leadership from all three branches of the federal government, presidents of the American Bar Association, and state and local bar groups. Lawyers for large corporations also have been especially active.

Five motives, often intermingled, spark most of the interest in alternatives to traditional litigation: 1. saving time and money, and possibly rescuing the judicial system from an overload; 2. having "better" processes — more open, flexible and responsive to the unique needs of the participants. (This motive often is connected with negative feelings toward law and lawyers.); 3. achieving "better" results — outcomes that serve the real needs of the participants or society; 4. enhancing community involvement in the dispute resolution process; and 5. broadening access to "justice." A sixth motive, sometimes subconscious, is to protect turf for oneself, an institution, or a profession. These motives influence which alternative dispute resolution (ADR) process one prefers and how one operates within a given process.

* For a discussion of previous periods of strong interest in "informal justice," see JEROLD S. AUERBACH, JUSTICE WITHOUT LAW? RESOLVING DISPUTES WITHOUT LAWYERS (1983). For a discussion of the use of arbitration, mediation, and negotiation in Anglo–Saxon England during the earliest stages of English legal history, see Valerie A. Sanchez, *Towards a History of ADR: The Dispute Processing Continuum in Anglo–Saxon England and Today*, 11 OHIO ST. J. ON DISP. RESOL. 1 (1996).

The Primary Dispute Resolution Processes*

	Court	Arbitration	Mediation	Negotiation
Nature	Formal hearings	Informal hearings	Informal meetings with parties or representatives	Informal meetings with parties or representatives
Decision Maker	Judge or jury	Arbitrator	Parties	Parties
Third Party Role	Decide based on application of law to facts	Decide based on terms of agreement to arbitrate	Facilitate negotiation between parties	NA
Basis for Decision	Law	Standards provided by arbitration agreement – e.g. industry practices	Interests or positions of parties	Interests or positions of parties
Desired Result	Reasoned decision	Award	Settlement agreement	Settlement agreement
Confidential	Generally no	Generally yes	Generally yes	Generally yes
Binding	Yes. Court decree	Yes. Confirmation of arbitration award	Yes. Settlement agreement enforced as a contract	Yes. Settlement agreement enforced as a contract
Appeal	Yes.	Generally no substantive review	NA	NA

* Note: This chart presents a simple overview of the primary dispute resolution processes. As we will see throughout the book, in actual practice there are many variations and nuances in the characteristics described above.

The motives are intricately intertwined in most people who are involved in ADR. The judge who considers annexing a dispute resolution program to speed up case processing, for instance, may be impelled in part by a perception that the public will not long tolerate extensive delays without imposing changes upon the courts. Her concern about judicial overload may be mixed with desire to protect the court's authority. She also may appreciate that informal processes outside the courts have reduced the court's caseload and sometimes have been more satisfying to participants and have yielded results better suited to their needs. Yet her enthusiasm for informal processes on all these counts may be tempered by a belief in the importance of courts as articulators of public policy and as guarantors of public and private rights. Lawyers involved with ADR, and their clients, experience similar motivations, similarly mixed.

Brief descriptions of the major methods of dispute processing are set forth below. We begin with the "primary processes" — adjudicative and consensual — and then describe "mixed processes," which combine features of the primary processes. We exclude other important forms of dispute processing such as voting, fighting, and avoidance.

1. ADJUDICATIVE PROCESSES

Court and Administrative Adjudication

This, the most familiar process to lawyers, features a third party with power to impose a solution upon the disputants, such as in public trials and appeals by courts and in administrative adjudication by government agencies. It usually produces a "win/lose" result. Participants are given the opportunity to present evidence and arguments, and usually they do so through representatives, ordinarily lawyers.

Arbitration

In arbitration, the parties agree to submit their dispute to a neutral party whom they have, at least theoretically, selected to make a decision. Arbitration is used extensively in industrial labor relations and in commercial and consumer disputes. The parties have an opportunity to select an arbitrator with background and experience suitable for dealing with the particular issues in dispute. Because the parties can customize the proceedings to suit their needs, arbitration has the potential to be less formal, faster, and less expensive than the judicial process. The parties can agree that less importance be given to following or establishing precedent and more importance be given to other factors, such as community, industry, or workplace norms or expectations.

All states have enacted statutes, most modeled after the Uniform Arbitration Act, that govern the validity and enforceability of arbitration agreements. In these and other jurisdictions, enforcement also may be available under the Federal Arbitration Act. 9 U.S.C. § 1 (2000). Enforcement of agreements to arbitrate labor disputes is available under

§ 301 of the Labor Management Relations Act of 1947 (codified at 29 U.S.C. § 185(a) (2000)). As a primary dispute resolution process, we devote Chapter V to a fuller consideration of the arbitration process.

Private Tribunals

Sometimes called "rent-a-judge," such processes are available in jurisdictions where statutes or rules of court permit a court to refer cases to privately selected and paid third-party neutrals. The private judge's decision is entered as the judgment of the court. Therefore, unlike an arbitrator's award, a judgment entered by a private judge may be appealed. The parties voluntarily submit to such tribunals in order to select their own decision maker, or in the hope of eliminating delay or gaining the ability to exclude the public from the proceedings. For further discussion, see Chapter VI.

2. CONSENSUAL PROCESSES

Negotiation

In negotiation, persons seek to resolve a disagreement or plan a transaction through discussions, which may include reasoned argument. The discussions may be conducted between the parties themselves or through representatives. Negotiation is used in all manners of disputes and transactions and is common in everyday life. It is a constant activity of lawyers, and is explored in Chapter III.

Much negotiation in law practice, particularly that involved in resolving disputes, is based on adversarial assumptions — i.e., that the purpose of the negotiation is to divide a limited resource. In recent years, however, scholars have argued that problem-solving approaches to negotiation, long-used in putting together business deals and other transactions, can and should be applied to dispute resolution. These problem-solving approaches, which emphasize the underlying interests and concerns of the parties, make up an important part of this book.

Mediation

Mediation is an informal process in which an impartial third party helps others resolve a dispute or plan a transaction but does not impose a solution. In other words, mediation is facilitated negotiation. The parties often enter into mediation voluntarily, but many courts have programs that require parties to mediate before proceeding to trial. *See, e.g.,* Fla. Stat. ch. 44.102 et seq. (Supp. 1996). The desired result is an agreement uniquely suited to the needs and interests of the parties. Normally the agreement is expressed in a contract or release and is enforceable according to the rules of contract law. Apart from negotiation, mediation has come to be the predominant alternative method of dispute resolution, and Chapter IV addresses it more comprehensively.

Conciliation

The term "conciliation" sometimes is used interchangeably with "mediation," particularly internationally. Often, however, it is meant to refer to a less formal process (e.g., where the neutral acts as a "go-between") or to a less active role for the neutral.

3. MIXED PROCESSES

Negotiation, mediation, and arbitration are the most commonly used methods of alternative dispute resolution. Still, disputing parties frequently use so-called mixed processes, which combine elements of more than one basic dispute resolution process. The following are the most common forms of mixed processes, and are considered more fully in Chapter VI.

Mediation–Arbitration

"Med-arb" begins as a mediation. If the parties do not reach an agreement, they proceed to arbitration, which may be performed either by the person who mediated or by another neutral. This process has found employment in various arenas, including labor-management relations and commercial disputes.

Arbitration–Mediation

"Arb-med" is similar to med-arb, except that it begins as an arbitration, but converts to a mediation after the presentation of evidence to the arbitrator. The arbitrator makes and records a decision, which is withheld from the parties while they attempt to mediate the dispute. If the parties settle, that ends the matter and the arbitrator's decision is never disclosed to the parties. If the parties do not settle, then the arbitrator's award is disclosed to the parties and is binding upon them.

Mini-trial

"Mini-trials," or "structured settlement negotiations," refer to specially designed processes, usually employed to resolve complex disputes that would otherwise be the subject of protracted litigation. The goal is for the parties to reach a mutually satisfactory resolution.

Mini-trials are tailored to the needs of the participants and may embody a number of dispute resolution processes. In one model, lawyers for both sides present their cases in abbreviated form to a panel composed of a neutral advisor, who usually is a lawyer with expertise in relevant areas of law, and decision-making executives of the two organizations. The neutral advisor then gives his opinion of what would happen if the matter were litigated. Next, the executives retire to negotiate a settlement, with or without the neutral advisor. In some mini-trials, however, the neutral lawyer does not render an opinion unless the principals fail to reach an agreement.

Sometimes the parties agree that the neutral lawyer's opinion will be binding. When that happens, the proceeding is really an adjudication. In other mini-trials, the neutral advisor acts as a facilitator after rendering his or her advisory opinion, and the proceeding is mainly a mediation. Neutral advisors also have acted as fact-finders. The mini-trial was a popular form of ADR in the early 1990s, but is costly and has been less common more recently as mediation and other processes have become more popular.

Summary Jury Trial

Summary jury trial is an adaptation of some mini-trial concepts to cases that would be tried before a jury. It consists of lawyers giving brief presentations of their cases to a jury that has no authority, but whose members are drawn from the same population as real jurors. The jury's non-binding verdict on liability and damages helps the parties better understand their cases, and, thus, it encourages settlement. Like the mini-trial, the summary judgment trial's popularity has waned since the early 1990s as mediation and other processes have become more popular.

Early Neutral Evaluation

Court-annexed early neutral evaluation seeks to reduce pretrial costs and delay by requiring the parties to confront the strengths and weaknesses of their cases at an early stage through the assistance of a skilled neutral. The neutral identifies issues on which the parties agree and disagree and provides an evaluation of each side's case. The neutral may predict the probable outcome if the case goes to trial and suggest a range of damages if the plaintiff wins. The neutral may also offer to assist the parties in settlement discussions. Early neutral evaluation combines elements of mediation and nonbinding court-annexed arbitration.

Factfinding

In this process, a neutral makes findings on contested issues of fact, such as the valuation of property. This can aid in negotiation, mediation, or adjudication.

Ombuds

An ombuds is an official, appointed by a public or private institution, whose job is to receive complaints and either prevent disputes or facilitate their resolution within that institution. Methods include investigating, publicizing, and recommending. Although ombuds sometimes mediate and perform other dispute resolution functions, the more classic model is to assist complainants, directing them to other processes that might be appropriate.

Other Processes

Some quite imaginative approaches have developed to deal with complex multiple-party cases such as asbestos-related personal injury suits. For example, Professors Francis McGovern and Eric Green, special masters appointed by Judge Thomas Lambros, developed a sophisticated plan to encourage settlements referred to as the Ohio Asbestos Litigation Plan. It used a computer model to provide the judge and the parties' attorneys with a historically-based case value for each case scheduled for a settlement conference based on selected information about the case. Similarly, to address other claims asbestos producers and their insurers established an Asbestos Claims Facility as a "one stop" system for compensating victims. In other contexts, law firms sometimes use a "settlement counsel" approach, in which teams of lawyers for the parties attempt to reach settlement while other lawyers handle the litigation. *See* William F. Coyne Jr., *The Case for Settlement Counsel,* 14 Ohio St. J. on Disp. Resol. 367 (1999).

4. CONFUSION ABOUT THE PROCESSES

Confusion about ADR terminology is rampant, for several reasons. Many people, including some lawyers, simply are not familiar with the different processes and therefore tend to lump nearly all non-litigious methods into one large ADR blob. Even people who have a passing acquaintance with alternatives tend to confuse them in speech and writing, in part because processes that are analytically distinct can, in particular cases, work almost identically in practice. Thus, a small claims court judge, who has authority to impose a solution, may in fact seek to facilitate an agreement between the parties and then announce it as his decision. Some arbitrators do the same. Lawyers representing individuals are said to "mediate" when they seek a fair solution. And there are "mediators" who in effect impose a solution through the force of their own convictions or techniques or because of the power they exercise outside the mediation. Additionally, within almost any institution that deals with disputes, many different dispute resolution processes are employed. Thus, administrative agencies not only adjudicate, they also make rules, and sometimes the rules are developed through negotiation or mediation. Similarly, under the auspices of courts we commonly find negotiation, mediation, and summary jury trials. Yves Dezalay and Bryant Garth assert that the character of the various processes is changed by professional competition for dispute resolution business. They suggest, for example, that American litigators helped transform international commercial arbitration into a process closer to U.S.-style litigation because they had the skills and resources needed in such a process. *See* Yves Dezalay & Bryant Garth, *Merchants of Law as Moral Entrepreneurs: Constructing International Justice from the Competition for Transnational Business Disputes,* 29 Law & Soc'y Rev. 27 (1995).

Despite these tendencies, and perhaps because of them, it is important to understand and maintain the distinctions, even though blurring these distinctions — when an arbitrator mediates, for instance — may occasionally help achieve desirable results. Consider the following: First, different legal consequences flow from the formal nature of certain processes. An arbitrator's award, for example, is enforceable in accordance with federal or state statutes, but an agreement reached through mediation is enforceable only if it satisfies the requirements of contract law. These legal consequences apply even if the arbitration is conducted in a mediation-like fashion or if the mediator acts like an arbitrator. Second, each process has characteristics that make it more or less helpful in a given kind of case. A focus on these characteristics can help the parties achieve their goals. They might not, for example, wish to select an arbitrator known for following the strict rules of evidence if they chose arbitration over litigation because of a preference for speed and informality. Similarly, if a mediator pushes the parties toward the solution he or she thinks best, the process may lose its potential for enhancing the participants' working relationship.

Other Distinctions

To understand more fully the differences among dispute resolution and management processes, a few key distinctions are worth noting at the outset. One distinction that permeates this book is essential: the distinction between positions and interests. A position is what someone says he wants or is entitled to have. For instance, a plaintiff in a personal injury case who asks for money damages or a monetary settlement of $100,000 is asserting a position. An interest is the need or motive that underlies the position. The plaintiff might be motivated by interests in self-respect, or clarifying or improving his relationship with the defendant or others; the plaintiff might also have interests, in the coverage of compensatory and non-economic damages, such as punishing the defendant, a faster settlement, or even an apology. The claim for money damages, even if it is successful, might not satisfy all of these interests (or corresponding interests of the defendant). In a position-based process, the parties' goals are strictly opposed. In an interest-based process, the object is to reconcile interests, so both can, in some sense, "win."

In this book, we will often label interest-based approaches as "problem-solving" (though others call them "collaborative," or "value-creating," or "integrative"). In contrast, we will often call position-based approaches "adversarial" (though others call them "competitive," "value-claiming," or "rights-based").

Some dispute resolution processes focus more naturally on positions than interests. Adjudication, for example, generally is position-based (although sometimes arbitration, a form of adjudication, will consider interests). Negotiation and mediation, however, can focus on positions (based on arguments about rights or power) or interests or both.

Much of the confusion and many of the arguments about alternative methods of dispute resolution stem from a failure to recognize, understand, or appreciate the distinction between positions and interests. Sometimes this results from the narrowness of traditional legal education, which produces a distinct way of looking at the world. An understanding of this distinction may help you function much more effectively as a lawyer, a dispute resolution neutral, and a person.

There are also different perspectives on how to use the acronym "ADR." Historically, it has been interpreted as we described it in the opening section of this chapter, as "Alternative Dispute Resolution"– that is, as a phrase that refers to methods of resolving disputes other than trial. DICTIONARY OF CONFLICT RESOLUTION 17–20 (Douglas H. Yarn ed., 1999). However, today some use "ADR" to stand for "Appropriate Dispute Resolution." *Id.* at 26. In our view, the best term to describe the full array of processes, including litigation, is probably just "dispute resolution." We recognize the value of all of these processes when selected and used appropriately. Viewed from this perspective, the lawyer's goal is to work with the client to select the best, or most appropriate, process for resolving the particular dispute at issue, which could be trial or an ADR method. This goal, to us, is appropriate dispute resolution. To avoid confusion, however, in this book we use the term "ADR" in its conventional sense — as referring to those methods other than trial.

C. WHAT PROCESS IS APPROPRIATE?

The real value of understanding the nature of conflict and disputes and the methods by which they may be addressed is that such understanding can inform the selection of the most appropriate method for a particular dispute. This proposition may seem simple at first blush, but it raises enormously deep and fundamental questions. How do we determine which method of resolution is appropriate for a particular dispute? Who should decide? What interests does society have in the resolution of disputes, particularly those between seemingly private disputants? What should be the relationship between "litigation" and "ADR"?

Further complicating these questions is the fact that we can see dispute resolution from several perspectives: those of the client, of individual lawyers, of the legal profession, of courts, and of society in general. Yet we must recognize that these are not distinct, unified perspectives. Every case, every client, and every judge is unique. While bar associations, for example, may adopt positions, individual lawyers have widely divergent opinions. Each dispute resolution process threatens or promotes different values or interests, and so one's attitude about each process depends, in part, on where one sits. Moreover, within each process we find many variations.

The readings in this section deal with this issue on a macro-level, and we explore them by focusing on the great settlement debate and the institutionalization of ADR. What kinds of cases, these excerpts ask, should move through which kinds of processes? In succeeding chapters, we consider "micro" decisions, such as how to choose or tailor or build a process for a particular dispute with its own wrinkles, rather than for a class of disputes.

As you read the pieces in this section, recall the principal goals (described in Part I–B. above) that seem to motivate people who are interested in ADR. What seems to animate the various writers?

1. THE GREAT DEBATE OVER SETTLEMENT AND ADR

ADR evokes a wide range of views on its desirability and the extent to which it is justified. Some, for example, might believe ADR is generally inappropriate when there is a public system of law available, while others might see the presumption falling the other way, generally favoring the use of alternative methods of dispute resolution as the first option. The issues and concerns that arise from this debate resonate throughout the many policy issues affecting ADR, and the materials that follow explore this important debate.

a. The Strong View

OWEN M. FISS, AGAINST SETTLEMENT
93 Yale L.J. 1073, 1075, 1076–78, 1082–90 (1984).

In a recent report to the Harvard Overseers, Derek Bok called for a new direction in legal education. He decried "the familiar tilt in the law curriculum toward preparing students for legal combat," and asked instead that law schools train their students "for the gentler arts of reconciliation and accommodation." He sought to turn our attention from the courts to "new voluntary mechanisms" for resolving disputes. In doing so, Bok echoed themes that have long been associated with the Chief Justice, and that have become a rallying point for the organized bar and the source of a new movement in the law. This movement is the subject of a new professional journal, a newly formed section of the American Association of Law Schools, and several well-funded institutes. It has even received its own acronym — ADR (Alternative Dispute Resolution).

The movement promises to reduce the amount of litigation initiated, and accordingly the bulk of its proposals are devoted to negotiation and mediation prior to suit. But the interest in the so-called "gentler arts" has not been so confined. It extends to ongoing litigation as well, and the advocates of ADR have sought new ways to facilitate and perhaps even pressure parties into settling pending cases.

* * *

The advocates of ADR are led to support such measures and to exalt the idea of settlement more generally because they view adjudication as a process to resolve disputes. They act as though courts arose to resolve quarrels between neighbors who had reached an impasse and turned to a stranger for help. Courts are seen as an institutionalization of the stranger and adjudication is viewed as the process by which the stranger exercises power. The very fact that the neighbors have turned to someone else to resolve their dispute signifies a breakdown in their social relations; the advocates of ADR acknowledge this, but nonetheless hope that the neighbors will be able to reach agreement before the stranger renders judgment. Settlement is that agreement. It is a truce more than a true reconciliation, but it seems preferable to judgment because it rests on the consent of both parties and avoids the cost of a lengthy trial.

In my view, however, this account of adjudication and the case for settlement rest on questionable premises. I do not believe that settlement as a generic practice is preferable to judgment or should be institutionalized on a wholesale and indiscriminate basis. It should be treated instead as a highly problematic technique for streamlining dockets. Settlement is for me the civil analogue of plea bargaining: Consent is often coerced; the bargain may be struck by someone without authority; the absence of a trial and judgment renders subsequent judicial involvement troublesome; and although dockets are trimmed, justice may not be done. Like plea bargaining, settlement is a capitulation to the conditions of mass society and should be neither encouraged nor praised.

* * *

The Imbalance of Power

By viewing the lawsuit as a quarrel between two neighbors, the dispute-resolution story that underlies ADR implicitly asks us to assume a rough equality between the contending parties. It treats settlement as the anticipation of the outcome of trial and assumes that the terms of settlement are simply a product of the parties' predictions of that outcome. In truth, however, settlement is also a function of the resources available to each party to finance the litigation, and those resources are frequently distributed unequally. Many lawsuits do not involve a property dispute between two neighbors, or between AT & T and the government (to update the story), but rather concern a struggle between a member of a racial minority and a municipal police department over alleged brutality, or a claim by a worker against a large corporation over work-related injuries. In these cases, the distribution of financial resources, or the ability of one party to pass along its costs, will invariably infect the bargaining process, and the settlement will be at odds with a conception of justice that seeks to make the wealth of the parties irrelevant.

The disparities in resources between the parties can influence the settlement in three ways. First, the poorer party may be less able to amass and analyze the information needed to predict the outcome of the litigation, and thus be disadvantaged in the bargaining process. Second, he may need the damages he seeks immediately and thus be induced to settle as a way of accelerating payment, even though he realizes he would get less now than he might if he awaited judgment. All plaintiffs want their damages immediately, but an indigent plaintiff may be exploited by a rich defendant because his need is so great that the defendant can force him to accept a sum that is less than the ordinary present value of the judgment. Third, the poorer party might be forced to settle because he does not have the resources to finance the litigation, to cover either his own projected expenses, such as his lawyer's time, or the expenses his opponent can impose through the manipulation of procedural mechanisms such as discovery. It might seem that settlement benefits the plaintiff by allowing him to avoid the costs of litigation, but this is not so. The defendant can anticipate the plaintiff's costs if the

case were to be tried fully and decrease his offer by that amount. The
indigent plaintiff is a victim of the costs of litigation even if he settles.

* * *

Of course, imbalances of power can distort judgment as well: Resources influence the quality of presentation, which in turn has an
important bearing on who wins and the terms of victory. We count,
however, on the guiding presence of the judge, who can employ a number
of measures to lessen the impact of distributional inequalities. He can,
for example, supplement the parties' presentations by asking questions,
calling his own witnesses, and inviting other persons and institutions to
participate as amici. These measures are likely to make only a small
contribution toward moderating the influence of distributional inequalities, but should not be ignored for that reason. Not even these small
steps are possible with settlement. There is, moreover, a critical difference between a process like settlement, which is based on bargaining and
accepts inequalities of wealth as an integral and legitimate component of
the process, and a process like judgment, which knowingly struggles
against those inequalities. Judgment aspires to an autonomy from distributional inequalities, and it gathers much of its appeal from this aspiration.

The Absence of Authoritative Consent

The argument for settlement presupposes that the contestants are
individuals. These individuals speak for themselves and should be bound
by the rules they generate. In many situations, however, individuals are
ensnared in contractual relationships that impair their autonomy: Lawyers or insurance companies might, for example, agree to settlements
that are in their interests but are not in the best interests of their
clients, and to which their clients would not agree if the choice were still
theirs. But a deeper and more intractable problem arises from the fact
that many parties are not individuals but rather organizations or groups.
We do not know who is entitled to speak for these entities and to give
the consent upon which so much of the appeal of settlement depends.

* * *

The Lack of a Foundation for Continuing Judicial Involvement

The dispute-resolution story trivializes the remedial dimensions of
lawsuits and mistakenly assumes judgment to be the end of the process.
It supposes that the judge's duty is to declare which neighbor is right
and which wrong, and that this declaration will end the judge's involvement (save in that most exceptional situation where it is also necessary
for him to issue a writ directing the sheriff to execute the declaration).
Under these assumptions, settlement appears as an almost perfect
substitute for judgment, for it too can declare the parties' rights. Often,
however, judgment is not the end of a lawsuit but only the beginning.
The involvement of the court may continue almost indefinitely. In these

cases, settlement cannot provide an adequate basis for that necessary continuing involvement, and thus is no substitute for judgment.

The parties may sometimes be locked in combat with one another and view the lawsuit as only one phase in a long continuing struggle. The entry of judgment will then not end the struggle, but rather change its terms and the balance of power. One of the parties will invariably return to the court and again ask for its assistance, not so much because conditions have changed, but because the conditions that preceded the lawsuit have unfortunately not changed. This often occurs in domestic-relations cases, where the divorce decree represents only the opening salvo in an endless series of skirmishes over custody and support.

The structural reform cases that play such a prominent role on the federal docket provide another occasion for continuing judicial involvement. In these cases, courts seek to safeguard public values by restructuring large-scale bureaucratic organizations. The task is enormous, and our knowledge of how to restructure on-going bureaucratic organizations is limited. As a consequence, courts must oversee and manage the remedial process for a long time — maybe forever. This, I fear, is true of most school desegregation cases, some of which have been pending for twenty or thirty years. It is also true of antitrust cases that seek divestiture or reorganization of an industry.

* * *

Settlement also impedes vigorous enforcement, which sometimes requires use of the contempt power. As a formal matter, contempt is available to punish violations of a consent decree. But courts hesitate to use that power to enforce decrees that rest solely on consent, especially when enforcement is aimed at high public officials, as became evident in the Willowbrook deinstitutionalization case and the recent Chicago desegregation case. Courts do not see a mere bargain between the parties as a sufficient foundation for the exercise of their coercive powers.

* * *

JUSTICE RATHER THAN PEACE

The dispute-resolution story makes settlement appear as a perfect substitute for judgment, as we just saw, by trivializing the remedial dimensions of a lawsuit, and also by reducing the social function of the lawsuit to one of resolving private disputes: In that story, settlement appears to achieve exactly the same purpose as judgment — peace between the parties — but at considerably less expense to society. The two quarreling neighbors turn to a court in order to resolve their dispute, and society makes courts available because it wants to aid in the achievement of their private ends or to secure the peace.

In my view, however, the purpose of adjudication should be understood in broader terms. Adjudication uses public resources, and employs not strangers chosen by the parties but public officials chosen by a process in which the public participates. These officials, like members of the legislative and executive branches, possess a power that has been defined and conferred by public law, not by private agreement. Their job is not to maximize the ends of private parties, nor simply to secure the peace, but to explicate and give force to the values embodied in authoritative texts such as the Constitution and statutes: to interpret those values and to bring reality into accord with them. This duty is not discharged when the parties settle.

In our political system, courts are reactive institutions. They do not search out interpretive occasions, but instead wait for others to bring matters to their attention. They also rely for the most part on others to investigate and present the law and facts. A settlement will thereby deprive a court of the occasion, and perhaps even the ability, to render an interpretation. A court cannot proceed (or not proceed very far) in the face of a settlement. To be against settlement is not to urge that parties be "forced" to litigate, since that would interfere with their autonomy and distort the adjudicative process; the parties will be inclined to make the court believe that their bargain is justice. To be against settlement is only to suggest that when the parties settle, society gets less than what appears, and for a price it does not know it is paying. Parties might settle while leaving justice undone. The settlement of a school suit might secure the peace, but not racial equality. Although the parties are prepared to live under the terms they bargained for, and although such peaceful coexistence may be a necessary precondition of justice, and itself a state of affairs to be valued, it is not justice itself. To settle for something means to accept less than some ideal.

* * *

THE REAL DIVIDE

To all this, one can readily imagine a simple response by way of confession and avoidance: We are not talking about *those* lawsuits. Advocates of ADR might insist that my account of adjudication, in contrast to the one implied by the dispute-resolution story, focuses on a rather narrow category of lawsuits. They could argue that while settlement may have only the most limited appeal with respect to those cases, I have not spoken to the "typical" case. My response is twofold.

First, even as a purely quantitative matter, I doubt that the number of cases I am referring to is trivial. My universe includes those cases in which there are significant distributional inequalities; those in which it is difficult to generate authoritative consent because organizations or social groups are parties or because the power to settle is vested in autonomous agents; those in which the court must continue to supervise the parties after judgment; and those in which justice needs to be done, or to put it more modestly, where there is a genuine social need for an authoritative interpretation of law. I imagine that the number of cases that satisfy one of these four criteria is considerable; in contrast to the kind of case portrayed in the dispute-resolution story, they probably dominate the docket of a modern court system.

Second, it demands a certain kind of myopia to be concerned only with the number of cases, as though all cases are equal simply because the clerk of the court assigns each a single docket number. All cases are not equal. The Los Angeles desegregation case, to take one example, is not equal to the allegedly more typical suit involving a property dispute or an automobile accident. The desegregation suit consumes more resources, affects more people, and provokes far greater challenges to the judicial power. The settlement movement must introduce a qualitative perspective; it must speak to these more "significant" cases, and demonstrate the propriety of settling them. Otherwise it will soon be seen as an irrelevance, dealing with trivia rather than responding to the very conditions that give the movement its greatest sway and saliency.

Nor would sorting cases into "two tracks," one for settlement, and another for judgment, avoid my objections. Settling automobile cases and leaving discrimination or antitrust cases for judgment might remove a large number of cases from the dockets, but the dockets will nevertheless remain burdened with the cases that consume the most judicial resources and represent the most controversial exercises of the judicial power. A "two track" strategy would drain the argument for settlement of much of its appeal. I also doubt whether the "two track" strategy can be sensibly implemented. It is impossible to formulate adequate criteria for prospectively sorting cases. * * *

* * *

Someone like Bok sees adjudication in essentially private terms: The purpose of lawsuits and the civil courts is to resolve disputes, and the amount of litigation we encounter is evidence of the needlessly combative and quarrelsome character of Americans. Or as Bok put it, using a more diplomatic idiom: "At bottom, ours is a society built on individualism, competition, and success." I, on the other hand, see adjudication in more public terms: Civil litigation is an institutional arrangement for using state power to bring a recalcitrant reality closer to our chosen ideals. We turn to the courts because we need to, not because of some quirk in our personalities. We train our students in the tougher arts so that they may help secure all that the law promises, not because we want them to become gladiators or because we take a special pleasure in combat.

To conceive of the civil lawsuit in public terms as America does might be unique. I am willing to assume that no other country — including Japan, Bok's new paragon — has a case like *Brown v. Board of Education* in which the judicial power is used to eradicate the caste structure. I am willing to assume that no other country conceives of law and uses law in quite the way we do. But this should be a source of pride rather than shame. What is unique is not the problem, that we live short of our ideals, but that we alone among the nations of the world seem willing to do something about it. Adjudication American-style is not a reflection of our combativeness but rather a tribute to our inventiveness and perhaps even more to our commitment.

* * *

b. The Responses

Fiss's powerful article, which articulates concerns about settlement and alternative methods of dispute resolution that continue to be felt throughout the legal community, drew a generation of responses. The following excerpt, for example, takes on a core component of Fiss's argument: that settlement is inappropriate because of the public's overriding interest in the resolution of private disputes for purposes of shaping future behavior. Other responses follow in the notes and questions.

CARRIE MENKEL–MEADOW, WHOSE DISPUTE IS IT ANYWAY?: A PHILOSOPHICAL AND DEMOCRATIC DEFENSE OF SETTLEMENT (IN SOME CASES)

83 Geo. L.J. 2663, 2663–71, 2692 (1995).

In the last decade or so, a polarized debate about how disputes should be resolved has demonstrated to me once again the difficulties of simplistic and adversarial arguments. Owen Fiss has argued "Against Settlement"; Trina Grillo and others have argued against mediation (in divorce cases and other family matters involving women); Richard Delgado and others have questioned whether informal processes are unfair to disempowered and subordinated groups; Judith Resnik has criticized the (federal) courts' unwillingness to do their basic job of adjudication; Stephen Yeazell has suggested that too much settlement localizes, decentralizes, and delegalizes dispute resolution and the making of public law; Kevin C. McMunigal has argued that too much settlement will make bad advocates; and David Luban and Jules Coleman, among other philosophers, have criticized the moral value of the compromises that are thought to constitute legal settlements. On the other side, vigorous proponents of alternative dispute resolution, including negotiation, mediation, arbitration, and various hybrids of these forms of preadjudication settlement, criticize the economic and emotional waste of adversarial processes and the cost, inefficiency, and political difficulties of adjudication, as well as its draconian unfairness in some cases.

In my view, this debate, while useful for explicitly framing the underlying values that support our legal system, has not effectively dealt with the realities of modern legal, political, and personal disputes. For me, the question is not "for or against" settlement (since settlement has become the "norm" for our system), but *when, how, and under what circumstances* should cases be settled? When do our legal system, our citizenry, and the parties in particular disputes need formal legal adjudication, and when are their respective interests served by settlement, *whether public or private?*

As several recent commentators have noted, the role of settlement in our legal system has increased: some think because it is actively promoted by such developments as the Civil Justice Reform Act; others by simple caseload pressures, and still others because of the desirability of party-initiated or consented-to agreements to resolve disputes. While court administrators, judges, and some lawyers suggest that we must continue to mine the advantages of settlement for caseload reduction, or equity among claimants, especially in mass torts or class action settings, many legal scholars continue to express concern with the use of settlement as a device for resolving our legal disputes.

The difficulty with the debate about settlement vs. adjudication is that there are many more than two processes, as well as other variables that affect the processes, to consider. The diverse interests of the participants in the dispute, the legal system, and society may not be the same. Issues of fairness, legitimacy, economic efficiency, privacy, publicity, emotional catharsis or empathy, access, equity among disputants, and lawmaking may differ in importance for different actors in the system, and they may vary by case — this is the strength of our common law system.

In his accompanying essay, David Luban argues that settlement is problematic because it reduces public participation in the business of dispute resolution and, consequently, reduces production of rules and precedents — in short, settlement leads to an "erosion of the public realm." Settlement works in favor of "private peace" and in opposition to "public justice." Luban, like other critics of settlement, suggests that the legal system is designed to engage us (and our judges, lawyers, and litigants) in the public discourse of lawmaking and policy debate that concerns itself with justice and self-defined societal values — in our case, democratic deliberation. By judging and enunciating rules, judges set baselines for political endowments and entitlements and alternately close and open debates by reviewing facts and articulating the rules and values that underlie particular legal positions. Settlements, on the other hand, represent cruder "compromises" of raw bargaining skill and extrajudicial power imbalances (economics, legal skill, and repeat play experience). Luban acknowledges that we can no longer imagine a "world without settlement." We need it simply to muddle through the hundreds of thousands of disputes our modern society produces. Unlike Fiss, he acknowledges that not all disputes are occasions for "structural transformation" or public elucidation of basic values. And, as he suggests realistically, "[t]oo many cases will make bad law." With an increase of cases, and trial and appeals courts making more and more law, there are likely to be irreconcilable inconsistencies in decisional law, producing a virtual "tower of Babel" of legal precedents.

Thus Luban shifts the focus to a consideration of *when and how* settlements should take place. His ultimate focus is on the need to keep settlements public and to decry the loss to democratic discourse when too many settlements are kept secret. Luban argues that secret settlements deprive us not only of "result" information, but the "facts" of discovery, necessarily "privatizing" information to which a democratic society should have access. He suggests that those who continue to favor secret settlements prefer the "problem-solving" (dispute resolution) conception of our legal system to "public production of rules and precedents" or the "public goods and discourse" function. Thus Luban is willing to tolerate settlement, but only if it is open to the "sunshine" laws and serves "at least some of the public values of adjudication," by keeping the settlement process and its information open to the public.

In this essay, I hope to explore some of the same questions that Professor Luban has framed for us — how can we decide which settlements to be for and which to be against? In other words, how can we tell good settlements from bad ones, and when should we prefer adjudication to settlement? Like others who have written on this subject, both recently and in the past, I do not think there are easy answers to this question; but more problematically, I want to suggest that it will be very difficult for us to specify in advance criteria for allocation to particular processes. In the words of current academic cachet, much depends on the context — of disputes, of disputants, and of the system being considered. I will here complexify and problematize Luban's seemingly easy proposition — that democratic discourse requires full disclosure of legal dispute information. In this essay, I will make a case for settlement by arguing that there are philosophical, as well as instrumental, democratic, ethical, and human justifications for settlements (at least in some cases).

Those who criticize settlement suffer from what I have called, in other contexts, "litigation romanticism," with empirically unverified assumptions about what courts can or will do. More important, those who privilege adjudication focus almost exclusively on structural and institutional values and often give short shrift to those who are actually involved in the litigation. I fear, but am not sure, that this debate can be reduced to those who care more about the people actually engaged in disputes versus those who care more about institutional and structural arrangements. I prefer to think that we need both adjudication and settlement. These processes can affect each other in positive, as well as negative ways, but in my view, settlement should not be seen as "second best" or "worst case" when adjudication fails. Settlement can be justified on its own moral grounds — there are important values, consistent with the fundamental values of our legal and political systems, that support the legitimacy of settlements of some, if not most, legal disputes. These values include consent, participation, empowerment, dignity, respect, empathy and emotional catharsis, privacy, efficiency, quality solutions, equity, access, and yes, even justice.

Though some have argued that compromise itself can be morally justified, I will here argue, as well, that compromise is not always necessary for settlement and that in fact, some settlements, by not requiring compromise, may produce better solutions than litigation. In particular, my own arguments for settlements (of particular kinds) have been often misstated or oversimplified, for the purpose of argument, so that they begin to strike me as strawpersons and cause me to question whether we are really able to understand each other when we "sharpen" the argument by "narrowing" it.

To summarize, it seems to me that the key questions implicated in the ongoing debate about settlement vs. adjudication are:

1. In a party-initiated legal system, when is it legitimate for the parties to settle their dispute themselves, or with what assistance from a court in which they have sought some legal-system support or service?

2. When is "consent" to a settlement legitimate and "real," and by what standards should we (courts and academic critics) judge and permit such consent?

3. When, in a party-initiated legal system, should party consent be "trumped" by other values — in other words, when should public, institutional, and structural needs and values override parties' desire to settle or courts' incentives to promote settlement? In short, when is the need for "public adjudication" or as Luban suggests, "public settlement" more important (to whom?) than what the parties may themselves desire?

* * *

I have here tried to make the following arguments on behalf of the "best" aspects of settlement:

1. Settlements that are in fact consensual represent the goals of democratic and party-initiated legal regimes by allowing the parties themselves to choose processes and outcomes for dispute resolution.

2. Settlements permit a broader range of possible solutions that may be more responsive to both party and system needs.

3. What some consider to be the worst of settlement, that is, compromise, may actually represent a moral commitment to equality, precision in justice, accommodation, and peaceful coexistence of conflicting interests.

4. Settlements may be based on important nonlegal principles or interests, which may, in any given case, be as important or more important to the parties than "legal" considerations. Laws made in the aggregate may not always be appropriate in particular cases, and thus settlements can be seen as yet another "principled" supplement to our common law system.

5. Settlement processes may be more humanely "real," democratic, participatory, and cathartic than more formalized processes, permitting in their best moments, transformative and educational opportunities for parties in dispute as well as for others.

6. Some settlement processes may be better adapted for the multiplex, multiparty issues that require solutions in our modern society than the binary form of plaintiff-defendant adjudication.

7. Despite the continuing and important debates about discovery and information exchange in the litigation process, some settlement processes (mediation and some forms of neutral case evaluation and scheduling) may actually provide both more and better (not just legally relevant) information for problem-solving, as well as "education" of the litigants.

8. When used appropriately, settlement may actually increase access to justice, not only by allowing more disputants to claim in different ways, but also by allowing greater varieties of case resolutions.

Notes and Questions

1. Do you think Fiss or Menkel–Meadow has the better view? How does one measure and compare the justice provided in adjudication and alternative processes? What does justice mean to you?

2. Professor Menkel-Meadow responds primarily to Fiss's public realm argument. Jethro Lieberman and James Henry offer several other critiques of Fiss's central thesis, emphasizing the uniqueness of individual cases and contexts, and the reasons for which ADR can be socially desirable in some cases.

> * * * One short answer to Fiss is that most ADR proponents make no claim for shunting all, or even most, litigation into alternative forums. The ADR movement of the 1980s does not suppose that every legal dispute has a non-judicial solution. Indeed, the ADR literature recognizes that some types of cases are not suited to resolution outside the courtroom, including particularly cases in which the plaintiff seeks a declaration of law by the court. Fiss overlooks this accepted limitation of ADR because he assumes, at least implicitly, that all cases resemble *Brown v. Board of Education.* But, of course, they do not. It seems obvious that large classes of cases are not so consequential, and do not call for the definitive ruling of a judge or the imprimatur of an official organ of the state. Automobile accidents, uncontested divorces, breaches of contract, and other common types of suits do not cry out to be memorialized in the official reports, and, in any event, most are settled far short of trial.
>
> A second response to Fiss's critique is that his "conspiracy theory" of ADR is dubious. Many people who seek to use ADR are scarcely "powerful" economic interests — ADR is not limited to adoption by Fortune 500 companies. Moreover, ADR does not dispense with community norms. All dispute resolution takes place with an eye toward existing alternatives — including litigation. Finally, the choice to employ ADR is made by parties who have determined that the injustice resulting from delay and the prohibitive costs of pursuing a case through the courts (direct expenditures for lawyers and expenses, as well as significant indirect expenditures, like lost opportunity costs) far outweigh any putative injustice stemming from the decision to forgo judgment by the court.

A third response to Fiss is that not all questions need to be answered. An open society needs the tension of open questions; parties who settle do not thereby foreclose answers at some later time when matters of principle are truly at stake and the issues cannot be compromised. Fiss agrees that avoidance has a value to society, "which sometimes thrives by masking its basic contradictions." He questions, however, whether settlement will result in too much avoidance. But we know of no way to measure the appropriateness of avoidance. Furthermore, Fiss's concern is one-sided. We should be equally concerned to prevent courts from rendering judgment when settlement is more appropriate.

Finally, Fiss's position is seriously weakened by his failure to offer proof that court judgments are more just. He says, for example, that "[a]djudication is more likely to do justice than conversation, mediation, arbitration, settlement, rent-a-judge, mini-trials, community moots or any other contrivance of ADR, precisely because it vests the power of the state in officials who act as trustees for the public, who are highly visible, and who are committed to reason."

Does ADR reach a just result or merely an expedient one? How can one measure the justice of a private settlement? The question is important, but it has not been well discussed in the ADR literature — no doubt because it is so difficult a proposition to test. Whatever the answer, it seems fair to ask the same questions of courts. In theory, courts are committed to reason, but in practice much stands in their way. Some judges are dispassionate and disinterested seekers after justice, but not all are. And all judges are busy; it is a fair assumption that they do not have sufficient time to devote to any single case. Moreover, the maneuvering of partisan lawyers alone is often enough to ensure that justice will *not* be done.

A perhaps more controversial response to Fiss's argument about the quality of outcomes is that in certain important classes of cases — cases involving public institutions like schools, hospitals, and prisons (the very cases that particularly interest Fiss) — courts themselves invoke processes that are firmly lodged in the ADR arsenal. Stories that describe litigation over unconstitutional prison conditions, inhumane mental hospital conditions, and segregated schools frequently depict the judge acting as mediator, helping the parties to negotiate the remedy the court will impose by consent decree. If the courts themselves find these processes useful or even necessary, chances are good that the same processes can be as beneficial when invoked outside the courts.

Jethro K. Lieberman & James F. Henry, *Lessons From the Alternative Dispute Resolution Movement*, 53 U. Chi. L. Rev. 424, 432, 433–35 (1986). How might Fiss respond to these arguments?

3. Fiss asserts that adjudication is more likely to do justice than ADR "because it vests the power of the state in officials who act as trustees for the public, who are highly visible, and who are committed to reason." Professor Jethro Lieberman and James Henry point to things that stand in the way of courts doing justice. In her excerpt, Professor Menkel–Meadow asserts that adjudication is often romanticized when compared with settlement, and gives reasons why settlement sometimes achieves more justice

than adjudication. Similarly, Marc Galanter maintains that the reality of ADR has never matched the hopes of its boosters. Richard C. Reuben, *The Lawyer Turns Peacemaker,* A.B.A. J., Aug. 1996, at 55.

4. The settlement debate raises important questions about the goals of ADR. In Section B of this chapter, we listed the goals of ADR as including the saving of time and money, having better processes, achieving better results, and broadening access to justice. Are these goals always consistent? Are they socially desirable? Consider, for example, the goals of efficiency and access to justice. Is it possible to construct a dispute resolution process that saves time and money but threatens the goal of access to justice? See the discussion of mandatory arbitration in Chapter V, beginning at page 554.

5. In his article, Fiss indicates that he believes the movement's principal objective is to relieve court congestion. In a response, Professors McThenia and Shaffer say Fiss missed the soundest argument in favor of ADR: its capacity to foster reconciliation. For them, justice is not something we get from government but something we give to each other. Andrew W. McThenia & Thomas L. Shaffer, *For Reconciliation,* 94 Yale L.J. 1660 (1985). In his reply, Fiss faults McThenia and Shaffer for giving a partial view of the ADR movement and for failing to understand that "the more general ADR version" is just another assault on the activist state, another form of the deregulation movement. Owen M. Fiss, *Out of Eden,* 94 Yale L.J. 1669 (1985). He pleads that the reader give credit to the aspirations behind litigation and asserts that adjudication is more likely than ADR to realize its aspirations. With which side do you agree?

6. ADR proponents often cast their arguments in terms of efficiency, especially the capacity of parties to save time and money through the use of ADR processes. However, such claims have not been easily supportable. *See, e.g.,* JAMES S. KAKALIK, TERENCE DUNWORTH, LAURAL A. HILL, DANIEL MCCAFFREY, MARIAN OSHIRO, NICHOLAS M. PACE & MARY E. VAIANA, AN EVALUATION OF MEDIATION AND EARLY NEUTRAL EVALUATION UNDER THE CIVIL JUSTICE REFORM ACT 48–53 (1996) (arguing that arbitration, mediation, and early neutral evaluation in the six federal district court programs they studied produced no "statistically significant" reductions in time to disposition, the costs of litigation, perceptions of fairness, or client satisfaction). This work (sometimes referred to as the "RAND Report") was criticized by some for focusing on under-developed or poorly designed programs, and for failing to show significant advantages over unmediated litigation. *See generally* Craig McEwen, *Managing Corporate Disputing: Overcoming Barriers to the Effective Use of Mediation for Reducing the Cost and Time of Litigation,* 14 Ohio St. J. on Disp. Resol. 1, 1–4 (1998). Moreover, some programs have reported considerable cost and time savings. *See, e.g.,* DONNA STIENSTRA, MOLLY JOHNSON & PATRICIA LOMBARD, A STUDY OF THE FIVE DEMONSTRATION PROGRAMS ESTABLISHED UNDER THE CIVIL JUSTICE REFORM ACT OF 1990 215–253 (1997); Kent Snapp, *Five Years of Random Testing Shows Early ADR Successful,* Disp. Resol. Mag., Summer 1997, at 16. Clearly the empirical evidence is mixed at best. Under what circumstances or conditions might a particular ADR method promote efficiency? Under what circumstances might an ADR method undermine efficiency? Should the desirability of ADR turn only on whether it is economically efficient, or are other factors equally or more important, such as party satisfaction and the quality of outcomes?

2. THE INSTITUTIONALIZATION OF ADR

Assuming, as we do, that settlement and ADR are legitimate, socially desirable processes and may be beneficial in appropriate cases, questions remain over whether and how they fit within our traditional system of law. Over time, the institutionalization of ADR has proceeded in both the public and private spheres, and has raised many significant questions that we touch briefly here and that are explored more deeply in later chapters.

a. Institutionalization in the Courts

Courts have been an important venue of ADR institutionalization. Today, significant ADR initiatives can be found in most federal and state trial courts, and in all federal and many state appellate courts as well. *See* Robert J. Niemic, Mediation & Conference Programs in the Federal Courts of Appeals (1997); Elizabeth Plapinger & Donna Stienstra, ADR and Settlement in the Federal District Courts (1996). Most of these are mediation programs, which deal with a wide range of civil disputes, including family, employment, commercial, and environmental matters. Many criminal courts also work with victim-offender mediation programs that bring perpetrators of crimes together with their victims, or the survivors of victims, to discuss restitution and other matters. We give more focused attention to the issues raised by court-annexed ADR in Chapter VI, after our consideration of the major ADR processes in Chapters II-V.

Judicial support for modern ADR has been crucial since its earliest days. Indeed, the birth of modern ADR is commonly pegged at 1976, the date of the so-called "Pound Conference," which was organized by U.S. Supreme Court Chief Justice Warren Burger. The conference invoked a speech presented to the ABA by Harvard Law School Dean Roscoe Pound on August 29, 1906, entitled "The Causes of Popular Dissatisfaction with the Administration of Justice." The 1976 conference revisited such causes, as well as ways in which the justice system could be made more efficient and effective. Burger was an important early supporter of the ADR movement, and called for its support in his 1982 state of the judiciary report to Congress, excerpted below. Burger's report is followed by an excerpt from a speech that called for lawyers to consider alternative methods for resolving disputes, by Harvard Law Professor Frank E.A. Sander at the Pound Conference. It is widely credited as heralding the dawn of the ADR movement. In the final excerpt, Professor Judith Resnik articulates concerns about the institutionalization of ADR within public adjudication.

WARREN E. BURGER, ISN'T THERE A BETTER WAY?: ANNUAL REPORT ON THE STATE OF THE JUDICIARY

(Jan. 24, 1982).

The obligation of our profession is, or long has been thought to be, to serve as healers of human conflicts. To fulfill our traditional obligation means that we should provide mechanisms that can produce an acceptable result in the shortest possible time, with the least possible expense and with a minimum of stress on the participants. That is what justice is all about.

The law is a tool, not an end in itself. Like any tool, particular judicial mechanisms, procedures, or rules can become obsolete. Just as the carpenter's handsaw was replaced by the power saw and his hammer was replaced by the stapler, we should be alert to the need for better tools to serve our purposes.

Many thoughtful people, within and outside our profession, question whether that is being done today. They ask whether our profession is fulfilling its historical and traditional obligation of being healers of human conflicts. Although it may be too much to say that we lawyers are becoming part of the problem instead of the means to a solution, I confess there is more to support our critics than I would have thought 15 or 20 years ago.

Today I address the administration of justice in civil matters, which shares with criminal justice both delay and lack of finality. Even when an acceptable result is finally achieved in a civil case, that result is often drained of much of its value because of the time-lapse, the expense and the emotional stress inescapable in the litigation process.

Abraham Lincoln once said: "Discourage litigation. Persuade your neighbors to compromise whenever you can. Point out to them how the nominal winner is often the real loser — in fees, expenses, and waste of time." In the same vein, Judge Learned Hand commented: "I must say that, as a litigant, I should dread a lawsuit beyond almost anything else short of sickness and death."

I was trained, as many of you were, with a generation of lawyers taught that the best service a lawyer could render a client was to keep away from the courts. Obviously that generalization needs qualifying, for often the courts are the only avenue to justice. In our search for "better ways," we must never forget that.

Law schools have traditionally steeped the students in the adversary tradition rather than the skills of resolving conflicts. And various factors in the past 20–25 years have combined to depict today's lawyer in the role of a knight in shining armor, whose courtroom lance strikes down all obstacles. But the emphasis on that role can be carried too far. * * * The adversary process is expensive. It is time-consuming. It often leaves a trail of stress and frustration.

One reason our courts have become overburdened is that Americans are increasingly turning to the courts for relief from a range of personal distresses and anxieties. Remedies for personal wrongs that once were considered the responsibility of institutions other than the courts are now boldly asserted as legal "entitlements." The courts have been expected to fill the void created by the decline of church, family, and neighborhood unity.

* * *

We, as lawyers, know that litigation is not only stressful and frustrating, but expensive and frequently unrewarding for litigants. A personal injury case, for example, diverts the claimants and entire families from their normal pursuits. Physicians increasingly take note of "litigation neuroses" in otherwise normal, well-adjusted people. This negative impact is not confined to litigants and lawyers. Lay and professional witnesses, chiefly the doctors who testify, are also adversely affected. The plaintive cry of many frustrated litigants echoes what Learned Hand implied: "There must be a better way."

We must now use the inventiveness, the ingenuity and the resource-fulness that have long characterized the American business and legal community, to shape new tools. The paradox is that we already have some very good tools and techniques ready and waiting for imaginative lawyers to adapt them to current needs. We need to consider moving some cases from the adversary system to administrative processes, like workmen's compensation, or to mediation, conciliation, and especially arbitration. Divorce, child custody, adoptions, personal injury, landlord and tenant cases, and probate of estates are prime candidates.

* * *

FRANK E.A. SANDER, VARIETIES OF DISPUTE PROCESSING
70 F.R.D. 111, 112, 130–133 (1976).

[One] concern to which we ought to address ourselves here is how we might escape from the specter projected [of ever-burgeoning court dockets]. This might be accomplished in various ways. First, we can try to prevent disputes from arising in the first place through appropriate changes in the substantive law, such as the adoption of a no-fault principle for automobile injuries or the removal of a criminal sanction for certain conduct. A less obvious substantive law issue that may have a bearing on the extent of litigation that arises is whether we opt for a discretionary rule or for one that aims to fix more or less firmly the consequences that will follow upon certain facts. For example, if a statute says that marital property on divorce will be divided in the court's discretion there is likely to be far more litigation than if the rule is, as in the community property states, that such property will normally be divided 50–50.

* * *

Another method of minimizing disputes is through greater emphasis on preventive law. Of course lawyers have traditionally devoted a large part of their time to anticipating various eventualities and seeking, through skillful drafting and planning, to provide for them in advance. But so far this approach has been resorted to primarily by the well-to-do. I suspect that with the advent of prepaid legal services this type of practice will be utilized more widely, resulting in a probable diminution of litigation.

A second way of reducing the judicial caseload is to explore alternative ways of resolving disputes outside the courts, and it is to this topic that I wish to devote my primary attention. By and large we lawyers and law teachers have been far too single-minded when it comes to dispute resolution. Of course, as pointed out earlier, good lawyers have always tried to prevent disputes from coming about, but when that was not possible, we have tended to assume that the courts are the natural and obvious dispute resolvers. In point of fact there is a rich variety of different processes, which, I would submit, singly or in combination, may provide far more "effective" conflict resolution.

* * *

What I am thus advocating is a flexible and diverse panoply of dispute resolution processes, with particular types of cases being assigned to differing processes (or combinations of processes), according to [previously-mentioned criteria: nature of dispute; relationship between disputants; amount in dispute; cost; and speed.] Conceivably such allocation might be accomplished for a particular class of cases at the outset by the legislature; that in effect is what was done by the Massachusetts legislature for malpractice cases. Alternatively one might envision by the year 2000 not simply a court house but a Dispute Resolution Center, where the grievant would first be channeled through a screening clerk who would then direct him to the process (or sequence of processes) most appropriate to his type of case. The room directory in the lobby of such a Center might look as follows:

Screening Clerk	Room 1
Mediation	Room 2
Arbitration	Room 3
Fact Finding	Room 4
Malpractice Screening Panel	Room 5
Superior Court	Room 6
Ombudsman	Room 7

Of one thing we can be certain: once such an eclectic method of dispute resolution is accepted there will be ample opportunity for everyone to play a part. Thus a court might decide of its own to refer a certain type of problem to a more suitable tribunal. Or a legislature might, in framing certain substantive rights, build in an appropriate dispute resolution process. Institutions such as prisons, schools, or mental hospitals also could get into the act by establishing indigenous dispute resolution processes. Here the grievance mechanism contained in the typical collective bargaining agreement stands as an enduring example of a successful model. Finally, once these patterns begin to take hold, the law schools, too, should shift from their preoccupation with the judicial process and begin to expose students to the broad range of dispute resolution processes.

* * *

I would be less than candid if I were to leave this idyllic picture without at least brief reference to some of the substantial impediments to reform in this area. To begin with there is always the deadening drag of status quoism. But I have reference to more specific problems. First, particularly in the criminal field, cries of "denial of due process" will undoubtedly be heard if an informal mediational process is sought to be substituted for the strict protections of the adversary process. In response to this objection it must be asserted candidly that many thoughtful commentators appear agreed that we may have over-judicialized the system, with concomitant adverse effects on its efficiency as well as its accessibility to powerless litigants. This is not the place to explore that difficult issue, but we clearly need to address ourselves more fully to that question.

A related concern is * * * the need to retain the courts as the ultimate agency capable of effectively protecting the rights of the disadvantaged. This is a legitimate concern which I believe to be consistent with the goals I have advocated. I am not maintaining that cases asserting novel constitutional claims ought to be diverted to mediation or arbitration. On the contrary, the goal is to reserve the courts for those activities for which they are best suited and to avoid swamping and paralyzing them with cases that do not require their unique capabilities.

Finally, we are robbed of much-needed flexibility by the constitutional requirement of jury trial. For present purposes this normally means that cases initially referred to binding arbitration (or some other nonjudicial process) must have the consent of both parties or else that a de novo trial must be permitted. Obviously we can live with such restrictions and still achieve considerable constructive change, especially if, as in Pennsylvania, the price of the de novo appeal from arbitration is to require the appellant to assume the cost of the arbitration. But one is bound to wonder whether, as an original matter, the requirement of jury trial still makes sense in the run-of-the-mill civil case, particularly if one keeps in mind the attendant increase in cost and time. In view of the desperate state of some of our civil calendars, it seems to me that the burden of persuasion should shift to those who maintain that the high costs are justified by unique advantages afforded by jury trials. Here again we must try to shun the endless abstract discussions of pros and cons, and seek instead to explore whether there are specific types of cases in which juries make more or less sense, so that we might opt ultimately for a constitutional amendment that would give greater flexibility to the legislature on this question.

* * *

Notes and Questions

1.   Professor Sander's idea of a Dispute Resolution Center has come to be known as the "multi-door courthouse." *See e.g.*, Jethro K. Lieberman & James F. Henry, *Lessons From the Alternative Dispute Resolution Movement*, 53 U. Chi. L. Rev. 424, 427 n.17 (1986). While the idea is attractive, few true multi-door courthouses have actually been established. Why do you suppose this is so? What barriers do you see to the creation of multi-door courthouses? How might they be overcome? For a discussion, see Gladys Kessler & Linda J. Finkelstein, *The Evolution of a Multi–Door Courthouse*, 37 Cath. U. L. Rev. 577 (1988); Jeffrey W. Stempel, *Reflections on Judicial ADR and the Multi–Door Courthouse at Twenty: Fait Accompli, Failed Overture, or Fledgling Adulthood?*, 11 Ohio St. J. on Disp. Resol. 297 (1996).

2.   Chief Justice Burger and Professor Sander pointed to a "litigation explosion" as one reason for turning to alternative dispute resolution processes. Dean Robel said that recent years "have seen a renewal of the claim that the federal courts are in a caseload crisis." Lauren K. Robel, Private *Justice and the Federal Bench*, 68 Ind. L.J. 891, 893 (1993). Indeed, this belief or perception has animated much of the contemporary tort reform debate. *See* Arthur R. Miller, *The Pretrial Rush to Judgment: Are The "Litigation Explosion," "Liability Crisis," and Efficiency Cliches Eroding Our Day in Court And Jury Trial Commitments?*, 78 N.Y.U. L. Rev. 982 (2003). Professor Marc Galanter challenged the idea that there is too much litigation in America, making empirical arguments that such formalization of disputes is relatively uncommon. Marc S. Galanter, *Reading the Landscape of Disputes: What We Know and Don't Know (and Think We Know) About Our Allegedly Contentious and Litigious Society,* 31 UCLA L. Rev. 4 (1983). Galanter's conclusions were challenged in several works. *See* RICHARD POSNER, THE FEDERAL COURTS: CRISIS AND REFORM 76–77 (1985); Kenyon P. Bunch & Richard J. Hardy, *A Re-examination of Litigation Trends In the United States: Galanter Reconsidered,* 1986 J. Disp. Resol. 87, 90–98. Professor Galanter renewed his defense of the civil justice system in Marc Galanter, *News from Nowhere: The Debased Debate on Civil Justice*, 71 Denv. U. L. Rev. 77 (1993). Bolstering Galanter's position, Professor Paul Carrington later observed that complaints about cost, delay, and the excessive use of litigation to solve problems are "seldom accompanied by empirical data." Paul D. Carrington, *A New Confederacy? Disunionism in the Federal Courts,* 45 Duke L.J. 929, 957 (1996).

3.   Professor Albert Alschuler suggested that "[t]he crisis in our courts that observers decry may be the product of an inadequate supply of adjudication rather than of the excessive litigiousness of our society." Albert W. Alschuler, *Mediation with a Mugger: The Shortage of Adjudicative Services and the Need for a Two–Tier Trial System in Civil Cases,* 99 Harv. L. Rev. 1808, 1818 (1986). He proposed a "two-tier" system of civil trials, which could make adjudication more accessible and also would encourage settlement. He criticized Judge Posner's argument that the current government subsidization of private litigation is too great, with the following.

> To assert that justice must be rationed by queue unless it is rationed by price is erroneous. Although the government has priced emergency firefighting services substantially below cost, these services

have not been rationed by queue to any great extent. People might be surprised to find this situation changed: "Thank you for calling 911. If your house is still burning in April 1987, a fire engine will come." Apart from the fact that they gradually have gotten used to it, Americans also might be shocked to discover that justice has been rationed both by price and by queue to the extent that it often is effectively unavailable.

In summary, the subsidization of private litigation can have at least three valuable consequences. It can create precedents that aid the settlement of disputes (an interest recognized by Judge Posner); it can discourage wrongful primary conduct (an interest neglected by Posner but recognized by Professor Shavell); and it can discourage violent self-help (an interest neglected by Posner and Shavell but recognized by John Locke). No list of consequences, however, can capture fully the reasons for the public provision of adjudication. In the end, some rights are sensed as rights, not merely as economically efficient arrangements. That rights imply remedies is not a fresh or transient idea. When adjudication is unavailable, a lumberjack may respond to an invasion of his rights with his fists. Nevertheless, society's obligation to provide adjudication to an elderly invalid who cannot fight is as strong as or stronger than its obligation to provide adjudication to a lumberjack. The provision of adjudication is the means by which society keeps the promises of its substantive law and assures both lumberjacks and invalids that their rights are taken seriously.

Id. at 1816.

* * *

JUDITH RESNIK, MANY DOORS? CLOSING DOORS? ALTERNATIVE DISPUTE RESOLUTION AND ADJUDICATION

10 Ohio St. J. on Disp. Resol. 211, 212, 216–18, 241–58, 261–65 (1995).

I turn back less than two decades, to 1976 and the Pound Conference, a meeting of some 250 judges, lawyers, court administrators, law professors, and non-lawyers at which Professor Frank Sander called for a "multi-doored" courthouse. Reviewing his published comments is useful, for what was written not yet twenty years ago seems like it was aimed at a group of people removed from us by many more than two decades.

Professor Sander took as his burden the need to explain the "significant characteristics of various alternative dispute resolution mechanisms." He assumed his readership's familiarity with adjudication; his task was to educate his readers on what else there was and then to persuade his readers of the desirability and utility of those "alternative dispute resolution forms." His purpose was to suggest "promising avenues to explore."

Professor Sander's key move was to focus the discussion not on substantive areas (i.e., should tax cases go to a specialized court?) but rather on *process*. He urged that across a wide variety of disputes, the process should be elaborated, and a mediation, conciliation, or alternative phase be *incorporated* into it. Professor Sander pointed to some experiments with these processes, labeled "alternative dispute resolution," as evidence of the plausibility of his proposals.

Pause to consider the metaphor that has come to encapsulate his ideas: a "multi-doored courthouse." The image has a good deal of appeal, stemming in part from its implicit reliance on the phrase "access to justice" to posit a structure with several doors of entry. In his reprinted speech, Frank Sander actually described a "lobby" in which a litigant could be "channelled through a screening clerk" to one of six doors, comprising "a diverse panoply of dispute resolution processes." Specifically, one might be sent to "mediation, arbitration, fact finding, malpractice screening panel, superior court," or an ombudsperson.

While "flexible," this model also assumed something presumably stable: the courthouse was a known, readily conjured-up entity. In fact, one of the doors in the Sander lobby was to something called the "superior court." Moreover, one of Professor Sander's goals was to "reserve the courts for those activities for which they are best suited and to avoid swamping and paralyzing them with cases that do not require their unique abilities." Whatever the number of doors, the call was for access to and preservation of the courthouse.

It is fair to say that, within a very short time period (less than two decades), Frank Sander's call has been heard. It is worth mapping that shift, from disinterest and some hostility toward ADR to the embrace of it as a mode of responding to disputes.

* * *

Two descriptions of ADR and adjudication can be identified, both assuming compatibility but for different reasons. Under one vision, ADR and adjudication are distinct and complementary; one supplements the other. Under the other, the two forms are more similar than distinct. ADR is sufficiently close to adjudication that the two are compatible.

I think that the claim of supplementation will not be long lasting and that the claim of similarity is more complex than usually stated. ADR functions less as a court's adjunct than as a competitor. My point here is not primarily turf, about private litigants with resources purchasing adjudication from sources other than the state. While federal and state judges perhaps should worry that they may lose in the competition for the "good" cases, these judges (and others) should also attend to the competition about and among values. ADR — and especially the embrace of settlement — is both a product of and the means by which adjudication is both reframed and devalued in this political system.

Despite a friendly facade, implicit in many of the claims for ADR as "better" is a deeply-held criticism of the contemporary version of adjudication: that the outcomes produced are too expensive, too time consuming, not close enough to the merits, not responsive to parties' interests, not (in sum) "worth it." The descriptive arguments on behalf of ADR make a normative claim about adjudication. One can track the relationship between the growth in interest in ADR and changes in adjudication as it has been conceived under the framework of the 1938 Federal Rules of Civil Procedure: the diminution of interest in adjudication's rights pronouncement and its capacity for fact finding and the pressures to transform adjudication, causing a melding of adjudication and ADR, sometimes into a simplified adjudication and sometimes into a settlement-oriented set of managerial procedures.

Having posited this relationship, I should also respond to questions about the links I have drawn between contemporary promotion of ADR and the frustration with and hostility to adjudication. One set of issues relates to causation, which (as I stated at the outset) is not my enterprise here. Instead, I am interested in the interaction of two generic modes of dispute resolution, one styled "adjudication" and one styled "alternative dispute resolution" — even as we know that both are constructs, with internal distinctions, a variety of expressions, and a good deal of overlap. Thus, the next question I need to explore is whether hostility to adjudication is *intrinsic* in the institutionalization at the end of the twentieth century of ADR by the state.

Several comments are in order. First, ADR proponents sought to embed ADR into the state's processes. In their advocacy, many expressly denigrated adjudicatory processes. It is possible that, had ADR proponents not gone that route, not attempted to make ADR a part of the state's justice apparatus but had sought instead only that the state recognize the validity of extra-judicial ADR, that the aggression toward adjudication might have been damped down; perhaps coexistence might then have resulted. One cannot tell how an unfettered market would have valued the two forms of dispute resolution because regulation has intervened to mandate that the state provide and litigants use ADR.

Second, ADR is by no means the only source of criticism about adjudication in general and its regulatory aspects in particular. The last two decades have witnessed a rise in anti-lawyer, anti-regulatory, anti-government rhetoric and sentiments. Had ADR emerged at a time when lawyers were not perceived as economically greedy, when the policy was celebrating governmental regulation, and when public and private officials lauded adjudication as the vehicle by which to police that regulation, the attitude toward ADR would likely have been different. What has occurred has taken place in the context of distrust of government and promotion of privatization. ADR has become linked to the general hostility to government decision making, and adjudication has been linked with the disdained regime of government as regulator.

Third, perhaps the negativity around adjudication could have been either submerged or unsuccessful, had adjudication proponents been themselves more visible and vocal. Intriguingly, many within the federal judiciary are participating in the ADR movement without having shaped the conversation to preserve much interest in the activities unique to judges. It is hard to find discussion of the value of elements attributed to adjudication: its attention paid to the individual instance, its effort to announce, explain, and generate public norms, its slowness, its labor intensive and messy activity of attempting to reconstruct events so as to attach the label "fact" from whence "law" and "judgment" can flow. Indeed, visible examples of rights announcement — in the context of school desegregation, criminal defendants' rights, and abortion — have been held up by some as exemplars of how adjudication fails.

I believe we are approaching a time when many a civil trial will be characterized as a "pathological event." One possibility is that this development is to be welcomed as an appropriate correction to what John Langbein calls the "too trial-centered" Anglo–American tradition. From this perspective, one must recall that a strong source of pressure for ADR comes from the judiciary. Judicial endorsement of ADR is a demonstration from individuals with firsthand knowledge of the weakness of adjudication, its failures and limitations. To the extent judicial support of ADR affects our understanding of the value of adjudication, judges may wisely be participating in a societal shove that will result in the demise of civil adjudication as it is currently understood. Further, the decline of civil adjudication — in law courts — and its shift to governmental agencies, claims facilities, and private dispute resolution centers may be the appropriate denouement of this cycle of procedural reform.

Alternatively, anxiety about the triumph of ADR can come from across the spectrum, from those perceived to be proponents of ADR as well as from those styled proponents of adjudication. Proponents of ADR have succeeded in making it "an integral part of our federal judicial system." In the process, they have helped to change both "our federal judicial system" and ADR.

For those who envisioned ADR as the blossoming of something different and generative, they should worry (as scholars such as Carrie Menkel–Meadow and Lucy Katz do) about its institutionalization and its transformation into the very adversarial processes that they had hoped to avoid. As courts make ADR their own, that formalization may well undermine the very attributes of ADR that prompted its praise. Further, as courts compel ADR, the relationship between ADR and volition weakens, pushing it ever closer to a state-imposed mode of resolution. On the other hand, when ADR mimes adjudication, the critique of ADR as a lawless or factless process loses strength.

Similarly, those who think adjudication has something to offer had better start explaining why one would aspire to a preserve for adjudication, and why relatively highly paid government officials (to wit federal and state judges) should be empowered to do some of it. If there is an important and affirmative — if not a cheerful — story to be told for the preservation of adjudicatory forms, with judges in distinctive roles, and why a culture would value, cherish, fund, encourage, and sometimes insist on adjudication, then those who believe so had better speak up soon, for it is becoming increasingly hard to hear those claims.

A vivid example of this problem is provided by turning to the work of one prominent adjudication advocate, Professor Albert Alschuler. In his essay, "Mediation with a Mugger," he examined the justifications for public subsidies for civil adjudication, concluded that the task of "[i]mpartial adjudication" was a central one for government to undertake, and worried about the "shortage of adjudicative services." He urged that adjudication be remodeled, to respond to problems of procedural complexity and the capacity of litigants to inflict wasteful costs on each other. His preferred solutions all seek "a simplified form of adjudication" — that would include the possibility of impartial factfinding. His preference is for "first instance" and "second instance" trials, scaled back in an effort to distribute adjudicatory services. When one reads the details of Alschuler's proposal, it sounds quite like court-annexed arbitration, albeit sometimes with public access.

But court-annexed arbitration, which could be described as scaled down adjudication, may also become vulnerable to the criticisms that animate its installation. Many of the rhetorical claims made on behalf of ADR may prompt policy makers to create settlement mechanisms rather than procedures that closely resemble adjudication. The emphasis placed on the quality of information possessed by the parties and on the cost and inefficiencies of transferring that information to a third party decision maker puts pressure on court-annexed arbitration, which could well be called "short trials." Moreover, empirical research has raised questions about whether court-annexed arbitration saves time or money. Robert MacCoun's study of court-annexed arbitration in New Jersey found that neither public costs were saved nor time to disposition shortened in the arbitration program. While court-annexed arbitration may be cheaper and quicker than trial, few cases in fact go to trial, and court-annexed arbitration is slower and more expensive than settlement. In short, the barrage of anti-adjudication claims in the promotion of state-run and state-mandated ADR may hit court-annexed arbitration as well. The interaction may well cause the ADR spectrum to narrow as well, because the ideological claims increasingly point toward settlement as *the* desired mode of dispute resolution.

As this century draws to its end, we can observe the melding of ADR into adjudication, and then the narrowing of ADR and its refocusing as a tool to produce contractual agreements among disputants. The focus is shifting from adjudication to resolution. Frank Sander's lovely image of the accessible, multi-doored courthouse — with one door wide open for adjudication — has now been eclipsed. The door to the twentieth century's version of adjudication is closing.

Notes and Questions

1.   Professor Resnik has long been an astute and sympathetic commentator on adjudication. *See, e.g.*, Judith Resnik, *For Owen M. Fiss, Reflections on the Triumph and Death of Adjudication*, 58 U. Miami L. Rev. 173 (2003); Judith Resnik, *Managerial Judges*, 96 Harv. L. Rev. 374 (1982); Judith

Resnik, *Procedural Innovations, Sloshing Over: A Comment on Deborah Hensler, A Glass Half Full, A Glass Half Empty: The Use of Alternative Dispute Resolution In Mass Personal Injury Litigation,* 73 Tex. L. Rev. 1627 (1995). She expressed the following concerns in a 1986 article:

> [T]he adjudicatory mode offers some theory of its own limits, of what counts as permissible and impermissible adjudication. The 'alternatives' to it have yet to articulate how we might assess the legitimacy of the outcomes rendered. Speed and superficial lack of expenses are, in themselves, incomplete answers.

Judith Resnik, *Failing Faith: Adjudicatory Procedure in Decline,* 53 U. Chi. L. Rev. 494, 546 (1986).

> Can we develop some process in between settlement and adjudication and describe the appropriate arena within it for judges? Or would (and does) the involvement of judges in anything less than adjudication diminish the legitimacy of adjudication and reduce the utility of settlement?

Id. at 553.

2.   Why are so many judges ADR advocates? Why might other judges remain skeptical? What does the great debate over ADR tell us about contemporary opinions of adjudication?

3.   Which of the claims on behalf of ADR do you find most and least persuasive?

4.   Why might some ADR proponents want to reduce the role of attorneys in dispute resolution?

5.   Recent empirical studies indicate that the percentage of trials decreased significantly in the second half of the twentieth century. A 2004 study by Marc Galanter has received a great deal of attention in particular, finding that between 1962 and 2002, dispositions by trial courts increased by factor of five — from 50,320 to 258,876 cases — but the number of actual civil trials dropped by more than 20%, from 5,802 in 1962 to 4,569 in 2002. Therefore, the portion of dispositions that were by trial in 2002 was less than one-sixth of what it was in 1962 — 1.8% in 2002 as opposed to 11.5% in 1962. Galanter further found:

> The drop in trials has been recent and steep. In the early part of our period, there was an increase in federal trials, peaking in 1985, when there were 12,529. From then to now, the number of trials in federal court has dropped by more than 60 percent and the portion of cases disposed of by trial has fallen from 4.7 percent to 1.8 percent.

> A substantial portion of the cases that reach the trial stage terminate before the trial is completed. In 1988 some 24 percent of all cases reaching trial were disposed of "during" trial — 28 percent of jury trials and 19 percent of bench trials. By 2002, when the number of cases reaching the trial stage dropped by 60 percent, the percentage disposed of "during" trial fell to 18 percent, with little difference between jury and bench trials. As fewer cases managed to survive until the trial stage, those that began a jury trial were more resistant to being deflected from pursuing the trial through to its conclusion.

Marc Galanter, *The Vanishing Trial: An Examination of Trials and Related Matters in State and Federal Courts,* 1 J. Empirical Leg. Stud. 459, 461 (2004).

Galanter has described the phenomenon as "the vanishing trial." His research has spawned much discussion in professional practice and scholarly communities. *See, e.g.,* Symposium, *The Vanishing Trial,* 1 J. Empirical Leg. Stud. v (2004); Symposium, *ADR and the Vanishing Trial,* Disp. Resol. Mag., Summer 2004, at 3. Galanter suggests the decline may be attributed to fewer complaints making it to trial, trial costs and complexity, and the diversion of cases to other venues, such as ADR. Do you see this as a positive or negative development? What systemic responses, if any, might be appropriate?

b. Institutionalization in Administrative Agencies

Alternative dispute resolution has become commonplace in federal and state agencies for a wide variety of disputes, ranging from disputes over internal employment and procurement matters to administrative rulemaking on public policy issues delegated to agencies by the legislature.

The federal government has seen increasing growth in the use of ADR. As Jeffrey M. Senger, senior counsel in the Office of Dispute Resolution at the U.S. Department of Justice, has observed:

> At the Justice Department, for example, parties used ADR in five hundred cases in 1995. Seven years later, however, ADR has grown to close to three thousand cases. The Equal Employment Opportunity Commission (EEOC) now uses mediation in about five thousand workplace cases annually, and the U.S. Postal Service mediates twice as many each year. The Environmental Protection Agency has eight full-time ADR staff members and pays private mediators millions of dollars in mediator fees each year. All told, more than four hundred people work now on ADR full time in the federal government, and agency ADR programs are funded by more than $36 million in dedicated budgets. The government's total commitment to ADR is even higher than these figures. Many agencies operate programs that are funded from other budgetary sources and staffed by employees who have part-time ADR responsibilities in addition to other duties.

Jeffrey M. Senger, Federal Dispute Resolution: Using ADR with the United States Government 2 (2004).

Notes

1. Senger estimates that administrative agencies have achieved significant time savings through the use of ADR.

> Federal administrative equal employment opportunity (EEO) complaints rose by more than 50 percent over a recent eight-year period. Over about the past ten years, agency EEO case backlogs have doubled, hearing backlogs at the EEOC have tripled, and appellate backlogs have increased sevenfold.

ADR reduces these delays by sidestepping the adjudicative process and its backlogs. For example, in workplace cases involving the Office of Special Counsel, ADR resolved complaints in an average of 115 days, while traditional adjudicatory process required an average of 465 days. In disputes with the Federal Aviation Administration, parties using ADR resolved bid protests in an average of 25 days, while those seeking a final agency decision typically waited 61 days.

Id. at 3–4

2. Senger further estimates ADR has also saved the federal government a substantial amount of money. He notes:

Estimates of the administrative costs for processing an EEO case range from $5,000 for an informal dispute up to $77,000 for a formal dispute that goes all of the way through to an appeal. * * * Justice Department attorneys estimated that ADR saved an average of $10,700 in litigation expenses in each case. The Office of Special Counsel estimated an average cost of $1,000 to process a case where ADR is used, compared with an average cost of $10,500 for a case that does not go to ADR. The U.S. Air Force examined travel and staff costs for base engineers, inspectors, contracting officers, pricers, auditors, and experts, and determined that ADR saved $40,000 per case for contract cases involving less than $1 million and $250,000 for cases over $1 million.

Id. at 4–5.

3. The U.S. Postal Service is widely held out as an example of the capacity of ADR to improve relationships within an agency. In 1998, the agency implemented a mediation program, REDRESS (Resolve Employment Disputes Reach Equitable Solutions Swiftly), to help managers and employees better understand each other. In the program's first year, formal complaints dropped by twenty-four percent from the preceding year. They dropped another twenty percent the following year. *See* FED. INTERAGENCY WORKING GROUP, REPORT TO THE PRESIDENT (MAY 8, 2000). For further discussion of the REDRESS program, see Chapter VI, beginning at page 741.

4. Administrative dispute resolution programs have been successful, yet the federal government continues to spend millions of dollars every year on traditional litigation and related formal processes. Why might a government agency be reluctant to use ADR processes? *See* JEFFREY M. SENGER, FEDERAL DISPUTE RESOLUTION: USING ADR WITH THE UNITED STATES GOVERNMENT 9–10 (2004).

5. All major branches of the U.S. military have instituted extensive ADR programs to deal with personnel, procurement, and other issues. The U.S. Air Force's program in particular has been singled out several times for national dispute resolution awards and honors. For more on the program, see its web site, http://www.adr.af.mil.

6. While states lag behind the federal government with respect to the use of administrative dispute resolution, there is still a considerable amount of activity. For an overview, see POL'Y CONSENSUS INST., GOVERNING TOOLS FOR THE 21ST CENTURY: HOW STATE LEADERS ARE USING COLLABORATIVE PROBLEM SOLVING AND DISPUTE RESOLUTION (2002).

7. These and other related administrative developments are discussed further in Chapter VI, beginning at page 731.

c. Institutionalization in the Private Sphere

The government has only been one vehicle of ADR's institutionalization. The private sector has also been an important focus of ADR institutionalization. Many businesses have incorporated alternative methods of dispute resolution into their workplace management systems, as well as their procedures for dealing with other types of disputes. The fundamental premise of this vehicle of institutionalization is contract — that is, parties privately agree to use ADR methods to resolve their differences, rather than turning to courts. The excerpt by former professor Thomas Stipanowich, now president of the CPR Institute for Dispute Resolution, highlights the enormous potential of private ordering through contract, but also hints at limits on this aspect of contractual freedom. In the following passage, Professor Reuben, echoing some of Resnik's concerns, argues that the line between public and private dispute resolution isn't always so clear, thus raising the important and pervasive question about the proper relationship between dispute resolution and law.

* * *

THOMAS J. STIPANOWICH, CONTRACT AND CONFLICT MANAGEMENT

2001 Wis. L. Rev. 831, 831–838.

We live in the era of the made-to-order issue resolution clause. A quarter century after Macaulay, Macneil, and others first explored systems of governance for contractual relationships, bargains have plumbed the breadth and depth of that universe. Agreements to arbitrate future disputes are broadly enforceable under federal and state statutes; a series of U.S. Supreme Court decisions have transformed the Federal Arbitration Act (FAA) into a source of burgeoning substantive arbitration law that preempts state initiatives aimed at restricting the enforceability of agreements to arbitrate. A quiet revolution in court and agency "ADR" — alternative or "appropriate" dispute resolution — has given official imprimatur to mediation, early neutral evaluation and other conflict resolution approaches and stimulated their use in the realm of private transactions. Taken together, these events are reshaping the way many people think about managing and resolving disputes.

As contract planners, lawyers do not simply respond to conflict; they have the opportunity to limit or manage problems prospectively through negotiation and drafting. They may tackle prospective conflict at its roots by encouraging clear and concise contract language, realistic risk assessment and allocation, and suitable issue and conflict resolution mechanisms for contractual relationships. For many businesses, for example, tailoring of dispute resolution approaches most appropriate to resolving particular issues "is an integral part of corporate policy" and an important measure for achieving corporate objectives. These include: saving time and money, adapting a problem solving approach to fit the problem and thereby assuring control and reducing uncertainty and risk, maintaining privacy and confidentiality, and preserving business relationships. In some cases, carefully crafted approaches may serve even higher values for individuals. In light of the great flexibility parties enjoy in adapting ADR approaches to their specific goals, there is considerable room for creativity in planning the process.

Much time and energy is now devoted to the design and implementation of multi-step contract-based conflict management programs to resolve disputes effectively, early, and informally, with relatively minor diversion of financial and human resources. Today, garden-variety arrangements for binding arbitration are increasingly joined by more exotic specimens reflecting the imaginativeness of the drafters and the need to fit procedures to specific needs, ends and contingencies. These include specialized variants (such as "Biblically based mediation"), complex mechanisms to "filter" disputes through a progression of discrete ADR processes, often culminating in binding arbitration, and even judgments by public "spectacle" in the form of a televised courtroom.

The spectrum will soon encompass a full range of "virtual" options made possible by the current revolution in information technology. A harbinger of these developments is SquareTrade's innovative multi-step voluntary dispute resolution process for parties to transactions on the E–Bay web site. In a little over a year, the online program for negotiation and mediation of buyer/seller disputes handled more than 20,000 cases involving parties from eighty countries.

Because each of these schemes is a creature of contract, its essential character and legal ramifications depend upon the expressed, implied, or presumed intent of the parties. Sometimes the latter convey their procedural intentions with great specificity; at other times they make do with the sketchiest of integrations. Well-counseled parties may make the most of the opportunity to craft their own dispute resolution procedure, weaving their way between the Scylla of ambiguity and the Charybdis of too-tight drafting.

* * *

* * * An important subtext of the discussion is the abiding tension between the need for judicial intervention and the desire for party autonomy implicit in private conflict resolution provisions. Indeed, from the flourishing of international merchant fairs, to the dawn of chancery jurisdiction, and to the present day, a recurring theme in the history of Anglo–American conflict resolution is the search for alternatives to the formalities and perceived limitations of traditional court adjudication. The norms of public law and procedural due process often give way to other priorities in bargaining; going to court is often precisely what parties are trying to avoid. Mindful of these realities, modern courts tend to afford wide berth to private conflict management arrangements.

That said, we must carve out for special treatment the growing universe of agreements that implicate significant disparities in bargaining power, including the power of information. Highly publicized cases such as a computer purchase contract which required consumers to arbitrate under the rules and fee structure of the Paris-based International Chamber of Commerce (ICC), and an HMO's in-house arbitration program that entailed more than two years of delay of a malpractice claim have drawn public attention to the abuses that can occur in private dispute resolution programs. It is fair to say that consumers, employees, and others may benefit from meaningful access to prompt, inexpensive, and effective out-of-court dispute resolution. On the other hand, non-dickered boilerplate making general reference to an arcane set of dispute resolution procedures may produce an unwelcome surprise to non-drafting parties, particularly where a clause purports to substitute binding arbitration for the right to go to court. Such concerns have spurred action or calls for action on many levels: policing by industry, association, or quasi-public groups or associations, legislative action, judicial oversight, or agency regulation.

* * *

RICHARD C. REUBEN, CONSTITUTIONAL GRAVITY: A UNITARY THEORY OF ALTERNATIVE DISPUTE RESOLUTION AND PUBLIC CIVIL JUSTICE

47 UCLA L. Rev. 949, 952–960 (2000).

Many have come to view ADR as "privatized justice," the devolution of public power to private authority that is a byproduct of the downsizing of government at the close of the twentieth century. This bipolar approach is the dominant view of courts, practitioners, and legal scholars. Under this view, disputants choose between public and private systems of dispute resolution, prompting some legal scholars to suggest that the advent of modern ADR has led to a "process pluralism" of dispute resolution choices for disputants. This is, of course, a positive development in light of the continuing popular dissatisfaction with the public justice system that has provided the basis for the ADR movement itself.

But it also raises serious questions, such as whether any constitutional procedural safeguards follow the dispute to the alternative hearing. Under the bipolar approach, the answer is "no"; the hearings are strictly private. But does that mean that the parties have no enforceable due process rights whatsoever in that hearing, such as the right to an impartial adjudicator, the right to present their side of the story, or the right to counsel?

The mere asking of such questions suggests a dark side to ADR, and one with all-too-human faces: a group of waitresses who were told that their sexual harassment claims had to be arbitrated before a panel selected by their employer, in a private rather than a public proceeding, and without compensatory or punitive damages available as remedies; a businessman who lost his business and his life's savings when a retired judge, brought in to mediate a minor partnership dispute, instead ordered the distribution of all partnership assets; a Utah housewife who, just moments before being wheeled into serious knee surgery, was told that she must sign a mandatory arbitration agreement in order to proceed with the operation.

In a recent article, I began to suggest a different understanding that may be far more consistent with the nuanced sophistication of modern ADR than the current bipolar model allows — a unitary theory of public justice that is predicated upon the recognition that a significant portion of the modern ADR movement is built upon the foundation of state action. That is, after analyzing the history of ADR, the state and federal statutory systems under which it primarily operates, and the U.S. Supreme Court's state action doctrine, I suggested that much of modern ADR may not be private at all, but rather may be public in nature and therefore subject to constitutional constraints, particularly due process, at least at some level. ADR programs that are operated by federal and state courts or administrative agencies provide the best example of seemingly private ADR that is more properly characterized as public dispute resolution — a particularly important realization considering Congress's massive 1998 expansion of ADR to every federal district court, the Clinton administration's equally extensive expansion of ADR in federal administrative agencies, and the significant push to expand the use of ADR in state administrative agencies. A strong, but more controversial, argument can also be made that contractual arbitration is also driven by state action.

The reasoning of that article is relatively straightforward and may be easily summarized. The many state and federal statutes, executive orders, and court rules that by necessity have provided the basic architecture for the modern movement have done so by establishing a structure in which public and private actors participate jointly in furthering the goal of binding dispute resolution. Public courts are actively involved in the administration, oversight, and execution of such processes in governmental ADR programs, often compelling or strongly encouraging parties into those programs, often using private neutrals to implement the programs, and often adopting the results of those ADR processes as their own legally binding judgments. The involvement of public courts is similarly woven into the fabric of the many federal and state contractual arbitration statutes that overturned the courts' historic refusal to enforce agreements to arbitrate. In such situations, state action would appear to be present under current doctrine, obliging compliance with constitutional safeguards for personal and property rights, at least at some level. Given the pivotal role that public courts and constitutional values play in the exercise of constitutional democracy, such an understanding may be essential to the facilitation of public confidence in the rule of law as a public institution that political scientists increasingly are recognizing as critical to the deepening and consolidation of constitutional democracies.

In sharp contrast with the bipolar approach to binding dispute resolution, then, recognizing state action in seemingly private ADR processes lays the foundation for an expanded notion of public civil justice — that is, dispute resolution that is administered and enforced by and through the public courts — rather than for its contraction through privatization. This foundation gives rise to a unitary theory of ADR and public civil justice, which recognizes that the rise of the ADR movement at the end of the twentieth century has created, perhaps inadvertently, a unified system of public civil justice in which trial, arbitration, mediation, evaluative techniques, and other forms of ADR all operate toward the single end of binding public civil dispute resolution. In this view, trial is but one end of a spectrum of public civil dispute resolution, rather than the exclusive method. The Constitution, after all, certainly permits other forms of binding dispute resolution; as long as constitutional values are respected, the type of dispute resolution process can be flexible. However, the fact that procedures must comply with due process when energized by state action establishes the unitary character of binding public civil dispute resolution.

* * *

[Constitutional due process must] . . . be incorporated into seemingly private ADR in a minimal but meaningful way that both preserves and enhances those processes, while remaining faithful to the core values of the Constitution. [It may be accomplished] by squaring the unique characteristics and of the various ADR processes with those values paying particular attention to the role being played by the neutral or the government actor in light of the state action doctrine. For arbitration, these minimal but meaningful standards include the right to a neutral forum, the right to present and confront evidence, and a qualified right to counsel. For mediation, they include the right to a neutral forum and a qualified right to counsel. For advisory evaluative and fact-finding processes, they are limited to a qualified right to counsel.

Under such an approach, the incorporation of such constitutional minimums would not disturb the settled law that governs these processes or interfere with their operation. To the contrary, these constitutional minimums are, for the most part, consistent with the best practices of ADR processes and enhance the value of these ADR programs by recognizing fundamental constitutional standards, beyond mere contractual norms, that may be vindicated in the context of specific and exceptional cases. The recognition of such a modest constitutional dimension can mitigate the need for greater governmental regulation of ADR that is currently being felt at the state and national levels and instead bring new and creative energy to our concept of public justice for this new millennium.

Notes and Questions

1. Professor Stipanowich paints a broad, exciting, and optimistic picture of private ADR as a function of contractual freedom. He acknowledges the need for the law to provide some constraints, however, such as in the consumer and employment contexts, where there can be significant disparities in bargaining power. However, Stipanowich stops short of saying just how the law should provide this constraint. Professor Reuben's excerpt, animated by similar concerns, picks up that gauntlet and suggests that constitutional due process norms provide a limiting force. What are the implications of Reuben's analysis for ADR processes? Would engrafting constitutional norms into seemingly private ADR processes destroy the virtues of those processes?

2. The Stipanowich and Reuben excerpts crystallize the question of the relationship between ADR and the law. Some ADR advocates think of these processes as ones that are wholly removed from the reach of the law, especially when the path into dispute resolution is through private contract. However, that plainly is not the case. All contracts are subject to judicial review and potential invalidation. Moreover, as the materials in the following chapters illustrate, all of these processes are subject to and/or influenced by other positive law that may affect the dispute. Even private negotiations are said to operate in the "shadow of the law," meaning that parties are assessing the desirability of their negotiated settlements against the possible outcomes before a court. Robert H. Mnookin & Lewis Kornhauser, *Bargaining in the Shadow of the Law: The Case of Divorce,* 88 Yale L.J. 950, 968–69 (1979). What other legal constraints might influence purely private negotiations? For further discussion, see Chapter III, beginning at page 233.

3. Sometimes the law operates in a way that is consistent with the fundamental principles of a given dispute resolution mechanism. For example, traditional rules of contract regarding the substance and content of contractual agreements, such as the law barring enforcement of contracts that are unconscionable, seem consistent with the notion of private ordering that lies at the heart of ADR. But are there other limits to this private power to contract? For example, consider the ramifications, discussed in Chapter V, beginning at page 582, of an adhesion contract that includes a dispute resolution provision, such as a provision in an employment contract requiring the arbitration of disputes arising under the contract. What are the arguments for and against the enforceability of such provisions? Should enforceability depend upon on the specific terms of the provision? For example, should arbitration provisions be enforced when they are too one sided, such as by limiting discovery, witnesses, or remedies? How should a court determine how much is too much?

4. Sometimes the law operates in a way that is at odds with the principles of a dispute resolution process. For example, confidentiality in mediation is often held out as the cornerstone of the process — and indeed part of the role of the mediator is to get parties to disclose information about their interests, aspirations, and concerns that they may be reluctant to disclose in a court of law. *See, e.g.,* Sarah R. Cole, Craig E. McEwen, & Nancy H. Rogers, Mediation: Law, Policy, Practice §§ 9:1, 9:2 (2d ed. 2001). But this process principle seems fundamentally inconsistent with the well-established

principle of evidence that every person is entitled to relevant evidence that will help prove their case in a court of law. Which principle should prevail when a party seeks to introduce evidence of statements made during an allegedly "confidential" alternative dispute resolution proceeding? On what factors should such a decision be made? For more discussion about mediation confidentiality, see Chapter IV, beginning at page 439.

3. CHOOSING A PROCESS

In selecting a dispute resolution process, careful consideration should be given to the nature and characteristics of the dispute at issue, as well as the unique needs, interests, and concerns of the client. The following excerpts offer three different perspectives on the question. In the first, Bernard Mayer suggests that the parties must reach resolution on three dimensions — behavioral, cognitive, and emotional — in order to fully resolve the dispute. Professors Robert Cochran, John DiPippa, and Martha Peters then describe several factors that lawyers should consider when assessing a client's goals with respect to the choice of a dispute resolution process. Finally, William Ury, Jeanne Brett, and Stephen Goldberg apply similar principles to the design of conflict management systems for businesses and other institutions. These themes, and others, are more fully explored in Chapter VII.

BERNARD MAYER, THE DYNAMICS OF CONFLICT RESOLUTION

98–102, 106–08 (2000).

The dimensions of resolution parallel the dimensions of conflict. The process of resolution occurs along cognitive, emotional, and behavioral dimensions. We can think of each dimension in terms of the individuals embroiled in conflict or in terms of the conflict system as a whole.

Cognitive Resolution

Whether disputants have reached resolution in a conflict depends to a large extent on how they view the situation. If they believe that the conflict is resolved, perceive that their key issues have been addressed, think that they have reached closure on the situation, and view the conflict as part of their past as opposed to their future, then an important aspect of resolution has been reached. Sometimes people make a deliberate that it is time to move beyond their conflict. They are resolved to be done with it, and if they can hold on to that resolve, they have to some extent willed themselves to resolution. Resolution at this level can precede or result from resolution of the emotional or behavioral components. Mostly, however, the cognitive dimension of resolution develops in tandem with the other dimensions. * * *

Resolution on the cognitive dimension is often the most difficult to attain because people tenaciously hang onto their perceptions and beliefs about a conflict. Disputants may be locked into a set of behaviors and anchored in an emotional response as well, but people can decide to change behavior, and emotional responses often vary quickly and repeatedly. Beliefs and perceptions are usually more rigid. They are often the cornerstone of a person's sense of stability and order, particularly in the midst of confusing and threatening situations. People cling to their beliefs and perceptions because to question them threatens to upset their sense of themselves and their world, and this sense is an essential guide during difficult times. Also, many people equate changing their views with admitting that they were wrong, something most people do not readily do. * * * Although difficult to reach, this is also the dimension in which some of the most profound change can occur during the process of conflict. When disputants change their essential view of the people with whom they are in conflict, the nature of the conflict, or the issues themselves, a long-lasting and important type of resolution can occur.

Emotional resolution

The emotional dimension of resolution involves both the way disputants feel about a conflict and the amount of emotional energy they put into it. When people no longer experience the feelings associated with a conflict, or at least not as often or at as high a level of intensity as when they were fully engaged, then the most important aspect of resolution has been reached. This may be the most volatile dimension of resolution because emotions change rapidly and repeatedly. Disputants may reach a great deal of emotional closure on a conflict, but then an event or interaction occurs that reawakens their feelings, and suddenly they feel right back in the middle of it.

People experience emotional resolution in very different ways. Some disputants process the conflict primarily through this dimension. If they feel better, the conflict must be resolved; if they do not, then no matter what else has occurred, the conflict is still as bad as ever. Others, however, tend to minimize or suppress this aspect of conflict and are often unaware whether they feel emotional closure. In any multiparty conflict a variety of approaches to this dimension are likely.

* * *

One of the best clues to a person's degree of emotional resolution is the amount of emotional energy he or she continues to put into the conflict. If a person continues to spend a great deal of time thinking about the conflict, cannot discuss it without lots of emotional intensity; or needs a great teal of ongoing support to cope with the emotional aftermath, he or she clearly has not reached emotional resolution along this dimension.

To some extent emotional disclosure is a natural result of time and distance, but it also occurs as disputants become more convinced that their needs have been addressed. Sometimes people cannot arrive at an agreement until they experience progress on this dimension, but at other times it is only through a settlement that they can gain the perspective and distance from a conflict that will allow an emotional resolution.

* * *

Behavioral resolution

When we think of resolution, it is the behavioral dimension we usually have in mind. We think of resolution as being about what people will do (or will not do) or what agreements they will make about what they will do. There are two aspects to behavioral resolution. One has to do with discontinuing the conflict behavior and the other with instituting actions to promote resolution. Stopping fighting is one part of behavioral resolution. Taking steps to meet each other's needs and to implement a new mode of interaction is another.

Sometimes there is a specific act that symbolizes or actualizes the cessation of conflict behavior and the initiation of resolution behavior. Formal agreements, peace treaties, contracts, and consent decrees are examples of this. Sometimes less formal or institutionalized acts function in the same way — a shake of the hands, a drink together, a hug, the initiation of a joint activity, giving flowers, and so forth. At other times, the conflict behavior simply ceases, sometimes gradually, sometimes abruptly, and the resolution behavior begins, without any obvious demarcation between the two. There are conflicts in which all that needs to occur is the cessation of conflict behavior. This is particularly true when the disputants will not have any relationship after the end of the conflict.

Full resolution of conflict only occurs when there is a resolution along all three dimensions: cognitive, emotional, and behavioral. But such closure does not often happen in a neat, orderly, synchronized manner. Sometimes disputants are happy to call a conflict resolved when they have achieved significant resolution on one or two dimensions. Not that people think of it in this way, but this is often how they experience it. Although resolution along one of these dimensions encourages resolution along the other dimensions, the reverse is also true. People in conflict may experience a significant setback in their progress toward resolution on one dimension when they do not experience progress along another. Furthermore, different disputants in a conflict often experience differing degrees of resolution along the various dimensions. Sometimes this difference becomes the basis of a trade-off that allows an agreement to be reached. People will often make a psychological concession, for example, in exchange for a behavioral agreement. Enduring resolution of deep conflicts, however, generally requires some significant progress along all three dimensions.

Notes and Questions

1. A deeper understanding of conflict is particularly helpful for attorneys in their roles as client counselors. Do you think it is appropriate for lawyers to explore all three dimensions with their clients? What dimensions, if any, may be best addressed through litigation? Which dimensions are ordinarily discussed in traditional law school courses?

2. Clients are often looking for something more than mere legal advice from their lawyers. They are seeking judgment and advice for resolving their

problem. How might a deeper understanding inform the kind of advice that a lawyer might give in a particular case, such as in the divorce situation of Bob and Mary described at the beginning of this chapter?

* * *

ROBERT F. COCHRAN, JR., JOHN M.A. DIPIPPA, & MARTHA M. PETERS, COUNSELING CONCERNING ALTERNATIVE DISPUTE RESOLUTION: THE COUNSELOR-AT-LAW: A COLLABORATIVE APPROACH TO CLIENT INTERVIEWING AND COUNSELING*

198–202 (1999).

Mediation and arbitration may differ from litigation in terms of time required before resolution of the dispute, cost, effect on the future relationship of the parties, likely result, and procedural protections. There are risks and potential benefits to each means of dispute resolution. The decision whether to pursue an alternative means of dispute resolution is an important one, and, just as medical patients, under the right of informed consent, are entitled to choose whether to pursue alternatives to surgery, legal clients should be entitled to pursue alternatives to litigation. Lawyers need to be able to explain the common means of dispute resolution and the risks and potential benefits of each. * * *

Time and Attorneys' Fees. Mediation and arbitration may save the client both time and money. They can save the client time in two respects. First, the parties generally can arrange to have the dispute mediated or arbitrated at a much earlier date than they could have a trial. In litigation, the delay between the filing of a complaint and the trial of a case can be substantial. In arbitration or mediation the parties can begin to mediate or arbitrate a dispute as soon as they agree on a mediator or arbitrator and arrange for a meeting. Second, once mediation or arbitration begins, it may require a shorter amount of attorney and client time than litigation or attorney negotiation. In some cases, mediation will resolve a dispute faster than attorney negotiation; in some cases it will not. * * *

Arbitration generally will require a shorter amount of time than litigation. The arbitrator is typically an expert in the subject matter of the dispute, and it may require less time for the arbitrator to understand the facts of the case than a judge or jury. Arbitration results also may not be subject to appeal, and this may prevent the long delay that may accompany appeal.

In addition to the potential savings of time, the parties may save attorneys fees. In some mediations, the parties meet alone with the mediator. If so, negotiations that take place with the opposing party during mediation will require less on the part of the parties than negotiation for a similar amount of time by attorneys. Mediation requires only one professional fee, the fee of the mediator, during the time of the mediation. This savings may be offset, to some extent, by the expense of having an attorney review the agreement. If the mediation is successful, the parties will probably save money. If the mediation is unsuccessful, however, the parties will bear the mediator's fees, as well as their future attorneys' fees. * * *

The attorneys' fees in arbitration are likely to be somewhat less than the attorneys' fees in litigation. In arbitration, attorneys represent the parties in hearings that are like trials in many respects. The arbitrator is typically an expert in the subject matter of the dispute, and so the hearing may be shorter, requiring less attorney fees than a trial. However, the parties will generally have to pay the expense of the arbitrator, and this may reduce the savings of attorneys' created by the shorter hearing. A big savings in time and attorneys' fees can result if the parties agree that the arbitrator's decision will be final. The parties can thereby avoid the great potential expense of an appeal.

The Future Relationship Between the Parties. Litigation discourages communication and encourages distrust. In litigation, the parties are adversaries: one party wins, the other party loses, and victory is reduced to a money judgment. Litigation is likely to increase friction and animosity between the parties. The friction that litigation creates can be especially troublesome in commercial cases in which the parties want to maintain a future business relationship, and in child custody cases in which the parties must maintain a future relationship. Possibly the greatest value of mediation is the likelihood that it will lead to a better future relationship between the parties than litigation. One of the central goals of mediation is to create trust and communication between the parties.

Results. Whether, for an individual client, mediation is likely to lead to a more favorable resolution than litigation or attorney negotiation will depend on the client, the other party, the case, and the mediator. Clients with good negotiation skills, i.e., clients that are intelligent, articulate, forceful, and meticulous, are likely to do well alone in mediation; clients that have poor negotiation skills are likely to do poorly. If the parties have had a relationship in which one party has dominated the other party — often the case in a domestic dispute — the dominant party may have a great advantage. The party with the greater knowledge of the subject of the litigation is likely to do better in mediation. Some mediators will attempt to equalize the bargaining strengths of the parties, and others will not. * * *

Studies comparing the attitudes of parties toward litigation and mediation show that the parties are more satisfied with the results that they achieve in mediation. They are more likely to comply with and less likely to litigate agreements that they have reached through mediation. An arbitrator may be more likely to give a correct decision than a judge or jury. The parties can choose the arbitrator based on experience, expertise in the subject of the dispute, and reputation for good judgment. The arbitrator's expertise may be especially beneficial if the resolution of the dispute depends on trade custom and usage. In a dispute concerning a complex area of business, it may be in the interest of a client who wants a correct decision to have an arbitrator with a background in the subject area resolve it.

Privacy. A final advantage to the parties of ADR is privacy. Mediation sessions and arbitration hearings generally are not open to the public. In some jurisdictions, the information that the parties convey in the meetings will not be a matter of public record unless the result later becomes the subject of a court proceedings. In other jurisdictions, information conveyed during ADR sessions is confidential as a matter of law. Privacy can be especially important to parties to a domestic dispute, who consider the matters discussed to be personal, or to parties to a business dispute, who want to avoid releasing information that might place them at a competitive disadvantage.

Lack of Procedural Protections. Since mediation often does not rely on rules of law, rules of procedure, or the other protections of the adversarial processes, less powerful individuals and groups may not fare as well under it. In litigation, judges may lessen the impact of inequalities, for example by asking questions at trial or inviting amici to participate. As noted previously, arbitration cases generally cannot be appealed; this can be cheaper, but the client loses the protections of the appeal process.

Lack of Precedent–Making Potential. In addition, cases resolved under ADR do not establish precedent. Sometimes a client may want to avoid having a case establish a precedent. But removing cases from the judicial system may reduce the ability of the system to develop just rules of law. This can especially be a problem if ADR becomes the predominant route for cases involving the poor. Courts will not be confronted with the opportunity and responsibility to develop precedents that will benefit the disadvantaged. For many issues, there is a genuine social need for an authoritative interpretation of law. * * *

* * *

WILLIAM L. URY, JEANNE M. BRETT, & STEPHEN B. GOLDBERG, GETTING DISPUTES RESOLVED: DESIGNING SYSTEMS TO CUT THE COSTS OF CONFLICT
169–173 (1988).

This book offers a simple framework for understanding the process of dispute resolution. Three major ways to resolve the dispute are to reconcile underlying interests, to determine who is right, and to determine who has more power. This framework allows us not only to classify such disparate dispute resolution procedure as negotiation, adjudication, and strikes but also to understand how they interrelate.

Our basic proposition is that, in general, it is less costly and more rewarding to focus on interests than to focus on rights, which in turn is less costly and more rewarding than to focus on power. The straightforward prescription that follows is to encourage the parties to resolve disputes by reconciling their interests wherever it is possible and, where it is not, to use low-cost methods to determine rights and power.

* * *

This book is about how to reduce the costs of resolving disputes: the hours wasted in futile quarreling, the ruinous expenses of lawsuits and strikes, and the strain on valued relationships. In organizations, these costs translate into losses in productivity and performance. In personal relationships, they translate into dissatisfaction and tension. At the extreme, the costs that designers seek to avoid are divorce, plant closings, injuries to life and limb, and the senseless destruction of war.

This book is also about gains: getting the most out of disputes. Conflict is a normal aspect of any relationship or organization. Resolving disputes effectively allows people and organizations to grow and change. The resolutions can result in mutual benefit, not only for the immediate disputants but for others who are affected by the same problem. Difficult trade-offs are faced and decisions made. Tensions are released and relationships strengthened. Productivity and performance are enhanced.

* * *

Any relationship or organization could benefit from a periodic dispute resolution diagnosis: a review of what kinds of disputes are occurring, how they are being resolved, and why some procedures are being used rather than others. Where the diagnosis indicates room for improvement, dispute systems design is in order: adding or altering procedures, strengthening motivation to use them, building skills, and adding resources. The great advantage of a systems approach is that it addresses not just a single dispute but the ongoing series of disputes that occur in any organization or relationship.

* * *

In this book, we set out six basic principles for designing an effective dispute resolution system. The first and most central principle is to put the focus on interests by encouraging the use of interests-based negotiation and mediation. The second is to provide rights and power "loopbacks" — procedures that turn the disputants' attention back to negotiation. The third principle is to provide rights and power "backups" — low-cost means for resolution if interests-based procedures fail. The fourth design principle — prevention — is to build in consultation to head off disputes before they arise and post-dispute feedback to prevent similar disputes in the future. The fifth principle is to arrange all these procedures in a low-to-high-cost sequence. And the final principle is to provide the motivation, skill, and resources necessary to make all the procedures work. Taken together, these six design principles form an integrated strategy for cutting the costs and achieving the potential gains of conflict.

* * *

This book is a first step. Dispute systems design needs to be developed in both theory and practice. As a field, it is now in its infancy. In the future, dispute systems design may join the ranks of other well-known dispute resolution methods, such as mediation and arbitration. For some, it may one day become a profession. For many — managers, lawyers, diplomats, and others — it should become, just as negotiation is now, an essential tool in their repertoire of skills.

Notes

1. The focus in the Ury, Brett, and Goldberg excerpt is on designing dispute resolution systems for institutions and organizations rather than for courts. The distinction between an interests-based approach and a rights- or power-based approach, however, is helpful in understanding and evaluating all of the processes considered in this book.

2. Your casebook authors also believe that interests-based approaches usually are better for the parties. However, one of the authors made the following comments about the Ury, Brett and Goldberg book:

> [M]y second reservation about Getting Disputes Resolved is grounded in a belief that professionals who serve clients should have a client bias rather than a process bias.

* * *

> When a lawyer advises a client on process choice, I believe that her professional responsibilities require her to consider the client's unique situation and combination of values and preferences. Individual clients vary in temperament, economic status, value orientation, and in many other ways. Vidmar and Schuller have found, for example, that some people are more inclined than others to perceive problems and make claims and that there is a statistically significant relationship between claim propensity and a preference for adjudication over mediation. Institutional clients also vary greatly in significant ways. Lawyers too often operate on the basis of stereo-types of what clients want or should do rather than on the basis of what a particular client wants and needs. This frequently involves steering the client toward litigation instead of one of the alternative processes. Process choice should instead be the product of a dialogue between lawyer and client, a dialogue that focuses on which process is most consistent with or would best promote that particular client's values, needs, and preferences. It would be as wrong for a lawyer to always steer clients toward an interests-based process as always to steer them toward a rights-based process.

James E. Westbrook, *The Problems with Process Bias,* 1989 J. Disp. Resol. 309, 313, 316.

* * *

Professor Goldberg responded as follows:

With regard to your second reservation, that a process bias is inappropriate for professionals who serve clients, I would stand by our advice that for clients who are engaged in an ongoing relationship, an interests-based system is best. That does not mean that it is always achievable since particular characteristics of either the parties or their interaction may make an interests-based system impracticable. Indeed, I believe that in dispute resolution, as in negotiation, the lowest common denominator in terms of approach will prevail. Our view, however, is that an interests-based approach is best, and that disputing parties in an ongoing relationship should use such an approach if possible. While I accept your view that it is the client's interests that should ultimately prevail, I think that the client's interests will normally best be served by the interests-based approach and that encouraging clients to consider that approach is sound professional behavior.

Letter from Stephen B. Goldberg to James E. Westbrook (Nov. 21, 1989).

D. WHAT ARE THE ROLES OF THE LAWYER?

Our goal is to prepare lawyers to help others (their clients and communities) choose or design the most appropriate methods to resolve a dispute or consummate a transaction and to be able to participate effectively in such a process once it is chosen. This, to us, is appropriate dispute resolution. This also means that we view lawyers as more than advocates. We see problem solving as the overriding function of the lawyer, the general mission of lawyering. In our view, advocacy — inside or outside of litigation — is simply one approach to dealing with a problem. In this regard, we see lawyers managing the dispute from the point at which it has escalated to its resolution, as well as continuing to manage, and perhaps even reverse, the dimensions of escalation to help contain the underlying conflict and to steer it toward as constructive of an outcome as circumstances will reasonably allow. In this sense, lawyers can be agents of conflict healing, as well as dispute resolution.

Lawyers deal with disputes in a great variety of ways. Practicing lawyers give advice about how to prevent and resolve disputes and take part in many dispute resolution processes. They represent or advise parties in arbitration, mediation, and negotiation. Lawyers also function in neutral capacities, as arbitrators, mediators, and fact-finders.

Lawyers affect dispute processing in many other capacities as well. As legislators or as leaders of the bar, community organizations, or government agencies, they define what conflicts will be addressed, as well as the means by which they will be addressed, including the design and implementation of programs for the resolution of particular disputes.

To perform well in any of these jobs, the lawyer must understand the processes and their advantages and disadvantages in different contexts. She also must appreciate the impact the process will have on those who will be affected — her clients, other involved or affected parties, or the community as a whole. Unless the lawyer has achieved this kind of understanding and appreciation, she will do poorly at helping clients or others choose or use the appropriate process. The danger of incomplete knowledge is substantial. The lawyer who considers arbitration the only alternative to litigation, for instance, may inappropriately steer too many of his clients into arbitration, or away from other alternatives.

There is an additional danger. As we suggested earlier, any of these processes can be carried out many different ways. Some mediations will look more like arbitration than some arbitrations. Thus, choosing the best process demands much more than simply deciding whether to negotiate, mediate, arbitrate, or use a mini-trial. The lawyer and client also must decide how to carry out a given process in order to achieve their objectives. When preparing for a mediation, for example, the lawyer and client should give careful consideration to the many choices available regarding the focus of the mediation, the procedures to be employed, and the roles of the mediator, the parties, and the lawyers. It is imperative that lawyers work with such choices based upon the needs of their client and with awareness of the needs of others.

1. HEADWINDS: OBSTACLES TO APPROPRIATE INVOLVE-MENT OF LAWYERS IN ALTERNATIVES TO TRADITIONAL LITIGATION

There are several obstacles to the appropriate involvement of lawyers in alternative dispute resolution. The first is unfamiliarity, which can breed either contempt or misjudgment. Many lawyers have little understanding of alternative methods because they lack either education or interest. This is changing as law schools, bar associations, and courts promote knowledge about alternatives, but in practice you may still find lawyers who are unaware of the differences among arbitration, mediation, and a mini-trial, or who will tell you they are opposed to arbitration because it means "splitting the difference." The second obstacle is generalized fear of the unknown, combined with the apprehension that the lawyer might make less money or lose control if he is involved in alternatives.

A third obstacle is that many lawyers view their role primarily as an advocate, narrowly defined, and this affects the way they see the world. The basic problem here is that the adversarial perspective, so valuable in some settings, often constricts the way lawyers function in settings where a problem-solving approach might be more appropriate. Finally, there is the culture of lawyering and law practice, which tends to inhibit a lawyer's effectiveness by sometimes discouraging a broad range of perspectives and diminishing self-awareness, social competency, and other aspects of emotional intelligence.

The excerpts below address the adversarial process and its costs. In the first excerpt, Lon Fuller and John Randall describe the purpose, value, and limits of the lawyer's role as an advocate on behalf of a client.

The following excerpt, by Monroe Freedman, takes an even stronger view, one of even fewer constraints on a legal advocacy. This adversarial perspective has a pervasive power, and Leonard Riskin in the next reading suggests that this perspective — or the "lawyer's standard philosophical map," which is its frequent companion — can keep lawyers from appreciating the value of negotiation, mediation, and other consensual models of dispute resolution. Marguite Millhauser's excerpt then addresses some unspoken, practice-related reasons that attorneys and law firms may resist ADR. Finally, this subsection concludes with an excerpt from Mark Twain's *War Prayer*, and related comments, which underscore the potential negative consequences of the adversarial process.

LON L. FULLER & JOHN D. RANDALL, PROFESSIONAL RESPONSIBILITY: REPORT OF THE JOINT CONFERENCE

44 A.B.A. J. 1159, 1160–61 (1958).

In modern society the legal profession may be said to perform three major services. The most obvious of these relates to the lawyer's role as advocate and counselor. The second has to do with the lawyer as one who designs a framework that will give form and direction to collaborative effort. His third service runs not to particular clients, but to the public as a whole.

THE LAWYER'S ROLE AS ADVOCATE IN OPEN COURT

The lawyer appearing as an advocate before a tribunal presents, as persuasively as he can, the facts and the law of the case as seen from the standpoint of his client's interest. It is essential that both the lawyer and the public understand clearly the nature of the role thus discharged. Such an understanding is required not only to appreciate the need for an adversary presentation of issues, but also in order to perceive truly the limits partisan advocacy must impose on itself if it is to remain wholesome and useful.

In a very real sense it may be said that the integrity of the adjudicative process itself depends upon the participation of the advocate. This becomes apparent when we contemplate the nature of the task assumed by any arbiter who attempts to decide a dispute without the aid of partisan advocacy.

Such an arbiter must undertake, not only the role of judge, but that of representative for both of the litigants. Each of these roles must be played to the full without being muted by qualifications derived from the others. When he is developing for each side the most effective statement of its case, the arbiter must put aside his neutrality and permit himself to be moved by a sympathetic identification sufficiently intense to draw from his mind all that it is capable of giving — in analysis, patience and creative power. When he resumes his neutral position, he must be able to view with distrust the fruits of this identification and be ready to reject the products of his own best mental efforts. The difficulties of this undertaking are obvious. If it is true that a man in his time must play many parts, it is scarcely given to him to play them all at once.

It is small wonder, then, that failure generally attends the attempt to dispense with the distinct roles traditionally implied in adjudication. What generally occurs in practice is that at some early point a familiar pattern will seem to emerge from the evidence; an accustomed label is waiting for the case and, without awaiting further proofs, this label is promptly assigned to it. It is a mistake to suppose that this premature cataloguing must necessarily result from impatience, prejudice or mental sloth. Often it proceeds from a very understandable desire to bring the hearing into some order and coherence, for without some tentative theory of the case there is no standard of relevance by which testimony may be measured. But what starts as a preliminary diagnosis designed to direct the inquiry tends, quickly and imperceptibly, to become a fixed conclusion, as all that confirms the diagnosis makes a strong imprint on the mind, while all that runs counter to it is received with diverted attention.

An adversary presentation seems the only effective means for combating this natural human tendency to judge too swiftly in terms of the familiar that which is not yet fully known. The arguments of counsel hold the case, as it were, in suspension between two opposing interpretations of it. While the proper classification of the case is thus kept unresolved, there is time to explore all of its peculiarities and nuances.

* * *

But here again the true significance of partisan advocacy lies deeper, touching once more the integrity of the adjudicative process itself. It is only through the advocate's participation that the hearing may remain in fact what it purports to be in theory: a public trial of the facts and issues.

* * *

These, then, are the reasons for believing that partisan advocacy plays a vital and essential role in one of the most fundamental procedures of a democratic society. But if we were to put all of these detailed considerations to one side, we should still be confronted by the fact that, in whatever form adjudication may appear, the experienced judge or arbitrator desires and actively seeks to obtain an adversary presentation of the issues. Only when he has had the benefit of intelligent and vigorous advocacy on both sides can he feel fully confident of his decision.

Viewed in this light, the role of the lawyer as a partisan advocate appears not as a regrettable necessity, but as an indispensable part of a larger ordering of affairs. The institution of advocacy is not a concession to the frailties of human nature, but an expression of human insight in the design of a social framework within which man's capacity for impartial judgment can attain its fullest realization.

When advocacy is thus viewed, it becomes clear by what principle limits must be set to partisanship. The advocate plays his role well when zeal for his client's cause promotes a wise and informed decision of the case. He plays his role badly, and trespasses against the obligations of professional responsibility, when his desire to win leads him to muddy the headwaters of decision, when, instead of lending a needed perspective to the controversy, he distorts and obscures its true nature.

MONROE FREEDMAN, LAWYERS' ETHICS IN AN ADVERSARY SYSTEM

9 (1975).*

[T]he adversary system assumes that the most efficient and fair way of determining the truth is by presenting the strongest possible case for each side of the controversy before an impartial judge or jury. Each advocate, therefore, must give "entire devotion to the interest of the client, warm zeal in the maintenance and defense of his rights and the exertion of his utmost learning and ability". The classic statement of that ideal is by Lord Brougham, in his representation of the Queen in *Queen Caroline's Case.* Threatening to defend his client on a ground that would, literally, have brought down the kingdom, Brougham stated:

> * * * An advocate, in the discharge of his duty, knows but one person in all the world, and that person is his client. To save that client by all means and expedients, and at all hazards and costs to other persons, and, amongst them, to himself, is his first and only duty; and in performing this duty he must not regard the alarm, the torments, the destruction which he may bring upon others. Separating the duty of a patriot from that of an advocate, he must go on reckless of the consequences, though it should be his unhappy fate to involve his country in confusion.

Let justice be done — that is, for my client let justice be done — though the heavens fall. That is the kind of advocacy that I would want as a client and that I feel bound to provide as an advocate. The rest of the picture, however, should not be ignored. The adversary system ensures an advocate on the other side, and an impartial judge over both. Despite the advocate's argument, therefore, the heavens do not really have to fall — not unless justice requires that they do.

LEONARD L. RISKIN, MEDIATION AND LAWYERS

43 Ohio St. L.J. 29, 43–48, 57–59 (1982).

Most lawyers neither understand nor perform mediation nor have a strong interest in doing either. At least three interrelated reasons account for this: the way most lawyers, as lawyers, look at the world; the economics and structure of contemporary law practice; and the lack of training in mediation for lawyers.

---

* For further elaboration on Professor Freedman's views, see Monroe Freedman, *Personal Responsibility in a Professional System,* 27 CATH. U. L. REV. 191 (1978).

A.   The Lawyer's Standard Philosophical Map

E.F. Schumacher begins his *Guide for the Perplexed* with the following story:

> On a visit to Leningrad some years ago, I consulted a map * * * but I could not make it out. From where I stood, I could see several enormous churches, yet there was no trace of them on my map. When finally an interpreter came to help me, he said: "We don't show churches on our maps." Contradicting him, I pointed to one that was very clearly marked. "That is a museum," he said, "not what we call a 'living church.' It is only the 'living churches' we don't show."

> It then occurred to me that this was not the first time I had been given a map which failed to show many things I could see right in front of my eyes. All through school and university I had been given maps of life and knowledge on which there was hardly a trace of many of the things that I most cared about and that seemed to me to be of the greatest possible importance to the conduct of my life.

The philosophical map employed by most practicing lawyers and law teachers, and displayed to the law student — which I will call the lawyer's standard philosophical map — differs radically from that which a mediator must use. What appears on this map is determined largely by the power of two assumptions about matters that lawyers handle: (1) that disputants are adversaries — *i.e.*, if one wins, the other must lose — and (2) that disputes may be resolved through application, by a third party, of some general rule of law. These assumptions, plainly, are polar opposites of those which underlie mediation: (1) that all parties can benefit through a creative solution to which each agrees; and (2) that the situation is unique and therefore not to be governed by any general principle except to the extent that the parties accept it.

The two assumptions of the lawyer's philosophical map (adversariness of parties and rule-solubility of dispute), along with the real demands of the adversary system and the expectations of many clients, tend to exclude mediation from most lawyers' repertoires. They also blind lawyers to other kinds of information that are essential for a mediator to see, primarily by riveting the lawyers' attention upon things that they must see in order to carry out their functions. The mediator must, for instance, be aware of the many interconnections between and among disputants and others, and of the qualities of these connections; he must be sensitive to emotional needs of all parties and recognize the importance of yearnings for mutual respect, equality, security, and other such non-material interests as may be present.

On the lawyer's standard philosophical map, however, the client's situation is seen atomistically; many links are not printed. The duty to represent the client zealously within the bounds of the law discourages concern with both the opponents' situation and the overall social effect of a given result.

Moreover, on the lawyer's standard philosophical map, quantities are bright and large while qualities appear dimly or not at all. When one party wins, in this vision, usually the other party loses, and, most often, the victory is reduced to a money judgment. This "reduction" of nonmaterial values — such as honor, respect, dignity, security, and love — to amounts of money, can have one of two effects. In some cases, these values are excluded from the decision makers' considerations, and thus from the consciousness of the lawyers, as irrelevant. In others, they are present but transmuted into something else — a justification for money damages. Much like the church that was allowed to appear on the map of Leningrad only because it was a museum, these interests — which may in fact be the principal motivations for a lawsuit — are recognizable in the legal dispute primarily to the extent that they have monetary value or fit into a clause of a rule governing liability.

The rule orientation also determines what appears on the map. The lawyer's standard world view is based upon a cognitive and rational outlook. Lawyers are trained to put people and events into categories that are legally meaningful, to think in terms of rights and duties established by rules, to focus on acts more than persons. This view requires a strong development of cognitive capabilities, which is often attended by the under-cultivation of emotional faculties. This combination of capacities joins with the practice of either reducing most nonmaterial values to amounts of money or sweeping them under the carpet, to restrict many lawyers' abilities to recognize the value of mediation or to serve as mediators.

The lawyer's standard philosophical map is useful primarily where the assumptions upon which it is based — adversariness and amenability to solution by a general rule imposed by a third party — are valid. But when mediation is appropriate, these assumptions do not fit. The problem is that many lawyers, because of their philosophical maps, tend to suppose that these assumptions are germane in nearly any situation that they confront as lawyers. The map, and the litigation paradigm on which it is based, has a power all out of proportion to its utility. Many lawyers, therefore, tend not to recognize mediation as a viable means of reaching a solution; and worse, they see the kinds of unique solutions that mediation can produce as threatening to the best interests of their clients.

* * *

I do not mean to imply that all lawyers see only what is displayed on the lawyer's standard philosophical map. The chart I have drawn exaggerates certain tendencies in the way many lawyers think. Any good lawyer will be alert to a range of nonmaterial values, emotional considerations, and interconnections. Many lawyers have "empathic, conciliatory" personalities that may incline them to work often in a mediative way. And other lawyers, though they may be more competitive, would recognize the value of mediation to their clients. I do submit, however, that most lawyers, most of the time, use this chart to navigate.

Notes and Questions

1.   Has law school pushed your thinking toward what Professor Riskin describes as the "lawyer's standard philosophical map"? Consider an example: Has law school changed the way you view injuries or catastrophes? Imagine that a neighbor tells you she just heard on the radio that a bus crashed in a part of the United States with which you have no connections. What are your subjective reactions? What questions would you ask? Would you try to elicit information that would enable you to place the event into a category you learned about in law school? Would you have had a similar reaction before law school?

Many lawyers and law students might see such a situation in terms of whether there is a cause of action. Would such a tendency impair a lawyer's ability to deal with a client's non-economic concerns? If so, would it impair the lawyer's ability to serve her client? What would it mean in this context for a lawyer to consider herself a problem solver?

2.   Consider these same questions in the context of large-scale accidents. For example, how do you react to news of large-scale accidents, such as the 1984 disaster in Bhopal, India in which over 2500 people died from exposure to methylisocyanite, a deadly chemical used in pesticide production, which escaped from a Union Carbide plant? For a discussion of how law schools do and should deal with such disasters, see Howard H. Lesnick, *Legal Education's Concern with Justice: A Conversation With a Critic*, 35 J. Legal Educ. 414 (1985).

3.   The role of the lawyer is the subject of much debate and controversy. Among the more interesting writings that call into question the adequacy of the adversarial perspective are: ELIZABETH DVORKIN, JACK HIMMELSTEIN & HOWARD LESNICK, BECOMING A LAWYER: A HUMANISTIC PERSPECTIVE ON LEGAL EDUCATION AND PROFESSIONALISM (1981); ROBERT H. MNOOKIN, SCOTT R. PEPPET & ANDREW S. TULUMELLO, BEYOND WINNING: NEGOTIATING TO CREATE VALUE IN DEALS AND DISPUTES (2000); THOMAS SHAFFER, ON BEING A CHRISTIAN AND A LAWYER (1981); Warren Lehman, *The Pursuit of a Client's Interest*, 77 Mich. L. Rev. 1078 (1979); William Simon, *The Ideology of Advocacy*, 1978 Wis. L. Rev. 29.

4.   Former Harvard University President and law professor Derek Bok sees a source of this problem, and a possible solution, in law school education:

> * * * [J]udges, lawmakers, scholars will all have to recognize that our conception of the role of law has fallen into disrepair. In its place, they will need to search for a new understanding that is no less sensitive to injustice but more realistic in accounting for the limits and costs of legal rules in ordering human affairs. Such an effort should result in fewer rules, but rules that are more fundamental, better understood, and more widely enforced throughout the society. Lacking such a vision, judges and regulators will continue to drift toward a general willingness to intervene whenever they feel that one person has suffered at the hands of another. That is the logical end of a process that concentrates so heavily on the plight of individual litigants and gives so little heed to the effects on the system as a whole. What emerges from this process is a spurious form of justice. In such a world, the law may seem enlight-

ened and humane, but its constant stream of rules will leave a wake strewn with the disappointed hopes of those who find the legal system too complicated to understand, too quixotic to command respect, and too expensive to be of much practical use.

* * *

If law schools are to do their share in attacking the basic problems of our legal system, they will need to adapt their teaching as well as their research. The hallmark of the curriculum continues to be its emphasis on training students to define the issues carefully and to marshal all of the arguments and counterarguments on either side. Law schools celebrate this effort by constantly telling students that they are being taught "to think like a lawyer." But one can admire the virtues of careful analysis and still believe that the times cry out for more than these traditional skills. As I have tried to point out, the capacity to think like a lawyer has produced many triumphs, but it has also helped to produce a legal system that is among the most expensive and least efficient in the world.

One example of this problem is the familiar tilt in the law curriculum toward preparing students for legal combat. Look at a typical catalogue. The bias is evident in the required first-year course in civil procedure, which is typically devoted entirely to the rules of federal courts with no suggestion of other methods for resolving disputes. Looking further, one can discover many courses in the intricacies of trial practice, appellate advocacy, litigation strategy, and the like — but few devoted to methods of mediation and negotiation. Throughout the curriculum, professors spend vast amounts of time examining the decisions of appellate courts, but make little effort to explore new voluntary mechanisms that might enable parties to resolve various types of disputes without going to court in the first place.

Many people have debated whether lawyers exacerbate controversy or help to prevent it from arising. Doubtless, they do some of each. But everyone must agree that law schools train their students more for conflict than for the gentler arts of reconciliation and accommodation. This emphasis is likely to serve the profession poorly. In fact, lawyers devote more time to negotiating conflicts than they spend in the library or the courtroom, and studies show that their bargaining efforts accomplish more for their clients. Over the next generation, I predict, society's greatest opportunities will lie in tapping human inclinations toward collaboration and compromise rather than stirring our proclivities for competition and rivalry. If lawyers are not leaders in marshaling cooperation and designing mechanisms that allow it to flourish, they will not be at the center of the most creative social experiments of our time.

Derek Bok, *A Flawed System of Law Practice and Law Teaching*, 33 J. Legal Educ. 570, 580, 582, 583 (1983).

The teaching of ADR in American Law Schools has increased dramatically since President Bok wrote his article. For an overview of developments and their significance, see Symposium, *Dispute Resolution: Raising the Bar and Enlarging the Canon*, 54 J. Legal Educ. 4 (2004).

5. Should lawyers be required to advise clients of alternative dispute resolution options? This issue is discussed in Chapter II, infra, beginning at page 152.

6. In addition, "new" approaches to law school and lawyering that generally embrace the goal of addressing clients' real needs and interests, in addition to their legal entitlements, have grown dramatically in recent years. These approaches provide a cause for optimism about lawyers' appropriate involvement in dispute resolution. These include therapeutic jurisprudence; preventive law; holistic lawyering; collaborative law; lawyering with an ethic of care; affective lawyering; the lawyer as problem solver; the lawyer as healer; and restorative justice. Professor Susan Daicoff considers these approaches, along with several ADR methods, "vectors" in what she calls the "comprehensive law movement." *See* SUSAN SWAIM DAICOFF, LAWYER, KNOW THYSELF: A PSYCHOLOGICAL ANALYSIS AT PERSONALITY STRENGTHS AND WEAKNESSES (2004). For further elaboration, see Chapter VIII, beginning at page 882.

* * *

MARGUERITE MILLHAUSER, THE UNSPOKEN RESISTANCE TO ALTERNATIVE DISPUTE RESOLUTION

3 Negotiation J. 29, 31–32 (1987).

* * *

Many of the individual inhibitions affecting clients are operative as well at the lawyer level. By the time most clients seek legal assistance, they have established in their own minds positions that they believe are at least defensible, if not correct. Notwithstanding the many unkind remarks made about lawyers, most clients, when it comes to their own matters, relish the concept of "lawyer as hired gun." Faced with these client expectations, lawyers are often reluctant to suggest approaches that do anything but vindicate their client's position. There is concern about appearing less than fully committed to their client's cause. There is also hesitance or lack of ability to diffuse the emotional attachment reflected in the client's position.

It takes certain skills to help people release or channel anger and use it to achieve more forward-looking results, and attorneys certainly are not trained for such tasks. In fact, almost the reverse is true. Lawyers are trained to represent their client's position zealously, as long as it is anything short of frivolous. The inclination, therefore, is not to look beyond the client's position to the underlying interests that could, perhaps, be better met in some alternative way, but to develop arguments and bases for advancing the client's position.

Finally, there is the ego of the lawyer who wants to think of and present himself or herself as able to deliver the result the client seeks, or better yet to exceed the client's expectations.

The same fears ultimately are likely to lurk beneath the lawyer's ego as underlie the ego of the client, thereby increasing the chances of commitment to protectionist strategies. What often occurs, in fact, is that the ego investment of the lawyers on both sides of a case becomes itself a driving force in strategy and other decisions.

For the lawyer on the other side of the case approached with a proposition suggesting some alternative methodology, there is yet another consideration. Given the training most lawyers have had and the adversarial atmosphere in which lawyers typically work, a not surprising first reaction to ADR often is suspicion. The ever-alert advocate is likely to assume, at least until proven wrong, that some trick or trap is involved. Feeling the same ego concerns and fears as the opposing counsel, this lawyer will want to insure that acceptance of such a proposal is neither a gullible action nor a disservice to his or her client. In addition to assuaging self doubts, the lawyer in such a situation also must convince the client of the benefits of this approach. The client is likely to have questions as to why the other side is proposing ADR or, why, if this step is so advisable, the client's own lawyer did not suggest it.

Because of self-doubts or client skepticism, the lawyer faced with a proposal to utilize an alternative means of dispute resolution may object or even aggressively oppose it. In that circumstance, it is incumbent on the side that initiated the idea to continue to support it calmly and resist the temptation to fight back. In many cases, after this initial testing period, the lawyer and client on the other side may be more willing to accept the proposal on its face value and embrace it as their own.

* * *

MARK TWAIN, *THE WAR PRAYER, IN* THE COMPLETE SHORT STORIES AND FAMOUS ESSAYS OF MARK TWAIN 861–863 (COLLIER 1928)*

202–205 (1981).

It was a time of great and exalting excitement. The country was up in arms, the war was on, in every breast burned the holy fire of patriotism; the drums were beating, the bands playing, the toy pistols popping, the bunched firecrackers hissing and spluttering; on every hand and far down the receding and fading spread of roofs and balconies a fluttering wilderness of flags flashed in the sun; daily the young volunteers marched down the wide avenue gay and fine in their new uniforms, the proud fathers and mothers and sisters and sweethearts cheering them with voices choked with happy emotion as they swung by; nightly the packed mass meetings listened, panting, to patriot oratory which stirred the deepest deeps of their hearts, and which they interrupted at briefest intervals with cyclones of applause, the tears running down their cheeks the while; in the churches the pastors preached devotion to flag and country, and invoked the God of Battles, beseeching His aid in our good cause in outpouring of fervid eloquence which moved every listener. It was indeed a glad and gracious time, and the half dozen rash spirits that ventured to disapprove of the war and cast a doubt upon its righteousness straightway got such a stern and angry warning that for their personal safety's sake they quickly shrank out of sight and offended no more in that way.

Sunday morning came — next day the battalions would leave for the front; the church was filled; the volunteers were there, their young faces alight with martial dreams — visions of the stern advance, the gathering momentum, the rushing charge, the flashing sabers, the flight of the foe, the tumult, the enveloping smoke, the fierce pursuit, the surrender! — then home from the war, bronzed heroes, welcomed, adored, submerged in golden seas of glory! With the volunteers sat their dear ones, proud, happy, and envied by the neighbors and friends who had no sons and brothers to send forth to the field of honor, there to win for the flag, or, failing, die the noblest of noble deaths. The service proceeded; a war chapter from the Old Testament was read; the first prayer was said; it was followed by an organ burst that shook the building, and with one impulse the house rose, with glowing eyes and beating hearts, and poured out that tremendous invocation —

"God the all-terrible! Thou who ordainest,

Thunder thy clarion and lightning thy sword!"

Then came the "long" prayer. None could remember the like of it for passionate pleading and moving and beautiful language. The burden of its supplication was, that an ever-merciful and benignant Father of us all would watch over our noble young soldiers, and aid, comfort, and encourage them in their patriotic work; bless them, shield them in the day of battle and the hour of peril, bear them in His mighty hand, make them strong and confident, invincible in the bloody onset; help them to crush the foe, grant to them and to their flag and country imperishable honor and glory —

An aged stranger entered and moved with slow and noiseless step up the main aisle, his eyes fixed upon the minister, his long body clothed in a robe that reached to his feet, his head bare, his white hair descending in a frothy cataract to his shoulders, his seamy face unnaturally pale, pale even to ghastliness. With all eyes following him and wondering, he made his silent way; without pausing, he ascended to the preacher's side and stood there, waiting. With shut lids the preacher, unconscious of his presence, continued his moving prayer, and at last finished it with the words, uttered in fervent appeal, "Bless our arms, grant us the victory, O Lord our God, Father and Protector of our land and flag!"

The stranger touched his arm, motioned him to step aside — which the startled minister did — and took his place. During some moments he surveyed the spellbound audience with solemn eyes, in which burned on uncanny light; then in a deep voice he said:

"I come from the Throne — bearing a message from Almighty God!" The words smote the house with a shock; if the stranger perceived it he gave no attention. "He has heard the prayer of His servant your shepherd, and will grant it if such shall be your desire after I, His messenger, shall have explained to you its import — that is to say, its full import. For it is like unto many of the prayers of men, in that it asks for more than he who utters it is aware of — except he pause and think.

"God's servant and yours has prayed his prayer. Has he paused and taken thought? Is it one prayer? No, it is two — one uttered, the other not. Both have reached the ear of Him Who heareth all supplications, the spoken and the unspoken. Ponder this — keep it in mind. If you would beseech a blessing upon yourself, beware! lest without intent you invoke a curse upon a neighbor at the same time. If you pray for the blessing of rain upon your crop which needs it, by that act you are possibly praying for a curse upon some neighbor's crop which may not need rain and can be injured by it.

"You have heard your servant's prayer — the uttered part of it. I am commissioned of God to put into words the other part of it — that part which the pastor — and also you in your hearts — fervently prayed silently. And ignorantly and unthinkingly? God grant that it was so! You heard these words: 'Grant us the victory, O Lord our God!' That is sufficient. The *whole* of the uttered prayer is compact into those pregnant words. Elaborations were not necessary. When you have prayed for victory you have prayed for many unmentioned results which follow victory — *must* follow it, cannot help but follow it. Upon the listening spirit of God the Father fell also the unspoken part of the prayer. He commandeth me to put it into words. Listen!

"O Lord our Father, our young patriots, idols of our hearts, go forth to battle — be Thou near them! With them — in spirit — we also go forth from the sweet peace of our beloved firesides to smite the foe. O Lord our God, help us to tear their soldiers to bloody shreds with our shells; help us to cover their smiling fields with the pale forms of their patriot dead; help us to drown the thunder of the guns with the shrieks of their wounded, writhing in pain; help us to lay waste their humble homes with a hurricane of fire; help us to wring the hearts of their unoffending widows with unavailing grief; help us to turn them out roofless with their little children to wander unfriended the wastes of their desolated land in rags and hunger and thirst, sports of the sun flames of summer and the icy winds of winter, broken in spirit, worn with travail, imploring Thee for the refuge of the grave and denied it — for our sakes who adore Thee, Lord, blast their hopes, blight their lives, protract their bitter pilgrimage, make heavy their steps, water their way with their tears, stain the white snow with the blood of their wounded feet! We ask it, in the spirit of love, of Him Who is the Source of Love, and Who is the ever-faithful refuge and friend of all that are sore beset and seek His aid with humble and contrite hearts. Amen."

(After a pause) "Ye have prayed it; if ye still desire it; speak! The messenger of the Most High waits."

Notes and Questions

1. Twain's story was written a century ago. Is it relevant to modern law practice? Consider the following comment on the passage that was written by a couple of ADR pioneers, at the dawn of the modern movement.

> I have often made a commitment to a client's cause, felt righteous and good about doing battle for my client, and then been shocked to notice that the object of my client's scorn, fear or righteousness was indeed a person. At these moments I have a slight sinking sensation, my own moral righteousness sagging ever so slightly until I am able to dismiss this perception from my mind as an unwanted distraction bent on keeping me from doing what I know should be done. There is something exhilarating about gearing up to prepare for a confrontation. The opponent is physically absent, and I am filled with empathy for my physically present client. I am like the soldier preparing his weapons for war; I pay little or no attention to the reality of the life of the person who stands in the way of our winning.

> Sometimes it is possible for me to go through an entire case without having to deal with this unwelcome perception. But the need usually arises, occurring in a completely unexpected way, often at a time when my fervor for my client's cause is running particularly high. It could be a look of vulnerability, a word that betrays the sense of hurt or pain, a humorous remark, any of the thousands of things that people do that reveal themselves to be more than the masks they wear. At these times, no matter what I want to be feeling, I cannot wholly suppress a sudden surge of sympathy — or simply a recognition of that other person as more than the adversary, the enemy. I am confused and threatened by these feelings. I am afraid that they will take over and that I will be engulfed by them. So I resist, pretending that I am not feeling what I feel and trying to rouse myself to a higher pitch of war readiness.

> Yet I know too that these reactions contain something important for me in my representation of my client. My responsibility as a lawyer cannot exclude my responsibility as a citizen or a person to the human dilemma that underlies not only my client's situation but the total human situation. It seems right that I be struggling with these reactions.

Gary J. Friedman, *Comment on the* War Prayer, *in* BECOMING A LAWYER: A HUMANISTIC PERSPECTIVE ON LEGAL EDUCATION AND PROFESSIONALISM 205–206 (Elizabeth Dvorkin, Jack Himmelstein, & Howard Lesnick eds., 1981).*

* * *

The popular injunction, "Sue the bastards," captures much of what is attractive to many of us in the adversary spirit: the lawyer identifying with a client seen as weak and wronged, who turns to law (in particular to adjudication) because of its promise of affording a fair hearing before a disinterested arbiter able and willing to call the mighty to account and to judge their conduct according to law. Thomas Shaffer has described advocacy "at its best [as] a form of reconciliation":

"It reconciles the advocate with those whose champion he proposes to be. It reconciles the advocate with his hearers. It reconciles the person whose cause is advocated with the persons who hear advocacy. It brings to community life a new sense of the interests of those the community neglects. It seeks to make things better. It is moral discourse."

Much is of course reserved by the opening qualification; advocacy is seldom encountered "at its best." For me, *The War Prayer* contains a powerful reminder of the danger in the moral fervor we incline toward as advocates, a fervor reinforced by the claims of autonomy and fairness of the adjudicatory system. All too often, that moral fervor legitimates a moral blindness toward "the bastards" on the other side, and toward the moral ambiguities and outright failures of our system of adjudicatory justice.

It would be all too easy to reserve Mark Twain's admonition for the occasions when we are representing an unworthy client; Gary Friedman brings us up short so arrestingly because he postulates a client no less appealing than his or her adversary. One of the painful difficulties of practicing law is maintaining the connection between the valid appeal of the values of adjudicatory adversariness and client-identification, and the need to remain aware and responsible about the true operation of the adversary system, the harms we do to our adversaries, and the ambivalence of the lawyer's own moral posture.

Howard Lesnick, *Comment on the War Prayer*, *in* ELIZABETH DVORKIN, JACK HIMMELSTEIN & HOWARD LESNICK, BECOMING A LAWYER: A HUMANISTIC PERSPECTIVE ON LEGAL EDUCATION AND PROFESSIONALISM 206–207 (1981).*

2. Ethical issues are often challenging for lawyers and the legal profession, but can be especially so in the context of alternative dispute resolution. This, in part, is because ethics rules have generally been drafted under an adversarial understanding of the practice of law. Consider, for example, Professor Carrie Menkel–Meadow's comment on a recent ABA proposal to modify the ABA Model Rules of Professional Conduct to allow an attorney who serves as a mediator in a law firm to be "screened" so that his or her partners may subsequently represent one of the parties in the mediator's matter without obtaining client consent.

* * * The newly proposed Rule 1.12 treats mediators as arbitrators and judges have been treated by the rules in the past. * * *

* * *

I am concerned that there still are complicated issues not covered by the current draft of the rule. As an illustration, a few months ago I was training some extremely sophisticated intellectual property lawyers in mediation, and I talked to them about these ethics issues. Professional responsibility teachers will be shocked to learn that when I described the proposed screen of the new Rule 1.12 as a positive phenomenon, these practicing intellectual property lawyers, who serve as both advocates and mediators, understood this new rule as prohibiting them from engaging in their current multiple kinds of practice, where they previously had not been cognizant of the potential conflicts of interests issues. In other words, they had not even conceptualized the possibility that when a lawyer serves as a mediator in one matter, his or her partner cannot represent one of the parties in that mediation in a related, or even an unrelated, litigation matter. * * *

It was surprising, given all the bar associations' continuing legal education requirements, how little these lawyers knew about conflicts of interest. Most of these quite prominent lawyers have been mediating and representing parties without using screens and thinking the entire time that this was perfectly permissible. When I said, "The good news is that now you are going to be able to perform both of these roles, provided you screen in appropriate cases," they looked at me in horror, realizing that they would now need to engage in all the complexities involved in screening, such as the segregation of files and fees and the prohibition on discussions with firm partners on screened matters.

I offer that example to demonstrate: (a) the lack of knowledge that still exists about our very basic rules of conflict of interest, and (b) the significant effort that will be required to apply the complex conflict of interest rules and screening to the ADR environment. * * *

Carrie Menkel–Meadow, *Ethics in ADR: The Many "Cs" of Professional Responsibility and Dispute Resolution*, 28 Fordham Urb. L.J. 979 (2001). Ethics issues are considered throughout this textbook.

2. TAILWINDS: REASONS FOR OPTIMISM ABOUT LAWYERS' APPROPRIATE INVOLVEMENT IN ALTERNATIVES TO LITIGATION

a. In General

As we can see, there are certainly legitimate reasons for skepticism about the embrace of ADR by the legal profession. However, there are many reasons for optimism, too. Lawyers today are bombarded with information about ADR, with pressure from judges and clients, and with the reality of court delays. Training is offered in law school courses and CLE programs. And no large bar association conference is complete today without a session on dispute resolution. Many major law firms are now publicizing their ADR capabilities. Many have established dispute resolution units and have assigned lawyers solely or principally to help their colleagues resolve disputes.

There are other reasons as well. Most lawyers want to respond to the needs of their clients and communities. These needs include material and economic factors as well as interpersonal and other psychological considerations. For this task, an understanding of the alternative processes is essential, and most lawyers are beginning to recognize this.

Much of the available education and training deals with when and to what extent it is preferable to use a problem-solving as opposed to — or along with — an adversarial approach. Plainly, lawyers who have "narrowed" their clients' disputes to fit legal categories have the capacity to restore them to what they were before — human problems — in order to achieve solutions that meet the client's needs. We hope that this book and the courses in which it is used will help law students and lawyers develop the knowledge, skills, and perspectives necessary to give their clients the most appropriate service.

b.   The Law's Embrace of ADR

The following excerpt, although it speaks to mediation, could as well be addressing education in negotiation and in designing and selecting appropriate dispute resolution processes.

LEONARD L. RISKIN, MEDIATION AND LAWYERS
43 Ohio St. L.J. 29, 57–59 (1982).

There are similar benefits — not very certain, but profoundly important — that could follow merely from the development of mediation education for lawyers. The provision of good quality mediation-cum-legal services could help lawyers, the bar, and the law schools fulfill the strong impulses — frequently shaded on the lawyer's standard philosophical map — to make law more responsive to the needs of individuals and society. Properly done, mediation training can enhance the learner's awareness of his own emotional needs and value orientations and those of others. It should expand his ability to understand both sides of a case — not just with his head but with his heart as well. These sensitivities can, of course, make the lawyer better able to perceive his clients' needs and, on a purely instrumental level, to work more effectively with all manner of people.

And there is much more to it. Mediation highlights the interconnectedness of human beings. Lawyers who notice the interconnectedness are less vulnerable to the kind of over-enthusiasm with the adversary role that has brought about much of its sinister reputation. Lawyers who can experience both sides of a controversy — not merely understand the legal arguments — will have an awareness of consequences that can become a guide to their conduct which can compete with the established rules of lawyers' behavior. This may, when appropriate, blunt the edge of their adversarialness. It may also help them recognize that although their individual clients may be doing fine, in many ways the judicial system is not serving most people well.

I do not mean to indict the lawyers' standard philosophical map. In many cases, lawyers must use it. Most clients and judges expect them to. Moreover, the adversary-rule perspective from which the standard map is drawn has real strengths. It promotes a loyalty to clients. It encourages vigorous presentation of competing positions and interests. The rule orientation fosters in the lawyer an allegiance to the system of laws, which in turn serves to unify society, to provide a measure of security of expectations, and to keep open possibilities of fairness between persons irrespective of status and of vindication of the rights of the downtrodden. But at the same time, the lawyer's conventional view of the world permits a great deal of misery. It does this by dominating the professional consciousness of most lawyers and legal educators too fully, crowding or crowding out other views.

An enormous percentage of potential consumers of legal services are either ill-served or not served at all by our legal system. Many people can afford a lawyer only when a contingent fee arrangement is feasible. Those who can get into the litigation process will find it enormously time consuming, expensive, uncertain, and unpleasant unless their lawyers can arrange settlements. And much of this results directly from the over-zealousness with which many lawyers routinely embrace their adversarial roles. Many lawyers tend to delay and obscure the truth in the service (usually) of their clients' financial interest. Often they "exacerbate and prolong the contest rather than * * * arrive at a quiet compromise."

That this situation persists can be attributed in no small measure to the strength of the lawyer's standard philosophical map. The atomistic perspective, the inclination to accept the adversary system as it is and assume that it is useful, the focus on legal rights and interests (often reduced to monetary terms), the assumption of an adversary stance — all these tendencies combine to permit the working lawyer to ignore, at least while he is working, the well-known adverse conditions that I set forth above.

A lawyer who has experienced the mediational perspective would have difficulty keeping on his adversarial blinders and would be more likely, therefore, to acknowledge the serious difficulties in our current adversary system. The mediation experience also may encourage the lawyer to come up with creative solutions to systemic as well as individual problems. Mediation training and practice can help lawyers question the many (often unconscious) value presuppositions that underlie normal lawyer behavior — for example, assumptions about adversariness and rules, how lawyers behave, and what clients want — from which we tend to operate automatically. Mediation training, in other words, may help lawyers break out of the "mental grooves and compartments" characteristic of the lawyer's conventional world view. This can lead not just to mediation but to legal services that are more responsive to the needs of clients and of society.

Notes

There are many additional reasons for optimism about the development of appropriate involvement of lawyers in alternative methods of dispute resolution.

1. The organized bar has been active in promoting the appropriate use of dispute resolution. One section of the American Bar Association focuses solely on dispute resolution, and at least eighteen other ABA sections have ADR committees. Richard C. Reuben, *Plethora of ABA resources for ADR*, A.B.A. J., Aug. 1996, at 62. The vast majority of state and local bar associations have committees or sections on ADR. Robert D. Raven & James M. Schurz, *The Expanding Role of Bar Associations in ADR*, ADR Currents, 1996, at 1. Many state and local bar associations also provide education and training in ADR and maintain programs that provide ADR services. *Id.*; *see also*, S. Gale Dick, *Bar Groups Offer Variety of ADR Services*, Alternatives to the High Cost of Litig., Nov. 1994, at 135. A powerful example of bar support for ADR occurred in 2001 and 2002, when the nation's two most significant legal reform organizations — the American Bar Association and the National Conference of Commissioners on Uniform State Laws — overwhelmingly voted to endorse the Uniform Mediation Act and revisions broadening the Uniform Arbitration Act. The UMA was particularly significant because it was a new act, and because its cornerstone is an evidentiary privilege for participants in mediation that makes statements made in mediation inadmissible in subsequent legal proceedings. Many of these statements would be admitted into evidence without the privilege, and the acceptance of this policy choice speaks volumes about the legal profession's embrace of mediation. For more on the privilege in the Uniform Mediation Act, see Chapter IV, beginning at page 448.

2. The federal government has been particularly active in promoting the appropriate use of alternative dispute resolution. *See generally* Jeffrey M. Senger, Federal Dispute Resolution: Using ADR With the United States Government (2003). For example, the Alternative Dispute Resolution Act of 1998 requires all federal district courts to offer at least one alternative dispute resolution option. 28 U.S.C. § 651 (2000). The Administrative Dispute Resolution Act of 1990 (ADRA) requires all federal agencies to adopt ADR policies and to provide departmental ADR leadership and training. 5 U.S.C. § 571 (2000). Significantly, Congress amended ADRA in 1996 to make its 1990 requirements permanent and to provide for a confidentiality privilege for most communications between parties and neutrals. 5 U.S.C. § 574(j) (2000). The Negotiated Rule-Making Act of 1990 also authorized "reg negs," a process in which federal agencies and private parties collaborate in developing regulations. 5 U.S.C. §§ 584–85 (2000).

In addition to these congressional initiatives, ADR has also had strong support in the White House since the early 1990s. In 1991, President George H. W. Bush issued an Executive Order requiring federal agencies to apply some of the proposals developed by the President's Council on Competitiveness in the "Agenda for Civil Justice Reform in America." Exec. Order No. 12,778, *reprinted in* 3 C.F.R. 359 (1992), 38 U.S.C. § 547. The order emphasized the need to consider alternative mechanisms before going to court. In 1995, President Clinton signed Exec. Order 12,979, which encouraged the use of alternative methods of dispute resolution in addressing protests over procurement decisions. And in 1996 he issued Exec. Order 12,988, entitled "Civil Justice Reform," which encouraged government lawyers to consider using ADR in all civil cases.

Such federal support for ADR has been bipartisan. President Clinton's Attorney General, Janet Reno, was a highly visible advocate of ADR whose pro bono activities included the mediation of cases. For a discussion, see Daniel Marcus & Jeffrey M. Senger, *ADR and the Federal Government: Not Such Strange Bedfellows After All*, 66 Mo. L. Rev. 709 (2001). Similarly, President George W. Bush's first attorney general, John Ashcroft, acknowledged that "today, perhaps more than any time in our history, it is vital that we aspire to a deeper understanding of justice." Kevin R. Kemper, *Ashcroft Sends Signal of Support for ADR in Justice Department*, Disp. Resol. Mag., Summer 2002, at 29. These and other related federal administrative developments are discussed further in Chapter VI, beginning at page 731.

3.   State courts and governments also have been active in promoting alternative dispute resolution. According to a 1996 survey, in all but five states, state courts have instituted ADR programs. Richard C. Reuben, *The Lawyer Turns Peacemaker*, A.B.A. J., Aug. 1996, at 56. A 2001 study by the Policy Consensus Initiative found more than 175 state ADR programs, including 39 state court ADR centers, six centers housed in the executive branch, and 32 offices of attorneys general that listed an ADR contact. For a discussion, see Christine M. Carlson, *ADR in the States: Great Progress, but There is Still Much to Do*, Disp. Resol. Mag., Summer 2001, at 4. Florida has one of the oldest statewide court ADR programs. For a history and discussion, see Sharon Press, *Institutionalization of Mediation in Florida: At the Crossroads*, 108 Penn. St. L. Rev. 43 (2003). More recently, the state of Maryland has been particularly innovative in state dispute resolution programs. *See* Rachel Wohl, *Resolving Disputes: MACRO Update,* 36–AUG Md. B.J. 14 (2003). State dispute resolution programs are discussed at further length in Chapter VI, beginning at page 684.

4.   In the private corporate context, ADR has been increasingly used since the 1980s, and the indications are that this trend can be expected to continue. A Cornell University study, for example, surveyed the corporate counsel of the 1000 largest U.S. corporations, and found that nearly all respondents reported having used some form of ADR, and that 97 percent of respondents felt mediation saved time and money. David B. Lipsky & Ronald L. Seeber, The Appropriate Resolution of Corporate Disputes: A Report on the Growing Use of ADR by U.S. Corporations (1998). Similarly, a study by the U.S. General Accounting Office indicated a 90% growth in the use of arbitration and more than 70% growth in the use of mediation for employment disputes studied between 1995 and 1997. U.S. GAO, Alternative Dispute Resolution: Employers' Experiences with ADR in the Workplace (1997). Approximately 4,000 operating companies have signed a "pledge," sponsored by the CPR Institute for Dispute Resolution, to consider ADR

options when confronting disputes with other companies that signed the pledge. The use of ADR in the private corporate context is discussed further in Chapter VI, beginning at page 755.

5.   Dispute resolution now occurs regularly in and about cyberspace, and is often called "online dispute resolution," or "ODR." Several providers have emerged as major players in ODR, tending to focus on particular types of disputes. For example, SquareTrade, one of the largest online providers, has partnership agreements with eBay, Verisign, and PayPal to offer dispute resolution services for e-commerce disputes. A critical feature of the program is its Seal Program, which is intended to provide public assurances about the fairness of the processes. Cybersettle, another major provider of online services, focuses primarily on insurance and workers' compensation disputes. Disputes over Internet domain names are also arbitrated online through the World Intellectual Property Organization's Uniform Domain Name Dispute Resolution Policy. For a general discussion, see ETHAN KATSH & JANET RIFKIN, ONLINE DISPUTE RESOLUTION 19 (2001); Joseph W. Goodman, *The Pros and Cons of Online Dispute Resolution: An Assessment of Cyber–Mediation Websites,* 2003 Duke L. & Tech. Rev. 4. For more on online dispute resolution, see Chapter VI, beginning at page 780.

Chapter II

THE ATTORNEY–CLIENT RELATIONSHIP: INTERVIEWING AND COUNSELING

This chapter introduces the lawyer-client relationship, a relationship that we will address repeatedly throughout the book. After introducing the lawyer-client relationship generally, we then explore two central components of that relationship: interviewing and counseling.

Interviewing and counseling appear in this book for several reasons. First, this book looks at most problems from the standpoint of the practicing lawyer. Interviewing is the principal means by which the lawyer comes to understand the client and the problems and issues that brought the client to her. In counseling, the lawyer helps the client decide whether and how to address the problems, which may include selecting a method for resolving a dispute or for planning a transaction.

Second, interviewing and counseling are dispute resolution processes in their own right. After an interview or a counseling session with a lawyer, for instance, many clients will drop their claim or concern or decide to seek other professional help or to delay action. In addition, many disputes are transformed or redefined during interviewing and counseling. Sometimes the transformation is from an ill-defined human problem to a legal dispute. Other times the reverse occurs: A client comes in wishing to sue, but learns that other approaches may be more appropriate.

Third, interviewing and counseling are important parts of other dispute resolution or planning processes, such as mediation and fact-finding, and important adjuncts to others, such as litigation and negotiation. Often the lawyer-negotiator will interview and counsel her client between negotiation sessions as she gains new insight into what negotiated outcomes are possible.

Interviewing and counseling are distinct but closely related activities. We study them separately in this chapter to better understand each process. But we also study them together because in practice they usually occur together, and ideally in sequence, as part of a process of problem solving.

Our main objective for this chapter is to introduce the goals, strategies, and techniques of interviewing and counseling. We also wish to give the reader a sense of the choices open to the lawyer and client in determining the nature of their relationship.

Section A describes three models of the attorney-client relationship and addresses the agency issues inherent in the relationship. Sections B and C provide a basic introduction to interviewing and counseling respectively. Because the two primary skills used in interviewing and counseling are the same — questioning and listening — Section D addresses those skills together. Finally, as a prelude to the remaining chapters in this book, Section E explores whether the lawyer, as part of her role as counselor, has a duty to advise her clients about dispute resolution alternatives. Section F provides the general instructions for a role play exercise for practicing the skills discussed in this chapter.

A.   THE ATTORNEY–CLIENT RELATIONSHIP

1. BASIC MODELS

Most of us carry a model or idealized vision of the attorney-client relationship around in our heads. Formed in various ways — from television, movies and books, to real encounters with lawyers and clients — it informs our understanding of the way lawyers and clients are supposed to relate to one another.

The following two excerpts explore three models of the lawyer-client relationship. In the first excerpt, Professor Robert Dinerstein describes both the traditional model, in which the lawyer exercises broad control over the relationship, and the client-centered model, in which the client plays a much larger role. In the second excerpt, Professors Robert Cochran, Jr., John DiPippa, and Martha Peters describe their more recently developed collaborative model of the lawyer-client relationship, which falls somewhere between the extremes of the traditional and client-centered approaches.

ROBERT D. DINERSTEIN, CLIENT–CENTERED COUNSELING: REAPPRAISAL AND REFINEMENT

32 Ariz. L. Rev. 501, 503–04, 506–09 (1990).

Legal counseling inevitably raises questions about the proper role of the lawyer with respect to her client and the degree of the client's participation in the decisionmaking process. Who should decide what actions to take — lawyer, client, or a combination of the two? Is the lawyer's professional role to make decisions for the client, advise the client about what decision the client should make, or simply lay out the options and let the client decide? Should client decisions be judged by an informed consent standard? These questions are not unique to the lawyer-client relationship — in some sense they arise in all professional/layperson relationships — but they have particular salience within that relationship.

The traditional view of legal counseling (and the lawyer-client relationship generally) maintains that the client should make the critical decisions concerning the overall goals of the representation, with the lawyer exercising a great deal of influence over how such decisions are made and what the actual decisions are. This view holds that the client should stand by passively while the lawyer lays out all relevant legal considerations for the decision and indicates what decision he believes, as a matter of his professional judgment, the client ought to make. The lawyer then urges the client to make the recommended decision. The client-centered or participatory model of counseling, with the client empowered to make decisions for him or herself, is a response to this traditional model.

* * *

A.   *The Traditional Model*

Traditional legal counseling reflects an absence of meaningful interchange between lawyer and client. The client comes to the lawyer with some idea about his problem. The lawyer asks questions designed to adduce the information necessary to place the client's problem within the appropriate conceptual box. At the proper time, he counsels the client by essentially conducting a monologue: the lawyer tells the client about the course of action he recommends. The lawyer may go into great detail about the rationale for his advice. Alternatively, she may provide a relatively terse recitation of technical advice and let the client decide how to proceed. The lawyer is concerned with the client's reaction to his advice but tends not to value client input, for he believes that the client has little of value to contribute to the resolution of his legal problem. Lawyer and client are likely to talk at, rather than with, each other. Any assurance that the lawyer provides to the client — and it could be substantial — is likely to be based on the client's perception that the lawyer is "taking care of matters" rather than on a belief that the lawyer truly tried to understand the client as a whole, complex person.

In general, the traditional legal counseling model assumes that clients should be passive and delegate decisionmaking responsibility to their lawyers; that ineffective professional service is relatively rare; that professionals give disinterested service and maintain high professional standards; that effective professional services are available to all who can pay; and that professional problems tend to call for technical solutions beyond the ken of laypersons.

B.   *The Binder and Price Counseling Model*

Client-centered counseling is a critical component of client-centered lawyering. Client-centered counseling may be defined as a legal counseling process designed to foster client-decisionmaking. Its goal is not only to provide opportunities for clients to make decisions themselves but also to enhance the likelihood that the decisions are truly the client's and not the lawyer's. To accomplish these goals, client-centered counselors must attend to the means they employ in the counseling process, as well as the end of client decisionmaking they attempt to achieve.

Binder and Price describe a relatively straightforward, but highly structured, legal counseling model to be used in litigation contexts. With respect to the basic decision about whether to litigate, the lawyer first sets out the legal alternatives for the client. Next, she solicits the client's input in generating additional alternatives. Then, the lawyer engages the client in a discussion of the positive and negative consequences of the options. These consequences include not only the legal consequences, as to which the lawyer is enjoined to make predictions of the most likely outcome of each alternative, but the social, psychological and economic consequences as well. Finally, the lawyer assists the client in weighing these consequences with an eye towards having the client make the final decision.

ROBERT F. COCHRAN, JR., JOHN M. A. DIPIPPA & MARTHA M. PETERS, THE COUNSELOR–AT–LAW: A COLLABORATIVE APPROACH TO CLIENT INTERVIEWING AND COUNSELING*

6–7 (1999).

We believe that the authoritarian [traditional] model provides too small a role for clients, the client-centered approach provides too small a role for lawyers, and that clients will be best served when lawyers and clients resolve problems in the law office through collaborative decision making. Under this model, the client would control decisions, but the lawyer would structure the process and provide advice in a manner that is likely to yield wise decisions.

This model would be likely to avoid the problems of the authoritarian model. The client's control of the decisions would ensure client dignity. It would also be likely to yield superior results to the authoritarian model. Rosenthal found that the more varied forms of client participation and the more persistently the client employed them, "the better his chances of protecting his emotional and economic interests in the case outcome." We share Rosenthal's call for lawyers and clients to engage in "mutual participation in a cooperative relationship in which the cooperating parties have relatively equal status, are equally dependent, and are engaged in activity 'that will be in some ways satisfying to both [parties].' "

A collaborative client counseling model would also avoid the weaknesses of the client-centered counselors. It would provide the lawyer and client with an opportunity to consider the effects of their decisions on other people. It would provide the flexibility to counsel the client in a wide variety of ways. Finally it would enable the client and lawyer to engage in a collaborative deliberation that would be likely to yield practical wisdom.

Notes and Questions

1. The distinction between the client-centered model and the collaborative model is subtle. Here is a helpful way to think about it:

The client-centered approach seeks to promote client autonomy by making the client an active participant in the decision-making process. The lawyer tries to identify the client's problem from the client's perspective and then enlists the client's aid in identifying potential solutions and the likely consequences of each solution. Ultimately, counsel encourages the client to make all decisions that are likely to have a substantial legal or non-legal impact on the client's case. The client-centered model emphasizes client feelings, stresses the importance of lawyer empathy, and insists that lawyers accept client values when rendering advice. Lawyers' recommendations, therefore, shall be designed to promote the client's best interests as defined by that client. As Cochran and his compatriots pointed out, "whereas the client has a very limited role in the authoritarian model, the lawyer has a very limited role in the client-centered model." * * *

[With the collaborative decision-making model, Cochran and his co-authors] looked to Douglas Rosenthal who urged lawyers and clients to engage in "mutual participation in a cooperative relationship." To Cochran and his colleagues, the collaborative model is superior to the client-centered model because it increases counsel's flexibility, promotes equality, and encourages a lawyer-client dialog about the effects that case decisions may have on others. Thus, in Cochran's collaborative model, "the client would control decisions, but the lawyer would structure the process and provide advice in a manner that is likely to yield wise decisions."

Cochran and his colleagues trumpet the collaborative model because they believe that lawyers following this approach are more likely to achieve what Dean Anthony Kronman calls practical wisdom. To Kronman, the key to being a good lawyer is the ability to exercise practical wisdom. To exercise such wisdom, a lawyer must "combine the opposing qualities of sympathy and detachment." Acting as a counselor and friend, the good lawyer strives to help her clients make sound judgments. To render the good advice her client needs, counsel must also seek to understand the client. Ultimately, "it is only through a process of joint deliberations, in which the lawyer imaginatively assumes his client's position, and with sympathetic detachment begins to examine the alternatives for himself, that the necessary understanding can emerge." Using this process then, the good lawyer is better able to assist her client in making the "deliberatively wise choice" among alternatives. Thus, not only does the good lawyer exercise practical wisdom, but she helps her client make wise judgments as well.

Rodney J. Uphoff, *Relations between Lawyer and Client in* Damages*: Model, Typical, or Dysfunctional?*, 2004 J. Disp. Resol. 145, 152–54.

2.   Which model of the attorney-client relationship do you think is most appropriate? Who should decide — you or your client — how you will carry out your representation of the client? What factors might help you decide which model is more appropriate? The type of client? The nature of your relationship with the client? The type of knowledge required to solve the problem? Your knowledge of your client's needs and goals? The client's ability or inability to make a decision?

3.   Recall Mayer's argument from Chapter I that it is helpful to understand conflict and conflict resolution along three dimensions: behavioral, cognitive, and emotional. Which model of the attorney-client relationship is most likely to address conflict along all three dimensions?

4.   What impact might the choice of model have on whether conflict de-escalates, stabilizes, or escalates?

5.   The client-centered model of *lawyering* is based on the client-centered model of *psychotherapy*, which Carl Rogers explains as follows:

> Client-centered therapy is built on two central hypotheses: (1) the individual has within him the capacity, at least latent, to understand the factors in his life that cause him unhappiness and pain, and to reorganize himself in such a way as to overcome those factors; (2) these powers will become effective if the therapist can establish with the client a relationship sufficiently warm, accepting and understanding. From these two convictions it follows that in practice we do not try to do something *to* the client. We do not diagnose his case, nor evaluate his personality; we do not prescribe treatment, nor determine what changes are to be effected, nor set the goal that shall be defined as a cure. Instead the therapist approaches the client with a genuine respect for the person he is now and with a continuing appreciation of him as he changes during association. He tries to see the client as the client sees himself, to look at problems through his eyes, to perceive with him his confusions, fears and ambitions. The therapist in such a relationship is not concerned with judging or making suggestions, but always strives to understand.

Carl R. Rogers, *"Client–Centered" Psychotherapy*, 187 Sci. Am. 66, 66–67 (1952).

6.   For the lawyer and client who wish to conduct their relationship in accord with the client-centered model or the collaborative model, what impediments might prevent them from doing so? From the client's side, active participation in the relationship may be difficult for several reasons. The client may not wish to devote the time or energy required for participation. He may strongly embrace a traditional model of lawyer-client relationships. He may be unable to master enough knowledge or muster enough judgment to make a wise decision.

The lawyer may also have problems helping the client participate effectively. The lawyer may assume that the client wants or needs the lawyer to take charge. She may worry about losing time or money. She may feel anxious about the possibility of losing control. As Douglas Rosenthal put it:

Lawyers, and perhaps most professionals, seem to have two human needs in disproportionately great measure: the desire to control their environment and aggressive (and competitive) feelings. * * * The traditional model serves the function of a professional ideology, justifying the control the lawyer wants, affirming his status and competence, and defining as legitimate a role of client passivity and uncritical trust. The traditional model resolves unilaterally the conflicts inherent in the lawyer's role. It is a way lawyers can cope with the strains of practice.

DOUGLAS ROSENTHAL, LAWYER AND CLIENT: WHO'S IN CHARGE? 173, 174 (1974).

7. The traditional model, in which the lawyer takes broad control over the decision-making process, might make sense if: (a) The solutions may require knowledge or expertise within the lawyer's exclusive control; (b) The lawyer fully understands the needs and values of the client; (c) The lawyer can be neutral; and (d) The client is unwilling or unable to make a decision. These factors exist in some situations, especially where the lawyer and the client have a continuing relationship. But in many other situations they may be absent.

8. Several of the current Model Rules of Professional Conduct address the appropriate role for the lawyer to play in the lawyer-client relationship. As you read through the following provisions, consider whether they are more compatible with the traditional model, the client-centered model, or the collaborative model of the lawyer-client relationship:

RULE 1.2 Scope of Representation and Allocation of Authority Between Client and Lawyer

(a) Subject to paragraphs (c) and (d), a lawyer shall abide by a client's decisions concerning the objectives of representation and, as required by Rule 1.4, shall consult with the client as to the means by which they are to be pursued. A lawyer may take such action on behalf of the client as is impliedly authorized to carry out the representation. A lawyer shall abide by a client's decision whether to settle a matter. In a criminal case, the lawyer shall abide by the client's decision, after consultation with the lawyer, as to a plea to be entered, whether to waive jury trial and whether the client will testify.

(b) A lawyer's representation of a client, including representation by appointment, does not constitute an endorsement of the client's political, economic, social or moral views or activities.

(c) A lawyer may limit the scope of the representation if the limitation is reasonable under the circumstances and the client gives informed consent.

(d) A lawyer shall not counsel a client to engage, or assist a client, in conduct that the lawyer knows is criminal or fraudulent, but a lawyer may discuss the legal consequences of any proposed course of conduct with a client and may counsel or assist a client to make a good faith effort to determine the validity, scope, meaning or application of the law.

MODEL RULES OF PROF'L CONDUCT R. 1.2 (2004).

RULE 1.4 Communications

(a) A lawyer shall:

(1) promptly inform the client of any decision or circumstance with respect to which the client's informed consent, as defined in Rule 1.0(e), is required by these Rules;

(2) reasonably consult with the client about the means by which the client's objectives are to be accomplished;

(3) keep the client reasonably informed about the status of the matter;

(4) promptly comply with reasonable requests for information; and

(5) consult with the client about any relevant limitation on the lawyer's conduct when the lawyer knows that the client expects assistance not permitted by the Rules of Professional Conduct or other law.

(b) A lawyer shall explain a matter to the extent reasonably necessary to permit the client to make informed decisions regarding the representation.

MODEL RULES OF PROF'L CONDUCT R. 1.4 (2004).

RULE 2.1 Advisor

In representing a client, a lawyer shall exercise independent professional judgment and render candid advice. In rendering advice, a lawyer may refer not only to law but to other considerations such as moral, economic, social, and political factors that may be relevant to the client's situation.

MODEL RULES OF PROF'L CONDUCT R. 2.1 (2004).

2. ATTORNEY–CLIENT RELATIONSHIPS IN ACTION

The next three readings explore lawyer-client relationships in action. In the first excerpt, Professor Herbert Kritzer describes the results of his study of lawyer-client relationships in civil litigation based on interviews with a very large sample of lawyers and litigants. In the second excerpt, Professor Gary Neustadter describes the results of his study of consumer bankruptcy attorneys and their clients. In the third reading, Professors Rodney Uphoff and Peter Wood describe the results of a study of public defenders based on a survey they administered to attorneys in five public defender offices.

Taken together, these readings suggest that the traditional model of lawyering still predominates, though a significant minority of lawyers attempts to follow the dictates of the other models:

HERBERT M. KRITZER, THE JUSTICE BROKER: LAWYERS AND ORDINARY LITIGATION

60–65 (1990).

The idea of professional autonomy suggests that it is the professional who is dominant in the [lawyer-client] relationship; [however,] norms for lawyer responsibility dictate that the client be advised and consulted at important junctures and that final decisions on important matters (e.g., filing a court case, rejecting or accepting an offer of settlement) be the responsibility of the client. While this ambiguity may suggest that it will be impossible to arrive at any kind of definitive statement on who dominates the relationship, the analysis shows very clearly that control rests largely with the lawyer, particularly when the client is an individual.

From the Lawyer's Viewpoint

* * *

THE NATURE OF CLIENT INVOLVEMENT

Concerning the nature of the explicit or ongoing understandings regarding the client's role, lawyers were asked to characterize them in terms of one of the following categories.

> The client would play a major decision-making role, providing (the lawyer) with instructions on some matters.

> The client would not play a major decision-making role, but (its) approval would be required on most decisions.

> (The lawyer) and the client would discuss matters, but (the lawyer) would make most of the decisions.

> The client would pretty much turn the case over to (the lawyer).

Not surprisingly, the largest groups of lawyers placed the understanding in the two intermediate categories (35 percent and 26 percent), with 19 percent describing the content as falling into each of the two extreme categories.

Things shift somewhat when the lawyers describe the actual role taken by their clients. The actual role taken in 90 percent or more of the dyads where there was an understanding was consistent with that understanding, but when there was a discrepancy, there was a slight tendency for the actual role to be one of less involvement than called for by the understanding. Client involvement tended to be substantially lower when no agreement about that involvement was reached:

> • Only 20 percent of clients having an understanding with their lawyers about their involvement played no significant role at all, while 44 percent of the clients without an understanding played no significant role.

- In 19 percent of the dyads where there was an understanding, the client's involvement fell at the high end versus only 8 percent where there was no understanding.

In general, the likely organizational clients tended to play a larger role than the likely individual clients, regardless of whether or not there was an explicit understanding ...

This pattern is confirmed, at least from the lawyer's viewpoint, by the responses to a second question: "To what degree was your client involved in determining case strategy other than in settlement negotiations?" Sixty-seven percent of the lawyers said that their clients had little or no role in determining case strategy, and only 13 percent said that the clients had been "very much" involved in strategic planning. Again, the level of involvement among likely individual litigants was much lower than that among likely organizational litigants, with 59 percent of the likely organizations having little or no involvement compared to 79 percent of the likely individuals.

* * *

From the Client's Viewpoint

* * *

ALLOCATING RESPONSIBILITY

If the picture from the lawyers' side of the relationship is described as a substantial amount of autonomy being retained by the lawyer, that picture is quite consistent with what the clients report in terms of allocation of responsibility, reporting, and decision making. First, a majority of both organizational (52 percent) and individual (78 percent) litigants report that there were *no* discussions at all concerning allocation of responsibilities between the lawyer and the litigant. At least a part of this may reflect the existence of a prior relationship between the lawyer and the client in which explicit discussions had taken place or implicit understandings had been arrived at regarding responsibilities. Ninety-five of the 141 organizational litigants who reported no discussions concerning responsibilities and 50 of the 180 individual litigants so situated had had a prior professional relationship with their lawyer. If one makes the strong (and probably unwarranted) assumption that some prior discussion or agreement about responsibilities governed the relationship if the lawyer had worked for the litigant previously (and there was no explicit discussion for this particular case), then only 15 percent of the organizations were dealing with a lawyer where allocation of responsibilities had not been brought up or previously settled; the comparable figure for individuals is much, much higher at 57 percent. In actuality, the two figures for each type of litigant (15 percent and 52 percent for organizations, and 57 percent and 78 percent for individuals), provide an upper and lower bound for the likelihood that allocation of responsibilities had been deal with "up front".

* * *

STAYING INVOLVED AND INFORMED

This picture of greater involved by organizations than individuals carries over to reporting practices from the lawyer to the client. Sixty-nine percent of the organizational litigants reported receiving regular written reports from their lawyer, compared to only 50 percent of the individual litigants. For the individuals receiving such reports, only 10 percent explicitly requested them — 90 percent of the time, the reports were sent on the lawyer's own initiative; only 51 percent of the organizations said that the lawyer took the initiative in sending reports, with the rest indicating that they requested written reports or that such reports were simply part of the standard procedure.

While the level of involvement of the litigants in the major decisions in the case (filing the lawsuit, going to trial) seems to be quite high, these are the kinds of decisions that the lawyer would expect the client to be involved with. In fact, it is somewhat surprising that clients reported decisions being made entirely, or mostly, by the lawyers as often as they were; it is not surprising, given the other patterns I have described here, that lawyer dominance was greater with individual clients than with organizational clients. Seventy-six organizations reported that the suit was filed on their behalf; only 20 percent said that their lawyer (or "mostly" their lawyer) made the decisions, and another 18 percent said that their own involvement had been equal to that of their lawyer. One hundred and sixty-four individuals reported that the suit had been filed on their behalf; 29 percent said it was their lawyer's decision (or "mostly" the lawyer's decision), and 22 percent reported equal involvement by themselves and their lawyer. Thus, the litigant dominated the decision to file 62 percent of the time when that litigant was an organization, but only 49 percent of the time when it was an individual.

GARY NEUSTADTER, WHEN LAWYER AND CLIENT MEET: OBSERVATIONS OF INTERVIEWING AND COUNSELING BEHAVIOR IN THE CONSUMER BANKRUPTCY LAW OFFICE

35 Buff. L. Rev. 177, 177–78, 229 (1986).

What happens when lawyer and client first meet? How do they talk, how do they listen, what do they say, and what do they do? The answers to these questions are generated, and then lost, in thousands of law offices daily. There is thus a treasure of information, but it is mostly hidden from our view by legal barriers that protect privacy and confidentiality and by other barriers, economic, psychological, and logistical, that inhibit or preclude third party observation of lawyer-client contact. This Article reports an exploratory journey in search of that treasure, a journey into six law offices in the metropolitan areas of two states.

In these offices I observed the initial consultation between consumer bankruptcy lawyers and individuals seeking legal assistance in connection with personal financial distress. The report of my observations introduces Lawyers A through F, each of whom devotes a significant portion of their time to consumer bankruptcy counseling. It describes the general structural characteristics and pertinent details of the consumer bankruptcy law practice of each lawyer. The report also identifies the differing attitudes of these lawyers about the alternative solutions to the financial distress of their consumer bankruptcy clients and reveals significant differences in the structure, content, and style of their interviewing and counseling behavior.

* * *

Much of the behavior of the lawyers and paralegals (hereafter "lawyers" for convenience) in the client interviews observed followed routine patterns. In all but two of the law offices, lawyers exercised virtually exclusive control over the structure, sequence, content, and length of the dialogue with clients. Most of the lawyers did not explain their design for the interview to the client at any point. Most did not invite clients to discuss various ways in which the lawyer might serve the client. Except for Lawyer C, lawyers did not regularly discuss solutions to financial distress other than solutions offered by federal bankruptcy law. However, the amount of information offered by the lawyers about the bankruptcy solutions, the degree of influence exercised by lawyers over the client's choice between solutions, and the systems adopted by the lawyers for gathering and dispensing information and implementing chosen solutions varied more widely.

RODNEY J. UPHOFF & PETER B. WOOD, THE ALLOCATION OF DECISIONMAKING BETWEEN COUNSEL AND CRIMINAL DEFENDANT: AN EMPIRICAL STUDY OF ATTORNEY–CLIENT DECISIONMAKING

47 U. Kan. L. Rev. 1, 6, 30–35, 59–60 (1998).

[W]e conducted an exploratory study of five public defender offices involving almost seven hundred public defenders.... We found that a majority of the lawyers studied adopt a more lawyer-centered approach to decisionmaking. Nevertheless we also found a significant number of public defenders who exhibit a more client-centered orientation, which allows their clients to make numerous strategic and tactical decisions.

* * *

We began by identifying twelve strategic and tactical decisions that repeatedly confront criminal defense lawyers and their clients. Some of these decisions — whether to accept a plea agreement, whether to waive a jury trial, whether the client will testify — unquestionably are the client's call. We anticipated that the responses to the survey would reflect the clear allocation of these decisions to the client. The other decisions * * * represent important pretrial and trial-related strategic choices that may significantly affect the outcome of a criminal case. Although these decisions are not constitutionally allocated to either the client or the lawyer, support can be found, to varying degrees, for giving the client or the lawyer the final say for each of these decisions.

We used two different sets of survey questions to determine the degree of support for client-centered lawyering. One set of questions asked whether the public defender agrees (strongly, somewhat) or disagrees (strongly, somewhat) with the proposition that "a lawyer should secure the client's consent" before making a particular decision. We termed this set of questions the "Belief" questions because they reveal the extent to which the lawyer respondents agree or disagree with securing the client's consent before making each of the twelve specific strategic or tactical decisions.

The second set of questions asked "how often do you secure your client's consent" (almost always, most of the time, sometimes, never) before making a particular decision. We termed this set of questions the "Practice" questions because they attempt to identify the extent to which lawyers actually secure the client's consent before making the same twelve strategic or tactical decisions. Using these two response formats enabled us to compare the attitudes of public defenders toward client-centered lawyering with their reported practices.

* * *

As noted above, we identified twelve strategic decisions that every lawyer who practices criminal law particularly as a public defender encounters regularly. Table 2 [omitted from this casebook] presents response frequencies to the items that have been labeled Belief items. The survey items are ranked according to the percent of respondents that "strongly agreed" with the survey item. These twelve items provide some evidence of the respondents' degrees of ideological support for client-centered decisionmaking.

The responses set forth in Table 2 reflect differing levels of commitment to the concept of client-centered decisionmaking. First, it is not surprising that there are four decisions that most respondents strongly agreed should involve the client's consent. Those decisions are: (1) making the decision to waive a jury trial; (2) making a decision regarding a plea bargain; (3) making the decision whether the client will testify at trial; and (4) making the decision to waive a preliminary hearing. When one adds in the "somewhat agree" responses, nearly all respondents agreed that a lawyer should secure a client's consent before making any of these four decisions.

Second, there are three decisions over which the attorney respondents seem sharply divided. Those decisions are: (1) deciding whether to talk to the prosecutor about a possible plea bargain; (2) deciding whether to raise an affirmative defense; and (3) deciding whether to request a lesser included instruction. When the response categories regarding these three decisions are collapsed into simple "agree" and "disagree" groupings, the respondents were almost evenly split over each item.

Finally, most of the respondents apparently believed that the remaining five decisions are the responsibility of counsel, and fewer than 10% of the respondents "strongly agreed" that the lawyer should secure the client's consent before making these decisions. In fact, a majority of the lawyers responding to the survey disagreed with the need to secure a client's consent before: (1) deciding to file a suppression motion; (2) deciding which defense witnesses to call at trial; or (3) exercising peremptory challenges at trial. An even greater majority of the respondents believed that the client's consent was unnecessary when making the decision to request the appointment of an expert witness or the decision to interview the prosecution's witness.

Just as Table 2 provides response frequencies for the Belief items, Table 3 [omitted from this casebook] shows response frequencies for what have been labeled the Practice items. Using the same set of questions, the respondents were asked to report how often they secured a client's consent before making a given decision. Table 3 lists the survey items in the same order as they appear in Table 2.

The response frequencies to the Practice items set forth in Table 3 roughly divide into three categories that are almost identical in composition to those generated by the Belief items. Again, the vast majority of the public defenders responding to the survey claimed they "almost always" secure their clients' consent before: (1) making the decision to waive a jury trial; (2) making the decision regarding a plea bargain; (3) making the decision whether the client will testify; and (4) making the decision to waive a preliminary hearing. Once again, the respondents were divided sharply over how often they actually secured their clients' consent before talking to a district attorney about plea bargaining, affirmative defenses, or requests for a lesser included instruction. In addition, almost 47% of the respondents contended that they secured their clients' consent before deciding which defense witnesses to call at trial. For each of these four items, then, anywhere from 40–60% of the attorneys claimed to secure the client's consent either "almost always" or "most of the time" before making the particular decision.

Finally, except for the decision regarding calling defense witnesses, the practices of the lawyers as reflected by the responses to the remaining items identified in Table 3 correspond to the beliefs expressed as set forth in Table 2. That is, in making the decision to file a suppression motion, to exercise peremptory challenges, to request the appointment of an expert witness, and to interview the prosecution's witnesses, a majority of the respondents stated that they obtain their clients' consent only "sometimes" or "rarely" before making such decisions.

* * *

As this Article demonstrates, many criminal defense lawyers still believe that as the "captain of the ship ... 'it is counsel, not defendant, who is in charge of the case.' " Most lawyers also believe that they generally have the right to control trial tactics and strategy even in the face of the defendant's contrary opinion or explicit objection. Yet, as our study shows, a significant minority of criminal defense lawyers are willing to share decisionmaking power with their clients in a number of important strategic case decisions. Unquestionably, both the commitment to, and the practice of, this client-centered approach varies significantly depending on the strategic or tactical decision to be made. Nonetheless, not only do a sizeable number of public defenders believe in a client-centered approach to decisionmaking, they also claim to practice such lawyering.

Notes and Questions

1.   Professors Uphoff and Wood observe that "a significant minority of criminal defense lawyers" adheres to the client-centered model of lawyering. Relying largely on a case decided by the U.S. Court of Appeals for the Second Circuit, Professor Steven Zeidman warns against the use of client-centered lawyering (at least in its most extreme form) in criminal cases:

> It is time to focus on the constitutional requirements of counseling criminal defendants. What must defense counsel do in order to satisfy the constitutional mandate of effective assistance of counsel in the context of the acceptance or rejection of a plea?

> The recent decision by the Court of Appeals for the Second Circuit in Boria v. Keane addresses this crucial question. This case's holding and analysis have profound implications for the caliber of representation provided to all criminal defendants, as well as for long-standing clinical legal educational notions of client-centered counseling. Oscar Boria was convicted after a jury trial and sentenced to twenty years to life imprisonment. He moved to set aside his conviction, claiming that his attorney, in failing to advise him to accept an offered plea bargain of one to three years incarceration, did not provide effective assistance of counsel. Defense counsel readily admitted that he never counseled the defendant whether or not to accept the plea — a decision, in his view, for a defendant to make. He did, however, discuss the plea repeatedly with the defendant, point out the implications of rejecting it, review the suppression hearing issues and inform the defendant that in his view the chances of prevailing at trial were slim. According to defense counsel, the defendant steadfastly maintained his innocence, and told him that he would not plead guilty, especially if a plea included a jail sentence.

> Granting the defendant's petition for a writ of habeas corpus, the court of appeals held that the Constitution requires that defense counsel provide an informed opinion on whether to plead guilty or go to trial. The court ruled that the defendant had a "constitutional right to be advised whether or not the offered bargain 'appeared to be desirable.' " Because the defense attorney never actually advised his client whether or not he should accept the plea offer, he failed to provide the requisite effective assistance of counsel.

Steven Zeidman, *To Plead or Not to Plead: Effective Assistance and Client–Centered Counseling*, 39 B.C. L. Rev. 841, 847–48 (1998). The case the authors referred to in the article is *Boria v. Keane*, 90 F.3d 36 (2d Cir. 1996).

2.   How would you have decided the *Boria* case? Why would you have reached that decision?

3.   Several courts have distinguished or disagreed with the *Boria* decision, including the Second Circuit in a subsequent case. *Purdy v. U.S.*, 208 F.3d 41 (2d Cir. 2000) (distinguishing and limiting the *Boria* holding)*; see also Jones v. Murray*, 947 F.2d 1106, 1110 (4th Cir. 1991) (refusing to find ineffective assistance of counsel in a capital case where defense counsel neither recommended nor attempted to persuade defendant to enter into a plea agreement); *Bright v. State*, 4 S.W.3d 568 (Mo. Ct. App. 1999) (distinguishing *Boria* and choosing explicitly not to adopt it as law).

3.   MANAGING THE ATTORNEY–CLIENT RELATIONSHIP

Whether traditional, client-centered, or collaborative, the relationship between a client and lawyer is a classic example of a principal-agent relationship. The client, as principal, retains the lawyer, as her agent, to carry out her wishes. As the following excerpt explains, agency relationships, including the lawyer-client relationship, require careful management.

ROBERT H. MNOOKIN, SCOTT R. PEPPET & ANDREW S. TULUMELLO, BEYOND WINNING: NEGOTIATING TO CREATE VALUE IN DEALS AND DISPUTES

70–71 (2000).

Agency relationships are everywhere. We constantly delegate authority to others so that they may act in our place. We ask lawyers to represent us; we give money managers authority to make our investments; we ask doctors to take responsibility for our medical care; we depend on employees to do the work we assign; and we elect public officials to legislate on our behalf. Indeed, it is hard to imagine how society could function at all without agents acting on behalf of principals — diplomats on behalf of nations; labor leaders on behalf of unions; sports agents on behalf of players; literary agents on behalf of authors.

When a principal hires an agent to act on his behalf in negotiations across the table with another party, he may expect — naively — that the agent will be motivated solely to serve the principal's interests. This is how principal-agent relations would work ideally. But in the real world, agents always have interests of their own. As a result, the principal-agent relationship is rife with potential conflicts that demand skillful management behind the table.

For example, a client and his lawyer may need to negotiate how the lawyer will be paid; how the other side will be approached; what information will be sought from or disclosed to the other side; at what point to accept the other side's offer, and so on. If these issues are left unacknowledged and unaddressed, they can adversely affect the negotiation across the table. For all of these reasons, effective negotiation requires a good understanding of the benefits and risks of the agency relationship and how it can best be managed.

Notes and Questions

1.   As the excerpt from Professor Mnookin and his colleagues suggests, clients hire lawyers because they offer certain advantages or benefits in dispute resolution. Below, we explore three "agency benefits" offered by lawyers: "rationality," expertise, and strategic advantages.

a.   *"Rationality."* Lawyers may offer their clients a more rational perspective, which may be of particular value in highly-charged disputes like contentious divorce disputes, employment disputes, and so on. Consider the following excerpt:

> Most lawyers, perhaps by personality as well as by training and practice, approach the world in an abstract, analytical way. Lawyers are deemed so rational and analytical, in fact, that "brain researchers have selected lawyers when they wished to test an occupational group that is characteristically analytical in its preferred mode of thought." Scholars using a variety of methodologies have demonstrated that lawyers are analytically inclined. Researchers using a brain-dominance testing instrument, for instance, have found that nearly 90% of lawyers are "left-brain dominant," indicating an analytical orientation. Researchers have also used the Myers–Briggs Type Indicator (MBTI) to assess lawyers' personalities. The MBTI, which is based on Jungian psychology, measures four dimensions of personality, including whether one is inclined toward "thinking" or "feeling." Thinkers "make decisions more analytically and impersonally" than Feelers. "When making decisions, they place more value on consistency and fairness than on how others will be affected. They look for flaws and fallacies, excelling at critiquing conclusions and pinpointing what is wrong with something." Researchers from the 1960s to the 1990s have found that lawyers are substantially more inclined toward the "thinking" orientation than the population as a whole. Lawyers, in short, "tend to be more logical, unemotional, rational, and objective" than others and place a "great emphasis on logic, thinking, rationality, justice, fairness, rights, and rules."

Chris Guthrie, *The Lawyer's Philosophical Map and the Disputant's Perceptual Map: Impediments to Facilitative Mediation and Lawyering*, 6 Harv. Negot. L. Rev. 145, 156–57 (2001).

b.   *Expertise.* Lawyers also offer their clients special knowledge. As the following excerpt explains, this expertise can take several forms:

> *Substantive knowledge.* A tax attorney or accountant knows things about the current tax code that make it more likely that negotiations with an IRS auditor will benefit the client as much as possible. Similarly, a divorce lawyer, an engineering consultant, and a real estate agent may have substantive knowledge in a rather narrow domain of expertise, and this expertise may redound to the client's benefit.

> *Process expertise.* Quite apart from the specific expertise they may have in particular content areas, agents may have skill at the negotiation

process, per se, thereby enhancing the prospects of a favorable agreement. A skillful negotiator — someone who understands how to obtain and reveal information about preferences, who is inventive, resourceful, firm on goals but flexible on means, etc. — is a valuable resource. Wise principals would do well to utilize the services of such skilled negotiators, unless they can find ways of developing such process skills themselves.

Special influence. A Washington lobbyist is paid to know the "right" people, to have access to the "corridors of power" that the principals themselves are unlikely to possess. Such "pull" can certainly help immensely, and is yet another form of expertise that agents may possess, although the lure of this "access" often outweighs in promise the special benefits that are confirmed in reality.

Jeffrey Z. Rubin & Frank E. A. Sander, *When Should We Use Agents? Direct vs. Representative Negotiation*, 4 Negotiation J. 395, 396 (1988).

c. *Strategic Advantages.* Lawyers also may offer their clients certain strategic advantages. The following excerpt identifies some specific strategic advantages lawyers might offer their clients in negotiation:

The use of agents allows various gambits to be played out by the principals, in an effort to ratchet as much as possible from the other side. For example, if a seller asserts that the bottom line is $100,000, the buyer can try to haggle, albeit at the risk of losing the deal. If the buyer employs an agent, however, the agent can profess willingness to pay that sum but plead lack of authority, thereby gaining valuable time and opportunity for fuller consideration of the situation together with the principal. Or an agent for the seller who senses that the buyer may be especially eager to buy the property can claim that it is necessary to go back to the seller for ratification of the deal, only to return and up the price, profusely apologizing all the while for the behavior of an "unreasonable" client. The client and agent can thus together play the hardhearted partner game.

Conversely, an agent may be used in order to push the other side in tough, even obnoxious, fashion, making it possible — in the best tradition of the "good cop/bad cop" ploy — for the client to intercede at last, and seem the essence of sweet reason in comparison with the agent. Or the agent may be used as a "stalking horse," to gather as much information about the adversary as possible, opening the way to proposals by the client that exploit the intelligence gathered.

Id. at 397–98.

2. Notwithstanding the benefits identified above, lawyers may impose certain disadvantages or costs on their clients as well. Below, we explore three agency costs: rationality, conflicting interests, and misaligned incentives.

a. *Rationality.* Lawyers are famously rational or analytical in their approach to disputes. As noted above, this orientation often works to the benefit of clients. In some circumstances, though, it can pose significant problems, as the following excerpt explains:

[L]awyers' analytical prowess is "purchased at the price of a loss of concrete information" because abstract analysis necessarily reduces complexity. When information is too complex or too subtle to lend itself to abstract reduction, lawyers often have difficulty understanding, interpreting, and working with such information. One task that requires "a gestalt appreciation of an unedited set of concrete data, rather than abstract analytical reduction," is the "recognition and interpretation of subtle displays of emotion."

For all their analytical skills, most lawyers seem fairly uninterested in, and unskilled at, dealing with emotional and interpersonal content. Researchers using the MBTI, for example, have found not only that lawyers are more inclined toward the "thinking" orientation than the population as a whole, but also that lawyers are substantially less inclined toward the "feeling" orientation. Feelers "make decisions more subjectively [than Thinkers], according to their values or what is more important to them. They also place greater emphasis on how other people will be affected by their choices and actions.... It is possible for them to decide whether something is acceptable or agreeable without needing logical reasons." Professors John Barkai and Virginia Fine administered the Truax Accurate Empathy Scale to law students and found that even after undergoing empathy training, law students obtained an average score below Level Five on the scale, "the minimum level of facilitative interpersonal functioning." Professor G. Andrew Benjamin and his colleagues, who undertook a comprehensive study of the mental health and well-being of law students and lawyers, found elevated levels of mental distress and speculated that this could be due to the "[u]nbalanced development of [law] student interpersonal skills." Professor James Hedegard, in his study of BYU law students found "drops in sociability and, more generally, interest in people" during the first year of law school. And Professor Sandra Janoff, who studied the moral reasoning of law students before and after the first year of law school, found that law students became less "caring" during their first year of formal legal education.

On balance, this research suggests that lawyers are "less interested in people, in emotions, and interpersonal concerns" than others. In fact, the research "suggests that humanistic, people-oriented individuals do not fare well, psychologically or academically, in law school or in the legal profession."

Chris Guthrie, *The Lawyer's Philosophical Map and the Disputant's Perceptual Map: Impediments to Facilitative Mediation and Lawyering*, 6 Harv. Negot. L. Rev. 145, 158–60 (2001).

b. *Conflicting Interests*. Rule 1.2 of the Model Rules of Professional Conduct requires lawyers to "abide by a client's decisions concerning the objectives of representation," to "consult with the client as to the means by which they are to be pursued," and to "abide by a client's decision whether to settle a matter." Despite this requirement that lawyers act on their clients' behalf, lawyers and clients may have conflicting interests, as the following excerpt suggests:

In theory, it is clear that the principal calls the shots. Imagine, however, an agent who is intent on applying the GETTING TO YES (Fisher and Ury, 1981) approach by searching for objective criteria and a fair outcome. Suppose the client simply wants the best possible outcome, perhaps because it is a one-shot deal not involving a future relationship with the other party. What if the agent (a lawyer, perhaps) *does* care about his future relationship with the other *agent,* and wants to be remembered as a fair and scrupulous bargainer? How *should* this conflict get resolved and how, in the absence of explicit discussion, *will* it be resolved, if at all? Conversely, the client, because of a valuable long-term relationship, may want to maintain good relations with the other side. But if the client simply looks for an agent who is renowned for an ability to pull out all the stops, the client's overall objectives may suffer as the result of an overzealous advocate.

This issue may arise in a number of contexts. Suppose that, in the course of a dispute settlement negotiation, a lawyer who is intent on getting the best possible deal for a client turns down an offer that was within the client's acceptable range. Is this proper behavior by the agent? The Model Rules of Professional Conduct for attorneys explicitly require (see Rules 1.2(a), 1.4) that every offer must be communicated to the principal, and perhaps a failure to do so might lead to a successful malpractice action against the attorney if the deal finally fell through.

Jeffrey Z. Rubin & Frank E. A. Sander, *When Should We Use Agents? Direct vs. Representative Negotiation*, 4 Negotiation J. 395, 399–40 (1988).

c. *Misaligned Incentives.* Conflicting interests can lead to conflicting economic incentives. Misaligned incentives, in turn, can lead lawyers to take actions that might not be in the client's best interests, as the following excerpt explains:

The economic literature on agency, and scholarship relating to transaction cost economics, teaches that an agent's incentives cannot be perfectly aligned with those of her principal. Using an agent allows the principal the benefits of the agent's special knowledge, skills, and resources. However, the interests of an agent negotiating on behalf of a principal may be a barrier to reaching an agreement that would benefit the principal. For example, critics often claim that litigators are themselves a barrier to the efficient resolution of business disputes through early settlement. High discovery costs surely contribute to the income of partners in many large American defense law firms. Similarly, the fact that plaintiffs' lawyers paid on contingency largely bear the costs of trial surely leads to some settlements that are not in the clients' interests.

Ronald J. Gilson & Robert H. Mnookin, *Foreword: Business Lawyers and Value Creation for Clients*, 74 Or. L. Rev. 1, 11–12 (1995)

3. In what circumstances do the agency benefits of the attorney-client relationship outweigh the agency costs? Which of the agency benefits is most important? Which of the agency costs is most troubling?

4. What strategies might clients and lawyers employ to maximize agency benefits but to minimize agency costs? Careful structuring of fee arrangements (e.g., hourly versus contingency)? Client monitoring of lawyer

behavior? Reliance on professional norms governing lawyers? Ongoing discussions between client and lawyer over the relationship?

5. Consider the following hypothetical. Jim, a solo practitioner specializing in personal injury, is representing Sandy, a retail department store clerk, in a personal injury matter on a contingency basis, in which Jim will keep 33% of Sandy's recovery. Sandy was in a car accident in which her car was totaled by the driver of a major overnight shipping company, who was hurrying to meet a drop-off deadline. Sandy's actual damages were $30,000 for the cost of replacing her car, plus another $10,000 in medical expenses. During the discovery process, however, Jim learns that the shipping company has very tight drop-off deadlines for drivers, and that the accident rate for the company's drivers is ten times higher than the industry standard. The shipping company has offered a settlement of $45,000, which Jim knows Sandy might be willing to accept to put the matter behind her. However, Jim thinks Sandy's claim will be more valuable if he uses it to pursue a class action against the shipper. How are Jim's and Sandy's interests aligned? How are they inconsistent?

B. INTERVIEWING

In this section, we introduce our version of client interviewing, which is based on insights developed by proponents of both the Binder, Bergman & Price client-centered model of interviewing and the Cochran, DiPippa & Peters collaborative model of interviewing.

We believe that the lawyer's primary task is to understand the client's situation and interests rather than focusing exclusively on legally relevant facts (i.e., facts that might help establish a cause of action or defense). Of course, it is typically important for the lawyer to understand and develop the relevant legal theories. However, too much emphasis on law — particularly in the early stages of the consultation — can obscure the client's interests and non-legal concerns, unduly narrow the subject matter of the lawyer-client relationship, and cut off opportunities for finding the best processes and solutions.

1. THE INTERVIEWING PROCESS

What follows is an overview of an interviewing process that will help you acquire the information you need to help your client define the problem and develop options that meet her interests (and perhaps the interests of others). The interviewing process we recommend has six stages: a. introduction; b. preliminary problem identification; c. detailed problem identification; d. exploration of interests; e. theory development; and f. next steps.*

a. Introduction

During the initial moments of the interview, the lawyer seeks to build trust and establish rapport with the client by introducing herself,

---

* Although we believe our approach is consistent with both the client-centered and collaborative models, we owe a special debt to the client-centered model developed by Professors Binder, Bergman, and Price. *See infra* Section C, beginning at page 112.

exchanging pleasantries (or "icebreaking"), and discussing the terms of the representation. The lawyer should take steps to put the client at ease without minimizing the concerns that may have brought the client to the lawyer's office.

b. Preliminary Problem Identification

During the preliminary problem identification stage of the interview, the lawyer seeks to develop a basic notion of what brought the client into the office and what the client would like to happen. Typically, the lawyer would use open-ended questions, such as, "How can I help you?" and "What brought you here?"

Suppose, for example, that a client explains he is an executive with Hays Corp., a manufacturer of water filtration equipment, and that the firm wants to sue Hovercamp Brewery for failure to make certain payments due under a contract. He wants you to tell him whether Hays has a strong claim. That's plenty of information for the preliminary problem identification, but it might not be enough for the lawyer to understand how she can most appropriately help the client.

Some lawyers might, at least temporarily, allow the client's first definition of the problem to set the parameters of the representation. Such lawyers might then gather the information needed to answer the client's question. This might lead to a discussion of solutions that focus narrowly on what would happen in court.

Under the approach we recommend, however, the lawyer would try to slow down the process in order to learn more about what happened and the client's situation, interests, and goals.

c. Detailed Problem Identification

During this stage, the lawyer asks the client to start at the beginning and describe the events that led to the situation at hand — whether an automobile accident or negotiations to start a new joint venture. Generally, the lawyer leads the client gently during this stage, interrupting principally to obtain essential clarifications or — if the client is rambling excessively (a reasonable amount of rambling is a good thing) — to get the client back on track. Ordinarily, this approach yields the bulk of the basic information that the lawyer will need.

During this stage, the Hays executive would describe the two corporations and the history of their relationship. He would set forth the events, as he saw them, leading up to the contract under which Hays developed and installed a water purification system for Hovercamp Brewing. He would explain that the system did not work as expected because the water contained debris of the sort that Hays did not anticipate; that Hovercamp knew of the debris but did not tell Hays; that Hays tried to correct the problem but was unable to do so; and that he has heard that Hovercamp eventually hired another company that was able to correct the problem. Finally, the Hays executive might explain that Hovercamp has withheld $100,000 of the payments due under the contract.

d. Exploration of Interests

During this stage, the lawyer probes to understand, and to make sure the client understands, not merely his *positions* but also his *interests*.

A client's *position* is what he says he wants. A client who feels he has been defamed, for instance, may demand $1 million. A client's *interests* are the motivations or needs that impel him to assert that position. He may be motivated to repair his reputation; to "punish" the newspaper editor; to get the newspaper to change its reporting practices; to support his family; to maintain his business; or to buy a new sailboat. These are interests. Looking at your client's interests along with the interests of the other side makes it easier to come up with solutions. For more on interests, see *infra* Section C, beginning at page 112.

It is clear that the Hays executive wishes to assert the *position* that Hays is legally entitled to the $100,000 payment that Hovercamp has withheld. But the lawyer should explore — to the extent the client is willing to do so — the client's underlying interests as well. So, for instance, the lawyer might ask the Hays executive about the firm's current situation, its short- and long-term goals, and any significant new developments in the services or products it provides. The client might explain that Hays wishes to expand its services to the brewing and bottling industries and that it has developed — but has not found an opportunity to test — a new technology that probably will deal with the problem in the system it installed for Hovercamp. As the lawyer and client discuss the situation, the client may reach a new understanding of the problem or at least recognize that the problem can be defined in a different way.

The lawyer might ask what attempts Hays has made to negotiate a settlement with Hovercamp, and what has stood in the way. Consequently, she might, for instance, learn about personality problems or communication difficulties or hurt feelings. The lawyer would seek to learn how the other side — the Hovercamp executives — might see this situation and what their interests and goals might be as well.

e. Theory Development

Now that the lawyer understands the client's interests, the lawyer is in a much better position to determine what she might do for the client. To the extent legal remedies seem appropriate — here, for instance, a breach of contract suit against Hovercamp may be a real possibility — the lawyer makes sure she has — or requests — the facts necessary to develop her legal theory. In this case, for instance, she would want a copy of the contract and any other relevant document, she would want to understand the course of dealings between Hays and Hovercamp, and she would want to know the customary practices in this industry.

f. Next Steps

Finally, before terminating the interview, the lawyer and client discuss what they will do next. In some instances, this will be the end of the matter; the interview may lead the client to determine that legal representation is not what he needs or may lead the lawyer to decide she will not represent the client. In other instances, the lawyer and client will decide to work together to address the client's problem. At this point, the lawyer makes clear what she intends to do next and may ask the client for assistance — e.g., providing documents and so forth.

Notes and Questions

1. Lawyers have to make judgments about the problem(s) confronting their clients. This task, which might be called "theory development" or "problem setting," is a demanding one:

> In real-world practice, problems do not present themselves to the practitioner as givens. They must be constructed from the materials of problematic situations which are puzzling, troubling, and uncertain. In order to convert a problematic situation to a problem, a practitioner must do a certain kind of work. He must make sense of an uncertain situation that initially makes no sense.

* * *

> When we set the problem, we select what we will treat as the "things" of the situation, we set the boundaries of our attention to it, and we impose upon it a coherence which allows us to say what is wrong and in what directions the situation needs to be changed. Problem setting is a process in which, interactively, we *name* the things to which we will attend and *frame* the context in which we will attend to them.

Donald A. Schon, The Reflective Practitioner: How Professionals Think in Action 40 (1983).

2. Although lawyers must help "set" or diagnose the client's problems, they must strive to avoid premature diagnosis. A physician-friend of ours, whom we will call Bud, tells a story that makes this point nicely:

> During an internship, Bud rode in an ambulance that was summoned to the scene of an accident. The ambulance screeched to a halt in front of a large group of people standing around a man lying in the street. Bud ran over to the man, examined him, and made his diagnosis. He called back to his colleagues on the ambulance, "It's a broken leg. Bring a splint and a stretcher." A nervous murmur passed through the crowd, until, finally, someone yelled out, "Hey, dummy, he's dead!"

> Bud's diagnosis was technically accurate, of course, but he saw only one part of the man's problem–obviously the less important part.

> Then there is another true story about a medical resident working in an emergency room who was interviewing a middle aged man who complained of chest pain. Immediately the resident asked, "Have you ever had heart trouble?"

> "No."

"Have your parents had heart trouble?"

"No."

"How about your siblings or other relatives?"

"No, Doc," the patient answered. "How come you're asking all these questions about heart trouble?"

"Because I think that the reason you are having chest pain is that you are having a heart attack," said the resident.

"Well, Doc," replied the patient, "I think the reason I am having chest pain is that a tractor ran over my chest this afternoon."

The same kind of premature diagnosis can take place in a law office. It is easy for a lawyer to mentally transform a client, a human being, into a "rear-ender" or a "breach of contract." The interviewing approach delineated above should help the lawyer avoid this problem.

3. Although it is important not to jump to conclusions about the problem confronting the client, it is also important to attend carefully to the disclosures the client makes early in the interview. In her empirical study of lawyer-client interviews, Professor Gay Gellhorn found "a pattern of revelation of key, emotion-laden information in the opening moments of the interview ... " Gay Gellhorn, *Law and Language: An Empirically–Based Model for the Opening Moments of Client Interviews*, 4 Clinical L. Rev. 321, 326 (1998).

4. The interview is often an ongoing process rather than a single event, with the lawyer and the client continuing to communicate about new issues as they arise, and preferences as they develop.

* * *

2. TAILORING THE INTERVIEW

Our proposed approach to interviewing is general. In some contexts, lawyers may want to deviate from this approach due to the unique characteristics of their client, the nature of their client's problem, and so forth. In the following excerpt, for example, Linda Lopez advises lawyers how to interview domestic-violence clients. As you read this excerpt, note the ways in which it is consistent (and inconsistent) with the general approach to interviewing we propose above.

LINDA LOPEZ, INTERVIEWING THE DOMESTIC VIOLENCE VICTIM, IN NEW YORK PRACTICE SKILLS COURSE HANDBOOK SERIES

345–48 (Sept. 27, 2000).

III. CONDUCTING THE INTERVIEW

- Begin the interview by introducing yourself and giving the client your business card. Explain your position in your office and the purpose of your meeting. If there is a translator or other third party present, introduce them and explain the purpose of their presence. Encourage the client to make herself comfortable and offer her something to drink.

- Explain issues of confidentiality and whether or not they apply to the information being provided to you. Explain whether or not you will consult with other staff members or interns and volunteers about the case.

- If you are male, be sensitive to the fact that some clients may not feel completely comfortable speaking with you about private matters. Many victims of domestic violence and sexual abuse are embarrassed to speak with anyone, but especially a man, about such experiences. There may also be cultural reasons that inhibit a client from speaking with a man about these circumstances. If you sense that your client is less than forthcoming about the information you need to know, ask if she will be more comfortable speaking with a woman, if a woman attorney is available. The most important thing is to get information about the domestic violence and make the client comfortable enough to provide as many of the relevant facts as possible.

- Some problems that you may encounter are:

  A. Some clients will not be forthcoming with relevant information. To address this, you can ask specific, focused questions such as:

      a. Have you ever gone to the hospital or a doctor as a result of your partner's behavior?

      b. Did you or anyone else ever call the police about problems occurring in your household?

      c. Has your partner ever been physical with any of the children?

      d. Are you or the children afraid of your partner? If so, why?

      e. Has your partner ever forced you to do any sexual acts that you are uncomfortable with?

      f. Have there been any incidents of violence during the holidays?

      g. Did your partner do or say things to you that made you feel embarrassed, humiliated, or belittled?

  B. Some clients will talk endlessly without providing the relevant information you need. Focus your questions so that the client will be encouraged to answer the questions you are asking. If she goes off on tangents, remind her that you need specific information. If she continues to ramble and appears to need someone to talk to, make a referral to an appropriate mental health provider or self-help group. Be mindful that some clients may resist such deferrals because of preconceived notions about therapy, which you should try to diffuse.

  C. Other suggestions:

- It is crucial to consider the impact of your body language and tone of voice during the interview.

- Be wary about asking the question "Why?" Many clients will become defensive and think that you are judging them.

- Make eye contact. This will help the client feel that you see her as a real and individual person.

- If your client becomes emotionally overwrought, interrupt the interview and give her an opportunity to compose herself.

- If you find that the interview has not been productive, schedule another meeting. It is not unusual to have to conduct several sessions to obtain all the information you need.

3. EVALUATING YOUR INTERVIEWING TECHNIQUES

In the following excerpt, Roy Sobelson offers lawyers a way to evaluate their client interviewing skills.

ROY M. SOBELSON, INTERVIEWING CLIENTS ETHICALLY
37 Prac. Law. 13, 18–21 (1991).

There are two common myths about interviewing. One is that everyone can do it and that training is unnecessary. This myth is encouraged by traditional legal training which makes no attempt to teach the three skills most often used in practice: interviewing, counseling, and negotiating. The second myth is that people are born as good or bad interviewers and that training is a waste of time.

My own experience tells me that neither one of these myths is true. You can and should learn proper interviewing techniques. Since it's never too late to learn, here are some questions that may prove helpful in evaluating your own interviewing techniques. Every "no" answer points to a potential problem.

Did I "Break the Ice" First?

Studies indicate that people may fear going to lawyers as much as opposing them. Lawyers need to "acknowledge" the fear by making explicit attempts to put people at ease by "reducing the strangeness" of the experience.

Did I Explain the Interview Process to the Client Before We Got Started?

Was there really a process at all? Once I explained the process, did I live up to the "contract" to conduct the interview in the manner promised? If not, did I acknowledge the reason for varying from my stated format?

Suggested Five "Stages" in the Process

My interviews are composed of the following five "stages":

- *Icebreaker.* Noncontroversial introductions, including an introduction to the process (i.e., methods, time limits, follow ups, etc). This is also a good place to initiate the "conflicts screening process."

You must get enough information to decide whether it is even appropriate to continue;

- *Initial problem identification.* Sometimes known as the "gush," this is where the client first gets to talk openly. In addition to identifying the "problem," the lawyer should ask the client about expectations and goals. Try to limit note taking to "trigger notes" (i.e., notes that will trigger later questioning);

- *Chronological overview.* This is the stage where the client retells the story, with an emphasis on chronological order. It's still too early to ask too many questions. Whatever questions are asked should be for clarification only;

- *Verification.* The aim here is to support potential solutions to the problem by filling in gaps. This is the point when you start to "funnel" your questions, using "secondary" or "follow up" questions;

- *Closure.* Where do we go from here? The most important question to deal with is whether you now have an attorney-client relationship.

Did I Explain Confidentiality?

There is little, if any, evidence that confidentiality plays a major role in the attorney-client relationship. Nevertheless, you must make the client understand that a relationship of trust is partly supported by the promise of confidentiality.

Did I Give the Client My Undivided Attention?

Think about possible distractions here. They may range from the papers on the desk to the ringing telephone to a client's peculiar habits, looks, speech, etc. Notes are often nothing more than a distracting crutch. Do you listen more than you talk?

Did I Control the Interview Without Being "Controlling"?

Lawyers often approach clients as if they were "cases" that can be handled by using a checklist, whether that list is in the lawyer's head or on paper. Consider who determined what subjects were covered in the interview and at what time.

Did I Ask Mostly Open–Ended Questions Before Closed–End Questions?

Open-ended questions and narrative answers elicit more information than closed-ended or directed questions and answers. Although open-ended questions are generally better at getting the conversation started, they may not always be preferable. Varying the types of questions is helpful.

Did I Periodically Check My Understanding with the Client?

Summaries are valuable. They tend to: show the client you are listening; keep the interview on track; aid memory; and clarify things for the speaker and the listener.

Did I Avoid Concluding Too Early in the Interview What the Problem Was?

The danger of the "premature diagnosis" is a very real one. It can mislead and stifle the process.

Did I Find Out What the Client's Real Objective Was?

Find out exactly what it is that the client wants. Lawyers think in terms of legal solutions and approach problems accordingly. The fact that a client has sought a lawyer's help does not mean that the best solution is a legal one.

Did the Client and I Nonjudgmentally Explore Alternative Solutions?

Did I Recognize the Existence of Non-legal Problems or Solutions?

Brainstorming with the client is essential.

Did I Communicate Empathy and Understanding?

The evidence is overwhelming that clients are more likely to be complete, accurate, and honest if they believe the listener is empathic.

Did I Effectively Handle Questions I Was Unable To Answer Immediately?

Did I Say "I Don't Know" When I Didn't Know? Did I Say "No" Instead of "Maybe" When the Answer Should Have Been "No"? Did I Make Sure That Important Questions or Concerns Were Adequately Addressed?

Did I "Hear" Things the Client Didn't Say?

Did I Pay Attention to "When" and "How" Things Were Said?

Pay particularly close attention to: word emphasis; unresponsiveness; adjectives; and gestures.

Did I Acknowledge and Respect My Client's Feelings?

Although you are not expected to be a therapist, remember that feelings are facts. Even if you can't make the problems go away, you can at least acknowledge them. This will help in your honest evaluation of your client's strengths and weaknesses, as well as showing the client that her feelings "count." Try to focus on "what" questions instead of "why" questions.

Did I Leave the Situation Where Fairness and Honesty Demand That It Be Left?

Sometimes the hardest thing to do is to say "no." Considerations of fairness and honesty, as well as potential liability, demand that you give clients the bad news when it is warranted.

Did I Deal With the "Hard Stuff" Myself?

Some lawyers don't like to talk about money with their clients, leaving fee agreements, etc. up to their secretaries, paralegals, assistants, or (even worse) the mail!

Did I Pay Attention to the "Environmental" Factors?

These factors include proximity, lighting, and seating. They are very powerful in communicating messages about importance, sharing of responsibilities, etc. Are they communicating the messages you want them to communicate?

Do My Client and I Have a Relationship Based on Mutual Respect, Trust, and Understanding?

Keep in mind that although the client is the boss and you are the employee, this relationship is unique and requires open communication.

Does My Client Know What His "Role" Is?

Clients should not be treated as passive recipients of services. Give them a stake in the enterprise and they will be more likely to help you. They'll also be more likely to accept responsibility if things don't turn out exactly as planned.

Notes and Questions

1. Sobelson dismisses the use of "checklists" during client interviews. However, if used properly, checklists can be quite valuable to lawyers, ensuring that they address topics they intend to address.

2. To practice the concepts addressed in this section, assume the role of a lawyer and interview a classmate or friend about a dispute in which he or she has been involved. Spend 15 minutes as the interviewer, then switch sides and spend 15 minutes being interviewed about a dispute in which you were involved. What factors made doing the interview challenging? How did it feel being interviewed? Did your counterpart think you fully understood the problem by the end of the interview? Did you feel you had enough information at the end of the interview to proceed in your representation?

C. COUNSELING

Interviewing and counseling are inextricably linked. Lawyers interview their clients to obtain information about the problems that have brought them to seek legal help. Armed with this information, lawyers then help clients in counseling sessions determine how to address the problems confronting them.

Here we propose a four-step counseling model, consistent with both the client-centered and collaborative models of lawyering. This model assumes that the lawyer has interviewed the client, perhaps multiple times, and understands the objectives of the representation. Armed with that information, the lawyer and client should follow a four-step counseling process: 1. clarifying interests; 2. identifying options; 3. exploring the likely consequences of each option; and 4. facilitating decision making.

1. CLARIFYING INTERESTS

The first step in the counseling process is to clarify the client's interests. If the counseling session occurs immediately after the client interview, the lawyer should have a good idea about the client's interests, particularly if the lawyer follows the interviewing model proposed above. Regardless, the lawyer should start by saying something like, "It seems to me that you hope to obtain *interest x, interest y, and interest z,* is that right?" Assuming the client confirms this, then the lawyer might ask, "Is there anything else that is important to you in this process, or is there anything I've missed?" Once the lawyer has clarified the client's interests, then the lawyer can move the counseling session into its problem-solving phase.

2. IDENTIFYING OPTIONS

During the second stage of the counseling process, the lawyer and client work together to identify alternative courses of action that might meet the client's interests. The following readings explore different ways of accomplishing this objective. Alex Osborn begins by describing what he calls "brainstorming" to identify options. Jennifer Gerarda Brown then discusses several other techniques that might be used to generate creative options. Finally, Robert Persig demonstrates how simply "being" with a problem can enable people to generate creative options, in an excerpt from his famous novel, ZEN AND THE ART OF MOTORCYCLE MAINTENANCE (1975).

ALEX F. OSBORN, APPLIED IMAGINATION: PRINCIPLES AND PROCEDURES OF CREATIVE PROBLEM–SOLVING

151–52, 155–56 (3d ed. 1963).

It was in 1938 when I first employed organized ideation in the company I then headed. The early participants dubbed our efforts "Brainstorm Sessions"; and quite aptly so because, in this case, "brainstorm" means using the *brain* to *storm* a problem.

Brainstorming has become so much a part of the American scene that the verb brainstorm, in the sense of creative effort, is now included in Webster's International Dictionary and defined as follows: "To practice a conference technique by which a group attempts to find a solution for a specific problem by amassing all the ideas spontaneously contributed by its members."

This kind of conference is not entirely new. A similar procedure is known to have been used in India for more than 400 years as part of the technique of Hindu teachers while working with religious groups. The Indian name for this method is *Prai-Barshana. Prai* means "outside yourself" and *Barshana* means "question." In such a session there is no discussion or criticism. Evaluation of ideas takes place at later meetings of the same group.

The modern brainstorm session is nothing more than a creative conference for the sole purpose of producing a checklist of ideas — ideas which can serve as leads to problem-solution — ideas which can *subsequently* be evaluated and further processed.

* * *

Idea-producing conferences are relatively fruitless unless certain rules are understood by all present, and are faithfully followed. Here are four basics:

(1) *Criticism is ruled out.* Adverse judgment of ideas must be withheld until later.

(2) *"Free-wheeling" is welcomed.* The wilder the idea, the better; it is easier to tame down than to think up.

(3) *Quantity is wanted.* The greater the number of ideas, the more the likelihood of useful ideas.

(4) *Combination and improvement are sought.* In addition to contributing ideas of their own, participants should suggest how ideas of others can be turned into *better* ideas; or how two or more ideas can be joined into still another idea.

JENNIFER GERARDA BROWN, CREATIVITY AND PROBLEM–SOLVING

87 Marq. L. Rev. 697, 699–702, 703–4, 705, 706 (2004).

A. WORDPLAY

Once an issue or problem is articulated, it is possible to play with the words expressing that problem in order to improve understanding and sometimes to yield new solutions.

1. Shifting Emphasis

To take a fairly simple example, suppose that two neighbors are in a dispute because cigarette butts and other small pieces of trash, deposited by Mr. Smith in his own front yard, are blowing into Mr. Jones's yard, and those that remain in Mr. Smith's yard are detracting from the appearance of the neighborhood (at least as Mr. Jones sees it). Mr. Jones might ask himself (or a mediator at the neighborhood justice center), "How can I get Mr. Smith to stop littering in his yard?" Shifting the emphasis in this sentence brings into focus various aspects of the problem and suggests possible solutions addressing those specific aspects. Consider the different meanings of the following sentences:

"How can *I* get Mr. Smith to stop littering in his yard?"

"How can I get *Mr. Smith* to stop littering in his yard?"

"How can I get Mr. Smith to stop *littering* in his yard?"

"How can I get Mr. Smith to stop littering in *his* yard?"

"How can I get Mr. Smith to stop littering in his *yard*?"

As the focus of the problem shifts, so too different potential solutions might emerge to address the problem as specifically articulated.

2.   Changing a Word

Sometimes changing a word in the sentence helps to reformulate the problem in a way that suggests new solutions. In the example above, Mr. Jones might change the phrase "littering in his yard" to something else, such as "neglecting his yard" or "hanging out in his yard." It may be that something besides littering lies at the root of the problem, and a solution will be found, for example, not in stopping the littering, but in more regularized yard work.

3.   Deleting a Word

Through word play, parties can delete words or phrases to see whether broadening the statement of the problem more accurately or helpfully captures its essence. Mr. Jones might delete the phrase "Mr. Smith" from his formulation of the problem, and thereby discover that it is not just Mr. Smith's yard, but the entire street, that is looking bad. Focusing on Mr. Smith as the source of the problem may be counterproductive; Mr. Jones might discover that he needs to organize all of the homeowners on his block to battle littering in order to make a difference. Deleting words sometimes spurs creativity by removing an overly restrictive focus on the issue or problem.

4.   Adding a New Word

A final form of word play that can spur creative thinking is sometimes called "random word association." Through this process, participants choose a word randomly and then think of ways to associate it with the problem. Suppose Mr. Jones and Mr. Smith were given the word "work" and asked how it might relate to their dispute. Here are some possible results:

> *Work (time, effort)*: Mr. Smith will try to work harder to keep his yard looking nice, and he will check Mr. Jones's yard every Saturday to make sure there are no cigarette butts or other pieces of trash in it.

> *Work (being operational or functional)*: What the neighborhood needs is a sense of cohesion; Mr. Jones and Mr. Smith will organize a neighborhood beautification project to try to instill a sense of community among their neighbors.

> *Work (job)*: Although Mr. Smith's odd working hours sometimes lead him to smoke on his front porch and chat with his friends or family late at night (after Mr. Jones has gone to bed), Mr. Smith will stay in the back of his house after 10 p.m., further from Mr. Jones's bedroom window.

As the different meanings and resulting associations of "work" are explored by the parties, they discover new ways to solve their shared problem. Other seemingly unrelated words might trigger still more associations and more potential solutions.

Adding words can also be helpful if participants insert adjectives that narrow the problem so it appears more manageable. Mr. Jones might ask, "How can I get Mr. Smith to stop littering in his *front* yard?" Narrowing the problem from all of Mr. Smith's property to the front yard might suggest agreements that could keep Mr. Smith's front yard looking nice but still permit him to use other parts of his property (such as a side or back yard) as he wishes. This approach to word play builds upon the insight that many creative solutions are incremental. The problem will not seem so daunting to the parties when it is narrowed, and they can address the larger issues step by step.

These techniques of word play (especially random word association) are designed to "force the mind to 'jump across' its usual pathways (mental ruts), or make new connections between old pathways in order to create a new idea out of two seemingly disparate ideas." The exercises might feel mechanical to the parties at first, but if adopted with some energy and good faith, they could help the parties to enhance the creativity of their thinking.

* * *

D. ATLAS OF APPROACHES

Another technique for stimulating creative ideas about a problem from a variety of perspectives is called the "Atlas of Approaches." Roger Fisher, Elizabeth Koppelman and Andrea Kupfer Schneider propose this approach in *Beyond Machiavelli*, their book on international negotiation. Using the Atlas of Approaches technique, participants adopt the perspectives of professionals from a variety of fields. By asking themselves, for example, "What would a journalist do?", "What would an economist do?", "How would a psychologist view this?", and so on, negotiators are able to form a more interdisciplinary view of their problem. With this more complete picture of the issues and potential outcomes, they might be able to connect disciplines in ways that give rise to creative solutions.

E. VISUALIZATION

When parties use the visualization technique, they take time to imagine the situation they desire, one in which their problem is solved. What do they see? What specific conditions exist, and how might each of those conditions be achieved? Weinstein and Morton suggest that parties can engage in visualization simply by closing their eyes and thinking about the problem in terms that are visual rather than abstract. Another approach is to "look at the problem from above, and see things otherwise invisible." The goal is to deploy a variety of the brain's cognitive pathways (verbal, visual, spatial and abstract), the better to make connections that give rise to creative solutions.

F. "WWCD": WHAT WOULD CROESES DO?

This process requires a participant to take the perspective of an unconstrained actor. What solutions suggest themselves if we assume no limit to available money, time, talent, technology, or effort? In some ways, one could think of the WWCD method as a more specific application of brainstorming. As the proponents of brainstorming are quick to point out, creativity and the free flow of ideas can be impeded by criticism or assessment. WWCD takes off the table any assessment based on constraints — financial, technological, etc. If we assume that we can afford and operationalize any solution we can come up with, what might we discover?

A second phase of this approach requires participants to think about the extent to which their unconstrained solution might be modified to make it workable given the existing constraints.

* * *

H. FLIPPING OR REVERSAL

With this technique, one asks whether flipping or reversing a given situation will work. As Edward de Bono explains:

> In the reversal method, one takes things as they are and then turns them round, inside out, upside down, back to front. Then one sees what happens ... one is not looking for the right answer but for a different arrangement of information which will provoke a different way of looking at the situation.

Chris Honeyman sometimes uses this technique in his work as a neutral when he asks parties to put forward some really *bad* ideas for resolving the conflict. When people offer ideas in response to a call for "bad" ideas, they may free themselves to offer the ideas they partially or secretly support; again, as in brainstorming, they disclaim ownership of the ideas. It is also possible that the instruction to offer bad ideas stimulates creative thinking because it can seem *funny* to people. Humor is a good stimulant for creativity.

* * *

I. IDEA ARBITRAGE

With idea arbitrage, parties see an existing solution in one context and ask themselves where else it might work. A great example of this from the field of consumer products design is the electric toothbrush with rotating bristles. Nalebuff and Ayres point out that this terrific invention actually grew out of a much more trivial discovery — the rotating lollipop! The inventors of the lollipop knew they had a good thing, so they looked for new places to put it to use. Similar stories can be told about velcro or polycarbonate wheels. This building upon prior discovery is the root of creativity in art and science. With idea arbitrage, the creativity stems from solutions — that is, expanding the problem to which an existing solution may be applied, rather than from a focus on the problems themselves. This approach assumes that there are solutions in search of problems, rather than the other way around.

ROBERT PIRSIG, ZEN AND THE ART OF MOTORCYCLE MAINTENANCE

278–79, 285–86 (1975).

Stuckness. That's what I want to talk about today ...

A screw sticks, for example, on a side cover assembly. You check the manual to see if there might be any special cause for this screw to come off so hard, but all it says is "Remove side cover plate" in that wonderful terse technical style that never tells you what you want to know. There's no earlier procedure left undone that might cause the cover screws to stick.

If you're experienced you'd probably apply a penetrating liquid and an impact driver at this point. But suppose you're inexperienced and you attach a self-locking plier wrench to the shank of your screwdriver and really twist it hard, a procedure you've had success with in the past, but which this time succeeds only in tearing the slot of the screw.

Your mind was already thinking ahead to what you would do when the cover plate was off, and so it takes a little time to realize that this irritating minor annoyance of a torn screw slot isn't just irritating and minor. You're stuck. Stopped. Terminated. It's absolutely stopped you from fixing the motorcycle.

This isn't a rare scene in science or technology. This is the commonest sense of all. Just plain *stuck*. In traditional maintenance this is the worst of all moments, so bad that you have avoided even thinking about it before you come to it.

* * *

The book's no good to you now. Neither is scientific reason. You don't need any scientific experiments to find out what's wrong. It's obvious what's wrong. What you need is an hypothesis for how you're going to get that slotless screw out of there and scientific method doesn't provide any of these hypotheses. It operates only after they're around.

This is the zero moment of consciousness. Stuck. No answer. Honked. Kaput. It's a miserable experience emotionally. You're losing time. You're incompetent. You don't know what you're doing. You should be ashamed of yourself. You should take the machine to a *real* mechanic who knows how to figure these things out.

* * *

Let's consider a reevaluation of the situation in which we assume that the stuckness now occurring, the zero of consciousness, isn't the worst of all possible situations, but the best possible situation you could be in. After all, it's exactly this stuckness that Zen Buddhists go to so much trouble to induce; through koans, deep breathing, sitting still and the like. Your mind is empty, you have a "hollow-flexible" attitude of "beginner's mind." You're right at the front end of the train of knowledge, at the track of reality itself. Consider, for a change, that this is a moment to be not feared but cultivated. If your mind is truly, profoundly stuck, then you may be much better off than when it was loaded with ideas.

* * *

But now consider the fact that no matter how hard you try to hang on to it, this stuckness is bound to disappear. Your mind will naturally and freely move toward a solution. Unless you are a real master at staying stuck you can't prevent this. The fear of stuckness is needless because the longer you stay stuck the more you see the Quality-reality that gets you unstuck every time. What's *really* been getting you stuck is the running from the stuckness through the cars of your train of knowledge looking for a solution that is out in front of the train.

Stuckness shouldn't be avoided. It's the ... predecessor of all real understanding. An egoless acceptance of stuckness is a key to an understanding of all Quality, in mechanical work as in other endeavors. It's this understanding of Quality as revealed by stuckness which so often makes self-taught mechanics appear so superior to institute-trained men who have learned how to handle everything except a new situation.

Notes and Questions

1. Brainstorming and the other processes described in the excerpts from Professor Brown's article and Robert Pirsig's novel are all devices that can enable lawyers and clients to generate options for the client. To illustrate, suppose you are a lawyer, and a new client, Albert, tells you he loaned his $600 mountain bicycle to Bernice and she has refused to return it. He wants to know what to do. Do you see any options immediately? Write them down.

Suppose you ask a few questions and learn that Albert and Bernice had been neighbors and close "platonic" friends for several years until Bernice moved to another town fifty miles away; that Bernice may be angry at Albert because he borrowed $200 from her several months ago, and that Albert is in debt, does not need the bicycle, and would like to resume a friendship with Bernice.

What options do you see now? Take two or three minutes to think about them. As you do, notice that the "interests" of your client have broadened from those he first mentioned. Although he would like the bicycle back, he also wants to resume a relationship with Bernice, and he owes her money.

2. To be a good problem solver, you also must learn and respond to Bernice's interests. Why is she keeping the bike? What does she want from Albert? Recognition? Money? Does she need transportation? Are there other ways for her to get around?

The following is a list of ideas that might have come from brainstorming or another process designed to stimulate creative thinking:

Albert helps himself and takes the bicycle.

Albert offers to pay the $200 in exchange for the bicycle.

Bernice keeps the bicycle.

Bernice keeps the bicycle and forgives the debt.

Bernice keeps the bicycle, forgives the debt, and gives some money ($200? $400?) to Albert.

Albert visits the D.A. and seeks to have Bernice prosecuted.

Albert ceases contact with Bernice and gives up trying to get the bicycle.

Negotiation

- Albert and Bernice negotiate.

- Albert's lawyer negotiates with Bernice.

- Albert's lawyer negotiates with Bernice's lawyer.

Letter writing

- Albert (or his lawyer) sends a letter to Bernice

  - asking for return of the bicycle.

  - asking to meet.

  - proposing one of the solutions described above.

- Albert or his lawyer writes or telephones others, such as Bernice's employer, parent, roommate

Third-party assistance

- Small claims court

- Mediation (formal)

  - Neighborhood justice center

  - Prosecutor's mediation program

  - Other forums as appropriate, such as Christian Conciliation Service

- Mediation (informal)

  - Intervention by a mutual friend

3.   Notice that this list is disorganized; it resulted from a free-association process. Sometimes you can enhance your creativity by ignoring rigid categories. But before analyzing the options, you would want to group them. Some of the items — such as Bernice keeping the bicycle and paying money to Albert — are proposals for specific solutions to the problem. Others suggest a process for developing a solution. Still others combine elements of process and content.

3. EXPLORING CONSEQUENCES

After identifying viable options, the lawyer and client should attempt to assess the likely consequences of each of these options and then determine whether each consequence is advantageous or disadvantageous to the client.

Lawyers normally are more skilled at predicting the likely outcome of legal processes like trials: How long they will take, how much they will cost, the chances of a judgment for a given amount, the degree of publicity, and the like. Clients typically are better able to characterize these consequences as advantages or disadvantages. Also the client may be better at predicting non-legal or social outcomes, such as the effect of various actions on her emotional state, employment, and family and social relationships. The lawyer's job is to help the client bring out, understand, and evaluate such outcomes.

Let us return to Albert, Bernice and the bicycle. Albert expresses interest in using the small claims court. How might he and the lawyer analyze this?

First, the lawyer could explain the process — how one goes about filing, the expense, time, and likely result. In abbreviated form, it might go something like this: "It would cost $100 for filing and service of process. The hearing would be held within three weeks. You probably would get an order against Bernice requiring that she return the bike. However, there is an excellent chance that she would assert her claim against you for the money you borrowed, and she probably would get a judgment against you for that amount." The lawyer also would help the client understand the process by which a judgment would be executed.

Next the lawyer might inquire about predictions the client could make. How is Bernice likely to react? Would the notice from the court soften her attitude in negotiations or harden her resistance, and increase her possible anger about the money? What is the likely impact of instituting this action upon your feelings toward Bernice? Your relationships with mutual friends?

In this example, the small claims court probably would not be the best initial choice, and an analysis of the consequences would make that plain to most clients. If the lawyer is to be a problem solver, he must help the client consider how the other side would interpret any action the client takes.

Lawyer and client might go through a similar dialogue regarding each of the alternatives that seemed superficially plausible. This would narrow the numerous options to a few: probably a contact through a mutual friend, a letter, or a telephone call by the client or attorney.

4. FACILITATING DECISION MAKING

a. Deciding How to Decide

Often, after the client and lawyer have developed options and identified likely consequences, the client can easily tell the lawyer his choice. Many times, however, the lawyer will have to review options, help the client revisit or re-clarify his objectives, or give the client time to think over the choices, perhaps after discussing them with friends, relatives or colleagues. And sometimes the client will ask the lawyer for his opinion about what to do.

Deciding how to decide as a pair can be difficult, as the following readings attest. The first, by Dr. Atul Gawande, tells a very personal story illustrating this difficulty in the doctor-patient relationship; the second, by Professors Binder, Bergman, and Price, describes this difficulty in the lawyer-client relationship.

ATUL GAWANDE, COMPLICATIONS: A SURGEON'S NOTES ON AN IMPERFECT SCIENCE
210–11, 211–12, 219–22 (2002).

Little more than a decade ago, doctors made the decisions; patients did what they were told. Doctors did not consult patients about their desires and priorities, and routinely withheld information — sometimes crucial information, such as what drugs they were on, what treatments they were being given, and what their diagnosis was. Patients were even forbidden to look at their own medical records: too fragile and simple-minded to handle the truth, let alone make decisions. And they suffered for it. People were put on machines, given drugs, and subjected to operations they would not have chosen. And they missed out on treatments that they might have preferred.

My father recounts that, through the 1970s and much of the 1980s, when men came to see him seeking vasectomies, it was accepted that he would judge whether the surgery was not only medicinally appropriate but also personally appropriate for them. He routinely refused to do the operation if the men were unmarried, married but without children, or "too young." In retrospect, he's not sure he did right by all these patients, and, he says, he'd never do things this way today. In fact, he can't even think of a patient in the last few years whom he has turned down for a vasectomy.

One of the reasons for this dramatic shift in how decisions are made in medicine was a 1984 book, THE SILENT WORLD OF DOCTOR AND PATIENT, by a Yale doctor and ethicist named Jay Katz. It was a devastating critique of traditional medical decision making, and it had wide influence. In the book, Katz argued that medical decisions could and should be made by the patients involved.

* * *

Eventually, medical schools came around to Katz's position. By the time I attended, in the early 1990s, we were taught to see patients as autonomous decision makers. "You work for them," I was often reminded. There are still many old-school doctors who try to dictate from on high, but they are finding that patients won't put up with that anymore. Most doctors, taking seriously the idea that patients should control their own fates, lay out the options and the risks involved. A few even refuse to make recommendations, for fear of improperly influencing patients. Patients ask questions, look up information on the Internet, seek second opinions. And they decide.

In practice, however, matters aren't so straightforward. Patients, it turns out, make bad decisions, too. Sometimes, of course, the difference between one option and another isn't especially significant. But when you see your patient making a grave mistake, should you simply do what the patient wants? The current medical orthodoxy says yes. After all, whose body is it, anyway?

* * *

The new orthodoxy about patient autonomy has a hard time acknowledging an awkward truth: patients frequently don't want the freedom that we've given them. That is, they're glad to have their autonomy respected, but the exercise of that autonomy means being able to relinquish it. Thus, it turns out that patients commonly prefer to have others make their medical decisions. One study found that although 64 percent of the general public thought they'd want to select their own treatment if they developed cancer, only 12 percent of newly diagnosed cancer patients actually did want to do so.

This dynamic is something I only came to understand recently. My youngest child, Hunter, was born five weeks early, weighing barely four pounds, and when she was eleven days old she stopped breathing. She had been home a week and doing well. That morning, however, she seemed irritable and fussy, and her nose ran. Thirty minutes after her feeding, her respiration became rapid, and she began making little grunting noises with each breath. Suddenly, Hunter stopped breathing. My wife, panicked, leaped up and shook Hunter awake, and the baby started breathing again. We rushed her to the hospital.

Fifteen minutes later, we were in a large, bright, emergency department examination room. With an oxygen mask on, Hunter didn't quite stabilize — she was still taking over sixty breaths a minute and expending all her energy to do it — but she regained normal oxygen levels in her blood and held her own. The doctors weren't sure what the cause of her trouble was. It could have been a heart defect, a bacterial infection, a virus. They took X rays, blood, and urine, did an electrocardiogram, and tapped her spinal fluid. They suspected — correctly, as it turned out — that the problem was an ordinary respiratory virus that her lungs were too little and immature to handle. But the results from the cultures wouldn't be back for a couple of days. They admitted her to the intensive care unit. That night, she began to tire out. She had several spells of apnea — periods of up to sixty seconds in which she stopped breathing, her heartbeat slowed, and she became pale and ominously still — but each time she came back, all by herself.

A decision needed to be made. Should she be intubated and put on a ventilator? Or should the doctors wait to see if she could recover without it? There were risks either way. If the team didn't intubate her now, under controlled circumstances, and she "crashed" — maybe the next time she would not wake up from an apneic spell — they would have to perform an emergency intubation, a tricky thing to do in a child so small. Delays could occur, the breathing tube could go down the wrong pipe, the doctors could inadvertently traumatize the airway and cause it to shut down, and then she might suffer brain damage or even die from lack of oxygen. The likelihood of such a disaster was slim but real. I myself had seen it happen. On the other hand, you don't want to put someone on a ventilator if you don't have to, least of all a small child. Serious and detrimental effects ... happen frequently. And, as people who have been hooked up to one of these contraptions will tell you, the machine shoots air into and out of you with terrifying, uncomfortable force; your mouth becomes sore; your lips crack. Sedation is given, but the drugs bring complications, too.

So who should have made the choice? In many ways, I was the ideal candidate to decide what was best. I was the father, so I cared more than any hospital staffer ever could about which risks were taken. And I was a doctor, so I understood the issues involved. I also knew how often problems like miscommunication, overwork, and plain hubris could lead physicians to make bad choices.

And yet when the team of doctors came to talk to me about whether to intubate Hunter, I wanted them to decide — doctors I had never met before. The ethicist Jay Katz and others have disparaged this kind of desire as "childlike regression." But that judgment seems heartless to me. The uncertainties were savage, and I could not bear the possibility of making the wrong call. Even if I made what I was sure was the right choice for her, I could not live with the guilt if something went wrong. Some believe that patients should be pushed to take responsibility for decisions. But that would have seemed equally like a kind of harsh paternalism in itself. I needed Hunter's physicians to bear the responsibility; they could live with the consequences, good or bad.

I let the doctors make the call, and they did so on the spot. They would keep Hunter off the ventilator, they told me. And, with that, the bleary-eyed, stethoscope-collared pack shuffled onward to their next patient. Still, there was the nagging question: if I wanted the best decision for Hunter, was relinquishing my hard-won autonomy really the right thing to do? Carl Schneider, a professor of law and medicine at the University of Michigan, recently published a book called THE PRACTICE OF AUTONOMY, in which he sorted through a welter of studies and data on medical decision making, even undertaking a systematic analysis of patients' memoirs. He found that the ill were often in a poor position to make good choices: they were frequently exhausted, irritable, shattered, or despondent. Often, they were just trying to get through their immediate pain, nausea, and fatigue; they could hardly think about major decisions. This rang true to me. I wasn't even the patient, and all I could do was sit and watch Hunter, worry, or distract myself with busywork. I did not have the concentration or the energy to weigh the treatment options properly.

Schneider found that physicians, being less emotionally engaged, are able to reason through the uncertainties without the distortions of fear and attachment. They work in a scientific culture that disciplines the way they make decisions. They have the benefit of "group rationality" — norms based on scholarly literature and refined practice. And they have the key relevant experience. Even though I am a doctor, I did not have the experience that Hunter's doctors had with her specific condition.

In the end, Hunter managed to stay off the ventilator, although she had a slow and sometimes scary recovery.

DAVID A. BINDER, PAUL BERGMAN & SUSAN C. PRICE, LAWYERS AS COUNSELORS: A CLIENT–CENTERED APPROACH*

348–50 (2d ed. 1991).

Responding to client requests for your opinion about what to do primarily concerns not whether, but how and when you give it.

A.   GIVING ADVICE BASED ON CLIENTS' VALUES

When you give an opinion, client-centeredness suggests that you usually do so on the basis of each client's unique mix of values and attitudes towards the consequences at stake. Thus, if a client asks for your opinion early on, you should normally withhold it until after you have engaged the client in a thorough counseling dialogue. However, explain your desire to postpone giving your opinion in an empathic manner which indicates that you are aware of the client's request and will respond to it. A dialogue conveying such an explanation may go as follows:

> Lawyer: Next, Diana, why don't we turn to the question I asked you to think about, whether to insist on a personal guarantee from the officers?

> Client: I've been thinking about it a lot, and I'm still not sure what to do. What do you suggest?

> Lawyer: I hate to sound like a lawyer, but there's not one right answer. A lot depends on the unique circumstances of your situation. What I suggest is this. Let's discuss the likely pros and cons both of having and not having personal guarantees. We'll even prepare a chart of the likely consequences. If you still want my opinion after we've done that, I'll certainly give it to you. But by postponing my view, I'll be able to take what you say into account in giving you my opinion. Does that sound all right?

> Client: Sure.

Sometimes clients will not agree to a counseling dialogue. For example, after the explanation above, instead of "Sure," Diana might have said:

> Client: That sounds like it'll take some time, and frankly I don't want to devote the time or money to it. You're a lawyer, and I'm

* With permission of the West Group.

sure you've come across these situations lots of times. I'll go along with what you think is best.

Here, the client refuses the invitation to go through the counseling process, and again asks for your opinion. Should you give it? The answer depends on whether the client has had a "reasonable opportunity" to make the decision. That, in turn, entails consideration of, among other things, the relative importance of the decision in the framework of the client's problem and the content and extent of your prior discussions with Diana. Assuming you believe that Diana has had a reasonable opportunity to decide, you might respond as follows:

Lawyer: I'm not sure that I know what's best. But you tell me if I'm wrong. My sense is that your primary objective is for this deal to go through and that you feel the company itself is pretty solid. If I'm right about those things, probably you're better off not insisting on personal guarantees. Is that a decision you're comfortable with?

Note that you couch the advice in terms of the client's apparent values, invite the client to disagree if you have the values wrong, and conclude by giving the client room to have the last word. Thus, when you do give advice, you do so as much as possible based on the client's values.

In a second type of scenario, clients make (or renew) requests for your opinion after a thorough counseling dialogue has taken place. In these situations, you are at least confident that a client has had a reasonable opportunity to decide. The advice-giving dialogue might proceed as follows:

Client: I know we've gone round and round on this, but I just can't decide. What do you think I ought to do?

Lawyer: Well, I agree that it's time to cut bait on this one. In the abstract, either decision might be proper, so primarily my advice grows out of what you've said as we've talked. I know your accountant has advised you to get personal guarantees, and I don't want to come between you and her. You can tell me if I'm wrong, but what you've indicated is that your primary objective is for this deal to go through, and that you feel the company itself is pretty solid. Also, you have some fear that insisting on guarantees might sour this deal and spoil future business opportunities. Based on these feelings, I think you'd be best off not insisting on personal guarantees. Does that seem sound?

As you can see, the advice remains tied to the client's values. But since a full counseling dialogue has already taken place, you have a richer data base from which to operate, and can give advice on what the client has actually said.

B.   OFFERING OPINIONS BASED ON YOUR PERSONAL VALUES

[C]lients may ask for and are entitled to receive opinions based on your own personal values. That is, they want to know what you personally would do if you faced the same decision as they do.

Assume that a client asks, "What would you do personally?" or, "I want to do what's right. Do you think I'm doing the right thing?" These questions are ambiguous in terms of what sort of reply the client expects. You should ask a question such as the following to clarify the ambiguity:

"Just so I'm clear, do you want to know what I'd do if I were in your shoes, or what I would personally do, given my own values and objectives?"

In response, a client may say one or the other, or both. In any event, when a client does want to know what you personally would do, be sure to mention the values and attitudes on which you rest your decision. That way, clients can compare their attitudes to yours when deciding how much weight to give your opinion.

For example, assume that you represent an employer who has to decide which form of non-competition clause to include in a contract proposal to a prospective employee, Huber. One option is a very restrictive clause which has an 80% chance of being held invalid; the other is a less restrictive provision which is in all likelihood valid. The latter provision would give Huber far more opportunity to seek other employment should Huber cease working for the employer after signing the contract. The client asks, "Which clause would you personally choose if you were in this situation?" You might respond,

> That's pretty difficult to say — I've never been in this exact situation. But in my experience people often go along with what they agree to. Also, I'm pretty willing to take risks, and here I'd be willing to take the risk that Huber will live up to the agreement rather than try to defy it and risk being sued. So based on that, I'd choose the more restrictive language. Now you may feel differently, in which case you might not want to do what I would do.

This statement tells the client that your opinion is based on your experience with how people generally behave and your willingness to take risks. The client can then compare her or his beliefs with yours and decide how much stock to put in your opinion.

Notes and Questions

1.   The foregoing approach to counseling should help the lawyer and client avoid selecting the first solution that occurs to them. This is one of the major problems facing both parties in the legal counseling situation and is a first cousin to the "premature diagnosis" problem in interviewing, which is discussed in Section B.

The crux of the problem is that a person who thinks he knows the answer is likely to pass up other opportunities. This is the point of the following story, familiar in religious circles, about a man sitting on the roof of his home as a flood swept through his town.

> The water was well up to the roof when along came a rescue team in a rowboat. They tried hard to reach him and finally when they did, they shouted, "Well, come on. Get into the boat!" And he said, "No, no. God will save me." So the water rose higher and higher and he climbed higher and higher on the roof. The water was very turbulent, but still another boat managed to make its way to him. Again they begged him to get into the boat and to save himself. And again he said, "No, no, no. God will save me! I'm praying. God will save me!" Finally the water was almost over him, just his head was sticking out. Then along came a helicopter. It came down right over him and they called, "Come on. This is your last chance! Get in here!" Still he said, "No, no, no. God will save me!" Finally his head went under the water and he drowned. When he got to heaven, he complained to God, "God, why didn't you try to save me?" And God said, "I did. I sent you two rowboats and a helicopter."

CHARLOTTE JOKO BECK, EVERYDAY ZEN 70 (1989).

2. When lawyers counsel clients, they must be attentive both to legal *and* non-legal considerations, as former Stanford Law School Dean Paul Brest explains:

> Counseling lies at the heart of the professional relationship between lawyer and client. A client comes to a lawyer — rather than, say, an accountant, an engineer, or a psychologist — because the client perceives his problem to have a legal component. But most real-world problems do not conform to the neat boundaries that define and divide different disciplines, and a good lawyer must be able to counsel clients and serve their interests beyond the confines of his technical expertise — to integrate legal considerations with the business, personal, political, and other nonlegal aspects of the matter.

> In counseling a client about a strategic decision, negotiating or drafting an agreement, or dealing with an organizational problem, the lawyer's work may be constrained, facilitated, or even driven, by the law; but it often calls for judgment and even expertise not of a strictly legal nature. Thus, good lawyers bring more to bear on a problem than legal knowledge and lawyering skills. They bring creativity, common sense, practical wisdom, and that most precious of attributes, good judgment.

Paul Brest, *The Responsibility of Law Schools: Educating Lawyers as Counselors and Problem Solvers*, 58 Law & Contemp. Probs. 5, 8 (1995).

Unfortunately, however, many lawyers choose to limit their counsel to legal matters, and this can work to the detriment of their clients. In the following reading, Professors Austin Sarat and William Felstiner describe findings from a study of lawyer-client interactions in divorce cases:

> Throughout their interactions, lawyers and clients mark conversational space as a way of defining the appropriate scope of the legal divorce. Clients often seek to expand the conversational agenda to encompass a broader picture of their lives, experiences, and needs. In so doing, they

contest the ideology of separate spheres that lawyers seek to maintain. Lawyers, on the other hand, passively resist such expansion. They close down the aperture; they are interested only in those portions of the client's life that have tactical significance for the prospective terms of the divorce settlement or the conduct of the case. Although O'Gorman reports that over two-thirds of the lawyers in his sample described themselves as counselors who considered it to be their "job ... to ascertain the nature of the client's problem and then work toward a solution that is fair to both parties," the lawyers that we studied did not take a broad perspective on their professional mission. They did not act as "counselors for the situation" nor did they try to provide psychological, emotional, or moral support or guidance for their clients.

Austin Sarat & William L. F. Felstiner, Divorce Lawyers and Their Clients: Power and Meaning in the Legal Process 144 (1995)

b. Moral Issues

Moral issues are among the most difficult non-legal issues that can arise in legal counseling. To what extent should a lawyer concern herself with the virtue of decisions to be made in lawyer-client relations? Should lawyers worry about the impact of the client's decisions on others?

In the following excerpt, Professor Robert Cochran describes three approaches to "morals" issues in legal counseling. As you review this reading, think about which approach — the directive, the client-centered, or the collaborative — you think is most appropriate.

ROBERT F. COCHRAN, JR., INTRODUCTION: THREE APPROACHES TO MORALS ISSUES IN LAW OFFICE COUNSELING

30 Pepp. L. Rev. 591, 592, 593, 594–95, 595–97, 597–98, 598–99, 600 (2003).

One of the most important challenges to lawyers and clients is addressing issues that are not controlled by law. Will the client take steps (legal steps) that will harm other people? Will the officers of a corporation consider the effects of its actions on workers, on consumers, on the community, on the environment? In a divorce, will the client take actions that will harm a child or spouse? What role should the lawyer play regarding these questions? The way lawyers address such issues may do more to determine whether their practice is socially useful or socially harmful than any rule governing the profession. The way lawyers address these issues is also likely to have a great deal to do with whether they find the practice of law personally satisfying.

* * *

Over recent decades, three schools of thought have emerged among legal ethicists and legal clinicians concerning the lawyer's role as to moral issues in the counseling relationship. Those approaches are directive, client-centered, and collaborative. Each provides a different combination of answers to the following questions: 1) Who controls the important decisions in the relationship? and 2) Are the interests of people other than the client taken into consideration in making those decisions?

* * *

A.   The Directive Approach

The first school of lawyering advocates a directive lawyer, a lawyer who is willing to assert control of moral issues that arise during legal representation. Along with Professors David Luban and William Simon, Professor Deborah Rhode, whose essay appears in this colloquium, has proposed a lawyer who is likely to take control of moral issues that arise during the representation. In her book, IN THE INTERESTS OF JUSTICE, Rhode argues that "[l]awyers can, and should, act on the basis of their own principled convictions, even when they recognize that others could in good faith hold different views." David Luban argues in his book, THE GOOD LAWYER, that "when professional and moral obligations conflict, moral obligations take precedence." Rhode and Luban provide little, if any, discussion of the role that the client might play in determining what moral standards should control the representation.

William Simon argues in his book, THE PRACTICE OF JUSTICE, that "[l]awyers should take those actions that, considering the relevant circumstances of the particular case, seem likely to promote justice." "Justice" here connotes the basic values of the legal system and subsumes many layers of more concrete norms. Decisions about justice are not assertions of personal preferences, nor are they applications of ordinary morality. They are legal judgments grounded in the methods and sources of authority of the professional culture. I use "justice" interchangeably with "legal merit."

Under Simon's model, the lawyer looks to the values underlying the law to resolve moral issues. This model clearly leaves the lawyer in charge of the moral issues that arise in legal representation. Simon's criteria for making decisions during the representation are beyond the understanding of the ordinary client. In Simon's formulation, "justice" is a technical issue for legal experts. Simon's model places moral judgments on the lawyer's turf.

* * *

There are troubling aspects of the directive approach. First, there is the danger that, as to moral issues arising in the representation, the lawyer will be wrong. Humility is justified when approaching such issues. These issues are likely to be difficult. I do not suggest that there are not objective moral standards, but none of us has perfect ability to discern those standards or to determine how they should apply. There is a danger that lawyers will be confident of their moral judgment when confidence is not justified. Generally, two consciences in conversation are more likely to get to moral truth than one.

A second concern is that the directive lawyer is likely to impose her values on the client. Directive lawyering is inconsistent with client dignity. There is no place in the directive lawyer's office for the morals of the client. The lawyer robs the client of the opportunity to grow morally. People grow morally through exercising moral judgment. They develop virtues through practice, as an athlete develops physical skills through practice. Lawyers who prevent clients from moral exercise — from deliberating, making moral judgments, and acting on them — deny clients the opportunity to become better people.

B. The Client–Centered Approach

"Client-centered counseling" is designed to craft legal solutions which satisfy client interests. David Binder, Paul Bergman, and Susan Price, the founders of the client-centered approach, in their LAWYERS AS COUNSELORS: A CLIENT-CENTERED APPROACH, state: "Because client autonomy is of paramount importance, decisions should be made on the basis of what choice is most likely to provide a client with maximum satisfaction." Paul Tremblay, who contributes an essay to this symposium, will join Binder, Bergman, and Price in the next edition of that book. Other leaders of the client-centered school include Robert Bastress and Joseph Harbaugh.

In the client-centered view, the lawyer should not act in ways that would influence the client's choice. The lawyer should be "neutral" and "nonjudgmental." Whereas the client has a very limited role in resolving moral issues under the directive model, the lawyer has a very limited role in resolving such issues under the client-centered model. The danger for the client-centered lawyer is that she becomes merely a hired gun in the hands of the client.

* * *

The client-centered counselors' framework claims to be neutral, but in fact, it steers the client toward a particular method of moral analysis, consequentialism. Decision-making under the client-centered counselor model is a matter of cost-benefit analysis. The client-centered counselors' framework excludes the moral imperatives and virtues that are a part of the moral framework of many. Under some standards of morality, one should do the right thing in spite of the negative consequences.

In addition, the client-centered counselors' framework steers clients toward making self-serving choices. The client considers only "Consequences to the Client." This ignores the importance of other people. In the illustration that only one client-centered book gives of its counseling method, a client is considering suing his neighbor over a zoning violation. Among the "consequences for client" of filing suit are: "Time and effort required," "[m]oney to pay for fees and expenses," "[e]xposure to deposition and trial examination," and "[s]train on relationship with [the neighbor]." The client is to consider the consequences to the neighbor solely in light of the effect that they will have on the client; the neighbor has no independent moral significance. The client-centered approach imposes a framework of client selfishness. It may advance the autonomy of clients, but that autonomy comes at the expense of the autonomy of other people. It is likely to advance the autonomy of those who can afford lawyers at the expense of those who cannot.

* * *

C.   The Collaborative Approach

The lawyering models discussed thus far each identify one party who dominates decisions raising moral concerns. Under the directive approach, the lawyer controls such decisions; under the client-centered approach, the client controls such decisions (and the lawyer is careful not to influence the client). Under the collaborative model, the lawyer and client resolve moral issues together through moral discourse. The client makes the ultimate decision, but the lawyer is actively involved in the process. Thomas Shaffer, who represents the collaborative approach in this symposium, uses the traditional notion of friendship to describe how a lawyer might raise and discuss moral issues with clients. A lawyer should approach moral issues with a client in the same way that she would approach such issues with a friend, raising such issues for serious discussion, but not imposing her will on the client. Other proponents of a collaborative approach to client counseling include Anthony Kronman, John DiPippa, Martha Peters, and me.

Lawyers cannot become friends with every client, but they might discuss moral issues with clients in the way that they discuss moral issues with friends. Central to the traditional notion of friendship was a moral component: friends help friends become better people. People today generally think of friendship in terms of pleasure, but the traditional notion of friendship as a moral relationship is not entirely lost. Imagine that a close friend comes to you and confesses that he has embezzled something from his employer. You are likely neither to push your friend to confess, nor to ignore the wrong that your friend has done. You are likely to try and help your friend think through the matter. You might offer an opinion, but you would be likely to do so in a tentative fashion, respecting the dignity of your friend. As Aristotle said, friends collaborate in the good. A friend is unlikely to impose his or her will on a friend, but neither will a friend sit by and let a friend go down a wrong path.

The lawyer as friend engages in moral conversation with the client but generally leaves decisions to the client. One of the best ways to raise such issues is by asking questions that come naturally in the course of decision-making. As to each alternative under consideration, the lawyer can ask the client, "what will be its effect on other people?" The lawyer and client should consider all of the consequences that might arise from various alternatives, not merely the consequences to the client. When it comes time to make a choice among alternatives, the lawyer can ask, "What would be fair?" Note that this question does not impose the lawyer's values on clients; it calls on clients to draw on their own sources of moral values.

* * *

As with other models of lawyering, there are difficulties with the collaborative model. To raise and discuss moral problems thoughtfully with another requires wisdom, a quality that comes in part with age and experience. It is difficult to combine the sympathy and detachment that is the heart of good lawyering (it may be that the lawyers for Enron erred too much on the side of sympathy and were not able to give the dispassionate advice that their clients needed). In addition, we live in an individualistic age — we do not collaborate very well. That may be why each of the other models of client counseling identifies one of the parties to the relationship as the party in charge. Moral counsel also requires time, a scarce commodity in the hourly billing-driven practice of the corporate lawyer or the heavy case-load practice of the legal aid lawyer.

In addition, differences in power between lawyer and client may make collaboration difficult. There is a danger that either the lawyer or the client will dominate the other. In many lawyer/client relationships, the lawyer is in the dominant position. The lawyer has the knowledge of the law and the trappings of power. The lawyer sits behind the big desk in the elevated chair. But in another world of lawyering, the client is likely to be in the position of power. The lawyer may be little more than an employee of the corporate client. If the lawyer is in-house counsel she is an employee of the corporate client. The CEO is likely to sit behind the bigger desk, in the more elevated chair. The power within the relationship can also be a function of a host of other factors: age, education, experience, sex, social class, race, and status. The lawyer in either situation may have to work to attain a level of mutuality with the client. She may need to empower the weak client; she may need to assert herself with the strong client.

Notes and Questions

1. Does Professor Cochran's analysis of moral issues in legal counseling prompt you to re-evaluate which of the three approaches is most appropriate? Does the situation or context matter?

2. We believe that the similarities between the client-centered and collaborative approaches are greater than their dissimilarities, and that either is generally preferable to the traditional or directive approach.

c. Giving Bad News

Sometimes lawyers are forced to give their clients bad news — perhaps the judicial approval of an unwanted divorce or the rejection of a final settlement offer or the prospect of incarceration. In the following excerpt, Professor Linda Smith borrows from medicine a model for delivering bad news to clients.

LINDA F. SMITH, MEDICAL PARADIGMS FOR COUNSELING: GIVING CLIENTS BAD NEWS

4 Clinical L. Rev. 391, 391–92, 417–19, 421–22, 423–24 (1998).

The dominant paradigm for legal counseling focuses on giving the client choice. The "Ethical Lawyer" explains the situation sufficiently for the client to make an informed decision. The "Client–Centered Lawyer" identifies alternatives, predicts consequences, and assists the client in choosing the course of action that best meets the client's goals. This orientation has been, no doubt, an appropriate corrective to the paradigm of the controlling professional who knows best and decides what the client needs.

But sometimes there are no choices that will achieve the client's goals. The abandoned spouse cannot prevent the divorce or avoid an order for visitation, the thief cannot stay out of jail, the business cannot escape paying damages, and the tenant will be evicted. Of course, the amount of the visitation, jail time or damages can be greater or smaller and the eviction may be delayed a bit; but the outcome the client wants to avoid is inevitable. These are particularly hard cases for the lawyer-counselor where the formula of identifying alternatives and predicting consequences can seem like a cruel joke. In these cases the lawyer must also be able to tell the client "bad news." At these junctures, the skill of informing and explaining empathically takes priority over the paradigm of offering the client choice.

* * *

B.   A Model for Legal Counseling About "Bad News"

* * *

1) Be Prepared. Because clients will usually desire (and may need) a good deal of information, the lawyer should avoid communicating "bad news" until she is prepared to fully explain the situation. In most instances, this may mean delaying the "bad news" counseling until after the interview and providing it during a follow-up counseling session. Even when the lawyer may know early in an interview that a client's goal cannot be achieved, it will be wise to delay that discussion. Time will allow the lawyer not only to prepare a comprehensive explanation, but to engage in creative problem-solving. The lawyer will be able to consider whether there may be alternatives to achieving the most important aspects of the client's goals.

If, during the interview, the lawyer hears a client insist upon an outcome that seems highly unlikely, the lawyer should decline to tell the client how hopeless the case is. Instead, the lawyer should empathize with the underlying feeling and encourage the client to explore what the most important aspects of a solution might be. For example, imagine a client whose spouse has left, telling the client he wants a divorce and intends to marry "the other woman":

> Client: There is no way I'll let him have a divorce. Let them live in sin, but there is no way I'm agreeing to a divorce.

> Lawyer: Well, since the "no fault" statute there really isn't anything you can do to prevent him from getting a divorce. If he files for divorce, he'll get one. Of course we can try to hit him up for alimony and the house, so he won't enjoy his freedom.

While the lawyer may be correct in this legal advice, providing this information to the client at this time is not necessary. The lawyer would be better advised to empathize and explore the rationale of the client's underlying goal of remaining married:

> Lawyer: I can tell you are quite angry at him and don't want to just agree to his demands. Could you tell me some more about what's gone on to get to this point? Have there been problems for some time? What if any counseling have you or he had?

Alternatively, the lawyer might discuss the client's immediate needs and offer her choices about short-term goals:

> Lawyer: I can see you are quite angry with him at this point. Can you tell me what's going on with the children and the bills, and what you'd like to see done in the immediate future to help you and your kids have some stability?

2) Be Self–Aware. Ironically, being overly prompt with bad news may come from the laudable goals of providing the client with information (e.g., no consent is required for a no-fault divorce) and performing effective service (e.g., obtaining alimony). Yet the client who is still in denial about the separation and divorce is not emotionally ready to consider this information or to make such a decision. The attorney must help her process the "bad news" that her marriage is over before they can consider various realistic options.

Sarat and Felstiner [*see supra* this section] criticize their domestic relations lawyers for just such a "tutorial posture toward the world of law" and their "strategic" movement of clients "toward positions they deem to be reasonable and appropriate." If these lawyers are to alter their counseling, it would be well if they understood why they feel the need to take such a posture and pursue such strategies. Similarly, Sarat and Felstiner conclude that these lawyers "resist" clients' attempts to "expand the conversation agenda to encompass a broader picture of their lives, experiences, and needs." In order to change such behavior, the lawyer must know how she reacts to clients in pain — whether she wants to rescue them or to "talk some sense into" them. Only by becoming self-aware will the lawyer be able to interact supportively with a client instead of reacting to a client in pain.

3) Conduct the counseling session in person, in private, and with sufficient time. Once it is clear that "bad news" must be conveyed and

the lawyer is prepared to do so, the lawyer should arrange a personal counseling session with ample time for the difficult conversation.

4) Be clear, direct and candid in giving information. The lawyer should open with a "warning shot," control the conversation and get to the point promptly.

* * *

5) Convey empathy and caring. Of course, while divulging this information, the lawyer should show empathy for the client and take note of the client's concerns and agendas. In fact, such empathy may be necessary to help the client take in the "bad news."

A counseling session with a tenant facing a certain eviction may include the following information exchange:

Lawyer: I need to explain the legal situation you face. Since your lease requires rent be paid on the first of the month, and you were unable to make that payment three weeks ago, under your lease, here in paragraph 15, your landlord is entitled to go to court and ask that the judge order you out of your apartment.

Client: But it is so unfair — I lost my job and couldn't possibly pay this month.

Lawyer: It certainly is unfortunate that you are facing an eviction on top of your job loss. And it certainly would be a decent thing for the landlord to give you a little while to get work and catch up on the rent. But I've talked to the landlord's lawyer and he says that unless you can come up with the rent by the end of the week, they want to go ahead with the eviction case.

Client: I've told you I have no cash, no job, no one to borrow from, and I'm behind on my utilities anyway. Why can't the judge understand that?

Lawyer: It seems like they're kicking you when you're down. But the judge is required to enforce the laws on the books. The statute says that if you are behind in your rent and don't immediately catch up, the landlord is entitled to his apartment back so he can rent it to someone else. And that is almost certainly what the judge will order, even if you explain your situation.

It is most important for the client to understand the legal standard and how it applies to his case. Linking the law with the facts allows the client to understand, and requires the client to rely less upon the lawyer's forcefulness or estimated risk (99%) of loss. Moreover, in those cases where the lawyer may have performed a perfunctory interview and misunderstood some crucial facts, this presentation will enable the client to correct the lawyer and the two to reach a better analysis.

6) Attend and respond to the client's level of knowledge.

7) Attend and respond to the client's emotional reactions. Once they hear "bad news," clients, like patients, will respond in a variety of ways. In fact, studies suggest that how much patients know about the condition or treatment influences their reaction and even whether they consider the news to be "bad." Accordingly, the lawyer should be calm and empathetic, but not signal an opinion that the legal situation is a dire one. For example, a career criminal may not see incarceration as so terrible, and a tenant who can move in with relatives may prefer moving out to keeping an apartment which she cannot afford. Instead, the lawyer must listen to the client's concerns during the counseling session.

Patients frequently respond with disbelief or denial; and clients who feel wronged may also respond by expressing disbelief. The lawyer should understand this as the client's emotional difficulty in accepting the situation, rather than an argument over the lawyer's analysis. Accordingly, the lawyer should empathize with the client who feels unfairly treated. The lawyer should explore the client's feelings if they are unclear. If the client needs further information to understand the law and how it applies in his case, of course the lawyer should explain.

* * *

8) Conclude with a proposed plan which takes into account the client's personal perspective. As doctors turn to the treatment plan following the information, once the lawyer has conveyed the essence of the "bad news" he should discuss how the case can be handled. Here alternatives will be discussed — but in light of the crucial information about the weakness of the client's case.

* * *

With this approach the lawyer-counselor should be able to engage in counseling sessions which, of necessity, involve telling clients that their goal is probably impossible and the outcome they most fear is likely to be ordained under the law.

D. INTERVIEWING AND COUNSELING TECHNIQUES: QUESTIONING AND LISTENING

Interviewing and counseling are structured conversations. In interviews, the lawyer attempts to obtain relevant information from the client about the problems that have brought her to the lawyer; in counseling sessions, the lawyer attempts to help the client determine how to address those problems. In both interviewing and counseling sessions, the lawyer is attentive to the client, strives to develop trust, and works to cultivate a productive relationship.

This means, of course, that lawyers need to develop good communication skills to become effective interviewers and counselors. The two communication skills most directly relevant to interviewing and counseling are questioning and listening. These two skills facilitate the information-gathering required of interviews and the advising required of counseling. At the same time, the lawyer who asks and listens well demonstrates empathy, which will facilitate the development of a trusting and productive working relationship between her and her client. Good questioning and listening skills are also important to other dispute resolution processes we will discuss in this book.

1. QUESTIONING

The primary purpose of client interviews is for the lawyer to elicit information from the client. To do so effectively, lawyers must cultivate their questioning skills. Generally speaking, lawyers should begin an interview with *open* or *open-ended* questions to gather general information and subsequently ask *specific* or *closed* questions to clarify understandings.

Open-ended questions. Open-ended questions are broad enough to permit the respondent to choose the subject matter:

"What prompted you to see a lawyer?"

"What brings you here today?"

"What happened?"

An open-ended question can enhance the client's willingness to talk and ability to choose the precise topics. It is likely, therefore, to increase rapport and bring out information that other forms of questions seldom would elicit. In the following reading, Professors Don and Martha Peters elaborate on some of the benefits of open-ended questions in client interviews:

> [The client-centered] models encourage frequent use of open questions which allow the client to select either the topic or aspects of a designated subject. Open inquiry is encouraged to take advantage of its potential to communicate that clients are important, essential resources in the information-gathering process. It also provides maximum opportunities for lawyers to listen to their clients and build rapport by demonstrating they heard and understood what was being said. Using open questions may avoid the damage to rapport resulting from focused inquiry posed prematurely on topics that are likely to threaten clients. Contemporary interviewing literature acknowledges that an effective interviewer must consider the motivational realities of human communication, and one of these realities is that questions seeking certain types of information can inhibit complete disclosure. Open inquiry is also recommended because it has the information-gathering advantage of letting clients respond from their frames of reference and relevance. Open inquiry is particularly suggested for beginning interviews when lawyers should invite their clients to talk freely about their situations and what they want to do about them.

DON PETERS & MARTHA M. PETERS, MAYBE THAT'S WHY I DO THAT: PSYCHOLOGI-
CAL TYPE THEORY, THE MYERS–BRIGGS TYPE INDICATOR, AND LEARNING LEGAL
INTERVIEWING 169, 186 (1990)

In some circumstances, however, open-ended questions may engender discomfort, or draw information that is not sufficiently precise.
When that happens, the lawyer should temporarily abandon such questions and opt for more specific or closed questions.

Closed questions are designed to elicit particular pieces of information.

"Where were you born?"

"How much is your rent?"

"What happened to your car after the accident?"

In some situations, closed questions may also increase the client's
comfort level, improve rapport, and stimulate recollections. In other
situations, however, they may stem the flow of information or make the
client feel cut off, particularly if they take the form of *leading questions*
(e.g., "The door was ajar, wasn't it?").

In the following reading, Sana Loue explores the relative advantages
and disadvantages of open-ended and closed questions in the context of
immigration interviews:

SANA LOUE, A GUIDE TO BETTER
CLIENT INTERVIEWS*

89–07 Immigration Briefings 1 (1989).

Probing for Information

You must be able to motivate your client to answer your questions,
and you must ask your questions in a way that allows your client to give
you the information you seek. The timing, form and direction of your
questions are all important.

Timing. Your opening question at the beginning of the interview is
crucial because your client does not know yet what is expected. Your
first question should not be difficult and should not touch on a traumatic
or embarrassing area. . . .

Form. Questions can be "open" or "closed." Open questions are
more appropriate if the client may not have formulated an opinion or if
you wish to learn about the client's frame of reference and how he or she
arrived at a particular point of view. A closed question is more appropriate if there is a known range of possible responses and within that range
there are clearly defined points representing each client's position.

> Case Illustration: You are interviewing an asylum applicant and
> want to determine if she fears persecution upon return to her
> country. Compare:

* With permission of West Publishing.

Open question: "What do you think will happen to you if you go back?"

Closed question: "Are you afraid of being persecuted upon your return?"

In this situation, the open question is likely to yield significantly more information. The closed question presumes that the client defines and understands "afraid" and "persecuted" as you do and will answer accurately. It further presumes that the only valid answers are "yes" and "no," thereby foreclosing further inquiry into the client's particular situation.

Case Illustration: You are interviewing a Section 212(c) applicant for evidence of rehabilitation.

Open question: "Have you had any trouble with the police since your last conviction?"

Closed question: "Have you been arrested or detained by any law enforcement officer since your last conviction?"

In this case, the closed question is more likely to yield an accurate answer, "yes" or "no." The open question may yield an inaccurate or partial response because the client's definition of "trouble" is not the same as yours.

Note

It is clear that lawyers can gather information through questioning. Lawyers can also gather information in other ways. Some clients will respond to a non-committal acknowledgment, such as an "I see" or "Uh-huh". Silence can also be powerful; most people will feel a need to speak to avoid the discomfort that silence evokes. Lawyers can also gather information through relevant document requests.

2. LISTENING

A lawyer's questioning skills are only as good as her listening skills; only if she listens well will she understand the facts and feelings a client communicates. Moreover, the lawyer who demonstrates that she is listening carefully conveys understanding, empathy, and interest in her client, and this, in turn, furthers the lawyer-client relationship.

a. Active Listening

Active listening is an especially effective device for conveying non-judgmental, empathetic understanding, and for eliciting information. In active listening, the interviewer restates both the content and the feelings she believes are associated with the statement. The following excerpt explains and illustrates active listening.

ROBERT DINERSTEIN, STEPHEN ELLMAN, ISABELLE GUNNING & ANN SHALLECK, CONNECTION, CAPACITY AND MORALITY IN LAWYER–CLIENT RELATIONSHIPS

10 Clinical L. Rev. 755, 758–62 (2004).

First and foremost, it is crucial to listen. There are many tools to aid in real listening, but here we focus on one of the most crucial: active listening. Active listening is a particular form of listening that involves conveying to the speaker, here your client, that you have heard both the substance of what she has said as well as its emotional content. You do this by "mirroring" or paraphrasing what you have heard said explicitly, and by putting into words the implicit feelings emanating from the speaker; sometimes you may answer on only one of these levels (addressing explicit content or implicit feelings, but not both), but often you will need to respond both to the client's words and to his emotions. It is important to note that you will or should use active listening from the moment you meet your client, and consistently thereafter, as a way to verify for yourself and your client that you understand what he has told you and as a way of demonstrating your respect for and sympathy with his concerns.

Consider these examples:

In the first dialogue, Harriet Long, a family lawyer, is a divorced African American woman in her 50's. Her client, Betty Ann Jackson, is also in her 50s, but Caucasian. Jackson seeks Long's help for a divorce and custody matter.

L1:   Mrs. Jackson, good to finally meet you in person. Please sit. How may I help you today?

C1:   Hello, Ms. Long. Well after 25 years of marriage, of putting him through dental school and raising his children, my husband has found someone younger, thinner and childless and I need to decide how to kill him and get away with it.

L2:   Ah Mrs. Jackson.... I see. After all you have done in this marriage, you fear this affair will break it up.

C2:   I guess that is fair. Although he has said that he wants to leave me for ... her, so it seems like the marriage is pretty much over.

(A few minutes later in the conversation):

L3:   So, Mrs. Jackson.... After many years of marriage where you have been an enormous support and helpmate to your husband and mother to his and your children, your husband has made it clear that this recent affair will break up your marriage and you are hurt and angry.

C3:   Yes. I can't believe that this is happening. He was never a cheat.... and I guess I thought if he did he would be like my

friends' husbands who will stay in the marriage but this.....
That he would really leave after all these years!

L4:   Okay. So you may well be facing a divorce. And we can talk
      about the specifics of that. I recognize that this kind of
      circumstance is bound to cause some very strong feelings in
      you and I want us to address those. But let's agree to put the
      killing issue aside, shall we? Tell me more about how you are
      feeling about what your husband said and what you think,
      now, you would like to do about it?

Here attorney Long immediately learns from her new client that a
divorce matter is the likely legal object of this representation and that
her client is quite bitter and unhappy. She uses active listening to show
her client that she has heard the gist of what the client has said. Long's
response at L2 both paraphrases some of the facts — "after all you have
done" — and names one of the possible emotions involved, fear. When
an attorney should do a summary of facts that appear most important,
along with a more complete restatement of the client's emotions as the
lawyer has heard them, is a judgment call that turns on how the rest of
the conversation has progressed, but you should certainly consider
making such a statement to your client. Attorney Long summarizes her
understanding of the facts and emotions at L3 where she paraphrases all
the facts — the marriage has been long, the wife has taken care of the
husband in some respects and there are children — and names the
emotions — hurt and anger — that underlie the assertion "I need to
decide how to kill him and get away with it."

The lawyer's restatement of "killing him" as "hurt and anger"
demonstrates several characteristics of active listening. First, her response was not a "stupid" or literal paraphrase of the client's statement.
Long does not say "Ah Mrs. Jackson, you want to take out a contract on
your husband's life and need my help in drawing up the particulars."
The lawyer understands that the client's words are much more likely an
expression of emotion than of criminal intent, and she rightly avoids
attributing to the client a literal meaning that is extreme and offensive.
Second, however, while the phrase "kill him" probably is a figure of
speech, the lawyer also picks up on the acute ethical issue that would be
raised if there is any literal truth to the assertion, and she puts herself
on record immediately as discouraging the client from even thinking
about pursuing such a course of action. And third, notice that in lightly
discouraging the client from thinking that killing would be appropriate,
the attorney is disagreeing with her client. Young lawyers and students
sometimes think that active listening and the support it conveys means
never disagreeing with your client. However, you will have occasions to
disagree with clients; and many of those times clients will expect to hear
your differing opinions.

Sometimes the client's feelings will be farther from the surface than
in our first example. In the following dialogue, Allen Anderson, an
employment discrimination attorney, is a white male in his 40's who,

due to a shooting, cannot walk and uses a wheel chair. His client, Anthony Braxton, is also a white male and in a wheel chair, but in his late 20's.

L1: Mr. Braxton, it is a pleasure to meet you. I see you were given coffee. So ... make yourself comfortable and please tell me what employment matter I can help you with?

C1: Well Mr. Anderson, where to begin? Well for one thing I just learned this morning that all of my coworkers at the brokerage firm I work at, Burnham and Block, make almost twice as much money as I do and I figured I should talk with a lawyer about my options.

L2: All right, Mr. Braxton. You learned something today that you had not known before, which is that you are apparently the lowest paid employee at your job and you feel that this fact, if true, is unfair and want to know if the law can help.

C2: Well it's true. And it's not just unfair. I have worked hard, gotten the highest evaluations and gone through ... well, just not gotten any kind of support at that office.

L3: It sounds as if with your work record and evaluations you should be at or near the top of the pay scale and so you are feeling quite angry and maybe even surprised by this revelation.

C3: Yes, but maybe not entirely surprised.

L4: Please tell me more. How did you discover this and why aren't you surprised?

Here attorney Anderson, while given facts, is not given much emotional content to work with based upon what his client tells him. In an actual interview, of course, there may be any number of nonverbal cues that convey the client's emotional state, like the tone or intensity of his voice, facial expressions, the color of the eyes or skin, and the movements of different parts of the body. Still, despite the (possible) paucity of information, the attorney forges ahead and both describes the facts he has heard ("you learned something today ... you are apparently the lowest paid") and attaches a likely emotional state ("you feel this is unfair"). The inferences the lawyer makes about the client's emotional reaction are plausible; they fit with the juxtaposition of the client's discovery of his low pay and his seemingly immediate consultation with a lawyer. But the lawyer could be wrong.

Indeed in this case, the client does not really feel that "unfair" quite captures his feelings. Like most clients, however, the client does not hold the lawyer's inability to "mind read" (or "heart read") against him. He corrects the lawyer by providing him with more information. That information still emerges as a factual account rather than a direct assertion of feelings. But the new facts — the client's hard work and excellent evaluations — lead the lawyer more confidently to identify and label some of Braxton's feelings as anger and surprise. In addition, the client's cryptic and incomplete reference to having "gone through" something, followed by a pause and then a statement about lack of "support," suggest to the attorney the strength and color of the client's emotions, despite the client's difficulty in speaking about them.

Although active listening is a critical tool to underscore that you are listening to your client, it is generally not seen by the novice as a very natural or comfortable way to respond. The young attorney or law student sometimes feels that it is difficult to come up with true active listening responses and that the client will view his awkward attempts as phoniness. Effective active listening responses are difficult for many new interviewers to imagine or to formulate on the spot and so require practice. While early and self-conscious efforts at active listening may have a feeling of "phoniness," it is our own view and experience that clients sense phoniness and can tell it apart from the authentic feeling communicated by the lawyer regardless of how smoothly or awkwardly she speaks. A sincere attempt to understand the client's factual statement and feelings, no matter how stiff and even off base, will usually be met with appreciation by clients for the effort made by the attorney — even if the client ends up having to correct what you have said.

Notes and Questions

1. We recommend a four-step approach to active listening called "looping" (borrowed from Gary Friedman and Jack Himmelstein) or the "empathy loop" (borrowed from Professor Robert Mnookin, Professor Scott Peppet, and Andrew Tulumello): First, the lawyer inquires of the client. Second, the client responds. Third, the lawyer attempts to demonstrate her understanding of what the client has said. Finally, if the client does not confirm the lawyer's understanding, the lawyer returns to step one. If the client does confirm the lawyer's understanding, the loop is closed, but the lawyer asks the client whether she has anything else she would like to discuss, thereby returning to the beginning of the loop. Upon completing this four-step process, the lawyer should understand the content and feelings conveyed by her client, and the client should understand that the lawyer understands. For more on this technique, see Chapter IV at page 348.

2. Active listening is a method of conveying empathy to a client. Empathy is a complicated construct with emotional, cognitive, and behavioral components. As the following reading explains, it is valuable in the doctor-patient relationship and no doubt in the lawyer-client relationship as well:

> Emotional empathy amounts to feeling what others feel; cognitive empathy amounts to understanding what others feel by virtue of first having an open-mind to attain that understanding; and behavioral empathy amounts to displaying emotional empathy to the other person with some measure of cognitive empathy.

> A completely "other-aware" person will be able to achieve the three dimensions of empathy in relation to another person. Numerous experiments in medical contexts suggest that the presence of emotional, cognitive, and behavioral empathy in doctors for their patients is crucial to patients' speedy recovery and healing, both emotionally and physical-

ly. Studies repeatedly prove that when doctors communicate with patients in a way that conveys understanding of the patient's feelings, patients are "enabled" to recover, and recover more readily. In her classic study on empathy and healing, Saint Edith Stein described this process as "grasp[ing] the Other as a living body and not merely as a physical body." Empathy thus enables physicians to "grasp the content of first-person reports of bodily disorder, and to comprehend the meaning of illness as lived." Appropriately, there is now a renewed call to incorporate empathy training into medical school curricula.

Valerie A. Sanchez, *Back to the Future of ADR: Negotiating Justice and Human Needs*, 18 Ohio St. J. on Disp. Resol. 669, 726–28 (2003).

3.   Some law students find active listening difficult because it feels artificial, contrived or manipulative. Consider this response by Professors Binder and Price:

> The use of active listening skills is in part the use of a technique to gain information. However, you do not employ active listening simply out of a voyeuristic interest in a client's private feelings. Rather, active listening is one among many techniques you employ in order to assist a client in finding an adequate solution to a problem. If any technique which produces information that a client might not otherwise reveal is to be denounced as "manipulative," then perhaps such standard practices as putting clients at ease with a bit of chit-chat and cup of coffee, eliciting information in chronological fashion, probing for details with closed rather than open questions, and showing clients documents to refresh their recollection are all unfairly "manipulative."

> For us, the answer to the claim that active listening is unfairly "manipulative" is this: Clients come to you for assistance and advice, and a client's full participation is necessary if you are to help a client find a solution that addresses all dimensions of a problem. Active listening, which provides non-judgmental understanding, is an essential technique for gaining full client participation.

David A. Binder & Susan C. Price, Legal Interviewing and Counseling: A Client Centered Approach 32–36 (1977).

4.   To practice the concepts addressed in this section, choose a classmate or friend and spend ten minutes actively listening to them as they describe a dispute in which they were involved. Then let them actively listen to you as you spend ten minutes describing a dispute in which you were involved. Was active listening easy or difficult? To the extent it was difficult, what made it difficult? How was it different from a normal conversation, or a more formal interview? Did you feel that your counterpart really understood your dispute and how you felt about it?

b.   Benefits of Listening

Listening is beneficial not only to clients but also to lawyers themselves. Consider the next two readings. The first, written by David Maister, Charles Green, and Robert Galford, explores some of the potential benefits to clients. The second, written by Steven Keeva, explores some of the potential benefits to the lawyers.

DAVID MAISTER, CHARLES GREEN & ROBERT GALFORD, THE TRUSTED ADVISOR*

Am. Law., Oct. 2000, at 65, 65–66.

Jack Welch, CEO of General Electric Company, has high praise for Steven Volk, a corporate lawyer to whom Welch turned when GE's subsidiary NBC acquired Financial News Network in 1991. "He is really a great adviser," says Welch. "He listens better than anybody else."

Effective, trusted advisers are (without a single exception, in our experience) very good listeners. Listening is not a sufficient condition by itself, but it is a necessary one. Listening is essential to earn the right to comment on and be involved with the client's issues. We must listen effectively, and be *perceived* to be listening effectively, *before* we can proceed with any advisory process. Cutting to the chase without having earned the right to do so will usually be interpreted as arrogance.

Jim Copeland is the CEO of Deloitte & Touche and someone who very effectively builds lasting, deep relationships. In 1989 Deloitte, Haskins & Sells merged with Touche, Ross & Co. Copeland had been with Deloitte. He describes the first five minutes of a nine-hour meeting with the CEO of a key Touche, Ross client, a fiery character who was not at all pleased at having to "train" a whole new accounting firm.

> He leads with power, energy, wants to overwhelm you, to let you know who's in charge. And I didn't fight that. I just kept saying, "Tell me more about that problem. How did it happen, how did it come about, what's going on?" I wanted to know why he was upset and what it would take to fix things. Basically I was there for him and let him know that. You just start with an attitude that, by gosh, you are going to set things right, and to do that you have to totally focus on the client and the client's problems.

There are many aspects of Copeland's demeanor in this meeting that explain why it was the genesis of a very long and successful relationship. But in that first meeting, none mattered more than his ability to listen. Listening earned him the right to deliver on quality content, to cross-sell, to demonstrate problem-solving capabilities, and to speak about his people. None of that would have happened had he not earned the right through listening (thereby finding out what was going on).

Why is "being listened to" so important? The answer is not only about the need for a rational understanding of the issues. Our desire to be heard also flows from our need for respect, empathy, and involvement. The trusted adviser recognizes this and always ensures that the self-esteem of the client is protected. A trusted adviser might say, "What I like about your idea is *X;* now help me understand how we can use it to accomplish *Y*." Through such language, the adviser constantly lets the client know that the client is respected and that the two of them are free to discuss with great candor the specific merits of the idea at hand.

In listening to earn the right, we have found advisers make two common mistakes. One is to listen only for the rational; the other is to listen too passively. The concept of "earning the right" may sound like a rational approach. After all, we send resumes in order to "earn the right" to interview. We send our firm's qualifications to "earn the right" to bid on a piece of work. The truth is, these rational processes only mimic the real action. Listening to earn the right is very much an emotional as well as a rational process. Here's the rest of Copeland's story:

> So he got the message that I cared about him, and wouldn't let things go by that weren't right for him. Years later, we had a chance to pitch a project to him, $5 million, a pretty big project in those days, and at the end of the pitch, he just looked at me and said, "Do *you* think I should do this?" Meaning that if I could look him in the eye and say, "You bet," then he had me on the line to do the right thing for him. And he knew that if I didn't believe that, I wouldn't look him in the eye and say so, because he knew he could trust me. And I was able to say, in this case, "Absolutely you should do it; you need this, and we'll do great work for you."

We have had clients (and you probably have, too) who insist that this listening stuff is all so much soft talk. "I want results, hard stuff, answers," they insist to us. "Don't give me the passive, listening stuff." Yet at the end of the day, that client (and nearly all clients) wants to be able to look someone in the eye and know that someone cares for him and won't "let things go by that [aren't] right for him." Is that "soft"? We don't think so.

The other (related) common mistake in listening to earn the right is to listen too passively. Tony Alessandra, in his audiotape THE DYNAMICS OF EFFECTIVE LISTENING, has a section titled "Giving the Gift of Acknowl-edgment." We would add, not only is it a gift, it is also a requirement. Good listening is active, not passive.

A key part of communication is the continual back-and-forth of acknowledging that each is being heard and understood. We all know the blank "uh-huh" and glazed-over look that comes from someone who we just *know* is not really listening to us. We need, in a normal conversa-tion, some kind of acknowledgment from the other party on a regular basis. Without that, we are forced to stop and either demand it, or stop our communicating.

But what is considered acknowledgment? Is it body language? Words? The answer is that it depends on the content of the message.

If the message is purely rational (for example, a senior lawyer imparting the fine points of an analysis to an associate), then the appropriate acknowledgment may be almost entirely verbal. An occasional "mm-hmm," with a slight nod of the head, is enough to let a teacher know he or she is being heard and understood and should continue.

But if the message carries any emotional flavor at all (and most do), then *not* to use emotive colorings or tones in our acknowledgments sends the message that we are not listening. A client who says, "We do 300,000 transactions a day here" has a feeling about that number. It is not enough to know whether 300,000 is above or below the competition, or higher or lower than last month. The client may be proud of that number, or proud simply of knowing it. Or he may be bored by the number, or embarrassed by it, or any number of things. The adviser who listens passively (using only "mm-hmm") is sending a message that only the rational content matters, that the feelings of the one conveying the information are irrelevant. The effective adviser knows that the emotional data is every bit as valid and important as the rational data. Each plays its role in successfully adding value and changing a client organization.

There are even circumstances when a reaction from the adviser is not just good to have, but essential. For example, a CEO who complains that a former key employee is selling trade secrets to the enemy deserves more than mere "mm-hmm." The adviser might appropriately respond, "You must be outraged. I wish I had a button to push to resolve this for you instantly, but I don't. I don't think anyone does."

LISTENING TO THE SEQUENCE

We have often conducted a real-time quiz to assess the frequency with which people's minds wander from the subject at hand. Our nonscientific study suggests that, on average, businesspeople can pay attention for no more than 30 to 60 seconds without being distracted by an unrelated thought. Listening is a process that requires skill and discipline.

Much of communication follows the model of a story. There is a beginning, a middle, and an end. There is setup, tension, and resolution. There is background, setup, and punch line. When we talk to someone (about almost anything), we choose our words to create some version of the story.

But if the listener breaks up our sense of story (insists on interrupting, or rearranging, or imposing his or her own sense of story line), the meaning we intend is disrupted. It feels inappropriate when someone jumps to a conclusion, or misses a connection, or gets things out of sequence. All these are forms of not "getting it." Good listening respects the speaker by respecting the sequence of the story he or she chooses to tell us.

Our good friends at the Ariel Group, a theater-based communications-training firm in Cambridge, Massachusetts, teach the idea of "reflective listening," followed by "supportive listening," and finally "listening for possibility."

- *Reflective listening* demonstrates clarity and communicates back to the speaker that his or her message has been heard and that the impact, implications, and emotions that are connected with the issue are also well understood. ("What I hear you saying is . . . ")

- *Supportive listening* demonstrates empathy and shows that the listener not only understands why the client feels a particular way about an issue or problem but also that he or she will help the client feel comfortable with that point of view. ("Gee, that must be tough!")

- *Listening for possibility* demonstrates insight and suggests to the client that a particular path or solution may help resolve the dilemma. ("So what have you thought about doing to deal with that?")

If we listen sequentially, we will hear the meaning the speaker intends. If we impose our own structure on what is being said, we will not hear the meaning that is being presented. We will hear some version of our own meaning, superimposed on the speaker.

Avoid asking questions such as, "What are the top three issues facing XYZ?" If you ask that question, you'll generally get your list of three. You may, however, miss the fact that one of those issues is far less significant that the other two, and that any unprompted question would have elicited only the two important issues.

Consider the situation of interviewing people you are thinking of hiring for your firm. When you interview candidates by asking them about their capabilities, you deprive them of the chance to tell you their very personal story. If you listen for their story, you will hear the meaning that *they* see in their lives and careers, not one that you may have assigned. You still have the right, of course, to hire or not to hire, but it makes sense to hear someone's idea about what makes them tick before forming your own opinions.

This is as true with clients as it is with interview candidates. If we conduct fact-finding sessions based on rigidly preconceived notions of the issues, we will miss the stories, the meaning, that our clients want to tell us. And thus we miss truth.

STEVEN KEEVA, HEART–HEALTHY CONVERSATIONS
A.B.A. J., Sept. 2003, at 73, 73–74.

Psychologist James J. Lynch has a rather unique, and persuasive, perspective on what really matters in the practice of law.

Here's how he encapsulates it: "If nothing else, lawyers need to know that they're in a talking profession, and nothing affects the body more than talking."

Lynch, author of A CRY UNHEARD: NEW INSIGHTS INTO THE MEDICAL CONSEQUENCES OF LONELINESS, began to understand this about 25 years ago. That's when he became one of the first researchers to use a new technology that allowed him to measure patients' blood pressure moment-to-moment while they were engaged in conversation.

He found that dialogue has a huge impact on the cardiovascular system. In fact, talking typically causes blood pressure to rise, at least until the speaker feels heard (if indeed he ever does), at which time it decreases. Why? Well, blood pressure fluctuations represent one way the body communicates. Lynch came to understand this by studying crying babies, whose blood pressure continued to rise the longer they cried. "At one point I realized that that's exactly what adult patients are doing, but their cries are inward. And that's when I realized that listening to people has the effect of lowering their blood pressure because we hear their cries."

Why should this matter to lawyers? As human beings in a talking profession, lawyers experience the same physical impact as anyone else, perhaps even more so. That's because of the way the legal profession is so narrowly focused on the life of the mind.

* * *

Another reason lawyers can benefit from Lynch's work is its great relevance to understanding and helping clients, who often complain of not feeling "seen" by their lawyers. While most of us may realize on some level that clients need to be heard in a nonjudgmental way, Lynch provides scientific evidence that the relationship between listener and speaker can be mutually healing.

* * *

[W]hen you listen to others, your blood pressure drops. By understanding this, you can help yourself while helping your clients (whose blood pressure you help lower by hearing them).

c. Developing Better Listening Skills

Several of the readings in this chapter, and in subsequent chapters, emphasize the value of listening. We believe law students and lawyers can — and indeed, must — become good listeners to be effective client interviewers and counselors. We acknowledge, though, that listening is hard, in large part because it is difficult to control the focus of our attention. This is due to at least two qualities of the human mind.

First, the human mind wanders, almost incessantly. As a result, we have trouble keeping our attention where we want it to be. If you have any doubt about this, think about a time you were reading a book or a case and, after a few pages, realized you had no idea what you had read. Your eyes covered the words, but your mind was elsewhere, perhaps on a beach, or in a supermarket, or in the bleachers watching a baseball game. Or try this: Get into a comfortable seated position and close your eyes. Bring your attention to your breath. Specifically, focus on either the sensation the breath makes when it enters or leaves your nostrils or the sensation of the rising and falling of your belly as you inhale and exhale. Once you have focused, begin counting your breaths. Count up to ten exhalations. Once you reach ten or lose track of your count, begin again at one and count up to ten. Do this for five minutes. If you are like many smart, disciplined people we know, you may have trouble reaching ten even one time!

Second, we not only have difficulty focusing our attention where we want it to be, we are often unaware of where our attention is actually focused. Our minds seem to have a mind of their own! To illustrate, try resuming the breathing exercise, but this time, when you become aware that your mind has wandered, notice where it has gone and then return your attention to your breath. To the extent you are able to do this exercise (and it is often surprisingly difficult), you probably will have noticed a wide range of thoughts, bodily sensations, and emotions. In addition, you may have observed that many of the thoughts were about you, and they concerned making things better for you — getting more pleasure or avoiding pain.

Since 1998, several scholars and practitioners have begun to teach law students and lawyers a way to pay attention called "mindfulness." This is a skill one develops in meditation and then deploys in everyday life, including law study or practice. Mindfulness meditation is given greater consideration in Chapter VIII, beginning at page 888. However, in the following excerpts Professor Riskin explains how mindfulness can facilitate better listening.

LEONARD L. RISKIN, THE CONTEMPLATIVE LAWYER: ON THE POTENTIAL CONTRIBUTIONS OF MINDFULNESS MEDITATION TO LAW STUDENTS, LAWYERS, AND THEIR CLIENTS

7 Harv. Negot. L. Rev. 1, 49–53 (2002).

Good listening means paying attention both to the interaction between the lawyer and client and to what is going on inside the lawyer. But this kind of attention takes a high degree of self-awareness and empathy, along with self-confidence, motivation, patience, and emotional self-control — the very capacities that mindfulness can produce. Thus, mindfulness could help lawyers improve their ability to listen deeply — to themselves and others — and to respond appropriately, rather than react automatically based on established mind-sets and habits. This is how mindfulness has improved the listening skills of one bankruptcy attorney:

> When Stacey is practicing mindfully and a colleague or opponent flies off the handle she tries to simply notice the feelings that come up for her without responding reflexively. Instead, she waits until she's ready. Oftentimes, she chooses to look more deeply, to consider what might be behind the outburst. Maybe there's an illness in the person's family, or perhaps someone just told him off.

In the past, when an interview with a client was getting off track, Stacey became self-critical; internal voices told her she really didn't know what she was doing and even questioned her choice of work. Now when that happens, she just watches it happening, often noticing that her stomach is knotting up. She lets herself be aware of it all without having to get attached to it. She doesn't fight the voices or the physical sensations, so they have no real power over her. Suddenly she becomes aware that she can choose to work with the client in a different way. She stops, takes a mindful breath, and thinks about how she might connect with the person in her office in a way that helps them both find their way.[213]

Simply by listening carefully, deeply, and openly, a lawyer can relieve some clients' suffering and establish a connection that would be satisfying to both. Such listening also can be essential if the lawyer is to help the client make wise decisions. Through such attentive listening, the lawyer can help the client understand her own needs and then select the most appropriate methods for addressing them. Mindfulness can help lawyers overcome barriers to attentive listening, including distracting thoughts and emotions, "personal agendas," and bias and prejudice based on the speaker's appearance, ethnicity, gender, speech or manner.

E.   A LAWYER'S DUTY TO ADVISE CLIENTS ABOUT DISPUTE RESOLUTION OPTIONS

The rest of this book is devoted to the various dispute resolution processes to which the client and her lawyer might turn, including negotiation, mediation, arbitration, and mixed processes. Do lawyers have an ethical duty to advise their clients about potential dispute resolution processes? Should they have such a duty?

In the following excerpt, Professor Marshall Breger explores whether there is such a duty, and if so, what shape that duty might take. As you read this excerpt, note the various sources of legal authority Breger cites.

MARSHALL J. BREGER, SHOULD AN ATTORNEY BE REQUIRED TO ADVISE A CLIENT OF ADR OPTIONS?

13 Geo. J. Legal Ethics 427, 430–31, 433–36, 439–41 (2000).

[T]he Model Rules [of Professional Conduct] do not provide explicit guidance regarding the mandatory quality of an ADR requirement. For many, however, the language of the Model Rules creates an implicit obligation to advise a client regarding ADR options. After all, the Model

---

213. Steven Keeva, Transforming Prac- Legal Life 70 (1999).
tices: Finding Joy and Satisfaction in the

Rules require that an attorney "consult with the client" to "explain a matter," to expedite litigation and to "render candid advice" on relevant matters, all seemingly consonant with the duty to consult with a client regarding ADR options.

In contrast, some have opposed mandatory ADR disclosure by arguing that it results in unnecessary client expense. "Such a rule would increase greatly malpractice liability and run up the meter on client expenses" suggests New Jersey lawyer, Michael L. Prigoff. Thus, he argues that in "small disputes" it is "counter productive to the goal of providing more satisfactory dispute resolution at an affordable price." Such proposals, Prigoff concludes, are "overkill and unfair micro-management of the practice of law."

* * *

II.   DOES SUCH A RULE OF CONSULTATION ALREADY EXIST?

Read literally, neither Model Rule 1.2 or 1.4(b) even mentions ADR. Model Rule 1.2 requires that attorneys consult as to "means" and Model Rule 1.4(b) provides only that "a lawyer shall explain a matter to the extent reasonably necessary to permit the client to make informed decisions regarding the representation." Reading "reasonably necessary" broadly, this rule may be construed as containing an inherent obligation for an attorney to provide an explanation of ADR processes sufficient to enable a client to make an "informed decision" as to whether to pursue ADR. Some commentators have suggested that a reasonable reading of state rules based on Model Rule 1.4 reveals such an implicit duty.

Besides reading Model Rule 1.4(b) broadly, an ADR obligation can often be inferred by referring to legal sources outside of the rules of professional conduct. For example, under the Louisiana Rules of Professional Conduct, Disciplinary Rule 1.4 reads that attorneys have a duty to "keep clients reasonably informed about the status of a matter." As in the case of the Model Rules, enforcement of this rule relies upon the meaning of "reasonably informed." It has been argued that in light of the Louisiana Mediation Act, enacted to encourage the use of ADR, the "reasonably informed" language of rule 1.4 should be read as including an obligation for attorneys to discuss ADR options with their clients. Model Rule 2.1 provides a different approach than rules 1.2 or 1.4(b). It requires that an attorney should render "candid advice," directing an attorney not only to consider legal, but also "moral, economic, social and political factors" that may impact the outcome of a client's dispute. If such "candid advice" includes a discussion regarding ADR options, then attorneys will have an affirmative obligation to discuss ADR options for a wide variety of reasons beyond the technically "legal." States such as Colorado, Hawaii and Georgia have taken this a step further to include the specific recommendation that an attorney consider alternative dispute resolution, in addition to these other considerations.

As clients are clearly the best interpreters of their "non-legal" interests, the proportion of disputes for which ADR consultation should be required has become exceedingly large. Thus, this analysis suggests that allowing an attorney to make the ADR decision for the client takes away the control over aspects of the case that should rightfully be in the client's hands. Even if one does not accept that a duty of consultation can be derived from a reading of Model Rules 1.4(b) or 2.4, it is possible to cobble together support from other textual sources for an existing rule of consultation. One may, as an example, treat an offer to pursue ADR as any other settlement offer and base the purported consultation requirement on Model Rule 1.4(b). Such an offer must be communicated to the client. Thus, a Kansas Bar Opinion states that "[i]f an ADR technique is proposed by opposing counsel or the court, the lawyer must advise the lawyer's client of the benefits and disadvantages of the ADR techniques proposed, and give the lawyer's professional advice to the client regarding use of the ADR in the particular case." The State Bars of Michigan and Pennsylvania adhere to a similar position.

Following this view, the State Bar of Virginia proposed a revised version of the Virginia Rules of Professional Conduct. Proposed Rule 1.4(c) provides, that "[a] lawyer shall inform the client of facts pertinent to the matter and of communications from another party that may significantly affect settlement or resolution of the matter." Driving home this specific point, Comment 1(a) to proposed Rule 1.4 explicitly provides that "[t]his continuing duty to keep the client informed includes a duty to advise the client about the availability of dispute resolution processes that might be more appropriate to the client's goals than the initial process chosen."

* * *

IV. WHAT EXACTLY DOES THE ATTORNEY'S DUTY TO ADVISE CLIENTS OF ADR OPTIONS ENCOMPASS?

The duty to consult with a client concerning ADR options may be understood in two ways: a "hard" sense, in which an attorney is required to analyze the case at hand and recommend an option to his client, or, a "weak" sense, in which he must simply inform his client that ADR is an option that the client may wish to explore.

Under the "hard" sense, analyzing and explaining all of the ADR options available to a client may require a level of attention to the details of a case that may often not occur until the parties are closer to trial. Thus, attorneys will be expected to "analyze" the "cash value" of a lawsuit far earlier than they might otherwise have done under existing customary practice. This "front-end" analysis may cost clients more. Whether the case value of the settlement or verdict will be worth the extra expense is an open question.

As one example, a Michigan Bar Opinion provides that an attorney must disclose "all information pertinent to a mediation decision," including "the cost, whether the decision-maker is a single individual or panel of individuals, the format of the presentation to the forum, whether the decision is binding, the length of time before a decision is rendered, and the general objective of the forum."

This view is undergirded by Model Rule 1.4(b) which requires that "a lawyer shall explain a matter to the extent reasonably necessary to permit the client to make informed decisions regarding the representation." The rule further states that "the client shall have sufficient information to participate intelligently in decisions concerning the objectives of representation and the means by which they are to be pursued." Issues such as how much information, how long an attorney must take in explaining alternatives and whether the costs of such an explanation are sufficient to comply with this rule will add to the cost of legal advice. A resolution of these issues will depend on what is encompassed by the general requirement to communicate with one's clients.

In contrast to the more detailed Model Rule 1.4(b), a Missouri Supreme Court Rule 17.02(b) merely provides that lawyers "shall advise their clients of the availability of alternative dispute resolution programs." This "weak" consultation is, of course, far less burdensome because it does not require an individual analysis of the case file, but merely a generic explanation of the ADR concept. Certainly, the transaction costs in such a "weak" consultation requirement would be less, but the utility to the client may be commensurably less as well. However, unless there is some specificity regarding the modality of disclosure, the consent process is likely to become both boilerplate and rote in short order.

Notes and Questions

1.   Does one's attitude toward whether such a duty should exist depend on the model of attorney-client relations that one holds?

2.   If the law is going to require lawyers to disclose, should it require "hard" disclosures or "weak" disclosures (to use Professor Breger's terminology)?

3.   Besides legal and ethical requirements, what other reasons would counsel in favor of a practice of discussing ADR options with clients?

4.   Should lawyers who fail to advise their clients face potential liability for legal malpractice? *See* Robert F. Cochran, *Must Lawyers Tell Their Clients About ADR?*, Arb. J., June 1993, at 8.

5.   Assuming you believe that it is necessary or appropriate to discuss dispute resolution options with a client, how would you do it? That question underlies much of what appears in this book, and we expect that your understanding of it will develop as you proceed through these materials. Chapter VII will provide suggestions on how to deploy — in a particular case — the knowledge you have developed about dispute resolution options.

F. INTERVIEWING AND COUNSELING

A FIGHT OVER AMY

The following are general instructions for an interviewing and counseling role play about child custody in the divorce context. The confidential instructions for Alice, Bob, and the attorneys are available from the instructor, and may also be downloaded from the casebook web site, at www.lawschool.westlaw.com. A password is required to download the confidential instructions.

General Information for All Parties

Alice and Bob divorced five years ago when their daughter, Amy, was three years old. They amicably reached an agreement, the terms of which the court entered in its decree ordering that: Alice was sole owner of the family home, Alice had the right of custody and the responsibility for bringing up Amy, and Bob had the "right of reasonable visitation with Amy, including full time for a two-week vacation period each summer."

For three years the family cooperated comfortably under this arrangement, but last year Alice objected to Bob taking Amy to Florida for two weeks in July, saying it was too hot. Alice refused to give up Amy at the last minute, and Bob went without her. This year Bob informed Alice a month in advance, when he bought the supersaver plane tickets, that he would take Amy to New York City during his vacation. Alice phoned him about two days ahead and indicated she did not think that was a good idea, but Bob told her he would pick Amy up at 7:00 p.m. the night before the scheduled plane departure. Alice said, "Don't come." When Bob arrived at 7:00 p.m., Alice met him at the edge of the front porch and told him not to come any further and that he could not take Amy to New York because it was too dangerous for her there. Bob could see Amy peering through the screen door and brushed by Alice, walking to the door. Alice stepped in front of him and gently pushed him back to the edge of the porch. When Bob tried to move forward again, Alice pushed harder, and Bob fell down the steps breaking his wrist. Amy was crying.

The next morning, both Alice and Bob called for appointments with their respective attorneys, who are *not* the same persons who represented them in the divorce. At the beginning of their office visit, both Alice and Bob recount the above sequence of events.

Chapter III

NEGOTIATION

Negotiation is an interpersonal process through which we make arrangements with others to resolve disputes or plan transactions, often by reconciling conflicting — or apparently conflicting — interests. It involves communication — through the use of words or actions — of demands, wishes, and perspectives.

Most lawyers spend a major part of their professional lives engaged in this process. Lawyers negotiate, usually with other lawyers, to plan transactions and to resolve disputes. In addition, negotiation makes up an important part of other dispute resolution processes. Mediation, for instance, is negotiation that is facilitated by a third party. Several of the mixed processes discussed in Chapter VI — court-annexed (non-binding) arbitration, the mini-trial, and the summary jury trial — are intended to help parties negotiate better. So many cases in litigation are actually settled through negotiation that Professor Marc Galanter finds it useful to consider the two processes as one "litigotiation" process. Marc Galanter, *World of Deals: Using Negotiation to Teach About Legal Process*, 34 J. Legal Educ. 268, 268 (1984). Professor Gary Goodpaster has gone a step further and suggested that we could learn much by looking at litigation as part of the negotiation process. Gary Goodpaster, *Lawsuits as Negotiations*, 8 Negotiation J. 221 (1992).

Lawyers do not merely negotiate with other lawyers, however. In their professional lives, lawyers also negotiate with their bosses, partners, subordinates, and with providers of supplies and services. Lawyers also spend a significant portion of their professional lives negotiating with their clients about various aspects of their representation. And in their personal lives, lawyers, like all people, negotiate constantly — with their family, friends, physicians, clergy, taxi drivers, and so on.

Because negotiation takes place in such a wide variety of situations, and relies significantly on intuition and judgment, some argue that negotiation skills cannot be taught. We believe, however, that anyone can improve his or her negotiating skills by learning from experience and by planning, practicing, and reflecting on negotiation.

In this chapter, we cannot hope to cover the many situations in which lawyers negotiate. For that reason, we attempt to deal with the basics — a set of concepts and suggestions that will help you understand the various negotiation situations in which you may find yourself. In Section A, we begin by focusing on individual negotiator style or personality. In Section B, we introduce the negotiation process and provide a basic framework for thinking about how a typical negotiation might proceed. Then, in Section C, we explore how negotiators might approach this process by setting forth two major approaches to (or conceptualizations of) negotiation, which we label "adversarial" and "problem-solving." The former approach focuses on positions while the latter focuses on the interests underlying the dispute. Believing that nothing is more practical than a good theory, we hope that this section will give you a solid foundation for understanding the approaches that you and your counterparts employ in negotiations. In Section D, we elaborate on these approaches by identifying strategies and tactics associated with each. In Section E, we turn our attention explicitly to "legal negotiations," exploring the roles of law, lawyers, and clients in the negotiation process. Finally, in Section F, we examine the potential impact of culture, race, and gender on the negotiation process.

A. NEGOTIATOR STYLE

Because negotiation is an interpersonal process, a negotiator's personality or style is a critically important component of successful negotiation. In an excerpt from BARGAINING FOR ADVANTAGE: NEGOTIATION STRATEGIES FOR REASONABLE PEOPLE, Professor G. Richard Shell provides the following thought experiment to help negotiators discern which of five personality types fits them.

G. RICHARD SHELL, BARGAINING FOR ADVANTAGE: NEGOTIATION STRATEGIES FOR REASONABLE PEOPLE
9–11 (1999).

Behind the bewildering array of personality differences, psychologists have isolated five basic negotiation personality types based on the way people prefer handling interpersonal conflict. The five types are, in descending order of aggressiveness: competitors, problem solvers, compromisers, accommodators, and conflict avoiders. No system of categorization is perfect, but this one is better than average because the potential for interpersonal conflict is what gives negotiation its characteristic "edge." If you can pinpoint how you feel about conflicts with other people, you are on the way toward understanding a lot about your preferred approach to negotiation.

* * *

As a simple test to see which of these styles you tend to use, try the following "thought experiment." Imagine you are one of ten people, all of whom are strangers, sitting at a big round table in a conference room. Someone comes into the room and makes the following offer: "I will give a prize of one thousand dollars to each of the first two people who can persuade the person sitting opposite to get up, come around the table, and stand behind his or her chair."

Do you have that picture in mind? You are one of the ten strangers at the table. You can see the person sitting opposite you, and that person is looking at you. The first two people who can persuade the person sitting opposite to get up, come around the table, and stand behind his or her chair get $1,000. Everyone else gets $0.

How will you respond to this strange offer? You will need to move quickly because everyone else at the table is also thinking about what to do.

Before reading on, close your eyes and let yourself respond. Don't think too hard; just note the first idea that occurs to you. When you have decided what you would do, read on.

One reaction is to do nothing, suspecting a trick or worrying that you might look like a fool running around a table in response to a stranger's offer. "I don't want to play," you might say. This is the response of an **"avoider"** — someone who strongly dislikes interpersonal conflict, has a distaste for games with winners and losers, and tries to dodge situations that hold the prospect for open disagreement. Avoiders prefer peace and quiet in both their personal and professional lives. They will go to considerable lengths to arrange their homes and offices so that conflict is at a minimum.

Perhaps the most obvious response is to offer the person sitting opposite you $500 to race around and stand behind your chair. But suppose the other person is yelling for you to do the same thing? Would you argue or jump up to run behind his or her chair? If your tendency is to concede this debate and start running, you are a **"compromiser."**

Compromisers are fair-minded people who are interested in maintaining productive relations with others. Compromisers favor agreements that give each party some equitable part of each and every item under discussion, but in a pinch, they are slightly more likely to favor a solution that preserves a relationship than one that yields them an advantageous result. If you are a compromiser, you like to split the difference as a routine method of concluding negotiations. You do not relish the negotiation process, but you do not shy away from it either. You are not greedy, nor are you timid. You look for quick, obvious, and fair solutions to bargaining problems. Compromise is not a bad choice in the table problem because you need to move quickly, and a 50–50 split of the money (assuming the other side keeps his or her promise) satisfies most people's criteria for a fair agreement.

A third response takes even less time than the compromise solution: You race around the table and stand behind your opposite's chair. You don't negotiate–you act to solve the problem. In this case, your opposite will get $1,000 because you were moving while everyone else was still talking. But notice the outcome. Your colleague, whom you do not know, now has $1,000 and you have $0. You are trusting that the other person will do the right thing and share the money with you.

This is the response of an **"accommodator."** You like to resolve interpersonal conflicts by solving the other person's problem. If the people you help are like you, they share the wealth and return the favor. If they are greedy and selfish, you get a pat on the back and end up with little or nothing.

The fourth approach is that of the **"competitor."** Above all, competitors like to win. That means they are willing to take chances to get more money than anyone else in the game. A competitor might yell to his counterpart, "Quick, get behind my chair! I'll share the money with you!" Then the competitor sits tight, hoping the other side gets moving. Unlike the compromiser, the competitor will argue over whether he or you should be the one to get up and race around the table. In fact, he may even lie a little and tell you he *can't* move because he has a sprained ankle.

If the ploy works, the competitor decides how to share the money. He will keep the lion's share. Competitors like to control negotiations, opening with ambitious demands, using threats and ultimatums, and walking out to demonstrate their commitment to their goals.

The final response is the most imaginative, given the terms of the offer. You get out of your chair and scream, "Let's both get behind each other's chairs! We can each make a thousand dollars!" This can work — if you are quick enough. It is the assertive response of the **"problem solver."** Instead of trying to figure out how to divide $1,000 two ways, the problem solver has the insight to see that there is a way for *both parties* to get $1,000 out of the situation.

* * *

Now take a moment to think — honestly — about which of the five conflict styles feel most comfortable for you. You probably have two or three preferred styles, not just one. And there is probably at least one that feels distinctly awkward to you.* * **

Whatever your answers, they reflect your style preferences. Different situations will bring out different aspects of your style. But, in the words of the Danish folk saying that led this chapter, "you must bake with the flour you have." Your attitudes about conflict are the emotional "stuff" you have to work with.

Notes and Questions

1.   What is *your* preferred negotiation style? Why?

2.   Learning about negotiation style generally, and one's own style specifically, is valuable not only because it helps negotiators appreciate their own tendencies, but also because it provides them with a framework for

understanding their counterparts and for making sense of the interactions between them.

3. Speaking of interactions between negotiators with different conflict styles, what do you think happens when two "competitors" negotiate with one another? Two "avoiders"? Two "compromisers"? How about a "competitor" and an "accommodator"? A "competitor" and an "avoider"?

4. Robert R. Blake and Jane Srygley Mouton identified these five styles — competing, accommodating, avoiding, compromising, and collaborating — in the mid–1960s. *See* ROBERT R. BLAKE & JANE SRYGLEY MOUTON, THE MANAGERIAL GRID: KEY ORIENTATIONS FOR ACHIEVING PRODUCTION THROUGH PEOPLE (1964). Professors Kenneth Thomas and Ralph Kilmann developed an instrument, called the Thomas–Kilmann Instrument or TKI, to test for these styles. *See* Ralph H. Kilmann & Kenneth W. Thomas, *Developing a Forced–Choice Measure of Conflict–Handling Behavior: The "Mode" Instrument*, 37 Educ. Testing & Measurement 309 (1977). Although this instrument is not behaviorally validated, some research suggests that negotiators do exhibit fairly consistent styles. *See* Robert H. Mnookin, Scott R. Peppet & Andrew S. Tulumello, *Negotiators' Empathy and Assertiveness*, 14 Alternatives to the High Cost of Litig. 133, 145 (1996).

5. That said, many negotiators find that their styles vary by context, and from situation to situation within a particular context. Do you think you exhibit the same style in professional settings that you exhibit in personal settings? Is your style the same when you are negotiating on your own behalf as when you are negotiating for someone else? What other contextual factors might influence your negotiation style?

6. Professor Robert Mnookin, Professor Scott Peppet, and Andrew S. Tulumello focus in BEYOND WINNING: NEGOTIATING TO CREATE VALUE IN DEALS AND DISPUTES (2000) on two components of conflict style: assertiveness and empathy. They define assertiveness as "the capacity to express and advocate for one's own interests," and empathy as the "capacity to demonstrate an accurate, nonjudgmental understanding of another person's concerns and perspective." Robert H. Mnookin, Scott R. Peppet & Andrew S. Tulumello, *The Tension Between Empathy and Assertiveness*, 12 Negotiation J. 217, 218 (1995). Is there any tension between assertiveness and empathy? Can negotiators exhibit both? The problem-solving (or collaborative) style reflects high degrees of both assertiveness and empathy. (It is worth observing that empathy has affective, cognitive, and behavioral dimensions. Professor Mnookin and his colleagues focus on the latter two dimensions.)

7. Much of the research on negotiation style has focused on a more basic difference — i.e., whether negotiators are competitive or cooperative. Consider the following:

● In the late 1970s, Professor Gerald Williams conducted a study of lawyer-negotiators in Denver and Phoenix. *See* GERALD WILLIAMS, LEGAL NEGOTIATION AND SETTLEMENT (1983). He asked them to recall their most recently completed negotiation and then to select from a lengthy list of adjectives those that best described the lawyer-negotiator who represented the other side. Williams performed a statistical analysis of the responses in an effort to categorize negotiators as "competitive" or "cooperative." He found that lawyers deemed 65% of their counterparts cooperative and 24% competitive (11% were not susceptible to categorization).

- More recently, Professor Andrea Kupfer Schneider replicated (and extended) the Williams study. She employed essentially the same methodology to assess the competitiveness and cooperativeness of lawyer-negotiators in Chicago and Milwaukee. She found that lawyers deemed 64% of their counterparts "cooperative" (or, to use her term, "problem-solving") and 36% "competitive" (or, to use her term, "adversarial"). Andrea Kupfer Schneider, *Shattering Negotiation Myths: Empirical Evidence on the Effectiveness of Negotiation Style*, 7 Harv. Negot. L. Rev. 143, 163 (2002)

- Both Professor Williams and Professor Schneider asked their subjects to evaluate the effectiveness of their counterparts. Both found that lawyer-negotiators rated "cooperative" were deemed more effective than those rated "competitive."

8. Other commentators have explored negotiation style through other lenses. Professor Don Peters has used the Myers–Briggs Type Indicator and its four personality dimensions (sensing-intuitive, thinking-feeling, judging-perceiving, and extraverted-introverted) as a way of understanding the impact personality variables can have on negotiation. *See* Don Peters, *Forever Jung: Psychological Type Theory, The Myers–Briggs Type Indicator and Learning Negotiation*, 42 Drake L. Rev. 1 (1993). Professors Bruce Barry and Raymond Friedman studied the impact of the "five-factor model" of personality on negotiation (extroversion, agreeableness, conscientiousness, emotional stability, and openness to experience) and found that two of the five factors — extroversion and agreeableness — can be liabilities in distributive negotiation (or negotiation involving the division of a good in which any gains one side gets are at the expense of the other). Bruce Barry & Raymond A. Friedman, *Bargainer Characteristics in Distributive and Integrative Negotiation*, 74 J. of Personality & Soc. Psychol. 345 (1998). Others have conducted even more comprehensive analyses of personality and negotiation behavior. *See, e.g.*, Roderick W. Gilkey & Leonard Greenhalgh, *The Role of Personality in Successful Negotiating*, 2 Negotiation J. 245 (1986).

9. Research suggests not only that personality can have an impact on the way we negotiate but also that something as ephemeral as mood can influence negotiation behavior. *See* Clark Freshman, Adele Hayes & Greg Feldman, *The Lawyer–Negotiator as Mood Scientist: What We Know and Don't Know About How Mood Relates to Successful Negotiation*, 2002 J. Disp. Resol. 1.

10. Recently, Professor Leonard Riskin has argued that negotiators who practice mindfulness meditation are likely to gain insight into their own personalities, moods, and the way they respond to conflict and, consequently, perform better. *See* Leonard L. Riskin, *The Contemplative Lawyer: On the Potential Contributions of Mindfulness Meditation to Law Students, Lawyers, and Their Clients*, 7 Harv. Negot. L. Rev. 1 (2002). For further discussion of mindfulness meditation, see Chapter VIII, beginning at page 888.

B. THE NEGOTIATION PROCESS

Every negotiation is unique, but most negotiations follow a fairly predictable path. In the following excerpt, Professor Shell argues that negotiations typically include four steps or stages.

G. RICHARD SHELL, BARGAINING FOR ADVANTAGE: NEGOTIATION STRATEGIES FOR REASONABLE PEOPLE

119 (1999).

Negotiation is a dance that moves through four stages or steps.... Let's look at a simple example from real life to see how the four-step sequence works in practice.

Imagine you are approaching a traffic intersection in your car. You notice that another car is nearing the intersection at the same time. What do you do?

Most experienced drivers start by slowing down to assess the situation. Next, they glance toward the other driver to make eye contact, hoping to establish communication with the other person. With eye contact established, one driver waves his or her hand toward the intersection in the universally recognized 'after you' signal. Perhaps both drivers wave. After a little hesitation, one driver moves ahead and the other follows.

Note the four-step process: preparation (slowing down), information exchange (making eye contact), proposing and concession making (waving your hand), and commitment (driving through). This may seem like a unique case, but anthropologists and other social scientists have observed a similar four-stage process at work in situations as diverse as rural African land disputes, British labor negotiations, and American business mergers. The four stages form an unstated and often unseen pattern just below the surface of negotiations.

Notes and Questions

1.   Professor Shell describes this four-step process as an "important truth" about negotiation. Do you think all negotiations include these four steps?

2.   The first step in Professor Shell's four-step process is preparation or planning. How should a negotiator prepare for an upcoming negotiation?

3.   Some negotiators focus their preparation primarily on the positions they expect to advocate — and the positions they expect their counterparts to advocate — in the negotiation. This approach to planning is more consistent with an "adversarial" approach to negotiation. *See infra* Chapter III, Section C, beginning at page 165.

4.   Other negotiators reject this approach to negotiation planning as too narrow:

Many people feel prepared if they know what they want and what they'll settle for. But if our preparation consists of creating a wish list, with a minimum fall-back position, the only thing we will be ready to do in the negotiation is to state demands and make concessions. Position preparation leads to positional negotiation. By focusing on what we will ask for and what we will give up, we set ourselves up for an adversarial, zero-sum kind of negotiation. But this kind of preparation often prevents us from finding creative solutions that expand the pie before splitting it, or from working side by side to solve some joint problem.

Positional preparation is the greatest source of stress and anxiety during negotiations. We might think that if we invest time and energy planning our demands and concessions we will feel more confident as we make them. But the reality of the matter is that a positional negotiator, even one who has thought about what positions to take and what concession to make, has little basis for deciding when to make a concession. Making a concession when the other side won't simply rewards their bad behavior. Yet not making one can precipitate a contest as to who can be more stubborn. Preparing only by making a list of demands and concessions is preparation for a bad negotiation.

Roger Fisher & Danny Ertel, Getting Ready to Negotiate: The "Getting to Yes" Workbook 5 (1995).

Professor Fisher and Mr. Ertel recommend, instead, that negotiators focus on seven keys during preparations: interests, options, alternatives, legitimacy, communication, relationship, and commitment. *Id.* at 6. Their approach to preparation is more consistent with a "problem-solving" approach to negotiation. *See* Chapter III, Section C, beginning on page 165.

5.   Is anything missing from Professor Shell's depiction of the negotiation process? Don't negotiators need to spend some time "ice-breaking" or "rapport building" prior to engaging in the processes of information exchange and concession making? For an analysis of the empirical evidence documenting the valuable role that rapport building can play in negotiation, see Janice Nadler, *Rapport in Negotiation and Conflict Resolution*, 87 Marq. L. Rev. 875 (2004). How might one develop rapport during a negotiation? *See* Robert Mnookin, Scott Peppet & Andrew S. Tulumello, Beyond Winning: Negotiating to Create Value in Deals and Disputes 209 (2000) (advising negotiators to "negotiate a process" for the negotiation).

6.   Professor Shell does acknowledge that negotiators might vary the sequencing and pacing of the process:

Of course, in complex bargaining encounters, people vary the sequence and pacing of these steps. They may reach an impasse in the concession-making stage, so they go back to exchanging information. And some aspects of a deal may move faster than others — commitments may come on issues "A" and "B" while information exchange and concession making continue on issue "C."

G. Richard Shell, Bargaining for Advantage: Negotiation Strategies for Reasonable People 119 (1999).

C. APPROACHES TO NEGOTIATION

The humorist Robert Benchly declared that "[t]here may be said to be two classes of people in the world: those who constantly divide the people of the world into two classes, and those who do not." Paul Dickson, *The Official Rules,* The Washingtonian, Nov. 1978, at 152. Many commentators have developed systems for dividing approaches to negotiation into two (and sometimes more) categories. For us, the most helpful dichotomy is that between two basic and widely held orientations toward negotiation: adversarial and problem solving. These two approaches are often in tension with one another.

The adversarial approach is grounded upon the assumption that there is a limited resource — such as money, golf balls, or lima beans — and the parties must decide whether and how to divide it. In such a situation, the parties' positions conflict; what one gains, the other must lose. An adversarial approach naturally fosters strategies designed to maximize the client's position with respect to the resource in question. And the typical tactics include those designed to uncover as much as possible about the other side's situation and simultaneously mislead the other side as to your own situation.

The problem-solving approach is quite different. It seeks to meet the interests or underlying needs of all parties to the dispute or transaction, and, accordingly, tends to produce strategies designed to promote the disclosure and relevance of these underlying needs. The recommended techniques include those intended to increase the number of issues for bargaining or to "expand the pie" before dividing it.

We introduce both approaches below. The first excerpt, by Professor Russell Korobkin, reflects an adversarial orientation to negotiation. The second excerpt, by Professor Carrie Menkel–Meadow, reflects a problem-solving orientation. Legal negotiators should be acquainted with both approaches because they certainly will encounter both during the course of their practices, and it is important to be able to respond appropriately. While we generally believe that the problem-solving approach is generally superior, we also recognize that there may be times when it is necessary to use adversarial tactics during a negotiation.

1. ADVERSARIAL NEGOTIATION

RUSSELL KOROBKIN, A POSITIVE THEORY OF LEGAL NEGOTIATION
88 Geo. L. J. 1789, 1792–94 (2000).

In any negotiation, the maximum amount that a buyer will pay for a good, service, or other legal entitlement is called his "reservation point" or, if the deal being negotiated is a monetary transaction, his "reservation price" (RP). The minimum amount that a seller would accept for that item is her RP. If the buyer's RP is higher than the seller's, the distance between the two points is called the "bargaining zone." Reaching agreement for any amount that lies within the bargaining zone is superior to not reaching an agreement for both parties, at least if they are concerned only with the transaction in question.

For example, suppose Esau, looking to get into business for himself, is willing to pay up to $200,000 for Jacob's catering business, while Jacob, interested in retiring, is willing to sell the business for any amount over $150,000. This difference between Esau's and Jacob's RPs creates a $50,000 bargaining zone. At any price between $150,000 and $200,000, both parties are better off agreeing to the sale of the business than they are reaching no agreement and going their separate ways.

The same structure used to describe a transactional negotiation can be used to describe a dispute resolution negotiation. Suppose that Goliath has filed suit against David for battery. David is willing to pay up to $90,000 to settle the case out of court — essentially, to buy Goliath's legal right to bring suit — while Goliath will "sell" his right for any amount over $60,000. These RPs create a $30,000 bargaining zone between $60,000 and $90,000. Any settlement in this range would leave both parties better off than they would be without a settlement.

In contrast, if the seller's RP is higher than the buyer's RP, there is no bargaining zone. In this circumstance, there is no sale price that would make both parties better off than they would be by not reaching a negotiated agreement. Put another way, the parties would be better off not reaching a negotiated agreement. If Jacob will not part with his business for less than $150,000 and Esau will not pay more than $100,000 for it, there is no bargaining zone. If David will pay up to $50,000 to settle Goliath's claim, but Goliath will not accept any amount less than $60,000, again there is no bargaining zone. An agreement in either case would leave at least one party, and possibly both parties, worse off than if they were to decide not to make a deal.

Knowledge of the parameters of the bargaining zone, which is created by the two parties' reservation points, is the most critical information for the negotiator to possess. Those parameters tell the negotiator both whether any agreement is possible and, if so, identify the range of possible deal points. At the same time, the negotiator has an interest in adjusting the parameters of the bargaining zone to his advantage. A buyer not only wants to know his and the seller's RP, he wishes to make both lower, or at least make both *appear* lower to the seller. This shifts the zone of possible deal points lower, increasing the chances that the seller will ultimately agree to a relatively low price. Experimental evidence in fact confirms that negotiators with more favorable RPs (that is, lower for buyers, higher for sellers) reach more profitable agreements than negotiators with less favorable RPs.

Esau wants to know his and Jacob's RPs, but he also would like to shift both numbers, and therefore the bargaining range, lower. Assuming Esau knows his RP is $200,000 and learns Jacob's is $150,000, Esau knows that an agreement is possible for some amount greater than the latter figure and less than the former. If he could reduce Jacob's RP to

$120,000 and his own to $170,000, however, the bargaining zone would remain the same size, but its changed parameters would suggest that Esau would be likely to buy the business for a lower price. Esau could achieve the same advantage if Jacob *believes* the parties' RPs are $120,000 and $170,000 respectively, even if the RPs objectively are $150,000 and $200,000.

The existence of a bargaining zone is necessary for a negotiated agreement, and the parameters of the bargaining zone — defined by both parties' RPs — define the set of possible "deal points."

Notes and Questions

1. Based on this excerpt, what assumptions appear to underlie the adversarial approach to negotiation:

- That the principal goal of each party is to maximize its own economic gain?
- That the outcome of the negotiation will likely be determined by two separate, individualistic cost-benefit analyses, rather than through any joint exploration of what is most suitable for both parties?
- That the process will be closed and deceptive, with each party trying to mislead or at least to conceal information about its own position while seeking to learn as much as it can about the other's position?
- That "deal points" fall along a continuum, and movement favorable to one party is inevitably unfavorable to the other?

2. We have labeled this the "adversarial" approach to negotiation. Other commentators have used other terms. For an example of the "adversarial" approach being described as "positional," see ROGER FISHER, WILLIAM URY & BRUCE PATTON, GETTING TO YES: NEGOTIATING AGREEMENT WITHOUT GIVING IN (2d ed. 1991). To see it described as "distributive," see DAVID LAX & JAMES SEBENIUS, THE MANAGER AS NEGOTIATOR: BARGAINING FOR COOPERATION AND COMPETITIVE GAIN (1986); HOWARD RAIFFA, THE ART AND SCIENCE OF NEGOTIATION (1982). For the term "value-claiming", see ROBERT H. MNOOKIN, SCOTT R. PEPPET & ANDREW S. TULUMELLO, BEYOND WINNING: NEGOTIATING TO CREATE VALUE IN DEALS AND DISPUTES (2000). Regardless of the label employed, this approach posits that negotiation is a zero-sum game in which the gains one side receives are at the expense of the other.

2. PROBLEM–SOLVING NEGOTIATION

CARRIE J. MENKEL–MEADOW, TOWARD ANOTHER VIEW OF LEGAL NEGOTIATION: THE STRUCTURE OF PROBLEM SOLVING
31 UCLA L. Rev. 754, 755–61, 795–801 (1984).

When people negotiate they engage in a particular kind of social behavior; they seek to do together what they cannot do alone. Those who negotiate are sometimes principals attempting to solve their own problems, or, more likely in legal negotiation, they are agents acting for clients, within the bounds of the law.

When lawyers write about this frequent social activity they join commentators from other disciplines in emphasizing an adversarial or zero-sum game approach to negotiation. In their view, what one party gains the other must lose. Resources are limited and must be divided. Information about one's real preferences must be jealously guarded. If the negotiation fails, the court will declare one party a winner, awarding money or an injunction. Successful negotiations represent a compromise of each party's position on an ordinal scale of numerical (usually monetary) values. This Article suggests that writers and negotiators who take such an adversarial approach limit themselves unnecessarily because they have not fully examined their assumptions.

Recently, several analysts have suggested that another approach to negotiation, an approach I will call problem-solving, might better accomplish the purposes of negotiation. This problem-solving model seeks to demonstrate how negotiators, on behalf of litigators or planners, can more effectively accomplish their goals by focusing on the parties' actual objectives and creatively attempting to satisfy the needs of both parties, rather than by focusing exclusively on the assumed objectives of maximizing individual gain. Unfortunately, some of this new literature tends to confuse collaborative negotiation styles or strategies with what must be antecedent to any negotiation behavior — a conception of negotiation goals. These recent analysts have also failed to fully explore their own assumptions concerning the objectives in negotiation. This Article explores those assumptions and elaborates on a framework for problem-solving negotiation that responds to the limitations of the adversarial model.

In order to contrast the adversarial model with the problem-solving model several key concepts must be defined and criteria for evaluation of the models made explicit. The negotiation models described here may seem unduly polarized, yet they represent the polarities of approach exemplified both by the conceptions of negotiation we construct as well as by the strategies and behaviors we choose. The models described here are based on orientations to negotiation, that is, how we approach our purpose in negotiation, rather than on the particular strategies or tactics we choose. It must be noted, however, that the tactics and strategies we choose may well be affected by our conception of negotiation. A general model demonstrates the relationship of negotiation orientations to negotiation results:

Orientation–> Mind-set–> Behavior–> Results.

The orientation (adversarial or problem solving) leads to a mind-set about what can be achieved (maximizing individual gain or solving the parties' problem by satisfying their underlying needs) which in turn affects the behavior chosen (competitive or solution searching) which in turn affects the solutions arrived at (narrow compromises or creative solutions).

The primary, but not exclusive, criterion for evaluation of a negotiation model is the quality of the solution produced. This includes the extent to which the process utilized contributes to or hinders the search for "quality" solutions.

In elaborating on approaches to negotiation I shall consider the following criteria of evaluation:

1. Does the solution reflect the client's total set of "real" needs, goals and objectives, in both the short and the long term?

2. Does the solution reflect the other party's full set of "real" needs, goals and objectives, in both the short and long term?

3. Does the solution promote the relationship the client desires with the other party?

4. Have the parties explored all the possible solutions that might either make each better off or one party better off with no adverse consequences to the other party?

5. Has the solution been achieved at the lowest possible transaction costs relative to the desirability of the result?

6. Is the solution achievable, or has it only raised more problems that need to be solved? Are the parties committed to the solution so it can be enforced without regret?

7. Has the solution been achieved in a manner congruent with the client's desire to participate in and affect the negotiation?

8. Is the solution "fair" or "just"? Have the parties considered the legitimacy of each other's claims and made any adjustments they feel are humanely or morally indicated?

A. The Underlying Principles of Problem Solving: Meeting Varied and Complementary Needs

Parties to a negotiation typically have underlying needs or objectives — what they hope to achieve, accomplish, and/or be compensated for as a result of the dispute or transaction. Although litigants typically ask for relief in the form of damages, this relief is actually a proxy for more basic needs or objectives. By attempting to uncover those underlying needs, the problem-solving model presents opportunities for discovering greater numbers of and better quality solutions. It offers the possibility of meeting a greater variety of needs both directly and by trading off different needs, rather than forcing a zero-sum battle over a single item.

The principle underlying such an approach is that unearthing a greater number of the actual needs of the parties will create more possible solutions because not all needs will be mutually exclusive. As a corollary, because not all individuals value the same things in the same way, the exploitation of differential or complementary needs will produce a wider variety of solutions which more closely meet the parties' needs.

A few examples may illustrate these points. In personal injury actions courts usually award monetary damages. Plaintiffs, however, commonly want this money for specific purposes. For instance, an individual who has been injured in a car accident may desire compensation for any or all of the following items: past and future medical expenses, rehabilitation and compensation for the cost of rehabilitation, replacement of damaged property such as a car and the costs of such replacement, lost income, compensation for lost time, pain and suffering, the loss of companionship with one's family, friends and fellow employees and employer, lost opportunities to engage in activities which may no longer be possible, such as backpacking or playing basketball with one's children, vindication or acknowledgment of fault by the responsible party, and retribution or punishment of the person who was at fault. In short, the injured person seeks to be returned to the same physical, psychological, social and economic state she was in before the accident occurred. Because this may be impossible, the plaintiff needs money in order to buy back as many of these things as possible.

In the commercial context, a breach of contract for failure to supply goods might involve compensation for the following: the cost of obtaining substitute goods, psychological damage resulting from loss of a steady source of supply, lost sales, loss of goodwill, any disruption in business which may have occurred, having to lay off employees as a result of decreased business, restoration of good business relationships, and retribution or punishment of the defaulting party. In [a] case described above, the litigation model structured the parties' goals in terms of the payment of money, when in fact one party sought to purchase and own a reliable form of transportation and the other sought a profit. It may be more useful in any contract case to think of the parties' needs in terms of what originally brought them together — the purpose of their relationship. Can the parties still realize their original goals? Charles Fried describes the classic function of contracts as attempts by the parties to mutually meet each other's needs:

> You want to accomplish purpose A and I want to accomplish purpose B. Neither of us can succeed without the cooperation of the other. Thus, I want to be able to commit myself to help you achieve A so that you will commit yourself to help me achieve B.

Some of the parties' needs may not be compensable, directly or indirectly. For example, some injuries may be impossible to fully rehabilitate. A physical disability, a scar, or damage to a personal or business reputation may never be fully eradicated. Thus, the underlying needs produced by these injuries may not be susceptible to full and/or monetary satisfaction. The need to be regarded as totally normal or completely honorable can probably never be met, but the party in a negotiation will be motivated by the desire to satisfy as fully as possible these underlying human needs. Some parties may have a need to get "as much X as possible," such as in demands for money for pain and suffering. This demand simply may represent the best proxy available for satisfying the unsatisfiable desire to be made truly whole — that is to be put back in the position of no accident at all. It also may represent a desire to save for a rainy day or to maximize power, fame or love.

It is also important to recognize that *both* parties have such needs. For example, in the personal injury case above, the defendant may have the same need for vindication or retribution if he believes he was not responsible for the accident. In addition, the defendant may need to be compensated for his damaged car and injured body. He will also have needs with respect to how much, when and how he may be able to pay the monetary damages because of other uses for the money. A contract breaching defendant may have specific financial needs such as payroll, advertising, purchases of supplies, etc.; defendants are not always simply trying to avoid paying a certain sum of money to plaintiffs. In the commercial case, the defendant may have needs similar to those of the plaintiff: lost income due to the plaintiff's failure to pay on the contract, and, to the extent the plaintiff may seek to terminate the relationship with the defendant, a steady source of future business.

* * *

To the extent that negotiators focus exclusively on "winning" the greatest amount of money, they focus on only one form of need. The only flexibility in tailoring an agreement may lie in the choice of ways to structure monetary solutions, including one shot payments, installments, and structured settlements. By looking, however, at what the parties desire money for, there may be a variety of solutions that will satisfy the parties more fully and directly. For example, when an injured plaintiff needs physical rehabilitation, if the defendant can provide the plaintiff directly with rehabilitation services, the defendant may save money and the plaintiff may gain the needed rehabilitation at lower cost. In addition, if the defendant can provide the plaintiff with a job that provides physical rehabilitation, the plaintiff may not only receive income which could be used to purchase more rehabilitation, but be further rehabilitated in the form of the psychological self-worth which accompanies such employment. Admittedly, none of these solutions may fully satisfy the injured plaintiff, but some or all may be equally beneficial to the plaintiff, and the latter two may be preferable to the defendant because they are less costly.

Understanding that the other party's needs are not necessarily as assumed may present an opportunity for arriving at creative solutions. Traditionally, lawyers approaching negotiations from the adversarial model view the other side as an enemy to be defeated. By examining the underlying needs of the other side, the lawyer may instead see opportunities for solutions that would not have existed before based upon the recognition of different, but not conflicting, preferences.

An example from the psychological literature illustrates this point. Suppose that a husband and wife have two weeks in which to take their vacation. The husband prefers the mountains and the wife prefers the seaside. If vacation time is limited and thus a scarce resource, the couple may engage in adversarial negotiation about where they should go. The simple compromise situation, if they engage in distributive bargaining, would be to split the two weeks of vacation time spending one week in the mountains and one week at the ocean. This solution is not likely to be satisfying, however, because of the lost time and money in moving from place to place and in getting used to a new hotel room and locale. In addition to being happy only half of the time, each party to the negotiation has incurred transaction costs associated with this solution. Other "compromise" solutions might include alternating preferences on a year to year basis, taking separate vacations, or taking a longer vacation at a loss of pay. Assuming that husband and wife want to vacation together, all of these solutions may leave something to be desired by at least one of the parties.

By examining their underlying preferences, however, the parties might find additional solutions that could make both happy at less cost. Perhaps the husband prefers the mountains because he likes to hike and engage in stream fishing. Perhaps the wife enjoys swimming, sunbathing and seafood. By exploring these underlying preferences the couple might find vacation spots that permit all of these activities: a mountain resort on a large lake, or a seaside resort at the foot of mountains. By examining their underlying needs the parties can see solutions that satisfy many more of their preferences, and the "sum of the utilities" to the couple as a whole is greater than what they would have achieved by compromising.

In addition, by exploring whether they attach different values to their preferences they may be able to arrive at other solutions by trading items. The wife in our example might be willing to give up ocean fresh seafood if she can have fresh stream or lake trout, and so, with very little cost to her, the couple can choose another waterspot where the hikes might be better for the husband. By examining the weight or value given to certain preferences the parties may realize that some desires are easily attainable because they are not of equal importance to the other side. Thus, one party can increase its utilities without reducing the other's. This differs from a zero-sum conception of negotiation because of the recognition that preferences may be totally different and are, therefore, neither scarce nor in competition with each other. In addition, if a preference is not used to "force" a concession from the other party (which as the example shows is not necessary), there are none of the forced reciprocal concessions of adversarial negotiation.

The exploitation of complementary interests occurs frequently in the legal context. For example, in a child custody case the lawyers may learn that both parties desire to have the children some of the time and neither of the parties wishes to have the children all of the time. It will be easy, therefore, to arrange for a joint custody agreement that satisfies the needs of both parties. Similarly, in a commercial matter, the defendant may want to make payment over time and the plaintiff, for tax purposes or to increase interest income, may desire deferred income.

Notes and Questions

1.   Based on this excerpt, what assumptions appear to underlie the problem-solving approach to negotiation:

- That the principal goal for each party is to meet its underlying needs and interests rather than maximizing economic gain?

- That the outcome of the negotiation will likely be determined by a joint exploration of what is most appropriate for both parties?

- That the process will be an open and creative one in which each party shares information with the other about its underlying needs and interests?

- That parties can produce joint gains by capitalizing on both shared and different interests?

2.   We have labeled this the "problem-solving" approach to negotiation. Other commentators have used different terms for this approach. To see the "problem-solving" approach referred to as "principled," see ROGER FISHER, WILLIAM URY & BRUCE PATTON, GETTING TO YES: NEGOTIATING AGREEMENT WITHOUT GIVING IN (2D ED. 1991). To see it described as "integrative," see DAVID LAX & JAMES SEBENIUS, THE MANAGER AS NEGOTIATOR: BARGAINING FOR COOPERATION AND COMPETITIVE GAIN (1986); HOWARD RAIFFA, THE ART AND SCIENCE OF NEGOTIATION (1982). To see it described as "value-creating," see ROBERT H. MNOOKIN, SCOTT R. PEPPET & ANDREW S. TULUMELLO, BEYOND WINNING: NEGOTIATING TO CREATE VALUE IN DEALS AND DISPUTES (2000). Regardless of the label employed, this approach posits that negotiation is a collaborative exercise in which the parties work together to satisfy their interests and create joint gains.

3.   Which of these approaches — adversarial or problem-solving — seems better able to address conflict on the different dimensions in which it operates (i.e., behavioral, cognitive, and emotional)?

D.   NEGOTIATION STRATEGY AND TACTICS

In this section, we move from general approaches to negotiation to the strategies and tactics deployed in the actual negotiation process. For our purposes, a "strategy" is an overall plan for achieving one's goals (or one's client's goals) in a negotiation. A "tactic" is a particular move designed to further that strategy. Below, we discuss strategies and tactics associated with both the adversarial approach to negotiation and the problem-solving approach to negotiation.

1.   ADVERSARIAL STRATEGY AND TACTICS

The adversarial approach assumes that negotiation is a zero-sum game in which any gains one side gets are inevitably at the expense of the other. This approach to negotiation suggests a straightforward strategy or plan of action: negotiators should attempt to maximize their gains at the bargaining table. The following excerpt by Professor Gary Goodpaster articulates this strategy and introduces the primary tactics associated with it.

GARY GOODPASTER, A PRIMER ON COMPETITIVE BARGAINING

1996 J. Disp. Resol. 325, 342–43.

In competitive negotiation or distributive bargaining, the parties' actual or perceived respective aims or goals conflict. In this context, the negotiator's aim is to maximize the realization of its goals. Since the goals conflict, either in fact or supposition, one party's gains are the other party's losses. Therefore, a negotiator's goal is to win by gaining as much value as possible from the other party. The basic idea is that the negotiation is about a fixed good or sum that must be divided between the parties. Not only is the competitive negotiator out to gain as much as he or she can, but he or she will take risks, even the risk of non-agreement, to secure a significant gain.

The competitive negotiator adopts a risky strategy which involves the taking of firm, almost extreme positions, making few and small concessions, and withholding information that may be useful to the other party. The intention, and hoped-for effect, behind this strategy is to persuade the other party that it must make concessions if it is to get agreement. In addition to this basic strategy, competitive negotiators may also use various ploys or tactics aimed at pressuring, unsettling, unbalancing or even misleading the other party to secure an agreement with its demands.

In an important sense, the competitive negotiator plays negotiation as an information game. In this game, the object is to get as much information from the other party as possible while disclosing as little information as possible. Alternatively, a competitive negotiator some-times provides the other party with misleading clues, bluffs, and ambiguous assertions with multiple meanings, which are not actually false, but nevertheless mislead the other party into drawing incorrect conclusions that are beneficial to the competitor.

The information the competitive negotiator seeks is the other party's bottom line. How much he will maximally give or minimally accept to make a deal. On the other hand, the competitive negotiator wants to persuade the other side about the firmness of the negotiator's own *asserted* bottom line. The competitive negotiator works to convince the other party that it will settle only at some point that is higher (or lower, as the case may be) than its *actual* and unrevealed bottom line.

Notes

1. Several tactics are commonly associated with the adversarial negotiation theory and strategy. For lists of adversarial tactics, see, for example, HARRY EDWARDS & JAMES J. WHITE, THE LAWYER AS NEGOTIATOR 112–21 (1977); ROBERT H. MNOOKIN, SCOTT R. PEPPET & ANDREW S. TULUMELLO, BEYOND WINNING: NEGOTIATING TO CREATE VALUE IN DEALS AND DISPUTES (2000); Michael Meltsner &

Philip G. Schrag, *Negotiating Tactics for Legal Services Lawyers*, 7 Clearinghouse Rev. 259 (1973).

2. Professor Goodpaster identifies the central adversarial tactics, including extreme opening positions, few and small concessions, withholding information, and staking out commitments. To be sure, all negotiations require some action along each of these dimensions, in that even problem-solving negotiators must make opening offers, concessions and manage the flow of information. It is the more extreme manner in which these tactics are used that gives them their adversarial character. Below, we examine each of these adversarial tactics in turn.

a. Extreme Opening Offers

Adversarial negotiators often begin with extremely self-serving positions at the bargaining table. Research suggests that negotiators who begin with extreme positions often fare quite well due to a phenomenon psychologists call "anchoring."

CHRIS GUTHRIE, JEFFREY J. RACHLINSKI & ANDREW J. WISTRICH, INSIDE THE JUDICIAL MIND

86 Cornell L. Rev. 777, 787–89 (2001).

When people make numerical estimates (e.g., the fair market value of a house), they commonly rely on the initial value available to them (e.g., the list price). That initial value tends to "anchor" their final estimates. In many situations, reliance on an anchor is reasonable because many anchors convey relevant information about the actual value of an item (although people might rely too heavily on anchors). The problem, however, is that anchors that do not provide any information about the actual value of an item may also influence judgment.

In one early study of anchoring, Professors Amos Tversky and Daniel Kahneman asked participants to estimate the percentage of African countries in the United Nations. Before asking for this estimate, they informed the participants that the number was either higher or lower than a numerical value identified by the spin of a "wheel of fortune." Tversky and Kahneman had secretly rigged this "wheel of fortune" to stop either on ten or sixty-five. When the wheel landed on ten, participants provided a median estimate of 25%; when the wheel landed on sixty-five, participants provided a median estimate of 45%. Even though the initial values were clearly irrelevant to the correct answer, the initial values had a pronounced impact on the participants' responses.

Anchors affect judgment by changing the standard of reference that people use when making numeric judgments. Anchors induce people to consider seriously the possibility that the real value is similar to the anchor, thereby leading them to envision circumstances under which the anchor would be correct. Even when people conclude that an anchor provides no useful information, mentally testing the validity of the anchor causes people to adjust their estimates upward or downward toward that anchor. As a consequence, even extreme, wholly absurd anchors can affect judgment. For example, students provided higher estimates of the average price of a college textbook when they were first asked to determine whether it was higher or lower than $7128.53. This anchor, although ridiculously high, forces students to consider the possibility that textbook pricetags are higher than they might have otherwise believed. Similarly, people provided higher estimates of the average annual temperature in San Francisco when first asked to determine whether it was higher or lower than 558 degrees. Such a high anchor induces people to consider the possibility that the real average is quite high.

Litigation frequently produces anchors. In settlement talks, for instance, litigants can be influenced by the opening offers that their adversaries make. Professors Russell Korobkin and Chris Guthrie found that people evaluating hypothetical settlement offers were more likely to accept a $12,000 final settlement offer when it followed a $2000 opening offer than when it followed a $10,000 opening offer. Korobkin and Guthrie hypothesized that those who received the $2000 opening offer expected to settle for a relatively small amount, so the $12,000 final offer seemed generous by comparison. On the other hand, those who received the $10,000 opening offer expected to settle for relatively more, so the $12,000 final offer seemed relatively stingy. The opening offers effectively "anchored subjects' expectations" and influenced their settlement preferences.

Notes and Questions

1. Psychological research indicates that anchoring may benefit negotiators in two ways. First, as the above excerpt suggests, one negotiator may use an extreme opening position as an anchor to induce her counterpart to agree to terms more favorable to the proposer. Second, a negotiator who anchors herself on a more optimistic goal is likely to fare relatively better than a negotiator who anchors on a less optimistic goal. *See* Russell Korobkin, *Aspirations and Settlement*, 88 Cornell L. Rev. 1 (2002).

2. Does the work on anchoring suggest that an adversarial negotiator should make the initial demand or offer in negotiation?

3. Professor Shell recommends that if a negotiator has decided to open, she should offer "the highest (or lowest) number for which there is a supporting standard or argument enabling [her] to make a presentable case." G. RICHARD SHELL, BARGAINING FOR ADVANTAGE: NEGOTIATING STRATEGIES FOR REASONABLE PEOPLE 161 (1999).

4. What are the risks associated with making an extreme opening offer?

5. Are there circumstances in which negotiators might profit by starting not with an extremely self-serving position but rather with a position that is extremely charitable to the other side? Consider the following excerpt:

A quotation on the cover of my Morocco travel guide reads, "From the moment you land, adventure assails you." This curiously ominous accolade turned out to be true: my fellow-travelers and I, conspicuously American tourists in an impoverished country, were continually beset by hucksters who wished to sell us undesirable goods or services. We were all at our most vulnerable in the ancient marketplaces, where, for a few pennies, you could have your photograph taken with a large snake draped over your shoulders, and then, for a few dollars, have the snake (now slowly wrapping itself around your neck) removed.

My guidebook also informed me that the prices in the markets are highly negotiable, and that tourists should haggle aggressively. I dutifully bargained a little at one vender's stall — and bought my son a key chain attached to a chunk of plastic in which a scorpion had been embedded–but I hated the feeling that I was fighting over a trivial sum with a man who clearly needed every dirham he could lay his hands on. Suddenly, I had a conceptual breakthrough: instead of bargaining down, why not bargain up? I tried my idea first in a taxi, which I was sharing with two other sportswriters. When the driver told us that the fare was eighty dirhams (about seven dollars), I said, "No! A hundred!" He did a perfect cartoon double take, then looked at me with deep suspicion. I said, in halting French, "You are an excellent driver. Eighty is not enough. A hundred and ten!" He then not only laughed but also drove us all the way across a busy intersection in the middle of which he had previously seemed inclined to abandon us. A little later, in a maze-like souk [marketplace], I reverse-haggled over the price of a leather purse for my daughter ("The work is so beautiful!" I said. "Your price is too low!") and ended up with a free second purse and an invitation to spend Ramadan with the family of the shopkeeper (I think).

David Owen, *Swinging in Morocco*, The New Yorker, May 21, 2001, at 52, 53–54.

b. Making Few and Small Concessions

Adversarial negotiators not only prefer to start with extreme opening positions, they also prefer to make few and small concessions from those opening positions. As Howard Raiffa explains it, "The most common pattern of concessions (for a maximizer) is monotone decreasing–that is, the intervals between your decreasing offers become successively smaller, signaling that you are approaching your limit." HOWARD RAIFFA, THE ART AND SCIENCE OF NEGOTIATION 128 (1982).

Concession making rests on the so-called "reciprocity norm," which Professor Robert Cialdini explains below.

ROBERT B. CIALDINI, INFLUENCE: SCIENCE AND PRACTICE*
36–39 (4th ed. 2001).

I was walking down the street when I was approached by an 11– or 12-year-old boy. He introduced himself and said he was selling tickets to the annual Boy Scouts Circus to be held on the upcoming Saturday night. He asked if I wished to buy any tickets at $5 apiece. Since one of the last places I wanted to spend Saturday evening was with the Boy Scouts, I declined. "Well," he said, "if you don't want to buy any tickets, how about buying some of our chocolate bars? They're only $1 each." I bought a couple and, right away, realized that something noteworthy had happened. I knew that to be the case because (a) I do not like chocolate bars; (b) I do like dollars; (c) I was standing there with two of his chocolate bars; and (d) he was walking away with two of my dollars.

To try to understand precisely what had happened, I went to my office and called a meeting of my research assistants. In discussing the situation, we began to see how the reciprocity rule was implicated in my compliance with the request to buy the candy bars. The general rule says that a person who acts in a certain way toward us is entitled to a similar return action. We have already seen that one consequence of the rule, however, is an obligation to make a concession to someone who has made a concession to us. As my research group thought about it, we realized that was exactly the position the Boy Scout had put me in. His request that I purchase some $1 chocolate bars had been put in the form of a concession on his part; it was presented as a retreat from his request that I buy some $5 tickets. If I were to live up to the dictates of the reciprocation rule, there had to be a concession on my part. As we have seen, there was such a concession: I changed from noncompliant to compliant when he moved from a larger to a smaller request, even though I was not really interested in *either* of the things he offered.

It was a classic example of the way a weapon of influence can infuse a compliance request with its power. I had been moved to buy something, not because of any favorable feelings toward the item, but because the purchase request had been presented in a way that drew force from the reciprocity rule. It had not mattered that I do not like chocolate bars; the Boy Scout had made a concession to me, *click*, and *whirr*, I responded with a concession of my own. Of course, the tendency to reciprocate with a concession is not so strong that it will work in all instances on all people; none of the weapons of influence considered in this book is that strong. However, in my exchange with the Boy Scout, the tendency had been sufficiently powerful to leave me in mystified possession of a pair of unwanted and overpriced candy bars.

Why should I feel obliged to reciprocate a concession? The answer rests once again in the benefit of such a tendency to the society. It is in the interest of any human group to have its members working together toward the achievement of common goals. However, in many social interactions the participants begin with requirements and demands that are unacceptable to one another. Thus, the society must arrange to have these initial, incompatible desires set aside for the sake of socially beneficial cooperation. This is accomplished through procedures that promote compromise. Mutual concession is one important such procedure.

The reciprocation rule brings about mutual concession in two ways. The first is obvious; it pressures the recipient of an already-made concession to respond in kind. The second, while not so obvious, is pivotally important. Because of a recipient's obligation to reciprocate, people are freed to make the *initial* concession and, thereby, to begin the beneficial process of exchange. After all, if there were no social obligation to reciprocate a concession, who would want to make the first sacrifice? To do so would be to risk giving up something and getting nothing back. However, with the rule in effect, we can feel safe making the first sacrifice to our partner, who is obligated to offer a return sacrifice.

Because the rule for reciprocation governs the compromise process, it is possible to use an initial concession as part of a highly effective compliance technique. The technique is a simple one that we will call the rejection-then-retreat technique, although it is also known as the door-in-the-face technique. Suppose you want me to agree to a certain request. One way to increase the chances that I will comply is first to make a larger request of me, one that I will most likely turn down. Then, after I have refused, you make the smaller request that you were really interested in all along. Provided that you structured your requests skillfully, I should view your second request as a concession to me and should feel inclined to respond with a concession of my own — compliance with your second request.

Was that the way the Boy Scout got me to buy his candy bars? Was his retreat from the $5 request to the $1 request an artificial one that was intentionally designed to sell candy bars? As one who has still refused to discard even his first Scout merit badge, I genuinely hope not. Whether or not the large-request-then-small-request sequence was planned, its effect was the same. It worked! Because it works, the rejection-then-retreat technique can and will be used *purposely* by certain people to get their way. First let's examine how this tactic can be used as a reliable compliance device. Later we will see how it is already being used. Finally we can turn to a pair of little-known features of the technique that make it one of the most influential compliance tactics available.

Remember that after my encounter with the Boy Scout, I called my research assistants together to try to understand what had happened to me — and, as it turned out, to eat the evidence. Actually, we did more than that. We designed an experiment to test the effectiveness of the procedure of moving to a desired request after a larger preliminary request had been refused. We had two purposes in conducting the experiment. First, we wanted to see whether this procedure worked on people besides me. (It certainly seemed that the tactic had been effective on me earlier in the day, but then I have a history of falling for compliance tricks of all sorts.) So the question remained, "Does the rejection-then-retreat technique work on enough people to make it a useful procedure for gaining compliance?" If so, it would definitely be something to be aware of in the future. Our second reason for doing the study was to determine how powerful a compliance device the technique was. Could it bring about compliance with a genuinely sizable request? In other words, did the *smaller* request to which the requester retreated have to be a *small* request? If our thinking about what caused the technique to be effective was correct, the second request did not actually have to be small; it only had to be smaller than the initial one. It was our suspicion that the critical aspect of a requester's retreat from a larger to a smaller favor was its appearance as a concession. So the second request could be an objectively large one — as long as it was smaller than the first request — and the technique would still work.

After a bit of thought, we decided to try the technique on a request that we felt few people would agree to perform. Posing as representatives of the "County Youth Counseling Program," we approached college students walking on campus and asked if they would be willing to chaperon a group of juvenile delinquents on a day trip to the zoo. This idea of being responsible for a group of juvenile delinquents of unspecified age for hours in a public place without pay was hardly an inviting one for these students. As we expected, the great majority (83 percent) refused. Yet we obtained very different results from a similar sample of college students who were asked the very same question with one difference. Before we invited them to serve as unpaid chaperons on the zoo trip, we asked them for an even larger favor — to spend two hours per week as counselors to juvenile delinquents for a minimum of two years. It was only after they refused this extreme request, as all did, that we made the small, zoo-trip request. But presenting the zoo trip as a retreat from our initial request, our success rate increased dramatically. Three times as many of the students approached in this manner volunteered to serve as zoo chaperons.

Be assured that any strategy able to triple the percentage of compliance with a substantial request (from 17 to 50 percent in our experiment) will be used often in a variety of natural settings. Labor negotiators, for instance, often use the tactic of making extreme demands that they do not expect to win but from which they can retreat and draw real concessions from the opposing side. It would appear, then, that the procedure would be more effective the larger the initial request, since there would be more room available for illusory concessions. This is true only up to a point, however. Research conducted at Bar Ilan University in Israel on the rejection-then-retreat technique shows that if the first set of demands is so extreme as to be seen as unreasonable, the tactic backfires. In such cases, the party who has made the extreme first request is not seen to be bargaining in good faith. Any subsequent retreat from that wholly unrealistic initial position is not viewed as a genuine concession and, thus, is not reciprocated. The truly gifted negotiator, then, is one whose initial position is exaggerated just enough to allow for a series of small reciprocal concessions and counteroffers that will yield a desirable final offer from the opponent.

Notes and Questions

1. Do you see how an adversarial negotiator can use both anchoring (starting with an extreme opening offer) and the reciprocity rule (specifically, the rejection-then-retreat strategy Cialdini describes above) to induce her counterpart to reach agreement?

2. Consider this rather unconventional example of the "rejection-then-retreat" tactic taken from network television negotiations between TV show creators/writers (who want to include racy language in their network shows) and network censors (who are employed by the networks to ensure that the shows are sufficiently wholesome):

> ABC employs twenty-seven Standards and Practices censors, or "editors," and the other broadcast networks have similar staffs. Most Standards editors have experience as lawyers, teachers, and members of the clergy. They scrutinize every show and commercial for vulgarity, sexuality, violence, and subject matter that could violate F.C.C. standards of obscenity, community standards of indecency, and, particularly, corporate standards of comfort.

* * *

> Standards departments typically have vague written guidelines but no lists of forbidden words or proscribed scenarios. Theirs is an oral culture, one whose strictures are handed down like Inuit tribal lore. The fiats that emerge from the Standards' editors' deliberations are scrupulous, nuanced, and often hilarious. The producers of the CBS drama "Delvecchio" were once told to amend the term "rat-doo-doo" to "rat-doo"; when a hunchback got knifed on "Get Smart," the censors decreed that "it would be better if the knife were to go into the part of his back which isn't hunched."

> Writers see Standards editors as Emily Posts who cling to archaic rules; the editors see themselves as Emily Dickinsons who strive to preserve a cultural standard. "We're accused of limiting creativity," a Standards editor told me. "But I feel we're challenging creativity. Instead of using 'damn' eleven times, can't you come up with some other word?" Censor-writer colloquies would delight William Safire: does "scumbag" connote a repellent individual, or will older viewers recall that it originally meant a condom? "Schmuck" means a jerk in Los Angeles, but is it still a synonym for "penis" in New York? "Dick" and "pussy" are now sometimes allowed, but only as insults (it may thus be permissible to say "You're a dick," but never "Your dick ... ")

* * *

> The rules of engagement in this routine warfare are understood by everyone involved. Standards editors often tell one another, "Give them seven notes so you can negotiate." The writers, in turn, put "asshole" in the script a few times as "censor bait," knowing they'll have to cut it but hoping to keep two "bitches" and a "balls" in exchange.

Tad Friend, *You Can't Say That*, The New Yorker, Nov. 19, 2001, at 44, 48–49.

3.   The rejection-then-retreat tactic that Cialdini describes above suggests that an adversarial negotiator can offer a concession as a way to induce her counterpart to do the same. In the following excerpt, however, Alexander Dobrev, relying largely on the work of Professors Amos Tversky and Daniel Kahneman, argues that each negotiator is likely to devalue the concessions she receives from her counterpart relative to the concessions she makes. This is because a negotiator experiences the concessions she makes as "losses" from her prior position and the concessions she receives as "gains." Psychologists have found that individuals experience more pain from a loss than they experience pleasure from a gain of the same size, as explained below.

> Imagine a Double Whopper with cheese. No onions. Now imagine your Whopper accompanying you to the negotiation table, where I, your counterpart, take it from you and eat it. You have just lost a Whopper.

> Imagine a second scenario. You come to the negotiation table with no food of your own and I, your counterpart, of my own accord, offer you that very same type of sandwich. You have just gained a Whopper. How would you value these otherwise identical sandwiches?

> A loss aversion approach would predict that most individuals would "hate" the loss of the Whopper in the first scenario considerably more than they would "love" the gain of an equivalent product in the second. You may be wondering, "How can anyone compare the value of the loss of a Whopper with the value of its gain in terms of 'love' and 'hate'?" Indeed, love and hate, although certainly expressing value, are not readily quantified. Consider, therefore, the following alternatives to a love-hate relationship with your sandwich:

> How much money would you require in order to lose your Whopper in the first scenario, if I asked for it?

> If, on the other hand, I offered you a Whopper when you did not have one, how much would you be willing to pay in order to gain it?

> The loss aversion prediction is that you would ask me to pay a considerably larger proportion of money to part with your Whopper than you would be willing to pay if I offered you mine.

Alexander Dobrev, *Concession Aversion: Can Fast Food Slow Down Successful Negotiations?*, Convenor Conflict Resolution, *available at* http://www.convenor.com/madison/dobrev.htm (last visited Feb. 17, 2005).

4.   There is ample experimental evidence supporting loss aversion in exchange. Consider the following example:

> The following classroom demonstration illustrates the principle of loss aversion. An attractive object (e.g., a decorated mug) is distributed to one-third of the students. The students who have been given mugs are *sellers* — perhaps better described as owners. They are informed that there will be an opportunity to exchange the mug for a predetermined amount of money. The subjects state what their choice will be for different amounts, and thereby indicate the minimal amount for which

they are willing to give up their mug. Another one-third of the students are *choosers*. They are told that they will have a choice between a mug like the one in the hands of their neighbor and an amount of cash; they indicate their choices for different amounts. The remaining students are *buyers*: they indicate whether they would pay each of the different amounts to acquire a mug. In a representative experiment, the median price set by sellers was $7.12, the median cash equivalent set by the choosers was $3.12, and the median buyer was willing to pay $2.88 for the mug.

Daniel Kahneman & Amos Tversky, *Conflict Resolution: A Cognitive Perspective*, in BARRIERS TO CONFLICT RESOLUTION 54–56 (Kenneth J. Arrow, Robert M. Mnookin, Lee Ross, Amos Tversky & Robert B. Wilson eds., 1995).

5. Note that loss aversion applies only when negotiators are trading "use goods," not when negotiating over "exchange goods".

Loss aversion does not affect all transactions: it applies to goods held for use, not goods held for exchange. Three categories of exchange goods are money held for spending, goods held specifically for sale, and "bargaining chips," goods that are valued only because they can be traded. The significance of missiles, for example, is substantially reduced when they are treated not as strategic assets but as bargaining chips. Concession aversion, we suggest, will only inhibit agreement in the latter case. Loss aversion plays little role in routine economic transactions, in which a seller and a buyer exchange a good and money, both of which are held for that purpose. In contrast, many of the objects of bargaining in labor negotiations (e.g., job security, benefits, grievance procedures) are "use goods" rather than exchange goods. Labor negotiations in which both sides seek to modify an existing contract to their advantage therefore provided the paradigm case of concession aversion.

Id. at 56–57.

6. What implications does concession aversion have for the rejection-then-retreat strategy Cialdini described above? In other words, are negotiators likely to accept proposals made by their counterparts if those proposals appear to be concessions (or "retreats") from prior proposals? Or will the concessions be devalued and therefore rejected?

7. Concession aversion is similar to "reactive devaluation." Research on this phenomenon suggests that negotiators may devalue proposals simply because they have been offered.

In one classic study conducted during the days of Apartheid, researchers solicited students' evaluations of two university plans for divestment from South Africa. The first plan called for partial divestment, and the second increased investments in companies that had left South Africa. Both plans, which fell short of the students' demand for full divestment, were rated before and after the university announced that it would adopt the partial divestment plan. The results were dramatic: students rated the university plan less positively after it was announced by the university and the alternative plan more positively.

We hasten to note that the source of an offer may be diagnostic of its quality. It may be reasonable to view an offer more critically when the source is one's opponent, particularly if there is an unpleasant history between the parties. However, evidence from the aforementioned studies suggests that people tend to experience a knee-jerk overreaction to the source of the offer. If negotiators routinely undervalue concessions made by their counterparts, it will inhibit their ability to exploit tradeoffs that might result in more valuable agreements.

Consider an example of how reactive devaluation might manifest itself in a negotiation between lawyers. Imagine a simplified environmental cleanup action in which the parties are a government enforcement agency (represented by a single person) and a single responsible polluter. There may be two solutions to their problem. In one, the government effectuates the cleanup and sends a bill to the polluter. In the second, the polluter does the cleanup and the government inspects. Perhaps solution one meets more of the polluters' interests than solution two. One might suppose that the polluter would prefer this solution regardless of how it emerges as the agreed method. However, studies of reactive devaluation suggest that once the government tentatively agrees to that particular solution, the polluter may view the alternative solution more favorably. The apparent thought process is 'if they held it back, it must be worse for them and therefore better for me than the one offered.' The polluter may irrationally reorder her priorities and reject a deal simply because it was offered freely by an opponent.

Richard Birke & Craig R. Fox, *Psychological Principles in Negotiating Civil Settlements*, 4 Harv. Negot. L. Rev. 1, 48–49 (1999).

c. Limited Disclosure of Information

Adversarial negotiators tend to keep their private information close to the vest, though they often seek to discover the private information their counterparts possess. In the following excerpt, Professors Ian Ayres and Jennifer Gerarda Brown describe the incentives negotiators face to limit information disclosure.

IAN AYRES & JENNIFER GERARDA BROWN, ECONOMIC RATIONALES FOR MEDIATION
80 Va. L. Rev. 324, 331–34 (1994).

Adverse selection causes many inefficiencies in negotiations and the resolution of disputes. Potential buyers and sellers, for example, often have private information about how much they individually value a particular good or service. Because each party's reservation price (or BATNA) is not publicly known, each party has "hidden information" that can give rise to adverse selection.

If parties had complete information about each other, bargaining would be much less costly. First, knowing each other's reservation price, they would immediately know whether there were gains from trade to bargain over. Second, if the parties knew their relative bargaining power, they would be more likely to avoid the inefficiencies of bargaining by quickly agreeing how to divide the gains from trade.

However, when the buyer and the seller have private information about their valuations or their costs of bargaining, the parties need to communicate — at least indirectly — something about their private information in order to determine whether there are in fact gains from trade. The parties' reports of information can take the form of either direct representations concerning the buyer's or seller's reservation price or, more commonly, the use of offers and counteroffers to signal indirectly one's own valuation.

The parties might strategically withhold or misrepresent the private information, however, in order to increase their private returns. When the parties have private knowledge of their own reservation prices, sellers will have an incentive to overstate their valuations in order to negotiate a higher price and buyers will have an incentive to understate their valuations in order to negotiate a lower price. Strategic misrepresentations of this kind and the contracts that result from them provide an important example of adverse selection. Just as sick people have an incentive to convince insurance companies that they are healthy when negotiating an insurance premium, high-valuing buyers have an incentive to convince sellers that they are low-valuing when negotiating the contract price. In both cases, the asymmetric information gives the party with private information an incentive to pretend to be a different type in negotiating a contract.

Adverse selection can consume a large percentage of the potential gains from trade. Strategic misrepresentation of value can induce parties to waste time bargaining when there are no gains from trade, and to bargain to impasse at times when there are no gains. And even when agreement is reached, real resources are consumed in the "negotiation dance" that might have been retained if the parties' valuations were public knowledge.

Notes and Questions

1. How can one change the negotiators' incentives to encourage them to disclose information? If one negotiator discloses private information to the other, will the other negotiator feel compelled to disclose due to the reciprocity norm described above?

2. What role might mediation — that is, assisted negotiation — play in overcoming the problems of asymmetric information that Ayres and Brown describe above?

d. Commitments

Adversarial negotiators also tend to make commitment statements in negotiation. Effective commitment statements are clear, specific, and final. For example, "we must have a 10% volume discount next month, or we will sign with an alternative supplier" is a more effective commitment statement than "if we don't get a volume discount, there will be trouble."

Consider the following excerpt on commitments:

THOMAS C. SCHELLING, THE STRATEGY OF CONFLICT

21–25, 27–28 (1980).

A bargain is struck when somebody makes a final, sufficient concession. Why does he concede? Because he thinks the other will not. "I must concede because he won't. He won't because he thinks I will. He thinks I will because he thinks I think he thinks so . . . . " There is some range of alternative outcomes in which any point is better for both sides than no agreement at all. To insist on any such point is pure bargaining, since one always *would* take less rather than reach no agreement at all, and since one always *can* recede if retreat proves necessary to agreement. Yet if both parties are aware of the limits to this range, *any* outcome is a point from which at least one party would have been willing to retreat and the other knows it! There is no resting place.

There is, however, an outcome; and if we cannot find it in the logic of the situation we may find it in the tactics employed. The purpose of this chapter is to call attention to an important class of tactics, of a kind that is peculiarly appropriate to the logic of indeterminate situations. The essence of these tactics is some voluntary but irreversible sacrifice of freedom of choice. They rest on the paradox that the power to constrain an adversary may depend on the power to bind oneself; that is, in bargaining, weakness is often strength, freedom may be freedom to capitulate, and to burn bridges behind one may suffice to undo an opponent.

* * *

How does one person make another believe something? The answer depends importantly on the factual question, "Is it true?" It is easier to prove the truth of something that is true than of something false. To prove the truth about our health we can call on a reputable doctor; to prove the truth about our costs or income we may let the person look at books that have been audited by a reputable firm or the Bureau of Internal Revenue. But to persuade him of something false we may have no such convincing evidence.

When one wishes to persuade someone that he would not pay more than $16,000 for a house that is really worth $20,000 to him, what can he do to take advantage of the usually superior credibility of the truth over a false assertion? Answer: make it true. How can a buyer make it true? If he likes the house because it is near his business, he might move his business, persuading the seller that the house is really now worth only $16,000 to him. This would be unprofitable; he is no better off than if he had paid the higher price.

But suppose the buyer could make an irrevocable and enforceable bet with some third party, duly recorded and certified, according to which he would pay for the house no more than $16,000, or forfeit

$5,000. The seller has lost; the buyer need simply present the truth. Unless the seller is enraged and withholds the house in sheer spite, the situation has been rigged against him; the "objective" situation — the buyer's true incentive — has been voluntarily, conspicuously, and irreversibly changed. The seller can take it or leave it. This example demonstrates that if the buyer can accept an irrevocable *commitment*, in a way that is unambiguously visible to the seller, he can squeeze the range of indeterminacy down to the point most favorable to him. It also suggests, by its artificiality, that the tactic is one that may or may not be available; whether the buyer can find an effective device for committing himself may depend on who he is, who the seller is, where they live, and a number of legal and institutional arrangements (including, in our artificial example, whether bets are legally enforceable).

If both men live in a culture where "cross my heart" is universally accepted as potent, all the buyer has to do is allege that he will pay no more than $16,000, using this invocation of penalty, and he wins — or at least he wins if the seller does not beat him to it by shouting "$19,000, cross my heart." If the buyer is an agent authorized by a board of directors to buy at $16,000 but not a cent more, and directors cannot constitutionally meet again for several months and the buyer cannot exceed his authority, and if all this can be made known to the seller, then the buyer "wins" — if, again, the seller has not tied himself up with a commitment to $19,000. Or, if the buyer can assert that he will pay no more than $16,000 so firmly that he would suffer intolerable loss of personal prestige or bargaining reputation by paying more, and if the fact of his paying more would necessarily be known, and if the seller appreciates all this, then a loud declaration by itself may provide the commitment. The device, of course, is a needless surrender of flexibility unless it can be made fully evident and understandable to the seller.

* * *

The foregoing discussion has tried to suggest both the plausibility and the logic of self-commitment. Some examples may suggest the relevance of the tactic, although an observer can seldom distinguish with confidence the consciously logical, the intuitive, or the inadvertent use of a visible tactic. First, it has not been uncommon for union officials to stir up excitement and determination on the part of the membership during or prior to a wage negotiation. If the union is going to insist on $2 and expects the management to counter with $1.60, an effort is made to persuade the membership not only that the management could pay $2 but even perhaps that the negotiators themselves are incompetent if they fail to obtain close to $2. The purpose — or, rather, a plausible purpose suggested by our analysis — is to make clear to the management that the negotiators could not accept less than $2 *even if they wished to* because they no longer control the members or because they would lose their own positions if they tried. In other words, the negotiators reduce the scope of their own authority and confront the management with the threat of a strike that the union itself cannot avert, even though it was the union's own action that eliminated its power to prevent the strike.

Something similar occurs when the United States Government negotiates with other governments on, say, the uses to which foreign assistance will be put, or tariff reduction. If the executive branch is free to negotiate the best arrangement it can, it may be unable to make any position stick and may end by conceding controversial points because its partners know, or believe obstinately, that the United States would rather concede than terminate the negotiations. But, if the executive branch negotiates under legislative authority, with its position constrained by law, and it is evident that Congress will not be reconvened to change the law within the necessary time period, then the executive branch has a firm position that is visible to its negotiating partners.

When national representatives go to international negotiations knowing that there is a wide range of potential agreement within which the outcome will depend on bargaining, they seem often to create a bargaining position by public statements, statements calculated to arouse a public opinion that permits no concessions to be made. If a binding public opinion can be cultivated and made evident to the other side, the initial position can thereby be made visibly "final."

These examples have certain characteristics in common. First, they clearly depend not only on incurring a commitment but on communicating it persuasively to the other party. Second, it is by no means easy to establish the commitment, nor is it entirely clear to either of the parties concerned just how strong the commitment is. Third, similar activity may be available to the parties on both sides. Fourth, the possibility of commitment, though perhaps available to both sides, is by no means equally available; the ability of a democratic government to get itself tied by public opinion may be different from the ability of a totalitarian government to incur such a commitment. Fifth, they all run the risk of establishing an immovable position that goes beyond the ability of the other to concede, and thereby provoke the likelihood of stalemate or breakdown.

Notes

1. The Schelling excerpt describes how adversarial negotiators can use commitment to constrain their own behavior in negotiation. As Mnookin and his colleagues explain it, a negotiator who commits to a particular position "ties one's hands, thus forcing the other side to accommodate." ROBERT MNOOKIN, SCOTT PEPPET & ANDREW S. TULUMELLO, BEYOND WINNING: NEGOTIATING TO CREATE VALUE IN DEALS AND DISPUTES 24 (2000).

2. In addition to using commitment tactics to constrain their own behavior, adversarial negotiators may also attempt to induce their counterparts to make commitments as a way of constraining their counterparts' behavior. Consider the following excerpt from Professor Cialdini:*

If I can get you to make a commitment (that is, to take a stand, to go on record), I will have set the stage for your automatic and ill-considered consistency with that earlier commitment. Once a stand is taken, there is a natural tendency to behave in ways that are stubbornly consistent with the stand.

* * *

Charitable organizations, for instance, will often use progressively escalating commitments to induce individuals to perform major favors. Research has shown that such trivial first commitments as agreeing to be interviewed can begin a "momentum of compliance" that induces such later behaviors as organ or bone marrow donations (Carducci, Deuser, Bauer, Large, & Ramaekers, 1989; Schwartz, 1970).

Many business organizations employ this approach regularly as well. For the salesperson, the strategy is to obtain a large purchase by starting with a small one. Almost any small sale will do because the purpose of that small transaction is not profit, it is commitment. Further purchases, even much larger ones, are expected to flow naturally from the commitment. * * *

* * *

The tactic of starting with a little request in order to gain eventual compliance with related larger requests has a name: the foot-in-the-door technique. Social scientists first became aware of its effectiveness in 1966 when psychologists Jonathan Freedman and Scott Fraser published an astonishing set of data. They reported the results of an experiment in which a researcher, posing as a volunteer worker, had gone door to door in a residential California neighborhood making a preposterous request of homeowners. The homeowners were asked to allow a public-service billboard to be installed on their front lawns. To get an idea of the way the sign would look, they were shown a photograph depicting an attractive house, the view of which was almost completely obscured by a very large, poorly lettered sign reading DRIVE CAREFULLY. Although the request was normally and understandably refused by the great majority of the residents in the area (only 17 percent complied), one particular group of people reacted quite favorably. A full 76 percent of them offered the use of their front yards.

The prime reason for their startling compliance has to do with something that had happened to them about two weeks earlier: They had made a small commitment to driver safety. A different "volunteer worker" had come to their doors and asked them to accept and display a little three-inch-square sign that read BE A SAFE DRIVER. It was such a trifling request that nearly all of them had agreed to it, but the effects of that request were enormous. Because they had innocently complied with a trivial safe-driving request a couple of weeks before, these homeowners became remarkably willing to comply with another such request that was massive in size.

ROBERT B. CIALDINI, INFLUENCE, SCIENCE AND PRACTICE 65 (4th ed. 2001).

3.   Although commitment tactics can help negotiators reach agreement on favorable terms, they can also backfire. Consider the following excerpt from Professor Jeffrey Rubin:

> Negotiators often find it tempting, particularly when discussions bog down and things appear not to be going the way they would like, to commit themselves to tough negotiating positions from which they swear they will never retreat. Like the players in the proverbial game of "chicken", each negotiator threatens not to turn aside (to concede) until the other does so first. There are several problems with such bold, seemingly irrevocable commitments. First, if they work — that is, if they succeed in eliciting some long-sought concession — the adversary is likely to think twice before sitting down to negotiate again. Why deliberately elect to walk into a buzz saw if one can help it? On the other hand, should the negotiation commitment fail to work — that is, should the adversary refuse to knuckle under — then the perpetrator is likely to be confronted with a nasty choice: To go back on one's stated commitment is to run the risk of losing credibility in the eyes of the adversary, while opening the way to subsequent exploitation by the other; on the other hand, to carry through a commitment to intransigence, in light of the adversary's determination to resist concession, is in turn to run the risk of engineering unnecessary havoc for both sides.

Jeffrey Rubin, *Negotiation: An Introduction to Some Issues and Themes*, 27 Am. Behav. Scientist 135, 142 (1983).

2.   PROBLEM–SOLVING STRATEGY AND TACTICS

In contrast to the adversarial approach to negotiation, which posits that negotiation is a zero-sum game in which any gains one side receives are necessarily at the expense of the other, the problem-solving approach views negotiation as a collaborative problem-solving exercise in which the parties work side-by-side to satisfy their interests and produce joint gains.

The most popular explanation of a problem-solving approach appears in ROGER FISHER, WILLIAM URY & BRUCE PATTON, GETTING TO YES: NEGOTIATING AGREEMENT WITHOUT GIVING IN (2d ed. 1991). The authors call their approach "principled negotiation" or "negotiation on the merits," and they contrast it with adversarial negotiation (which they label "hard positional bargaining" and "soft positional bargaining"). They describe the problem-solving strategy and its primary tactics in the following excerpt.

ROGER FISHER, WILLIAM URY & BRUCE PATTON, GETTING TO YES: NEGOTIATING AGREEMENT WITHOUT GIVING IN
10–12, 14 (2d ed. 1991).

At the Harvard Negotiation Project we have been developing an alternative to positional bargaining: a method of negotiation explicitly designed to produce wise outcomes efficiently and amicably. This method, called *principled negotiation* or *negotiation on the merits*, can be boiled down to four basic points.

These four points define a straightforward method of negotiation that can be used under almost any circumstance. Each point deals with a basic element of negotiation, and suggests what you should do about it.

People: Separate the people from the problem.

Interests: Focus on interests, not positions.

Options: Generate a variety of possibilities before deciding what to do.

Criteria: Insist that the result be based on some objective standard.

The first point responds to the fact that human beings are not computers. We are creatures of strong emotions who often have radically different perceptions and have difficulty communicating clearly. Emotions typically become entangled with the objective merits of the problem. Taking positions just makes this worse because people's egos become identified with their positions. Hence, before working on the substantive problem, the "people problem" should be disentangled from it and dealt with separately. Figuratively if not literally, the participants should come to see themselves as working side by side, attacking the problem, not each other. Hence the first proposition: *Separate the people from the problem.*

The second point is designed to overcome the drawback of focusing on people's stated positions when the object of a negotiation is to satisfy their underlying interests. A negotiating position often obscures what you really want. Compromising between positions is not likely to produce an agreement which will effectively take care of the human needs that led people to adopt those positions. The second basic element of the method is: *Focus on interests, not positions.*

The third point responds to the difficulty of designing optimal solutions while under pressure. Trying to decide in the presence of an adversary narrows your vision. Having a lot at stake inhibits creativity. So does searching for the one right solution. You can offset these constraints by setting aside a designated time within which to think up a wide range of possible solutions that advance shared interests and creatively reconcile differing interests. Hence the third basic point: Before trying to reach agreement, *invent options for mutual gain.*

Where interests are directly opposed, a negotiator may be able to obtain a favorable result simply by being stubborn. That method tends to reward intransigence and produce arbitrary results. However, you can counter such a negotiator by insisting that his single say-so is not enough and that the agreement must reflect some fair standard independent of the naked will of either side. This does not mean insisting that the terms be based on the standard you select, but only that some fair standard such as market value, expert opinion, custom, or law determine the outcome. By discussing such criteria rather than what the parties are willing or unwilling to do, neither party need give in to the other; both can defer to a fair solution. Hence the fourth basic point: *Insist on using objective criteria*.

* * *

To sum up, in contrast to positional bargaining, the principled negotiation method of focusing on basic interests, mutually satisfying options, and fair standards typically results in a *wise* agreement. The method permits you to reach a gradual consensus on a joint decision *efficiently* without all the transactional costs of digging in to positions only to have to dig yourself out of them. And separating the people from the problem allows you to deal directly and empathetically with the other negotiator as a human being, thus making possible an *amicable* agreement.

Notes

1. As formulated by Professor Fisher, and Mssrs. Ury & Patton, problem-solving negotiators should attempt to achieve a wise, efficient, and amicable outcome, not merely to maximize gains. In contrast to the adversarial strategy — which focuses solely on the substance of the negotiation — the problem-solving strategy focuses on the substance, the process, and the relationship between the negotiators.

2. Below, we focus on the four primary tactics, or principles, of the problem-solving approach. With respect to each, we identify what we believe is the key (though certainly not the only) skill a negotiator needs to develop to use the tactic successfully.

a. "Separating the People from the Problem" (Listening)

Problem-solving negotiators recognize that negotiators are people first and that "people problems" can become entangled with the substantive issues under discussion. To minimize entanglement, problem-solving negotiators are attentive to the people and relationship issues inherent in negotiation.

People problems can arise due to misconceptions on the part of the negotiators, emotional issues, or communication difficulties. Regardless of the source of these problems, problem-solving negotiators can best address them by attempting to listen carefully to their counterparts. Through good listening, problem-solving negotiators can identify and overcome misperceptions, acknowledge emotional issues, and facilitate good communication.

DOUGLAS STONE, BRUCE PATTON & SHEILA HEEN, DIFFICULT CONVERSATIONS: HOW TO DISCUSS WHAT MATTERS MOST

163–67 (1999).

Andrew is visiting his Uncle Doug. While Doug is on the phone, Andrew tugs on his uncle's pant leg, saying, "Uncle Doug, I want to go outside."

"Not now, Andrew, I'm on the phone," says Doug.

Andrew persists: "But Uncle Doug, I want to go outside!"

"Not now Andrew!" comes Doug's response.

"But I want to go out!" Andrew repeats.

After several more rounds, Doug tries a different approach: "Hey, Andrew. You really want to go outside, don't you?"

"Yes," says Andrew. Then without further comment, Andrew walks off and begins playing by himself. Andrew, it turns out, just wanted to know that his uncle understood him. He wanted to know he'd been heard.

Andrew's story demonstrates something that is true for all of us: we have a deep desire to feel heard, and to know that others care enough to listen.

Some people think they are already good listeners. Others know they are not, but don't much care. If you're in either group you might be tempted to skip this chapter. Don't. Listening well is one of the most powerful skills you can bring to a difficult conversation. It helps you understand the other person. And, importantly, it helps them understand you.

LISTENING TRANSFORMS THE CONVERSATION

A year ago, Greta's mother learned she had diabetes and was ordered to follow a strict regimen of medication, diet, and exercise. Greta is concerned that her mother is not following the regimen, but Greta has had little success encouraging her mother to do so. A typical conversation between them goes like this:

GRETA: Mom, you need to stay on the exercise plan. I worry that you don't understand how important it is.

MOM: Greta, please stop hounding me about this. You don't understand. I'm doing the best I can.

GRETA: Mom, I do understand. I know that exercising can be difficult, but I want you to stay well. I want you to be around for your grandchildren.

MOM: Greta, I really don't like these conversations. It's all very hard for me, the diet, the exercise.

GRETA: I know it's hard. Exercising is no fun, but the thing is, after a week or two, it gets easier, and you start to look forward to it. We can find you some sort of activity that you'll really enjoy.

MOM: [choked up] You don't realize.... It's very stressful. I'm just not going to talk about it anymore. That's all there is to it!

Not surprisingly, these conversations leave Greta feeling frustrated, powerless, and deeply sad. Greta wonders how she might be more assertive, how she can persuade her mother to change.

But assertiveness isn't Greta's problem. What's missing from her stance is curiosity. In a follow-up conversation, Greta shifts her goal from persuasion to learning. To do this she limits herself to listening, asking questions, and acknowledging her mother's feelings:

GRETA: I know you don't like talking about your diabetes and exercising.

MOM: I really don't. It's very upsetting to me.

GRETA: When you say it's upsetting, what do you mean? In what ways?

MOM: Greta, the whole thing. Do you think it's fun for me?

GRETA: No, Mom, I know it's really hard. I just don't know much about what you think about it, what it means to you, what you feel about it.

MOM: I'll tell you, if your father were alive, it would be different. He was so sweet when I would get sick. Having to follow all these complicated rules, that's what he would have been good at. He would have taken care of the whole thing. Being sick, it just makes me miss him so much.

GRETA: It sounds like you've been feeling really lonely without Dad.

MOM: I have friends, and you've been wonderful, but it's not the same as having your father here to help. I suppose I really do feel lonely, but I hate to talk about that. I don't want to be a burden on you kids.

GRETA: You feel like if you tell us you're lonely, it will be a burden? We'll worry?

MOM: I just don't want you to have to go through what my mother went through. You know *her* mother died of diabetes.

GRETA: I didn't know. Wow.

MOM: It's scary to be told you have what your grandmother died of. It's hard for me to accept. I know the medications are better now, which is why I should be following all those rules, but if I follow all those rules, it just makes me feel like some sick old lady.

GRETA: So keeping to the regimen would feel like accepting something that you don't totally accept yet?

MOM: It's irrational. I'm not saying it's not. [choked up] It's just very frightening and overwhelming.

GRETA: I know it is, Mom.

MOM: I'll tell you something else. I don't even understand what I'm supposed to be doing. The eating, the exercise. If you do one, it affects the other, and you have to keep track. It's complicated, and the doctor isn't terribly helpful in explaining it. I don't know where to begin. Your father would know.

GRETA: Maybe that's something I could help you with.

MOM: Greta, I don't want to be a burden.

GRETA: I want to help. It would actually make me feel better. Not so powerless.

MOM: If you could, that would take a big load off my mind....

Greta was astonished and delighted at how much better her conversations became after she began truly listening to her mother. She came to see the issues from her mother's point of view, how much deeper they ran than she suspected, and how she might be able to help her mother in ways that her mother wanted to be helped. This is perhaps the most obvious benefit of listening: learning about the other person. But there is a second, more surprising benefit as well.

LISTENING TO THEM HELPS THEM LISTEN TO YOU

Ironically, when Greta shifted away from trying to persuade her mother to exercise and toward simply listening and acknowledging, she ended up achieving the goal that had eluded her up to that point. This is not an accident. One of the most common complaints we hear from people engaged in difficult conversations is that the other person won't listen. And when we hear that, our standard advice is "*You* need to spend more time listening to *them*."

When the other person is not listening, you may imagine it is because they're stubborn or don't understand what you're trying to say (If they did, they'd understand why they should listen to it.) so you may try to break through that by repeating, trying new ways to explain yourself, talking more loudly, and so forth.

On the face of it, these would seem to be good strategies. But they're not. Why? Because in the great majority of cases, the reason the other person is not listening to you is not because they are stubborn, but because *they* don't feel heard. In other words, they aren't listening to you for the same reason you aren't listening to them: they think *you* are slow or stubborn. So they repeat themselves, find new ways to say things, talk more loudly, and so forth.

If the block to their listening is that they don't feel heard, then the way to remove that block is by helping them feel heard — by bending over backwards to listen to what they have to say, and perhaps most important, by demonstrating that you understand what they are saying and how they are feeling.

If you don't quite believe this, try it. Find the most stubborn person you know, the person who never seems to take in anything you say, the person who repeats himself or herself in every conversation you ever have — and listen to them. Especially, listen for feelings, like frustration or pride or fear, and acknowledges those feelings. See whether that person doesn't become a better listener after all.

Notes and Questions

1. The focus of the above excerpt is on "difficult conversations" in general. Is the authors' advice applicable to negotiation? Negotiations involving strangers? Negotiations between lawyers representing clients who are in conflict?

2. Proponents of the problem-solving approach advise negotiators to engage in a particular type of listening called "active listening" or "looping" (a term coined by Gary Friedman and Jack Himmelstein). Professor Mnookin and his colleagues explain the looping process below.

The Empathy Loop:

Step 1 You inquire

Step 2 The other side responds

Step 3 You demonstrate your understanding and test with the other side

Step 4 If they confirm your understanding, the loop is complete. If not, go to Step 1

* * *

There is no single formula for demonstrating understanding. But we *can* suggest some helpful questions for eliciting the other person's story and showing them that you're trying to understand. These include:

- "Is this the problem as you see it?"
- "Will you clarify what you mean by ... My understanding is ... Is that right?"
- "What I understand you to say is ... Is that right?"
- "As I understand it, the problem is ... Am I hearing you correctly?"
- "To summarize, the main points as I heard them are ... Have I understood you right?"
- "What am I missing?"
- "Is there anything about how you see this that we haven't talked about yet?"

The precise formulation is less important than trying to check the accuracy of what you have understood. Demonstrating understanding requires paraphrasing, checking your understanding, and giving the other person a chance to respond.

ROBERT MNOOKIN, SCOTT PEPPET & ANDREW S. TULUMELLO, BEYOND WINNING: NEGOTIATING TO CREATE VALUE IN DEALS AND DISPUTES 64–65 (2000).

3. Despite the benefits of active listening in negotiation (and other settings), Stone and his colleagues offer the following warning:

> Scores of workshops and books on "active listening" teach you what you should *do* to be a good listener. Their advice is relatively similar — ask questions, paraphrase back what the other person has said, acknowledge their view, sit attentively and look them in the eye — all good advice. You emerge from these courses eager to try out your new skills, only to become discouraged when your friends or colleagues complain that you sound phony or mechanical. "Don't use that active listening stuff on me," they say.

> The problem is this: you are taught what to say and how to sit, but the heart of good listening is authenticity. People "read" not only your words and posture, but what's going on inside of you. If your "stance" isn't genuine, the words won't matter. What will be communicated almost invariably is whether you are genuinely curious, whether you genuinely care about the other person. If your intentions are false, no amount of careful wording or good posture will help. If your intentions are good, even clumsy language won't hinder you.

> Listening is only powerful and effective if it is authentic. Authenticity means that you are listening because you are curious and because you care, not just because you are supposed to. The issue, then, is this: Are you curious? Do you care?

DOUGLAS STONE, BRUCE PATTON & SHEILA HEEN, DIFFICULT CONVERSATIONS: HOW TO DISCUSS WHAT MATTERS MOST 167–68 (1999).

For Stone and his colleagues, then, negotiators should adopt a "learning stance" and attempt to have "learning conversations" where the goal is to understand, not dispute, the other side.

b. "Focus on Interests" (Asking)

Problem-solving negotiators focus on interests rather than positions in negotiation. As we discussed in Chapter I, beginning at page 19, interests are a negotiator's underlying needs, wants, fears, and motivations; positions are the negotiator's translation of those interests into particular demands or offers. In a personal injury dispute, for instance, a plaintiff might demand $500,000 to settle the case (her position). The plaintiff may have adopted that position in order to satisfy such interests as paying her medical bills, obtaining a measure of financial security, receiving some vindication for the pain she has suffered, and so on. In short, interests are a negotiator's *ends*, while the position she adopts is merely one *means* of obtaining those ends:

> Before entering a negotiation, one needs to be clear what it is that one seeks from the deal. Although this may appear to be simple, most knowledgeable observers suggest that it is not. Goals determi-

nation involves more than describing a desired end position; it also requires assessing why one seeks a particular goal or goals. As Roger Fisher and William Ury, in their classic exposition on negotiation, *Getting to Yes*, so insightfully observe, those who negotiate over positions without focusing on the underlying interests behind the positions, create enormous and unnecessary obstacles to reaching effective agreements. Identifying and sharing interests with one's opponent injects a substantial degree of flexibility into a negotiation because there are typically a number of ways to satisfy interests, many of which both sides find completely compatible. For example, two sides that vie for a tract of land may find that one wants it for logging purposes and the other to convert it into a pasture for raising livestock. In this case, the parties should be able to accommodate each other's interests without substantial conflict. Unless they reveal their interests to one another, however, they may never get past their competing positions.

Robert S. Adler & Elliot M. Silverstein, *When David Meets Goliath: Dealing with Power Differentials in Negotiations,* 5 Harv. Negot. L. Rev. 1, 62–63 (2000).

i. Open and Closed Questions

Negotiators often become so caught up in the positions they are advancing that they neglect to identify their own interests and to elicit their counterparts' interests. To identify interests, negotiators need to become skilled questioners.

As we saw in Chapter II there are two basic types of questions: open and closed. Negotiators ask open questions to elicit broad information. For example, "what do you hope to accomplish?" or "what can we do for you?" or "what will enable us to put this deal together?" are examples of open questions.

Negotiators ask closed questions to discover more specific information and to clarify their understanding of previously elicited information. Some closed questions are subject-specific — for example, "what are your client's medical bills?" Other closed questions call for yes-no answers — for example, "has your client incurred any medical bills?" is a yes-no question. Finally, some closed questions seek to lead one's counterpart to a particular answer — for example, "your client has incurred $10,000 in medical bills, right?" is a leading question.

Fisher, Ury & Patton contend that two questions, in particular, are likely to help negotiators uncover their own and their counterparts' interests in negotiation: "why?" and "why not?" Consider the following excerpt:

ROGER FISHER, WILLIAM URY & BRUCE PATTON, GETTING TO YES: NEGOTIATING AGREEMENT WITHOUT GIVING IN
44 (2d ed. 1991).

The benefit of looking behind positions for interests is clear. How to go about it is less clear. A position is likely to be concrete and explicit; the interests underlying it may well be unexpressed, intangible, and perhaps inconsistent. How do you go about understanding the interests involved in a negotiation, remembering that figuring out *their* interests will be at least as important as figuring out *yours*?

Ask "Why?" One basic technique is to put yourself in their shoes. Examine each position they take, and ask yourself "Why?" Why, for instance, does your landlord prefer to fix the rent — in a five-year lease — year by year? The answer you may come up with, to be protected against increasing costs, is probably one of his interests. You can also ask the landlord himself why he takes a particular position. If you do, make clear that you are asking not for justification of this position, but for an understanding of the needs, hopes, fears, or desires that it serves. "What's your basic concern, Mr. Jones, in wanting the lease to run for no more than three years?"

Ask "Why not?" Think about their choice. One of the most useful ways to uncover interests is first to identify the basic decision that those on the other side probably see you asking them for, and then to ask yourself why they have not made that decision. What interests of theirs stand in the way? If you are trying to change their minds, the starting point is to figure out where their minds are now.

ii. Knowing What We Want

The advice to focus on interests assumes that negotiators are able to identify what it is they want to get out of a negotiation. When asked why they want something, negotiators are expected to know this (even if they choose not to disclose it). Is this assumption usually valid? Are negotiators likely to know what they want? Consider the following excerpt, which suggests that people may not be very good at identifying what they really want in negotiation:

CHRIS GUTHRIE & DAVID SALLY, THE IMPACT OF THE IMPACT BIAS ON NEGOTIATION
87 Marq. L. Rev. 817, 817–22 (2004).

The defining feature of "principled" or "problem-solving" negotiation is its emphasis on "interests" rather than "positions." In negotiation parlance, "positions" are what disputants declare they want. "Interests," on the other hand, "are the silent movers behind the hubbub of positions." They are the "needs, desires, concerns, and fears" that underlie stated positions.

Disputants routinely negotiate over positions. "Each side takes a position, argues for it, and makes concessions to reach a compromise."

Unfortunately, however, "[c]ompromising between positions [is] not likely to produce an agreement which will effectively take care of the human needs that led people to adopt those positions."

Proponents of problem-solving negotiation thus argue that disputants should strive not merely to assert positions but rather to identify and satisfy their underlying interests. Indeed, according to the proponents of this approach to negotiation, "the object of a negotiation is to satisfy underlying interests." On this view, disputants should try to get what they *really* want at the bargaining table.

But what if they do not know what they *really* want?

I. Impact Bias

Researchers from an emerging movement within psychology — variously labeled "positive psychology" or "hedonic psychology" or "affective forecasting" — have learned a great deal in recent years about what people really want. Of greatest relevance to this essay, researchers studying affective forecasting have discovered that people are often mistaken about what they want or what will make them happy. In more technical terms, people often find that what they predict they want or how they predict they will feel — i.e., their "predicted utility" — is different from their actual experience — i.e., their "experienced utility."

It is not that people are entirely unaware of what they want or how they will feel. In fact, people are generally quite skilled at predicting whether they will feel positively or negatively about some event or item. People accurately predict, for example, that they will feel favorably about a promotion and unfavorably about a demotion. Similarly, people are generally pretty good at predicting the specific emotion(s) they will experience upon obtaining some item or experiencing some event. People anticipate, for instance, that they will feel pride and joy upon being promoted and anger and embarrassment upon being demoted.

What people struggle with, however, is predicting both the *intensity* and *duration* of their emotional reactions to an event or outcome. One's sense of well-being turns significantly on this kind of prediction.

> Often people predict correctly the valence of their emotional reactions ('I'll feel good if I get the job') and correctly predict the specific emotions they will experience (e.g., joy). Even when achieving such accuracy, however, it is important for people to predict what the initial intensity of the reaction will be (how much joy they will experience) and the duration of that emotion (how long they will feel this way). It is useful to know that we will feel happy on our first day at a new job, but better to know how happy and how long this feeling will last, before committing ourselves to a lifetime of work as a tax attorney. It is helpful to know that it will be painful to end a long-term relationship, but better to know how painful and whether the pain will last half a second or half a decade.

Unfortunately, people have a tendency "to overestimate the impact of future events on their emotional lives." Psychologists Daniel Gilbert and Timothy Wilson refer to this phenomenon as the "impact bias."

Researchers have found that the impact bias influences reactions to all kinds of life events, including "romantic breakups, personal insults, sports victories, electoral defeats, parachute jumps, failures to lose weight, reading tragic stories, and learning the results of pregnancy and HIV tests." With few exceptions, people tend to overestimate the emotional impact such events will have on their lives.

Researchers are not entirely sure why people overestimate the emotional impact of various life events and outcomes, but they have identified at least two phenomena that systematically point people in this direction. First, when predicting reactions to a future event, people tend to ignore the impact that *other* events are likely to have on their sense of well-being. People, in other words, are prone to "focalism" or a "focusing illusion." Second, people underestimate the extent to which they process an experience or outcome psychologically to dampen its emotional impact. Upon experiencing some event or outcome, people engage in what Wilson and Gilbert call "sense-making processes"; that is, they "inexorably explain and understand events that were initially surprising and unpredictable, and this process lowers the intensity of emotional reactions to the events." In advance, however, they fail to "anticipate how much they will transform events psychologically in ways that reduce their emotional power."

Other phenomena undoubtedly contribute to the impact bias. For example, people may fall prey to the impact bias because they fail to recognize that they have something akin to a happiness "set point" which does not fluctuate too much regardless of life events. Also, research suggests that people in a "hot" emotional state have a hard time anticipating how they will react when they are in a "cold" emotional state, again suggesting that they may overestimate the emotional impact of future events and outcomes.

Whatever its source, the existence of the impact bias means that people often "miswant." Writing in a *New York Times Magazine* article, Jon Gertner explains this as follows:

> [W]e might believe that a new BMW will make life perfect. But it will almost certainly be less exciting than we anticipated; nor will it excite us for as long as predicted .... Gilbert and his collaborator Tim Wilson call the gap between what we predict and what we ultimately experience the 'impact bias' — 'impact' meaning the errors we make in estimating both the intensity and duration of our emotions and 'bias' our tendency to err. The phrase characterizes how we experience the dimming excitement over not just a BMW but also over any object or event that we presume will make us happy. Would a 20 percent raise or winning the lottery result in a contented life? You may predict it will, but almost surely it will not turn out that way. And a new plasma television? You may have high

hopes, but the impact bias suggests that it will almost certainly be less cool, and in a shorter time, than you imagine. Worse, Gilbert has noted that these mistakes of expectation can lead directly to mistakes in choosing what we think will give us pleasure. He calls this 'miswanting.'

II.   "Miswanting" in Negotiation

The potential impact of the impact bias on negotiation is straightforward. If people in general are likely to have difficulty determining what they really want because of a tendency to overestimate how attaining that item will affect their sense of well-being, disputants are also likely to have difficulty identifying what they really want in negotiation for the very same reason. Just like the consumer who erroneously believes he will be much happier if he purchases a new BMW, the disputant seeking to obtain vindication from the other side or financial security or whatever else may very well overestimate how much obtaining it will contribute to her sense of well-being. Indeed, it seems reasonable to speculate that the added complexity of a negotiation — in particular, the tension and conflict between the negotiators — will make it even more difficult for disputants to discern what they really want.

This has important implications for lawyers (and other agents) who represent disputants in negotiation. Under the prevailing model of the lawyer-client relationship — the so-called 'client-centered' counseling model — the client is viewed as a fully competent and autonomous actor who retains full decisional authority over her case. The lawyer, by contrast, is a largely passive and objective advisor who strives to avoid encroaching on client autonomy in the decision-making process.

* * *

The client-centered approach to lawyering — both in theory and as reflected in various ethical rules — is both sensible and respectful. After all, the client is the principal, and the lawyer is merely the agent hired by the client. The client "owns" the problem, and she will reap the primary benefit (or bear the primary brunt) of the outcome. Thus, it seems appropriate to vest decision-making power solely in her hands.

Research on the impact bias gives one pause, however, because it suggests that clients may have great difficulty predicting accurately what they want out of a negotiation. Even given this difficulty, the client will generally know better than anyone else what she wants. But in some circumstances, her lawyer may have insight into her wants that even she does not. Namely, in those cases where the client is a "one-shotter" (perhaps in a divorce case or a personal injury suit), and the lawyer is a "repeat-player" who has represented dozens or even hundreds of similarly situated clients in like cases, it seems *possible* that the lawyer might know better than the client what the client really wants.

iii.   Creating Value Through Differences

Problem-solving negotiation theorists encourage negotiators to try to uncover each other's interests in order to "create value" in negotiation. Negotiators can create value by capitalizing on "shared" interests. Divorcing spouses, for example, are likely to share an interest in the physical, emotional, and mental well-being of their children, and they may be able to use this shared interest to construct a value-creating divorce settlement.

Less intuitively, though perhaps more importantly, negotiators can also create value by capitalizing on "different" or "conflicting" interests. Consider the following excerpt:

ROBERT H. MNOOKIN, SCOTT R. PEPPET & ANDREW S. TULUMELLO, BEYOND WINNING: NEGOTIATING TO CREATE VALUE IN DEALS AND DISPUTES

14–15 (2000).

The notion that differences can create value is counter-intuitive to many negotiators, who believe that they can reach agreement only by finding common ground. But the truth is that differences are often more useful than similarities in helping parties reach a deal. Differences set the stage for possible gains from trade, and it is through trades that value is most commonly created. Consider the following five types of differences:

Different Resources: In the simplest example, two parties may simply trade resources. A vegetarian with a chicken and a carnivore with a large vegetable garden may find it useful to swap what they have....

Different Relative Valuations: Even if both parties have chickens and vegetables, and both prefer chicken to some extent, they can still make useful trades. To put it in economic terms, if the two parties attach different *relative* valuations to the goods in question, trades should occur that make both better off. The party who more strongly prefers chicken to vegetables should be willing to pay a high enough price — in terms of vegetables — to induce the other party to give up at least some of her chickens.

Different Forecasts: Parties may have different beliefs about what the future will hold. In the entertainment industry, for example, performers, agents, and concert halls often have different predictions about the likelihood of various attendance levels. Performers are often convinced of their ability to draw huge crowds, while concert halls may be much less sanguine. By trading on these different forecasts — perhaps through contingent fee arrangements — the parties can resolve these differences to mutual advantage. A singer who expects to draw a standing-room-only crowd might agree to a guaranteed fee based on 80 percent attendance, plus a percentage of any profits earned from higher attendance. Such arrangements allow the parties to place bets on their different beliefs about the future.

Different Risk Preferences: Even if the parties have identical fore-casts about a particular event, they might not be equally risk-tolerant with regard to that event. My life insurance company and I might have similar expectations about what the odds are that someone my age will die within the next year. But we will probably have very different risk preferences regarding that possibility. I will be risk-averse, knowing that my family will face financial hardship if I die. Therefore, I might pay the insurance company to absorb that risk. The insurance company, by pooling my risk with the risk of others, can offer me insurance based on costs averaged over the entire pool. In effect, I have shifted the risk of my early demise to the more efficient risk carrier — the insurance company. Negotiators often create value in this way. A car buyer might purchase an extended warranty, or a start-up company might sell shares to a wealthy investor in exchange for needed capital. In each case, by allocating risk to the more risk-tolerant party for an acceptable price, the parties create a more beneficial agreement.

Different Time Preferences: Negotiators often value issues of timing differently — when an event will occur or a payment will be made. For example, a law school graduate and his wife fell in love with a condomin-ium in Washington, D.C. Because he was going to be clerking for a federal judge for two years, his salary during that time was not sufficient to cover the mortgage payments. After the clerkship, however, he knew that he would be joining a large D.C. law firm, at more than twice his clerkship salary. He could then easily afford the house. The solution lay in structuring a mortgage schedule so that there were small payments for the first two years — less than even the interest costs — and larger payments thereafter. Although he had to pay a premium for agreeing to this tiered payment schedule, in the meantime he was able to "afford" his dream home.

* * *

These five types of differences — in resources, relative valuations, forecasts, risk preferences, and time preferences — are all potential sources of value creation. They all support the same basic principal: trades can create value.

Notes

1. A value-creating deal seeks to approach a "Pareto-optimal" or "Pareto-efficient" outcome, i.e., one in which the negotiated deal, "when compared to other possible *negotiated* outcomes, either makes both parties better off or makes one party better off without making the other party worse off." *Id.* at 12.

2. Despite the widespread endorsement of value creation in negotia-tion, some scholars have questioned the problem-solving theorists' conten-tion that opportunities for value creation are as abundant as suggested. *See, e.g.*, Russell Korobkin, *A Positive Theory of Legal Negotiation*, 88 Geo. L.J. 1789 (2000); Gerald Wetlaufer, *The Limits of Integrative Bargaining*, 85 Geo. L.J. 369 (1996).

c. "Consider a Variety of Options" (Inventing)

Problem-solving negotiators seek to generate a variety of options in negotiation to increase the likelihood they have mutually attractive options from which to choose. Consider the following excerpt by Professor Menkel–Meadow:

CARRIE MENKEL–MEADOW, AHA? IS CREATIVITY POSSIBLE IN LEGAL PROBLEM SOLVING AND TEACHING IN LEGAL EDUCATION?

6 Harv. Negot. L. Rev. 97, 105–06, 109–11 (2001).

How do lawyers generate options, find alternative courses of action, consider potential or alternative clauses in documents and deals, discover sources of financing, create rules of deal or organizational governance, risk allocation, profit allocation, admissions of wrongdoing, compensation, policy changes and the literally dozens of legal "tropes" or solutions that constitute legal problems?

Dispute negotiation too often looks for its solutions among the legal precedents or outcomes thought likely in the "shadow of the courthouse" (these days most often compromise of some monetary values), and deal negotiations too often seek solutions in the boilerplate language of form contracts for transactions. Ironically, these litigated outcomes and boilerplate clauses were once the creative ideas of some lawyers who developed a new reading of a statute, a novel argument before a common law or Constitutional court, developed a new scheme of risk allocation, or found a new source of capital or drafted a new clause for a deal document.

Solutions to legal problems, then, come from creative lawyers, as well as legal or practice precedent. The challenge for negotiation theorists, practitioners and teachers is to find systematic ways to teach solution devising, short of reading thousands of cases, transactional documents, statutes or other legal documents that will show us not only what already has been done, but also what might be done. . . .

* * *

One can structure a problem solving approach to negotiation by focusing on a three step process in which first, the lawyer identifies multiple classes of needs, objectives, interests or goals from one's own client. Then, s/he proceeds to do the same for other parties involved, using information available from public knowledge, research, client knowledge and from the negotiation session. Finally, the negotiator examines and matches loci of complementary and then conflicting needs and interests of the parties, in a systematic way, in order to craft solutions that maximize joint gain or Pareto-optimal solutions. . . .

* * *

Often a solution to a negotiated problem may be illuminated by exploring the characteristics of the "problem" mapped over parties' particular needs and interests. WHAT is the problem about? (What is the res? What is at stake? Can the thing itself be altered in any way?) WHO is involved? Are there stakeholders other than the parties formally at the table? Does adding parties facilitate a solution, or, as in the case of bringing in an insurer, does one increase those who can contribute to a solution, or, as in the case of the IRS, which is always a party to a legal negotiation, do tax concerns change the dynamics and suggest other solutions? WHERE is the transaction/dispute/res located? Does jurisdiction matter for the problem? What about the location is alterable? (e.g. employment disputes with multiple offices or government agencies can offer transfer opportunities). WHEN does the dispute or transaction have to be resolved? This factor has led to the important and structural solutions of annuity payments in tort cases, installment payment contracts, contingency pricing and risk allocations, as well as continuing options, accelerated or graduated payments and duties and a whole host of substantive time-based solutions for trials, contingencies and terminable-upon-conditions arrangements. HOW may the matter be negotiated? Must solutions be conventional payments of money? Are other more creative solutions possible? In-kind trades? Apologies? Percentage of gross or net, instead of fixed sums? Contingent agreements? Secured obligations? Guarantors? Third party reviews? Can dispute resolution procedures themselves be altered? These framing questions for legal solutions to negotiated problems are a way of increasing the resources available for solving problems and probing for non-obvious solutions.

Note and Questions

1. One way that problem-solving negotiators can generate options is through the brainstorming process to which we were introduced in Chapter II. In this process, negotiators generate as many options as possible, without judging them. For more on brainstorming, see Chapter II, beginning at page 113.

2. Should parties brainstorm prior to negotiation as a way of preparing for the negotiation? Should they brainstorm with their counterparts at the bargaining table? Both?

3. What are the advantages of option-generation processes like brainstorming?

4. Do you see any potential drawbacks? Consider the following excerpt:

CHRIS GUTHRIE, PANACEA OR PANDORA'S BOX? THE COSTS OF OPTIONS IN NEGOTIATION

88 Iowa L. Rev. 601, 607–08 (2003).

The prescriptive literature on negotiation seeks to help negotiators obtain better outcomes at the bargaining table. To do so, the prescriptive literature advises negotiators to generate as many options as possible to enable them to satisfy their "interests" in negotiation. Negotiators who generate multiple options will "open doors and produce a range of potential agreements satisfactory to each side."[1] Having done so, they need only decide which of the available options to select.

The prescriptive literature assumes that negotiators will make rational decisions when selecting from these options. What it means to decide "rationally" is a subject of some dispute, but generally speaking, rational models of choice assume that negotiators will assign a subjective value to each option based solely on the characteristics of that option, rank-order the options in the choice set, and then select the one they should prefer. Rational models assume, in other words, that irrelevant options or irrelevant characteristics of a set of options will *not* induce negotiators to select an option other than the one they most prefer. Unfortunately, however, this assumption is often wrong because the addition of options to a choice set can induce negotiators to make non-value-maximizing decisions. Specifically, the addition of options can give rise to four phenomena that tend to occur in the following order:

The first phenomenon arises when a choice set grows from one option to two or more options. When a choice set expands from the original option under consideration to more than one option, negotiators tend to devalue the initial option (assuming that the options in the set have both advantages and disadvantages relative to one another). Thus, the first option cost the Article explores below is *option devaluation*.

The second phenomenon arises when a choice set consisting of two or more options grows by one. When an option is added to a choice set consisting of two or more options, negotiators tend to reconsider their relative ranking of the options already under consideration even when the additional option sheds no new light on those options. Negotiators do *not*, in other words, make context-*in*dependent decisions. Thus, the second option cost the Article explores below is *context dependence*.

The third phenomenon arises when a choice set grows to include a large number of options, perhaps ten, fifteen, or twenty options. When a choice set includes a large number of options, negotiators tend to abandon compensatory decision-making strategies that take all options and attributes into account in favor of simplified decision strategies that consider only some of the available information. Thus, the third option cost the Article explores below is *non-compensatory* or *partial decision making*.

The fourth and final phenomenon arises after the decision has been made. Following a decision, negotiators tend to feel greater regret when they have selected one option over another than when they have simply selected the sole available option. Thus, the fourth option cost the Article explores below is *decision regret*.

---

1. [ROGER FISHER ET AL., GETTING TO YES: (2d ed. 1991)] at 80.
NEGOTIATING AGREEMENT WITHOUT GIVING IN

Although the prescriptive literature on negotiation is certainly correct that option generation offers potential benefits to negotiators, the four phenomena identified above and described below suggest that option generation poses potential costs as well. Negotiators who generate multiple options may be induced by the very availability of those options to make decisions that run contrary to their true preferences and that induce negative post-decision emotions.

d. "Insist on Outcomes Tied to Objective Criteria" (Referencing)

The problem-solving approach advises negotiators to tie their proposed outcomes to legitimate, objective criteria, like fair market value, precedent, professional standards, and the like. Rather than rely solely on pressure to persuade their counterparts to reach agreement, problem-solving negotiators appeal to principle. In the following excerpt, Professor Shell explains why negotiators can benefit by tying their proposed outcomes to legitimate, objective criteria.

G. RICHARD SHELL, BARGAINING FOR ADVANTAGE: NEGOTIATION STRATEGIES FOR REASONABLE PEOPLE

42–43 (1999).

Why are standards and norms — particularly standards the other side has adopted — such an important part of bargaining? Because, all else being equal, people like to be seen as consistent and rational in the way they make decisions.

Psychologists have a name for this need-to-appear-reasonable phenomenon. They call it "the consistency principle." Social psychologists have discovered that people have a deep need to avoid the disjointed, erratic, and uncomfortable psychological states that arise when our actions are manifestly inconsistent with previously expressed, long-held, or widely shared standards and beliefs.

Most of us have complex "consistency webs" that are interconnected at many levels of our personality. Because we like to keep these webs intact, we rationalize our actions so they appear (at least in our own eyes) to be consistent with our prior beliefs. We are also more open to persuasion when we see a proposed course of action as being consistent with a course we have already adopted.

Negotiations are fertile ground for observing the consistency principle at work. Whether we are aware of it or not, we sometimes feel a tug to agree with the other party when the standards or norms he or she articulates are consistent with prior statements and positions we ourselves have taken. We also feel uncomfortable (though we may keep this to ourselves) when the other side correctly points out that we have been inconsistent in one of our positions or arguments. In short, standards and norms are — or can be — more than just intellectual pawns in bargaining debates. They can be strong, motivating factors in the way negotiations proceed.

Question

What should problem-solving negotiators do when they disagree over the appropriate objective criterion to use to resolve a particular issue in negotiation? According to Professor Fisher, Ury & Patton, "When each party is advancing a different standard, look for an objective basis for deciding between them, such as which standard has been used by the parties in the past or which standard is more widely applied. Just as the substantive issue itself should not be settled on the basis of will, neither should the question of which standard applies." ROGER FISHER, WILLIAM URY & BRUCE PATTON, GETTING TO YES: NEGOTIATING AGREEMENT WITHOUT GIVING IN 89–90 (2d ed. 1991).

e.   The BATNA and Power in Negotiation

Objective criteria provide problem-solving negotiators with some power in negotiation. So, too, does the negotiator's "best alternative to a negotiated agreement," or BATNA. As Professor Fisher, and Mssrs. Ury & Patton put it, "People think of negotiating power as being determined by resources like wealth, political connections, physical strength, friends, and military might. In fact, the relative negotiating power of two parties depends primarily upon how attractive to each is the option of not reaching agreement." *Id.* at 102. Assume, for example, that you are a tourist wishing to buy a certain kind of brass pot. You can give yourself additional power in negotiations with a particular vendor by learning how much you will have to pay to get the item elsewhere. Similarly, you have more power in a job interview if you have other job offers than if you do not.

In the following excerpt, Professor Korobkin offers the important observation that it is one's *perceived* BATNA, as opposed to one's *actual* BATNA, that is the true source of power in negotiation.

Strictly speaking, it is not the actual, objective quality of the negotiator's BATNA that determines his degree of bargaining power, but what the counterpart believes that the negotiator believes about the quality of his BATNA. For example, when an employee receives a job offer from a competing firm and asks his boss for a raise, whether the employee has power depends on whether the boss believes that the employee believes it is in the employee's best interest to accept the competing offer if the demand for a raise is not met. The credibility of the employee's threat to walk away from the negotiation and accept the competing offer if his demand is not met is unaffected by the fact that neither the boss nor any of the employee's colleagues would prefer the competing offer to the employee's current job at his current salary. Where power is concerned, the beauty of a BATNA is in the eye of the beholder, and eccentricity is not penalized as long as it is perceived to be genuine. The employee's threat of impasse will be credible to the boss, thus giving the employee power, even if the employee himself actually would not prefer the competing offer, so long as the boss thinks the employee would prefer that offer.

An objectively strong BATNA is helpful, of course, because a BATNA that appears strong renders the negotiator's claim that he *believes* his BATNA is strong more credible. The employee's threat of impasse will more likely translate into bargaining power if his competing job offer is a $300,000 per year CEO position than if it is a $15,000 per year mailroom attendant position. But either a phantom BATNA (i.e., a nonexistent alternative) or a real BATNA with phantom *value* (i.e., an existent but undesirable alternative) can be a source of power in the hands of a persuasive negotiator.

Russell Korobkin, *Bargaining Power as Threat of Impasse*, 87 Marq. L. Rev. 867, 869–70 (2004).

Note

1.   Despite the importance of BATNA to problem-solving negotiation, it is not the only source of power available to a problem-solving negotiator. *See, e.g.*, ROGER FISHER, WILLIAM URY & BRUCE PATTON, GETTING TO YES: NEGOTIATING AGREEMENT WITHOUT GIVING IN 177–87 (2d ed. 1991) (responding to questions about power in principled negotiation); Roger Fisher, *Negotiating Power: Getting and Using Influence*, 27 Am. Behav. Scientist 149 (1983) (proposing six different sources of power in negotiation).

Professor Shell offers the following easy-to-remember test to assess which party has more power or leverage in a negotiation:

> *Ask yourself, as of the moment when you make the assessment, which party has the most to lose from no deal. The party with the most to lose has the* least *leverage; the party with the least to lose has the* most *leverage; and both parties have roughly equal leverage when they both stand to lose equivalent amounts should the deal fall through.*

G.   RICHARD SHELL, BARGAINING FOR ADVANTAGE: NEGOTIATION STRATEGIES FOR REASONABLE PEOPLE 105 (1999) (emphasis in original).

f.   Critiques

Now that you know the two primary theoretical approaches to negotiation and the strategies and tactics that accompany them, which approach do you intend to use? Under what circumstances are you more likely to prefer one over the other? When would you, by necessity, employ some combination of the two approaches? This section critically explores each approach to enable you to make better-informed decisions about which to employ or when to favor one approach over the other.

In the following exchange — which occurred after the first edition of GETTING TO YES was published — Professors James White and Roger Fisher debate the relative merits of adversarial and problem-solving approaches.

JAMES J. WHITE, THE PROS AND CONS OF "GETTING TO YES"

34 J. Legal Educ. 115–16 (1984).

GETTING TO YES is a puzzling book. On the one hand it offers a forceful and persuasive criticism of much traditional negotiating behavior. It suggests a variety of negotiating techniques that are both clever and likely to facilitate effective negotiation. On the other hand, the authors seem to deny the existence of a significant part of the negotiation process, and to oversimplify or explain away many of the most troublesome problems inherent in the art and practice of negotiation. The book is frequently naive, occasionally self-righteous, but often helpful.

* * *

The book's thesis is well summarized by the following passage:

> Behind opposed positions lie shared and compatible interests, as well as conflicting ones. We tend to assume that because the other side's positions are opposed to ours, their interests must also be opposed. If we have an interest in defending ourselves, then they must want to attack us. If we have an interest in minimizing the rent, then their interest must be to maximize it. In many negotiations, however, a close examination of the underlying interests will reveal the existence of many more interests that are shared or compatible than ones that are opposed (p. 43).

This point is useful for all who teach or think about negotiation. The tendency of those deeply involved in negotiation or its teaching is probably to exaggerate the importance of negotiation on issues where the parties are diametrically opposed and to ignore situations where the parties' interests are compatible. By emphasizing that fact, and by making a clear articulation of the importance of cooperation, imagination, and the search for alternative solutions, the authors teach helpful lessons. The book therefore provides worthwhile reading for every professional negotiator and will make sound instruction for every tyro.

Unfortunately the book's emphasis upon mutually profitable adjustment, on the "problem solving" aspect of bargaining, is also the book's weakness. It is a weakness because emphasis of this aspect of bargaining is done to almost total exclusion of the other aspect of bargaining, "distributional bargaining," where one for me is minus one for you. Schelling, Karrass and other students of negotiation have long distinguished between that aspect of bargaining in which modification of the parties' positions can produce benefits for one without significant cost to the other, and on the other hand, cases where benefits to one come only at significant cost to the other. They have variously described the former as "exploring for mutual profitable adjustments," "the efficiency aspect of bargaining," or "problem solving." The other has been characterized as "distributional bargaining" or "share bargaining." Thus some would describe a typical negotiation as one in which the parties initially begin by cooperative or efficiency bargaining, in which each gains something with each new adjustment without the other losing any significant benefit. Eventually, however, one comes to bargaining in which added benefits to one impose corresponding significant costs on the other. For example, in a labor contract one might engage in cooperative bargaining by the modification of a medical plan so that the employer could engage a less expensive medical insurance provider, yet one that offered improved services. Each side gains by that change from the old contract. Ultimately parties in a labor negotiation will come to a raw economic exchange in which additional wage dollars for the employees will be dollars subtracted from the corporate profits, dollars that cannot be paid in dividends to the shareholders.

One can concede the authors' thesis (that too many negotiators are incapable of engaging in problem solving or in finding adequate options for mutual gain), yet still maintain that the most demanding aspect of nearly every negotiation is the distributional one in which one seeks more at the expense of the other. My principal criticism of the book is that it seems to overlook the ultimate hard bargaining. Had the authors stated that they were dividing the negotiation process in two and were dealing with only part of it, that omission would be excusable. That is not what they have done. Rather they seem to assume that a clever negotiator can make any negotiation into problem solving and thus completely avoid the difficult distribution of which Karrass and Schelling speak. To my mind this is naive. By so distorting reality, they detract from their powerful and central thesis.

ROGER FISHER, COMMENT

34 J. Legal Educ. 120, 121–23 (1984).

Are distributional issues amenable to joint problem solving? The most fundamental difference between White's way of thinking and mine seems to concern the negotiation of distributional issues "where one for me is minus one for you." We agree on the importance of cooperation, imagination, and the search for creative options where the task is to reconcile substantive interests that are compatible. White, however, sees the joint problem-solving approach as limited to that area. In his view, the most demanding aspect of nearly every negotiation is the distributional one in which one seeks more at the expense of the other. Distributional matters, in his view, must be settled by the ultimate hard bargaining. He regards it as a distortion of reality to suggest that problem solving is relevant to distributional negotiation.

Here we differ. By focusing on the substantive issues (where the parties' interests may be directly opposed), White overlooks the shared interest that the parties continue to have in the process for resolving that substantive difference. How to resolve the substantive difference is a shared problem. Both parties have an interest in identifying quickly and amicably a result acceptable to each, if one is possible. How to do so is a problem. A good solution to that process-problem requires joint action.

The guts of the negotiation problem, in my view, is not who gets the last dollar, but what is the best process for resolving that issue. It is certainly a mistake to assume that the only process available for resolving distributional questions is hard bargaining over positions. In my judgment it is also a mistake to assume that such hard bargaining is the best process for resolving differences efficiently and in the long-term interest of either side.

Two men in a lifeboat quarreling over limited rations have a distributional problem. One approach to resolving that problem is to engage in hard bargaining. *A* can insist that he will sink the boat unless he gets 60 percent of the rations. *B* can insist that he will sink the boat unless he gets 80 percent of the rations. But *A*'s and *B*'s shared problem is not just how to divide the rations; rather it is how to divide the rations without tipping over the boat and while getting the boat to safer waters. In my view, to treat the distributional issue as a shared problem is a better approach than to treat it as a contest of will in which a more deceptive, more stubborn, and less rational negotiator will tend to fare better. Treating the distributional issue as a problem to be solved ("How about dividing the rations in proportion to our respective weights?" or "How about a fixed portion of the rations for each hour that one of us rows?") is likely to be better for both than a contest over who is more willing to sink the boat.

Objective criteria. It is precisely in deciding such distributional issues that objective criteria can play their most useful role. Here is a second area of significant disagreement. White finds it useful to deny the existence of objective standards: "The suggestion that one can find objective criteria (as opposed to persuasive rationalizations) seems quite inaccurate." To his way of thinking the only approach is for a negotiator first to adopt a position and later to develop rationalizations for it: " . . . every able negotiator rationalizes every position that he takes."

No one has suggested that in most negotiations there is a single objective criterion that both parties will quickly accept as determinative. The question is rather what should be treated as the essence of the negotiation, and what attitude should be taken toward arguments advanced in the discussion. White thinks it better to treat positions of the parties as the essence of the negotiation, and objective standards advanced by either party as mere rationalizations. That is one approach. A different approach is possible and, I believe, preferable.

Two judges, in trying to reach agreement, will be looking for standards that should decide the case. They may have their predispositions and even strongly-held views, but they will jointly look for an agreed basis for decision. Each will typically advance law, precedent, and evidence not simply as rationalizations for positions adopted for other reasons, but honestly, as providing a fair basis for decision. White's example of litigation is the very one I would advance to demonstrate that however great the disagreement, the wise approach is to insist upon using objective criteria as the basis for decision. It is better for the parties in court to be advancing objective standards which they suggest ought to be determinative than to be telling the court that they won't take less (or pay more) than so many dollars. The same, I believe, is true for negotiators.

Two negotiators can be compared with two judges, trying to decide a case. There won't be a decision unless they agree. It is perfectly possible for fellow negotiators, despite their self-interest, to behave like fellow judges, in that they advance reasoned arguments seriously, and are open to persuasion by better arguments. They need not advance standards simply as rationalizations for positions, but as providing a genuine basis for joint decision.

What we are suggesting is that in general a negotiator should seek to persuade by coming up with better arguments on the merits rather than by simply trying to convince the other side that he is the more stubborn. A good guideline is for a negotiator to advance arguments as though presenting them to an impartial arbitrator, to press favorable bases for decision, but none so extreme as to damage credibility. (On the receiving side, a good guideline is for a negotiator to listen to arguments as though he were an impartial arbitrator, remaining open to persuasion despite self-interest and preconceptions.) My experience suggests that this method is often more efficient and amicable than hard positional bargaining and more often leads to satisfactory results for both parties.

Notes and Questions

1. Who gets it right? Is problem-solving negotiation hopelessly naive? Or is adversarial negotiation hopelessly pessimistic? Neither? Both?

2. William Ury published a book addressing concerns, like those raised by White, about problem-solving negotiation. *See* WILLIAM URY, GETTING PAST NO: NEGOTIATING WITH DIFFICULT PEOPLE (1991). Professor James Westbrook explains Ury's recommendations for dealing with so-called hard-bargaining in a book review:

> One of the most persistent questions about [GETTING TO YES] has been whether the principled negotiation approach will work if the other side takes an adversarial approach. Will the proponent of principled negotiation have to change to an adversarial approach? If she doesn't, will an impasse result? Will a negotiator using the adversarial approach take advantage of a negotiator who tries to engage in principled negotiations? Ury wrote GETTING PAST NO to respond to questions such as these. Of course, not everyone who takes an adversarial approach to negotiation is a jerk. I used the word jerk in my title to get your attention and because I believe it sums up a fear by many persons who are called upon to negotiate but who want to do so in a way that is consistent with their notion of appropriate conduct. Approaches such as principled negotiation appeal to these persons, but they fear that they or their client will

be taken advantage of if they take such an approach. I suspect that one of their greatest concerns is that they may have to act like a jerk in order to deal effectively with a bully, a liar, or someone who is both astute and obnoxious. *Getting Past No* asserts that there is an effective alternative to relying on techniques such as deception, stonewalling, or threatening.

AN OVERVIEW OF THE BREAKTHROUGH STRATEGY

Ury recommends what he calls a "breakthrough strategy" for overcoming barriers to cooperation. He concedes that this strategy is counter-intuitive. You are called upon to do the opposite of what you might naturally do. You go around your opponent's resistance instead of meeting it head on.

The first step in the breakthrough strategy is to "go to the balcony." Instead of reacting to your opponent's tactics without thinking, you find a way to buy time. Use the time to recognize your opponent's tactics, figure out your interests, and identify your best alternative to a negotiated agreement. Much of the discussion in the chapter on going to the balcony is about the danger of making important decisions without adequate reflection and about ways of buying time for this reflection.

Second, you "step to their side" in order to create a more favorable negotiating climate. You disarm your opponent before discussing substantive issues. Ury provides a variety of ways to do this, such as asking for more information and reflecting back what you hear, acknowledging points without agreeing with them, focusing on issues on which you agree, and speaking about yourself rather than your opponent by describing the impact of the problem on yourself or your client. The chapter includes an interesting discussion about the value of an apology.

Third, reframe whatever your opponent has said as an attempt to deal with the problem. Since rejecting your opponent's position will usually reinforce it, recast what she says in a way that directs attention to satisfying interests. Ask her for advice, ask why she wants something, bring up what you think her interests are and ask her to correct you if you are wrong, ask "what if" questions, reframe your opponent's position as one possible option among many, and ask why she thinks her position is fair. Throughout, ask questions that cannot be answered by "no" by prefacing them with "how," "why," and "who." Not only do you reframe positions, but you reframe tactics. For example, if your opponent lays down a rigid deadline, reinterpret it as a target to strive for. If this cannot be done, you turn from negotiating substance to negotiating how the negotiations are to proceed. The goal here is to change the game from positional to problem-solving negotiation.

Fourth, make it easy for your opponents to say yes by "building them a golden bridge." The golden bridge chapter contains a multitude of ideas and techniques for involving your opponent in developing your proposal and for presenting it in a way that makes it easier for her to accept. Guide rather than push her toward an agreement. Consider her interests, involve her in developing your proposal, ask for and use her ideas where possible, and offer her choices. Ury suggests ways of expanding the pie by looking for low-cost, high-benefit trades and using an "if-then" formula, which deals with difficult issues by building flexible provisions into the agreement. Help her save face by showing how circumstances have changed since she adopted her position, asking for a third party recommendation, or urging reliance on a standard of fairness. Ury explains the dangers of trying to go too fast and the value of breaking the negotiation into steps.

The fifth and final step is to "make it hard to say no." This chapter contains a discussion of what to do if your opponent still resists your proposals after you have gone through the first four steps. Ury emphasizes persuasion rather than force or threats. He argues that force or threats often backfire. He suggests that you educate your opponent about the costs of not agreeing, that you warn rather than threaten, and that you demonstrate your best alternative to a negotiated agreement (BATNA). Such a demonstration shows what you will do without your actually carrying it out. Ury points out that,

> Power, like beauty, exists in the eyes of the beholder. If your BATNA is to have its intended educational effect of bringing your opponent back to the table, he needs to be impressed with its reality.

If you must use your BATNA, Ury recommends using as little power as possible, exhausting alternatives before escalating, and using only legitimate means. He explains the value of employing third parties where possible. As you try to persuade your opponent and as you resort to your BATNA, you need to remind her regularly of the golden bridge available to her.

James E. Westbrook, *How to Negotiate With a Jerk Without Being One*, 1992 J. Disp. Resol. 443, 444–46.

3.   What approach are lawyer-negotiators most likely to use in practice? In her recent study, Professor Schneider found widespread evidence of problem-solving negotiation among the lawyers she studied. In another recent study of lawyer-negotiators, however, Professor Jonathan Hyman and his colleagues found that adversarial negotiation was more common in settlement negotiations, even though this was not their preference.

> [O]ur study revealed a widespread desire to use more problem solving methods in settlement. Fully 61 percent of the litigators responding to the questionnaire said that problem solving methods should be used more than they are now. Fifty seven percent of the judges agreed. Both lawyers and judges expressed this preference in the face of a system of settlement negotiation that they described as overwhelmingly positional in its methods. The lawyers thought that, on average, 71 percent of cases were settled through positional, not problem solving, methods, and judges pegged the figure at 69 percent.

Jonathan M. Hyman, Milton Heumann, Kenneth J. Dautrich & Harold L. Rubenstein, Civil Settlement: Styles of Negotiation in Dispute Resolution 165 (parentheticals omitted) (New Jersey Administrative Office of the Courts, 1995)

4.   Most commentators agree that "although competition and collaboration are antagonistic processes, both necessarily occur in virtually all negoti-

ations." Gary Lowenthal, *A General Theory of Negotiation Process, Strategy and Behavior*, 31 U. Kan. L. Rev. 69, 75 n.31 (1982). Professors Lax and Sebenius conceptualize this as the "negotiator's dilemma," that is, the constant tension between creating value on the one hand and claiming it on the other. DAVID LAX & JAMES SEBENIUS, THE MANAGER AS NEGOTIATOR: BARGAINING FOR COOPERATION AND COMPETITIVE GAIN (1986); *see also* ROBERT MNOOKIN, SCOTT PEPPET & ANDREW S. TULUMELLO, BEYOND WINNING: NEGOTIATING TO CREATE VALUE IN DEALS AND DISPUTES 11–43 (2000). Like these commentators, we believe that many negotiations require negotiators to use both problem-solving and adversarial approaches to resolve a dispute successfully. We also believe that negotiators should look for certain reasons to determine whether to favor one approach over the other as they almost invariably balance the two. What factors do you think are likely to suggest adversarial negotiation is more appropriate? What factors are likely to point toward problem-solving negotiation?

E.   LAW, LAWYERS, AND CLIENTS IN NEGOTIATION

Most people conduct most of their negotiations without help from lawyers or other agents. *See, e.g.*, ROBERT C. ELLICKSON, ORDER WITHOUT LAW: HOW NEIGHBORS SETTLE DISPUTES (1991). Even in disputes involving potentially legally actionable claims, people seldom retain lawyers to represent them. One famous study is illustrative. Richard Miller and Austin Sarat contacted individuals by telephone to inquire about potentially legally remediable injuries that members of their households had suffered. Out of every 1,000 such instances, individuals hired lawyers on only 100 occasions. *See* Richard E. Miller & Austin Sarat, *Grievances, Claims, and Disputes: Assessing the Adversary Culture*, 15 Law & Soc'y Rev. 525, 534–46 (1980–81). A more detailed discussion and charts based on this research appear in Chapter I, beginning at page 9.

Despite the relative infrequency with which lawyers are involved, the disputes of greatest relevance to us are those in which disputants do retain lawyers to represent them. Thus, this section explores the role of lawyer-negotiators in dispute resolution. We begin in Subsection 1 below by exploring the primary domain in which lawyers represent disputants, i.e., in litigation and settlement. In Subsection 2, we explore some of the ethical obligations imposed upon lawyer-negotiators.

1.   SETTLEMENT

a.   In General

Clients often retain lawyers to represent them in litigation. In civil litigation, our primary thrust, lawyers are retained either to file claims against another party or to defend against same. Most civil cases — something on the order of two-thirds of them — settle through negotiation.

MARC GALANTER & MIA CAHILL, "MOST CASES SETTLE": JUDICIAL PROMOTION AND REGULATION OF SETTLEMENTS

46 Stan. L. Rev. 1339, 1339–40, 1341–42 (1999).

"Most cases settle" has become a commonplace in discussions of civil justice. It is a welcome corrective to the naive tendency to speak as if every case were tried and subjected to appellate review.

* * *

[I]t should be noted that the simple observation 'most cases settle' requires some qualification. While settlement is the most frequent disposition of civil cases in the United States, its predominance should not be exaggerated. Oft-cited figures estimating settlement rates of between 85 and 95 percent are misleading; those figures represent all civil cases that do not go to trial. But that is not quite the same as limiting the definition of cases that 'settle' to those resolved solely by agreement between the parties without any decision by an authoritative decisionmaker. Cases may be disposed of by authoritative decisions in ways other than by trial. Herbert Kritzer, analyzing 1649 cases in five federal judicial districts and seven state courts, found that although only 7 percent of cases went to trial and reached a jury verdict or court decision, another 15 percent terminated through some other form of adjudication, such as arbitration or dismissal. Another 9 percent settled following a ruling on a significant motion.

In the two-thirds of cases that do settle without a definitive judicial ruling, judges are by no means absent. Rather, they are a ghostly but influential presence, through their rulings in adjudicated cases and their anticipated response to the case at hand.

* * *

[M]ost cases that enter the system are resolved short of full-dress adjudication by a process of maneuver and bargaining 'in the shadow of the law.' Rather than two separate tracks — adjudication on the one hand and negotiation and settlement on the other — there is a single process of pursuing remedies in the presence of courts. For mnemonic purposes, we attach to it the fanciful neologism 'litigotiation.'

The whole 'litigotiation' system has been growing as part of a general expansion of the legal world. As the legal system has grown, the settlement component has increased in prominence while the portion of cases that run the whole course to trial has shrunk.

Notes and Questions

1. Settlement is now so common and trials are so rare that the ABA Section on Litigation recently commissioned a report entitled "The Vanish-

ing Trial," and the *Dispute Resolution Magazine* devoted much of its Summer 2004 issue to this topic. For more on this topic, review the discussion in Chapter I, beginning at page 45.

2. Settlement is so common, in fact, that many participants in the civil justice system view trials as failures. According to Professors Gross and Syverud:

> A trial is a failure. Although we celebrate it as the centerpiece of our system of justice, we know that trial is not only an uncommon method of resolving disputes, but a disfavored one. With some notable exceptions, lawyers, judges, and commentators agree that pretrial settlement is almost always cheaper, faster, and better than trial. Much of our civil procedure is justified by the desire to promote settlement and avoid trial. More important, the nature of our civil process drives parties to settle so as to avoid the costs, delays, and uncertainties of trial, and, in many cases, to agree upon terms that are beyond the power or competence of courts to dictate. These are powerful forces, and they produce settlement in a very high proportion of litigated disputes.

Samuel R. Gross & Kent D. Syverud, *Getting to No: A Study of Settlement Negotiations and the Selection of Cases for Trial*, 90 Mich. L. Rev. 319, 320 (1991).

3. Because the civil justice system favors settlement and disfavors trial, several procedural and evidentiary rules are designed to encourage settlement. Consider, for example, the following:

- Rule 16 of the Federal Rules of Civil Procedure encourages judges to facilitate settlements during pretrial conferences.

- Rule 68 of the Federal Rules of Civil Procedure provides that a defendant may make a settlement offer to the plaintiff. If the plaintiff rejects the offer and fares less well at trial, she must pay the post-offer costs the defendant incurred.

- Rule 408 of the Federal Rules of Evidence generally excludes settlement discussions from admission at trial.

4. Judicial intervention in settlement has received substantial attention. As we saw in Chapter I, beginning at page 40. Professor Judith Resnik describes this function as "managerial judging," and notes:

> Many federal judges have departed from their earlier attitudes; they have dropped the relatively disinterested pose to adopt a more active, 'managerial' stance. In growing numbers, judges are not only adjudicating the merits of issues presented to them by litigants, but also are meeting with parties in chambers to encourage settlement of disputes and to supervise case preparation. Both before and after the trial, judges are playing a critical role in shaping litigation and influencing results.

Judith Resnik, *Managerial Judging*, 96 Harv. L. Rev. 376, 376–77 (1982).

b. Approaches to Settlement

Lawyers generally play a central role in settling civil cases. Professor Mnookin and his colleagues distinguish between two approaches to settlement negotiations: the dominant "net-expected-outcome" or "expected value" approach and the "interest-based" approach. ROBERT MNOOKIN, SCOTT PEPPET & ANDREW S. TULUMELLO, BEYOND WINNING: NEGOTIATING TO CREATE VALUE IN DEALS AND DISPUTES 226 (2000). These roughly parallel the styles of negotiation we have been discussing. The former approach is generally more consistent with the adversarial approach to negotiation, while the latter is more consistent with the problem-solving approach to negotiation. We consider both below.

i. The Expected–Value Approach to Settlement

Lawyers who use an expected-value approach rely on basic economic principles to determine whether, or under what circumstances, their clients should settle. Using this approach, lawyers calculate the expected value of trial and then attempt to negotiate a settlement for their clients higher than that value.

To illustrate, suppose that a plaintiff has filed a breach of contract suit against a defendant for $100,000. Suppose further that the lawyers representing both litigants believe based on the facts of the case and the legal research they have conducted that the plaintiff has a 50% of winning. Finally, suppose that both litigants will have to spend $10,000 more to litigate the case to a verdict than they will to settle.

To calculate the expected value of trial for the plaintiff, her lawyer multiplies the probability of prevailing (50%) by the anticipated judgment ($100,000) and subtracts the costs of trial ($10,000). The expected value of trial for the plaintiff is thus $40,000 [(50% x $100,000) + (50% x $0) — $10,000].

To calculate the expected value of trial for the defendant, her lawyer multiplies the probability of the plaintiff prevailing (50%) by the anticipated judgment (-$100,000) and subtracts the costs of trial ($10,000). The expected value of trial for the defendant under these circumstances is thus -$60,000 [(50% x – $100,000) + (50% x $0) — $10,000].

Based on these calculations, the plaintiff should be willing to settle for a minimum of $40,000, and the defendant should be willing to pay a maximum of $60,000 to settle. Thus, the lawyers should attempt to negotiate a settlement within this $20,000 bargaining range.

Notes and Questions

1.   To calculate the expected value of trial, a lawyer must predict how a judge or jury will apply governing principles of law to the facts of the case. If a settlement offer exceeds that expected value, she will advise her client to settle; if it does not, she will recommend trial. Thus, a lawyer employing the expected-value approach to settlement bargains "in the shadow of the law." Robert H. Mnookin & Lewis Kornhauser, *Bargaining in the Shadow of the Law: The Case of Divorce*, 88 Yale L.J. 950 (1979).

2.   Because the costs of trial are generally so much greater than the costs of settlement, proponents of the expected-value approach assume that virtually all civil cases will settle. What, then, accounts for those cases that fail to settle and go forward to trial? In the following excerpt, Professors

Russell Korobkin and Chris Guthrie observe that scholars have proposed three explanations for settlement breakdowns:

> In attempting to create a general framework for explaining why settlement attempts fail and trials occur, commentators have developed two primary explanations, both of which assume that disputants are rational actors. Proponents of the standard economic models of settlement hypothesize that because settlement is almost always less costly than trial, parties will reach agreement out of court as long as they agree on the expected value of a trial; the litigation costs they save represent joint gains of trade achieved through settlement, which the litigants can then distribute between themselves. Conversely, trials will occur when one or both parties miscalculate the likely outcome of the trial. Other commentators — focusing on the distributive bargaining issues that arise when the parties recognize that they would create joint gains by reaching out-of-court agreement but must determine how to divide that savings — hypothesize that disputants fail to settle when one or both parties employ rational distributive bargaining strategies that lead to impasse, as they will on some occasions.

> We have no quarrel with either of these theories, but we believe that they fail to explain the full range of litigation negotiation failures. While they are elegant in their simplicity, their explanatory power is limited by the narrow assumptions about human behavior on which they rely. When individuals engaged in litigation must choose between settling a lawsuit out of court and seeking a trial verdict, we predict that they will not always act in the rational way that the economic and strategic bargaining models assume. We hypothesize that even in the absence of miscalculation and strategic bargaining, psychological processes create barriers that preclude out-of-court settlements in some cases.

Russell Korobkin & Chris Guthrie, *Psychological Barriers to Litigation Settlement: An Experimental Approach*, 93 Mich. L. Rev. 107, 108–09 (1994).

3. Professors Korobkin and Guthrie argue that psychological processes might prevent cases from settling. The following notes identify three distinct psychological processes that may work to undermine settlement: framing effects, self-serving bias, and equity seeking.

a. *Framing Effects.* When faced with risk or uncertainty — like when deciding whether to settle a case or go forward to trial — people tend to make risk-averse decisions when choosing between options that appear to be gains and risk-seeking decisions when choosing between options that appear to be losses. Professor Jeffrey Rachlinski and other legal scholars have applied this insight — formalized by Professors Daniel Kahneman and Amos Tversky in "prospect theory" — to litigation and settlement.

> Most decisions concerning the course of litigation involve risk. As a result, litigation decisions are influenced by the risk preferences of the parties, which, in turn, are determined by the character of the decision as a gain or as a loss. Predicting the behavior of litigants therefore requires an understanding of whether a party views their decision from the perspective of a gain or loss.

Settlement choices seem particularly vulnerable to framing effects. Consider the litigation setting . . .

Version 1.

Imagine you are the plaintiff in a copyright infringement lawsuit. You are suing for the $400,000 that the defendant allegedly earned by violating the copyright. Trial is in two days and the defendant has offered to pay $200,000 as a final settlement. If you turn it down, you believe that you will face a trial where you have a 50% chance of winning a $400,000 award. Do you agree to accept the settlement?

Version 2.

Imagine you are the defendant in a copyright infringement lawsuit. You are being sued for the $400,000 that the defendant allegedly earned by violating the copyright. Trial is in two days and the plaintiff has offered to accept $200,000 as a final settlement. If you turn it down, you believe that you will face a trial where you have a 50% chance of losing a $400,000 award. Do you agree to pay the settlement?

[B]oth versions represent economically identical outcomes. Both parties in the problem above choose between keeping $200,000 for sure and a gamble with a 50% chance of winning $400,000 or $0. The context of litigation, however, sets up the defendant as the stakeholder, making it appear that the defendant chooses among losses while the plaintiff chooses among gains.

As a simple demonstration that framing influences risk preferences in litigation, I presented this hypothetical to first-year law school students at Cornell Law School. Of the 13 students evaluating the plaintiff's perspective, 10, or 77%, chose to settle, while only 4 of the 13, or 31%, of the students evaluating the defendant's perspective chose to settle. Despite the small sample size, the difference in settlement rates was both striking and statistically significant.

Jeffrey J. Rachlinski, *Gains, Losses, and the Psychology of Litigation*, 70 S. Cal. L. Rev. 113, 128–29 (1996)

b. *Self-Serving Biases*. When evaluating their respective cases, litigants and lawyers may overestimate their chances of prevailing at trial due to "self-serving" or "egocentric" biases. The following excerpt explains:

People tend to make judgments about themselves and their abilities that are "egocentric" or "self-serving." People routinely estimate, for example, that they are above average on a variety of desirable characteristics, including health, driving, professional skills, and likelihood of having a successful marriage. Moreover, people overestimate their contribution to joint activities. For example, after a conversation both parties will estimate that they spoke more than half the time. Similarly, when married couples are asked to estimate the percentage of household tasks they perform, their estimates typically add up to more than 100%.

Egocentric biases occur for several reasons. First, of course, is self-presentation. People may not really believe that they are better than average, but they will nonetheless tell researchers that they are. Second, people engage in confirmatory mental searches for evidence that supports a theory they want to believe, such as that their marriage will succeed. They have no comparable data on the nature of strangers' marriages, so the only evidence they find suggests that theirs is more likely than others' to be successful. Third, memory is egocentric in that people remember their own actions better than others' actions. Thus, when asked to recall the percentage of housework they perform, people remember their own contribution more easily and, consequently tend to overestimate it. Finally, many of the constructs involved in egocentric biases are ambiguous, and thus, people can define success differently. For example, safe driving means different things to different people, and as a result, everyone really can drive safer than average, at least as measured by their own standards.

Egocentric biases can be adaptive, but they can also have an unfortunate influence on the litigation process. Due to egocentric biases, litigants and their lawyers might overestimate their own abilities, the quality of their advocacy, and the relative merits of their cases. These views, in turn, are likely to undermine settlement efforts. In one study, for example, Professor George Loewenstein and his colleagues asked undergraduates and law students to assess the value of a tort case in which the plaintiff had sued the defendant for $100,000 in damages arising from an automobile-motorcycle collision. These researchers assigned some participants to play the role of plaintiff and others the role of defendant, but they provided both sets of participants with identical information about the case. Nevertheless, the participants interpreted the facts in self-serving ways. When asked to predict the amount they thought the judge would award in the case, the participants evaluating the case from the perspective of the plaintiff predicted that the judge would award $14,527 more than the defendant-participants predicted. When asked to identify what they perceived to be a fair settlement value, plaintiff-participants selected a value $17,709 higher than the value selected by defendant-participants. These results suggest that self-serving or egocentric biases can lead to bargaining impasse and wasteful litigation.

Chris Guthrie, Jeffrey J. Rachlinski & Andrew J. Wistrich, *Inside the Judicial Mind*, 86 Cornell L. Rev. 777, 811–13 (2001).

c. *Equity-Seeking*. Even litigants and lawyers attempting to maximize their net-expected-outcomes in litigation may seek to accomplish non-monetary objectives, such as obtaining vindication from the other side or restoring equity to a damaged relationship. As the following excerpt indicates, concerns for these non-monetary goods may prevent litigants from maximizing their net-expected outcomes.

Many researchers assume, quite logically, that litigants seeking to restore equity may behave "irrationally" — that is, they may fail to select options with the highest expected monetary value. We attempted to bolster these assumptions with empirical data. Accordingly, we designed a hypothetical litigation scenario to study the extent to which a litigant's sense that she has been treated unjustly by an adversary, in and of itself, impedes the resolution of legal disputes. Such a study would be difficult to conduct using actual litigation data because in many legal disputes the relative blameworthiness of the disputants affects their legal rights and remedies. Using our experimental method, however, we were able to test for the effects of perceived inequitable treatment while controlling for legal rights.

We provided subjects with a simple landlord-tenant dispute. Subjects were told that they signed a six-month lease to live in an off-campus apartment beginning September 1. After two months the heater broke down. Although they immediately notified the landlord and requested repair, the landlord failed to fix the heater. As a result, according to the scenario, the subjects spent four winter months in a cold apartment attempting to keep warm with a space heater before moving out at the end of the lease period. Throughout this time period, the subjects had continued to pay $1,000 per month in rent. After moving out, they learned from a student legal service lawyer that "there was a good chance" of recovering a portion of the $4,000 in rent paid over that four-month period of time. The lawyer gave neither a specific prediction of the likelihood of success nor any estimate of the exact magnitude of a judgment. Subjects learned that, with the assistance of their attorney, they had filed an action in small claims court against the landlord. Prior to the court date, the landlord offered to settle the case out of court for $900.

The variable tested in this scenario was the landlord's reason for failing to repair the heater in spite of the tenant's prompt request that he do so. Group A subjects learned that they had made a number of calls to the landlord, to no avail. "The landlord promised to fix your heater, but he never did. A week later, you called him again. Again, he promised to fix it, but he never did. Over the next several weeks, you called him a half-dozen times, but he did not return your calls." Group B participants received a different explanation: After the second call to the landlord, "[y]ou learned that he had left the country unexpectedly due to a family emergency and that he was expected to be gone for several months . . . ."

The given explanation had a significant impact on how likely subjects were to accept the settlement offer and forgo their day in court. Knowing that the landlord did not fix the heater because he was out of the country due to a family emergency, most Group B (Family Emergency) subjects were willing to accept the landlord's offer and let the matter rest. Their mean response was 3.41 [on a 5–point scale where 1 = "definitely reject" and 5 = "definitely accept"]. Group A subjects (Broken Promise), in contrast, were more likely to reject the $900 offer and risk a less favorable decision in small claims court than to accept the offer. Their average score was 2.60. The difference between the two groups is highly significant. Fifty-nine percent of the Family Emergency subjects said they would "definitely" or "probably" accept the settlement offer, while only 35% of the Broken Promise subjects provided those same responses. Thirty percent of the Broken Promise subjects said they would "definitely reject" the $900 settlement offer in favor of small claims court, while only 9% of the Family Emergency subjects would "definitely reject" the offer....

The very different responses of the Family Emergency and Broken Promise subjects provide empirical support for the hypothesis that litigant victims seek more than just monetary damages from the legal system. They seek to restore equity to inequitable relationships. When litigants feel they have been treated badly by the other side, the chances of settlement decrease because litigants are more likely to seek retaliation or vindication of their moral position in addition to monetary damages.

Russell Korobkin & Chris Guthrie, *Psychological Barriers to Litigation Settlement: An Experimental Approach*, 93 Mich. L. Rev. 107, 144–47.

4. One way a wrongdoer may be able to provide vindication to an injured party and increase the chances that a reasonable financial settlement offer will be accepted is to apologize. Consider the following excerpt from Professor Jennifer Robbennolt:

Recently, I conducted a series of experimental studies designed to begin a systematic examination of whether, in what ways and under what conditions apologies might affect settlement decisionmaking. The findings described here are based on the results of two experimental studies in which 506 participants were asked to read a vignette describing a pedestrian-bicycle accident, to take on the role of the injured party, to indicate whether or not they were likely to accept a settlement offer and to respond to a series of questions about the situation.

All participants reviewed the same basic scenario and evaluated the same settlement offer. However, some participants evaluated a version of the scenario in which no apology was offered; a second group evaluated a version of the scenario in which the other party offered a partial apology that merely expressed sympathy for the potential claimant's injuries (i.e., 'I am so sorry that you were hurt.'); and a third group of participants evaluated a version of the scenario in which the other party offered a full apology that took responsibility for causing the injuries (i.e., 'I am so sorry that you were hurt. The accident was all my fault.'). Thus, the only difference between the three groups was the nature of the apology offered.

Apologies Affect Settlement

In the first, study, even though all participants were told that they had suffered the same injuries and received the same offer of settlement, the nature of the apology offered influenced recipients' willingness to accept the offer. Receipt of a full, responsibility-accepting apology increased the likelihood that the offer would be accepted. In contrast, a partial, sympathy-expressing apology increased participants' uncertainty about whether or not to accept the offer.

Specifically, when no apology was offered, 52 percent of respondents indicated that they would definitely or probably accept the offer, while 43 percent would definitely or probably reject the offer, and 5 percent were unsure. When a partial apology was offered, only 35 percent of respondents were inclined to accept the offer, 25 percent were inclined to reject it and 40 percent indicated that they were unsure. In contrast, when a full apology was offered, 73 percent of respondents were inclined to accept the offer, with only 14 percent inclined to reject it and 14 percent unsure.

In addition, a full apology resulted in more positive ratings of numerous variables that are thought to underlie settlement decision making than did either a partial apology or no apology. Where there were differences in participants' responses across conditions, the differences follow a strikingly similar pattern: failing to offer an apology or offering a partial apology elicited equivalent responses on these measures that were both different from the responses elicited when a full apology was offered.

Thus, as compared to offenders who offered either a partial apology or no apology, an offender who offered a full apology was seen as:

- having offered a more sufficient apology
- experiencing more regret
- being more moral
- being more likely to be careful in the future
- believing that he or she was more responsible for the incident, and
- having behaved less badly.

In addition, participants who received a full apology, as opposed to a partial apology or no apology, expressed:

- greater sympathy for the offender
- less anger, and
- more willingness to forgive the offender.

Finally, participants who received a full apology, as opposed to a partial apology or no apology, anticipated:

- less damage to the parties' relationship, and
- that the settlement offer would better make up for their injuries.

These underlying judgments provided the mechanism by which apologies influenced settlement decisions. Beyond their effect on decisions regarding a particular offer, such judgments might also be expected to influence the willingness and ability of litigants to engage in settlement negotiations more generally.

Jennifer K. Robbennolt, *Apology — Help or Hindrance? An Empirical Analysis of Apologies' Influence on Settlement Decision Making*, Disp. Resol. Mag., Spring 2004, at 33–34. For a fuller discussion, see Jennifer K. Robbennolt, *Apologies and Legal Settlement: An Empirical Examination*, 102 Mich. L. Rev. 460 (2003).

5.   Given various impediments to economically rational settlements — i.e., rational miscalculation, strategic behavior, and such psychological barriers as framing effects, self-serving biases, and equity-seeking lawyers may

find it helpful to use the tools of formal decision analysis to guide their clients through an expected-value approach to litigation. Consider the following explanation by David Hoffer:

DAVID P. HOFFER, DECISION ANALYSIS AS A MEDIATOR'S TOOL

1 Harv. Negot. L. Rev. 113, 134–37 (1996).

A decision tree is a graphical representation of a complex decision. Developed in the 1960s for use in business education, decision trees are flexible enough to be used for many types of decisions. Professionals in the fields of business, economics, medicine, public policy, engineering, and law all use decision trees when multiple uncertainties complicate the decision process.

A. *Structure*

Decision trees are organized chronologically, from left to right. They contain "nodes" of three different types: decision, chance, and terminal. A decision node (represented by a square) denotes a point at which the decision-maker must choose between two or more options. A chance node (represented by a circle) denotes a point where the decision-maker has no control over the outcome; each event following a chance node has a probability associated with it that reflects how likely it is to occur. Terminal nodes (represented by triangles) denote final outcomes, after which no events relevant to the decision are considered.

The following simple decision tree represents a situation in which a personal injury plaintiff must decide whether to proceed to trial with a chance of recovering $1,000 or settle for $500. (See Fig. A.) Assume that you represent the plaintiff in this lawsuit.

FIGURE A

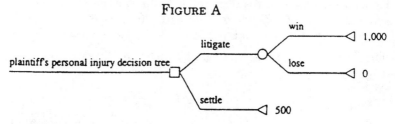

The plaintiff faces two choices — litigate or settle — which are represented by branches emanating from the decision node at the left. If the plaintiff settles, the inquiry is complete: he gets $500 and the dispute ends. If he chooses to litigate, there are two possible outcomes: win (a terminal node with a payoff of $1,000) and lose (a terminal node with a payoff of zero). For purposes of this example, all of the uncertainties associated with litigation (other than liability), as well as costs, are ignored.

To make this decision intelligently, the plaintiff must assess how likely he is to win if litigation is pursued. A $500 settlement offer may seem inadequate if the plaintiff has an excellent chance of winning $1,000; however, the offer may be very attractive if a successful outcome is less certain. In order to be more precise, we must assign probabilities to the uncertain events modeled by the tree. In this simple case, we must assess the likelihood that the plaintiff will win at trial.

Assume that, in your professional judgment, your client has a 40% (.4) chance of winning at trial. This probability would be displayed beneath the node labeled "win." Accordingly, a probability of 60% (.6) would be displayed beneath the node labeled "lose." (See Fig. B.)

FIGURE B

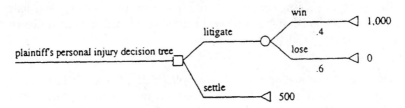

B. *Calculation*

Settlement is apparently preferable to litigation in this case because the probability of winning is not high enough to risk the gamble of trial. This evaluation is based on a concept called expected value or expected monetary value. The expected value of a node is defined as the sum of the products of the probabilities and payoffs of its branches. In other words, the expected value of a course of action is the average value of taking that course of action many times. If one were to try cases identical to this case one hundred times, about forty would result in a victory while sixty would result in a loss. The average recovery would be 40 victories at $1,000 per victory, or $40,000, plus 60 losses at $0 per loss, divided by 100 cases tried, for an average recovery of $400.[2]

Thus, the expected value associated with the "litigate" node is $400. (See Fig. C.)

FIGURE C

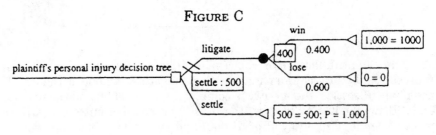

---

2. The same result can be reached by (1) multiplying the probability of victory, 0.4, by the payoff associated with one victory; (2) multiplying the probability of defeat, 0.6, by the payoff associated with one defeat; and (3) adding the two together, for an expected value of $400 + $0 = $400.

C. *Different Kinds of Trees*

A distinction must be drawn between decision trees and chance trees. A decision tree is a tree whose first node (the "root" node) is a decision node; thus, it models a situation in which the events being modeled are triggered by an initial decision to be made by the decision-maker. A chance tree (or "event tree") is a tree whose root is a chance node; in other words, no decision is required. It is used to model events over which the decision-maker has no control, and its value represents the value of being faced with the modeled set of uncertainties.

Chance trees are often embedded in decision trees. For example, one can examine the chance tree that represents the litigation alternative in the example above. Its expected value, $400, represents the expected value of litigation. (See Fig. D.)

FIGURE D

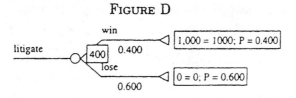

D. *More Complex Trees*

The concept of expected value is at the core of all decision analysis. In more complex trees, the expected value is calculated in stages. In the example below, a motion for summary judgment is interposed between the decision to litigate and the outcome of the trial. (See Fig. E.)

FIGURE E

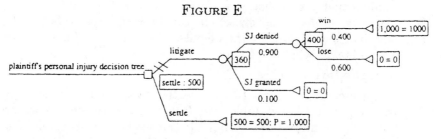

If your client chooses to litigate, the defendant will move for summary judgment, with a 10% chance of winning. If summary judgment is denied, the same win/lose chance tree from Figure D follows the denial of summary judgment.

To calculate the expected value of this tree, the decision analyst starts at the right side. As discussed above, by multiplying the probability of winning by the damage award, multiplying the probability of defeat at trial by the payoff, and adding the two figures together, an expected value of $400 is calculated and displayed next to the node "SJ denied." Thus, the expected value of the case upon denial of summary judgment is $400.

The plaintiff's expected value of litigation must also take into account the possibility of losing on summary judgment. Thus, the expected value of litigation is calculated by multiplying the expected value associated with the denial of summary judgment, $400, by the probability that summary judgment will be denied, 90 percent. This figure, $360, is added to the product of the zero value of losing on summary judgment and the 10% probability of losing on summary judgment. The expected value of litigation is thus $360. The $40 difference between this expected value and the expected value in the simpler example reflects the risk that the plaintiff will lose on summary judgment. Since a $500 settlement offer is preferable to a litigation alternative whose expected value is $360, your client would be well-advised to settle the case.

ii. The Interest–Based Approach to Settlement

Lawyers who pursue the interest-based approach to settlement attempt to convert the litigation into a deal-making opportunity by focusing on the parties' underlying interests and attempting to make value-creating trades. Professor Mnookin and his colleagues describe this approach as follows.

ROBERT H. MNOOKIN, SCOTT R. PEPPET & ANDREW S. TULUMELLO, BEYOND WINNING: NEGOTIATING TO CREATE VALUE IN DEALS AND DISPUTES

240–42 (2000).

Assuming that your negotiations at the net-expected-outcome table are under way, how do you switch to the interest-based table if the situation might permit turning the dispute into a deal? And once at the interest-based table, what do you do?

Moving to the Interest–Based Table

Inviting opposing counsel to explore the opportunity for creating value at the interest-based table can feel risky. Both sides may be reluctant to share interests once they are entrenched in litigation. The interest-based table presents a new concept that may be difficult for some lawyers and clients to accept: that dispute resolution may be an opportunity to find value-creating trades as well as a time for waging war.

For this reason, we advise lawyers interested in moving to the interest-based table to deliver three explicit messages to their counterparts. First, looking for trades may be good for both sides. Moving to the interest-based table may strengthen the parties' relationship, facilitate value-creating deals, and ease distributive tensions at the net-expected-outcome table. Second, looking for trades does not require or imply a ceasefire. Litigation can continue, and a party need not disclose information at the interest-based table that he feels will undermine his position at the net-expected-outcome table. Finally, discussing interests does not signal weakness. Indeed, a willingness to broaden the scope of negotiations can be framed as a sign of strength and confidence.

Searching for Trades

If the other side is willing to try to convert your dispute into a deal, you must first negotiate a process. If you have thought carefully about the other side's interests and come up with options that meet those interests, you may be tempted to unveil all your ideas at once, as in: "I know what you really want, and I've got the solution that gives you what you want." This is a dangerous tendency, and it is unlikely to work. Even if you have guessed right about the other side's interests, he is likely to reject what you propose, either because he has not been given an opportunity to speak for himself or because of reactive devaluation.

Instead, jointly explore what each side cares about and why, and what each side hopes the lawsuit will accomplish. Think broadly — don't just include obvious interests related to the lawsuit, such as "settle quickly" or "receive fair compensation." Also consider interests beyond the scope of the litigation. If two businesses are involved, what are their general business interests? To sell more product? Attract more customers? Expand geographically? Specialize in some area? Reduce costs? What are the interests of the individuals who run those businesses? What synergies exist? Can one side provide the other side with goods or services in a mutually advantageous way? What differences exist between the parties in resources, capabilities, and preferences? How can they trade on those differences?

In some cases, the parties may have important interests beyond the dollar amount of damages at issue. A defendant in an employment discrimination suit may worry about its reputation. Plaintiffs bringing a civil rights complaint against a police department may be interested in an admission of wrongdoing and changing police practices and policies in the future. The seller in a long-term supply contract may have an interest in establishing a more flexible delivery schedule in order to respond to market changes.

Also consider involving clients more at the interest-based table than at the net-expected-outcome table. Of course, if an attorney is accustomed to negotiations that focus on assessing the net expected outcome of litigation, she may not be comfortable with having her clients play an active role at the bargaining table. Relinquishing control can be difficult. But as we have noted, clients often understand their interests and the relative priorities among those interests better than their lawyers do, and they can often be very helpful at the interest-based table.

Finally, consider involving nonparties in searching for trades. The tendency in legal dispute resolution is to focus only on those people or institutions that are named parties in the litigation and to forget that each side has many other relationships that may be affected by the lawsuit. Adding some of these players at the interest-based table can be helpful. If, for example, a building owner and a general contractor are having a dispute over payment, they might bring in an official from the lending institution underwriting the project to assist with their negotiation. If they find a value-creating trade that requires additional lending, this official will be indispensable to making their creative solution possible. Similarly, in a dispute among coauthors over copyright issues, it may be helpful to bring in a representative of the publisher. As the frame of the negotiation widens, outside parties may be essential to devising sophisticated trades.

Notes and Questions

1. Under what circumstances are lawyer-negotiators most likely to employ the interest-based approach to settlement discussions? What difference might it make if the disputing clients expect to have an ongoing relationship? Will it matter whether the litigants are "one-shotters" or "repeat players" in litigation? What difference might the relationship between the attorneys make?

2. Does law play a more prominent role in interest-based settlement negotiations or in expected-value settlement negotiations? Relative to other factors — such as the economic consequences of each course of action, the relationship between the parties, psychological factors, time constraints, and so on — how important is law likely to be to the settlement process?

3. Is the dichotomy between the expected-value approach to settlement and the interest-based approach to settlement a false one? In other words, do skilled lawyer-negotiators use both approaches? Should they?

4. How central *should* law be to the settlement process? Some believe that settlements should reflect what a court of law would decide; others believe that settlement should simply reflect the parties' preferences. Like lawyer-mediator Gary Friedman, we believe that law (in both negotiation and mediation) is relevant but that it should not be determinative.

> In addition to being used as a concrete resource, "the law" may point to relevant principles or values which the parties might want to consider in approaching their own resolution of the issues. So, the fact that spousal support is often awarded reflects some underlying view of obligations between spouses.

Gary J. Friedman, Center for the Development of Mediation in Law Training Materials, Memo #6 (1983).

5. Professor Mnookin and his colleagues recommend that clients play a more active role in interest-based settlement discussions than in expected-value settlement negotiations. For a detailed discussion of the benefits and costs of including clients in settlement negotiations, see Leonard L. Riskin, *The Represented Client in a Settlement Conference: The Lessons of* G. Heileman Brewing Co. v. Joseph Oat Corp., 69 Wash. U. L.Q. 1059, 1097–1105 (1991).

6. Some commentators have argued that the mindset required for litigating a case to verdict is so different from the mindset required for settlement that clients might benefit from hiring special "settlement counsel." Indeed, some clients do retain counsel to play this sole role. Consider the following excerpt:

Clients, courts, and the public yearn for a less adversarial approach to dispute resolution. Lawyers are frequently blamed for the current state of affairs. However, lawyers are, for the most part, reacting rationally and in good faith to existing incentives and expectations. The current approach imposes a duty on lawyers to resolve cases quickly, while ignoring the real constraints on settlement and incentives to delay resolution.

The constraints are of several sorts. One is our view of how lawyers resolve disputes. Some people see lawyers romantically — as knights in shining armor, or as hired guns. Others see them realistically, using the litigation process to try to pound opponents into a favorable settlement. But each of these models has elements that make it difficult to settle cases quickly. Conversely, the model of the lawyer as a problem-solver, which could encourage efficient resolution, is neither as clearly defined nor as widely known.

Aside from the fact that problem-solvers are breaking new ground, there are significant incentives for lawyers not to embrace early settlement. These incentives include the need to market services, the desire not to appear weak, the obligation to represent a client zealously, the thirst for justice, and last, but perhaps not least, the desire to maximize income. In addition, it is extremely difficult, psychologically, for an attorney to act as an effective advocate and, at the same time, to encourage settlement. In the face of these obstacles, a poorly defined and toothless "duty to settle" is not likely to bring about the behavior which critics seek.

When a lawyer is hired for the sole purpose of determining if a fair resolution is possible without litigation — i.e., to act as settlement counsel — the lawyer's interests are aligned with the goal of achieving early settlement. Settlement counsel should be in a better position to use interest-based bargaining techniques and should be better able to avoid some of the common obstacles to early settlement. Because settlement counsel is encouraged to use "value-creating" techniques before "value-claiming" begins, the prospect of early settlement should improve.

William F. Coyne, Jr., *The Case for Settlement Counsel*, 14 Ohio St. J. on Disp. Resol. 367, 369–70 (1999).

7. What about an arrangement in which both clients hire settlement counsel only? This arrangement captures the essence of "collaborative lawyering," a controversial interest-based approach to dispute settlement that has begun to emerge in some family law practices. See Chapter VI, beginning at page 773, for more on this innovative approach to dispute resolution.

2. LEGAL AND ETHICAL OBLIGATIONS

a. In General

When negotiating, lawyers are subject to several rules governing their conduct, including common law rules, certain context-specific rules, and the ethical rules governing the legal profession. The following excerpt introduces these three sources of regulation of lawyer-negotiator behavior.

RUSSELL KOROBKIN, MICHAEL MOFFITT & NANCY WELSH, THE LAW OF BARGAINING

87 Marq. L. Rev. 839, 839–44 (2004).

I. COMMON LAW LIMITS ON BARGAINING BEHAVIOR

When a negotiated agreement results from false statements made during the bargaining process, the common law of tort and contract sometimes holds negotiators liable for damages or makes their resulting agreements subject to rescission. The common law does not, however, amount to a blanket prohibition of all lying. Instead, the common law principles are subject to the caveats that false statements must be material, the opposing negotiator must rely on the false statements, and such reliance must be justified. Whether reliance is justified depends on the type of statement at issue and the statement's specificity. A seller's specific false claim ("this car gets eighty miles per gallon gas mileage") is actionable, but his more general claim ("this car gets good gas mileage") is probably not, because the latter statement is acknowledged as the type of "puffing" or "sales talk" on which no reasonable buyer would rely.

While it is often said that misrepresentations of fact are actionable but misrepresentations of opinion are not, this statement is not strictly accurate. Statements of opinions can be false, either because the speaker does not actually have the claimed opinion ("I think this Hyundai is the best car built in the world today") or because the statement implies facts that are untrue ("I think this Hyundai gets the best gas mileage of any car"). But statements of opinion are less likely to induce justified reliance than are statements of specific facts, especially when they are very general, such as a claim that an item is one of "good quality."

Whether reliance on a statement of fact or opinion is justified depends significantly on the context of the negotiation and whether the speaker has access to information that the recipient does not. A seller "aggressively" promoting his product whose stated opinions imply facts that are not true is less likely to find himself in legal difficulty if the veracity of his claims are easily investigated by an equally knowledgeable buyer than if his customer is a consumer unable to evaluate the factual basis of the claims. The case for liability is stronger still when the negotiator holds himself out as being particularly knowledgeable about the subject matter that the expressed opinion concerns. Whether a false statement can be insulated from liability by a subsequent disclaimer depends on the strength and clarity of the disclaimer, as well as on the nature of the false statement. Again, the standard is whether the reasonable recipient of the information in total would rely on the statement at issue when deciding whether to enter into an agreement.

It is universally recognized that a negotiator's false statements concerning how valuable an agreement is to her or the maximum she is willing to give up or exchange in order to seal an agreement (the negotiator's "reservation point," or "bottom line") are not actionable, again on the ground that such false statements are common and no reasonable negotiator would rely upon them. So an insurance adjuster who claimed that $900 was "all he could pay" to settle a claim is not liable for fraud, even if the statement was false. The law is less settled regarding the status of false statements concerning the existence of outside alternatives for a negotiator. A false claim of an offer from a third party is relevant because it implies a strong reservation point, so a negotiator might logically argue that such a claim is no more actionable than a claim as to the reservation point itself. But courts have occasionally ruled that false claims of a specific outside offer are actionable, on the ground that they are material to the negotiation and that the speaker has access to information that cannot be easily verified by the listener's independent investigation.

The most inscrutable area of the law of deception concerns when a negotiator may be held legally liable for failing to disclose information that might weaken his bargaining position (rather than affirmatively asserting a false claim). The traditional laissez-faire rule of caveat emptor eroded in the twentieth century, with courts placing greater disclosure responsibility on negotiators. It is clear that any affirmative action taken to conceal a fact, including the statement of a "half-truth" that implies a false fact, will be treated as if it were an affirmative false statement. Beyond this point, however, the law becomes murky. Although the general rule is probably still that negotiators have no general disclosure obligation, some courts require bargainers (especially sellers) to disclose known material facts not easily discovered by the other party.

Just as the law places some limits on the use of deceptive behavior to seal a bargain, so too does it place some limits upon negotiators' ability to use superior bargaining power to coerce acquiescence with their demands. In general, negotiators may threaten to withhold their goods and services from those who will not agree to their terms. Courts can invoke the doctrine of duress, however, to protect parties who are the victims of a threat that is "improper" and have "no reasonable alternative" but to acquiesce to the other party's demand, such as when one party procures an agreement through the threat of violence, or through the threat to breach a prior agreement after using the relationship created by that agreement to place the victim in a position in which breach would cause noncompensable damage. Judicial intervention is most likely when the bargaining parties' relationship was not arms-length. For example, the common law provides the defense of undue influence to negotiators who can show that they were dependent upon and thus vulnerable to the other, dominant negotiator.

II.   Context-Specific Regulation of Negotiators' Behavior

Beyond the general common law constraints on negotiators' behavior, the law imposes particularized parameters on bargainers engaged in negotiations in some specific contexts. For example, labor law places a number of procedural restrictions on negotiating behavior. Compared with their counterparts in non-unionized settings, employers, employees, and their representatives involved in collective bargaining all have considerable limits on their ability to adopt certain approaches to negotiating the terms and conditions of employment.

While federal and state laws proscribe a range of behaviors in collective bargaining contexts, the most vivid encapsulation of these requirements is the duty imposed on both sides by the National Labor Relations Act to bargain in "good faith." The concept of "good faith" bargaining lacks clear parameters, but a "totality of conduct" standard has given way to a list of proscribed behaviors, such as disengaging from the negotiations and presenting take-it-or-leave-it offers.

In other contexts, the law imposes affirmative duties of disclosure rather than attempting to define the parameters of negotiation behavior. For example, in residential real estate transactions in many states, sellers have a legal obligation to disclose a range of information even if the buyer does not request it. Supplanting the baseline principle of caveat emptor, many states have judged that real estate transactions require different foundational principles.

Finally, in certain bargaining contexts that seem unusually prone to exploitation, the law provides paternalistic protection for potential victims. For example, certain legal disputes involving seamen on the high seas and their employers require judicial approval, because of the perceived power imbalance between seamen and ship owners. Similarly, most jurisdictions require court ratification of divorce agreements. To protect principal parties with little ability to monitor their agents, settlements of class action and shareholder derivative suits also require a judicial finding of fairness. Rather than judicial oversight, many jurisdictions give consumers in certain vulnerable contexts the self-help remedy of unilaterally rescinding an agreement within several days of acceptance, such as when they accept a bargain proposed by telemarketers or door-to-door salespersons. Finally, the law sometimes establishes alternative dispute resolution mechanisms for contexts frequently characterized by dissatisfaction with negotiated agreements. For example, lemon laws anticipate that some percentage of negotiations over used car purchases will result in unhappy consumers. In states with lemon laws, consumers who are dissatisfied with their purchase need not establish one of the traditional bases for rescinding a contract or ceasing performance (for example fraud, duress, or material breach). Instead, consumers have a streamlined system for demonstrating eligibility for the laws' protection after the fact.

III.   Professional and Organizational Constraints on Bargaining Behavior

Some negotiators operate not only within the legal constraints applicable to the general public, but also within the parameters of professional or organizational codes of conduct. These parameters can provide another layer of substantive constraints on negotiating behavior (in addition to those provided by generally applicable law), additional or enhanced enforcement mechanisms, or both.

As an example, attorneys are subject not only to generally applicable legal constraints on negotiating behavior but also to [applicable rules of professional responsibility, which in most jurisdictions are based upon] the American Bar Association's *Model Rules of Professional Conduct.* Model Rule 4.1(a) provides that "[i]n the course of representing a client a lawyer shall not knowingly ... Make a false statement of material fact or law to a third person." The commentary to the rule suggests that the scope of the rule roughly parallels the common law. For example, estimates of "price or value" are not considered material, thus permitting lawyers in general to "puff" as well as lie outright about their reservation prices. One important difference, however, between the administrative law governing lawyer-negotiators and the common law governing all bargainers is the absence of the requirements of reliance and damages in the regulatory context. To sustain a tort or contract action, the victim must actually suffer harm. Although punishment for transgressions in bargaining outside of the doors of the courthouse is a relatively rare occurrence, lawyers can face disciplinary action for making material misrepresentations even if no legally cognizable damage results.

Notes

1. As the last section of the excerpt from Professor Korobkin and his colleagues indicates, lawyers are subject to ethical rules governing the profession. These rules impose obligations on the lawyer-as-negotiator which may appear to be in tension with the obligations the lawyer faces as an advocate for her client.

Attorneys are required to comply with the professional responsibility rules adopted by the state where the attorney is licensed. More than forty states have now patterned their professional responsibility rules after the ABA's Model Rules of Professional Conduct. For more information, see JAMES R. DEVINE, WILLIAM FISCH & STEPHEN EASTON, PROBLEMS, CASES AND MATERIALS IN PROFESSIONAL RESPONSIBILITY 7–12 (3d ed. 2004). The preamble to the Model Rules requires that: "As advocate, a lawyer zealously asserts the client's position under the rules of the adversary system. As negotiator, a lawyer seeks a result advantageous to the client but consistent with the requirements of honest dealing with others."

2. As Korobkin and his colleagues explain, the requirements of honest dealing are embedded in Model Rule 4.1, quoted in full below:

Rule 4.1 Truthfulness in Statements to Others

In the course of representing a client a lawyer shall not knowingly:

(a) make a false statement of a material fact or law to a third person; or

(b) fail to disclose a material fact to a third person when disclosure is necessary to avoid assisting a criminal or fraudulent act by a client, unless disclosure is prohibited by Rule 1.6 [which deals with the lawyer's obligation to keep client confidences.]

MODEL RULES OF PROF'L CONDUCT R. 4.1 (2002).

The Comments accompanying this rule attempt to define two of the most vexing terms included in Rule 4.1: "misrepresentation" and "statements of fact":

Misrepresentation

[1]   A lawyer is required to be truthful when dealing with others on a client's behalf, but generally has no affirmative duty to inform an opposing party of relevant facts. A misrepresentation can occur if the lawyer incorporates or affirms a statement of another person that the lawyer knows is false. Misrepresentations can occur by failure to act. Misrepresentations can also occur by partially true but misleading statements or omissions that are the equivalent of affirmative false statements * * *

Statements of Fact

[2]   This Rule refers to statements of fact. Whether a particular statement should be regarded as one of fact can depend on the circumstances. Under generally accepted conventions in negotiation, certain types of statements ordinarily are not taken as statements of material fact. Estimates of price or value placed on the subject of a transaction and a party's intentions as to an acceptable settlement of a claim are ordinarily in this category, and so is the existence of an undisclosed principal except where nondisclosure of the principal would constitute fraud. Lawyers should be mindful of their obligations under applicable law to avoid criminal and tortious misrepresentation.

MODEL RULES OF PROF'L CONDUCT R. 4.1 cmts. (2004).

b.   Confidentiality in Negotiation

A lawyer involved in negotiations will often divulge information that could be detrimental if widely disseminated, particularly if the lawyer is using a problem-solving approach in her negotiation. The law allows for the protection of negotiation communications in two ways. The first is by allowing negotiating parties to agree not to disclose statements made during the negotiation to the general public, such as to friends, spouses, business associates, or others who might have an interest in learning about what was said in the negotiation. Courts routinely uphold such private agreements. *See, e.g., Cohen v. Cowles Media Co.*, 501 U.S. 663, 111 S.Ct. 2513, 115 L.Ed.2d 586 (1991) (First Amendment does not bar recovery against a newspaper's breach of promise of confidentiality); *Horne v. Patton*, 291 Ala. 701, 287 So.2d 824 (1973) (physician disclosure may be invasion of privacy, breach of fiduciary duty, breach of contract).

The second way the law protects the confidentiality of legal negotiations is through the regulation of their admissibility in judicial proceedings by certain evidentiary rules. The most significant of these rules is the rule regarding settlement discussions or offers of compromise on legal claims — a common type of legal negotiation — which generally prohibits statements made in settlement discussions from being introduced in a later trial or other legal proceeding to establish the validity or amount of a legal claim. The purpose of the rule is generally to promote settlement by encouraging the parties to be candid during settlement discussions by rendering information exchanged during the settlement discussion inadmissible in subsequent proceedings. The rule is of common law origin, but has been codified by many states, and at the federal level by Rule 408 of the Federal Rules of Evidence, which provides:

> Evidence of (1) furnishing or offering or promising to furnish, or (2) accepting or offering or promising to accept, a valuable consideration in compromising or attempting to compromise a claim which was disputed as to either validity or amount, is not admissible to prove liability for or invalidity of the claim or its amount. Evidence of conduct or statements made in compromise negotiations is likewise not admissible. This rule does not require the exclusion of any evidence otherwise discoverable merely because it is presented in the course of compromise negotiations. This rule also does not require exclusion when the evidence is offered for another purpose, such as proving bias or prejudice of a witness, negativing a contention of undue delay, or proving an effort to obstruct a criminal investigation or prosecution.

In the following excerpt, Professor Rambo discusses the history and codification of Rule 408, as well as the uncertainty over whether it bars the use of statements made during a negotiation from being used to establish that a witness was lying during a later legal proceeding.

LYNNE H. RAMBO, IMPEACHING LYING PARTIES WITH THEIR STATEMENTS DURING NEGOTIATION: DEMYSTICIZING THE PUBLIC POLICY RATIONALE BEHIND EVIDENCE RULE 408 AND THE MEDIATION–PRIVILEGE STATUTES

75 Wash. L. Rev. 1037, 1046–49, 1051–54, 1056–57, 1066–73, 1075–77 (2000).

* * *

1.   The Drafting and Enactment of Rule 408

The first sentence of Rule 408, excluding offers to compromise and completed compromises, reflects essentially a codification of the common law as it stood in 1975 when the Federal Rules of Evidence were adopted. Offers to compromise and completed compromises had long been held inadmissible by federal and state courts, at least to the extent that they were tendered as an admission that a party's position was invalid. In excluding evidence of compromise, the courts had relied on what has come to be known as the "relevance" rationale: proposals to compromise are irrelevant for the purpose of disproving a claim or defense, because they do not necessarily signify any admission of weakness by the proposing party. Parties compromise claims and defenses for a variety of reasons other than in belief that those claims and defenses are not sound. The courts had also recognized what has come to be known as the public policy rationale: negotiated compromises should be encouraged, and litigants will be discouraged from attempting compromises if their proposals can be used against them in the event negotiation fails. Indeed, at the time Rule 408 was enacted, commentators had come to view the latter rationale as bearing greater force.* * *

In contrast to Rule 408's treatment of offers to compromise and completed compromises, the Rule's second sentence, excluding statements and conduct in compromise negotiations, worked at least a partial reversal of the common law. Prior to enactment of the Rule, a party's unconditional statements of fact had rarely been excluded from evidence, whether they were made in the course of compromise negotiations or not. What were called "independent admissions of fact" were freely admissible; the only way a negotiating party could protect its statements in the course of negotiations was to state facts in hypothetical terms or expressly state that its pronouncements were made "without prejudice." The Advisory Committee became convinced that this formalism both "inhibited freedom of communication with respect to compromise, even among lawyers," and generated excessive "controversy over whether a given statement falls within or without the protected area."

* * *

3. *Judicial Reliance on the Public Policy Rationale To Prohibit Impeachment by Inconsistent Statements During Negotiation*

It may be that the Rule's drafters simply assumed that if a party represented the facts one way during negotiations and presented a different version of the facts at trial, impeachment by prior inconsistent statement would be available. * * *

Unfortunately, if there was such an assumption, it remained unexpressed in all of the official sources. As a result, several courts apparently have considered the Rule inconclusive on the point and have turned to the broad policy behind Rule 408 to provide the answer. These courts have noted that the primary reason negotiation statements are excluded under Rule 408 is to promote candor in the pursuit of settlements, and reflexively concluded that permitting a party to be impeached with its inconsistent negotiation statement will discourage that candor.

The Tenth Circuit Court of Appeals' decision in EEOC v. Gear Petroleum, Inc., is the leading example. In Gear Petroleum, the EEOC brought an action under the Age Discrimination in Employment Act (ADEA), alleging that 66-year-old Donald Trowbridge's employment had been improperly terminated on the basis of his age. Prior to the lawsuit, the employer's counsel had written two letters to the EEOC in the course of discussing a negotiated resolution. The first letter stated that Mr. Trowbridge had been laid off not only because the company was generally reducing its staff and the employee had not performed well, but also because the company was "moving toward mandatory retirement at 65." In the second letter, counsel stated that the company considered age to be a bona fide occupational qualification for Mr. Trowbridge's job, which would permit age to be taken into account without violating the ADEA.

During discovery depositions, however, the employer's story changed. The employer's executives testified that there was no mandatory-retirement policy and that age was not a factor in their termination of Mr. Trowbridge's employment. The employer's counsel claimed that he had simply been mistaken in the two letters written to the EEOC. Prior to trial, the company moved in limine to exclude the letters and any testimony about them, and the district court granted the motion.

At trial, the employer's executives once again testified that there was no mandatory-retirement policy and that age had not been a factor in Mr. Trowbridge's firing. The EEOC was prepared to show that the executives had actually conferred with their attorney in producing the letters to the EEOC and thereby had knowledge of the attorney's statements, but the court still refused to allow the EEOC to impeach the executives with the letters. The Tenth Circuit affirmed the judgment in favor of the employer, holding that the district court was not "clearly erroneous" in excluding the attorneys' letters.

The Tenth Circuit acknowledged that Rule 408 allows the admission of statements made in negotiations for purposes other than proving the validity or invalidity of a claim or its amount. The court concluded, however, that the policy behind Rule 408 required exclusion of the letters even though they impeached the employer's defense. Quoting a legal commentator, the court wrote:

> "The philosophy of the Rule is to allow the parties to drop their guard and to talk freely and loosely without fear that a concession made to advance negotiations will be used at trial. Opening the door to impeachment evidence on a regular basis may well result in more restricted negotiations."[69]

* * *

[This] holding that Rule 408 does not allow negotiation statements to be used to impeach by prior inconsistent statement (and several other cases suggesting that result, if not directly so holding) [is] not the only case[] to address the question. The courts have divided on the issue, and a somewhat greater number have either held or suggested that Rule 408 allows for impeachment by prior inconsistent statement, because the Rule identifies the purposes for which compromise evidence cannot be used, and impeachment by prior inconsistent statement is not among them. Legal commentators are likewise split on the question, and their division mirrors the courts' difficulty in deciding whether Rule 408's purpose limitations, or the policy behind the Rule, should govern. * * *

[Courts that have precluded the use of negotiation statements under Rule 408 have generally applied a public policy rationale for the excep-

---

69. Id. at 1545–46 (quoting Stephen A. Saltzburg & Kenneth R. Redden, Federal   Rules of Evidence Manual 286 (4th ed. 1986)). * * *

tion: that the benefit to be gained from admitting evidence in one particular suit is outweighed by the cost to the public at large.] The exclusion of negotiation statements of fact (as a category separate from compromises or offers to compromise) by Rule 408 * * * reflects the same sort of reasoning. The factual statements a party makes in a negotiation will in most instances be relevant, but Rule 408 * * * exclude[s] them on the public policy rationale that to do otherwise would inhibit the "free and frank discussion" necessary to render negotiations * * * effective in producing settlement.

* * *

The premise for this conclusion, what will hereafter be referred to as the public policy rationale, has been almost universally accepted, without question. As Justice O'Connor recently stated, however, "[a] privilege should operate ... only where 'necessary to achieve its purpose,' and an invocation of [a] privilege should not go unexamined 'when it is shown that the interests of the administration of justice can only be frustrated by [its] exercise.' " This Article posits that when one examines negotiation confidentiality against the rationale that supposedly supports it, there is little reason to believe that confidentiality with respect to statements of fact actually promotes settlement, and even less reason to believe that prohibiting impeachment does.

First, there is no empirical evidence to support the public policy rationale even generally, much less with respect to impeachment. For example, the author is unaware of any studies to suggest that the enactment of Rule 408 — which reversed the common law on the admissibility of statements made during negotiation — led to an increase in the amount of negotiated settlements. While this absence of empirical evidence is not conclusive in and of itself, it does suggest that the theory warrants greater scrutiny than it has heretofore received.

Second, the courts and legislatures relying on the rationale that admitting negotiation statements will inhibit successful negotiation fail to distinguish between the different types of statements parties make during negotiations. * * * [T]his lack of precision is significant, because the inhibiting effect of admitting negotiation statements is likely to differ markedly depending on what type of statement is involved.

Third, the notion that admitting negotiation statements would discourage settlements appears to be based on two assumptions: that settlements most often result when the parties admit the weaknesses in their cases, and that a negotiating party will feel free to admit the weaknesses in his or her case so long as a confidentiality rule is in place. As described below, these assumptions are unrealistic. The truth is that many settlements result even without the parties' admissions of weakness, and the admissions that are made would usually be made even without confidentiality, because the substance of the admissions will be revealed by other evidence in any event.

Finally, when one considers the types of statements that are actually made during negotiations, it becomes clear that confidentiality is necessary in largest measure only to protect statements that are not related to the underlying facts: the type of statements that address the parties' reasons for wanting to settle, such as a party's financial status or fear of proceeding. This type of statement, however, is not the type of statement that would even be used for impeachment, because the subject matter would not be relevant at trial, and thus there would be no relevant testimony to impeach.

* * *

II. THE MYTHICAL NATURE OF THE PUBLIC POLICY RATIONALE AS APPLIED TO NEGOTIATION STATEMENTS OF FACT

* * *

A. *Distinguishing the Types of Statements Parties Make During Negotiations*

The premise on which Rule 408 * * * [is] based is that admitting any statement whatsoever made during negotiations will inhibit the type of communication necessary for cases to settle. The jurisdictions that have adopted Rule 408 have recognized that there are circumstances when negotiation statements should be admitted — for example, when they are used to show bias, obstruction of justice, or that a party has not engaged in undue delay — but these jurisdictions appear to have done so not on any belief that admitting only certain types of statements will inhibit settlement. Rather, they seem to have concluded, as a matter of policy, that the need to admit negotiation statements for certain purposes outweighs what is nonetheless believed to be the settlement-inhibiting effect of admitting any statement whatsoever. * * *

* * *

* * * [T]he public policy rationale is overbroad, [however,] because the rationale fails to account for the difference in inhibiting effect of admitting different types of statements. The contrast further suggests that to determine whether the public policy rationale is accurate even in the majority of cases, it is necessary to break the overbroad category of "negotiation statements" into the different types of statements that might be made during negotiations.

2. *Identifying the Different Types of Negotiation Statements*

The first, broad level of differentiation among the types of statements that might be made during negotiations would distinguish (1) admissions of liability, (2) statements that relate to the facts underlying the dispute, and (3) statements that may aid resolution of the dispute but do not actually relate to the dispute. * * *

Once these distinctions are drawn, further distinctions can be drawn within the second category of statements of fact related to the underlying dispute. One such distinction would be between statements of fact that the speaker perceives as supporting the speaker's position, and statements of fact that the speaker acknowledges weaken the speaker's position. * * *

Thus, the universe of possible factual statements during negotiations can be charted initially as follows:

1. Pure admissions of liability or non-liability

2. Statements of fact related to the underlying dispute

   a. Statements of fact perceived to support the speaker's position

   b. Statements of fact perceived to weaken the speaker's position

3. Statements of fact relevant to resolving the dispute but not related to the underlying dispute.

When the types of negotiation statements are distinguished this way, the public policy rationale, at first blush, appears accurate. It is clear, as described above, that even if there were no confidentiality, parties would not be inhibited from making the types of statements that fall within category 2.a (statements of fact that support their position) because no party would mind having the strengths of its case repeated outside the negotiation session. Negotiating parties might be inhibited, however, from making the types of statements that fall within categories 1, 2.b, and 3. If no other considerations were in play, negotiating parties would theoretically be less likely to admit liability (category 1), admit the weakness in their cases (category 2.b), or discuss the business or personal reasons that they want to settle (category 3) if they knew that these statements would be disclosed outside the negotiating session.

B. Confidentiality's Limited Effect on the Statements Parties Make in Negotiation

Of course, it is one thing to consider the effect of confidentiality in the abstract, and quite another to consider the effect of confidentiality in context. To measure the effect of confidentiality in context, one has to look at all of the other forces that come into play in a negotiation to determine what a party says. When these forces are considered, it becomes clear that confidentiality does not in fact promote the types of statements in categories 1 or 2 (admissions of liability or non-liability, or statements of fact related to the dispute), but only those statements falling within category 3.

1. Admissions of Liability

Common sense dictates that statements in category 1, pure admissions of liability or non-liability, are neither encouraged nor discouraged by confidentiality. It could be argued, as a theoretical matter, that parties would be less likely to make such statements if their statements could be admitted at trial. In the actual negotiation context, however, it is clear that confidentiality has no effect whatsoever on a party's willingness to admit liability or non-liability. The reality is that regardless of whether their statements will later be disclosed or not, parties do not generally go into any negotiation and admit that they are liable or that their opponent is not. * * * The public policy rationale thus fails because these statements almost certainly will not be made even when absolute confidentiality is in place.

The only exception would be a negotiation in which one party had already conceded liability and the amount owing was the only question. In that instance, however, even in the absence of confidentiality, parties would not be inhibited from admitting liability if they knew their statements could be used against them, because their admissions of liability would already be a matter of record. * * * Thus, to the extent that negotiation statements are excluded on the thought that parties need to be free in negotiations to admit their liability, the public policy rationale on which the exclusion is based is a mirage. Because the kinds of statements in category 1 either are not made, or are made in situations where the party making them would not be affected by whether they were admissible or not, the public policy rationale that admitting negotiations statements would inhibit settlements does not apply.

2. *Admissions of "Bad Facts"*

Much the same might be said with respect to category 2.b (statements of fact that the speaker perceives are weaknesses in his or her case). It is unrealistic to assume that parties regularly admit facts during negotiation that they perceive will weaken their position. Fundamental negotiation strategy suggests that a party will seek to capitalize on the other party's risk of failing at trial, because even a party with a very strong case must fear the unpredictability of the factfinder. For that reason, the usual approach to a negotiation is to emphasize the strengths of one's case and leave assertions of one's weaknesses to the other side. This is not to say that a party will never admit the weaknesses in its case. Certainly, in the give-and-take of a negotiation * * * parties will sometimes acknowledge what might be called "bad facts." And sometimes these admissions are what enable parties to meet in the middle and reach a negotiated solution.

* * *

3. *Admission of Statements of Fact Unrelated to the Underlying Dispute*

Thus, all that remains for consideration is whether the public policy rationale serves its purpose with respect to category 3, statements of fact relevant to resolving the dispute but unrelated to the underlying dispute. This category covers a variety of statements made during negotiations that address issues beyond the transactional facts. * * *

With respect to this category of statements, the public policy rationale works well. Certainly, if a negotiating party were told that these statements would be disclosed outside the confines of the negotiation, the party would be less likely to make them. The party would not necessarily fear the admission of such statements at trial, because they are by definition unrelated to the transactional facts, and thus the content of any such statement would be irrelevant. The party might well fear disclosure other than at trial, however, because of the impact disclosure would have outside the context of the existing litigation. * * *

All told, then, the public policy rationale may well be accurate with respect to statements in category 3 (those relevant to resolution of the dispute but not related to the underlying facts), but is not likely to be accurate with respect to any of the categories of statements addressed to the underlying facts. Returning to the chart of statements potentially made during negotiations, it now looks as follows:

1. Pure admissions of liability or non-liability: *exclusion does not promote settlement because parties will not make these statements even when there is confidentiality*

2. Statements of fact related to the underlying dispute

    a. Statements of fact perceived to support the speaker's position: *exclusion does not promote settlement because parties will make these statements even when there is not confidentiality*

    b. Statements of fact perceived to weaken the speaker's position * * *

3. Statements of fact relevant to resolving the dispute but not related to the underlying dispute: *exclusion does promote settlement because parties will be inhibited in making these statements and fewer settlements will result* * * *

* * *

The law currently extends confidentiality to the parties to a negotiation * * * on the nearly universally accepted public policy rationale that confidentiality is necessary to ensure that parties can communicate freely enough to reach settlements. That rationale is undeserving of its widespread application, however, because it is only partly correct. Although confidentiality does help parties discuss their needs in settling or their hesitation in settling, it is not what determines whether an honest party will divulge the facts needed to resolve the case. Thus, when confidentiality is extended so far as to preclude impeachment by inconsistent statement, it operates only to protect dishonest parties, those who would represent the facts one way during negotiation or a mediation and deliberately represent the facts differently during subsequent litigation. The honest parties on the other side of the table may then become the unknowing victims of an unjust settlement, or the knowing, but helpless, victims of a false trial outcome.* * *

Notes and Comments

1. The settlement discussion rule is broad in that it protects not only statements made during settlement, but also evidence of conduct during a settlement discussion. Thus, for example, if the plaintiff in a personal injury case was walking fine during a settlement discussion, but was limping at trial, the settlement discussion rule would prohibit the defendant from establishing this point at trial.

2. Professor Rambo mentions some of the exceptions to the settlement discussion rule, specifically to show the bias or prejudice of a witness, obstruction of justice, or that a party has not engaged in undue delay. The plain language of Rule 408 also reflects another exception commonly recog-

nized in the states: that the rule does not preclude the use of statements made, or conduct engaged in, during a settlement discussion if the information was "otherwise discoverable." This exception prevents the settlement discussion from being used to shield otherwise discoverable evidence. In the personal injury example described in Note 1, for example, the defendant would be able to establish that the plaintiff was walking without a limp at times other than during the settlement discussion.

3.   Professor Rambo chides the courts for disregarding the settlement discussion exception for bias and using principles of public policy to exclude statements made during a settlement discussion as prior inconsistent statements at trial. Do you agree?

4.   Professor Rambo generally asserts that Rule 408 is unnecessary to shield many of the statements of fact that are routinely made during a settlement discussion, such as admissions of liability and bad facts, because litigants can't be expected to disclose these during a settlement discussion. Do you agree? Would your answer depend upon the style of the negotiation — i.e., whether it was more adversarial or more problem-solving?

c. Lying

The aforementioned rules governing candor and deception take a lawyer only so far, of course. Most lawyer-negotiators base their conduct not only on the governing ethical rules but also on their own sense of right and wrong. In the following reading, Professor James White describes the circumstances under which he thinks it is acceptable for a lawyer-negotiator to deceive his counterpart.

JAMES J. WHITE, MACHIAVELLI AND THE BAR: ETHICAL LIMITATIONS ON LYING IN NEGOTIATION

1980 Am. B. Found. Res. J. 926, 927–29, 931–35.

[In this excerpt, Professor White is commenting on a proposed ethical rule that would have required, in part, that lawyers "be fair in dealing with others."]

On the one hand the negotiator must be fair and truthful; on the other he must mislead his opponent. Like the poker player, a negotiator hopes that his opponent will overestimate the value of his hand. Like the poker player, in a variety of ways he must facilitate his opponent's inaccurate assessment. The critical difference between those who are successful negotiators and those who are not lies in this capacity both to mislead and not to be misled.

Some experienced negotiators will deny the accuracy of this assertion, but they will be wrong. I submit that a careful examination of the behavior of even the most forthright, honest, and trustworthy negotiators will show them actively engaged in misleading their opponents about their true positions. That is true of both the plaintiff and the defendant in a lawsuit. It is true of both labor and management in a collective bargaining agreement. It is true as well of both the buyer and the seller in a wide variety of sales transactions. To conceal one's true position, to mislead an opponent about one's true settling point, is the essence of negotiation.

Of course there are limits on acceptable deceptive behavior in negotiation, but there is the paradox. How can one be "fair" but also mislead? Can we ask the negotiator to mislead, but fairly, like the soldier who must kill, but humanely?

TRUTHTELLING IN GENERAL

The obligation to behave truthfully in negotiation is embodied in the requirement of Rule 4.2(a) that directs the lawyer to "be fair in dealing with other participants."

* * *

The comment on fairness under Rule 4.2 makes explicit what is implicit in the rule itself by the following sentence: "Fairness in negotiation implies that representations by or on behalf of one party to the other party be truthful." Standing alone that statement is too broad. Even the Comments contemplate activities such as puffing which, in the broadest sense, are untruthful. It seems quite unlikely that the drafters intend or can realistically hope to outlaw a variety of other nontruthful behavior in negotiations.

* * *

FIVE CASES

[I]t is probably important to give more than the simple disclaimer about the impossibility of defining the appropriate limits of puffing that the drafters have given in the current Comments. To test these limits, consider five cases. Easiest is the question that arises when one misrepresents his true opinion about the meaning of a case or a statute. Presumably such a misrepresentation is accepted lawyer behavior both in and out of court and is not intended to be precluded by the requirement that the lawyer be "truthful." In writing his briefs, arguing his case, and attempting to persuade the opposing party in negotiation, it is the lawyer's right and probably his responsibility to argue for plausible interpretations of cases and statutes which favor his client's interest, even in circumstances where privately he has advised his client that those are not his true interpretations of the cases and statutes.

A second form of distortion that the Comments plainly envision as permissible is distortion concerning the value of one's case or of the other subject matter involved in the negotiation. Thus the Comments make explicit reference to "puffery." Presumably they are attempting to draw the same line that one draws in commercial law between express warranties and "mere puffing" under section 2–313 of the Uniform Commercial Code. While this line is not easy to draw, it generally means that the seller of a product has the right to make general statements concerning the value of his product without having the law treat those statements as warranties and without having liability if they turn out to be inaccurate estimates of the value. As the statements descend toward greater and greater particularity, as the ignorance of the person receiving the statements increases, the courts are likely to find them to be not puffing but express warranties. By the same token a lawyer could make assertions about his case or about the subject matter of his negotiation in general terms, and if those proved to be inaccurate, they would not be a violation of the ethical standards. Presumably such statements are not violations of the ethical standards even when they conflict with the lawyer's dispassionate analysis of the value of his case.

A third case is related to puffing but different from it. This is the use of the so-called false demand. It is a standard negotiating technique in collective bargaining negotiation and in some other multiple-issue negotiations for one side to include a series of demands about which it cares little or not at all. The purpose of including these demands is to increase one's supply of negotiating currency. One hopes to convince the other party that one or more of these false demands is important and thus successfully to trade it for some significant concession. The assertion of and argument for a false demand involves the same kind of distortion that is involved in puffing or in arguing the merits of cases or statutes that are not really controlling. The proponent of a false demand implicitly or explicitly states his interest in the demand and his estimation of it. Such behavior is untruthful in the broadest sense; yet at least in collective bargaining negotiation its use is a standard part of the process and is not thought to be inappropriate by any experienced bargainer.

Two final examples may be more troublesome. The first involves the response of a lawyer to a question from the other side. Assume that the defendant has instructed his lawyer to accept any settlement offer under $100,000. Having received that instruction, how does the defendant's lawyer respond to the plaintiff's question, "I think $90,000 will settle this case. Will your client give $90,000?" Do you see the dilemma that question poses for the defense lawyer? It calls for information that would not have to be disclosed. A truthful answer to it concludes the negotiation and dashes any possibility of negotiating a lower settlement even in circumstances in which the plaintiff might be willing to accept half of $90,000. Even a moment's hesitation in response to the question may be a nonverbal communication to a clever plaintiff's lawyer that the defendant has given such authority. Yet a negative response is a lie.

It is no answer that a clever lawyer will answer all such questions about authority by refusing to answer them, nor is it an answer that some lawyers will be clever enough to tell their clients not to grant them authority to accept a given sum until the final stages in negotiation. Most of us are not that careful or that clever. Few will routinely refuse to answer such questions in cases in which the client has granted a much lower limit than that discussed by the other party, for in that case an honest answer about the absence of authority is a quick and effective method of changing the opponent's settling point, and it is one that few of us will forego when our authority is far below that requested by the other party. Thus despite the fact that a clever negotiator can avoid having to lie or to reveal his settling point, many lawyers, perhaps most, will sometime be forced by such a question either to lie or to reveal that they have been granted such authority by saying so or by their silence in response to a direct question. Is it fair to lie in such a case?

Before one examines the possible justifications for a lie in that circumstance, consider a final example recently suggested to me by a lawyer in practice. There the lawyer represented three persons who had been charged with shoplifting. Having satisfied himself that there was no significant conflict of interest, the defense lawyer told the prosecutor that two of the three would plead guilty only if the case was dismissed against the third. Previously those two had told the defense counsel that they would plead guilty irrespective of what the third did, and the third had said that he wished to go to trial unless the charges were dropped. Thus the defense lawyer lied to the prosecutor by stating that the two would plead only if the third were allowed to go free. Can the lie be justified in this case?

How does one distinguish the cases where truthfulness is not required and those where it is required? Why do the first three cases seem easy? I suggest they are easy cases because the rules of the game are explicit and well developed in those areas. Everyone expects a lawyer to distort the value of his own case, of his own facts and arguments, and to deprecate those of his opponent. No one is surprised by that, and the system accepts and expects that behavior. To a lesser extent the same is true of the false demand procedure in labor-management negotiations where the ploy is sufficiently widely used to be explicitly identified in the literature. A layman might say that this behavior falls within the ambit of "exaggeration," a form of behavior that while not necessarily respected is not regarded as morally reprehensible in our society.

The last two cases are more difficult. In one the lawyer lies about his authority; in the other he lies about the intention of his clients. It would be more difficult to justify the lies in those cases by arguing that the rules of the game explicitly permit that sort of behavior. Some might say that the rules of the game provide for such distortion, but I suspect that many lawyers would say that such lies are out of bounds and are not part of the rules of the game. Can the lie about authority be justified on the ground that the question itself was improper? Put another way, if I have a right to keep certain information to myself, and if any behavior but a lie will reveal that information to the other side, am I justified in lying? I think not. Particularly in the case in which there are other avenues open to the respondent, should we not ask him to take those avenues? That is, the careful negotiator here can turn aside all such questions and by doing so avoid any inference from his failure to answer such questions.

What makes the last case a close one? Conceivably it is the idea that one accused by the state is entitled to greater leeway in making his case.

Possibly one can argue that there is no injury to the state when such a person, particularly an innocent person, goes free. Is it conceivable that the act can be justified on the ground that it is part of the game in this context, that prosecutors as well as defense lawyers routinely misstate what they, their witnesses, and their clients can and will do? None of these arguments seems persuasive. Justice is not served by freeing a guilty person. The system does not necessarily achieve better results by trading two guilty pleas for a dismissal. Perhaps its justification has its roots in the same idea that formerly held that a misrepresentation of one's state of mind was not actionable for it was not a misrepresentation of fact.

In a sense rules governing these cases may simply arise from a recognition by the law of its limited power to shape human behavior. By tolerating exaggeration and puffing in the sales transaction, by refusing to make misstatement of one's intention actionable, the law may simply have recognized the bounds of its control over human behavior. Having said that, one is still left with the question, Are the lies permissible in the last two cases? My general conclusion is that they are not, but I am not nearly as comfortable with that conclusion as I am with the conclusion about the first three cases.

Taken together, the five foregoing cases show me that we do not and cannot intend that a negotiator be "truthful" in the broadest sense of that term. At the minimum we allow him some deviation from truthfulness in asserting his true opinion about cases, statutes, or the value of the subject of the negotiation in other respects. In addition some of us are likely to allow him to lie in response to certain questions that are regarded as out of bounds, and possibly to lie in circumstances where his interest is great and the injury seems small. It would be unfortunate, therefore, for the rule that requires "fairness" to be interpreted to require that a negotiator be truthful in every respect and in all of his dealings. It should be read to allow at least those kinds of untruthfulness that are implicitly and explicitly recognized as acceptable in his forum, a forum defined both by the subject matter and by the participants.

Notes and Questions

1.   Is Professor White right that a negotiator "must be fair and truthful" on the one hand but that he "must mislead his opponent" on the other?

2.   Do you agree with Professor White's view that there are permissible and impermissible lies? Consider the following excerpt from Professor Gerald Wetlaufer arguing that lawyer-negotiators cannot distinguish between types of lies:

> For purposes of this Article, 'lying' will be defined to include all means by which one might attempt to create in some audience a belief at variance with one's own. These means include intentional communicative acts, concealments and omissions. The exact boundaries of 'lying' as defined, is a subject to which we will, in due course, devote a good deal of attention.

It has been suggested that this definition of lying is too broad and that one should, at this early stage of the inquiry, acknowledge a distinction between lying and other lesser deceptions. My reasons for not doing so are three. First, it is perfectly appropriate, at least in American usage, to define lying as I have done. Second, as is made clear in the new OXFORD ENGLISH DICTIONARY, there is a strong measure of euphemism in our habit of reserving 'lying' for only the most serious offenses. This tendency toward euphemism can bring considerable confusion to the inquiry at hand. Third, the desire to distinguish lying from lesser deceptions rests on the assumption that there is a moral or ethical distinction between these two categories of conduct.

Gerald Wetlaufer, *The Ethics of Lying in Negotiations*, 75 Iowa L. Rev. 1219, 1223 (1990).

3. In each of the five cases Professor White discusses, do you agree with his conclusions about whether it is permissible to mislead your opponent? For a discussion of similar issues focusing on the lawyer's obligation, see Rex R. Perschbacher, *Regulating Lawyers' Negotiations*, 27 Ariz. L. Rev. 75 (1985).

4. From Professor White's perspective, how would you respond to the following: Assume you represent a plaintiff in a personal injury case who sustained a back injury. You have had a series of negotiations with the insurance company claims adjuster in which you indicated, truthfully, that because of the back injury, your client has had to give up all vigorous activity for an indefinite period of time. Yesterday, your client told you he had played two sets of tennis in each of the last two weeks, with only minor soreness. This indicates he is recovering much more quickly than anyone anticipated. Would you volunteer this information at the next meeting with the claims adjuster? How would you respond if the claims adjuster asked, "Is your client able to exercise at all?" *See* Thomas F. Guernsey, *Truthfulness in Negotiation*, 17 U. Rich. L. Rev. 99, 113–23 (1982); David Luban, *Bargaining and Compromise: Recent Work on Negotiation and Informal Justice*, 14 Phil. & Pub. Aff. 397 (1985).

d. Moral Obligation

Does the lawyer-negotiator's obligation to her counterpart extend beyond merely being truthful? According to Professor Jonathan Cohen, lawyer-negotiators have a moral obligation to treat one another with respect.

JONATHAN R. COHEN, WHEN PEOPLE ARE THE MEANS: NEGOTIATING WITH RESPECT

14 Geo. J. Legal Ethics 739, 741–43, 749–51 (2001).

The topic of negotiation ethics is by no means new. Negotiation has long been a hallmark of social development, and from ancient times writers have been concerned with how negotiation should be practiced. Were the Biblical characters Rebecca and Jacob wrong to deceive Isaac, by masquerading and outright lying, so as to ensure that Isaac's blessing passed to Jacob rather than Esau? If a merchant porting grain by ship from Alexandria to famine-stricken Rhodes overtakes at sea several other vessels also porting grain to Rhodes, should he, upon arriving in Rhodes, reveal the imminent arrival of those other vessels, or should he bargain without revealing that information? To this day the puzzles of deception and disclosure have remained at the heart of most discussions of negotiation ethics within the American legal community, with occasional attention paid to the topic of fairness. Yet there is a fundamental domain within negotiation ethics that relates to, but is distinct from, these topics that has been largely unaddressed. I call this the ethics of orientation. The purpose of this Article is to explore that domain.

To introduce this domain, consider the following question: What distinguishes negotiation from interpersonal interactions generally? A basic difference is that in negotiation, each party attempts to get the other party to do something, or at least explores that possibility. Put differently, in negotiation the other party is a potential means towards one's ends. If two people are chatting about the weather, rarely will their conversation end with an exchange of promises. If they are negotiating the sale of a car, it very well may.

This basic difference between negotiation and most social interactions points to a core question, or tension, lying within the domain of orientation ethics. Usually we think of other people as, well, people. Yet negotiation may pull us towards seeing others as mere instruments for achieving our purposes. To borrow from the language of Martin Buber, in negotiation we are drawn towards reducing the other person from a "Thou" to an "It." Negotiation thus presents an apparent ethical tension that I call the object-subject tension: when negotiating, how is one to reconcile the impulse to treat the other person as a mere means toward one's ends with general ethical requirements for treating people? In response, I argue that in negotiation one should see the other party both as a means toward one's ends and as a person deserving respect. More specifically, the act of negotiation does not relieve one of the moral duty to respect others. This duty of respect implicates both the traditional negotiation ethics topics of deception, disclosure and fairness and also topics such as manipulation, coercion, listening, and autonomy.

* * *

What orientation should one take towards the other party in a negotiation?

A hard-nosed "realist" might claim that, in a negotiation, the other party is a possible means to one's ends, an instrument toward one's goals. This is undoubtedly true and relevant. However, it is only a partial picture. One's stance towards the other party in negotiation should recognize more than just that person's instrumentality.

Sometimes one's relationship with the other party affects what orientation one should take when negotiating. If a parent and child are negotiating over the child's bedtime, one would hope that they see themselves not as adversaries but rather as members of a loving family. A good parent should ask both "What will work for me?" and "What will be best for my child?" Athletes in team sports often face similar situations. "If I pass the ball, my individual scoring 'stats' may be lower, but it might help the team to win. What should I do?" Implicitly, the issue faced is whether the athlete sees her teammates as rivals or as partners, or as a combination of both.

Even if one does not have a prior relationship with the other party, the other party is still a human being, and it is morally relevant to see the other party as such. Skeptics might argue, "What difference does it make what orientation I take towards the other party? That's just a matter of my internal beliefs." Yet beliefs affect actions. Is it wrong to intimidate another person? Then prima facie it should be wrong to intimidate that other person in negotiation. The same applies to deception, coercion, threats, incivility, psychological assaults, manipulation, and so on. If it is wrong to treat people in these ways, then, unless compelling justification is given (e.g., few would say that it was wrong for the Allies to deceive the Nazis about where the Normandy invasion would occur), it remains wrong to do so in negotiation. A fundamental moral challenge in negotiation is seeing the fundamental dignity of people despite their instrumentality.

Note the linkage here between orientation ethics and more traditional topics within negotiation ethics, such as lying, failing to disclose material information, or substantive unfairness in bargaining outcomes. Seeing the other party as a person with fundamental dignity provides a moral basis for refraining from acts such as treating him unfairly, deceiving him, and so on. Derived from the concept of fundamental human dignity, a very high level of care should attach to our interactions with one another. It is no excuse for a hard-nosed person to say, "I treat people as objects, and that is how I expect them to treat me." There may well be other possible moral bases for refraining from such immoral acts (e.g., religious beliefs that God will punish you if you lie), but seeing the other party as a person deserving of respect provides a solid one.

Notes and Questions

1. How does a lawyer-negotiator both see "the other party as a person deserving of respect" and attempt to secure the greatest advantage possible for her client? Is there an irreconcilable tension between a lawyer-negotiator's duty to her client and her ethical obligations to the human being on the other side of the table?

2. What other moral obligations might a negotiator owe her counterpart, in addition to the respect that Professor Cohen suggests?

3. How might the cultivation of mindfulness discussed in Chapter II, beginning at page 150, affect a negotiator's morals and choices with respect to her style of negotiation? *See* Scott R. Peppet, *Can Saints Negotiate? A Brief Introduction to the Problems of Perfect Ethics in Bargaining*, 7 Harv. Negot. L. Rev. 83, 84–90 (2002).

F. THE ROLES OF CULTURE, GENDER, AND RACE IN NEGOTIATION

When negotiating, people often make assumptions about the motives and goals of their counterparts. Sometimes these assumptions are grounded on substantial experience in negotiating with that person or others who seem similar to her. In other cases, these assumptions are grounded on stereotypes, which themselves may be based on experience or common understandings about characteristics of people who belong to a certain gender or cultural group. Other times these stereotypes will prove useful; sometimes, however, they will mislead. This section's readings focus on actual and perceived differences based on culture, gender, and race at the bargaining table.

1. CULTURE

"Culture" is not a simple concept. In the following readings, Professor Jayne Seminare Docherty, an anthropologist, describes three different ways of thinking about culture and negotiation. Moving from what she considers to be the least sophisticated to the most sophisticated, these three approaches are the "tip of the iceberg" approach, the "patterns" approach, and the "symmetrical anthropology" approach. Below, we consider each of these in turn and then explore subcultures as well. Seminare's "tip of the iceberg" is followed by two excerpts, the first of which advises Australians on negotiating with Chinese and the second of which advises Japanese on negotiating with Americans. Assuming you are familiar with either Chinese or American culture, ask yourself how helpful you think these characterizations really are as you read those excerpts.

a. The "Tip of the Iceberg" Approach to Culture

JAYNE SEMINARE DOCHERTY, CULTURE AND NEGOTIATION: SYMMETRICAL ANTHRO- POLOGY FOR NEGOTIATORS

87 Marq. L. Rev. 711, 712–13 (2004).

Unfortunately, some negotiation texts — particularly but not exclusively popular books on negotiation — focus almost entirely on the part of the iceberg visible above the surface. In these texts, cultures are presented as lists of do's and don'ts. These lists are rooted in stereotypes and are of dubious value. Teaching negotiators about culture in this manner is of limited value and might actually be dangerous in some settings.

Furthermore, this approach contains a number of faulty assumptions about human beings and about culture. Lists of do's and don'ts: Do not offer your left hand to an Arab; learn how to deeply bow to a Japanese negotiator; understand the protocols for offering refreshment to a Turkish counterpart; treat culture as a superficial overlay that covers a universal human nature or perhaps a universal human culture; deep down, where it counts, all persons are fundamentally the same when it comes to reasoning, emotionality, needs, and desires. This confusion arises because there is a generic human culture, 'a species-specific attribute of Homo sapiens, an adaptive feature of our kind on this planet for at least a million years or so.' But there are also local cultures — 'those complex systems of meanings created, shared, and transmitted (socially inherited) by individuals in particular social groups'. It is local cultures that can create problems in negotiation.

IYLA DAVIES & GAY CLARKE, THE ART OF WAR BETWEEN FRIENDS: SUCCESSFULLY NEGOTIATING WITH THE CHINESE

L. Soc'y J. (Australia), Mar. 1994, at 38, 38–40, 42.

The purpose of this article is to familiarise Australian lawyers with the Chinese negotiating style. This analysis will provide only a general overview of the style utilised. However, it should be noted that because of China's sheer size (with a population of over one billion people), regional variations will occur. National variations are also evident between Chinese residents of mainland China, Hong Kong and Taiwan.

The cultural aspects of negotiation strategies will be focused upon. The political aspects will of course be important in negotiating with mainland Chinese officials. However, such matters are beyond the scope of this article.

The time factor

The Chinese negotiating style is traditionally time consuming. The need to take time in negotiating has been linked to the Chinese need to construct a firm relationship with the other party.

Three cultural factors are referred to in explaining the need to be patient in negotiating with the Chinese. The first acknowledges that the Chinese "have a long-range view of things and are therefore in less of a hurry". The second explanation relies upon the Chinese desire for perfection as they "want to be exactly sure of everything and avoid all possible mistakes". The third explanation emanates from the Chinese desire to personally 'invest' in the business relationship, accordingly they "distrust fast talkers who want to make quick deals".

For those who wish to conduct business quickly and impersonally, negotiations with the Chinese will be a frustrating experience. In Hong Kong and Taiwan the pace of life has been affected by substantial contact with the West, whereas in mainland China things continue to move at a slower pace.

Chin–Ning Chu, in her book *The Chinese Mind Game: The Best Kept Trade Secrets of the East,* suggests that the tradition of the "scholarly way of being" lies behind the slow pace. Historically, great wisdom was thought only to emanate from slow and laborious study. Scholars who worked as if time were eternal were revered and honoured and mimicked in business.

Time management is not a major consideration in Chinese business and the priority placed upon speed and efficiency by Western business practices is frowned upon by the Chinese. Time is often more important than money to Westerners, and this is clearly not the case for the Chinese: "Time has never been equal to money as it tends to be in the West. In China, money is money and time is time". One Western businessman who has conducted a considerable amount of business in China has gone so far as to conclude that Western haste has cost companies dearly in dealing with the Chinese and that taking the time to conduct business at the "Chinese pace" may be the single most important thing for Westerners to learn.

Consensus and harmony

In Western business culture the 'secrets of success' are often thought to emanate from certain characteristics. Rampant individualism, an aggressive manner and confrontationalist behaviour are often thought to be the traits of successful entrepreneurs in the West. The Chinese, however, do not value these characteristics. Instead, the attainment of objectives through group effort and the maintenance of harmonious relations are very important. Aggressive and confrontationalist behaviour is perceived as a weakness of character by the Chinese.

Chinese societies are not litigious. The Chinese prefer to resort to other means of dispute resolution such as negotiation and mediation. Various forms of mediation proceedings have been used by the Chinese for centuries. The Chinese will go to extreme lengths to avoid direct confrontation.

The Chinese ideals of consensus and harmony are thought to be connected to the main principles of Chinese religion and philosophy.

One of the main symbols of Chinese philosophy, the Yin and Yang, embodies the concept of harmony. The Yin and Yang symbol portrays the perfect balance between the female and the male, the light and darkness, the positive and the negative and the balance between all things in the universe. Harmony in every aspect of life is considered the ideal.

At the negotiating table

At the negotiating table the ideal of harmony is evidenced by the consensual style of decision-making. A Chinese negotiating team will often temporarily adjourn proceedings in order to meet privately and ascertain what the consensus of the group is. The process of consensus-gathering may also involve important people who are outside the negotiating team. The Chinese do not consider it necessary to have all interested parties at the negotiating table. This may be contrasted with the importance placed upon face-to-face negotiating in the West. The pattern of consensus-gathering also contrasts with the individualist behaviour exhibited by Western negotiators.

Confrontationalist behaviour between members of a negotiating group is avoided as the members of the group will go along with whatever decision is reached by the consensus process. Chinese negotiators are not impressed by the competitive behaviour via which the individualist attempts to be noticed, and such displays of overtly aggressive and competitive behaviour usually have an adverse effect upon negotiation proceedings with the Chinese. Negotiators from the West would be well advised to curtail such behaviour when negotiating with people from a culture which idealises consensus and harmony.

Friendship or guanxi

The Chinese concept of *guanxi* or 'friendship' is very different to the Western concept. To the Chinese, the sharing of *guanxi* entails the creation of a special relationship between individuals or groups of individuals. The relationship implies that each party will be able to make unlimited demands upon the other.

The party to whom the request is made is obliged to respond positively to the demands. The concept of *guanxi* has been linked to the Chinese sense of dependency and accordingly the subordinate party in the *guanxi* relationship gains extensive rights over the superior party.

The Chinese often welcome Westerners with offers of friendship and flattery including asides about their own inferiority. In these circumstances the *guanxi* relationship may arise without any conscious effort on the part of the visitor from the West.

In the West if a friend is unable to be helpful in relation to one matter it is quite acceptable for them to seek out another way to compensate the friend. Pursuant to the Chinese concept of *guanxi* such conduct is unacceptable and is considered to be of "questionable morality". The attempted trade-off implicit in such conduct is a denial of the total commitment which is inherent in the *guanxi* relationship.

At the negotiating table

The difference between the Western and the Chinese concept of friendship may give rise to many problems at the negotiating table. The Chinese will invariably try to establish a *guanxi* relationship by offering friendship and complimenting the other party at the beginning of the negotiating process.

A Western negotiator may believe that such conduct is merely a meaningless formality or simply a form of traditional Chinese custom. The negotiator may be totally unaware of the obligation which is created when giving a response which includes an exchange of friendship and an intimation of helpfulness in the future. A negotiator who is aware of the commitment involved in the *guanxi* relationship will be able to consciously accept the relationship with all of its ramifications or to deliberately and overtly avoid the creation of the bond. It is interesting to note that Japanese negotiators usually resist the establishment of a *guanxi* relationship.

Face

The Chinese concept of 'face' is well-known throughout the West and much has been written about it. It has been described as an "extreme sensitivity to personal dignity". Any incident or matter which injures an individual's pride or reduces one's status is seen as a loss of face.

At the negotiating table

A negotiator from the West needs to be sensitive to the potential for loss of face throughout the negotiation process. An incident which causes nothing more than embarrassment to a negotiator from the West may constitute a loss of face for a Chinese negotiator and accordingly form an obstacle in future proceedings.

One concept relating to face which is not as well known in the West is the counterpart of the 'losing of face' namely, the 'gaining of face' or the 'granting of face'. Much may be gained by flattering a Chinese negotiator and deliberately trying to boost the negotiator's self-esteem. In the West such conduct may be seen as insincere or meaningless. However, in this context it will help alleviate any anxieties about self-esteem which the Chinese negotiator may have.

The concept of face may be linked to the concept of *guanxi*, in fact it will be extremely difficult to grant face to a Chinese negotiator without entering the commitment of *guanxi*. A negotiator who is unwilling to establish the *guanxi* relationship will probably have to forego the positive advantages to be gained from the giving of face. The negotiator in such circumstances may still avoid causing any loss of face by being sensitive to the Chinese vulnerability in self-esteem.

* * *

Conclusion

Australian lawyers have much to gain from an understanding of the Chinese cultural traits which affect negotiation proceedings. Recognition of their own negotiating style will further enhance the likelihood of successful negotiations with the Chinese. The temptation for Australian negotiators to employ Chinese strategies in order to attempt to out-manoeuvre their Chinese counterparts must be resisted.

"It is impossible to out-Chinese the Chinese. It is foolish to try to."

However, it is imperative that Australian negotiators are sensitive to the cultural differences in order to ensure that effective negotiations take place.

ANONYMOUS, A JAPANESE VIEW OF AMERICAN NEGOTIATORS*

Negotiators from the United States are difficult to understand because they come from a background of different nationalities and

---

* This reading, purportedly written by a Japanese person who has negotiated with Americans, has appeared previously in several publications. We first encountered it in the materials for a CLE program conducted by Professor John Haley of the University of Washington and sponsored by the Washington Law Foundation in 1996. It was also reprinted in Yukio Yanagida, et al., Law and Investment in Japan 219, 220–22 (1994), which gives a publication history.

experiences. Unlike Japanese, the Americans are not racially or culturally homogeneous. Even their way of speaking English varies. Gaining a
good understanding of one U.S. representative is only a little help in
understanding others. Americans from large cities are different from
those coming from small towns. There are differences between East,
West, North and South, as well as in religion and national origin.

Thus, much of what they do is truly unpredictable and erratic. At
the same time, there is no reason to suspect that beneath the rather
disorderly appearance of U.S. negotiating teams, whose members often
seem to not be listening to each other and who may not even dress in the
same style, there is a calculated set of tactics and objectives that guides
them. Sometimes U.S. representatives seem to make mistakes or to be
ignorant of commonly known facts, but their lack of humility in such
cases may mean that they really know what they are doing.

* * *

Adversarial Approach

Americans also highly value what they call adversary proceedings.
This seems to come from their court system, where two sides argue their
cases in a direct confrontation with no effort made to find any harmony
at all. Then the judge issues a ruling one way or the other without
private consultation with the two sides and with no value given to
conciliating the feelings of those in the case. Americans believe this
undemocratic system is the best way to learn the truth and impose
justice.

Americans sometimes say "truth is relative," or that "there is no
such thing as black and white, only shades of grey," but often they act
differently. They are seekers of truth and morality, just as we are, but
they think truth and morality exist apart from the practical world
around them. So in a negotiation it is common for American negotiators
to say what basic principles are important. Later they may reject a sound
practical idea because it violates principle. Therefore, it is necessary to
be cautious about agreeing to any statement of principles and always
point out the need for workable understandings. One possibility is that
their fixed ideas about truth come from the Christian religion, which
promises perfection at some future time or after death, so many American negotiators try to negotiate perfect and final agreements, which they
think will never need reinterpretation or adjustment. Indeed, once an
agreement is signed they may be very rigid about it because they think it
is perfect. * * *

They often talk about how hard we Japanese work, but many
Americans work hard and they can be extremely clever sometimes.
However, they seem to attribute their leadership status not to hard work
but to the idea that they know the truth and are moral. Thus, they are
convinced that their ideas are right and others must follow or reveal

themselves as fools or knaves. This may seem a harsh judgment, and it is overstated, but Americans are often ethnocentric without knowing it.

U.S. Negotiating Preparations

Without access to their secrets, I can only guess, from their behavior and what they tell me, how the Americans prepare for negotiations. Often they argue among themselves in public, so it is safe to assume that they argue even more in private. This is part of their idea of adversary proceedings and they seem to feel no shame about such embarrassing behavior.

The procedures they use include careful study of the Japanese position, the reasons for it, and the negotiating pressure each side can apply. They spend the most time on their own position. Like the Japanese government, they have many different agencies with different interests that must be reconciled. This is done by circulating draft papers and holding meetings at which middle level officials discuss what to do. Each of these officials represents his own superiors and has limited power to express his own ideas, unlike Japanese officials at that level whose advice is usually accepted since they have more time to study and become experts on detailed matters.

U.S. negotiators often have fallback positions which they can use if they do not win agreement to first proposals. These fallbacks are worked out in advance almost as if they knew their first offers were unreasonable. They do not prepare one approach as the best under the circumstances, while giving their negotiators the authority to approach the matter flexibly. Therefore, it is necessary for us to learn what the final fallback is as early as possible. Once that information is obtained, it is often possible to get the U.S. side to offer its fallback proposal in return for a concession of no consequence.

The Americans also try to predict what our reactions will be. They prepare contingency plans, which they hope will counter our statements, again believing that confrontation and rebuttal are necessary. They seem to value highly winning such arguments. When arguments do develop, U.S. negotiators may become tense; after that they may try to distract attention from a difficult situation by resorting to humor. Their humor is hard to understand since it is based on their own rather strange cultural experience, but it is safe to laugh when they do.

In the Negotiating Room

U.S. negotiating teams are sometimes small and are sometimes large. Their delegations are often large when the internal disagreements between agencies have not been reconciled before the meeting, and therefore each department must send an agent, or, on the other hand, perhaps because of internal jealousy. They do not always admit observers from interested agencies and seldom have anyone present for training purposes or as an extra notetaker. Thus our delegation is usually larger.

Americans are quite conscious of protocol, so it is necessary to consider seating and the matters of introductions and entertainment. They often say that rank means nothing to them, but it really does. On the other hand, when mistakes are made they adapt easily and are not offended if the matter is quietly corrected. In short, they want the proper gestures made but are satisfied with that. They also like to be invited to social events where they say they dislike discussing business and then in fact they easily agree to do so. Such occasions are useful for testing compromises and obtaining information on their fallback positions.

The Progress of Talks

Americans are energetic and persistent. They are enthusiastic negotiators who seldom take naps during talks even if the topic at hand is of no real concern. They enjoy arguing the logic of their position, which they like to describe as good for all and not just for them. They have a disturbing habit, however, of passing over very quickly the areas of agreement and giving high emphasis to disagreements. In fact, they talk about little else, as if that were the most important subject.

Americans like to concentrate on one problem at a time. They seem not to understand that the whole picture is more important, and they spend little time on developing a general understanding of the views and interests of both sides. Since their habit of focusing on one issue often forces a direct disagreement, they often propose setting the issue aside, but they come back to it later with the same attitude and concentration. A negotiation with them may therefore become a series of small conflicts and we must always make a special effort to give proper attention to the large areas of agreement and common interest.

b. The "Patterns" Approach to Culture

JAYNE SEMINARE DOCHERTY, CULTURE AND NEGOTIATION: SYMMETRICAL ANTHRO-POLOGY FOR NEGOTIATORS

87 Marq. L. Rev. 711, 713–14 (2004).

A more sophisticated approach to culture in negotiation involves identifying patterns or types of cultures by studying a large group of cultures. Instead of getting inside of a specific culture to understand it, this approach stands outside of cultures and looks for patterns or cultural styles. These are often presented as a list of dichotomous characteristics including: high context/low context; individualism/collectivism; and egalitarian/hierarchical. A high-context culture often relies on indirect communication, because the participants are expected to understand the complex meaning of relatively small non-verbal gestures. A low-context culture will tend to rely on direct statements and formal, clear ratification of written negotiated agreements. Negotiators from individualist cultures may worry less about preserving relationships than negotiators from collectivist cultures. And, negotiators from egalitarian cultures are likely to be less concerned about issues of rank and privilege than negotiators from hierarchical cultures.

* * *

The goal in identifying types of cultures or developing cultural profiles is to alert negotiators to communication patterns and to provide cautionary advice about how to communicate in a particular cultural context or with someone from a particular culture. This way of thinking about culture is more useful for negotiators than lists of traits as long as they recognize the following: these dichotomies are actually continua; within cultures, changes in context (e.g., family versus business setting) will lead people to locate in different places along the continua; there are subcultural variations within any culture; and not all individuals carry their culture in exactly the same way.

At least this approach to culture alerts people to the fact that *they* have a culture too! The issue is not what is wrong with that person from another culture, but where the mismatches are between our cultures. On the other hand, describing cultures as a collection of styles or preferences that impact communication and therefore negotiation still does not get us at the deepest part of the iceberg. Many people who talk about culture this way miss the point that conflict as a domain of social interaction and negotiation as a mechanism for communicating about conflict are both culturally constructed. All cultures have conflict, but not all cultures see the same problems as conflicts, nor do they make the same assumptions about how human beings should respond to conflict. All cultures have processes we can identify as negotiation, but they do not all negotiate the same way.

Notes and Questions

1.   Professor Docherty refers to three different dichotomies that researchers have studied: high-context versus low-context, individualist versus collectivist, and egalitarian versus hierarchical. Researchers categorize the United States as low-context, individualist, and egalitarian. For more on this in the context of negotiation, see JEANNE M. BRETT, NEGOTIATING GLOBALLY (2001).

2.   Using these dichotomies, how would you describe the culture of a workplace in which you have been employed? Your law school? The legal profession in general?

c.   "Symmetrical Anthropology" Approach to Culture

JAYNE SEMINARE DOCHERTY, CULTURE AND NEGOTIATION: SYMMETRICAL ANTHRO-POLOGY FOR NEGOTIATORS

87 Marq. L. Rev. 711, 714–17 (2004).

The most complete and sophisticated way of thinking about culture and negotiation requires that we greatly enrich our definition of culture.

Avruch offers the following definition: 'For our purposes, *culture* refers to the socially transmitted values, beliefs and symbols that are more or less shared by members of a social group, and by means of which members interpret and make meaningful their experience and behavior (including the behavior of 'others').' He also points out that this definition includes a number of assumptions. First, individuals belong to multiple groups and therefore carry multiple cultures. The implication is that an encounter between two individuals is likely to be a *multicultural* encounter since each participant can draw on more than one culture to make sense of the situation. This includes negotiation encounters. Second, it is important to understand the institutions and mechanisms that transmit culture. Third, culture is almost never perfectly shared by all members of a community or group. Individuals have the capacity to selectively adopt and adapt their multiple cultures, so you cannot assume that a person from culture X will do Y. Each party can draw from, adapt, and modify a multifaceted set of cultural norms and rules; therefore every intercultural encounter is a complex improvisational experience.

It is critically important to remember that our own cultures are largely invisible to us; they are simply our 'common sense' understandings of the world. Hence, 'conflict is, at essence, the construction of a special type of reality. Most of the time we assume and take for granted that we share a single reality with others, but we do not.' We see culture when we are forced to recognize that not everyone experiences and lives in the world the way we do. Perhaps we experience 'language shock' when we recognize that someone may be speaking the same language, but we are not sure they live on the same planet we do. Or, we may encounter someone whose 'moral order' — their 'pattern of ... compulsions and permissions to act in certain ways and [their] prohibitions against acting in other ways' — differs from our own. In negotiations, these moments of shock and surprise may occur around issues of risk because risk is very much a cultural construct. We may also experience surprise when people use the same language, even the same metaphors, but we discover that their shared language is actually covering over profound differences in their sense of reality. What *we* assume is negotiable may not be negotiable to another person and vice versa.

As negotiators, the recognition that we have a culture too reshapes the reality within which we work. We are forced to grapple with the fact that the very domain of our work — social conflict — is culturally constructed.

* * *

When we encounter cultural differences about when and how to negotiate, we can focus on what the other person is doing 'wrong' compared to us.... Or, instead of focusing on what is wrong with the other culture, we can become adept at a form of 'symmetrical anthropology' that is 'capable of confronting not beliefs that do not touch us directly — we are always critical enough of them — but the true knowledge to which we adhere totally.' We can subject our own culture(s) to the same scrutiny we apply to the culture(s) of others. That means we will need to become critically aware of our own assumptions about negotiation. What does it mean to say 'get beneath positions to interests?' Does everyone share the assumptions about human nature and social relationships on which this approach to finding a 'win-win' solution rests?

Notes and Questions

1. Professor Docherty offers several suggestions to those who would like to improve their skills as "symmetrical anthropologists," including broadening one's expectations, attempting to understand our own and others' worldviews, and exploring the metaphors that people embroiled in conflict use in their speech.

2. How might one handle cultural differences in negotiation? Consider the following suggestion:

> What, then, are some implications of this brief essay for more effective negotiation across cultural/national boundaries? First, while cultural/national boundaries clearly *do* exist, much of what passes for such differences may well be the result of expectations and perceptions which, when acted upon, help to bring about a form of self-fulfilling prophecy. Perhaps the best way to combat such expectations is to go out of one's way to acquire as much information as one can beforehand about the way people in other cultures view the kind of problem under consideration. Thus, if we are negotiating with a German about a health care contract, we should try to find out whatever we can about how Germans tend to view health care. Of course, in large countries, there may be regional variations that also need to be taken into account.

> Second, it is important to enter into such negotiations with self-conscious awareness of the powerful tendency we share toward stereotyping; this kind of consciousness-raising may, in its own right, help make it a bit less likely that we will slip into a set of perceptual biases that overdetermine what transpires in the negotiations proper.

> Third, it is important to enter into negotiations across cultural/national lines by trying to give your counterpart the (cultural) benefit of the doubt. Just as you would not wish others to assume that you are nothing more than an exemplar of people from your culture, try similarly to avoid making the same mistaken assumption about the other person.

Jeffrey Z. Rubin & Frank E. A. Sander, *Culture, Negotiation, and the Eye of the Beholder*, 7 NEGOTIATION J. 249, 252 (1991).

3. Professor Ilhyung Lee argues that cross-cultural negotiation should be taught in more law schools. Ilhyung Lee, *In re Culture: The Cross-cultural Negotiations Course in the Law School Curriculum*, 20 Ohio St. J. on Disp. Resol. 375 (2005). Do you agree?

d. Subcultures

When negotiating with a person from a substantially different culture, it may be easy to spot some differences in basic approaches to negotiation. However, when negotiating with someone from our own culture but a different subculture — a different ethnic group, business, organization, or even law school — it may be more difficult to observe such differences. The following excerpt illustrates this problem.

LEONARD L. RISKIN, OBEY THE RULE: JUST SAY "NO, NO, NO,"

Chi. Trib., June 25, 1992, at C19.

Right after my speech, a tall woman in a gray business suit rushed forward and said she'd like to meet me for breakfast to discuss professional collaboration. The next morning, before I had tasted my fresh-squeezed orange juice, we both realized that our interests did not match. As I wiped the last bits of the $14.25 Eggs Benedict from my beard, my companion did something that brightened my day immeasurably: She asked the waiter to put both checks on one bill. But when she fumbled awkwardly for her cash, I was impelled to ask whether she would be reimbursed. "Yes," she replied, "but it's from a very limited fund." Reflexively, I blurted out, "I'd be glad to pay my share." And she snapped up my offer.

I was stunned. I quickly recovered my composure, however, when I realized that she accepted my offer only because she thought I meant it. And this misapprehension was in no way her fault.

To grasp the complexity of my state of mind, the woman would have had to drop in on a gathering in my parents' plushly carpeted living room in the 1950s, when I was a schoolboy learning the basics of manners.

There she would schmooze with my relatives and my parents' friends, locked into an irregular circle — formed by a shiny green sofa (from which the plastic cover had been removed for the occasion), three folding "bridge" chairs, two wing-back chairs and an old piano bench — with each guest clutching a tall glass embellished with a frosted flower and brimming with what was known in Milwaukee as "white soda." About 9:15, just as my Tante Nettie mumbles, "Time to go home," my mother throws open the sliding door from the kitchen, steps into the living room and announces she's prepared "a little something to eat." This draws a negative cacophony: "Why did you go to all that trouble?" "My stomach has been bothering me." "I'm on a diet." My mother deftly undercuts their positions: "I've done it already. I had everything in the house. It will all go to waste. Just have a bite." Because of the logic and force of my mother's arguments, most of the group moves, with only mild grumbling, into the kitchen, there to encounter a semi-lavish and overabundant presentation of homemade strudel, sweet rolls, cheese, bread and coffee.

Although my mother has won the major battle, she must carry out several "mopping up" operations — one-on-one combat, to ensure that the guests don't just sit there, but eat! At this point, the players act out the principle that muddled up the end of my breakfast: The Rule of Threes. In its simplest formulation, the rule provides that "Any offer worth making — or any refusal meant sincerely — must be extended three times, unless it is accepted first." For instance:

My mother: "Have some strudel." Her friend Rose (who eats like a bird): "No thanks." My mother: "You eat like a bird." Rose: "I am full, and I've been having stomach trouble." My mother: "Oh, a little bit won't hurt you." Rose: "I am really full." My mother: "Are you sure you won't have just a little?" Rose: "Well, maybe a tiny bit."

Rose proceeds to eat more than my cousins Donny and Delores combined.

Now the Rule of Threes was never meant to be followed woodenly. Its legitimate purpose is simply to help you find out what the other person really wants. Since we can never truly understand another person, the Rule of Threes substitutes for that understanding in the same sense that the adversary process in a court substitutes for truth or justice.

But I've seen friends and relatives twist the rule and employ it to serve another precept — that "It is better, much better, to give than to receive." For instance, any time my parents gave my maternal grandmother a gift, she replied (even before she saw the gift): "That's ridiculous. Why did you spend money on me?" After she opened the box and saw the dress — it was always a dress — she insisted that she didn't need it. After protesting for at least five minutes in at least three languages, she caved in: "All right, if it will make you happy, I will keep it."

My analysis: Giving a gift creates an indebtedness from the recipient (my grandmother) to the giver (my mother). This means that the giver has "won" and the recipient lost. But the recipient can dilute the victory by saying she did not need the gift, that she is accepting it only to please the gift giver. In other words, she in fact is bestowing a good on the gift giver, and — by thus demonstrating that she is a superior person — has "won."

In restaurants, dining with friends and relatives, the rules were more complex — because the stakes were much higher. In a restaurant, the question of who picked up the check could have significant financial consequences. So all the rituals were subservient to the general principle that "He who is best off should pay." Usually, this meant my cousin Joe, who was single and almost wealthy, or my Uncle Max, who could sell aluminum siding to homeless people.

But not before virtually everyone at the table reached for that check, or snatched at it with the same blend of aggression and reticence displayed by two golden retrievers locked in a ritualistic battle — lots of snarling and snapping, but no real attempt to make contact.

On at least one occasion, I manipulated the Rule of Threes in a way that now seems cruel, deploying it against a person who was unaware of the rule, an unarmed civilian, so to speak. It was my friend Isidore, from Montreal, who was visiting my wife and me for a week in Washington. Playing the gracious host (and the prosperous American lawyer), I paid for all the food, at home and in restaurants. But on the last night of Isidore's visit, the three of us were sitting in Luigi's restaurant, playing with the hot wax that dripped onto the gingham tablecloth from the candle stuck into the top of a chianti bottle (this was the early '70s). Isidore said he wanted to pay the bill, and he reached for it. But he was no match for me. I snatched the bill before he could get it. And when he protested that I had paid for all the meals, I said he could reciprocate — when we visited him in Montreal. I expected him to keep offering, but he did not; and so I paid.

He looked surprised, as I recall, perhaps hurt. He really wanted to pay, I guess, but he didn't know what it took. I regretted my behavior almost immediately and have continued to regret it for almost 20 years. This is partly because I wanted him to pay, too, and partly because I thought I had robbed him of a measure of dignity. But there is another reason: I went to Montreal last summer with my family, and I thought Isidore would repay my largesse in a good French restaurant. I tried to call him, but he is not listed in the telephone book.

Notes and Questions

1. This excerpt suggests that, in a variety of settings, people will not always say what they mean or mean what they say. In fact, sometimes a negotiator may say the opposite of what he or she means. Accordingly, the listener, even if he comes from the same general culture, may often misinterpret the intended message. This is less likely to happen when the negotiation is conducted by lawyers or other agents who share a common negotiation culture.

2. How could you interpret the negotiation described in the foregoing excerpt in terms of the distinction between high and low context cultures? Consider Riskin's "offer" to pay for his breakfast. In the high-context culture of his family, would that offer have been interpreted in the way that he intended it? Why did he assume, if he did, that his breakfast companion would understand his intention?

Can you recall negotiations or even conversations in which you misunderstood or were misunderstood because of the differing assumptions about the context or meaning of a something said or done? How can you, as a negotiator, determine that your counterpart means what he or she says? How can you enhance the likelihood that your counterpart will understand what you mean to convey?

3. For another example of negotiation problems between persons from the same culture but different subcultures, see TRACEY KIDDER, HOUSE 31–47 (1985).

2. GENDER

Gender may also play a role in negotiation. The following excerpt explores some empirically documented differences in the negotiation behavior of men and women. The first portion of the reading highlights an alleged weakness in the negotiation behavior of many women; the second portion of the reading highlights an alleged strength in the negotiation behavior of many women. As you read this, whether you are male or female, consider whether, in your experience, this rings true.

LINDA BABCOCK & SARA LASCHEVER, WOMEN DON'T ASK: NEGOTIATION AND THE GENDER DIVIDE

1–3, 9–10, 165–66, 167–69, 170, 171–72 (2003).

Could it be that women don't get more of the things they want in life in part because they don't think to ask for them? Are there external pressures that discourage women from asking as much as men do — and even keep them from realizing what they can ask? Are women really less likely than men to ask for what they want?

To explore this question, Linda conducted a study that looked at the starting salaries of students graduating from Carnegie Mellon University with their master's degrees. When Linda looked exclusively at gender, the difference was fairly large: The starting salaries of the men were 7.6 percent or almost $4,000 higher on average than those of the women. Trying to explain this difference, Linda looked next at who had negotiated his or her salary (who had asked for more money) and who had simply accepted the initial offer he or she had received. It turned out that only 7 percent of the female students had negotiated but 57 percent (eight times as many) of the men had asked for more money. Linda was particularly surprised to find such a dramatic difference between men and women at Carnegie Mellon because graduating students are strongly advised by the school's Career Services department to negotiate their job offers. Nonetheless, hardly any of the women had done so. The most striking finding, however, was that the students who had negotiated (most of them men) were able to increase their starting salaries by 7.4 percent on average, or $4,053 — almost exactly the difference between men's and women's average starting pay. This suggests that the salary differences between the men and the women might have been eliminated if the women had negotiated their offers.

Spurred on by this finding, Linda and two colleagues, Deborah Small and Michele Gelfand, designed another study to look at the propensity of men and women to ask for more than they are offered. They recruited students at Carnegie Mellon for an experiment and told them that they would be paid between three and ten dollars for playing *Boggle* ™, a game by Milton Bradley. In *Boggle*, players shake a cube of tile letters until all the letters fall into a grid at the bottom of the cube. They must then identify words that can be formed from the letters vertically, horizontally, or diagonally. Each research subject was asked to play four rounds of the game, and then an experimenter handed him or her three dollars and said, "Here's three dollars. Is three dollars okay?" If a subject asked for more money, the experimenters would pay that participant ten dollars, but they would not give anyone more money if he or she just complained about the compensation (an indirect method of asking). The results were striking — almost *nine times* as many male as female subjects asked for more money. Both male and female subjects rated how well they'd played the game about equally, meaning that women didn't feel they should be paid less or should accept less because they'd played poorly. There were also no gender differences in how much men and women complained about the compensation (there was plenty of complaining all around). The significant factor seemed to be that for men, unhappiness with what they were offered was more likely to make them try to fix their unhappiness — by asking for more.

In a much larger study, Linda, Michele Gelfand, Deborah Small, and another colleague, Heidi Stayn, conducted a survey of several hundred people with access to the Internet (subjects were paid ten dollars to log on to a website and answer a series of questions). The survey asked respondents about the most recent negotiations they'd attempted or initiated (as opposed to negotiations they'd participated in that had been prompted or initiated by others). For the men, the most recent negotiation they'd initiated themselves had occurred two weeks earlier on average, while for the women the most recent negotiation they'd initiated had occurred a full month before. Averages for the second-most-recent negotiations attempted or initiated were about seven weeks earlier for men and twenty-four weeks earlier for women.

These results suggest that men are asking for things they want and initiating negotiations much more often than women — two to three times as often. Linda and her colleagues wanted to be sure that this discrepancy was not produced simply by memory lapses, however, so the survey also asked people about the *next* negotiation they planned to initiate. In keeping with the earlier findings, the negotiations planned by the women were much further in the future than those being planned by the men — one month ahead for the women but only one week ahead for the men. This means that men may be initiating *four* times as many negotiations as women. The sheer magnitude of this difference is dramatic, especially since respondents to the survey included people of all ages, from a wide range of professions, and with varied levels of education. It confirms that men really do take a more active approach than women to getting what they want by asking for it.

* * *

Besides not realizing that asking is possible, many women avoid negotiating even in situations in which they know that negotiation is appropriate and expected (like the female students in the starting salary study). In another one of Linda's studies, 20 percent of the women polled said that they never negotiate at all. Although this seems unlikely (perhaps these women think of their negotiations as something else, such as "problem-solving" or "compromising" or even "going along to get along"), their statement conveys a strong antipathy toward negotiating among a huge number of women. (In the United States alone, 20 percent of the female adult population equals 22 million people.)

That many women feel uncomfortable using negotiation to advance their interests — and feel more uncomfortable on average than men — was confirmed by a section of Linda's Internet survey. This part of the survey asked respondents to consider various scenarios and indicate whether they thought negotiation would be appropriate in the situations described. In situations in which they thought negotiation was appropriate, respondents were also asked to report how likely they would be to negotiate in that situation. Particularly around work scenarios, such as thinking they were due for a promotion or a salary increase, women as a group were less likely to try to negotiate than men — even though they recognized that negotiation was appropriate and probably even necessary.

These findings are momentous because until now research on negotiation has mostly ignored the issue of when and why people attempt to negotiate, focusing instead on tactics that are successful once a negotiation is underway–what kinds of offers to make, when to concede, and which strategies are most effective in different types of negotiations. With few exceptions, researchers have ignored the crucial fact that the most important step in any negotiation process must be deciding to negotiate in the first place. Asking for what you want is the essential first step that "kicks off" a negotiation. If you miss your chance to negotiate, the best negotiation advice in the world isn't going to help you much. And women simply aren't "asking" at the same rate as men.

* * *

Up to this point in the book we've focused on the socialization that often prevents women from asking for more of life's bounty — and on the discouraging responses they often get when they do negotiate. But women also have some advantages that can make them outshine men at negotiating. Although the more aggressive approach favored by many men can win good short-term results, women's focus on cooperation and relationship building can be a huge advantage. This is because a multitude of negotiation studies in the past two decades have shown that a cooperative approach, aimed at finding good outcomes for all parties rather than just trying to "win," actually produces solutions that are objectively superior to those produced by more competitive tactics. The influence of this line of research has been so profound, and the behaviors it recommends dovetail so nicely with women's strengths, that negotiation experts often joke that the goal of many negotiation courses today is to train people to negotiate like women. This chapter looks at how powerful the female approach to negotiating can be.

Cooperative Advantage

Why would taking a cooperative approach to a negotiation produce a better solution than just trying to get as much as you can for yourself or "your side?" The answer lies in understanding something negotiation scholars have dubbed "the mythical fixed-pie bias." Many people walk into a negotiation mistakenly assuming that their interests are in direct conflict with those of the other negotiator or negotiators. This attitude, "the mythical fixed-pie bias," creates the belief that "what is good for the other side must be bad for us." Although this is occasionally true, particularly in negotiations in which there's only one issue to be decided ("distributive" negotiations), the vast majority of negotiations are not single-issue negotiations. Much more common are multi-issue negotiations (called "integrative" negotiations), in which more than one issue needs to be decided or more than one problem needs to be solved, and the negotiators typically have different priorities. Because more issues are "in play" in an integrative negotiation, this type of negotiation allows participants to trade things they value less for other things that matter to them more, a practice called "logrolling." Perhaps most important, integrative negotiations allow for resolutions that can be good for both sides.

* * *

Real Differences

We've said that women take a more cooperative approach to negotiation and that men are usually more competitive in their attitude. But do we know this for a fact? Although this area of research is relatively new, a few studies have found that women do indeed behave differently from men when they negotiate.

In one of the earliest studies to look at this question, the researchers divided subjects into same-sex pairs to conduct a negotiation that could be settled in a distributive (i.e., competitive — I win, you lose) fashion but could also be settled more creatively so that both sides would benefit. They observed that men used distributive tactics (making threats, insulting the other side, and staking out inflexible positions) much more than women did. In two other studies that compared the characteristics of male and female managers, the business writer and consultant Sally Hegelsen found that men were much less likely than women to share information. A meta-analysis that quantified the results of numerous research studies also found differences in the ways in which men and women behave in negotiations, with women more likely to behave cooperatively than men.

Another study, by the negotiation scholars Jennifer Halperon and Judi McLean Parks, also separated subjects (undergraduates in a negotiations class) into same-sex groups of two. These all-male or all-female pairs were asked to conduct a negotiation about allocating public money to build a children's playground. One member in each pair played the role of a representative from the Parks Department and the other played a representative of a community volunteer organization.

The differences between the all-male and all-female pairs were dramatic. Males were more likely than females to talk about their positions (how much they wanted to see allocated to the project), with all of the male pairs discussing their positions but only 17 percent of the female pairs doing so. Males also used confrontational bargaining techniques (making threats or posing ultimatums) more, with men using confrontational tactics nine times as much as women did. (Only two of the 12 female pairs became confrontational at all.)

On the other side of the equation, the female pairs talked about personal information far more than the males (92 percent of the females compared to 23 percent of the males introduced information about themselves into the negotiation). The women weren't simply making small talk, however, or asking random questions about each other's private lives. The personal information the women discussed was directly relevant to what each side wanted, and introducing this information into their negotiations helped expand their shared understanding of the goals on both sides. In addition, when the women discussed personal information, they did so within the first five minutes of the negotiation (suggesting a more efficient process) but the men who introduced personal information did so only after 20 minutes of negotiation, and only when they were having difficulty reaching an agreement.

Another interesting finding from this study involved the different ways in which the male and female negotiating teams used the case information provided to them. Whereas 50 percent of the female pairs discussed how the playground would affect a senior citizen's home nearby (falling in line with women's prescribed role as caretakers who look out for the interests of others), none of the male pairs took notice of this factor. On the other hand, 58 percent of the males but only 8 percent of the females discussed legal liability issues. This was particularly noteworthy because legal issues were not part of the case materials — the men introduced them on their own.

The results of the playground study strongly suggest that men typically focus more on the competitive elements of a negotiation (discussing their positions from the outset, resorting to confrontational behavior, talking about each side's legal responsibilities) while women focus more on the relational aspects — the needs of both sides and how the outcome of the negotiation will affect other people, such as the senior citizens. Because increasing the flow of information between the negotiators is essential to achieving a superior solution in an integrative bargain, and the female pairs exchanged much more information than the male pairs, this study suggests that women not only employ a more productive process when they negotiate — they're more likely to produce better agreements for both sides.

* * *

Women Are Better

If integrative bargaining methods produce superior results in many types of negotiations, and women are more likely than men to use these methods, this should mean that women actually make better negotiators than men. Actually, this appears to be true — at least in situations in which women's cooperative overtures are reciprocated. In one of Linda's negotiation experiments, she and her colleague Hannah Riley asked pairs of MBAs to conduct a multi-issue negotiation that possessed integrative potential. Some possible negotiated agreements could be terrific for both parties, with a wide range of alternatives in between. Linda and Hannah Riley had chosen the issues to be negotiated so that finding the better outcomes requires the negotiators to share information, and when they compared outcomes they discovered that the all-female pairs had outperformed the all-male pairs. The agreements reached by the all-female pairs were better for both negotiators than those reached by the all-male pairs on average. This strongly suggests that the female pairs shared more information and that the male and female pairs used different techniques and behaviors to achieve these results.

* * *

When Advantage Breaks Down

Although we know that the more cooperative approach women bring to negotiation can produce superior results, a good outcome using this approach is not guaranteed. When both negotiators don't share this view of a negotiation — if a man and woman take different "scripts" into a negotiation, with the man approaching it as a win/lose situation and the woman seeing it as a search for outcomes to benefit both parties — the woman's strategy, though potentially superior, can leave her vulnerable.

Linda and Hannah Riley's study mentioned above, in which the all-female pairs outperformed the all-male pairs, produced another interesting finding: The mixed female-male pairs produced agreements that were no better than those produced by the all-male pairs. Not only did the females fare much worse when they were negotiating against men than when they were negotiating with women, but the "pies" that the female/male pairs slit up were *smaller* than the "pies" divided by the all-female pairs. In other words, by sharing information and working together, the all-female pairs were able essentially to "enlarge the pie." By "logrolling" and together taking an integrative approach to the process, they were able to identify hidden benefits for both sides that went unnoticed by the pairs that took a more competitive approach. This suggests that the best outcomes are produced in situations in which both negotiators take a cooperative rather than an adversarial approach to working out a solution — that it takes two women, in other words, or two people trained to "negotiate like women," to produce a superior outcome.

Notes and Questions

1. Professor Carol Rose argues that "women's *actual* taste for cooperation — if such a taste exists — is much less important than something else: people *think* women are likely to be cooperative types." Carol M. Rose,

Bargaining and Gender, 18 Harv. J.L. & Pub. Pol'y 547, 549 (1995). Do you agree?

2.   For more on actual and assumed gender differences in negotiation, see Charles B. Craver & David W. Barnes, *Gender, Risk Taking, and Negotiation Performance*, 5 Mich. J. Gender & L. 299 (1999).

3.   What should a female do when she encounters gender-based stereotypes? Professor Andrea Schneider offers some suggestions. Her counsel is directed at the problem of offensive comments, but as you read this excerpt consider whether it has broader application.

ANDREA SCHNEIDER, EFFECTIVE RESPONSES TO OFFENSIVE COMMENTS

10 Negotiation J. 107, 111–13 (1994).

Responding

There are four major responses a negotiator can make to an offensive comment-ignoring, confronting, deflecting, or engaging. The response you choose should be based on a number of factors, including an analysis of your own assumptions and the other side's motivation for making such a comment.

Other factors — such as whether there is an audience for the comment, whether it has been repeated over time, and how much the comment personally offends you — may also be important. But the question of most significance in these situations is: What is your purpose in responding and what do you hope to achieve?

The response of ignoring the comment needs little explanation — you choose not to respond in any way. Many people end up doing this automatically in response to a comment that makes them uncomfortable. Instead, ignoring a comment should be a conscious, affirmative decision by you that either the comment does not bother you that much or it is just not worth your time and effort to deal with it.

Similarly, the response of confronting the comment is also relatively simple theoretically. Confronting is a counterattack either on the person or the comment (e.g., "That's racist! How can you say that?" or "What a stupid thing to say!") This response should also be a conscious one, a response made to achieve a purpose, not a response made just because you cannot think of anything else to say. At times, confronting is wholly appropriate and is often a highly useful response, particularly with bullies.

Deflecting means acknowledging the comment and moving on. For example, in response to someone who is bragging, about his or her grandiose office space compared with yours (which could be interpreted as demeaning), you might respond, "Yes, your office is lovely and perhaps we might now move to the subject at hand." Or, in response to someone asking you to get coffee, you might respond, "I'll call my secretary to bring us refreshments. In the meantime, can we review the contract?" Deflecting, more than any other response, is a question of personal style and comfort level. It often demands a sense of humor and even quicker thinking than other responses.

Engaging is the fourth type of response one can make to an inflammatory remark. Engaging means having a conversation about the other side's purpose in making the remark and your feelings upon hearing it. First, you check your assumptions about their intentions by asking what their purpose was in making the comment. After they respond, you can gather additional data about their intentions and ask further questions.

Finally, when you think that you understand their point of view and also have demonstrated the ability to listen to them, you share your perceptions. Explain your reaction and your reasoning (e.g., "When I hear that comment, I usually assume.... And it makes me feel, think, etc. ..."). The purpose of entering into this type of conversation is both to check your own perceptions and to educate the other side about your perceptions in a way that is nonconfrontational and nonthreatening.

Engaging the other side with regard to the objectionable comment has several advantages over the other responses. Since engaging follows a pattern, it can be a learned skill. Having a practiced reaction to a comment that throws you off balance in a negotiation can be a great advantage. Engaging also gives you more time to think since you are asking questions — another advantage when you are surprised.

Engaging allows you the opportunity to check your perceptions and assumptions once again. In particular, if you do not know the other side, running through charts and decision trees in your own mind may not be helpful when you have very little data on which to base your conclusions. Engaging them can help you determine if the comment was conscious or unconscious, prejudice or ignorance.

Since engaging is nonconfrontational, it is more appropriate for professional and long-term relationships. Engaging allows both you and the other side to rethink assumptions without escalating the conflict. The two of you can agree that there was a misunderstanding and move on to the substance of the negotiation rather than continue to disagree about the comment and each other's worth as a person. It is better for the relationship than confronting since it may provide each side with a way out of the conflict. It is also better than ignoring the comment if the comment will fester within you and color your future interactions.

Engaging can be particularly useful with someone using biased comments as a tactic for two reasons. First, it throws them off to be asked a question about why they made the comment, and second, your question lets them know that you know the game they are playing. Engaging also gives you back control over the conversation since you are directing it through your questions.

Engaging does not preclude the responses of confronting or deflecting. Once you learn more about what they are thinking, you can still decide to confront them or deflect the comment based on that additional knowledge.

Engaging is also something that you can do at later date after further reflections upon the comment. You can still bring the comment up the next day if you initially ignored it or deflected it and it continues to bother you or if you confronted the comment but are not pleased with the outcome of that conversation.

For example, a black person responding to a question about his or her family's educational history could start an engaging conversation by asking , "Why did you ask me if I was the first person in my family to graduate college?" The other side might respond, "Well, I just think that it's wonderful that you went to college and did so well." The black person might follow up by acknowledging the compliment and then asking the other negotiator if he or she thinks that it is so rare for black people to go to college. The other side may respond, "No, but when they come from disadvantaged backgrounds, it's much more of an achievement."

Now that the black person understands the other side's intentions and reasoning, he or she can share their feeling:" Well, when people ask me if I am the first in my family it makes me feel as if I were somehow less worthy to go to college because of my race and background. Rather than take it as a compliment, which is how you intended it, I interpret that question as a slur on my family." If the exchange has gone well, the other side may respond, "I never realized that. I did not intend to insult you in any way."

Engaging conversations can be as explosive as confronting situations, depending on the tone of the engager and the attitude of the person who made the original comment. Yet they have the possibility to educate and to change behavior in the future.

A key difference between confronting and engaging is the acceptance of responsibility for whatever feelings or thoughts you may have. For example, in confronting, you often accuse the other side of having a certain type of character or intention. This, of course, can be disputed by them. When you discuss how the comment makes you feel (engaging), there is no room for disagreement. The issue is not what they intended — of which you cannot really be sure — but what you feel — which they cannot dispute.

* * *

3. RACE

Like culture and gender, race may influence negotiation behavior. The following excerpt reports the results of a study of negotiations at car dealerships. Professor Ian Ayres found significant differences in outcomes based on the race and gender of the prospective car buyers.

IAN AYRES, FAIR DRIVING: GENDER AND
RACE DISCRIMINATION IN RETAIL
CAR NEGOTIATIONS

104 Harv. L. Rev. 817, 817–19, 827–33 (1991).

The civil rights laws of the 1960s prohibit race and gender discrimination in the handful of markets — employment, housing, and public
accommodations — in which discrimination was perceived to be particularly acute. In recent years, lawsuits have increasingly presented claims
of more subtle and subjective forms of discrimination within these
protected markets. Both legislators and commentators, however, have
largely ignored the possibility of discrimination in the much broader
range of markets left uncovered by civil rights laws. Housing and
employment may be the two most important markets in which people
participate, but women and racial minorities may also be susceptible to
discrimination when spending billions of dollars on other goods and
services. Of these unprotected markets, the market for new cars is
particularly ripe for scrutiny because, for most Americans, new car
purchases represent their largest consumer investment after buying a
home. In 1986, for example, more than $100 billion was spent on new
cars in the United States.

This Article examines whether the process of negotiating for a new
car disadvantages women and minorities. More than 180 independent
negotiations at ninety dealerships were conducted in the Chicago area to
examine how dealerships bargain. Testers of different races and genders
entered new car dealerships separately and bargained to buy a new car,
using a uniform negotiation strategy. The study tests whether automobile retailers react differently to this uniform strategy when potential
buyers differ only by gender or race.

The tests reveal that white males receive significantly better prices
than blacks and women. As detailed below, white women had to pay
forty percent higher markups than white men; black men had to pay
more than twice the markup, and black women had to pay more than
three times the markup of white male testers. Moreover, the study
reveals that testers of different race and gender are subjected to several
forms of nonprice discrimination. Specifically, testers were systematically
steered to salespeople of their own race and gender (who then gave them
worse deals) and were asked different questions and told about different
qualities of the car.

* * *

II. RESULTS OF THE TEST

The results from the tester surveys provide a rich database for
investigating how salespeople bargain and whether they treat testers of a
different race or gender differently. This Part presents the results of
these tests in three sections. The first section reports disparate treat-

ment regarding the prices that dealerships were willing to offer the testers. This section includes an analysis of both initial and final offers as well as refusals to bargain and differences in the bargaining paths (the sequence of offers made in succeeding rounds). In the second section, nonprice dimensions of the bargaining process are analyzed. The tests reveal that salespeople asked testers different types of questions and used different tactics in attempting to sell the cars. Finally, the third section uses multivariate regression analysis to analyze the determinants of the final offers. The regressions reveal a fairly sophisticated seller strategy. In particular, the size of final offers is sensitive not only to the race and gender of both the tester and the salesperson, but also to the information revealed by the tester in the course of bargaining.

A. Price Discrimination

1. *Final Offers.* — The final offer of each test was the lowest price offered by a dealer after the multiple rounds of bargaining. By comparing these final offers with independent estimates of dealer cost, it was possible to calculate the dealer profit associated with each final offer (final offer minus dealer cost). For a sample of 165 tester visits, the average dealer profits for the different classes of tester are presented in Table 1.

TABLE 1:
Average Dealer Profit for Final Offers

White Male	$ 362
White Female	504
Black Male	783
Black Female	1237

Black female testers were asked to pay over three times the markup of white male testers, and black male testers were asked to pay over twice the white male markup. Moreover, race and gender discrimination were synergistic or superadditive: the discrimination against the black female tester was greater than the combined discrimination against both the white female and the black male tester.

The reliability of these results is buttressed by an analysis of the relative unimportance of individual effects. The average dealer profits on the non-white male testers were statistically different from the average profits on the white males at a five percent significance level. The average profits for the three individual white males were, however, not significantly different from each other. This last result lends support to the proposition that the idiosyncratic characteristics of at least the white male testers did not affect the results.

To determine whether the final offer discrimination stemmed from disparate treatment in sellers' initial offers or from disparate treatment in the sellers' subsequent concession rates, we calculated the average offers testers received in each round of bargaining. Graphically, the differences in final offers can be decomposed into differences in the intercept and differences in the slope: different intercepts represent disparate initial offers; different slopes represent disparate rates of concession. We found that the concession rates do not significantly differ across tester type or across bargaining rounds. The average dealer offers in the initial and subsequent rounds of bargaining, however, differed significantly. For example, the average dealer offers made to black females were significantly higher than those made to white males, but the rate of concession was virtually the same. These results indicate that discrimination in early rounds tends to be perpetuated in later rounds: final offer discrimination is caused by disparate initial offers and not by disparate concession rates. Sellers quoted testers disparate initial offers and then made roughly equal concessions.

Arguably, this perpetuation effect may be an artifact of the testers' split the difference bargaining strategy. In particular, the script instructs testers, in calculating their second counteroffer, to split the difference between dealer's cost (the testers' first counteroffer) and the dealer's second offer. Dealer discrimination in early rounds will cause disparate concessions by testers that may preclude equal treatment in final rounds. The possibility that early offers matter, however, is not an embarrassment of design. Bargainers engage in time-consuming initial rounds of bargaining because they individually believe that these rounds will affect the final price. The tests provide strong evidence that if consumers use the same split the difference strategy, they will receive different final offers that are determined by their race and gender.

2. *Initial Offers.* This study also constructed a test of disparate treatment on the basis of the initial offers sellers made to the testers. As noted above, this short test offers more experimental control because the testers asked only a single question. The average dealer profit on initial offers are presented in Table 2.

TABLE 2:
Average Dealer Profit for Initial Offers

White Male	$ 818
White Female	828
Black Male	1534
Black Female	2169

The average dealer profit on offers made to white female testers was not significantly different from the average profit on offers made to white male testers. Sellers, however, offered both black males and black females significantly higher prices: sellers asked black males to pay almost twice the markups they charged white males, and they asked females to pay two and one-half times that markup.

3. *Willingness to Bargain.* Another potentially important form of disparate treatment concerns the sellers' willingness to bargain. Consumers are hurt if the sellers either refuse to bargain or force the consumers to spend more time bargaining to achieve the same price. An analysis of the number of bargaining rounds reveals that the average number of rounds for different types of testers did not differ significant-

ly, as shown in Table 3. The amount of time black male and white female testers spent bargaining (both total and per round) was not statistically longer than the amount spent by white male testers. Although black female testers clearly had to pay the most for cars, it was not because dealers refused to spend time bargaining with them.

TABLE 3:
Differences in Rounds

	Average # Rounds	Average Length of Test (Minutes)	Average Length per Round (Minutes)
White Male	2.43	35.8	14.8
White Female	2.21	32.9	14.9
Black Male	2.32	49.1	21.2
Black Female	3.08	34.6	11.2

Indeed, the sellers' willingness to bargain longer with black men (or for more rounds with black women) may be an indirect attempt to enhance their market power by reducing their potential competition. If the hourly costs to consumers of searching for a car increase with the time spent searching, then the longer a dealership keeps customers bargaining in its showroom, the smaller the possibility that the consumers will visit additional dealerships. In other words, dealers may intentionally try to bargain for more rounds with certain types of consumers, if doing so is particularly like to reduce the chance that they will visit other dealerships.

Notes and Questions

1. One of the acknowledged limitations of Professor Ayres's study is that it involved only six testers. To address this limitation, Professor Ayres conducted an elaborate follow-up study involving 38 testers. In it, he replicated his earlier results, with one notable exception:

> The results of the expanded audit confirm the previous finding that dealers systematically offer lower prices to white males than to other tester types. But the more comprehensive data reveal a different ordering of discrimination than in the prior study: as in the original study, dealers offered all black testers significantly higher prices than white males, but unlike the original study, the black male testers were charged higher prices than the black female testers.

Ian Ayres, *Further Evidence of Discrimination in New Car Negotiations and Estimates of its Cause*, 94 Mich. L. Rev. 109, 110 (1995).

2. What do you think accounts for the observed differences in the two studies by Professor Ayres?

3. Several noted scholars have expressed concerns about how less powerful parties or members of disadvantaged groups are likely to fare in consensual dispute resolution processes like negotiation or mediation. *See supra* Chapter I, beginning at page 21; *infra* Chapter IV, beginning at page 464. Does the Ayres excerpt corroborate their concerns? Or is a transactional

negotiation like this likely to be different from a negotiation or mediation involving a dispute between the parties?

4. In a study of outcomes obtained in negotiation simulations in his "Legal Negotiation" course, Professor Charles Craver found that race did not have a statistically significant impact on negotiation outcomes. *See* Charles B. Craver, *Race and Negotiation Performance*, Disp. Resol. Mag., Fall 2001, at 22.

G. NEGOTIATION EXERCISES

1. A TRANSACTION NEGOTIATION: THE CARTON CONTRACT[1]

Glasco Corporation of Cincinnati, Ohio, manufactures and sells glass jars for use in home canning. The company has asked its lawyer to meet with the lawyer for Quality Carton Company of Springfield, Missouri, to negotiate a contract for the delivery of a particular model of honeycomb fiber carton used for shipping the cartons.

If you were one of these lawyers, how would you decide which approach or approaches to use in negotiating this contract?

2. A DISPUTE NEGOTIATION: THE THOMPSON v. DECKER MEDICAL MALPRACTICE CLAIM[2]

GENERAL INFORMATION FOR ALL PARTICIPANTS

This is a summary of the information the attorneys in this case have stipulated to and the information the attorneys still hold in contention.

A. Statement of Claim:

Plaintiff claims $500,000 compensatory and $500,000 punitive damages against defendant for defendant's alleged negligence and battery during the course of medical treatment. Defendant denies liability on both the negligence and battery claims.

B. Undisputed Facts:

1. Ten months ago, plaintiff, a jazz pianist, consulted defendant doctor, a hand specialist, regarding a pain in her right hand. The defendant doctor diagnosed the condition as the early onset of an arthritic condition.

---

1. This exercise is based upon The Carton Contract, Videotape II in the Dispute Resolution and Lawyers Videotape Series (Distributed by West Publishing Co. (1991)), which was based upon William H. Henning, "The Mason–Dixon (Product) Line: A Transaction Negotiation Exercise" in Leonard L. Riskin and James E. Westbrook, Instructor's Manual for Dispute Resolution and Lawyers 336 (West Publishing Co. 1992). Confidential Information for the role players appears in the Instructor's Manual, and on the casebook TWEN web site at www.lawschool.westlaw.com.

2. This simulation was developed by Deborah Doxsee for the role players in Videotape I: The Thompson v. Decker Medical Malpractice Claim Negotiation (West Publishing Co. 1991). It is based upon Robert M. Ackerman, "The Case of the Weary Hand: A Negotiation Exercise for Torts" in Leonard L. Riskin and James Westbrook, Instructor's Manual for Dispute Resolution and Lawyers (West Publishing Co. 1987). Confidential instructions for the role players appear in the Instructor's Manual, and on the casebook TWEN web site at www.lawschool.westlaw.com.

2. Defendant treated plaintiff's arthritis by injecting the drug polynuvoarthromaleate (AR–21) into the palm of plaintiff's right hand.

3. Prior to injecting the AR–21, defendant told plaintiff that she might feel "a little numbness" for a short while after treatment.

4. AR–21 has recently been approved for use by the U.S. Food and Drug Administration. Approximately 10% of all practicing hand specialists use the drug for the treatment of arthritic conditions.

5. Approximately twelve hours after injection of the AR–21 the plaintiff noted a "slight tingling" in her hand, and within thirty-six hours after injection of the drug, plaintiff experienced total numbness in the fingers of her right hand. This numbness lasted eight weeks, during which plaintiff missed twenty-four scheduled performances.

6. Plaintiff received extensive therapy. The numbness has disappeared, and the plaintiff has regained the use of her right hand. Her arthritic condition continues to bother her as it did prior to her consultation with the defendant.

C. Disputed Issues of Fact:

1. Whether defendant was negligent in treating plaintiff's arthritis with an injection of AR–21.

2. Whether defendant utilized the correct procedures in injecting the AR–21.

3. Whether defendant's injection of AR–21 caused the numbness in the fingers of plaintiff's right hand.

4. Whether defendant fully and adequately informed plaintiff of the risks attendant to the use of AR–21.

D. Damages: Plaintiff claims the following damages:

1. Medical Expenses: Plaintiff claims $20,000 in damages for the cost of therapy for her right hand. Defendant contends that this sum is an unreasonable amount for the twenty therapy sessions attended by plaintiff, and that the numbness would have disappeared in three months time without therapy.

2. Lost Income: Plaintiff claims lost income of $60,000, representing the twenty–four canceled engagements, each of which would have netted the plaintiff $2,500.

3. Pain and suffering: Plaintiff claims pain and suffering in the amount of $420,000.

4. Punitive Damages: Plaintiff claims punitive damages in the amount of $500,000 in connection with her battery claim.

Additional Information:

Plaintiff's Witnesses:

1. Plaintiff will testify on her own behalf as to the treatment performed by the defendant, the therapy she underwent to restore feeling in her right hand, her pain and suffering, and her lost income.

2. An orthopedic surgeon, Dennis Waller, M.D., from a University Hospital on one side of the state, will testify as to the proper treatment of arthritis. He will state that he never uses AR–21 because the drug often causes numbness in the extremities.

3. A physical therapist, Rick Abernathy, R.P.T., will testify to the therapy he performed to restore feeling to the plaintiff's right hand, and to the reasonableness of the costs incurred for such therapy.

Defendant's Witnesses:

1. Defendant will testify as to the appropriateness of the AR–21 for the treatment of arthritis, the care she utilized in injecting the AR–21 into the plaintiff's hand, and the warning she gave the plaintiff as to the possible risks associated with the use of AR–21.

2. An orthopedic surgeon, John Sullivan, M.D., from a University Hospital on the other side of the state will testify as to the appropriateness of the use of AR–21, the risks associated with the use of AR–21, and the prognosis for persons whose fingers have been numbed by AR–21.

Discovery:

Discovery is now complete. The parties have exchanged interrogatories and summaries of testimony of medical witnesses. Both plaintiff and defendant and all witnesses have been deposed.

Stipulations:

The parties have stipulated that statements made during the course of settlement negotiations shall not be admissible at trial.

Pretrial Conference:

A pretrial conference is scheduled for one week from today. Extensive negotiations are expected prior to that time.

* * *

The following is a "copy" of the brief drug insert enclosed in the packaging of each vial of the drug. Additionally there is a longer drug description included in the vial with the specific pharmacologic properties of the drug, which fulfills the FDA regulations pertaining to the drug inserts.

POLYNUVOARTHROMALEATE

"AR–21"

ANTIRHEUMATIC & ANTI–INFLAMMATORY

Actions and Uses:

A new water soluble synthetic nonionizable preparation consisting of 50% Polynuvoarthro, a low density metallic alloy. Mechanism of action unknown, though recent research indicates that perhaps some disruption of the degenerative process occurs on a cellular level via individual cellular coating by the alloy. The major effect is a reduction of the inflammatory process early on after the onset of the arthritic condition.

There is no reparative effect. Usefulness limited to those with active rheumatoid arthritis or debilitating degenerative joint disease. Particularly good results have been reported with use in the hands and feet.

Absorption and Fate:

Readily absorbed from site of injection with limited dissemination to other soft tissues. Rapidly excreted through urine and feces with maximum of 20% remaining in tissue for prolonged period (greater than 48 hours after injection). This drug has an extremely short half-life and is most beneficial for the treatment of acute rheumatic episodes, though prolonged use is not contraindicated, and bi-weekly treatment for extended periods is not uncommon.

Contraindications and Cautions:

Similar to other synthetic low density metallic alloys. Renal insufficiency, diabetes, recent or ongoing radiation therapy, severe impairment of the hepatic, integumentary, hematopoietic or cardiac systems, presence of other chronic debilitating diseases. Safe use in pregnancy is not established.

Adverse Reactions:

G.I. — diarrhea, gastritis, colic. **Dermatologic** — skin rash, urticaria, pruritus. **G.U.** — urinary insufficiency. **CNS** — headache, dizziness, vertigo, nervousness, tinnitus, polyneuritis, transient neuralgias, occasional paralysis reported. **GENERAL** — Disruptions of the hematopoietic system (rate), and angina, hypertension, syncope, anaphylactoid response.

Route and Dosage:

Intramuscular injection; "Z" — track if possible. Adults only. Single dosage administration 25–50 mg weekly or 5–20 mg three times a week. Prolonged continuous use for 6 mos. or more is not recommended.

Chapter IV

MEDIATION

In mediation, an impartial third party helps others negotiate to resolve a dispute or plan a transaction. Unlike a judge or arbitrator, the mediator lacks authority to impose a solution. In many cultures, mediation is the predominant means of resolving disputes. So, ordinarily, a mediation is a meeting or series of meetings that are informal (compared to court or arbitration proceedings) in which the mediator helps the parties understand the matter at issue and develop ways to address it.

In the United States, the use of mediation has grown enormously since the late 1970s — much faster than other methods of dispute resolution. Thousands of disputes — from virtually every realm of human activity — are mediated each day. We find mediation of disputes involving child-custody, labor and employment relations, personal injury claims, environmental and other public issues, special education, workers compensation, business transactions, professional-client relations, bankruptcy, international relations, racial and ethnic concerns, and many other issues. Mediation, and its close cousin, facilitation, also are used by government administrative agencies, legislatures, and community and political organizations to develop plans, proposals and agreements on a huge range of issues. Formal mediation programs are sponsored by trial and appellate courts, government agencies, bar associations, business organizations, civic and religious groups, and other organizations. Many individuals and firms offer mediation services. Usually entry into mediation is voluntary, but many courts order cases, or categories of cases, into mediation — a practice that is both common and controversial.

In this chapter, we cannot hope to provide a detailed picture of mediation in the U.S. today. We will, however, present a basic introduction to mediation and help you consider the process from the perspectives of various participants:

• A lawyer, who might recommend for or against mediation to a client, represent a client in a mediation, serve as a mediator, or help to develop, promote or regulate the practice of mediation;

• A party to a dispute or potential transaction, who might (or might not) seek advice or representation from a lawyer in connection with a mediation;

- A judge or other public official, who might establish a mediation program or refer cases to mediation; and

- A mediator, who might offer services for a fee or on a pro bono basis.

In viewing mediation from each of these perspectives, this chapter seeks to emphasize three major ideas about mediation:

First, mediation has certain core characteristics: It is a non-binding process in which a third party, aspiring to be impartial, seeks to help others resolve or settle a dispute or plan a transaction.

Second, mediation comes in a huge variety of forms. Thus, mediation can be as varied as dancing, sports, or music. An aspect of the variety is captured through a number of "models" of mediation, but they can only hint at the richness and diversity of actual mediation processes. In addition, the precise characteristics of a particular mediation depend on a combination of factors, such as:

- The setting in which the dispute or potential transaction arose or is being mediated. For example, the fact that a dispute is already the subject of a lawsuit may incline the process toward a focus on legal issues.

- The attitudes and beliefs of the participants about the nature and significance of the dispute, about the nature of mediation, about their respective roles. For example, beliefs about how much the mediator should direct the process or outcome affect the mediator's behavior, which will influence the nature of the mediation.

Third, any of the participants potentially can exercise great influence over the procedures and outcomes of a mediation.

Despite the variety, which we mention above and will explore below, most mediation processes have certain common elements: The participants can include one or more mediators, who preside; parties to the dispute, or representatives (e.g., executives) of organizational parties, such as corporations or government agencies; and, in certain kinds of cases, lawyers representing the parties. Usually mediations are private and confidential, but sometimes observers are allowed. Procedures usually include presentations by the parties or lawyers or both; explorations of the parties' legal claims and underlying interests; development of options for resolution; evaluation of such options; and attempts to reach an agreement that settles the dispute and, ideally, resolves the conflict. Many mediations center around private "caucuses" between the mediator and participants on each side, though some mediators never use such private meetings.

The Chapter is organized as follows: Section A sets out the wide variety of approaches to mediation, sometimes called "models." Section B presents a more detailed look at typical mediation processes. In Section C, we take a closer look at mediation processes by examining the participants — the mediator, the parties, and the lawyers — as well as the mechanisms and forces that regulate their participation in mediation. Section D considers the circumstances in which one should use, refuse or adjust mediation, in the context of the potential risks and advantages of the informality of mediation. Section E contains instructions for three mediation exercises.

A. APPROACHES TO MEDIATION

One way to understand mediation is through "models" that commentators have developed to categorize or promote various approaches to mediation. Usually these models focus on the mediator's idea of the nature of the dispute and the mediator's role in addressing it. It is important that all participants be aware of any mental models that the mediator brings to the table, for a variety of reasons that will appear throughout this Chapter. We begin, in Section 1, with Leonard Riskin's mediation "grid," which suggests four mediator "orientations" based on (1) the extent to which the mediator tends to define the problem narrowly or broadly; and (2) whether the mediator sees her role as mainly to "evaluate" or "facilitate." In Section 2, we review other models of mediation.

1. THE "GRID" SYSTEM FOR UNDERSTANDING MEDIATOR ORIENTATIONS

LEONARD L. RISKIN, UNDERSTANDING MEDIATORS' ORIENTATIONS, STRATEGIES, AND TECHNIQUES: A GRID FOR THE PERPLEXED

1 Harv. Negot. L. Rev. 7, 8–13, 17–39 (1996).

Not long ago, a lawyer asked me to conduct a workshop, for his firm and its clients, on how to participate in a mediation. As I began to prepare this program, I realized that my co-trainers and I could not talk sensibly about how, or even whether, to participate in a mediation without knowing the nature of the process the mediator would conduct. But a bewildering variety of activities fall within the broad, generally-accepted definition of mediation — a process in which an impartial third party, who lacks authority to impose a solution, helps others resolve a dispute or plan a transaction. Some of these processes have little in common with one another. And there is no comprehensive or widely-accepted system for identifying, describing, or classifying them. Yet most commentators, as well as mediators, lawyers, and others familiar with mediation, have a definite image of what mediation is and should be.

For these reasons, almost every conversation about mediation suffers from ambiguity, a confusion of the "is" and the "ought." This creates great difficulties when people try to determine whether and how to participate in mediation, and when they grapple with how to select, train, evaluate, or regulate mediators.

The largest cloud of confusion and contention surrounds the issue of whether a mediator may evaluate. "Effective mediation," claims lawyer-mediator Gerald S. Clay, "almost always requires some analysis of the strengths and weaknesses of each party's position should the dispute be arbitrated or litigated." But law school Dean James Alfini disagrees, arguing that "lawyer-mediators should be prohibited from offering legal advice or evaluations." Formal ethical standards have spoken neither clearly nor consistently on this issue.

Other issues also bedevil the mediation field. People of good will argue about whether mediation should be employed in cases involving constitutional rights, domestic violence, or criminal activity. Program planners differ on how to select mediators. Trainers disagree on the place of the private caucus. Commentators debate whether the mediator should bear responsibility for the outcome of environmental mediation. Lawyers and judges argue about whether a judge may order a represented client to attend a settlement conference along with her or his lawyer. Disputants selecting a mediator worry about bias and whether the neutral should have "subject-matter expertise." And many lawyers and clients wonder about what exactly mediation is and how it differs from other dispute resolution processes.

The bulk of these disagreements arise out of clashing assumptions — often unarticulated — about the nature and goals of mediation. Nearly everyone would agree that mediation is a process in which an impartial third party helps others resolve a dispute or plan a transaction. Yet in real mediations, goals and methods vary so greatly that generalization becomes misleading. This is not simply because mediators practice differently according to the type of dispute or transaction; even within a particular field, one finds a wide range of practices. For example, in studying farm-credit mediation, I discerned two patterns of mediation, which I called "broad" and "narrow." These patterns differed so radically that they could both be called mediation only in the sense that noon meals at McDonald's and at Sardi's could both be called lunch.

The confusion is especially pernicious because many people do not recognize it; they describe one form of mediation and ignore other forms, or they claim that such forms do not truly constitute mediation. I do not aim in this Article to favor one type of mediation over another, although, like most mediators, I incline toward a certain approach. Instead, I hope to facilitate discussions and to help clarify arguments by providing a system for categorizing and understanding approaches to mediation. I try to include in my system most activities that are commonly called mediation and arguably fall within the broad definition of the term. I know that some mediators object to such inclusiveness, and fear that somehow it will legitimize activities that are inconsistent with the goals that they associate with mediation. Although I sympathize with this view, I also disagree with it. Usage determines meaning. It is too late for commentators or mediation organizations to tell practitioners who are widely recognized as mediators that they are not, in the same sense that it is too late for the Pizza Association of Naples, Italy to tell Domino's that its product is not the genuine article. Such an effort would both cause acrimony and increase the confusion that I am trying to diminish. Instead, I propose that we try to categorize the various approaches to mediation so that we can better understand and choose among them.

* * *

II. THE PROPOSED SYSTEM

The system I propose describes mediations by reference to two related characteristics, each of which appears along a continuum. One continuum concerns the goals of the mediation. In other words, it measures the scope of the problem or problems that the mediation seeks to address or resolve. At one end of this continuum sit narrow problems, such as how much one party should pay the other. At the other end lie very broad problems, such as how to improve the conditions in a given community or industry. In the middle of this continuum are problems of intermediate breadth, such as how to address the interests of the parties or how to transform the parties involved in the dispute.

The second continuum concerns the mediator's activities. It measures the strategies and techniques that the mediator employs in attempting to address or resolve the problems that comprise the subject matter of the mediation. One end of this continuum contains strategies and techniques that *facilitate* the parties' negotiation; at the other end lie strategies and techniques intended to *evaluate* matters that are important to the mediation.

The following hypothetical, developed by Professor Charles Wiggins, will help illustrate the system of categorization that I propose.

COMPUTEC

Golden State Savings & Loan NTC is the second largest savings and loan association in the state. Just over a year ago, it contracted with Computec, a computer consulting firm, to organize and computerize its data processing system and to operate that system for a period of ten years. Computec thus became responsible for all of the computer-related activities of the savings and loan, such as account management, loan processing, investment activity, and payroll. Golden State agreed to pay Computec a consulting and administration fee of over one million dollars per year for the term of the contract.

At the end of the first year of operation under this contract, Computec presented Golden State with a bill for approximately $30,000 in addition to the agreed-upon fee. This bill represented costs incurred by Computec staff in attending seminars and meetings related to the installation of computer technology in banks, and costs incurred while meeting with various outside consultants on aspects of the contract with Golden State. Upon receipt of this bill, Golden State wrote to Computec, advising Computec that because Golden State could find no express term in the contract requiring reimbursement for these charges, and because the bank had a strict policy against reimbursement for such expenses incurred by its own employees, it would not reimburse Computec staff for similar expenses. Computec responded quickly, informing Golden State that this type of charge was universally reimbursed by the purchaser of computer consulting services, and that it would continue to look to Golden State for reimbursement.

The conflict is generating angry feelings between these two businesses, who must work together closely for a number of years. Neither party can see any way of compromising on the costs already incurred by Computec, and of course Computec expects to be reimbursed for such charges in the future as well. Under applicable law, reasonable expenses directly related to the performance of a professional service contract are recoverable as an implied term of the contract if it is industry practice that they be so paid. It is unclear, however, whether the purchaser of these services must be aware of the industry practice at the time of contracting.*

A. *The Problem–Definition Continuum: Goals, Assumptions, and Focuses*

The focus of a mediation — its subject matter and the problems or issues it seeks to address — can range from narrow to broad. Here, I identify four "levels" of a mediation that correspond to different degrees of breadth.

1. *Level I: Litigation Issues*

In very narrow mediations, the primary goal is to settle the matter in dispute though an agreement that approximates the result that would be produced by the likely alternative process, such as a trial, without the delay or expense of using that alternative process. The most important issue tends to be the likely outcome of litigation. "Level I" mediations, accordingly, focus on the strengths and weaknesses of each side's case.

In a "Level I" mediation of the Computec case, the goal would be to decide how much, if any, of the disputed $30,000 Golden State would pay to Computec. The parties would make this decision "in the shadow of the law."[116] Discussions would center on the strengths and weaknesses of each side's case and on how the judge or jury would likely determine the relevant issues of fact and law.

2. *Level II: "Business" Interests*

At this level, the mediation would attend to any of a number of issues that a court would probably not reach. The object would be to satisfy business interests. For example, it might be that Golden State is displeased with the overall fee structure or with the quality or quantity of Computec's performance under the contract, and the mediation might address these concerns. Recognizing their mutual interest in maintaining a good working relationship, in part because they are mutually

---

116. See Robert H. Mnookin & Lewis Kornhauser, Bargaining in the Shadow of the Law: The Case of Divorce, 88 Yale L.J. 950 (1979).

dependent, the companies might make other adjustments to the contract.

Broadening the focus a bit, the mediation might consider more fundamental business interests, such as both firms' need to continue doing business, make profits, and develop and maintain a good reputation. Such a mediation might produce an agreement that, in addition to disposing of the $30,000 question, develops a plan to collaborate on a new business venture. Thus, by exploring their mutual business interests, both companies have the opportunity to improve their situations in ways they might not have considered but for the negotiations prompted by the dispute.

3. *Level III: Personal/Professional/Relational Issues*

"Level III" mediations focus attention on more personal issues and interests. For example, during the development of the $30,000 dispute, each firm's executives might have developed animosities toward or felt insulted by executives from the other firm. This animosity might have produced great anxiety or a loss of self-esteem. On a purely instrumental level, such personal reactions can act as barriers to settlement. Although Fisher, Ury and Patton tell us to "separate the people from the problem," sometimes the people *are* the problem. Thus, mediation participants often must address the relational and emotional aspects of their interactions in order to pave the way for settlement of the narrower economic issues. In addition, addressing these relational problems may help the parties work together more effectively in carrying out their mediated agreement.

Apart from these instrumental justifications, addressing these personal and relational problems can be valuable in its own right. Focusing on such issues may be important even if the mediation does not produce a solution to the narrower problems. In other words, a principal goal of mediation could be to give the participants an opportunity to learn or to change. This could take the form of moral growth or a "transformation," as understood by Bush and Folger to include "empowerment" (a sense of "their own capacity to handle life's problems") and "recognition" (acknowledging or empathizing with others' situations). In addition, the parties might repair their relationship by learning to forgive one another or by recognizing their connectedness. They might learn to understand themselves better, to give up their anger or desire for revenge, to work for inner peace, or to otherwise improve themselves. They also might learn to live in accord with the teachings or values of a community to which they belong.

4. *Level IV: Community Interests*

"Level IV" mediations consider an even broader array of interests, including those of communities or entities that are not parties to the immediate dispute. For example, perhaps the ambiguity in legal principles relevant to the Computec case has caused problems for other companies; the participants might consider ways to clarify the law, such as working with their trade associations to promote legislation or to produce a model contract provision. In other kinds of disputes, parties might focus on improving, or "transforming," communities.

Figure 1 illustrates and summarizes the type of problems that appear along the problem-definition continuum. Of course, mediations that employ broader problem-definitions can include resolution of narrower problems that appear to the left on the continuum. Thus, a mediation of the Computec case that addresses the underlying business interests also could resolve the distributive issue — how much of the $30,000, if any, does Golden State pay to Computec? As the problem broadens, however, the distributive issue could become less important. Thus, if the two feuding executives learn to understand each other, instead of deciding how much Golden State will pay to Computec, they might arrive at an agreement that washes away that distributive issue. For example, they might decide to serve the firms' underlying business interests by creating a joint venture to market computer services to financial institutions, with a $30,000 seed-money contribution from Golden State and an employee loaned by Computec. In other words, in moving from narrow to broad definitions of the subject matter of a mediation, one's view of the conflict can change from that of a problem to be eliminated to that of an opportunity for improvement.

FIGURE 1

PROBLEM–DEFINITION CONTINUUM

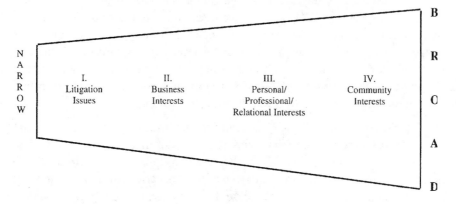

Within a given mediation, a particular problem or issue can have either primary or secondary significance. In a very narrow mediation of Computec, for example, the primary focus is on how much of the $30,000, if any, Golden State will pay. Yet, even in such a mediation, the participants might benefit in secondary, broader ways. They could, for example, feel vindicated, satisfied, or enlightened as to their own situation or that of their counterpart. This might permit greater empathy and the ability to rebuild their working relationship. And any of these developments could transform them, in ways large or small. In a narrow mediation, however, such outcomes claim only secondary importance, as occasional by-products of solving the central, distributive issue. The participants — including the mediator — may not think or care about such outcomes.

B. *The Mediator's Role: Goals and Assumptions Along The Facilitative–Evaluative Continuum*

The second continuum describes the strategies and techniques that the mediator employs to achieve her goal of helping the parties address and resolve the problems at issue. At one end of this continuum are strategies and techniques that *evaluate* issues important to the dispute or transaction. At the extreme of this evaluative end of the continuum fall behaviors intended to direct some or all of the outcomes of the mediation. At the other end of the continuum are beliefs and behaviors that *facilitate* the parties' negotiation. At the extreme of this facilitative end is conduct intended simply to allow the parties to communicate with and understand one another.

The mediator who evaluates assumes that the participants want and need her to provide some guidance as to the appropriate grounds for settlement — based on law, industry practice or technology — and that she is qualified to give such guidance by virtue of her training, experience, and objectivity.

The mediator who facilitates assumes that the parties are intelligent, able to work with their counterparts, and capable of understanding their situations better than the mediator and, perhaps, better than their lawyers. Accordingly, the parties can develop better solutions than any the mediator might create. Thus, the facilitative mediator assumes that his principal mission is to clarify and to enhance communication between the parties in order to help them decide what to do.

To explain the facilitative-evaluative continuum more fully, I must demonstrate how it relates to the problem-definition continuum. The relationship is clearest if we show the problem-definition continuum on a horizontal axis and the facilitative-evaluative continuum on a vertical axis, as depicted in Figure 2. The four quadrants each represent a general orientation toward mediation: evaluative-narrow, facilitative-narrow, evaluative-broad, and facilitative-broad.

FIGURE 2

MEDIATOR ORIENTATIONS

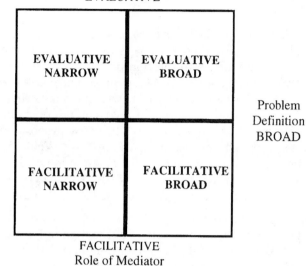

C. *The Four Orientations: Strategies and Techniques*

Most mediators operate from a predominant, presumptive or default orientation (although, as explained later, many mediators move along continuums and among quadrants). For purposes of the following explication of mediator orientations, I will assume that the mediator is acting from such a predominant orientation. For this reason, and for convenience, I will refer to the "evaluative-narrow mediator" rather than the more precise, but more awkward, "mediator operating with an evaluative-narrow approach."

A mediator employs strategies — plans — to conduct a mediation. And a mediator uses techniques — particular moves or behaviors — to effectuate those strategies. Here are selected strategies and techniques that typify each mediation orientation.

1. *Evaluative–Narrow*

A principal strategy of the evaluative-narrow approach is to help the parties understand the strengths and weaknesses of their positions and the likely outcome of litigation or whatever other process they will use if they do not reach a resolution in mediation. But the evaluative-narrow mediator stresses her own education at least as much as that of the parties. * * *

a. *Assess the strengths and weaknesses of each side's case.* — In the Computec case, an evaluative mediator might tell Computec's representatives that, even if a court were to interpret the law as they hoped, the firm would have trouble meeting its burden of establishing the existence of an industry custom that purchasers of such services normally pay the related travel expenses of their suppliers. The mediator would explain her reasoning, invoking her experience and knowledge.

b. *Predict outcomes of court or other processes.* — In Computec, the mediator might predict for Golden State the likely rulings on issues of law and fact, the likely outcome at trial and appeal, and the associated costs.

c. *Propose position-based compromise agreements.* — A mediator can make such proposals with varying degrees of directiveness. Some mediators might suggest resolution points so gently that they are barely evaluative — for instance, throwing out a figure at which she thinks the parties might be willing to settle, without suggesting that this corresponds to what would happen in court or is otherwise an appropriate settlement point. A slightly more directive proposal might be to ask Computec, "Would you accept $12,000?" or "What about $12,000?" A still more directive proposal would be to suggest that the case might settle within a certain range, say $10,000–$15,000. An even more directive move would be to say, "I think $12,000 would be a good offer."

d. *Urge or push the parties to settle or to accept a particular settlement proposal or range.* — In the Computec case, the mediator might tell Computec that she thinks Computec "should" accept a settlement offer of $12,000 because that would protect it against the risk and expense of litigation or because it is "right" or "fair" or "reasonable." If the mediator has any sort of "clout," she may threaten to use it. Or she may engage in "head-banging."

2. *Facilitative–Narrow*

The facilitative-narrow mediator shares the evaluative-narrow mediator's general strategy — to educate the parties about the strengths and weaknesses of their claims and the likely consequences of failing to settle. But he employs different techniques to carry out this strategy. He does not use his own assessments, predictions, or proposals. Nor does he apply pressure. He is less likely than the evaluative-narrow mediator to request or to study relevant documents. Instead, believing that the burden of decision-making should rest with the parties, the facilitative-narrow mediator might engage in any of the following activities.

a. *Ask questions.* — The mediator may ask questions — generally in private caucuses — to help the participants understand both sides' legal positions and the consequences of non-settlement. The questions ordinarily would concern the very issues about which the evaluative-narrow mediator makes statements — the strengths and weaknesses of each side's case and the likely consequences of non-settlement, as well as the costs of litigation (including expense, delay, and inconvenience).

b. *Help the parties develop their own narrow proposals.* — In the Computec case, for instance, a facilitative-narrow mediator would help each party develop proposals as to how much of the $30,000 Golden State would pay.

c. *Help the parties exchange proposals.* — The mediator might present party proposals in private caucuses or encourage parties to make such proposals in a joint session. In either event, he would encourage participants to provide a rationale for each proposal that might help the other side accept it.

d. *Help the parties evaluate proposals.* — To do this, the mediator might ask questions that would help the parties weigh the costs and benefits of each proposal against the likely consequences of non-settlement.

The facilitative nature of this mediation approach might also produce a degree of education or transformation. The process itself, which encourages the parties to develop their own understandings and outcomes, might educate the parties, or "empower" them by helping them to develop a sense of their own ability to deal with the problems and choices in life. The parties also might acknowledge or empathize with each other's situation. However, in a narrowly-focused mediation, even a facilitative one, the subject matter normally produces fewer opportunities for such developments than does a facilitative-broad mediation.

3. *Evaluative–Broad*

It is more difficult to describe the strategies and techniques of the evaluative-broad mediator. Mediations conducted with such an orientation vary tremendously in scope, often including many narrow, distributive issues, as the previous discussion of the problem-definition continuum illustrates. In addition, evaluative-broad mediators can be more-or-less evaluative, with the evaluative moves touching all or only some of the issues.

The evaluative-broad mediator's principal strategy is to learn about the circumstances and underlying interests of the parties and other affected individuals or groups, and then to use that knowledge to direct the parties toward an outcome that responds to such interests. To carry out this strategy, the evaluative-broad mediator will employ various techniques, including the following (listed from least to most evaluative).

a. *Educate herself about underlying interests.* — The evaluative-broad mediator seeks to understand the underlying legal and other distributive issues by studying pleadings, depositions, and other documents, as well as by allowing the parties (usually through their lawyers) to argue their cases during the mediation. Unlike the narrow mediator, however, the broad mediator emphasizes the parties' underlying interests rather than their positions, and seeks to uncover needs that typically are not revealed in documents. Pleadings in the Computec case, for instance, would not indicate that one of the causes of the dispute was Golden State's interest in protecting the sanctity of its internal policy against reimbursing convention travel expenses of its own employees, let alone that the policy was born when the CEO observed staff members, at a convention in Bermuda, frolicking instead of attending seminars.

* * *

Evaluative-broad mediators expect to construct proposed agreements. For that reason, they generally emphasize their own education over that of the parties. Accordingly, they typically will restrict or control direct communication between the parties; thus, for example, the evaluative-broad mediator would spend more time in private caucuses than in joint sessions.

b. *Predict impact (on interests) of not settling.* — After determining the parties' underlying interests and setting the scope of the problems to be addressed in the mediation, some evaluative-broad mediators would predict how failure to settle would impact important interests. In the Computec case, an evaluative-broad mediator might tell Golden State that unless it reaches an agreement that allows Computec executives to feel appreciated and effective, relations will sour and Computec might become less diligent, thereby impairing Golden State's ability to compete and to serve its customers.

An evaluative-broad mediator also might try to persuade the participants that her assessments are correct by providing objective criteria or additional data.

c. *Develop and offer broad (interest-based) proposals.* — An evaluative-broad mediator's goal is to develop a proposal that satisfies as many of the parties' interests, both narrow and broad, as feasible. Proposals in the Computec case, for example, might range from a payment scheme for Golden State (based on an allocation of costs), to a system for the submission and approval of travel and education expenses in future years, to the formation of a new joint venture.

d. *Urge parties to accept the mediator's or another proposal.* — The evaluative-broad mediator (like the evaluative-narrow mediator) might present her proposal with varying degrees of force or intended impact. If the mediator has clout (the ability to bring pressure to bear on one or more of the parties), she might warn them or threaten to use it.

If the mediator has concluded that the goal of the mediation should include changing the people involved, she might take measures to effectuate that goal, such as appealing to shared values, lecturing, or applying pressure.

4. *Facilitative–Broad*

The facilitative-broad mediator's principal strategy is to help the participants define the subject matter of the mediation in terms of underlying interests and to help them develop and choose their own solutions that respond to such interests. In addition, many facilitative-broad mediators will help participants find opportunities to educate or change themselves, their institutions, or their communities. To carry out such strategies, the facilitative-broad mediator may use techniques such as the following.

a. *Help parties understand underlying interests.* — To accomplish this task, the facilitative-broad mediator will engage in many of the same activities as the evaluative-broad mediator, such as encouraging attendance and participation by the real parties, not just their lawyers, and explaining the importance of interests. Because he expects the parties to generate their own proposals, the facilitative-broad mediator emphasizes the need for the parties to educate themselves and each other more than the mediator. * * *

The facilitative-broad mediator also will help the parties define the scope of the problem to be addressed in the mediation, often encouraging them to explore underlying interests to the extent that they wish to do so. This behavior stands in sharp contrast to that of narrow mediators (even most facilitative-narrow mediators), who tend to accept the obvious problem presented, and that of evaluative-broad mediators, who often define the scope of the problem to be addressed themselves.

Many facilitative-broad mediators especially value mediation's potential for helping parties grow through an understanding of one another and of themselves. These mediators tend to offer the participants opportunities for positive change. One way to look at this is through Bush and Folger's concept of "transformation." In this view, by encouraging the parties to develop their own understandings, options, and proposals, the facilitative-broad mediator "empowers" them; by helping the parties to understand one another's situation, the facilitative-broad mediator provides them opportunities to give "recognition" to one another.

b. *Help parties develop and propose broad, interest-based options for settlement.* — The facilitative-broad mediator would keep the parties focused on the relevant interests and ask them to generate options that might respond to these interests. In the Computec case, the options may include various systems through which the already-incurred expenses could be allocated to the Golden State contract, methods for handling the same issue in the future (informally or by contract amendment), and opportunities to collaborate on other projects (an example of positive change). Next, he would encourage the parties to use these options — perhaps combining or modifying them — to develop and present their own interest-based proposals.

c. *Help parties evaluate proposals.* — The facilitative-broad mediator uses questions principally to help the parties evaluate the impact on various interests of proposals and of non-settlement. In Computec, for instance, a facilitative-broad mediator might ask the Computec representative how a specific settlement would affect the parties' working relationship and how it would alter Computec's ability to deliver appropriate services.

* * *

D. *Movement Along the Continuums and Among the Quadrants: Limitations on the Descriptive Capabilities of the Grid*

Like a map, the grid has a static quality that limits its utility in depicting the conduct of some mediators.

It is true that most mediators — whether they know it or not — generally conduct mediations with a presumptive or predominant orientation. Usually, this orientation is grounded in the mediator's personality, education, training, and experience. For example, most retired judges tend toward an extremely evaluative-narrow orientation, depicted in the far northwest corner of the grid. Many divorce mediators with backgrounds or strong interests in psychology or counseling — and who serve affluent or well-educated couples — lean toward a facilitative-broad approach. Sometimes, the expectations of a given program dictate an orientation; for example, narrow mediation tends to dominate many public programs with heavy caseloads.

Yet many mediators employ strategies and techniques that make it difficult to fit their practices neatly into a particular quadrant. First, some mediators deliberately try to avoid attachment to a particular orientation. Instead, they emphasize flexibility and attempt to develop their orientation in a given case based on the participants' needs or other circumstances in the mediation.

Second, for a variety of reasons, some mediators who have a predominant orientation do not always behave consistently with it. They occasionally deviate from their presumptive orientation in response to circumstances arising in the course of a mediation. * * *

In other cases, a mediator might seek to foster her dominant approach using a technique normally associated with another quadrant. * * *

A narrow mediator who runs into an impasse might offer the parties a chance to broaden the problem by exploring underlying interests. This might lead to an interest-based agreement that would enable the parties to compromise on the distributive issue as part of a more comprehensive settlement. Similarly, a broad mediator might encourage the parties to narrow their focus if the broad approach seems unlikely to produce a satisfactory outcome.

For these reasons it is often difficult to categorize the orientation, strategies, or techniques of a given mediator in a particular case.

Notes and Questions

1. Professor Riskin recently critiqued and revised this system. *See* Leonard L. Riskin, *Decisionmaking in Mediation: The New Old Grid and the New New Grid System*, 79 Notre Dame L. Rev. 1 (2003), an excerpt from which appears infra in Chapter IV, beginning at page 422.

2. Do you think the "grid" can classify all approaches to mediation? Consider that question as you read the following materials about other approaches to mediation.

3. The question of whether a mediator may properly "evaluate" the legal or other aspects of a dispute — e.g., make and communicate assessments of the strengths and weaknesses of one or both parties' sides of a dispute, or predict a judicial outcome — has generated much controversy.

Many mediators and commentators believe that such conduct is necessarily inconsistent with the nature of mediation and the mediator's role. Kimberlee K. Kovach & Lela P. Love, *"Evaluative Mediation" is an Oxymoron,* 14 Alternatives to High Cost Litig. 31 (1996). We cover this issue infra, Chapter IV, beginning at page 367.

2. OTHER MODELS OF MEDIATION

The mediator orientations described in the grid article—evaluative-narrow, facilitative-narrow, evaluative-broad, facilitative-broad—were meant to describe common models of mediation practice. Other writers, however, have described and promoted different models that may not fit neatly into the grid. This section begins with a description of two such models — Transformative Mediation and Understanding–Based Mediation. Each of these models emphasizes what we think of as humanistic aspects of mediation — while also maintaining a focus on resolving specific issues — and draws upon perspectives that motivated many in the early days of the modern mediation movement.

ROBERT A. BARUCH BUSH & JOSEPH FOLGER, THE PROMISE OF MEDIATION: THE TRANSFORMATIVE APPROACH TO CONFLICT

45–46, 49–56, 59, 60, 62, 65–66, 68, 72, 75, 78–81 (Revised ed. 2005).

The Transformative Theory of Conflict

The transformative theory of conflict starts by offering its own answer to the foundational question of what conflict means to the people involved. According to transformative theory, what people find most significant about conflict is not that it frustrates their satisfaction of some right, interest, or pursuit, no matter how important, but that it leads and even forces them to behave toward themselves and others in ways that they find uncomfortable and even repellent. More specifically, it alienates them from their sense of their own strength and their sense of connection to others, thereby disrupting and undermining the interaction between them as human beings. This crisis of deterioration in human interaction is what parties find most affecting, significant — and disturbing — about the experience of conflict.

* * *

The transformative theory starts from the premise that interactional crisis is what conflict means to people. And help in overcoming that crisis is a major part of what parties want from a mediator.

* * *

The Picture of Negative Conflict Interaction — and the Evidence Behind It

... Conflict, along with whatever else it does, affects people's experience of both self and other. First, conflict generates, for almost anyone it touches, a sense of their own *weakness* and incapacity.... This overall sense of "weakening" is something that occurs as a very natural human response to conflict; almost no one is immune to it, regardless of their initial "power position." At the very same time, conflict generates a sense of *self-absorption*: compared to before, each party becomes more focused on self alone — more protective of self, and more suspicious, hostile, closed and impervious to the perspective of the other person. In sum, no matter how strong a person is, conflict propels them into relative weakness. No matter how considerate of others people are, conflict propels them into self-absorption, self-centeredness.

Support for this account of the human experience of conflict comes from work in the fields of cognitive and social psychology, and neurophysiology, among others...

* * *

...[T]he experiences of weakness and self-absorption...reinforce each other in a feedback loop: the weaker I feel myself becoming, the more hostile and closed I am toward you; and the more hostile I am toward you, the more you react to me in kind, the weaker I feel, the more hostile and closed I become, and so on. This vicious circle of *disempowerment* and *demonization* is exactly what scholars mean when they talk about *conflict escalation*. The transformative theory looks at it more as *interactional degeneration*. Before a conflict begins, whatever the context, parties are engaged in some form of decent, perhaps even loving, human interaction. Then the conflict arises and, propelled by the vicious circle of disempowerment and demonization, what started as a decent interaction spirals down into an interaction that is negative, destructive, alienating and demonizing, on all sides.

* * *

What Parties Want From a Mediator: Help in Reversing the Negative Spiral

Taking the transformative view of what conflict entails and means to parties, one is led to a different assumption, compared to other theories of conflict, about what parties want, need and expect from a mediator. If what bothers parties most about conflict is the interactional degeneration itself, then what they will most want from an intervenor is help in reversing the downward spiral and restoring constructive interaction. Parties may not express this in so many words when they first come to a mediator. More commonly, they explain that they what they want is not just agreement but "closure," to get past their bitter conflict experience and "move on" with their lives. However, it should be clear that, to help parties achieve closure and move on, the mediator's intervention must directly address the interactional crisis itself.

The reason for this conclusion is straightforward: if the negative conflict cycle is not reversed, if parties don't regenerate some sense of their own strength and some degree of understanding of the other, it is unlikely they can move on and be at peace with themselves, much less each other. In effect, without a change in the conflict interaction between them, parties are left disabled, even if an agreement on concrete issues is reached. The parties' confidence in their own competence to handle life's challenges remains weakened, and their ability to trust others remains compromised. The result can be permanent damage to the parties' ability to function, whether in the family, the workplace, the boardroom, or the community (Folger and others, 2001). Recognition of this possibility and its ramifications for the workplace was the main reason for the United States Postal Service's decision to employ the transformative model exclusively in their REDRESS Program for mediating workplace conflicts (Bush, 2001; Hallberlin, 2001). * * *

From the perspective of transformative theory, reversing the downward spiral is the primary value mediation offers to parties in conflict. That value goes beyond the dimension of helping parties reach agreement on disputed issues. With or without the achievement of agreement, the help parties most want, in all types of conflict, involves helping them end the vicious circle of disempowerment, disconnection and demonization, alienation from both self and other. Because without ending or changing that cycle, the parties cannot move beyond the negative interaction that has entrapped them and cannot escape its crippling effects.

* * *

The Theory of Mediation as Conflict Transformation

* * * [T]ransformative mediation can best be understood as a process of *conflict transformation* — that is, changing the quality of conflict interaction. In the transformative mediation process, parties can recapture their sense of competence and connection, reverse the negative conflict cycle, re-establish a constructive (or at least neutral) interaction and move forward on a positive footing, with the mediator's help.

Party Capacity for Conflict Transformation: Human Nature and Capacity

To explain this view of mediation, we first return to the concept of interactional degeneration in conflict. How does mediation help parties in conflict reverse the negative conflict spiral? Out of what resource is that kind of transformation generated, and what is the mediator's role in doing so? The first part of the theoretical answer to this question points not to the mediator at all, but to the parties themselves. The critical resource in conflict transformation is the parties' own basic humanity — their essential strength, decency and compassion, as human beings. As discussed earlier, the transformative theory of conflict recognizes that conflict tends to escalate as interaction degenerates, because of the susceptibility we have as human beings to experience weakness and self-absorption in the face of sudden challenge.

However, the theory also posits, based on what many call a *relational theory* of human nature, that human beings have inherent capacities for *strength* (agency/autonomy) and *responsiveness* (connection/understanding), and an inherent *social* or *moral impulse* that activates these capacities when people are challenged by negative conflict, ultimately working to counteract the tendencies to weakness and self-absorption. (Della Noce, 1999) The transformational theory asserts that when these capacities are activated, the conflict spiral can reverse and interaction can regenerate, even without the presence of a mediator as intervenor.

* * *

Conflict is not static. It is an emergent, dynamic phenomenon, in which parties can — and do — move and shift in remarkable ways, even when no third party is involved. They move out of weakness, becoming calmer, clearer, more confident, more articulate and more decisive — in general, *shifting from weakness to strength*. They shift away from self-absorption, becoming more attentive, open, trusting, and understanding of the other party — in general, shifting from self-centeredness to responsiveness to other.

* * *

In transformative theory, these dynamic shifts are called *empowerment* and *recognition* (Bush, 1989a; Bush, 1989b). * * * The stronger I become, the more open I am to you. The more open I am to you, the stronger you feel, the more open you become to me, and the stronger I feel. Indeed the more open I become to you, the stronger I feel in myself, simply because I'm more open; that is, openness not only requires but creates a sense of strength, of magnanimity. So there is also a circling between strength and responsiveness once they begin to emerge. But this is not a vicious circle, it is a "virtuous circle" — a virtuous circle of conflict transformation.

Why conflict transformation? Because as the parties make empowerment and recognition shifts, and as those shifts gradually reinforce in a virtuous circle, the interaction as a whole begins to transform and regenerate. It changes back from a negative, destructive, alienating and demonizing interaction to one that becomes positive, constructive, connecting and humanizing, even while conflict and disagreement are still continuing.

* * *

Mediation as Conflict Transformation: Definitions and Guiding Principles

The previous discussion brings us to the definition of mediation itself, and the mediator's role, in the transformative model. Both of these definitions differ markedly from the normal definitions found in training materials and practice literature — in which mediation is usually defined as a process in which a neutral third party helps the parties to reach a mutually acceptable resolution of some or all the issues in dispute, and the mediator's role is defined as establishing ground rules, defining issues, establishing an agenda, generating options, and ultimately persuading the parties to accept terms of agreement (Stulberg, 1980; Alfini et al., 2003; Moore, 1986; Folberg & Taylor, 1984).

By contrast, in the transformative model

- Mediation is defined as a process in which a third party works with parties in conflict to help them change the quality of their conflict interaction from negative and destructive to positive and constructive, as they explore and discuss issues and possibilities for resolution.

- The mediator's role is to help the parties make positive interactional shifts (empowerment and recognition shifts) by supporting the exercise of their capacities for strength and responsiveness through their deliberation, decision-making, communication, perspective-taking, and other party activities.

- The mediator's primary goals are: (1) to support empowerment shifts, by supporting — but never supplanting — each party's deliberation and decision-making, at every point in the session where choices arise (regarding either process or outcome) and (2) to support recognition shifts, by encouraging and supporting — but never forcing — each party's freely chosen efforts to achieve new understandings of the other's perspective.

* * *

Fourth, even though the mediator's job is to support empowerment and recognition shifts, the transformative model does not ignore the significance of resolving specific issues. Rather, it assumes that, if mediators do the job just described, the parties themselves will very likely make positive changes in their interaction and find acceptable terms of resolution for themselves where such terms genuinely exist.* * *

Empowerment and Recognition: What the Terms Do and Do Not Mean

* * *

[E]mpowerment and recognition are not end states or products of the conflict transformation process. They are *dynamic shifts* from one mode of experiencing self or other to a different mode. In fact, we make it a point today to always use the words empowerment and recognition as *adjectives* attached to the word *"shift."* In an *empowerment shift*, the party moves from weakness to greater strength. In a *recognition shift*, a party moves from self-absorption to greater understanding of other. * * *

The Value of Conflict Transformation: Private and Public

* * *

... [W]hen conflict transformation occurs — because empowerment and recognition shifts were made during mediation — there may also be long term benefits to the parties. These are what some have called *upstream effects* of conflict transformation: impacts of the mediation experience that carry over into future situations. (Hallberlin, 2000) For example, from having made empowerment shifts from confusion to clarity in mediation, parties may carry forward an increased confidence in their ability to clarify and express their views in future situations. Or, having made recognition shifts from suspicion to greater openness, parties may be more willing and able, in other situations, to withhold judgment and give others the benefit of the doubt. The result is that they are more likely to avoid the negative conflict spiral in the future, or to have greater ability to reverse it on their own — important long term benefits of mediation for the parties themselves. * * *

The public value of conflict transformation is overlooked in most discussions of the public benefits of mediation.* * * [S]ome fifteen years ago, one of the authors of this volume explained the public benefits of mediation — beyond systemic efficiency — in the following terms:

> Parties to mediation [are affected] in two ways: in terms of their ... capacity for self-determination, and in terms of their ... capacity for consideration and respect for others. And *that itself* is the public value that mediation promotes. In other words, going through mediation is a direct education and growth experience, as to self-determination on the one hand and consideration for others on the other ... Simply put, it is the value of providing a moral and political education for citizens, in responsibility for themselves and respect for others.

Notes and Questions

1. Professors Bush and Folger first elaborated their theory of Transformative Mediation in ROBERT A. BARUCH BUSH & JOSEPH FOLGER, THE PROMISE OF MEDIATION: RESOLVING CONFLICT THROUGH EMPOWERMENT AND RECOGNITION (1994). That book, and numerous writings that promoted transformative mediation, have inspired great enthusiasm for and efforts to implement this approach. The most notable example is the REDRESS program of the U.S. Postal Service, under which thousands of employment disputes have been mediated. Why do you suppose the Postal Service chose transformative mediation as opposed to, say, the narrow-evaluative approach described in the Riskin excerpt, supra? For an analysis of this program, see Chapter VI, beginning at page 741.

2. Bush and Folger assert that "interactional crisis is what conflict means to people. And help in overcoming that crisis is a major part of what parties want from a mediator." Do Bush and Folger mean that everyone in every conflict experiences it in this way? To what extent are these thoughts consistent with your own experiences with conflict? With experiences of others with whom you are familiar?

3. For other information about the uses of Transformative Mediation, see Dorothy J. Della Noce, *Special Series: Assuring Mediator Quality: From Practice to Theory to Practice: A Brief Retrospective on the Transformative Mediation Model*, 19 Ohio St. J. on Disp. Resol. 925 (2004); and the web site of the Institute for the Study of Conflict Transformation, Inc., http://www.transformativemediation.org. Although the approach elaborated in the first edition of the Bush & Folger book has attracted many enthusiastic adherents, it also has drawn substantial criticism. Can you imagine what some of those criticisms might be? *See* Carrie Menkel–Meadow, *The Many Ways of Mediation: The Transformation of Traditions, Ideologies, Paradigms, and Practices*, 11 Negotiation J. 217 (1995). How well does legal training prepare one for transformative mediation?

4. For a demonstration of the Transformative Model of mediation, see THE "PURPLE" HOUSE CONVERSATIONS: A DEMONSTRATION OF TRANSFORMATIVE MEDIATION IN ACTION (2003) (video or DVD), available from the web site of the Institute for the Study of Conflict Transformation, Inc., supra.

———

GARY J. FRIEDMAN & JACK HIMMELSTEIN, RESOLVING CONFLICT TOGETHER: THE UNDERSTANDING–BASED APPROACH TO MEDIATION

(forthcoming 2006).

The Understanding–Based Model of Mediation

The overarching goal of this approach to mediation is to resolve conflict through understanding. Deeper understanding by the parties of their own and each other's perspectives, priorities and concerns enables them to work through their conflict together. With an enhanced understanding of the whole situation, the parties are able to shape creative and mutually rewarding solutions that reflect their personal, business and economic interests. To these ends, the mediator meets directly and simultaneously (rather than separately) with both sides and, if the parties desire, with their lawyers present as well.

The Center's model shares much in common with a number of other approaches to mediation. For example, we stress the importance of articulating interests that underlie the parties conflicting positions and developing solutions that will serve those interests. There is also much that distinguishes this approach.

Parties' Responsibility and Non-caucus Approach

In the Understanding–Based Model, the emphasis is on the parties' responsibility for the decisions they will make. Many models of mediation assume that the mediator should take a strong role in crafting a solution to the parties' dispute and persuading them to adopt it. In this approach, the assumption is that it is the parties, not the professionals, who have the best understanding of what underlies the dispute and are in the best position to find the solution. It is <u>their</u> conflict, and <u>they</u> hold the key to reaching a solution that best serves them both.

Meeting together with the parties (and counsel) follows from these assumptions about parties' responsibility. Many other approaches to mediation recommend that the mediator shuttle back and forth between the parties (caucusing), gaining information that he or she holds confidential. Our central problem with caucusing is that the mediator ends up with the fullest picture of the problem and is therefore in the best position to solve it. The mediator, armed with that fuller view, can readily urge or manipulate the parties to the end he or she shapes. The emphasis here, in contrast, is on understanding and voluntariness as the basis for resolving the conflict rather than persuasion or coercion.

We view the mediator's role in the Understanding-based approach as assisting the parties to gain sufficient understanding of their own and each other's perspective so as to be able to decide together how to resolve their dispute. The parties not only know first hand everything that transpires, they have control over fashioning an outcome that will work for both. And they also participate with the mediator (and counsel) in designing a process by which they can honor what they each value and help them reach a result that reflects what is important to both of them. As mediators, our goal is to support the parties in working through their conflict together — in ways that respect their differing perspectives, needs and interests as well as their common goals.

To work in this way is challenging for both the mediator and the parties. The parties' motivation and willingness to work together is critical to the success of this approach. Mediators often assume that the parties (and their counsel) simply do not want to work together, and therefore keep the parties apart. In our experience, many parties (and counsel) simply accept that they will not work together and that the mediator will be responsible for crafting the solution. But once educated how staying in the same room might be valuable, many are motivated to do so. If the parties (and the mediator) are willing, working together throughout can be as rewarding as it is demanding.

Notes and Questions

1. What appear to be the similarities and differences between the transformative and understanding–based approaches?

2. The understanding–based approach is particularly influential in Germany, Austria, and Switzerland, where Friedman and Himmelstein have done a great deal of training.

For a demonstration of the understanding–based approach in action, see *Videotape: Saving the Last Dance: Resolving Conflict Through Understanding* (Harvard Law School Program on Negotiation & The Center for Mediation in Law 2001).

3. Other commentators have developed other systems for classifying approaches to mediation. Professor Ellen Waldman, for instance, has relied

on the role played by norms, by describing "norm-generating," "norm-educating," and "norm-advocating" models. Ellen A. Waldman, *Identifying the Role of Social Norms in Mediation: A Multiple Model Approach,* 48 Hastings L. J. 703, 707–10 (1997). Other models include "trashing, bashing and hashing it out" (James J. Alfini, *Trashing, Bashing, and Hashing it Out: Is This the End of "Good Mediation?,"* 19 Fla. St. U. L. Rev. 47 (1991)); the "problem-solving — transformative" approach to mediation (BARBARA ASHLEY PHILLIPS, THE MEDIATION FIELD GUIDE: TRANSCENDING LITIGATION AND RESOLVING CONFLICTS IN YOUR BUSINESS OR ORGANIZATION 59 (2001)); narrative mediation (JOHN WINSLADE & GERALD MONK, NARRATIVE MEDIATION: A NEW APPROACH TO CONFLICT RESOLUTION 31–41 (2000)); the "insight" approach to mediation (CHERYL PICARD, PETER BISHOP, RENA RAMKAY & NEIL SARGENT, THE ART AND SCIENCE OF MEDIATION 120–24 (2004)). For other categorizations, see Leonard L. Riskin, *Understanding Mediators' Orientations, Strategies, and Techniques: A Grid for the Perplexed,* 1 Harv. Negot. L. Rev. 7, 14–16 (1996).

Each of the models rests on different assumptions about the goals and purposes of a mediation. In terms of the ideas of conflict and conflict resolution described in Chapter I, each has different aspirations and assumptions about which elements of conflict — behavioral, emotional and cognitive — that mediation should address, and how deeply beneath the surface of the dispute the mediation could or should reach. And although each has value for these purposes and others, none of them can fully describe what happens in a real mediation; in that sense, they all distort reality. As many commentators have put it, "[t]he map is not the territory." In George Box's terms, "All models are wrong, but some are useful." G.E.P. Box, *Robustness in the Strategy of Scientific Model Building, in* ROBUSTNESS IN STATISTICS 201, 202 (Robert L. Launer & Graham N. Wilkinson eds., 1979).

For purposes of learning about mediation, however, the models are important for at least three reasons. First, they provide a way of understanding the mental conceptions of mediation — conscious or subconscious — that often influence participants in mediation as well as observers, potential supporters, sponsors, opponents and critics. Second, they should help us begin to think about what kind of process is most appropriate in a particular dispute or category of disputes (e.g., family disputes, "barking dog" cases). And third, they can help us be aware of how various participants can influence the development of a particular mediation. In short, as lawyers we need to be aware of the potential variations in mediation processes so we can promote the most appropriate method in particular situations.

4.   Recently, Professor Michael Moffit examined the challenges of defining mediation and categorizing different forms of mediation. Michael L. Moffit, *Schmediation and the Dimensions of Definition*, 10 Harv. Negot. L. Rev. 69 (2005).

B.   BRIEF TAKES ON REAL MEDIATIONS

As we hope you can imagine from the forgoing, describing "mediation" generically is nearly as daunting as generically describing dancing or sports. One challenge — in addition to dealing with various models, such as those described above — is that mediation takes place in many different settings, with variations in the types of problems and parties involved, and good mediators respond to these variations, sometimes in ways that do not fit into standard mediation models. For these reasons and others, some mediation processes are so dissimilar that they all can be called mediation only in the same sense that bowling, football, and golf can all be called sports.

Still, for you to understand mediation, it helps to have some sense of how the process works in practice. So, in this section, we set out brief descriptions of four mediations, each from a different field, followed by information about that field and commentary and questions about the issues raised in the mediation described. Within each area in which mediation is practiced, of course, there is so much variety that reading one case study can give you only a small amount of insight. Accordingly, each case study represents the field from which it was drawn only in the limited sense in which an individual "Granny Smith" apple represents the world of apples.

1. PROFESSIONAL MALPRACTICE

HANK DE ZUTTER, PROPONENTS SAY ADR SPELLS RELIEF

Ill. Legal Times, Jan. 1988, at 1.

The 62-year-old man had one good testicle and one bad one. A urologist operated and mistakenly removed the good one. The man and wife were outraged: he was impotent.

Time for a lawsuit? Most Americans would think so. An insult so grave, so horrible — mistake or not — would seem to require the most dramatic response: take this doctor to the cleaners. Take him to court.

Then the doctor's insurance company talked them into mediating the matter. Nothing would be binding. Nothing said to the mediator could be part of a future lawsuit, and something might be worked out.

A lawsuit may provide a form of cathartic revenge, but it would prolong the bitterness as well as payment of the claim. The man was 62, and he did have health problems. A trial in the log-jammed Cook County courts was three to five years away. That's three to five years of hating the doctor, hating the insurance company, hating the doctor's lawyer, and wondering about his own lawyer. It would be three to five years of living with the case, of endlessly discussing this hatred and the injustice of it all with sympathetic friends. It would also be three to five years of waiting for financial compensation.

So the man, his wife, and their lawyer showed up earlier this year at the Huron Street office of Resolve Dispute Management Inc., a private dispute settlement firm organized by Brian Muldoon, a successful trial lawyer turned professional mediator.

* * *

Mediation can be seen as a way of improving the quality of our lives. It builds satisfaction in an area that ordinarily mass-produces frustration: it gives clients and their lawyers greater control over their professional and personal lives.

* * *

Though educated and licensed as a lawyer, Muldoon now sees himself as a member of a different profession — a professional in dispute resolution, or a professional mediator.

* * *

He was one of three ADR consultants who recently spoke to a standing-room-only luncheon workshop of the Chicago Bar Association's committee on Arbitration and Alternative Dispute Resolution. And all three described the shift in warm, glowing terms that usually accompany tales of personal transformation.

* * *

The case of the mistaken testicle was resolved one week after the first mediation session. The man accepted a settlement of $75,900. Both parties were happy, Muldoon says, to put the matter behind them and move on.

* * *

The satisfaction, Muldoon says, involved much more than the money. Because the parties — the man, his wife and the doctor — got to resolve the bitter, awkward feelings involved.

Says Muldoon, "The man and his wife got the chance to vent their anger and frustration with the doctor — not just a lawyer or insurance adjustor — there to hear it. It is not very often that you get to tell off a doctor you've sued for malpractice. They had a chance to get it off their chest, a very important step in resolving any conflict. They felt tremendous relief just to get a chance to tell their story."

The doctor, likewise, got a chance to apologize, saying he was proud of his reputation but absolutely mortified that he had made such an error. He said he was wrong and apologized.

The plaintiff then said to the doctor, "I have wanted to hate you and have hated you, but the truth of the matter is that you have been an excellent doctor and I would refer anyone to you. I forgive you." The doctor was so moved that he stayed around to make sure that his insurance company settled the claim.

Muldoon says lawyers, as well as clients, have much to gain through ADR — though some defense lawyers may not think so. "Defense attorneys who charge clients on an hourly fee basis may feel threatened by quick settlements, but once they work out the economics — by charging a flat settlement fee — they will be pushing for it like crazy.

"Lawyers who incorporate mediation as part of their business have more control of their lives, are personally happier, and get paid more regularly," he adds.

"We lawyers have enough problems in our own lives without going through the psychodramas of someone else's life. These psychodramas are exaggerated because of the nature of the adversary system. Every battle we get engaged in is totally black or totally white; we are trained to exaggerate our client's case. The trouble is we begin to believe our exaggerations by the time we get to court. We see our opponents as personal enemies. I've known cases where some lawyers will leave a restaurant if they see an opposition lawyer there."

"Stress infects their lives," Muldoon says. "Divorce among trial lawyers is common. The toll is especially heavy among divorce lawyers."

"Those who seek to avoid the stress through emotional detachment also pay a price. Lawyers are supposed to be their clients' champions, and if they stop seeing themselves that way, they can stop caring for their clients. They can stop caring in other parts of their life — at home — as well. Lawyers have not been very open about the personal price paid in the current advocacy system."

Muldoon says he was initiated to the joys of negotiating settlements when he was appointed by the mayor of Phoenix, where he had his law practice, to head a downtown redevelopment commission. With the help of a veteran lawyer and ace negotiator, Muldoon says in 60 days he negotiated a redevelopment plan involving all the conflicting interests: developers, existing businesses, historic preservationists, and others who were affected.

"It was so exciting I wanted to try to resolve all pending cases in litigation, about a half dozen in all. So I called up my clients, told them I was going to change my system of billing from hourly fees to a 'results achieved' basis, and within 60 days all cases were settled. This done, I needed to figure out a way to make a living. So I took a sabbatical in Puerto Rico and started designing standardized systems for reaching agreement. Then I came back to Chicago [where he had clerked for the U.S. Attorney's office] to start a business specializing in dispute settlement."

* * *

Despite all his talk about the therapeutic benefits of mediating settlements, Muldoon says it's a mistake to regard ADR and mediation as a "dreamy California, let's be nice approach."

It is still a very tough — gentlemanly, but tough — confrontational business. Disputes don't get resolved through mediation because people want to be nice, but because they become educated through the process about the best results available. Mediation takes something that is a matter of principle that people want to fight about and turns it into a business deal-making opportunity.

Notes and Questions

1. Recall our discussion of apology in Chapter III, beginning on page 225. How common do you suppose it is for parties to apologize in mediation or negotiation? Mediator Brian Muldoon states that although explicit apologies are rare, in most cases a kind of implicit forgiveness occurs when a culpable party explains the circumstances. Telephone interview by Leonard L. Riskin with Brain Muldoon (Sept. 8, 1989).

2. A mediator can control the process of a mediation so as to allow for personal exchanges such as the one described in the foregoing article, or to discourage them. Some mediators do not encourage the presence of the real defendant in personal injury claims, believing that the insurance company representative is sufficient. In what circumstances should a mediator encourage or, if the mediator is a judge and has authority to do so, compel a party to attend? If the party is present, and also is represented by a lawyer, what should their respective roles be? *See* Leonard L. Riskin, *The Represented Client in a Settlement Conference: The Lessons of* G. Heileman Brewing Co. v. Joseph Oat Corp., 69 Wash. U. L.Q. 1059 (1991), a relevant portion of which is reprinted infra in Chapter IV, beginning at page 416.

3. This "brief take" involved medical malpractice. Might some people who are involved in automobile or slip and fall accidents have emotional needs to interact with the other parties? Do our legal system and legal profession discourage fulfillment of these needs? See Jonathan R. Cohen, *Advising Clients to Apologize,* 72 So. Calif. L. Rev. 1009 (1999).

Damages in some civil suits substitute for other kinds of relief, such as an apology, which courts cannot grant. *See* Richard L. Abel, *A Critique of American Tort Law*, 8 Brit. J. of L. & Soc'y 199 (1981).

Assume you were a lawyer representing an insurance company who's insured was a defendant in a negligence suit involving an automobile accident. If the insured wanted to call the plaintiff to apologize or to ask about the plaintiff's condition, would you object? Do you think an apology might be appropriate in the settlement of such a case? Listen to Professors Wagatsuma and Rosett:

> The important point here is that while there are some injuries that cannot be repaired just by saying you are sorry, there are others that can only be repaired by an apology. Such injuries are the very ones that most trouble American law. They include defamation, insult, degradation, loss of status and the emotional distress and dislocation that accompany conflict. To the extent that a place may be found for apology in the resolution of such conflicts, American law would be enriched and better able to deal with the heart of what brought the controversy to public attention. It would also be relieved of some of the pressure to convert all damages into dollars — a pressure that produces absurdly large punitive damage judgments when a trier of fact sympathetically identifies with the claim of degradation and emotional distress but the economic loss is fictive. More to the point, society at large might be better off and better able to advance social peace if, instead of discouraging apology in such situations by treating them as admissions of liability, the law encouraged people to apologize to those they have wronged

and to compensate them for their losses. Lawsuits may never be filed in such situations.

Hiroshi Wagatsuma & Arthur Rosett, *The Implications of Apology: Law and Culture in Japan and the United States,* 20 Law & Soc'y Rev. 461, 487–88 (1986). Since Wagatsuma and Rosett wrote, apology has come to prominence both in mediation practice and in negotiation scholarship. For recent writings on the role of apology in dispute resolution, see Chapter III, beginning at page 225.

4. Mediation has come to play an important role in addressing disputes between professionals and their clients. Some writers have praised the possibilities for education and healing. *E.g.,* Ann J. Kellett, Comment, *Healing Angry Wounds: The Roles of Apology and Mediation in Disputes Between Physicians and Patients,* 1987 Mo. J. Disp. Resol. 111. Others have been less optimistic. Andrew McMullen, Comment, *Mediation and Medical Malpractice Disputes: Potential Obstacles in the Traditional Lawyer's Perspective,* 1990 J. Disp. Resol. 371. Bar associations have established mediation and arbitration programs to deal with fee disputes between lawyers and their clients, and disciplinary bodies have created programs to mediate grievances (generally minor ones) against lawyers. See Alan Scott Rau, *Resolving Disputes Over Attorneys Fees: The Role of ADR,* 46 SMU L. Rev. 2005 (1993). Mediation also has found employment with a more prospective outlook in matters of bioethics. See Nancy N. Dubler & Carol B. Liebman, Bioethics Mediation: A Guide to Shaping Shared Solutions (2004).

2. A SHAREHOLDER-MANAGEMENT DISPUTE

FRANK J. SCARDILLI,*

SISTERS OF THE PRECIOUS BLOOD v. BRISTOL–MYERS CO.

This case was on appeal from a grant of summary judgment in favor of Bristol–Myers Co., defendant-appellee (hereinafter "Bristol") and against the Sisters of the Precious Blood, plaintiff-appellant (hereinafter "Sisters"). The latter, who owned 500 shares of Bristol stock, started a lawsuit against Bristol under the proxy solicitation section of the Securities Exchange Act of 1934 alleging that a shareholder resolution they proposed was defeated because Bristol's stated opposition to the resolution in the proxy materials distributed to the shareholders was based on serious misrepresentations of fact.

The Sisters were concerned that the company's sales practices in the third world of its infant baby formula were contributing to serious illness, malnutrition and death of infants because of the unsanitary conditions often prevailing there. Frequently the formula is mixed with contaminated water, there is no refrigeration and its use discourages breastfeeding which is clearly healthier in most instances than is the formula.

---

* Frank J. Scardilli is a mediator employed by the Second Circuit Court of Appeals. Mr. Scardilli presented this at a Harvard Faculty Seminar on negotiation on April 13, 1982.

The Sisters' proposed resolution requested that management report to the shareholders the full extent of its marketing practices of the infant formula in the third world to alert other shareholders to what they perceived was irresponsible business behavior. Their lawsuit was aimed at getting the company to come up with a corrected proxy solicitation to be submitted to a special meeting of the shareholders to be called specifically for that purpose rather than await the next annual meeting of shareholders.

The court declined to grant the relief sought by the Sisters, stating:

> Defendant's proxy solicitation did not result in or have the tendency to threaten or cause plaintiffs irreparable harm sufficient to warrant injunctive relief. Plaintiffs' proposal was precatory only; it sought merely stockholder approval of a "request" that Bristol management issue a report covering the marketing of infant baby formula products in developing countries. Regardless of the outcome of the shareholder vote, management was entirely privileged to ignore the request and retained complete discretion not to make such a report.

The court refused to reach the question of whether Bristol had actually lied in its recommendation to the shareholders to reject the Sisters' proposed resolution, stating:

> To proceed further with the lawsuit would be 'an empty exercise resulting, at most, in a judicial declaration of no practical import.' An evaluation of the objective accuracy of the proxy statement regarding plaintiff's shareholder proposal would be an empty exercise of semantics in the circumstances of this case.

Mediation Efforts on Appeal

The first of four conferences seeking to mediate this dispute was held on July 19, 1977. (The subject of abuses involving infant formulas in the third world seemed relatively new in 1977 but has obviously had considerable media exposure since then.)

First Conference

Apparently because they believed no amicable resolution was possible, counsel who appeared for the parties were very able but had virtually no settlement authority. (The parties' previous negotiations had broken down despite the best efforts of a very able judge who tried to resolve their differences.)

Legal Merits

As is customary, I first explored the arguments of counsel relative to the strengths and weaknesses of their legal positions on appeal. The parties seemed genuinely far apart in their assessment of the likely outcome in our court. The issue on appeal involved some complexity because of the rather technical requirements for suits under Section 14 of the Securities Exchange Act of 1934. While generally appellees have a distinct advantage, if for no other reason than that only about one out of eight cases is reversed on appeal in our court, the outcome of this particular case was hard to predict. Even if the district court decision were deemed technically correct, this could have disturbing policy implications because the decision appeared to create a license for management to lie with impunity whenever it sought to defeat a proposed shareholder resolution, which would virtually always be precatory. The SEC was apparently disturbed by this implication and advised me it was seriously considering filing a brief amicus curiae urging our court to reverse the decision below. In addition, as I pointed out to counsel for Bristol, although a shareholder resolution is precatory in law, in the real world it can and often does have a serious impact on managerial decisions.

Predictably, the parties' respective positions on what might constitute a satisfactory settlement were far apart. The Sisters were adamant on the principle that no settlement terms could be discussed unless Bristol openly admitted that it had lied in its earlier proxy solicitation and that this fact had to be communicated through new proxy solicitations at a special meeting of the shareholders to be convened solely for that purpose. Bristol, of course, insisted it had been truthful all along. It offered, however, to permit the Sisters to make any written statement they wished at the next annual shareholders' meeting, and Bristol would simply state its opposition to the proposal without elaboration. This was unacceptable to the Sisters. Because it was clear I needed parties with more authority and flexibility, I set up a second conference requiring senior counsel to come in with their clients.

Second Conference

The second conference held in the middle of August, 1977 was attended by senior counsel for both sides, the inside General Counsel of Bristol, and a representative of the Advisory Committee of the Interfaith Group for Corporate Responsibility, which was the real moving force behind the Sisters' litigation.

It soon became apparent that there was very deep hostility and profound distrust between the parties. Each was convinced the other was acting in bad faith. The Sisters were outraged by Bristol's insistence that it had not lied. Its distrust of Bristol was total and uncompromising.

At this conference, the Sisters, for the first time, insisted that they would have to be reimbursed for their litigation expenses of approximately $15,000 before any settlement could be effected. After checking with top management, counsel for management flatly refused to pay anything at all to the Sisters.

As a still further condition of settlement, the Sisters wanted Bristol to provide them with a list of the 1000 largest shareholders of the company prior to the next annual meeting. Bristol refused to give the list. I finally disposed of this issue by convincing both parties to allow Delaware law to determine the Sisters' entitlement to the list (Delaware was the state of Bristol's incorporation).

The Parties' Perceptions of Themselves and of Each Other

It became clear that the respective parties' self-image was significantly at variance with the image each had of the other.

Bristol regarded itself as by far the most responsible marketer of infant formula in the third world, far more so than its three major American competitors and the giant Swiss company, Nestle. It claimed it put out a quality nutritional product that was very useful when mothers either could not or chose not to breast feed their infants; that it did not advertise its infant formulas directly to consumers in the third world; that the company policy already sought to minimize the danger or improper use by its labeling. In short, it was convinced that its business practices were both prudent and responsible. Therefore, they were furious that they had been singled out as "baby killers" by the Sisters who had so testified before a Congressional Committee and who had lost few opportunities to criticize them in the media. It was clear they viewed the Sisters as wild-eyed, misguided religious fanatics who were themselves engaging in a distortion of the facts and reckless character assassination.

The Sisters, on the other hand, had spent years accumulating data in affidavits taken throughout the world regarding the enormous peril to infants created by the indiscriminate use of infant formula in the third world. They had witnessed suffering and death and were suffused with the self-righteousness of avenging angels. To them, Bristol was a monster who cared only about profits and not at all about the lives and health of infants.

Restructuring Perceptions of "Bad Faith"

As negotiations proceeded, it became apparent that no meaningful communication could take place until each of the parties realized that its view of the other was a grossly distorted caricature and counter-productive.

I struck often at the theme that it was dangerous to assume that one with whom you disagree violently is necessarily acting in bad faith. Moreover, I stressed to both that I had become fully and firmly convinced that each of the parties was acting in complete good faith, albeit from a different perspective. I strove to get each to view the matter through the eyes of the other.

I found that before I could get the parties to trust each other I had first to get them to trust me. I was aided in this by able and responsible counsel on both sides who though powerful and often uncompromising advocates were more reasonable than their respective constituencies.

Interest of the Parties — Illusion of "Winning" at Law

It was necessary to convince each that its interests were not nearly as incompatible as they perceived them and that the interest of each would be best served by a cooperative problem-solving attitude rather than a litigious one.

I stressed that neither party's true interest would be served by "winning" the appeal.

A "win" by Bristol would not be likely to stop the public attacks in the media which so angered and disturbed them. Likewise, a "win" by the Sisters could mean a remand for an expensive trial with no assurance whatever thereafter that Bristol's marketing practices would be altered in any way.

The point was made forcibly to the Sisters that their insistence that Bristol admit that it had lied was totally unrealistic and that progress was impossible so long as they insisted on humiliating the company's management. They were reminded that their real interest lay in effecting marketing changes in the third world and they could best achieve this in a climate of cooperative good will with management. So long as management perceived them as vindictive it was likely to simply dig in its heels and refuse to budge. I urged that a softening of their attitude would in turn create a more flexible attitude in management.

Bristol in turn was forced to concede that notwithstanding what they viewed as the distasteful stridency of the Sisters there was indeed a real moral issue to be faced and they had a real interest in being perceived as highly ethical, responsible businessmen who were not insensitive to the human tragedy which could result from the improper use of their product in the third world.

Agreement at Last

After considerable negotiation in four face-to-face conferences supplemented by numerous telephone conferences over a period of nearly six months, in the course of which Bristol voluntarily changed some of its marketing practices, the parties finally agreed to resolve their differences as follows:

1. The Sisters were satisfied that Bristol had already changed some of its marketing practices which the Sisters had regarded as particularly offensive.

2. The Sisters would be given direct access to Bristol's Board of Directors and other representatives of the company at various times for the purpose of maintaining a first-hand continuing dialogue on the problems of marketing infant formula in the third world.

3. Bristol and the Sisters would each prepare a separate written statement of its views not to exceed 1500 words to be presented to the shareholders in the next quarterly report of the Company. This would be preceded by an agreed-upon joint preamble which would recite the background of the litigation, its resolution by the parties and that the Sisters and Bristol planned to continue to exchange views in an atmosphere of mutual respect for each other's good faith.

To insure that the statements would not be inflammatory each side was given the right to veto the statement of the other. Agreeing on the principle, however, was easier than its implementation. Numerous drafts were exchanged and when appropriate I mediated between their respective versions.

The final agreement on language was arrived at as a result of a 4½–hour drafting session involving 8 people sitting around a conference table in the court in the afternoon of Christmas Eve of 1977. In a sense of relief and elation, the Chairperson of the Interfaith Group for Corporate Responsibility stated, "It is fitting and perhaps prophetic that we have finally resolved our differences on how best to protect tender infants on this eve when we prepare to celebrate the birth of an Infant who has meant so much to millions of Christians all over the world."

Notes and Questions

1. Notice that the mediator helped each party see the dispute from the other's perspective and recognize both sides' underlying *interests* in addition to *positions*. Thus, he moved the negotiations from adversarial to problem solving, and the mediation produced an agreement that seemed to respond to the underlying interests. This broadening of the "problem definition" was necessary to achieving a settlement.

2. Is it socially desirable that this case was settled before the court of appeals had an opportunity to make law? In this case, the mediator pointed out that a victory in court would have benefited neither party. Would "society" have gained if the court had had an opportunity to clarify or make law? In answering this question, consider again the perspective of Professor Owen M. Fiss, *Against Settlement*, 93 Yale L.J. 1073 (1984), a portion of which is reprinted in Chapter I, beginning at page 21.

3. To what extent did the mediator seem to employ evaluative techniques?

4. This mediation involved a dispute between a company's management and shareholders. In a recent article, Professor Scott Peppet argues, using economics and psychology, that a mediator can "add value" to transactions in the same way that a mediator can add value to disputes. The mediator can do this by helping the parties overcome "information asymmetries," which will enable them to reach a more efficient agreement, and to overcome psychological barriers. Scott R. Peppet, *Contract Formation in Imperfect Markets: Should We Use Mediators in Deals?*, 19 Ohio St. J. on Disp. Resol. 283 (2004).

3. REGULATORY NEGOTIATION

ALANA S. KNASTER & PHILIP J. HARTER,
THE CLEAN FUELS REGULATORY
NEGOTIATION

Intergovernmental Perspective, Summer 1992, at 20.

Within days after passage of the *Clean Air Act Amendments of 1990,* officials of the U.S. Environmental Protection Agency were confronted with the onerous task of drafting complicated gasoline regulations to meet the November 15, 1991, deadline for promulgation. The act's clean fuels provisions required EPA to issue regulations for the certification of reformulated gasoline, which is to be made available for sale by 1995 in the nine cities experiencing the worst ozone pollution in the country. Other nonattainment areas may take part in this program on petition of the governor to the EPA administrator.

The regulations are intended to reduce emissions of toxic and ozone producing chemicals, to establish procedures for ensuring that the gasoline sold outside these areas is not any worse than that sold before 1990 (the anti-dumping provision), and to address the problem of carbon monoxide. The carbon monoxide rules were to be issued in August 1991 and the program is to be in place by the end of 1992. Adding oxygen to motor fuels reduces the emission of carbon monoxide. The 1990 amendments, therefore, require certain carbon monoxide nonattainment areas to implement a program to secure the use of fuels with an average oxygen content of 2.7 percent. Because only an average is required, the rules needed to provide a means by which it would operate — something easy to describe in principle but difficult to implement in regulations.

The debates over passage of the legislation had been contentious, and it was felt that developing the regulations would be equally controversial. William Rosenberg, EPA's Assistant Administrator for Air Programs, decided to consider using regulatory negotiation to develop the rules. Even though negotiation would be time consuming and would preclude staff from beginning drafting immediately, Rosenberg determined that the process would provide EPA with the expertise, experience, and practical insight of these parties in sorting through the complex issues. And, at least as important, it would develop a consensus on the rules.

Regulatory negotiation — known as "reg neg" — had been used several times by EPA to address difficult, controversial rules. The Congress recently endorsed the process by enacting the *Negotiated Rulemaking Act of 1990* as an amendment to the *Administrative Procedure Act*. Essentially, it provides a structured process by which representatives of the interests that would be substantially affected, including a senior representative of the regulatory agency, come together to negotiate an agreement on the terms of a rule. The negotiations are conducted under the *Federal Advisory Committee Act*, which requires that the meetings be announced in advance and be open to the public.

A consensus in this case means that each interest concurs in the recommended rule when considered as a whole; each interest, therefore, has a veto over the proposal. The agreement also provides that no one participating in the negotiations will do anything to inhibit its adoption or, to the extent the final rule is consistent with the recommended rule, challenge the rule in court. No rule that has been the subject of such a consensus has resulted in court action. The parties participate because they have a direct hand in crafting the rule.

The Convening

EPA contacted the authors, both of whom had experience conducting complex, technical regulatory negotiations, to undertake a feasibility study. This is done during the convening phase of a regulatory negotiation, during which a neutral third party — the convener — identifies potential interests, interviews representatives of those interests, determines what issues they believe will need to be considered and what information is necessary to resolve those issues, determines the willingness of the interests to participate, and ascertains the likelihood that an accommodation can be reached on the key provisions.

EPA initially chose to treat the oxygenated fuels rule and the reformulated gasoline rule separately, with the mediators each assigned the convening for one rule. Since some parties were interested in both rules, interviews and analyses were coordinated as much as possible. The process began with extensive interviews of EPA's Office of Mobile Sources. Using an initial list of potential interests supplied by EPA, the conveners contacted each of the parties to acquaint them with the regulatory negotiations process. The limited amount of time before the rule had to be published was a key concern of nearly all the parties. EPA estimated that the negotiations phase would have to be completed in approximately three months — by mid-June — to give agency staff sufficient time to draft a rule based on the recommendations of the group. The effort would necessitate almost a full-time commitment by many of the participants. The turnaround time for staff to produce notes of the deliberations and draft proposals would be very short.

There was an almost equal concern that the negotiations not reopen the issues that had been debated and resolved during the legislative process. It would be incumbent on the neutral facilitators and the participants themselves to keep the talks productive. Accordingly, the parties were asked to provide their assessment of the feasibility of concluding negotiations in the limited time, the desirability of combining the negotiations, and the willingness to participate in a negotiation of a subset of issues if time constraints or technical complexities made a negotiation of all the issues proposed infeasible.

Accommodating the Interests

It is important to include all the key interests in regulatory negotiation. While one can never hope to get representatives of all the affected interests around the same table, the convener seeks representatives of the major interests and enough others to ensure that the issues will be adequately raised and resolved. In the case of clean fuels, the difficulty lay not in determining what interests needed to be included but in keeping a manageable number of direct participants.

There are several approaches for accommodating additional participants while still keeping the number of negotiators to a minimum, including:

1) Designating alternates to attend as many deliberation sessions as possible and to be ready to substitute for the representative;

2) Setting up technical work groups or subcommittees to do the preparatory work and submit proposals for consideration by the larger advisory committee;

3) Selecting a participating organization's executive director, chief attorney, or another appropriate staff person to represent the group, with staff to serve with one or more member representatives and coordinate the team during the negotiations; and

4) Selecting spokespersons in situations when the parties remain adamant about retaining a greater number of representatives than is ideal for the functioning of the advisory committee, especially when there is great diversity within an interest group and the members reach a compromise.

The *Negotiated Rulemaking Act* suggests that there be a maximum number of 25 members on the Federal Advisory Committee established for each negotiation. In this case, the conveners initial recommendations were in that range, but the parties insisted that the number of "seats at the table" be expanded so that all the key sub-interests within each major organization were represented.

The diversity among members in several key interest groups became an important consideration in the final design of the clean fuels negotiations process. For example, the petroleum refiners had two trade associations, one representing a broad spectrum of the industry, including numerous small refiners, and the other representing major refiners. Differences in market share, geography, and organizational structure between the large and small refiners necessitated that both associations be seated at the table. Representation was complicated further by the diversity among the major refiners, ranging from significant differences in the composition of the crude oil they used to a wide variety of investment strategies that affected companies' position on the content of the regulation. Moreover, several of the major companies were further along in their product reformulations in response to changing, stringent regulations.

To accommodate these differences, it became necessary to allot nine seats for the refining industry on the negotiating committee. Additional representation was afforded through the use of alternates and working group members. Commitments by the facilitators to ensure that alternates were accorded an equal voice in decisionmaking were important in keeping the number to nine.

The oxygenate producers — makers of MBTE, ethanol, and methanol — presented a similar representation problem. Again, although there was considerable overlap in membership among the trade associations, the significance of the rule for individual companies mandated that their representation be expanded to five. One interest, for example, requested a seat even though it was represented by another, broader trade association. With nine major cities subject to the reformulated gasoline provisions (as well as opt-in possibilities) and 40 cities affected by the winter oxygenate requirements, it was important to keep the state and local government interest caucus to a manageable size without sacrificing the ability of the representatives to speak for all the cities and states. The time commitment convinced several cities and states to allow others to participate in the negotiations on their behalf. The willingness of the executive director of the Association of State and Local Air Pollution Control Officials to coordinate the caucus effort and to obtain member input meant that this caucus could accept five seats on the advisory committee. Total representation was expanded in the work groups.

Final Process Design

EPA published a notice in the *Federal Register* announcing its intention to use negotiated rulemaking, outlining the issues involved, and describing the interests that would be represented during the negotiations. The notice made clear that any party that believed it would be significantly affected but was not otherwise represented could request to participate on the committee. A public meeting was held on February 21–22 in Washington. Because of the extensive convening phase, there were no surprises with respect to new interests demanding representation. Two hundred people attended the meeting, at which the conveners presented the results of their interviews, including recommendations for process design and membership on the advisory committee and technical work groups.

"Umbrella" Committee and Work Groups. The conveners proposed that EPA establish an overall policy or "umbrella" committee that would be responsible for developing a consensus on a total package. The conveners recommended allocating the seats on the committee among the various interests that needed to be represented, with the designation of individual representatives left up to the interests (members would be appointed formally by the EPA administrator to form a Federal Advisory Committee). The conveners initially recommended 23 members for the committee, but this was expanded to 31 members. Advisory committee members would designate alternates and work group members. The work groups would develop consensus recommendations for review and consideration by the umbrella committee. The concept of an "umbrella" therefore connoted an oversight role.

Work Group Topics. The participants at the public meeting chose to establish four work groups — fuel certification (combining the issues of testing and modeling); anti-dumping; supply and distribution of oxygenates; and averaging, credits, and enforcement. The participants agreed to schedule meetings to ensure that participants could observe the sessions that were most important to them. After considerable debate, membership on the work groups, with minor exceptions, was kept at approximately 15 individuals. The facilitators agreed to keep observers from usurping the role of official work group members.

The Negotiations Phase

After an initial meeting of the advisory committee in mid-March, the work groups began their discussions in earnest. Each session was scheduled for a full day. Often, meetings would extend into the evening. Progress varied considerably among the different groups, especially in instances when they were waiting for data from EPA researchers and Auto/Oil, the major research consortium jointly sponsored by the petroleum and auto industries. The work groups also enabled the technical experts from the respective interest groups to solve problems collaboratively. Although the members had numerous ideological differences, they were able to develop several key provisions.

In light of the ongoing development of several EPA models and requirements, the negotiators developed provisions for accommodating these changes once they were final, including scheduling future meetings of the key participants to review the EPA products. These types of compromise approaches are unique to negotiated rulemaking.

The debate over the role of modeling versus testing of proposed gasoline formulas was a critical aspect of the negotiations. A strong case could be made that laboratory testing of each gasoline formula to ensure that it met the standard would be both time consuming and costly for the refiners — to the point of making the 1995 deadline difficult to achieve. On the other hand, modeling was not wholeheartedly accepted by all interests because of the gap in existing data on which to base the model. The final agreement incorporated a simpler model than had originally been contemplated. However, the parties established a process for incorporating new data and corresponding time frames that would result in Phase II reformulated gasoline being in the marketplace earlier than was required by the law.

The anti-dumping deliberations clearly demonstrated the advantages of negotiations over the traditional rulemaking process for accommodating the diverse needs of affected interests. The negotiators crafted a hierarchy of approaches for establishing baseline gasoline — against which the anti-dumping provisions in the law would be measured — that began with the use of actual 1990 gasoline data, allowed for variations in the recordkeeping systems of a large number of refiners, and addressed the unique problems of companies that were retrofitting their plants to meet other new gasoline requirements and therefore might not be producing gasoline in 1990. A realistic and enforceable regulatory approach emerged.

Finally, the negotiators crafted an important compromise that enabled the oil companies to agree to reductions that were greater than those contemplated when the process began. To take account of the enormously complex distribution system for gasoline and to enable refineries to smooth out production runs, the committee developed a system by which the standards could be met on an annual average, as opposed to a gallon-by-gallon basis. To meet the concern that one locality could end up with all the dirty fuel, a means was developed by which samples would be taken from around the country, and specific action would be taken if this problem occurred. That provided a creative means of meeting a standard that itself had many creative aspects.

The committee negotiated late into the night of its final meeting, putting together an outline of an entire standard. The various interests could then see the standard as a whole and decide whether they were better off with negotiation or with traditional rulemaking. They also could see how to make the standard work for them — what changes would have to be made and how to package proposed changes so that others would agree to them.

Following that marathon session, the negotiators went back to their constituents for their reactions. Each decided to continue. The bare bones of the outline were fleshed out in a series of smaller meetings that addressed individual issues. The effort culminated in an agreement that was signed by representatives of all the parties on August 16, 1991. Each party "concur[red] in principle to the outline of the proposed rules . . . when considered as a whole," and "not to challenge the . . . rules in court to the extent that the final rules and their preambles have the same substance and effect as the . . . outline concurred in by the Advisory Committee." With the major issues settled by the agreement, the parties could work together to develop specific regulatory language to implement their handiwork.

This rule clearly demonstrated the power of the process: without the direct negotiations among the affected interests, there is very little chance that the rules would have been developed anywhere close to the schedule necessary to meet the ambitious goals of the *Clean Air Act Amendments of 1990*. Although each interest could point to sections they would have preferred to craft differently, the benefits of the final rule in addressing their most important needs clearly outweighed what would otherwise be considered negative features of the resulting regulations.

Notes and Questions

1. For further background on negotiated rulemaking (which is often called "reg-neg"), see Chapter VI, beginning at page 736; *Reg.Neg.*, NIDR News, Aug. 1995, at 6; Stephen B. Goldberg, *Reflections on Negotiated Rulemaking: From Conflict to Consensus*, Wash. Law., Sept.–Oct. 1994, at 42.

2. For a critique of negotiated rulemaking, see Cary Coglianese, *Assessing Consensus: The Promise and Performance of Negotiated Rulemaking*, 46 Duke L. J. 1255 (1997), arguing that the process does not save time or reduce litigation. Professor Harter criticized Coglianese's methods and conclusions in Philip J. Harter, *Assessing the Assessors: The Actual Performance of Negotiated Rulemaking*, 9 N.Y.U. Envtl. L.J. 32 (2000). Other positive assessments of the process appear in Laura I. Langbein & Cornelius M. Kerwin, *Regulatory Negotiation versus Conventional Rule Making: Claims, Counterclaims, and Empirical Evidence*, 10 J. Pub. Admin. Res. & Theory 599 (2000); Jody Freeman & Laura I. Langbein, *Regulatory Negotiation and the Legitimacy Benefit*, 9 N.Y.U. Envtl. L. J. 60 (2000).

3.   If you were selecting a mediator for a regulatory negotiation, what background and orientation would you seek?

4.   VICTIM OFFENDER MEDIATION

TEXAS CASE STUDY ONE: MURDER–VICTIM AND OFFENDER PERSPECTIVES, *IN* MARK S. UMBREIT, ET AL., FACING VIOLENCE: THE PATH OF RESTORATIVE JUSTICE AND DIALOGUE

45–52 (2003).

The Experience of the Event

Billie Lee Blair, divorced mother of an only child, was awakened by a phone call at 1:00 a.m. The male voice on the other end of the line opened with "Do you know a Bryan Blair?" When she responded with "yes, he's my son," the voice went on: "Somebody shot him a couple of hours ago. You'll need to come to San Antonio to pick up the body." Billie Lee lived alone in a small town some 200 miles from her son's college town. She called her best friend, who drove 50 miles and arrived by 4:00 a.m. Together they made the drive to San Antonio, and began making funeral arrangements.

Billie Lee stood up for herself at the funeral home and insisted on an uninterrupted time alone with her son's body. "It's very important, I feel, that a crime victim get that private time. I personally needed that time with Bryan, that was our time to say goodbye." Her loss was devastating, and there were times she felt suicidal. She had always taken care of Bryan and done what she was supposed to as a mother; now there was nothing more she could do for him. But there were important things she could do for herself. So many things went wrong at the trial of her son's murderer that Billie Lee became an advocate and got involved in victim organizations. She was concerned when she heard that a mediation program for victims of violent crime was being considered. "What if you go talk to that murderer and they tell you, 'Yes, I held that gun on your son, and yes, he was afraid?' And that crime victim that's so alone can't deal with it and they go commit suicide? What if the offender goes back and hangs himself in his cell?"

And, she focused on keeping the offender, James, in prison. Every six months she was at the parole board to make sure he wouldn't be released. James was often moved from one institution to another because of his unruly behavior. Billie Lee wanted to know why they couldn't put him in a more violent prison, where somebody might kill him. She even said they could fix prison overcrowding by just giving them all a loaded gun, locking the door and letting them see who survived.

The offender, James Lewis, who was 17 at the time, tells his experience of that night's events: "I was selling drugs and had two warrants out against me ... I knew right then they were lookin' for me." So he decided, "I'm gonna try and leave now, I'm not gonna stay and let the law catch me." His plan: to steal a car and flee Texas. He cruised a video arcade; upon seeing Bryan engrossed in a game, he approached him with "say, man, can I get a ride from you?" and told him his mother was sick. Bryan said yes but wanted to finish his game. While Bryan wasn't looking, James pulled his gun out, put three shells in it, and put it back under his shirt. They left together.

As James's directions began getting more and more complicated, Bryan finally protested and pulled the car to a stop, asking James to get out. "I tried to convince him to cut the engine, but he wouldn't. So I guess I was gonna try to wrestle him out of the car, but he reached up like he was gonna get a knife or a pistol or something, and I just blacked out and I turned around and pulled the trigger twice." The car, still running and in gear, crashed into a brick wall. When James regained consciousness he fled the scene, quickly wrapping the pistol in his jacket and stuffing both down a nearby sewer.

James ran home to his mother's house. "She knew I had a burglary warrant but I wasn't man enough to tell her that I just shot somebody." Within three days, police came to the home while he was still sleeping. "I woke up and rolled over and there was two detectives ... they asked me my name, gave me my rights and told me to get my clothes on." They didn't tell his mother what they were taking him to jail for. At the jail, officers presented him with his pistol and his jacket, both with his fingerprints on them.

James had no idea what he was in for. He heard his victim's mother was trying to get him sentenced to death, but stated he knew she couldn't do it, "because I didn't take nothing from him." He thought he might get 10 years or 15 at the most. He was shocked when his lawyer told him the best he could get was a plea bargain for 40 years, but he took it. And he added, "I don't blame her. Somebody kills my child, I wouldn't feel too much different. In my situation, justice was served."

Introduction to Mediation and Reasons for Participating

For a long time Billie Lee was adamantly against meeting with James. She watched videos of other mediations but felt if she were to meet with James, "nothing's gonna change and I'm not gonna know any more when I leave than when I started." But as her own healing progressed, her anger abated and she began to have reasons to meet with him. She wanted him to know how she felt about her son, and she wanted to make a change in his life. As she put it, "I wanted to make such an impression on him that his life would never, ever be the same. Mine's not, Bryan's isn't, and I told him, 'When you asked Bryan for a ride, our three lives were cemented together for eternity.'"

James was approached by a mediator from the Texas Victim Offender Mediation/Dialogue Program and invited to participate in dialogue with his victim's mother. The mediator was able to bring him a videotape of Billie Lee talking about her experience: "She just explained how she felt, she is real emotional — it's not real easy." It took him a long time to decide he would be willing to meet with her, but he began the preparation process with the mediator and felt this was what changed his mind.

He didn't really think there would be any benefits for himself. He felt the only thing he could give his victim's mother was "answers to why her son was murdered," and to let her know that when he got out he wasn't going to stalk her. He wasn't even sure that telling her he was sorry would make any difference: " 'That's gonna change what happened to her child? That ain't gonna change nothin'."

Preparation

The preparation phase in this case lasted for over two years, largely because James was continually in trouble in the prison, was frequently in lock-down, and often had to be moved from one prison to another.

As part of her preparation, Billie Lee studied James's life in detail. She learned where he grew up, read books on the slums he had come out of, and garnered tidbits of information from every source she could find. She came to understand that he had grown up in anger and violence and had never known the kinds of things she had so carefully taught her own son. She learned that as a very young boy he had seen his older brother kill a man. And she felt that his excessive infraction record in the institution was a result of having no life skills, no way of handling any feelings. Out of all this material she carefully drafted an opening statement that she hoped would cause James to *feel* the pain he had created.

Billie Lee found the process of her preparation to be very helpful and deeply appreciated the support of her mediator throughout. She rated her evaluation of the preparation as "somewhat satisfied" because she wished she had been given more detail about the physical setting. She was shocked to discover how tiny the table was separating herself from James in the conference room — it placed her much too close to him for comfort, and she had nowhere to set all the things she had brought with her to share. She recommended that victims be given a chance to see the meeting set-up ahead of time, get a feel for it, and have the opportunity to make changes if possible.

James and the mediator met sporadically over the two-year stretch of the preparation phase. Interruptions were frequent due to his being in lock-down, but at other times they met as often as twice a month. Over time James came to trust the mediator and the process. "He told me, 'I've been doing this quite a while, and so far we never had no one attack their offender.'"

For James, the preparation process was "a healing process, it's like a therapy." He felt preparation was as good as it could have been, though he still was unprepared for how emotional both he and Billie Lee became. The most helpful thing the mediator did was bringing videos of other mediations. "I seen from my own eyes that he's not new at this, he's pretty professional."

The Mediation/Dialogue Session

The session lasted for eight hours, with small breaks and a break for lunch. Present were only Billie Lee, James, the mediator, and the camera crew.

According to Billie Lee, James had brought no opening statement. She began with hers, and shared Bryan's baby book and a large photograph of him. "I asked him if he remembered what Bryan looked like and he said, 'No.' How can you kill somebody that you don't even know?" Fairly quickly she knew she had him where she wanted him. He hung his head and began to cry — and, to her own surprise, she reached for a tissue and wiped his eyes. "I felt compassion for him — my child had those skills, my child was nurtured, this young man had no life skills at all. He was lost." Later in the interview Billie Lee described an even more surprising moment: she herself was crying, and James reached over with a tissue and wiped her tears.

Billie Lee reported that at one point in the mediation James said, "But I don't have anything to give you," and she responded, "Yes you do. You can change. You can be different. I know what your I.Q. is, You're capable of learning." And she gave him a book she had found written by someone else who had grown up in the same ghetto and succeeded. She described his response: "He just cradled the book in his arms, and he said, 'I ain't never had no book come to me before. You can get 'em, but I ain't never had no book.'"

Billie Lee received a lot of information from James and found it very helpful. He told her how the events of the crime unfolded and he shared Bryan's last words. And she came to understand that he didn't set out to commit murder. "He really didn't want to kill him. He got scared, he panicked. And you can't say it was an accident, because he did have a loaded gun. But I think he thought he'd just shoot Bryan in the arm."

James was surprised that Billie Lee looked almost exactly as he had remembered her from the courtroom many years earlier. He said Billie Lee explained to him all the things she'd been through: her own experience with a violent husband and then raising Bryan without a father, Bryan's life and hopes and dreams, his photograph, and all his baby pictures. When James was asked how this affected him, he responded "There's no way I can sit here and try to describe the feeling, it was so emotional, I looked into her eyes and I couldn't say nothing, for about ten minutes."

James reported that when he told Billie Lee that his own mother had advised him against doing the mediation, she was concerned that he had gone against what his mother said. He responded, "My mother got five kids, all her boys in prison. You only had one son, he's gone forever. She'll probably never know how you feel. That's why I disregarded what she said."

James described how Billie Lee confronted him about his prison behavior. "She said, 'You got a hundred cases, why do you have all these cases?' I explained how when I came to prison I just didn't care. But now I care." And, he told her about his own childhood, about moving from a small town to an urban ghetto as a 10-year-old and getting hooked on drugs. He was stunned when she pulled out a book by someone from his own neighborhood: "She found out how it is livin' in the ghetto and livin' on the streets, 80% of the black families they don't have no father — she gave me this big twenty-one dollar book." She told him she wanted to help him, that she wanted him to get back in the class and get his G.E.D. And when she left, "She smiled, she laughed, and she said, 'James, I could go off filled with hatred — I just don't hate you no more.' "

Outcome and Evaluation

Billie Lee accomplished what she set out to do. James felt the pain she wanted him to feel — perhaps, she thinks, for the first time in his life. She was able to bring him what she had given her own son, and what she felt no one in his life had been able to do for him. And she got a commitment out of him to change. At the time of the interview, she reported James's prison infractions had completely ceased. She worried that he wasn't going as deep as he needed to but was very glad for his behavior change.

When asked to evaluate the impact of the mediation on her outlook on life, Billie Lee rated her outlook as only "somewhat" changed, because of the changes she had already undergone. In particular she felt her spiritual journey had both helped her heal and helped prepare her for her meeting with James. "I just inhale books ... I began learning tolerance, not so much for Bryan's murder, as for other people. We are all the children of the world, and my spiritual belief is that the power that created us all has put us here to learn lessons."

Billie Lee was extremely pleased with her mediator's role during the session. She knew there were times when he might have wanted to jump in and was impressed that he held back and let her and James handle the process in their own way. She did report that she found it difficult to bring the session to an end, and rated her satisfaction level as "somewhat satisfied." This led her to recommend that preparation could also include thinking about a closing statement: "What would be the last words the victim would want to leave in the offender's ears?" She also found it somewhat unfair that for the preparation phase, mediators can travel to where the offenders are located to meet with them, but victims have to travel to where the mediators are. "It's not balanced."

James could hardly find words for how impactful the meeting has been in his life. "And wow, you know, wow, if I ever get my class back, I'll be helpin' a bunch of kids, so they don't follow in my footprints ... she's always wanting me to help change other people's lives." Later he added, "I made a commitment. I'm not gonna mess up, I'm gonna do what she told me."

James was deeply impressed with Billie Lee: "She's the strongest woman I ever met." He has seen a video of Billie Lee's debriefing and was very moved: "She was concerned about me, she asked the mediator, 'do you think he'll be all right?' just like I was her child." In fact, he felt she was more concerned about him than his own mother, who had made no contact for two years. "She calls up here every week."

Advice to Others

Billie Lee's words: "I'd encourage anybody to do it if it's appropriate, but not with somebody that's still going to be angry." She felt anyone who decides to meet their offender should get as fully informed about the person and the crime as possible, much in the way she did. She also encouraged participants to ask for a picture of the offender so they won't be surprised at the beginning of the session.

James thought perhaps it might depend on the crime, but in general felt offenders should participate in mediation if their victim wants to, because they never know what they can accomplish — "If you don't try to change your life in here, you're just wasting your time, and when you get out you're gonna come right back. So if you got somebody out there trying to help you, you'd be a fool not to take up on it."

Notes and Questions

1. More than 300 victim offender mediation (VOM) programs operate in the U.S. and at least 1100 operate abroad. Most focus on juvenile rather than adult crime and tend to address less serious offenses. MARK S. UMBREIT, BETTY VOS, ROBERT B. COATES & KATHERINE A. BROWN, FACING VIOLENCE: THE PATH OF RESTORATIVE JUSTICE AND DIALOGUE 11 (2003). Umbreit and his co-authors describe the usual procedures:

> The process undertaken by most VOM programs is very similar. Trained mediators or facilitators, who may be paid staff members but are more often community volunteers, make contact with the offenders and victims who have been referred and invite their participation, which is always voluntary for the victim and most often voluntary for the offender. If both parties express interest in meeting, facilitators typically provide at least one "preparation" meeting for both the victim and the offender, in which they explore the participant's experience of the event, the nature of the harm caused, and potential avenues for repairing the harm. Victim and offender are then brought together in a meeting that usually opens with sharing the experience of the crime, and then turns to a discussion of restitution or other resolution. Often family members, support persons, and/or other community members may also be present. Facilitators remain "neutral" in the sense that they support both the victim and the offender in sharing their experience and working toward a resolution. Some programs remain in contact with participants afterwards to monitor compliance with any negotiated agreement; in other programs the referring jurisdiction retains this responsibility.
>
> There is a growing body of empirical research on VOM worldwide * * * [B]oth victims and offenders who have participated in VOM have

consistently reported high levels of satisfaction with the process and with the outcome of their meetings. Some studies have found that victims reported reduced levels of fear as a result of their meetings with offenders. In some instances, offender participants have higher rates of restitution compliance than similar offenders whose restitution require- ments were not mutually negotiated with victims. And there are en- couraging reports of reduced offender recidivism among many VOM programs. It is becoming increasingly clear that the VOM process hu- manizes the criminal justice experience for both victim and offender, holds offenders directly accountable to the people they victimized, al- lows for more active involvement of crime victims and community members (as participants or as volunteer mediators) in the justice process,, and can potentially suppress further criminal behaviors in offenders.

Id. at 11–12.

As this excerpt suggests, the parties are not mediating the question of the defendant's guilt or innocence in a victim offender mediation. Many VOM programs require an admission or adjudication of guilt. What is being mediated is restitution, the relationship between the victim and the defen- dant, or other terms that may be appropriate to the particular case.

2.   Victim offender mediation has faced criticism, too. Professor Jenni- fer Brown has criticized victim-offender mediation because it inappropriately allows the victim to have some control over the offender's fate. She recom- mends a complete separation between victim offender mediation and the criminal justice system. Jennifer Gerarda Brown, *The Use of Mediation to Resolve Criminal Cases: A Procedural Critique*, 43 Emory L.J. 1247 (1994). And Professor Annalise Acorn has provided an extensive critique of "restora- tive justice," of which victim offender mediation is a part. She criticizes "much of [the] rhetoric [of restorative justice] and the aspirations it inspires as culpably sentimental and dangerously naïve." Annalise Acorn, Compulsory Compassion: A Critique of Restorative Justice 19 (2004). For a thorough analysis of restorative justice, see John Braithwaite, Restorative Justice and Responsible Regulation (2002).

3.   Which dimensions of conflict — behavioral, cognitive, emotional — are typically (or best) addressed through a criminal prosecution? Through a victim offender mediation?

4.   Another way to think about these issues is in terms of what the problem-definition is or should be, in a given mediation. In a victim-offender mediation, such as the one described by Umbreit and his colleagues, to what extent do or should the various participants — the victim, the offender, the mediator — influence the development of the problem-definition? *See* Leon- ard L. Riskin, *Decisionmaking in Mediation: The New Old Grid and the New New Grid System,* 79 Notre Dame L. Rev. 1 (2003), an excerpt from which appears infra in Chapter IV, beginning at page 423.

5.   For further information on victim-offender mediation, see generally Mark S. Umbreit, Victim Meets Offender: The Impact of Restorative Justice and Mediation (1994) and the Victim Offender Mediation Association web site, www.voma.org.

Note: Mediation in Other Contexts and by Other Names

1. In the U.S., mediation takes place in a great variety of arenas, in addition to those mentioned in this section and in the introduction to this chapter. To give yourself a fuller picture, see JAMES J. ALFINI, SHARON B. PRESS, JEAN R. STERNLIGHT & JOSEPH B. STULBERG, MEDIATION THEORY AND PRACTICE 513–89 (2001); DONNA CRAWFORD & RICHARD BODINE, CONFLICT RESOLUTION EDUCATION: A GUIDE TO IMPLEMENTING PROGRAMS IN SCHOOLS, YOUTH SERVING ORGANIZATIONS, AND COMMUNITY AND JUVENILE JUSTICE SETTINGS (1996); WHEN TALK WORKS: PROFILES OF MEDIATORS (Deborah M. Kolb ed., 1993); ROGER RICHMAN, ORION F. WHITE, JR. & MICHAUX H. WILKINSON, INTERGOVERNMENTAL MEDIATION: NEGOTIATIONS IN LOCAL GOVERNMENT DISPUTES (1986); JEFFREY M. SENGER, FEDERAL DISPUTE RESOLUTION: USING ADR WITH THE UNITED STATES GOVERNMENT (2004); COMMUNITY MEDIATION: A HANDBOOK FOR PRACTITIONERS AND RESEARCHERS (Karen Grover Duffy, James W. Grosch & Paul V. Olczak eds., 1991); Wallace Warfield, *Building Consensus for Racial Harmony in American Cities: A Case Model Approach*, 1996 J. Disp. Resol. 151.

2. It is common for federal district courts to appoint mediators, sometimes calling them special masters, in complex institutional reform cases, such as those involving segregation in public schools and overcrowding of prisons. *See* Vincent M. Nathan, *The Use of Special Masters in Institutional Reform Litigation*, 10 U. Tol. L. Rev. 419 (1979). For other examples of mediations of cases involving constitutional rights, see THE PROMISE AND PERFORMANCE OF ENVIRONMENTAL CONFLICT RESOLUTION (Rosemary O'Leary & Lisa B. Bingham eds., 2003); Lela Love, *Glen Cove: Mediation Achieves What Litigation Cannot*, CONSENSUS, Oct. 1993, at 1.

3. It is increasingly common for mediators to facilitate negotiations among participants on one side of a dispute. Sometimes — generally when many individuals will be involved in a mediation — mediators also will provide negotiation training before a mediation begins.

4. Culture affects mediation, just as it affects negotiation, as we saw in Chapter III. One reason for the variety of mediation practices in the U.S. is that mediations take place among different cultures or subcultures. The culture of personal injury lawyers and their clients is likely to shape a mediation process differently than would the culture of divorce lawyers and clients or the culture of business lawyers and their clients.

It should not be surprising, therefore, that in cultures radically different from ours, "mediation" would have a radically different character. For some examples, see JOHN PAUL LEDERACH, PREPARING FOR PEACE: CONFLICT TRANSFORMATION ACROSS CULTURES (1995); Bruce E. Barnes, *Conflict Resolution Across Cultures: A Hawaii Perspective and a Pacific Mediation Model*, 12 Med. Q. 117 (1995); Fu Hualing, *Understanding People's Mediation in Post–Mao China*, 6 J. Chinese L. 211 (1992); Michelle LeBaron, *Conflict Resolution in Native Cultures: An Overview*, NIDR Forum, Spr. 1995, at 1; James A. Wall, Jr., *Community Mediation in China and Korea: Some Similarities and Differences*, 9 Negotiation J. 141 (1993); Robert Yazzie, *Traditional Navajo Dispute Resolution in the Navajo Peacemaker Court*, NIDR Forum, Spr. 1994, at 5.

5. An increasingly important application of mediation is in the fostering of democracy. *See Special Issue: Developing Mediation Processes in the New Democracies*, 10 Mediation Q. 225 (1993); *Symposium: The Lawyer's Role(s) in Deliberative Democracy: A Commentary by and Responses to Carrie Menkel–Meadow*, 5 Nev. L.J. 347 (2005); Richard C. Reuben, *Democracy and Dispute Resolution: The Problem of Arbitration*, 67 L. & Contemp. Probs. 279 (Winter/Spring 2004).

And, of course, mediation has always been an essential feature of international relations. *See* Marieke Kleiboer, The Multiple Realities of International Mediation (1998).

Not surprisingly, mediation and other forms of dispute resolution also take place on-line. See Chapter VI, beginning at page 780.

6. The terms "conciliation" and "facilitation" sometimes are used to describe processes that we would call mediation. However, sometimes the terms have different meanings. For example, in some programs, conciliation refers to the process of helping parties agree to mediation. And often facilitation refers to processes that are less focused (or not focused) on resolving a particular dispute. For background on facilitation, and different notions of that process, see Sam Kaner, Lenny Lind, Catherine Toldi, Sarah Fisk & Duane Berger, Facilitator's Guide to Participatory Decision-Making (1996); Roger M. Schwarz, The Skilled Facilitator: Practical Wisdom for Developing Effective Groups (1994).

C. THE PARTICIPANTS AND PROCESSES

In Part C, we try to understand the mediation process more fully. We do this by focusing in Section 1 on the Mediator and in Section 2, on the parties. In Section 3, we examine the issue of confidentiality in mediation, which has spawned much controversy, and some legislation in recent years.

1. THE MEDIATOR

A mediator's behavior in and about mediation is affected by many factors, including their personalities, professional training and experience, mediation training and education, their philosophies, beliefs and assumptions about mediation, and potential sources of professional regulation, such as the market for mediation, codes of conduct, and risks of malpractice liability. In this section, we survey a number of these elements.

a. Sources and Backgrounds

Mediators come in many varieties. In community mediation programs and some small-claims court mediation programs, volunteer mediators are drawn from nearly all walks of life and vary greatly in terms of education, socio-economic status, and occupation. In many court-connected mediation programs, however, the mediators must be lawyers or have other specialized education. Government and business organizations that sponsor mediation programs often have special requirements.

For consideration of such requirements, see Chapter VI, beginning at page 687.

Many private providers of dispute resolution services maintain rosters of mediators. Some of these are non-profit organizations, such as the American Arbitration Association, the CPR Institute for Dispute Resolution, and state and local bar associations. Others, such as JAMS and U.S. Arbitration & Mediation Service, are organized for profit. Until it merged with Endispute in 1994, JAMS (Judicial Arbitration and Mediation Services) included only retired judges on its panels. Nearly all mediation programs and providers have substantial training requirements, ranging from sixteen to forty-eight hours, though many of these have "grandfather" exceptions that cover judges or others with substantial dispute resolution experience.

Numerous law firms now provide neutral services, and many small groups have organized solely to offer such services. In addition thousands of people across the U.S. have been trained in mediation. Many of these offer their services directly to the public; some are very busy, while others have little or no mediation work.

b. Training of Mediators

A mediator's training is likely to have a significant impact on her or his performance — though not as significant as many trainers would hope. There are many varieties of mediation training. Organizations offer specialized training to deal with disputes involving such fields as divorce, environmental protection, special education, victim-offender, and attorney-client fee disputes. The training programs vary to some extent with the specialty and with the philosophies of the trainers, including their mental models of mediation, such as those described supra in Chapter IV, Section A. These programs generally include certain core elements, however. The following reading comes from a mediation training guide intended to be "generic," but which is based largely on assumptions associated with the mediation of civil, non-family disputes, which are, or might be, in litigation.

LEONARD L. RISKIN, MEDIATION TRAINING GUIDE

(excerpts) (2004).

A. THE MEDIATOR'S ROLE

The following list provides a way to understand the range of functions a mediator can perform; it arranges the "interventions" very roughly from the least to the most active:

- urging participants to agree to talk
- helping participants understand the mediation process
- providing a suitable environment for negotiation
- carrying messages between participants
- helping participants agree upon an agenda

- setting an agenda
- maintaining order
- clarifying misunderstandings
- identifying issues
- helping participants understand the problem(s)
- defusing unrealistic expectations
- carrying offers back and forth
- rephrasing one participant's perspective or proposals into a form that is understandable and acceptable to the others
- helping participants develop their own proposals
- helping participants negotiate
- expanding resources
- proposing possible solutions
- persuading participants to accept a particular solution

Disagreement abounds concerning the mediator's role, and commentators have described and promoted a variety of models of mediation, each grounded on a particular ideology of mediation or assumptions about what goals are appropriate. [We cover such issues primarily in Section A of this Chapter, though they also arise in many other spots.]

* * *

B. OVERVIEW OF STAGES, STRATEGIES, AND TACTICS IN MEDIATION

To explain mediation, most writers conceptualize it in terms of stages. For simplicity, I suggest an alternative approach — to understand mediation in terms of five tasks that must be accomplished:

1. Agreeing to mediate;
2. Understanding the problem(s);
3. Generating options;
4. Reaching agreement;
5. Implementing the agreement.

A mediation usually addresses these tasks in the above order, hence the implication of stages. On the other hand, sometimes the parties cannot really agree to mediate until they understand the problems or generate options. In any multi-session mediation, each of these tasks is addressed in virtually every session. The agreement to mediate, for instance, almost always is tentative and subject to recission; a party can walk out at any time. Thus, every session involves a new commitment. Participants begin to work at "understanding the problems" immediately; however, new understandings develop continually. Even after fifteen hours of mediation, with the parties on the verge of agreement, or at impasse, suddenly a new insight can emerge. Similarly, parties can reach tentative accords on some issues in the earliest stages, subject to later developments.

Joint Sessions or Private Sessions (Caucuses)

Before explaining the mediation process in more detail, it is important to describe the private caucus. Most mediators use a combination of joint sessions and private sessions (caucuses). A caucus can be employed during any stage of a mediation. It can give a mediator a good chance to develop trust and rapport with a party, to learn the party's real interests or positions, to defuse unrealistic expectations, and to help the party develop or assess proposals. If you caucus with one party, always caucus with the other(s) before returning to a joint session.

Some mediators use the caucus routinely in the belief that parties will speak freely only in private. Other mediators tend to use caucuses only as needed, which often means when the parties are at impasse or the mediator suspects a party is holding back. Mediators who avoid the caucus do so on the theory that one of the great values of mediation is to facilitate direct communication between the parties, which can lead to new understandings and improved relationships. Private meetings can inhibit such direct communication, and something nearly always is lost in the mediator's translation. (One lawyer-mediator feels so strongly about this that he tells parties they may call a caucus with him but that he will not keep from the other party information revealed in a caucus. Gary J. Friedman, A Guide to Divorce Mediation 36–37 (1993)).

1.   Agreeing to Mediate

a.   Pre-mediation

Some mediations typically begin with or are preceded by private sessions — in person or by telephone — involving the mediator and the individual lawyers or parties. Sometimes the parties do not agree to mediate until after such sessions. Much depends on the nature of the dispute and the types of parties. In most cases, however, it is best to begin with a joint session.

b.   The First Joint Session

Goals for the first joint session include: 1) ensuring that the parties understand mediation; 2) helping the parties decide whether they wish to continue with mediation; 3) allowing the mediator to decide whether mediation seems appropriate and whether the mediator can work with these parties and what problems they will face; and 4) setting the tone and structure for future sessions. To achieve these goals, the mediator should undertake the following tasks, while treating all participants equally and with respect:

(1)   Seat the participants

Decide in advance where the parties should sit, so as not to exacerbate adversarial tendencies. If the group is small and the room suitable — and tensions are not terribly high — consider sitting in comfortable chairs in a circle rather than at a rectangular table. The seating should reflect equality. For example, the mediator generally should not sit behind a desk. To encourage participation by clients, seat them close to the mediator and put their lawyers further away.

(2) Introduce self and others present

Raise the question of how participants will address one another — by first names or by "Mr.," "Ms.," and the like.

(3) Identify basic nature of dispute

The mediator should ask the parties to state briefly the nature of the dispute and the parties' relationship, for two reasons: first, to be sure the dispute that brought the parties into mediation is still a problem, and, second, to give them an opportunity to speak early in the process, which could relieve tension and reflect the participatory nature of the process. In some cases, especially if the mediator has been in touch with the parties during the pre-mediation process, this step may be unnecessary.

Beware of premature diagnosis of the problem. Avoid letting the parties' initial definition of the problem restrict the issues that later become relevant for discussion, as this might inhibit creativity. In most cases, parties initially will conceive of the problem in adversarial, "win-lose" terms. Sometimes, particularly in a dispute over money, that approach may be appropriate; but the mediator should remain open to the possibilities of expanding the pie, of reaching a problem-solving solution that goes beyond the parties' stated positions and responds to their underlying interests.

(4) Educate Parties About Nature of Mediation Process: The Mediator's Opening Statement and Initial Dialogue

Explain how mediation generally works and allow opportunities for questions, dialogue, and negotiation about the mediation process. This education process should include information on the following:

(a) Basic explanation of mediation

Mediation is a voluntary process in which a neutral third party helps the disputants reach their own resolution. The mediator (unlike a judge or arbitrator) will not decide the case.

In my view, the appropriate goal is to reach an agreement that satisfies the parties' underlying interests, that is fair to the parties, and that is not unfair to affected third parties. Other mediators have different, sometimes narrower or broader, ideas about the appropriate goals.

(b) The mediator's role

The mediator is impartial. The mediator keeps order, facilitates communication, clarifies issues, and keeps participants moving toward their own agreement. The mediator, unlike judge or arbitrator, does not decide the case.

(c) The roles of lawyers and clients

Address the role of the lawyer. Much will depend on the nature of the case. Some mediations will involve only lawyers, not clients. Other mediations — such as the typical divorce or community mediation — will involve only parties, not lawyers. In private divorce mediations, however, the parties often consult lawyers before finalizing an agreement, whereas this is rarely done in community mediation.

In many mediations, especially those arising in cases in which a lawsuit has been filed, both lawyers and clients attend. It generally facilitates settlement if the clients can speak directly to one another for at least part of the session. Lawyers can play supporting, advisory roles. In some cases, mediators will ask lawyers not to sit at the table, thereby encouraging greater client communication. Another possibility is that the lawyers do some of the talking — e.g., present the clients' legal argument — and the clients do the rest. Many variations are possible.

It is important that the mediator raise the question of the roles of lawyers and clients, so that the parties and lawyers understand that they have to make decisions about this.

The mediator — especially if she is a lawyer — should inform the parties that she does not represent any party, and cannot represent either party in any related matter.

If the mediator determines that one or more of the parties needs legal counsel, she should tell them so and offer to help them find a lawyer, if necessary.

(d) Other participants

As appropriate, the parties or the mediator may include witnesses to an event or other individuals, such as an expert, who might help resolve the conflict.

(e) Mediation procedure

The mediator should present an outline of the steps in mediation, which should include:

[1] Each side has uninterrupted time to make an opening statement about the case and how he would like to see it resolved.

[2] Mediator and other participants discuss what issues must be addressed and how best to address them, i.e., plan an agenda.

[3] Parties (or their lawyers) gather and present in more detail the necessary information (unless it is presented in sufficient detail above).

[4] Parties, lawyers, and mediator develop options to meet the parties' needs.

[5] Parties negotiate and choose among options.

[6] Parties, lawyers, or mediator may incorporate the agreement into a contract.

(f) Agreement to mediate

In some circumstances, and in some jurisdictions, it will be advisable to ask the parties to sign an agreement to mediate. Some agreements — such as those commonly used in private divorce mediation — will include detailed rules of mediation, an explanation of fees, and the like. Others will be brief and will simply state that the parties submit the case to mediation.

(g) Caucuses

Either the mediator or a party may call a private caucus. Statements made during caucuses will be kept confidential except to the extent that the caucusing party permits the mediator to reveal the information. If you plan to hold caucuses immediately after the initial session, it is advisable to announce it at this time.

(h) Confidentiality

Mediation thrives best in an atmosphere of free and open discussion. To foster such discussion requires that information revealed during a mediation be shielded, at least to some extent, against subsequent disclosure both in and out of court. Thus, it may be desirable to protect information against:

1. Admissibility or discoverability in a subsequent judicial proceeding in the same case;

2. Revelation and admissibility through subpoena or depositions in other cases; and

3. Revelation to third parties.

In most jurisdictions, some or all of these results may be achieved by virtue of court rules, statutes, or agreement between the parties. The mediator should ensure that the parties and their lawyers are aware of the protections available and the limitations on these protections. In many jurisdictions, for example, laws that mandate reporting of child abuse may affect the mediator's obligations as to confidentiality. And the mediator may have duties to protect the interests of other third parties. Often mediators ask parties to sign a confidentiality agreement that incorporates applicable rules or establishes additional obligations. Sometimes parties wish to negotiate their own confidentiality agreement. [Confidentiality in mediation is discussed more fully in this book in Chapter IV, beginning at page 439.]

(i) Evidence

Stress informality of the process. Rules of evidence do not apply. Information may be presented by witnesses, documents, or narrative of parties. Within reason, anything the parties deem relevant is relevant. For example, the fact that one party feels offended by the other's conduct toward her is relevant in a mediation though it might not be relevant in a court or arbitration proceeding.

(j) Fees

The mediator should be certain the parties understand the fee arrangements. Most mediators in private practice charge an hourly fee that close to (or the same as) the fee they charge for their other professional services such as law or psychotherapy. Some mediators charge a flat daily rate or an additional administrative fee. Normally mediators who are required to travel expect reimbursement for travel expenses.

Some court connected or community oriented mediation programs charge no fees or minimal fees. Some private mediators will waive or reduce fees in appropriate cases.

(k) Questions

Be sure to allow time for parties to ask questions about the process and to participate in planning how the process will work.

By this point, the parties should have a fundamental understanding of mediation and the mediator should have some insight into the problem and how the parties relate to one another. The mediator should not be surprised at having to repeat much of the above information later.

2. Understanding the Problems

After the introductory stage, the task is to begin understanding the problems, which can be divided into two types:

Problems inside the mediation. These are problems that will affect the mediation process, such as how well the parties can work with one another or with the mediator. Issues of power imbalance and emotions such as anger, hurt, and pride are important here. In dealing with internal problems, the mediator should consider such questions as:

How will the parties' relationship affect their ability to negotiate?

How openly will the parties speak?

How adversarial or problem-solving are the parties' likely perspectives and behaviors?

How well do the parties understand the difficulties they will face in the mediation process?

What strategies might the mediator employ to deal with problems that affect the process?

Problems that gave rise to the mediation. These are the basic facts, feelings, and perceptions relevant to the conflict. The mediator should consider such questions as:

How do the parties perceive what happened?

How well do they understand each other's perceptions?

What resolution does each party want?

If the parties are taking adversarial "positions," what are the chances of converting the negotiation into a joint problem-solving effort?

Feelings and perceptions are as important as more objective facts, such as how much rent is owed or who did what when. Moreover, in the usual case, the mediator should not only try to understand both sets of problems described above, he also should help all parties understand these problems so that the mediation can foster joint problem-solving.

The mediator should begin gathering information about these problems as soon as he gets involved in the case. The introductory phase, described above, will be a rich source of impressions. A more formal procedure for "understanding the problems" is described below.

a.   Parties' opening statements

Each party is allowed time to present his or her view of the problem and to indicate his or her preferred resolution. The other parties should not interrupt the presentation. It is important to allow each speaker room express feelings and raise issues. The mediator may, however, interrupt to keep the presentation focused and to clarify important facts or issues. In making such interventions, the mediator should bear in mind suggestions about interviewing techniques described in Chapter II.

In particular the mediator should strive to identify and make relevant the parties' underlying interests. Thoughtful questioning and active listening will help.

During this time, the mediator should take notes, using brief phrases that will remind him of the ideas he is trying to capture, and try to keep eye contact with the speaker. If there are only two or three parties, you might try having a separate column for each on your note pad, so you may readily compare their outlooks. Do not try to make your own transcript.

b.   Post statement information gathering, issue identification, and agenda setting

After the opening presentations, the mediator should work with the parties to identify the issues that must be addressed and to begin to develop a process for addressing them. This may be done by continuing the joint session or by adjourning to private caucuses.

The mediator and the parties should jointly determine the issues to be addressed and the order in which to take them up — i.e., the agenda. The mediator should list the issues on a flip chart or blackboard and work with the parties to order them. Reaching agreement on these points can encourage the parties and help them learn to negotiate.

Ordinarily it is best to begin with the easier issues, so as to generate momentum. Sometimes, however, this is not feasible. It may be essential, for substantive reasons, to settle a difficult issue — at least tentatively—before addressing others. Sometimes a party may wish to address a particularly difficult issue first because it is of overriding importance to her. If the mediator thinks it preferable to postpone this issue, he could acknowledge its importance and explain why he thinks postponement is likely to be beneficial. But a mediator should be flexible and willing to change his thinking as he learns from the parties.

In addition, the mediators should help the parties

• Identify any decisions that must be made immediately.

- Identify additional information that is needed, e.g., written agreements, receipts, depositions. Decide who will provide such information and set deadlines.

- Decide if any witnesses or other participants are needed for the mediation.

- Decide if all the necessary parties are present.

c. Underlying interests

Here are a number of techniques for bringing out underlying interests that the mediator can use at various points.

- Explain and illustrate the difference between interests and positions and the advantages of interest-based bargaining.

- As part of active listening, try to identify interests that lie behind statements made by the parties. In joint sessions, such active listening can help each participant understand the other's interests.

- Ask questions about plans and then speculate, with the participant, about the participants' interests.

- Float proposals for resolution and measure the parties' responses in terms of the likely interests represented.

- When dealing with a given proposal, ask what interests it fosters or impedes.

- Listen for understanding. [For more on listening, see Chapter II, Section D.2., beginning at page 137, and Note 1, following this excerpt.]

d. Other Approaches to Understanding the Problems.

(1) Orienting toward future.

At many points during a mediation, a party may talk at great length about what another party did wrong. Although this is sometimes useful, often it causes tensions and non-productive arguments to escalate. The mediator should remind the parties that the purpose of mediation is to plan for the future and that too much rehashing the past can interfere with that goal.

(2) Understanding other perspectives.

Often a party will not understand the way another party perceives the situation. The mediator can help him do so by stressing that the other person's perspective is itself a fact, regardless of whether he agrees with that perspective. The mediator also can ask each party to explain how they think the other actually sees the situation (not how they should see it), and then ask the other to comment. Sometimes it is effective to ask the parties to reverse roles: "Joe, make believe you are Robert. Tell us, in Robert's words, how you think Robert sees this." Such moments may allow for the "recognition" that is a cornerstone of Bush and Folger's notion of "transformation," which they promote as a goal of mediation. ROBERT A. BARUCH BUSH & JOSEPH FOLGER, THE PROMISE

OF MEDIATION: THE TRANSFORMATIVE APPROACH TO CONFLICT 2D ED. (2005). [A portion of this book is reprinted supra at Chapter IV, Section B, beginning at page 300.]

There are, of course, situations in which one participant is unwilling to understand the perspectives of the other; sometimes this occurs when the participant cannot control his rage or fear. In other situations, a participant may fear that if he understood his counterpart's perspective, he might empathize, and, as a decent person, have to change his position. Although many would consider this an important form of moral growth, not everyone wants it. For instance, if you are negotiating with an apparently impoverished merchant, do you really want to know how desperately his large family needs the money? Would you get a "worse" deal, financially, if you did?

(3) Defining the problems to be addressed.

Activities such as the foregoing can help clarify the scope of the problem to be addressed in the mediation. For our purposes, problems may be defined along a continuum ranging from broad to narrow. See Leonard L. Riskin, *Understanding Mediators' Orientations, Strategies and Techniques: A Grid for the Perplexed,* 1 Harv. Negot. L. Rev. 7, 18–23 (1997). [A portion of this article appears earlier in this chapter, beginning at page 288.]

A narrowly defined problem ordinarily involves just one issue, such as who gets how much of something — money, coffee, cheese. In such a "distributive" negotiation, what one party wins the other loses; there is a fixed pie, so to speak. In these cases, one party may demand $100,000 and the other may offer $20,000. Ideally, and perhaps with the help of the mediator, each will have a rationale for his "position."

A broad conceptualization of the problem may involve more than one issue. Accordingly, there may be room for trade-offs to recognize that parties may attach different values to the same issue. "Problem-solving" negotiation (or "integrative bargaining") seeks to satisfy underlying interests. Thus, if issues of money, prestige, safety, and specific pieces of property are present, many more solutions are possible than if money is the only issue.

In many mediations, parties enter not only with an adversarial attitude but also with a distributive concept of the problem. Often the mediator can best serve the parties by helping them expand the number of issues, and thus the possible solutions.

Sometimes the mediator can help the parties broaden a narrow distributive problem. Imagine a dispute over whether back rent is due. The tenant believes she owes only $300 for one month's rent while the landlord believes she is entitled to $600. Using a distributive approach, the parties cannot settle; their settlement ranges do not overlap. The mediator can help the parties introduce another factor, such as time, which the parties might value differently. A tenant might need her security deposit back before 30 days but might be willing to move immediately. The landlord might want to rent the apartment immediately and would be willing to return the tenant's deposit. Similarly the tenant might be willing to pay more than $300.00 if the payments were extended over time. By making the parties' underlying interests relevant, the mediator can increase the likelihood of agreement.

Even in disputes that obviously have many facets, the mediator can increase the likelihood of an integrative settlement by getting the parties to consider their own and each other's underlying interests and then focusing on developing options that meet them. [See the discussion of underlying interests supra, beginning at pages 19, 112, and 197.]

3. Generating Options

The mediator has a number of strategies and techniques for developing options and moving the parties toward solution. For most of these to work, the parties must have some understanding of "problem-solving" negotiation and the differences between positions and interests (discussed supra). The mediator may have to explain and illustrate these matters more than once. In addition, it must be clear that the goal is to separate option development from option selection. Because judging, selecting, and choosing interfere with creativity, we postpone them.

Here are some strategies for developing options and moving parties toward agreement.

a. Dealing with specific proposals by the parties

In true distributive problems, specific proposals about amounts of money (or goods or materials) will be important and often dominant. And note that in late stages of most negotiations, the time comes when distributive questions must be answered; after enlarging the pie, it must be divided.

Sometimes in the early stages of mediation, specific proposals can be counter-productive. On the other hand it is usually more desirable if the parties — rather than the mediator — initiate proposals; this gives the parties a greater sense of psychological "ownership" and allows the mediator to remain more detached and objective. What the mediator should do when a party wishes to make a specific proposal depends upon factors too numerous and subtle to describe, but here are a few suggestions.

1. Treat the proposal as one option.

2. Examine and discuss the proposal to learn what underlying interests of the proponent it is designed to serve and how it affects the underlying interests of others.

3. Listen to the proposal in private caucus and help the party decide whether to (a) modify the proposal to better address underlying needs; (b) present it to the other parties, either directly or through the mediator; (c) delay its presentation; or (d) drop it.

4. Discuss the proposal with the other parties in a joint session or caucus.

b. Brainstorming

In brainstorming the parties are encouraged to suggest virtually any possible solution that comes to mind, and, what is most important, no one — not even the proposer — is allowed to assess or judge any proposal. The mediator should list the ideas on a blackboard or flip chart and then, when brainstorming is completed, lead the parties through assessing the extent to which each alternative meets the parties' underlying needs. Many suggestions will be obviously inappropriate, but sometimes elements of proposals can be combined into new proposals. More likely, the process will reveal several options the parties think are worth further discussion. Brainstorming also may help identify underlying interests.

4. Reaching Agreement

Once various options have been suggested, the next task is deciding about them. Formulas will not help, because everything depends on the precise situation. Here are a number of strategies and tactics:

a. The single negotiating text

The group starts out with one proposal that speaks to all the issues and negotiates to modify it to meet the interests of all concerned. This technique can be very effective in managing negotiations with multiple parties, all of whom might have their own proposals.

b. The BATNA (Best Alternative to a Negotiated Agreement)

The mediator encourages and helps the parties realistically assess their settlement opportunities by understanding and developing their best alternative, such as court or arbitration. (Roger Fisher, William Ury & Bruce Patton, Getting to Yes: Negotiating Agreement without Giving In 97–107 (2d ed. 1991).)

c. Creating doubts

A mediator can encourage a party to be more flexible by creating doubts about the validity of its position. This normally should be done in private — and with great care — so as not to mislead a party or weaken the parties confidence in the mediator or the mediation process.

d. Assessing proposed agreements

The mediator can help the parties evaluate the consequences of particular proposals. It is important to help the parties consider social, psychological, and moral consequences as well as financial ones.

e. Explaining proposals

The mediator should help each party understand the other's proposals and view of the problem. This can be achieved either in joint or private sessions. Again, normally it is best if the parties explain their own ideas, but sometimes the mediator should rephrase ideas to make them easier for the other parties to understand or cope with. For instance, if Party A says, "I think B is a filthy liar and I can't believe a word he says," the mediator can explain that to B as follows: "A has doubts about whether she can rely upon your promises."

f.   Using objective criteria

Fair market value, customary practices, and the like may be readily agreed upon as bases for decision. Experts often will be needed to establish these measures, and the parties may agree on an expert or a process for selecting an expert. Note that there may be a tension between using objective criteria and finding a solution that meets the parties' underlying needs and is fair in the context of their own relationship.

g.   Logrolling

By breaking down the dispute into several issues, the mediator can encourage the parties to trade or "logroll": "I'll give you A and D, if you'll give me B and two-thirds of C." If parties have complementary interests, both might be better off through such a process.

h.   Using deadlines

People ordinarily will not make decisions before they must, so the mediator often can help parties by creating or emphasizing deadlines.

i.   Different types of agreements

Parties may agree to a resolution that deals with some or all the issues. They may agree to negotiate further and they may set up processes — such as mediation — to deal with issues that may arise in the future. In some cases, it may be appropriate for the mediator to encourage the parties to consider using further professional services, such as those of a counselor or an appraiser.

5.   Implementing the agreement

Implementing the agreement means putting it in writing and carrying it out. If the parties consent, a written agreement may be prepared either by the mediator, a party, or a lawyer. Often the parties will reach an oral understanding and will not desire a written agreement. In some cases the parties will agree on the terms and prepare a short memorandum of agreement during the mediation session and plan to work out the precise language later.

In the agreement, the parties should provide for resolving disputes that arise in implementation. Normally, it makes sense to include a clause in the agreement providing that, in the event of a dispute, the parties will return to mediation and, perhaps, if the mediation fails, that they will try another dispute resolution method.

C.   REFERRALS AND OUTSIDE EXPERTS

During the course of the mediation it may become apparent that one or all of the parties in the mediation need additional help in resolving their problems or that the mediator can not adequately address the parties' conflict. In these cases the mediator should refer the parties to appropriate outside agencies or services. It may also be appropriate to arrange for certain kinds of experts — such as accountants or real estate appraisers — to perform their services for both parties.

Notes and Questions

1.   Many other commentators have described how a mediator should go about mediating. Most mediation trainers have their own manuals. But a wide variety of books are available that provide guides to mediation practice. These include: JAMES J. ALFINI, SHARON B. PRESS, JEAN R. STERNLIGHT & JOSEPH B. STULBERG, MEDIATION THEORY AND PRACTICE (2001); MARK D. BENNETT & MICHELE S.G. HERMANN, THE ART OF MEDIATION (1996); DWIGHT GOLANN, MEDIATING LEGAL DISPUTES: EFFECTIVE STRATEGIES FOR LAWYERS AND MEDIATORS (1996); KIMBERLEE R. KOVACH, MEDIATION PRINCIPLES AND PRACTICES (2nd ed. 2000); CHRISTOPHER W. MOORE: THE MEDIATION PROCESS: PRACTICAL STRATEGIES FOR RESOLVING CONFLICT (3d ed. 2003).

2.   One of the mediator's most important activities is listening, a topic we covered in Chapter II, beginning at page 137, where we briefly mentioned a method of active listening known as "looping." Here is a fuller explanation of that process in the mediation context, as explained by Gary Friedman and Jack Himmelstein, who originated it as part of their Understanding–Based approach to mediation.

THE LOOP OF UNDERSTANDING

Central to the Understanding-based approach to mediation is the search for understanding. The 'Loop of Understanding,' as we have come to call it, gives form and substance to that effort. "Looping" is a technique but it is also much more than a technique. The goal is to *Develop Understanding* systematically, authentically and compassionately throughout the mediation.

Looping builds on the mediator's intention. Just as successful mediation must build on the parties' intention to work through their conflict together, looping proceeds from the mediator's intention to understand the parties and to build a ground of understanding between the mediator and the parties.

The Steps of Looping

Although the approach is similar to and borrows much from what others have referred to as "active listening," "looping" captures a fuller sense of it for us. We term it the "loop" of understanding because the goal is to complete a loop.

For the mediator, the simple steps are to try within him or herself to understand each party, to try to express that understanding to that party, and to seek and receive confirmation from the party that he/she feels understood. The last step is crucial. When a party confirms that the mediator understands what he or she has been trying to express, that loop is complete. Until then, it is not.

Step 1: M inquires of   ⟶ P
Step 2: P responds, asserts   ⟶ M
Step 3: M demonstrates and confirms understanding   ⟶ P
Step 4: P responds   ⟶ M

> *If yes, loop is complete.*
> *If no, go back to Step 1 and ask: "What am I missing?"*

By bringing <u>looping</u> to the exchange between him/herself and each of the principal antagonists to the conflict, the mediator the mediator has begun to understand each of them. And while they likely do not feel understood by each other, they feel at least somewhat understood by the mediator. He has also begun to clarify the essence of the dispute.

The goal is to understand the speaker <u>and</u> to demonstrate that you understand. Already this is much more than many mediators (and others) will do in the effort to listen. Even when we make a sincere effort to understand another, that effort is often evidenced by silent attention, a nod of agreement, or a statement such as: "I understand what you are saying." These are not bad. But when it comes to the goal of resolving conflict through understanding, much more is possible. Stating what you hear the other to have said goes further. It shows that you understand (if you do).

So far we have a partial loop — statement by the loopee and response (restatement) by the looper. The next step begins to close the loop. If done with the intent of fostering understanding, it tests whether the mediator has truly understood. The mediator asks the party whether the response captured the meaning of what he was trying to communicate.

The loopee's response can close the loop. If "yes" — if the speaker confirms that he/she feels understood — this one loop is complete. If the speaker does not feel fully understood by the looper's words (whether because the looper missed something or simply because the speaker has the need to clarify what he/she meant), the loop is not complete. The party can then clarify what he/she meant, the mediator loops back and again seeks confirmation. When the party confirms that the mediator correctly has understood, that loop is complete.

The point is not to convince, nor to contradict, nor to take exception to, nor explain away. The point is to understand.

From the start, we are saying to the parties in word and in deed:

"I am going to do my best to understand each of you. My hope is that if we work together in this way, and it makes sense to you, we can together try to understand what is going on — and from that understanding appreciate what the conflict is about and hopefully enable you to resolve it."

The honest attempt by the mediator to understand each party begins to point to an alternative to the confines of a most basic element that keeps people ensnared in a Conflict Trap. For when people are locked in conflict, they typically tend to want to defend their position, blame the other, try to convince a third party that they are right and the other wrong. The mode is one of defense, persuasion, coercion.

When conflict takes that form, understanding is at a minimum. Misunderstanding prevails. The more the parties to conflict feel blamed or vilified by the other, the more they feel misunderstood. The more that they feel misunderstood, the more they tend to justify, blame and vilify. The cycle is well known and yet, once within its grasp, very powerful. Understanding, from the get-go, can help begin to soften the strictures and be the beginning of pointing the way out.

A caution: our recommendation for looping from the start applies to the mediator looping the parties, not to asking the parties to loop each other. Many mediators, drawn by the desire to increase understanding, will turn to the parties early on and ask: what did you understand the other to say? Our advice, generally, is: NOT YET. People are much more willing and able to understand another when they feel understood themselves. To put it another way, being mired in feelings of being misunderstood is not a good place from which to be asked to understand another. And parties to conflict are often mired in just such feelings. By establishing some understanding at the start (by the mediator of the parties), the mediator can begin to help break the cycle of misunderstanding. The invitation to the parties to loop each other can also prove essential, but it rarely comes at the start.

Looping from the inside out.

As the description we have been giving about looping may suggest, it is both a skill and much more than a skill. To understand looping and its place in this approach to mediation is to realize that understanding has an inner life. And it is in that inner life that the essential spirit of looping is grounded. The mediator needs to want to loop (and learn to loop) as more than a useful skill. The hard work is to truly want to understand the people before you — to reach inside oneself when each speaker is speaking and make the effort to understand how the other (each of them) really experiences the situation–even (and particularly) when you find it difficult to understand them. That inner desire to understand is key.

Focusing too much on the outer skill, on getting the words right, on learning to rephrase or reframe (which are important skills to learn) can miss the essential point. That point is truly to want to understand — to connect within oneself to one's own intention to do that. If the inner intent is there, you may at times miss some of the basic steps and still move toward understanding. Like with the "Inner Game of Tennis," this one needs to be played from the inside.

GARY J. FRIEDMAN & JACK HIMMELSTEIN, RESOLVING CONFLICT TOGETHER: THE UNDERSTANDING-BASED APPROACH TO MEDIATION (forthcoming 2006).

3.   Private Caucuses (i.e., private meetings between mediator and parties or lawyers on one side of dispute) are common. The Mediation Training Guide reprinted earlier in this chapter describes various attitudes and practices regarding the use of the private caucus, and the excerpt by Friedman and Himmelstein on the Understanding–Based model of media-

tion, in Chapter IV, Section A.2., beginning at page 307, supra, makes the case for not caucusing. For excellent explanations of when and how the mediator should use a private caucus, which have obvious implications for lawyers in mediation, see Dwight Golann, Mediating Legal Disputes: Effective Strategies for Lawyers and Mediators 68–81 (1996); J. Michael Keating, Jr., *In Mediation, Caucus Can be a Powerful Tool*, 14 Alternatives to High Cost Litig. 85 (1996). And recall that Professors Jennifer Brown and Ian Ayres have argued that the economic rationale for the use of mediation is based entirely on the use of private caucuses:

> * * * mediators can create value by controlling the flow of private information (variously eliminating, translating, or even creating it) to mitigate adverse selection and moral hazard. Adverse selection is caused by hidden information that distorts the terms of a contract; because of adverse selection, for example, unhealthy people are more likely than healthy people to opt for life insurance. Moral hazard is caused by hidden conduct; because of moral hazard, insured people are more likely than uninsured people to take risks. Thus, adverse selection problems involve hidden precontractual information; moral hazard problems involve hidden postcontractual conduct. Both adverse selection and moral hazard are caused by the disputants' ability to hide information about themselves or their conduct. Adverse selection can create inefficiency in negotiation when parties hide information about their valuation or other characteristics prior to agreement. Moral hazard can create inefficiency when one or both parties take hidden actions after an agreement that reduce the joint gains from trade. Moral hazard in the ADR setting is a problem of coordination, because the parties' inability to directly observe each other's postcontractual conduct makes it difficult for the parties to coordinate their performance.
>
> Sequential caucusing is particularly adept at responding to informational problems because it is a uniquely mediative way to elicit and channel private information. * * * [M]ediators can reduce adverse selection in three ways:
>
> (1) by committing parties to break off negotiations when private representations to a mediator indicate that there are no gains from trade;
>
> (2) by committing parties to equally divide the gains from trade; and
>
> (3) by committing to send noisy translations of information disclosed during private caucuses.
>
> Each of these commitments allows a mediator to increase the amount and accuracy of disclosure and thus decrease the impact of the parties' private information. Our third conclusion — that mediators can enhance communication by adding imprecision (or "noise") to privately disclosed information — is especially illuminating. Although adding noise would seem to degrade the quality of information communicated, this result is only true if one mistakenly assumes that the amount of information disclosed is unaffected by the mediator's commitments. When a mediator commits to translate imprecisely the private disclosures of one party, the mediator may induce that party to make more precise disclosures to the mediator, because the mediator's imprecise translation reduces the ability of the other side to use the disclosure to

the detriment of the disclosing party. We also show that noisy (but correlated) signals can help mediators mitigate the inefficiencies of moral hazard.

Jennifer Gerarda Brown & Ian Ayres, *Economic Rationales for Mediation*, 80 Va. L. Rev. 323, 327–29 (1994).

Should the decision whether to hold a private caucus be solely that of the mediator? *See* Leonard L. Riskin, *Decisionmaking in Mediation: The New Old Grid and the New New Grid System,* 79 Notre Dame L. Rev. 1, 42–46 (2003), a portion of which is reprinted, infra, beginning at page 423.

c. Regulation of Mediator Performance

No state requires mediators to be licensed, though virtually all states require licenses for a range of professions and occupations, including taxi-drivers, hairdressers, and accountants. So, as a practical matter, anyone can hold herself out as a mediator. In that sense, people become mediators by doing mediation. But such independence carries costs, for in mediation, as in other areas of regulation, there exists a tension between freedom of contract for the parties and the mediator, on the one hand, and, on the other, protecting the parties and other mediation participants. In addition, regulation raises questions about barriers to entry into the "profession" of mediation, while the lack of regulation raises questions about the integrity of the process, which in many contexts is supported by the apparatus of public law. This section provides insight into the principal methods of regulating mediator performance by focusing on credentials, ethics standards, evaluation by a mediator, malpractice liability, and mediator conflicts of interest.

i. Credentials

SOCIETY OF PROFESSIONALS IN DISPUTE RESOLUTION, REPORT OF THE SPIDR COMMISSION ON QUALIFICATIONS
(1989).

RATIONALE

The most commonly discussed purposes of setting criteria for individuals to practice as neutrals are (1) to protect the consumer and (2) to protect the integrity of various dispute resolution processes. Many policy makers and professionals in the field are concerned about individuals with little information about or skill in dispute resolution simply "hanging out a shingle" and offering to mediate or arbitrate anyone's dispute. Further, concerns are being raised about poorly trained and inexperienced neutrals offering training to others. The risks are several — the interest of parties may be harmed by incompetent practice and the public's understanding of what it means to request specific dispute resolution services may become confused, leading to public dissatisfaction with the field and claims that mediation and arbitration are merely a form of second class justice.

Proposals to establish qualifications for neutrals also raise considerable controversy, however. Some of the reaction appears to be anxiety among members of a profession newly faced with regulation. Many substantive concerns also have been raised, particularly about mandatory standards of certification, including: (1) creating inappropriate barriers to entry into the field, thus, (2) hampering the innovative quality of the profession, and (3) limiting the broad dissemination of peacemaking skills in society. Even many of those who are persuaded that there is a need for some mandatory standards are concerned that it may not be possible yet to define and measure competence.

* * *

POLICY OPTIONS

There is no single way to promote quality in any professional practice. Among the options are:

A. free market

B. disclosure requirements

C. public/consumer education

D. "after the fact" controls, such as malpractice lawsuits

E. rosters

F. voluntary standards

G. codes of professional ethics

H. mandatory standards for neutrals

I. mandatory standards for programs

J. improvements in training for neutrals, including apprenticeship programs

* * *

IV. PRINCIPLES

There is no single answer to what constitutes a qualified neutral or which of the policy options described is appropriate to ensure that those who practice are qualified to do so. SPIDR recommends the following central principles:

A. that no single entity (rather, a variety of organizations) should establish qualifications for neutrals;

B. that the greater the degree of choice the parties have over the dispute resolution process, program or neutral, the less mandatory should be the qualification requirements; and

C. that qualification criteria should be based on performance, rather than paper credentials.

* * *

7. Knowledge acquired in obtaining various degrees can be useful in the practice of dispute resolution. At this time and for the foreseeable future, however, no such degree in itself ensures competence as a neutral. Furthermore, requiring a degree would foreclose alternative avenues of demonstrating dispute resolution competence. Consequently, no degree should be considered a prerequisite for service as a neutral.

C. Performance-based qualifications

* * *

8–10. SPIDR believes that performance criteria (such as neutrality, demonstrated knowledge of relevant practices and procedures, ability to listen and understand, and ability to write a considered opinion for arbitrators) are more useful and appropriate in setting qualifications to practice than is the manner in which one achieves those criteria (such as formal degrees, training, or experience). * * *

Note

After issuing this report, SPIDR continued its interest in competence and qualifications. SOCIETY OF PROFESSIONALS IN DISPUTE RESOLUTION, ENSURING COMPETENCE AND QUALITY IN DISPUTE RESOLUTION PRACTICE (REPORT NO. 2 OF THE SPIDR COMMISSION ON QUALIFICATION 1995). Another report of a SPIDR subcommittee proposed competencies for mediators of public disputes. PUBLIC DISPUTES SECTOR, SOCIETY OF PROFESSIONALS IN DISPUTE RESOLUTION, COMPETENCIES FOR MEDIATORS OF COMPLEX, PUBLIC DISPUTES (1992).

ELLEN WALDMAN, CREDENTIALING APPROACHES: THE SLOW MOVEMENT TOWARD SKILLS– BASED TESTING

Disp. Resol. Mag., Fall 2001, at 13, 13–14, 16.

The three faces of credentialing

Degree-based approaches

A brief glance at the credentialing land-scape reveals several different approaches. The first approach relies on education and degree requirements to distinguish between those who can and cannot mediate. This approach has been almost unanimously rejected by the mediation community. Theorists and practitioners alike maintain that quality mediation does not flow from a particular educational track or professional status. Nonetheless, degree requirements are common in court-annexed mediation programs.

A number of states have adopted Maryland's requirement that civil mediators possess "at least a bachelor's degree from an accredited college or university." Other states, like Florida and Indiana, require their civil mediators to possess a law degree. And even states that impose no degree requirement on mediators serving the general trial courts do require professional degrees when the dispute involves specialized subject matter such as divorce, probate or malpractice.

Training, experience-based approaches

The second approach looks to training and experience to measure mediator competence. This approach is popular among court-annexed programs, private mediation providers and trade organizations. And perhaps this popularity is unsurprising. Grounding credentialing efforts in training and/or experience is both administratively simple and intuitively attractive. Administering a credentialing program based on training and experience requires only a simple review of the application form that candidates submit. And, intuitively, it makes sense to assume that mediators who have received didactic training and refined their skills in the mediation trenches would be at least minimally competent.

However, this intuitive appeal may be misleading. No data exist to support the notion that training and experience requirements guarantee or are even substantially related to enhanced skills or effectiveness. Indeed, the limited data available suggest that training and experience are only indirectly related to mediator performance. And, despite the innumerable experiments with mediation credentialing taking place throughout the "laboratory of the states," no specific amount of training or experience has emerged as an adequate or suitable method of assessing or ensuring quality. Indeed, training and experience requirements vary dramatically from jurisdiction and from program to program.

If one is an attorney, a four-hour mediation training is sufficient to mediate civil cases in York County, Pennsylvania. In Massachusetts, court mediators must attend 30 hours of training. Many states, including Georgia, Tennessee, and Indiana to name just a few, demand attendance at a 40–hour mediation training. Experience requirements are similarly variable, ranging from the minimum of three cases required of the court mediators in Kansas to the 125 hours of experience required of those who wish to be credentialed by the Texas Credentialing Association, a consortium of mediation providers, judicial and consumer representatives.

Skills-based evaluation

A small minority of mediation providers, trade organizations and state courts have adopted a third cutting-edge approach that marries training and experience requirements with skills-based evaluation. The San Diego Mediation Center (SDMC), the Maryland Council for Dispute Resolution (MCDR), and Family Mediation Canada (FMC) offer voluntary certification programs. The Department of the Navy (DON) strongly encourages and the Massachusetts Office of Dispute Resolution (MODR) and the District and Circuit Courts of Virginia require their mediators to obtain certification in order to participate in their programs. * * *

Performance testing

Early efforts–defining mediator effectiveness, evaluating per-formance

The skills-based approach to assessing mediator competence was first conceptualized in the mid–1980s. In 1988 mediator Chris Honeyman began the first effort to isolate the particular skills required for effective mediation. Honeyman articulated seven core mediator competencies: investigation, empathy, inventiveness and problem-solving, persuasion and presentation skills, distraction, managing the interaction, and substantive knowledge. Honeyman also developed a performance exam that ranked mediators on a scale of one to nine on each of the seven parameters. While relatively simple in structure, Honeyman's test was not designed as a one-size-fits-all invention, but as a flexible instrument that programs could modify to fit their particular needs. Honeyman's work then continued in more elaborate form by empaneling the Test Design Project, an initiative sponsored by the National Institute of Dispute Resolution. The Project's performance exam was adopted in modified form by a number of different institutions, including the Massachusetts Office of Dispute Resolution (MODR), operating in the Suffolk County Superior Court, and the San Diego Mediation Center (SDMC), a full-service Mediation center. * * *

Notes and Questions

1. Which approach or approaches to regulation seem most appropriate in connection with mediators who focus on matters of divorce, environmental protection and land use, and personal injury claims?

2. Assume you were creating a private for-profit organization that would offer services of a number of mediators on a roster that the organization would establish. What credentials would you impose for people to appear on your roster?

3. Professor Waldman also describes "second-generation" performance-testing initiatives established the U.S. Department of the Navy, the Maryland Council for Dispute Resolution, and Family Mediation Canada (FMC). The FMC program requires substantially more training than U.S. programs of which we are aware: 180 hours for mediating relational issues in family disputes; 230 hours for mediating financial issues in divorce. These resemble mediation certification programs in Germany, Austria, and Switzerland, which have 240–hour training requirements. What would account for this apparent disparity in training obligations between these countries and the U.S.? In what circumstances should mediation training include training in substantive law?

4. In 2003, an Association for Conflict Resolutions (ACR) task force recommended the establishment of a voluntary mediator certification program based on the "presentation of a 'portfolio' of years of experience and training," a test of knowledge, provisions for recertification and the possibility of decertification for ethical violations. ASSOCIATION FOR CONFLICT RESOLUTION, ACR MEDIATOR CERTIFICATION TASK FORCE: REPORT AND RECOMMENDA-

TIONS TO THE ACR BOARD OF DIRECTORS (2004), *available at* http://www.acrnet.org/about/taskforces/certification.htm. The Task force chose not to include performance testing. Other organizations recently established efforts to address the certification issue. Both the ABA and the ACR have expressed interest in creating a separate entity to offer a voluntary certification program. James B. McGuire, *Joint Certification: An Idea Whose Time Has Come,* Disp. Resol. Mag., Summer 2004, at 22.

ii. Ethics

This section includes material on ethics standards and on court enforcement of rules dealing with mediator conflicts of interest.

a) Ethics Standards

Numerous organizations and courts have promulgated standards of practice and ethics for mediators. One of the most broadly accepted and influential standards appears below. It is similar to many other standards of conduct and includes the obligations that most believe are essential for mediators. A version of these standards with an Introductory Note, a Preface, and Comments appears in Appendix C.

MODEL STANDARDS OF CONDUCT FOR MEDIATORS

(Approved by the American Arbitration Association, American Bar Association Sections of Dispute Resolution and Litigation, and the Society of Professionals in Dispute Resolution, 1994).

* * *

Mediation is a process in which an impartial third party — a mediator — facilitates the resolution of a dispute by promoting voluntary agreement (or "self-determination") by the parties to the dispute. A mediator facilitates communications, promotes understanding, focuses the parties on their interests, and seeks creative problem solving to enable the parties to reach their own agreement. These standards give meaning to this definition of mediation.

I. **Self–Determination: A Mediator Shall Recognize that Mediation is Based on the Principle of Self–Determination by the Parties.**

II. **Impartiality: A Mediator Shall Conduct the Mediation in an Impartial Manner.**

III. **Conflicts of Interest: A Mediator Shall Disclose all Actual and Potential Conflicts of Interest Reasonably Known to the Mediator. After Disclosure, the Mediator Shall Decline to Mediate Unless all Parties Choose to Retain the Mediator. The Need to Protect Against Conflicts of Interest Also Governs Conduct that Occurs During and After the Mediation.**

IV. **Competence: A Mediator Shall Mediate Only When the Mediator Has the Necessary Qualifications to Satisfy the Reasonable Expectations of the Parties.**

V.   Confidentiality: A Mediator Shall Maintain the Reasonable Expectations of the Parties with Regard to Confidentiality.

VI.   Quality of the Process: A Mediator Shall Conduct the Mediation Fairly, Diligently, and in a Manner Consistent with the Principle of Self–Determination by the Parties.

VII.   Advertising and Solicitation: A Mediator Shall Be Truthful in Advertising and Solicitation for Mediation.

VIII.   Fees: A Mediator Shall Fully Disclose and Explain the Basis of Compensation, Fees, and Charges to the Parties.

IX.   Obligations to the Mediation Process.

Notes and Questions

1.   For more on the Standards of Conduct for Mediators (commonly called the "Joint Standards" or the "Model Standards") and the documents from which the drafters drew, see John D. Feerick, *Toward Uniform Standards of Conduct for Mediators*, 38 So. Tex. L. Rev. 455 (1997); *Symposium: Standards of Professional Conduct in Alternative Dispute Resolution,* 1995 J. Disp. Resol. 95. The American Bar Association Standards on Family Law and Divorce Mediation (2001), which can be found in the online appendix on the TWEN web site for this casebook at www.lawschool.westlaw.com. As this book went to press, a joint committee of the American Arbitration Association, the ABA Section of Dispute Resolution, and the Association for Conflict Resolution had drafted a revision of these Model Standards that was approved by the ABA House of Delegates in August 2005, and was to be considered for approval by AAA and ACR later that year. A copy of that revision can be found on the casebook web site, at www.lawschool.westlaw.com.

2.   Florida has established an elaborate system to regulate the practice of mediation in the court system. For a comprehensive review, see Robert B. Moberly, *Ethical Standards for Court–Appointed Mediators and Florida's Mandatory Mediation Experiment,* 21 Fla. St. U. L. Rev. 701 (1994). In addition to rules for mediator conduct (FLA. R. FOR CERTIFIED & COURT APPOINTED MEDIATORS 10.410 (2000)), the system includes a Mediator Qualifications Advisory Panel, which provides advice to mediators, and a Mediator Qualifications Board, which handles discipline of certified mediators. Mattox Hair, Sharon Press & Brooks Rathet, *Ethics Within the Mediation Process,* 1 Am. Arb. Ass'n *ADR Currents*, No. 1, at 9 (1996). The Advisory Board has issued opinions dealing with, inter alia, confidentiality, advertising, and the billing process. *Id.* at 10–11. *See also* Bruce A. Blitman, *Mediator Ethics: Florida's Ethics Advisory Panel Breaks New Ground,* Disp. Resol. Mag., Spring 2001, at 10 (describing operations of Florida Ethics Review Panel); Sharon Press, *Standards ... and Results: Florida Provides Forum for Grievances Against Mediators*, Disp. Resol. Mag, Spring 2001, at 8 (discussing Florida's general system of regulating mediators).

Minnesota has an ADR Review Board that has promulgated ethics and practice standards as well as dealing with evaluation and other issues. Barbara McAdoo & Nancy Welsh, *The Times They Are a Changin' — Or Are*

They? An Update on Rule 114, The Hennepin Lawyer, July–Aug. 1996, at 8; Duane W. Krohnke, *Minnesota Takes up ADR Ethics Challenge*, 14 Alternatives to High Cost Litig. 121 (1996); Duane W. Krohnke, *Conflicts Rules for ADR Neutrals,* 14 Alternatives to High Cost Litig. 135 (1996); Duane W. Krohnke, *Decisions Standards Raise Policy Issues as Minnesota Drafts ADR Code of Ethics*, 15 Alternatives to High Cost Litig. 3 (1997). Other state supreme courts have developed codes of ethics for mediators. *E.g.*, Virginia Supreme Court, Standards of Ethics and Professional Responsibility for Certified Mediators (1993). Legislatures in many states have considered numerous bills dealing with certification. *E.g., see, Symposium: Certification of Mediators in California*, 30 U.S.F. L. Rev. 609 (1996).

3.   Some professional organizations, such as the Association for Conflict Resolution, also consider ethics complaints against members. Several attempts to systematize processes of selecting, training, and evaluating mediators have emerged in recent years. THE TEST DESIGN PROJECT, PERFORMANCE-BASED ASSESSMENT: A METHODOLOGY FOR USE IN SELECTING, TRAINING, AND EVALUATING MEDIATIONS (National Institute for Dispute Resolution ed., 1995); SAN DIEGO MEDIATION CENTER, MEDIATOR CREDENTIAL: AN IMPLEMENTATION GUIDE (1992). Mediator Charles Pou, Jr. recently argued that we don't need more rules, but better ways of encouraging and helping mediators behave ethically. He suggested, among other things, the creating "ethics hotlines," building support systems, and focusing on the system, rather than just the mediator. Charles Pou, Jr., *Making Ethical Dispute Resolution a Reality*, Disp. Resol. Mag., Winter 2004, at 19.

4.   Whether mediation is a profession — or "a set of executive life skills" — is the subject of some debate. *See* Juliana Birkhoff & Robert Rack, *Points of View: Is Mediation Really a Profession?*, Disp. Resol. Mag., Fall 2001, at 10. Is it helpful to frame this as an either-or question? What do you think mediation is, or should be? Mediators who are members of other professions, including law, may be subject to other regulatory regimes. The regulation of mediation practice by lawyers is covered infra, Chapter IV, Section C.1.c.2) and 3).b).

5.   Should mediators be able to use contingent fee arrangements? In an effort to protect parties through fostering mediator neutrality, many ethics codes and court rules prohibit "contingent fee" mediation, an agreement under which the mediator's fee depends upon the outcome of the mediation. Professor Scott Peppet, however, has argued against such rigid prohibitions. Scott R. Peppet, *Contractarian Economics and Mediation Ethics: The Case for Customizing Neutrality Through Contingent Fee Mediation*, 82 Tex. L. Rev. 227 (2003). He suggests that parties should be allowed to contract for contingent mediator fees in circumstances where such an agreement would not interfere with the three core functions through which the mediator "adds value": "by discovering whether settlement is possible; by optimizing settlement; and by helping to manage psychological, emotional, and relational barriers." *Id.* at 262. Peppet proposes the following rule as a guide to future ethics codes:

A mediator shall not take a fee contingent on any aspect of a mediation unless

(a) the mediator discloses, in writing, the fee arrangement and its potential consequences, the mediator recommends that the parties consult with counsel about the fee arrangement, and, prior to the mediation, all parties provide informed consent in writing and after an opportunity to consult with counsel;

(b) in court-ordered mediation, the fee arrangement is disclosed to and approved by the court prior to the mediation; and

(c) the fee arrangement does not create an appearance or actuality of partiality toward one party.

Id. at 276.

Does this rule satisfy concerns about the risk that the mediator will overreach? Would it actually protect against partiality?

b) Mediator Conflicts of Interest

It is widely understood that, in order to foster impartiality, a mediator may not mediate a case as to which the mediator has a conflict of interest unless the mediator discloses that conflict of interest and the parties give a knowing consent to the mediation after such disclosure. The Uniform Mediation Act addresses the matter as follows:

SECTION 9. MEDIATOR'S DISCLOSURE OF CONFLICTS OF INTEREST; BACKGROUND.

(a) Before accepting a mediation, an individual who is requested to serve as a mediator shall:

   (1) make an inquiry that is reasonable under the circumstances to determine whether there are any known facts that a reasonable individual would consider likely to affect the impartiality of the mediator, including a financial or personal interest in the outcome of the mediation and an existing or past relationship with a mediation party or foreseeable participant in the mediation; and

   (2) disclose any such known fact to the mediation parties as soon as is practical before accepting a mediation.

(b) If a mediator learns any fact described in subsection (a)(1) after accepting a mediation, the mediator shall disclose it as soon as is practicable.

(c) At the request of a mediation party, an individual who is requested to serve as a mediator shall disclose the mediator's qualifications to mediate a dispute.

(d) A person that violates subsection [(a) or (b)][(a), (b), or (g)] is precluded by the violation from asserting a privilege under Section 4. * * *

Similar disclosure obligations appear in ethical standards. *See, e.g.,* MODEL STANDARDS OF CONDUCT FOR MEDIATORS (AAA, ABA, SPIDR 1994), Standard III, which are reprinted in Appendix C; FLA. RULES FOR CERTIFIED AND COURT-APPOINTED MEDIATORS, Rule 10.340 (2000).

Mediators also must be concerned about conflicts of interest that arise during or after a mediation. The Model Standards of Conduct for Mediators, for instance, provide that "The need to protect against conflicts of interest also governs conduct that occurs during and after the mediation." MODEL STANDARDS OF CONDUCT FOR MEDIATORS, STANDARD III (1994). The Comments provide that "[w]ithout the consent of all parties, a mediator shall not subsequently establish a professional relationship with one of the parties in a related matter, or in an unrelated matter under circumstances which would raise legitimate question about the integrity of the mediation process." *Id.* Comments. If the mediator is a lawyer, the situation sometimes can become more complicated as the following materials show.

* * *

McKENZIE CONSTRUCTION
v. ST. CROIX STORAGE

District Court of the Virgin Islands, Div. of St. Croix, 1997.
961 F.Supp. 857.

RESNICK, United States Magistrate Judge.

Plaintiff McKenzie Construction is a local lumber retail company who brought this damages action against defendants St. Croix Storage Corp. for conversion of lumber. The Court ordered the matter submitted to mediation and later appointed Attorney Lisa Moorehead as mediator.* * * Mediation was unsuccessful and the parties have resumed preparation for trial.

In seeking to disqualify the firm of Rohn & Cusick, defendants claim that the firm's hiring of Attorney Moorehead, who was the mediator appointed by the Court to settle this case, presents an irreparable conflict of interest in contravention of the rules governing the conduct of mediators and attorneys alike. Defendants reason that Moorehead's position as mediator allowed her access to "a wide range of confidential information derived from her private consultations" with the parties. Plaintiffs responded that although Moorehead may be subject to disqualification, she is simply "of counsel" to the law firm of Rohn & Cusick and that, under Virgin Islands law, the disqualification of the law firm is not automatic. Moreover, plaintiffs assert that although no confidences were exchanged in the mediation, the firm had created a "cone of silence" around Moorehead, insulating her from the case. However, defendants countered that since being hired by Rohn & Cusick in September of 1996, Moorehead had inserted herself into the case by meeting with an investigator for defendants concerning the investigator's contact with plaintiff about the case. The Court requested that plaintiffs file a direct response to defendants' allegation. In their response, plaintiffs submit an affidavit of Attorney Moorehead in which she avers that a "cone of silence" has been erected at Rohn & Cusick and admits that she met with the investigator in order to advise him that he could be civilly liable for attempting to settle a case with a represented party. She claims that she did not discuss the merits of the instant case. Defendants also seek the imposition of sanctions against plaintiffs' law firm for filing false affidavits.

After review of the record and the submissions of the parties, this Court concludes that there exists a sufficient basis for resolution of this issue on the pleadings alone. Accordingly, the request for a hearing is denied.

A motion to disqualify counsel requires the court to balance the right of a party to retain counsel of his choice and the substantial hardship which might result from disqualification as against the public perception of and the public trust in the judicial system. *Powell v. Alabama,* 287 U.S. 45, 53, 53 S.Ct. 55, 58, 77 L.Ed. 158 (1932). The underlying principle in considering motions to disqualify counsel is safeguarding the integrity of the court proceedings and the purpose of granting such motions is to eliminate the threat that the litigation will be tainted. *United States Football League v. National Football League,* 605 F.Supp. 1448, 1464 (S.D.N.Y.1985). The district court's power to disqualify an attorney derives from its inherent authority to supervise the professional conduct of attorneys appearing before it. *Richardson v. Hamilton International Corp.,* 469 F.2d 1382, 1385–86 (3d Cir.1972), *cert. denied* 411 U.S. 986, 93 S.Ct. 2271, 36 L.Ed.2d 964 (1973). Disqualification issues must be decided on a case by case basis. *Rogers v. Pittston Co.,* 800 F.Supp. 350, 353 (W.D.Va.1992); *In re Asbestos Cases,* 514 F.Supp. 914, 924 (E.D.Va 1981).

This case presents the question whether a law firm must be disqualified from representing a party when it employs an attorney who was formerly the mediator in the identical litigation. Plaintiffs essentially concede that Attorney Moorehead should be screened from involvement in the case. Indeed, they "do not dispute that Ms. Moorehead, herself, may be subject to disqualification." Plaintiffs' Opposition, page 1. They argue, however, that the "cone of silence" erected around Attorney Moorehead is sufficient under the rules and case law, and that the facts do not warrant disqualification of the entire firm. Defendants maintain that Moorehead's contact with the investigator, subsequent to the date that the "cone of silence" was reportedly constructed, constitutes a violation of the relevant ethical standards and presents a more compelling case for disqualification.

The leading case on attorney disqualification in this district is *Bluebeard's Castle, Inc. v. Delmar Marketing, Inc.,* 886 F.Supp. 1204, 1207 (D.V.I.1995). In that case, this Court ruled that where an attorney accepts representation of a party adverse to a former client in a substantially related matter, the Court "presumes that confidences were disclosed during the previous relationship and that such confidences would be used against the former client ... [and] does not require that the moving party be able to show that confidences actually were passed on or to detail their contents." (citations omitted.) The Court went on to find that an attorney faced with such a prospect should, at the least, fully disclose the fact to that party or, at most, refuse such representation. Failure to honor such conflict would result in the disqualification of the attorney and his entire firm. *Id.* at 1208–1210. The Court relied on the Model Rules of Professional Conduct in disqualifying the attorney and his law firm.

* * *

[In footnote 2, p. 859, the court quoted Rule 1.9 of the ABA MODEL RULES OF PROFESSIONAL CONDUCT:

CONFLICT OF INTEREST: FORMER CLIENT

(a) A lawyer who has formerly represented a client in a matter shall not thereafter represent another person in the same or a substantially related matter in which that person's interests are materially adverse to the interests of the former client unless the former client consents after consultation.

(b) A lawyer shall not knowingly represent a person in the same or substantially related matter in which a firm with which the lawyer formerly was associated had previously represented a client

(1) whose interests are materially adverse to that person; and

(2) about whom the lawyer had acquired information protected by rules 1.6 and 1.9(c) that is material to the matter; (c) A lawyer who has formerly represented a client in a matter or whose present or former firm has formerly represented a client in a matter shall not thereafter

(1) use information relating to the representation to the disadvantage of the former client except as Rule 1.6 or Rule 3.3 would permit or require with respect to a client, or when the information has become generally known; or (2) reveal information relating to the representation except as rule 1.6 or Rule 3.3 would permit or require with respect to a client.]

* * *

The recent case of *Poly Software International, Inc. v. Su,* 880 F.Supp. 1487 (D.Utah 1995), discusses the identical issue presented in the case *sub judice.* In that case, two parties agreed to mediate a copyright action which they were defending. However, soon after the mediated settlement the parties sued each other. One of the parties retained the mediator as his counsel. The other party moved to disqualify the mediator-turned-attorney in light of his prior status as mediator in the previous action. The District Court disqualified the attorney and his law firm from participating in the litigation and held that an attorney who serves as a mediator cannot subsequently represent anyone in a substantially related matter without the consent of the original parties. The court reasoned that mediators routinely receive and preserve confidences in much the same manner as an attorney. The court referred to the Model Rules of Professional Conduct and concluded that where the mediator was privy to confidential information, the applicable ethical rules imposed the same responsibilities as the rules relating to an attorney's subsequent representation of a former client. The court also considered the rule prohibiting judges and other adjudicative officers from representing anyone in connection with a matter in which he or she participated "personally and substantially." Model Rule 1.2.

Likewise, in *Cho v. Superior Court,* 39 Cal.App.4th 113, 45 Cal. Rptr.2d 863 (1995), a former judge and his law firm were disqualified from representing a party in an action in which the former judge had participated in settlement conferences. That court relied on ABA Model Rule 1.12 which prohibits a lawyer who has participated personally and substantially in a matter as a judge or adjudicative officer, from representing anyone in connection with the same matter. *Id.* 45 Cal.Rptr.2d at 867. The Court compared the judge's role in the proceedings to that of a mediator, and found that the position necessarily involved the exchange of confidences going to the merits of the case. The court cautioned that "no amount of assurances or screening procedures, no 'cone of silence' could ever convince the opposing party that the confidences would not be used to its disadvantage." *Id.* 45 Cal.Rptr.2d at 869. The Court concluded that based on the nature of the attorney's prior participation, there is a presumption that confidences were revealed, and the attorney should not have "to engage in subtle evaluation of the extent to which he acquired relevant information in the first representation and of the actual use of that representation." *Id.* Thus, the rule of the cases is that a mediator should never represent a party to the mediation in a subsequent related or similar matter.

It is against this backdrop that this Court must determine whether Attorney Moorehead, who was the mediator in this identical action, may have received confidences which may be used to the disadvantage of defendant in this case, warranting her disqualification and that of her law firm. Guided by the case law and experience, this Court notes that the very nature of mediation requires that confidences be exchanged. Hence, Local Rule of Civil Procedure 3.2(c)(2) provides that a mediator appointed in this jurisdiction must be impartial and is required to disqualify himself or herself "in any action in which he/she would be required under Title 28, USC sec. 455 to disqualify him/herself if he/she were a judge or Magistrate Judge." Title 28, USC sec. 455 requires such a judicial officer to disqualify himself or herself (1) where the attorney served as a lawyer, the associate lawyer, a witness or a judge in the case; or (2) where the attorney has served in governmental employment and participated in the case as a counsel, adviser or material witness.

John Landers, Vice President of defendant St. Croix Storage Corp., states by affidavit that he was present during the mediation conference and met with Attorney Moorehead separately and together with the other parties. He states that he openly discussed "the facts of the matter, the financial status and capability of Sun Storage to either pay a settlement figure or to pay a verdict, the status and degree of involvement of certain of the partners ... in the management and operation

... and the trial strategy that was to be employed in the absence of settlement of this matter." Plaintiffs claim that all discussions in the case were done in a group setting and not "confidential". They further argue that any information received would have been discovered during the normal course of litigation.

Plaintiffs' entire argument against disqualification lacks credibility, is unsupported by legal analysis, and completely ignores the existing standards governing attorney conduct. This Court finds, and many commentators agree, that during mediation parties are encouraged to disclose the strengths and weaknesses of their positions, in an effort to arrive at a settlement, Protection of confidences in such a setting strengthens the incentive of parties to negotiate without fear that the mediator will subsequently use the information against them. Additionally, the rules regulating attorney conduct place the onus on the attorney to "remain conscious of the obligation to preserve confidences and maintain loyalty." 886 F.Supp. at 1207. It is clear from the record that the parties met to negotiate a settlement. It is undisputed that the mediation lasted at least one hour. It is not unreasonable to assume that in light of the nature and purpose of the proceeding, that confidential information was disclosed by the parties. Notwithstanding Attorney Moorehead's statements to the contrary, the present situation presents such a serious affront to the policy that forms the basis of the rules, that this Court has no choice but to conclude that Attorney Moorehead must be disqualified.

DISQUALIFICATION OF THE FIRM

This Court further finds that disqualification of Attorney Moorehead should be imputed to the other members of the firm. The cases and Model Rule 1.10(a)[117] require such disqualification. * * *

In addition, the Court is disturbed by Attorney Moorehead's contact with Mr. Pierre Tepie, an investigator associated with this case. Partly in response to a Motion for Sanctions filed by plaintiffs, Mr. Tepie, who is a self-employed investigator and process server, stated, via affidavit that he was hired by Shirryl Hughes, on behalf of a defendant in this case, to attempt to negotiate an out of court settlement. He further stated that after such attempted negotiation, he was contacted by Attorney Moorehead, who attempted to persuade him to discontinue his efforts. Attorney Moorehead responded, also via affidavit, that she contacted Tepie with regard to his attempted negotiation because she "thought it was wise to inform him that he could be civilly liable for contacting a represented party." She claims she did not know whom he worked for. Moorehead, who was reportedly excluded from the case, does not explain in her affidavit, the manner in which she learned about Tepie's involvement. In any event, this court finds that Moorehead's contact with an agent of the defendants in this very case, implicates the

---

117. The rule states: "While lawyers are associated in a firm, none of them shall knowingly represent a client when any one of them practicing alone would be prohibited from doing so by Rule 1.7, 1.8(c), 1.9 or 2.2."

effectiveness of the measures allegedly adopted by her employer to avoid her involvement in this matter. Accordingly, disqualification of the law firm of Rohn & Cusick is necessary to safeguard the integrity of the ongoing litigation and to eliminate the threat that the proceedings will be tainted.

* * *

CONCLUSION

Based on the foregoing, this Court finds that, as the mediator in this case, Attorney Moorehead is presumed to have received confidential information going to the merits of the case and must be disqualified. This Court also finds that in addition to the mandate of the Model Rules, the screening procedure reportedly employed at the law firm of Rohn & Cusick failed to prevent Moorehead's subsequent involvement in this matter, further bolstering the court's conclusion that the law firm of Rohn & Cusick must also be disqualified. Finally, the Court finds that plaintiffs' affidavits herein do not warrant the imposition of sanctions. Accordingly, none will be imposed.

Notes and Questions

1. The *McKenzie* opinion assumed that the mediator had obtained confidential information during the mediation. Do you suppose the judge assumed that the mediator held private caucuses? If so, does that mean that the result might have been different if there had been no private caucuses, i.e., if the parties, lawyers, and mediator had stayed in joint session at all times, as is the practice in Understanding–Based Mediation?

2. If you were a partner in a large law firm, would you discourage other members of the firm from acting as mediators or arbitrators out of a concern that such practices might disqualify the firm from some potential representations? Or would you prefer to establish procedures that would avoid running afoul of conflict of interest provisions?

For an example of conflict of interest concerns prompting the break up of a law firm that included lawyer-mediators, see *With Conflicts at Issue, Florida Firm and Its Former Partners Restructure ADR — Again*, 15 Alternatives to High Cost Litig. 131 (1997).

For a review of conflict-of-interest issues (along with the question of whether a lawyer-mediator has an obligation to report unethical behavior by a lawyer in connection with a mediation), see D. Alan Rudlin, Greer D. Saunders & Barbara L. Hulburt, *Attorney–Mediators Face Important Ethical Issues*, Nat'l L.J., Nov. 18, 1996, at D9. John Bickerman makes useful suggestions about dealing with conflict of interest issues. John Bickerman, *Handling Potential Conflicts in Mediation*, 14 Alternatives to High Cost Litig. 83 (1996).

3. Lawyer-mediators also must pay attention to rules of professional responsibility dealing with advertising. *See* Nancy H. Rogers & Craig McEwen,

MEDIATION: LAW, POLICY, PRACTICE, Sec. 10.3 (2d ed. 2003), and practicing jointly with a non-lawyer. *Id*. at Sec. 10.4.

* * *

In 2002, the ABA modified Model Rule 1.12, which previously dealt only with former judges and arbitrators, so as to include mediators and other third-party neutrals. It now reads as follows:

ABA MODEL RULE 1.12 FORMER JUDGE, ARBITRATOR, MEDIATOR OR OTHER THIRD–PARTY NEUTRAL

(2004).

(a) Except as stated in paragraph (d), a lawyer shall not represent anyone in connection with a matter in which the lawyer participated personally and substantially as a judge or other adjudicative officer or law clerk to such a person or as an arbitrator, mediator or other third-party neutral, unless all parties to the proceeding give informed consent, confirmed in writing.

(b) A lawyer shall not negotiate for employment with any person who is involved as a party or as lawyer for a party in a matter in which the lawyer is participating personally and substantially as a judge or other adjudicative officer or as an arbitrator, mediator or other third-party neutral. A lawyer serving as a law clerk to a judge or other adjudicative officer may negotiate for employment with a party or lawyer involved in a matter in which the clerk is participating personally and substantially, but only after the lawyer has notified the judge or other adjudicative officer.

(c) If a lawyer is disqualified by paragraph (a), no lawyer in a firm with which that lawyer is associated may knowingly undertake or continue representation in the matter unless:

(1) The disqualified lawyer is timely screened from any participation in the matter and is apportioned no part of the fee therefrom; and

(2) Written notice is promptly given to the parties and any appropriate tribunal to enable them to ascertain compliance with the provisions of this rule.

(d) An arbitrator selected as a partisan of a party in a multimember arbitration panel is not prohibited from subsequently representing that party.

Notes and Questions

1.   Recall that the ABA Model Rules of Professional Responsibility have no binding effect until a particular rule is adopted by an appropriate ethics body, usually a state supreme court.

2.   The Model Rule for the Lawyer as Third–Party Neutral, developed by the CPR–Georgetown Commission on Ethics and Standards in ADR in 2002 address this issue in a similar fashion in proposed Rule 2.4. These materials can be found in the online Appendix on the TWEN web site for this casebook, at www.lawschool.westlaw.com.

3.   Do you think the screening and notice provisions in Model Rules of Professional Conduct Rule 1.12 provide adequate protection? The Georgia Dispute Resolution Commission thought that even less protection was needed. Because a mediator is pledged to maintain confidentiality, the commission held that it was not appropriate to impute such knowledge to his firm. *See* Georgia Dispute Resolution Commission, Committee on Ethics, Advisory Opinion 4 (1997).

4.   Assume that the chief judge of your local trial court appoints you to a committee to study and recommend ways to regulate mediators in the court-ordered mediation program the court is planning to establish. Under that program, judges could order any civil case into mediation, and the parties would be encouraged to select mediators from a roster that the court would maintain. At your upcoming committee meeting, which methods of regulation, if any, would you recommend?

In particular, would you require that mediators have certain degrees? Training?

Would your answer depend on whether parties would have a choice of mediators? On whether parties would pay the mediators, and, if so, how such fees would be determined?

Would you have different requirements for mediators who would deal with family or divorce cases and for those who would handle general civil matters?

If you recommend specific training requirements, would you exempt or "grandfather" retired judges, who have served more than a certain number of years? Why or why not?

What kind of conflict of interest provisions would you use?

Would your answer to any of these questions depend on your own background and expectations about providing or using mediation services?

iii.   Limitations on What Mediators May Say About Law

The question of what a mediator may say about law is hotly debated among some academics, practitioners, and mediation program developers and administrators. To provide windows on such issues, we focus first in subsection a) on a "debate" over whether a mediator may properly "evaluate" — i.e., make predictions about what would happen in court or assessments of how the law applies. In subsection b), we consider whether certain practices by a mediator, lawyer or non-lawyer, might constitute the practice of law.

a)   The Facilitative–Evaluative Debate

The question of whether a mediator may properly "evaluate" the legal or other aspects of a dispute — e.g., make and communicate assessments of the strengths and weaknesses of one or both parties' sides of a dispute, or predict a judicial outcome — has generated much controversy. *See* Leonard L. Riskin, *Decisionmaking in Mediation: The New Old Grid and the New New Grid System*, 79 Notre Dame L. Rev. 1, 11–21 (2003). Many mediators and commentators believe that such conduct is necessarily inconsistent with the nature of mediation and the mediator's role. Kimberlee K. Kovach & Lela P. Love, *"Evaluative" Mediation is an Oxymoron*, 14 Alternatives to High Cost Litig. 31 (1996). In this view, evaluation is a separate process, and therefore should be called by a different name, such as neutral evaluation or non-binding arbitration (these are "mixed" processes, which we cover infra in Chapter VI). Professor Love lists 10 reasons why mediators should not evaluate. However, she allows that

> [m]ediators are not foreclosed from engaging in some other process or helping parties design a mixed process. Whatever the service being provided, however, it should be requested by the parties and accurately labeled. When a process is "mixed" and the neutral has multiple roles, he or she is bound by more than one code of ethics, charged with separate goals and tasks. A properly labeled process — or conversely, a label that has a clear meaning — promotes integrity, disputant satisfaction [because expectations are met], and uniform practice.

Lela P. Love, *The Top Ten Reasons that Mediators Should Not Evaluate*, 24 Fla. St. U. L. Rev. 937, 948 (1997).

Is the idea of treating evaluation as a separate process consistent with the approach taken in the model Standards of Conduct for Mediators, Standard VI, supra, at page 358?

Many proponents of evaluation in mediation also see its potential problems. Mediator Marjorie Corman Aaron, for instance, lists the risks associated with evaluation as follows:

— perceived loss of neutrality;

— assumption of an adversarial relationship;

— loss of "face";

— alienation or division of counsel and client;

— entrenchment of at least one party's bargaining position;

— reduction in the parties' sense of process and outcome ownership; and

— shift in the focus toward winning and away from solving the problem.

Marjorie Corman Aaron, *Evaluation in Mediation*, in Dwight Golann, Mediating Legal Disputes: Effective Strategies for Lawyers and Mediators 267, 279 (1996).

Aaron thinks that "the mediation community has been somewhat coy on the issues of mediators providing evaluation of legal disputes." *Id.*

at 269. And she argues that a mediator may evaluate, if that is what the parties' desire, but only where evaluation is appropriate.

> While evaluation has a place in mediation, it is appropriate only where necessary. Where it is not necessary, evaluation should not be provided. The mediator should not include an evaluation in such cases on the theory that "it won't hurt and it might help." In fact, evaluation can hurt the process, making it inherently risky. And, if one accepts the notion that the benefits of mediation are optimized when the participants have found their own path to resolution, less substantive intervention may indeed be better.

> The fundamental diagnostic question a mediator must consider when planning a mediation process and strategy is "What are the barriers to negotiated resolution here?" Where the central barriers to resolution are found in the negotiation dynamics, in poor communication patterns, in asymmetrical information, or in the parties' lack of a sense of empowerment, the mediator should structure the process to address these issues; no evaluation is needed.

Id. at 271.

Aaron supplies thoughtful guidelines for a mediator to consider in attempting to provide a necessary evaluation in such a way as to minimize these risks. These include presenting evaluations in private sessions (after asking and receiving permission), "maintaining a distance" from the evaluation, and acknowledging the limits of the mediator's expertise.

Can you imagine circumstances in which evaluation might foster party self-determination and autonomy? *See* Jacqueline M. Nolan–Haley, *Informed Consent in Mediation: A Guiding Principle for Truly Educated Decisionmaking*, 74 Notre Dame L. Rev. 775 (1999).

In other writings, Professor Aaron and David Hoffer have described how a mediator can use decision-tree analysis to help create an evaluation of the case using the parties' own assessments — a real blend of elicitive and evaluative techniques. *See* David P. Hoffer, *Decision Analysis as a Mediator's Tool*, 1 Harv. Negot. L. Rev. 113 (1996), a portion of which is reprinted in Chapter III, beginning at page 227; Marjorie Corman Aaron, *The Value of Decision Analysis in Mediation Practice*, 11 Negot. J. 123 (1995); Marjorie Corman Aaron & David P. Hoffer, *Decision Analysis as a Method of Evaluating the Trial Alternative*, in Dwight Golann, Mediating Legal Disputes: Effective Strategies for Lawyers and Mediators 307 (1996).

For a strong argument against mediator evaluation, see Lela P. Love, *The Top Ten Reasons Why Mediators Should Not Evaluate*, 24 Fla. St. U. L. Rev. 937 (1997).

Commentators on both sides of this debate share a concern over whether the participants in a mediation get what they expect. Yves Dezalay and Bryant Garth have argued, however, that neither mediation nor arbitration has a fixed meaning and that debates over their definitions derive partially from the desires of practitioners and scholars to promote the forms of these processes that they use or support. Yves Dezalay & Bryant Garth, *Fussing About the Forum: Categories and Definitions as Stakes in a Professional Competition,* 21 Law & Soc. Inquiry 285 (1996).

Dean James Alfini recently presented nuanced discussion of this issue in relation to various standards of ethics for mediators. James J. Alfini, *Mediator Ethics, in* DISPUTE RESOLUTION ETHICS: A COMPREHENSIVE GUIDE 65, 76–77 (Phyllis Bernard & Bryant Garth, eds., 2002).

Issues related to evaluation by a mediator — whether, when, how and why — also arise outside the ethics context. We address such issues, and others, below in discussions of mediation as the practice of law, malpractice by mediators, and party self-determination.

b) Is Mediation the Practice of Law?

The foregoing section dealt with the question of whether a mediator may properly evaluate, as a matter of ethics. In this section we look at a range of mediator activities, including evaluation, in terms of whether the activity might constitute the practice of law. To the extent that mediator activity constitutes the practice of law, it subjects the mediator to regulation by authorities that control the practice of law — ordinarily, regulatory bodies established by the supreme court in each jurisdiction. Lawyers are subject to the ethical obligations of their profession while they are mediating. So they must be concerned about how their conduct is restricted by the rules of the jurisdictions in which they are admitted. In addition, when they are mediating in another jurisdiction, they could *conceivably* be subject to criminal charges for engaging in the unauthorized practice of law. When someone claims that mediation could constitute the practice of law, usually they are imagining that the mediator is not a lawyer.

i) The Rules

Ordinarily, mediators — even if they are lawyers — do not believe that they are forming a lawyer-client relationship, with the attendant obligations, when they undertake a mediation. However, there has been a good deal of disagreement or confusion on this issue among commentators and ethics authorities. Virtually all state supreme courts — which regulate the conduct of lawyers — have adopted ethical provisions based on one of two ABA documents: the Model Code of Professional Responsibility, first adopted by the ABA in 1969, and its successor, the Model Rules of Professional Conduct, adopted by the ABA in 1983 and most recently amended in 2003. One initial cause of confusion about the relationship between the lawyer-mediator and the parties was the fact that the only provisions in these two documents that seemed to touch on the mediator-party relationship assumed it was a lawyer-client relationship. See Model Rules of Professional Conduct EC 5–20, DR 5–105(B), DR 5–105(C)(1983).

Until 2002, Rule 2.2 of the Model Rules of Professional Conduct provided:

RULE 2.2 Intermediary

(a) A lawyer may act as intermediary between clients if:

(1) the lawyer consults with each client concerning the implications of the common representation, including the advantages and risks involved, and the effect on the attorney-client privileges, and obtains each client's consent to the common representation;

(2) the lawyer reasonably believes that the matter can be resolved on terms compatible with the clients' best interests, that each client will be able to make adequately informed decisions in the matter and that there is little risk of material prejudice to the interest of any of the clients if the contemplated resolution is unsuccessful; and

(3) the lawyer reasonably believes that the common representation can be undertaken impartially and without improper effect on other responsibilities the lawyer has to any of the clients.

(b) While acting as intermediary, the lawyer shall consult with each client concerning the decisions to be made and the considerations relevant in making them, so that each client can make adequately informed decisions.

(c) A lawyer shall withdraw as intermediary if any of the clients so request, or if any of the conditions stated in paragraph (a) is no longer satisfied. Upon withdrawal, the lawyer shall not continue to represent any of the clients in the matter that was the subject of the intermediation.

ABA, MODEL RULES OF PROFESSIONAL CONDUCT RULE 2.2 (2001).

Not surprisingly, numerous ethics opinions dealt with the question of whether a lawyer could mediate a given case in the context of whether the lawyer could represent both parties and draft documents or otherwise provide legal advice. The principal questions included whether the parties' interests conflicted and whether the parties' knowing consent was sufficient to allow the joint representation. *See* SARA COLE, NANCY H. ROGERS & CRAIG A. MCEWEN, MEDIATION: LAW, POLICY & PRACTICE 10:2 (2d ed. 2001). Some ethics opinions, however, recognized that these provisions did not apply because mediation by a lawyer, under certain conditions, did not constitute legal representation. *See id.* Fortunately, most commentators, dispute resolution organizations and ethics authorities recently have come to recognize that mediation ordinarily does not involve legal representation.

The so-called Joint Standards (1994) (MODEL STANDARDS OF CONDUCT FOR MEDIATORS, adopted by the AAA, ABA, and SPIDR), provide, in Comments to Standard VI, that

[t]he primary purpose of a mediator is to facilitate the parties' voluntary agreement. This role differs substantially from other professional-client relationships. Mixing the role of a mediator

and the role of a professional advising a client is problematic, and mediators must strive to distinguish between the roles. A mediator should therefore refrain from providing professional advice. Where appropriate, a mediator should recommend that parties seek outside professional advice, or consider resolving their dispute through arbitration, counseling, neutral evaluation or other processes. A mediator who undertakes, at the request of the parties, an additional dispute resolution role in the same matter assumes increased responsibilities and obligations that may be governed by the standards of other professions.

ABA, SPIDR, AFCC, MODEL STANDARDS OF CONDUCT FOR MEDIATORS, Standard VI, Comments (1994).

The ABA Model Standards of Practice for Family and Divorce Mediation use the dichotomy between legal information and legal advice: "Consistent with standards of impartiality and preserving participants' self-determination, a mediator may provide the participant with information that the mediator is qualified by training and experience to provide. The mediator shall not provide therapy or legal advice." MODEL STANDARDS OF PRACTICE FOR FAMILY AND DIVORCE MEDIATION, Standard VI, Comment B (2001).

In 2002, the American Bar Association finally addressed the confusion directly, by amending the Model Rules of Professional Conduct. First, it deleted the following language from the Preamble: "As an intermediary between clients, a lawyer seeks to reconcile their divergent interests as an advisor and to a limited extent, as a spokesperson for each client." It also deleted Rule 2.2 Intermediary, which appears above. And it added the following language to the Preamble: "In addition to these representational functions [advisor, advocate, and negotiator] a lawyer may serve as a third-party neutral, a nonrepresentational role helping the parties to resolve a dispute or other matter." ABA MODEL RULES OF PROFESSIONAL CONDUCT, Preamble [3] (2002). And it further clarified its stance on whether a lawyer who is mediating is representing the parties, by deleting Rule 2.2 Lawyer as Intermediary, supra, and adopting the following new Rule 2.4.

RULE 2.4 LAWYER SERVING AS THIRD–PARTY NEUTRAL

(a) A lawyer serves as a third-party neutral when the lawyer assists two or more persons who are not clients of the lawyer to reach a resolution of a dispute or other matter that has arisen between them. Service as a third-party neutral may include service as an arbitrator, a mediator or in such other capacity as will enable the lawyer to assist the parties to resolve the matter.

(b) A lawyer serving as a third-party neutral shall inform unrepresented parties that the lawyer is not representing them. When the lawyer knows or reasonably should know that a party does not understand the lawyer's role in the matter, the lawyer shall explain the difference between the lawyer's role as a third-party neutral and a lawyer's role as one who represents a client.

ABA, MODEL RULES OF PROFESSIONAL CONDUCT, Rule 2.4 (2003).

Of course new provisions such as these do not become binding until they are adopted by the highest court in a jurisdiction.

Important aspects of the debate over whether mediation was the unauthorized practice of law took place *before* the ABA made these changes in 1992. Professor Carrie Menkel–Meadow, e.g., argued that "evaluative mediation" constitutes the practice of law. Carrie Menkel–Meadow, *Is Mediation the Practice of Law?* 14 Alternatives to High Cost Litig. 57, 61 (1996). Lawyer-mediator Bruce Meyerson disagreed with Menkel–Meadow. Bruce Myerson, *Lawyers Who Mediate Are Not Practicing Law*, 14 Alternatives to High Cost Litig. 74 (1996).

ii) A Proposed Solution

ABA SECTION OF DISPUTE RESOLUTION, RESOLUTION ON MEDIATION AND THE UNAUTHORIZED PRACTICE OF LAW

(Feb. 2, 2002).

The ABA Section of Dispute Resolution has noted the wide range of views expressed by scholars, mediators, and regulators concerning the question of whether mediation constitutes the practice of law. The Section believes that both the public interest and the practice of mediation would benefit from greater clarity with respect to this issue in the statutes and regulations governing the unauthorized practice of law ("UPL"). The Section believes that such statutes and regulations should be interpreted and applied in such a manner as to permit all individuals, regardless of whether they are lawyers, to serve as mediators. The enforcement of such statutes and regulations should be informed by the following principles:

Mediation is not the practice of law. Mediation is a process in which an impartial individual assists the parties in reaching a voluntary settlement. Such assistance does not constitute the practice of law. The parties to the mediation are not represented by the mediator.

Mediators' discussion of legal issues. In disputes where the parties' legal rights or obligations are at issue, the mediator's discussions with the parties may involve legal issues. Such discussions do not create an attorney-client relationship, and do not constitute legal advice, whether or not the mediator is an attorney.

Drafting settlement agreements. When an agreement is reached in a mediation, the parties often request assistance from the mediator in memorializing their agreement. The preparation of a memorandum of understanding or settlement agreement by a mediator, incorporating the terms of settlement specified by the parties, does not constitute the practice of law. If the mediator drafts an agreement that goes beyond the terms specified by the parties, he or she may be engaged in the practice of law. However, in such a case, a mediator shall not be engaged in the practice of law if (a) all parties are represented by counsel and (b) the mediator discloses that any proposal that he or she makes with respect to the terms of settlement is informational as opposed to the practice of law, and that the parties should not view or rely upon such proposals as advice of counsel, but merely consider them in consultation with their own attorneys.

Mediators' responsibilities. Mediators have a responsibility to inform the parties in a mediation about the nature of the mediator's role in the process and the limits of that role. Mediators should inform the parties: (a) that the mediator's role is not to provide them with legal representation, but rather to assist them in reaching a voluntary agreement; (b) that a settlement agreement may affect the parties' legal rights; and (c) that each of the parties has the right to seek the advice of independent legal counsel throughout the mediation process and should seek such counsel before signing a settlement agreement.

* * *

4. *UPL and multi-jurisdictional practice of lawyer-mediators.* Lawyer-mediators should be aware that, unless they are admitted to the bar in every state, they too are potentially affected by the issue of UPL and mediation. Many lawyer-mediators provide mediation services in more than one jurisdiction. If mediation is considered the practice of law, lawyer-mediators could be accused of violating UPL statutes when they serve in a jurisdiction in which they are not admitted to the bar. Although a lawyer may petition for temporary admission, requiring such admission substantially and unnecessarily burdens the practice of mediation outside of the mediator's local area.

This problem is compounded for lawyer-mediators who have ceased practicing law, serve only as a neutral, and later relocate to different states. These lawyer-mediators may face difficult bar admission issues, as a state may require a certain minimum years of active engagement in the practice of law to qualify for admission to the bar without examination. This problem arises because bar regulators' definitions of the active practice of law may not include the activities typical of mediation, whereas the regulators who enforce UPL statutes (typically the state Attorney General, local district attorneys, or a bar committee) may include such activities as the practice of law in their interpretation of UPL statutes. It would seem to be a perverse result if transplanted lawyers clearly engaged in the practice of law could do so without proving their command of their new jurisdiction's laws, while a mediator who has no intention of practicing law would be required to take the new jurisdiction's bar exam.

The ABA's Commission on Multi-jurisdictional Practice is currently considering proposals for modification of the Model Rules of Professional Conduct that would, if adopted by the ABA and enacted by the states, eliminate, or at least reduce, concerns about lawyer-mediators engaging in a multi-jurisdictional practice.

5. *Guidelines on legal advice.* The Virginia Guidelines on Mediation and the Unauthorized Practice of Law, drafted by the Department of Dispute Resolution Services of the Supreme Court of Virginia, and the North Carolina Guidelines for the Ethical Practice of Mediation and to Prevent the Unauthorized Practice of Law, adopted by the North Carolina Bar in 1999, articulate a UPL standard for mediators that differs from the standard articulated in this Resolution. According to those Guidelines, a mediator may provide the parties with legal information but may not give legal advice. The Guidelines define legal advice as applying the law to the facts of the case in such a way as to (a) predict the outcome of the case or an issue in the case, or (b) recommend a course of action based on the mediator's analysis. The Section believes that adoption of the Virginia and North Carolina standards in other jurisdictions would be harmful to the growth and development of mediation.

It is important that mediators who are competent to engage in discussion about the strengths and weaknesses of a party's case be free to do so without running afoul of UPL statutes. Indeed, many parties, and their counsel, hire mediators precisely to obtain feedback about their case. Even though mediators who engage in these discussions do sometimes aid the parties by discussing possible outcomes of the dispute if a settlement is not reached and providing evaluative feedback about the parties' positions, this conduct is not the practice of law because the parties have no reasonable basis for believing that the mediator will provide advice solely on behalf of any individual party. This is the important distinction between the mediator's role and the role of an attorney. Parties expect their attorney to represent solely their interests and to provide advice and counsel only for them. On the other hand, a mediator is a neutral, with no duty of loyalty to the individual parties. (Thus, for example, when a judge conducts a settlement conference, acting in a manner analogous to that of a mediator and providing evaluation to the parties about their case, no one suggests that the judge is practicing law.)

6. *Discussion of legal issues.* This Resolution seeks to avoid the problem of a mediator determining, in the midst of a discussion of relevant legal issues, which particular phrasings would constitute legal advice and which would not. For example, during mediation of a medical malpractice case, if a mediator comments that the video of the newborn (deceased shortly after birth) has considerable emotional impact and makes the newborn more real, is this legal advice or prediction or simply stating the obvious? In context, the mediator is implicitly or explicitly suggesting that it may affect a jury's damage award, and thus settlement value. S/he is raising, from the neutral's perspective, a point the parties (presumably the defendants) may have missed, which may distinguish this case from others (e.g., cases in which a baby died *in utero* or where there was no video of the newborn) in which lower settlement amounts

were offered and accepted. Is the mediator absolved if s/he phrases the point as a "probing question"?

In their article, "A Well–Founded Fear of Prosecution: Mediation and the Unauthorized Practice of Law" (6 *Dispute Resolution Magazine* 20 (Winter 2000)), authors David A. Hoffman and Natasha A. Affolder illustrate this problem across a broader mediation context, setting out numerous alternative ways a mediator might phrase a point. They note that there would likely be very little professional consensus about which phrasings would constitute the practice of law and which would not. Even if mediators could agree as to where the line would be drawn among suggested phrasings, the intended meaning and impact of any particular statement might vary with the context and how the statement was delivered. Because mediation is almost always an informal and confidential process, it is virtually impossible, without an audio or video recording of a mediation, for regulators to police the nuances of the mediator's communications with the parties. Such recording would clearly be anathema to the mediation process.

7. *Settlement agreements.* The Virginia and North Carolina Guidelines' approach to the drafting of settlement agreements by a mediator is similar to the approach outlined in this Resolution. See "Guidelines on Mediation and the Unauthorized Practice of Law," Department of Dispute Resolution Services of the Supreme Court of Virginia, at 27–28 ("Mediators who prepare written agreements for disputing parties should strive to use the parties' own words whenever possible and in all cases should write agreements in a manner that comports with the wishes of the disputants .... Unless required by law, a mediator should not add provisions to an agreement beyond those specified by the disputants.") Ethics opinions in some states have approved the drafting of formal settlement agreements by mediators who are lawyers, even where the mediator incorporates language that goes beyond the words specified by the parties, provided that the mediator has encouraged the parties to seek independent legal advice. *See, e.g.,* Massachusetts Bar Association Opinion 85–3 (attorney acting as mediator may draft a marital settlement agreement, "but must advise the parties of the advantages of having independent legal counsel review any such agreement, and must obtain the informed consent of the parties to such joint representation").

* * *

Notes and Questions

1. The comments to the Resolution disagree with provisions in the Virginia and North Carolina standards on mediation and unauthorized practice of law. The Virginia Standards of Ethics and Professional Responsibility for Certified Mediators require the mediator to inform the parties in writing that "[t]he mediator does not provide legal advice." JUDICIAL COUNCIL OF VIRGINIA, STANDARDS OF ETHICS AND PROFESSIONAL RESPONSIBILITY FOR CERTIFIED MEDIATORS, Standard D.2.a)1 (2002). Virginia's Guidelines on Mediation and

the Unauthorized Practice of Law explain legal advice as follows: "A mediator provides legal advice whenever, in the mediation context, he or she
applies legal principles to facts in a manner that (1) predicts a specific
resolution of a legal issue or (2) directs, urges, or recommends a course of
action by a disputant or disputants."

Do you prefer the ABA approach or the Virginia approach?

2.   In 2000, lawyer-mediators David Hoffman and Natasha A. Affolder
thoroughly examined the issue of whether mediation could or should constitute the practice of law. They caution about the difficulty of distinguishing — in practice — between legal information and legal advice, the
approach in the Virginia and North Carolina UPL standards, and recommend a uniform approach that distinguishes between drafting settlement
agreements — which would be treated as the practice of law and regulated
by the state supreme courts; and providing "advice," which is part of the
mediation process and would be regulated through mediation ethics. David
A. Hoffman & Natasha A. Affolder, *Mediation and UPL: Do Mediators Have
a Well–Founded Fear of Prosecution?*, Disp. Resol. Mag., Winter 2000, at 20.
Would your answer to the question in the title depend on whether you are
considering a jurisdiction, such as Florida or Minnesota, that has a formal
regulatory process for mediators?

For a range of practitioner views on whether a mediator should draft a
settlement agreement, see Harry N. Mazadoorian, *To Draft or Not to Draft:
The Rights and Wrongs of Drafting and Signing Settlement Agreements*,
Disp. Resol. Mag., Spring 2004, at 31.

3.   In a jurisdiction that adopts Rule 2.4 of the ABA Model Rules of
Professional Conduct, does the rule obviate any claims that mediation
constitutes the practice of law? In a jurisdiction that has neither adopted nor
rejected that rule, would the rule nonetheless have some persuasive effect?

Would the rule, if adopted in a jurisdiction, affect the risk that a lawyer-
mediator who makes an "incorrect" prediction about a judicial outcome
could, in a malpractice action, be held to have breached a duty of care owed
to the parties?

4.   For further discussion of the unauthorized practice of law issue in
the context of mediation, see SARA R. COLE, NANCY H. ROGERS & CRAIG A.
MCEWEN, MEDIATION: LAW, POLICY AND PRACTICE 10:5 (2d ed. 2001); Geetha
Ravindra, *Balancing Mediation with Rules on Unauthorized Practice*, 18
Alternatives to High Cost Litig. 2 (2000).

iv. Malpractice Liability

Mediator malpractice liability has not been a significant factor in
regulating mediator behavior, for a least two reasons that are explained
below: (1) some mediators are immune from liability (as appears in the
first case below, *Wagshal v. Foster*); (2) it generally is very difficult to
establish the standard of care and a breach of that standard of care,
causation, and damages. Nonetheless, the theoretical possibility of liability exists and most people in the field assume that someday an appropriate case for imposition of liability may arise. The second case in this
section, *Tapoohi v. Lowenberg*, raises issues about whether certain kinds

of conduct by a mediator violate the standard of care as well as questions of causation.

WAGSHAL v. FOSTER

United States Court of Appeals, District of Columbia Circuit, 1994.
28 F.3d 1249.

Before: SILBERMAN, WILLIAMS and RANDOLPH, Circuit Judges.

Opinion for the Court filed by Circuit Judge WILLIAMS.

STEPHEN F. WILLIAMS, Circuit Judge:

This case presents the issue of whether a court-appointed mediator or neutral case evaluator, performing tasks within the scope of his official duties, is entitled to absolute immunity from damages in a suit brought by a disappointed litigant. The district court found such immunity and we agree.

* * *

In June 1990, appellant Jerome S. Wagshal filed suit in D.C. Superior Court against Charles E. Sheetz, the manager of real property owned by Wagshal. In October 1991 the assigned judge, Judge Richard A. Levie, referred the case to alternative dispute resolution pursuant to Superior Court Civil Rule 16[1] and the Superior Court's alternative dispute resolution ("ADR") program. While the program does not bind the parties (except when they agree to binding arbitration), participation is mandatory. See Superior Court Rules of Civil Procedure 16(j).

Judge Levie chose "neutral case evaluation" from among the available ADR options, and appointed Mark W. Foster as case evaluator.[2] Pursuant to the order of appointment, the parties signed a "statement of understanding" providing (among other things) that the proceedings would be confidential and privileged, and that the evaluator would serve as a "neutral party". Moreover, the parties were not allowed to subpoena the evaluator or any documents submitted in the course of evaluation, and "[i]n no event [could the] mediator or evaluator voluntarily testify on behalf of a party." Wagshal signed in January 1992 (under protest, he alleges).

After Foster held his first session with the parties, Wagshal questioned his neutrality. Foster then asked that Wagshal either waive his objection or pursue it; if Wagshal made no response waiving the objec-

---

1. Superior Court Rule 16(b) provides in part: "At [the initial scheduling and settlement] conference the judge will ... explore the possibilities for early resolution through settlement or alternative dispute resolution techniques...."

2. We use the terms "case evaluator" and "mediator" interchangeably in this opinion. Each acts as a neutral third party assisting the parties to a dispute in explor-

ing the possibility of settlement, the principal difference being that implicit in the name: the case evaluator focuses on helping the parties assess their cases, while the mediator acts more directly to explore settlement possibilities. See Melinda Ostermeyer, Alternative Dispute Resolution Programs 6 (Superior Court of the District of Columbia, Multi–Door Dispute Resolution Division 1992).

tion, Foster would treat it as a definite objection. Receiving no response by the deadline set, and later receiving a communication that he regarded as equivocal, Foster wrote to Judge Levie in February 1992, with copies to counsel, recusing himself. The letter also reported to the judge on his efforts in the case and recommended continuation of ADR proceedings. In particular, Foster said that the case was one "that can and should be settled if the parties are willing to act reasonably", and urged the court to order Wagshal, "as a precondition to any further proceedings in his case, to engage in a good faith attempt at mediation." He also urged Judge Levie to "consider who should bear the defendant's costs in participating" in the mediation to date.

Judge Levie then conducted a telephone conference call hearing in which he excused Foster. Wagshal's counsel voiced the claim that underlies this suit — that he thought Foster's withdrawal letter "indicates that he had certain feelings about the case. Now, I'm not familiar with the mediation process but as I understood, the mediator is not supposed to say, give his opinion as to where the merits are." On that subject, Judge Levie said, "I don't know what his opinions are and I'm not going to ask him because that's part of the confidentiality of the process." Neither Wagshal nor his counsel made any objection or motion for Judge Levie's own recusal.

Judge Levie soon after appointed another case evaluator, and Wagshal and the other parties settled the *Sheetz* case in June 1992. In September 1992, however, Wagshal sued Foster and sixteen others (whom he identified as members of Foster's law firm) in federal district court, claiming that Foster's behavior as mediator had violated his rights to due process and to a jury trial under the Fifth and Seventh Amendments, and seeking injunctive relief and damages under 42 U.S.C. § 1983. Besides the federal claims, he threw in a variety of local law theories such as defamation, invasion of privacy, and intentional infliction of emotional distress. His theory is that Foster's conduct as case evaluator forced him to settle the case against his will, resulting in a far lower recovery than if he had pursued the claim.

The district court granted the defendants' motion to dismiss with prejudice, holding that Foster, like judges, was shielded by absolute immunity. We affirm.

* * *

Foster's first line of defense against the damages claim was the assertion of quasi-judicial immunity. The immunity will block the suit if it extends to case evaluators and mediators, so long as Foster's alleged actions were taken within the scope of his duties as a case evaluator.

Courts have extended absolute immunity to a wide range of persons playing a role in the judicial process. These have included prosecutors, *Imbler v. Pachtman,* 424 U.S. 409, 430, 96 S.Ct. 984, 994–95, 47 L.Ed.2d 128 (1976); law clerks, *Sindram v. Suda,* 986 F.2d 1459, 1460 (D.C.Cir. 1993); probation officers, *Turner v. Barry,* 856 F.2d 1539, 1541 (D.C.Cir.

1988); a court-appointed committee monitoring the unauthorized practice of law, *Simons v. Bellinger,* 643 F.2d 774, 779–82 (D.C.Cir.1980); a psychiatrist who interviewed a criminal defendant to assist a trial judge, *Schinner v. Strathmann,* 711 F.Supp. 1143 (D.D.C.1989); persons performing binding arbitration, *Austern v. Chicago Bd. Options Exch., Inc.,* 898 F.2d 882, 886 (2d Cir.1990); and a psychologist performing dispute resolution services in connection with a lawsuit over custody and visitation rights, *Howard v. Drapkin,* 222 Cal.App.3d 843, 271 Cal.Rptr. 893, 905 (Ct.App.1990). On the other hand, the Supreme Court has rejected absolute immunity for judges acting in an administrative capacity, *Forrester v. White,* 484 U.S. 219, 229, 108 S.Ct. 538, 545, 98 L.Ed.2d 555 (1988), court reporters charged with creating a verbatim transcript of trial proceedings, *Antoine v. Byers & Anderson, Inc.,* 508 U.S. 429, 113 S.Ct. 2167, 124 L.Ed.2d 391 (1993), and prosecutors in relation to legal advice they may give state police, *Burns v. Reed,* 500 U.S. 478, 111 S.Ct. 1934, 114 L.Ed.2d 547 (1991). The official claiming the immunity "bears the burden of showing that such immunity is justified for the function in question." *Antoine,* 508 U.S. at 432-33 n. 4, 113 S.Ct. at 2169–70 n. 4 (citing *Burns v. Reed,* 500 U.S. at 486, 111 S.Ct. at 1939).

We have distilled the Supreme Court's approach to quasi-judicial immunity into a consideration of three main factors: (1) whether the functions of the official in question are comparable to those of a judge; (2) whether the nature of the controversy is intense enough that future harassment or intimidation by litigants is a realistic prospect; and (3) whether the system contains safeguards which are adequate to justify dispensing with private damage suits to control unconstitutional conduct. *Simons v. Bellinger,* 643 F.2d at 778 (citing *Butz v. Economou,* 438 U.S. 478, 512, 98 S.Ct. 2894, 2913–14, 57 L.Ed.2d 895 (1978)).

In certain respects it seems plain that a case evaluator in the Superior Court's system performs judicial functions. Foster's assigned tasks included identifying factual and legal issues, scheduling discovery and motions with the parties, and coordinating settlement efforts. These obviously involve substantial discretion, a key feature of the tasks sheltered by judicial immunity and the one whose absence was fatal to the court reporter's assertion of immunity in *Antoine.* See 508 U.S. at ___, 113 S.Ct. at 2170–71. Further, viewed as mental activities, the tasks appear precisely the same as those judges perform going about the business of adjudication and case management.

Wagshal protests, however, that mediation is altogether different from authoritative adjudication, citing observations to that effect in radically dissimilar contexts. See, e.g., *General Comm. of Adjustment v. Missouri–Kan.–Tex. R.,* 320 U.S. 323, 337, 64 S.Ct. 146, 152–53, 88 L.Ed. 76 (1943) ("The concept of mediation is the antithesis of justiciability."). However true his point may be as an abstract matter, the general process of encouraging settlement is a natural, almost inevitable, concomitant of adjudication. Rule 16 of the Federal Rules of Civil Procedure, for example, institutionalizes the relation, designating as subjects for pre-trial conferences a series of issues that appear to encompass all the tasks of a case evaluator in the Superior Court system: "formulation and simplification of the issues", "the possibility of obtaining admissions of fact and of documents", "the control and scheduling of discovery", and a catch-all, "such other matters as facilitate the just, speedy, and inexpensive disposition of the action." Fed.R.Civ.P. 16(c). Wagshal points to nothing in Foster's role that a Superior Court judge might not have performed under Superior Court Rule 16(c), which substantially tracks the federal model. Although practice appears to vary widely, and some variations raise very serious issues, see, e.g., *G. Heileman Brewing Co. v. Joseph Oat Corp.*, 871 F.2d 648 (7th Cir.1989) (en banc), it is quite apparent that intensive involvement in settlement is now by no means uncommon among federal district judges. See, e.g., Robert J. Keenan, *Rule 16 and Pretrial Conferences: Have We Forgotten the Most Important Ingredient?*, 63 S.Cal.L.Rev. 1449 (1990); Symposium, *The Role of the Judge in the Settlement Process,* 75 F.R.D. 203 (1976).

Wagshal does not assert that a case evaluator is performing a purely administrative task, such as the personnel decisions — demotion and discharge of a probation officer — at issue in *Forrester v. White.* Because the sort of pre-trial tasks performed by a case evaluator are so integrally related to adjudication proper, we do not think that their somewhat managerial character renders them administrative for these purposes.

Conduct of pre-trial case evaluation and mediation also seems likely to inspire efforts by disappointed litigants to recoup their losses, or at any rate harass the mediator, in a second forum. Cf. *Butz v. Economou,* 438 U.S. at 512, 98 S.Ct. at 2913 ("The loser in one forum will frequently seek another, charging the participants in the first with unconstitutional animus."). Although a mediator or case evaluator makes no final adjudication, he must often be the bearer of unpleasant news — that a claim or defense may be far weaker than the party supposed. Especially as the losing party will be blocked by judicial immunity from suing the judge, there may be great temptation to sue the messenger whose words foreshadowed the final loss. Cf. *Sindram v. Suda,* 986 F.2d at 1461 (noting that loser may turn on clerks because unable to reach the judge).

The third of the Supreme Court's criteria, the existence of adequate safeguards to control unconstitutional conduct where absolute immunity is granted, is also present. Here, Wagshal was free to seek relief from any misconduct by Foster by applying to Judge Levie. Alternatively, if he thought Foster's communications might prejudice Judge Levie, he could have sought Levie's recusal under Superior Court R.Civ.P. 63–I, Bias or Prejudice of a Judge. The avenues of relief institutionalized in the ADR program and its judicial context provide adequate safeguards.

Wagshal claims that even if mediators may be generally entitled to absolute immunity, Foster may not invoke the immunity because his action was not taken in a judicial capacity, see *Mireles v. Waco,* 502 U.S. 9, ___, 112 S.Ct. 286, 288, 116 L.Ed.2d 9 (1991) (citing *Forrester,* 484 U.S. at 227–29, 108 S.Ct. at 544–45; *Stump,* 435 U.S. at 360, 98 S.Ct. at

1106–07), and because he acted in complete absence of jurisdiction, see *id.* (citing *Stump,* 435 U.S. at 356–57, 98 S.Ct. at 1104–05; *Bradley,* 13 Wall. at 351). Neither exception applies.

Wagshal's argument that the acts for which he has sued Foster are not judicial (apart from the claim against mediators generally) rests simply on his claim that Foster's letter to Judge Levie, stating that he felt he "must recuse" himself and giving his thoughts on possible further mediation efforts and allocation of costs, breached Foster's obligations of neutrality and confidentiality. We assume such a breach for purposes of analysis. But "if judicial immunity means anything, it means that a judge 'will not be deprived of immunity because the action he took was in error . . . or was in excess of his authority.' " *Mireles,* 502 U.S. at ___, 112 S.Ct. at 288 (quoting *Stump,* 435 U.S. at 356, 98 S.Ct. at 1104–05). Accordingly "we look to the particular act's relation to a general function normally performed by a judge". *Mireles,* 502 U.S. 9–___, 112 S.Ct. at 288–89. Applying the same principle to case evaluators, we have no doubt that Foster's announcing his recusal, reporting in a general way on the past course of mediation, and making suggestions for future mediation were the sort of things that case evaluators would properly do.

Wagshal finally argues that Foster cannot be immune for the statements in his letter made after he stated that he "must recuse" himself. This is frivolous. Even if the letter alone effected a recusal (which is doubtful — Judge Levie clearly saw himself as later excusing Foster from service), the simultaneous delivery of an account of his work was the type of act a case evaluator could properly perform on the way out. In fact, we doubt very much if a modest gap in time between effective recusal and recounting of the events would take the latter out of the immunity.

Nor were Foster's actions "taken in the complete absence of all jurisdiction." Wagshal's claim to the contrary rests primarily on the theory that, although Superior Court Rule of Civil Procedure 16(j) requires parties to "attend . . . any alternative dispute resolution session ordered by the court", there is no explicit authority to *appoint* case evaluators. This contrasts, says Wagshal, with explicit District law authorizing appointment of masters and hearing commissioners. See, Superior Court R.Civ.P. 53(a) & (b) (masters); D.C.Code § 11–1732(a) (hearing commissioners).

Whatever merit this claim may have under District law, it does not come within a country mile of showing complete absence of jurisdiction. For such a showing, the judicial officer must "know[ ] that he lacks jurisdiction, or act[ ] despite a clearly valid statute or case law expressly depriving him of jurisdiction." *Mills v. Killebrew,* 765 F.2d 69, 71 (6th Cir.1985) (citing *Rankin v. Howard,* 633 F.2d 844, 849 (9th Cir.1980)). Similarly, in *White by Swafford v. Gerbitz,* 892 F.2d 457, 462 (6th Cir.1989), the court held that a judge enjoyed judicial immunity when, despite procedural defects in his appointment, he "possessed the office of

Special City Judge and was discharging the duties of that position under color of authority." Foster was similarly discharging the duties of case evaluator under color of authority.

At no point does Wagshal develop his constitutional attacks on Foster's jurisdiction, which evidently rest on the theory that the District's use of case evaluators for mandatory but non-binding dispute resolution violates the due process clause of the Fifth Amendment and the right to jury trial guaranteed by the Seventh Amendment. We do not normally pass upon claims that a party fails to articulate intelligibly. *Int'l Brotherhood of Teamsters v. Pena,* 17 F.3d 1478, 1487 (D.C.Cir. 1994).

* * *

We hold that absolute quasi-judicial immunity extends to mediators and case evaluators in the Superior Court's ADR process, and that Foster's actions were taken within the scope of his official duties. The judgment of the district court is

    Affirmed.

Notes and Questions

1. The idea that mediators should be immune from liability is not widely shared in the mediation community. Caroline Turner English argues, based upon a review of U.S. Supreme Court cases dealing with judicial immunity, that mediators should not have absolute quasi-judicial immunity. She proposes a compromise — qualified immunity, under which they could be held liable for acts that violate the rights of parties. Caroline Turner English, *Mediator Immunity*, 63 Geo. Wash. L. Rev. 759 (1995). Professor Michael Moffitt also believes that *Wagshal v. Foster* was wrong in extending quasi-judicial immunity to court-appointed evaluators and mediators, and believes that if any kind of immunity is appropriate, it should be a qualified one. Michael Moffitt, *Suing Mediators*, 83 B.U. L. Rev. 147, 204 (2003). He writes:

> Former mediation parties are not currently using private litigation as a means to address dissatisfaction with mediators' practices. The fact that there have been no successful lawsuits against mediators for their mediation conduct should not be mistaken as evidence that mediators are not making mistakes during their service. Instead, the lack of post-mediation legal activity is principally a product of the extraordinary legal obstacles facing any prospective plaintiff. Some mediators enjoy immunity from suits. The difficulty of establishing liability and damages protect mediators who do not enjoy immunity. The challenge of accessing information related to mediations further complicates matters. No traditional basis of recovery is readily available to unhappy mediation consumers and, as a result, lawsuits against mediators are rare.

> The uncertainty and rarity of lawsuits against mediators is, in some ways, costly. Victims of substandard mediation practices remain uncompensated for their injuries. Mediators who adopt offensive or harmful approaches to mediation may never be educated about, much less

deterred from, those practices. Furthermore, the public — including prospective mediation consumers, potential regulators, and other practitioners — may never learn about the current state of mediation practice in any meaningful way.

The solution to the lack of lawsuits, however, is not a wholesale broadening of liability exposure for all mediators. Instead, appropriate liability treatment demands recognition of some of the unique aspects of mediation practice. Mediation has very few, if any, practices so universally embraced that they would be considered customary. As a result, mediators should face significant exposure only to suits alleging a breach of a duty articulated or established by something other than customary practice. This would shield mediators from excessive second-guessing of those mediation decisions that are fundamentally discretionary judgments. At the same time, shielding mediators from liability in cases in which they breach a duty articulated outside of customary practice serves no persuasive policy. A mediator who engages in egregious behavior, violates contractual or statutory obligations, or breaches separately articulated duties should enjoy no legal or de facto immunity from lawsuits. Simultaneously, courts should favor lawsuits from parties who exercised their judgment in terminating an inadequate mediation. Wise policy and respect for autonomy demand deference both to mediators' subjective judgments and to parties' decisions regarding their continued participation in mediations.

Id. at 206–07.

Do you agree with Moffitt's proposal? Would your answer depend upon any of the following factors: Whether the mediation took place as part of a court program? Was court-ordered? Whether the mediator was a volunteer or was compensated?

The National Standards for Court–Connected Mediation Programs provide:

14.0   Courts should not develop rules for mediators to whom they refer cases that are designed to protect these mediators from liability. Legislators and courts should provide the same indemnity or insurance for those mediators who volunteer their services or are employed by the court that they provide for non-judicial court employees.

NATIONAL STANDARDS FOR COURT-CONNECTED MEDIATION PROGRAMS, STANDARD 14.0, CENTER FOR DISPUTE SETTLEMENT AND THE INSTITUTE FOR JUDICIAL ADMINISTRATION (1992). These standards can be found in the online appendix on the TWEN web site for this casebook, at www.lawschool.westlaw.com.

The drafters of the Uniform Mediation Act assumed mediators would be subject to liability for professional malpractice. Indeed, an early draft included a provision expressly repudiating the possibility of a mediator including a waiver of this liability. Section 4(b) of the NCCUSL Annual Meeting Draft of 1999 stated "[u]nless immunity from liability is extended to mediators by common law, rules of court, or other law of this State, a contractual term purporting to disclaim a mediator's liability is void as a matter of public policy." *See* UNIFORM MEDIATION ACT (1999), *at* http://www.law.upenn.edu/bll/ulc/mediat/medam99.htm. The provision, which would have been presented to the states as an optional paragraph, was later deleted as being unnecessary in that it merely restated current law.

2. Professors Cole, McEwen, and Rogers review possible bases for mediator liability, including negligence and breach of confidentiality, and note that other commentators have suggested that a mediator might be held liable for fraud, false advertising, outrageous conduct, breach of fiduciary duty, or tortious interference with contractual relations. SARAH R. COLE, NANCY H. ROGERS & CRAIG A. McEWEN, MEDIATION: LAW, POLICY AND PRACTICE 11:2, at 6–21 (3d ed. 2001). They conclude that "[e]xcept as a vague threat, mediator liability to the parties for malfeasance has not assumed a major role as a means of quality control. As mediation use grows, however, it is likely that some mediators will be held liable for acts that would subject other service providers to liability as well." *Id*. at 8. Some jurisdictions have enacted immunities for mediators in specific programs. *Id*. at 8–9.

3. The proposed revision of the joint standards expressly contemplates the possibility that the standards may be used to establish a standard of care for purposes of mediator liability. See the proposed revision in the online appendix on the TWEN web site for this casebook, at www.lawschool.west-law.com.

4. Would a mediator who gave an erroneous evaluation be negligent? Would it matter if the parties had lawyers? Can you imagine circumstances in which a party could establish causation and damages?

* * *

In the following opinion, the Supreme Court of Victoria, Australia recognizes the possibility of causes of action for breach of contract and tort duties of care against a mediator, on alleged facts that bear further study. As you read this opinion, pay particular attention to the behavior of the mediator and the lawyers and consider whether, in any of those roles, you might have behaved as they did, or differently.

TAPOOHI v. LEWENBERG

2003 VSC 410 (2003) Supreme Court of Victoria, Australia.
[Victorian Unreported Judgments].

[This dispute between sisters Regina Tapoohi and Halina Lewenberg over the disposition of their deceased mother's estate led to a voluntary (i.e., not court-ordered) mediation. At the conclusion of the mediation the mediator dictated an agreement, which was faxed to Tapoohi in Israel, who signed it on the advice of her solicitors (who were at the mediation), had it notarized, and faxed it back. Under this agreement, Tapoohi undertook to pay Mrs Lewenberg $1.4 million and to receive certain properties in exchange. In addition, Mrs Tapoohi was to transfer her shares in EOS Holdings to Mrs Lewenberg. Subsequently Mrs Tapoohi asked the court to set aside this written agreement, essentially on the grounds that it was subject to an oral agreement "that the parties would seek taxation advice concerning the settlement" of the matters in dispute and thereafter "would negotiate in good faith the form of any settlement reached." She also brought a claim against her solicitors, alleging that, if the agreement was binding upon her, the solicitors had breached a duty of care toward her by advising her to sign the agreement and telling her it was not binding. The solicitors, in turn, asserted claims for breach of tort and contract duties against their barrister and the mediator.

The mediator asked the court to dismiss the duty-based claims and moved for summary judgment. In ruling on these motions of the mediator, the court said it had to accept the allegations in the solicitors' affidavits. According to these affidavits,]

[25]   At approximately 8.00 pm the parties reached agreement in principle concerning the commercial settlement proposal, which provided that the properties would be transferred to Mrs Tapoohi in return for the payment of $1.4 million and that Mrs Tapoohi would relinquish her interest in the family companies. Mr Shiff [Tapoohi's solicitor] said that these were the only matters agreed and that many others remained outstanding. * * *

[26]   Mr Shiff said in his affidavit that when agreement in principle had been reached he said to Mr Denton [his barrister] and Ms Adams [his co-solicitor] that he thought they had done enough for the day. Mr Denton agreed. Both Mr Denton and Mr Shiff said that they did not want to stay late. Mr Shiff said in his affidavit that he was hungry, tired and worn out and did not think that he could deal constructively with the many outstanding issues.

[27]   Shortly thereafter, there was a discussion between Mr Golvan [the mediator] and Mr Shiff and Ms Adams. Mr Golvan stated in substance that everyone was to return to the main room so that they could get something down for the parties to sign. Mr Golvan indicated to Mr Shiff that terms of settlement would be drawn up, which Mr Shiff understood to mean that Mr Golvan was going to reduce to writing the terms of the commercial settlement proposal that had been reached in principle. Either Mr Shiff or Ms Adams said to Mr Golvan words to the effect that it was late. In the ensuing discussion Mr Golvan said such things as:

"You have got to stay, you have got to do the terms of settlement tonight.

No, we are doing it now. We are signing up tonight as that is the way that I do it, that's how I conduct mediations.

Given the acrimony between these two sisters we must go away with something that is written. It is in the interests of all the parties to sign up tonight."

These statements were made forcefully. Both Mr Shiff and Ms Adams took them as a direction from the mediator. Mr Shiff stated that he told Mr Golvan that he was not comfortable with signing that night. Ms Adams said Mr Shiff told Mr Golvan that it had been their intention to leave the mediation at that stage.

[28]   Mr Denton also indicated to Mr Golvan that he wished to leave the mediation, however, according to Mr Denton, Mr Golvan asked him to stay to "get down in writing the bones of the commercial agreement." Mr Denton stayed on as requested.

[29]   As a result of Mr Golvan's statements, Mr Denton, Mr Shiff and Ms Adams joined the remaining lawyers in the conference room. Mr Shiff said in his affidavit that he "decided to defer to Golvan's advice". He said that he knew Mr Golvan was an experienced mediator and that "his firmness of position weighed heavily on me". He regarded what Mr Golvan had said "as a direction from the mediator about which, effectively, I did not have any choice". Mr Shiff also said that he relied heavily upon both Mr Golvan and Mr Denton agreeing "to proceed to reduce the agreement in principle (to the extent that there was one) to writing because of their experience in these matters". Ms Adams stated that but for Mr Golvan's insistence that terms of settlement be signed that night, she would have departed the mediation when the agreement in principle was reached regarding the transfer of the properties and the payment of $1.4 million.

[30]   When he parties had reassembled, Mr Golvan said:

"We will now put together the terms of settlement and I will dictate them."

He also said that someone was needed to write down the terms and Ms Lewenberg agreed to do this. Mr Golvan then proceeded to dictate the proposed terms of settlement. Mr Shiff attempted to raise with Mr Golvan that all terms were subject to seeking taxation advice. Mr Denton and Ms Adam confirmed this. However, Mr Golvan interrupted Mr Shiff and stated that he wished to continue to dictate the terms. Despite Mr Golvan's assertive dictation of the terms, Mr Shiff reluctantly offered limited observations regarding the terms. Mr Shiff did not accept that the legal representatives of the parties really contributed to the drafting by making alterations to the terms. According to Mr Shiff, Mr Denton and Mr Tsalanidis effectively took no active role in the drafting process. Mr Shiff also stated that Mr Golvan went into far more detail than he had expected in dictating the Terms of Settlement.

[31]   Part of the Terms of Settlement included the transfer of shares in EOS Holdings from Mrs Tapoohi to Mrs Lewenberg. When Mr Golvan came to this issue in his dictating, the question of price was raised by him. Ms Lewenberg stated that the amount of consideration for the shares had not yet been addressed. Mr Shiff replied that the amount of consideration could be not be dealt with until advice on the tax implications was sought. Mr Golvan suggested that a figure of $1.00 be provided as nominal consideration for the share transfer. Mr Shiff stated that it was "all subject to review". Although no-one said that the figure of $1.00 was appropriate it was inserted in the Terms. Mr Shiff regarded the insertion of the nominal figure as an indication that there was no binding agreement between the parties, a position that he understood Mr Golvan and Ms Lewenberg to accept because he recollected stating to

both of them that he needed to obtain tax advice in relation to the appropriate amount of consideration before any amount could be agreed upon.

[32]   Mr Shiff said that after the Terms of Settlement had been drafted they were read "briefly" by both Mr Denton and himself and some minor changes were made. On the contrary, Mr Denton said that he left the mediation without reading or advising on the draft Terms of Settlement. According to Ms Adams, she and Mr Shiff reviewed the Terms of Settlement in private. She said that she did not read the Terms "thoroughly" on that night because she believed that "what was being agreed was only an agreement in principle and not a legally binding agreement". Mr Denton did not join in this private discussion because he had by then left the mediation. According to Mr Shiff, there was no objection to Mr Denton's departure as Mr Shiff did not believe he had to obtain any further instructions from Mrs Tapoohi in relation to a binding agreement.

[33]   Ms Adams said that she faxed the Terms of Settlement to Mrs Tapoohi in Israel, on the direction of Mr Golvan. Mr Shiff and Ms Adams discussed the Terms of Settlement with Mrs Tapoohi by telephone. No further amendments were made. The Terms were returned, signed by Mrs Tapoohi.

[34]   At the conclusion of the mediation, Mr Golvan provided each party with a copy of the Terms of Settlement, signed by all parties to the Settlement, including the signature of Ms Vivien Lewenberg on behalf of Mr Lewenberg. Mr Golvan then terminated the mediation conference. At this point Ms Adams had a conversation with Ms Vivien Lewenberg, who expressed her concern that her client would be "burdened with tax issues because Tapoohi was an overseas resident." In response, Ms Adams stated that Ms Lewenberg's position would be taken into account once the tax issues had been considered. This conversation took place in the same room in which the Terms of Settlement were prepared.

[35]   Thus, Mr Shiff maintained that, at the mediation, he repeatedly informed Mr Golvan that Mrs Tapoohi was not willing to enter into a binding agreement as the matters required expert tax advice that the legal representatives for Mrs Tapoohi were not qualified to provide.

[36]   Both Mr Shiff and Ms Adams agreed that that the Terms of Settlement did not contain the express term. Mr Shiff said that he expected that Ms Lewenberg would have recorded the requirement, indicated by Mrs Tapoohi's legal representatives, that tax advice was still to be obtained and was a condition of the Terms of Settlement. However, Mr Shiff stated that given the late hour and the length of time taken to conduct the mediation he failed to observe, when reading over the Terms of Settlement, that such a condition was not included. Mr Shiff did not realise the omission of this condition until some period of time after the mediation's conclusion. Mr Shiff accepted that he did not state to Mr Golvan that there was an express term which had to be included in the Terms of Settlement, but rather indicated to Mr Golvan repeatedly that

the Terms were subject to the parties getting tax advice and that once that advice was obtained the Terms required further discussion. Ms Adams said that she did not notice the failure to include the express terms in the Terms of Settlement on the night of the mediation.

[37] According to Mr Shiff, at no time during the mediation did he contemplate that a binding agreement would be entered into. If he had thought that the Terms of Settlement would be considered a binding agreement, Mr Shiff would not have put the document to Mrs Tapoohi. He only did so in reliance on Mr Golvan's firmly expressed views.

[38] Mr Shiff stated that he was aware of Mr Golvan's reputation, when conducting mediations, of being extremely determined to get the parties to reach settlement. However, Mr Shiff said that he did not expect that this approach would result in an agreement being prepared which did not reflect what had been agreed between the respective parties.

* * *

[Tapoohi asserted that the mediator owed and breached contractual and similar common law claims to:]

"(a) exercise all the due care and skill of a senior barrister specialising in commercial litigation and related matters;

(b) exercise all the due care and skill of a senior expert mediator;

(c) reasonably protect the interests of the Parties;

(d) not act in a manner patently contrary to the interests of the Parties, or any of them;

(e) act impartially as between the Parties;

(f) carry out his instructions from the Parties by all proper means;and further or alternatively

(g) not coerce or induce the Parties into settling the Earlier Proceeding when, at the relevant time or times, there was a real and substantial risk that settlement would be contrary to the interests of the Parties, or any of them."

* * *

[In denying the mediator's motions to dismiss and for summary judgment, the court concluded]

it is not beyond argument that some at least of the breaches of the contractual and tortious duties might be made out. I consider that it is possible that a court could find that there was such a breach constituted by the imposition of undue pressure upon resistant parties, at the end of a long and tiring mediation, to execute an unconditional final agreement settling their disputes where it was apparent that they, or one of them, wanted to seek further advice upon aspects of it, or where it was apparent that the agreement was not unconditional, or where the agreement was of such complexity that it required further consideration. I emphasise that it is not for me to conclude that any of these things occurred in the present case and I do not do so. It is sufficient that I conclude, as I do, that on the evidence before me such a contention is not plainly hopeless.

* * *

[The opinion also noted that in the trial, plaintiff Tapoohi would face major causation issues.]

Notes and Questions

1. Professor John Wade used the factual allegations in *Tapoohi* to describe "familiar negotiation and mediation dynamics":

> 12. The facts alleged in the case of *Tapoohi v. Lewenberg* provide a microcosm of events familiar to evaluative and other kinds of mediators, and to lawyers negotiating at the door-of a-court around the planet. For example:

- Big dollar disputes attract groups of lawyers to share the work and spread the professional risks.

- Ironically, often an essential person (e.g. accountant) or key piece of information (e.g. potential tax liabilities) is missing at early mediation meetings.

- Having assembled so many key people, negotiations tend to go on into the night. Usually, the costs and emotions of adjourning and "meeting again" are daunting. In this case, "night" negotiations had been arranged for the convenience of Mrs T who was in Israeli time zone.

- Mediators (and usually lawyers) make insistent speeches about the necessity of recording any agreements before "ending" the meeting.

- Nevertheless, several participants depart before the final document is signed (in this case, two people left "early").

- Drafting and amending the terms of settlement occurs when people are tired; and in a hurry to go home (though no "tiredness" was alleged by anyone in this initial reported case).

- Inevitably, every written settlement overlooks certain contingencies.

- Invariably, those present have different memories of what was said. A memory-battle lurks.

- Large numbers of people present mean that there are numerous conversations occurring, especially during the focussed work of drafting (e.g. para 34). Potential "side-bar" or collateral contracts can proliferate.

- All mediated conflicts require some degree of "pressure" or "risk analysis" in order to settle. Without the "pressures" of escalating legal and investigative costs, late hours, inconvenience of missed work, peer disapproval, the fear of post-settlement regrets, the door of the court, uncertain judicial behaviour, delay, adverse publicity etc., someone in the room can procrastinate and plead for "more time to think it over" indefinitely. That is, the concept of "free" consent is illusory. But when does inevitable (and desirable) decision-making pressure cross the line to become "improper"? These judgments about what is "improper" pressure vary between individuals and fact situations. What useful guidelines can emerge on what is "appropriate" pressure from lawyers, judges and mediators in the thousands of different door-of-the-court or mediated settlements which take place around the country each day?

- How much pressure, advice and risk analysis should a mediator offer? Competing answers to this question can be based upon habit, personal ethics, social utility, organisational ethics, market expectation, market reputation and legal risks for the mediator.

    There is no such thing as an "adviceless mediator".

- For mediators, organising meetings with multiple people present is often like herding cats. How far is the mediator (or lawyer at the door of the court) being hired to drive the acrimonious, wavering personalities and agendas to an outcome? . . .

- When should the mediator take the lead and dictate or write the first draft, or assist by suggesting wording to be first draft, of any settlement? It is common practice in many parts of Australia, USA, Asia and New Zealand for mediators to assist with drafting. Moreover, in the majority of mediations which take place around Australia and the world, there are no lawyers or professional wordsmiths present. The multi-skilled mediator has no realistic choice but to draft or dictate the first, and often the final draft. To do otherwise would usually disenfranchise the poor and middle class from *any* dispute resolution services. It is folly to suggest that everyone can choose to dine at the Ritz. A few mediators in California dictate settlement terms for unrepresented parties themselves to write out. This appears to be a vain attempt to transfer liability for omissions or commissions from the dictator to the secretary. Nor will reversing the scribe-dictator roles absolve an experienced secretarial mediator from *allegations* or conclusions of blame for scribing "holey" settlements. Nor will exiting the room and leaving inexperienced parties to draft alone create a bright line of moral or legal righteousness for a defensive though experienced mediator.

- When a mediator makes procedural suggestions, younger lawyers and less-experienced clients are often reluctant to assertively question or oppose those suggestions.

J.H. Wade, *Liability of Mediators for Pressure, Drafting and Advice:* Tapoohi v Lewenberg, Bond Dispute Resolution News (Jan. 2004), *at* http://www.bond.edu.au/law/centres/drc/newsletter/Vol16Jan04.doc.*

2. Assuming the facts alleged are true, how do you assess mediator Golvan's behavior in terms of the duty of reasonable care that he owed Ms. Tapoohi? In terms of ethics? How does any possible breach of duty by Golvan relate to possible breaches of duty by the lawyers?

3. Jeff Kichaven, a well-known mediator based in Los Angeles, has strong feelings about this:

---

* Professor Wade understands that this claim against the mediator and the lawyers was subsequently settled on undisclosed terms.

If the court's facts as recited are true, we should feel bad for Mr. Golvan personally. He was trying to help and he thought that what he did was right.

But he deserves to be sued. He probably deserves to lose. * * *

As improper as Golvan's bullying was, he still may win this case. That's because the extent to which Golvan was unethical is exceeded only by the extent to which Tapoohi's lawyer was incompetent. How dare the lawyer abdicate his responsibilities so completely to a mediator? Didn't he realize that while he owed his client a duty of undivided loyalty, the mediator did not?

* * *

In California, as a matter of law, a client represented by counsel cannot "reasonably" or even "actually" rely on the advice of anyone else on matters within the scope of that counsel's representation * * *

Tapoohi's attorney was profoundly wrong when he allowed, or maybe even required, his client to rely on the advice of another on matters within the scope of his representation. * * *

Jeff Kichaven, *Avoidable Sins: When a Mediator Steps Beyond the Boundaries*, 22 Alternatives to High Cost Litig. 77, 89–90 (2004).

The authors of this book have learned from mediators in Australia that mediator Golvan was in high demand before this case and remained in high demand after it. What would explain that?

4. If somehow you found yourself representing a client like Ms. Tapoohi in a mediation situation such as that alleged in the Tapoohi case, what might you do to protect your client's interests? See the excerpt from Kichaven, supra Note 3.

5. If you were selecting a mediator for a personal injury case in which you were representing the plaintiff, would you prefer to have the mediator potentially liable for negligence?

6. If you were offering your services as a mediator, would your standard form mediation agreement include a provision in which the parties agree not to hold you liable for negligence? Would courts enforce such an exculpatory clause? Liability insurance for mediation is readily available at rates much lower than for law practice.

7. If you were a judge planning to establish a court-connected mediation program, would you want the mediators to be personally liable for misconduct? Would your answer depend at all on whether the mediators were to volunteer their time or be paid?

2. PARTIES, LAWYERS, AND MEDIATION ADVOCACY

In 1998, when one of the authors was standing in the conference room of the Jerusalem Mediation Center in Israel, which was attached to a small law firm, he noticed two lounge chairs, in full reclining positions, sitting in the corner, some distance from the table. When he inquired about the purpose of this arrangement, the director replied, "That's where we put the lawyers." This reminds us that at the dawn of the "modern mediation movement" in the U.S. — in the late 1970's and early 1980's — many mediation proponents were motivated by anti-lawyer sentiments. The fundamental idea was that mediation had the potential of freeing people from the narrowness of a traditional legal perspective and from the potentially harmful effects of excessive adversarialism that they thought typified traditional lawyers. (This perspective has been characterized as the "lawyer's standard philosophical map." Leonard L. Riskin, *Mediation and Lawyers*, 43 Ohio St. L.J. 29, 43–48 (1982), which is excerpted in Chapter I, beginning at page 66, supra.) In response to such perspectives, some mediation programs have excluded lawyers or limited their roles. And in some mediation arenas — such as family and community mediation — lawyers' roles are still limited, either for these reasons, or for reasons of economy.

In the last twenty-five years, however, mediation has become a routine part of law practice in most parts of the U.S. By and large, lawyers have played constructive roles in these processes. Yet, there is still much debate and confusion about the role of the lawyer for a party in a mediation. The materials in this Section address the roles of lawyers and clients in preparing for and participating in a mediation. For convenience, we divide the subject into five categories: Getting into Mediation, which we cover in section a); Selecting a mediator, the focus of section b); Advocacy and Problem-solving, section c); Good Faith Participation, which we introduce in section d) and elaborate in Chapter VI, infra; and the Consulting Lawyer's Role, section e). As you read these materials, keep in mind the tension between adversarial and problem-solving perspectives in negotiation that we discussed in Chapter III, supra.

a. Getting into Mediation

Disputes get into mediation in a variety of ways. Very often, courts order cases into mediation — though in many such programs, parties have opportunities to opt out. In other cases, parties have agreed in advance to mediate disputes that arise under a contract. Sometimes the parties or their lawyers decide to mediate after a dispute has arisen. It is quite common, however, for lawyers to find themselves or their clients wanting to mediate, but facing an adversary who may be unwilling or reluctant. If you were in such a situation, how would you deal with it? In the following excerpt, Michael Keating, a lawyer who has been mediating full time for more than 25 years, offers suggestions.

J. MICHAEL KEATING, JR., GETTING RELUCTANT
PARTIES TO MEDIATE: A GUIDE FOR
ADVOCATES

13 Alternatives to High Cost Litig. 9 (CPR Institute
for Dispute Resolution, 1995).*

Once parties agree to mediate a dispute, they stand at least a 75 percent chance of resolving the conflict without litigation. Yet persuading reluctant parties in business disputes to try mediation may require as much creativity, persuasiveness and flexibility as the mediation process itself. The following guide for advocates outlines some persuasive gambits to convince disputants and their counsel to consider mediation.

NATURE OF THE PROCESS

A first group of inducements to mediate relate to the nature of the process.

Control over the substantive outcome. Because mediation is not a binding process (the parties settle their dispute only if the outcome is mutually acceptable), the disputants never have to surrender control over the result to an outsider who may not understand the nature and context of their confrontation. Mediation is facilitated negotiation, and one of the cardinal rules of negotiation is that you do not accept the proffered outcome unless it is as good as or better than any available alternative. That central understanding ensures that the parties, not the neutral, will decide the outcome.

Parties retain control over the outcome in two senses. First, they retain for themselves the power to define the final result. In addition, they avoid the necessity of handing over to randomly-selected judges or barely-known arbitrators responsibility for crafting a resolution. Binding adversarial processes, on the other hand, deprive the parties of control in both of these senses. Even non-binding adversarial procedures, like court-annexed arbitration, exclude the parties from an active role in formulating a resolution.

In many commercial disputes, retaining control over the outcome is critical. Astute business people don't want to delegate the resolution of complex and potentially expensive commercial disputes to outsiders who can be ignorant of or indifferent to the realities of business life. The more control business executives preserve over the outcome of their disputes, the more fully a company's interests are likely to be served.

Control over the process. The procedural flexibility of mediation allows parties to fashion a process that responds directly to their needs and concerns. Parties decide whether they prefer an evaluative or a facilitative process. They can dictate the characteristics and experience of the mediator; they identify the issues they want the mediator to help them decide; and they can limit the duration of the mediation process. They also can prescribe such details as scheduling, logistics, fees and the scope of pre-mediation and mediation presentations.

Mediation eliminates the lock-step ritual of traditional adversarial approaches. Instead, lawyers become the true architects of conflict resolution, able to fashion creative dispute resolution procedures. No one is happier about this development than lawyers' business clients, who see procedural design as a key component in containing the cost of resolving commercial disputes.

Opposition to mediation often springs from attorneys' ignorance about its intricacies. One way to overcome that kind of reluctance is by engaging opposing counsel directly in the design of a custom-tailored process. If the other side is convinced that some legal issue needs to be thoroughly aired in the course of the mediation, include the opportunity to do so in the framework of mediation proposed. A competent mediator will be responsive to such concerns and help to incorporate the procedural requirements of parties into the process.

Opportunity for better solutions. The most powerful argument for the use of mediation is the opportunity it offers, particularly in the business context, for generating better solutions to complex problems. A Chinese proverb observes, "Conflict is opportunity riding on the crest of a dangerous wave." Mediation provides a unique vehicle for capturing that opportunity.

By shifting the focus and energy of disputants away from the purely legal aspects of their confrontation, facilitative mediation promotes a search for settlement options directly responsive to the commercial interests and concerns of the parties. Mediation promotes a full understanding of underlying business interests and a search for resolutions that best meet those interests.

NATURE OF THE DISPUTE

Another set of reasons for using mediation in particular cases relates to the nature of the dispute.

Relationship of the parties. Whenever the parties to a dispute anticipate a relationship that will outlast the particular confrontation, mediation ought to be the dispute resolution process of choice. Adversarial alternatives are too divisive and rely too exclusively on demonstrating culpability and liability. Mediation eschews the placing of blame, and concentrates instead on finding solutions that meet the parties' interests, preserve the relationship and cut further losses. The relationships may include business people locked in some continuing commercial embrace, sibling heirs, landlords and tenants, merchants and customers, service providers and clients. Whenever there is an important stake in future cooperation, only fools will leap to litigation without an attempt at mediation.

Complexity of the dispute. Some disputes are so factually dense that litigation would inevitably be prolonged and dubiously probative. Almost always such disputes involve an orgy of documentary discovery that drives the transactional cost of the case into orbit. Mediation is not a substitute for discovery, but it can be useful for identifying real disclosure needs. It also can limit abuses, especially in cases when the parties seek genuinely to establish and control compensable losses.

Another measure of complexity may be the number of parties on one or another side of a dispute. Most commercial cases involve insurers — at least for one party — and many, such as environmental cases, bring a dozen or more parties to the table. These sorts of cases often involve co-plaintiffs and co-defendants who often differ amongst themselves, as well as with their mutual opponent. When defendants' intramural efforts to fix blame on each other help make the plaintiff's case, mediation clearly makes sense. If you represent one of the defendants in such a situation, you would do well to persuade your fellow counsel to cooperate to draw the plaintiff into mediation.

Time imperative. Disputes that involve continuing damage to business interests in the absence of quick resolution are particularly appropriate for mediation. When attorneys ponder the evils of litigation, they think most often in terms of transactional costs, but the hemor-rhaging of business interests and opportunities is often the principal concern of their business clients. Mediation can be activated quickly and is far removed from the plodding pace of litigation, making it powerfully attractive to business adversaries.

Containing damage to reputation. In addition to the direct damage to the bottom line of business entities caught up in litigation, the adversarial struggle often seriously harms the combatants' reputa-tions within their immediate business communities. * * *

The literature on mediation is full of wildly optimistic emphasis on the capacity of the process to deliver "win-win" resolutions. More accurately, mediation may help develop "lose-less-lose-less" resolutions to contain costs and minimize the future adverse impact associated with current disputes. Many business clients know that once suit is filed — or even before suit is filed if an important deal has already fallen apart — any process for cleaning up the mess will involve a struggle simply to keep losses at some acceptable level.

General Benefits of ADR

Some more general advantages of mediation accrue from its status as one alternative to the judicial process. [Here Keating describes bene-fits such as privacy, speed, lower transactions costs, developing a better understanding. He also identifies a series of potential resources, includ-ing individual judges, whom you may be able to persuade to order the case into mediation; court-annexed mediation programs, private provid-ers, literature and videotapes; contract clauses, and financial incen-tives — including offering to pay for the mediator]

* * *

Selection of the mediator. Another desperate measure is to let your adversary select the mediator, whom you may reject only if there is a conflict of interest. Such an offer is a testament to your understanding of the process of mediation, and your confidence that mediation cannot compel you to enter an agreement against your client's interest.

Notes and Questions

1. Some lawyers have expressed concern about initiating discussions with clients or opposing counsel about mediation or other alternative meth-

ods of dispute resolution based on a fear that that the client will consider them less than fully committed to vigorous representation. For demonstrations of how to hold such a conversation, see *Overview of ADR*, Tape IV in the DISPUTE RESOLUTION AND LAWYERS VIDEOTAPE SERIES (West Publishing Co. 1991); *How to Prepare Your Client and Yourself for Mediation,* Tape 2 in WHAT EVERY LITIGATOR NEEDS TO KNOW ABOUT MEDIATION (AMERICAN BAR ASSOCIATION 1993).

2.   If a lawyer on the opposite side of a case offered to pay for all or part of the mediator's fees and expenses in order to induce you to agree to mediate, what concerns would you have? To what extent does your response derive from an adversarial assumption about the motivation behind that lawyer's offer?

3.   Some anecdotal reports and research studies indicate that lawyers who have experienced mediation — even if they were ordered into such mediation — are more likely to recommend mediation to their clients in the future. *See* Roselle L. Wissler, *Court–Connected Mediation in General Civil Cases: What We Know from Empirical Research,* 17 Ohio St. J. on Disp. Resol. 641, 695 (2002). Wissler reached a similar conclusion as to lawyers recommending ADR. Rosselle L. Wissler, *When Does Familiarity Breed Content? A Study of the Role of Different Forms of ADR Education and Experience in Attorneys' ADR Recommendations,* 2 Pepp. Disp. Resol. J. 199 (2002). Does that argue in favor of mandatory mediation programs in courts? For a discussion of court-ordered mediation, see Chapter VI, beginning at page 692.

b.   Selecting a Mediator
i.   Mediator Background and Approach

Who chooses the mediator, or the mediator's approach? Sometimes a court or mediation service provider will propose one or more mediators, giving the parties the opportunity to select or reject any of them. And often parties or lawyers select mediators on their own, either from a list developed by a court or service provider, or simply based on the neutral's reputation. Assuming you have a choice, here are some considerations to keep in mind. The following excerpt is based on the "old grid" of mediator orientations, which assumes that the mediator's "orientation" could be the most significant factor in determining how the mediator will behave in a mediation (an assumption that we question in subsequent readings.) This reading describes potential advantages and disadvantages of various mediator behaviors and perspectives.

LEONARD L. RISKIN, UNDERSTANDING MEDIATORS' ORIENTATIONS, STRATEGIES, AND TECHNIQUES: A GRID FOR THE PERPLEXED

1 Harv. Negot. L. Rev. 7, 41–48 (1996).

* * *

[An earlier portion of this article, which appears supra at page 288, sets forth the "Computec" hypothetical, which involves a dispute that arose under a service contract between Golden State Savings and Loan and Computec, a computer services company, over Golden State's refusal to reimburse certain travel expenses submitted by Computec.]

A. *The Potential Advantages and Disadvantages of the Various Approaches to Mediation*

Assume that you represent Computec in its dispute with Golden State and that you and your counterpart have agreed (with the consent of both clients) to try mediation. Before considering the characteristics that you would like to see in the mediator and in the mediation process, you need to ask yourself two questions: first, what has blocked the success of the negotiations to date; and, second, what do you hope to achieve through mediation? You must find a mediator whose approach to mediation and other characteristics are most likely to remove obstacles to settlement or otherwise help you accomplish your goals.

To know which orientation on the grid is most appropriate, one must comprehend a great deal about the origins and nature of the dispute, the relationships among the concerned individuals and organizations (both behind and across party lines), and their fears, levels of competence, and goals. Before mediation begins, however, parties and lawyers often will not fully understand these matters; individuals are likely to have different perceptions of what is needed, possible, or desirable in the mediation. These divergent perceptions may interfere with the parties' ability to select the most appropriate form of mediation. Accordingly, and because mediators may fail to test their assumptions about the parties' needs and may thus exercise what Felstiner and Sarat have called "power by indirection," it is important for parties to understand the potential advantages and disadvantages of various points on the two continuums.

1. *The Problem–Definition Continuum*

a. *Narrow Problem–Definition.* — A narrow problem-definition can increase the chances of resolution and reduce the time needed for the mediation. The focus on a small number of issues limits the range of relevant information, thus keeping the proceeding relatively simple. In addition, a narrow focus can avoid a danger inherent in broader approaches — that personal relations or other "extraneous issues" might exacerbate the conflict and make it more difficult to settle.

On the other hand, in some cases the narrow approach can increase the chance of impasse because it allows little room for creative option-generation or other means of addressing underlying interests, which, if unsatisfied, could block agreement. Also, a narrow approach to mediation might preclude the parties from addressing other long-term mutual interests that could lead to long-lasting, mutually-beneficial arrangements.

b. *Broad Problem–Definition.* — A broad problem-definition can produce an agreement that accommodates the parties' underlying interests, as well as the interests of other affected individuals or groups. Such an agreement is substantively superior. Broadening the problem-definition also can both increase the likelihood of settlement and reduce the time necessary for the mediation; when such a process addresses the parties' needs and allows room for creativity, it reduces the likelihood of impasse. In addition, it can provide opportunities for personal change.

In some situations, however, a broad problem-definition can have the opposite effect: it can increase both the probability of an impasse and the time and expense required for mediation by focusing the parties on issues that are unnecessary to the resolution of the narrow issues and that might exacerbate conflict. In addition, broad problem-definition can make parties and lawyers uncomfortable with the process. They may fear the expression of strong emotions and doubt their own abilities to collaborate with the other side and still protect their own interests.

In the Computec case, the parties' mutual dependence and need to work together suggest the desirability of a broad problem-definition. One could also imagine, however, that it might be best simply to resolve the narrow issue, so that the disputants could get on with their work. If we change the facts slightly, we could see the possible virtue of a narrow focus. For instance, if the contract had already terminated, if the parties had no interest in future relations, and if they both believed that the matter could best be handled simply by addressing the issue of whether and how much Golden State should pay, a narrow approach might make great sense. (Of course, the danger here is that the person carrying this narrow vision of the dispute does not fully understand the situations of all concerned, and, for that reason, is unaware of the possibilities for future collaboration.)

2. *The Mediator Role Continuum*

a. *The Evaluative Approach.* — The evaluative mediator, by providing assessments, predictions, or direction, removes some of the decision-making burden from the parties and their lawyers. In some cases, this makes it easier for the parties to reach an agreement. Evaluations by the mediator can give a participant a better understanding of his "Best Alternative to a Negotiated Agreement" (BATNA), a feeling of vindication, or an enhanced ability to deal with his constituency. If you were Computec's lawyer, for example, and were having trouble educating your client about the weaknesses of its case, you might want a mediator willing to predict credibly what would happen in court.

Yet, in some situations an assessment, prediction, or recommendation can make it more difficult for the parties to reach agreement by impairing a party's faith in the mediator's neutrality or restricting a party's flexibility. As Arthur Chaykin of Sprint Corp. has written:

> Parties often feel [an evaluation] is what they want, until they get it. Once the "opinion" is given, the parties often feel that the mediator betrayed them. They will feel that the mediator's decision on the merits may have been influenced by perceptions of what they would be willing to swallow, not on the "merits" of the case....

Nevertheless, the parties should understand that once they involve a third party, and allow that "neutral" to give an opinion on the merits, that determination will almost always have a powerful impact on all further negotiations. After all, how could the "prevailing party" take much less than what the mediator recommended?[118]

Moreover, these evaluative techniques decrease the extent of the parties' participation, and thereby may lower the participants' satisfaction with both the process and the outcome. Of course, such techniques also reduce opportunities for change and growth.

In addition, if the parties or lawyers know that the mediator will evaluate, they are less likely to be candid either with their counterparts or with the mediator. When a mediator asks such parties (in private caucus, for example) to analyze the strengths and weaknesses of their own case or to describe their situation and interests, they may be disinclined to respond honestly. Thus, the prospect that the mediator will render an evaluation can interfere with the parties' coming to understand fully their own and each other's positions and interests, and thereby render the process more adversarial.

b. *The Facilitative Approach.* — On the one hand, the facilitative approach offers many advantages, particularly if the parties are capable of understanding both sides' interests or developing potential solutions. It can give them and their lawyers a greater feeling of participation and more control over the resolution of the case. They can fine-tune the problem-definition and any resulting agreement to suit their interests. The facilitative approach also offers greater potential for educating parties about their own and each other's position, interests, and situation. In this way, it can help parties improve their ability to work with others and to understand and improve themselves.

On the other hand, when participants are not sufficiently knowledgeable or capable of developing proposals or negotiating with one another, the facilitative approach holds certain risks. The participants might fail to recognize relevant issues or interests, to fully develop options, or to reach an agreement that is as "good" — by whatever standards — as they would reach with a more evaluative mediator. In addition, a poorly-conducted facilitative approach might waste a great deal of time if it does not respond to underlying interests either in the process or in the outcome.

B. *The Importance of Subject–Matter Expertise*

In selecting a mediator, one would want to consider the relative importance of "subject-matter expertise" as compared to expertise in the mediation process. "Subject-matter expertise" means substantial understanding of the legal or administrative procedures, customary practices, or technology associated with the dispute. In the Computec case, for

---

118. Arthur A. Chaykin, Selecting the Right Mediator, Disp. Resol. J., Sept. 1994, at 65 n.5.

instance, a neutral with subject-matter expertise could be familiar with the litigation of computer services contract disputes; with the structure, economics, and customary practices of the savings and loan or computer services industries; with computer technology (especially as related to financial services industries); or with all of these.

The need for subject-matter expertise typically increases in direct proportion to the parties' need for the mediator's evaluations. In addition, the kind of subject-matter expertise needed depends on the kind of evaluation or direction the parties seek. If they want a prediction about what could happen in court, they might prefer an evaluative mediator with a strong background in related litigation. If they want ideas about how to structure future business relations, perhaps the mediator should understand the relevant industries. If they want suggestions about how to allocate costs, they may need a mediator who understands the relevant technology. If they need help in sorting out interpersonal-relations problems, they would benefit from a mediator oriented toward such issues, rather than one inclined to shy away from them. If they want to propose new government regulations, they might wish to retain a mediator who understands administrative law and procedure.

In contrast, to the extent that the parties feel capable of understanding their circumstances and developing potential solutions — singly, jointly, or with assistance from outside experts — they might, if they had to choose, prefer a mediator with great skill in the mediation process, even if she lacks subject-matter expertise.

The complexity and importance of a technical issue should influence the nature and extent of the required subject-matter expertise. In almost any mediation, the neutral must at least be able quickly to acquire a minimal level of familiarity with technical matters in order to facilitate discussions or propose areas of inquiry. But to the extent that other participants have this expertise, the need for the mediator to possess it diminishes. In fact, too much subject-matter expertise could incline some mediators toward a more evaluative role, thereby interfering with the development of creative solutions.

C.   *The Importance of Impartiality*

The idea that the mediator should be neutral or impartial — both in fact and in appearance — is deeply imbedded in the ethos of mediation, even though observers disagree about the meaning and achievability of the notion. The need for impartiality increases in direct proportion to the extent to which the mediator will evaluate. In other words, the greater the mediator's direct influence on the substantive outcome of the mediation, the greater the risk that one side will suffer as a result of the mediator's biases.

Imagine that you represent Computec and propose mediation to the lawyer representing Golden State. After considering the matter for a few days, she says she is ambivalent but that she would be inclined to agree to mediation if she could be satisfied with the mediator. Eventually, she proposes a neutral who is a lawyer, with substantial practice experience in both the financial services and computer industries, as well as an experienced mediator. She also tells you that the proposed mediator and she were close friends in college and that they occasionally get together for lunch or dinner. You do not know the mediator but are familiar with her fine reputation.

Your response to this proposal likely would depend in part upon your expectation as to the role the mediator would take in the process. If you wanted or expected evaluation, you might worry about this mediator's possible partiality. If you expected facilitation, this mediator might be just what you need, especially since her selection may be the only way to get the case into mediation. Of course, you would want to be certain that the proposed mediator is willing and able to commit to and carry out a facilitative process.

Notes and Questions

1.   Lawyers often want mediators to give their impressions of the strengths and weakness of their cases. *See* Bobbi McAdoo, *A Report to the Minnesota Supreme Court: The Impact of Rule 114 on Civil Litigation Practice in Minnesota*, 25 Hamline L. Rev. 401 (2002); Bobbi McAdoo & Art Hinshaw, *The Challenge of Institutionalizing Alternative Dispute Resolution: Attorney Perspectives on the Effect of Rule 17 on Civil Litigation in Missouri*, 67 Mo. L. Rev. 473, 530–31 (2002). Given the complex set of potential advantages and disadvantages described in the foregoing excerpt, why do you suppose this is the case?

2.   A recent study of 645 mediations of employment discrimination claims that were conducted under the U.S. Equal Employment Opportunity Commission's mediation program concluded that participants (both claimants and respondents) were more satisfied with facilitative mediation than with evaluative mediation but that claimants got more money in evaluative mediations. E. Patrick McDermott & Ruth Obar, *"What's Going On" in Mediation: An Empirical Analysis of the Influence of the Mediator's Style on Party Satisfaction and Monetary Benefit*, 9 Harv. Negot. L. Rev. 75 (2004). Not everyone in the field would agree with the way in which McDermott and Obar determined whether the mediator's self reports showed evaluative or facilitative mediation. Assuming you take their finding seriously, if you were a lawyer representing an employee in an employment discrimination claim, would you necessarily want a mediator who would evaluate? Is evaluation inconsistent with facilitation?

3.   When entering into a mediation, one of a lawyer's major concerns should be to know and have some control over what you and your client are getting into. This is true even though mediations frequently produce unexpected and unforeseeable activities and insights that redound to the benefit of all the parties. But there is a danger. Suppose you assume, based on what you have read about mediation, that the mediator will not evaluate, i.e., assess the strengths or weaknesses of each side's claims or predict the outcome in court. If your assumption were valid, you might justifiably tell the mediator, in a private caucus, something about your client's underlying interests. In a negligence claim against a physician and hospital, for in-

stance, you or your client might let the mediator know that your client really cares more about reforming hospital procedures than about the money. But if the mediator winds up evaluating — say, recommending a monetary settlement — such information might reduce the ultimate financial outcome for your client.

A contrasting situation presents a contrasting risk. The lawyer or client might assume that the mediator will evaluate; such an assumption could be based on prior experience with mediators who evaluate, or on confusion with arbitration or early neutral evaluation. One or both sides might have chosen mediation precisely because they wanted to get such an assessment in an informal atmosphere. Similarly, an individual who files a complaint in a small claims court or another informal court, and finds the matter referred to a court-connected mediation program, might expect that law will play some role in the resolution and that she will somehow be advised of how a court would likely determine the matter. Jacquelyn M. Nolan–Haley, *Court Mediation and the Search for Justice Through Law*, 74 Wash. U. L.Q. 47 (1996). In both of these situations, the parties might be disadvantaged, or at least disappointed, by a mediator who does not provide such a service. (On the other hand, a well-conducted facilitation often can provide the parties and lawyers with virtually the same information — or perhaps more valid information — than an evaluation. *See* Marjorie Corman Aaron, *Evaluation in Mediation, in* Dwight Golann, Mediating Legal Disputes 267 (1996)).

So, how might you control for such risks? There are two basic approaches. One is to select a mediator known to take the approach that you desire. The other is to select a mediator who is willing to provide the kind of service that the parties want or need. However, it may be difficult to know in advance what kind of mediation would be most appropriate; generally parties and lawyers learn a great deal during mediations.

How would you find out about a mediator's tendencies and practices and willingness to negotiate about procedures and about issues such as the problem-definition? First, it is generally acceptable for parties to have *ex parte* contact with mediators both before and during a mediation. (A few court-connected programs do not allow this, however.) Thus, you could contact a potential mediator and ask about his practices and ask for references. You might also contact other lawyers, mediators, or mediation trainers who are familiar with the mediator's practices. For a list of questions you might ask a mediator, see Layn R. Phillips, *Laying the Foundation for Successful Mediation: Questions Neutrals and Parties Need to Ask,* 13 Alternatives to High Cost Litig. 132 (1995). For various views of who should decide what kind of mediation should take place, see Kimberlee K. Kovach, *What is Real Mediation, and Who Should Decide*, Disp. Resol. Mag., Summer 1996, at 5. In large, complex mediations it has become commonplace for the parties to conduct extensive joint interviews with several candidates before selecting a mediator.

Assuming you have a mediator who is flexible, how would you work with the mediator to decide whether the mediator will evaluate, and if so, how and when? This raises the question of who should or can have influence over a variety of decisions in a mediation (an issue discussed in the next section). Such decisions can be difficult. For instance, what should happen if one side wants evaluation and the other does not — and the mediator tends to evaluate? *See* Joseph B. Stulberg, *Facilitative versus Evaluative Mediator Orientations: Piercing the "Grid"lock,* 24 Fla. St. U. L. Rev. 985, 992–93 (1997) and the excerpt from Riskin's New New Grid article in the next section.

ii. Mediator "Presence"

Have you ever noticed that you feel different in the presence of different people? Do you feel calm, excited, bored, or anxious depending on the person with whom you are having lunch, taking a walk, or playing tennis? Does this experience extend to your contacts in a professional context, with physicians or lawyers? More significantly for our purposes, how can this quality affect a mediation? In the following excerpt, lawyer-mediators Daniel Bowling and David Hoffman explore the importance of the mediator's presence.

DANIEL BOWLING AND DAVID A. HOFFMAN, BRINGING PEACE INTO THE ROOM: HOW THE PERSONAL QUALITIES OF THE MEDIATOR IMPACT THE PROCESS OF CONFLICT RESOLUTION
14, 17–18, 21–24 (2003).

* * *

[A]s mediators, we have noticed that, when we are feeling at peace with ourselves and the world around us, we are better able to bring peace into the room. Moreover, doing so, in our experience, has a significant impact on the mediation process. What may be more complex and difficult to explain is how we, as mediators, can maintain a sense of peacefulness while working with people who are deeply enmeshed in seemingly intractable conflict. Often the disputes that we deal with in mediation trigger feelings in us about conflicts in our own lives. However, we believe that successful mediators have an ability to transcend those conflicts, or perhaps to use the insight derived from them, to help the parties in the mediation reach a genuine resolution of the dispute that brought them there. This ability arises, in our view, not so much from a particular set of words or behaviors but instead from an array of personal qualities of the mediator that create an atmosphere conducive to resolution.

* * *

PERSONAL QUALITIES OF THE MEDIATOR

More than a decade ago, mediators William E. Simkin and Nicholas A. Fidandis (1986) catalogued what they believed to be the necessary qualities for an effective mediator. We assume, for purposes of this discussion, that these qualities, and the others discussed in this chapter, are not entirely innate and can be developed. Simkin and Fidandis included in their list, which was no doubt partly tongue-in-cheek:

- The patience of Job

- The sincerity and bulldog characteristics of the English
- The wit of the Irish
- The physical endurance of a marathon runner
- The broken-field dodging abilities of a halfback
- The guile of Machiavelli
- The personality-probing skills of a good psychiatrist
- The hide of a rhinoceros
- The wisdom of Solomon

Another writer (Boulie, 1996) suggested, in a more serious vein, that successful mediators are empathetic, nonjudgmental, patient, persuasive, optimistic, persistent, trustworthy, intelligent, creative, and flexible, and that they have a good sense of humor and common sense.

Such catalogues of qualities — which are anecdotal, not scientific — help us identify some of the characteristics that we may want to foster in ourselves and look for in other mediators. However, we believe there is some deeper and more fundamental quality that the most effective mediators have: a quality that may include such attributes as patience, wisdom, or wit but that involves other attributes that are not in these lists. As we try to identify that quality, we focus on both the subtle influences of the mediator (those that may operate beneath the level of conscious awareness), and those where the mediator's influence is readily apparent.

* * *

THE MEDIATOR'S "PRESENCE"

This brings us to the heart of our thesis: there are certain qualities that the mediator's presence brings to the mediation process that exert a powerful influence and enhance the impact of the interventions employed by the mediator. The term presence, of course, has at least two meanings here: (1) the fact that the mediator is physically present and (2) the qualities that his or her physical presence brings into the room. It is the second meaning we are interested in as we explore how the mediator's presence influences the mediation.

As part of that exploration, it is important to recognize that the personal qualities of the *parties* may influence the mediator, just as the mediator's personal qualities affect the parties. Trying to understand the effect of the mediator's presence, without considering the impact of the parties on the mediator* * * is to look at only half of the picture. In traditional psychoanalytic terms, a similar phenomenon might be described as countertransference, the term used to describe feelings evoked in the therapist by the client. * * * Just as it is important for a psychotherapist to be aware of those feelings so that they do not inappropriately influence the course of treatment, mediators need to be aware of the feelings evoked in them by their clients and the nature of the dispute in order to make productive use of those feelings. In Gestalt psychology, the phenomena we are examining would be viewed as being comprehensible only by looking at the whole set of interactions of the parties and the mediator, the qualities that each brings to the process, and the changes wrought by those interactions. Gestalt psychologists assert that "living organisms ... perceive things not in terms of isolated elements, but as integrated perceptual patterns — meaningful organized wholes, which exhibit qualities that are absent in their parts." * * *

These analogies from the field of psychology point to the utility of considering mediation from a systemic perspective, one in which we shift our focus from the interests of the individual parties to the set of interactions and relationships of the parties and the mediator. On the basis of systems theory, the essential properties of an organism, or living system, are properties of the whole, which none of the parts have. They arise from the interactions and relationships among the parts. These properties are destroyed when the system is dissected, either physically or theoretically, into isolated elements. Although we can discern individual parts in any system, these parts are not isolated, and the nature of the whole is always different from the mere sum of its parts. * * * Central to this way of looking at mediation is the recognition that the mediator is not extrinsic to the conflict (any more than the therapist is wholly separate from the issues addressed in therapy).

Such an approach is, to some extent, at odds with prevailing norms in the mediation field, in which the independence (or separateness) of the mediator is viewed as professionally appropriate, perhaps even necessary, if one is to be effective. These norms are expressed in ethical codes that articulate a vision of mediation in which mediators, for the most part, have no prior connections with the parties and maintain a stance of rigorous impartiality.

The view that mediators need to maintain a certain distance from the parties may stem from the professional norms of psychotherapy, law, and other disciplines where ethical principles require the professional to avoid personal involvement that might impair the ability to render independent professional judgments.

However, the values and norms of those other professions may not be completely applicable in the context of mediation. One important difference in the professional roles is that a psychotherapist or lawyer must, in some cases, take responsibility for directing the client's actions by giving professional advice. Most codes of ethics for mediators proscribe offering professional advice. * * *

We are not suggesting abandonment of neutrality or impartiality; far from it. However, being neutral or impartial does not mean that conflict resolvers are separate from the conflict systems they are seeking to help resolve. Because mediators are inextricably involved in the conflicts they mediate, impartial may not be as accurate a description of the mediator's role as the term "omnipartial," which has been proposed by mediator Kenneth Cloke * * *.

While reconceptualizing the process as one in which the mediator is personally involved — being influenced by the process as much as influencing it — the mediator must manage the tension between his or her own objectives and those of the parties. The mediator has a professional duty to the clients, whose interests and needs are of paramount importance. Yet at the same time, the mediator cannot fully serve the clients without being cognizant of (1) the evolution of relationships between and among the participants in the mediation, including the mediator, and (2) the impact of the mediation process on the mediator himself or herself.

We are not suggesting that the mediator redirect the attention of the parties from their needs or interests to his or her own. However, we are suggesting a departure from what we believe is the norm in much of the training of mediators with respect to managing their own feelings in the mediation process. Mediators are taught, for the most part, to contain whatever feelings they may have about the parties to maintain neutrality and communicate, by word and deed, their impartiality. We suggest that the feelings the mediator experiences may be important and useful material that the mediator can use — albeit judiciously — in helping the parties reach a resolution. In using such an intervention, a mediator must also maintain appropriate professional boundaries so that purely personal matters are not interjected into the process.

We are also suggesting that the mediator use his or her own self-awareness by adopting a deeply reflective practice, including the careful observation of the impact that the mediation, the conflict, and the parties have on her or him. Through such a practice, outside the mediation room, the mediator may substantially aid his or her progress in * * * mastering mediation to develop those personal qualities desirable for assisting in the resolution of conflicts. In doing so, mediators should seek to increase their awareness of how they resolve conflict in their own lives in order to lessen any unintended impact of unresolved personal conflict on the mediation process.

Notes and Questions

1. What are some of the characteristics of the "peaceful quality" that Bowling and Hoffman describe? As a lawyer selecting a mediator, would you look for such a quality in a mediator? If so, how? Would you look for such a quality in the mediator for every case, or would it depend on the nature of the conflict and the participants or other factors?

What factors would make it more appropriate to find a mediator with a very different kind of "presence"?

2. If you were responsible for the selection and training of mediators for a program, would you either look for mediators who were at peace with themselves or promote training that would develop such qualities? One way to develop such qualities is mindfulness meditation, which recently has been

incorporated into mediation training. *See* Leonard L. Riskin, *Mindfulness: Foundational Training for Dispute Resolution,* 54 J. Legal Educ. 79 (2004) (which is excerpted in Chapter VIII, beginning at page 889; Leonard L. Riskin, *The Contemplative Lawyer: On the Potential Contributions of Mindfulness Meditation to Law Students, Lawyers, and their Clients,* 7 Harv. Negot. L. Rev. 1 (2002); the Harvard Negotiation Insight Initiative, *at* http://www.pon.harvard.edu/hnii; the Initiative on Mindfulness in Law and Dispute Resolution, *at* www.law.missouri.edu/csdr/mindfulness.htm.

c. Working with the Mediator (and the Other Participants): Advocacy and Problem–Solving

Parties and their lawyers can exercise influence, even control in a mediation, in many ways. This section begins with an article by Tom Arnold, an intellectual property lawyer and mediator based in Houston, on ways in which they commonly miss opportunities to exercise influence. It is followed by a piece by Leonard Riskin that addresses the advantages and disadvantages of client participation in settlement conferences, a form of mediation. Next, Jeff Kichaven, a lawyer-mediator in Los Angeles, gives advice on what to do when a mediator tries to assert too much power. And in the final excerpt, Leonard Riskin revisits the "grid" of mediator orientations, which appeared at page 288, and proposes a new system that pays less attention to mediator orientations and more attention to the influence that all mediation participants — not just the mediator — can exert.

TOM ARNOLD, 20 COMMON ERRORS IN MEDIATION ADVOCACY

13 Alternatives to High Cost Litig. 69 (CPR Institute
for Dispute Resolution, 1995).*

Trial lawyers who are unaccustomed to being mediation advocates often miss important arguments. Here are 20 common errors, and ways to correct them.

Problem 1: Wrong client in the room

CEOs settle more cases than vice presidents, house counsel or other agents. Why? For one thing, they don't need to worry about criticism back at the office. Any lesser agent, even with explicit "authority," typically must please a constituency which was not a participant in the give and take of the mediation. That makes it hard to settle cases.

A client's personality also can be a factor. A "Rambo," who is aggressive, critical, unforgiving, or self-righteous doesn't tend to be conciliatory. The best peace-makers show creativity, and tolerance for the mistakes of others. Of course, it also helps to know the subject.

Problem 2: Wrong lawyer in the room

Many capable trial lawyers are so confident that they can persuade a jury of anything (after all, they've done it before), that they discount the importance of preserving relationships, as well as the exorbitant costs and emotional drain of litigation. They can smell a "win" in the court room, and so approach mediation with a measure of ambivalence.

Transaction lawyers, in contrast, tend to be better mediation counsel. At a minimum, parties should look for sensitive, flexible, understanding people who will do their homework, no matter their job experience. Good preparation makes for more and better settlements. A lawyer who won't prepare is the wrong lawyer.

Problem 3: Wrong mediator in the room

Some mediators are generous about lending their conference rooms but bring nothing to the table. Some of them determine their view of the case and urge the parties to accept that view without exploring likely win-win alternatives.

The best mediators can work within a range of styles that Leonard L. Riskin developed in a recent issue of Alternatives (September 1994 at p. 111). As Mr. Riskin described them, these styles fall along a continuum, from being totally facilitative, to offering an evaluation of the case. Ideally, mediators should fit the mediation style to the case and the parties before them, often moving from style to style as a mediation progresses.

Masters of the process can render valuable services whether or not they have substantive expertise. When do the parties need an expert? When they want an evaluative mediator, or someone who can cast meaningful lights and shadows on the merits of the case and alternative settlements.

It may not always be possible to know and evaluate a mediator and fit the choice of mediator to your case. But the wrong mediator may fail to get a settlement another mediator might have finessed.

Problem 4: Wrong case

Almost every type of case, from anti-trust or patent infringement to unfair competition and employment disputes, is a likely candidate for mediation. Occasionally, cases don't fit the mold, not because of the substance of the dispute, but because one or both parties want to set a precedent.

For example, a franchisor that needs a legal precedent construing a key clause that is found in 3,000 franchise agreements might not want to submit the case to mediation. Likewise, an infringement suit early in the life of an uncertain patent might be better resolved in court; getting the

Federal Circuit stamp of validity could generate industry respect not obtainable from ADR.

Problem 5: Omitting client preparation

Lawyers should educate their clients about the process. Clients need to know the answers to the types of questions the mediator is likely to ask. At the same time, they need to understand that the other party (rather than the mediator) should be the focus of each side's presentation.

In addition, lawyers should interview clients about the client's and the adversary's "best alternative to negotiated agreement," and "worst alternative to negotiated agreement," terms coined by William Ury and Roger Fisher in their book, *Getting to Yes*. A party should accept any offer better than his perceived BATNA and reject any offer seen as worse than his perceived WATNA. So the BATNAs and WATNAs are critical frames of reference for accepting offers and for determining what offers to propose to the other parties. A weak or false understanding of either party's BATNA or WATNA obstructs settlements and begets bad settlements.

Other topics to cover with the client:

- the difference between their interests and their legal positions;
- the variety of options that might settle the case;
- the strengths and weaknesses of their case;
- objective independent standards of evaluation;
- the importance of apology and empathy.

Problem 6: Not letting a client open for herself

At least as often as not, letting the properly coached client do most, or even all, of the opening and tell the story in her own words works much better than lengthy openings by the lawyer.

Problem 7: Addressing the mediator instead of the other side

Most lawyers open the mediation with a statement directed at the mediator, comparable to opening statements to a judge or jury. Highly adversarial in tone, it overlooks the interests of the other side that gave rise to the dispute.

Why is this strategy a mistake? The "judge or jury" you should be trying to persuade in a mediation is not the mediator, but the adversary. If you want to make the other party sympathetic to your cause, don't hurt him.

For the same reason, plenary sessions should demonstrate your client's humanity, respect, warmth, apologies and sympathy. Stay away from inflammatory issues, which are better addressed by the mediator in private caucuses with the other side.

Problem 8: Making the lawyer the center of the process

Unless the client is highly unappealing or inarticulate, the client should be the center of the process. The company representative for the other side may not have attended depositions, so is unaware of the impact your client could have on a judge or jury if the mediation fails. People pay more attention to appealing plaintiffs, so show them off.

Prepare the client to speak and be spoken to by the mediator and the adversary. He should be able to explain why he feels the way he does, why he is or is not responsible, and why any damages he *caused* are great or only peanuts. But he should also extend empathy to the other party.

Problem 9: Failure to use advocacy tools effectively

You'll want to prepare your materials for maximum persuasive impact. Exhibits, charts, and copies of relevant cases or contracts with key phrases highlighted can be valuable visual aids. A 90–second video showing key witnesses in depositions making important admissions, followed by a readable size copy of an important document with some relevant language underlined, can pack a punch.

Problem 10: Timing mistakes

Get and give critical discovery, but don't spend exorbitant time or sums in discovery and trial prep before seeking mediation.

Mediation can identify what's truly necessary discovery and avoid unnecessary discovery. One of my own war stories: With a mediation under way and both parties relying on their perception of the views of a certain vice president, I leaned over, picked up the phone, called the vice president, introduced myself as the mediator, and asked whether he could give us a deposition the following morning. "No," said he, "I've got a Board meeting at 10:00."

"How about 7:30 a.m., with a one-hour limit?" I asked. "It really is pretty important that this decision not be delayed." The parties took the deposition and settled the case before the 10:00 board meeting.

Problem 11: Failure to listen to the other side

Many lawyers and clients seem incapable of giving open-minded attention to what the other side is saying. That could cost a settlement.

Problem 12: Failure to identify perceptions and motivations

Seek first to understand, only then to be understood. Messrs. Fisher and Ury suggest you brainstorm to determine the other party's motivations and perceptions. Prepare a chart summarizing how your adversary sees the issues.*

---

* See chart at the end of this excerpt.

Problem 13: Hurting, humiliating, threatening, or commanding

Don't poison the well from which you must drink to get a settlement. That means you don't hurt, humiliate or ridicule the other folks. Avoid pejoratives like "malingerer," "fraud," "cheat," "crook," or "liar." You can be strong on what your evidence will be and still be a decent human being.

All settlements are based upon trust to some degree. If you anger the other side, they won't trust you. This inhibits settlement.

The same can be said for threats, like a threat to get the other lawyer's license revoked for pursuing such a frivolous cause, or for his grossly inaccurate pleadings.

Ultimatums destroy the process, and destroy credibility. Yes, there is a time in mediation to walk out — whether or not you plan to return. But a series of ultimatums, or even one ultimatum, most often is very counterproductive.

Problem 14: The backwards step

A party who offered to pay $300,000 before the mediation, and comes to the mediation table willing to offer only $200,000, injures its own credibility and engenders bad feelings from the other side. Without some clear and dramatic reasons for the reduction in the offer, it can be hard to overcome the damage done.

The backwards step is a powerful card to play at the right time — a walk away without yet walking out. But powerful devices are also dangerous. There are few productive occasions to use this one, and they tend to come late in a mediation. A rule of thumb: unless you're an expert negotiator, don't do it.

Problem 15: Too many people

Advisors — people to whom the decision-maker must display respect and courtesy, people who feel that since they are there they must put in their two bits worth — all delay a mediation immeasurably. A caucus that with only one lawyer and vice president would take 20 minutes, with five people could take an hour and 20 minutes. What could have been a one-day mediation stretches to two or three.

This is one context in which I use the "one martini lunch." Once I think that everyone present understands all the issues, I will send principals who have been respectful out to negotiate alone. Most come back with an expression of oral settlement within three hours. Of course, the next step is to brush up on details they overlooked, draw up a written agreement and get it signed. But usually those finishing touches don't ruin the deal.

Problem 16: Closing too fast

A party who opens at $1 million, and moves immediately to $500,000, gives the impression of having more to give. Rightly or wrongly, the other side probably will not accept the $500,000 offer because they expect more give.

By contrast, moving from $1 million to $750,000, $600,000, $575,000, $560,000, $550,000, sends no message of yield below $500,000, and may induce a $500,000 proposal that can be accepted.

The "dance" is part of communication. Skip the dance, lose the communication, and risk losing settlement at your own figure.

Problem 17: Failure to truly close

Unless parties have strong reasons to "sleep on" their agreement, to further evaluate the deal, or to check on possibly forgotten details, it is better to get some sort of enforceable contract written and signed before the parties separate. Too often, when left to think overnight and draft tomorrow, the parties think of new ideas that delay or prevent closing.

Problem 18: Breaching a confidentiality

Sometimes parties to a mediation unthinkingly, or irresponsibly, disclose in open court information revealed confidentially in a mediation.

When information is highly sensitive, consider keeping it confidential with the mediator. Or if revealed to the adversary in a mediation where the case did not settle, consider moving before the trial begins for an order in limine to bind both sides to the confidentiality agreement.

Problem 19: Lack of patience and perseverance

The mediation "dance" takes time. Good mediation advocates have patience and perseverance.

Problem 20: Misunderstanding conflict

A dispute is a problem to be solved together, not a combat to be won.

To prepare for mediation, rehearse answers to the following questions, which the mediator is likely to ask:

- How do you feel about this dispute or about the other party?
- What do you really want in the resolution of this dispute?
- What are your expectations from a trial? Are they realistic?
- What are the weaknesses in your case?
- What law or fact in your case would you like to change?
- What scares you most?
- What would it feel like to be in your adversary's shoes?
- What specific evidence do you have to support each element of your case?
- What will the jury charge and interrogatories probably be?
- What is the probability of a verdict your way on liability?

- What is the range of damages you think a jury would return in this case if it found liability?

- What are the likely settlement structures, from among the following possibilities: Terms, dollars, injunction, services, performance, product, recision, apology, costs, attorney fees, releases.

- What constituency pressures burden the other party? Which ones burden you?

Part of preparing for mediation is understanding your adversary's perceptions and motivations, perhaps even listing them in chart form. Here is an example, taken from a recent technology dispute.

Plaintiff's Perceptions	Defendant's Perceptions
Defendant entered the business because of my sound analysis of the market, my good judgment and convictions about the technology.	I entered the business based on my own independent analysis of the market and the appropriate technology that was different from Plaintiff's.
Defendant's business plan was based upon confidential information that I provided. He never would have considered it, but for me.	I interviewed nearly 100 market participants before arriving at my market, plan, using my own judgment.
Defendant used me by pretending to be interested in doing business with me.	Plaintiff misled me with exaggerated claims that turned out to be false.
Defendant made a low-ball offer for my valuable technology. Another company paid me my asking price.	I made Plaintiff a fair offer; I later paid less for alternative technology that was better.

———

If you are ordered into mediation, the terms of the order may dictate whether the lawyer or the client must or may attend, and, perhaps, the nature of the participation required. The next excerpt describes various ways in which clients can participate along with their lawyer in settlement conferences, a form of mediation.

LEONARD L. RISKIN, THE REPRESENTED CLIENT IN A SETTLEMENT CONFERENCE: THE LESSONS OF *G. HEILEMANN BREWING CO. v. JOSEPH OAT CORP.*

69 Wash. U. L.Q. 1059, 1098–1106 (1991).

A. *Advantages and Disadvantages of Client Attendance in Settlement Conferences*

A client's attendance at a settlement conference can take numerous forms. The following continuum describes one aspect of such involvement:

— Client is available by telephone.

— Client waits outside the conference room.

— Client waits outside the conference room part of the time and sits in on the conference part of the time.

— Client sits in on the conference but does not speak, except perhaps to his lawyer.

— Client sits in on the conference and speaks in response to questions from his lawyer or in response to questions from the other lawyer or judge.

— Client sits in on the conference and speaks and asks questions relatively freely.

— Client and lawyer meet privately with judge.

— Client(s) meet with judge without lawyers.

— Client meets privately with other client, without lawyers.

Add to these variables differences in attorney-client, client-client, and judge-attorney relationships, in the nature of the case, in the type of negotiation conducted and the judicial host's intervention, and you have an inkling of the complexity of the idea of client involvement in a settlement conference. Still, lawyers, judges, and commentators tend to argue about the advantages and disadvantages of client involvement based largely upon unarticulated assumptions about some of these variables.

1. *"Client–Centered" Arguments*

One area of debate concerns the effect of the client's participation on the client's own interests. For each potential advantage trumpeted, a corresponding risk or potential disadvantage waits to be sounded:

— The client's presence increases the likelihood that her lawyer will be well-prepared. [But: the client's presence may incline some lawyers to posture, to "show off." In addition, the client may become a great bother, interfering with the lawyer's ability to accomplish her or his work.]

— The client's presence can reduce the risk that interests of the lawyer will prevail over those of the client. For instance, a lawyer might recommend for or against a particular settlement because of the lawyer's own financial or professional needs, which could be related to excessive pressure from the judge. [But: The client's presence may remove tactical advantages. For example, often a lawyer will falsely attribute a stubbornness to the client that will give the lawyer negotiating strength. In addition, it may be strategically useful to delay consideration of an offer from the other side; this is easier to do with an absent client.]

* * *

— The client will feel he has had a chance to tell his story, in his own words, by participating in a settlement conference. [But: to the extent that such a feeling makes it easier for the client to settle, he loses a real day in court.]

— The client can learn much about the strengths and weaknesses of both sides of the case by observing the conduct of the other parties, the lawyers, and the judge; this can soften his attitudes or positions. [But: Some clients might be angered or hardened by exposure to the other side's behavior, making settlement more difficult.]

— If the client actually observes the exchange of monetary offers, he can better assess the strength of the other side's commitment to a position; he may notice things the lawyer misses. Although there may be some lawyers who can fully appreciate and convey to their client the nuances of a settlement negotiation, many are vulnerable to misreading, to oversimplifying, and to too-warmly embracing the virtues of their own side's case. [But: the client may misinterpret the events and affect the lawyer's judgment in an erroneous direction or become more difficult to "control."]

— The client's presence permits more rounds of offers and counter-offers. It permits him to act on new information and allows cooperation and momentum to build. In addition, attendance requires the client to pay attention to the case, which, in itself makes settlement more likely. [But: The client may lose his resolve because of the "crucible effect."]

— The client can clear up miscommunications about facts and interests between lawyers. [But: The client may be too emotionally involved to see the facts clearly.]

— Direct communication between clients can lead to better understanding of each other or of the events that transpired, perhaps even allow a healing of the rift between them. [But: direct communication may cause a flare-up and loss of objectivity. Parties may harden their resolve.]

—   The client, because he is more familiar with his situation, may be more able to spot opportunities for problem-solving solutions, which could lead to quicker and more satisfying agreements. [But: the client may give away information about his underlying interests that could leave him vulnerable to exploitation. Moreover, the client might not be sufficiently objective. A lawyer knowledgeable about the client's situation might do a better job at developing problem-solving solutions.]

—   Because the client's presence increases the likelihood of a settlement, and a settlement that will be satisfactory to the client, the client's participation will likely result in a savings of time and money for the client. [But: If some of the risks described above materialize, his presence will have caused him to lose time and money.]

—   The client would not consider an order to attend a settlement conference as coercive, but rather as an opportunity to participate. [But: the client might react negatively to the coercive nature of the order and be uncooperative.]

These arguments bear two important implications. First, the assertions of both risk and benefit gain strength as the client's actual participation increases. Thus, the client who not only observes the settlement conference, but also talks, may enhance his or her opportunities for developing a problem-solving solution, while simultaneously increasing his or her risks of being exploited, of angering the opponent, or of revealing potentially damaging information. * * *

Second, all the arguments in favor of including the client presume that the client is a competent, reasonably intelligent person with good judgment who will not be pushed into making an agreement. Conversely, the arguments against including the client assume he lacks one or more of these qualities, and that the client's lawyer has them. In other words, the arguments against inclusion of clients are more consistent with Model I perspectives: a traditional lawyer-client relationship, adversarial negotiation, and coercive intervention by the judicial host. The pro-inclusion arguments are generally consistent with the assumptions that undergird the Model II perspectives: a participatory lawyer-client relationship, problem-solving negotiation, and facilitative intervention by the judicial host.

2.   *Lawyers' and Judges' Perspectives*

Although most lawyers apparently believe that the client's presence enhances the prospects for settlement, many judges and lawyers are inclined to exclude clients from active participation in settlement conferences. This inclination is anchored in large part on Model I assumptions: traditional lawyer-client relations and adversarial negotiations under a judge's heavy thumb. These assumptions gain strength from the "lawyer's standard philosophical map" and induce many lawyers and judges to credit the arguments against including clients. Thus, a lawyer may have a reflexive aversion to direct contact between clients because he fears the client may make damaging disclosure. In turn, this fear may impair the lawyer's ability to imagine opportunities for creative problem solving.

Other, more subtle factors also may incline both lawyers and judges toward excluding clients. The client's presence threatens customary hierarchical professional practices. It creates a risk, for instance, that the judge's comments could embarrass the lawyer, a risk that could restrict the judge's perception of his freedom to speak with counsel. It also appears to threaten the lawyer-client relationship. Both lawyer and judge may wish to save the time required to explain to the client what is going on. Lawyers also may resent the loss of certain negotiating techniques, such as the "good-cop/bad-cop" routine.

On the other hand, good lawyers and wise settlement judges do not approach settlement discussions woodenly. Many will recognize particular circumstances in which client involvement, even if contrary to their general predilections, is appropriate. This may occur, for example, when the lawyer encounters "client control problems" or when he recognized that unique characteristics of the case or the client make the client's presence essential.

In addition, the psychological needs of lawyers and judges may be factors in the decision to exclude clients or to suggest, directly or indirectly, that the clients not participate. Take, for example, the personal injury insurance claim mediation described in the beginning of this Article. [Omitted] The clients' presence impaired my ability as mediator to predict and control events. That made me anxious. It called into question my own professional expertise, and, I imagine, that of both of the lawyers. In the mediation of the police brutality claim, at which only professionals were present, we could define the problem simply: finding a settlement agreement acceptable to the clients. The session included only matters that we could handle, in our professional roles, better than could the clients: arguments and discussions about law and fact and predictions about how a judge or jury would behave. The emotional relationship between the parties, which resides in a sphere typically beyond the lawyer's expertise, did not seem important.

Many settlement conferences are sufficiently similar to this kind of nonjudicial mediation that lawyers and judges in those conferences often will have experiences resembling those that the lawyers and I encountered. A lawyer who embraces a Model I vision of professional-client relations may be unsettled by the participation or mere presence of a client in a settlement conference. The lawyer who wants to maintain the mystique of expertise could feel severely threatened by the presence of a client. The client might interpret his uncertainty as incompetence, or, worse, notice that he is unprepared, that the other lawyer is more clever, or that the judge seems not to respect his opinion. Similarly, some judges might feel discomfort about interfering with lawyer-client relations or the possibility of being challenged, questioned, or evaluated by a client who, not being legally trained, might behave less predictably than the lawyer. In short, the presence of clients may breed anxiety and interfere with the lawyers' and judge's feelings of competence and control. This anxiety may cause an unspoken and, perhaps, unconscious conspiracy between lawyers and judges to exclude clients from all or important parts of settlement conferences.

B. When Should a Judge Mandate or Otherwise Encourage a Represented Client to Attend a Settlement Conference?

To the extent that a client's attendance at a settlement conference is likely to be useful to the client, it is more appropriate, and less likely to be an abuse of discretion, for a judicial host to compel such attendance. To the extent that the settlement conference provides for client participation (as opposed to mere attendance) the client's attendance more likely will benefit the client. Additionally, a client more likely will participate in a settlement conference that includes ... participatory lawyer-client relationships, problem-solving negotiation, and judicial interventions emphasizing facilitation rather than pressure. Conversely, the client is less likely to participate when the conference is dominated by ... traditional lawyer-client relations and adversarial bargaining under threats or pressure from the judicial host.

Many of the potential benefits of client involvement, however, are available even in such conferences. Even in a conference in which clients observe but do not speak, in which lawyers dominate, and in which the host attempts to pressure a settlement, the client may feel he benefits from observing both sides' lawyers in action. Such observation may improve his understanding of his legal position. It also may soften his impression of the other side, which could lead to righting the balance between them, to a psychological healing, and perhaps to a final settlement. In addition, the client's "presence," even in the hallway, permits more rounds of offers.

Notes and Questions

1. Obviously, how one prepares for a mediation must depend on one's expectations about the process. What kind of mediation process do you suppose Tom Arnold imagined when he wrote the article about common errors in mediation advocacy? For demonstrations and discussions of preparing and representing mediation clients, see the videotape, WHAT EVERY LITIGATOR NEEDS TO KNOW ABOUT MEDIATION (American Bar Association Division of Professional Education and Section of Litigation 1993).

2. As a lawyer, how might your expectations about whether the mediator will evaluate affect how you prepare for and behave during a mediation?

3. Many of the foregoing readings in this section have related to the issue of the extent to which a lawyer representing a client in a mediation should use adversarial as opposed to problem-solving approaches. You will recall that in Chapter III, we emphasized that an alert negotiator will be constantly aware of a "tension" between adversarial and problem solving moves. In a recent, comprehensive book on mediation advocacy, Professor Harold Abramson emphasizes problem-solving, as opposed to adversarial,

perspectives in mediation advocacy. HAROLD I. ABRAMSON, MEDIATION REPRESEN-
TATION: ADVOCACY IN A PROBLEM-SOLVING PROCESS (2004). Other commentators on
mediation advocacy have paid less attention to that perspective. *See* JOHN W.
COOLEY, MEDIATION ADVOCACY (1996); ERIC GALTON, REPRESENTING CLIENTS IN
MEDIATION (1994); Jean R. Sternlight, *Lawyers' Representation of Clients in
Mediation: Using Economics and Psychology to Structure Advocacy in a
Nonadversarial Setting,* 14 Ohio St. J. on Disp. Resol. 269 (1999).

4.   Is a lawyer's obligation to be truthful any different in a mediation
than in other processes, such as negotiation or court. As you will recall from
Chapter III, Rule 4.1 prohibits a lawyer, while representing a client (which
includes negotiating for a client), from making "a false statement of material
fact or law to a third person" or failing "to disclose a material fact when
disclosure is necessary to avoid assisting a criminal or fraudulent act by a
client..." ABA MODEL RULES OF PROFESSIONAL RESPONSIBILITY, RULE 4.1 (2003).
The Rules, however, provide a higher standard for a lawyer's communication
with a tribunal. *Id.* Rule 3.3. Commentators have discussed whether mediation constitutes a tribunal for these purposes. However in 2002, an amendment to the Model Rules defined tribunal for the first time. It "denotes a
court, an arbitrator, in a binding arbitration proceeding or a legislative body,
administrative agency or other body acting in an adjudicative capacity..."
Id. Rule 1.0(m).

JEFF KICHAVEN, AVOIDABLE SINS: WHEN A MEDIATOR STEPS BEYOND THE BOUNDARIES,

22 Alternatives to High Cost Litig.
77, 91–92 (2004).

[In the 2003 Australian case, *Tapoohi v. Lowenberg,* 2003 VSC 410
(2003), Supreme Court of Victoria, Australia [Victorian Unreported
Judgments], which is described supra, beginning at page 386, lawyers
who were sued for malpractice made a claim for contribution against the
mediator, George Golvan, whom they accused of a variety inappropriately directive behavior, such as insisting that the lawyers stay into the
evening to reduce the agreement to writing even though they wanted to
leave, and even controlling some of the content of that agreement. In the
following excerpt, Los Angeles lawyer-mediator Jeff Kichaven draws
some lessons for lawyers from this case, about selecting and working
with mediations.]

1.   Never hire a mediator who believes that "the client is the deal."
This Jekyll-and-Hyde character has the capacity to turn into a mon-
strous bully at the drop of a hat. This bully does not owe your client the
same duty of undivided loyalty that you, her lawyer, do. And his hat is
likely to be dropped when you are physically and emotionally least able
to protect your client from his mindless pursuit of settlement for
settlement's sake.

2.   Never ask a mediator to draft a settlement agreement. That's
your job, if you are there as a lawyer. If a mediator starts to do so,
politely but firmly tell him to stop. Don't even ask the mediator for a

form. Bring your own form. Your form is designed to protect your client's interests; the mediator's is not. Your job is to create a settlement agreement that protects your client's rights and promotes her interests. Whatever the mediator's job is, it's not the same as yours.

3.   Limit the help a mediator gives you in drafting a settlement agreement. Good mediators know how to help without crossing the line. Better mediators will use better mediation techniques, asking questions rather than making statements. If the lawyers had been drafting the settlement agreement and hit a snag on this point, Golvan might have asked, "Can we put in a price?" or "What about $1 as a price?"

Of course, these questions must be posed in a spirit of honest curiosity. The lawyers must be free to answer in any way that is consistent with the discharge of their fiduciary obligations to their clients. If the answer is, "I don't know, I have to check with the tax expert and I can't do that until tomorrow, maybe we can't sign this tonight, let's move on to the next point for now," the mediator might just have to accept that.

4.   Know when to call it a day. In some cases, it is appropriate for a mediator to be firm in encouraging — but never forcing — parties to stay until an agreement is signed. In cases where the only, or dominant, issue is "What must the defendant pay as the price of a release from the plaintiff?" the firm approach generally works well. These include, for example, most employment, personal injury, medical malpractice and other cases with consumer plaintiffs. If the mediation of such a case adjourns without a signed "deal," it generally takes all the king's horses and all the king's men to put the deal back together again, even if the adjournment is only overnight. When these plaintiffs go home for the evening and say to their significant others, "I'm about to make a deal," those others rarely say "I'm so happy for you!" Rather, they almost always say "WHAT? After what they have put you through?" and all progress is lost.

But Tapoohi is different. It's more of a business-to-business case, and its settlement involved the negotiation and documentation of a "commercial transaction." It's not good lawyering — or even common sense — to try to document most commercial transactions late at night on the back of a napkin, a legal pad, a laptop computer, or otherwise "on one foot." Neither is it necessary. In the commercial, as opposed to the consumer, context, parties generally are better able to prevent their buyer's or seller's remorse from becoming so severe that it undoes the deal.

And if the deal becomes undone? Well, as mediate.com's Jim Melamed sagely said in one of the first mediation trainings this author attended, "If the deal isn't right on Tuesday, it probably wasn't really right on Monday, either." What kind of lawyer would you be if you allow a mediator to bully you and your client into signing a deal that isn't really right? * * *

LEONARD L. RISKIN, DECISIONMAKING IN
MEDIATION: THE NEW OLD GRID AND
THE NEW NEW GRID SYSTEM

79 Notre Dame L. Rev. 1, 29–30, 32–47 (2003).

* * *

II. The Proposed New Grids and New Understandings

In Part I, I noted a series of problems with or limitations of the old grid. I suggested that both the structure and terminology of the facilitative-evaluative/role-of-the-mediator continuum have caused confusion and that the narrow-broad/problem-definition continuum remains useful, even though it may not be capable of describing certain kinds of mediation behaviors, and even though many commentators have ignored or misunderstood it. In addition, I suggested that the grid misses important issues because it: fails to distinguish between the mediator's behaviors with respect to substance and process; has a static quality that ignores both the interactive nature of mediation decision making and the elements of time and persistence; is grounded on the idea of overall mediator orientations — an unrealistic notion that excludes attention to many other issues in mediator behavior, obscures much about what mediators do, and ignores the role and influence of parties.

In this Part, I offer two proposals. The first revises the old grid to deal with the terminological problem discussed above; on this "New Old Grid," "elicitive" and "directive" fill in for "facilitative" and "evaluative." The second proposal replaces both the old and the new mediator orientation grids with a new grid system, a series of grids meant to address most of the problems associated with the old grid.

A. Revising the Grid: A "New Old Grid" of Mediator Orientations Using "Directive" and "Elicitive"

For reasons given above, I believe the terms "directive" and "elicitive" would serve better than "evaluative" and "facilitative" to anchor the role-of-the-mediator continuum. First, they more closely approximate my goal for this continuum, which was to focus on the impact of the mediator's behavior on party self-determination. Second, the term "directive" is more general and abstract than "evaluative" and therefore may cover a wider range of mediator behaviors. Figure 3 [omitted] shows a "new old grid" on which the terms "directive" and "elicitive substitute" for "evaluative" and "facilitative."

* * *

Although I proffer this "New Old Grid" of mediator orientations, I have substantial reservations about using it, because it retains many of the limitations of the old grid. First, the very idea of an overall orientation could imply, to some, a kind of rigidity in a mediator, an unwillingness to respond to circumstances. Thus, it may impair the mediator's ability, and that of the parties and their lawyers, to approach situations with an open mind. Second, as demonstrated above in connection with the old grid, it is nearly impossible — and generally unwise — to label a particular mediator with an overall orientation. * * *

In other words, there is a complex, dynamic quality in the relationships between directive and elicitive mediator moves. They often travel in tandem, and a particular move can have both directive and elicitive motives and effects. And there's more to say: Directive and elicitive moves each contain the seeds of the other and yield to the other. For example, as a mediator becomes very directive — say, pushing parties to reach an agreement — if such direction does not produce an agreement, she may need to become more elicitive in order to allow the parties to provide their own "direction" in working out a solution. In other words, too much directive behavior must yield to elicitive behavior.

Such mediator moves also have a dynamic relationship with the problem-definition and with the contributions of the parties. * * *

The "New Old Grid" of mediator orientations is more useful than the old one in providing a quick overview. Yet, like the old grid, it resembles a map that shows only major highways and large cities. On such a map, additional information — such as smaller towns, smaller roads, rivers, airports, recreation areas and ball parks, topography, and weather — could inform and remind travelers of choices and decisions that can enrich their journeys. People concerned about mediation — mediators, consumers, trainers, regulators — also could benefit from maps of mediation that highlight particular issues. With this in mind, I put forth a series of other new grids in Part II.B.

B. Replacing the Mediator Orientation Grids: The "New New Grid" System

I intend the "New New Grid" System to facilitate good mediation decisionmaking by bringing attention to two matters: an enormous range of potential decisions in and about a mediation, and the extent to which various participants could affect these decisions. The system works through a series of grids that — rather than focusing exclusively on the mediator, as did the old grids — give equal attention to all the participants, which ordinarily means the mediator, the parties, and the lawyers. In addition, the grids allow us to take account of time and the potentially dynamic nature of decisionmaking.

The system makes central the idea of participant "influence" with respect to particular issues. It provides a method for considering the influence that participants aspire to exert, actually exert, and expect others to exert, with respect to any of a wide range of decisions. It does this by dividing mediation decisionmaking into three categories: substantive, procedural, and meta-procedural.

1. Types of Decisionmaking

Substantive decisionmaking includes trying to understand substantive issues, such as what happened to give rise to the dispute, and trying to make agreements intended to resolve the dispute. It also includes establishing the problem-definition, i.e., the subject of the mediation.

Procedural decisionmaking means deciding what procedures will be employed to reach or address the substantive issues. Here is a list of potential procedural issues, which overlap to some extent.

Logistics:

Location.

Time (dates, starting and ending times, number and length of sessions).

Pre-mediation submissions:

Required or optional?

Short letters, mediation briefs, litigation or other documents.

Should submissions include: legal analyses, underlying interests, goals for the mediation, or obstacles to achieving these goals?

Who receives the submissions: just the mediator, or all participants?

Attendance and participation:

Who attends?

Roles of lawyers, clients, experts, others.

Procedure during the mediation:

Opening statements — Which side goes first? Do lawyers and clients speak? What is the focus of these statements?

Caucuses — Whether, when, why, and how to call caucuses. Who can call them? Whether to maintain confidentiality of communications?

Ending the mediation. Who decides?

Expressing the agreement in writing:

Whether, when, why, how, and by whom? How formal or legally-binding should the document be? Who decides?

Procedures for defining the problem(s) to be mediated (and/or deciding on the purposes of the mediation):

To what extent, if any, will the problem be defined by: The parties, e.g., through pre-mediation statements, pre-mediation briefs, or statements made during the mediation? The mediator, e.g., through the questions he asks the other participants? The mediation program managers, designers or sponsors, implicitly or explicitly? All the participants, through dialogue?

Developing options:

Will it happen? If so, when, how, and by whom?

Developing and presenting proposals:

By whom, when, how, where?

Evaluation:

Will/should the mediator evaluate or arrange for evaluation? If so, how, what, why, and under what conditions and standards?

Reaching agreement:

Will the mediator apply pressure on the parties or lawyers to reach a particular settlement? Settlement in general?

The mediator's role:

> Will the mediator direct or elicit as to particular procedural and substantive issues?
>
> Will the mediator be transparent or obscure about the mediator's behavior?
>
> Will the mediator provide food?

Meta-procedural decisionmaking means deciding how subsequent procedural decisions will be made. The participants could make agreements, for instance, about who or what would determine any of a range of procedural issues, such as those mentioned above.

A series of grids appears below. Each grid deals with a particular kind of decision and provides an example of an array of grids we could prepare that would shed light on particular aspects of decisionmaking in mediation. The concept that unifies the system is participant "influence" — the degree of influence that various participants either aspire to exert or actually exert with respect to a particular issue. On each of these grids, that concept is depicted on the north-south continuum. The north end of that continuum shows that most of the influence comes from the mediator; the south end shows parties and lawyers exerting most of the influence. The east-west axis would depict a particular issue. Thus, the purpose of each grid in this series is to bring attention to the influence that each participant exerts (or would like to exert) with respect to a particular issue. A generic version of this grid appears in Figure 4.

FIGURE 4. PARTICIPANT INFLUENCE (GENERIC GRID)

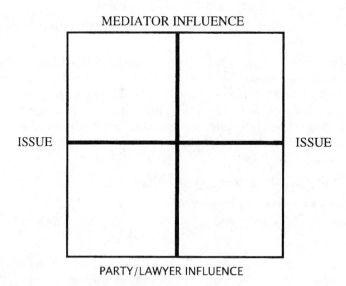

2.   Types of Decisionmaking Grids

Here are some examples of how grids could illuminate each of the three kinds of decisionmaking.

a. Substantive Decisionmaking Grids

Grids of substantive decisionmaking could deal with establishing the problem-definition or with understanding or resolving particular substantive issues. In addressing each of these focuses, I propose the use of two kinds of grids: one deals with participants' predispositions as to how that issue should be resolved and who should contribute to its resolution, the second grid focuses on actual influence. The first grid would depict the participants' beliefs, attitudes or aspirations about a particular issue before the mediation or before the issue arises. Figure 5, for example, shows participant predispositions with respect to the substantive issue of problem-definition and their assumptions about the degree of influence they would, or would like to, exert with respect to this issue.

FIGURE 5. SUBSTANTIVE DECISIONMAKING: PREDISPOSITION
REGARDING PROBLEM-DEFINITION

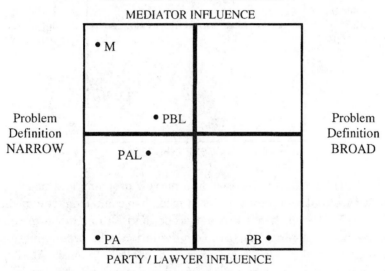

Point M shows that the mediator is predisposed to a narrow problem-definition and assumes that he or she would heavily influence the development of such a problem-definition. Point PA shows that party A is predisposed toward a narrow problem and definition and believes (or assumes) that he would exercise much influence in establishing that problem-definition. PAL shows that party A's lawyer was predisposed toward a slightly broader problem-definition and assumed that his influence, combined with that of the mediator, would move the process toward it. PB shows that party B was predisposed to a broader definition of the problem and assumed that the parties or lawyers would exercise much influence or control over the process of reaching that problem definition. PBL would show that party B's lawyer was predisposed toward a problem-definition of the same breadth as was party A's lawyer and expected the mediator to play the strongest role in setting that definition.

The second kind of substantive decisionmaking grid would focus on actual influence. For instance, grids could show the operative problem-definition at various times during a mediation and the influences of the participants in setting that problem-definition, as illustrated in Figure 6.

FIGURE 6. SUBSTANTIVE DECISIONMAKING: INFLUENCE
ON PROBLEM-DEFINITION AT VARIOUS TIMES

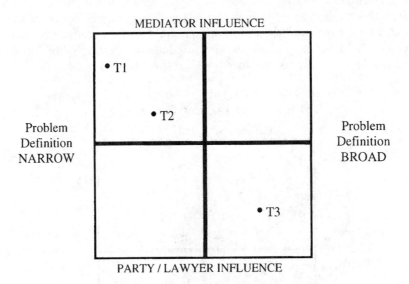

At T1, the mediation focuses on a narrow problem, and nearly all of the influence to develop that problem focus has come from the mediator. At T2, the mediation has a broader scope, and although the mediator's influence in developing that problem-definition still predominates, the parties and lawyers also have exercised some influence. At T3, the parties and lawyers have more substantially influenced the development of a broader problem-definition.

Alternatively, we could use separate grids to show the problem-definition at various times. By using individual grids to depict particular moments in a mediation, and considering each as a frame in a motion picture, it would be possible to get a sense of the flow of a mediation with respect to individual issues.

* * *

* * *[I]n Figure 8, point A shows the parties or lawyers heavily influencing the resolution of a narrow issue and point B shows the mediator heavily influencing the resolution of a broad issue.

FIGURE 8. SUBSTANTIVE DECISIONMAKING: INFLUENCE
ON RESOLVING PARTICULAR PROBLEMS

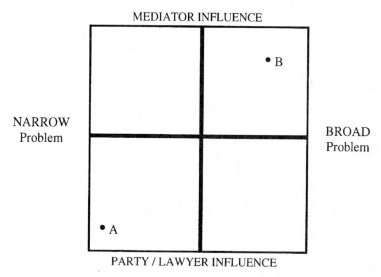

b.   Procedural Decisionmaking Grids

I intend procedural decisionmaking to include choices about a variety of issues made before or, sometimes moment-to-moment, during a mediation. Obviously, in making procedural decisions such as these, influence can come from mediators, parties, and participating lawyers. Sometimes, program administrators or designers make such procedural decisions. Some of these decisions are explicit and carefully determined — part of a formal dispute resolution design process.

In some situations, mediators themselves direct the outcome of certain process decisions, either before the mediation or at its inception or during the process; in terms of the "New New Grid" System, we would say that the mediator exercised virtually all the influence over such decisions. In other situations, the mediator might elicit the parties' perspectives and desires, and make a decision that responds either fully or partially to such party desires or perspectives. The new grids would show that both the mediator and the parties exercised some influence over this decision. Sometimes, the parties assert their desires even if the mediator does not "elicit," and the new grids would allow us to depict the influence associated with such assertions.

Procedural decisionmaking grids could address any of a range of procedural issues, such as those listed above. Figure 9, for example, shows the influence of the parties/lawyers and the mediator as to whether the mediator would provide an evaluation.

FIGURE 9. PROCEDURAL DECISIONMAKING: INFLUENCE
ON EVALUATION BY MEDIATOR

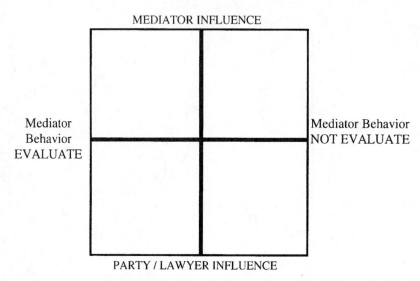

Another version of that grid could show predispositions around that issue. And Figure 10 shows influences on decisionmaking about the use of private caucuses. Point A shows a decision to use caucuses heavily that was reached through a process in which the mediator and the parties and their lawyers exercised equal influence. Point B depicts a decision to have no caucuses, influenced entirely by the mediator.

FIGURE 10. PROCEDURAL DECISIONMAKING: INFLUENCE ON USE OF CAUCUS

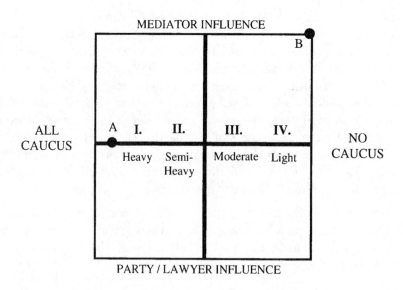

c.   Meta–Procedural Decisionmaking Grids

Meta-procedural decisionmaking refers to deciding how subsequent procedural decisions will be made. One major issue in meta-procedural decisionmaking is what degree of influence various participants will have over specific procedural issues or over procedural issues in general. * * *

3.   The "New New Grid" System in Perspective

The grids I have set forth are examples only. The system would allow for the development of other grids for specialized purposes. Thus, some may find it useful to produce problem-definition grids that focus on the depth of the problem, rather than on the breadth; the extent to which the mediation would focus on various dimensions of the conflict, such as cognitive, emotional and behavioral; and the extent to which the process would focus on settling the dispute, resolving the dispute, or transforming the parties. Other procedural decisionmaking grids could address the issue of how and when (as opposed to whether) the mediator would evaluate, or on questions regarding the rules under which caucuses would be conducted.

A series of specifically focused grids, such as these, could help foster a high degree of awareness — among mediators, parties, lawyers, program designers, administrators, and evaluators — of the many possible issues for decision and the various degrees to which participants could contribute to understanding or resolving such issues. This awareness would support more active and sophisticated decisionmaking in and about mediation. Such grids also could be useful in evaluating, studying, or reflecting on completed mediations.

* * *

Notes and Questions

1.   Figure 5 represents a quite common situation, in which participants in a mediation have different pre-dispositions as to problem-definition and as to who should have influence over it. *Damages*, by Barry Werth, an in-depth case study of a Connecticut medical malpractice claim involving a baby born severely damaged, provides a good example. Barry Werth, Damages: One Family's Legal Struggles in the World of Medicine (2001).

In the first mediation described in the book, the parents wanted a broad problem-definition that would afford them recognition for how much they had suffered and how well they had coped, and give them some understanding of what really caused the damage to their child. *See id*. at 310–25. On the other hand, their lawyers seemed to want a narrow problem-definition, limited principally to what was likely to happen in court. *Id*. This desire doubtless was based, at least in part, on the assumption that this focus was best for the client. *Id*. It also seems clear that all the other participants — the mediator, the defendants, and their insurers and lawyers — shared the plaintiffs' lawyers' perspective. *Id*. As a result, the parents exercised no influence over the problem-definition and received none of the recognition they sought. For a fuller discussion of the two mediations described in this book, see Leonard L. Riskin, *Teaching and Learning from the Mediations in Barry Werth's* Damages, 2004 J. Disp. Resol. 119.

Professor Nancy Welsh describes common attitudes and practices in mediation that could allow for the kind of situation described in the *Damages* book:

> Research reveals that attorneys prefer and select experienced litigators with substantive expertise to serve as the mediators. Attorneys want mediators who, like judges, have the knowledge and experience that will permit them to understand the parties' legal arguments, assess the merits of their cases, and even give their view of settlement ranges. In these mediation sessions, the attorneys often dominate the process, while their clients — the disputants — play minimal roles. The mediators increasingly bypass or marginalize the joint session to move quickly to caucuses and bargaining. In caucus, these mediators often assess the legal merits of each side's case and share their valuations of the cases. Attorneys apparently value these mediator interventions because they view mediation primarily as a settlement tool that can provide opposing counsel and their own clients with a needed "reality check." Few attorneys choose mediation because they perceive that their clients might like it or experience greater satisfaction or control.

Nancy A. Welsh, *Stepping Back Through the Looking Glass: Real Conversations with Real Disputants about Institutionalized Mediation and Its Value*, 19 Ohio St. J. on Disp. Resol. 573, 589–91 (2004).

The purpose of the new grid system, of course, is not to promote any particular behaviors in mediation. Instead, the intention behind the system is to enhance awareness of the choices that will be made, explicitly or implicitly, and of the degrees of influence that the any of the participants potentially could exercise, so that the participants can make better choices about how to make such decisions. Some of these decisions — procedural and meta-procedural — could be made during the process of selecting a mediator, which can involve dialogue or negotiation over such issues. More commonly, such decisions, as well as the substantive decisions, are made during the mediation. The new grid system could help participants decide whether to bring up certain issues and try to exercise influence over their determination.

2. As you observe mediations and mediation demonstrations (live or on the screen), try to notice who seems to be exerting influence on various decisions. It will not always be easy to notice. For example, if things are moving in a direction desired by a particular participant, she may exercise influence, in a sense, taking advantage of the existing momentum, by doing nothing.

3. Section A of this chapter presented readings on two approaches to mediation that commonly reach beyond narrow problem-definitions, "Transformative Mediation" and "Understanding–Based Mediation." What, if anything, do these excerpts tell you about the influence of various participants — with respect to substantive, procedural and meta-procedural decisionmaking under these two approaches? For a given mediation, which participants should exercise influence over whether either of these approaches will be employed? Under each approach, do you have a sense of

who has influence over whether the mediation will address all three dimensions of conflict — behavioral, cognitive, and emotional? Can you tell who will influence the level of depth?

4. In some mediations, the mediator or the mediation provider organization simply announces what the procedures will be. In others, the procedures are developed through discussion and dialogue. As a lawyer, what do you think should be the proper distribution of influence in substantive, procedural, and meta-procedural decisionmaking in the following kinds of cases:

    a. An automobile accident claim in which you represent

        1. The plaintiff?

        2. The defendant?

    b. A divorce case in which the parties have been married for ten years, have two young children, and are very bitter toward each other?

    c. An anti-trust claim by the U.S. government against a large corporation based on a claim of restraint of trade?

    d. A breach of contract claim between two corporations?

    e. A victim offender mediation? *E.g.*, a session involving the victim of a crime, say a burglary, and a person who has been convicted of, or has confessed to, committing the crime.

5. Assume you represent the parents of a woman who was murdered along with her child. Her husband was prosecuted. Although he was acquitted, the case was notorious in your community, and most residents assume he committed the crime. Your clients think he probably did it, but are not certain; he has never explicitly denied that he did it. You have filed a wrongful death action. The money at issue is the proceeds of several life insurance policies totaling $1 million, which has been paid into the court. The defendant's lawyer has proposed mediation of this civil claim. Obviously, the plaintiffs are likely to decline such an offer; they may be more concerned about showing that the defendant committed the crime than about getting the money. But suppose they agree to it because they understand that the defendant may receive the $1 million if their civil action fails. What qualities and approach would you seek in a mediator? In considering this question, recall two suggestions made by Bernard Mayer in the excerpt reprinted in Chapter I, beginning at page 6: That it is helpful to consider conflict and conflict resolution along three dimensions — behavioral, cognitive and emotional — and that it is important to try to address each conflict at the appropriate depth. Which dimensions do you suppose your clients would want, or be willing or able to address? How confident should you be of their perspectives on this question *before* the mediation begins?

In this case, would you want a mediator who was able and inclined to elicit the problem-definition from the parties or would you prefer a mediator who would tell them what the problem-definition should be? What would be more important in the mediator — substantive expertise in wrongful death litigation or experience as a counselor for bereaved people? How important would you think joint sessions — as opposed to private ones — would be and who should have influence over deciding the extent to which joint and separate sessions would be used?

How would you view these questions if you were on the defense side of this matter?

6.   Assume that you represent a neighborhood association in an area near the airport in Metropolis, a city of three million people. The neighborhood association, along with six other nearby neighborhood associations, has been in a dispute for the last ten years with the airport authority, which wants to build new runways and parking facilities. The associations have tied up the project in court for a long time, but now many members see that expansion is inevitable. Each association is concerned about the following issues: increased noise and air pollution from airplane take-offs and increased automobile traffic; damage to windows from airplane take-offs; and changes in the nature of the neighborhood, including condemnation of buildings. They wish to influence the plan as much as possible, to reduce harmful effects of the expansion, and to get appropriate compensation for any harm caused by the expansion.

The airport authority and the neighborhood groups have agreed to mediation, and the state office of dispute resolution has arranged for several mediators to come in for a group interview with representatives of the airport authority and the neighborhood associations.

Here are some salient facts that came out in the interviews:

Mediator A: A graduated five years ago from an elite law school and has been a mediator and mediation trainer for four years since he finished his one-year appointment as a law clerk to a state supreme court justice. He has never practiced law. He has mediated one dispute involving an airport expansion in a smaller city. He has lived in Metropolis all his life. When asked about his approach to mediation, Mediator A replied that he likes to empower the parties to help themselves and to help them learn to work together. He does not "evaluate," that is, make predictions about court outcomes or tell the parties what to do.

Mediator B: B retired from a position as a trial court judge in another part of the country two years ago, after sitting on the bench for twenty years. Before that she was a prosecutor and practiced family law for five years. She has developed a reputation as an effective mediator in commercial cases. In the interview, she says that, as a judge and as a lawyer, she "mediated all the time." She also says, "I generally know what's right and don't hesitate to give my opinion."

Assume the choice is between these two candidates. What are the advantages and disadvantages of each? What else would you want to know about them and about the dispute in order to decide which one to support?

7.   Assume that you are the director of two new programs sponsored by the state bar association. One will offer mediation services for lawyer-client fee disputes; the other will offer mediation services for "minor" ethics complaints against lawyers by their clients. You will have separate training programs. Would the differences in subject matter in these two programs incline you to seek different emphases in terms of the problem-definition continuum?

8.   Assume you are not a lawyer, but are advising a friend who is about to enter a divorce mediation. She has decided, for reasons of economics and philosophy, not to hire a lawyer. In your opinion, her husband has tended to dominate her and is much more familiar with matters of finance than she. If you cannot talk her into hiring a lawyer, what background or qualities would you suggest she seek in a mediator? Would you want a mediator with a transformative orientation? *See* ROBERT A. BARUCH BUSH & JOSEPH P. FOLGER, THE PROMISE OF MEDIATION: THE TRANSFORMATIVE APPROACH TO CONFLICT (Rev. ed. 2005), which is excerpted, *supra*, beginning at page 301.

9.   Your client is an elderly woman who sustained slight but permanent injuries when her truck was rear-ended. Liability is clear, but the extent of damages is not. If both sides agree to mediation, what background, orientation, and strategies would you seek in a mediator?

d.   Good Faith Participation

Given the range of ideas about whether and how to participate in mediation and the range of mediator practices, it is not surprising that questions have arisen about whether a party to a mediation, usually a court-ordered mediation, has an obligation to participate in "good faith," and if so, what such an obligation might mean and whether a party has met it. A number of commentators support establishment and enforcement of strict behavioral standards on good faith participation. *See, e.g.,* Maureen A. Weston, *Checks on Participant Conduct in Compulsory ADR: Reconciling the Tension in the Need for Good–Faith Participation, Autonomy, and Confidentiality,* 76 Ind. L. J. 591 (2001); Kimberlee K. Kovach, *Good Faith in Mediation — Requested, Recommended, or Required? A New Ethic,* 38 S. Tex. L. Rev. 575, 591–96 (1997). Others have cautioned against such rigid standards. *See, e.g,* Edward F. Sherman, *Court-Mandated Alternative Dispute Resolution: What Form of Participation Should be Required?,* 46 SMU L. Rev. 2079 (1993), arguing that we should see good faith as an aspiration. Professor John Lande emphasized the importance of process in seeking to fulfill the goals of good faith requirements. John Lande, *Using Dispute System Design Methods to Promote Good–Faith Participation in Court–Connected Mediation Programs,* 50 UCLA L. Rev. 69 (2002). The issue of good faith participation in mediation is complex and important, and we cover it in detail in Chapter VI, infra, beginning at page 705.

e.   The Consulting Lawyer

In most of the foregoing materials in this Section C, we have assumed that lawyers were intimately involved in the decision to mediate and that they participated in the mediation. Frequently, however, that is not the case. In many mediations lawyers are involved in limited ways, or not at all. This happens most often in community mediation and in family and divorce mediation. In many such cases, as well as others, parties may have a specially-tailored relationship with a lawyer. Sometimes, for instance, a party may consult with a lawyer before, during, or after a mediation. When that happens, especially when the consultation comes *after* the mediation, some lawyers may wonder how to serve the client most appropriately. Lawyer-mediators Gary Friedman and Jack Himmelstein provide some advice in the following excerpt.

GARY FRIEDMAN & JACK HIMMELSTEIN, DEAL KILLER OR DEAL SAVER: THE CONSULTING LAWYER'S DILEMMA

Disp. Resol. Mag., Winter 1997, at 7.

A client walks into your office, pulls out a document, thrusts it onto your desk and says: "I have just finished mediating a dispute that has been a source of great aggravation to me, and this is our agreement. I just want you to look this over before I sign it. What do you think?"

You glance quickly at the document, and ask your client a few questions. Your first impression is that your client has made a deal that leaves her considerably worse off than if she were to go to court or to have left the negotiation in your hands.

What are you to do? "Simple," you think to yourself: "I should just help my client recognize that she's getting screwed in this mediation. If she leaves this matter in the hands of a competent professional, someone like you who is an expert negotiator, she is much more likely to end up with a better deal."

That's the problem with mediation, you have long suspected. Would your client consider piloting an airplane without sufficient training? This is really no different, and you know it. Important decisions are being made and they require more than a cursory glance at an agreement. They require professional negotiation. That is what you as a lawyer do for a living, and you decide to give her your best legal advice: Bag the deal.

Or maybe you are a lawyer with a different attitude, have taken a mediation training and even meditated with the monks in Marin. After all, you certainly have had enough experience as a litigator to know that not all clients are satisfied with the litigation results, or even negotiation results, that you have been able to obtain for them. And, being honest with yourself, you also know that lawyers on the other side tend to see the likely result as much from what is in their clients' interests as you do from yours, and both of you can't be right at the same time.

While it is true that your client has agreed to a deal that leaves her worse off than what you think you could have gotten, she seems to be pretty satisfied, and she is the one who will have to live with the consequences. Besides, you don't like continually being cast as part of the Evil Empire, the "deal killer." You would like to support the mediation process and are ready, after gulping hard, to soft-pedal your concern about the poor result your client obtained on her own.

Tough Problem, Basic Principles

Whether you are more inclined to deal with the situation as the first lawyer did or the second, from the point of view of a mediator, you have not in either instance served your client well. The job of the consulting lawyer, as we view it, is not to yield to the temptation of either killing the deal because it is different than what you would have recommended, or blindly supporting the mediation process by rubber-stamping the result.

This dilemma is very real, and worthy of much more consideration than is possible here. Still, a few basic principles help begin pointing the way out.

First, you need to have a clear understanding about your role as a consulting lawyer. That role, as we see it, is to be a resource for your client: providing the perspective of an advocate without assuming the role of an advocate.

Second, and this is critical, you need to communicate that understanding to your client and come to a decision together about the parameters of your role. Mediation, correctly done, empowers clients. Supporting mediation as a consulting attorney can do likewise. In litigation, lawyers and clients generally take the lawyer's role for granted. In mediation, it is best that the lawyer's role be the result of explicit agreement. Rather than make assumptions about what your client wants from you, explore directly which responsibilities you can offer and which the client wants you to perform.

Third, you need to carry out those responsibilities in a manner that supports your client's responsibility in the mediation process and for the decisions that she is making. Your responsibilities can include:

- Informing your client of the applicable law, the principles underlying the law, and the likely outcomes in court. Your client is entitled to all of the knowledge of what you think would likely happen in court — and of the risks and costs associated with that strategy. But she is also entitled to your respect and support for her choice to participate in mediation, and to your assessment of how much weight to give to the legal perspective. The law is part of the picture, not the whole picture.

- Assisting your client (to the extent needed) in understanding the practical and legal consequences of what is considered in the mediation, and "reality testing" a proposed agreement to make sure that it will work over time.

- Assisting your client in developing an understanding of what is centrally important to her in the resolution of the dispute, and clarifying the priorities that need to be met for a successful outcome.

- Supporting your client in assuming the responsibility she chooses to take for participation in mediation and the decisions reached there, including advising the client about the negotiation process.

- Ensuring that the written agreement coincides with her understanding of what she thought she agreed to in the mediation.

The Already Done Deal

"So what!" You might say. "All of this would have been great if the client had come in at the start of the mediation, and I'll tell her that the next time she has a mediation. But she walked into my office with an agreement already in hand."

Certainly, it would have been better if the client had come in much earlier. Your task is harder, but it's not too late. And the same basic principles apply.

You need to explain how you see your role and the difficulty of assuming that role in a way that does not appear that you are out to upset the mediation or simply rubber-stamp it. Ascertain your client's priorities and how the proposed agreement does and does not meet them. Explain the applicable law, and respect that it is for your client to decide whether what is important to her in resolving the conflict is the same or differs from what might happen in court. In other words, make sure that the agreement captures what your client intended.

If after that, your client concludes that the agreement really does fail to meet what she intended or what she values, then explore with her how she might, with your support, bring her concerns into the mediation. That must be done with sensitivity to the other party's likely concern that your client could be seen as reneging on the agreement, with you as the deal killer cheering her on.

Your client will then have the difficult task of explaining to her counterpart that she is still willing to negotiate an agreement that serves what is important to both of them. With your help, she might be able to do it in a way that is responsible and seeks to do justice to both of them.

If they have a good mediator, he or she would have counseled them that nothing is final until it is final and this is an opportunity for assuring that they find an agreement that will work for both of them in the future. And, if you have played a part in helping that to come about, you have found a productive way to deal with the tension that you experienced in the beginning.

Notes and Questions

1. Notice that Friedman and Himmelstein are distinguishing between two accepted roles of the lawyer — advisor and advocate. *See* ABA Model Rules of Professional Conduct, Preamble, Rule 2.1 (2004). As a lawyer, would you be comfortable playing the limited role that Friedman and Himmelstein describe? If not, what would be the sources of your discomfort?

2. Do you agree with this advice? Would your answer depend upon which model of the lawyer-client relationship, discussed in Chapter II, that you use?

———

3. CONFIDENTIALITY

a. A Cornerstone, and a Challenge

Confidentiality is often said to be a cornerstone of mediation, for reasons that highlight the uniqueness of mediation as a dispute resolution process. Recall that judges, arbitrators, and other adjudicators preside over the receipt of evidence that the parties present to them, and ultimately make decisions on those cases. Mediators, however, work actively with the parties to help identify, understand, and assess the various underlying interests and concerns that are animating the dispute so that the parties can decide how to resolve the dispute themselves. For this reason, parties in adjudication are likely to guard sensitive information zealously, but in mediation they are encouraged to be more candid about underlying interests, concerns, and other information that is relevant to the dispute.

This candor is often necessary in mediation to get beyond the parties' positions, but can bring to the surface important information that the parties may not want to air publicly. For example, a divorce mediation may uncover such raw emotions as anger and resentment, perhaps even involving third parties, or inappropriate conduct that may be necessary to address in the mediation, but which could be highly prejudicial if the mediation fails and the divorce is litigated. Similarly, businesses engaged in a commercial mediation may need to discuss trade secrets or other proprietary information, the wider dissemination of which could threaten their interests, in order to resolve their immediate dispute. And a participant in a mediation may want or need to disclose information in the mediation that he simply doesn't want to be made public for fear of stigmatization or reputational harm, such as a mental health condition or certain lifestyle issues.

For these reasons and more, candor can be challenging, requiring skill by the mediator and confidence, courage, and commitment by the parties — especially if they are to address underlying interests and achieve resolution along the cognitive and emotional dimensions of the dispute as well as the behavioral dimension. To encourage such candor, the parties and mediator often agree not to disclose the mediation discussions to others outside of the room.

Actually achieving such confidentiality is difficult, however. As a practical matter, mediation confidentiality is in fundamental tension with some basic human instincts in dealing with conflict. As we discussed in Chapter I, beginning at page 9, a dispute that has been formalized to the point of being mediated has been percolating for some time, building its own energy as well as generating collateral effects. Many people have a felt need to discuss the resolution of the dispute with family members, friends, or others who may have been consulted or drawn into the dispute along the way. This can be a salutary development, allowing catharsis for the parties involved in conflict. Yet, such disclosures are at odds with the assurance of confidentiality that is so often necessary to facilitate the mediation.

More significantly for lawyers, confidentiality in mediation also implicates in a very direct way the often uneasy relationship between mediation and the law. Some participants in the mediation process like to think of mediation as removed from the law, and in many important respects it is. However, mediation is not wholly removed from the law. The results of a mediated settlement agreement are a contract that may be enforced in a court of law, and sometimes are. Moreover, mediations sometimes are unsuccessful, in which case the dispute can continue to formalize, perhaps ultimately requiring resolution in court. It's at that point where the tension between the public law and private mediation is most acute, because a cardinal value of the judicial process is the right of the parties to all of the relevant evidence available to prove their cases — evidence that could include admissions or other statements made during the mediation to prove, for example, that a witness is lying in a trial that follows an unsuccessful mediation.

This tension between the judicial system's demand for evidence in the pursuit of truth, and the mediation process' demand for confidentiality to promote understanding and resolution permeates this area of the law. The complexity this tension creates is compounded by the variety of the different types and contexts of mediation, as well as the recognition that different mediation participants — parties, mediators, support persons and experts — have different and sometimes competing interests with respect to disclosures of mediation communications outside the mediation.

This section provides some initial exposure to the challenges associated with mediation confidentiality, and the way in which the law has responded to them. The first excerpt, from the Prefatory Note for the recently promulgated Uniform Mediation Act, lays out the need for confidentiality in mediation and addresses the various policy interests relevant to its legal regulation. The Prefatory Note is followed by notes and questions that address the nuanced meaning of confidentiality, and discuss the mechanisms that have been used to protect mediation confidentiality, including both contract law and various evidentiary rules prohibiting the discovery or admissibility of mediation communications. These structures include evidentiary privileges, settlement discussion rules, rules of categorical exclusion, and rules rendering mediators incompetent to testify about cases they have mediated.

We proceed to take a closer look at excerpts from the Uniform Mediation Act, the centerpiece of which is an evidentiary privilege that can be invoked to prevent later discovery of or testimony about mediation communications. Finally, this section concludes with a case from California that dramatically demonstrates the tension between mediation values and rule of law values, and addresses the question of whether a mediator should be required to testify about what happened in a mediation when both parties want the mediator to testify, but the mediator does not want to provide such testimony.

As you read these materials, think about how they might shape your approach to mediation in your role as a lawyer representing a party or as a mediator.

b. The Policies Supporting Mediation Confidentiality, and Their Implementation

The following excerpt from the Uniform Mediation Act sets forth the central justifications for the legal protection of mediation confidentiality: the promotion of party candor and public confidence in mediation.

UNIFORM MEDIATION ACT
(2003) Prefatory Note.

[The UMA was enacted by the National Conference of Commissioners on Uniform State Laws in 2001, endorsed by the American Bar Association in 2002, and amended by NCCUSL in 2003 to include a provision on international commercial mediation. The UMA was the result of a four-year national drafting effort by dispute resolution scholars, practitioners, and lawyers from a variety of practice areas, led by NCCUSL and the ABA, to provide states with a uniform law for certain aspects of mediation, especially confidentiality. By the end of May 2005, it had already been enacted in six states — Illinois, Iowa, Nebraska, New Jersey, Ohio, and Washington — and was being actively considered in many more. The UMA is reprinted in full text in Appendix B.]

* * *

1. Promoting candor

Candor during mediation is encouraged by maintaining the parties' and mediators' expectations regarding confidentiality of mediation communications. *See* Sections 4–6. Virtually all state legislatures have recognized the necessity of protecting mediation confidentiality to encourage the effective use of mediation to resolve disputes. Indeed, state legislatures have enacted more than 250 mediation privilege statutes. Approximately half of the States have enacted privilege statutes that apply generally to mediations in the State, while the other half include privileges within the provisions of statutes establishing mediation programs for specific substantive legal issues, such as employment or human rights.

The Drafters recognize that mediators typically promote a candid and informal exchange regarding events in the past, as well as the parties' perceptions of and attitudes toward these events, and that mediators encourage parties to think constructively and creatively about ways in which their differences might be resolved. This frank exchange can be achieved only if the participants know that what is said in the mediation will not be used to their detriment through later court proceedings and other adjudicatory processes. Such party-candor justifications for mediation confidentiality resemble those supporting other communications privileges, such as the attorney-client privilege, the doctor-patient privilege, and various other counseling privileges. This rationale has sometimes been extended to mediators to encourage mediators to be candid with the parties by allowing the mediator to block evidence of the mediator's notes and other statements by the mediator.

Similarly, public confidence in and the voluntary use of mediation can be expected to expand if people have confidence that the mediator will not take sides or disclose their statements, particularly in the context of other investigations or judicial processes. The public confidence rationale has been extended to permit the mediator to object to testifying, so that the mediator will not be viewed as biased in future mediation sessions that involve comparable parties. To maintain public confidence in the fairness of mediation, a number of States prohibit a mediator from disclosing mediation communications to a judge or other officials in a position to affect the decision in a case. This justification also is reflected in standards against the use of a threat of disclosure or recommendation to pressure the parties to accept a particular settlement. *See, e.g.*, Center for Dispute Settlement, National Standards for Court–Connected Mediation Programs (1994); Society for Professionals in Dispute Resolution, Mandated Participation and Settlement Coercion: Dispute Resolution as it Relates to the Courts (1991).

A statute is required only to assure that aspect of confidentiality that relates to evidence compelled in a judicial and other legal proceeding. The parties can rely on the mediator's assurance of confidentiality in terms of mediator disclosures outside the proceedings, as the mediator would be liable for a breach of such an assurance. Also, the parties can expect enforcement of their agreement to keep things confidential through contract damages and sometimes specific enforcement. The courts have also enforced court orders or rules regarding nondisclosure through orders striking pleadings and fining lawyers. Promises, contracts, and court rules or orders are unavailing, however, with respect to discovery, trial, and otherwise compelled or subpoenaed evidence. Assurance with respect to this aspect of confidentiality has rarely been accorded by common law. Thus, the major contribution of the Act is to provide a privilege in legal proceedings, where it would otherwise either not be available or would not be available in a uniform way across the States.

As with other privileges, the mediation privilege must have limits, and nearly all existing state mediation statutes provide them. Definitions and exceptions primarily are necessary to give appropriate weight to other valid justice system values, in addition to those already discussed in this Section. They often apply to situations that arise only rarely, but might produce grave injustice in that unusual case if not excepted from the privilege.

In this regard, the Drafters recognize that the credibility and integrity of the mediation process is almost always dependent upon the neutrality and the impartiality of the mediator. The provisions of this Act are not intended to provide the parties with an unwarranted means to bring mediators into the discovery or trial process to testify about matters that occurred during a court ordered or agreed mediation. There are of course exceptions and they are specifically provided for in Section 5(a)(1) (express waiver by the mediator) or pursuant to Section 6's narrow exceptions such as 6(b)(1) (felony). Contrary use of the provisions of this Act to involve mediators in the discovery or trial process would have a destructive effect on the mediation process and would not be in keeping with the intent and purpose of the Act.

Finally, these exceptions need not significantly hamper candor. Once the parties and mediators know the protections and limits, they can adjust their conduct accordingly. For example, if the parties understand that they will not be able to establish in court an oral agreement reached in mediation, they can reduce the agreement to a record or writing before relying on it. Although it is important to note that mediation is not essentially a truth-seeking process in our justice system such as discovery, if the parties realize that they will be unable to show that another party lied during mediation, they can ask for corroboration of the statement made in mediation prior to relying on the accuracy of it. A uniform and generic privilege makes it easier for the parties and mediators to understand what law will apply and therefore to understand the coverage and limits of the Act, so that they can conduct themselves in a mediation accordingly.

* * *

Notes and Questions

1. The Prefatory Note articulates a majority view within the dispute resolution community about the importance of confidentiality to the mediation process. For thoughtful critiques of this viewpoint, see Eric D. Green, *A Heretical View of the Mediation Privilege*, 2 Ohio St. J. on Disp. Resol. 1 (1986); Scott H. Hughes, *The Uniform Mediation Act: To the Spoiled Go the Privileges*, 85 Marq. L. Rev. 9 (2001); Christopher Honeyman, *Confidentiality, More or Less: The Reality and Importance of Confidentiality is Often Oversold by Mediators and the Profession*, Disp. Resol. Mag., Winter 1998, at 20.

2. In laying out a justification for the uniform law, the Prefatory Note takes care to distinguish between the types of disclosures of mediation communications that it is appropriate for law to regulate, and those disclosures that may be adequately regulated by the parties themselves. This discussion bears on the very meaning of confidentiality and reflects the fact that the concept of mediation confidentiality embraces two very different contexts in which mediation communications may be revealed during an ongoing mediation, or after a mediation has ended.

The first context can be thought of as the disclosure of mediation communications outside of formal judicial or governmental proceedings — such as to spouses and other family members, friends, business associates, the news media or others in the general public. The law typically addresses this type of mediation confidentiality through private contract. That is to say, the parties agree in a contract (typically their agreement to mediate) whether or not to disclose mediation communications to third parties outside of the mediation, and the conditions under which such disclosures may be made if the parties do agree to permit such disclosures. This practice furthers party autonomy, and courts have generally been willing to enforce such contracts as a matter of legitimate private ordering. *See, e.g., Cohen v. Cowles Media Co.*, 501 U.S. 663, 111 S.Ct. 2513, 115 L.Ed.2d 586 (1991) (First Amendment does not bar recovery against a newspaper's breach of promise of confidentiality); *Horne v. Patton*, 291 Ala. 701, 287 So.2d 824 (1973) (physician disclosure may be invasion of privacy, breach of fiduciary duty, breach of contract). Why might parties want to agree to permit disclosures of mediation communications? Why might mediation advocates be concerned about such disclosures?

A few states have enacted statutes and court rules that could arguably reach and prohibit these kinds of disclosures. For example, OK. ST. DISPUTE RES APP. C, Rule 10 (A), provides that "All persons attending a mediation session shall respect and maintain the total confidentiality of the session." Would such an interpretation foster or inhibit party self-determination in mediation?

The UMA defers to these personal and state law choices in Section 8, stating "Unless subject to the [insert statutory references to open meetings act and open records act], mediation communications are confidential to the extent agreed by the parties or provided by other law or rule of this State."

The second disclosure context deals with the use of mediation communications in subsequent legal or other formal governmental proceedings, and related discovery proceedings, where the tension between mediation and rule of law values is implicated most directly. While parties could, theoretically, contractually agree not to testify in such situations, courts are generally reluctant to uphold such agreements as a matter of public policy. The law generally permits parties the right to relevant evidence to prove their cases, and encroachments on this fundamental principle are generally disfavored and narrowly construed. 8 WIGMORE, EVIDENCE § 2192, at 70 (McNaughton Rev. 1961); *see* SARAH R. COLE, CRAIG A. MCEWEN & NANCY H. ROGERS, MEDIATION: LAW, POLICY, PRACTICE §§ 9.23, 9.25 (2d ed. and 2001 Supp.). There are occasionally situations in which a court has upheld agreements not to testify, such as *Simrin v. Simrin*, 233 Cal.App.2d 90, 43 Cal.Rptr. 376 (1965), in which the court enforced such an agreement between a rabbi acting as marriage counselor and couple seeking his services. However, such situations are very much the exception, not the rule.

On the other hand, the law does provide some protection against the disclosure of mediation communications in formal legal proceedings. One way is by extending the law of privilege to the mediation context, which a few courts have done in particular cases. *See, e.g., Folb v. Motion Picture Industry Pension & Health Plans*, 16 F.Supp.2d 1164, 1181 (C.D.Cal. 1998) (" ... encouraging mediation by adopting a federal mediation privilege ... will provide a 'public good transcending the normally dominant principle of utilizing all rational means for ascertaining the truth.' "); *United States v. Gullo*, 672 F.Supp. 99 (W.D.N.Y. 1987) (suppressing mediation communications in a criminal proceeding); *NLRB v. Macaluso*, 618 F.2d 51 (9th Cir. 1980) (public interest in maintaining the perceived and actual impartiality of mediators outweighs the benefits derivable from a given mediator's testimony). These courts have generally relied upon Rule 501 of the Federal Rules of Evidence, which provides that " ... the privilege of a witness ... shall be governed by the principles of the common law ... ," as well as a key U.S. Supreme Court decision interpreting that provision, *Jaffee v. Redmond*, 518 U.S. 1, 116 S.Ct. 1923, 135 L.Ed.2d 337 (1996). In weighing whether to grant a privilege, *Jaffee* calls upon courts to consider whether the asserted privilege is "rooted in the imperative need for confidence and trust," whether the privilege would serve public ends, whether the evidentiary detriment caused by the exercise of the privilege is modest, and whether the denial of the federal privilege would frustrate a parallel privilege adopted by the states.

However, judicial decisions such as these that recognize a mediation privilege are relatively rare, as the weight of the presumption of party access to relevant evidence more commonly will lead courts to permit mediation communications if necessary to permit parties to establish their cases. *See Branzburg v. Hayes*, 408 U.S. 665, 682 n.21, 92 S.Ct. 2646, 33 L.Ed.2d 626 (1972) (quoting 8 JOHN H. WIGMORE, EVIDENCE § 2286, at 543 (McNaughton rev. 1961)) ("In general, then, the mere fact that a communication was made in express confidence, or in the implied confidence of a confidential relation, does not create a privilege [for the media under the First Amendment] ... No pledge of privacy or oath of secrecy can avail against the demand for the truth in a court of justice."); *see also, In re Grand Jury Subpoena Duces Tecum*, 112 F.3d 910, 923 (8th Cir. 1997) (former First Lady Hillary "Clinton's reasonable belief that her conversations with White House lawyers were privileged is insufficient to prevent their disclosure."); Charles Ehrhardt, *Confidentiality, Privilege and Rule 408: The Protection of Mediation Proceedings in Federal Court,* 60 La. L. Rev. 91 (1999). Because courts are, understandably, unreliable protectors of mediation confidentiality, the federal government and the states have enacted statutes or court rules to provide explicit protection for mediation communications.

3. The Prefatory Note observes that there are approximately 250 state statutes and court rules affecting mediation confidentiality, all of which vary widely in scope, application, and exceptions. They may be generally classified according to type and structure.

A. *Type.* There are two general classifications of confidentiality rules based on type. The first of these classes includes those rules that are embedded in substantive statutes or court rules and only apply to mediations covered by such provisions. These would include, for instance, statutes in some jurisdictions that deal with the mediation of particular kinds of disputes, such as farmer-lender or employment disputes, as well as court rules that apply to cases (or certain kinds of cases) that are litigated in affected courts. The second of these classifications according to type includes those rules that apply to all mediations conducted in that state. Many states have both types of regulations. In states that only have context-specific mediation confidentiality protections, lawyers should be aware that mediation communications are generally not protected from subsequent discovery and admissibility at trial unless they are of the type specified by statute. For example, in a context-specific state in which the only mediation confidentiality provision is in a statute regulating farmer-lender relations, the mediation of a domestic relations dispute would have no direct confidentiality protections. Attorneys in such a case may argue for a privilege, but may not be successful, as noted above.

B. *Structure*. In addition to type, the 250 statutes and court rules also vary by structure, which is significant because the scope, exceptions, and other factors will vary depending upon the structure of the protection.

The vast majority of the state protections are structured as privileges, such as the Uniform Mediation Act. *See, e.g.*, ARIZ. REV. STAT. ANN. § 12–2238 (West 1993); NEB. REV. STAT. § 25–2914 (1997); WASH. REV. CODE § 5.60.070 (1993). One reason is that the privilege structure is the most common way that the law has historically protected communications between persons in a special relationship from later discovery or admissibility, such as the lawyer-client privilege, the doctor-patient privilege, the priest-penitent privilege, and the spousal privilege. Courts therefore can be presumed to be familiar with the policies that guide such privileges, and the well-established exceptions to them, when applying a relatively new mediation privilege. *See*, UNIF. MEDIATION ACT § 4, Comment 2(a) (2001). Another advantage of the privilege structure is that it results in a narrow exclusion of potentially relevant evidence. In addition, a party must be a valid holder of the privilege in order to raise or waive it. For example, a spousal privilege may be asserted by spouses, not by their children. Moreover, the law over time has carved out exceptions in which the value of fostering the confidential relationship give way to other interests, such as the need for personal safety. Holder and exception issues for mediation are discussed further below, beginning at page 448, in the context of the Uniform Mediation Act.

While the privilege structure is clearly the majority rule, a few states have enacted mediation communications protections modeled on the protections traditionally provided for settlement discussions. For example, a Missouri confidentiality statute includes a provision stating "Arbitration, conciliation and mediation proceedings shall be regarded as settlement negotiations ... " MO. REV. STAT. § 435.014(2) (2000). The settlement discussion rule is of common law origin, but has been codified by many states, and at the federal level by Rule 408 of the Federal Rules of Evidence, which provides:

> Evidence of (1) furnishing or offering or promising to furnish, or (2) accepting or offering or promising to accept, a valuable consideration in compromising or attempting to compromise a claim which was disputed as to either validity or amount, is not admissible to prove liability for or invalidity of the claim or its amount. Evidence of conduct or statements made in compromise negotiations is likewise not admissible. This rule does not require the exclusion of any evidence otherwise discoverable merely because it is presented in the course of compromise negotiations. This rule also does not require exclusion when the evidence is offered for another purpose, such as proving bias or prejudice of a witness, negativing a contention of undue delay, or proving an effort to obstruct a criminal investigation or prosecution.

States adopting the settlement discussion model essentially extend the settlement discussions protection to mediation. This approach has the benefit of familiarity, but has been generally disfavored by legislative drafters because of the broad array of exceptions that have been carved out for settlement discussions at common law. These include exceptions to permit statements made in settlement discussions to be used for impeachment, to prove bias, and for the admission of other relevant statements of fact that are not offers of compromise specifically mentioned in the settlement discussion rule. Several of these exceptions may be seen in the black letter of Rule 408. States may of course address this problem in the drafting of their statutes and court rules. Missouri's statute, for example, removes some exceptions by providing "No admission, representation, statement or other confidential communication made in setting up or conducting such proceedings not otherwise discoverable or obtainable shall be admissible as evidence or subject to discovery." Mo. Rev. Stat. § 435.014(2).

A third, relatively rare model is one that simply makes the mediator incompetent to testify as a matter of law and provides no other protections. For example, the Missouri statute noted above also includes such a provision, stating "If all the parties to a dispute agree in writing to submit their dispute to any forum for arbitration, conciliation, or mediation, then no person who serves as arbitrator, conciliator or mediator, nor any agent or employee of that person, shall be subpoenaed or otherwise compelled to disclose any matter disclosed in the process of setting up or conducting the arbitration, conciliation or mediation." Mo. Rev. Stat. § 435.014(1); see also; Minn. Stat. § 595.02 (Subd. 1a) (2000).

While the mediator incompetency approach has the benefit of simplicity, standing alone it also has at least two significant weaknesses. First, it provides no protections for the parties against the later use of mediation communications evidence. Second, if the mediator is sued for mediator malpractice, he or she would not be able to testify in his or her own defense, if the statute is taken seriously. While courts could carve out an exception to cover this situation, such a move would seem to invite other exceptions as circumstances arise, thus undermining the law's certainty, and ultimately the public's confidence in mediation.

Finally, as we will see in the *Olam* case excerpted below, California has adopted yet another, unique approach, which may be thought of as a categorical exclusion. Cal. Evid. Code § 1119 provides:

> Except as otherwise provided in this chapter: (a) No evidence of anything said or any admission made ... in the course of, or pursuant to, a mediation ... is admissible or subject to discovery, and disclosure of the evidence shall not be compelled, in any ... noncriminal proceeding ... (b) No writing ... prepared in the course of, or pursuant to, a mediation ... is admissible or subject to discovery, and disclosure of the writing shall not be compelled in any, ... noncriminal proceeding ... (c) All communications ... by and between participants in the course of a mediation ... shall remain confidential.

This approach seeks to effectively build a cocoon around the mediation, and to prevent any communication made in the mediation from getting out. Not surprisingly, considering the fundamental tension between mediation and rule of law values, California's categorical exclusion statute has been the most litigated of all the vehicles of mediation confidentiality.

The statute has been met with mixed success in the lower state and federal courts, but the California Supreme Court has generally been more supportive. *See, e.g., Foxgate Homeowners' Ass'n v. Bramalea California Inc.*, 26 Cal.4th 1, 108 Cal.Rptr.2d 642, 25 P.3d 1117 (2001) (ruling that a court may not issue sanctions based on mediation communications); *Rojas v. Superior Court*, 33 Cal.4th 407, 15 Cal.Rptr.3d 643, 93 P.3d 260 (2004) (finding photographs and reports of construction damage used in mediation not discoverable or admissible in later trial). The *Rojas* case spurred considerable controversy, with the trial bar, joined by some mediators, moving to have the statute amended to reverse the decision. Why do you suppose it generated this level of controversy? Why would some mediators join the trial bar in trying to scale back this protection of mediation confidentiality?

4. If you were drafting a statute, which of these approaches would you use?

5. As a practical matter, the evidentiary approaches described above apply only in proceedings in which the rules of evidence apply, such as judicial proceedings. They do not apply, however, to bar the use of mediation evidence in proceedings in which the rules of evidence do not apply, such as most administrative and legislative proceedings. State legislatures may provide a broader sweep to their mediation confidentiality protections. For example, the UMA expressly applies to "(A) a judicial, administrative, arbitral, or other adjudicative process, including related pre-hearing and post-hearing motions, conferences, and discovery; or (B) a legislative hearing or similar process."

6. A broadly applicable mediation privilege has not yet been recognized by the federal courts. However, Congress has created a statutory privilege for mediations that take place in the various federal agencies. The federal privilege, found in the ALTERNATIVE DISPUTE RESOLUTION ACT OF 1996, 5 U.S.C. § 574 (1996), is narrower than many state privileges. For example, it applies only to the caucus sessions between the mediator and a party, and does not apply to general sessions in which the mediator meets jointly with the parties. It includes exceptions for disclosures that are "necessary to (A) prevent a manifest injustice; (B) help establish a violation of law; or (C) prevent harm to the public health and safety. . . . " These exceptions are few, but are they too broad to provide parties with meaningful assurance of confidentiality protection? Can courts be counted on to narrow the statute? The act can be found in the online appendix on the TWEN web site for this casebook, at www.lawschool.westlaw.com.

7. Look up the protections for mediation confidentiality in your state. Are they found in a statute or court rule, or both? Do they apply to all mediations, or are they subject-matter specific? How are they structured? How have any courts construed the provisions? What exceptions are there to the general rule of confidentiality?

c. A Closer Look at Privilege

Since privilege is the primary structure by which mediation communications are kept from disclosure in subsequent discovery or testimony, it is worth taking a closer look at the privilege structure. The UMA is particularly helpful here because it was drafted at the national level for consideration by individual states, and because it draws upon the experience of the many state privileges. Notes detailing the operation of the act, how it relates to the larger fabric of state law in this area, and raising questions to consider, follow this excerpt.

UNIFORM MEDIATION ACT
(2003).

* * *

SECTION 4. PRIVILEGE AGAINST DISCLOSURE; ADMISSIBILITY; DISCOVERY.

(a) Except as otherwise provided in Section 6, a mediation communication is privileged as provided in subsection (b) and is not subject to discovery or admissible in evidence in a proceeding unless waived or precluded as provided by Section 5.

(b) In a proceeding, the following privileges apply:

(1) A mediation party may refuse to disclose, and may prevent any other person from disclosing, a mediation communication.

(2) A mediator may refuse to disclose a mediation communication, and may prevent any other person from disclosing a mediation communication of the mediator.

(3) A nonparty participant may refuse to disclose, and may prevent any other person from disclosing, a mediation communication of the nonparty participant.

(c) Evidence or information that is otherwise admissible or subject to discovery does not become inadmissible or protected from discovery solely by reason of its disclosure or use in a mediation.

Legislative Note: The Act does not supersede existing state statutes that make mediators incompetent to testify, or that provide for costs and attorney fees to mediators who are wrongfully subpoenaed. See, e.g., Cal. Evid. Code Section 703.5 (West 1994).

* * *

SECTION 5. WAIVER AND PRECLUSION OF PRIVILEGE.

(a) A privilege under Section 4 may be waived in a record or orally during a proceeding if it is expressly waived by all parties to the mediation and:

(1) in the case of the privilege of a mediator, it is expressly waived by the mediator; and

(2) in the case of the privilege of a nonparty participant, it is expressly waived by the nonparty participant.

(b) A person that discloses or makes a representation about a mediation communication which prejudices another person in a proceeding is precluded from asserting a privilege under Section 4, but only to the extent necessary for the person prejudiced to respond to the representation or disclosure.

(c) A person that intentionally uses a mediation to plan, attempt to commit or commit a crime, or to conceal an ongoing crime or ongoing criminal activity is precluded from asserting a privilege under Section 4.

* * *

SECTION 6. EXCEPTIONS TO PRIVILEGE.

(a) There is no privilege under Section 4 for a mediation communication that is:

   (1) in an agreement evidenced by a record signed by all parties to the agreement;

   (2) available to the public under [insert statutory reference to open records act] or made during a session of a mediation which is open, or is required by law to be open, to the public;

   (3) a threat or statement of a plan to inflict bodily injury or commit a crime of violence;

   (4) intentionally used to plan a crime, attempt to commit or commit a crime, or to conceal an ongoing crime or ongoing criminal activity;

   (5) sought or offered to prove or disprove a claim or complaint of professional misconduct or malpractice filed against a mediator;

   (6) except as otherwise provided in subsection (c), sought or offered to prove or disprove a claim or complaint of professional misconduct or malpractice filed against a mediation party, nonparty participant, or representative of a party based on conduct occurring during a mediation; or

   (7) sought or offered to prove or disprove abuse, neglect, abandonment, or exploitation in a proceeding in which a child or adult protective services agency is a party, unless the

    [Alternative A: [State to insert, for example, child or adult protection] case is referred by a court to mediation and a public agency participates.]

    [Alternative B: public agency participates in the [State to insert, for example, child or adult protection] mediation].

(b) There is no privilege under Section 4 if a court, administrative agency, or arbitrator finds, after a hearing in camera, that the party seeking discovery or the proponent of the evidence has shown that the evidence is not otherwise available, that there is a need for the evidence that substantially outweighs the interest in protecting confidentiality, and that the mediation communication is sought or offered in:

(1) a court proceeding involving a felony [or misdemeanor]; or

(2) except as otherwise provided in subsection (c), a proceeding to prove a claim to rescind or reform or a defense to avoid liability on a contract arising out of the mediation.

(c) A mediator may not be compelled to provide evidence of a mediation communication referred to in subsection (a)(6) or (b)(2).

(d) If a mediation communication is not privileged under subsection (a) or (b), only the portion of the communication necessary for the application of the exception from nondisclosure may be admitted. Admission of evidence under subsection (a) or (b) does not render the evidence, or any other mediation communication, discoverable or admissible for any other purpose.

Legislative Note: If the enacting state does not have an open records act, the following language in paragraph (2) of subsection (a) needs to be deleted: "available to the public under [insert statutory reference to open records act] or".

Notes and Questions

1.   The mediation privilege in the UMA is unique in that it expressly provides for three separate holders: the parties, the mediator(s), and any non-party participants, such as support persons or witnesses. Many mediation statutes and court rules are either silent as to the holders, or specify only the parties, and, occasionally the mediator; courts, too, sometimes will construe an ambiguous statute to include mediators, as we will see in the *Olam* case below. The UMA is the only mediation statute or court rule to expressly cover non-party participants.

2.   Under Section 4, holders of the UMA privilege are entitled to refuse to testify, and in some circumstances may affirmatively prevent, or block, another person from testifying about mediation communications. *See* UNIF. MEDIATION ACT § 4, Comment 4(b) (2001).

Parties have the greatest blocking power under the UMA, and may block discovery or testimony about mediation communications made by anyone in the mediation — including another party, a mediator, or any other participant. Mediators and non-party participants have a more limited privilege. A mediator may block testimony of her own mediation communications, regardless of whether that testimony is being offered by a party or non-party participant. The mediator privilege allows the mediator to block any testimony about the mediator's mediation communications, even if both parties consent to the testimony. Finally, a non-party participant may block evidence of that individual's mediation communications, regardless of who provides the evidence and whether the parties or mediator consent.

3.   Assume an employment discrimination mediation in which Jim, an African–American, claims that he did not receive a promotion because of his race. During the mediation, Jim's boss, Bill, admitted that Jim's race was a factor in the decision not to promote Jim. The mediation is unsuccessful, and a trial ensues in a jurisdiction has adopted the UMA. Can Bill block Jim from testifying about Bill's admission? Can Bill stop the mediator from

similarly testifying? Can Bill, Jim, or the mediator prevent similar testimony by Jim's union steward, who was at the mediation and heard the admission?

4. The UMA exceptions are consistent with mediation privilege exceptions that have been recognized in most jurisdictions by statute or common law. What is unique about the UMA exceptions is that they are divided into two classes, referred to during the drafting process as "above the line" and "below the line" exceptions. The "above the line" exceptions are found in Section 6 (a)(1)-(7), and do not require judicial balancing as a condition of admissibility. If one of these exceptions applies, the mediation communications evidence will be admitted. These include exceptions that would allow the admission of a mediated settlement agreement, evidence of the abuse of vulnerable parties, and evidence of criminal activities.

The "below the line" exceptions, UMA Section 6(b)(1)-(2), require a court to determine the admissibility of the evidence under the unique facts and circumstances of the case in an *in camera* proceeding. Significantly, the statute sets a high standard for admissibility, requiring the proponent of the evidence to show that the evidence is "otherwise unavailable" and "substantially outweighs" the state's strong presumption favoring the confidentiality of mediation communications. This includes exceptions that would allow testimony of mediation communications to be used to establish guilt or innocence in at least felony criminal proceedings (and misdemeanors if states elect to adopt this bracketed language), and that would permit a party to establish that she signed the mediated settlement agreement because of fraud, duress, or some other basis that would render the agreement legally invalid as a matter of contract law. What is the benefit of requiring judicial balancing before the evidence can be admitted in the matters covered by these two exceptions?

5. The Section 5 waiver provision is unusual among privileges in that it does not provide waiver by conduct. UNIF. MEDIATION ACT § 5(a). Why might the drafters have made this policy choice?

6. The drafting of the Uniform Mediation Act was an often stormy process, as it implicated some of most cherished values of mediation, and the broad range of views on those issues that are held by mediators, litigators, judges, and other interested parties. There were more than a dozen public meetings in locations around the country over the four year drafting period, with new drafts circulated for public comment before each meeting. In the end, however, the final act was endorsed without opposition by the Uniform Law Commission, the American Bar Association (on the strength of more than a dozen co-sponsoring ABA sections), all major dispute resolution professional organizations, and by all major providers of dispute resolution services. For a history of the drafting process, see Richard C. Reuben, *The Sound of Dust Settling: A Response to Critics of the UMA*, 2003 J. Disp. Resol. 99.

7. Professor Scott Hughes has strongly criticized the UMA. Hughes questions the need for a mediation privilege in general, and criticizes the UMA's treatment of the issue in particular, writing:

> To the extent that mediation confidentiality impairs the parties' self-determination, the mediation privilege should yield to self-determination and to the court's ability to determine the truth. If the party's

access to justice is hampered, or is so restricted by the UMA as to be virtually non-existent, any relationship between the results achieved in mediation and self-determination will be merely coincidental. This is not acceptable. . . .

If it is necessary to have a privilege for mediation, certain elements should be adopted. First, the mediation process is not well served by a separate privilege for mediators. Second, clear exceptions should be drafted to cover contractual misconduct. Third, although a procedural step prior to accessing testimony (such as an in camera hearing or sealed proceedings) is appropriate, no substantive hurdles should hinder access to normal common law contract remedies or impair self-determination. Finally, when challenges arise to an agreement reached in mediation, the mediator should be treated like all other mediation participants — he or she should be required to testify. The UMA should not allow the artificial distinction between the mediator malpractice and the contractual misconduct exceptions.

Scott H. Hughes, *The Uniform Mediation Act: To the Spoiled Go the Privileges*, 85 Marq. L. Rev. 9, 77 (2001).

Do you agree? If not, how would you respond to Professor Hughes?

8.   Compare the mediation statute(s) and/or court rule(s) in your state to the UMA. What are the differences between the rules? Which is stronger?

9.   Casey Brewery Works (CBW) and Pat Smith asked you to mediate an employment dispute. Smith, a production employee with two years seniority, claimed that CBW terminated her employment in violation of the Americans with Disabilities Act and the state workers compensation statute as a result of her missing work due to a back injury that she suffered caused by an on-the-job injury.

CBW's position was that Smith was terminated for cause as a result of missing more than one-half of the workdays in the prior year and for failure to list on her employment application that she had filed a back-injury claim against her prior employer. CBW produced an orthopedic specialist in back injuries at the mediation who stated that, based on his examinations of Smith, she did not suffer the injury while at work but rather that her back problems were due to a pre-existing injury she suffered while working for a previous employer.

During a caucus, Smith admitted to you that she had hurt her back while working for the previous company but had re-injured it while working on the CBW production line. She said that she did not list the prior injury on the employment application because she knew CBW would not hire her. In a caucus with CBW, its manager stated that although Smith was a good worker, she was no longer dependable and the company could not condone the employment falsification.

After six hours in mediation, Smith authorized you to tell CBW that she would drop her claims if CBW would give her back pay for the time she missed and a good recommendation for the work she performed. She also allowed you to tell CBW that she knew she should have listed the prior injury but did not because she was afraid CBW would not hire her. After two more hours of negotiations, the parties concluded that they could not reach a settlement.

You have just been served with a subpoena from CBW's attorney to attend a deposition to testify as to Smith's comments about her statements during the mediation concerning her pre-existing injury and admission about her employment-application falsification. If your state has adopted the Uniform Mediation Act, what would be the outcome of your motion to quash CBW's subpoena? If your state has not adopted the UMA, what would be the outcome under the current law of your state?

d. Should the Mediator Be Compelled to Testify?

Mediation confidentiality is often thought of in terms of the parties, but what about the mediator? Under what circumstances, if any, should a mediator be compelled to testify about what went on in a mediation? The following case explores this difficult problem.

OLAM v. CONGRESS MORTGAGE CO.

United States District Court, N.D. California, 1999.
68 F.Supp.2d 1110.

BRAZIL, U.S. MAGISTRATE JUDGE.

The court addresses in this opinion several difficult issues about the relationship between a court-sponsored voluntary mediation and subsequent proceedings whose purpose is to determine whether the parties entered an enforceable agreement at the close of the mediation session.
* * *

One of the principal issues with which the court wrestles, below, is whether evidence about what occurred during the mediation proceedings, including testimony from the mediator, may be used to help resolve this dispute. * * *

[In 1992, Donna Olam applied for and received a loan from Congress Mortgage in the amount of $187,000, which was secured by two single-family homes located in San Francisco. Ms. Olam later said that she never read the 1992 loan documentation, and simply signed where Congress Mortgage's agent told her to sign. She also said she could not afford the monthly payments on the 1992 loan, and when she eventually defaulted, Congress Mortgage began foreclosure proceedings on the properties. After several different follow-up agreements between the parties, and changes of counsel by Mrs. Olam, the matter proceeded to litigation before Judge Brazil.

Pursuant to a local court rule, the matter was referred to mediation by the court's ADR program counsel, Howard Herman, an accomplished mediator. The mediation began on September 9, 1998, and lasted more than 12 hours, ending at approximately 1 a.m. with a memorandum of understanding between the parties that was to be later memorialized into a formal settlement agreement. That formal settlement agreement never materialized, however, and several months after the mediation, Congress Mortgage moved to enforce the original Memorandum of Understanding (MOU).

Olam opposed the motion, alleging, *inter alia*, that the MOU was unconscionable and that she was incapable — intellectually, emotionally, and physically — of giving legally viable consent. In particular, Olam, 65 years old at the time of the mediation and allegedly suffering a variety of ailments, claimed she didn't understand the mediation process, and didn't actively participate in the mediation. She further claimed she was pressured into signing the MOU, and that her physical and emotional distress rendered her unduly susceptible to this pressure. As a result, she says, she signed the MOU against her will and without reading and/or understanding its terms.]

* * *

After receiving additional papers from the parties addressing these matters, the court held another status conference on July 21, 1999. At that time counsel for plaintiff confirmed that plaintiff agreed to waive any attorney-client privilege that would attach between her and her former counsel, Phyllis Voisenat. Plaintiff also waived any "mediation privilege" that might attach to any and all communications made during the mediation. Defendants agreed to a limited waiver of their mediation privileges — so that testimony could be taken about both the mediator's and the defendants' interaction with plaintiff and her attorney during the mediation.

As we explain below, it is not at all clear that the waivers by the parties were sufficient to make it lawful to compel testimony from the mediator. * * *

PERTINENT CALIFORNIA PRIVILEGE LAW

The California legislature has crafted two sets of statutory provisions that must be addressed by courts considering whether they may use in a subsequent civil proceeding any evidence about what occurred or was said during a mediation.

Section 703.5 of the California Evidence Code states, in pertinent part: "No person presiding at any judicial or quasi-judicial proceeding, and no arbitrator or mediator, shall be competent to testify, in any subsequent civil proceeding, as to any statement, conduct, decision, or ruling, occurring at or in conjunction with the prior proceeding, except as to a statement or conduct that could [give rise to contempt, constitute a crime, trigger investigation by the State Bar or the Commission on Judicial Performance, or give rise to disqualification proceedings]."

We note, before proceeding, that by its express terms § 703.5 applies (as pertinent here) only to statements or decisions made, or conduct occurring, in connection with a mediation. Read literally, this statute would not apply to perceptions of participants' appearance, demeanor, or physical condition during a mediation. We also note, however, that compelling mediators to testify or otherwise offer evidence about *anything* that occurred or was perceived during a mediation threatens confidentiality expectations of the participants and imposes burdens on mediators — and that such threats and burdens tend, at least in some measure, to undermine interests that the California legislature likely sought to protect when it enacted this statute. In construing and applying this statute, we endeavor to honor the purposes that drive it.

The other directly pertinent provision from the California Evidence Code is § 1119. It states, in pertinent part: "Except as otherwise provided in this chapter: (a) No evidence of anything said or any admission made ... in the course of, or pursuant to, a mediation ... is admissible or subject to discovery, and disclosure of the evidence shall not be compelled, in any ... noncriminal proceeding ... (b) No writing ... prepared in the course of, or pursuant to, a mediation ... is admissible or subject to discovery, and disclosure of the writing shall not be compelled in any, ... noncriminal proceeding ... (c) All communications ... by and between participants in the course of a mediation ... shall remain confidential."

* * *

As noted above, the "Memorandum of Understanding" that the parties executed at the end of the mediation session in this case states expressly that it "is intended as a binding document itself." No party contends that this MOU is inadmissible.

* * *

THE MEDIATOR'S PRIVILEGE

California law confers on mediators a privilege that is independent of the privilege conferred on parties to a mediation. By declaring that, subject to exceptions not applicable here, mediators are incompetent to testify "as to any statement, conduct, decision, or ruling, occurring at or in conjunction with [the mediation]," section 703.5 of the Evidence Code has the effect of making a mediator the holder of an independent privilege. Section 1119 of the Evidence Code appears to have the same effect — as it prohibits courts from compelling disclosure of evidence about mediation communications and directs that all such communications "shall remain confidential." * * *

In the case at bar, the mediator (Mr. Herman) was and is an employee of the federal court (a "staff neutral"). He hosted the mediation at the behest of the court and under this court's ADR rules. These facts are not sufficient to justify ordering him to testify about what occurred during the mediation — even when the parties have waived their mediation privilege and want the mediator to testify. Mr. Herman is a member of the California bar — and no doubt feels bound to honor the directives of California law. He also is a professional in mediation — and feels a moral obligation to preserve the essential integrity of the mediation process — an integrity to which he believes the promise of confidentiality is fundamental.

Out of respect for these feelings, the court chose not to put Mr. Herman in an awkward position where he might have felt he had to choose between being a loyal employee of the court, on the one hand,

and, on the other, asserting the mediator's privilege under California law. Instead, the court announced that it would proceed on the assumption that Mr. Herman was respectfully and appropriately asserting the mediator's privilege and was formally objecting to being called to testify about anything said or done during the mediation.

* * *

We turn to the issue of whether, under California law, we should compel the mediator to testify — despite the statutory prohibitions set forth in sections 703.5 and 1119 of the Evidence Code. The most important opinion by a California court in this arena is *Rinaker v. Superior Court*, 62 Cal. App. 4th 155 (Third District 1998). In that case the Court of Appeal held that there may be circumstances in which a trial court, over vigorous objection by a party and by the mediator, could compel testimony from the mediator in a juvenile delinquency proceeding (deemed a "civil" matter under California law). * * *

In essence, the *Rinaker* court instructs California trial judges to conduct a two-stage balancing analysis. The goal of the first stage balancing is to determine whether to compel the mediator to appear at an *in camera* proceeding to determine precisely what her testimony would be. In this first stage, the judge considers all the circumstances and weighs all the competing rights and interests, including the values that would be threatened not by public disclosure of mediation communications, but by ordering the mediator to appear at an *in camera* proceeding to disclose only to the court and counsel, out of public view, what she would say the parties said during the mediation. At this juncture the goal is to determine whether the harm that would be done to the values that underlie the mediation privileges[29] simply by ordering the mediator to participate in the *in camera* proceedings can be justified — by the prospect that her testimony might well make a singular and substantial contribution to protecting or advancing competing interests of comparable or greater magnitude.

The trial judge reaches the second stage of balancing analysis only if the product of the first stage is a decision to order the mediator to detail, *in camera,* what her testimony would be. A court that orders the *in camera* disclosure gains precise and reliable knowledge of what the mediator's testimony would be — and only with that knowledge is the court positioned to launch its second balancing analysis. In this second stage the court is to weigh and comparatively assess (1) the importance of the values and interests that would be harmed if the mediator was compelled to testify (perhaps subject to a sealing or protective order, if appropriate), (2) the magnitude of the harm that compelling the testimony would cause to those values and interests, (3) the importance of the rights or interests that would be jeopardized if the mediator's testimony was not accessible in the specific proceedings in question, and (4) how much the testimony would contribute toward protecting those rights or

---

29.   Cal. Evid. Code §§ 703.5 and 1119.

advancing those interests — an inquiry that includes, among other things, an assessment of whether there are alternative sources of evidence of comparable probative value.

* * *

As indicated in an earlier section, the product of the first stage of the analysis was my decision that it was necessary to determine (through sealed proceedings) what Mr. Herman's testimony would be. Reaching that determination involved the following considerations. First, I acknowledge squarely that a decision to require a mediator to give evidence, even *in camera* or under seal, about what occurred during a mediation threatens values underlying the mediation privileges. As the *Rinaker* court suggested, the California legislature adopted these privileges in the belief that without the promise of confidentiality it would be appreciably more difficult to achieve the goals of mediation programs.

* * *

While this court has no occasion or power to quarrel with these generally applicable pronouncements of state policy, we observe that they appear to have appreciably less force when, as here, the parties to the mediation have waived confidentiality protections, indeed have asked the court to compel the mediator to testify — so that justice can be done.

* * *

As the *Rinaker* court pointed out, ordering mediators to participate in proceedings arising out of mediations imposes economic and psychic burdens that could make some people reluctant to agree to serve as a mediator, especially in programs where that service is pro bono or poorly compensated.

This is not a matter of time and money only. Good mediators are likely to feel violated by being compelled to give evidence that could be used against a party with whom they tried to establish a relationship of trust during a mediation. Good mediators are deeply committed to being and remaining neutral and non-judgmental, and to building and preserving relationships with parties. To force them to give evidence that hurts someone from whom they actively solicited trust (during the mediation) rips the fabric of their work and can threaten their sense of the center of their professional integrity. These are not inconsequential matters.

Like many other variables in this kind of analysis, however, the magnitude of these risks can vary with the circumstances. Here, for instance, all parties to the mediation want the mediator to testify about things that occurred during the mediation — so ordering the testimony would do less harm to the actual relationships developed than it would in a case where one of the parties to the mediation objected to the use of evidence from the mediator.

We acknowledge, however, that the possibility that a mediator might be forced to testify over objection could harm the capacity of mediators in general to create the environment of trust that they feel maximizes the likelihood that constructive communication will occur during the mediation session. But the level of harm to that interest likely varies, at least in some measure, with the perception within the community of mediators and litigants about how likely it is that any given mediation will be followed at some point by an order compelling the neutral to offer evidence about what occurred during the session. I know of no studies or statistics that purport to reflect how often courts or parties seek evidence from mediators — and I suspect that the incidence of this issue arising would not be identical across the broad spectrum of mediation programs and settings. What I can report is that this case represents the first time that I have been called upon to address these kinds of questions in the more than fifteen years that I have been responsible for ADR programs in this court. Nor am I aware of the issue arising before other judges here. Based on that experience, my partially educated guess is that the likelihood that a mediator or the parties in any given case need fear that the mediator would later be constrained to testify is extraordinarily small.

* * *

The magnitude of the risk to values underlying the mediation privileges that can be created by ordering a mediator to testify also can vary with the nature of the testimony that is sought. Comparing the kind of testimony sought in *Rinaker* with the kind of testimony sought in the case at bar illustrates this point. In *Rinaker,* one party wanted to use the mediator's recollection about what another party said during the mediation to impeach subsequent trial testimony. So the mediator was to serve as a source of evidence about what words a party to the mediation uttered, what statements or admissions that party made.

As the Court of Appeal appeared to recognize, this kind of testimony could be particularly threatening to the spirit and methods that some people believe are important both to the philosophy and the success of some mediation processes. Under one approach to mediation, the primary goal is not to establish "the truth" or to determine reliably what the historical facts actually were. Rather, the goal is to go both deeper than and beyond history — to emphasize feelings, underlying interests, and a search for means for social repair or reorientation. In this kind of mediation, what happened between the parties in the past can be appreciably less important than why, than what needs drove what happened or were exposed or defined by what happened, than how the parties feel about it, and than what they can bring themselves to do to move on.

Moreover, the methods some mediators use to explore underlying interests and feelings and to build settlement bridges are in some instances intentionally distanced from the actual historical facts. In some mediations, the focus is on feelings rather than facts. The neutral may ask the parties to set aside pre-occupations with what happened as she tries to help the parties understand underlying motivations and needs and to remove emotional obstacles through exercises in venting. Some mediators use hypotheticals that are expressly and intentionally not presented as accurate reflections of reality — in order to help the parties explore their situation and the range of solution options that might be available. A mediator might encourage parties to "try on" certain ideas or feelings that the parties would contend have little connection with past conduct, to experiment with the effects on themselves and others of expressions of emotions or of openness to concessions or proposals that, outside the special environment of the mediation, the parties would not entertain or admit. All of this, as mediator Rinaker herself pointed out, can have precious little to do with historical accuracy or "truth."[119]

Given these features of some mediations, it could be both threatening and unfair to hold a participant to the literal meaning of at least some of the words she uttered during the course of a mediation. And testimony from the mediator about what those words were during the mediation might constitute very unreliable (actively misleading) evidence about what the earlier historical facts were.

For these reasons, a court conducting the kind of balancing analysis called for by the *Rinaker* court should try to determine what kind of techniques and processes were used in the particular mediation in issue. The more like the processes just described, the more harm would be done by trying to use evidence about what was said or done during the mediation to help prove what the earlier historical facts really were. On the other hand, if the mediation process was closer to an adjudicate/evaluative model, with a clear focus (understood by all participants) on evidence, law, and traditional analysis of liability, damages, and settlement options, use of evidence from the mediation in subsequent civil proceedings might be less vulnerable to criticism for being unfair and unreliable.

*   *   *

The interests that are likely to be advanced by compelling the mediator to testify in this case are of considerable importance. Moreover, as we shall see, some of those interests parallel and reinforce the objectives the legislature sought to advance by providing for confidentiality in mediation.

The first interest we identify is the interest in doing justice. Here is what we mean. For reasons described below, the mediator is positioned in this case to offer what could be crucial, certainly very probative,

---

119. I found the descriptions in Rinaker's briefs of her mediation process articulate and instructive. *See, Rinaker,* 62 Cal. App. 4th at 170 and 166 (quotations from Ms. Rinaker's briefs).

It is important to acknowledge, however, that there is a broad range of approaches to mediation (people attach the label "mediation" to many different kinds of processes and methods) — and that the "mediations" that occur in at least some federal court ADR programs are likely to be quite a bit more "evaluative" than the purely facilitative model would contemplate. In fact, I suspect that in a good many "mediations" of cases filed in federal court, the parties and the neutral pay considerable attention to evidence and law — and that the negotiations revolve around fairly traditional analysis of positions — as much as the mediators might want to shift focus to underlying interests and to searches for creative solutions.

evidence about the central factual issues in this matter. There is a strong possibility that his testimony will greatly improve the court's ability to determine reliably what the pertinent historical facts actually were. Establishing reliably what the facts were is critical to doing justice (here, justice means this: applying the law correctly to the real historical facts). It is the fundamental duty of a public court in our society to do justice — to resolve disputes in accordance with the law when the parties don't. Confidence in our system of justice as a whole, in our government as a whole, turns in no small measure on confidence in the courts' ability to do justice in individual cases. So doing justice in individual cases is an interest of considerable magnitude.

When we put case-specific flesh on these abstract bones, we see that "doing justice" implicates interests of considerable importance to the parties — all of whom want the mediator to testify. From the plaintiff's perspective, the interests that the defendants' motion threatens could hardly be more fundamental. According to Ms. Olam, the mediation process was fundamentally unfair to her — and resulted in an apparent agreement whose terms are literally unconscionable and whose enforcement would render her homeless and virtually destitute. To her, doing justice in this setting means protecting her from these fundamental wrongs.

From the defendants' perspective, doing justice in this case means, among other things, bringing to a lawful close disputes with Ms. Olam that have been on-going for about seven years — disputes that the defendants' believe have cost them, without justification, at least scores of thousands of dollars. The defendants believe that Ms. Olam has breached no fewer than three separate contractual commitments with them (not counting the agreement reached at the end of the mediation) — and that those breaches are the product of a calculated effort not only to avoid meeting legitimate obligations, but also to make unfair use, for years, of the defendants' money.

* * *

And they are not the only interests that could be advanced by compelling the mediator to testify. According to the defendants' pre-hearing proffers, the mediator's testimony would establish clearly that the mediation process was fair and that the plaintiff's consent to the settlement agreement was legally viable. Thus the mediator's testimony, according to the defendants, would re-assure the community and the court about the integrity of the mediation process that the court sponsored.

That testimony also would provide the court with the evidentiary confidence it needs to enforce the agreement. A publicly announced decision to enforce the settlement would, in turn, encourage parties who want to try to settle their cases to use the court's mediation program for that purpose. An order appropriately enforcing an agreement reached through the mediation also would encourage parties in the future to take mediations seriously, to understand that they represent real opportunities to reach closure and avoid trial, and to attend carefully to terms of agreements proposed in mediations. In these important ways, taking testimony from the mediator could strengthen the mediation program.

In sharp contrast, refusing to compel the mediator to testify might well deprive the court of the evidence it needs to rule reliably on the plaintiff's contentions — and thus might either cause the court to impose an unjust outcome on the plaintiff or disable the court from enforcing the settlement. In this setting, refusing to compel testimony from the mediator might end up being tantamount to denying the motion to enforce the agreement — because a crucial source of evidence about the plaintiff's condition and capacities would be missing. Following that course, defendants suggest, would do considerable harm not only to the court's mediation program but also to fundamental fairness. If parties believed that courts routinely would refuse to compel mediators to testify, and that the absence of evidence from mediators would enhance the viability of a contention that apparent consent to a settlement contract was not legally viable, cynical parties would be encouraged either to try to escape commitments they made during mediations or to use threats of such escapes to try to re-negotiate, after the mediation, more favorable terms — terms that they never would have been able to secure without this artificial and unfair leverage.

* * *

In short, there was a substantial likelihood that testimony from the mediator would be the most reliable and probative on the central issues raised by the plaintiff in response to the defendants' motion. And there was no likely alternative source of evidence on these issues that would be of comparable probative utility. So it appeared that testimony from the mediator would be crucial to the court's capacity to do its job — and that refusing to compel that testimony posed a serious threat to every value identified above. In this setting, California courts clearly would conclude the first stage balancing analysis by ordering the mediator to testify *in camera* or under seal — so that the court, aided by inputs from the parties, could make a refined and reliable judgment about whether to use that testimony to help resolve the substantive issues raised by the pending motion. * * *

[The court concluded that Olam's signature on the MOU was not the result of undue influence because California law does not permit undue influence to be satisfied by a showing that a party's lawyer pressured her into signing the contract. The court further ordered the mediator's testimony to be unsealed because it revealed that Mrs. Olam was competent to participate in the mediation, participated in the mediation actively, and understood the terms and the nature of the final mediated settlement agreement.] * * *

Notes and Questions

1. In his discussion, Judge Brazil repeatedly stressed that both of the parties wanted the mediator to testify, albeit for different reasons. What

rationales might support an independent power of the mediator to refuse to testify, despite contrary preferences of the parties? Are they sufficient in your mind to justify a categorical rule that trumps the right of the parties to the mediator's evidence in all cases? Would a more nuanced approach be preferable?

2. Construing California law, Judge Brazil's opinion seeks to stake a middle ground between the competing needs for confidentiality in mediation and for evidence at trial by hearing the mediator's testimony in an *in camera* proceeding — that is, in a private, out-of-court proceeding, perhaps in the judge's chambers — and under seal, so that the evidence wouldn't be received into evidence unless the court determined that the seal should be lifted. Brazil then applied a two-part balancing test to determine if the mediator's testimony should be unsealed. In the first part, he identified the interests that might be threatened by ordering the mediator to testify, and then assessed the magnitude of the harm that might be done to those interests by ordering the testimony. In the second stage, he identified the interests that the mediator's testimony might advance, assessed their importance, and tried to predict the significance of the mediator's testimony to the fulfillment of those interests.

Applying these considerations, Brazil said he needed the mediator's testimony to assess Mrs. Olam's claim that she didn't have the capacity to enter into the mediation agreement, and that she didn't actually participate in the mediation. If these judicial needs were significant enough to overcome the mediator's interests in not testifying in this case, in what type of case might the balance come out the other way?

3. Citing *Rinaker*, Brazil notes that mediation evidence may not be very reliable because the mediation process is aimed at resolving competing interests rather than the truth-finding function of courts. Why might this distinction between the processes lead mediation evidence to be potentially unreliable? As you reflect back on the Riskin grid of mediator orientations, how might a mediator's behavior affect the reliability of mediation communications as an evidentiary matter? Does it matter whether the communication is made by the parties or the mediator?

4. Notice that Judge Brazil discusses two of the four vehicles for protecting mediation confidentiality that we addressed in the previous notes: CAL. EVID. CODE § 703.5, which renders the mediator incompetent to testify, and the CAL. EVID. CODE § 1119, which bars courts from hearing or using mediation evidence. Brazil reads these together to conclude that the nature of mediation protection in California is actually a privilege, which is both narrower than the categorical exclusion of § 1119 and broader than a mediator incompetency rule of § 703.5. This was a crucial decision, because it forced him to consider whether the mediator, as a holder of the privilege, could be compelled to testify. He ultimately decided in the affirmative. Do you think he was correct in determining that the California law effectively created a privilege? What other results could he have reached in attempting to square the two statutory provisions? What would have been the effect on the admissibility of the mediator's testimony?

5. Early in his decision, Judge Brazil observes that CAL. EVID. CODE § 703.5 applies only to exclude from discovery and admissibility evidence of

statements made during a mediation — and does not apply to evidence that may be observed or perceived, such as demeanor, physical condition during a mediation, as well as unspoken conduct. For example, if a party in mediation wore a Santa suit to the mediation but no one commented upon it, the party could be compelled to testify in a subsequent proceeding that he wore the Santa suit. Similarly, a party to a personal injury lawsuit who appeared in court with a noticeable limp would not be able to use the privilege to block the admission of testimony that he did not limp at the mediation proceeding, unless there was comment upon it. This is because a privilege generally protects only communications, not conduct or other verifiable facts that can be observed outside of the context of the privileged communications.

With few exceptions, this understanding is consistent with the general law of privileged communications, and is also the position adopted by the Uniform Mediation Act. *See* Unif. Mediation Act § 2(2), and related comments. But is it appropriate for mediation? Recall that it was the mediator's observation evidence — his impressions of Mrs. Olam's demeanor, participation, and competency — that Judge Brazil felt he needed most in order to be able to rule on her claim that the MOU should not be enforced because she did not really participate in the mediation and was incompetent to do so at the time. What are the arguments for and against excluding such mediation evidence from the privilege?

6. Consider the posture of the *Olam* case with an eye toward ethics. Mrs. Olam's original claim was brought to Judge Brazil, who in turn appointed a mediator, the court's ADR program administrator, who works closely with Brazil in that capacity. Should Brazil have decided the question of whether the mediator should be compelled to testify? Should he have recused himself?

D. SELECTING, REJECTING, OR MODIFYING MEDIATION: FAIRNESS, SELF–DETERMI-NATION, AND FORMALITY

The question of whether to use mediation in a given case or category of cases is important and complex; although we have referred to it repeatedly in this Chapter, we defer it mainly to Chapter VII, infra. In this section, however, we address one of the controversial issues that arises in this connection: the extent to which mediation threatens or promotes fairness to less powerful individuals or groups or to important public interests.

This issue arises most strikingly in so-called mandatory mediation, that is, where a court orders parties in a particular case or category of cases to mediate. (We cover mandatory mediation — a common but controversial practice — along with other forms of mandatory dispute resolution in Chapter VI, beginning at page 695.) On one hand, mediation has been widely touted for its informality and the possibilities it can offer the parties for self-determination, including the ability to uncover and address their real interests (in addition to their positions, which is the focus of litigation). On the other had, some argue that mediation is less able to protect the less powerful, because it typically lacks at least some of the formal protections associated with court — such as a neutral decision-maker and the ability to invoke and even establish legal entitlements and set public policy.

Recall the great settlement debate excerpted in Chapter I, beginning at page 21. Professor Fiss argued that, as a society we should not encourage settlement of lawsuits because it often deprives the parties of "justice." In response, however, Professors McThenia and Shaffer maintained that justice is not necessarily what people get from courts, but "what we discover — you and I, Socrates said — when we walk together, listen together, and even love one another, in our curiosity about what justice is and where justice comes from." Andrew W. McThenia & Thomas L. Shaffer, *For Reconciliation*, 94 Yale L. J. 1660, 1665 (1985). This debate was prompted in part by different policy goals, of course, but the two sides also have different ideas about the meaning and source of justice. And more important for our purposes, they have different ideas about what mediation actually is. This should not be surprising, for as we have seen frequently in this chapter, mediation comes in a bewildering array of forms.

Commentators have maintained that mediation is not well-suited for certain kinds of people (e.g., women, minorities, or members of other less powerful groups) or for particular kinds of cases (such as divorce, civil rights, environmental, or other public policy cases). These arguments — as well as the counter-arguments — assume the primacy of certain values. They also assume that mediation has certain relatively fixed characteristics, an assumption that is necessarily wrong much of the time. In this section, we showcase the issue of how to address the fairness issue with respect to mediation.

The underlying question is how to address the potential for unfairness or other risks posed by mediation. There are two basic answers: (1) to discourage or forbid the use of mediation by certain kinds of people or in certain kinds of cases; or (2) to customize mediation so as to lessen or eliminate the risks. We see many examples of the first category in court-connected mediation programs. Courts can allow parties to opt out without cause, or may exclude categories of cases, such as those involving civil rights claims. In addition, the court could refuse to enforce an agreement made in mediation, based on coercion or other reasons that could serve as the basis for rescinding any contract.

Outside the court-ordered mediation context, parties only mediate by agreement, so they can avoid mediation simply by not agreeing to mediate. However, it is common to have mediation agreements in contracts, and these agreements could cover a variety of terms, such as how to choose the mediator and what procedures to follow. Courts typically enforce such agreements. *See* Sarah Cole, Nancy H. Rogers & Craig A. McEwen, Mediation: Law, Policy, and Practice Sections §§ 8.1–8.4 (2d ed. 2001).

This section focuses most heavily on the second type of response to the problem of what to do about risks posed by mediation: design the mediation process in order to address its potentially undesirable aspects or outcomes. It begins with an article by Professor Nancy Welsh, who argues that in court-connected mediations, the parties' self-determination is severely limited and recommends a series of measures for addressing this problem. The next two excerpts — by Professors Richard Delgado and Michele Hermann and their colleagues — at one level seem to argue that that mediation is appropriate only where disputants are equally powerful and knowledgeable. However, both articles suggest ways in which mediation can be modified to reduce the risks of unfairness. Then, Professor Trina Grillo cautions about the risks associated with a certain form of mandatory child custody mediation, and Professor Joshua Rosenberg attacks her argument, although each of them may have in mind a different form of mediation. In the final excerpt, Professors McEwen, Rogers, and Maiman argue that many of the risks of divorce mediation can be cured by including lawyers.

NANCY A. WELSH, THE THINNING VISION OF SELF–DETERMINATION IN COURT–CONNECTED MEDIATION: THE INEVITABLE PRICE OF INSTITUTIONALIZATION?

6 Harv. Negot. L. Rev. 1, 3–7 (2001).

Ethical codes for mediators describe party self-determination as "the fundamental principle of mediation," regardless of the context within which the mediation is occurring. But what exactly does "party self-determination" mean? Does it mean the same thing now in the context of court-connected mediation as it did when it inspired many people to become involved in the "contemporary mediation movement" that arose in the 1970s and early 1980s? Most importantly, if the meaning of this "fundamental" term is changing as mediation adapts to its home in the courthouse, does it matter?

Based on a review of the debate surrounding recently promulgated or revised ethical codes for court-connected mediators in Florida and Minnesota, this Article will demonstrate that the originally dominant vision of self-determination, which borrowed heavily from concepts of party empowerment, is yielding to a different vision in the court-connected context. Perhaps not surprisingly, this vision is more consistent with the culture of the courts.

Believers in the originally dominant vision of self-determination assumed that the disputing parties would be the principal actors and creators within the mediation process. The parties would: 1) actively and directly participate in the communication and negotiation that occurs during mediation, 2) choose and control the substantive norms to guide their decision-making, 3) create the options for settlement, and 4) control the final decision regarding whether or not to settle. The mediator's role was to enable the parties' will to emerge and thus support their exercise of self-determination. Many mediation advocates continue to adhere to this vision.

However, as mediation has been institutionalized in the courts and as evaluation has become an acknowledged and accepted part of the mediator's function, the original vision of self-determination is giving way to a vision in which the disputing parties play a less central role. The parties are still responsible for making the final decision regarding settlement, but they are cast in the role of consumers, largely limited to selecting from among the settlement options developed by their attorneys. Indeed, it is the parties' attorneys, often aided by mediators who are also attorneys, who assume responsibility for actively and directly participating in the mediation process, invoking the substantive (i.e., legal) norms to be applied and creating settlement options. Thus, even as most mediators and many courts continue to name party self-determination as the "fundamental principle" underlying court-connected mediation, the party-centered empowerment concepts that anchored the original vision of self-determination are being replaced with concepts that are more reflective of the norms and traditional practices of lawyers and judges, as well as the courts' strong orientation to efficiency and closure of cases through settlement.

It can be argued that this thinning of the vision of self-determination does not matter. After all, even in its reduced form, self-determination still promises that the mediator will respect, support, and protect the parties' control over the final decision regarding settlement. Unfortunately, however, a disconnect is surfacing between even this more limited promise and the reality of court-connected mediation.

It is quite clear that court-connected mediators are providing evaluations of the parties' positions (e.g., estimates of the strengths and weaknesses of the parties' cases, suggestions regarding settlement options, etc.). When offered in the context of a party-centered, facilitative mediation, evaluation can serve a useful educational function and can aid party self-determination by assisting the parties in making informed decisions. There is growing evidence, however, that at least some court-connected mediators are engaging in very aggressive evaluations of parties' cases and settlement options (i.e., "muscle mediation") with the goal of winning a settlement, rather than supporting parties in their exercise of self-determination. As mediation has become increasingly institutionalized in the courts, a small but growing number of disputants have approached courts and ethical boards, claiming that mediators' aggressive evaluation or advocacy for particular settlements actually coerced them into a settlement.

In response to this challenge to party self-determination, ethical boards in some states have established mechanisms intended to keep evaluative mediation in check. Specifically, Florida and Minnesota, while permitting mediator evaluation in their ethical guidelines, have incorporated safeguards that pronounce party self-determination as the paramount goal of mediators and clearly prohibit coercion by the mediator.

These mechanisms are unlikely to be effective in taming mediator evaluation and in protecting even the narrowed vision of party self-determination. Despite the aspirational language and the good intentions underlying Florida's and Minnesota's ethical guidelines, the narrowed vision of party self-determination that is now institutionalized in these guidelines will be understood as no different than the free will which is to be exercised by parties involved in judicially-hosted settlement conferences. In that context, when parties have alleged that the judge or magistrate presiding over their settlement conference coerced them into reaching a settlement agreement by evaluating the parties' cases or urging a particular settlement, the courts have generally refused to find coercion unless the judge or magistrate engaged in outright threats or issued sanctions. Indeed, one court has written, "We do not agree that a judge should refrain from offering his or her assessment of a case on the eve of trial, solely to avoid the appearance of impropriety. Such a policy would effectively render meaningless a judge's role in the settlement process." It is unlikely that the courts or ethical boards responsible for interpreting and enforcing mediators' ethical guidelines will judge aggressive evaluation as coercive just because it occurred within the context of a mediation rather than in a judicially-hosted settlement conference, especially if the vision of party self-determination in mediation is no longer anchored in the concept of party empowerment.

This Article examines possible means to protect parties' self-determination in mediation and advocates for a particular solution. Specifically, the proposal suggests modifying the current presumptions regarding the finality of mediated settlement agreements and urges the adoption of a three-day, non-waivable cooling-off period before mediated settlement agreements may become enforceable. This modification would permit the continued use of evaluative techniques as a means to educate parties and inform their decision-making while rewarding the use of techniques (often facilitative) that increase parties' commitment to their settlement. The more committed parties are to their settlement, the less likely it is that they will withdraw from the settlement during the cooling-off period. Ultimately, this proposal has the potential to keep "muscle mediation" in check while also allowing the return to a vision of self-determination which is closer to that which first dominated (and inspired) the contemporary mediation movement.

Notes and Questions

1. In order to address concerns about self-determination, Professor Welsh makes several proposals. The first would seek to "clarify the definition of self-determination":

> In response to the concern that the original rich vision of self-determination is being lost, there may be a need to clarify the definition of self-determination in statutes, rules and ethical guidelines. It must be made clear that self-determination is different than parties' free will and requires more protection than parties' free will has received in traditional negotiation or in judicially-hosted settlement conferences. Specifically,

statutes, rules, and ethical guidelines regarding self-determination could be rewritten to include: the parties' active and direct participation, communication, and negotiation; the parties' identification and selection of the interests and substantive norms which should guide the creation of settlement options; the parties' creation of potential settlement options; and the parties' control over the final outcome. In other words, the definitions should reference the indicia of party empowerment.

Welsh, *supra* at 80.

Do you think such a provisions are likely to affect actual practices?

2. If the Minnesota rules had been in force in Australia, would the behavior of the mediator in the *Tapoohi* case, beginning at page 386, have been influenced by this provision: "A mediator shall not require a party to stay in the mediation against the party's will"?

Professor Welsh also recommends, among other things, education of mediators and the public, changing the presumption against coercion, focusing on undue influence rather than coercion, and the implementation of a three-day "cooling-off" period. *Id.* at 23–26. To what extent do you think the imposition of any of these requirements would be helpful?

3. Professor Welsh's concept of self-determination is consistent with larger concepts of more democratic dispute resolution methods and processes. Personal autonomy is a central value of democratic governance and civil society, and when fostered in a dispute resolution method, as generally in mediation, helps to legitimize that method. Would this help explain why mediation, even court-ordered mediation, has proven satisfying for participants in terms of both process and outcome? *See* Richard C. Reuben, *Democracy and Dispute Resolution: The Problem of Arbitration,* 67 Law & Contemp. Probs. 279 (2004).

RICHARD DELGADO, CHRIS DUNN, PAMELA BROWN, HELENA LEE & DAVID HUBBERT, FAIRNESS AND FORMALITY: MINIMIZING THE RISK OF PREJUDICE IN ALTERNATIVE DISPUTE RESOLUTION

1985 Wis. L. Rev. 1359, 1387–91, 1400–04.

E. *The Optimal Setting for the Reduction of Prejudice: Formal vs. Informal Dispute Resolution*

The selection of one mode or another of dispute resolution can do little, at least in the short run, to counter prejudice that stems from authoritarian personalities or historical currents. Prejudice that results from social-psychological factors is, however, relatively controllable. Much prejudice is environmental — people express it because the setting encourages or tolerates it. In some settings people feel free to vent hostile or denigrating attitudes toward members of minority groups; in others they do not.

Our review of social-psychological theories of prejudice indicates that prejudiced persons are least likely to act on their beliefs if the immediate environment confronts them with the discrepancy between their professed ideals and their personal hostilities against out-groups. According to social psychologists, once most persons realize that their attitudes and behavior deviate from what is expected, they will change or suppress them.

Given this human tendency to conform, American institutions have structured and defined situations to encourage appropriate behavior. Our judicial system, in particular, has incorporated societal norms of fairness and even-handedness into institutional expectations and rules of procedure at many points. These norms create a "public conscience and a standard for expected behavior that check *overt* signs of prejudice."[120] They do this in a variety of ways. First, the formalities of a court trial — the flag, the black robes, the ritual — remind those present that the occasion calls for the higher, "public" values, rather than the lesser values embraced during moments of informality and intimacy. In a courtroom trial the American Creed, with its emphasis on fairness, equality, and respect for personhood, governs. Equality of status, or something approaching it, is preserved — each party is represented by an attorney and has a prescribed time and manner for speaking, putting on evidence, and questioning the other side. Equally important, formal adjudication avoids the unstructured, intimate interactions that, according to social scientists, foster prejudice. The rules of procedure maintain distance between the parties. Counsel for the parties do not address one another, but present the issue to the trier of fact. The rules preserve the formality of the setting by dictating in detail how this confrontation is to be conducted.

That the formality of adversarial adjudication deters prejudice is borne out by the few empirical studies that have investigated the question. An experiment conducted by Walker and his colleagues showed that subjects viewed adversarial procedures as "the most preferable and the fairest mode of dispute resolution,"[121] a preference that may even extend to persons in countries that do not use an adversarial system of justice. Another experiment placed subjects in a laboratory setting behind a "veil of ignorance" and asked them to choose among a variety of procedural alternatives. Almost all the subjects chose the adversarial system. The authors concluded that the adversary system introduces a systematic evidentiary bias in favor of the weaker party.

Another experiment showed that the "competitive presentation of evidence counteracts decisionmaker bias ..."[227] In one experiment, subjects were presented with a test case; they were given a list of both "lawful" and "unlawful" factors, but were told to consider only the "lawful" ones in making a decision. The results showed that in a simulated adversarial framework, even those subjects predetermined to be biased gave less weight to unlawful factors in their decisionmaking.

120. G. ALLPORT, THE NATURE OF PREJUDICE 7, 470 (25th Anniv.Ed.1979).

121. Thibaut, Walker, LaTour & Houlden, *Procedural Justice as Fairness*, 26 STAN. L.REV. 1271, 1288 (1974).

227. Thibaut, Walker & Lind, *Adversary Presentation & Bias in Legal Decisionmaking*, 86 HARV.L.REV. 386, 401 (1972).

The authors hypothesized that adversarial procedure counteracts decisionmaker bias because it combats the natural human tendency to "judge too swiftly in terms of the familiar that which is not yet fully known."[230] The human propensity to prejudge and make irrational categorizations is thus checked by procedural safeguards found in an adversarial system.

Formality and adversarial procedures thus counteract bias among legal decisionmakers and disputants. But it seems likely that those factors increase fairness in yet a third way — by strengthening the resolve of minority disputants to pursue their legal rights.

F. DISPUTE RESOLUTION AND THE MINORITY DISPUTANT

Early in life, minority children become aware of themselves as different, especially with respect to skin color. This awareness is often not merely neutral, but associated with feelings of inferiority. Separate studies by psychologists Kenneth Clark and Mary Goodman in which minority children were presented with dolls of various colors illustrate this graphically. For example, when asked to make a choice between a white and black doll, "the doll that looks like you," most black children chose the white doll. A black child justified his choice of the white doll over the black doll as friend because "his feet, hands, ears, elbows, knees, and hair are clean."[235] In another experiment, a black child hated her skin color so much that she "vigorously lathered her arms and face with soap in an effort to wash away the dirt."[236] As minority children grow, they are "likely to experience a long series of events, from exclusion from play groups and cliques to violence and threats of violence, that are far less likely to be experienced by the average member of the majority group."[237] Against a background of "slights, rebuffs, forbidden opportunities, restraints, and often violence ... the minority group member shapes that fundamental aspect of personality — a sense of oneself and one's place in the total scheme of things."[238]

Discriminatory treatment can trigger a variety of responses. Writers identify three main reactions: avoidance, aggression, and acceptance. A minority group member may display one or more of these responses, depending on the setting. In some situations, victims of discrimination are likely to respond with apathy or defeatism; in others, the same individuals may forthrightly and effectively assert their interests. In general, when a person feels "he is the master of his fate, that he can control to some extent his own destiny, that if he works hard things will

---

230. *Id.* at 390, 401.

235. Clark & Clark, *Racial Identification and Preference in Negro Children*, in READINGS IN SOCIAL PSYCHOLOGY 602, 611 (E. Maccoby, T. Newcomb & E. Hartley, eds. 1958).

236. M. GOODMAN, RACE AWARENESS IN YOUNG CHILDREN 56 (rev. ed. 1964) (discussing and citing studies).

237. G. SIMPSON & J. YINGER, RACIAL AND CULTURAL MINORITIES: AN ANALYSIS OF PREJUDICE AND DISCRIMINATION 168 (4th ed. 1972).

238. *Id.* at 192.

go better for him, he is then likely to achieve more...."[242] That is, minority group members are more apt to participate in processes which they believe will respond to reasonable efforts. They are understandably less likely to participate in proceedings where the results are random and unpredictable.

Thus, it is not surprising that a favored forum for redress of race-based wrongs has been the traditional adjudicatory setting. Minorities recognize that public institutions, with their defined rules and formal structure, are more subject to rational control than private or informal structures. Informal settings allow wider scope for the participants' emotional and behavioral idiosyncrasies; in these settings majority group members are most likely to exhibit prejudicial behavior. Thus, a formal adjudicative forum increases the minority group member's sense of control and, therefore, may be seen as the fairer forum. This perception becomes self-fulfilling: minority persons are encouraged to pursue their legal rights as though prejudice were unlikely and thus the possibility of prejudice is in fact lessened.

IV. The Left Critique of ADR

Many commentators who have criticized ADR have expressed concerns associated with the "left" — concerns for the unempowered, the poor and other disadvantaged groups. This section canvasses the thoughts of these commentators, in particular objections that informalism (i) solidifies control by capital and the state; (ii) disadvantages "weaker" parties; (iii) expands state control; (iv) deflects energy away from collective action; and (v) promotes law without justice. As we shall see, the political critique of ADR, although based on different premises and couched in different terms, comes to the same general conclusion as the psychological critique: ADR is no safe haven for the poor and powerless.

* * *

ADR increases the risk of prejudice toward vulnerable disputants. Our review of social science writings on prejudice reveals that the rules and structures of formal justice tend to suppress bias, whereas informality tends to increase it. The social science findings are reinforced, on a sociopolitical level, by ADR's leftwing critics, who see ADR as increasing the power of authoritarian social institutions over individuals, extending state coercive power into new areas of citizens' lives, and discouraging collective action.

This Part assumes that the social-science and leftwing critiques are at least partly valid — that ADR does indeed increase the risk of unfair treatment for minority disputants, women and the poor. From this it proceeds to address two final questions: (i) How much weight should be

242. Grambs, *Negro Self–Concept Reappraised*, in Black Self-Concept: Implications For Education and Social Science 184 (J. Banks & J. Grambs, eds. 1972).

assigned to such a risk? and (ii) Can the risk be minimized without forfeiting the benefits and advantages of ADR?

A. The Ideal of Fairness in American Procedure

If ADR increases the risk of prejudice or bias in adjudication, it does not follow immediately that ADR should be curtailed. Equity concerns are only one value among many; conceivably, the gains in flexibility, speed, and economy that ADR's proponents cite could override moderate losses in fairness. A survey of the role of the ideal of fairness in American procedural law suggests, however, that the balance should be struck on the side of fairness.

American procedural law's history evidences a strong and steady evolution toward fairness, an evolution that has at times overshadowed the impulse toward economy and efficiency. Over a century ago, the Field code simplified pleading rules, largely to eliminate traps for the unwary and to render legal paper work intelligible to ordinary persons. The great procedural reforms of this century, civil discovery and long-arm jurisdiction, were likewise intended to equalize power and opportunity among litigants. Discovery enables litigants of modest means to learn facts about the dispute that might otherwise remain in the exclusive possession of the more powerful party. Long-arm jurisdiction enables citizens injured by corporations and other powerful entities to bring them to account where the injury occurred, instead of being forced to sue where the defendant is found.

Civil and criminal reforms have made access to court cheaper and more readily available to all. * * *

B. Striking the Balance: Protecting against Prejudice without Sacrificing the Benefits of ADR

ADR offers a number of clear-cut benefits. It can shape a decree flexibly so as to protect a continuing relationship between the parties. It is low-cost, speedy, and, for some at least, nonintimidating. Yet there is little benefit for a minority disputant in a quick, painless hearing that renders an adverse decision tainted by prejudice.

Part III showed that the risk of prejudice is greatest when a member of an in-group confronts a member of an out-group; when that confrontation is direct, rather than through intermediaries; when there are few rules to constrain conduct; when the setting is closed and does not make clear that "public" values are to preponderate; and when the controversy concerns an intimate, personal matter rather than some impersonal question. Our review also indicated that many minority participants will press their claims most vigorously when they believe that what they do and say will make a difference, that the structure will respond, and that the outcome is predictable and related to effort and merit.

It follows that ADR is most apt to incorporate prejudice when a person of low status and power confronts a person or institution of high status and power. In such situations, the party of high status is more likely than in other situations to attempt to call up prejudiced responses; at the same time, the individual of low status is less likely to press his or her claim energetically. The dangers increase when the mediator or other third party is a member of the superior group or class. Examples of ADR settings that may contain these characteristics are prison and other institutional review boards, consumer complaint panels, and certain types of cases referred to an ombudsman. In these situations, minorities and members of other out-groups should opt for formal in-court adjudication, and the justice system ought to avoid pressuring them to accept an alternate procedure. ADR should be reserved for cases in which parties of comparable power and status confront each other.

ADR also poses heightened risks of prejudice when the issue to be adjudicated touches a sensitive or intimate area of life, for example, housing or culture-based conduct. Thus, many landlord-tenant, inter-neighbor, and intrafamilial disputes are poor candidates for ADR. When the parties are of unequal status and the question litigated concerns a sensitive, intimate area, the risks of an outcome colored by prejudice are especially great. If, for reasons of economy or efficiency ADR must be resorted to in these situations, the likelihood of bias can be reduced by providing rules that clearly specify the scope of the proceedings and forbid irrelevant or intrusive inquiries, by requiring open proceedings, and by providing some form of higher review. The third-party facilitator or decisionmaker should be a professional and be acceptable to both parties. Any party desiring one should be provided with an advocate, ideally an attorney, experienced with representation before the forum in question. To avoid atomization and lost opportunities to aggregate claims and inject public values into dispute resolution, ADR mechanisms should not be used in cases that have a broad societal dimension, but forward them to court for appropriate treatment.

Would measures like these destroy the very advantages of economy, simplicity, speed, and flexibility that make ADR attractive? Would such measures render ADR proceedings as expensive, time-consuming, formalistic, and inflexible as trials? These measures do increase the costs, but, on balance, those costs seem worth incurring. The ideal of equality before the law is too insistent a value to be compromised in the name of more mundane advantages. Continued growth of ADR consistent with goals of basic fairness will require two essential adjustments: (1) It will be necessary to identify those areas and types of ADR in which the dangers of prejudice are greatest and to direct those grievances to formal court adjudication; (2) In those areas in which the risk of prejudice exists, but is not so great as to require an absolute ban, checks and formalities must be built into ADR to ameliorate these risks as much as possible. With both inquiries, the preliminary investigations and tentative identifications of troublesome areas made in this Article may prove useful starting points.

MICHELE HERMANN ET AL., METROCOURT PROJECT FINAL REPORT: A STUDY OF THE EFFECTS OF ETHNICITY AND GENDER IN MEDIATED AND ADJUDICATED CASES AT THE METROPOLITAN COURT MEDIATION CENTER

viii-xii (1993).

INTRODUCTION

This study was funded by the Fund for Research in Dispute Resolution to examine how women and minorities fared in mediated and adjudicated small claims civil cases in Albuquerque, New Mexico. The research hypotheses that we examined were:

(1) Whether women and minorities achieve worse results than males and non-minorities in both adjudicated and mediated small claims cases,

(2) Whether that disparity is greater in mediated than in adjudicated cases, and

(3) Whether that disparity is reduced or eliminated when the mediators are women and/or minorities.

These hypotheses were suggested by theoretical writings postulating that informal, flexible, private settings of alternative dispute resolution processes such as mediation are more susceptible to bias and prejudice which impacts disproportionately on ethnic minorities and women.

BACKGROUND

The study was conducted in the Bernalillo County Metropolitan Court, a non-record court which has jurisdiction to hear civil cases where the amount in controversy is $5,000 or less. The court has 3 judges in the civil division who hear a total caseload of approximately 9,000 cases per year. All three judges are male; one is African American, one Hispanic, and one Caucasian. The court contracts with the Albuquerque Mediation Center to administer and operate the court's mediation program.

With the cooperation of the court and the Mediation Center, civil cases were randomly assigned to either adjudication or mediation and followed by the study. The total final sample was 603 cases, 323 of which were adjudicated and 280 of which were mediated. Cases were co-mediated by a pool of mediators who were combined in all-female, all-male, or mixed gender pairs, and all-minority, all-white, or mixed ethnicity pairs.

Telephone interviews were conducted with parties in both mediated and adjudicated cases as soon as possible after the hearing or mediation. A follow-up questionnaire was mailed approximately six months after the initial interview. Parties who did not respond to the follow-up mailings were called on the telephone. A number of mediation sessions and adjudicated hearings also were observed by study researchers.

We sought to evaluate results in mediation and adjudication using two measures: (1) the objective formula for outcome developed by Vidmar, and (2) subjective measures of satisfaction. Vidmar's objective measure defines monetary outcome as the ratio of the final award minus admitted liability divided by the amount claimed minus admitted liability.

RESULTS

As measured by the objective Vidmar outcome ratio, minority claimants consistently received less money than non-minorities in our study cases, while minority respondents consistently paid more. These disparate results were more extreme in mediated than in adjudicated cases. Statistical analysis of the adjudicated cases showed that monetary outcomes were due primarily to case characteristics and secondarily to the ethnicity of the participants, with strong inter-relationships between the two. In mediated cases, however, ethnicity remained significantly more important for predicting outcome, even with the addition of case characteristic variables.

Having found that minority claimants received less and minority respondents paid more in mediated cases, we then explored whether these effects were counteracted by the ethnicity of the mediators. Our results were quite startling, showing that having two minority mediators eliminated the negative impact on the size of monetary outcomes for minorities in mediation. The combination of one minority mediator and one white mediator, however, did not produce a similar result.

The negative outcomes found for minority participants were not replicated when the data were analyzed for gender. Neither the gender of the claimant nor that of the respondent had an effect on monetary outcomes in either adjudicated or mediated cases. The only statistically reliable tendency we found was for female respondents to pay less in mediated than in adjudicated cases, i.e., to do better than males in mediation.

Our examination of subjective outcome and procedural satisfaction produced interesting contrasts to the objective outcome analysis. Despite their tendency to achieve lower monetary awards as claimants and to pay more as respondents, minority claimants were more likely than non-minority claimants to express satisfaction with mediation. Minority claimants and respondents consistently were more positive about mediation than they were about adjudication on all satisfaction and fairness measures. They also reported process satisfaction significantly more often than non-minorities in mediation.

Minority claimants were most satisfied with the mediation process when the two mediators were also minorities. In fact, white as well as minority claimants were more likely to report procedural satisfaction when the mediation involved a minority respondent and two minority mediators.

Looking at satisfaction levels of women, we found very different responses. As both claimants and respondents, compared to all other ethnic/gender groups, white women reported greater satisfaction with adjudicated rather than mediated outcomes. While white female respondents achieved significantly more favorable outcomes in mediation than the other three groups, they actually reported the lowest levels of satisfaction. Furthermore, compared to other mediation respondents, white women were less likely to see the mediation process as fair and unbiased. Minority women, on the other hand, reported the highest level of satisfaction with mediation, despite their tendency to receive less as claimants and to pay more as respondents.

CONCLUSION

The evidence that minority participants generally fare worse than whites in both mediation and adjudication, and that these effects are most severe in mediation, although they are coupled with higher levels of satisfaction in that forum, raises numerous questions concerning cause and implications. While the temptation is to jump to conclusions about bias, prejudice and cultural blindness, the underlying effects may be considerably more complex and should be the subject of further study, analysis and reflection. Similarly, the fact that women fare well in mediation in small claims court does not dispel the concerns about gender bias in mediation in other forums, such as family court in the context of marital dissolution. More study and analysis is required as well to understand the broader implications of gender differences in mediation. Such study also needs to examine the preference which women expressed for adjudication over mediation, and the disproportionate level of dissatisfaction with the mediation process which we found among white females.

Notes and Questions

1.   Does the analysis in the study by Professor Michele Hermann and her colleagues suggest that we can reduce or eliminate concerns about mediation's potential risks for members of minority groups by using a co-mediation model and making sure that one or both of the mediators are also a member of a minority group? Do you suppose that would always be feasible or appropriate? Would it present other problems?

2.   The New Mexico study concluded that minority women found mediation more satisfying than adjudication even though they seemed to do worse financially. Some would explain that finding by suggesting that these women were deceived. Can you think of other explanations? Professor Laura Nader suggests, for example, that ADR values harmony over justice, and tends to pacify the discontented rather than help them assert or enforce rights they may have. *See* Laura Nader, *Controlling Processes in the Practice of Law: Hierarchy and Pacification in the Movement to Re–Form Dispute Ideology,* 9 Ohio St. J. on Disp. Resol. 1 (1993).

3.   Professor Emily Calhoun recently proposed a variation in mediation procedure for cases involving allegations of individual employment discrimi-

nation. She suggests the use of a "first-phase" private caucus with plaintiffs in such cases as a way to make it likely that the mediation will include an awareness of the interests of the plaintiff's minority group and of the plaintiff's relationships with that group as well as the plaintiff's relationship with the workplace community. In addition, she argues that cultivation of "group presence" in such cases would enhance the plaintiff's prospects of self-determination and would foster improved problem-solving. Emily M. Calhoun, *Workplace Mediation: The First–Phase, Private Caucus in Individual Discrimination Disputes,* 9 Harv. Negot. L. Rev. 187 (2004). Thus, she urges that "mediators and civil rights advocates should take seriously the group presence in an individual discrimination dispute and take appropriate advantage of the opportunities offered by first-phase caucuses to work with that presence." *Id.* at 219. Would implementation of that proposal ameliorate some of the concerns expressed in the foregoing excerpts by Professor Delgado and his colleagues and by Professor Hermann and her colleagues?

4. For further related reading, see Isabelle R. Gunning, *Diversity Issues in Mediation: Controlling Negative Cultural Myths,* 1995 J. Disp. Resol. 55. For an overview of critical scholarship on ADR, see Eric K. Yamamoto, *ADR: Where have All the Critics Gone?,* 36 Santa Clara L. Rev. 1055 (1996).

TRINA GRILLO, THE MEDIATION ALTERNATIVE: PROCESS DANGERS FOR WOMEN

100 Yale L.J. 1545, 1549–50, 1600–08, 1610 (1991).

[California is one of numerous states that require mediation of disputed child custody issues in divorce cases. CAL. CIV. CODE § 4607(a) (West Supp.1990). In this excerpt, Professor Trina Grillo — at the time of this writing an active family mediator handling private, voluntary cases — criticizes California's mandatory system, which often excludes lawyers from the mediation sessions.]

[Custody mediation under the California system] provides neither a more just nor a more humane alternative to the adversarial system of adjudication of custody, and, therefore, does not fulfill its promises. In particular * * * mandatory mediation can be destructive to many women and some men because it requires them to speak in a setting they have not chosen and often imposes a rigid orthodoxy as to how they should speak, make decisions, and be. This orthodoxy is imposed through subtle and not-so-subtle messages about appropriate conduct and about what may be said in mediation. It is an orthodoxy that often excludes the possibility of the parties speaking with their authentic voices.

* * *

III. MANDATORY MEDIATION AND THE DANGERS OF FORCED ENGAGEMENT

Emma has been in a marriage which in its early years seemed to be a good one for both Emma and her husband. She has been the primary caretaker of the children, and she is very committed to them. She has lived much of her life through her husband and her children, and has not worked outside her home. Increasingly, however, she has begun to feel that she and her husband have grown apart, and that he does not see her as a person but rather as a repository of various roles. After much agony, she has decided to end her marriage. Her departure from the marriage is a first step toward seeing her life as having separate dimensions from her husband's and children's, but her right to individuation does not seem clear to her; in fact, there are many times when it seems selfish and wrong. It is hard for her even to find the language to describe what is propelling her to turn her life, and her children's lives, upside down, but propelling she is. The marital separation was an early step toward defining her own physical and psychological boundaries. She now finds herself, however, feeling guilty, frightened, and unsure of how she will survive in the world alone.

Joan has been in a marriage in which she has been physically abused for ten years. She and her husband David have two children, whom David has never abused. She is afraid, however, that if she leaves David, he will begin to abuse the children whenever he is caring for them. Joan has been afraid to leave her marriage because David has threatened to harm her if she does so. When she separated briefly from him previously, he followed her and continually harassed her. Each time David beats Joan he shows great remorse afterwards and promises never to do it again. He is a man of considerable charm, and she has often believed him on these occasions. Nonetheless, Joan has finally decided to leave her husband. She is worried about what will happen, economically and physically, to her children and herself.

It might be that mediation would help Emma's family disengage and discover ways of relating to one another. Mediation could be useful, even transformative, during the divorce process. Significant possibilities of damage to Emma also exist, however. For example, she might find herself traumatized by a forced engagement with her husband. Or, in the intimate mediation setting, she might find it difficult to withstand criticism of how she is conducting herself in life or in the mediation.

For Joan, the direct confrontation with her husband, with the safety of her children and herself at stake, would surely be psychologically traumatizing and might also put her in physical danger. Because of these possibilities, the chance — even the substantial one — of a beneficial result cannot justify the sort of intrusion by the state that occurs when mediation is mandatory.

While some of mandatory mediation's dangers affect men and women equally, others fall disproportionately on women. A study that compared people who chose to mediate with those who rejected the opportunity found that 44% of the reasons given by women who rejected mediation services offered to them center around their mistrust of, fear of, or desire to avoid their ex-spouse. In contrast, those men who rejected mediation appeared to do so because they were skeptical of the mediation process or convinced they could win in court. Thus, the requirement of mandatory mediation that the parties meet personally with one another, usually without a lawyer present, presents troubling issues for women. Feminist analyses, looked at alone and together, clarify why this is so.

A.   The Ethic of Care in Mediation

As discussed earlier, several feminist scholars have suggested that women have a more "relational" sense of self than do men. The most influential of these researchers, Carol Gilligan, describes two different, gendered modes of thought. The female mode is characterized by an "ethic of care" which emphasizes nurturance, connection with others, and contextual thinking. The male mode is characterized by an "ethic of justice" which emphasizes individualism, the use of rules to resolve moral dilemmas, and equality. Under Gilligan's view, the male mode leads one to strive for individualism and autonomy, while the female mode leads one to strive for connection with and caring for others. Some writers, seeing a positive virtue in the ethic of care, have applied Gilligan's work to the legal system. * * *

The "ethic of care" has also been viewed as the manifestation of a system of gender domination. Nevertheless, it is clear that those who operate in a "female mode" — whether biologically male or female — will respond more "selflessly" to the demands of mediation.

Whether the ethic of care is to be enshrined as a positive virtue, or criticized as a characteristic not belonging to all women and contributing to their oppression, one truth emerges: many women see themselves, and judge their own worth, primarily in terms of relationships. This perspective on themselves has consequences for how they function in mediation.

Carrie Menkel–Meadow has suggested that the ethic of care can and should be brought into the practice of law — that the world of lawyering would look very different from the perspective of that ethic. Some commentators have identified mediation as a way to incorporate the ethic of care into the legal system and thereby modify the harshness of the adversary process. And, indeed, at first glance, mediation in the context of divorce might be seen as a way of bringing the woman-identified values of intimacy, nurturance, and care into a legal system that is concerned with the most fundamental aspects of women's and men's lives.

If mediation does not successfully introduce an ethic of care, however, but instead merely sells itself on that promise while delivering something coercive in its place, the consequences will be disastrous for a woman who embraces a relational sense of self. If she is easily persuaded to be cooperative, but her partner is not, she can only lose. If it is indeed her disposition to be caring and focused on relationships, and she has been rewarded for that focus and characterized as "unfeminine" when she departs from it, the language of relationship, caring, and cooperation will be appealing to her and make her vulnerable. Moreover, the intimation that she is not being cooperative and caring, that she is thinking of herself instead of thinking selflessly of the children can shatter self-esteem and make her lose faith in herself. In short, in mediation, such a woman may be encouraged to repeat exactly those behaviors that have proven hazardous to her in the past.

In the story above, Emma is asked to undergo a forced engagement with the very person from whom she is trying to differentiate herself at a difficult stage in her life. She may find it impossible to think of herself as a separate entity during mediation, while her husband may easily be able to act on behalf of his separate self. "When a separate self must be asserted, women have trouble asserting it. Women's separation from the other in adult life, and the tension between that separation and our fundamental state of connection, is felt most acutely when a woman must make choices, and when she must speak the truth."[122]

Emma will be asked to talk about her needs and feelings, and respond to her husband's needs and feelings. Although in the past her valuing relationships above all else may have worked to the detriment of her separate self, Emma will now be urged to work on the future relationship between herself and her ex-husband. Above all, she will be asked to put the well-being of the children before her own, as if she and her children's well-being were entirely separate. Her problem in addressing her future alone, however, may be that she reflexively puts her children before herself, even when she truly needs to take care of herself in order to take care of her children. For Emma, mediation may play on what are already her vulnerable spots, and put her at a disadvantage. She may begin to think of herself as unfeminine, or simply bad, if she puts her own needs forward. Emma may feel the need to couch every proposal she makes in terms of the needs of her children. In sum, if she articulates her needs accurately, she may end up feeling guilty, selfish, confused, and embarrassed; if she does not, she will be moving backwards to the unbounded self that is at the source of her difficulties.

For Joan, the prescription of mediation might be disastrous. She has always been susceptible to her husband's charm, and has believed him when he has said that he would stop abusing her. She has always been afraid of him. She is likely, in mediation, to be susceptible and afraid once again. She may continue to care for her husband, and to think that she was responsible for his behavior toward her. Joan, and not her husband, will be susceptible to any pressure to compromise, and to compromise in her situation might be very dangerous for both her and her children.

B.   Sexual Domination and Judicial Violence

Women who have been through mandatory mediation often describe it as an experience of sexual domination, comparing mandatory mediation to rape. Catharine MacKinnon's work provides a basis for explaining why, for some women, this characterization is appropriate. MacKinnon has analyzed gender as a system of power relations, evidenced

---

122. West, *Jurisprudence and Gender*, 55 U.Chi.L.Rev. 1, 55 (1988).

primarily with respect to the control of women's sexuality. While Mac-Kinnon recognizes the sense in which women are fundamentally connected to others, she does not celebrate it. Rather, she sees the potential for connection as invasive and intrusive. It is precisely the potential for physical connection that permits invasion into the integrity of women's bodies. It is precisely the potential for emotional connection that permits intrusion into the integrity of women's lives.

Men do not experience this same fear of sexual domination, according to MacKinnon; they do not live in constant fear of having the very integrity of their lives intruded upon. Men may not comprehend their role in this system of sexual domination any more than women may be able to articulate the source of their feeling of disempowerment. Yet both of these dynamics are at work in the mediation setting. It may seem a large leap, from acts of physical violence and invasion to the apparently simple requirement that a woman sit in a room with her spouse working toward the resolution of an issue of mutual concern. But that which may be at stake in a court-ordered custody mediation — access to one's children — may be the main reason one has for living, as well as all one's hope for the future. And because mandatory mediation is a *forced* engagement, ordinarily without attorneys or even friends or supporters present, it may amount to a form of "psychic breaking and entering" or, put another way, psychic rape.

There is always the potential for violence in the legal system: "a judge articulates her understanding of a text, and as a result, somebody loses his freedom, his property, his children, even his life ... When interpreters have finished their work, they frequently leave behind victims whose lives have been torn apart by these organized, social practices of violence." [123]

The reality of this background of judicial violence cannot be discounted when measuring the potential trauma of the mandatory mediation setting. Although the mediation system is purportedly designed in part to help participants *avoid* contact with the violence that must come from judicial decisions, in significant ways the violence of the contact is more direct. Since the parties are obliged to speak for themselves in a setting to which the culture has not introduced them and in which the rules are not clear (and in fact vary from mediator to mediator), the potential violence of the legal result, combined with the invasiveness of the setting, may indeed end up feeling to the unwilling participant very much like a kind of rape. Moreover, in judging, it is understood that the critical view of the quarrel is that of the judge, the professional third party. Mediation is described as a form of intervention that reflects the *disputants'* view of the quarrel. But having the mediation take place on court premises with a mediator who might or might not inject her prejudices into the process may make it unlikely that the disputants' view will control. Thus, a further sense of violation may arise from

123. Cover, *Violence and the Word*, 95 YALE L.J. 1601, 1601 (1986).

having another person's view of the dispute characterized and treated as one's own.

That many reportedly find mediation helpful does not mean everyone does. Consensual sex may take place in a certain setting in one instance but that does not make all sex in that setting consensual; sometimes it is rape. And sometimes it may only seem to be consensual because forced sex is considered par for the course — that is, it is all we know or can imagine.

When I have suggested to mediators that even being forced to sit across the table and negotiate, unassisted, with a spouse might be traumatic, their reaction has been almost uniformly dismissive. Some mediators have denied that this could possibly be the case. Even mediators who acknowledge the possibility of trauma have said, in effect, "So what?" A few hours of discomfort seems not so much to ask in return for a system that, to their mind, serves the courts and the children much better than the alternative. But a few hours of discomfort may not be all that is at stake; the trauma inflicted upon a vulnerable party during mediation can be as great as that which occurs in other psychologically violent confrontations. As such, it should not be minimized. People frequently take months or years to recover from physical or mental abuse, rape, and other traumatic events. Given the psychological vulnerability of people at the time of a divorce, it is likely that some people may be similarly debilitated by a mandatory mediation process.

Moreover, because the mandatory mediation system is more problematic for women than for men, forcing unwilling women to take part in a process which involves much personal exposure sends a powerful social message: it is permissible to discount the real experience of women in the service of someone else's idea of what will be good for them, good for their children, or good for the system.

IV.   ALTERNATIVES TO MANDATORY MEDIATION

* * *

With respect to institutional changes, an adequate mediation scheme should not only be voluntary rather than mandatory, but should also allow people's emotions to be part of the process, allow their values and principles to matter in the discussion, allow parties' attorneys to participate if requested by the parties, allow parties to choose a mediator and the location for the mediation, allow parties to choose the issues to mediate, and require that divorcing couples be educated about the availability and logistics of mediation so as to enable them to make an intelligent choice as to whether to engage in it.

The second aspect of reform represents more of a personal dynamic, one which is harder to institutionalize or to regulate. But the mediator must learn to respect each client's struggles, including her timing, anger, and resistance to having certain issues mediated, and also learn to refrain, to the extent he is capable, from imposing his own substantive agenda on the mediation.

CONCLUSION

Although mediation can be useful and empowering, it presents some serious process dangers that need to be addressed, rather than ignored. When mediation is imposed rather than voluntarily engaged in, its virtues are lost. More than lost: mediation becomes a wolf in sheep's clothing. It relies on force and disregards the context of the dispute, while masquerading as a gentler, more empowering alternative to adversarial litigation. Sadly, when mediation is mandatory it becomes like the patriarchal paradigm of law it is supposed to supplant. Seen in this light, mandatory mediation is especially harmful: its messages disproportionately affect those who are already subordinated in our society, those to whom society has already given the message, in far too many ways, that they are not leading proper lives.

Of course, subordinated people can go to court and lose; in fact, they usually do. But if mediation is to be introduced into the court system, it should provide a better alternative. It is not enough to say that the adversary system is so flawed that even a misguided, intrusive, and disempowering system of mediation should be embraced. If mediation as currently instituted constitutes a fundamentally flawed process in the way I have described, it is more, not less, disempowering than the adversary system — for it is then a process in which people are told they are being empowered, but in fact are being forced to acquiesce in their oppression.

———

Professor Joshua D. Rosenberg, a colleague of Professor Grillo's and formerly a mediator in a mandatory court mediation program in California, provides an extensive rebuttal to Grillo's argument. A short excerpt follows:

JOSHUA D. ROSENBERG, IN DEFENSE OF MEDIATION
33 Ariz. L. Rev. 467, 468–69, 492–500, 503–05 (1991).*

Professor Grillo's article paints a very effective and very dramatic picture of mediation as a misguided and destructive process. As both a teacher and a student of mediation, I have found that the process is supportive, empowering and enlightening to the participants. Helping parties to feel better about themselves and their interests is one of the most important and most valued of skills among mediators. Studies regularly show that people who go through mandatory mediation are pleased with the process.

How does my colleague's picture of mediation as a monster emerge? Professor Grillo's article distorts the mediation process in four ways: (1)

the article tells stories about mediation that are the equivalent of using a series of stories about physicians' rape of patients to paint a picture of the practice of medicine in this country; (2) the article subjects mediation to a series of double-binds, in which anything a mediator does is characterized as bad; (3) mediation is blamed for problems which existed long before mediation; and (4) the article portrays mediation as being both more powerful and more dangerous than it really is.

* * *

Indeed, most of Professor Grillo's mediation horror stories are not from mediation at all. Instead, they involve mediation/evaluation, a process in which the "mediator" also functions as an evaluator and quasi-decision-maker. This process is often more like an informal arbitration or settlement conference than like mediation, a process in which the mediator has no decision-making authority at all. An overwhelming percentage of the mandatory participants (especially the women) prefer even mediation/evaluation to litigation. Nonetheless, it is significantly different from mediation.

* * *

GIVING IN

Another criticism of mediation stems from Professor Grillo's assertion that women are more "relational" than men. In essence, Professor Grillo asserts that women are more concerned with relating to and working with people, while men are often more concerned with dominating other people. Indeed, while Professor Grillo talks about psychological history as a basis for this difference, there is also biological evidence to support the proposition that some of men's tendencies toward dominance and aggression are hormonal. The truth of this proposition, however, does not lead, directly or indirectly, to the conclusion that mandatory mediation should be abandoned.

* * *

While it is true that one parent may do "better" than the other in mediation, it is equally true that the same parent is likely to do better in non-mediated settlements. Indeed, it is likely that during the entire marriage that spouse got things his or her way to a greater extent. Of course, the same reasoning is not limited to marriage. We all know some people who are more strong-willed and who seem able to get what they want; and we know others who, though perhaps equally or more capable, and perhaps more worthy, seem always to just miss getting what they want. Several surveys indicate that negotiating success correlates more highly with certain personality constructs (usually referred to as those that make someone "strong-willed") than it does with intelligence. It was suggested long ago that life is not fair, but it is more fair to those who stand up for what they want.

While it may not be news to suggest that life is not fair, it is no answer for Professor Grillo to suggest that the state should, as a result, be content to sit by and let things proceed unfairly. The state has an undeniably strong interest in intervening to change pre-existing power imbalances (indeed, that is what the state does every time it acts). An action between divorcing spouses engaged in child custody determinations, therefore, might simply be one of many occasions when state intervention is appropriate. An objective analysis of the situation, however, would indicate that it is not. In all relationships, and, as a result, in all marriages, there is, to a greater or lesser extent, some power imbalance caused solely by personality differences (in addition to whatever situation specific external power imbalances might also exist). These imbalances are often most dramatic in intact marriages, because the very filing for divorce is often a sign of change in the power imbalance, and it often acts to drastically realign relationships even more. Despite the relatively high divorce rate of recent years, many people go through years or an entire lifetime feeling stuck in relationships they find oppressive. Either because of feared financial hardship, or because they are afraid of what else might happen if they leave their spouses, people often endure relationships which give them little of what they want or need, and in which they feel at the mercy of their spouses. This kind of relationship is both intolerable for the person and potentially harmful to children of the marriage.

People who remain in these relationships need more assistance in asserting themselves than do people who are leaving them, or than people who are divorcing for other reasons. Unfortunately, this same lack of assertiveness, combined with a lack of understanding of its true roots and consequences, prevents those individuals most in need of assistance from obtaining it. Absent actual or threatened physical abuse, the state does not even consider intervening to help in these cases, where help may be most needed.

* * *

Professor Grillo asserts that some people will nonetheless feel compelled to abide by a tentative agreement. If so, it is only because the mediator does not adequately explain the party's options and the mediator's expectation that the party will take care to evaluate the tentative agreement outside of the mediation session. Concern that a mediator make that expectation clear is appropriate and helpful. To suggest that mandatory mediation ought to be eliminated because of a mediator might not do so is too drastic a remedy.

Professor Grillo suggests that some women may, nonetheless, resist mediation because they fear that they will give in. These women need protection because once in mediation, they will feel obligated to reach an agreement, and once having reached an agreement, they will feel obligated to stick to it regardless of whether or not it is actually binding at that point. In fact, those who become aware prior to mediation of a self-defeating tendency to acquiesce become less likely to actually capitulate once in the mediation. Anyone who is sufficiently aware of her tendency to give in so that she would, if given the opportunity, refuse to participate in mediation, is unlikely to feel compelled to adhere to an admittedly tentative agreement when she is directly advised that she ought to consider the agreement only tentative. This may happen on rare occasions, but to eliminate mandatory mediation would be to take drastic action that affects numerous individuals, to provide only limited benefit for a very small number of individuals who likely need assistance in many areas.

* * *

Finally, even if mediation were impermissible, there would be no guarantee that a court would order a more fair or just result in court. Court determinations on a given set of facts depend on the particular judge and on the quality of the attorney representing each party. Since there is as much fluctuation in the quality and the negotiating ability of attorneys as there is among non-attorneys, judicial results are subject to the same kinds of variation that result from bargaining between the parties.

FORCED ENGAGEMENT AS HORROR

Professor Grillo's final criticism of mandatory mediation is that the very experience of sitting in a room with her former husband may be awful for some women, and the state ought not to require women to go through that experience. Women would have to negotiate with their husbands over the future of their children even in the absence of state intervention, but they might not otherwise have to come in close physical proximity to them in a setting in which they are encouraged to be open and honest, so that mandatory mediation does, in this respect, affirmatively create a problem for some women. The problem, suggests Professor Grillo, is that women are expected to sit across from their husbands, expose their desires, needs and feelings, and listen to the desires, needs and feelings of their husbands. They are also expected to absorb an assortment of judgments from their husbands and the mediator about their ways of being inside and outside the mediation process.

Indeed, goes the argument, some women will find mediation traumatic and will experience it as being as terrible as rape. * * * The analogy of mandatory mediation to rape is somewhat less than compelling. First of all, while mandatory mediation may require a women to sit in the same room as her husband, it cannot be merely the physical proximity that makes the session feel like rape. If it were, the judicial hearing with the parties present would have the same result. What makes the situation so oppressive, according to Professor Grillo, is that a woman may subject herself to listening to and absorbing her husband's concerns and may feel guilty about standing up for her own desires. The choices available to the woman, according to Professor Grillo, are to either stand up for herself and feel intolerably guilty, or to give in and thereby give up what is most important to her — another classic double-bind. Fortunately, much more appealing alternatives are not only available, but are likely. The woman who cooperates for the good of the children is likely to feel good about herself for being concerned with her children and their best interests. She may, for the first time in her life, find her more relational stance being validated and even adopted, and her husband's competitive and noncommunicative stance being rejected by the mediator, a representative of the state. She may be encouraged, for the first time in her life, to stand up to her husband for the good of herself and her children. Her assertion (as opposed to watching someone else attempt to stand up for her) may be a transformative experience. Indeed, if the mediator is any good, the woman will find that she can stand up for herself *and* have her relational stance validated at the same time. If the mother is angry, the mediation is likely to allow her to feel justified in being angry and to encourage her to protect herself in the future.

* * *

Professor Grillo suggests that, at least in court, each party expects that the proceedings will be rough. Each party is therefore likely to have her guard up and be less vulnerable to the judicial violence. In a mediation session, however, the expectation is of cooperation. There, the woman is more likely to be hit with her defenses down. Of course, the woman who is getting divorced and fighting with her husband about child custody is less than likely to go into any kind of session aimed at resolving custody disputes expecting only cooperation and pleasantness. Hopefully, the mediator will be able to de-escalate conflict and allow cooperation to emerge in time. However, neither party is likely [to] be surprised to confront a spouse who is hostile in the beginning of the session, or even a spouse who remains hostile throughout.

Admittedly, one significant difference between court hearings and most mediation sessions is the presence of attorneys at one and not the other. The attorney's presence in court, claims Professor Grillo, protects the women from the psychological damage that a mediation session might cause. Initially, it is important to note that the role of an attorney is limited in a hearing. While she can object to certain questions from the other side, she can do so only for the reasons provided in the rules of evidence, not simply because the questions may cause some psychological harm to her client. Indeed, if anything, the mediator is generally more aware of the parties' psychological states than is a judge. The mediator is trained to attend to that state rather than to the rules of evidence in determining how far to allow questioning to go.

Nor is the presence of an attorney always a good thing for the person who habitually accommodates herself to the wishes of others. The woman who would accommodate the former husband who now opposes her is even more likely to accommodate the wishes of the attorney who is represented as her savior. * * *

On the other hand, the best of both worlds exists when the parties can better negotiate with help from a third party, who sees her role as both protecting the parties and facilitating creative problem-solving, and can also consult with their attorneys prior to making any commitments. This process allows the parties to explore solutions, and to adequately consider those proposed solutions before committing to them.

WHY MANDATORY

The vast majority of women who participate in mandatory mediation are satisfied with the experience and are glad that they have gone through mediation as opposed to a judicial hearing. Nor is there any indication that these women are somehow being duped. They come out with agreements that they believe are good for themselves and for their children. Statistics indicate that court hearings are likely to bring about arrangements that are worse. Not only do fathers "win" contested cases as often as do women, but also even those cases that women "win" are not as tailored or as personalized as are mediated agreements. In addition, mediated agreements are more likely to remain satisfactory to the parties and to continue to be respected and followed than are court-mandated arrangements.

But, goes the argument, if mediation is good, it should not have to be mandatory. All we need to do is tell people about it, or show them a videotape, and those for whom it is helpful will choose it. The unfortunate truth about human behavior, however, is that left to our own devices, we often choose to act in ways that are not profoundly wise.
* * *

To the extent that people's views about mediation are subject to influence outside of the judicial system, it is not the educational media, but the opinions of their lawyers, that seems to impact most noticeably. Where mediation is not mandatory, it is likely to be chosen by those whose lawyers recommend it and likely to be rejected by those advised by their attorneys to do so.

In addition, if mediation is not mandatory, it is not then voluntary in any real sense of the word. Instead, under a system of non-mandatory mediation, either parent could force the case to trial by refusing to mediate, regardless of the other party's preference. Evidence indicates that women would not be more likely than men to opt out of mediation. Instead, those most likely to reject mediation are those who are unfamiliar with the process and are generally hesitant to try anything new. Whether those represented by attorneys are likely to accept or reject mediation seems to depend more on the attitudes of the local bar than on any insight on the parties' part. Studies have shown that while in some areas one third of divorcing parents would reject mediation if given the opportunity, when those parents are required to mediate, 75% to 80% of them are satisfied with the process and glad they were ordered to participate. Courts satisfy about half that many. Many people find custody mediation to be tense and unpleasant. These same people find court more tense and more unpleasant, and of those who find the mediation process unpleasant, over three-quarters nonetheless remain satisfied with the process.

Notes and Questions

1. Notice that Professor Grillo is condemning a particular child custody mediation program with certain characteristics: the mediation is mandatory, the parties have little or no choice of mediators, the mediators have little time to spend on each case and often make recommendations to the court, and lawyers usually are excluded from the mediation sessions. Currently, custody mediation programs in California display great variety. *See* Joan B. Kelly, *Family Mediation Research: Is There Empirical Support for the Field?*, Conflict Resol. Q., Fall–Winter 2004, at 3. Kelly reports that "in thirty-four of California's fifty-eight counties (C. Depner, personal communication, Dec. 8, 2003), mediators are authorized to make recommendations to the court for custody and visitation when parents are at impasse." *Id*. at 5. Donald T. Saposnek, explaining the difficulty of doing empirical research on such programs, states that

> [w]ithin the court system, the definition of and the actual current practices of what is called mediation have parted ways, resulting in serious theoretical and practical inconsistencies. The mandate to mediate is being interpreted and implemented in practice as if the statute read: *Parties in dispute must attend a session with a court counselor who may mediate, arbitrate, recommend, refer or terminate the case.*

Donald T. Saposnek, *Commentary: The Future of the History of Family Mediation Research,* Conflict Resol. Q., Fall 2004, at 37, 43 (2004). And although parties have a right to legal representation, in more than half of such cases, at least one parent does not have legal counsel. Kelly, *supra* at 6. In one brief study, in 76 percent of cases at least one parent reported "interparental violence." *Id*. According to Kelly, "[s]ubsequent legislation provided for separate sessions, opt-outs for parents, and special assessment for families where domestic violence was alleged or had occurred." *Id*. at 5. Would such changes make mediation less objectionable to Grillo? To you? What other changes might you want?

Because of the great variety in mediation processes, in this and other settings, the question of whether a particular dispute ought to be mediated cannot be addressed without considering the types of mediation that might be available.

2. Do you think Professor Rosenberg would have found Professor Grillo's conclusions less objectionable if she had hedged her language more? Here is the second to last paragraph of that article into which we have inserted qualifiers in brackets:

> Although mediation can be useful and empowering, it presents some serious process dangers that need to be addressed, rather than ignored. When mediation is imposed rather than voluntarily engaged in, its virtues are [often] lost. More than lost: mediation becomes [can become; sometimes becomes] a wolf in sheep's clothing. It relies on force and [often] disregards [can disregard] the context of the dispute, while masquerading as a gentler, more empowering alternative to adversarial

litigation. Sadly, when mediation is mandatory it becomes [can become] like the patriarchal paradigm of law it is supposed to supplant. Seen in that light, mandatory mediation is [has the potential to be] especially harmful: its messages [may] disproportionately affect those who are already subordinated in our society, those to whom society has already given the message, in far too many ways, that they are not leading proper lives.

Rosenberg, 33 Ariz. L. Rev., at 505.

In suggesting these modifications are the authors of this book trying to mediate between Professors Grillo and Rosenberg? Does the solution proposed attempt to cover up real differences in their beliefs?

3.   For an elaboration of the risks of women's participation in divorce mediation, see Penelope E. Bryan, *Killing Us Softly: Divorce Mediation and the Politics of Power,* 40 Buff. L. Rev. 441 (1992). For a review of studies dealing with whether women tend to be more risk averse and more altruistic than men, see Margaret F. Brinig, *Does Mediation Systematically Disadvantage Women?,* 2 Wm. & Mary J. Women & L. 1 (1995). Professor Brinig concludes that

[b]ecause mediation is swifter, less expensive and easier on children, it is a good alternative to litigation in many divorce cases. Many women who have tried mediation liked it. However, congested courts cannot justify mandatory mediation in cases where one spouse holds a monopoly on marital power. No one should order mediation when there has been abuse within the family, substance abuse, or systematic hiding of assets.

Id. at 34.

Professor Nancy Ver Steegh, writing in the context of the mediation of divorces for couples that have encountered domestic abuse, suggests ways in which a divorce mediator can address problems of power imbalance:

In some cases, the power imbalance is too severe for mediation to take place. However, in less extreme cases, skilled mediators are equipped to deal with moderate power differentials. One way that mediators deal with power imbalance is through their own exercise of power. The mediator controls the process by:

1.   Creating the ground rules.

2.   Choosing the topic.

3.   Deciding who may speak.

4.   Controlling the length of time each person may speak.

5.   Allowing and timing the person's response.

6.   Determining which spouse may present a proposal to the other.

7.   Presenting an interpretation of what the spouse said.

8.   Ending the discussion.

9.   Writing down the agreement.

The mediator gradually transfers power from himself or herself to the divorcing couple as they become able to use it appropriately. If the mediator retains too much power the couple will not "own" the agreement, but if the mediator relinquishes power prematurely, sessions are unproductive and, in the case of domestic violence, potentially dangerous. Because knowledge is a form of power, special care is taken to share information and verify facts. Power can also be balanced in a neutral fashion by asking probing questions and validating the concerns of the less powerful party. Separate caucuses give the mediator a chance to obtain direct feedback on power and safety issues.

Mediators watch for specific behaviors that indicate power imbalances. These include but are not limited to tone of voice, glaring, insults, passivity, threats, outbursts, and refusal to speak. In addition to behavioral cues, mediators watch for lopsided agreements. "Even if we concede that a mediator will not be able to see how the husband is maneuvering his wife to where he wants to get her, it is simply impossible for the mediator not to see where her husband has brought her."

Additional safeguards in such situations include independent legal advice and, to some extent, judicial review. If necessary, the mediator can end the mediation "on behalf" of the less empowered person.

Some have argued that mediators cannot deal with power imbalance without jeopardizing their neutrality and impartiality. Mediators do remain neutral with respect to the outcome of the mediation but they are not "value-free" with respect to the process and the safety of the participants. For example, as a part of the process of balancing power, mediators ask probing questions and suggest that legal counsel be sought to ensure that the parties are equally informed and fully understand the implications of agreements being considered. The alternative to ignoring power imbalances would essentially amount to siding with the more powerful party. Obviously, the experience of the mediator is key.

Nancy Ver Steegh, *Yes, No, and Maybe: Informed Decision Making about Divorce Mediation in the Presence of Domestic Violence*, 9 Wm & Mary J. Women & L. 145, 186–88 (2003).

She concludes this extensive study as follows:

Should abuse victims mediate their divorces? In some cases, the answer is "no." In others, the answer is "maybe" but only on a voluntary basis with a highly skilled mediator using a specialized procedure. Even then, the decision regarding mediation must be made with regard for the victim's particular situation and the options realistically available. * * *

Thus, mediation should be offered as one option among many. Abuse survivors must be informed of choices, educated about the advantages and disadvantages of each, and counseled with respect to what might work for them. They and their families deserve no less.

Id. at 204.

4. A study by psychologist Joan Kelly compared attitudes of couples who mediated all their divorce issues (not just the custody issues as in the mandatory custody mediation program that was the subject of the Grillo–Rosenberg debate) with those who used a traditional "adversary" process

with two lawyers. On most measures, the mediation groups tended to be happier with its process and outcomes than the adversarial group. Here is an excerpt from that study:

> On a separate, global measure of satisfaction, the mediation group was significantly more satisfied with the mediation process and outcomes than the adversarial group was with the adversarial process. At final divorce, 69 percent of mediation respondents were somewhat to very satisfied, compared to only 47 percent of adversarial men and women. There were no significant sex differences.

Discussion

> The findings reported in this chapter consistently favor mediation as a method for reaching comprehensive divorce agreements when compared to the adversarial process. All but two of the eighteen significant group differences indicated that those in mediation had more positive perceptions of and greater satisfaction with their divorce experience. Men and women in the adversarial group did not report their divorce process as better, fairer, smoother, more empowering, or more satisfactory on any measure.

> In this study, mediation spouses believed that the mediation process had a more beneficial effect on their ability to be reasonable and communicative with each other compared to adversarial respondents who used attorneys.... The respondents in the current study also perceived that the mediators had led them to more workable compromises. Whether these perceptions of improved communication will result in reduced conflict and enhanced coparental communication and cooperation postdivorce will be determined in future analyses. We have reported elsewhere (Kelly, Gigy, and Hausman, 1988) that the mediation intervention resulted in greater increases in cooperation between mediation spouses at time 2 than did the adversarial experience. Pearson, Thoennes, and Vanderkooi and Emery and Jackson have also found small improvements in the parental relationship reported by mediation respondents. Preliminary time–3 analyses indicate that while mediation and adversarial clients do not differ in their level of anger at their spouses at final divorce, the mediation group reported less conflict during the divorce, were significantly more cooperative, and perceived their spouses as less angry than did the adversarial group.

> The absence of significant group differences on a number of crucial process variables begins to address some of the criticisms leveled against mediation by those who believe that divorcing spouses will be disadvantaged unless they have the legal representation inherent to the adversarial process. The questions assessing adequacy of information produced in the mediation process indicated that, in these particular mediation interventions, mediation respondents did not feel any less informed, unprotected, or heard than did the adversarial group; neither did they believe that their spouses had an advantage over them in the negotiations.

> With the exception of child support agreements, the mediation group was more satisfied with all of the outcomes reached. Fairer spousal support, more satisfactory property agreements, and better

custody and visiting agreements were more often reported by the mediation group, when compared to the adversarial group. There were no significant sex differences or interaction effects for these variables. The finding that the mediation group was significantly more likely to perceive that they had equal influence over the terms of these agreements compared to adversarial men and women suggests that the mediators did a competent job of balancing power and spouses' needs. Clearly, for some adversarial respondents, the presumed condition of equal power through legal representation was not met.

* * *

Much opposition to mediation currently expressed by legal and political advocates for women derives from the belief that women are less powerful and knowledgeable than men and therefore likely to be disadvantaged in all types of divorce mediation. The findings of this study do not support these concerns. On no single items measuring process or outcome did adversarial women express more satisfaction or more favorable perception of their attorneys, their divorce process, or their agreements. Mediation women are significantly more satisfied than adversarial women on eighteen process and outcome items. Further, women in mediation were equally as satisfied as men with the overall process, mediator impartiality, adequacy and clarity of data, and various mediator techniques.

Joan B. Kelly, *Mediated and Adversarial Divorce: Respondents' Perceptions of Their Processes and Outcomes,* Mediation Q., Summer 1989, at 71, 84–86.

Social scientist Jessica Pearson interviewed more than 300 people who mediated at least some of the issues in their divorce (the other issues were resolved by a judge, by negotiations between the parties' lawyers or by negotiations directly between the parties); all of these respondents — both those in public and in private mediation efforts — were enrolled in programs that were open to mediating more than just the custody issue. Jessica Pearson, *The Equity of Mediated Divorce Agreements*, Mediation Q., Winter 1991, at 179, 180. One of her goals was to determine whether adversarial processes or mediation "produce more equitable results for women" — an issue on which studies had produced conflicting results. Pearson concluded that "mediation is not worse than adversarial and independent decision-making in generating agreements that are perceived to be equitable and fair." *Id.* at 192–93.

5. For further reading on exceptions to compelled participation in mediation, with special relevance to domestic relations and violence, see Chapter VI, beginning at page 697.

6. Lawyers did not participate in the mediations discussed by Grillo and Rosenberg. In most parts of the U.S., even when divorcing parties have retained lawyers, the lawyers typically do not attend the divorce or custody mediations. In the following reading, Craig McEwen, Nancy Rogers, and Richard Maiman challenge the wisdom of continuing that practice.

CRAIG A. McEWEN, NANCY H. ROGERS & RICHARD J.
MAIMAN, BRING IN THE LAWYERS: CHALLENGING
THE DOMINANT APPROACHES TO ENSURING
FAIRNESS IN DIVORCE MEDIATION

79 Minn. L. Rev. 1317, 1319–23, 1347–51, 1373–78 (1995).

Mandatory divorce mediation is under attack. According to some critical commentators, divorce mediation reinforces bargaining imbalances between parties and places women at a disadvantage. * * *

Mediation proponents respond that mandatory mediation can produce results as fair as or more fair than those achieved through a traditional divorce system, and they praise mediation's benefits as compared to litigation. To insure fairness, however, proponents sometimes advocate regulation. Under this view, the elaborate scheme of statutes and court rules enacted to ensure that mediation is "done right" should produce uniformly high quality, and thus fair mandatory divorce mediation. This "regulatory" approach to mandated mediation often includes mediator duties to assure fairness (such as a duty to assure a balanced dialogue); exemption of some cases from compulsory mediation; limitation of the scope of discussion during sessions to custody and visitation issues; requirement of advanced degrees and mediation training for mediators; requirement that the parties' lawyers and the court review mediated agreements; and prohibitions against the mediator making recommendations to the court.

This "regulatory" approach to assuring fairness in divorce mediation contrasts with the "voluntary participation" approach often favored by those most critical of mediation. * * *

In this Article, we argue that the debate about fairness in divorce mediation, as well as the resulting legal schemes based on either the "regulatory" or "voluntary participation" approaches, results from the view that one must choose between a "lawyered" process ending in the courtroom, and an informal, problem-solving process involving parties but not lawyers in the mediation room. In our view, this dichotomy has unnecessarily narrowed the policy choices underlying mediation schemes, because it assumes that lawyers either cause conflict or act as mouthpieces for clients with a cause; that the divorce process is one in which, absent mediation (where lawyers do not appear), aggressive lawyers contest custody cases at hearings; and that mediators either protect parties' interests or pressure them toward a particular (and sometimes unjust) settlement.

We challenge these assumptions and the two approaches in statutes and court rules that follow from them — the "regulatory" and the "voluntary participation" approaches. We argue that the mediation scheme in Maine, where attorneys participate regularly and vigorously in mandated divorce mediation, provides a third avenue — one we call the "lawyer-participant" approach. Research evidence about this third approach undermines the assumptions that have confined the debate about fairness. * * *

In this Article we critique these assumptions and seek to demonstrate that the "lawyer-participant" approach in fact promotes fairness more effectively than the two dominant legal schemes for divorce mediation.

* * *

The "regulatory" approach attempts to insure fairness in the absence of lawyer participation in mediation sessions. Only one type of regulatory provision — judicial review — is relatively low in cost. Only one type of provision — prohibition of mediator reports on the merits — seems likely to increase the fairness of divorce mediation. The others — issue limitations, case selection procedures, high mediator qualifications, mediator duties, and lawyer review — threaten to make mediation more expensive and, in some cases, more rigid and less effective, with little prospect of positive effects on fairness. In short, substituting regulation for lawyer-participation threatens to undermine important qualities of mediation without doing much to insure fairness.

In addition, regulation fails to address the deepest concerns of critics of mediation — that even the best mediators can never be "neutral" and will play a powerful role in shaping outcomes that may create disadvantages for the parties. Lawyers who participate in mediation can address these concerns. Lawyer representation does not guarantee equity, but critics of mediation tend not to criticize as unfair divorce outcomes resulting from lawyer negotiations. Their confidence in lawyer-negotiated outcomes suggests a general agreement that attorney representation provides the best insurance of fairness that we know. The research in Maine, discussed below, indicates that in practice, lawyers play just such a role in protecting client interests in mediation.

B. THE "VOLUNTARY PARTICIPATION" APPROACH

* * *

In Maine, as elsewhere, lawyers encourage divorcing clients to do part of the negotiating themselves. Thus encouragement appears much more likely on some issues (the division of personal property and visitation schedules) and for some clients (those with less income). Such encouragement probably stems from a concern about controlling costs, especially when there are insufficient resources to pay attorneys. It also arises from a desire by some lawyers to avoid "pots and pans issues." According to these lawyers, these matters do not require legal expertise, unlike matters involving real property, alimony, and pensions. Parties, however, may well need as much support and guidance on these issues as they do on more legally relevant topics, but may find themselves referred either to party-to-party negotiation or mediation without lawyers, if it is available. Thus, a statutory approach that relies wholly on voluntary participation may indirectly exacerbate problems of unfairness by delegating difficult and important "nonlegal" issues to mediation without lawyers present.

Voluntary participation, as a means of assuring fairness, may also entail costs if voluntary mediation programs are party-paid. This makes mediation an option primarily for the well-to-do. For instance, in an Ohio study of contested cases, while only forty percent of all divorcing parties with contested cases had incomes over $20,000, seventy-three percent of those attending voluntary, party-paid mediation had incomes over $20,000.

Experience indicates that mediation does not occur frequently unless states require that parties participate or require attendance at a session where parties are urged to participate. One parent may reject the option when it is (or because it is) favored by the other parent. At least one of the parties rejected even free mediation services in half of the cases reported by one custody mediation study and even more in another. Thus, if reduced use of mediation constitutes a cost, voluntary mediation carries with it an additional disadvantage.

Under the voluntary approach, parties would rarely use mediation and would have little assistance of counsel when they did. Requiring the divorcing parties to attend a mediation session at which their lawyers actively participate would seem to promote fairness more effectively. Regulators and commentators, however, assume that this would destroy mediation. Furthermore, those advocating voluntary mediation often assert that trial will obviate fairness concerns, assuming trial is the alternative to attending mediation sessions.

* * *

III. ASSUMPTIONS UNDERLYING THE DOMINANT APPROACHES

Four assumptions are implicit in the two dominant statutory approaches to assuring fairness in mediation, and also in the commentary for and against mandatory mediation: (1) lawyers do not attend mediation sessions but do attend trials; (2) divorce mediation sessions are all alike; (3) lawyers spoil mediation if they attend and participate in the sessions; and (4) trial represents the typical alternative to mediation. We address the assumptions in turn, and in the next section show them to be myths.

* * *

5. Conclusions: The Myths and Maine Mediation

Many advocates of divorce mediation assume that lawyers create conflict and persist in legal argument and positional negotiation so that problem-solving negotiation cannot occur when they are present. Lawyers, presumably, speak in place of their clients and resist settlement. Under this view, if lawyers remind clients of legal rights, any negotiations will focus exclusively on these issues, and lawyers will dominate discussions. In order to preserve party participation and enable problem-solving negotiation, these advocates assume that mediation must take place without lawyers. To protect rights under these circumstances, these advocates argue that well-regulated mediation will balance bargaining inequalities and insure uniformly high-quality mediation. As a consequence, they argue, such mediation offers better resolution of cases than does a trial.

Critics of mandatory mediation similarly assume that mediation precludes discussion of rights and presupposes the absence of lawyers. They conclude, however, that mediators cannot effectively protect weaker parties and regularly insert their own biases in pressuring for settlements. As a consequence, parties lose out in mediation, faring less well than they would in court. All mediation systems share these qualities and thus mandatory mediation — perhaps all mediation — is generically bad, especially for women.

What has occurred under Maine's mandatory mediation scheme challenges these assumptions. First, lawyers who appear at negotiation sessions or trial typically appear at mediation sessions as well. Second, mandatory divorce mediation is highly variable. The existence of a program like Maine's — and similar programs elsewhere — challenges the assumption that all mandatory mediation systems are identical. Operating under few regulations and with the active participation of lawyers, Maine's divorce mediation differs strikingly from the versions portrayed by critics and advocates.

Differentiation does not end with the structure of the system. Mediators and mediation sessions also vary substantially within any system. Because of its dependence on relatively unguided participation of parties, mediation varies substantially with the interests, attributes, and relationships of the participants, as well as the issues at play in a divorce. Mediators must interpret, innovate, and improvise. It is too much to expect that even the best-trained and most perceptive mediators will always understand fully the range of issues and priorities of each party. Inevitably, mediation sessions unfold differently.

Furthermore, the participation of attorneys in Maine mediation helps to assert the rights of and provide support for parties at a disadvantage. It also provides for considerable levels of client involvement, expression of feeling, and personal control. Lawyers see themselves protecting clients against choosing a result because of the pressure of the process, the other party, or the mediator. Yet lawyer attendance does not interfere with settlement rates or with substantial client participation. The active roles of lawyers "spoil" neither advocacy nor the mediation process.

Finally, mandatory mediation in Maine does not usually replace trial. Instead, its major role is to structure and formalize negotiation and to place parties at the center of those negotiations.

The evidence from Maine thus challenges the myths implicit in much of the debate about how best to protect fairness in divorce mediation. Recognizing that mandatory mediation programs vary, that lawyers can participate actively in mediation without either spoiling mediation or neglecting advocacy, and that mandatory mediation serves largely as an adjunct to negotiation rather than as a substitute for trial, we examine anew the alternatives for achieving fairness in divorce mediation.

V. BRING IN THE LAWYERS

Absent the faulty assumptions discussed above, one can look anew at a regulatory scheme in which lawyers participate in mandatory mediation. This scheme achieves fairness primarily by encouraging lawyers to attend and participate. Legislators could accomplish this result by prohibiting exclusion of lawyers from mediation sessions and, in fact, broadening the issues covered in mediation to include matters of real property, alimony, and other financial issues that stimulate lawyer participation. This scheme includes only two other key regulatory provisions — court review of mediated agreements and a prohibition against the mediator's recommendation to the court. It is possible that some extra provision for domestic violence cases, such as the right to refuse joint sessions with the attacker, ought to be included as well.

A. Compared to the "Regulatory" Approach

Most fairness concerns evaporate if lawyers attend mediation sessions with the parties or if the parties opt out of the process when unrepresented. Less intrusive regulations, such as judicial review of agreements, prohibition of settlement pressures, and provisions for unrepresented parties, may moderate the remaining fairness issues. The detailed rules of the "regulatory approach" largely become unnecessary to preserve fairness if lawyers are present.

By encouraging lawyer presence and permitting modification of the mediation ground rules, this scheme is more flexible and certain in responding to the problems of bargaining imbalances and mediator pressures. Especially given the unpredictability and changing situational character of these challenges to fairness, the presence of lawyers in the process can assure necessary help in those unpredictable circumstances. The Maine research shows that with lawyers present as advisors and potentially as spokespersons, the risks of unfairness decline, even in the most unbalanced situations. By permitting adjustment of the mediation process (for example, allowing shuttle mediation), mediation can be tailored to fit particular relationships and issues in each case.

Lawyers prevent or moderate the effects of a face to face encounter with an abuser, thus diminishing the likelihood of unfairness in domestic violence cases. Maine lawyers attending mediation sessions with their clients report arranging separate sessions, time-outs, and other measures to protect their clients. Past violence, which may be a key factor in determining whether the parties will submit to an unfair settlement or will be forced into a frightening situation, becomes less of a bargaining factor if the parties attend with their lawyers. Lawyers can advise clients to avoid settlements that will allow further opportunities for abuse, or that are unlikely to be obeyed, or that are bad deals. Lawyers can also advise their clients to terminate mediation sessions. Although some suggest that mediation should also be avoided because divorce settlement condones violence, research indicates that in the prime alternative to mediation — negotiation — settlements occur with about the same frequency as in mediation. Thus, in domestic violence cases, mediation probably encourages settlement more quickly rather than more often.

Issue limitations also become unnecessary if lawyers attend and can advise on economic trade-offs and legal issues. There is no more danger in combining the issues in mediation than exists if disposition of all issues occurs outside of mediation.

So, too, an assumption that lawyers will be absent underlies reliance on mediator qualifications as a means to ensure fairness. Absent lawyers, mediators must have at least some of the skills and knowledge that lawyers would otherwise provide. In fact, Maine divorce lawyers acknowledge that they sometimes get poor mediators. In these cases, the lawyers simply take charge and use the sessions as four-way negotiation sessions. Although mediator qualifications involving advanced educational degrees may help increase settlements or party confidence, they are unnecessary to protect against unfairness under the "lawyer-participant" approach, because mediators need not substitute their knowledge for that of lawyers. Lawyers can intervene (as discussed above) to compensate for inferior mediators and can request their removal.

Mediator duties to appraise parties of various legal rights, to terminate mediation, and to moderate bargaining imbalances also rest on the assumption that lawyers are absent in mediation. Obviously, requirements for post-mediation review of settlements by lawyers rest on the assumption that the lawyer does not take part in the give-and-take of negotiations.

In other words, lawyer participation reduces substantially the need for regulation. Probably, a mediation model should allow domestic violence victims to opt out of joint sessions. This model should also prohibit mediator recommendations to the court. Such low-cost requirements as court review of the agreement and brief mediation training should be incorporated into this third model. Finally, because this model assumes lawyer participation, perhaps unrepresented parties should be able to avoid mediation.

* * *

Notes and Questions

1. The foregoing reading should underscore an important theme of this book — that dispute resolution processes can be adjusted in many ways to meet actual needs. This means, as we have mentioned, that the question of whether to use mediation in a particular case or category of cases is intricately interconnected with questions about what will happen in a mediation and how much influence the various participants are able to exert.

2.   A recent study of 645 mediations of employment discrimination claims that were conducted under the U.S. Equal Employment Opportunity Commission's mediation program found that claimants who were represented in "evaluative mediations" received much larger settlements than claimants who were not represented. E. Patrick McDermott & Ruth Obar, *"What's Going On" in Mediation: An Empirical Analysis of the Influence of the Mediator's Style on Party Satisfaction and Monetary Benefit,* 9 Harv. Negot. L. Rev. 75 (2004). Of course in these cases, as opposed to many civil suits, only one party is seeking monetary recovery.

3.   If you were a member of a state supreme court committee charged with developing proposals for establishing divorce mediation programs, how would you answer the following questions:

   a.   Should participation be voluntary or mandatory? If mandatory, should some kinds of cases be excluded?

   b.   Who should pay for such services — the parties or the courts?

   c.   Should the mediation include financial and property issues or only child custody issues?

   d.   Should the participation of lawyers in mediation sessions be encouraged or discouraged?

   e.   Should all meetings be joint, or should private caucuses be routine?

   f.   Should mediators evaluate, i.e., make predictions about what would happen in court? Would your answer depend on whether the mediator was a lawyer? Whether the parties had lawyers? Whether the lawyers attended the mediation?

4.   Would your views on the above questions differ if you were a divorce lawyer? A divorce mediator in private practice?

5.   Rogers, McEwen, and Maiman mention that if the mediator does not perform well, the lawyers can step up and "simply take charge and use the sessions as four-way negotiation sessions." It is also true that sometimes mediators can help make up for poor lawyering. Mediators might, e.g., facilitate communications between clients and their lawyers, about law, facts, or underlying interests; encourage or help lawyers to become more familiar with relevant law or local court practices; play devil's advocate; help lawyers and clients prepare for negotiation and conduct negotiations; and "translate" and explain offers.

6.   For an argument that state statutes and court rules barring lawyers from attending court-annexed mediations are unconstitutional, see Richard C. Reuben, *Constitutional Gravity: A Unitary Theory of Alternative Dispute Resolution and Public Civil Justice,* 47 UCLA L. Rev. 949, 1079–82 (2000).

E.   MEDIATION EXERCISES

1.   THE RED DEVIL DOG MEDIATION ROLE PLAY*

General Information for the Mediator

You are an attorney in private practice and have agreed to mediate a dispute between a commercial landlord and a prospective tenant. The

---

* This role play was prepared by Professor Nancy Rogers and is based on the facts of Videotape III in the *Dispute Resolution and Lawyers Videotape Series* (West Pub-

referral came from the landlord's lawyer. The landlord will pay for the first two hours of mediation. The prospective tenant, who apparently has no lawyer, has agreed to attend, as long as the landlord does not bring a lawyer. Piecing together information provided by the referring lawyer and the prospective tenant, you surmise that the prospective tenant had agreed to rent the premises to operate a local franchise of the well-known Red Devil Dog Restaurant chain. The lease provides for payment of $1,000 per month plus 3 percent of gross sales for a 5–year period. After the landlord made $2,500 in modifications and the tenant moved in boxes of equipment, the news broke that the Red Devil Dog chain had filed for bankruptcy. The prospective tenant then called to cancel the lease and the landlord responded with a letter demanding $80,000. The mediation has been scheduled in the early evening because the prospective tenant works days as a nurse. Your secretary reports that the prospective tenant sounded angry.

Before you begin the mediation, think out your approach. Do you expect any bargaining imbalances? If so, should your approach change in any way? If the disputing parties are angry, how can you get them to focus on possible solutions?

2. PROSANDO v. HIGH–TECH: GENERAL INFORMATION*

Prosando, a German–Argentine joint venture based in Argentina, is a distributor of office and business equipment. High–Tech is a large, well-established computer manufacturer, with its headquarters in southern California.

In January 1990** Prosando entered into an exclusive five-year distribution contract with High–Tech. Prosando agreed to establish a distribution network for High–Tech's Futura A and B minicomputers throughout South America and to use High–Tech's trademark in doing so.

Immediately after the contract was signed, Prosando ordered 50 Futura A computers. High–Tech, however, refused to ship until its legal department had reviewed the contract. Following that review, in June

lishing Co. 1991) and Dale A. Whitman, *The Missing Tenant: A Negotiation Exercise for Property Law, in* LEONARD L. RISKIN AND JAMES E. WESTBROOK, INSTRUCTOR'S MANUAL FOR DISPUTE RESOLUTION AND LAWYERS, 3rd ed. (2005). Confidential information for the landlord and the tenant may be found in the Instructor's Manual for this book, in the Instructor's Manual for Videotape III, supra, at 43 and on the casebook's TWEN web site at www.lawschool.westlaw.com.

 * This exercise was created for the CPR Institute for Dispute Resolution by Cathy Cronin-Harris, Vice President, and Profes-

sor Stephen Goldberg as a basis for CPR's 36–minute videotape, *Mediation in Action: Resolving a Complex Business Dispute* (1994). The videotape is available from CPR, 575 Lexington Avenue, 14th floor, New York, NY 10022 (212) 949–6490. Copyright 1994 by the CPR Institute for Dispute Resolution. Reprinted with the permission of CPR. Confidential information for attorneys and business executives appears in the Instructor's Manual, and on the casebook's TWEN web site at www.lawschool.westlaw.com.

 ** Assume this mediation takes place in 1994.

1990, High–Tech insisted that it retain the right to sell directly in South America. Prosando reluctantly agreed, and in August 1990, High–Tech shipped 50 Futura A computers to Prosando.

In October 1990, Prosando ordered another 20 Futura A computers, which were delivered in December 1990. In January 1991, High–Tech discontinued the Futura A and introduced the Century series, but refused initially to allow Prosando to distribute that series. According to High–Tech, Prosando's distribution contract was limited to the Futura series. In June 1991 (one and one-half years into the contract), High–Tech agreed to allow Prosando to distribute the Century series. In February 1992, Prosando ordered 18 Century series computers.

In June 1992, without prior warning, High–Tech notified Prosando that the contract would be terminated in 30 days because of Prosando's clear and unequivocal breach of contract. According to High–Tech, Prosando had:

1. Failed to use its best efforts to sell the product within the assigned territory to the total dissatisfaction of the Seller, since Prosando had placed orders for only 88 units of product in 24 months.

2. Failed to establish a "distributor" network on or before June 30, 1991. As of June 1992, Prosando had established a total of four distributors, all in Chile.

3. Failed to submit or negotiate annual purchase commitments.

The relevant provisions of the contract are these:

A. Prosando shall have the sole right (except for High–Tech) to sell High–Tech Futura A and Futura B minicomputers, and any updates thereto (hereafter "the product") within the assigned territory.

B. Prosando shall use its best efforts to sell within the assigned territory.

C. Prosando shall establish a distribution network within the assigned territory to the satisfaction of High–Tech.

D. Prosando shall have its distribution network in place by June 1991. If it fails to do so, High–Tech shall have the right to terminate Prosando's status as exclusive South American distributor of the product, and to engage other distributors in addition to Prosando.

E. Prosando must place a noncancellable blanket order for 100 of the product totalling one million U.S. dollars upon execution of this agreement for delivery on or after _____. (Left blank in the contract.)

F. On each calendar year commencing in _____ (left blank in the contract) the parties will agree on the minimum purchase requirements for the subsequent twelve-month period. If agreement is not achieved, either party may terminate this agreement upon prior 90 days' written notice.

G. Upon termination of this Agreement becoming effective: (a) Neither party shall be liable to the other for loss of profits or prospective profits of any kind or nature sustained or arising out of or alleged to have arisen out of such termination.

On receiving High–Tech's June 1992 notice of termination, Prosando continued to sell its remaining High–Tech equipment.

In September 1992, Prosando initiated litigation in the U.S. District Court for the Southern District of California, claiming damages for breach of contract and fraud: $1 million for loss of business reputation; $6 million for lost profits; and actual reliance damages of $3 million expended on the contract (including capitalized loans, leasing of premises, personnel, promoting and advertising the product, travel, etc.), a total of $10 million.

High–Tech denied all allegations and counterclaimed for $126,000 for equipment shipped and not paid for.

At the suggestion of the district court, the parties have agreed to attempt to resolve this dispute through mediation.

3. DANCE INNOVATION

Mediator's Instructions*

You had a short conference call with the two lawyers, Joe and Connie, in which you learned the following information prior to your first mediation session. Two years ago, Jackie (who had been a dancer and then a choreographer) was working as an assistant Director for a large New York Dance Company. At that point, Dance Innovation, a smaller Boston Company, hired her/him to become its Artistic Director and resident choreographer (when its founder and previous Artistic Director, Peter George, died suddenly). The three-year contract provided that any works Jackie produced as part of her/his employment were to be considered "work for hire." S/he could be fired with six months' notice.

The mission of Dance Innovation is to support the work of new choreographers. Jackie brought with her/him a work in progress that s/he had been creating (on the side) while at (and with the permission of) her/his former employer. S/he completed that work, MOTIF, while at Dance Innovation (and the company produced it). S/he created a second work, CHORALE, during her/his first year at Dance Innovation (and the company produced it). S/he was working on a third major work, ENSEMBLE, (which was to be produced in the upcoming season) when s/he was fired.

Mickey, Dance Innovation's Chairman and Executive Director, sent Jackie a letter notifying her/him of her/his dismissal on the grounds that

* Copyright © 2001, Center for Mediation in Law. Reprinted with permission. Confidential information for lawyers and parties appears in the Instructors Manual for this book, and on this casebook's TWEN web site at www.lawschool.westlaw.com. A video tape of a mediation based on the information in these instructions, Saving the Last Dance: Mediation Through Understanding, is available from the Program on Negotiation at Harvard Law School, www.pon.org.

s/he focused almost exclusively on the creation of her/his own work (rather than devoting attention to her/his own work <u>and</u> supporting the work of new choreographers) and because s/he was consistently over budget. Mickey also informed Jackie that he/she considered ENSEMBLE virtually complete when Jackie left, needing at most a little final polishing and refinement and that the company is going forward with completing ENSEMBLE which will be the centerpiece of its upcoming season. Mickey further maintained that any works completed by Jackie or that s/he was working on while employed are exclusively the property of Dance Innovation.

The Company views all the works as owned by the company under the contract language and the work-for-hire doctrine. Connie views the works as belonging to Jackie as the creator and threatens to enjoin the upcoming season of Dance Innovation, which has ENSEMBLE as its centerpiece.

The lawyers have agreed to come into mediation with their clients.

Chapter V

ARBITRATION

Arbitration is a form of adjudication in which the neutral decision maker is not a judge or an official of an administrative agency. Arbitration is normally a private proceeding based on the parties' agreement to arbitrate, although a few state and federal courts have arbitration programs, which is discussed more fully in Chapter VI beginning at page 677. Unlike in negotiation or mediation, where the disputing parties determine the outcome, in arbitration the arbitrator decides the parties' rights based on evidence or other submissions from them. Thus, an arbitration proceeding is more like litigation than negotiation or mediation. Arbitration is, however, less formal than litigation in that it generally is not conducted according to the same rules of law and procedure as public adjudication.

Arbitration also differs from negotiation and mediation in that it is based more on statutes and case law. In general, there are three types of arbitration that we will discuss in this chapter and each has its own legal basis. The first type are arbitrations between employers and unions, which are governed by § 301 of the National Labor Relations (Taft–Hartley) Act, 29 U.S.C. § 185 (2000). The second type are commercial arbitrations between (i) two or more business entities, (ii) businesses and consumers, or (iii) employers and non-unionized employees, which are generally governed by the Federal Arbitration Act (FAA), 9 U.S.C. § 1, *et. seq.* (2000), and related state arbitration laws. The third type are international arbitrations, which are governed primarily by the 1958 U.N. Convention on the Recognition and Enforcement of Foreign Arbitral Awards as adopted by Congress in 9 U.S.C. § 201, *et. seq* (2000). Most states (thirty-nine jurisdictions) either have adopted or based their arbitration statutes on the Uniform Arbitration Act (UAA), which was promulgated by the National Conference of Commissioners on Uniform State Laws (NCCUSL) in 1955. The UAA was revised in 2000, and 10 states have passed the revised Uniform Arbitration Act (RUAA). *See* Timothy J. Heinsz, *The Revised Uniform Arbitration Act: Modernizing, Revising, and Clarifying Arbitration Law*, 2001 J. Disp. Resol. 1. Our emphasis will be on commercial, employment, and consumer arbitration because these are the areas of greatest growth and the areas lawyers are most likely to encounter in practice. Unlike prior chapters, Chapter V will use more statutory and case analysis.

The use of arbitration has grown tremendously in recent years. At one time, most arbitrations involved either employers and unions or two or more commercial entities. Today arbitration clauses have become ubiquitous — particularly in adhesion situations. (*See* infra, beginning at page 582. Undoubtedly any reader who has a credit card or has made an on-line purchase of a product is a party to an arbitration agreement and subject to an arbitration process to resolve any disputes arising under it.

Private arbitration is based on contract and the parties may shape the contours of their arbitration agreement to meet their needs. Typically, parties either agree in advance that designated categories of disputes will be arbitrated (pre-dispute arbitration) or they enter into an ad hoc agreement to arbitrate after a dispute has arisen (post-dispute arbitration). Most private arbitration systems allow the parties to select the arbitrator jointly. Generally, arbitration clauses provide that the arbitrator's decision will be final and binding. Although courts enforce agreements to arbitrate and confirm or vacate arbitration awards, they typically do not review the merits of an arbitrator's decision. Arbitration is normally a confidential process. Because one of the features of private arbitration is that the parties have considerable autonomy in designing the process, the arbitration agreements can provide the substantive standards that arbitrators use in making a decision. Arbitrators do not consider themselves bound by the doctrine of precedent. Arbitration awards in some fields are published and arbitrators often look to such awards for guidance, even if they are not binding.

Section A of this chapter surveys the practice and procedures used in voluntary private arbitration. Section B reviews the legal framework of the arbitration process. Section C looks at international commercial arbitration. Section D examines the considerations involved in deciding whether to use arbitration and how to construct arbitration systems.

A.   THE PRACTICE AND PROCEDURES OF PRIVATE ARBITRATION

Arbitration is very different than the other processes we have discussed thus far, and in this section, we provide a general orientation to the arbitration process. We begin with a discussion of the contexts in which arbitration is used, and then provide some insight into the people who serve as arbitrators, and conclude Section A with a discussion of the mechanics of the arbitration process.

1. THE USES AND GROWTH OF ARBITRATION

Arbitration has an ancient lineage and an active present. King Solomon, Phillip II of Macedon, and George Washington employed arbitration. *See* ELKOURI & ELKOURI, HOW ARBITRATION WORKS 3–4 Alan Miles

Rubin ed., 6th ed. (2003). Commercial arbitration has been used in England and the United States for hundreds of years. Labor-management arbitration, which has its roots in the late nineteenth century, came to the fore after World War II, as companies expanded and employees unionized. "International commercial arbitration has to a great extent now been institutionalized as the generally accepted private legal process applicable to transnational business disputes." Yves Dezalay & Bryant Garth, *Merchants of Law as Moral Entrepreneurs: Constructing International Justice from the Competition for Transnational Business Disputes*, 29 Law & Soc'y Rev. 27, 59 (1995).

Arbitration takes place in three different institutional contexts: the disputing parties create their own process and make all the arrangements in processing the arbitration; trade associations or exchanges establish arbitration systems to deal with disputes among their members; and groups such as the American Arbitration Association, JAMS, the Federal Mediation & Conciliation Service, and the International Chamber of Commerce provide ready-made systems and panels of arbitrators for disputing parties who agree to use arbitration.

Arbitration is widely used to resolve construction, insurance, securities, and maritime disputes. Arbitration is also used to settle disputes between employers and unions, manufacturers and consumers, shareholders in close corporations, members of families, banks and their customers, attorneys and clients, major league baseball players and their employers, brokers and customers in the securities industry, and physicians and hospitals. Employers have promulgated arbitration plans that cover non-union employees.

The underlying reasons that many parties choose arbitration over litigation are the relative capacities for speed, cost savings, and greater efficiency in the arbitral process. These benefits primarily occur because, unlike trial practice, discovery either does not exist or is much more limited in arbitration. Additionally, most arbitration clauses specify that the arbitrator's decision will be final. As we will see, arbitration statutes provide only limited grounds for a court to overturn an arbitral award. The arbitration process usually is less formal than court proceedings. For instance, in many cases parties represent themselves or are represented by non-lawyers; and the arbitrator need not be a lawyer. Finally, parties often opt for arbitration because they can pick their decision maker, who will likely have expertise in the field in which their dispute arises.

Another factor causing significant growth in arbitration is the favorable legal framework for the process. For many years courts in the United States were hostile to arbitration and refused to enforce arbitration agreements. The underlying basis for this antagonism was that courts looked upon arbitration tribunals as competition that improperly ousted courts of their jurisdiction to hear cases decided under the law of the land, and provided an inferior form of justice. The legal doctrine courts used was that arbitration agreements were executory promises and thus unenforceable. *See, e.g., Red Cross Line v. Atlantic Fruit Co.,* 264 U.S. 109, 120–21, 44 S.Ct. 274, 68 L.Ed. 582 (1924) (noting that "federal courts — like those of the states and of England — have, both in equity and at law, denied, in large measure, the aid of their processes to those seeking to enforce executory agreements to arbitrate disputes."); *Home Insurance Co. v. Morse,* 87 U.S. (20 Wall.) 445, 455, 22 L.Ed. 365 (1874) (adopting so-called English "ouster doctrine" and refusing to enforce pre-dispute agreements to arbitrate). This hostility could be seen at the U.S. Supreme Court, which in *Wilko v. Swann,* 346 U.S. 427, 74 S.Ct. 182, 98 L.Ed. 168 (1953), again refused to enforce a pre-dispute arbitration provision because, it held, the right to a judicial forum could not be waived. *Id.* at 435.

This judicial antagonism first changed in labor-management arbitration when the U.S. Supreme Court in 1957 decided that arbitration agreements were enforceable under § 301 of the NLRA. *Textile Workers Union v. Lincoln Mills,* 353 U.S. 448, 451, 77 S.Ct. 912, 1 L.Ed.2d 972 (1957). Then in 1960, in three cases involving the United Steelworkers Union (referred to as the "Steelworkers Trilogy"), the Court held that the judiciary should favor labor arbitration and give only limited review to the decisions of arbitrators. *United Steelworkers v. American Manufacturing Co.,* 363 U.S. 564, 568–69, 80 S.Ct. 1343, 4 L.Ed.2d 1403 (1960); *United Steelworkers v. Warrior & Gulf Navigation Co.,* 363 U.S. 574, 585, 80 S.Ct. 1347, 4 L.Ed.2d 1409 (1960); *United Steelworkers v. Enterprise Wheel & Car Corp.,* 363 U.S. 593, 599, 80 S.Ct. 1358, 4 L.Ed.2d 1424 (1960).

In the 1980's, in a series of cases beginning with *Southland Corp. v. Keating,* see infra beginning at page 517, the U.S. Supreme Court applied the same pro-arbitration policy developed in the labor-management area to commercial disputes in interstate commerce subject to the Federal Arbitration Act, and formally overruled *Wilko v. Swan* in the late 1980s. *Rodriguez de Quijas v. Shearson/American Express, Inc.,* 490 U.S. 477, 484, 109 S.Ct. 1917, 104 L.Ed.2d 526 (1989). Today, rather than viewing arbitration as unfriendly competition, federal and state courts have embraced arbitration as a means parties may choose to resolve their disputes and as a beneficial mechanism to divert cases from crowded court dockets. This substantial judicial change, referred to by some as an "arbitration revolution," has fostered the substantial development of this dispute-resolution mechanism. *See* STEPHEN K. HUBER & E. WENDY TRACHTE-HUBER, ARBITRATION: CASES AND MATERIALS 5–6 (1998).

The success of traditional private arbitration has stimulated calls for increased reliance on arbitration. Arbitration has been used or proposed for use in connection with prisoner grievances, environmental disputes, civil rights disputes, divorce proceedings, and medical malpractice cases. The rapid increase in electronic commerce has been accompanied by the development of a number of on-line arbitration systems. As improvements in technology, transportation, and communications make for a global marketplace of goods and services, the role of arbitration can be expected to continue to grow and evolve.

2. THE ARBITRATOR

A primary reason parties decide to use arbitration rather than litigation is because they can select their decision maker. If the parties do not have a particular individual in mind to serve as an arbitrator, they may turn to a number of organizations for assistance in selecting arbitrators. Major providers of arbitration services, such as the American Arbitration Association (AAA) and the Judicial Arbitration and Mediation Service (JAMS), have separate panels of arbitrators for many areas, including, for example, commercial, labor-management, consumer, e-commerce, health care, mass claims, construction, and international arbitration. The CPR Institute for Dispute Resolution has national and regional panels of neutrals who serve as arbitrators. CPR focuses on major commercial disputes and, consequently, has fewer neutrals on its panels than AAA. The National Association of Securities Dealers and the New York Stock Exchange maintain panels of arbitrators for securities disputes. The Federal Mediation and Conciliation Service (FMCS) provides panels of labor-management arbitrators. The National Arbitration Forum emphasizes its expertise in providing arbitrators for intellectual property and on-line dispute resolution. In addition to arbitration provider agencies, there are also professional organizations to which arbitrators belong. Perhaps the best known is the National Academy of Arbitrators (NAA) for arbiters in the labor-management field. The NAA, founded in 1947, includes the most experienced arbitrators in the profession; its mission is to foster high ethical standards and promote education in labor-management arbitration.

There is no single, monolithic arbitration profession. To be an arbitrator does not require special training or education. Unlike lawyers, physicians, or accountants, arbitrators are not credentialed by state or national boards. As a result, and because arbitrators are involved in so many diverse areas, their backgrounds vary widely. Professors, attorneys, architects, accountants, clergy, and many others serve as arbitrators. The key to becoming an arbitrator is acceptability by the parties. While some make arbitration a full-time occupation, others devote only part of their time to arbitration.

A recent study by the NAA is indicative of the make-up of the arbitration profession. MICHEL PICHER, RONALD L. SEEBER & DAVID B. LIPSKY, THE ARBITRATION PROFESSION IN TRANSITION: A SURVEY OF THE NATIONAL ACADEMY OF ARBITRATORS (2000). About 40% reported that arbitration was their full-time activity. The average Academy arbitrator was sixty-three years old and had been arbitrating for twenty-six years. Only 12% of NAA arbitrators were women and less than 6% were nonwhite. The predominant education of this group of arbitrators was law. More than 60% had law degrees, while 35% of the remaining NAA arbitrators had master or doctorate degrees in various fields.

Ethical codes for arbitrators have been developed by several organizations. The American Bar Association and AAA have promulgated a Code of Ethics for Arbitrators in Commercial Disputes. A Code of Professional Responsibility for Arbitrators of Labor–Management Disputes has been instituted by AAA, FMCS, and NAA. (See casebook website at www.lawschool.westlaw.com for these materials.) The NAA's Committee on Professional Responsibility and Grievances issues formal advisory opinions on the ethical responsibilities of labor arbitrators.

Arbitrators, like judges, are granted immunity from civil liability when they act in their adjudicative capacity. This immunity is generally based on the common law, but has been codified in the RUAA § 14. (See casebook website at www.lawschool.westlaw.com.) In *Reexamining Arbitral Immunity In an Age of Mandatory and Professional Arbitration*, 88 Minn. L. Rev. 449 (2004), Professor Maureen H. Weston argues for a qualified immunity that balances the arbitrator's need for protection in their decisional roles against the public's need to hold the arbitration industry accountable.

3. THE ARBITRATION PROCESS

Generalizing about the arbitration process is difficult because the parties have the autonomy to design their arbitration system. The system proposed in the Commercial Arbitration Rules of the American Arbitration Association is one of those most widely used. (See casebook website at www.lawschool.westlaw.com.) AAA has a separate set of rules for labor arbitration and for a number of special situations such as health care, wills and trusts, patents, the wireless industry, real estate valuation, securities, and domain name disputes.

As an adjudicative process, arbitration is much more akin to litigation than is either negotiation or mediation. Most arbitrations involve a hearing in which attorneys may represent the parties; witnesses are sworn, examined and cross-examined; and exhibits are entered into evidence. In many cases, parties request a transcript of the proceedings and file post-hearing briefs. After all of the evidence and briefs (if filed) are in, the arbitrator will issue a decision. In some instances, such as commercial or securities cases, it is customary for arbitrators to write only an award finding in favor of the claimant or the respondent; in others, such as labor-management or international arbitration, arbitrators will include a reasoned decision along with their award.

Arbitration and litigation differ primarily in the areas of pre-hearing matters, such as discovery, and the applicability of the rules of evidence. The materials that follow discuss these two areas and some of the institutions and persons involved in international commercial arbitration.

STEPHEN HAYFORD AND RALPH PEEPLES, COMMERCIAL ARBITRATION: AN ASSESSMENT AND CALL FOR DIALOGUE

10 Ohio St. J. on Disp. Resol. 343, 367–71, 375–76 (1995).

1. *Pleadings and Pre–Hearing Motions*

The first major distinguishing characteristic of the commercial arbitration process is the comparative simplicity and brevity of the pleadings and pre-hearing stage. * * *

In a manner analogous to traditional litigation, the commercial arbitration proceeding commences with the filing of the moving party's (claimant's) demand for arbitration, setting forth a concise description of the facts pertinent to the underlying dispute and a description of the relief the claimant seeks. Subsequently, the respondent in arbitration files an answer to the claimant's submission, taking issue with any disputed factual allegations, setting forth any defenses, and articulating any * * * controversy. This pleadings process is largely mechanical and does not require any active intervention by the arbitrator. In fact, the pleadings process is usually complete before the arbitrator is selected.

There is no formal analog in commercial arbitration to the pre-trial motion practice in traditional litigation. This characteristic of the process accounts for a substantial portion of the cost and time savings that can be realized in arbitration. Rule 10 of the AAA Commercial Arbitration Rules does provide for pre-hearing proceedings, including a "preliminary hearing." However, Rule 10 does not expressly contemplate pre-hearing motions addressing the form and content of the pleadings, questions of proper parties and jurisdiction, or attempts to avoid a hearing by achieving dismissal as a matter of law or through an adjudication based on undisputed facts.

Rule 4 of the AAA Supplementary Procedures for Large, Complex Disputes does speak to a more extensive preliminary hearing dealing with, among other matters: service by the parties on one another of detailed statements of claims, damages, and defenses; specification of the issues before the arbitrator; and stipulations of fact. Even though this proceeding is labeled a "preliminary hearing," on its face, Rule 4 does not contemplate any form of adjudication by a neutral in the nature of a motion to dismiss or a motion for summary judgment. In the same manner, the emphasis of the relevant pre-hearing portion of the Endispute Comprehensive Arbitration Rules is on the submission of claim, answer, and counterclaim.

The omission of a surrogate for pre-hearing motion practice from the existing framework for commercial arbitration does not mean the concerns underlying that dimension of traditional litigation are not at times present in commercial arbitration. Rather, the Authors believe this circumstance is due to the fact that, to date, the parties and their attorneys generally have been willing to forego pre-hearing motion practice and present their entire cases at hearing. This is likely to continue to be the case in the commercial disputes submitted to arbitration that present relatively simple questions of law (and contract) and application of law to fact.

However, as larger numbers of more complex cases are submitted to arbitration, arbitrators will find themselves frequently confronted with the type of complicated questions of law and application of law to fact that give rise to the pre-trial motions in traditional litigation. These cases seldom turn on simple questions of contract interpretation. Rather, they typically involve numerous and interrelated claims based in common law doctrine or statutory law, or both. Consequently, questions of law and mixed questions of law and fact are often crucial determinations that competent adjudication requires to be made in some fashion, tacitly or expressly, by the arbitration tribunal.

* * *

2. *The Role and Nature of Discovery*

As with most all of the dimensions of commercial arbitration, it is difficult to generalize as to the extent and nature of pre-hearing discovery. The only reference to pre-hearing discovery contained in the AAA Commercial Arbitration Rules is found at Rule 10 which addresses the Preliminary Conference. Rule 10 authorizes the arbitrator to "establish ... the extent of and schedule for the production of relevant documents and other information, [and to establish] the identification of any witnesses to be called." Rule 5 (b)-(d) of the Association's Supplementary Procedures for Large, Complex Cases grants the arbitrator(s) authority to: direct an exchange of documents, exhibits, and information; limit the nature and extent of discovery; and order the deposition of, or the propounding of written interrogatories to a person possessing material knowledge if that person will not be available to testify at the arbitration hearing. In addition to these matters, Endispute's Comprehensive Arbitration Rule C–13 speaks directly to interrogatories, document exchange, expert witnesses, and the parties' continuing obligation to provide one another with documents they rely upon to supplement their post-pleading responses.

The discovery-related promulgations cited above contemplate a pre-hearing discovery process that focuses on the production of documents and data. Depositions and written interrogatories are accorded a lower level of significance, generally being deemed warranted only if the deponent or the subject of the interrogatories is not able to testify at the hearing, or if the party seeking to depose a hostile witness can convince the arbitrator of a reasonable need for the deposition(s).

* * *

4. *Hearing Advocacy Tactics and The Rules of Evidence*

One of the primary selling points for the commercial arbitration alternative to traditional litigation is its relative simplicity of procedure and substance. At hearing, this characteristic is reflected by the absence of rigid standards for the admission of evidence. Rule 31 of the AAA Commercial Arbitration Rules states that "conformity to legal rules of evidence shall not be necessary." Instead, the arbitrator is instructed to judge the relevance and materiality of the proffered evidence. Rule 31 does not expressly establish relevance or materiality as criteria for the admissibility of evidence.

* * *

Despite the fluid nature of the evidentiary standards in commercial arbitration, the Authors' collective experience indicates that litigators are seldom able or willing to abandon the standard jury trial *modus operandi*, including the compulsion to continually test the boundaries of the rules of evidence applicable in court while strenuously challenging the same maneuvers by opposing counsel. Generally, admonitions from the arbitrator to counsel to remember that rigid adherence to the rules of evidence is not necessary (because the case is not being presented to a jury of laypersons) go unheeded. At times this adherence to traditional jury trial tactics can result in a highly dysfunctional and unnecessary extension of the proceeding, and a significant diminution in arbitral attention span. It also leads to the application of a wide range of *de facto* evidentiary standards at hearing, depending in large part on the proclivities and the decisional consistency of the presiding arbitrator.

The roadblocks to expeditious adjudication and the inconsistency in *de facto* evidentiary standards that frequently arise at hearings are troubling and indicate a need for a careful scrutiny of this key dimension of the commercial arbitration process. Litigators, arbitrators, and neutral appointing authorities are obliged to confront this reality and openly and thoughtfully debate the utility of the current rudimentary evidentiary standards. If a consensus emerges in favor of a simplified evidentiary standard, it needs to be more clearly defined and attorneys and arbitrators alike must deem themselves obliged to abide by it. If the result is general agreement that something more than the existing evidentiary framework is called for, new standards need to be drafted that fully contemplate the presence of an expert adjudicator who need not be shielded in the same manner as a lay jury.

Note

The typical labor arbitration process is quite similar to the Hayford and Peeples description of the commercial process, except that labor arbitrators usually prepare a written opinion explaining their award. Professor Hayford summarized the labor arbitration process as follows in 1992:

> Though there are exceptions, when compared to litigation, the typical private-sector arbitration tribunal is a relatively informal proceeding. But, for contractual provisions requiring full disclosure at the latter stages of the grievance procedure, there is no analog to prehearing discovery. Similarly, prehearing submissions/briefs are an anomaly. The rules of evidence are not applied in any formal sense. The relevant

FMCS statistic indicates that transcripts are made in only one of four cases. Further, in most cases we need not be concerned with potential reversal on the merits by an appellate body.

[Professor] St. Antoine's conceptualization of the arbitrator as the parties' "official contract reader" provides an apt description of the arbitrator's function in the private sector * * *.

Stephen L. Hayford, *The Changing Character of Labor Arbitration, in* ARBITRATION 1992, IMPROVING ARBITRAL AND ADVOCACY SKILLS, PROCEEDINGS OF THE FORTY-FIFTH ANNUAL MEETING, NATIONAL ACADEMY OF ARBITRATORS 73–74 (Gladys W. Gruenberg ed., 1992).

The material in Section C suggests that international commercial arbitration is somewhat more formal than either domestic commercial arbitration or labor arbitration.

YVES DEZALAY AND BRYANT GARTH, MERCHANTS OF LAW AS MORAL ENTREPRENEURS: CONSTRUCTING INTERNATIONAL JUSTICE FROM COMPETITION FOR TRANSNATIONAL BUSINESS DISPUTES

29 Law & Soc'y Rev. 27, 30–31 (1995).

When businesses enter into transnational relationships such as contracts for the sale of goods, joint ventures, construction projects, or distributorships, the contract typically calls for arbitration in the event of any dispute arising from the contractual arrangement. The main reason given today for this choice is that it allows each party to avoid being forced to submit to the courts of the other. Another is the secrecy of the process. International arbitration can be "institutional," following the procedural rules of the International Chamber of Commerce in Paris, the American Arbitration Association, the London Court of International Commercial Arbitration, or many others; or it can be ad hoc, often following the rules of the United Nations Commission on International Trade Law (UNCITRAL) used also for the arbitrations by the Iran Claims Tribunal at the Hague.

The arbitrators are private individuals selected by the parties, and usually there are three arbitrators. The parties each select one, and the parties jointly, the arbitrators, or an institutional appointing authority select the third. They act as private judges, holding hearings and issuing judgments. There are few grounds for appeal to courts, and the final decision of the arbitrators, under the terms of a widely adopted 1958 New York Convention, is more easily enforced among signatory countries than would be a court judgment.

There is considerable competition for the business of representing parties, providing institutional support, and serving as arbitrators. The increasing competition is an important aspect of international arbitration today, but it is also essential to see that there are a relatively small number of important institutions, chief among them the International Chamber of Commerce, and of individuals in each country who are the key players both as counsel and as arbitrators. There is a kind of "international arbitration community" — quite often referred to as a "club" — connected by personal and professional relations cemented by conferences, journals, and actual arbitrations. * * *

Questions

1. Would you feel comfortable as a lawyer presenting a case to an arbitrator without some of the procedural rights available in litigation? Would it depend on the type of case?

B. THE LEGAL FRAMEWORK FOR ARBITRATION UNDER THE FAA

In this section, we focus on the legal framework for arbitrations conducted under the Federal Arbitration Act, which will include most commercial, employment, and consumer arbitrations. As we shall see in Section 2, the U.S. Supreme Court has given the FAA broad preemptive effect over related state arbitration law. As you read these materials, ask yourself what policy interests are served and disserved by such a posture. Section 3 then looks at the difficult problem of arbitrability, which is, generally, the question of whether a dispute is subject to an arbitration provision, and who decides that question. In Section 4, we focus on the controversial problem of so-called mandatory, or unilaterally imposed arbitration, with a series of important cases that in part chronicle the U.S. Supreme Court's initial unwillingness to enforce pre-dispute agreements to arbitrate in *Wilko v. Swan*, to the Court's apparent modern embrace of mandatory arbitration in *Gilmer v. Interstate Johnson/Lane*, 500 U.S. 20, 111 S.Ct. 1647, 114 L.Ed.2d 26 (1991), and the related problems of forum fees and class actions.

1. A BRIEF SUMMARY OF THE FEDERAL ARBITRATION ACT

The FAA, 9 U.S.C. § 1 *et seq.* (2000), was enacted in 1925 primarily to reverse legislatively the historic "ouster doctrine," a centuries-old common law doctrine under which courts refused to enforce agreements to arbitrate. For a definitive legislative history of the FAA, see IAN R. MACNEIL, AMERICAN ARBITRATION LAW: REFORMATION, NATIONALIZATION, INTERNATIONALIZATION (1992). In particular, Section 2 of the Act provides that arbitration agreements will be enforced just like any other agreement, as long as the agreement is enforceable as a matter of contract law. Section 4 of the Act further permits a court to compel an unwilling party into arbitration if it is satisfied that there is an enforceable agreement to arbitrate, and Section 3 permits it to stay related legal proceedings. Section 7 of the FAA permits an arbitrator to summon and hear witnesses during the arbitration, while Sections 9 and 13 permit the arbitrator to issue an award that may be entered as a court judgment. After an arbitration, Section 11 authorizes a court to modify or correct an award, while Section 10 allows a court to vacate an award where there was corruption, partiality, or other misconduct by the arbitrator, or where the arbitrator exceeded the scope of his or her authority.

2. WHAT LAW APPLIES? THE FAA AND THE PREEMPTION OF STATE LAW

Whether courts will enforce an agreement to arbitrate is a crucial issue. At one time, United States courts would not enforce such an agreement until the arbitrator had issued the award. Thomas E. Carbonneau, *The Reception of Arbitration In United States Law*, 40 Me. L. Rev. 263, 267 (1988). This meant that parties could withdraw from a proceeding at any time prior to the award if they thought they were going to lose. Arbitration proponents secured the passage of federal and state statutes changing this rule. As noted above, the Federal Arbitration Act (see Appendix D) was adopted in 1925, and was initially called the U.S. Arbitration Act. The promulgation in 1955 of the Uniform Arbitration Act (see Appendix E) was an important impetus for state action. Peter H. Berge, *The Uniform Arbitration Act: A Retrospective On Its Thirty-Fifth Anniversary*, 14 Hamline L. Rev. 301, 305 (1991). Section 301 of the Taft–Hartley Act was interpreted as authorizing enforcement of agreements to arbitrate labor-management contract disputes. *Textile Workers Union v. Lincoln Mills,* 353 U.S. 448, 451, 77 S.Ct. 912, 1 L.Ed.2d 972 (1957). Although there is cross citing of precedent between labor and commercial arbitration cases, labor arbitration law is rooted in Section 301, and commercial arbitration law is rooted in the FAA.

The original assumption was that the FAA applied only in federal courts. Ian R. Macneil, Richard E. Speidel, Thomas J. Stipanowich, Federal Arbitration Law §§ 10.2, 10.3.1, 10.3.2 (1994 ed. & Supp. 1999). This was significant because the FAA authorized enforcement of a broader range of arbitration agreements than most states. Numerous issues were excluded from arbitration by state arbitration statutes or other state statutes or decisions. Application of the FAA in state courts had the potential of invalidating a wide range of state statutes and decisions hostile to arbitration. The Supreme Court indicated in its 1967 decision in *Prima Paint Corp. v. Flood & Conklin Manufacturing Co.,* 388 U.S. 395, 87 S.Ct. 1801, 18 L.Ed.2d 1270 (1967), that the FAA created a body of federal substantive law. *Id.* at 404–05. This conclusion was reaffirmed in the Court's 1983 decision in *Moses H. Cone Memorial Hospital v. Mercury Construction Corp.,* 460 U.S. 1, 103 S.Ct. 927, 74 L.Ed.2d 765 (1983). The significance of these decisions became clear in the case that follows.

SOUTHLAND CORP. v. KEATING

Supreme Court of the United States, 1984.
465 U.S. 1, 104 S.Ct. 852, 79 L.Ed.2d 1.

Chief Justice Burger delivered the opinion of the Court.

This case presents the questions (a) whether the California Franchise Investment Law, which invalidates certain arbitration agreements covered by the Federal Arbitration Act, violates the Supremacy Clause and (b) whether arbitration under the Federal Act is impaired when a class-action structure is imposed on the process by the state courts.

I

Appellant Southland Corp. is the owner and franchisor of 7–Eleven convenience stores. Southland's standard franchise agreement provides each franchisee with a license to use certain registered trademarks, a lease or sublease of a convenience store owned or leased by Southland, inventory financing, and assistance in advertising and merchandising. The franchisees operate the stores, supply bookkeeping data, and pay Southland a fixed percentage of gross profits. The franchise agreement also contains the following provision requiring arbitration:

> Any controversy or claim arising out of or relating to this Agreement or the breach hereof shall be settled by arbitration in accordance with the Rules of the American Arbitration Association ... and judgment upon any award rendered by the arbitrator may be entered in any court having jurisdiction thereof.

Appellees are 7–Eleven franchisees. Between September 1975 and January 1977, several appellees filed individual actions against Southland in California Superior Court alleging, among other things, fraud, oral misrepresentation, breach of contract, breach of fiduciary duty, and violation of the disclosure requirements of the California Franchise Investment Law, Cal.Corp.Code § 31000 *et seq.* (West 1977). Southland's answer, in all but one of the individual actions, included the affirmative defense of failure to arbitrate.

In May 1977, appellee Keating filed a class action against Southland on behalf of a class that assertedly includes approximately 800 California franchisees. Keating's principal claims were substantially the same as those asserted by the other franchisees. After the various actions were consolidated, Southland petitioned to compel arbitration of the claims in all cases, and appellees moved for class certification.

The Superior Court granted Southland's motion to compel arbitration of all claims except those claims based on the [California] Franchise Investment Law. The court did not pass on appellees' request for class certification. Southland appealed from the order insofar as it excluded from arbitration the claims based on the California statute. Appellees filed a petition for a writ of mandamus or prohibition in the California Court of Appeal arguing that the arbitration should proceed as a class action.

The California Court of Appeal reversed the trial court's refusal to compel arbitration of appellees' claims under the Franchise Investment Law. That court interpreted the arbitration clause to require arbitration of all claims asserted under the Franchise Investment Law, and construed the Franchise Investment Law not to invalidate such agreements to arbitrate. Alternatively, the court concluded that if the Franchise Investment Law rendered arbitration agreements involving commerce unenforceable, it would conflict with § 2 of the Federal Arbitration Act, 9 U.S.C. § 2 (1976), and therefore be invalid under the Supremacy Clause. The Court of Appeal also determined that there was no "insurmountable obstacle" to conducting an arbitration on a classwide basis, and issued a writ of mandate directing the trial court to conduct class certification proceedings.

The California Supreme Court, by a vote of 4–2, reversed the ruling that claims asserted under the Franchise Investment Law are arbitrable. The California Supreme Court interpreted the Franchise Investment Law to require judicial consideration of claims brought under that statute and concluded that the California statute did not contravene the federal Act. The court also remanded the case to the trial court for consideration of appellees' request for classwide arbitration.

We postponed consideration of the question of jurisdiction pending argument on the merits. We reverse in part and dismiss in part.

* * *

The California Franchise Investment Law provides:

> Any condition, stipulation or provision purporting to bind any person acquiring any franchise to waive compliance with any provision of this law or any rule or order hereunder is void. Cal.Corp. Code § 31512 (West 1977).

The California Supreme Court interpreted this statute to require judicial consideration of claims brought under the state statute and accordingly refused to enforce the parties' contract to arbitrate such claims. So interpreted the California Franchise Investment Law directly conflicts with § 2 of the Federal Arbitration Act and violates the Supremacy Clause.

In enacting § 2 of the federal act, Congress declared a national policy favoring arbitration and withdrew the power of the states to require a judicial forum for the resolution of claims which the contracting parties agreed to resolve by arbitration. The Federal Arbitration Act provides:

> A written provision in any maritime transaction or a contract evidencing a transaction involving commerce to settle by arbitration a controversy thereafter arising out of such contract or transaction, or the refusal to perform the whole or any part thereof, or an agreement in writing to submit to arbitration an existing controversy arising out of such a contract, transaction, or refusal, shall be valid, irrevocable, and enforceable, save upon such grounds as exist at law or in equity for the revocation of any contract. 9 U.S.C. § 2 (1976).

Congress has thus mandated the enforcement of arbitration agreements.

We discern only two limitations on the enforceability of arbitration provisions governed by the Federal Arbitration Act: they must be part of a written maritime contract or a contract "evidencing a transaction involving commerce" and such clauses may be revoked upon "grounds as exist at law or in equity for the revocation of any contract." We see nothing in the Act indicating that the broad principle of enforceability is subject to any additional limitations under state law.

The Federal Arbitration Act rests on the authority of Congress to enact substantive rules under the Commerce Clause. In *Prima Paint Corp. v. Flood & Conklin Manufacturing Corp.*, 388 U.S. 395 (1967), the Court examined the legislative history of the Act and concluded that the statute "is based upon . . . the incontestable federal foundations of 'control over interstate commerce and over admiralty.' " *Id.*, at 405 (quoting H.R.Rep. No. 96, 68th Cong., 1st Sess. 1 (1924)). The contract in *Prima Paint,* as here, contained an arbitration clause. One party in that case alleged that the other had committed fraud in the inducement of the contract, although not of the arbitration clause in particular, and sought to have the claim of fraud adjudicated in federal court. The Court held that, notwithstanding a contrary state rule, consideration of a claim of fraud in the inducement of a contract "is for the arbitrators and not for the courts," 388 U.S. at 400. The Court relied for this holding on Congress' broad power to fashion substantive rules under the Commerce Clause.

At least since 1824 Congress' authority under the Commerce Clause has been held plenary. In the words of Chief Justice Marshall, the authority of Congress is "the power to regulate; that is, to prescribe the rule by which commerce is to be governed." *Ibid.* The statements of the Court in *Prima Paint* that the Arbitration Act was an exercise of the Commerce Clause power clearly implied that the substantive rules of the Act were to apply in state as well as federal courts. As Justice Black observed in his dissent, when Congress exercises its authority to enact substantive federal law under the Commerce Clause, it normally creates rules that are enforceable in state as well as federal courts.

In *Moses H. Cone Memorial Hospital v. Mercury Construction* Corp., 460 U.S., at 1, 25, and n. 32, we reaffirmed our view that the Arbitration Act "creates a body of federal substantive law" and expressly stated what was implicit in *Prima Paint, i.e.,* the substantive law the Act created was applicable in state and federal court. *Moses H. Cone* began with a petition for an order to compel arbitration. The District Court stayed the action pending resolution of a concurrent state-court suit. In holding that the District Court had abused its discretion, we found no showing of exceptional circumstances justifying the stay and recognized "the presence of federal-law issues" under the federal Act as "a major consideration weighing against surrender [of federal jurisdiction]." We thus read the underlying issue of arbitrability to be a question of substantive federal law: "Federal law in the terms of the Arbitration Act governs that issue in either state or federal court."

Although the legislative history is not without ambiguities, there are strong indications that Congress had in mind something more than making arbitration agreements enforceable only in the federal courts. The House Report plainly suggests the more comprehensive objectives:

> The purpose of this bill is to make valid and enforcible [sic] agreements for arbitration contained *in contracts involving interstate commerce* or within the jurisdiction or [sic] admiralty, *or* which may be the subject of litigation in the Federal courts.

This broader purpose can also be inferred from the reality that Congress would be less likely to address a problem whose impact was confined to federal courts than a problem of large significance in the field of commerce. The Arbitration Act sought to "overcome the rule of equity, that equity will not specifically enforce [any] arbitration agreement." The House Report accompanying the bill stated:

> The need for the law arises from ... the jealousy of the English courts for their own jurisdiction. ... This jealousy survived for so [long] a period that the principle became firmly embedded in the English common law and was adopted with it by the American courts. The courts have felt that the precedent was too strongly fixed to be overturned without legislative enactment....

Surely this makes clear that the House Report contemplated a broad reach of the Act, unencumbered by state-law constraints. As was stated in *Metro Industrial Painting Corp. v. Terminal Construction Co.*, "the purpose of the act was to assure those who desired arbitration and whose contracts related to interstate commerce that their expectations would not be undermined by federal judges, or ... by state courts or legislatures." Congress also showed its awareness of the widespread unwillingness of state courts to enforce arbitration agreements, and that such courts were bound by state laws inadequately providing for "technical arbitration by which, if you agree to arbitrate under the method provided by the statute, you have an arbitration by statute[;] but [the statutes] [had] nothing to do with validating the contract to arbitrate."

The problems Congress faced were therefore twofold: the old common law hostility toward arbitration, and the failure of state arbitration statutes to mandate enforcement of arbitration agreements. To confine the scope of the Act to arbitrations sought to be enforced in federal courts would frustrate what we believe Congress intended to be a broad enactment appropriate in scope to meet the large problems Congress was addressing.

Justice O'Connor argues that Congress viewed the Arbitration Act "as a procedural statute, applicable only in federal courts." If it is correct that Congress sought only to create a procedural remedy in the federal courts, there can be no explanation for the express limitation in the Arbitration Act to contracts "involving commerce." 9 U.S.C. § 2. For example, when Congress has authorized this Court to prescribe the rules of procedure in the federal courts of appeals, district courts, and bankruptcy courts, it has not limited the power of the Court to prescribe rules applicable only to causes of action involving commerce. We would expect that if Congress, in enacting the Arbitration Act, was creating what it thought to be a procedural rule applicable only in federal courts, it would not so limit the Act to transactions involving commerce. On the other hand, Congress would need to call on the Commerce Clause if it intended the Act to apply in state courts. Yet at the same time, its reach would be limited to transactions involving interstate commerce. We therefore view the "involving commerce" requirement in § 2, not as an inexplicable limitation on the power of the federal courts, but as a necessary qualification on a statute intended to apply in state and federal courts.

Under the interpretation of the Arbitration Act urged by Justice O'Connor, claims brought under the California Franchise Investment Law are not arbitrable when they are raised in state court. Yet it is clear beyond question that if this suit had been brought as a diversity action in a federal district court, the arbitration clause would have been enforceable. *Prima Paint, supra.* The interpretation given to the Arbitration Act by the California Supreme Court would therefore encourage and reward forum shopping. We are unwilling to attribute to Congress the intent, in drawing on the comprehensive powers of the Commerce Clause, to create a right to enforce an arbitration contract and yet make the right dependent for its enforcement on the particular forum in which it is asserted. And since the overwhelming proportion of all civil litigation in this country is in the state courts, we cannot believe Congress intended to limit the Arbitration Act to disputes subject only to *federal-court* jurisdiction. Such an interpretation would frustrate congressional intent to place "[an] arbitration agreement ... upon the same footing as other contracts, where it belongs."

In creating a substantive rule applicable in state as well as federal courts, Congress intended to foreclose state legislative attempts to undercut the enforceability of arbitration agreements.[11] We hold that § 31512 of the California Franchise Investment Law violates the Supremacy Clause.

* * *

Justice O'Connor, with whom Justice Rehnquist joins in dissenting.

* * *

One rarely finds a legislative history as unambiguous as the FAA's. That history establishes conclusively that the 1925 Congress viewed the FAA as a procedural statute, applicable only in federal courts, derived, Congress believed, largely from the federal power to control the jurisdiction of the federal courts.

---

11. Justice Steven dissents in part on the ground that § 2 of the Arbitration Act permits a party to nullify an agreement to arbitrate on "such grounds as exist at law or in equity for the revocation of any contract." We agree, of course, that a party may assert general contract defenses such as fraud to avoid enforcement of an arbitration agreement. We conclude, however, that the defense to arbitration found in the California Franchise Investment Law is not a ground that exists at law or in equity "for the revocation of *any* contract" but merely a ground that exists for the revocation of arbitration provisions in contracts subject to the California Franchise Investment Law. * * *

In 1925 Congress emphatically believed arbitration to be a matter of "procedure." At hearings on the Act congressional Subcommittees were told: "The theory on which you do this is that you have the right to tell the Federal courts how to proceed." The House Report on the FAA stated: "Whether an agreement for arbitration shall be enforced or not is a question of procedure ..." On the floor of the House Congressman Graham assured his fellow members that the FAA

> Does not involve any new principle of law except to provide a simple method ... in order to give enforcement ... It creates no new legislation, grants no new rights, except a remedy to enforce an agreement in commercial contracts and in admiralty contracts.

A month after the Act was signed into law the American Bar Association Committee that had drafted and pressed for passage of the federal legislation wrote:

> The statute establishes a procedure in the Federal courts for the enforcement of arbitration agreements ... A Federal statute providing for the enforcement of arbitration agreements does relate solely to procedure in the Federal courts ... [Whether] or not an arbitration agreement is to be enforced is a question of the law of procedure and is determined by the law of the jurisdiction wherein the remedy is sought. That the enforcement of arbitration contracts is within the law of procedure as distinguished from substantive law is well settled by the decisions of our courts.

* * *

The Court, *ante*, at 15–16, rejects the idea of requiring the FAA to be applied only in federal courts partly out of concern with the problem of forum shopping. The concern is unfounded. Because the FAA makes the federal courts equally accessible to both parties to a dispute, no forum shopping would be possible even if we gave the FAA a construction faithful to the congressional intent. * * *

[The court's discussion of jurisdiction and the propriety of superimposing class action procedures on a contract arbitration is omitted. Also omitted is the opinion of Justice Stevens, who concurred in part and dissented in part.]

Notes and Questions

1. *Southland* was one of the more important of a group of Supreme Court decisions that federalized arbitration law and gave a strong impetus to arbitration. Not only is the FAA a substantive statute that governs in state as well as federal courts, superseding conflicting state law, but "any doubts concerning the scope of arbitrable issues should be resolved in favor of arbitration, whether the problem at hand is the construction of the contract language itself or an allegation of waiver, delay, or a like defense to arbitrability." *Moses H. Cone Memorial Hospital v. Mercury Construction Corp.*, 460 U.S. 1, 24–25, 103 S.Ct. 927, 74 L.Ed.2d 765 (1983).

2. *Southland* was and remains controversial. If you were a state attorney general charged with enforcing your states' civil laws, what would be your reaction to the decision? *See* Barbara A. Atwood, *Issues in Federal–State Relations Under the Federal Arbitration Act*, 37 U. Fla. L. Rev. 61, 102–03 (1985).

If you were a United States Senator would you support legislation that would overrule Southland? *See* Jean R. Sternlight, *Panacea or Corporate Tool?: Debunking the Supreme Court's Preference for Binding Arbitration*, 74 Wash. U. L.Q. 637, at 697–701 (1996).

3. The FAA does not apply unless an arbitration provision is part of a written maritime contract or a contract evidencing a transaction involving commerce. Following *Southland*, the lower courts differed on whether this language extended the FAA's coverage to the constitutional limits of Congress' power.

The Supreme Court adopted the expansive interpretation in *Allied-Bruce Terminix Cos. v. Dobson*, 513 U.S. 265, 115 S.Ct. 834, 130 L.Ed.2d 753 (1995). Writing for the Court, Justice Breyer stated that:

> ... a broad interpretation of this language is consistent with the Act's basic purpose, to put arbitration provisions on "the same footing" as a contract's other terms ... Conversely, a narrower interpretation ... would create a new, unfamiliar test lying somewhere in the no-man's land between "in commerce" and "affecting commerce," thereby unnecessarily complicating the law and breeding litigation from a statute that seeks to avoid it.

513 U.S. at 275.

In a concurring opinion in *Allied-Bruce*, Justice O'Connor said, "I continue to believe that Congress never intended the Federal Arbitration Act to apply in state courts..." (513 U.S. at 283) but then went on to state that:

> Were we writing on a clean slate, I would adhere to that view and affirm the Alabama court's decision. But, as the Court points out, more than 10 years have passed since *Southland*, several subsequent cases have built upon its reasoning, and parties have undoubtedly made contracts in reliance on the Court's interpretation of the Act in the interim. After reflection, I am persuaded by considerations of *stare decisis*, which we have said "have special force in the area of statutory interpretation," ... to acquiesce in today's judgment. Though wrong, *Southland* has not proved unworkable, and, as always, "Congress remains free to alter what we have done."

Id. at 283–84.

Do you find Justice O'Connor's argument persuasive?

4. For an extended and authoritative critique of *Southland*, see IAN R. MACNEIL, AMERICAN ARBITRATION LAW: REFORMATION, NATIONALIZATION, INTERNATIONALIZATION 92–121 (1992). *See also*, Paul D. Carrington, *Contract and Jurisdiction*, 1996 S. Ct. Rev. 331; David S. Schwartz, *Correcting Federalism Mistakes In Statutory Interpretation: The Supreme Court and the Federal Arbitration Act*, 67 Law & Contemp. Probs. 5 (2004), and Jean R. Sternlight, *Rethinking the Constitutionality of the Supreme Court's Preference for*

Binding Arbitration: A Fresh Assessment of Jury Trial, Separation of Powers, and Due Process Concerns, 72 Tul. L. Rev. 1 (1997). Professor David Schwartz argues that the FAA is unconstitutional as it has been applied in Southland and its progeny. He asserts that "the FAA is the only federal statute that is 'substantive' for preemption purposes even though it is really procedural, and procedural for every other purpose." David Schwartz, *The Federal Arbitration Act and the Power of Congress Over State Courts,* 83 Oregon L. Rev. 541, 628 (2004).

Professor Christopher R. Drahozal acknowledges the weakness of Justice Burger's arguments in his *Southland* analysis, but offers alternative rationales in arguing that the court reached the right result in the case. *See* Christopher R. Drahozal, *In Defense of Southland: Reexamining the Legislative History of the Federal Arbitration Act,* 78 Notre Dame L. Rev. 101 (2002).

DOCTOR'S ASSOCIATES, INC. v. CASAROTTO

Supreme Court of the United States, 1996.
517 U.S. 681, 116 S.Ct. 1652, 134 L.Ed.2d 902.

Justice Ginsburg delivered the opinion of the Court.

This case concerns a standard form franchise agreement for the operation of a Subway sandwich shop in Montana. When a dispute arose between parties to the agreement, franchisee Paul Casarotto sued franchisor Doctor's Associates, Inc. (DAI), and DAI's Montana development agent, Nick Lombardi, in a Montana state court. DAI and Lombardi sought to stop the litigation pending arbitration pursuant to the arbitration clause set out on page nine of the franchise agreement.

The Federal Arbitration Act (FAA or Act) declares written provisions for arbitration "valid, irrevocable, and enforceable, save upon such grounds as exist at law or in equity for the revocation of any contract." 9 U.S.C. § 2. Montana law, however, declares an arbitration clause unenforceable unless "notice that [the] contract is subject to arbitration" is "typed in underlined capital letters on the first page of the contract." Mont.Code Ann. § 27–5–114(4) (1995). The question here presented is whether Montana's law is compatible with the federal Act. We hold that Montana's first-page notice requirement, which governs not "any contract," but specifically and solely contracts "subject to arbitration," conflicts with the FAA and is therefore displaced by the federal measure.

I

Petitioner DAI is the national franchisor of Subway sandwich shops. In April 1988, DAI entered a franchise agreement with respondent Paul Casarotto, which permitted Casarotto to open a Subway shop in Great Falls, Montana. The franchise agreement stated, on page nine and in ordinary type: "Any controversy or claim arising out of or relating to this contract or the breach thereof shall be settled by Arbitration ...."

In October 1992, Casarotto sued DAI and its agent, Nick Lombardi, in Montana state court, alleging state-law contract and tort claims relating to the franchise agreement. DAI demanded arbitration of those claims, and successfully moved in the Montana trial court to stay the lawsuit pending arbitration.

The Montana Supreme Court reversed. That court left undisturbed the trial court's findings that the franchise agreement fell within the scope of the FAA and covered the claims Casarotto stated against DAI and Lombardi. The Montana Supreme Court held, however, that Mont. Code Ann. § 27–5–114(4) rendered the agreement's arbitration clause unenforceable. The Montana statute provides:

> "Notice that a contract is subject to arbitration ... shall be typed in underlined capital letters on the first page of the contract; and unless such notice is displayed thereon, the contract may not be subject to arbitration."

Notice of the arbitration clause in the franchise agreement did not appear on the first page of the contract. Nor was anything relating to the clause typed in underlined capital letters. Because the State's statutory notice requirement had not been met, the Montana Supreme Court declared the parties' dispute "not subject to arbitration."

DAI and Lombardi unsuccessfully argued before the Montana Supreme Court that § 27–5–114(4) was preempted by § 2 of the FAA.[1] DAI and Lombardi dominantly relied on our decisions in *Southland Corp. v. Keating,* and *Perry v. Thomas.* In *Southland,* we held that § 2 of the FAA applies in state as well as federal courts, see 465 U.S. at 12, and "withdr[aws] the power of the states to require a judicial forum for the resolution of claims which the contracting parties agreed to resolve by arbitration." We noted in the pathmarking *Southland* decision that the FAA established a "broad principle of enforceability," and that § 2 of the federal Act provided for revocation of arbitration agreements only upon "grounds as exist at law or in equity for the revocation of any contract." In *Perry,* we reiterated: "State law, whether of legislative or judicial origin, is applicable *if* that law arose to govern issues concerning the validity, revocability, and enforceability of contracts generally. A state-law principle that takes its meaning precisely from the fact that a contract to arbitrate is at issue does not comport with [the text of § 2]."

The Montana Supreme Court, however, read our decision in *Volt Information Sciences, Inc. v. Board of Trustees of Leland Stanford Junior Univ.,* 489 U.S. 468, 103 L. Ed. 2d 488, 109 S. Ct. 1248 (1989), as limiting the preemptive force of § 2 and correspondingly qualifying *Southland* and *Perry.* As the Montana Supreme Court comprehended *Volt,* the proper inquiry here should focus not on the bare words of § 2, but on this question: Would the application of Montana's notice requirement, contained in § 27–5–114(4), "undermine the goals and policies of

---

1. Section 2 provides, in relevant part: "A written provision in ... a contract evidencing a transaction involving commerce to settle by arbitration a controversy thereafter arising out of such contract or trans- action, or the refusal to perform the whole or any part thereof, ... shall be valid, irrevocable, and enforceable, save upon such grounds as exist at law or in equity for the revocation of any contract."

the FAA." Section 27–5–114(4), in the Montana court's judgment, did not undermine the goals and policies of the FAA, for the notice requirement did not preclude arbitration agreements altogether; it simply prescribed "that before arbitration agreements are enforceable, they be entered knowingly."

DAI and Lombardi petitioned for certiorari. Last Term, we granted their petition, vacated the judgment of the Montana Supreme Court, and remanded for further consideration in light of *Allied-Bruce Terminix Cos. v. Dobson*, 513 U.S. 265, 130 L. Ed. 2d 753, 115 S. Ct. 834 (1995). See 515 U.S. 1129 (1995). In *Allied-Bruce,* we restated what our decisions in *Southland* and *Perry* had established:

> "States may regulate contracts, including arbitration clauses, under general contract law principles and they may invalidate an arbitration clause 'upon such grounds as exist at law or in equity for the revocation of *any* contract.' 9 U.S.C. § 2 (emphasis added). What States may not do is decide that a contract is fair enough to enforce all its basic terms (price, service, credit), but not fair enough to enforce its arbitration clause. The Act makes any such state policy unlawful, for that kind of policy would place arbitration clauses on an unequal 'footing,' directly contrary to the Act's language and Congress's intent."

On remand, without inviting or permitting further briefing or oral argument, the Montana Supreme Court adhered to its original ruling. The court stated: "After careful review, we can find nothing in the *[Allied–Bruce]* decision which relates to the issues presented to this Court in this case." Elaborating, the Montana court said it found "no suggestion in *[Allied–Bruce]* that the principles from *Volt* on which we relied [to uphold § 27–5–114(4)] have been modified in any way." We again granted certiorari, and now reverse.

II

Section 2 of the FAA provides that written arbitration agreements "shall be valid, irrevocable, and enforceable, save upon such grounds as exist at law or in equity for the revocation of *any* contract." Repeating our observation in *Perry,* the text of § 2 declares that state law may be applied "*if* that law arose to govern issues concerning the validity, revocability, and enforceability of contracts generally." Thus, generally applicable contract defenses, such as fraud, duress, or unconscionability, may be applied to invalidate arbitration agreements without contravening § 2. * * *

Courts may not, however, invalidate arbitration agreements under state laws applicable *only* to arbitration provisions. See *Allied-Bruce*; *Perry.* By enacting § 2, we have several times said, Congress precluded States from singling out arbitration provisions for suspect status, requiring instead that such provisions be placed "upon the same footing as other contracts." Montana's § 27–5–114(4) directly conflicts with § 2 of the FAA because the State's law conditions the enforceability of arbitration agreements on compliance with a special notice requirement not applicable to contracts generally. The FAA thus displaces the Montana statute with respect to arbitration agreements covered by the Act. * * *

The Montana Supreme Court misread our *Volt* decision and therefore reached a conclusion in this case at odds with our rulings. *Volt* involved an arbitration agreement that incorporated state procedural rules, one of which, on the facts of that case, called for arbitration to be stayed pending the resolution of a related judicial proceeding. The state rule examined in *Volt* determined only the efficient order of proceedings; it did not affect the enforceability of the arbitration agreement itself. We held that applying the state rule would not "undermine the goals and policies of the FAA," because the very purpose of the Act was to "ensur[e] that private agreements to arbitrate are enforced according to their terms."

Applying § 27–5–114(4) here, in contrast, would not enforce the arbitration clause in the contract between DAI and Casarotto; instead, Montana's first-page notice requirement would invalidate the clause. The "goals and policies" of the FAA, this Court's precedent indicates, are antithetical to threshold limitations placed specifically and solely on arbitration provisions. Section 2 "mandate[s] the enforcement of arbitration agreements, "save upon such grounds as exist at law or in equity for the revocation of any contract."* * * Montana's law places arbitration agreements in a class apart from "any contract," and singularly limits their validity. The State's prescription is thus inconsonant with, and is therefore preempted by, the federal law.

* * *

For the reasons stated, the judgment of the Supreme Court of Montana is reversed, and the case is remanded for further proceedings not inconsistent with this opinion.

It is so ordered.

Justice Thomas, dissenting. For the reasons given in my dissent last Term in *Allied-Bruce Terminix Cos. v. Dobson*, I remain of the view that § 2 of the Federal Arbitration Act, does not apply to proceedings in state courts. Accordingly, I respectfully dissent.

Notes and Questions

1. The *Casarotto* case is an example of the breadth of the preemption doctrine. Does the case make you more or less supportive of *Southland* and *Allied-Bruce*?

2. Would any of the following state laws or decisions be invalid under the principles laid down in *Southland* and *Allied-Bruce*?

a) Massachusetts regulations prohibited securities firms from requiring customers to agree to arbitration as a condition precedent to account relationships. *See Securities Industry Ass'n v. Connolly*, 883 F.2d 1114 (1st Cir. 1989).

(b) New York law required arbitration agreements to be express and unequivocal. *See Continental Group, Inc. v. NPS Communications, Inc.*, 873 F.2d 613, 619 n.3 (2d Cir. 1989); and IAN R. MACNEIL, RICHARD E. SPEIDEL & THOMAS J. STIPANOWICH, FEDERAL ARBITRATION LAW § 10.8.3.3, text accompanying n.103 (1994 ed. & Supp. 1999).

(c) A Pennsylvania rule precluded arbitration of bad faith claims against insurance companies. *Brayman Construction Co. v. Home Insurance Co.*, 319 F.3d 622, 627 (3rd Cir. 2003).

STEPHEN L. HAYFORD, FEDERAL PREEMPTION AND VACATUR: THE BOOKEND ISSUES UNDER THE REVISED UNIFORM ARBITRATION ACT

2001 J. Disp. Resol. 67, 67–76, 78–80.

I. INTRODUCTION

As one of the two Academic Advisors to the Drafting Committee appointed by the National Conference of Commissioners on Uniform State Laws ("NCCUSL") to revise the Uniform Arbitration Act, I was assigned primary responsibility for the two most important issues pertinent to the Drafting Committee's framing of the Revised Uniform Arbitration Act ("RUAA"). The first — the issue of federal preemption — set the baseline for the scope and character of the RUAA by defining for the Drafting Committee the areas of the substantive law of arbitration in which the states are free to regulate, the Federal Arbitration Act ("FAA") notwithstanding. The second — the issue of vacatur — is by far the most significant dimension of substantive arbitration law open to state regulation. This article describes the manner in which the RUAA Drafting Committee engaged and resolved the issues of federal preemption and vacatur.

II. THE RUAA AND FEDERAL PREEMPTION

When NCCUSL promulgated the original Uniform Arbitration Act ("UAA") in 1955, the preemptive effect of the FAA and attendant federal case law on state arbitration statutes was not a major concern. The FAA was moribund, having been effectively subsumed by the long-standing common law rule whereby executory agreements to arbitrate were deemed unenforceable. Even if the FAA had not been hamstrung, the UAA presented no significant preemption concerns because its substantive provisions did little more than mimic the terms of the FAA.

American arbitration, circa 1955, was for the most part limited to a few business-to-business venues and arbitration arising under collective-bargaining agreements between employers and the unions representing their employees. These were comparatively simple arbitration mechanisms that were not considered surrogates for adjudication in a court of law. Consequently, NCCUSL, in its quest to provide the states with a uniform framework for legislation that would override the common law rule of non-enforceability, saw no need for state arbitration statutes to address any matters beyond the very basic concerns of enforceability and vacatur that are the core of the FAA regulatory scheme.

A. Commercial Arbitration Circa 1996 — A Whole New World

In 1996, when the RUAA Drafting Committee was charged with fashioning a replacement for the forty-plus year old UAA, the arbitration landscape had changed drastically. In a remarkable series of fourteen opinions handed down from 1983 through 1996, the Supreme Court eviscerated the common law rule rendering executory arbitration agreements unenforceable and resuscitated the FAA. The Court divined in the FAA a sweeping pro-arbitration public policy that, once recognized, it deemed sufficient to override many decades of judicial hostility toward the arbitration process outside the labor-management sphere. An integral dimension of this new legal framework for commercial arbitration is the Supreme Court's emphatic and repeated assertion that the pro-arbitration public policy of the FAA preempts contrary state law.

As a result of this drastic alteration in the federal legal landscape, the use of arbitration as an alternative to litigation in a court of law in the commercial sector (including non-union employment arbitration) exploded in the last decade of the twentieth century. The intersection of these two dynamics has greatly increased the demands placed on the law regulating commercial arbitration, revealing the gaps in the FAA's skeletal structure. Arbitration organizations like the American Arbitration Association and Judicial Arbitration and Mediation Services ("JAMS") have attempted to fill the interstices in the FAA by revising and expanding their commercial arbitration rules. Admirable as those efforts are, they are not an effective substitute for well thought-out legislative reform.

* * * Because it was the first public policy-making body charged with fashioning a statutory template for regulating an arbitration process that has morphed into a full-blown surrogate for litigation in the courts, the Drafting Committee confronted a question that had never before demanded an answer. That question asks: When undertaking to frame and enact a comprehensive legal framework for today's complex, high stakes arbitration process, what aspects of arbitration law remain open to regulation by the states in the face of the preemptive effect of the Federal Arbitration Act as identified and defined by the Supreme Court?

* * *

B. The Essential Predicate: The Supreme Court's Take on FAA Preemption

The six recent Supreme Court opinions defining the law of preemption under the FAA spring from the Court's earlier opinions in *Prima Paint Corp. v. Flood & Conklin Manufacturing Corp.* and *Moses H. Cone Memorial Hospital v. Mercury Construction Corp.* In those cases, the Court stated its belief that the FAA is an exercise of the Commerce

Clause authority creating a body of federal substantive law governing arbitration, applicable in both the federal and state courts. There are two dimensions to the law of preemption. The first concerns the direct preemption of conflicting state laws by the FAA and is represented by *Southland Corp. v. Keating, Perry v. Thomas, Allied-Bruce Terminix Cos. v. Dobson* and *Doctor's Associates v. Casarotto*. The second element of the law of FAA preemption centers on interpretation of the parties' contractual agreements to arbitrate in the course of determining the effect of those agreements on the state law-FAA interaction. It is embodied in *Volt Information Sciences, Inc. v. Board of Trustees of Leland Stanford Junior University*, and *Mastrobuono v. Shearson Lehman Hutton, Inc.* Each element is examined separately below.

1. The Direct Interface Between the Federal Arbitration Act and State Law

* * *

Read in concert, *Southland, Perry, Terminix* and *Casarotto* confirm that the FAA preempts state law conflicting with any of its terms. The substantive law of commercial arbitration is that set out in the Federal Arbitration Act, at least with regard to the issues expressly addressed in the FAA. The state courts are obliged to apply that law, even in the face of contrary state statutory or case law. This line of cases repeatedly signals that the Supreme Court will not tolerate efforts by state legislatures or state courts to undermine the seminal purpose of the FAA — the enforcement of contractual agreements to arbitrate. Further evidence that the Court views commercial arbitration under the FAA as a matter of contract, and the role of the judiciary under the FAA primarily to be a simple matter of enforcing otherwise valid agreements to arbitrate, is provided by the two cases discussed immediately below.

2. The Contract–Based Caveat to the Broad Rule of FAA Preemption

An important caveat to the general rule of FAA preemption is found in *Volt Information Sciences, Inc.* and *Mastrobuono*. The focus here is on the effect of FAA preemption on the choice of law provisions frequently included in commercial contracts. Plain and simple, in *Volt* the Supreme Court held that the intent of the parties to an arbitration agreement, as expressed in the contract between them, to conduct their arbitration under state law rules effectively trumps the preemptive effect of the FAA. [*Volt*, 489 U.S. 468 at 478 (1989)]. State law controls even when the contractual choice of law provision results in an arbitration conducted in a manner inconsistent with the substantive law of commercial arbitration set out in the FAA.

In *Volt*, the Court did not view the choice of law provision in the parties' contract as constituting a waiver of the federally-guaranteed right to compel arbitration of their dispute, a matter undoubtedly controlled by federal rather than state law. It stated: "§ 4 of the FAA does not confer a right to compel arbitration of any dispute at any time;

it confers only the right to obtain an order directing that 'arbitration proceed in the manner provided for in [the parties'] agreement.' " The Court observed there is no federal policy requiring commercial arbitration to be conducted under any particular set of rules. It stated: "arbitration under the FAA is a matter of consent, not coercion, and parties are generally free to structure their arbitration agreements as they see fit, just as they may limit by contract the issue which they will arbitrate, so too may they specify by contract the rules under which that arbitration will be conducted." Thus, if the parties elect to govern their contractual arbitration mechanism by the law of a particular state and thereby limit the issues they will arbitrate or the procedures under which the arbitration will be conducted, their bargain will be honored — as long as the state law principles invoked by the choice of law provision do not conflict with the FAA's prime directive that agreements to arbitrate be enforced.

In *Mastrobuono*, the Supreme Court further clarified its view of the circumstances when a contractual choice of law provision can block FAA preemption and permit an arbitration to be conducted under procedures or other terms not consistent with the FAA. In *Mastrobuono*, the Court was asked to decide whether a boilerplate contractual choice of law provision (not specific to the arbitration agreement contained in the underlying contract) invoking New York law rendered inarbitrable the claimant's prayer for punitive damages. [*Mastrobuono*, 514 U.S. 52 at 56 (1995)]. Unlike *Volt*, where great deference was paid a state court's interpretation of the effect of a choice of law clause, *Mastrobuono* gave the Court an opportunity to engage in a de novo analysis of the proper interpretation and effect of the disputed contract provisions. The way the Court analyzed the choice of law provision in the subject contract, juxtaposing it with the contractual arbitration clause, reveals it is willing to go to some length to avoid applying the rule of *Volt* in a manner that results in a contractual choice of law provision precluding an arbitral award of punitive damages.

The court achieved that result by characterizing the issue before it as a question of what the parties' contract had to say about the arbitrability of the claimant's prayer for punitive damages. In its effort to ascertain the mutual intent of the parties in that regard, the Court looked first to the choice of law provision (which made no reference to arbitration). It found there no indication that the parties, by virtue of their general invocation of New York law, intended to preclude arbitral awards of punitive damages. The Court next moved to an interpretation of the arbitration clause of the parties' contract, finding there strong implication that an arbitral award of punitive damages was appropriate. It ultimately concluded that "at most, the choice of law provision introduced an ambiguity into an arbitration agreement that would otherwise allow punitive damages awards." Citing to *Volt*, the Court asserted that in an arbitration agreement governed by the FAA due regard must be given to the strong federal policy favoring arbitration, and consequently, ambiguities as to the scope of the arbitration clause itself should be resolved in favor of arbitration.

Mastrobuono sends a forceful message as to the manner in which the Court believes the rule of *Volt* should be applied in the course of interpreting contractual choice of law provisions. By electing to read the choice of law provision before it in conjunction with the arbitration clause of the parties' contract, the *Mastrobuono* Court evidenced its belief that judicial interpretation of choice of law provisions designating state law inconsistent with the FAA should be glossed with a predisposition toward the strong federal policy favoring arbitration and a concomitant rule of (statutory and contract) interpretation which teaches that ambiguities as to the reach of the arbitration clause are to be resolved in favor of arbitration (and application of the FAA).

Thus, *Mastrobuono* establishes that choice of law provisions are properly interpreted to exclude a particular matter from arbitration, or to limit the arbitration proceeding in a manner inconsistent with the FAA, only when the parties' contract clearly and unequivocally evidences a mutual intent to that effect and where the state law doctrine contrary to the FAA is indisputable. Given the pro forma nature and vague wording of the typical contractual choice of law provision, that result seems unlikely in most cases. The mode of contract interpretation approved in *Mastrobuono* will, in the absence of a definitive decision by the parties to invoke state law inconsistent with the FAA, serve to ensure that the law of commercial arbitration remains a matter of federal substantive law controlled first by the FAA. That standard for application of the rule of *Volt* is entirely consistent with the position taken by the Court in *Southland, Perry,* and *Terminix* regarding preemption of state law by the FAA.

* * *

Notes and Questions

1. Explain how the *Volt* decision enables parties to structure their agreement so that they can conduct their arbitration proceeding in a manner inconsistent with the FAA substantive law.

2. Explain how *Mastrobuono* limits the practical effect of *Volt*.

CHRISTOPHER R. DRAHOZAL, FEDERAL ARBITRATION ACT PREEMPTION

79 Ind. L.J. 393, 393–395, 407–408, 420, 423–424 (2004).

Courts are now facing the second generation of Federal Arbitration Act ("FAA") preemption cases. "First generation" cases of FAA preemption involve state laws that invalidate parties' agreements to arbitrate. Courts now routinely hold such laws preempted, as required by a line of Supreme Court cases dating from Southland Corp. v. Keating. With those efforts to restrict the ongoing "consumerization" of arbitration stymied, state legislatures have begun adopting laws that modify the parties' arbitration agreement rather than invalidating it, regulating the arbitration process rather than the parties' obligation to arbitrate. California, for example, now requires extensive disclosures by neutral arbitrators of potential conflicts of interest and has enacted statutes regulating the conduct of institutions that administer consumer arbitrations. New Mexico, in adopting the Revised Uniform Arbitration Act ("RUAA"), added a provision making a "disabling civil dispute clause" — which the statute defines as including a provision that provides for a less convenient forum, reduced access to discovery, a limited right to appeal, the inability to join class actions, or the like- voidable by consumers, borrowers, tenants and employees in arbitration.

* * *

FAA Preemption: An Analytical Framework

Given the Supreme Court's cases to date, how should one analyze whether the FAA preempts a particular state law? The starting point is that preemption under the FAA is a form of conflict preemption, with state laws preempted when they conflict with the dictate of § § 2 that arbitration agreements be "valid, irrevocable, and enforceable." Then the question is: when do state arbitration laws conflict with the FAA? The focus here is on FAA preemption issues as they arise in state courts, the issue addressed by the Supreme Court in virtually all of its FAA preemption cases. In some respects, the analysis may differ in federal courts (as noted when appropriate).

This Part sets out a basic framework for analyzing FAA preemption, taking as given the Supreme Court's cases to date. The analytical framework consists of four steps:

1.   Does the state law apply to contracts generally or does it "single out" arbitration agreements for different treatment than other contracts? If the law applies to contracts generally, it is not preempted. If it singles out arbitration agreements for different treatment than other contracts, continue with the next step.

2.   Have the parties expressly contracted for application of the state law to the arbitration proceeding? If so, the law is not preempted. If not, continue with the next step.

3.   Does the state law invalidate the parties' arbitration agreement, in whole or in part, conditionally or unconditionally (i.e., does application of the state law result in the parties going to court even though they have agreed to arbitrate their dispute)? If so, the law is preempted. If not, continue with the final step.

4.   Evaluate the state law under one of the following alternative preemption theories (described below): the *Keystone* Theory; the RUAA Theory; the Anti–FAA Theory; the Pro–Contract Theory; or the FAA Exclusivity Theory.

* * *

The Supreme Court has not yet determined how to analyze FAA preemption of state laws that regulate the arbitration process rather than invalidate the arbitration agreement-what I have called "second generation" FAA preemption cases. Commentators and lower courts have set out a number of possible theories that might be applied to such laws. I label these theories: (1) the *Keystone* Theory; (2) the RUAA Theory; (3) the Anti–FAA Theory; (4) the Pro–Contract Theory; and (5) the FAA Exclusivity Theory.

1. *Keystone* Theory

A state law is not preempted, even if it singles out arbitration, so long as the law does not invalidate the parties' arbitration agreement. The Keystone Theory is named after the Montana Supreme Court's decision in *Keystone, Inc. v. Triad Systems Corp.*, in which the court held that a Montana statute requiring arbitration to take place in Montana was not preempted because it did not "nullif[y] either party's obligation to arbitrate their dispute." The theory can be categorized as involving a very narrow form of obstacle preemption, with the state law standing as an obstacle to Congress's purpose of overcoming common law barriers to the enforcement of arbitration agreements. (Alternatively, it might be characterized as impossibility preemption under the broader view of impossibility.) The Keystone Theory is the narrowest theory described here, as it essentially limits FAA preemption to the sorts of state laws the Supreme Court already has held preempted.

2. RUAA Theory

A state law that does not invalidate the parties' arbitration agreement is preempted if the state law conflicts with terms in the arbitration agreement addressing "the most essential dimensions of the commercial arbitration process" — that is, that "go to the essence of the agreement to arbitrate and the role of the judiciary in holding parties to those agreements." The theory is called the RUAA Theory because it is the view of FAA preemption used by the drafters of the Revised Uniform Arbitration Act ("RUAA"). In determining the provisions to be included in RUAA, the drafters identified a "preemption continuum." At one end of the continuum, state laws that deal with "front-end" issues (the agreement to arbitrate and the arbitrability of a dispute) and "back-end" issues (modification, confirmation, and vacatur of awards) are most likely to be preempted. At the other end of the continuum, state laws that deal with "procedural" issues in the arbitration proceeding (e.g., discovery, consolidation, and the immunity of arbitrators from suit) are least likely to be preempted. In between are "borderline" issues (such as the authority of arbitrators to award punitive damages and provisional remedies, arbitrator disclosure of conflicts of interest, and the right to counsel in arbitration proceedings).

Although not articulated by the RUAA drafters, a possible rationale for the RUAA Theory might go as follows: Section 2 of the FAA, the provision that applies in state court and preempts state law, provides that agreements to arbitrate shall be "valid, irrevocable, and enforceable." A state law can conflict with this provision in two ways. First, the law can make an arbitration agreement invalid, revocable, or unenforceable, such that the parties must go to court instead of arbitration to resolve their dispute. This describes the Supreme Court's cases to date. Second, the law can alter the terms of the parties' agreement such that the procedure being enforced is no longer "arbitration." For example, a state law providing that all arbitration proceedings shall be presided over by a state court judge would be preempted under this theory, even though the parties proceeded to "arbitration." This theory might be categorized as a form of obstacle preemption, under which state laws are preempted when they conflict with Congress's purpose of making arbitration agreements as enforceable as other contract terms.

3. Anti–FAA Theory

A state law that does not invalidate the parties' arbitration agreement is preempted if it "limit[s] or obstruct[s] explicit FAA provisions or general federal arbitration law" (such as the doctrine that arbitration agreements should be construed in favor of finding a dispute within their scope) — in other words, if the state law is "anti-FAA." This theory comes from Professors Ian Macneil et al. in their *Federal Arbitration Law* treatise. They acknowledge that most provisions of the FAA by their terms apply only in federal court, but they find preemptive force in "emanations from FAA § 2" as well as in general principles of federal arbitration law derived from the "pro-arbitration" policy of the FAA. Macneil et al. seem to suggest that a state law is preempted when it provides for a different rule than the FAA does (including an FAA provision that does not by its terms apply in state court), at least when the FAA provision is "an essential aspect of any modern arbitration statute." On this view, the Anti–FAA Theory differs from the RUAA Theory because the Anti–FAA Theory focuses on what is essential to a modern arbitration law rather than on the essential aspects of the parties' obligation to arbitrate. This theory might be characterized as a form of obstacle preemption based on Congress's purpose of establishing a national policy in favor of arbitration. A variation on this theory would require state laws to be less favorable than, rather than simply different from, the FAA in order to be preempted.

4. Pro–Contract Theory

A state law that does not invalidate the parties' arbitration agreement is preempted if it conflicts with a provision in that agreement. Professor Stephen J. Ware is a proponent of the Pro–Contract Theory. He argues that the FAA takes a "resolutely pro-contract stance" and that Section 2 of the FAA "gives the terms of arbitration agreements the force of federal law." According to Professor Ware, "if one can imagine an arbitration agreement that might be rendered unenforceable by the state law then that state law is almost sure to be preempted unless it falls into the 'general contract law' category." The Pro–Contract Theory is similar to the RUAA Theory, only broader. Under the Pro-Contract Theory, any state law that conflicts with a term in the parties' arbitration agreement (by singling out arbitration) is preempted. By comparison, under the RUAA Theory, only state laws that conflict with a term "essential" to arbitration are preempted. The preemption theory relied on by the dissenting Justices in Bazzle most closely resembles the Pro–Contract Theory.

5.   FAA Exclusivity Theory

All state laws that single out arbitration are preempted. Macneil et al. identify "strong arguments for interpreting the FAA as both exclusive and unitary and, when it is applicable, preempting entirely all state arbitration law." As such, according to Macneil et al., "the better course would be for the Supreme Court to hold that where the FAA governs a case, state arbitration law is entirely preempted." The argument is that the FAA occupies (or at least should be held to occupy) the field of arbitration law. As Macneil et al. recognize, however, current case law does not support this theory. Indeed, the Supreme Court flatly stated in Volt that the FAA does not "reflect a congressional intent to occupy the entire field of arbitration." Nonetheless, it is useful to consider the FAA Exclusivity Theory for purposes of comparing it with the other theories.

Notes and Questions

1.   Which approach is the most protective of state sovereignty? Which is the least protective? Which makes the most sense to you?

2.   The states have resisted broad FAA preemption. In *Doctor's Associates, Inc. v. Casarotto, supra* at page 525, two Montana Supreme Court justices refused to sign the order remanding the case from the U.S. Supreme Court down to the lower Montana courts for further proceedings, stating: "We cannot in good conscience be an instrument of a policy which is as legally unfounded, socially detrimental and philosophically misguided as the United States Supreme Court's decision in this and other cases which interpret and apply the Federal Arbitration Act." Richard C. Reuben, *Western Showdown: Two Montana Judges Buck the U.S. Supreme Court*, 82 ABA J. 16 (October 1996). A year earlier, in *Allied–Bruce Terminix Cos. v. Dobson*, 513 U.S. 265, 115 S.Ct. 834, 130 L.Ed.2d 753 (1995), more than 20 state attorneys general signed on to an amicus brief asking the Supreme Court to reverse its ruling in *Southland*. The Supreme Court declined.

3.   ARBITRABILITY

Arbitration is a contractual process. With few exceptions, parties arbitrate because they have agreed to do so, either in a contract entered into before the dispute arose or in an ad hoc agreement after the dispute arose.

In considering arbitrability, it is essential to distinguish between two different levels of analysis. The first level is the substantive issue of *whether* the parties agreed to arbitrate a dispute, and the scope of that agreement. The second level is the more "arcane" procedural level of *who decides* the existence and scope of an arbitration agreement: the "who decides" question.

Unfortunately, the term "arbitrability" has come to embrace — and confuse — a series of similar but analytically distinct issues relating to agreements to arbitrate. The analytical abyss that has inevitably followed does not permit easy synthesis; even simple discussion is often inhibited by the frailty of language in allowing for nuance. As a result, one leading arbitration scholar has mused wistfully that " 'arbitrability' is a word that might well be banned from our vocabulary entirely — or at least restricted, a in other legal systems, to the notion of what society will permit arbitrators to do."

It is therefore helpful to identify the major related but clearly distinct questions that are commonly and crudely clumped together under the general heading of "arbitrability," and to recognize that they operate at both the substantive level and the "who decides" level. These questions principally include:

1. Whether the parties entered into an agreement to arbitrate (and who decides);

2. Whether a specific issue or dispute is included within the scope of the arbitration agreement (and who decides);

3. Whether any conditions that might be necessary to trigger the contractual duty to arbitrate have been satisfied (and who decides).

A related and important concept that is also sometimes included within the rubric of "arbitrability" is the question of whether an arbitrator may decide his or her own jurisdiction, a concept know in international and comparative commercial arbitration as *competence-competence*, or *kompetenz-kompetenz.* * * *

Richard C. Reuben, *First Options, Consent to Arbitration, and the Demise of Separability: Restoring Access to Justice for Contracts with Arbitration Provisions*, 56 SMU L. Rev. 819, 832–33 (2003)(emphasis added).

Arbitrability issues usually arise in court when petitions are filed under § 3 of the FAA to stay litigation or under § 4 to compel arbitration.

a. Who Decides Issues of Arbitrability?

PRIMA PAINT CORP. v. FLOOD & CONKLIN MANUFACTURING CO.

Supreme Court of the United States, 1967.
388 U.S. 395, 87 S.Ct. 1801, 18 L.Ed.2d 1270.

Mr. Justice Fortas delivered the opinion of the Court.

This case presents the question whether the federal court or an arbitrator is to resolve a claim of "fraud in the inducement," under a contract governed by the United States Arbitration Act of 1925, where there is no evidence that the contracting parties intended to withhold that issue from arbitration.

The question arises from the following set of facts. On October 7, 1964, respondent, Flood & Conklin Manufacturing Company, a New Jersey corporation, entered into what was styled a "Consulting Agreement," with petitioner, Prima Paint Corporation, a Maryland corporation. This agreement followed by less than three weeks the execution of a contract pursuant to which Prima Paint purchased F & C's paint business. The consulting agreement provided that for a six-year period F & C was to furnish advice and consultation "in connection with the formulae, manufacturing operations, sales and servicing of Prima Trade Sales accounts." These services were to be performed personally by F & C's chairman, Jerome K. Jelin, "except in the event of his death or disability." F & C bound itself for the duration of the contractual period to make no "Trade Sales" of paint or paint products in its existing sales territory or to current customers. To the consulting agreement were appended lists of F & C customers, whose patronage was to be taken over by Prima Paint. In return for these lists, the covenant not to compete, and the services of Mr. Jelin, Prima Paint agreed to pay F & C certain percentages of its receipts from the listed customers and from all others, such payments not to exceed $225,000 over the life of the agreement. The agreement took into account the possibility that Prima Paint might encounter financial difficulties, including bankruptcy, but no corresponding reference was made to possible financial problems which might be encountered by F & C. The agreement stated that it "embodies the entire understanding of the parties on the subject matter." Finally, the parties agreed to a broad arbitration clause, which read in part:

> "Any controversy or claim arising out of or relating to this Agreement, or the breach thereof, shall be settled by arbitration in the City of New York, in accordance with the rules then obtaining of the American Arbitration Association . . . ."

The first payment by Prima Paint to F & C under the consulting agreement was due on September 1, 1965. None was made on that date. Seventeen days later, Prima Paint did pay the appropriate amount, but into escrow. It notified attorneys for F & C that in various enumerated respects their client had broken both the consulting agreement and the earlier purchase agreement. Prima Paint's principal contention, so far as presently relevant, was that F & C had fraudulently represented that it was solvent and able to perform its contractual obligations, whereas it was in fact insolvent and intended to file a petition under Chapter XI of the Bankruptcy Act, shortly after execution of the consulting agreement. Prima Paint noted that such a petition was filed by F & C on October 14, 1964, one week after the contract had been signed. F & C's response, on October 25, was to serve a "notice of intention to arbitrate." On November 12, three days before expiration of its time to answer this "notice," Prima Paint filed suit in the United States District Court for the Southern District of New York, seeking rescission of the consulting agreement on the basis of the alleged fraudulent inducement. The complaint asserted that the federal court had diversity jurisdiction.

Contemporaneously with the filing of its complaint, Prima Paint petitioned the District Court for an order enjoining F & C from proceeding with the arbitration. F & C cross-moved to stay the court action pending arbitration. F & C contended that the issue presented — whether there was fraud in the inducement of the consulting agreement — was a question for the arbitrators and not for the District Court. Cross-affidavits were filed on the merits. On behalf of Prima Paint, the charges in the complaint were reiterated. Affiants for F & C attacked the sufficiency of Prima Paint's allegations of fraud, denied that misrepresentations had been made during negotiations, and asserted that Prima Paint had relied exclusively upon delivery of the lists, the promise not to compete, and the availability of Mr. Jelin. They contended that Prima Paint had availed itself of these considerations for nearly a year without claiming "fraud," noting that Prima Paint was in no position to claim ignorance of the bankruptcy proceeding since it had participated therein in February of 1965. They added that F & C was revested with its assets in March of 1965.

The District Court, granted F & C's motion to stay the action pending arbitration, holding that a charge of fraud in the inducement of a contract containing an arbitration clause as broad as this one was a question for the arbitrators and not for the court. For this proposition it relied on *Robert Lawrence Co. v. Devonshire Fabrics, Inc.*, 271 F.2d 402 (C.A.2d Cir. 1959), cert. granted, 362 U.S. 909, dismissed under Rule 60, 364 U.S. 801 (1960). The Court of Appeals for the Second Circuit dismissed Prima Paint's appeal. It held that the contract in question evidenced a transaction involving interstate commerce; that under the controlling *Robert Lawrence Co.* decision a claim of fraud in the inducement of the contract generally — as opposed to the arbitration clause itself — is for the arbitrators and not for the courts; and that this rule — one of "national substantive law" — governs even in the face of a contrary state rule. We agree, albeit for somewhat different reasons, and we affirm the decision below.

The key statutory provisions are §§ 2, 3, and 4 of the United States Arbitration Act of 1925. Section 2 provides that a written provision for arbitration "in any maritime transaction or a contract evidencing a transaction involving commerce ... shall be valid, irrevocable, and enforceable, save upon such grounds as exist at law or in equity for the revocation of any contract." Section 3 requires a federal court in which suit has been brought "upon any issue referable to arbitration under an agreement in writing for such arbitration" to stay the court action pending arbitration once it is satisfied that the issue is arbitrable under the agreement. Section 4 provides a federal remedy for a party "aggrieved by the alleged failure, neglect, or refusal of another to arbitrate under a written agreement for arbitration,"and directs the federal court to order arbitration once it is satisfied that an agreement for arbitration has been made and has not been honored.

* * *

Having determined that the contract in question is within the coverage of the Arbitration Act, we turn to the central issue in this case: whether a claim of fraud in the inducement of the entire contract is to be resolved by the federal court, or whether the matter is to be referred to the arbitrators. The courts of appeals have differed in their approach to this question. The view of the Court of Appeals for the Second Circuit, as expressed in this case and in others, is that — *except where the parties otherwise intend* — arbitration clauses as a matter of federal law are "separable" from the contracts in which they are embedded, and that where no claim is made that fraud was directed to the arbitration clause itself, a broad arbitration clause will be held to encompass arbitration of the claim that the contract itself was induced by fraud. The Court of Appeals for the First Circuit, on the other hand, has taken the view that the question of "severability" is one of state law, and that where a State regards such a clause as inseparable a claim of fraud in the inducement must be decided by the court.

With respect to cases brought in federal court involving maritime contracts or those evidencing transactions in "commerce," we think that Congress has provided an explicit answer. That answer is to be found in § 4 of the Act, which provides a remedy to a party seeking to compel compliance with an arbitration agreement. Under § 4, with respect to a matter within the jurisdiction of the federal courts save for the existence of an arbitration clause, the federal court is instructed to order arbitration to proceed once it is satisfied that "the making of the agreement for arbitration or the failure to comply [with the arbitration agreement] is not in issue." Accordingly, if the claim is fraud in the inducement of the arbitration clause itself — an issue which goes to the "making" of the agreement to arbitrate — the federal court may proceed to adjudicate it. But the statutory language does not permit the federal court to consider claims of fraud in the inducement of the contract generally. Section 4 does not expressly relate to situations like the present in which a stay is sought of a federal action in order that arbitration may proceed. But it is inconceivable that Congress intended the rule to differ depending upon which party to the arbitration agreement first invokes the assistance of a federal court. We hold, therefore, that in passing upon a § 3 application for a stay while the parties arbitrate, a federal court may consider only issues relating to the making and performance of the agreement to arbitrate. In so concluding, we not only honor the plain meaning of the statute but also the unmistakably clear congressional purpose that the arbitration procedure, when selected by the parties to a contract, be speedy and not subject to delay and obstruction in the courts.

There remains the question whether such a rule is constitutionally permissible. The point is made that, whatever the nature of the contract involved here, this case is in federal court solely by reason of diversity of citizenship, and that since the decision in *Erie R. Co. v. Tompkins*, federal courts are bound in diversity cases to follow state rules of decision in matters which are "substantive" rather than "procedural," or where the matter is "outcome determinative." The question in this case, however, is not whether Congress may fashion federal substantive rules to govern questions arising in simple diversity cases. Rather, the question is whether Congress may prescribe how federal courts are to conduct themselves with respect to subject matter over which Congress plainly has power to legislate. The answer to that can only be in the affirmative. And it is clear beyond dispute that the federal arbitration statute is based upon and confined to the incontestable federal foundations of "control over interstate commerce and over admiralty."

In the present case no claim has been advanced by Prima Paint that F & C fraudulently induced it to enter into the agreement to arbitrate "(a)ny controversy or claim arising out of or relating to this Agreement, or the breach thereof." This contractual language is easily broad enough to encompass Prima Paint's claim that both execution and acceleration of the consulting agreement itself were procured by fraud. Indeed, no claim is made that Prima Paint ever intended that "legal" issues relating to the contract be excluded from arbitration, or that it was not entirely free so to contract. Federal courts are bound to apply rules enacted by Congress with respect to matters — here, a contract involving commerce — over which it has legislative power. The question which Prima Paint requested the District Court to adjudicate preliminarily to allowing arbitration to proceed is one not intended by Congress to delay the granting of a § 3 stay. Accordingly, the decision below dismissing Prima Paint's appeal is

Affirmed.

[The concurring opinion of Mr. Justice Harlan is omitted.]

* * *

Mr. Justice Black, with whom Mr. Justice Douglas and Mr. Justice Stewart join, dissenting.

The Court here holds that the United States Arbitration Act, 9 U.S.C. §§ 1–14, as a matter of federal substantive law, compels a party to a contract containing a written arbitration provision to carry out his "arbitration agreement" even though a court might, after a fair trial, hold the entire contract — including the arbitration agreement — void because of fraud in the inducement. The Court holds, what is to me fantastic, that the legal issue of a contract's voidness because of fraud is to be decided by persons designated to arbitrate factual controversies arising out of a valid contract between the parties. And the arbitrators who the Court holds are to adjudicate the legal validity of the contract need not even be lawyers, and in all probability will be nonlawyers, wholly unqualified to decide legal issues, and even if qualified to apply the law, not bound to do so. I am by no means sure that thus forcing a person to forgo his opportunity to try his legal issues in the courts where, unlike the situation in arbitration, he may have a jury trial and right to appeal, is not a denial of due process of law. I am satisfied, however, that Congress did not impose any such procedures in the Arbitration Act. And I am fully satisfied that a reasonable and fair reading of that Act's language and history shows that both Congress and the framers of the Act were at great pains to emphasize that nonlawyers designated to adjust and arbitrate factual controversies arising out of valid contracts would not trespass upon the courts' prerogative to decide the legal question of whether any legal contract exists upon which to base an arbitration.

* * *

I would reverse this case.

Notes and Questions

1. Arbitration under the FAA is predicated upon the law of contract. What is the majority's theory of contractual assent?

2. Do you agree with the majority or the dissent? Why?

3. The doctrine of separability announced in *Prima Paint* has been widely criticized by many legal scholars.

According to Professor Stempel, "[m]uch of the atrophy of contract revocation defenses results from *Prima Paint Corp. v. Flood & Conklin Manufactuing Co*. . . . To be heard by courts after *Prima Paint*, a contract revocation defense must specifically address the arbitration clause rather than the entire contract, which at least in the first instance, made the vast bulk of fraud, misrepresentation, illegality, and other traditional recision defenses the province of the arbitrator." Jeffrey W. Stempel, *A Better Approach to Arbitrability,* 65 Tul. L. Rev. 1377, 1390–91 (1991).

Professor Sternlight has argued that "it is difficult to imagine a factual scenario in which a party would use fraud solely to impose an arbitration clause and not to affect other essential terms of a contract." Jean R. Sternlight, *Rethinking the Constitutionality of the Supreme Court's Preference for Binding Arbitration: A Fresh Assessment of Jury Trial, Separation of Powers, and Due Process Concerns,* 72 Tul. L. Rev. 1, 24 (1997).

Professor Reuben had this to say about *Prima Paint:* "For a society steeped in the belief in the right to one's 'day in court,' the separability doctrine is counter-intuitive, and as a result has been difficult for many lower courts to implement, and has simply been rejected by others as bad policy. This has led to massive doctrinal complexity, confusion, and uncertainty. . . ." Richard C. Reuben, *First Options, Consent to Arbitration, and the Demise of Separability: Restoring Access to Justice for Contracts With Arbitration Provisions,* 56 SMU L. Rev. 819, 825 (2003). Professor Reuben provides numerous arguments for the repudiation of separability and points to *First Options,* the next case, as an indication that the Supreme Court may be moving toward a different approach. *Id.* at 883. The Wyoming Supreme Court adopted Professor Reuben's reasoning on separability in *Fox v. Tanner,* 101 P.3d 939 (Wyo. 2004).

State cases recognizing and refusing to recognize some form of the separability doctrine are collected in Comment 4 of Section 6 of RUAA, infra Section B (2)(a) following the *Howsam* case, beginning at page 549.

For a comprehensive defense of *Prima Paint*, see Alan Scott Rau, *Everything You Really Need to Know About "Separability" In Seventeen Simple Propositions*, 14 Am. Int'l Rev. Arb. 1 (2003). Professor Rau asserts that "[i]t should be obvious how frequently the issue of contract validity will be intertwined with the substantive issues underlying the 'merits' of the dispute: The arbitral determination that the parties unquestionably bargained for .... Here we can say how abundantly sensible it would be to impute to contracting parties a preference for what has neatly been termed 'the practical advantages of one-stop adjudication.'" *Id.* at 33–34.

FIRST OPTIONS OF CHICAGO, INC. v. KAPLAN

Supreme Court of the United States, 1965.
514 U.S. 938, 115 S.Ct. 1920, 131 L.Ed.2d 985.

Justice Breyer delivered the opinion of the Court.

In this case we consider two questions about how courts should review certain matters under the federal Arbitration Act, 9 U.S.C. § 1 *et seq.* (1988 Ed. and Supp. V): (1) how a district court should review an arbitrator's decision that the parties agreed to arbitrate a dispute, and (2) how a court of appeals should review a district court's decision confirming, or refusing to vacate, an arbitration award.

I.

The case concerns several related disputes between, on one side, First Options of Chicago, Inc., a firm that clears stock trades on the Philadelphia Stock Exchange, and, on the other side, three parties: Manuel Kaplan; his wife, Carol Kaplan; and his wholly owned investment company, MK Investments, Inc. (MKI), whose trading account First Options cleared. The disputes center on a "workout" agreement, embodied in four separate documents, which governs the "working out" of debts to First Options that MKI and the Kaplans incurred as a result of the October 1987 stock market crash. In 1989, after entering into the agreement, MKI lost an additional $1.5 million. First Options then took control of, and liquidated, certain MKI assets; demanded immediate payment of the entire MKI debt; and insisted that the Kaplans personally pay any deficiency. When its demands went unsatisfied, First Options sought arbitration by a panel of the Philadelphia Stock Exchange.

MKI, having signed the only workout document (out of four) that contained an arbitration clause, accepted arbitration. The Kaplans, however, who had not personally signed that document, denied that their disagreement with First Options was arbitrable and filed written objections to that effect with the arbitration panel. The arbitrators decided that they had the power to rule on the merits of the parties' dispute, and did so in favor of First Options. The Kaplans then asked the Federal District Court to vacate the arbitration award, and First Options requested its confirmation. The court confirmed the award. Nonetheless, on appeal the Court of Appeals for the Third Circuit agreed with the Kaplans that their dispute was not arbitrable; and it reversed the District Court's confirmation of the award against them.

We granted certiorari to consider two questions regarding the standards that the Court of Appeals used to review the determination that the Kaplans' dispute with First Options was arbitrable. First, the Court of Appeals said that courts "should *independently* decide whether an arbitration panel has jurisdiction over the merits of any particular dispute." First Options asked us to decide whether this is so (*i.e.,* whether courts, in "reviewing the arbitrators' decision on arbitrability," should "apply a *de novo* standard of review or the more deferential standard applied to arbitrators' decisions on the merits") when the objecting party "submitted the issue to the arbitrators for decision." Second, the Court of Appeals stated that it would review a district court's denial of a motion to vacate a commercial arbitration award (and the correlative grant of a motion to confirm it) "*de novo.*" First Options argues that the Court of Appeals instead should have applied an "abuse of discretion" standard.

II

The first question — the standard of review applied to an arbitrator's decision about arbitrability — is a narrow one. To understand just how narrow, consider three types of disagreement present in this case. First, the Kaplans and First Options disagree about whether the Kaplans are personally liable for MKI's debt to First Options. That disagreement makes up the *merits* of the dispute. Second, they disagree about whether they agreed to arbitrate the merits. That disagreement is about the *arbitrability* of the dispute. Third, they disagree about *who should have the primary power to decide the second matter.* Does that power belong primarily to the arbitrators (because the court reviews their arbitrability decision deferentially) or to the court (because the court makes up its mind about arbitrability independently)? We consider here only this third question.

Although the question is a narrow one, it has a certain practical importance. That is because a party who has not agreed to arbitrate will normally have a right to a court's decision about the merits of its dispute (say, as here, its obligation under a contract). But, where the party has agreed to arbitrate, he or she, in effect, has relinquished much of that right's practical value. The party still can ask a court to review the arbitrator's decision, but the court will set that decision aside only in very unusual circumstances. Hence, who — court or arbitrator — has the primary authority to decide whether a party has agreed to arbitrate can make a critical difference to a party resisting arbitration.

We believe the answer to the "who" question (*i.e.,* the standard-of-review question) is fairly simple. Just as the arbitrability of the merits of a dispute depends upon whether the parties agreed to arbitrate that dispute, so the question "who has the primary power to decide arbitrability" turns upon what the parties agreed about *that* matter. Did the parties agree to submit the arbitrability question itself to arbitration? If so, then the court's standard for reviewing the arbitrator's decision about *that* matter should not differ from the standard courts apply when they review any other matter that parties have agreed to arbitrate. That is to say, the court should give considerable leeway to the arbitrator, setting aside his or her decision only in certain narrow circumstances. If, on the other hand, the parties did *not* agree to submit the arbitrability question itself to arbitration, then the court should decide that question just as it would decide any other question that the parties did not submit to arbitration, namely, independently. These two answers flow inexorably from the fact that arbitration is simply a matter of contract between the parties; it is a way to resolve those disputes — but only those disputes — that the parties have agreed to submit to arbitration.

We agree with First Options, therefore, that a court must defer to an arbitrator's arbitrability decision when the parties submitted that matter to arbitration. Nevertheless, that conclusion does not help First Options win this case. That is because a fair and complete answer to the standard-of-review question requires a word about how a court should decide whether the parties have agreed to submit the arbitrability issue to arbitration. And, that word makes clear that the Kaplans did not agree to arbitrate arbitrability here.

When deciding whether the parties agreed to arbitrate a certain matter (including arbitrability), courts generally (though with a qualification we discuss below) should apply ordinary state-law principles that govern the formation of contracts. The relevant state law here, for example, would require the court to see whether the parties objectively revealed an intent to submit the arbitrability issue to arbitration.

This Court, however, has (as we just said) added an important qualification, applicable when courts decide whether a party has agreed that arbitrators should decide arbitrability: Courts should not assume that the parties agreed to arbitrate arbitrability unless there is "clear and unmistakable" evidence that they did so. In this manner the law treats silence or ambiguity about the question "*who* (primarily) should decide arbitrability" differently from the way it treats silence or ambiguity about the question "*whether* a particular merits-related dispute is arbitrable because it is within the scope of a valid arbitration agreement" — for in respect to this latter question the law reverses the presumption. * * * (" '[A]ny doubts concerning the scope of arbitrable issues should be resolved in favor of arbitration' ").

But, this difference in treatment is understandable. The latter question arises when the parties have a contract that provides for arbitration of some issues. In such circumstances, the parties likely gave at least some thought to the scope of arbitration. And, given the law's permissive policies in respect to arbitration, one can understand why the law would insist upon clarity before concluding that the parties did *not* want to arbitrate a related matter. See Domke § 12.02, p. 156 (issues will be deemed arbitrable unless "it is clear that the arbitration clause has not included" them). On the other hand, the former question — the "who (primarily) should decide arbitrability" question — is rather arcane. A party often might not focus upon that question or upon the significance of having arbitrators decide the scope of their own powers. And, given the principle that a party can be forced to arbitrate only those issues it specifically has agreed to submit to arbitration, one can understand why courts might hesitate to interpret silence or ambiguity on the "who should decide arbitrability" point as giving the arbitrators that power, for doing so might too often force unwilling parties to arbitrate a matter they reasonably would have thought a judge, not an arbitrator, would decide.

On the record before us, First Options cannot show that the Kaplans clearly agreed to have the arbitrators decide (*i.e.,* to arbitrate) the question of arbitrability. First Options relies on the Kaplans' filing with the arbitrators a written memorandum objecting to the arbitrators' jurisdiction. But merely arguing the arbitrability issue to an arbitrator does not indicate a clear willingness to arbitrate that issue, *i.e.,* a willingness to be effectively bound by the arbitrator's decision on that point. To the contrary, insofar as the Kaplans were forcefully objecting to the arbitrators deciding their dispute with First Options, one naturally would think that they did *not* want the arbitrators to have binding authority over them. This conclusion draws added support from (1) an obvious explanation for the Kaplans' presence before the arbitrators (*i.e.,* that MKI, Mr. Kaplan's wholly owned firm, was arbitrating workout agreement matters); and (2) Third Circuit law that suggested that the Kaplans might argue arbitrability to the arbitrators without losing their right to independent court review.

* * *

We conclude that, because the Kaplans did not clearly agree to submit the question of arbitrability to arbitration, the Court of Appeals was correct in finding that the arbitrability of the Kaplan/First Options dispute was subject to independent review by the courts.

* * *

The judgment of the Court of Appeals is affirmed.

Notes and Questions

1. Why do you think the Kaplans wanted to avoid arbitration? The choice between arbitration and court litigation is discussed in Section D, *infra,* beginning at page 651.

2. In deciding whether the parties have agreed to arbitrate a dispute, the federal courts are to resolve doubts in favor of arbitration. As the Court stated in *Mitsubishi Motors Corp. v. Soler Chrysler–Plymouth Inc.,* "the parties' intentions control, but those intentions are generously construed as to issues of arbitrability." 473 U.S. 614, 626, 105 S.Ct. 3346, 87 L.Ed.2d 444

(1985). See cases collected in Stephen Hayford & Ralph Peeples, *Commercial Arbitration in Evolution: An Assessment and Call for Dialogue*, 10 Ohio St. J. on Disp. Resol. 343, 357 n.48 (1995).

The presumption of arbitrability in labor-management contract disputes was established in the "Steelworkers Trilogy" in 1960. It was reaffirmed in *AT & T Technologies, Inc. v. Communications Workers*, 475 U.S. 643, 106 S.Ct. 1415, 89 L.Ed.2d 648 (1986), where the Court quoted with approval the following language from *United Steelworkers v. Warrior & Gulf Navigation Co.*, 363 U.S. 574, 80 S.Ct. 1347, 4 L.Ed.2d 1409 (1960), one of the Trilogy cases: "[a]n order to arbitrate the particular grievance should not be denied unless it may be said with positive assurance that the arbitration clause is not susceptible of an interpretation that covers the asserted dispute. Doubts should be resolved in favor of coverage." 475 U.S. at 650, quoting *United Steelworkers v. Warrior & Gulf Navigation Co.*, 363 U.S. at 582–83.

In *First Options*, however, the Court held that "courts should not assume that the parties agreed to arbitrate arbitrability unless there is 'clear and unmistakable' evidence that they did so." 514 U.S. at 994. Does *First Options* represent a retreat from the expansive conception of arbitrability expressed in *Mitsubishi Motors* and *Prima Paint*? Professor Reuben asserts that the *First Options* opinion " ... seems to support the suggestion that a judicial interpretation of 'clear and unmistakable' waiver cannot be based on implied consent, as *Prima Paint* and following cases had permitted." Richard C. Reuben, *First Options, Consent to Arbitration, and the Demise of Separability: Restoring Access to Justice for Contract With Arbitration Provisions*, 56 SMU L. Rev. 819, 859 (2003). He further argues that the move to a "clear and unmistakable" waiver standard may also reflect a shift to an actual consent theory of assent to arbitration, one that is fundamentally inconsistent with the implied consent theory that lies at the heart of Prima Paint. As Professor Reuben explained the importance of implied consent to separability:

> [S]eparability imputes assent and consideration from the container contract to the 'separated' contract for arbitration by virtue of the construction of the FAA, not by the conduct of the parties. * * * It is this imputed consent that makes it theoretically possible for the arbitration provision to survive as an independent contract when the larger contract that contains it is found to be defective by an arbitrator.

Id. at 849–50.

Professor Rau argues that there is no conflict between *Prima Paint* and *First Options* because *First Options* dealt with the question of who decides arbitrability issues while *Prima Paint* dealt with the question of who decides the merits of fraudulent inducement claims. Alan Scott Rau, *The Arbitrability Question Itself*, 10 Am. Rev. Int'l Arb. 287, 331, 339 (1999). In another article, Rau says Reuben "seems to me to get the point of *Prima Paint* precisely backwards: Any supposed difficulty completely evaporates once one understands that the doctrine's presumption of intent — for example, its presumption of a willingness to entrust a fraudulent inducement claim to arbitration — has no role at all in the absence of a prior finding of an 'agreement' to arbitrate. It is always a court, acting at the threshold as a gatekeeper, that passes on this requisite to arbitral jurisdiction." Alan Scott

Rau, *Everything You Really Needed to Know About "Separability" in Seventeen Simple Propositions,* 14 Am. Rev. Int'l. Arb. 1, 29–30 (2003).

Do you agree with Professor Reuben or Professor Rau?

3. Suppose a court asked to enforce an agreement to arbitrate concludes that the contract claim asserted by the party seeking arbitration is a "frivolous, patently baseless claim" because the contract provision on which the claim is based "clearly" favors the party resisting arbitration. Should the court refuse to order arbitration? The opinion for the court in *United Steelworkers v. American Manufacturing Co.,* 363 U.S. 564, 80 S.Ct. 1343, 4 L.Ed.2d 1403 (1960), states on page 568 that "[t]he courts * * * have no business weighing the merits of the grievance, considering whether there is equity in a particular claim, or determining whether there is particular language in the written instrument which will support the claim. The agreement is to submit all grievances to arbitration, not merely those which the court will deem meritorious." Do you agree that the courts should not consider the merits of the dispute in deciding whether the dispute is arbitrable? *See* Harry H. Wellington, *Judicial Review of the Promise to Arbitrate,* 37 N.Y.U. L. Rev. 471, 472–77 (1962).

HOWSAM v. DEAN WITTER REYNOLDS, INC.

Supreme Court of the United States, 2002.
537 U.S. 79, 123 S.Ct. 588, 154 L.Ed.2d 491.

Justice Breyer delivered the opinion of the Court.

This case focuses upon an arbitration rule of the National Association of Securities Dealers (NASD). The rule states that no dispute "shall be eligible for submission to arbitration ... where six (6) years have elapsed from the occurrence or event giving rise to the ... dispute." NASD Code of Arbitration Procedure § 10304 (1984) (NASD Code or Code). We must decide whether a court or an NASD arbitrator should apply the rule to the underlying controversy. We conclude that the matter is for the arbitrator.

I

The underlying controversy arises out of investment advice that Dean Witter Reynolds, Inc. (Dean Witter), provided its client, Karen Howsam, when, some time between 1986 and 1994, it recommended that she buy and hold interests in four limited partnerships. Howsam says that Dean Witter misrepresented the virtues of the partnerships. The resulting controversy falls within their standard Client Service Agreement's arbitration clause, which provides:

> all controversies ... concerning or arising from ... any account ...,
> any transaction ..., or ... the construction, performance or breach
> of ... any ... agreement between us ... shall be determined by
> arbitration before any self-regulatory organization or exchange of
> which Dean Witter is a member.

The agreement also provides that Howsam can select the arbitration forum. And Howsam chose arbitration before the NASD.

To obtain NASD arbitration, Howsam signed the NASD's Uniform Submission Agreement. That agreement specified that the "present matter in controversy" was submitted for arbitration "in accordance with" the NASD's "Code of Arbitration Procedure." And that Code contains the provision at issue here, a provision stating that no dispute "shall be eligible for submission ... where six (6) years have elapsed from the occurrence or event giving rise to the ... dispute."

After the Uniform Submission Agreement was executed, Dean Witter filed this lawsuit in Federal District Court. It asked the court to declare that the dispute was "ineligible for arbitration" because it was more than six years old. And it sought an injunction that would prohibit Howsam from proceeding in arbitration. The District Court dismissed the action on the ground that the NASD arbitrator, not the court, should interpret and apply the NASD rule. The Court of Appeals for the Tenth Circuit, however, reversed. In its view, application of the NASD rule presented a question of the underlying dispute's "arbitrability"; and the presumption is that a court, not an arbitrator, will ordinarily decide an "arbitrability" question.

The Courts of Appeals have reached different conclusions about whether a court or an arbitrator primarily should interpret and apply this particular NASD rule. We granted Howsam's petition for certiorari to resolve this disagreement. And we now hold that the matter is for the arbitrator.

II

This Court has determined that arbitration is a matter of contract and a party cannot be required to submit to arbitration any dispute which he has not agreed so to submit. Although the Court has also long recognized and enforced a "liberal federal policy favoring arbitration agreements," it has made clear that there is an exception to this policy: The question whether the parties have submitted a particular dispute to arbitration, *i.e.*, the *"question of arbitrability,"* is "an issue for judicial determination unless the parties clearly and unmistakably provide otherwise." We must decide here whether application of the NASD time limit provision falls into the scope of this last-mentioned interpretive rule.

Linguistically speaking, one might call any potentially dispositive gateway question a "question of arbitrability," for its answer will determine whether the underlying controversy will proceed to arbitration on the merits. The Court's case law, however, makes clear that, for purposes of applying the interpretive rule, the phrase "question of arbitrability" has a far more limited scope. The Court has found the phrase applicable in the kind of narrow circumstance where contracting parties would likely have expected a court to have decided the gateway matter, where they are not likely to have thought that they had agreed that an arbitrator would do so, and, consequently, where reference of the gateway dispute to the court avoids the risk of forcing parties to arbitrate a matter that they may well not have agreed to arbitrate.

Thus, a gateway dispute about whether the parties are bound by a given arbitration clause raises a "question of arbitrability" for a court to decide. Similarly, a disagreement about whether an arbitration clause in a concededly binding contract applies to a particular type of controversy is for the court.

At the same time the Court has found the phrase "question of arbitrability" *not* applicable in other kinds of general circumstance where parties would likely expect that an arbitrator would decide the gateway matter. Thus " 'procedural' questions which grow out of the dispute and bear on its final disposition" are presumptively *not* for the judge, but for an arbitrator, to decide. * * * Indeed, the Revised Uniform Arbitration Act of 2000 (RUAA), seeking to "incorporate the holdings of the vast majority of state courts and the law that has developed under the [Federal Arbitration Act]," states that an "arbitrator shall decide whether a condition precedent to arbitrability has been fulfilled." And the comments add that "in the absence of an agreement to the contrary, issues of substantive arbitrability ... are for a court to decide and issues of procedural arbitrability, *i.e.,* whether prerequisites such as *time limits,* notice, laches, estoppel, and other conditions precedent to an obligation to arbitrate have been met, are for the arbitrators to decide."

Following this precedent, we find that the applicability of the NASD time limit rule is a matter presumptively for the arbitrator, not for the judge. The time limit rule closely resembles the gateway questions that this Court has found not to be "questions of arbitrability." Such a dispute seems an "aspec[t] of the [controversy] which called the grievance procedures into play."

Moreover, the NASD arbitrators, comparatively more expert about the meaning of their own rule, are comparatively better able to interpret and to apply it. In the absence of any statement to the contrary in the arbitration agreement, it is reasonable to infer that the parties intended the agreement to reflect that understanding. And for the law to assume an expectation that aligns (1) decisionmaker with (2) comparative expertise will help better to secure a fair and expeditious resolution of the underlying controversy — a goal of arbitration systems and judicial systems alike.

We consequently conclude that the NASD's time limit rule falls within the class of gateway procedural disputes that do not present what our cases have called "questions of arbitrability." And the strong pro-court presumption as to the parties' likely intent does not apply.

* * *

IV

For these reasons, the judgment of the Tenth Circuit is

Reversed.

Justice O'Connor took no part in the consideration or decision of this case. * * *

[Justice Thomas' concurring opinion is omitted.]

Notes and Questions

1. The *Howsam* court draws the distinction between "substantive" arbitrability and "procedural" arbitrability. Substantive arbitrability generally addresses the question of whether a particular dispute is covered by an arbitration clause. Procedural arbitrability generally addresses the question of whether the conditions that would trigger the arbitration provision have been met. *See John Wiley & Sons, Inc. v. Livingston*, 376 U.S. 543, 84 S.Ct. 909, 11 L.Ed.2d 898 (1964). For a discussion, see Richard C. Reuben, *First Options, Consent to Arbitration, and the Demise of Separability: Restoring Access to Justice for Contracts With Arbitration Provisions*, 56 SMU L. Rev. 819, 835–36 (2003).

The distinction is widely recognized at common law, and is codified in § 6 of the revised Uniform Arbitration Act (2000), which had been adopted in 12 states as of the publication of this book.

SECTION 6. VALIDITY OF AGREEMENT TO ARBITRATE.

(a) An agreement contained in a record to submit to arbitration any existing or subsequent controversy arising between the parties to the agreement is valid, enforceable, and irrevocable except upon a ground that exists at law or in equity for the revocation of a contract.

(b) The court shall decide whether an agreement to arbitrate exists or a controversy is subject to an agreement to arbitrate.

(c) An arbitrator shall decide whether a condition precedent to arbitrability has been fulfilled and whether a contract containing a valid agreement to arbitrate is enforceable.

(d) If a party to a judicial proceeding challenges the existence of, or claims that a controversy is not subject to, an agreement to arbitrate, the arbitration proceeding may continue pending final resolution of the issue by the court, unless the court otherwise orders.

Comment

1. The language in Section 6(a) as to the validity of arbitration agreements is the same as UAA Section 1 and almost the same as the language of FAA Section 2 which states that arbitration agreements "shall be valid irrevocable, and enforceable, save upon such grounds as exist at law or in equity for the revocation of any contract." Because of the significant body of case law that has developed over the interpretation of this language in both the UAA and the FAA, this section, for the most part, is intact.

* * *

2. Subsections (b) and (c) of Section 6 are intended to incorporate the holdings of the vast majority of state courts and the law that has developed under the FAA that, in the absence of an agreement to the

contrary, issues of substantive arbitrability, *i.e.*, whether a dispute is encompassed by an agreement to arbitrate, are for a court to decide and issues of procedural arbitrability, *i.e.*, whether prerequisites such as time limits, notice, laches, estoppel, and other conditions precedent to an obligation to arbitrate have been met, are for the arbitrators to decide. * * *

In particular it should be noted that Section 6(b), which provides for courts to decide substantive arbitrability, is subject to waiver under Section 4(a). This approach is not only the law in most States but also follows Supreme Court precedent under the FAA that if there is no agreement to the contrary, questions of substantive arbitrability are for the courts to decide. Some arbitration organizations, such as the American Arbitration Association in its rules on commercial arbitration disputes, provide that arbitrators, rather than courts, make the initial determination as to substantive arbitrability. AAA, Commercial Disp. Resolution Pro. R–8(b); * * *

Sections 6(c) and (d) are also waivable under Section 4(a).

* * *

4.   The language in Section 6(c), "whether a contract containing a valid agreement to arbitrate is enforceable," is intended to follow the "separability" doctrine outlined in *Prima Paint Corp. v. Flood & Conklin Manufacturing Co.*, 388 U.S. 395 (1967). * * * A majority of States recognize some form of the separability doctrine under their state arbitration laws. * * *

Other States have either limited or declined to follow the *Prima Paint* doctrine on separability. * * *

5.   Waiver is one area where courts, rather than arbitrators, often make the decision as to enforceability of an arbitration clause. However, because of the public policy favoring arbitration, a court normally will only find a waiver of a right to arbitrate where a party claiming waiver meets the burden of proving that the waiver has caused prejudice. For instance, where a plaintiff brings an action against a defendant in court, engages in extensive discovery and then attempts to dismiss the lawsuit on the grounds of an arbitration clause, a defendant might challenge the dismissal on the grounds that the plaintiff has waived any right to use of the arbitration clause. *S & R Co. of Kingston v. Latona Trucking, Inc.*, 159 F.3d 80 (2d Cir. 1998). Allowing the court to decide this issue of arbitrability comports with the separability doctrine because in most instances waiver concerns only the arbitration clause itself and not an attack on the underlying contract. It is also a matter of judicial economy to require that a party, who pursues an action in a court proceeding but later claims arbitrability, be held to a decision of the court on waiver.

6.   Section 6(d) follows the practice of the American Arbitration Association and most other arbitration organizations that if a party challenges the arbitrability of a dispute in a court proceeding, the arbitration organization or arbitrators in their discretion may continue with the arbitration unless a court issues an order to stay the arbitration or makes a final determination that the matter is not arbitrable.

2. Are courts or arbitrators better qualified to decide questions of procedural arbitrability? *See John Wiley & Sons, Inc. v. Livingston*, 376 U.S. 543, 555–59, 84 S.Ct. 909, 11 L.Ed.2d 898 (1964).

3. What are the arguments for and against a court compelling arbitration under Section 6 of the RUAA in the following situation?

American Italian Pasta Company (American Pasta) entered into a contract with Austin under which Austin agreed to design and build a pasta factory. Article 16 of the contract provides:

> In the event of any dispute or disagreement arising under this contract, it is mutually agreed, that upon written notice of either to the other party, both Owner and Austin will use their best efforts to settle such disputes or disagreement in a manner that is fair and equitable to both parties before either party can exercise the right of any legal action.

> If both parties agree that a dispute or disagreement is of such nature that it cannot be settled as provided for above, then such dispute or disagreement may be submitted to arbitration in accordance with the Rules of The American Arbitration Association in which event, the decision of the arbitrators shall be final and binding upon the parties.

A dispute arose between the parties, and settlement negotiations were unsuccessful. Austin notified the American Arbitration Association to proceed with arbitration. American Pasta filed an application for stay of arbitration in state court.

[See *American Italian Pasta Co. v. Austin Co.*, 914 F.2d 1103, 1104–08 (8th Cir. 1990).]

b. Statutory Claims and the Problem of Mandatory Arbitration

The use of arbitration in the statutory context has been controversial over the last decade, largely because of the rise of so-called mandatory, or unilaterally imposed, arbitration in employment and consumer contracts. In these contracts, the employer or providers of consumer goods and services typically will include a broad arbitration provision in their standard form contract or other documents governing the relationship between the parties stating, for example, that "all disputes arising under this contract will be decided by binding arbitration." The question is whether such clauses are enforceable, since the effect is to foreclose the ability of the parties to have their dispute heard by a court of law. While the question may be raised for all legal claims, some judges and scholars would contend that it is particularly significant for statutory claims because these are legislatively conferred rights, such as the right to be free from job discrimination or to pursue remedies against a particular party. Does this make a difference? What policy interests are advanced by permitting the enforcement of mandatory arbitration provisions, and what are diminished by such enforcement? These materials also recall issues we have already addressed, such as what is the meaning of consent to arbitration? Who should decide whether these clauses are enforceable? The courts? The legislature? What law should apply? State? Federal? These questions and others permeate these pro-vocative materials.

1. The Shift in Judicial Attitudes

WILKO v. SWAN

Supreme Court of the United States, 1953.
346 U.S. 427, 74 S.Ct. 182, 98 L.Ed. 168.

[A customer of a securities brokerage firm sought damages under the Securities Act of 1933 in a United States District Court. The customer alleged that he was induced to buy stock because of false representations and a failure to provide relevant information. The bro-kerage firm argued that the customers agreement to arbitrate waived his right to sue under the Securities Act. The U.S. Supreme Court rejected the waiver argument.]

Mr. Justice Reed delivered the opinion of the Court.

. . . [W]e think the right to select the judicial forum is the kind of 'provision' that cannot be waived under § 14 of the Securities Act. * * *

Even though the provisions of the Securities Act, advantageous to the buyer, apply, their effectiveness in application is lessened in arbitra-tion as compared to judicial proceedings. Determination of the quality of a commodity or the amount of money due under a contract is not the type of issue here involved. This case requires subjective findings on the purpose and knowledge of an alleged violator of the Act. They must be not only determined but applied by the arbitrators without judicial instruction on the law. As their award may be made without explanation of their reasons and without a complete record of their proceedings, the arbitrators' conception of the legal meaning of such statutory require-ments as 'burden of proof,' 'reasonable care' or 'material fact,' * * * cannot be examined. * * * While it may be true, as the Court of Appeals thought, that a failure of the arbitrators to decide in accordance with the provisions of the Securities Act would 'constitute grounds for vacating the award pursuant to section 10 of the Federal Arbitration Act,' that failure would need to be made clearly to appear. In unrestricted submis-sion, such as the present margin agreements envisage, the interpreta-tions of the law by the arbitrators in contrast to manifest disregard are not subject, in the federal courts, to judicial review for error in interpre-tation. The United States Arbitration Act contains no provision for judicial determination of legal issues such as is found in the English law. As the protective provisions of the Securities Act require the exercise of judicial direction to fairly assure their effectiveness, it seems to us that congress must have intended § 14 note 6, supra, to apply to waiver of judicial trial and review.

* * *

Recognizing the advantages that prior agreements for arbitration may provide for the solution of commercial controversies, we decide that the intention of Congress concerning the sale of securities is better carried out by holding invalid such agreement for arbitration of issues arising under the act.

Reversed.

[Mr. Justice Jackson's concurring opinion and Mr. Justice Frankfurter's dissenting opinion have been omitted.]

Note

In *Shearson/American Express, Inc. v. McMahon*, 482 U.S. 220, 233, 107 S.Ct. 2332, 96 L.Ed.2d 185 (1987), the U.S. Supreme Court stated that " . . . the mistrust of arbitration that formed the basis for the *Wilko* opinion in 1953 is difficult to square with the assessment of arbitration that has prevailed since that time." *Wilko* was specifically overruled in *Rodriguez de Quijas v. Shearson/American Express, Inc*, 490 U.S. 477, 485, 109 S.Ct. 1917, 104 L.Ed.2d 526 (1989). For an interesting behind-the-scenes account of the court's shifting view of *Wilko*, see Ellen E. Deason, *Arbitrability of Statutory Claims: Perspectives from the Blackmun Papers*, 2005 J. Disp. Resol. (forthcoming 2005).

GILMER v. INTERSTATE/JOHNSON LANE CORP.

Supreme Court of the United States, 1991.
500 U.S. 20, 111 S.Ct. 1647, 114 L.Ed.2d 26.

Justice White delivered the opinion of the Court.

The question presented in this case is whether a claim under the Age Discrimination in Employment Act of 1967 (ADEA), as amended, can be subjected to compulsory arbitration pursuant to an arbitration agreement in a securities registration application. The Court of Appeals held that it could, and we affirm.

I

Respondent Interstate/Johnson Lane Corporation (Interstate) hired petitioner Robert Gilmer as a Manager of Financial Services in May 1981. As required by his employment, Gilmer registered as a securities representative with several stock exchanges, including the New York Stock Exchange (NYSE). His registration application, entitled "Uniform Application for Securities Industry Registration or Transfer," provided, among other things, that Gilmer "agreed to arbitrate any dispute, claim or controversy" arising between him and Interstate "that is required to be arbitrated under the rules, constitution or by-laws of the organizations with which I register." Of relevance to this case, NYSE Rule 347 provides for arbitration of "any controversy between a registered representative and any member or member organization arising out of the employment or termination of employment of such registered representative."

Interstate terminated Gilmer's employment in 1987, at which time Gilmer was 62 years of age. After first filing an age discrimination charge with the Equal Employment Opportunity Commission (EEOC), Gilmer subsequently brought suit in the United States District Court for the Western District of North Carolina, alleging that Interstate had discharged him because of his age, in violation of the ADEA. In response to Gilmer's complaint, Interstate filed in the District Court a motion to compel arbitration of the ADEA claim. In its motion, Interstate relied upon the arbitration agreement in Gilmer's registration application, as well as the Federal Arbitration Act (FAA). The District Court denied Interstate's motion, based on this Court's decision in *Alexander v. Gardner–Denver Co.,* and because it concluded that "Congress intended to protect ADEA claimants from the waiver of a judicial forum." The United States Court of Appeals for the Fourth Circuit reversed, finding "nothing in the text, legislative history, or underlying purposes of the ADEA indicating a congressional intent to preclude enforcement of arbitration agreements." We granted certiorari, to resolve a conflict among the Courts of Appeals regarding the arbitrability of ADEA claims.

II

* * *

It is by now clear that statutory claims may be the subject of an arbitration agreement, enforceable pursuant to the FAA. Indeed, in recent years we have held enforceable arbitration agreements relating to claims arising under the Sherman Act, § 10(b) of the Securities Exchange Act of 1934; the civil provisions of the Racketeer Influenced and Corrupt Organizations Act (RICO)*;* and § 12(2) of the Securities Act of 1933. In these cases we recognized that "by agreeing to arbitrate a statutory claim, a party does not forgo the substantive rights afforded by the statute; it only submits to their resolution in an arbitral, rather than a judicial, forum."

Although all statutory claims may not be appropriate for arbitration, "having made the bargain to arbitrate, the party should be held to it unless Congress itself has evinced an intention to preclude a waiver of judicial remedies for the statutory rights at issue." In this regard, we note that the burden is on Gilmer to show that Congress intended to preclude a waiver of a judicial forum for ADEA claims. If such an intention exists, it will be discoverable in the text of the ADEA, its legislative history, or an "inherent conflict" between arbitration and the ADEA's underlying purposes. Throughout such an inquiry, it should be kept in mind that "questions of arbitrability must be addressed with a healthy regard for the federal policy favoring arbitration."

III

Gilmer concedes that nothing in the text of the ADEA or its legislative history explicitly precludes arbitration. He argues, however, that compulsory arbitration of ADEA claims pursuant to arbitration agreements would be inconsistent with the statutory framework and purposes of the ADEA. Like the Court of Appeals, we disagree.

A

Congress enacted the ADEA in 1967 "to promote employment of older persons based on their ability rather than age; to prohibit arbitrary age discrimination in employment; [and] to help employers and workers find ways of meeting problems arising from the impact of age on employment." To achieve those goals, the ADEA, among other things, makes it unlawful for an employer "to fail or refuse to hire or to discharge any individual or otherwise discriminate against any individual with respect to his compensation, terms, conditions, or privileges of employment, because of such individual's age." This proscription is enforced both by private suits and by the EEOC. * * *

As Gilmer contends, the ADEA is designed not only to address individual grievances, but also to further important social policies. We do not perceive any inherent inconsistency between those policies, however, and enforcing agreements to arbitrate age discrimination claims. It is true that arbitration focuses on specific disputes between the parties involved. The same can be said, however, of judicial resolution of claims. Both of these dispute resolution mechanisms nevertheless also can further broader social purposes. The Sherman Act, the Securities Exchange Act of 1934, RICO and the Securities Act of 1933 all are designed to advance important public policies, but as noted above, claims under those statutes are appropriate for arbitration. "So long as the prospective litigant effectively may vindicate [his or her] statutory cause of action in the arbitral forum, the statute will continue to serve both its remedial and deterrent function."

We also are unpersuaded by the argument that arbitration will undermine the role of the EEOC in enforcing the ADEA. An individual ADEA claimant subject to an arbitration agreement will still be free to file a charge with the EEOC, even though the claimant is not able to institute a private judicial action. Indeed, Gilmer filed a charge with the EEOC in this case. In any event, the EEOC's role in combating age discrimination is not dependent on the filing of a charge; the agency may receive information concerning alleged violations of the ADEA "from any source," and it has independent authority to investigate age discrimination. Moreover, nothing in the ADEA indicates that Congress intended that the EEOC be involved in all employment disputes. Such disputes can be settled, for example, without any EEOC involvement. Finally, the mere involvement of an administrative agency in the enforcement of a statute is not sufficient to preclude arbitration. For example, the Securities Exchange Commission is heavily involved in the enforcement of the Securities Exchange Act of 1934 and the Securities Act of 1933, but we held that claims under both of those statutes may be subject to compulsory arbitration.

Gilmer also argues that compulsory arbitration is improper because it deprives claimants of the judicial forum provided for by the ADEA. Congress, however, did not explicitly preclude arbitration or other nonjudicial resolution of claims, even in its recent amendments to the ADEA.

"If Congress intended the substantive protection afforded [by the ADEA] to include protection against waiver of the right to a judicial forum, that intention will be deducible from text or legislative history." Moreover, Gilmer's argument ignores the ADEA's flexible approach to resolution of claims. The EEOC, for example, is directed to pursue "informal methods of conciliation, conference, and persuasion," which suggests that out-of-court dispute resolution, such as arbitration, is consistent with the statutory scheme established by Congress. In addition, arbitration is consistent with Congress' grant of concurrent jurisdiction over ADEA claims to state and federal courts, because arbitration agreements, "like the provision for concurrent jurisdiction, serve to advance the objective of allowing [claimants] a broader right to select the forum for resolving disputes, whether it be judicial or otherwise."

B

In arguing that arbitration is inconsistent with the ADEA, Gilmer also raises a host of challenges to the adequacy of arbitration procedures. Initially, we note that in our recent arbitration cases we have already rejected most of these arguments as insufficient to preclude arbitration of statutory claims. Such generalized attacks on arbitration "rest on suspicion of arbitration as a method of weakening the protections afforded in the substantive law to would-be complainants," and as such, they are "far out of step with our current strong endorsement of the federal statute favoring this method of resolving disputes." Consequently, we address these arguments only briefly.

Gilmer first speculates that arbitration panels will be biased. However, "we decline to indulge the presumption that the parties and arbitral body conducting a proceeding will be unable or unwilling to retain competent, conscientious and impartial arbitrators." In any event, we note that the NYSE arbitration rules, which are applicable to the dispute in this case, provide protections against biased panels. The rules require, for example, that the parties be informed of the employment histories of the arbitrators, and that they be allowed to make further inquiries into the arbitrators' backgrounds. In addition, each party is allowed one peremptory challenge and unlimited challenges for cause. Moreover, the arbitrators are required to disclose "any circumstances which might preclude [them] from rendering an objective and impartial determination." The FAA also protects against bias, by providing that courts may overturn arbitration decisions "where there was evident partiality or corruption in the arbitrators." There has been no showing in this case that those provisions are inadequate to guard against potential bias.

Gilmer also complains that the discovery allowed in arbitration is more limited than in the federal courts, which he contends will make it difficult to prove discrimination. It is unlikely, however, that age discrimination claims require more extensive discovery than other claims that we have found to be arbitrable, such as RICO and antitrust claims. Moreover, there has been no showing in this case that the NYSE discovery provisions, which allow for document production, information requests, depositions, and subpoenas, will prove insufficient to allow ADEA claimants such as Gilmer a fair opportunity to present their claims. Although those procedures might not be as extensive as in the federal courts, by agreeing to arbitrate, a party "trades the procedures and opportunity for review of the courtroom for the simplicity, informality, and expedition of arbitration." Indeed, an important counterweight to the reduced discovery in NYSE arbitration is that arbitrators are not bound by the rules of evidence.

A further alleged deficiency of arbitration is that arbitrators often will not issue written opinions, resulting, Gilmer contends, in a lack of public knowledge of employers' discriminatory policies, an inability to obtain effective appellate review, and a stifling of the development of the law. The NYSE rules, however, do require that all arbitration awards be in writing, and that the awards contain the names of the parties, a summary of the issues in controversy, and a description of the award issued. In addition, the award decisions are made available to the public. Furthermore, judicial decisions addressing ADEA claims will continue to be issued because it is unlikely that all or even most ADEA claimants will be subject to arbitration agreements. Finally, Gilmer's concerns apply equally to settlements of ADEA claims, which, as noted above, are clearly allowed.

It is also argued that arbitration procedures cannot adequately further the purposes of the ADEA because they do not provide for broad equitable relief and class actions. As the court below noted, however, arbitrators do have the power to fashion equitable relief. Indeed, the NYSE rules applicable here do not restrict the types of relief an arbitrator may award, but merely refer to "damages and/or other relief." The NYSE rules also provide for collective proceedings. But "even if the arbitration could not go forward as a class action or class relief could not be granted by the arbitrator, the fact that the [ADEA] provides for the possibility of bringing a collective action does not mean that individual attempts at conciliation were intended to be barred." Finally, it should be remembered that arbitration agreements will not preclude the EEOC from bringing actions seeking class-wide and equitable relief.

C

An additional reason advanced by Gilmer for refusing to enforce arbitration agreements relating to ADEA claims is his contention that there often will be unequal bargaining power between employers and employees. Mere inequality in bargaining power, however, is not a sufficient reason to hold that arbitration agreements are never enforceable in the employment context. Relationships between securities dealers and investors, for example, may involve unequal bargaining power, but we nevertheless held in *Rodriguez de Quijas* and *McMahon* that agreements to arbitrate in that context are enforceable. As discussed above, the FAA's purpose was to place arbitration agreements on the same footing as other contracts. Thus, arbitration agreements are enforceable "save upon such grounds as exist at law or in equity for the revocation of any contract." "Of course, courts should remain attuned to well-supported claims that the agreement to arbitrate resulted from the sort of fraud or overwhelming economic power that would provide grounds 'for the revocation of any contract.'" There is no indication in this case, however, that Gilmer, an experienced businessman, was coerced or defrauded into agreeing to the arbitration clause in his registration application. As with the claimed procedural inadequacies discussed above, this claim of unequal bargaining power is best left for resolution in specific cases.

IV

In addition to the arguments discussed above, Gilmer vigorously asserts that our decision in *Alexander v. Gardner–Denver Co.*, and its progeny preclude arbitration of employment discrimination claims. Gilmer's reliance on these cases, however, is misplaced.

In *Gardner–Denver,* the issue was whether a discharged employee whose grievance had been arbitrated pursuant to an arbitration clause in a collective-bargaining agreement was precluded from subsequently bringing a Title VII action based upon the conduct that was the subject of the grievance. In holding that the employee was not foreclosed from bringing the Title VII claim, we stressed that an employee's contractual rights under the collective-bargaining agreement are distinct from the employee's statutory Title VII rights:

> In submitting his grievance to arbitration, an employee seeks to vindicate his contractual right under a collective-bargaining agreement. By contrast, in filing a lawsuit under Title VII, an employee asserts independent statutory rights accorded by Congress. The distinctly separate nature of these contractual and statutory rights is not vitiated merely because both were violated as a result of the same factual occurrence.

We also noted that a labor arbitrator has authority only to resolve questions of contractual rights. The arbitrator's "task is to effectuate the intent of the parties" and he or she does not have the "general authority to invoke public laws that conflict with the bargain between the parties." By contrast, "in instituting an action under Title VII, the employee is not seeking review of the arbitrator's decision. Rather, he is asserting a statutory right independent of the arbitration process." We further expressed concern that in collective-bargaining arbitration "the interests of the individual employee may be subordinated to the collective interest of all employees in the bargaining unit."

Berrentine and *McDonald* similarly involved the issue whether arbitration under a collective-bargaining agreement precluded a subsequent statutory claim. In holding that the statutory claims there were not precluded, we noted, as in *Gardner–Denver,* the difference between contractual rights under a collective-bargaining agreement and individual statutory rights, the potential disparity in interests between a union and an employee, and the limited authority and power of labor arbitrators.

There are several important distinctions between the *Gardner–Denver* line of cases and the case before us. First, those cases did not involve the issue of the enforceability of an agreement to arbitrate statutory claims. Rather, they involved the quite different issue whether arbitration of contract-based claims precluded subsequent judicial resolution of statutory claims. Since the employees there had not agreed to arbitrate their statutory claims, and the labor arbitrators were not authorized to resolve such claims, the arbitration in those cases understandably was held not to preclude subsequent statutory actions. Second, because the arbitration in those cases occurred in the context of a collective-bargaining agreement, the claimants there were represented by their unions in the arbitration proceedings. An important concern therefore was the tension between collective representation and individual statutory rights, a concern not applicable to the present case. Finally, those cases were not decided under the FAA, which, as discussed above, reflects a "liberal federal policy favoring arbitration agreements." Therefore, those cases provide no basis for refusing to enforce Gilmer's agreement to arbitrate his ADEA claim.

V

We conclude that Gilmer has not met his burden of showing that Congress, in enacting the ADEA, intended to preclude arbitration of claims under the Act. Accordingly, the judgment of the Court of Appeals is

Affirmed.

Justice Stevens, with whom Justice Marshall joins, dissenting.

* * *

III

Not only would I find that the FAA does not apply to employment-related disputes between employers and employees in general, but also I would hold that compulsory arbitration conflicts with the congressional purpose animating the ADEA, in particular. As the Court previously has noted, authorizing the courts to issue broad injunctive relief is the cornerstone to eliminating discrimination in society. The ADEA, like Title VII, authorizes courts to award broad, class-based injunctive relief to achieve the purposes of the Act. Because commercial arbitration is typically limited to a specific dispute between the particular parties and because the available remedies in arbitral forums generally do not provide for class-wide injunctive relief, I would conclude that an essential purpose of the ADEA is frustrated by compulsory arbitration of employment discrimination claims. Moreover, as Chief Justice Burger explained:

Plainly, it would not comport with the congressional objectives behind a statute seeking to enforce civil rights protected by Title VII to allow the very forces that had practiced discrimination to contract away the right to enforce civil rights in the courts. For federal courts to defer to arbitral decisions reached by the same combination of forces that had long perpetuated invidious discrimination would have made the foxes guardians of the chickens.

In my opinion the same concerns expressed by Chief Justice Burger with regard to compulsory arbitration of Title VII claims may be said of claims arising under the ADEA. The Court's holding today clearly eviscerates the important role played by an independent judiciary in eradicating employment discrimination.

IV

When the FAA was passed in 1925, I doubt that any legislators who voted for it expected it to apply to statutory claims, to form contracts between parties of unequal bargaining power, or to the arbitration of disputes arising out of the employment relationship. In recent years, however, the Court "has effectively rewritten the statute," and abandoned its earlier view that statutory claims were not appropriate subjects for arbitration. Although I remain persuaded that it erred in doing so, the Court has also put to one side any concern about the inequality of bargaining power between an entire industry, on the one hand, and an individual customer or employee, on the other. Until today, however, the Court has not read § 2 of the FAA as broadly encompassing disputes arising out of the employment relationship. I believe that additional extension of the FAA is erroneous. Accordingly, I respectfully dissent.

Notes and Questions

1. One of the recurring arguments against compelling the arbitration of a statutory claim is that the arbitration process is "an inferior system of justice, structured without due process, rules of evidence, accountability of judgment or rule of law." The relative merits of litigation and alternative processes is a continuing issue. Arbitration is criticized by Professor Stephen Goldberg in Section D, infra, beginning at page 654, for being too much like litigation. Defenses of arbitration focus at times on ways that arbitration systems are similar to the legal system. Recall, for example, Justice White's discussion in *Gilmer* of NYSE rules on discovery and the powers of arbitrators to fashion equitable relief. Is arbitration too much like litigation or not enough like litigation? If your answer is "it depends," on what does it depend? This issue is explored in Section D, infra, beginning at page 651.

2. The court's opinion in *Gilmer* was viewed by many practitioners as a broad endorsement of mandatory arbitration. Do you read it that broadly? Could one argue that it is more of a case about presumptions regarding arbitration and the evidence that is required to support or refute such assumptions? *See* Joseph R. Grodin, *Arbitration of Employment Discrimination Claims: Doctrine and Policy in the Wake of* Gilmer, 14 Hofstra Lab. L.J. 1 (1996). The scholarly literature critical of *Gilmer* is voluminous. *See, e.g.,*

David S. Schwartz, *Enforcing Small Print to Protect Big Business: Employee and Consumer Rights Claims in an Age of Compelled Arbitration*, 1997 Wis. L. Rev. 33; Jean R. Sternlight, *Panacea or Corporate Tool?: Debunking the Supreme Court's Preference for Binding Arbitration*, 74 Wash. U. L.Q. 637 (1996); Katherine Van Wezel Stone, *Mandatory Arbitration of Individual Employment Rights: The Yellow Dog Contract of the 1990's*, 73 Denv. U. L. Rev. 1017 (1996); Reginald Alleyne, *Statutory Discrimination Claims: Rights "Waived" and Lost in the Arbitration Forum*, 13 Hofstra Lab. L. J. 381 (1996); Robert A. Gorman, *The Gilmer Decision and the Private Arbitration of Public–Law Disputes*, 1995 U. Ill. L. Rev. 635. For scholarly commentary defending *Gilmer*, see Dennis R. Nolan, *Employment Arbitration After* Circuit City, 41 Brandeis L.J. 853 (2003); Samuel Estreicher, *Pre-dispute Agreements to Arbitrate Statutory Employment Claims*, 72 N.Y.U. L. Rev. 1344 (1997).

3.   Mandatory arbitration provisions are now common in a wide variety of areas, including securities, health care, financial services, consumer goods and service, and employment, to name just a few. Professor Hensler and Linda Demaine analyzed 161 consumer contracts in a variety of industries, and discovered nearly a third of them, fifty-one, included mandatory arbitration provisions. *See* Linda J. Demaine & Deborah R. Hensler, *"Volunteering" to Arbitrate through Pre-dispute Arbitration Clauses: The Average Consumer's Experience*, 67 Law & Contemp. Probs. 55, 61 (2004). Demaine and Hensler further found:

> The prevalence of arbitration clauses is highest (69.2%) in the financial category (credit cards, banking, investment, and accounting/tax consulting), and lowest (0) in the food and entertainment category (grocery stores, restaurants, theme parks, and cultural/sports events). This pattern is not surprising, as the financial category is characterized by industries that rely heavily on written contracts, often for ongoing services, whereas the food and entertainment category is characterized by industries that engage in isolated transactions with no written contract between businesses and consumers. A similar pattern holds to some extent across industries. The auto insurance and health insurance industries, for example — both of which typically provide ongoing services under written contract — are more likely to require arbitration than are the auto repair/maintenance and health-care-provider industries. This pattern is not universal, however. For example, none of the home protection companies and only one health club surveyed required arbitration, although consumers usually contract in writing for these ongoing services. Customary practice and industry regulations likely explain some of the patterns found.

Id. at 62.

4.   There were differences of opinion among lower courts about the effect of *Gilmer* on *Gardner–Denver*. *Wright v. Universal Maritime Service Corp.*, 525 U.S. 70, 119 S.Ct. 391, 142 L.Ed.2d 361 (1998), answered some questions and raised others. While *Gardner–Denver* held that "there can be no prospective waiver of an employees' rights under Title VII," (415 U.S. 36, 51, 94 S.Ct. 1011, 39 L.Ed.2d 147 (1974)), the opinion in *Wright* stated that any waiver of statutory rights resulting from a collective bargaining contract

must be "explicitly stated" and "clear and unmistakable." 525 U.S. at 80. Speaking for the Court, Justice Scalia said there was "obviously some tension between" *Gardner–Denver* and *Gilmer,* (*Id.* at 76), but went on to assert that, "whether or not *Garner–Denver*'s seemingly absolute prohibition of union waiver of employees' federal forum rights survives *Gilmer, Gardner–Denver* at least stands for the proposition that the right to a federal judicial forum is of sufficient importance to be protected against less-than-explicit union waiver in a CBA." *Id.* at 80. Concluding that the CBA in *Wright* did not contain a clear and unmistakable waiver, Justice Scalia indicated that the Court did not "reach the question whether such a waiver would be enforceable." *Id.* at 82. In an article published in 2003, Mary K. O'Melverny, of counsel to a law firm that represents unions, said that most courts since *Wright* have held that ". . . the contractual grievance machinery was insufficient to establish a 'clear and unmistakable waiver' of statutory rights." Mary K. O'Melverny, *One Bite of the Apple and One of the Orange: Interpreting Claims That Collective Bargaining Agreements Should Waive the Individual Employee's Statutory Right,* 19 Lab. Law 185, 198 (2003).

5.   Congress endorsed arbitration and other alternative processes in the Civil Rights Act of 1991, 42 U.S.C. § 1981 (2000), and the Americans with Disabilities Act, 42 U.S.C. § 12212 (2000). Referring to the Civil Rights Act of 1991, the D.C. Circuit stated that "the language of the statute in no way suggests that the rule of *Gilmer* should no longer apply." *Benefits Communication Corp. v. Klieforth,* 642 A.2d 1299, 1305 (D.C. 1994).

6.   Consider the following arguments prompted by the *Gilmer* decision:

Gilmer thus represents the Supreme Court's endorsement of delegating the interpretation of public law to privately accountable adjudicators subject only to minimal oversight by the judiciary. The justification for employment arbitration is thus the same as for other types of ADR — speed, informality and cost-effectiveness — rather than the promotion of a private system of workplace self-government. Furthermore, it is presumed that arbitration will further the public interest by reducing overcrowded judicial and administrative dockets.

Both those who hail and those who dread the growing ADR movement recognize that there is a tension between speedy, efficient dispute resolution and publicly accountable lawmaking. ADR opponents maintain that gains in efficiency, if any, cannot justify what they decry as a privatization of public justice. ADR proponents minimize the public justice concerns and maintain that without ADR's efficiency gains there will be no justice at all, only judicial and administrative gridlock. Some have sought to resolve this seemingly insolvable debate by supporting ADR generally, while carving out certain types of cases heavily laden with public value choices and requiring that those be litigated in a public forum. * * *

Title VII represents a public justice value judgment that the elimination of racial discrimination is so important that forcing employers to bear some of the cost of pursuing that goal is justified. The extent of the costs that employers must bear is not specified in the statute. That issue is delegated to politically accountable judges and administrative agencies to determine as a matter of interpretation. Under a system in which employment arbitrators make final and binding decisions in cases involving charges of discrimination based on Title VII, there will be serious concern about whether those decisions adequately reflect the public justice values at the heart of the statute.

Martin H. Malin and Robert F. Ladenson, *Privatizing Justice: A Jurisprudential Perspective on Labor and Employment Arbitration From the Steelworkers Trilogy to* Gilmer, 44 Hastings L.J. 1187, 1207–08, 1229 (1993).

Also consider the following remarks by Theodore O. Rogers, Jr., a management lawyer, and Judith P. Vladeck, an attorney who represents employees, in *Symposium on Arbitration in the Securities Industry*, 63 Fordham L. Rev. 1507 (1995).

I believe there has been a well-orchestrated public relations campaign over the course of the last nine or ten months against arbitration of employment discrimination claims. I think it has been unfair and I think the motives of many of the people who are behind it are quite suspect.

* * *

What the Exchange's arbitration facility does, and I believe does well, is consider and resolve individual claims — employment claims. It has considered employment claims for years. What's new, in light of the Supreme Court's decision in *Gilmer* in 1991, is the consideration of employment discrimination claims. The General Accounting Office's March 1994 report on securities arbitration, about which I'm sure many here are familiar, noted, for example, that in 1991 and 1992 the New York Stock Exchange arbitrated 312 employment cases, and only sixteen of those were discrimination cases.

* * *

One of the reasons that I think it is so vital for the exchange and the other self-regulatory organizations to continue their good work in arbitration, including arbitration of employment discrimination claims, is that the court system is broken.

Page one of today's New York Times reports on the U.S. Judicial conference's recommendation that employment discriminations claims somehow be thrown out of the federal courts or at least be subject to some preliminary screenings by the Equal Employment Opportunity Commission.

The federal judges realize that they cannot handle the tidal wave of employment discrimination claims. Their suggestion that the EEOC handle it is a difficult one to fathom because those of us with experience with the EEOC know that they're swamped and what they're doing is trying to shuttle cases over to the federal courts.

The Dunlop Commission, the commission formed by the current administration to consider worker-management relations, issued a fact-finding report in May of 1994.

* * *

[T]he report found that litigation is expensive and that complicated court processes make it difficult for employees to pursue claims; the report also found that from 1971 to 1991 the overall number of civil cases brought in federal court has risen by 110%, but the number of employment claims rose by 430%. And those figures are from before the Americans with Disabilities Act and the 1991 Civil Rights Act became effective, so by now presumably, the increase in discrimination cases is much larger.

As for costs, the Commission found that substantially over one dollar in costs, attorneys' fees, and other just wasted money is spent for each one dollar that goes to a claimant in compensation for a court finding of discrimination. The Commission found that the costs, the difficulty, and the complication of employment litigation ultimately restrict litigation to upper-level professionals, usually complaining of their termination.

Jury verdicts, the Commission noted, are often lottery-like in their results. The problem of unpredictable jury decisions is one that everyone seems to be considering these days. Last night on the eleven o'clock news, I saw a report that the City of New York is going to propose some way whereby claims against the City could be determined in a forum without a jury.

In other words, the current litigation process is just broken. * * *

Now, I want to address a few of the specific criticisms that have been raised against arbitration of employment discrimination claims. First, it is often claimed that arbitrators have no training in employment law. That's wrong. The NYSE does train arbitrators in the law. The NASD, I know, does an excellent job in its training efforts. * * *

Those who criticize the supposed lack of legal training by arbitrators ignore the fact that juries have no training in discrimination law, and there is no reason to suppose that a judge's instruction to a jury concerning the law leaves the jury any more informed on these issues than arbitrators who have received some training and have the benefit of the competing arguments and evidence submitted by counsel. In short, I don't believe that discrimination law presents any more complications than other legal claims that have been handled here in arbitration successfully for years.

The second criticism that's been raised in this ongoing P.R. campaign against arbitration is that arbitration rules are unfair to employees. That's wrong again. The New York Stock Exchange bends over backwards to afford employees an opportunity to present their case. * * *

Finally, another subtext that underlies all of the criticisms of arbitration is the claim that employees cannot win. Mr. Clemente may have more accurate or more updated statistics, but the ones I have prove this is just not right. The GAO report from March of 1994 studied eighteen cases that went to a decision, and of those the claimant won in ten of them. A fifty-five percent success rate for claimants is not evidence of a biased forum. Now, some may try to minimize that substantial success by claimants by stating that a number of the winning employees may have wanted more than they even got. But I don't think that's anything that distinguishes arbitration from any other litigation forum.

The short of it is that the criticisms of arbitration are readily rebutted. I can speak from current and personal experience. * * *

Theodore O. Rogers Jr., *Employment Discrimination,* 63 Fordham L. Rev. 1613, at 1617–22.

If I take a woman into the federal court who has a legitimate, meritorious case of discrimination, she is entitled to certain protection, she is entitled to a fair hearing, entitled to due process. If she wins, she gets whatever money she's lost in back wages, she gets enough in attorneys' fees so that she nets whatever it is of the damages provided, and if she has suffered emotional distress, under the Act she can get damages for that. * * *

Let me ask you all: How ready are you to let all of your IRS matters be arbitrated? The IRS doesn't like some filing you've done. It gives it to an arbitrator. You don't get to pick. You don't get to choose. The arbitrator doesn't have to be bound by the law. He thinks you earn too damn much money anyway. Not only don't you get a refund, but you get a penalty imposed with no explanation and no right to appeal. What are we doing with our public rights, giving them to untrained arbitrators? Do you really want to do that with major pieces of your life? You know, you could be there some day. This is not simply for women who complain of sexual harassment. It is for executives, too, who have been cheated.

Judith P. Vladeck, *Employment Discrimination*, 63 Fordham L. Rev. 1613, 1625–26.

ii. The Costs of Arbitration

One of the differences between public adjudication and private arbitration is that with public adjudication the costs of the judge, the courtroom, the clerk's office, and the other necessary components of a public court are paid by the government. With private arbitration, however, those costs must be borne by the parties, including the costs of the arbitrator's time and the costs of administering the case. The *Cole* and the *Green Tree* cases that follow examine the implications of this dynamic in the context of mandatory arbitration.

COLE v. BURNS INTERNATIONAL SECURITY SERVICES

United States Court of Appeals, District of Columbia Circuit, 1997.
105 F.3d 1465.

Harry T. Edwards, Chief Judge:

This case raises important issues regarding whether and to what extent a person can be required, *as a condition of employment,* to (1) waive all rights to a trial by jury in a court of competent jurisdiction with respect to any dispute relating to recruitment, employment, or termination, including claims involving laws against discrimination, and (2) sign an agreement providing that, at the employer's option, any such employment disputes must be arbitrated. At its core, this appeal challenges the enforceability of conditions of employment requiring individuals to arbitrate claims resting on statutory rights. The issues at hand bring into focus the seminal decision of *Gilmer v. Interstate/Johnson Lane Corp.*, and call into question the limits of the Supreme Court's holdings in that case.

In this case, the appellant, Clinton Cole, seeks to overturn an order of the District Court dismissing his complaint under Title VII of the Civil Rights Act of 1964, as amended, and compelling arbitration of his disputes with Burns International Security Services ("Burns" or "Burns Security"). Although Cole seemingly raised a viable action under Title VII, the District Court held that his statutory claims of employment discrimination should be dismissed pursuant to the Federal Arbitration Act ("FAA" or "Act"). The District Court held that section 1 of the Act does not exempt *all* "employment" contracts and that Cole's job was not in an exempt category, and, therefore, Cole was bound by the agreement he had signed with Burns allowing the employer to opt for arbitration. In reaching this conclusion, the trial court found that the arbitration agreement was a valid and enforceable contract.

We agree with the District Court that section 1 of the FAA does not exclude all contracts of employment from the coverage of the FAA. Every circuit court to squarely address this issue has held that section 1 excludes from the coverage of the FAA only the employment contracts of workers actually engaged in the movement of goods in interstate commerce. Additionally, the Supreme Court's interpretation of section 2 of the FAA in *Allied–Bruce Terminix Cos. v. Dobson*, strongly supports this narrow interpretation of section 1. Finally, although the Supreme Court did not address the issue of section 1's scope in *Gilmer,* the majority's decision suggests that the Court would be inclined to accept the narrow interpretation we adopt.

Second, we find that the disputed arbitration agreement is valid. In doing so, we are mindful of the clear distinctions between arbitration of labor disputes under a collective bargaining agreement and mandatory arbitration of individual statutory claims outside of the context of collective bargaining. We are also cognizant of the numerous concerns that have been voiced by arbitrators, legal commentators, the Equal Employment Opportunity Commission ("EEOC"), and National Labor Relations Board ("NLRB") regarding the potential inequities and inadequacies of arbitration in individual employment cases, as well as their concerns about the competence of arbitrators and the arbitral forum to enforce effectively the myriad of public laws protecting workers and regulating the workplace. Nonetheless, in this case, we are constrained by *Gilmer* to find the arbitration agreement enforceable. We do not read *Gilmer* as mandating the enforcement of *all* mandatory agreements to arbitrate statutory claims; rather, we read *Gilmer* as requiring the enforcement of arbitration agreements that do not undermine the relevant statutory scheme. The agreement in this case meets that standard.

We note that this case raises an issue not directly presented in *Gilmer* or any other Supreme Court case to date: can an employer require an employee to arbitrate all disputes and also require the employee to pay all or part of the arbitrators' fees? We hold that it cannot. In *Gilmer* and other securities industry cases, the employers routinely paid *all* arbitrators' fees, so the matter was not in dispute. However, there is no reason to think that the Court would have approved a program of mandatory arbitration of statutory claims in *Gilmer* in the absence of employer agreement to pay arbitrators' fees. Because public law confers both substantive rights and a reasonable right of access to a neutral forum in which those rights can be vindicated, we find that employees cannot be *required* to pay for the services of a "judge" in order to pursue their statutory rights. In this case, the parties' contract does not address explicitly the payment of the arbitrators' fees; however, because ambiguity in a contract should be resolved against the drafter — here, the employer — and ambiguity should be resolved in favor of a legal construction of the parties' agreement, we interpret the arbitration agreement at issue as requiring Burns to pay all arbitrators' fees associated with the resolution of Cole's claims. So construed, the contract is valid.

The dissent objects to our reaching the question as to who bears the burden of paying for an arbitrator's services, presumably because in *some* cases an employee might not be required to pay the arbitrator's compensation. This argument clearly misses the point. In our view, an employee can never be required, as a condition of employment, to pay an arbitrator's compensation in order to secure the resolution of statutory claims under Title VII (any more than an employee can be made to pay a judge's salary). If there is any risk that an arbitration agreement can be construed to require this result, this would surely deter the bringing of arbitration and constitute a *de facto* forfeiture of the employee's statutory rights. The only way that an arbitration agreement of the sort at issue here can be lawful is if the employer assumes responsibility for the payment of the arbitrator's compensation.

Cole has also argued that the arbitration agreement should not be enforced because the arbitrator's rulings, even as to the meaning of public law under Title VII, will not be subject to judicial review. Cole is wrong on this point. The nearly unlimited deference paid to arbitration awards in the context of collective bargaining is not required, and not appropriate, in the context of employees' statutory claims. In this context, the Supreme Court has assumed that arbitration awards are subject to judicial review sufficiently rigorous to ensure compliance with statutory law. Indeed, Burns has conceded such review in this case. Because the courts will always remain available to ensure that arbitrators properly interpret the dictates of public law, an agreement to arbitrate statutory claims of discrimination is not unconscionable or otherwise unenforceable.

* * *

Obviously, *Gilmer* cannot be read as holding that an arbitration agreement is enforceable no matter what rights it waives or what burdens it imposes. *See* Gorman, 1995 U. Ill. L. Rev. at 644 ("The Supreme Court in the *Gilmer* case did not hold that *any* sort of arbitration procedure before *any* manner of arbitrator would be satisfactory in the adjudication of public rights."). Such a holding would be fundamentally at odds with our understanding of the rights accorded to persons protected by public statutes like the ADEA and Title VII. The beneficiaries of public statutes are entitled to the rights and protections provided by the law. Clearly, it would be unlawful for an employer to condition employment on an employee's agreement to give up the right to be free from racial or gender discrimination. *See Gardner–Denver,* ("There can be no prospective waiver of an employee's rights under Title VII.... Title VII's strictures are absolute and represent a congressional command that each employee be free from discriminatory practices.... Waiver of these rights would defeat the paramount congressional purpose behind Title VII."). Any such condition of employment would violate Title VII, regardless of whether or not the agreement was viewed as a contract of adhesion. Thus, in a subsequent suit by the employee raising a viable claim of racial discrimination or sexual harassment, it would be no defense that the employee had signed a contract giving up her right to be free from discrimination.

Similarly, an employee cannot be required as a condition of employment to waive access to a neutral forum in which statutory employment discrimination claims may be heard. For example, an employee could not be required to sign an agreement waiving the right to bring Title VII claims in any forum. Although the employer could argue that such an agreement does not waive the substantive protections of the statute, surely such an agreement would nonetheless violate the law by leaving the employee's substantive rights at the mercy of the employer's good faith in adhering to the law. At a minimum, statutory rights include both a substantive protection *and* access to a neutral forum in which to enforce those protections. * * *

We believe that all of the factors addressed in *Gilmer* are satisfied here. In particular, we note that the arbitration arrangement (1) provides for neutral arbitrators, (2) provides for more than minimal discovery, (3) requires a written award, (4) provides for all of the types of relief that would otherwise be available in court, and (5) does not require employees to pay either unreasonable costs *or* any arbitrators' fees or expenses as a condition of access to the arbitration forum. * * *

Although we find that the disputed arbitration agreement is legally valid, there is one point that requires amplification. The arbitration agreement in this case presents an issue not raised by the agreement in *Gilmer:* can an employer condition employment on acceptance of an arbitration agreement that requires the employee to submit his or her statutory claims to arbitration and then requires the employee to pay all or part of the arbitrators' fees? * * *

[W]e are unaware of any situation in American jurisprudence in which a beneficiary of a federal statute has been required to pay for the services of the judge assigned to hear her or his case. Under *Gilmer,* arbitration is supposed to be a reasonable substitute for a judicial forum. Therefore, it would undermine Congress's intent to prevent employees who are seeking to vindicate statutory rights from gaining access to a judicial forum and then require them to pay for the services of an arbitrator when they would never be required to pay for a judge in court.

* * *

In sum, we hold that Cole could not be required to agree to arbitrate his public law claims as a condition of employment if the arbitration agreement required him to pay all or part of the arbitrator's fees and expenses. In light of this holding, we find that the arbitration agreement in this case is valid and enforceable. We do so because we interpret the agreement as requiring Burns Security to pay all of the arbitrator's fees necessary for a full and fair resolution of Cole's statutory claims.

* * *

The final issue in this case concerns the scope of judicial review of arbitral awards in cases of this sort, where an employee is compelled as a condition of employment to arbitrate statutory claims. Cole has argued that the arbitration agreement is unconscionable, because any arbitrator's rulings, even as to the meaning of public law under Title VII, will not be subject to judicial review. Cole is wrong on this point.

* * *

The value and finality of an employer's arbitration system will not be undermined by focused review of arbitral legal determinations. Most employment discrimination claims are entirely factual in nature and involve well-settled legal principles. * * * As a result, in the vast majority of cases, judicial review of legal determinations to ensure compliance with public law should have no adverse impact on the arbitration process. Nonetheless, there will be some cases in which novel or difficult legal issues are presented demanding judicial judgment. In such cases, the courts are empowered to review an arbitrator's award to ensure that its resolution of public law issues is correct. Indeed, at oral argument, Burns conceded the courts' authority to engage in such review. Because meaningful judicial review of public law issues is available, Cole's agreement to arbitrate is not unconscionable or otherwise unenforceable.

* * *

For the foregoing reasons, we affirm the District Court's order dismissing the complaint and compelling arbitration.

Karen LeCraft Henderson, Circuit Judge, concurring in part and dissenting in part:

* * *

By conditioning arbitration on the employer's assumption of arbitrator costs, the majority engages in pure judicial fee shifting which finds no support in the FAA, *Gilmer* or the parties' agreement, not one of which addresses arbitration fee allocation. Yet, relying on this very silence, the majority now declares that the employer must bear the costs, regardless of the outcome or the merits of the parties' positions, because of the majority's own speculation on what the arbitration costs will be and who will be required to pay them — factual matters never presented to the district court or even argued by the parties on appeal. * * *

The primary justification offered for the majority's contract reformation is to preserve the employee's statutory rights which, the majority asserts, will be lost if he is subjected to all the onerous expenses of arbitration. * * *

The majority also rationalizes its contractual modification as a counter to the employer's commanding position in the employment relationship: "Arbitration will occur in this case only because it has been mandated by the employer as a condition of employment." Maj. Op. at 152. I would suggest that the appellant's claims will be arbitrated, if at all, because each party agreed that the employer could so elect. In any event, if the majority believes that the arbitration agreement was reached under duress or that it is unconscionable, it should say so straight out and declare it unenforceable, as the appellant requests. On the other hand, if the majority truly believes the agreement is enforceable, as it maintains, it should enforce the agreement as written without judicial reformation.

For the foregoing reasons I dissent from the majority's holding that contractually required arbitration is conditioned on the employer's agreement to pay all arbitrator expenses.

Notes

1. The *Cole* case appears to be an example of what Professor Gorman recommended in 1995, when he said a code of due process for public law arbitration should be "articulated by the courts through a 'common law' type of evolutionary development." Robert A. Gorman, *The Gilmer Decision and the Private Arbitration of Public Law Disputes*, 1995 U. Ill. L. R. 635, 639.

2. You will have an opportunity to revisit the holding in *Cole* after you read the next case.

GREEN TREE FINANCIAL CORP. v. RANDOLPH

Supreme Court of the United States, 2000.
531 U.S. 79, 121 S.Ct. 513, 148 L.Ed.2d 373.

Chief Justice Rehnquist delivered the opinion of the Court.

In this case we first address whether an order compelling arbitration and dismissing a party's underlying claims is a "final decision with respect to an arbitration" within the meaning of § 16(a)(3) of the Federal Arbitration Act, 9 U.S.C. § 16(a)(3), and thus is immediately appealable pursuant to that Act. Because we decide that question in the affirmative, we also address the question whether an arbitration agreement that does not mention arbitration costs and fees is unenforceable because it fails to affirmatively protect a party from potentially steep arbitration costs. We conclude that an arbitration agreement's silence with respect to such matters does not render the agreement unenforceable.

I

Respondent Larketta Randolph purchased a mobile home from Better Cents Home Builders, Inc., in Opelika, Alabama. She financed this purchase through petitioners Green Tree Financial Corporation and its wholly owned subsidiary, Green Tree Financial Corp.–Alabama. Petitioners' Manufactured Home Retail Installment Contract and Security Agreement required that Randolph buy Vendor's Single Interest insurance, which protects the vendor or lienholder against the costs of repossession in the event of default. The agreement also provided that all disputes arising from, or relating to, the contract, whether arising under case law or statutory law, would be resolved by binding arbitration.

Randolph later sued petitioners, alleging that they violated the Truth in Lending Act (TILA), 15 U.S.C. § 1601 *et seq.,* by failing to disclose as a finance charge the Vendor's Single Interest insurance requirement. She later amended her complaint to add a claim that petitioners violated the Equal Credit Opportunity Act, 15 U.S.C. §§ 1691–1691f, by requiring her to arbitrate her statutory causes of action. She brought this action on behalf of a similarly situated class. In lieu of an answer, petitioners filed a motion to compel arbitration, to stay the action, or, in the alternative, to dismiss. The District Court granted petitioners' motion to compel arbitration, denied the motion to stay, and dismissed Randolph's claims with prejudice. The District Court also denied her request to certify a class. She requested reconsideration, asserting that she lacked the resources to arbitrate, and as a result, would have to forgo her claims against petitioners. The District Court denied reconsideration. Randolph appealed.

The Court of Appeals for the Eleventh Circuit first held that it had jurisdiction to review the District Court's order because that order was a final decision. The Court of Appeals looked to § 16 of the Federal

Arbitration Act (FAA), which governs appeal from a district court's arbitration order, and specifically § 16(a)(3), which allows appeal from "a final decision with respect to an arbitration that is subject to this title." The court determined that a final, appealable order within the meaning of the FAA is one that disposes of all the issues framed by the litigation, leaving nothing to be done but execute the order. The Court of Appeals found the District Court's order within that definition.

The court then determined that the arbitration agreement failed to provide the minimum guarantees that respondent could vindicate her statutory rights under the TILA. Critical to this determination was the court's observation that the arbitration agreement was silent with respect to payment of filing fees, arbitrators' costs, and other arbitration expenses. On that basis, the court held that the agreement to arbitrate posed a risk that respondent's ability to vindicate her statutory rights would be undone by "steep" arbitration costs, and therefore was unenforceable. We granted certiorari, and we now affirm the Court of Appeals with respect to the first conclusion, and reverse it with respect to the second.

II

* * *

The District Court's order directed that the dispute be resolved by arbitration and dismissed respondent's claims with prejudice, leaving the court nothing to do but execute the judgment. That order plainly disposed of the entire case on the merits and left no part of it pending before the court. The FAA does permit parties to arbitration agreements to bring a separate proceeding in a district court to enter judgment on an arbitration award once it is made (or to vacate or modify it), but the existence of that remedy does not vitiate the finality of the District Court's resolution of the claims in the instant proceeding. The District Court's order was therefore "a final decision with respect to an arbitration" within the meaning of § 16(a)(3), and an appeal may be taken.

* * *

III

We now turn to the question whether Randolph's agreement to arbitrate is unenforceable because it says nothing about the costs of arbitration, and thus fails to provide her protection from potentially substantial costs of pursuing her federal statutory claims in the arbitral forum. Section 2 of the FAA provides that "[a] written provision in any maritime transaction or a contract evidencing a transaction involving commerce to settle by arbitration a controversy thereafter arising out of such contract ... shall be valid, irrevocable, and enforceable, save upon such grounds as exist at law or in equity for the revocation of any contract." In considering whether respondent's agreement to arbitrate is unenforceable, we are mindful of the FAA's purpose "to reverse the longstanding judicial hostility to arbitration agreements ... and to place arbitration agreements upon the same footing as other contracts."

In light of that purpose, we have recognized that federal statutory claims can be appropriately resolved through arbitration, and we have enforced agreements to arbitrate that involve such claims. We have likewise rejected generalized attacks on arbitration that rest on "suspicion of arbitration as a method of weakening the protections afforded in the substantive law to would-be complainants." These cases demonstrate that even claims arising under a statute designed to further important social policies may be arbitrated because " 'so long as the prospective litigant effectively may vindicate [his or her] statutory cause of action in the arbitral forum,' " the statute serves its functions.

In determining whether statutory claims may be arbitrated, we first ask whether the parties agreed to submit their claims to arbitration, and then ask whether Congress has evinced an intention to preclude a waiver of judicial remedies for the statutory rights at issue. In this case, it is undisputed that the parties agreed to arbitrate all claims relating to their contract, including claims involving statutory rights. Nor does Randolph contend that the TILA evinces an intention to preclude a waiver of judicial remedies. She contends instead that the arbitration agreement's silence with respect to costs and fees creates a "risk" that she will be required to bear prohibitive arbitration costs if she pursues her claims in an arbitral forum, and thereby forces her to forgo any claims she may have against petitioners. Therefore, she argues, she is unable to vindicate her statutory rights in arbitration.

It may well be that the existence of large arbitration costs could preclude a litigant such as Randolph from effectively vindicating her federal statutory rights in the arbitral forum. But the record does not show that Randolph will bear such costs if she goes to arbitration. Indeed, it contains hardly any information on the matter. As the Court of Appeals recognized, "we lack ... information about how claimants fare under Green Tree's arbitration clause." The record reveals only the arbitration agreement's silence on the subject, and that fact alone is plainly insufficient to render it unenforceable. The "risk" that Randolph will be saddled with prohibitive costs is too speculative to justify the invalidation of an arbitration agreement.

To invalidate the agreement on that basis would undermine the "liberal federal policy favoring arbitration agreements." It would also conflict with our prior holdings that the party resisting arbitration bears the burden of proving that the claims at issue are unsuitable for arbitration. We have held that the party seeking to avoid arbitration bears the burden of establishing that Congress intended to preclude arbitration of the statutory claims at issue. Similarly, we believe that where, as here, a party seeks to invalidate an arbitration agreement on the ground that arbitration would be prohibitively expensive, that party bears the burden of showing the likelihood of incurring such costs. Randolph did not meet that burden. How detailed the showing of prohibitive expense must be before the party seeking arbitration must come forward with contrary evidence is a matter we need not discuss; for in this case neither during discovery nor when the case was presented on the merits was there any timely showing at all on the point. The Court of Appeals therefore erred in deciding that the arbitration agreement's silence with respect to costs and fees rendered it unenforceable.

The judgment of the Court of Appeals is affirmed in part and reversed in part.

It is so ordered.

Justice Ginsburg, with whom Justice Stevens and Justice Souter join, and with whom Justice Breyer joins as to Parts I and III, concurring in part and dissenting in part.

I

I join Part II of the Court's opinion, which holds that the District Court's order, dismissing all the claims before it, was a "final," and therefore immediately appealable, decision. *Ante,* at 4–8. On the matter the Court airs in Part III, *ante,* at 8–12 — allocation of the costs of arbitration — I would not rule definitively. Instead, I would vacate the Eleventh Circuit's decision, which dispositively declared the arbitration clause unenforceable, and remand the case for closer consideration of the arbitral forum's accessibility.

II

The Court today deals with a "who pays" question, specifically, who pays for the arbitral forum. The Court holds that Larketta Randolph bears the burden of demonstrating that the arbitral forum is financially inaccessible to her. Essentially, the Court requires a party, situated as Randolph is, either to submit to arbitration without knowing who will pay for the forum or to demonstrate up front that the costs, if imposed on her, will be prohibitive. As I see it, the case in its current posture is not ripe for such a disposition.

The Court recognizes that "the existence of large arbitration costs could preclude a litigant such as Randolph from effectively vindicating her federal statutory rights in the arbitral forum." But, the Court next determines, "the party resisting arbitration bears the burden of proving that the claims at issue are unsuitable for arbitration" and "Randolph did not meet that burden." In so ruling, the Court blends two discrete inquiries: First, is the arbitral forum *adequate* to adjudicate the claims at issue; second, is that forum *accessible* to the party resisting arbitration.

Our past decisions deal with the first question, the *adequacy* of the arbitral forum to adjudicate various statutory claims. These decisions hold that the party resisting arbitration bears the burden of establishing the inadequacy of the arbitral forum for adjudication of claims of a particular genre. It does not follow like the night the day, however, that the party resisting arbitration should also bear the burden of showing that the arbitral forum would be financially inaccessible to her.

The arbitration agreement at issue is contained in a form contract drawn by a commercial party and presented to an individual consumer on a take-it-or-leave-it basis. The case on which the Court dominantly relies, *Gilmer,* also involved a nonnegotiated arbitration clause. But the "who pays" question presented in this case did not arise in *Gilmer.* Under the rules that governed in *Gilmer* — those of the New York Stock Exchange — it was the standard practice for securities industry parties, arbitrating employment disputes, to pay all of the arbitrators' fees. Regarding that practice, the Court of Appeals for the District of Columbia Circuit recently commented:

> In *Gilmer,* the Supreme Court endorsed a system of arbitration in which employees are not required to pay for the arbitrator assigned to hear their statutory claims. There is no reason to think that the Court would have approved arbitration in the absence of this arrangement. Indeed, we are unaware of any situation in American jurisprudence in which a beneficiary of a federal statute has been required to pay for the services of the judge assigned to hear her or his case.

Id. at 1484.

III

The form contract in this case provides no indication of the rules under which arbitration will proceed or the costs a consumer is likely to incur in arbitration. Green Tree, drafter of the contract, could have filled the void by specifying, for instance, that arbitration would be governed by the rules of the American Arbitration Association (AAA). Under the AAA's Consumer Arbitration Rules, consumers in small-claims arbitration incur no filing fee and pay only $125 of the total fees charged by the arbitrator. All other fees and costs are to be paid by the business party. Other national arbitration organizations have developed similar models for fair cost and fee allocation. It may be that in this case, as in *Gilmer,* there is a standard practice on arbitrators' fees and expenses, one that fills the blank space in the arbitration agreement. Counsel for Green Tree offered a hint in that direction. ("Green Tree does pay [arbitration] costs in a lot of instances . . . ."). But there is no reliable indication in this record that Randolph's claim will be arbitrated under any consumer-protective fee arrangement.

As a repeat player in the arbitration required by its form contract, Green Tree has superior information about the cost to consumers of pursuing arbitration. In these circumstances, it is hardly clear that Randolph should bear the burden of demonstrating up front the arbitral forum's inaccessibility, or that she should be required to submit to arbitration without knowing how much it will cost her.

As I see it, the Court has reached out prematurely to resolve the matter in the lender's favor. If Green Tree's practice under the form contract with retail installment sales purchasers resembles that of the employer in *Gilmer,* Randolph would be insulated from prohibitive costs.

And if the arbitral forum were in this case financially accessible to Randolph, there would be no occasion to reach the decision today rendered by the Court. Before writing a term into the form contract, as the District of Columbia Circuit did, see *Cole,* 105 F.3d, at 1485, or leaving cost allocation initially to each arbitrator, as the Court does, I would remand for clarification of Green Tree's practice.

The Court's opinion, if I comprehend it correctly, does not prevent Randolph from returning to court, postarbitration, if she then has a complaint about cost allocation. If that is so, the issue reduces to when, not whether, she can be spared from payment of excessive costs. Neither certainty nor judicial economy is served by leaving that issue unsettled until the end of the line.

For the reasons stated, I dissent from the Court's reversal of the Eleventh Circuit's decision on the cost question. I would instead vacate and remand for further consideration of the accessibility of the arbitral forum to Randolph.

Notes and Questions

1.   Does the decision of the Supreme Court in *Green Tree Financial Corp.* cast doubt on the *Cole* opinion and Professor Gorman's argument for development by the courts of a code of due process for public law arbitration?

2.   An important question is whether an arbitration clause can be used to defeat a class action. Those who try to use arbitration clauses to defeat class actions assert that class actions are used to extort settlements from innocent defendants. They argue that arbitration cases must proceed individually and they sometimes draft arbitration clauses that specifically prohibit class actions. Employee and consumer advocates point out that many claimants lack the resources to pursue individual claims and that allowing arbitration to defeat class actions will allow defendants guilty of illegal conduct to defeat valid claims. These advocates argue for allowing class actions in arbitration and against foreclosing class actions when defendants have succeeded in inserting an arbitration clause in their contract with the claimant.

This question has been litigated often in cases involving a wide variety of law-fact patterns. When faced with a standard arbitration clause that does not mention class actions, some courts appear to assume that assent to arbitration "indicates waiver of the right to bring a class action." Lindsay R. Androski, *A Contested Merger: The Intersection of Class Actions and Mandatory Arbitration Clauses,* 2003 U. Chi. Legal F. 631, 639. Professor Jean Sternlight concluded after a comprehensive survey of the cases that, " ... existing federal statutes and traditional contract doctrines should sometimes, but not always, prohibit companies from entirely precluding consumers or others from bringing class actions." Jean R. Sternlight, *As Mandatory Binding Arbitration Meets the Class Action, Will the Class Action Survive?,* 42 Wm. & Mary L. Rev. 1, 78 (2000) [hereinafter Sternlight, *Class Action*]. Professor Sternlight argued forcefully for legislative reform to protect consumers, employees, and others from companies' efforts to eliminate class actions. *Id.* at 121–26.

3. In *Paying the Price of Process: Judicial Regulation of Consumer Arbitration Agreements*, 2001 J. Disp. Resol. 89, 99–100, Professor Stephen J. Ware contends that arguments for greater regulation of consumer arbitration should factor into their analysis the effect of such regulations on consumer prices.

> The previous section of this article discussed judicial decisions that raise prices (and interest rates) by requiring arbitration to: (1) allow for class actions, (2) subsidize the consumer's fees, (3) include substantial discovery, and (4) encompass both parties' claims. Whether these price increases are worth incurring, i.e., whether the judicial decisions are good policy, plainly depends on a number of factors including the amount of the price increase caused by each category of judicial decision. And different observers will certainly have different views about the value of, for example, class actions and litigation-like discovery. This article makes no attempt to assess the merits of those different views. Rather it argues that any such assessment should consider the influence consumer arbitration law has on the prices consumers pay. Failure to address price inevitably biases any assessment of consumer arbitration law. It is easy to insist upon "due process" in consumer arbitration, indeed "due process is as widely-cherished as 'mom and apple pie,' but the hard thinking begins when one asks who pays the price of process and how much they pay."

See also Christopher R. Drahozal, *Privatizing Civil Justice: Commercial Arbitration and the Civil Justice System*, 9 Kan. J.L. & Pub. Pol'y. 578, 587–88 (2000); but see Jean R. Sternlight & Elizabeth J. Jensen *Using Arbitration To Eliminate Consumer Class Actions: Efficient Business Practice or Unconscionable Abuse?* 67 Law & Contemp. Probs. 75, 92–99 (2004); (repudiating that argument).

Professor Mark E. Budnitz concluded as follows in *The High Cost of Mandatory Consumer Arbitration*, 67 Law & Contemp. Probs. 133, 161 (2004):

> The costs of arbitration can be so high that they deny consumers access to a forum in which to air their disputes. Costs can be excessive whether one considers the consumer's ability to pay, the absolute cost of arbitration, or the cost of arbitration compared to the cost of litigation. The problem is only exacerbated by agreement terms restricting remedies, class actions, and venue that make the actual cost of arbitration greater than the direct fees charged. Nevertheless, consumers face tremendous obstacles in proving that arbitration agreements should not be enforced because of those high costs. These obstacles arise from several sources. First, to avoid having to pay costs, the consumer must mount her challenge before the arbitration takes place, forcing her in many situations to estimate what the costs might be. In addition, the rules and fee schedules of the arbitration service providers and the common terms of arbitration agreements often makes this estimation extremely difficult, if not impossible. This is only made worse by the courts' disagreement

over what factors to consider in estimating the costs of arbitration and what standard to use in determining if those costs are too high.

4. In *Green Tree*, supra, the Supreme Court recognized that arbitration costs could preclude a claimant from effectively vindicating her statutory rights, but went on to hold that a plaintiff has the burden of showing a likelihood of incurring a prohibitively expensive financial burden.

Could you fashion an effective argument under *Green Tree* that an arbitration clause cannot be used to prohibit a class action by a large number of consumers with small claims? *See* Sternlight, *Class Action*, at 57–65.

5. The U.S. Supreme Court has not yet spoken on the class action issue, although it came tantalizingly close in *Green Tree Financial Corp. v. Bazzle*, 539 U.S. 444, 123 S.Ct. 2402, 156 L.Ed.2d 414 (2003).

The case involved a challenge to a consumer lender's mandatory arbitration provision that provided "[a]ll disputes, claims, or controversies arising from or relating to the contract or the relationships which result from this contract ... shall be resolved by binding arbitration by one arbitrator selected by us with consent of you." *Id. at 456.*

The South Carolina plaintiffs contended that the Green Tree form violated South Carolina law because it did not specify the right to name their own counsel and insurance agents. The Bazzles moved for class certification, and Green Tree responded with a motion to compel the arbitration. The trial court granted both requests, certifying the class and compelling the arbitration. The arbitrator later decided in favor of the plaintiffs, awarding the class damages and attorneys fees. The trial court confirmed the award, but Green Tree appealed, contending the arbitration provision did not authorize the arbitrator to decide class actions. A key question on appeal was whether the arbitration provision was silent on the question of its application to class actions, and who was to make that decision. Reversing the South Carolina Supreme Court, the U.S. Supreme Court held that the decision about whether the arbitration provision included the authority to decide class actions should have been made by the arbitrator, rather than the courts. Justices Rehnquist, O'Connor, and Kennedy, dissented, with the tacit agreement of Justice Stevens, arguing that the decision about whether the scope of the arbitration agreement included class actions was properly decided by the South Carolina Courts.

6. Choose one of the positions described below and be prepared to defend your position in class.

(a) *Gilmer* should be overturned by the U.S. Supreme Court or by an amendment to the FAA.

(b) The FAA should be amended to:

(1) prohibit enforcement of pre-dispute arbitration agreements that employees are required to accept in order to obtain a job; or

(2) prohibit companies from using arbitration clauses to preclude class actions; or

(3) require arbitrators to prepare a written opinion giving reasons for their award when cases turn on the interpretation and application of federal statutes; or *specifically authorize*,

(4) de novo review of arbitral interpretations of federal statutes.

(c) There is no need to amend the FAA. However, the courts should develop a code of due process for public law arbitration on a case by case basis.

See Thomas J. Stipanowich, *Contract and Conflict Management*, 2001 Wisc. L. Rev. 831, 909–916, for discussion of some of the issues underlying these choices.

c. Unconscionability and Adhesion

Like other contracts, arbitration agreements are subject to standard contractual formation defenses. Perhaps the most common defense associated with arbitration provisions is that of unconscionability — that the provision is substantively and procedurally too one-sided or unfair to be enforced by a court of law as a matter of policy. In recent years, the courts have become increasingly receptive to claims that mandatory arbitration provisions are unconscionable and therefore unenforceable. For a discussion with extensive case citations, see F. PAUL BLAND JR. ET AL., NATIONAL CONSUMER LAW CENTER, CONSUMER ARBITRATION AGREEMENTS §§ 4.1–4.4 (3d ed. 2003). In this Section, we look at unconscionability claims in the contexts of employment and consumer goods and services. All of the excerpted cases arise from mandatory arbitration situations, but it is certainly possible for unconscionability claims to be presented in situations in which there has been actual bilateral agreement to arbitration.

i. Employment Agreements

We pointed out earlier that collective bargaining arbitration is governed by § 301 of the Labor Management Relations Act (with courts cross-citing cases under § 301 and the FAA). Individual employment contracts that meet the commerce or maritime requirements are covered by the FAA. Such contracts are, however, subject to the following language in § 1 of the FAA: " . . . nothing herein contained shall apply to contracts of employment of seamen, railroad employees, or any other class of workers engaged in foreign or interstate commerce." Should this be read to exclude employment arbitration from the FAA?

CIRCUIT CITY STORES, INC. v. ADAMS

Supreme Court of the United States, 2001.
532 U.S. 105, 121 S.Ct. 1302, 149 L.Ed.2d 234.

Justice Kennedy delivered the opinion of the Court.

Section 1 of the Federal Arbitration Act (FAA or Act) excludes from the Act's coverage "contracts of employment of seamen, railroad employees, or any other class of workers engaged in foreign or interstate commerce." All but one of the Courts of Appeals which have addressed the issue interpret this provision as exempting contracts of employment of transportation workers, but not other employment contracts, from the FAA's coverage. A different interpretation has been adopted by the Court of Appeals for the Ninth Circuit, which construes the exemption so that all contracts of employment are beyond the FAA's reach, whether or not the worker is engaged in transportation. It applied that rule to the instant case. We now decide that the better interpretation is to construe the statute, as most of the Courts of Appeals have done, to confine the exemption to transportation workers. * * *

In October 1995, respondent Saint Clair Adams applied for a job at petitioner Circuit City Stores, Inc., a national retailer of consumer electronics. Adams signed an employment application which included the following provision:

> "I agree that I will settle any and all previously unasserted claims, disputes or controversies arising out of or relating to my application or candidacy for employment, employment and/or cessation of employment with Circuit City, *exclusively* by final and binding *arbitration* before a neutral Arbitrator. By way of example only, such claims include claims under federal, state, and local statutory or common law, such as the Age Discrimination in Employment Act, Title VII of the Civil Rights Act of 1964, as amended, including the amendments of the Civil Rights Act of 1991, the Americans with Disabilities Act, the law of contract and [the] law of tort."

Adams was hired as a sales counselor in Circuit City's store in Santa Rosa, California.

Two years later, Adams filed an employment discrimination lawsuit against Circuit City in state court, asserting claims under California's Fair Employment and Housing Act, and other claims based on general tort theories under California law. Circuit City filed suit in the United States District Court for the Northern District of California, seeking to enjoin the state-court action and to compel arbitration of respondent's claims pursuant to the FAA, 9 U.S.C. §§ 1–16. The District Court entered the requested order. Respondent, the court concluded, was obligated by the arbitration agreement to submit his claims against the employer to binding arbitration. An appeal followed.

While respondent's appeal was pending in the Court of Appeals for the Ninth Circuit, the court ruled on the key issue in an unrelated case. The court held the FAA does not apply to contracts of employment. In the instant case, following the rule announced in *Craft*, the Court of Appeals held the arbitration agreement between Adams and Circuit City was contained in a "contract of employment," and so was not subject to the FAA. Circuit City petitioned this Court, noting that the Ninth Circuit's conclusion that all employment contracts are excluded from the FAA conflicts with every other Court of Appeals to have addressed the question.

* * *

The instant case, of course, involves not the basic coverage authorization under § 2 of the Act, but the exemption from coverage under § 1. The exemption clause provides the Act shall not apply "to contracts of employment of seamen, railroad employees, or any other class of workers engaged in foreign or interstate commerce." Most Courts of Appeals conclude the exclusion provision is limited to transportation workers, defined, for instance, as those workers " 'actually engaged in the movement of goods in interstate commerce.' "As we stated at the outset, the Court of Appeals for the Ninth Circuit takes a different view and interprets the § 1 exception to exclude all contracts of employment from the reach of the FAA.

* * *

Respondent, at the outset, contends that we need not address the meaning of the § 1 exclusion provision to decide the case in his favor. In his view, an employment contract is not a "contract evidencing a transaction involving interstate commerce" at all, since the word "transaction" in § 2 extends only to commercial contracts. See *Craft,* 177 F.3d, at 1085 (concluding that § 2 covers only "commercial deal[s] or merchant's sale [s]"). This line of reasoning proves too much, for it would make the § 1 exclusion provision superfluous. If all contracts of employment are beyond the scope of the Act under the § 2 coverage provision, the separate exemption for "contracts of employment of seamen, railroad employees, or any other class of workers engaged in . . . interstate commerce" would be pointless. The proffered interpretation of "evidencing a transaction involving commerce," furthermore, would be inconsistent with *Gilmer v. Interstate/Johnson Lane Corp.* where we held that § 2 required the arbitration of an age discrimination claim based on an agreement in a securities registration application, a dispute that did not arise from a "commercial deal or merchant's sale." Nor could respondent's construction of § 2 be reconciled with the expansive reading of those words adopted in *Allied–Bruce,* 513 U.S., at 277, 279–280. If, then, there is an argument to be made that arbitration agreements in employment contracts are not covered by the Act, it must be premised on the language of the § 1 exclusion provision itself.

Respondent, endorsing the reasoning of the Court of Appeals for the Ninth Circuit that the provision excludes all employment contracts, relies on the asserted breadth of the words "contracts of employment of . . . any other class of workers engaged in . . . commerce." Referring to our construction of § 2's coverage provision in *Allied–Bruce* — concluding that the words "involving commerce" evidence the congressional intent to regulate to the full extent of its commerce power — respondent contends § 1's interpretation should have a like reach, thus exempting all employment contracts. The two provisions, it is argued, are coterminous; under this view the "involving commerce" provision brings within the FAA's scope all contracts within the Congress' commerce power, and the "engaged in . . . commerce" language in § 1 in turn exempts from the FAA all employment contracts falling within that authority.

This reading of § 1, however, runs into an immediate and, in our view, insurmountable textual obstacle. Unlike the "involving commerce" language in § 2, the words "any other class of workers engaged in . . . commerce" constitute a residual phrase, following, in the same sentence, explicit reference to "seamen" and "railroad employees." Construing the residual phrase to exclude all employment contracts fails to give independent effect to the statute's enumeration of the specific categories of workers which precedes it; there would be no need for Congress to use the phrases "seamen" and "railroad employees" if those same classes of workers were subsumed within the meaning of the "engaged in . . . commerce" residual clause. The wording of § 1 calls for the application of the maxim *ejusdem generis,* the statutory canon that "[w]here general words follow specific words in a statutory enumeration, the general words are construed to embrace only objects similar in nature to those objects enumerated by the preceding specific words." Under this rule of construction the residual clause should be read to give effect to the terms "seamen" and "railroad employees," and should itself be controlled and defined by reference to the enumerated categories of workers which are recited just before it; the interpretation of the clause pressed by respondent fails to produce these results.

Canons of construction need not be conclusive and are often countered, of course, by some maxim pointing in a different direction. The application of the rule *ejusdem generis* in this case, however, is in full accord with other sound considerations bearing upon the proper interpretation of the clause. For even if the term "engaged in commerce" stood alone in § 1, we would not construe the provision to exclude all contracts of employment from the FAA. Congress uses different modifiers to the word "commerce" in the design and enactment of its statutes. The phrase "affecting commerce" indicates Congress' intent to regulate to the outer limits of its authority under the Commerce Clause. The "involving commerce" phrase, the operative words for the reach of the basic coverage provision in § 2, was at issue in *Allied–Bruce.* That particular phrase had not been interpreted before by this Court. Considering the usual meaning of the word "involving," and the pro-arbitration purposes of the FAA, *Allied–Bruce* held the "word 'involving,' like 'affecting,' signals an intent to exercise Congress' commerce power to the full." Unlike those phrases, however, the general words "in commerce" and the specific phrase "engaged in commerce" are understood to have a more limited reach. In *Allied–Bruce* itself the Court said the words "in commerce" are "often-found words of art" that we have not read as expressing congressional intent to regulate to the outer limits of authority under the Commerce Clause.

It is argued that we should assess the meaning of the phrase "engaged in commerce" in a different manner here, because the FAA was enacted when congressional authority to regulate under the commerce power was to a large extent confined by our decisions. When the FAA was enacted in 1925, respondent reasons, the phrase "engaged in commerce" was not a term of art indicating a limited assertion of congressional jurisdiction; to the contrary, it is said, the formulation came close to expressing the outer limits of Congress' power as then understood. Were this mode of interpretation to prevail, we would take into account the scope of the Commerce Clause, as then elaborated by the Court, at the date of the FAA's enactment in order to interpret what the statute means now.

A variable standard for interpreting common, jurisdictional phrases would contradict our earlier cases and bring instability to statutory interpretation. The Court has declined in past cases to afford significance, in construing the meaning of the statutory jurisdictional provisions "in commerce" and "engaged in commerce," to the circumstance that the statute predated shifts in the Court's Commerce Clause cases.

* * *

The Court's reluctance to accept contentions that Congress used the words "in commerce" or "engaged in commerce" to regulate to the full extent of its commerce power rests on sound foundation, as it affords objective and consistent significance to the meaning of the words Congress uses when it defines the reach of a statute. To say that the statutory words "engaged in commerce" are subject to variable interpretations depending upon the date of adoption, even a date before the phrase became a term of art, ignores the reason why the formulation became a term of art in the first place: The plain meaning of the words "engaged in commerce" is narrower than the more open-ended formulations "affecting commerce" and "involving commerce." It would be unwieldy for Congress, for the Court, and for litigants to be required to deconstruct statutory Commerce Clause phrases depending upon the year of a particular statutory enactment.

* * *

In sum, the text of the FAA forecloses the construction of § 1 followed by the Court of Appeals in the case under review, a construction which would exclude all employment contracts from the FAA. While the historical arguments respecting Congress' understanding of its power in 1925 are not insubstantial, this fact alone does not give us basis to adopt, "by judicial decision rather than amendatory legislation" an expansive construction of the FAA's exclusion provision that goes beyond the meaning of the words Congress used. While it is of course possible to speculate that Congress might have chosen a different jurisdictional formulation had it known that the Court would soon embrace a less restrictive reading of the Commerce Clause, the text of § 1 precludes interpreting the exclusion provision to defeat the language of § 2 as to all employment contracts. Section 1 exempts from the FAA only contracts of employment of transportation workers. * * *

As the conclusion we reach today is directed by the text of § 1, we need not assess the legislative history of the exclusion provision. See *Ratzlaf v. United States*, 510 U.S. 135, 147–148, 114 S.Ct. 655, 126 L.Ed.2d 615 (1994) ("[W]e do not resort to legislative history to cloud a statutory text that is clear''). We do note, however, that the legislative record on the § 1 exemption is quite sparse. Respondent points to no language in either Committee Report addressing the meaning of the provision, nor to any mention of the § 1 exclusion during debate on the FAA on the floor of the House or Senate.

* * *

Various *amici,* including the attorneys general of 21 States, object that the reading of the § 1 exclusion provision adopted today intrudes upon the policies of the separate States. They point out that, by requiring arbitration agreements in most employment contracts to be covered by the FAA, the statute in effect pre-empts those state employment laws which restrict or limit the ability of employees and employers to enter into arbitration agreements. It is argued that States should be permitted, pursuant to their traditional role in regulating employment relationships, to prohibit employees like respondent from contracting away their right to pursue state-law discrimination claims in court.

It is not our holding today which is the proper target of this criticism. The line of argument is relevant instead to the Court's decision in *Southland Corp. v. Keating,* holding that Congress intended the FAA to apply in state courts, and to pre-empt state antiarbitration laws to the contrary.

The question of *Southland's* continuing vitality was given explicit consideration in *Allied–Bruce,* and the Court declined to overrule it. The decision, furthermore, is not directly implicated in this case, which concerns the application of the FAA in a federal, rather than in a state, court. The Court should not chip away at *Southland* by indirection, especially by the adoption of the variable statutory interpretation theory advanced by the respondent in the instant case. Not all of the Justices who join today's holding agreed with *Allied–Bruce,* see 513 U.S., at 284, 115 S.Ct. 834 (SCALIA, J., dissenting); *id.,* at 285, 115 S.Ct. 834 (THOMAS, J., dissenting), but it would be incongruous to adopt, as we did in *Allied–Bruce,* a conventional reading of the FAA's coverage in § 2 in order to implement proarbitration policies and an unconventional reading of the reach of § 1 in order to undo the same coverage. In *Allied–Bruce* the Court noted that Congress had not moved to overturn *Southland,* and we now note that it has not done so in response to *Allied–Bruce* itself.

Furthermore, for parties to employment contracts not involving the specific exempted categories set forth in § 1, it is true here, just as it was for the parties to the contract at issue in *Allied–Bruce,* that there are real benefits to the enforcement of arbitration provisions. We have been clear in rejecting the supposition that the advantages of the arbitration process somehow disappear when transferred to the employment context. Arbitration agreements allow parties to avoid the costs of litigation, a benefit that may be of particular importance in employment litigation, which often involves smaller sums of money than disputes concerning commercial contracts. These litigation costs to parties (and the accompanying burden to the courts) would be compounded by the difficult choice-of-law questions that are often presented in disputes arising from the employment relationship. The Court has been quite specific in holding that arbitration agreements can be enforced under the FAA without contravening the policies of congressional enactments giving employees specific protection against discrimination prohibited by federal law; as we noted in *Gilmer,* " '[b]y agreeing to arbitrate a statutory claim, a party does not forgo the substantive rights afforded by the statute; it only submits to their resolution in an arbitral, rather than a judicial, forum.' " *Gilmer,* of course, involved a federal statute, while the argument here is that a state statute ought not be denied state judicial enforcement while awaiting the outcome of arbitration. That matter, though, was addressed in *Southland* and *Allied–Bruce,* and we do not revisit the question here.

* * *

For the foregoing reasons, the judgment of the Court of Appeals for the Ninth Circuit is reversed, and the case is remanded for further proceedings consistent with this opinion.

It is so ordered.

Justice Stevens, with whom Justice Ginsburg and Justice Breyer join, and with whom Justice Souter joins as to Parts II and III, dissenting. [The dissenting opinions of Justices Stevens and Souter are omitted.]

* * *

Questions

1. Are you persuaded by the majority's textual argument? Why didn't the majority opinion devote more attention to legislative history? For a discussion of that legislative history, and an argument that the relevant language of Section 1 of the FAA was intended to exclude all employment cases, see Matthew W. Finkin, *"Workers' Contracts" Under the United States Arbitration Act: An Essay in Historical Clarification,* 17 Berkeley J. Empl. & Lab. L. 282 (1996).

2. What is *Circuit City's* significance?

HOOTERS OF AMERICA, INC. v. PHILLIPS

United States Court of Appeals, Fourth Circuit, 1999.
173 F.3d 933.

Wilkinson, Chief Judge:

Annette R. Phillips alleges that she was sexually harassed while working at a Hooters restaurant. After quitting her job, Phillips threatened to sue Hooters in court. Alleging that Phillips agreed to arbitrate employment-related disputes, Hooters preemptively filed suit to compel arbitration under the Federal Arbitration Act. Because Hooters set up a dispute resolution process utterly lacking in the rudiments of even-handedness, we hold that Hooters breached its agreement to arbitrate. Thus, we affirm the district court's refusal to compel arbitration.

I.

Appellee Annette R. Phillips worked as a bartender at a Hooters restaurant in Myrtle Beach, South Carolina. She was employed since 1989 by appellant Hooters of Myrtle Beach (HOMB), a franchisee of appellant Hooters of America (collectively Hooters).

Phillips alleges that in June 1996, Gerald Brooks, a Hooters official and the brother of HOMB's principal owner, sexually harassed her by grabbing and slapping her buttocks. After appealing to her manager for help and being told to "let it go," she quit her job. Phillips then contacted Hooters through an attorney claiming that the attack and the restaurant's failure to address it violated her Title VII rights. Hooters responded that she was required to submit her claims to arbitration according to a binding agreement to arbitrate between the parties.

This agreement arose in 1994 during the implementation of Hooters' alternative dispute resolution program. As part of that program, the company conditioned eligibility for raises, transfers, and promotions upon an employee signing an "Agreement to arbitrate employment-related disputes." The agreement provides that Hooters and the employee each agree to arbitrate all disputes arising out of employment, including "any claim of discrimination, sexual harassment, retaliation, or wrongful discharge, whether arising under federal or state law." The agreement further states that

> the employee and the company agree to resolve any claims pursuant to the company's rules and procedures for alternative resolution of employment-related disputes, as promulgated by the company from time to time ("the rules"). Company will make available or provide a copy of the rules upon written request of the employee.

The employees of HOMB were initially given a copy of this agreement at an all-staff meeting held on November 20, 1994. HOMB's general manager, Gene Fulcher, told the employees to review the agreement for five days and that they would then be asked to accept or reject the agreement. No employee, however, was given a copy of Hooters' arbitration rules and procedures. Phillips signed the agreement on November 25, 1994. When her personnel file was updated in April 1995, Phillips again signed the agreement.

After Phillips quit her job in June 1996, Hooters sent to her attorney a copy of the Hooters rules then in effect. Phillips refused to arbitrate the dispute.

Hooters filed suit in November 1996 to compel arbitration under 9 U.S.C. § 4. Phillips defended on the grounds that the agreement to arbitrate was unenforceable. Phillips also asserted individual and class counterclaims against Hooters for violations of Title VII and for a declaration that the arbitration agreements were unenforceable against the class. In response, Hooters requested that the district court stay the proceedings on the counterclaims until after arbitration.

In March 1998, the district court denied Hooters' motions to compel arbitration and stay proceedings on the counterclaims. The court found that there was no meeting of the minds on all of the material terms of the agreement and even if there were, Hooters' promise to arbitrate was illusory. In addition, the court found that the arbitration agreement was unconscionable and void for reasons of public policy. Hooters filed this interlocutory appeal, 9 U.S.C. § 16.

II.

* * *

The threshold question is whether claims such as Phillips' are even arbitrable. The EEOC as amicus curiae contends that employees cannot agree to arbitrate Title VII claims in predispute agreements. We disagree. The Supreme Court has made it plain that judicial protection of arbitral agreements extends to agreements to arbitrate statutory discrimination claims. In *Gilmer v. Interstate/Johnson Lane Corp.,* the Court noted that " '[b]y agreeing to arbitrate a statutory claim, a party does not forgo the substantive rights afforded by the statute; it only submits to their resolution in an arbitral, rather than a judicial, forum.' " Thus, a party must be held to the terms of its bargain unless Congress intends to preclude waiver of a judicial forum for the statutory claims at issue. Such an intent, however, must "be discoverable in the text of the [substantive statute], its legislative history, or an 'inherent conflict' between arbitration and the [statute's] underlying purposes." *Id.*

The EEOC argues that in passing the Civil Rights Act of 1991, Congress evinced an intent to prohibit predispute agreements to arbitrate claims arising under Title VII. This circuit, however, has already rejected this argument. The Civil Rights Act of 1991 provided that "Where appropriate and to the extent authorized by law, the use of alternative means of dispute resolution, including ... arbitration, is encouraged to resolve disputes arising under [Title VII]." In *Austin,* we stated that this language "could not be any more clear in showing Congressional favor towards arbitration." We also noted that the legislative history did not establish a contrary intent nor was there an "inherent conflict" between the Civil Rights Act and arbitration. This holding is in step with our sister circuits which have also rejected the EEOC's argument.

III.

Predispute agreements to arbitrate Title VII claims are thus valid and enforceable. The question remains whether a binding arbitration agreement between Phillips and Hooters exists and compels Phillips to submit her Title VII claims to arbitration. The FAA provides that agreements "to settle by arbitration a controversy thereafter arising out of such contract or transaction ... shall be valid, irrevocable, and enforceable, save upon such grounds as exist at law or in equity for the revocation of any contract." 9 U.S.C. § 2. "It [i]s for the court, not the arbitrator, to decide in the first instance whether the dispute [i]s to be resolved through arbitration." In so deciding, we " 'engage in a limited review to ensure that the dispute is arbitrable — i.e., that a valid agreement to arbitrate exists between the parties and that the specific dispute falls within the substantive scope of that agreement.' " Glass v. Kidder Peabody & Co., 114 F.3d 446, 453 (4th Cir.1997) (quoting PaineWebber Inc. v. Hartmann, 921 F.2d 507, 511 (3d Cir.1990)).

Hooters argues that Phillips gave her assent to a bilateral agreement to arbitrate. That contract provided for the resolution by arbitration of all employment-related disputes, including claims arising under Title VII. Hooters claims the agreement to arbitrate is valid because Phillips twice signed it voluntarily. Thus, it argues the courts are bound to enforce it and compel arbitration.

We disagree. The judicial inquiry, while highly circumscribed, is not focused solely on an examination for contractual formation defects such as lack of mutual assent and want of consideration. Courts also can investigate the existence of "such grounds as exist at law or in equity for the revocation of any contract." 9 U.S.C. § 2. However, the grounds for revocation must relate specifically to the arbitration clause and not just to the contract as a whole. In this case, the challenge goes to the validity of the arbitration agreement itself. Hooters materially breached the arbitration agreement by promulgating rules so egregiously unfair as to constitute a complete default of its contractual obligation to draft arbitration rules and to do so in good faith.

Hooters and Phillips agreed to settle any disputes between them not in a judicial forum, but in another neutral forum — arbitration. Their agreement provided that Hooters was responsible for setting up such a forum by promulgating arbitration rules and procedures. To this end, Hooters instituted a set of rules in July 1996.

The Hooters rules when taken as a whole, however, are so one-sided that their only possible purpose is to undermine the neutrality of the proceeding. The rules require the employee to provide the company notice of her claim at the outset, including "the nature of the Claim" and "the specific act(s) or omissions(s) which are the basis of the Claim." Hooters, on the other hand, is not required to file any responsive pleadings or to notice its defenses. Additionally, at the time of filing this notice, the employee must provide the company with a list of all fact witnesses with a brief summary of the facts known to each. The company, however, is not required to reciprocate.

The Hooters rules also provide a mechanism for selecting a panel of three arbitrators that is crafted to ensure a biased decisionmaker. The employee and Hooters each select an arbitrator, and the two arbitrators in turn select a third. Good enough, except that the employee's arbitrator and the third arbitrator must be selected from a list of arbitrators created exclusively by Hooters. This gives Hooters control over the entire panel and places no limits whatsoever on whom Hooters can put on the list. Under the rules, Hooters is free to devise lists of partial arbitrators who have existing relationships, financial or familial, with Hooters and its management. In fact, the rules do not even prohibit Hooters from placing its managers themselves on the list. Further, nothing in the rules restricts Hooters from punishing arbitrators who rule against the company by removing them from the list. Given the unrestricted control that one party (Hooters) has over the panel, the selection of an impartial decision maker would be a surprising result.

Nor is fairness to be found once the proceedings are begun. Although Hooters may expand the scope of arbitration to any matter, "whether related or not to the Employee's Claim," the employee cannot raise "any matter not included in the Notice of Claim." Similarly, Hooters is permitted to move for summary dismissal of employee claims before a hearing is held whereas the employee is not permitted to seek summary judgment. Hooters, but not the employee, may record the arbitration hearing "by audio or videotaping or by verbatim transcription." The rules also grant Hooters the right to bring suit in court to vacate or modify an arbitral award when it can show, by a preponderance of the evidence, that the panel exceeded its authority. No such right is granted to the employee.

In addition, the rules provide that upon 30 days notice Hooters, but not the employee, may cancel the agreement to arbitrate. Moreover, Hooters reserves the right to modify the rules, "in whole or in part," whenever it wishes and "without notice" to the employee. Nothing in the rules even prohibits Hooters from changing the rules in the middle of an arbitration proceeding.

If by odd chance the unfairness of these rules were not apparent on their face, leading arbitration experts have decried their one-sidedness. George Friedman, senior vice president of the American Arbitration Association (AAA), testified that the system established by the Hooters rules so deviated from minimum due process standards that the Association would refuse to arbitrate under those rules. George Nicolau, former president of both the National Academy of Arbitrators and the International Society of Professionals in Dispute Resolution, attested that the Hooters rules "are inconsistent with the concept of fair and impartial arbitration." He also testified that he was "certain that reputable designating agencies, such as the AAA and Jams/Endispute, would refuse to administer a program so unfair and one-sided as this one." Additionally, Dennis Nolan, professor of labor law at the University of South Carolina, declared that the Hooters rules "do not satisfy the minimum requirements of a fair arbitration system." He found that the "most serious flaw" was that the "mechanism [for selecting arbitrators] violates the most fundamental aspect of justice, namely an impartial decision maker." Finally, Lewis Maltby, member of the Board of Directors of the AAA, testified that "This is without a doubt the most unfair arbitration program I have ever encountered."

In a similar vein, two major arbitration associations have filed amicus briefs with this court. The National Academy of Arbitrators stated that the Hooters rules "violate fundamental concepts of fairness ... and the integrity of the arbitration process." Likewise, the Society of Professionals in Dispute Resolution noted that "[i]t would be hard to imagine a more unfair method of selecting a panel of arbitrators." It characterized the Hooters arbitration system as "deficient to the point of illegitimacy" and "so one sided, it is hard to believe that it was even intended to be fair."

We hold that the promulgation of so many biased rules — especially the scheme whereby one party to the proceeding so controls the arbitral panel — breaches the contract entered into by the parties. The parties agreed to submit their claims to arbitration — a system whereby disputes are fairly resolved by an impartial third party. Hooters by contract took on the obligation of establishing such a system. By creating a sham system unworthy even of the name of arbitration, Hooters completely failed in performing its contractual duty.

Moreover, Hooters had a duty to perform its obligations in good faith. * * * By agreeing to settle disputes in arbitration, Phillips agreed to the prompt and economical resolution of her claims. She could legitimately expect that arbitration would not entail procedures so wholly one-sided as to present a stacked deck. Thus we conclude that the Hooters rules also violate the contractual obligation of good faith.

Given Hooters' breaches of the arbitration agreement and Phillips' desire not to be bound by it, we hold that rescission is the proper remedy. Generally, "rescission will not be granted for a minor or casual breach of a contract, but only for those breaches which defeat the object of the contracting parties." As we have explained, Hooters' breach is by no means insubstantial; its performance under the contract was so egregious that the result was hardly recognizable as arbitration at all. We therefore permit Phillips to cancel the agreement and thus Hooters' suit to compel arbitration must fail.

IV.

We respect fully the Supreme Court's pronouncement that "questions of arbitrability must be addressed with a healthy regard for the federal policy favoring arbitration." Our decision should not be misread: We are not holding that the agreement before us is unenforceable because the arbitral proceedings are too abbreviated. An arbitral forum need not replicate the judicial forum. "[W]e are well past the time when judicial suspicion of the desirability of arbitration and of the competence of arbitral tribunals inhibited the development of arbitration as an alternative means of dispute resolution."

Nor should our decision be misunderstood as permitting a full-scale assault on the fairness of proceedings before the matter is submitted to arbitration. Generally, objections to the nature of arbitral proceedings are for the arbitrator to decide in the first instance. Only after arbitration may a party then raise such challenges if they meet the narrow grounds set out in 9 U.S.C. § 10 for vacating an arbitral award. In the case before us, we only reach the content of the arbitration rules because their promulgation was the duty of one party under the contract. The material breach of this duty warranting rescission is an issue of substantive arbitrability and thus is reviewable before arbitration. This case, however, is the exception that proves the rule: fairness objections should generally be made to the arbitrator, subject only to limited post-arbitration judicial review as set forth in section 10 of the FAA.

By promulgating this system of warped rules, Hooters so skewed the process in its favor that Phillips has been denied arbitration in any meaningful sense of the word. To uphold the promulgation of this aberrational scheme under the heading of arbitration would undermine, not advance, the federal policy favoring alternative dispute resolution. This we refuse to do.

The judgment of the district court is affirmed, and the case is remanded for further proceedings consistent with this opinion.

Note and Questions

1. In Jean R. Sternlight, *Panacea or Corporate Tool? Debunking the Supreme Court's Preference for Binding Arbitration*, 74 Wash. U. L.Q. 637 (1996), Professor Sternlight argues at length that large companies can use arbitration clauses to take advantage of employees and consumers. Id. at 677–97. She says that, "(1) procedural factors influence and sometimes determine substantive outcomes; (2) the party that drafts an agreement will try to draft it so as to achieve maximum advantage for itself, which may well entail imposing disadvantage on the opposing party; and (3) competitors will neither prevent businesses from taking advantage of little guys nor insure that gains from lower liability exposure will be passed on to the little guys." *Id.* at 680. For an argument that employees should unionize to deal with the power imbalance, see Michael Z. Green, *Opposing Executive Use of Employer Bargaining Power in Mandatory Arbitration Agreements Through Collective Employee Actions*, 10 Tex. Wesleyan L.Rev. 77

2. Which of the shortcomings in the *Hooters* arbitral process would have been sufficient, standing alone, to justify granting the rescission remedy? Which do you find most offensive? Least troubling?

3. Assuming that Hooters' management wanted a strong arbitration clause during the drafting of the provision at issue in this case, how might Hooters' lawyers have drafted the clause to have avoided this result? What arguments would it have made to management?

ii. Unconscionability in Consumer Goods and Services

HILL v. GATEWAY 2000, INC.
United States Court of Appeals, Seventh Circuit, 1997.
105 F.3d 1147.

Easterbrook, Circuit Judge.

A customer picks up the phone, orders a computer, and gives a credit card number. Presently a box arrives, containing the computer and a list of terms, said to govern unless the customer returns the computer within 30 days. Are these terms effective as the parties' contract, or is the contract term-free because the order-taker did not read any terms over the phone and elicit the customer's assent?

One of the terms in the box containing a Gateway 2000 system was an arbitration clause. Rich and Enza Hill, the customers, kept the computer more than 30 days before complaining about its components and performance. They filed suit in federal court arguing, among other things, that the product's shortcomings make Gateway a racketeer (mail and wire fraud are said to be the predicate offenses), leading to treble damages under RICO for the Hills and a class of all other purchasers. Gateway asked the district court to enforce the arbitration clause; the judge refused, writing that "[t]he present record is insufficient to support a finding of a valid arbitration agreement between the parties or that the plaintiffs were given adequate notice of the arbitration clause." Gateway took an immediate appeal, as is its right.

The Hills say that the arbitration clause did not stand out: they concede noticing the statement of terms but deny reading it closely enough to discover the agreement to arbitrate, and they ask us to conclude that they therefore may go to court. Yet an agreement to arbitrate must be enforced "save upon such grounds as exist at law or in equity for the revocation of any contract." 9 U.S.C. § 2. *Doctor's Associates, Inc. v. Casarotto* holds that this provision of the Federal Arbitration Act is inconsistent with any requirement that an arbitration clause be prominent. A contract need not be read to be effective; people who accept take the risk that the unread terms may in retrospect prove unwelcome. Terms inside Gateway's box stand or fall together. If they constitute the parties' contract because the Hills had an opportunity to return the computer after reading them, then all must be enforced.

ProCD, Inc. v. Zeidenberg holds that terms inside a box of software bind consumers who use the software after an opportunity to read the terms and to reject them by returning the product. Likewise, *Carnival Cruise Lines, Inc. v. Shute* enforces a forum-selection clause that was included among three pages of terms attached to a cruise ship ticket. *ProCD* and *Carnival Cruise Lines* exemplify the many commercial transactions in which people pay for products with terms to follow; *ProCD* discusses others. The district court concluded in *ProCD* that the contract is formed when the consumer pays for the software; as a result, the court held, only terms known to the consumer at that moment are part of the contract, and provisos inside the box do not count. Although this is one way a contract could be formed, it is not the only way: "A vendor, as master of the offer, may invite acceptance by conduct, and may propose limitations on the kind of conduct that constitutes acceptance. A buyer may accept by performing the acts the vendor proposes to treat as acceptance." Gateway shipped computers with the same sort of accept-or-return offer ProCD made to users of its software. *ProCD* relied on the Uniform Commercial Code rather than any peculiarities of Wisconsin law; both Illinois and South Dakota, the two states whose law might govern relations between Gateway and the Hills, have adopted the UCC; neither side has pointed us to any atypical doctrines in those states that might be pertinent; *ProCD* therefore applies to this dispute.

Plaintiffs ask us to limit *ProCD* to software, but where's the sense in that? *ProCD* is about the law of contract, not the law of software. Payment preceding the revelation of full terms is common for air transportation, insurance, and many other endeavors. Practical considerations support allowing vendors to enclose the full legal terms with their products. Cashiers cannot be expected to read legal documents to customers before ringing up sales. If the staff at the other end of the phone for direct-sales operations such as Gateway's had to read the four-page statement of terms before taking the buyer's credit card number, the droning voice would anesthetize rather than enlighten many potential buyers. Others would hang up in a rage over the waste of their time. And oral recitation would not avoid customers' assertions (whether true or feigned) that the clerk did not read term X to them, or that they did not remember or understand it. Writing provides benefits for both sides of commercial transactions. Customers as a group are better off when vendors skip costly and ineffectual steps such as telephonic recitation, and use instead a simple approve-or-return device. Competent adults are bound by such documents, read or unread. For what little it is worth, we add that the box from Gateway was crammed with software. The computer came with an operating system, without which it was useful only as a boat anchor. Gateway also included many application programs. So the Hills' effort to limit *ProCD* to software would not avail them factually, even if it were sound legally — which it is not.

For their second sally, the Hills contend that ProCD should be limited to executory contracts (to licenses in particular), and therefore does not apply because both parties' performance of this contract was complete when the box arrived at their home. This is legally and factually wrong: legally because the question at hand concerns the *formation* of the contract rather than its *performance*, and factually because both contracts were incompletely performed. *ProCD* did not depend on the fact that the seller characterized the transaction as a license rather than as a contract; we treated it as a contract for the sale of goods and reserved the question whether for other purposes a "license" characterization might be preferable. All debates about characterization to one side, the transaction in *ProCD* was no more executory than the one here: Zeidenberg paid for the software and walked out of the store with a box under his arm, so if arrival of the box with the product ends the time for revelation of contractual terms, then the time ended in *ProCD* before Zeidenberg opened the box. But of course ProCD had not completed performance with delivery of the box, and neither had Gateway. One element of the transaction was the warranty, which obliges sellers to fix defects in their products. The Hills have invoked Gateway's warranty and are not satisfied with its response, so they are not well positioned to say that Gateway's obligations were fulfilled when the motor carrier unloaded the box. What is more, both ProCD and

Gateway promised to help customers to use their products. Long-term service and information obligations are common in the computer business, on both hardware and software sides. Gateway offers "lifetime service" and has a round-the-clock telephone hotline to fulfil this promise. Some vendors spend more money helping customers use their products than on developing and manufacturing them. The document in Gateway's box includes promises of future performance that some consumers value highly; these promises bind Gateway just as the arbitration clause binds the Hills.

* * *

At oral argument the Hills propounded still another distinction: the box containing ProCD's software displayed a notice that additional terms were within, while the box containing Gateway's computer did not. The difference is functional, not legal. Consumers browsing the aisles of a store can look at the box, and if they are unwilling to deal with the prospect of additional terms can leave the box alone, avoiding the transactions costs of returning the package after reviewing its contents. Gateway's box, by contrast, is just a shipping carton; it is not on display anywhere. Its function is to protect the product during transit, and the information on its sides is for the use of handlers * * * rather than would-be purchasers.

Perhaps the Hills would have had a better argument if they were first alerted to the bundling of hardware and legal-ware after opening the box and wanted to return the computer in order to avoid disagreeable terms, but were dissuaded by the expense of shipping. What the remedy would be in such a case — could it exceed the shipping charges? — is an interesting question, but one that need not detain us because the Hills knew before they ordered the computer that the carton would include *some* important terms, and they did not seek to discover these in advance. Gateway's ads state that their products come with limited warranties and lifetime support. How limited was the warranty — 30 days, with service contingent on shipping the computer back, or five years, with free onsite service? What sort of support was offered? Shoppers have three principal ways to discover these things. First, they can ask the vendor to send a copy before deciding whether to buy. The Magnuson–Moss Warranty Act requires firms to distribute their warranty terms on request; the Hills do not contend that Gateway would have refused to enclose the remaining terms too. Concealment would be bad for business, scaring some customers away and leading to excess returns from others. Second, shoppers can consult public sources (computer magazines, the Web sites of vendors) that may contain this information. Third, they may inspect the documents after the product's delivery. Like Zeidenberg, the Hills took the third option. By keeping the computer beyond 30 days, the Hills accepted Gateway's offer, including the arbitration clause.

The Hills' remaining arguments, including a contention that the arbitration clause is unenforceable as part of a scheme to defraud, do not require more than a citation to *Prima Paint Corp. v. Flood & Conklin Mfg. Co.* Whatever may be said pro and con about the cost and efficacy of arbitration (which the Hills disparage) is for Congress and the contracting parties to consider. Claims based on RICO are no less arbitrable than those founded on the contract or the law of torts. The decision of the district court is vacated, and this case is remanded with instructions to compel the Hills to submit their dispute to arbitration.

Notes and Questions

1. The *ProCD* case relied upon by the majority, also an Easterbrook opinion, has not been widely followed by the other circuits, which generally have not issued decisions on this question.

2. What arguments would you make on behalf of the Hills?

3. Unconscionability law often distinguishes between substantive unconscionability (the unfairness of the term) and procedural unconscionability (the lack of choice about whether to accept the term). Many courts require arbitration clauses to be both substantively unconscionable and procedurally unconscionable in order to be invalidated as unconscionable. See e.g. *Graham v. Scissor–Tail*, 28 Cal.3d 807 (1981); *see generally* IAN R. MACNEIL, RICHARD E. SPEIDEL & THOMAS J. STIPANOWICH, FEDERAL ARBITRATION LAW § 19.3 (1994 ed. and Supp. 1999).

4. Recall the earlier discussion about class actions. Should an arbitration provision that precludes class actions be held unconscionable? *See Ting v. AT&T Corp.*, 319 F.3d 1126 (9th Cir. 2003), *cert. denied* 540 U.S. 811 (2003); *Discover Bank v. Superior Court*, 30 Cal.Rptr.3d 76, 113 P.3d 1100 (2005). See Notes 2–5 following *Green Tree Financial Services v. Randolph* in Section V(B)(3)(b)(ii), supra, beginning at page 574.

iii. Adhesion in Consumer Goods and Services

BROEMMER v. ABORTION SERVICES OF PHOENIX, LTD.

Supreme Court of Arizona, En Banc, 1992.
173 Ariz. 148, 840 P.2d 1013.

Moeller, Vice Chief Justice.

STATEMENT OF THE CASE

Melinda Kay Broemmer (plaintiff) asks this court to review a court of appeals opinion that held that an "Agreement to Arbitrate" which she signed prior to undergoing a clinical abortion is an enforceable, albeit an adhesive, contract. The opinion affirmed the trial court's grant of summary judgment in favor of Abortion Services of Phoenix and Dr. Otto (defendants). Because we hold the agreement to arbitrate is unenforceable as against plaintiff, we reverse the trial court and vacate in part the court of appeals opinion. We have jurisdiction pursuant to Ariz. Const. art. 6, § 5(3) and A.R.S. § 12–120.24.

FACTS AND PROCEDURAL HISTORY

In December 1986, plaintiff, an Iowa resident, was 21 years old, unmarried, and 16 or 17 weeks pregnant. She was a high school graduate earning less than $100.00 a week and had no medical benefits. The father-to-be insisted that plaintiff have an abortion, but her parents advised against it. Plaintiff's uncontested affidavit describes the time as one of considerable confusion and emotional and physical turmoil for her.

Plaintiff's mother contacted Abortion Services of Phoenix and made an appointment for her daughter for December 29, 1986. During their visit to the clinic that day, plaintiff and her mother expected, but did not receive, information and counseling on alternatives to abortion and the nature of the operation. When plaintiff and her mother arrived at the clinic, plaintiff was escorted into an adjoining room and asked to complete three forms, one of which is the agreement to arbitrate at issue in this case. The agreement to arbitrate included language that "any dispute aris[ing] between the Parties as a result of the fees and/or services" would be settled by binding arbitration and that "any arbitrators appointed by the AAA [American Arbitration Association] shall be licensed medical doctors who specialize in obstetrics/gynecology." The two other documents plaintiff completed at the same time were a 2–page consent-to-operate form and a questionnaire asking for a detailed medical history. Plaintiff completed all three forms in less than 5 minutes and returned them to the front desk. Clinic staff made no attempt to explain the agreement to plaintiff before or after she signed, and did not provide plaintiff with copies of the forms.

After plaintiff returned the forms to the front desk, she was taken into an examination room where pre-operation procedures were performed. She was then instructed to return at 7:00 a.m. the next morning for the termination procedure. Plaintiff returned the following day and Doctor Otto performed the abortion. As a result of the procedure, plaintiff suffered a punctured uterus that required medical treatment.

Plaintiff filed a malpractice complaint in June 1988, approximately 1 1/2 years after the medical procedure. By the time litigation commenced, plaintiff could recall completing and signing the medical history and consent-to-operate forms, but could not recall signing the agreement to arbitrate. Defendants moved to dismiss, contending that the trial court lacked subject matter jurisdiction because arbitration was required. In opposition, plaintiff submitted affidavits that remain uncontroverted. The trial court considered the affidavits, apparently treated the motion to dismiss as one for summary judgment, and granted summary judgment to the defendants. Plaintiff's motion to vacate, quash or set aside the order, or to stay the claim pending arbitration, was denied.

On appeal, the court of appeals held that although the contract was one of adhesion, it was nevertheless enforceable because it did not fall outside plaintiff's reasonable expectations and was not unconscionable. Following the court of appeals opinion, the parties stipulated to dismiss the Ottos from the lawsuit and from this appeal. We granted plaintiff's petition for review.

Issue

Plaintiff presents 5 potential issues in her petition for review. Some of the parties and amici have urged us to announce a "bright-line" rule of broad applicability concerning the enforceability of arbitration agreements. Arbitration proceedings are statutorily authorized in Arizona, and arbitration plays an important role in dispute resolution, as do other salutary methods of alternative dispute resolution. Important principles of contract law and of freedom of contract are intertwined with questions relating to agreements to utilize alternative methods of dispute resolution. We conclude it would be unwise to accept the invitation to attempt to establish some "bright-line" rule of broad applicability in this case. We will instead resolve the one issue which is dispositive: Under the undisputed facts in this case, is the agreement to arbitrate enforceable against plaintiff? We hold that it is not.

Discussion

I.   The Contract is One of Adhesion

When the facts are undisputed, this court is not bound by the trial court's conclusions and may make its own analysis of the facts or legal instruments on which the case turns. A.R.S. § 12–1501 authorizes written agreements to arbitrate and provides that they are "valid, enforceable and irrevocable, save upon such grounds as exist at law or in equity for the revocation of any contract." Thus, the enforceability of the agreement to arbitrate is determined by principles of general contract law. The court of appeals concluded, and we agree, that, under those principles, the contract in this case was one of adhesion.

An adhesion contract is typically a standardized form "offered to consumers of goods and services on essentially a 'take it or leave it' basis without affording the consumer a realistic opportunity to bargain and under such conditions that the consumer cannot obtain the desired product or services except by acquiescing in the form contract." The *Wheeler* court further stated that "[t]he distinctive feature of a contract of adhesion is that the weaker party has no realistic choice as to its terms."

The printed form agreement signed by plaintiff in this case possesses all the characteristics of a contract of adhesion. The form is a standardized contract offered to plaintiff on a "take it or leave it" basis. In addition to removing from the courts any potential dispute concerning fees or services, the drafter inserted additional terms potentially advantageous to itself requiring that any arbitrator appointed by the American Arbitration Association be a licensed medical doctor specializing in obstetrics/gynecology. The contract was not negotiated but was, instead, prepared by defendant and presented to plaintiff as a condition of treatment. Staff at the clinic neither explained its terms to plaintiff nor indicated that she was free to refuse to sign the form; they merely represented to plaintiff that she had to complete the three forms. The conditions under which the clinic offered plaintiff the services were on a "take it or leave it" basis, and the terms of service were not negotiable. Applying general contract law to the undisputed facts, the court of appeals correctly held that the contract was one of adhesion.

II.   Reasonable Expectations

Our conclusion that the contract was one of adhesion is not, of itself, determinative of its enforceability. "[A] contract of adhesion is fully enforceable according to its terms [citations omitted] unless certain other factors are present which, under established legal rules — legislative or judicial — operate to render it otherwise." To determine whether this contract of adhesion is enforceable, we look to two factors: the reasonable expectations of the adhering party and whether the contract is unconscionable. As the court stated in *Graham:*

> Generally speaking, there are two judicially imposed limitations on the enforcement of adhesion contracts or provisions thereof. The first is that such a contract or provision which does not fall within the reasonable expectations of the weaker or "adhering" party will not be enforced against him. The second — a principle of equity applicable to all contracts generally — is that a contract or provision, even if consistent with the reasonable expectations of the parties, will be denied enforcement if, considered in its context, it is unduly oppressive or "unconscionable."

* * *

Clearly, the issues of knowing consent and reasonable expectations are closely related and intertwined. Although customers typically adhere to standardized agreements and are bound by them without even appearing to know the standard terms in detail, they are not bound to unknown terms which are beyond the range of reasonable expectation.

The Restatement focuses our attention on whether it was beyond plaintiff's reasonable expectations to expect to arbitrate her medical malpractice claims, which includes waiving her right to a jury trial, as part of the filling out of the three forms under the facts and circumstances of this case. Clearly, there was no conspicuous or explicit waiver of the fundamental right to a jury trial or any evidence that such rights were knowingly, voluntarily and intelligently waived. The only evidence presented compels a finding that waiver of such fundamental rights was beyond the reasonable expectations of plaintiff. Moreover, as Professor Henderson writes, "[i]n attempting to effectuate reasonable expectations consistent with a standardized medical contract, a court will find less reason to regard the bargaining process as suspect if there are no terms unreasonably favorable to the stronger party." In this case failure to explain to plaintiff that the agreement required all potential disputes, including malpractice disputes, to be heard only by an arbitrator who was a licensed obstetrician/gynecologist requires us to view the "bargaining" process with suspicion. It would be unreasonable to enforce such a critical term against plaintiff when it is not a negotiated term and defendant failed to explain it to her or call her attention to it.

Plaintiff was under a great deal of emotional stress, had only a high school education, was not experienced in commercial matters, and is still not sure "what arbitration is." Given the circumstances under which the agreement was signed and the nature of the terms included therein, our reading of *Pepper, Darner,* the Restatement and the affidavits in this case compel us to conclude that the contract fell outside plaintiff's reasonable expectations and is, therefore, unenforceable. Because of this holding, it is unnecessary for us to determine whether the contract is also unconscionable.

* * *

DISPOSITION

Those portions of the opinion of the court of appeals inconsistent with this opinion are vacated. The judgment of the trial court is reversed and this case is remanded for further proceedings consistent with this opinion. Because plaintiff has successfully overcome defendant's claimed contractual defense, the trial court may entertain an application for fees incurred at the trial court and appellate level. Feldman, C.J., and Corcoran and Zlaket, JJ., concur.

Martone, Justice, dissenting.

The court's conclusion that the agreement to arbitrate was outside the plaintiff's reasonable expectations is without basis in law or fact. I fear today's decision reflects a preference for litigation over alternative dispute resolution that I had thought was behind us. I would affirm the court of appeals.

We begin with the undisputed facts that the court ignores. Appendix "A" to this dissent is the agreement to arbitrate. At the top it states in bold capital letters "PLEASE READ THIS CONTRACT CAREFULLY AS IT EFFECTS [sic] YOUR LEGAL RIGHTS." Directly under that in all capital letters are the words "AGREEMENT TO ARBITRATE." The recitals indicate that "the Parties deem it to be in their respective best interest to settle any such dispute as expeditiously and economically as possible." The parties agreed that disputes over services provided would be settled by arbitration in accordance with the rules of the American Arbitration Association. They further agreed that the arbitrators appointed by the American Arbitration Association would be licensed medical doctors who specialize in obstetrics/gynecology. Plaintiff, an adult, signed the document.

Under A.R.S. § 12–1501, a written contract to submit to arbitration *any* controversy that might arise between the parties is "valid, enforceable and irrevocable, save upon such grounds as exist at law or in equity for the revocation of any contract." The statute applies to any controversy. Under A.R.S. § 12–1503, if the arbitration agreement provides a method of appointment of arbitrators, "this method shall be followed." Under A.R.S. § 12–1518, the American Arbitration Association is expressly acknowledged as an entity that the state itself may use in connection with arbitration. There is judicial review of any award. A.R.S. § 12–1512. Thus, on the face of it, the contract to arbitrate is plainly reasonable and enforceable unless there are grounds to revoke it. A.R.S. § 12–1501.

The court seizes upon the doctrine of reasonable expectations to revoke this contract. But there is nothing in this record that would warrant a finding that an agreement to arbitrate a malpractice claim was not within the reasonable expectations of the parties. On this record, the exact opposite is likely to be true. For all we know, both sides in this case might wish to avoid litigation like the plague and seek the more harmonious waters of alternative dispute resolution. Nor is there anything in this record that would suggest that arbitration is bad. Where is the harm? In the end, today's decision reflects a preference in favor of litigation that is not shared by the courts of other states and the courts of the United States.

* * *

An agreement to arbitrate is hardly bizarre or oppressive. It is a preferred method of alternative dispute resolution that our legislature has expressly acknowledged in A.R.S. § 12–1501. Arbitration does not eviscerate any agreed terms. Nor does it eliminate the dominant purpose of the transaction. The plaintiff here had an opportunity to read the document, the document was legible and was hardly hidden from plaintiff's view. This arbitration agreement was in bold capital letters. Thus, the reasonable expectations standard of the *Restatement (Second) of Contracts* § 211 does not support this court's conclusion.

There is another reason why § 211(3) fails to support the court's conclusion. The *Restatement (Second) of Contracts* chapter 8 describes the whole range of unenforceable contracts. Its introductory note states:

> A particularly important change has been effected by statutes relating to arbitration, which have now been enacted in so many jurisdictions that it seems likely that even in the remaining states, there has been a change in the former judicial attitude of hostility toward agreements to arbitrate future disputes.... Such agreements are now widely used and serve the public interest by saving court time. *The rules stated in this Chapter do not preclude their enforcement even in the absence of legislation.*

It is difficult to reconcile the court's reliance on the *Restatement* in light of this.

* * *

At bottom, all that could explain the court's decision is a preference for litigation over arbitration.

* * *

The court says it will enforce arbitration agreements "freely and fairly entered," and that "the document involved is a contract of adhesion." But the court's own framework of analysis acknowledges that its "conclusion that the contract was one of adhesion is not, of itself, determinative of its enforceability." It acknowledges that once it is determined that an adhesive contract exists, one looks to (1) reasonable expectations and (2) conscionability. No one doubts that this was a contract of adhesion. And the court holds that because "the contract fell outside plaintiff's reasonable expectations" it is unenforceable, and therefore it is not necessary "to determine whether the contract is also unconscionable." Thus the court does not reach conscionability.

The only basis for the court's decision is "reasonable expectations," but words such as "freely and fairly entered," or "contract of adhesion" are irrelevant to that inquiry. * * * In the end we are left to conclude that people reasonably expect litigation over alternative dispute resolution. For all these reasons, I dissent.

Notes and Questions

1. The *Broemmer* decision has not been followed in other jurisdictions. Is *Broemmer* a stronger case for a plaintiff than *Hill*?

2. Was an arbitration clause really beyond the *Broemmer* plaintiff's reasonable expectations? Explain how you would go about ascertaining the plaintiff's reasonable expectations.

3. The implied duty of good faith and fair dealing is another contract doctrine that has been used to address unilaterally imposed arbitration provisions, in addition to the reasonable expectations doctrine. In one closely watched case arising in the financial services industry, *Badie v. Bank of America*, 67 Cal.App.4th 779, 79 Cal.Rptr.2d 273 (1998), the California Court of Appeals used this good faith duty as a basis for refusing to enforce the addition of a mandatory arbitration provision to the "terms and conditions" of the customer's deposit account signature card, ruling that a change in the dispute resolution forum was not consistent with the terms to which the customer had initially agreed when signing the deposit card. *Id.* at 790–97.

Since the initial customer agreement had not included a dispute resolution term, it was beyond the customer's reasonable expectation that the lender's right to change the terms of the signature agreement unilaterally would include a term limiting the presumptive right to court access. Rather, the court held that the Bank's right to change terms unilaterally was limited to those terms expressly included within the initial agreement, such as purchases and cash advances requirements and limitations, credit limits, finance charges, membership fees, late charges and other fees, calculation of balances and finance charges, payments, etc.

> Where, as in this case, a party has the unilateral right to change the terms of a contract, it does not act in an 'objectively reasonable' manner when it attempts to 'recapture' a forgone opportunity by adding an entirely new term which has no bearing on any subject, issue, right, or obligation addressed in the original contract and which was not within the reasonable contemplation of the parties when the contract was

entered into. That is particularly true where the new term deprives the other party of the right to a jury trial and the right to select a judicial forum for dispute resolution.

Id. at 796.

4. In Paul D. Carrington and Paul Y. Castle *The Revocability of Contract Provisions Controlling Resolution of Future Disputes Between the Parties*, 67 Law & Contemp. Probs. 207 (2004), the authors argued that pre-dispute arbitration agreements should be revocable when contained in contracts of adhesion, "at least until a dispute to which they purport to apply has been submitted in writing to the specified forum or procedure." *Id.* at 207.

5. Consider the Hill and Broemmer cases in light of Section 6, comment 7 of the revised Uniform Arbitration Act, excerpted below.

SECTION 6, Comment 7

Contracts of adhesion and unconscionability: Unequal bargaining power often affects contracts containing arbitration provisions involving employers and employees, sellers and consumers, health maintenance organizations and patients, franchisors and franchisees, and others.

Despite some recent developments to the contrary, courts do not often find contracts unenforceable for unconscionability. To determine whether to void a contract on this ground, courts examine a number of factors. These factors include: unequal bargaining power, whether the weaker party may opt out of arbitration, the clarity and conspicuousness of the arbitration clause, whether an unfair advantage is obtained, whether the arbitration clause is negotiable, whether the arbitration provision is boilerplate, whether the aggrieved party had a meaningful choice or was compelled to accept arbitration, whether the arbitration agreement is within the reasonable expectations of the weaker party, and whether the stronger party used deceptive tactics. *See, e.g., We Care Hair Dev., Inc. v. Engen*, 180 F.3d 838 (7th Cir. 1999); *Harris v. Green Tree Fin. Corp.*, 183 F.3d 173 (3d Cir. 1999); *Broemmer v. Abortion Serv. of Phoenix, Ltd.*, 173 Ariz. 148, 840 P.2d 1013 (1992); *Chor v. Piper, Jaffray & Hopwood, Inc.*, 261 Mont. 143, 862 P.2d 26 (1993); *Buraczynski v. Eyring*, 919 S.W.2d 314 (Tenn. 1996); *Sosa v. Paulos*, 924 P.2d 357 (Utah 1996); *Powers v. Dickson, Carlson & Campillo*, 54 Cal. App.4th 1102, 63 Cal.Rptr.2d 261 (1997); *Beldon Roofing & Remodeling Co. v. Tanner*, 1997 WL 280482 (Tex. Ct. App. May 28, 1997).

Despite these many factors, courts have been reluctant to find arbitration agreements unconscionable. II Macneil Treatise § 19.3; David S. Schwartz, *Enforcing Small Print to Protect Big Business: Employee and Consumer Rights Claims in an Age of Compelled Arbitration*, 1997 Wis. L. Rev. 33 (1997); Stephen J. Ware, *Arbitration and Unconscionability After Doctor's Associates, Inc. v. Cassarotto*, 31 Wake Forest L. Rev. 1001 (1996). However, in the last few years, some cases have gone the other way and courts have begun to scrutinize more closely the enforceability of arbitration agreements. *Hooters of Am., Inc. v. Phillips*, 173 F.3d 933 (4th Cir. 1999) (stating that one-sided arbitration agreement that takes away numerous substantive rights and remedies of employee under Title VII is so egregious as to constitute a complete default of employer's contractual obligation to draft arbitration rules in good faith); *Shankle v. B–G Maint. Mgt., Inc.*, 163 F.3d 1230 (10th Cir. 1999) (finding that an arbitration clause does not apply to employee's discrimination claims where employee is required to pay portion of arbitrator's fee that is a prohibitive cost for him so as to substantially limit his use of arbitral forum); *Randolph v. Green Tree Fin. Corp.*, 178 F.3d 1149 (11th Cir. 1999), cert. granted, 529 U.S. 1052, 120 S.Ct. 1552, 146 L.Ed.2d 458 (2000) (holding that consumer not required to arbitrate where arbitration clause is silent on subject of arbitration fees and costs due to risk that imposition of large fees and costs on consumer may defeat remedial purposes of Truth in Lending Act) [*but cf. Dobbins v. Hawk's Enter.*, 198 F.3d 715 (8th Cir. 1999) (finding that before court can determine if administrative costs make arbitration clause unconscionable, purchasers must explore whether arbitration organization will waive or diminish its fees or whether seller will offer to pay the fees)]; *Paladino v. Avnet Computer Tech., Inc.*, 134 F.3d 1054 (11th Cir. 1998) (employee not required to arbitrate Title VII claim where the contract limits damages below that allowed by the statute); *Broemmer v. Abortion Serv. of Phoenix, Ltd., supra* (stating that arbitration agreement unenforceable because it required a patient to arbitrate a malpractice claim and to waive the right to jury trial and was beyond the patient's reasonable expectations where drafter inserted potentially advantageous term requiring arbitrator of malpractice claims to be a licensed medical doctor); *Armendariz v. Foundation Health Psychcare Serv. Inc.*, 24 Cal.4th 83, 6 P.3d 669, 99 Cal.Rptr.2d 745 (2000) (concluding that clause in arbitration agreement limiting employee's remedies in state anti-discrimination claims is cause to void arbitration agreement on grounds of unconscionability); * * *

As a result of concerns over fairness in arbitration involving those with unequal bargaining power, organizations and individuals involved in employment, consumer, and health-care arbitration have determined common standards for arbitration in these fields. In 1995, a broad-based coalition representing interests of employers, employees, arbitrators and arbitration organizations agreed upon a Due Process Protocol for Mediation and Arbitration of Statutory Disputes Arising Out of the Employment Relationship; *see also* National Academy of Arbitrators, Guidelines on Arbitration of Statutory Claims under Employer–Promulgated Systems (May 21, 1997). In 1998, a similar group representing the views of consumers, industry, arbitrators, and arbitration organizations formed the National Consumer Disputes Advisory Committee under the auspices of the American Arbitration Association and adopted a Due Process Protocol for Mediation and Arbitration of Consumer Disputes. Also in 1998 the Commission on Health Care Dispute Resolution, comprised of representatives from the American Arbitration Association, the American Bar Association and the American Medical Association endorsed a Due Process Protocol for Mediation and Arbitration of Health Care Disputes. The purpose of these protocols is to ensure both procedural and substantive fairness in arbitrations involving employees, consumers and patients. The arbitration of employment, consumer and health-care disputes in accordance with these standards will be a legitimate and meaningful alternative to litigation. *See, e.g., Cole v. Burns Int'l Sec. Serv.*, 105 F.3d 1465 (D.C. Cir. 1997) (referring specifically to the due process protocol in the employment relationship in a case involving the arbitration of an employee's rights under Title VII).

The Drafting Committee determined to leave the issue of adhesion contracts and unconscionability to developing law because (1) the doctrine of unconscionability reflects so much the substantive law of the States and not just arbitration, (2) the case law, statutes, and arbitration standards are rapidly changing, and (3) treating arbitration clauses differently from other contract provisions would raise significant preemption issues under the Federal Arbitration Act. However, it should be pointed out that a primary purpose of Section 4, which provides that some sections of the RUAA are not waivable, is to address the problem of contracts of adhesion in the statute while taking into account the limitations caused by federal preemption.

Because an arbitration agreement effectively waives a party's right to a jury trial, courts should ensure the fairness of an agreement to arbitrate, particularly in instances involving statutory rights that provide claimants with important remedies. Courts should determine that an arbitration process is adequate to protect important rights. Without these safeguards, arbitration loses credibility as an appropriate alternative to litigation.

R.U.A.A. § 6, cmt. 7 (2000).

6.   Comment 7 to Section 6 of the RUAA concludes by stressing that courts should ensure that the arbitration agreement at issue is adequate to protect important rights. How does this differ from the approach in *Hill* and *Broemmer*? What does it mean for an agreement to be adequate?

7.   Should courts be more willing to find arbitration agreements unconscionable? Less willing? Is there something different about arbitration provisions? See Richard C. Reuben, Democracy and Dispute Resolution: The Problem of Arbitration, 67 Law & Contemp. Probs. 279 (Winter/Spring 2004).

4. JUDICIAL REVIEW OF ARBITRATION AWARDS

Most parties voluntarily comply with arbitration awards. Courts impose sanctions for failure to comply with an award only if it has been confirmed by a court. Federal and state statutes authorize courts to confirm, vacate, and modify awards. Courts do not routinely review the merits of an award in deciding whether to confirm, vacate, or modify. If they did, agreements to arbitrate would result in more rather than less time and money being devoted to processing disputes. As the Supreme Court said in a labor arbitration case, the "policy of settling labor disputes by arbitration would be undermined if courts had the final say on the merits of the awards." *United Steelworkers v. Enterprise Wheel & Car Corp.*, 363 U.S. 593, 80 S.Ct. 1358, 4 L.Ed.2d 1424 (1960). Limitation of judicial review is part of the strong federal pro-arbitration policy. *See* Ian R. Macneil, Richard E. Speidel, Thomas J. Stipanowich, Federal

ARBITRATION LAW § 40.14 (1994 ed. & Supp. 1999). Successful challenges of arbitration awards are relatively rare. Yet courts and commentators agree that there is a need at times to modify or vacate arbitration awards. The materials that follow focus on the difficult issues raised by attacks in court on arbitration awards.

SOBEL v. HERTZ, WARNER & CO.

United States Court of Appeals, Second Circuit, 1972.
469 F.2d 1211.

Before MOORE, FEINBERG and MULLIGAN, CIRCUIT JUDGES.

FEINBERG, CIRCUIT JUDGE:

This is an interlocutory appeal from an order of the United States District Court for the Southern District of New York, Milton Pollack, J., that remanded an arbitration proceeding to the arbitrators to fulfill their "obligation to furnish some explanation of the ultimate findings embodied in their decision." We hold that in the circumstances of this case the arbitrators have no such obligation to explain their award, and we reverse the order of the district court.

I

The arbitration that led to this appeal was first requested in November 1967 by appellee Herbert Sobel, who was a customer of appellant Hertz, Warner & Co., a stock brokerage firm and a member of the New York Stock Exchange. As a customer, Sobel had the right under Article VIII of the Constitution of the New York Stock Exchange to demand arbitration of any controversy he might have with a member firm growing out of its "business." Briefly, Sobel claimed that between December 1965 and March 1966 he had purchased 10,200 shares of the common stock of Hercules Galion Products, Inc., upon the recommendation of his long-time broker, Edward Wetzel, and Michael Geier, both then employed by Hertz, Warner, and that Wetzel and Geier had made fraudulent misstatements and omissions of material facts on which Sobel had relied to his detriment. As their employer, Hertz, Warner was, according to Sobel, liable for the damages he had suffered. Sobel continued to hold his Hercules shares until Hertz, Warner demanded, in connection with the arbitration, that they be sold to fix damages. This was done in May 1968, and Sobel thereafter claimed a direct loss of about $34,000.

In 1970, both parties signed a formal submission to arbitration pursuant to the provisions of the Stock Exchange Constitution and the rules of the Board of Governors. Under the Constitution, Sobel's claim was heard by a panel consisting of two persons "engaged in the securities business" and three not so engaged. The panel held two hearings at which it heard the testimony of three witnesses and received documentary evidence. At the hearings, of which there is a full transcript, both sides were ably represented by counsel.

In May 1971, the panel issued the following decision:

We, the undersigned, being the arbitrators selected to hear and determine a matter in controversy between the above-mentioned claimant and respondents set forth in a submission to arbitration signed by the parties on April 6, 1970 and April 10, 1970 respectively;

And having heard and considered the proofs of the parties, have decided and determined that the claim of the claimant be and hereby is in all respects dismissed;

That the costs, $240.00, be and hereby are assessed against the claimant.

After an unsuccessful request to the arbitrators for reconsideration, Sobel moved in the Southern District under 9 U.S.C. § 10 to vacate the arbitration award on the grounds that it had been "procured by undue means" and "that the Award is contrary to public policy, in that the arbitrators refused to make their Award in accordance with the applicable Federal Securities laws." Judge Pollack heard argument on the motion to vacate and concluded, in an exhaustive opinion, that he could not decide the question without "an indication, now wholly lacking from the record, of the basis on which the petitioner's claim was dismissed." Holding that "a District Court is justified in requiring some statement of the facts the arbitrators found decisive," the judge remanded the controversy to the arbitrators for that purpose. Thereafter, he certified as an interlocutory appeal the question whether his action was proper, and we permitted the appeal.

II

Although Sobel's claims before the arbitrators rested on state statutory law and common law fraud concepts, as well as on federal securities acts, only the last are significant on this appeal. The district judge was clearly disturbed by Sobel's claim that the arbitrators must have ignored the prohibitions of sections 12(2) and 17(a) of the Securities Act of 1933, 15 U.S.C. §§ 77l(2), 77q(a), section 10(b) of the Securities Exchange Act of 1934, 15 U.S.C. § 78j(b), and Rule 10b–5 promulgated thereunder. The judge's opinion emphasized that Wetzel and Geier had been indicted in 1967 — not long after the transactions complained of by Sobel — for conspiring to create market activity in the Hercules shares and to induce the purchase of the security by others, and that in 1971 Wetzel had pleaded guilty to the conspiracy charge and Geier had been found guilty of that and other counts after a jury trial. Sobel argued to the district court that unless the arbitrators explained their decision, there was no way of telling whether it was in "manifest disregard" of the provisions of the securities acts. The quotation is from *Wilko v. Swan*, which — oddly enough, in the context of Sobel's use of it here — stands primarily for the proposition that certain kinds of cláims cannot be forced to arbitration despite a pre-dispute agreement to arbitrate. *Wilko v. Swan* held that an agreement to arbitrate future controversies was an impermissible waiver of the plaintiff-customer's right to have his claim of securities act violations heard in court. In the course of its opinion, however, the Court also said:

> Power to vacate an award is limited. While it may be true, as the Court of Appeals thought, that a failure of the arbitrators to decide in accordance with the provisions of the Securities Act would "constitute grounds for vacating the award pursuant to section 10 of the Federal Arbitration Act," that failure would need to be made clearly to appear. In unrestricted submissions, such as the present margin agreements envisage, the interpretations of the law by the arbitrators *in contrast to manifest disregard* are not subject, in the federal courts, to judicial review for error in interpretation.

The district judge agreed with Sobel that unless the arbitrators in this case stated the basis of their decision, the judge could not determine whether it was in "manifest disregard" of the law.

The first issue before us is what is the issue before us. In one portion of his memorandum opinion certifying an interlocutory appeal, the district judge described the question as

> whether an arbitration award in a case involving federal securities law standards which fails to provide some indication of the basis of the arbitration panel's decision may be set aside and resubmitted to the arbitration panel pursuant to 9 U.S.C. § 10(d) and (e), * * *.

* * *

From this, Sobel argues that Judge Pollack's order merely requires a clarification from the arbitrators when the court finds no indication of the basis of the decision and that Judge Pollack's decision does not require arbitrators to write opinions in the first instance. Such a ruling, says Sobel, is not at all unusual. The latter part of the argument puzzles us. It does not make any real difference whether an arbitrator is ordered to write an opinion in the first instance or in the second instance. The issue is whether the requirement is proper in either case. As to the point that the judge sought only "clarification," if this version of the question were correct we doubt whether the appeal would have been certified by the district judge or accepted by this court. Sobel's description of the narrow effect of Judge Pollack's order is at variance with other portions of both his original opinion and his supplemental memorandum. In the latter, the judge phrased the question in the manner set forth in the first paragraph of this opinion. And, in the judge's earlier opinion before certifying the interlocutory appeal, he characterized the arbitrators' decision several times as inadequate because lacking an explanation of its basis. (sic) Moreover, whatever may be the power of a court to require clarification of an arbitration award, on the ample record in this case "clarification" can only mean setting forth the reasons for decision. Under these circumstances, we believe that the issue before us is whether the arbitrators here are required to disclose the reasoning underlying their award.

The question so phrased, of course, is still a narrow one. We are not asked to decide whether arbitration was an inappropriate forum here in the first place. Nor must we determine all the circumstances in which a court may vacate an arbitrator's award.

Nonetheless, the extent of an arbitrator's obligation to explain his award is necessarily related to the scope of judicial review of it. That issue, insofar as it leads to attempts to define "manifest disregard," is particularly troublesome. But if the arbitrators simply ignore the applicable law, the literal application of a "manifest disregard" standard should presumably compel vacation of the award. The problem is how a court is to be made aware of the erring conduct of the arbitrators. Obviously, a requirement that arbitrators explain their reasoning in every case would help to uncover egregious failures to apply the law to an arbitrated dispute. But such a rule would undermine the very purpose of arbitration, which is to provide a relatively quick, efficient and informal means of private dispute settlement. The sacrifice that arbitration entails in terms of legal precision is recognized, and is implicitly accepted in the initial assumption that certain disputes are arbitrable. Given that acceptance, the primary consideration for the courts must be that the system operate expeditiously as well as fairly.

Presumably based upon the foregoing considerations, the Supreme Court has made it clear that there is no general requirement that arbitrators explain the reasons for their award. In *Wilko v. Swan*, supra, just before the language quoted above the Court pointed out that an award by arbitrators "may be made without explanation of their reasons and without a complete record of their proceedings * * *." This statement is especially significant because Mr. Justice Frankfurter in dissent made exactly the opposite point. A little over two years later, the Court observed that "Arbitrators * * * need not give their reasons for their results. * * *." These statements were, of course, known to the district judge; he even quoted them in his opinion. The argument, then, must be that there is something about this particular case that justifies the extraordinary requirement of the district court's order. We fail to see what that is. There was a complete transcript here of the arbitration proceeding. The arbitrators — and the district court — also had the benefit of an extremely detailed submission to arbitration, including Sobel's Statement of Claim and Hertz, Warner's Reply, excellent memoranda of law and summations of counsel, all of which indicate a number of theories upon which the arbitrators may have decided. It is true that claims under the securities acts are frequently complicated, although those made here seem less so than usual. And the same public interest that led to the enactment of the securities acts makes it desirable that such claims be decided correctly. But there is also a public interest, manifested in the United States Arbitration Act, in the proper functioning of the arbitral process. It would be destructive of that process if we approved the district judge's requirement here that the arbitrators give reasons for their decision. Arbitration may not always be the speedy and economical remedy its admirers claim it is — this case is proof enough of that. But forcing arbitrators to explain their award even when grounds for it can be gleaned from the record will unjustifiably diminish whatever efficiency the process now achieves.

Sobel cites a number of cases in support of the district court order. Courts have, on occasion, remanded awards to arbitrators for clarification, but they generally have done so to find out whether an issue has already been decided in arbitration rather than to discover whether the arbitrators had good reasons for their award.

* * *

In short, we believe that the district court erred in remanding the arbitration proceeding to the arbitrators. We do not agree with its conclusion that "the present state of the record is not sufficient to justify final determination of the issues petitioner has raised." Those issues are whether the arbitration award was procured by "undue means," 9 U.S.C. § 10(a), or is void as against public policy. Both parties have urged us to decide those questions. While we are tempted to do so in order to bring this litigation to an end, orderly administration suggests that the district court should rule upon them first.

Case remanded for further proceedings consistent with this opinion.

Notes and Questions

1. Written and reasoned opinions are becoming more common, and are expressly provided for in rules of major providers of arbitration services. *See, e.g.,* AM. ARBITRATION ASSOC., NATIONAL RULES FOR THE RESOLUTION OF EMPLOYMENT DISPUTES § 34(c) (1999); CPR INST. FOR DISPUTE RESOLUTION, NON-ADMINISTERED ARBITRATION RULES, Rule 14.2 (rev. ed. 2000); JUDICIAL ARBITRATION AND MEDIATION SERVS., COMPREHENSIVE ARBITRATION RULES AND PROCEDURES, Rule 24(g) (rev. ed. 2003). Why might these providers have taken this step? What are the arguments for and against requiring arbitrators to explain an award?

2. The principal case indicates that arbitration awards will not be vacated for a mistaken interpretation of law — even a mistaken interpretation of a federal statute — but only will vacate an award where there has been manifest disregard of the law. The case also indicates that there is no general requirement that arbitrators explain the reasons for their award. *See, e.g., Monscharsh v. Heily & Blase,* 3 Cal.4th 1, 10 Cal.Rptr.2d 183, 832 P.2d 899 (1992) (arbitrator's decision is not generally reviewable for errors of fact or law, whether or not such error appears on the face of the award and causes substantial injustice to the parties). Findings of fact by arbitrators receive the same deference.

In Comment C of Section 23, the Drafting Committee of the RUAA explained why it decided against attempting to fashion unambiguous tests for the "manifest disregard" or "public policy" standards of court review of arbitral awards and summarized the experience with these tests:

> 1. The Drafting Committee also considered the advisability of adding two new subsections to Section 23(a) sanctioning vacatur of awards that result from a "manifest disregard of the law" or for an

award that violates "public policy." Neither of these two standards is presently codified in the FAA or in any of the state arbitration acts. However, all of the federal circuit courts of appeals have embraced one or both of these standards in commercial arbitration cases. *See* Stephen L. Hayford, *Law in Disarray: Judicial Standards for Vacatur of Commercial Arbitration Awards*, 30 Ga. L. Rev. 734 (1996).

2. "Manifest disregard of the law" is the seminal nonstatutory ground for vacatur of commercial arbitration awards. The relevant case law from the federal circuit courts of appeals establishes that "a party seeking to vacate an arbitration award on the ground of 'manifest disregard of the law' may not proceed by merely objecting to the results of the arbitration." *O.R. Securities, Inc. v. Professional Planning Associates, Inc.*, 857 F.2d 742, 747 (11th Cir. 1988). "Manifest disregard of the law" "clearly means more than [an arbitral] error or misunderstanding with respect to the law." *Carte Blanche (Singapore) Pte., Ltd. v. Carte Blanche Int'l.*, 888 F.2d 260, 265 (2d Cir. 1989) (quoting *Merrill Lynch, Pierce, Fenner & Smith, Inc. v. Bobker*, 808 F.2d 930, 933 (2d Cir. 1986)).

The numerous other articulations of the "manifest disregard of law" standard reflected in the circuit appeals court case law reveal its two constituent elements. One element looks to the result reached in arbitration and evaluates whether it is clearly consistent or inconsistent with controlling law. For this element to be satisfied, a reviewing court must conclude that the arbitrator misapplied the relevant law touching upon the dispute before the arbitrator in a manner that constitutes something akin to a blatant, gross error of law that is apparent on the face of the award.

The other element of the "manifest disregard of the law" standard requires a reviewing court to evaluate the arbitrator's knowledge of the relevant law. Even if a reviewing court finds a clear error of law, vacatur is warranted under the "manifest disregard of the law" ground only if the court is able to conclude that the arbitrator knew the correct law but nevertheless "made a conscious decision" to ignore it in fashioning the award. *See M & C Corp. v. Erwin Behr & Co.*, 87 F.3d 844, 851 (6th Cir. 1996). For a full discussion of the "manifest disregard of the law" standard, *see* Stephen L. Hayford, *Reining in the Manifest Disregard of the Law Standard: The Key to Stabilizing the Law of Commercial Arbitration*, 1999 J. Disp. Resol. 117. [Professor Hayford stated in a 1996 article, after a review of relevant circuit court case law, that, "no commercial arbitration award has been vacated on this ground." Stephen L. Hayford, *Law in Disarray: Judicial Standards for Vacatur of Commercial Arbitration Awards*, 30 Ga. L. Rev. 731, 776 (1996).]

3. The origin and essence of the "public policy" ground for vacatur is well captured in the Tenth Circuit's opinion in *Seymour v. Blue Cross/Blue Shield*, 988 F.2d 1020,1023 (10th Cir. 1993). *Seymour* observed: "[I]n determining whether an arbitration award violates public policy, a court must assess whether 'the specific terms contained in [the contract] violate public policy, by creating an explicit conflict with other

'laws and legal precedents.' " *Id.* at 1024 (citing *United Paperworkers Int'l Union v. Misco*, 484 U.S. 29, 43 (1987)).

Like the "manifest disregard of the law" nonstatutory ground, vacatur under the "public policy" ground requires something more than a mere error or misunderstanding of the relevant law by the arbitrator. Under all of the articulations of this nonstatutory ground, the public policy at issue must be a clearly defined, dominant, undisputed rule of law. However, the language employed by the various circuits to describe and apply this ground in the commercial arbitration milieu reflects two distinct, different thresholds for vacatur being used by those courts. First, the Tenth Circuit in *Seymour* and the Eighth Circuit in *Paine-Webber, Inc. v. Agron*, 49 F.3d 347 (8th Cir. 1995) contemplate that an award can be vacated when it "explicitly" conflicts with, violates, or is contrary to the subject public policy. The judicial inquiry under this variant of the "public policy" ground obliges the court to delve into the merits of the arbitration award in order to ascertain whether the arbitrator's analysis and application of the parties' contract or relevant law "violates" or "conflicts" with the subject public policy.

Second, the Eleventh Circuit in *Brown v. Rauscher Pierce Refsnes, Inc.*, 994 F.2d 775 (11th Cir. 1994) and the Second Circuit in *Diapulse Corp. of America v. Carba, Ltd.*, 626 F.2d 1108 (2d Cir. 1980) trigger vacatur only when a court concludes that implementation of the arbitral result (typically, effectuation of the remedy directed by the arbitrator) compels one of the parties to violate a well-defined and dominant public policy, a determination which does not require a reviewing court to evaluate the merits of the arbitration award. Instead, the court need only ascertain whether confirmation of, or refusal to vacate an arbitration award, and a judicial order directing compliance with its terms, will place one or both of the parties to the award in violation of the subject public policy. If it would, the award must be vacated. If it does not, vacatur is not warranted. For a full discussion of the evolution and application of the public policy exception in the labor arbitration sphere, *see* Stephen L. Hayford and Anthony V. Sinicropi, *The Labor Contract and External Law: Revisiting the Arbitrator's Scope of Authority*, 1993 J. Disp. Resol. 249.

4. States have rarely addressed "manifest disregard of the law" or "public policy" as grounds for vacatur.

* * *

One area in which state courts have considered it appropriate to review the awards of arbitrators on public-policy grounds is family law and, in particular, statutes or case law requiring consideration of the "best interest" of children.

* * *

5. There are reasons for the RUAA not to embrace either the "manifest disregard" or the "public policy" standards of court review of arbitral awards. The first is presented by the omission from the FAA of either standard. Given that omission, there is a very significant question of possible FAA preemption of such a provision in the RUAA, should the

Supreme Court or Congress eventually confirm that the four narrow grounds for vacatur set out in Section 10(a) of the federal act are the exclusive grounds for vacatur. The second reason for not including these vacatur grounds is the dilemma in attempting to fashion unambiguous, "bright line" tests for these two standards. The case law on both vacatur grounds is not just unsettled but also is conflicting and indicates further evolution in the courts. As a result, the Drafting Committee concluded not to add these two grounds for vacatur in the statute. A motion to include the ground of "manifest disregard" in Section 23(a) was defeated by the Committee of the Whole at the July, 2000, meeting of the National Conference of Commissioners on Uniform State Laws.

R.U.A.A. § 23, cmt. C (2000).

3. As the preceding note observes, courts rarely find arbitration decisions in manifest regard of the law. However, the U.S. Court of Appeal for the Seventh Circuit indicated a potential willingness to seriously entertain the question. *Halligan v. Piper Jaffray, Inc.*, 148 F.3d 197, 198 (1998). The court indicated it was "inclined to hold that [the arbitrators] ignored the law or the evidence or both," but remanded on other issues. *Id.* at 202. For a discussion, see Norman S. Poser, *Judicial Review of Arbitration Awards: Manifest Disregard of the Law*, 64 Brook. L. Rev. 471 (1998).

4. Section 10 of the Federal Arbitration Act (FAA) provides that awards maybe vacated in the following circumstances:

(1) Where the award was procured by corruption, fraud, or undue means.

(2) Where there was evident partiality or corruption in the arbitrators, or either of them.

(3) Where the arbitrators were guilty of misconduct in refusing to postpone the hearing, upon sufficient cause shown, or in refusing to hear evidence pertinent and material to the controversy; or of any other misbehavior by which the rights of any party have been prejudiced.

(4) Where the arbitrators exceeded their powers, or so imperfectly executed them that a mutual, final, and definite award upon the subject matter submitted was not made.

(5) Where an award is vacated and the time within which the agreement required the award to be made has not expired the court may, in its discretion, direct a rehearing by the arbitrators.

Section 11 of the FAA authorizes modification or correction of an award in the following circumstances:

(a) Where there was an evident material miscalculation of figures or an evident material mistake in the description of any person, thing, or property referred to in the award.

(b) Where the arbitrators have awarded upon a matter not submitted to them, unless it is a matter not affecting the merits of the decision upon the matter submitted.

(c) Where the award is imperfect in matter of form not affecting the merits of the controversy.

The order may modify and correct the award, so as to effect the intent thereof and promote justice between the parties.

See IAN R. MACNEIL, RICHARD E. SPEIDEL, THOMAS J. STIPANOWICH, FEDERAL ARBITRATION LAW § 40 (1994 ed. & Supp. 1999) for an overview of the grounds for attacking arbitration awards. See Brad A. Galbraith, *Vacatur of Commercial Arbitration Awards in Federal Court: Contemplating the Use and Utility of the "Manifest Disregard" of the Law Standard*, 27 Ind.L.Rev. 242 (1993), for a discussion of whether the statutory grounds for vacation should be exclusive or whether additional judicially created grounds are needed. Stephen L. Hayford has argued that "with the arguable exception of the 'manifest disregard' of the law standard and the 'public policy' ground, the non-statutory grounds for vacatur of commercial arbitration awards are without a legitimate legal, doctrinal or theoretical basis." Stephen L. Hayford, *Law in Disarray: Judicial Standards For Vacatur of Commercial Arbitration Awards,* 30 Ga. L. Rev. 731, 833 (1996).

In *Gilmer v. Interstate/Johnson Lane Corporation*, 500 U.S. 20, 111 S.Ct. 1647, 114 L.Ed.2d 26 (1991), the Court indicated that limited judicial scrutiny of arbitration awards was "sufficient to ensure that arbitrators comply with" statutory requirements. *Id.* at 31 n.4 (quoting *Shearson American Express, Inc. v. McMahon*, 482 U.S. 220, 232, 107 S.Ct. 2332, 96 L.Ed.2d 185 (1987)). Under the "manifest disregard" standard of review, it appears that a court could confirm an arbitrator's award that was based on an erroneous interpretation of a federal statute as long as the arbitrator did not know that the award conflicted with the statute. Does the obvious tension between such a result and the statements in *Gilmer* and *McMahon* suggest that the "manifest disregard" standard will be modified in cases where arbitrators base awards on federal statutes? See *Cole v. Burns International Security Services*, 105 F.3d 1465 (D.C. Cir. 1997), where the Court indicated that in cases involving novel or difficult legal issues, courts can review an arbitrator's award to ensure that its resolution of public law issues is correct. Would such a result support or undermine the arbitration process?

5. Labor arbitration awards may be vacated for reasons similar to those set forth in Sections 10 and 11 of the FAA. *See, e.g., Ludwig Honold Manufacturing. Co. v. Fletcher*, 405 F.2d 1123, 1127 (3d Cir. 1969). Another important basis for judicial review of labor arbitration awards is the "essence" test laid down in *United Steelworkers v. Enterprise Wheel & Car Corp.*, 363 U.S. 593, 80 S.Ct. 1358, 4 L.Ed.2d 1424 (1960). The fundamental responsibility of a labor arbitrator is to interpret the collective bargaining contract negotiated by labor and management. The Supreme Court repeatedly has stressed that when courts are asked to enforce or vacate a labor arbitration award, they should not overturn the award merely because they believe the arbitrator was mistaken in his interpretation of the contract. This deference to the arbitrator's decision on the merits has limits. The "essence" test, found in *Enterprise Wheel*, articulates these limits:

> [A]n arbitrator is confined to interpretation and application of the collective bargaining agreement; he does not sit to dispense his own brand of industrial justice. He may of course look for guidance from many sources, yet his award is legitimate only so long as it draws its

essence from the collective bargaining agreement. When the arbitrator's words manifest an infidelity to his obligation, courts have no choice but to refuse enforcement of the award.

Id. at 597.

The case reports are filled with decisions that have applied the "essence" test to challenged labor arbitration awards. Numerous commentators have interpreted and evaluated these decisions. *See, e.g.,* Charles Morris, *Twenty Years of Trilogy: A Celebration, Proceedings of the 33rd Annual Meeting,* Nat'l Acad. of Arbitrators, 331, 355–56 (1981); Dennis R. Nolan & Roger I. Abrams, *American Labor Arbitration: The Maturing Years,* 35 U. Fla. L. Rev. 557, 591 (1983); Theodore J. St. Antoine, *Judicial Review of Labor Arbitration Awards: A Second Look at* Enterprise Wheel *and Its Progeny,* 75 Mich. L. Rev. 1137, 1148–49 (1977). Some of the commentators have concluded that the courts frequently fail to honor the policy underlying the "essence" test. Instead they scrutinize the merits of an arbitration award under the guise of determining whether the award drew its "essence" from the contract. *See, e.g.,* Lewis B. Kaden, *Judges and Arbitrators: Observations on the Scope of Judicial Review,* 80 Colum. L. Rev. 267, 270–71, 274 (1980). On the other hand, there are cases in which courts vigorously resist requests by losing parties to reconsider the merits. *See Hill v. Norfolk & Western Railway Co.,* 814 F.2d 1192, 1194–95 (7th Cir. 1987).

Courts also refuse to enforce labor arbitration awards when they are contrary to public policy. In *United Paperworkers International Union, AFL–CIO v. Misco, Inc.,* 484 U.S. 29, 108 S.Ct. 364, 98 L.Ed.2d 286 (1987), the Supreme Court limited the public policy doctrine to situations where, "the contract as interpreted would violate 'some explicit public policy' that is 'well defined and dominant, and is to be ascertained' by reference to the law and legal precedents and not from general considerations of supposed public interest.' " *Id.* at 43. Lower courts don't always adhere to the Supreme Court's admonition not to rely on general considerations of public interest. *See, e.g., U.S. Postal Service v. National Ass'n of Letter Carriers,* 839 F.2d 146 (3d Cir. 1988). The federal courts disagree on the meaning of *Misco.* For example, the D.C. and Eleventh Circuits reached opposite conclusions in two cases that were indistinguishable on the facts. In *Northwest Airlines, Inc. v. Air Line Pilots Ass'n,* 808 F.2d 76 (D.C. Cir. 1987), an arbitration panel reinstated an airline pilot who had served as a co-pilot while intoxicated on condition that he regain FAA certification to fly, concluding that the award did not violate public policy as expressed in positive law. The court said that "[i]t would be the height of judicial chutzpa for us to second-guess the present judgment of the FAA recertifying Morrison for flight duty." *Id.* at 83. The Eleventh Circuit, on the other hand, held that enforcement of an award arising out of a similar situation would violate public policy. *Delta Air Lines, Inc. v. Air Line Pilots Ass'n,* 861 F.2d 665 (11th Cir. 1988). These two cases and others are analyzed in Arlus J. Stephens, Note, *The Sixth Circuit's Approach to the Public–Policy Exception to the Enforcement of Labor Arbitration Awards: A Tale of Two Trilogies?,* 11 Ohio St. J. on Disp. Resol. 441 (1996).

6.   In 2001, the U.S. Supreme Court again admonished the lower courts not to review arbitrator's decisions on the merits even when faced with

serious errors on the arbitrator's part. *Major League Baseball Players Assoc. v. Garvey*, 532 U.S. 504, 121 S.Ct. 1724, 149 L.Ed.2d 740 (2001). The following is from the per curium opinion for the Court:

> Judicial review of a labor-arbitration decision pursuant to such an agreement is very limited. Courts are not authorized to review the arbitrator's decision on the merits despite allegations that the decision rests on factual errors or misinterprets the parties' agreement. * * * We recently reiterated that if an " 'arbitrator is even arguably construing or applying the contract and acting within the scope of his authority,' the fact that 'a court is convinced he committed serious error does not suffice to overturn his decision.' " * * * (quoting *Misco, supra*, at 38, 108 S.Ct. 364). It is only when the arbitrator strays from interpretation and application of the agreement and effectively "dispense [s] his own brand of industrial justice" that his decision may be unenforceable. * * * When an arbitrator resolves disputes regarding the application of a contract, and no dishonesty is alleged, the arbitrator's "improvident, even silly, factfinding" does not provide a basis for a reviewing court to refuse to enforce the award. * * *

> In discussing the courts' limited role in reviewing the merits of arbitration awards, we have stated that "courts ... have no business weighing the merits of the grievance [or] considering whether there is equity in a particular claim." * * * When judiciary does so, "it usurps a function which ... is entrusted to the arbitration tribunal." ("It is the arbitrator's construction [of the agreement] which was bargained for....") Consistent with this role, we said in *Misco* that "[e]ven in the very rare instances when an arbitrator's procedural aberrations rise to the level of affirmative misconduct, as a rule the court must not foreclose further proceedings by settling the merits according to its own judgment of the appropriate result." * * * That step, we explained, "would improperly substitute a judicial determination for the arbitrator's decision that the parties bargained for" in their agreement. Instead, the court should "simply vacate the award, thus leaving open the possibility of further proceedings if they are permitted under the terms of the agreement."

> To be sure, the Court of Appeals here recited these principles, but its application of them is nothing short of baffling. The substance of the court's discussion reveals that it overturned the arbitrator's decision because it disagreed with the arbitrator's factual findings, particularly those with respect to credibility. The Court of Appeals, it appears, would have credited Smith's 1996 letter, and found the arbitrator's refusal to do so at worst "irrational" and best "bizarre." *Garvey I*, 203 F.3d, at 590–91. But even "serious error" on the arbitrator's part does not justify overturning his decision, where as here, he is construing a contract and acting within the scope of his authority.

Id. at 509–10.

7. David Feller, a former president of the National Academy of Arbitrators, has asserted that courts are more apt to set aside labor arbitration awards than commercial arbitration awards. DAVID E. FELLER, *Presidential Address, Proceedings of the 46th Annual Meeting*, NAT'L ACAD. OF ARBITRATORS

6–9 (1993). Although there are differences between labor and FAA arbitration, courts use concepts developed in one category in cases arising in the other. For example, the "essence" test, developed in labor arbitration cases, is used in commercial arbitration cases. *See, e.g., Michigan Mutual Insurance Co. v. Unigard Security Insurance Co.*, 44 F.3d 826, 830–32 (9th Cir. 1995); *Maxus, Inc. v. Sciacca*, 598 So.2d 1376, 1381 (Ala. 1992). Under the essence test, the arbitral award will be deemed within the scope of the arbitration agreement if it draws its essence from that agreement. The public policy rationale developed in *United Paperworkers International Union, AFL–CIO v. Misco, Inc.*, 484 U.S. 29, 108 S.Ct. 364, 98 L.Ed.2d 286 (1987), a labor arbitration case, was relied on in *PaineWebber, Inc. v. Agron*, 49 F.3d 347, 350 (8th Cir. 1995), a securities arbitration case. Ian R. Macneil, Richard E. Speidel & Thomas J. Stipanowich, Federal Arbitration Law § 40 (1994 ed. & Supp. 1999) urges caution in cross citing FAA and labor arbitration cases. "The purposes lying behind a number of LMRA § 301 principles respecting vacation are simply not applicable to the typical FAA arbitration." *Id.* at § 40.51. What about voluntariness? Are there justifications that would support mandatory arbitration in the labor context that would not be applicable in the commercial or consumer contexts?

8.   Arbitrators routinely award punitive damages even when the agreement of the parties does not expressly authorize them. Stephen J. Ware, Alternative Dispute Resolution 85 (2001). However, some courts, following New York's lead, have held that arbitrators can never award punitive damages. Some have held that arbitrators can award punitive damages only if they are specifically provided for in the parties' agreement. Others have held that arbitrators can award punitive damages unless they are explicitly excluded in the parties' agreement. See the discussion of case law in *Ratheon Co. v. Automated Business Systems, Inc.*, 882 F.2d 6, 11–12 (1st Cir.1989), and the discussion of policy issues in Thomas J. Stipanowich, *Punitive Damages in Arbitration:* Garrity v. Lyle Stuart, Inc. *Reconsidered*, 66 B.U. L. Rev. 953, 998–1010 (1986). Writing in 1994, Stephen J. Ware argued that the New York rule was preempted by the FAA. Steven J. Ware, *Punitive Damages in Arbitration: Contracting Out of Government's Role in Punishment and Federal Preemption of State Law*, 63 Fordham L. Rev. 529, 571 (1994). In *Mastrobuono v. Shearson Lehman Hutton, Inc.*, 514 U.S. 52, 115 S.Ct. 1212, 131 L.Ed.2d 76 (1995), the Supreme Court indicated that courts cannot use state law as a basis for refusing to enforce arbitral punitive damage awards unless the parties incorporate state arbitration law to this effect into their agreement. The Court said that, "in the absence of contractual intent to the contrary, the FAA would preempt the *Garrity* rule [the New York rule holding arbitrators cannot award punitive damages]." *Id.* at 59.

For a discussion of a proposal by the National Association of Securities Dealers to modify its arbitration rules to impose multiple caps on punitive damages by NASD arbitrators, see Thomas J. Stipanowich, *Punitive Damages and the Consumerization of Arbitration*, 92 Nw. U. L. Rev. 1 (1997).

Section 21 (C) of RUAA provides that if the arbitrator awards punitive damages, she shall "specify in the award that basis in fact justifying and the basis in law authorizing the award and state separately the amount of the punitive damages or other exemplary relief."

9. Do you agree that an arbitration award should receive less review than a decision of a lower court? Would a more expansive review "destroy the very thing the parties bargained for, namely, a non-judicial process"? Dan B. Dobbs, Handbook on the Law of Remedies 942 (1973). Would it result in greater delay and higher costs? See Jon O. Newman, *Rethinking Fairness: Perspectives on the Litigation Process*, 94 Yale L.J. 1643 (1985), in which a judge on the U.S. Court of Appeals for the Second Circuit argues that our litigation system has become slower and more expensive in part because of the elaborate lengths to which we go to avoid making a mistake in individual cases.

Compare the following from Jay R. Sever, *The Relaxation of Inarbitrability and Public Policy Checks on U.S. and Foreign Arbitration: Arbitration Out of Control?*, 65 Tul. L. Rev. 1661, 1696–97 (1991):

> Yet, limited judicial review may prove essential to the health and survival of both domestic and international arbitration. The most progressive arbitration statutes, such as France's statute of 1981, openly recognize this reality. There is no reason why the very threat of limited judicial review cannot benefit arbitration. As one commentator has noted:
>
>> The national court judge as 'guarantor of arbitral integrity' remains an indispensable factor in the international arbitration system. * * * Review of arbitral awards * * * involves an important psychological aspect. The constant threat of judicial review along clearly defined criteria leads arbitrators to pay due regard to the interests of the parties and factual and legal setting of the case, thus further contributing to more legality in arbitral proceedings.

10. Claim and issue preclusion are the two parts of res judicata law. They promote the policy of finality — putting an end to disputes. Claim preclusion prohibits relitigation of a claim or cause of action that was dealt with in a proceeding that produced a final judgment on the merits. Courts give claim preclusion effect to arbitration awards under appropriate circumstances. If they did not, parties could ignore demands to arbitrate and could relitigate when they lose in arbitration. Ian R. Macneil, Richard E. Speidel & Thomas J. Stipanowich, Federal Arbitration Law § 39.2.3 (1994 ed. & Supp. 1999).

Issue preclusion (collateral estoppel) prohibits relitigation of issues argued and decided in a prior proceeding. It is more difficult to determine when an arbitration award should be given an issue preclusion effect. Courts do give issue preclusion effect to arbitration awards at times, but the relative informality of arbitration proceedings and the fact that arbitrators don't always explain their awards make it more difficult to generalize about when it is appropriate to do so. Courts have considerable discretion and proceed case by case in deciding whether an award should have issue preclusion effect. *Id.* at § 39.3.1.2–1.5. Professor Motomura argues that "a better approach to arbitral collateral estoppel than the case-by-case method is a rule that arbitral findings never have collateral estoppel effect, unless the arbitration agreement clearly and expressly provides for it. Hiroshi Motomura, *Arbitration and Collateral Estoppel: Using Preclusion to Shape Procedural Choices*, 63 Tul. L. Rev. 29, 81 (1988). Compare Professor Motomura's views with G. Richard Shell, *Res Judicata and Collateral Estoppel Effects of Commercial Arbitration*, 35 UCLA L. Rev. 623, 673–74 (1988).

11.   In the excerpt that follows, Professor Edward Brunet discusses the relationship between arbitration and constitutional rights and suggests that parts of the FAA text quoted in note 2 above could be relied upon to expand the rights of parties in arbitration proceedings:

> The relationship between constitutional rights and arbitration is uneasy. Classical arbitration theory rejects the application of definite constitutional rights in an arbitration hearing. Such rights would needlessly judicialize what is supposed to be an informal process. Moreover, the parties have opted out of the formal, judicial process by contracting to arbitrate and have voluntarily removed any "state action" nexus which would mandate the application of constitutional rights.
>
> The classical view holds true when applied to parties who are experienced, repeat players in arbitration. Any argument of wholesale waiver of procedural rights, however, which applies to all arbitration fails to account for the explosive growth of arbitration. Arbitration has grown into areas such as consumer purchases or consumer loans where rookie signatories to arbitration clauses are unlikely to waive constitutional rights intentionally or intelligently. The doctrine of waiver of constitutional rights is, at this time, simply inadequate to explain the absence of constitutional rights in all arbitration settings.
>
> How can increased procedural protections find their way into both the arbitration hearing and judicial review of arbitration awards? The lack of a traditional basis of state action makes it improbable that courts will mandate the application of constitutional rights. A much more attractive legal ground is an historically accurate reading of the FAA which requires courts to protect "rights" of arbitral parties. The FAA's text provides a basis for vacating awards obtained by "undue means" and to safeguard "the rights" of parties to an arbitration. To date, courts have largely ignored these phrases, perhaps because of a general feeling that courts should avoid review of arbitral awards.

Edward Brunet, *Arbitration and Constitutional Rights*, 71 N.C. L. Rev. 81, 119 (1992).

Professor Reuben challenges the traditional distinction between public and private processes and asserts that contract-based arbitration under the FAA is state action. After discussing what he describes as "minimal but meaningful due process standards," Professor Reuben concludes that:

> Despite the arguments against its adoption, there is an air of inevitability about the recognition of state action in some seemingly private ADR processes, if not the embrace of a more fully developed unitary theory of public civil dispute resolution. The more court-related ADR expands, the more reasonable it is to expect questions to be raised in judicial forums over due process, the First Amendment, equal protection, and possibly other constitutional issues. The more those constitutional questions are raised in the court-related context, the greater the likelihood that courts will recognize that those processes are driven by state action and therefore compel at least rudimentary notions of due process as a

constitutional imperative. In time, the illogic of having different standards of fundamental fairness applicable in the court-related and contractual contexts — especially given that the same neutrals frequently serve in both spheres — may lead to the crumbling of that wall in practice if not in theory. At that point, the wall between the public and private dispute resolution systems will become imperceptibly thin, the elements of a unitary system of dispute resolution will begin to align, and the best promises of ADR will be well on their way to being finally fulfilled.

Richard C. Reuben, *Constitutional Gravity: A Unitary Theory of Alternative Dispute Resolution and Public Civil Justice*, 47 UCLA L. Rev. 949, 1104 (2000).

What would be the consequences of accepting the proposals of Brunet and Reuben?

12. The Drafting Committee of the RUAA considered whether the RUAA should explicitly sanction contractual provisions for "opt-in" review of challenged arbitration awards. The Prefatory Note to RUAA said that two types of opt-in provisions are in limited use today: (1) where parties can petition a designated state court to vacate an award for errors of law or fact; and (2) where an appellate arbitral mechanism is established to review for errors of law or fact. The Drafting Committee decided not to include an opt-in provision because of legal and policy concerns. The Committee pointed out that parties remain free to agree to contractual provisions for review of challenged awards within the constraints imposed by existing and developing law.

See Christopher R. Drahozal, *Contracting Around RUAA: Default Rules, Mandatory Rules, and Judicial Review of Arbitral Awards*, 3 Pepp. Disp. Res. L.J. 419, 427–29 (2003), for a suggestion that the RUAA created uncertainty regarding the enforceability of expanded review provisions.

13. One other question considered by the RUAA drafters was whether parties should be permitted to contract for greater judicial review of arbitration awards than those narrow grounds provided by the FAA or the UAA. At the time, several circuits, led by the Ninth Circuit, had endorsed the power of the parties to contract for substantive judicial review by the courts, while other circuits, led by the Seventh Circuit, refused to allow parties to contract for expanded judicial review. Compare *Lapine Technology Corp. v. Kyocera Corp.*, 130 F.3d 884 (9th Cir. 1997) with *Chicago Typographical Union No. 16 v. Chicago Sun–Times Inc.*, 935 F.2d 1501 (7th Cir. 1991). What problems do you see with such a proposal? Consider Judge Kozinski's concurring opinion in *Kyocera*, in which he said:

> The review to which the parties have agreed is no different from that performed by the district courts in appeals from administrative agencies and bankruptcy courts, or on habeas corpus. I would call the case differently if the agreement provided that the district judge would review the award by flipping a coin or studying the entrails of a dead fowl. Given the strong policy of party empowerment embodied in the Arbitration Act, I see no reason why Congress would object to enforcement of this agreement. This is not quite an express congressional

authorization but, given the Arbitration Act's policy, it's probably enough.

Kyocera, 130 F.3d at 390.

The drafters ultimately rejected the Ninth Circuit's position and did not provide for expanded judicial review in the RUAA. For a discussion of cases supporting and opposing contractual expansion of judicial review, see Lee Goldman, *Contractually Expanded Review of Arbitration Awards*, 8 Harv. Negot. L. Rev. 171, 194–79 (2003); *see also* Sarah Rudolph Cole, *Managerial Litigants: The Overlooked Problem of Party Autonomy in Dispute Resolution*, 51 Hastings L.J. 1199 (2000). The Ninth Circuit later reversed its position. *Kyocera v. Prudential–Bache Trade Services, Inc.*, 341 F.3d 987 (9th Cir. 2003) (en banc).

C. INTERNATIONAL COMMERCIAL ARBITRATION

Thus far we have been discussing arbitration in the domestic context, and even then primarily under the Federal Arbitration Act. However, arbitration is also widely used in the international commercial context, and, apart from negotiation, may be the most commonly used dispute resolution mechanism for settling private international disputes. While international commercial arbitration shares many of the same characteristics as domestic arbitration, there are also very significant differences.

Section 1 provides a general overview of the field, beginning with a comparison of international and domestic arbitration. The first two excerpts by W. Laurence Craig and Charles Brower, help explain the popularity of arbitration for resolving international commercial disputes, and introduce us to the key treaty affecting the area, the Convention on the Recognition and Enforcement of Foreign Arbitral Awards (the New York Convention). The article by Yves Dezalay and Bryant Garth describes the culture of international commercial arbitration, as well as the unique form of precedent known as the *lex mercatoria*.

Section 2 then discusses the legal framework of international commercial arbitration, focusing first on arbitrability, forum selection, and choice of law issues, and then concluding with discussion of enforceability and review of international commercial arbitration awards. As you work through these materials, consider how the similarities and differences between the domestic and international contexts would affect your decision to recommend arbitration to a client, and how it might affect your preparation for the arbitration.

1. OVERVIEW AND COMPARISON OF INTERNATIONAL AND DOMESTIC ARBITRATION

"[I]nternational arbitration is a consensual means of dispute resolution, by a non-governmental decision maker, that produces a legally binding and enforceable ruling." GARY BORN, INTERNATIONAL COMMERCIAL

ARBITRATION IN THE UNITED STATES 2 (1994). Although international arbitration is based on an agreement of the disputing parties, it works as well as it does because of national arbitration legislation, international conventions and treaties, several institutions, such as the International Chamber of Commerce (ICC), that administer international commercial arbitration proceedings, and a group of experienced advocates and arbitrators.

International arbitration is similar to domestic arbitration in many ways. Both are based on an agreement of the disputing parties, are normally conducted in private, and require the assistance of courts at times. Issues of arbitrability and judicial enforcement and review of awards arise in both kinds of arbitration. Both international and domestic arbitration have experienced explosive growth in recent years.

As noted earlier in this chapter, domestic arbitration is often sold on the basis of alleged speed, lower costs, and greater informality. That is hardly the case with respect to international arbitration. Indeed, the differences between international arbitration and other kinds of arbitration illustrate our point in Section D, infra, that each type of arbitration should be analyzed and evaluated in light of the context in which the process will be used. Although arbitration occurs between nations and between nations and private parties, the emphasis in this section is primarily on arbitration between private parties, where the great bulk of cases likely to confront lawyers arise.

The materials that follow illustrate differences between domestic and international arbitration, indicate why arbitration is the preferred method of dealing with international commercial disputes, and provide background on relevant sources of law and those who practice in this field.

W. LAURENCE CRAIG, SOME TRENDS AND DEVELOPMENTS IN THE LAWS AND PRACTICE OF INTERNATIONAL COMMERCIAL ARBITRATION

30 Tex. Int'l L.J. 1, 3–4, 6–7, 8–9, 10, 11, 57 (1995).

I. HISTORICAL MILESTONES

A. Normalcy of International Commercial Arbitration

* * *

[W]hile speed, informality, and economy have had some influence on the growth of international commercial arbitration, the essential driving force has been the desire of each party to avoid having its case determined in a foreign judicial forum. Parties seek to avoid these forums for fear that they will be at a disadvantage due to unfamiliarity with the jurisdiction's language and procedures, preferences of the judge, and possibly even national bias.

While the viewpoint outlined above may be stark and simplified, it seems likely that thoughts of this nature, if not necessarily of this degree, frequently motivate parties to choose international arbitration. Concerns about litigation in a foreign country are not limited to the result obtained in the court of first instance. There is the additional risk that a national court judgment will be subject to one or more layers of appellate review, causing further delay and uncertainty in the ultimate disposition of the matter. And even if a foreign court's decision is satisfactory, there is often doubt about whether the decision can be enforced in another country.

The absence of any multilateral convention for the recognition of foreign judgments, and the existence of very few bilateral treaties with such provisions, makes the arbitral solution not only attractive but compelling. This is due to the existence of an international mechanism for the enforcement of foreign arbitral awards. The Convention on the Recognition and Enforcement of Foreign Arbitral Awards (New York Convention), which entered into effect in 1958, has put into place a system which assures the recognition in member countries of arbitral awards rendered abroad and which excludes any judicial review of the merits of the arbitral award by the court where enforcement is sought. In the absence of any international court for the resolution of private international disputes, arbitration has provided the participants in international commerce with a decision-making process which, if not international in the legal sense, is a least internationalized, and which leads to an award which will ordinarily be enforceable internationally. It is for this reason that commercial arbitration is much more common in international dispute resolution than in domestic dispute resolution. Nicholas Katzenbach, former Attorney General of the United States and former General Counsel for IBM, commented on the importance of the private international dispute resolution system in dealing with the increase in world trade, investment, and finance, and the underlying technological developments which made multinational activities both inevitable and desirable:

> As national laws of contract, property, commercial paper developed and grew domestically to make a variety of types of promises enforceable in national courts in accordance with common commercial understanding, so too has it become essential to the same activities that promises and understandings on international or transnational scale be enforced in the same way. While we have experienced commercial arbitration in domestic trade for many years and this has been successful and helpful in a variety of ways, I suggest that arbitration in international commerce is really of a wholly different order of importance. Here to get effective and reasonably predictable and fair resolutions arbitration has become essential in a way it never has been in domestic matters. It is fair to say that arbitration in international commercial matters is today — and certainly should be — the norm, not the exception.

> ... While much can be said for arbitration in domestic transactions as an effective alternative to litigation, it is an alternative — a choice. Commercial promises can usually be effectively enforced in

national courts. But in international matters the risks of failure of effective enforcement are considerable and the existence of predictable commercial results far less.... [L]awyers and businessmen who are not experts in international transactions must acquire an understanding of the enormous advantages of arbitration in most circumstances.

* * *

B.   *Arbitration as a Self–Contained Process*

* * *

Especially in the case of arbitration under the auspices of a specialized arbitral institution between members of a close-knit trade or professional group, it is intended and confidently expected that the contractually chosen procedure will be definitive and will replace all recourse to courts. These arbitration proceedings are viewed by the parties as being an essentially independent process, and not the adjunct of any court system. Having agreed to participate in an arbitral process to resolve a dispute, the parties agree to carry out the resulting award, and to respect that award as final and binding between them. Indeed, where two parties have agreed to submit their dispute to a wise outsider for resolution, how can one of them later refuse to defer to the wisdom applied?

The same spirit which motivated the choice of arbitration by close-knit professional groups has also motivated its promotion by broader arbitration associations. In its early attempts to promote arbitration, the International Chamber of Commerce (ICC), which has become the foremost international arbitration association in the world, did not foresee the need to provide for judicial enforcement of awards. The ICC Arbitration Rules of 1923 provided only that the parties were "honor bound" to carry out the award of the arbitrators. It was expected that moral norms and "the force that businessmen of a country can bring to bear upon a recalcitrant neighbor" would be sufficient to ensure respect of arbitral awards.

While this view may seem somewhat quaint today, the success of international arbitration as a self-contained process should not be underestimated. The vast majority of disputes which go to arbitration are resolved without any judicial recourse whatsoever. This may be due to settlement negotiations during the course of the proceedings or by the rendition of an award and its satisfaction. The ICC estimates that more than 90% of its awards are satisfied voluntarily. Evidence is not available as to the voluntary settlement of awards in ad hoc arbitrations, but at least where these arbitration proceedings are specifically agreed to after the dispute arises — and hence where the parties have agreed to submit a defined dispute to a designated tribunal — it would stand to reason that voluntary respect of awards would be even greater than in the case of arbitration pursuant to a preexisting arbitration clause.

* * *

Conceptually, the desire to obtain an award enforceable by the courts — both nationally and internationally — lies at the heart of a conflict inherent in the arbitral process. Designed as a system of private justice, arbitration is a creation of contract, and parties may, through arbitration agreements, dispose of their right to sue in court to the same extent that they can, through other contracts, dispose of other legal rights. The contractual origin of arbitration proceedings allows for great flexibility. This flexibility is threatened, however, by the desire of the winning party to enlist the power of the state to compel compliance with the award. This requires recourse to the courts because only national courts have the power of the state to compel performance and execute against a party's assets. * * * The requirement of enforceability has both national and international consequences. During the early postwar period, the first priority of the international business community was to assure international recognition of agreements to arbitrate and of arbitral awards. On the international level this could be accomplished only by treaty.

* * *

The New York Convention was prepared and entered into force in 1959. Among the early parties to the Convention were France, Russia, Morocco, India, Israel, Egypt, Czechoslovakia, and the Federal Republic of Germany. The United States was a relative latecomer, ratifying the New York Convention only in 1970. As of April 1994, ninety-six states have ratified the New York Convention, making it the cornerstone upon which the value of international arbitral awards is based.

The New York Convention requires both the recognition of agreements to arbitrate and the recognition and enforcement of arbitral awards. The means for assuring recognition of arbitration agreements is the Convention's requirement that national litigation be stayed in favor of Convention arbitration and that the parties be referred to arbitration. This is spelled out in article II(3), which provides: "The court of a Contracting State, when seized of an action in a matter in respect of which the parties have made an agreement within the meaning of this article, shall, at the request of one of the parties, refer the parties to arbitration, unless it finds that the said agreement is null and void, inoperative or incapable of being performed."

* * *

The New York Convention was designed to give international currency to arbitral awards. Any award rendered and binding in a New York Convention country can, under the Convention, be enforced in any other New York Convention signatory. What the Convention did not do, however, was provide any international mechanism to insure the validity of the award where rendered. This was left to the provisions of local law.

The Convention provides no restraint whatsoever on the control functions of local courts at the seat of arbitration.

* * *

Concluding Points: Diversity or Convergence?

1. Despite all the developments in arbitration laws and practice, most international arbitrations will proceed as a self-contained process. The parties will conduct their proceedings according to rules that they have agreed to by contract. These actions will not be substantially impacted by the contents of national procedural law at the seat of arbitration or elsewhere. This will be particularly the case where the counsel who assisted in drafting the arbitration clause took care to choose as the seat of arbitration a jurisdiction whose arbitration law gives wide freedom to the parties, or to the arbitrators, to determine how arbitral proceedings shall be conducted. International arbitrations can in this respect be compared to an iceberg: Above the surface is a small visible mass representing those cases where arbitrations intersect with national courts through ancillary proceedings, judicial recourse, enforcement actions, and disputed issues of applicable procedural law. Below the surface is the great preponderance of cases which proceed in a self-contained private system of justice, as they were intended to do.

2. This very partial survey shows substantial convergence in modern arbitration laws with respect to the procedures to be followed in arbitration and the standards for judicial recourse therefrom. The common denominator is the specific recognition, by the law of the place of arbitration, of a wide degree of party autonomy to agree to rules of arbitral procedure. This degree of convergence may be explained by the fact that the laws have been designed to accommodate themselves to international arbitral practices, and not vice versa. These arbitral practices have been developed under both institutional rules, such as the ICC Rules, and noninstitutional rules, such as the UNCITRAL Rules, and have been designed to accommodate the specific needs of international business. This is not only true of the Model Law but also of a number of the recently modified arbitration laws in countries such as France, Switzerland, and the Netherlands.

3. One of the surprising effects of the legislative reform movement has been to reinforce the concept of the territorial application of arbitration law and the importance of the law of the seat of arbitration. The insistence on the application of the arbitration law of the place of arbitration has not, however, been deleterious to international arbitration, because the contents of the law have been designed to attract international arbitration, to be user-friendly, and to specifically empower the parties to contractually specify arbitral procedures.

* * *

CHARLES N. BROWER, THE GLOBAL COURT: THE INTERNATIONALIZATION OF COMMERCIAL ADJUDICATION AND ARBITRATION

26 U. Balt. L. Rev. 9, 11–12, 13 (1997).

* * *

Any arbitration necessarily is subject to the national law of the state in which it takes place. Statutes in major industrial jurisdictions have been modernized so as to minimize state intervention in the arbitral process itself, while offering judicial review to the extent necessary to ensure the integrity of the process by which the arbitral tribunal arrived at its award. To the same end UNCITRAL in 1985 fashioned a Model Law on International Commercial Arbitration designed to provide an "off the shelf" statute for adoption by less sophisticated jurisdictions and to encourage greater convergence, if not uniformity, on the part of others. It has been adopted, albeit with variations, in a considerable number of jurisdictions.

At the same time, the international community has adopted a series of conventions and treaties ensuring mutual and uniform enforcement of agreements to arbitrate, and also of the resulting awards, of which the New York Convention of 1958 is the most prominent. In 1965 the World Bank went so far as to establish, pursuant to convention, the International Centre for Settlement of Investment Disputes (ICSID), and with it, a completely self-contained regime for deciding investment disputes. So effective are these systems that today an international arbitral award is worth far more than a judgment of a national court abroad; the former is subject to comparatively automatic enforcement, whereas the latter must be made the subject of a plenary suit.

This three-tiered and essentially global system, consisting of private adjudication under agreed rules, supported by only the most limited national regulation necessary to ensure its integrity, and an international exercise of state power to the extent required to guarantee enforcement of the results, is based on the parties' reciprocal mistrust of state power. This mistrust takes a special form, however. It is not mistrust of state power per se; rather it is the lack of faith on the part of each party that the courts of the other party's state of nationality in fact will administer justice fairly and impartially. In short, neither party wishes to be judged in the other's "backyard." In addition, relative detachment of the process from state power facilitates a degree of internationalization, and consequent uniformity, which has its own merits for international commerce, but which otherwise would be unattainable.

This trend goes much deeper, however, than the adjudicatory process itself; it goes also to the heart of the matter, the applicable substantive law. Just as trading partners who are foreign to each other eschew each other's courts, so, too, do they prefer not to be judged by each other's national legal norms. This concern is highest, of course, where one of the parties is itself a state or a peristaltic enterprise. In such circumstances the parties, with increasing frequency, will concoct for themselves a jurisprudential corpus that either is divorced from any national system of law or combines a relevant national legal system with another body of law to supplement or modify it and which any national court system would have considerable difficulty to apply. For example, under the 1955 Libyan Petroleum Law, the law applicable to oil concession agreements in that country (some of which still are in effect), it is provided that the applicable law is "the law[] of Libya and such rules and principles of international law as may be relevant but only to the extent that such rules and principles are not inconsistent with and do not conflict with the laws of Libya."

* * *

The fact that this "global court" works, and works well, is proven by its consistent triumph over adversity. Numerous arbitrations against foreign parties, including pariah governments such as, in recent years, Libya, have proceeded to a conclusion, with payment being achieved, notwithstanding the most determined efforts of some defendants to disrupt, or even to abort, the proceedings. Tactics to this end have included failure to appoint an arbitrator, or appointment of a patently biased arbitrator; refusal to appear, or alternating sporadic appearances with demonstrative "walkouts" and other intentional absences; unwarranted objections to jurisdiction; unjustified challenges to the service of particular arbitrators, or even attempts to intimidate them; and all manner of lesser forms of abuse of the process. In one famous case at the Iran–United States Claims Tribunal two Iranian judges even assaulted an elderly Swedish colleague. In the end, none of these tactics succeeds, however, because all modern sets of arbitral rules provide the means for demolishing or overlooking such obstacles and are backed, as noted a moment ago, by indispensable attachment to state power.

* * *

Notes and Questions

1. Stephen R. Bond wrote in the ICC International Court of Arbitration Bulletin that, "The parties appear to desire a resolution based on a specified, predictable legal system." Christopher R. Drahozal, Commercial Arbitration: Cases and Problems 609 (2002). Charles Brower and Laurence Craig, practitioners in the field of international arbitration, give several reasons why parties prefer international arbitration. "Neither party wishes to be judged in the other's backyard." Brower, *supra* at page 11. They also mentioned a desire for uniformity and doubts about the enforcement of judgments by courts from other countries. Nicholas Katzenback, quoted in Craig, *supra* at page 4, said, "to get effective and reasonably predictable and fair resolutions arbitration has become essential in a way it never has been in domestic matters." Ian MacNeil and his co-authors point out other reasons: international arbitration allows parties to select a location for

arbitration most beneficial to the parties; the international arbitration establishment is used to handling problems arising from differing languages; and arbitration provides a way to avoid problems created by judges unfamiliar with the applicable law by selecting arbitrators who are experts in the applicable law. IAN R. MACNEIL, RICHARD E. SPEIDEL & THOMAS J. STIPANOWICH, FEDERAL ARBITRATION LAW § 44.3 (1994 ed. & Supp. 1999).

2. Why is enforcement of international arbitration awards generally more effective than enforcement of judgments of courts from various countries? *See* Christine Tecuyer–Thieffry & Patrick Thieffry, *Negotiating Settlement of Disputes Provisions in International Business Contracts: Recent Developments in Arbitration and Other Processes*, 45 Bus. Law. 577, 585–88 (1990); W. Lawrence Craig, *Some Trends and Developments in the Laws and Practice of International Commercial Arbitration*, 30 Tex. Int'l L.J. 1 (1995).

YVES DEZALAY & BRYANT GARTH, FUSSING ABOUT THE FORUM: CATEGORIES AND DEFINITIONS AS STAKES IN A PROFESSIONAL COMPETITION

21 Law & Soc. Inquiry 285, 295–99 (1996).

In the past 20 years, "international commercial arbitration" has shifted from an informal, compromise-oriented justice dominated by European academics to a U.S.-style, formalized, "offshore litigation." Despite dramatic practical changes, it is still called "international commercial arbitration," and the major institutions still have the same identities. The specific term of arbitration and some of the most general characteristics are, after all, passed on through the activities of individual carriers and through the activities of the institutions long identified with arbitration. Scholarly accounts of international commercial arbitration, furthermore, reinforce the story of continuity by counting cases and discussing growth as if the process has essentially remained the same. It is clear, however, that what is now generally understood by the term is significantly different.

International commercial arbitration's recent history began with the activities after World War II of a small group of gentlemen idealists — mainly Continental legal academics schooled in international law — connected with the International Chamber of Commerce in Paris. These idealists cultivated good relations with the business world and promoted the distinctiveness of international commercial arbitration as an alternative to national litigation. Through academic writing, conferences, and activity that promoted the virtues of arbitration, they gained credibility for arbitration as a means to resolve transnational business disputes. They promoted arbitration as relatively inexpensive, informal, and capable of meeting the needs of businesses increasing their international activities and investing in third world countries. They developed an elegant academic legal doctrine, which they termed the new *lex mercatoria,* and they also sought to make their decisions conform to the particular needs of business. One need they met was the business desire to avoid giving state enterprises advantages over private parties. The *lex mercatoria* governed all such business relations by the private norms of contract.

The promoters of the *lex mercatoria* also emphasized the importance of using arbitration as a way to bring the parties to an acceptable solution consistent with general business expectations. The success of these academic mediators reveals the advantage of a portfolio combining high status and academic sophistication. The formulators of the *lex mercatoria* could play a rather successful double game in dispute resolution. As academic authors of the rules of the game applicable substantively, they would also be the best ones to decide when the rules did and did not apply. Accordingly, they could shape their rulings to particular situations without losing the claim of universalism for the *lex mercatoria*. The success at finding tailored solutions was such that commentators active in international arbitration could emphasize that, in contrast to litigation, arbitration could help parties preserve a long-term contractual or other business relationship. Tailored settlements and the *lex mercatoria* coexisted perfectly.

There were not many arbitrations, however, even though the pioneers did succeed in promoting the idea and placing arbitration clauses in many contracts. They developed a niche, but no one could have predicted that business disputes that invoked these clauses would suddenly proliferate and open up this very small market. External factors helped bolster the demand.

The large construction and infrastructure projects that took place after the increase in the price of oil in the early 1970s can be seen as a key catalyst for change. The projects gave rise to numerous disputes and — because of the success of the pioneers in promoting arbitration clauses — many more international commercial arbitrations. New entrants sought to gain a foothold in the growing arbitration market, and they began to compete with the senior generation of gentlemen arbitrators. The terms of the competition, however, reflected the particular kind of market that existed and the way that arbitration had been defined by the gentlemen scholars.

Those pioneer idealists, who still possessed considerable power in the arbitral institutions and in the recommending of arbitrators, had succeeded in defining the terms of entry into the field of arbitration so that entry was virtually barred to individuals who did not purport to promote the long term interests of arbitration as a dispute resolution device for international conflicts. Under these rules, for example, it was difficult for self-promoters to gain the credibility to advance as arbitrators or lawyers in arbitration. There was no explicit advertising, and it would not have helped to gain entry into this cartelized community — sometimes termed a club or even a mafia.

The competition was therefore expressed in terms of what would best make arbitration legitimate and acceptable to businesses and to other potential constituencies. It was a competition in ideas organized around theoretical and scholarly debates about what international commercial arbitration must be in order to retain its legitimacy. The ideas were also closely related to the individuals seeking dominance in the business. Theorists and practitioners — quite often the same people — debated in academic terms that also reflected their own positions in arbitration.

Competitors thus sought to define international commercial arbitration — and the leading institutions, especially the ICC — in terms that privileged their own skills and attributes. The senior generation defended the status quo of informal, compromise-oriented arbitration close to business and the *lex mercatoria,* insisting that only very experienced and scholarly individuals, selected on the basis of their excellent legal careers, had the stature and judgment to resolve such cases. A younger generation criticized the vagueness and uncertainty of the *lex mercatoria* on scholarly grounds and emphasized the vital importance of technical sophistication about arbitration. The technocrats argued that arbitration could only be successful and legitimate if practiced in a more legalized fashion. Common law lawyers bolstered the technocrats by adding their criticisms of the vagueness of the academic *lex mercatoria* that was supposedly being applied by the Continental academics, and they hinted strongly that the English commercial court was a better forum for commercial disputes. Continental academics, in turn, emphasized the importance of arbitration detached from any national laws and legal systems.

Most significantly, however, American litigators — whose domestic power was just becoming established — insisted in this domain that the arbitrators needed to pay more attention to the facts, indulge more motions and adversarial behavior in the interests of their clients, and in general allow the litigators to employ their legal weaponry as if they were arguing in a U.S. court. They promoted the idea that arbitration could serve legitimately for international business transactions only if it became a courtlike substitute for national (meaning, to them, U.S.) courts.

Each group, in short, competed with theory and practice on behalf of the characteristics that its members had to offer to resolve international business disputes. The already-established prominence of international commercial arbitration led them to play within the rules of the arbitration field rather than to challenge it directly with some newly minted and defined process. They promoted their visions and theories of arbitration as what arbitration was and was supposed to be — in particular, offshore litigation on the side of one major group, a compromise-oriented academic affair on the other.

As it turned out, an alliance between the U.S. litigators and the technocrats gained the upper hand, although the other groups remain far from absent, and the competition continues. The champions of formalism succeeded in part because they promoted a kind of arbitration that could process more cases than could be handled by the charisma of the grand old men. They also succeeded because they were allied with the U.S. litigators empowered both by the resources of the large law firms and the powerful clients who employed those firms.

International commercial arbitration therefore became something very different from what it had been in the 1950s and 1960s. The center of power shifted from the small group of Continental academics to the U.S. law firms and their allies. Despite this important shift, however, it is important also to recognize the continuity. The International Chamber of Commerce remained the central institution, even though redefined by battles fought from within the institution. The practice of appointing private individuals to serve as "arbitrators" charged with deciding the cases also continued, but "international commercial arbitration" undeniably changed fundamentally from 1970 to 1990.

During this period of intense competition, furthermore, there was also cooperation. All the players in this field — and those who wanted to be taken seriously in the field — continued in their writing and activities to promote "international commercial arbitration" as the preferred method for resolving transnational business disputes. They adhered to the rules of the game while they fought to modify the rules to favor the position or positions that they occupied. Indeed, outsiders impressed by the public shows of unanimity about international commercial arbitration might believe that the members of the club were united around a stable set of practices.

On the contrary, practices were not stable, and as the practice of arbitration changed, so finally even the accepted definition of arbitration changed so as to define an almost entirely different process. The terminology — now reified in many scholarly publications and definitions — reflected the change in practice and in the balance of power. We now tend to accept the fact that international commercial arbitration is simply a quasi-judicial form of dispute resolution that substitutes for national courts but not court-like processes. The point, to repeat, is that we should not accept the latest scholarly representation as the essence of arbitration — as if such a thing existed in the abstract. The definition is but the linguistic evidence of the power of the promoters of that particular representation of international commercial arbitration. They played within the rules — established by the pioneers who built up the modern institutions — until they succeeded in redefining the game and the key institutions.

The legitimacy of international commercial arbitration is no longer built on the fact that arbitration is informal and close to the needs of business; rather legitimacy now comes more from a recognition that arbitration is *formal* and close to the kind of resolution that would be produced through litigation — more precisely, through the negotiation that takes place in the context of U.S.-style litigation. Litigators, in other words, maintained the name of international commercial arbitration, but they appropriated it as a place for the practice of large commercial litigation.

Notes and Questions

1. Dezalay and Garth suggest that processes such as arbitration do not have a fixed content. They believe that the process is changed as parties try to change rules and practices to help them compete for business. They view the increased formalism of international arbitration as one indication of the success of U.S. litigators in persuading affected parties that arbitration should become more like national courts (especially U.S. courts).

2. Is there an analogous situation with respect to the way mediation is conducted? See John Lande, *How Will Lawyering and Mediation Practices Transform Each Other?*, 24 Fla. St. U. L. Rev. 839, 849–54 (1997).

2. LEGAL FRAMEWORK

a. Arbitrability, Forum Selection, and Choice of Law

ROBY v. CORPORATION OF LLOYD'S

United States Court of Appeals, Second Circuit, 1993.
996 F.2d 1353.

MESKILL, Chief Judge:

[A group of American citizen or residents (referred to as "Roby Names" in the Court's opinion) sued the corporation of Lloyds (Loyds) in a United States District Court, alleging that they had suffered severe financial loss as a result of violations by Loyds and Lloyds entities of the 1933 Securities Act, the 1934 Securities Exchange Act, and the Racketeer Influenced and Corrupt Organizations Act. The Roby Names argued that their claim should be litigated in the United States in spite of contract clauses that provided for arbitration in England under English law. Syndicates, compete within Loyds for insurance underwriting business. The plaintiffs Roby Names were solicited in the United States by various Lloyds entities and representatives. Eighty percent of Lloyds 26,000 Names are English; about 2,500 Names are American. Roby Names selected from a list of syndicates and decided how much to invest in each one. Names earn profits in proportion to their capital contributions and bear unlimited liability for their proportionate losses in each syndicate they join.

The District Court dismissed the Roby Names complaint and its judgment and order was affirmed on appeal.]

* * *

Discussion

The Roby Names present us with two basic arguments as to why these suits should be litigated in the United States: (1) the contract clauses, by their terms, apply neither to the substance of their claims nor to certain defendants; and (2) the clauses are unenforceable due to the public policy codified in the securities laws. We find neither of these arguments persuasive.

* * *

Paragraph 2.2 of the General Undertaking states, in pertinent part:

Each party hereto irrevocably agrees that the courts of England shall have exclusive jurisdiction to settle any dispute and/or controversy of whatsoever nature arising out of or relating to the [Name's] membership of, and/or underwriting of insurance business at, Lloyd's.

Paragraph 2.1 is equally broad and provides for the application of English law. The syndicates are third-party beneficiaries of this agreement.

* * *

Disputes Covered

"[A] party cannot be required to submit to arbitration any dispute which he has not agreed so to submit." The Roby Names contend essentially that the forum selection and arbitration clauses apply only to disputes arising from the conduct of the defendants as managers, representatives or regulators. Because this conduct can occur only *after* the "securities" have been sold, the Roby Names claim that they did not agree to arbitration of, or English jurisdiction over, complaints pertaining to the sale of those "securities." They present two basic arguments: (1) because the choice of law clauses require the application of English law, the Roby Names' United States statutory claims cannot possibly be covered under the agreements, and (2) resolution of their claims does not require the construction of the agreements because the Roby Names have not alleged any breach of contract, and the language of the arbitration and forum selection clauses is not broad enough to cover their claims. We reject both arguments.

1. *Application of English Law*

It defies reason to suggest that a plaintiff may circumvent forum selection and arbitration clauses merely by stating claims under laws not recognized by the forum selected in the agreement. A plaintiff simply would have to allege violations of *his country's* tort law or *his country's* statutory law or *his country's* property law in order to render nugatory any forum selection clause that implicitly or explicitly required the application of the law of another jurisdiction. We refuse to allow a party's solemn promise to be defeated by artful pleading. In the absence of other considerations, the agreement to submit to arbitration or the jurisdiction of the English courts must be enforced even if that agreement tacitly includes the forfeiture of some claims that could have been brought in a different forum.

2. *Scope of the Agreements*

Of course, the Roby Names are quite right that if the *substance* of their claims, stripped of their labels, does not fall within the scope of the clauses, the clauses cannot apply. However, they must make this argument in the face of strong public policy in favor of forum selection and arbitration clauses. Indeed, an order to arbitrate "should not be denied unless it may be said with positive assurance that the arbitration clause is not susceptible of an interpretation that covers the asserted dispute."

There is ample precedent that the scope of clauses similar to those at issue here is not restricted to pure breaches of the contracts containing the clauses. * * *

In the instant case the conduct surrounding the underwriting activities at Lloyd's is integrally related to the sale of Lloyd's "securities" because the "security" is essentially equivalent to the underwriting of risk or the pledging of capital. * * *

It is perhaps even more persuasive that the agreements are in fact not limited to the conduct of business but also cover the raising of capital. * * *

Similarly, and even more forcefully, the broad language of the forum selection clause of the General Undertaking covers the Roby Names' claims at least against Lloyd's' governing bodies. Those claims are undoubtedly related to the Roby Names' "membership of, and/or underwriting of insurance business at, Lloyd's."

Application of the Securities Laws

The Roby Names argue that the public policy codified in the antiwaiver provisions of the securities laws renders unenforceable any agreement that effectively eliminates compliance with those laws. The Securities Act provides that "[a]ny ... stipulation ... binding any person acquiring any security to waive compliance with any provision of this subchapter ... shall be void." Similarly, the Securities Exchange Act states, "[a]ny ... stipulation ... binding any person to waive compliance with any provision of this chapter or of any rule or regulation thereunder ... shall be void." According to the undisputed testimony of a British attorney, neither an English court nor an English arbitrator would apply the United States securities laws, because English conflict of law rules do not permit recognition of foreign tort or statutory law. From this, the Roby Names conclude that the contract clauses work to waive compliance with the securities laws and therefore are void.

We note at the outset that *Wilko v. Swan* held that an agreement to arbitrate future controversies was void under the antiwaiver provision of the Securities Act. We do not doubt that judicial hostility to arbitration has receded dramatically since 1953 and that the arbitral forum is perfectly competent to protect litigants' substantive rights. In the words of the *Mitsubishi* Court, quoted by both the *Rodriguez* and *McMahon* Courts, "[b]y agreeing to arbitrate a statutory claim, a party does not forgo the substantive rights afforded by the statute; it only submits to their resolution in an arbitral, rather than a judicial, forum." 473 U.S. at

628, 105 S.Ct. at 3354. If the Roby Names objected merely to the choice of an arbitral rather than a judicial forum, we would reject their claim immediately, citing *Rodriguez* and *McMahon*. However, the Roby Names argue that they have been forced to forgo the *substantive* protections afforded by the securities laws, not simply the judicial forum. We therefore do not believe that *Rodriguez* and *McMahon* are controlling and must look elsewhere to determine whether parties may contract away their substantive rights under the securities laws.

The Tenth Circuit recently addressed this exact issue in a similar context in *Riley v. Kingsley Underwriting Agencies, Ltd.*, 969 F.2d 953 (10th Cir.). Relying primarily on four Supreme Court precedents, the *Riley* Court concluded that "[w]hen an agreement is truly international, as here, and reflects numerous contacts with the foreign forum, the Supreme Court has quite clearly held that the parties' choice of law and forum selection provisions will be given effect." While we agree with the ultimate result in *Riley*, we are reluctant to interpret the Supreme Court's precedent quite so broadly.

A. *Presumption of Validity*

The Supreme Court certainly has indicated that forum selection and choice of law clauses are presumptively valid where the underlying transaction is fundamentally international in character. In *The Bremen*, the Court explained that American parochialism would hinder the expansion of American business and trade, and more generally, interfere with the smooth functioning and growth of global commerce. Forum selection and choice of law clauses eliminate uncertainty in international commerce and insure that the parties are not unexpectedly subjected to hostile forums and laws. Moreover, international comity dictates that American courts enforce these sorts of clauses out of respect for the integrity and competence of foreign tribunals. In addition to these rationales for the presumptive validity of forum selection and choice of law clauses, the Court has noted that contracts entered into freely generally should be enforced because the financial effect of forum selection and choice of law clauses likely will be reflected in the value of the contract as a whole.

This presumption of validity may be overcome, however, by a clear showing that the clauses are " 'unreasonable' under the circumstances." The Supreme Court has construed this exception narrowly: forum selection and choice of law clauses are "unreasonable" (1) if their incorporation into the agreement was the result of fraud or overreaching; (2) if the complaining party "will for all practical purposes be deprived of his day in court," due to the grave inconvenience or unfairness of the selected forum; (3) if the fundamental unfairness of the chosen law may deprive the plaintiff of a remedy; or (4) if the clauses contravene a strong public policy of the forum state.

In this case, we can easily dispose of the first two factors. The Roby Names do not contend that they were fraudulently induced into agreeing to the forum selection, choice of law or arbitration clauses. Nor do we believe it gravely inconvenient for the Roby Names to litigate in London; they found it convenient enough to travel there for their mandatory interviews, and, in any event, many of them presently are prosecuting actions there. Moreover, nothing in the record suggests that the English courts would be biased or otherwise unfair, and United States courts consistently have found them to be neutral and just forums. Finally, the Roby Names have not presented any convincing evidence that the chosen arbitral forum would be biased in any way.

As to the third factor, we note that it is not enough that the foreign law or procedure merely be different or less favorable than that of the United States. Instead, the question is whether the application of the foreign law presents a danger that the Roby Names "will be deprived of *any* remedy or treated unfairly." As we explain below in section C, we believe the Roby Names have ample remedies under English law.

B. *Public Policy*

We depart somewhat from the *Riley* Court with respect to the fourth factor. We believe that there is a serious question whether United States public policy has been subverted by the Lloyd's clauses. In this section we explain our concerns; in section C below we resolve those concerns. Ultimately, we hold that the presumption of validity has not been overcome.

The Supreme Court in *The Bremen* wrote, "[a] contractual choice-of-forum clause should be held unenforceable if enforcement would contravene a strong public policy of the forum in which suit is brought." By including antiwaiver provisions in the securities laws, Congress made clear its intention that the public policies incorporated into those laws should not be thwarted.

The framers of the securities laws were concerned principally with reversing the common law rule favoring "caveat emptor." To this end, the securities laws are aimed at prospectively protecting American investors from injury by demanding "full and fair disclosure" from issuers. Private actions exist under the securities laws not because Congress had an overwhelming desire to shift losses after the fact, but rather because private actions provide a potent means of deterring the exploitation of American investors. We believe therefore that the public policies of the securities laws would be contravened if the applicable foreign law failed adequately to deter issuers from exploiting American investors.

* * *

We are concerned in the present case that the Roby Names' contract clauses may operate "in tandem" as a prospective waiver of the statutory remedies for securities violations, thereby circumventing the strong and expansive public policy in deterring such violations. We are cognizant of the important reasons for enforcing such clauses in Lloyd's' agreements. Lloyd's is a British concern which raises capital in over 80 nations. Its operations are clearly international in scope. There can be no doubt that the contract clauses mitigate the uncertainty regarding choice of law and forum inherent in the multinational affairs of Lloyd's. Comity also weighs in favor of enforcing the clauses. Yet we do not believe that a United States court can in good conscience enforce clauses that subvert a strong national policy, particularly one that for over fifty years has served as the foundation for the United States financial markets and business community. In this case, the victims of Lloyd's' alleged securities violations are hundreds of individual American investors, most of whom were actively solicited in the United States by Lloyd's representatives. We believe that if the Roby Names were able to show that available remedies in England are insufficient to deter British issuers from exploiting American investors through fraud, misrepresentation or inadequate disclosure, we would not hesitate to condemn the choice of law, forum selection and arbitration clauses as against public policy. For the reasons set forth in section C below, however, we conclude that the Roby Names have failed to make such a showing.

C. *Availability of Adequate Remedies*

We are satisfied not only that the Roby Names have several adequate remedies in England to vindicate their substantive rights, but also that in *this* case the policies of ensuring full and fair disclosure and deterring the exploitation of United States investors have not been subverted. We address the fraud and misrepresentation claims first.

1. *Fraud and Misrepresentation*

English common law provides remedies for knowing or reckless deceit, negligent misrepresentation, and even innocent misrepresentation. Moreover, the Misrepresentation Act of 1967 provides some additional statutory remedies. *Id.* * * *

In any event, the available remedies are adequate and the potential recoveries substantial. This is particularly true given the low scienter requirements under English misrepresentation law (*e.g.,* negligence, "innocence"). Moreover, together with the contractual obligations imposing certain fiduciary and similar duties on Members' and Managing Agents, we believe that the available remedies and potential damages recoveries suffice to deter deception of American investors.

* * *

Moreover, even the Corporation of Lloyd's is not exempt for acts "done in bad faith." Furthermore, as a self-regulating organization, we cannot say that Lloyd's' own bylaws will not insure the honesty and forthrightness that American investors deserve and expect. We conclude that the Roby Names have adequate remedies in England to vindicate their statutory fraud and misrepresentation claims.

2. *Disclosure*

We turn now to address whether adequate remedies are available to deter issuers from issuing securities without disclosing sufficient information to permit investors to make informed decisions. We believe that this policy concern is somewhat diluted in this case because the SEC consistently has exempted Lloyd's from the registration requirements of the securities laws. Apparently the SEC has decided that Lloyd's' means test meets the requirements of Regulation D. We are extremely reluctant to dispute the SEC's apparent judgment that the Roby Names are sophisticated enough that they do not need the disclosure protections of the securities laws.

* * *

While we do not doubt that the United States securities laws would provide the Roby Names with a greater variety of defendants and a greater chance of success due to lighter scienter and causation requirements, we are convinced that there are ample and just remedies under English law. Moreover, we cannot say that the policies underlying our securities laws will be offended by the application of English law. In this case, the Roby Names have entered into contracts that require substantial disclosure by both the Members' and Managing Agents. The specter of liability for breach of contract should act as an adequate deterrent to the exploitation of American investors. The well developed English law of fraud and misrepresentation likewise adequately requires that the disclosure be "fair."

* * *

CONCLUSION

For the foregoing reasons we hold that the Roby Names' contract clauses cover the scope of, and the parties named in, the complaint and that the Roby Names have remedies under English law adequate not only to vindicate their substantive rights but also to protect the public policies established by the United States securities laws.

The judgment and order of the district court are affirmed.

Notes and Questions

1. In *Mitsubishi Motors Corp. v. Soler Chrysler–Plymouth*, 473 U.S. 614, 105 S.Ct. 3346, 87 L.Ed.2d 444 (1985), the U.S. Supreme Court said that the liberal federal policy favoring arbitration applied with special force in international commerce. "Concerns of international comity, respect for the capacities of foreign and transnational tribunals, and sensitivity to the need of the international commercial system for predictability in the resolution of disputes, all require enforcement of the arbitration clause in question, even assuming a contrary result would be forthcoming in a domestic context." *Id*. at 629. Do you agree?

2. Why was it important for Lloyds' to provide for the arbitration of disputes in England with English law governing the disputes?

The International Chamber of Commerce recommends that parties stipulate in the arbitration clause the law governing the contract, the location of the arbitration, and the language of the hearing. COMMERCIAL ARBITRATION AT ITS BEST: SUCCESSFUL STRATEGIES FOR BUSINESS USES 331 (STIPANOWICH AND KASKELL EDS, CPR INST. DISP. RES. AND ABA SECTIONS OF BUSINESS LAW AND DISPUTE RESOLUTION) (2001).

3.   See CHARLES S. BALDWIN IV, RONALD A. BRAND, DAVID EPSTEIN, & MICHAEL WALLACE GORDON, INTERNATIONAL CIVIL DISPUTE RESOLUTION 627 (2004) for a list of issues to consider in drafting an arbitration provision for an international business contract. IAN R. MACNEIL, RICHARD E. SPEIDEL & THOMAS J. STIPANOWICH, FEDERAL ARBITRATION LAW § 44.7 (1994 ed. & Supp. 1999) also discusses issues to consider and cite to numerous articles and treatises that would be helpful in drafting such an arbitration provision.

b.   Enforcement and Review of Awards

Section 13 of the Federal Arbitration Act permits federal courts to enforce valid arbitration awards, and to review them for arbitral misconduct and ultra vires acts. As we know from the readings in the preceding section, however, international commercial arbitration is not supported by a unified judicial system. The following readings explore the problems created by the interplay between international treaties and the domestic law of a particular nation with respect to enforcement and review of international commercial arbitration awards.

YUSUF AHMED ALGHANIM & SONS v. TOYS "R" US, INC.

United States Court of Appeals, Second Circuit, 1997.
126 F.3d 15.

MINER, Circuit Judge.

Appeal from a judgment entered in the United States District Court for the Southern District of New York (McKenna, J.) denying respondents' cross-motion to vacate or modify an arbitration award and granting the petition to confirm the award. The court found that while the petition for confirmation was brought under the Convention on the Recognition and Enforcement of Foreign Arbitral Awards, respondents' cross-motion to vacate or modify the award was properly brought under the Federal Arbitration Act, and thus those claims were governed by the Federal Arbitration Act's implied grounds for vacatur. Nonetheless, the court granted the petition to confirm the award, finding that respondents' allegations of error in the arbitral award were without merit.

For the reasons that follow, we affirm.

BACKGROUND

In November of 1982, respondent-appellant Toys "R" Us, Inc. (collectively with respondent-appellant TRU (HK) Limited, "Toys 'R' Us") and petitioner-appellee Yusuf Ahmed Alghanim & Sons, W.L.L. ("Alghanim"), a privately owned Kuwaiti business, entered into a License and Technical Assistance Agreement (the "agreement") and a Supply Agreement. Through the agreement, Toys "R" Us granted Alghanim a limited right to open Toys "R" Us stores and use its trademarks in Kuwait and 13 other countries located in and around the Middle East (the "territory"). Toys "R" Us further agreed to supply Alghanim with its technology, expertise and assistance in the toy business.

From 1982 to the December 1993 commencement of the arbitration giving rise to this appeal, Alghanim opened four toy stores, all in Kuwait. According to Toys "R" Us, the first such store, opened in 1983, resembled a Toys "R" Us store in the United States, but the other three, two of which were opened in 1985 and one in 1988, were small storefronts with only limited merchandise. It is uncontested that Alghanim's stores lost some $6.65 million over the 11–year period from 1982 to 1993, and turned a profit only in one year of this period.

* * *

On July 20, 1992, Toys "R" Us purported to exercise its right to terminate the agreement, sending Alghanim a notice of non-renewal stating that the agreement would terminate on January 31, 1993. Alghanim responded on July 30, 1992, stating that because its most recently opened toy store had opened on January 16, 1988, the initial term of the agreement ended on January 16, 1993. Alghanim asserted that Toys "R" Us's notice of non-renewal was four days late in providing notice six months before the end of the initial period. According to Alghanim, under the termination provision of the agreement, Toys "R" Us's failure to provide notice more than six months before the fifth year after the opening of the most recent store automatically extended the term of the agreement for an additional two years, until January 16, 1995.

On September 2, 1992, Toys "R" Us sent a second letter. Toys "R" Us explained that, on further inspection of the agreement, it had determined that the initial term of the agreement expired on December 31, 1993, and it again gave notice of non-renewal. In this letter, Toys "R" Us also directed Alghanim not to open any new toy stores and warned that failure to comply with that direction could constitute a breach of the agreement.

* * *

On December 20, 1993, Toys "R" Us invoked the dispute-resolution mechanism in the agreement, initiating an arbitration before the American Arbitration Association. Toys "R" Us sought a declaration that the agreement was terminated on December 31, 1993. Alghanim responded by counterclaiming for breach of contract.

On May 4, 1994, the arbitrator denied Toys "R" Us's request for declaratory judgment. The arbitrator found that, under the termination provisions of the agreement, Alghanim had the absolute right to open toy stores, even after being given notice of termination, as long as the last toy store was opened within five years. The parties then engaged in substantial document and expert discovery, motion practice, and a 29–day evidentiary hearing on Alghanim's counterclaims.On July 11, 1996, the arbitrator awarded Alghanim $46.44 million for lost profits under the agreement, plus 9 percent interest to accrue from December 31, 1994. The arbitrator's findings and legal conclusions were set forth in a 47–page opinion.

Alghanim petitioned the district court to confirm the award under the Convention on the Recognition and Enforcement of Foreign Arbitral Awards of June 10, 1958 ("Convention"). Toys "R" Us cross-moved to vacate or modify the award under the Federal Arbitration Act ("FAA"), arguing that the award was clearly irrational, in manifest disregard of the law, and in manifest disregard of the terms of the agreement. The district court concluded that "[t]he Convention and the FAA afford overlapping coverage, and the fact that a petition to confirm is brought under the Convention does not foreclose a cross-motion to vacate under the FAA, and the Court will consider [Toys "R" Us's] cross-motion under the standards of the FAA." By judgment entered December 20, 1996, the district court confirmed the award, finding Toys "R" Us's objections to the award to be without merit. This appeal followed.

DISCUSSION

I. Availability of the FAA's Grounds for Relief in Confirmation Under the Convention

Toys "R" Us argues that the district court correctly determined that the provisions of the FAA apply to its cross-motion to vacate or modify the arbitral award. In particular, Toys "R" Us contends that the FAA and the Convention have overlapping coverage. Thus, Toys "R" Us argues, even though the petition to confirm the arbitral award was brought under the Convention, the FAA's implied grounds for vacatur should apply to Toys "R" Us's cross-motion to vacate or modify because the cross-motion was brought under the FAA. We agree that the FAA governs Toys "R" Us's cross-motion.

A. Applicability of the Convention

Neither party seriously disputes the applicability of the Convention to this case and it is clear to us that the Convention does apply. The Convention provides that it will apply to the recognition and enforcement of arbitral awards made in the territory of a State other than the State where the recognition and enforcement of such awards are sought, and arising out of differences between persons, whether physical or legal. It shall also apply to arbitral awards *not considered as domestic awards* in the State where their recognition and enforcement are sought.

* * *

The Convention's applicability in this case is clear. The dispute giving rise to this appeal involved two nondomestic parties and one United States corporation, and principally involved conduct and contract performance in the Middle East. Thus, we consider the arbitral award leading to this action a non-domestic award and thus within the scope of the Convention.

B. Authority Under the Convention to Set Aside An Award Under Domestic Arbitral Law

Toys "R" Us argues that the district court properly found that it had the authority under the Convention to apply the FAA's implied grounds for setting aside the award. We agree. Under the Convention, the district court's role in reviewing a foreign arbitral award is strictly limited: "The court shall confirm the award unless it finds one of the grounds for refusal or deferral of recognition or enforcement of the award specified in the said Convention." Under Article V of the Convention, the grounds for refusing to recognize or enforce an arbitral award are:

> (a) The parties to the agreement ... were ... under some incapacity, or the said agreement is not valid under the law ... ; or (b) The party against whom the award is invoked was not given proper notice of the appointment of the arbitrator or of the arbitration proceedings ... ; or (c) The award deals with a difference not contemplated by or not falling within the terms of the submission to arbitration, or it contains decisions on matters beyond the scope of the submission to arbitration ... ; or (d) The composition of the arbitral authority or the arbitral procedure was not in accordance with the agreement of the parties ... ; or (e) The award has not yet become binding on the parties, or has been set aside or suspended by a competent authority of the country in which, or under the law of which, that award was made.

Convention art. V(1). Enforcement may also be refused if "[t]he subject matter of the difference is not capable of settlement by arbitration," or if "recognition or enforcement of the award would be contrary to the public policy" of the country in which enforcement or recognition is sought. *Id.* art. V(2). These seven grounds are the only grounds explicitly provided under the Convention.

In determining the availability of the FAA's implied grounds for setting aside, the text of the Convention leaves us with two questions: (1) whether, in addition to the Convention's express grounds for refusal, other grounds can be read into the Convention by implication, much as American courts have read implied grounds for relief into the FAA, and (2) whether, under Article V(1)(e), the courts of the United States are authorized to apply United States procedural arbitral law, i.e., the FAA, to nondomestic awards rendered in the United States. We answer the first question in the negative and the second in the affirmative.

1. Availability Under the Convention of Implied Grounds for Refusal

We have held that the FAA and the Convention have "overlapping coverage" to the extent that they do not conflict. However, by that same token, to the extent that the Convention prescribes the exclusive grounds for relief from an award under the Convention, that application of the FAA's implied grounds would be in conflict, and is thus precluded.

In *Parsons & Whittemore Overseas Co. v. Societe Generale de L'Industrie du Papier (RAKTA)*, 508 F.2d 969 (2d Cir.1974), we declined to decide whether the implied defense of "manifest disregard" applies under the Convention, having decided that even if it did, appellant's claim would fail. *See id.* at 977. Nonetheless, we noted that "[b]oth the legislative history of Article V and the statute enacted to implement the United States' accession to the Convention are strong authority for treating as exclusive the bases set forth in the Convention for vacating an award." *Id.* (citation and footnote omitted).

There is now considerable caselaw holding that, in an action to confirm an award rendered in, or under the law of, a foreign jurisdiction, the grounds for relief enumerated in Article V of the Convention are the only grounds available for setting aside an arbitral award. This conclusion is consistent with the Convention's pro-enforcement bias. We join these courts in declining to read into the Convention the FAA's implied defenses to confirmation of an arbitral award.

2. *Nondomestic Award Rendered in the United States*

Although Article V provides the exclusive grounds for refusing confirmation under the Convention, one of those exclusive grounds is where "[t]he award ... has been set aside or suspended by a competent authority of the country in which, or under the law of which, that award was made." Convention art. V(1)(e). Those courts holding that implied defenses were inapplicable under the Convention did so in the context of petitions to confirm awards rendered abroad. These courts were not presented with the question whether Article V(1)(e) authorizes an action to set aside an arbitral award under the domestic law of the state in which, or under which, the award was rendered. We, however, are faced head-on with that question in the case before us, because the arbitral award in this case was rendered in the United States, and both confirmation and vacatur were then sought in the United States.

We read Article V(1)(e) of the Convention to allow a court in the country under whose law the arbitration was conducted to apply domestic arbitral law, in this case the FAA, to a motion to set aside or vacate that arbitral award. The district court in *Spector v. Torenberg*, reached the same conclusion as we do now, reasoning that, because the Convention allows the district court to refuse to enforce an award that has been vacated by a competent authority in the country where the award was rendered, the court may apply FAA standards to a motion to vacate a nondomestic award rendered in the United States.

The Seventh Circuit has agreed, albeit in passing, that the Convention "contemplates the possibility of the award's being set aside in a proceeding under local law." Likewise, the United States District Court for the District of Columbia has found that, in an arbitration conducted in Egypt and under Egyptian law, nullification of the award by the Egyptian courts falls within Article V(1)(e).

Our conclusion also is consistent with the reasoning of courts that have refused to apply non-Convention grounds for relief where awards were rendered outside the United States. For example, the Sixth Circuit in *M & C* concluded that it should not apply the FAA's implied grounds for vacatur, because the United States did not provide the law of the arbitration for the purposes of Article V(1)(e) of the Convention. Similarly, in *International Standard,* the district court decided that only the state under whose procedural law the arbitration was conducted has jurisdiction under Article V(1)(e) to vacate the award, whereas on a petition for confirmation made in any other state, only the defenses to confirmation listed in Article V of the Convention are available.

This interpretation of Article V(1)(e) also finds support in the scholarly work of commentators on the Convention and in the judicial decisions of our sister signatories to the Convention. There appears to be no dispute among these authorities that an action to set aside an international arbitral award, as contemplated by Article V(1)(e), is controlled by the domestic law of the rendering state. As one commentator has explained:

> The possible effect of this ground for refusal [Article V(1)(e)] is that, as the award can be set aside in the country of origin on *all* grounds contained in the arbitration law of that country, including the public policy of that country, the grounds for refusal of enforcement under the Convention may indirectly be extended to include all kinds of particularities of the arbitration law of the country of origin. This might undermine the limitative character of the grounds for refusal listed in Article V ... and thus decrease the degree of uniformity existing under the Convention.

van den Berg, *supra,* at 355 * * *. The defense in Article V(1)(e) incorporates the entire body of review rights in the issuing jurisdiction.... If the scope of judicial review in the rendering state extends beyond the other six defenses allowed under the New York Convention, the losing party's opportunity to avoid enforcement is automatically enhanced: The losing party can first attempt to derail the award on appeal on grounds that would not be permitted elsewhere during enforcement proceedings.

Indeed, many commentators and foreign courts have concluded that an action to set aside an award can be brought *only* under the domestic law of the arbitral forum, and can never be made under the Convention. ("[T]he fact is that setting aside awards under the New York Convention can take place only in the country in which the award was made.").

There is no indication in the Convention of any intention to deprive the rendering state of its supervisory authority over an arbitral award, including its authority to set aside that award under domestic law. The Convention succeeded and replaced the Convention on the Execution of Foreign Arbitral Awards ("Geneva Convention"), Sept. 26, 1927. The primary defect of the Geneva Convention was that it required an award first to be recognized in the rendering state before it could be enforced abroad, * * *.

The Convention eliminated this problem by eradicating the requirement that a court in the rendering state recognize an award before it could be taken and enforced abroad. In so doing, the Convention intentionally "liberalized procedures for enforcing foreign arbitral awards."

Nonetheless, under the Convention, the power and authority of the local courts of the rendering state remain of paramount importance. "What the Convention did not do ... was provide any international mechanism to insure the validity of the award where rendered. This was left to the provisions of local law. The Convention provides no restraint whatsoever on the control functions of local courts at the seat of arbitration." Another commentator explained:

> Significantly, [Article V(1)(e)] fails to specify the grounds upon which the rendering State may set aside or suspend the award. While it would have provided greater reliability to the enforcement of awards under the Convention had the available grounds been defined in some way, such action would have constituted meddling with national procedure for handling domestic awards, a subject beyond the competence of the Conference.

Leonard V. Quigley, *Accession by the United States to the United Nations Convention on the Recognition and Enforcement of Foreign Arbitral Awards,* 70 Yale L.J. 1049, 1070 (1961). From the plain language and history of the Convention, it is thus apparent that a party may seek to vacate or set aside an award in the state in which, or under the law of which, the award is rendered. Moreover, the language and history of the Convention make it clear that such a motion is to be governed by domestic law of the rendering state, despite the fact that the award is nondomestic within the meaning of the Convention as we have interpreted it in *Bergesen.* * * *

In sum, we conclude that the Convention mandates very different regimes for the review of arbitral awards (1) in the state in which, or under the law of which, the award was made, and (2) in other states where recognition and enforcement are sought. The Convention specifically contemplates that the state in which, or under the law of which, the award is made, will be free to set aside or modify an award in accordance with its domestic arbitral law and its full panoply of express and implied grounds for relief. *See* Convention art. V(1)(e). However, the Convention is equally clear that when an action for enforcement is brought in a foreign state, the state may refuse to enforce the award only on the grounds explicitly set forth in Article V of the Convention.

II. Application of FAA Grounds for Relief

Having determined that the FAA does govern Toys "R" Us's cross-motion to vacate, our application of the FAA's implied grounds for vacatur is swift. The Supreme Court has stated "that courts of appeals should apply ordinary, not special, standards when reviewing district court decisions upholding arbitration awards." We review the district court's findings of fact for clear error and its conclusions of law *de novo*.

"[T]he confirmation of an arbitration award is a summary proceeding that merely makes what is already a final arbitration award a judgment of the court." The review of arbitration awards is "very limited ... in order to avoid undermining the twin goals of arbitration, namely, settling disputes efficiently and avoiding long and expensive litigation." Accordingly, "the showing required to avoid summary confirmance is high."

More particularly, "[t]his court has generally refused to second guess an arbitrator's resolution of a contract dispute." As we have explained: "An arbitrator's decision is entitled to substantial deference, and the arbitrator need only explicate his reasoning under the contract 'in terms that offer even a barely colorable justification for the outcome reached' in order to withstand judicial scrutiny."

However, awards may be vacated, *see* 9 U.S.C. § 10, or modified, *see id.* § 11, in the limited circumstances where the arbitrator's award is in manifest disregard of the terms of the agreement, or where the award is in "manifest disregard of the law." We find that neither of these implied grounds is met in the present case.

A. *Manifest Disregard of the Law*

Toys "R" Us argues that the arbitrator manifestly disregarded New York law on lost profits awards for breach of contract by returning a speculative award. This contention is without merit. "[M]ere error in the law or failure on the part of the arbitrator[ ] to understand or apply the law" is not sufficient to establish manifest disregard of the law. For an award to be in "manifest disregard of the law,"

> [t]he error must have been obvious and capable of being readily and instantly perceived by the average person qualified to serve as an arbitrator. Moreover, the term "disregard" implies that the arbitrator appreciates the existence of a clearly governing legal principle but decides to ignore or pay no attention to it.

In the instant case, the arbitrator was well aware of and carefully applied New York's law on lost profits. The arbitrator specifically addressed *Kenford Co. v. County of Erie,* which contains New York's law on the subject and upon which Toys "R" Us relied in its arguments, and concluded:

> I do not think the Kenford case rules out damages in this case. Kenford disallowed damages based on future profits from concessions in a domed stadium that was never built.... In this case [Alghanim], which is forced into the estimating posture because of [Toys "R" Us's] breach, bases its damages not on its own experience but on [Toys "R" Us's]. [Toys "R" Us] has hundreds of toy stores worldwide. Since it has been found that the Agreements require

[Toys "R" Us] to provide a wide variety of services, similar to what it provides its own toy stores, I find that [Alghanim's] method of estimating damages is reasonable and believable, and provides a sound basis on which to fashion the award.

We find no manifest disregard of the law in this analysis.

* * *

B. Manifest Disregard of the Agreement

Toys "R" Us also argues that the district court erred in refusing to vacate the award because the arbitrator manifestly disregarded the terms of the agreement. In particular, Toys "R" Us disputes the arbitrator's interpretation of four contract terms: (1) the termination provision; (2) the conforming stores provision; (3) the non-assignment provision; and (4) the deletion provision. We find no error.

Interpretation of these contract terms is within the province of the arbitrator and will not be overruled simply because we disagree with that interpretation. We will overturn an award where the arbitrator merely "mak[es] the right noises — noises of contract interpretation — " while ignoring the clear meaning of contract terms. We apply a notion of "manifest disregard" to the terms of the agreement analogous to that employed in the context of manifest disregard of the law.

As to each of these contract provisions, Toys "R" Us merely takes issue with the arbitrator's well-reasoned interpretations of those provisions, and simply offers its own contrary interpretations. Toys "R" Us does not advance a convincing argument that the arbitrator manifestly disregarded the agreement. We will not overturn the arbitrator's award merely because we do not concur with the arbitrator's reading of the agreement. For the reasons stated by the district court, we find the arbitrator's interpretation of the contractual provisions supportable.

We have carefully considered Toys "R" Us's remaining contentions and find them all to be without merit.

Conclusion

For the foregoing reasons, the judgment of the district court is affirmed.

Notes and Questions

1. What was the primary defect in the Geneva Convention that was eliminated in the New York Convention?

2. In what situations does the New York Convention apply? See Convention Art. 1(1) cited in the *Yusuf* case. Grounds for non-enforcement of the Convention are set out in Article VI. American courts construe these grounds for non-enforcement narrowly. *See* Christopher R. Drahozal, Commercial Arbitration: Cases and Problems 536 (2002).

3. Chapter 2 of the FAA implements the U.S. obligations under the New York Convention. Section 207 of the FAA provides that any court having jurisdiction may confirm an arbitrator's award unless the award falls

under one of the grounds for refusal of recognition set out in the Convention. Section 203 of the FAA grants subject matter jurisdiction in federal court over an action falling under the convention. Section 205 of the FAA authorizes removal from state courts of cases falling under the Convention.

On the other hand, an action to vacate an international award can be brought only at the arbitration situs or in the country whose law was selected by the parties. *See* Drahozal, *supra* note 2, at 555. For discussions of the notion of "de-localizing" arbitration awards, a criticism of the arbitral situs rule, see *id*. at 555; William W. Park, *Book Review*, 82 Am. J. Int'l L. 616, at 622–23 (1988) (reviewing ALAN REDFERN & MARTIN HUNTER, LAW AND THE PRACTICE OF INTERNATIONAL COMMERCIAL ARBITRATION (1996)).

4.   Where does one look for the applicable standards for vacating an arbitration award? Is it proper to consider both explicit and implied grounds when deciding whether to vacate an award?

Where does one look for the applicable standards for confirmation and enforcement of an arbitration award? Is it proper to consider both explicit and implied grounds in deciding whether to confirm and enforce an arbitration award?

D.   DECIDING WHETHER AND HOW TO USE ARBITRATION

It is necessary to understand arbitration and its legal environment in order to make good decisions about whether and how it should be used. The preceding sections focused on the law and practice of arbitration. This section carries the analysis a step further and focuses on how arbitration differs from other dispute resolution processes. This subject is not easy to discuss because of the great variety in arbitration systems. Those who debate arbitration's advantages do not always focus on the same issues because their praise or criticism is based on experience with different kinds of arbitration. Evaluations of arbitration also are colored by the perspective from which its characteristics are viewed. Different considerations are important when deciding whether society should encourage the use of arbitration than are significant when disputing parties choose between arbitration and other processes. Still other considerations come into play when parties decide whether to create their own system for resolving disputes or use the courts or other dispute resolution systems of government or private organizations.

We agree with Professor Getman's assertion that arbitration's success in labor relations does not guarantee its success in all contexts. Julius G. Getman, *Labor Arbitration and Dispute Settlement,* 88 Yale L.J. 916, 916–18 (1979). Whether arbitration is appropriate for particular disputes or categories of disputes depends upon such factors as the nature of the dispute, the nature and goals of the parties, and the relationship between the parties. Each proposed use of arbitration should be analyzed in light of the specific context in which the process will be used. In making decisions on whether and how to use arbitration, it is helpful to ask what kinds of disputes are suited for a process with arbitration's characteristics. It also is helpful to focus on the unique features of the dispute and parties and ask what this implies in terms of process choice. *See* EDWARD A. DAUER, MANUAL OF DISPUTE RESOLUTION 7–3 (1994). It is important to remember that the issue is not just whether arbitration should be used, but also how arbitration should be structured in order to maximize its advantages in specific circumstances.

We begin with a discussion of arbitration's characteristics. We follow with excerpts that view arbitration from four different perspectives. In arguing for increased reliance on mediation in collective bargaining, Professor Stephen B. Goldberg criticizes what he believes are excessive delay, costs, and formality in arbitration. Professors Stephen Hayford and Ralph Peeples assert, in effect, that commercial arbitration will not receive long-run deference from the courts if it does not become more like litigation. Lewis Maltby, then director of the National Task Force on Civil Liberties in the Workforce, American Civil Liberties Union, writes of both the threats and potential benefits of private dispute resolution. Professor Judith Resnik details the Supreme Court's changing attitude toward arbitration's characteristics as it has dealt with agreements to arbitration disputes involving federal statutory rights.

1. THE CHARACTERISTICS OF ARBITRATION

Speed, lower costs, informality, the ability to obtain a more suitable neutral decision maker, and privacy are the advantages usually cited in support of arbitration. Many of arbitration's alleged advantages result from the autonomy parties gain when they decide to arbitrate rather than go to court. When parties arbitrate, they have power to decide for themselves many substantive and procedural issues over which they would have no control if they used the court system. The characteristic of autonomy overlaps the other characteristics. The power to choose the neutral decision maker, for example, is perhaps the most significant aspect of party autonomy. Even the characteristics of speed, lower costs, and informality relate to autonomy. These alleged advantages are potential rather than guaranteed, and will be fully realized only if the parties cooperate in using their freedom to pursue them. For a case study see Lisa Bernstein, *Opting Out of the Legal System: Extralegal Contractual Relations in the Diamond Industry,* 21 J. Leg. Stud. 115 (1992). For a discussion of ways to expedite the arbitration process, see Robert S. Peckar, *Making Commercial Arbitration Faster and More Efficient,* Arb. J., Dec. 1991, at 5. There may be times when the relative informality of arbitration results in less economy and more delay. *See* Thomas J. Stipanowich, *Arbitration and the Multiparty Dispute: The Search for Workable Solutions,* 72 Iowa L. Rev. 473, 476–82 (1987).

Speed, Lower Costs and Informality. One of the most frequent claims made on behalf of arbitration is that it can be faster and cheaper than the courts. Its proponents often focus on the long waiting time for a trial in some jurisdictions and the large legal and expert witness fees generated by extensive pre-trial discovery and long, complex trials. However, proponents of the diversion of more disputes from the courts into arbitration don't always view this primarily as a way to save the disputing parties' time and money. They may believe instead that additional public resources will not be available, should not be made available to add the judges and court personnel needed to process an increasing caseload, or that adding additional judges and court personnel will dilute the quality of the judiciary and create a large judicial bureaucracy which will provide an inferior quality of justice.

Informality is praised because it is one of the reasons arbitration can be faster and cheaper than the courts and because it is considered a desirable goal in itself. Although discovery is available in some arbitration systems, it typically is not used as much as in court proceedings. Although evidentiary objections are made in arbitration hearings, most arbitrators do not apply the strict rules of evidence, thus permitting the parties to introduce evidence in an arbitration that might be deemed inadmissible in a court of law because of hearsay, relevance, or other bars to admissibility. *See* W. Michael Tupman, *Discovery and Evidence in U.S. Arbitration: The Prevailing Views,* Arb. J., March 1989, at 27 (1989). The practice of filing numerous motions is not widespread in arbitration. The limited review of arbitration awards by courts discourages costly and time-consuming appeals. These and other differences between arbitration and traditional litigation create the potential for saving time and money.

It has been argued that adjudication that is less formal also can promote a perception of greater fairness and increase the satisfaction of those who participate in the proceedings. For example, non-lawyers do not normally communicate in a way that consistently satisfies the rules of evidence. One study indicated that frustration and dissatisfaction result from constraints placed on witnesses' ability to tell their stories in their own way and that they do not understand courts' explanations about why their narratives are unacceptable. William O'Barr & John M. Conley, *Litigant Satisfaction Versus Legal Adequacy in Small Claims Court Narratives,* 19 Law & Soc'y Rev. 661, 665–72 (1985).

A More Suitable Decisionmaker. This claim on arbitration's behalf is usually stated in terms of the decision maker's expertise. It is helpful to shift the focus somewhat and emphasize the ability of the parties to decide the characteristics desired in the decision maker. In one case the parties may want a person with in-depth specialized knowledge — an engineer for instance — to decide a technical issue in a dispute over a construction contract. Sometimes only general background is needed and might be provided by a businesswoman or lawyer from the same industry who is familiar with industry practices. In other cases the parties might prefer an arbitrator who knows nothing of the subject matter but has a reputation for good judgment and objectivity. It could be argued that even more fundamental than the ability to decide what characteristics the decision maker should have is the unstated message communicated by the decision to arbitrate rather than litigate. David Feller has said that "[t]he arbitrator's so-called expertise is not so much expertise as it is knowledge of the fact that the parties have not called upon him to act like a court in adjudicating a breach of contract action, but rather to act as — perhaps there is no better word — an arbitrator." David E. Feller, *Arbitration: The Days of Its Glory are Numbered*, 2 Indus. Rel. L.J. 97, 104 (1977). Most commentators believe the ability of the parties to choose the decision maker is one of arbitration's principal advantages. It is the best insurance the parties have that the arbitrator not only will make an objective decision based upon the evidence and argument, but will be sensitive to the needs of the parties and their relationship. An arbitrator who consistently fails to satisfy the parties' expectations becomes unacceptable and is not used in future cases. Others view the power to choose the decision maker as one of arbitration's principal weaknesses because it encourages arbitrators to make compromise decisions in order to remain acceptable.

Privacy. The arbitration hearing is typically conducted in private and the parties have some control over who has access to the arbitrator's opinion and award. This degree of privacy is not typical in the courts. Parties who believe that public access to the hearing or decision might result in competitive or other disadvantages consider arbitration's relative privacy one of its significant advantages.

Party Autonomy. In general, the parties have more control over the handling of their dispute when they arbitrate than when they go to court. As already noted, arbitrating parties have the power to choose the neutral decision maker. The parties also may, within limits, select the substantive standards that govern the arbitrator's decision, usually incorporated in a contract, and the procedure for processing the dispute. Party autonomy is enhanced by the limited court review of arbitration awards.

From the disputants' viewpoint, their freedom requires them to consider what is important to them in building and implementing their dispute resolution system. For example, is saving time and money more important than having an opinion explaining the basis of the arbitrator's award? From society's perspective, on the other hand, it is important to ask how much autonomy the parties should be permitted to have in building and implementing their system. This issue arises when courts are asked to enforce or vacate arbitration awards. Broad court review of awards limits party autonomy and narrow review expands it.

2. PERSPECTIVES ON ARBITRATION

STEPHEN GOLDBERG, THE MEDIATION OF GRIEVANCES UNDER A COLLECTIVE BARGAINING CONTRACT: AN ALTERNATIVE TO ARBITRATION
77 Nw. U. L. Rev. 270, 272–78 (1982).

Commentators have long agreed that, in order to fulfill its dual functions of avoiding strikes and providing a satisfactory alternative to litigation, arbitration should be speedy and inexpensive. Procedural informality is also generally thought to be a desirable aspect of arbitration for two reasons. First, the existence of a formal procedure implies that, if procedural requirements are not satisfied, the arbitrator's decision may rest on that non-compliance. Employees, however, may refuse to accept a decision not based upon the merits of the dispute. Thus, a lack of procedural formality may bring about employee acceptance of the results of the arbitration process. Second, procedural informality promotes the cathartic value of labor arbitration. The employee who is not intimidated by the formalities of judicial proceedings feels free to tell his or her own story as he or she wishes. The opportunity to do so, and to have both the employer and a neutral arbitrator listen, has a cathartic value that results in employee satisfaction with the arbitration process regardless of its outcome.

* * *

Nonetheless, the arbitration process fails to achieve many of its other goals. Costs in excess of $2,000 for arbitrating a single grievance are not uncommon. Delay also presents a serious problem. According to the most recent report of the Federal Mediation and Conciliation Service (FMCS), an average of 163 days — over five months — elapsed from the conclusion of the internal steps of the grievance procedure to the issuance of the arbitrator's award. Finally, the tendency to increased formality in the arbitration process has been reported by many commentators to have led to substantial employee dissatisfaction.

Perhaps the most significant aspect of these criticisms of the arbitration process is their early appearance and persistence. Arbitration did not become widespread until the 1940's, yet, by 1951, the process already was considered both too formal and too expensive. Complaints about excessive delay can be found as early as 1954, and in 1965 Robben Fleming wrote that cost, delay, and formality were the major problems of the arbitration process.

The long-standing nature of these criticisms suggests that those characteristics of the arbitration process that are criticized may be inherent in the process. Indeed, at least to some extent, I believe this to be the case. I further believe that the crucial element of the arbitration process that leads, in many instances, to its failure to meet the goals of being speedy, inexpensive, and informal, is the prevalence of the adjudicatory model of arbitration over the mediatory model. The essential element of the adjudicatory model is that a party can "win" a grievance, can have its position sustained, without obtaining the consent of the other party. This breeds an interest in "winning," which, in substantial part, is responsible for the delay, high cost, and formality that have come to characterize much of arbitration.

An analysis of the elements which contribute to delay, high cost, and formality supports this conclusion. If one focuses first on delay, the average time of 163 days from the conclusion of the internal steps of the grievance procedure to the issuance of the arbitrator's award is accounted for as follows: selection of an arbitrator (40 days); finding a mutually acceptable hearing date (60–90 days); preparation of a hearing transcript

(15–45 days); preparation of post-hearing briefs (15–30 days); and preparation of the arbitrator's decision (30–60 days).

The substantial time involved in selecting an arbitrator and agreeing upon a hearing date are both due, at least in part, to the importance each party attaches to the identity of the arbitrator. Each tends to believe that a potential arbitrator's decision on a particular grievance can be predicted from his or her prior decisions and therefore seeks an arbitrator whose prior decisions suggest a decision favorable to it on the pending grievance. This creates delay in reaching agreement on an arbitrator. In addition, outcome prediction is apt to be considered easier if the arbitrator has issued prior decisions on similar grievances, so the parties prefer arbitrators with substantial arbitral experience. Such arbitrators are also viewed as less likely, because of their accumulated knowledge, to render an egregiously erroneous decision. The selection of an inexperienced arbitrator also renders the representatives subject to criticism in the event that the grievance is lost. The preference for experienced arbitrators creates great demand for the services of a limited number of arbitrators and requires that the parties who wish the services of such an arbitrator wait, frequently for 60–90 days, until he or she is available. However, because the parties believe that a grievance can be "won" or "lost" depending on the identity of the arbitrator, each is willing to pay a substantial price in time to maximize its chances of victory.

A similar analysis applies to the other elements of delay in the arbitration process. One or both parties may believe that it is worth waiting for a transcript, because the possession of a transcript may be helpful in preparing a post-hearing brief. The post-hearing brief also takes time but may persuade the arbitrator to issue a favorable decision. The time involved in writing the arbitrator's decision is extended somewhat by the necessity of dealing with the issues raised in post-hearing briefs, but more by the limited time available to busy arbitrators. Delay in the arbitration process is thus caused primarily by the desire to prevail in that process.

The same factors that contribute to delay in arbitration also contribute to the high cost of arbitration. The parties' choice of an experienced arbitrator is likely to mean a relatively high-priced arbitrator, and transcripts and briefs may also be expensive. In addition, the desire to win frequently leads one or both parties to be represented by an attorney, a factor that substantially increases costs. Furthermore, an attorney, in an effort to increase his or her client's chances of victory, may broaden the scope of the arbitration proceedings by introducing procedural issues of which a non-lawyer might be unaware. This increases not only the time and costs of the attorney, but also those of the arbitrator, who must consider additional issues in order to dispose of the grievance.

The relationship between the interest in "winning" at arbitration and the reliance on procedural, technical, or formal arguments is clear.

The goal of victory encourages each party to use any legitimate argument available. If, for example, the contract provides that the union must request arbitration within ten days of the final step of the internal grievance procedure, and it fails to do so, the employer is likely to rely upon the untimely request for arbitration. Similarly, if the only evidence in support of an employer's argument that an employee was discharged for cause is hearsay, the union is likely to argue that such evidence should be excluded. The same is true for each of the other practices sometimes attacked as bringing excessive formalism into arbitration, including arguments about arbitrability, swearing of witnesses, and use of stenographic transcripts. Each is used to win the grievance, and each is likely to be used as long as winning is the goal.

The tendency to rely on procedural or technical arguments in arbitration might be checked by a concern for the effect of such arguments on the relationship of the parties. A union that loses an otherwise valid claim because of the employer's defense of untimeliness may be slow to respond to the employer's requests for cooperation in other matters. So, too, an employer thwarted in discharging a thoroughly unsatisfactory employee by the union's invocation of the hearsay rule may react by preventing the union from obtaining important objectives. The focus on winning the particular grievance, however, tends to distract the parties from their long-term relational interests. This tendency is sometimes aggravated by the parties' use of attorneys or other outsiders as representatives. To the extent that these representatives are not involved in the parties' day-to-day relationship, they are apt to be less sensitive to the importance of relational considerations, and less constrained by them, than the parties.

Notes and Questions

1. There seems to be less criticism of labor arbitration and international commercial arbitration than of other uses of arbitration. Does the excerpt which follows help explain why this is so?

There is widespread perception that our judicial system needs changing. It is expensive, unnecessarily technical, intrusive on private relations, and it gives unfair advantage to the wealthy and powerful. Labor arbitration, by contract, is frequently pointed to as a paradigm of private justice.

* * *

The perception that labor arbitration successfully achieves these various purposes has led some commentators to the erroneous conclusion that it offers a technique for dispute resolution that can be routinely applied, with only minor adjustments, in other situations. This conclusion, which has been fostered by prominent labor arbitrators and by prestigious groups such as the American Arbitration Association and the National Academy of Arbitrators, overlooks the idiosyncratic nature of labor arbitration and its crucial interrelationship with unionization and collective bargaining.

Collective bargaining shapes labor arbitration and gives it power. The collective-bargaining relationship itself reflects the strength and purpose of unions. It is only when unions are powerful, well established, and responsive to the needs of their members that labor arbitration works successfully. Without unions and collective bargaining, key aspects of labor arbitration would become meaningless or counter-productive. Therefore, proposals to utilize arbitration in various contexts cannot be justified by reference to the labor experience, although the effort to do so is common.

* * *

Disparities of power in the relationship that is the focus of a dispute are bound to be reflected in the mechanism used to resolve the dispute. When labor arbitration has been successful, it is because collective bargaining has established a rough equality and mutual respect between the parties. The key to changes in labor relations has been the pervasive role of the union in promulgating and administering rules, and not in the establishment of a particular system of dispute resolution. When unions are powerful, the form of grievance mechanism may vary, but it will reflect the essential nature of the relationship.

Julius Getman, *Labor Arbitration and Dispute Settlement*, 88 Yale L.J. 916, 916–17, 933–34 (1979).

2. Professor Goldberg is not alone in complaining about cost, delay and formality in the labor arbitration process. The 1980–81 President of the National Academy of Arbitrators stated in her presidential address that in every meeting of the Academy since 1959, the presentations had included one or more references to "the growing formalization of arbitration and what appeared to some to be a growing effort to convert arbitration into a litigation-type process" and "the increasing cost of arbitration and the delays in arbitration." Eva Robins, *Threats to Arbitration, Proceedings of the 34th Annual Meeting*, NAT'L ACAD. OF ARBITRATORS 3 (1982). The 1979–80 President of the Academy had this to say:

> What I really am concerned about is the rather easy time lawyers seem to have had in persuading so many parties, almost by default and without half trying, to join in their assumption that because a certain procedure, motion or objection is appropriate to litigation, it automatically and almost in the very nature of things should be applied in arbitration. * * * [I]t often happens that as soon as a lawyer makes a motion or objection in arbitration, everybody in the room acts as if they were in court and begins to deal with the motion or objection as would the law.

Clare B. McDermott, *An Exercise in Dialectic: Should Arbitration Behave as Does Litigation?, Proceedings of the 33rd Annual Meeting*, NAT'L ACAD. OF ARBITRATORS 12 (1981).

There also have been complaints about the impact of lawyers on commercial arbitration:

> While attorneys tend to complain about certain formal inadequacies of arbitration, many in the business community feel that the most significant problem with modern arbitration is the increasing formalization of

the process brought about by the legal profession. Many charge that in their zeal to make arbitration a carbon copy of traditional litigation, lawyers have robbed the process of its essential attributes.

Thomas J. Stipanowich, *Rethinking American Arbitration*, 63 Ind. L.J. 425, 445 (1988). Professor Stipanowich points out that empirical studies in the mid–1950s, in 1961, and in 1985–86 indicated that the presence of attorneys in arbitration tends to delay the process. *Id.* at 445 n.117, 461 nn.204–05, 473.

3.   Professor Goldberg makes a good case for increased reliance upon mediation in collective bargaining. To make his case, he relies upon evidence of delay, costs and formality in arbitration. This evidence does not demonstrate that arbitration is inferior to court litigation when mediation fails and a binding decision is desired. The evidence cited measures arbitration against an ideal of what it should be rather than against comparable litigation in the courts.

4.   Three variations on traditional arbitration are "final-offer," "high-low," and "incentive" arbitration. In final-offer arbitration, the arbitrator must choose one of the parties' final offers. Identified most closely with major league baseball salary disputes, final-offer arbitration is also used in various commercial disputes. In high-low arbitration, the parties agree in advance on the limits of recovery and loss. The parties are bound if the award falls within the range they have agreed upon. High-low arbitration reduces the risk to both sides. Incentive arbitration is not binding but imposes penalties on parties who reject the award. *See* STEPHEN B. GOLDBERG, FRANK E.A. SANDER & NANCY H. ROGERS, DISPUTE RESOLUTION: NEGOTIATION, MEDIATION AND OTHER PROCESSES 288–90 (4th ed. 2003); *The ABCs of ADR: A Dispute Resolution Glossary*, Alternatives to the High Cost of Litig., Nov. 1995, at 147, 147–48.

STEPHEN HAYFORD AND RALPH PEEPLES, COMMERCIAL ARBITRATION: AN ASSESSMENT AND CALL FOR DIALOGUE

10 Ohio St. J. on Disp. Resol. 343, 381, 394, 396, 397–98, 399, 400, 401, 403, 405, 413–14 (1995).

It is the Authors' belief that the institution of commercial arbitration is in need of retooling. Many of the dimensions of the existing mechanism do not adequately contemplate the emerging new reality of alternative dispute resolution and the demands that reality will place on the arbitration process and arbitrators. Commercial arbitration must be brought to a new, heightened level of rigor and sophistication of the nature required by the increasingly complex and significant disputes it is being routinely called upon to resolve.

* * *

In recent years, as the amounts in controversy and complexity of many of the disputes submitted to arbitration have increased, recognition has emerged of the need to provide some manner of enhanced structure and discipline to the pre-hearing discovery process. As observed earlier, today's commercial arbitration rules pertaining to discovery are of a very general nature. The Authors assert that rudimentary rules of the type reflected in AAA Commercial Arbitration Rule 10 and Rule 5(b)–(d) of the Association's Supplementary Procedures for Large, Complex Cases are not sufficient to facilitate effective, consistent arbitral oversight of the discovery process.

Instead, the Authors suggest that in all commercial arbitration cases, especially those of a more complex nature, the process would be aided by the promulgation of more detailed discovery rules loosely modeled after the new Federal Rules of Civil Procedure 26, 30, 33, and 37.

* * *

The primary areas of concern pertaining to the actual arbitration hearing that merit discussion go to the mode of arbitral conduct of the hearing, advocacy tactics and the rules of evidence. The contemporary commercial arbitrator is provided little in the way of procedural guidelines as to the manner in which the hearing is to be conducted. The conventional wisdom underlying this general lack of structure centers on the belief that arbitration can remain a relatively simple, expeditious process only if the rules governing it are kept to a minimum. This premise is generally sound. Nevertheless, the Authors assert that the time has come for a rethinking of the balance between the simplicity and succinctness of the procedural framework for commercial arbitration and the need to supplement that framework in order to ensure that arbitrators conduct hearings that truly are acceptable surrogates for the due process guarantees and the rigor inherent in court trials.

* * *

The Authors advocate supplementing the current evidentiary paradigm for commercial arbitration by adding the following:

● a more adequate description and working definition of the evidentiary standard of relevancy that articulates the "probative value/prejudice to the non-proffering party" standard;

● a highly-simplified version of the hearsay evidence rule, incorporating a clear definition of "hearsay evidence" and specifying certain, limited exceptions thereto that are particularly relevant in a commercial arbitration context (e.g., the exception pertaining to records kept in the customary course of business);

● a rule encouraging the use of fact stipulations by the parties and specifically empowering the arbitrator to request same where warranted;

● a rule sanctioning arbitral notice of adjudicative facts not in dispute;

● a rule clearly defining cumulative evidence, which grants the arbitrator authority either to exclude such evidence, or take arbitral notice of it.

* * *

The conventional wisdom is that post-hearing briefs are not necessary or appropriate in most commercial arbitration cases.

* * *

The Authors maintain that the process of commercial arbitration and the interest of the parties would benefit from a methodical determination, on a case-by-case basis as to whether post-hearing briefs are warranted. * * * However, when in a particular case post-hearing briefs would significantly elevate the quality of argument, and thereby enhance the rigor of arbitral analysis, the long-standing presumption in commercial arbitration that briefs are not warranted should not control.

* * *

The conventional wisdom of commercial arbitration dictates that the arbitrator's award should be kept as brief as possible and reveal as little as possible of the analytical process that leads the arbitrator to the result achieved. The Authors assert that as commercial arbitration moves toward maturity, this conventional wisdom needs to be reexamined.

* * *

There are several significant value-added factors that can be reached by giving the parties the option to request a written award. First, it will provide concrete notice to the arbitrator of the parties' expectation that the resolution of their dispute will be founded on careful, thoughtful efforts at: (1) identifying the relevant law and contract language; (2) evaluating the hearing record in order to discern the material facts adduced at hearing; and (3) applying the relevant law and contract language to the material facts. This increased assurance of thoughtful analysis should do much to encourage the belief that arbitration produces accurate and correct results. Second, the decision to require something more than a summary award will surely oblige arbitrators to pay careful attention and remain fully engaged throughout the proceedings.

* * *

Undoubtedly, it is the absence of a substantive guarantee of accurate and correct results that causes many experienced litigators to be reluctant to embrace commercial arbitration as an acceptable alternative to traditional litigation. That fact prompts speculation as to the feasibility of the parties to a given dispute agreeing contractually, at the outset of the arbitration proceeding, to some form of appellate arbitration mechanism that would provide a check on the otherwise unreviewable nature of the commercial arbitration award. As incongruous as such a proposition may seem to those who praise the relative simplicity and expediency of arbitration, the Authors maintain it merits consideration.

* * *

There remains today substantial question as to whether the process of commercial arbitration will achieve the level of rigor and reliability necessary to justify the continued, long-run deference of the judiciary in business disputes that otherwise would be appropriate for adjudication in the state or federal courts. If it does not, the window of opportunity created by the interaction of the U.S. Supreme Court's current charitable view of the process, the logjam in the courts, and the concerns of business decision makers with the costs and other problems associated with traditional litigation may prove to be short-lived.

* * *

The blessing recently granted the process of commercial arbitration by the U.S. Supreme Court is both a boon and a challenge. By taking the process from the fringes of litigation and placing it squarely in the forefront of the commercial dispute resolution arena, *Mitsubishi* and its progeny have vastly accelerated and indeed compelled the maturation of commercial arbitration. The challenge of creating in a short period of time a system of private adjudication that leaves disputants and their attorneys satisfied that they would have gained nothing of importance by utilizing the highly-developed system of civil justice provided by the federal and state courts is daunting to say the least.

The Authors assert that the institutionalization, the permanence of commercial arbitration, is by no means assured. The present absence of a true core, a sense of identity and mission, a gestalt around which to build the profession of commercial arbitration indicates a certain shallowness, a lack of substance that does not bode well for the ability of the process to stand in the place of the state and federal judiciaries, especially in complex, high-stakes disputes. There are serious concerns about the ability of a few high-entrepreneurial, unregulated private organizations and a large group of essentially self-labeled "arbitrators" of widely-divergent qualifications, competencies, and perspectives to lead the task of securing commercial arbitration's long-run viability and establishing the foundation for a bona fide profession.

Notes and Questions

1. Stephen Goldberg argued that labor arbitration is becoming too formal and expensive. Stephen Hayford and Ralph Peeples argued for changes that would make commercial arbitration more formal and expensive. Who is right? If you believe they are dealing with different issues and situations, in what ways are the issues and situations different?

2. Evaluate each of Hayford and Peeple's recommendations in light of the alleged advantages of arbitration, as discussed in the introduction of this Section under "The Characteristics of Arbitration."

LEWIS MALTBY, PRIVATE JUSTICE: EMPLOYMENT ARBITRATION AND CIVIL RIGHTS
30 Colum. Hum. Rts. L. Rev. 29, 29–34, 39–43,
45–48, 49, 54–55, 56–58, 63–64 (1998).

These are difficult times for civil rights. Affirmative action is under siege and losing ground. The Equal Employment Opportunity Commission (EEOC) has been forced onto a starvation diet by a hostile Congress. Some of the most venerable civil rights institutions are in a state of disarray.

But among all the serious and visible threats to civil rights is possibly an even greater danger that has gone almost unnoticed. This is the privatization of civil justice. Thousands of employers are abandoning the civil justice system, establishing their own systems of resolving disputes, and requiring employees to use them.

The implications of this trend could not be more important. One of the most profound lessons of the civil rights struggle is that rights without remedies are meaningless. Title VII and our other civil rights laws have been reasonably effective because the judiciary has generally been willing to enforce them. But if employers are able to establish private court systems under employer control, equal employment opportunity laws may become completely unenforceable.

Paradoxically, the trend toward private justice may have potential benefits for employees. The cost of public civil justice has grown dramatically in recent years. Many people with legitimate claims against their employers never receive justice because they are unable to afford lawyers. Private dispute resolution, which relies on mediation and arbitration, is generally much less expensive than litigation, and may bring justice within the reach of many to whom it is currently denied.

* * *

In a study conducted in 1979, the Bureau of National Affairs found that only two out of 128 employers surveyed used outside arbitration for employment disputes. In the late 1980s, however, many employers turned away from the civil justice system, and established private arbitration systems. By 1995, another survey conducted by the United States General Accounting Office (GAO) found that ten percent of employers were using arbitration for employment disputes, and 8.4% were considering establishing such a system. In 1997, the GAO found that nineteen percent of employers surveyed were using arbitration for employment disputes-an increase of almost ninety percent in only two years. Presently, the American Arbitration Association (AAA) alone administers plans covering over three million employees. The AAA's employment dispute caseload more than doubled between 1993 and 1996. At this rate of increase, the majority of employers will have established private justice systems within the near future.

The primary motivation of employers for creating such systems appears to be reducing legal expenses. The Rand Institute estimated in 1988 that defense costs in wrongful discharge actions averaged over $80,000. By 1994, costs were estimated to have increased to $124,000. In one recent survey by Bickner, Ver Ploeg, and Feigenbaum of employers who adopted alternate dispute resolution systems, the number one reason employers gave for this decision was the desire to reduce defense costs in employment cases. Employers responding to the GAO surveys also indicated that reducing litigation costs was their primary reason for turning to arbitration.

There is certainly room for a healthy dose of skepticism concerning the accuracy of such reports. One would hardly expect an employer whose motive was to create a more favorable captive forum to say so even if only the aggregate results were published. There are indications, however, that employers' self-reported motivation is accurate. First, according to the Conference Board, the desire to minimize the involvement of unions is the second most common motivating factor in the development of complaint systems. The reporting of this less flattering motive is some indication of candor. Second, employers are turning to arbitration to resolve other disputes as well. For example, Cornell University's Institute on Conflict Resolution recently reported that seventy-nine percent of America's 1,000 largest corporations have used arbitration in the last three years. Of these, thirty-three percent have used arbitration to resolve personal injury disputes and twenty-four percent have used arbitration in product liability cases. The AAA reports that its caseload of disputes between corporations grew twenty-five percent in the last three years. The growing use of arbitration in contexts where the employer cannot shape the procedure to its advantage suggests that the temptation to use arbitration because it is a more easily controlled forum is a factor but that it is not the primary motivation.

Due Process Issues

Whatever the employer's motivation, the potential due process problems arising from private justice are staggering. Unlike collective bargaining arbitration, in which the union must agree to all aspects of the system, non-union employment arbitration is an exercise in which one party to a dispute has the unilateral ability to shape the resolution system. * * *

The most direct manner in which an employer can stack the deck in its favor is by controlling the choice of arbitrator. Rather than giving both parties an equal voice in selecting the arbitrator and requiring that the person selected be neutral, the employer can design a system in which it unilaterally chooses the arbitrator. In the worst possible case, the employer could choose an arbitrator with whom it has an economic relationship. Even if this is avoided, the employer could select someone whose views on the issue predispose him or her to rule in the employer's favor. An employer could also bend the system to its advantage by specifying the substantive law the arbitrator must apply, or by denying the arbitrator the ability to award remedies which would be available in a court of law.

* * *

Even if the employer scrupulously avoids all of these temptations, there is still the potential for great unfairness. One of the great dangers to employee-plaintiffs is the "repeat player syndrome." In the traditional labor arbitration context, the arbitrators know that they will receive future business only if both the union and management believe they are fair. An arbitrator who always rules for one side will not prosper. But when the union and its institutional memory are removed, the arbitrator's incentives change dramatically. There is no need to satisfy the employee, who is highly unlikely to have another opportunity to choose an arbitrator. The employer, however, is likely to be a repeat player, with the opportunity to reject arbitrators whose previous rulings displeased it. The arbitrator thus has a financial incentive to rule in favor of the employer. Professor Lisa Bingham of Indiana University recently examined the results of employment arbitrations in which the employer was a repeat player, and found that employees fared very poorly in such situations.

These problems would be severe enough even if employees were theoretically free to accept or reject their employer's arbitration system. But where the employer's system is a condition of employment, and employees must "agree" to use it or lose their jobs, the potential for abuse is multiplied. Unfortunately, this is the approach most employers have elected to take. In the Bickner survey, approximately seventy-five percent of employers with arbitration systems made their use a condition of employment for new hires. Many experts believe the number is even higher, perhaps exceeding ninety percent.

* * *

RESULTS OF PRIVATE ARBITRATION

The ultimate test of private arbitration is whether it provides justice to the employees who use it. Do employees who take their cases to arbitration receive the same justice they would have received had their cases gone to court?

The most exhaustive analysis of arbitration results has been conducted by Professor Lisa Bingham. Professor Bingham's first study analyzed the results of all employment arbitrations conducted by the AAA in 1992. She found that employees won seventy-three percent of the cases they filed, and sixty-four percent of all cases. While this finding is useful, comparative data is needed. It is not enough to know that employees often win in arbitration. The ultimate question is whether they win as frequently in arbitration as they do in court.

Comparisons of the result rates in arbitration versus litigation reveal that, contrary to what many would expect, employees prevail more often in arbitration than in court. For example, an AAA survey of employment arbitration results from 1993–95 shows that employees who arbitrated their claims won sixty-three percent of the time. In comparison, according to federal district court records for 1994, only 14.9% of the employees who took their claims to court won their cases.

Other studies have also found fewer employees prevailing in litigation than arbitration. Burstein and Monaghan surveyed all EEOC trials published in Fair Employment Practice Cases (Bureau of National Affairs) between 1974 and 1983. In these cases, employee-plaintiffs won only 16.8% of the time.

Even when the plaintiff is the federal government rather than an individual employee, the pattern does not change — the EEOC prevails far less often in litigation than do plaintiffs in arbitration. A study by Baxter found that the EEOC won only twenty-four percent of its employment cases, whereas individual employees in arbitration won fifty-one percent of the time. This distinction is impressive considering the relatively superior resources of the EEOC. The EEOC is very selective in the cases it litigates, and the EEOC also has far greater resources than an individual plaintiff to prepare and present a case. In addition, the EEOC brings the credibility and prestige of the federal government to the case. One explanation for the EEOC's low success rate in litigation may be that the EEOC brings a higher percentage of "test" cases which are designed to expand the law using new theories than the private bar, and that this artificially depresses its success rate relative to private arbitration. There is probably some truth to this explanation. However, even if one looked only at EEOC cases that are not test cases, the EEOC's success rate in court would fall short of that which is achieved in private arbitration.

The infrequency with which employee-plaintiffs prevail in the civil justice system is surprising. The common perception is that juries are extremely sympathetic to employees. This perception is not entirely accurate. For example, employee-plaintiffs won only forty-four percent of jury verdicts in employment civil rights cases in 1994. Far more important, however, is the number of cases that never reach the jury. Of the 3,419 employment discrimination cases in 1994 in which the federal courts made a definitive judgment, sixty percent were disposed of by pretrial motion. Employers won virtually all of these decisions (ninety-eight percent). Taken together, these figures present a civil justice system far less sympathetic to employees than is commonly believed.

Scattered information from the arbitration systems of individual companies presents similar results. Hughes Aircraft Corporation established a binding arbitration program in 1993. During the first year of operation, 235 cases were closed. Of these, the employees won 141, a success rate of sixty percent.

It is not sufficient, however, to look at how often employees win in arbitration. Justice requires not merely that employees who have been wronged receive some compensation, but that they receive the amount of compensation they deserve. An employee who has suffered great financial loss and emotional injury because of employer discrimination is denied justice if the arbitrator rules in her favor but makes an award far less than her loss.

To examine this aspect of justice, one must compare the relative size of the awards rendered by arbitrators and courts. In another study based on cases from January 1993 to December 1995, Bingham found that the mean damages awarded by arbitrators was $49,030. The mean damages awarded by district courts was $530,611. A direct comparison of these results would be meaningful if the actual harm to the plaintiffs in these two groups were comparable. This, however, is not the case. The district court cases all involved statutory civil rights claims for which the law provides emotional distress and punitive damages (and have facts which will often cause a court to award such damages). Many of the AAA cases, by contrast, were contract claims with only economic damages.

To construct a more meaningful comparison, one can compare the mean damages awarded in arbitration and litigation as a percentage of the damages demanded. The mean damages received in arbitration were approximately twenty-five percent of the amount demanded. The mean received in court was seventy percent of the amount demanded. Thus, even using this rough comparison of the numbers, employee-plaintiffs are far more likely to win in arbitration than if they go to court, but employees who win in court receive higher awards than those who prevail in arbitration.

These findings do not answer the ultimate question of whether employees fare better in arbitration or litigation. A comparison of the total adjusted outcomes of arbitration and litigation is instructive. The "adjusted outcome" is the total amount received by all plaintiffs in arbitration or in court-not merely those who were successful — as a percentage of their demands. This "adjusted outcome" for arbitration-plaintiffs is eighteen percent (i.e., plaintiffs as a whole in arbitration received eighteen percent of their demands). For plaintiffs in litigation, the adjusted outcome is only 10.4%.

* * *

William M. Howard conducted a similar analysis of arbitration and litigation. He analyzed AAA results for 1993–94 and compared them to the results of federal employment litigation for 1992–94. Howard also found that plaintiffs prevailed more often in arbitration. Plaintiffs won sixty-eight percent of their cases in arbitration. Plaintiffs in litigation won only twenty-eight percent of their cases.

The only set of available arbitration data in which employees did not fare well is a set of thirteen discrimination cases from the 1996 caseload of the AAA. Employees won only one of these cases. The sample is so small, however, that it is difficult to attribute great significance to this report.

Even arbitration systems that provide inadequate due process have relatively high rates of employee success. The securities industry is one of the major industries with an established arbitration system. Its system has been highly criticized for its lack of impartiality. The roster of arbitrators for the securities industry's arbitration system is dominated by elderly white males, many of whom are former securities industry executives. Worst of all, the system does nothing to eliminate the repeat player problem.

Even in such a flawed system, employees did reasonably well. In the earliest study of this system, Bompey and Pappas found that employees prevailed in forty-three percent of the cases between 1989 and 1992. In a slightly more recent study, the GAO found that employees won fifty-five percent of their cases. While these results are predictably lower than the success rates in the more fair AAA system, even this flawed version of arbitration has higher employee success rates than the courts.

* * *

Thus, the data furnishes little support for the idea that arbitration shortchanges employees. All of the studies find that employees prevail more often in arbitration than they do in court. And while successful plaintiffs receive less in arbitration than in court, plaintiffs as a whole recover more. There is no evidence of arbitral bias against employees-employee-plaintiffs win more often, and receive a higher percentage of their demands than employer-plaintiffs. In addition, employees seldom appeal arbitrators' decisions, even when they have the right to. Moreover, employee response to employer dispute resolution systems as a whole indicates a substantial amount of satisfaction. This does not mean that private arbitration is always fair. There are many ways in which employers can and do structure arbitration systems to deny justice to employees. It does mean, however, that private arbitration is not inherently unfair to employees, and that arbitration often does a good job of providing workplace justice. In some cases, arbitration does a better job than the civil courts.

While there is not yet systematic data on this subject, it is likely that legal fees in arbitration may be far lower than in civil cases. One analysis suggests that legal fees in arbitration could run as little as $3,000. The GAO also found that legal fees among its respondents were generally lower in arbitration. Since the one area in which the civil courts outperformed private arbitration was in the size of the awards to successful litigants, to the extent that employees in arbitration have to spend less of their awards on legal fees, this advantage would be considerably reduced.

* * *

ACCESS TO JUSTICE

The greatest issue in workplace justice today, however, is not the quality of justice rendered by our civil courts, or the speed with which it is provided, but the ability of workers to gain access to the justice system.

Many people believe that the civil justice system adequately protects the rights of workers, and that the situation is getting better over time. The sources of this perception are not difficult to discover. Newspapers and television carry a continual stream of stories about multimillion dollar jury verdicts against employers. Every session of Congress produces new laws improving the legal rights of employees, even when opponents of employment rights are in power. Best-selling books by pro-management authors claim that employee rights have risen to the level where management's rights have been eclipsed.

The painful reality, however, is that the civil justice system has failed American employees. It has failed, not by unfairly resolving the cases it handles, but by denying most workers access to the system entirely. The economic hurdles facing an employee who seeks justice in court are staggering. The cost of litigating an employment dispute is at least $10,000, even if the case is resolved without trial. If a trial is required, the cost increases to at least $50,000. Costs of this magnitude represent several years' pay for most employees and far exceed their ability to pay under the best of circumstances.

Most employment disputes do not arise under the best of circumstances. The majority of employment disputes arise when the employee has been terminated. It is nearly impossible for a worker to raise thousands of dollars for an attorney when she is struggling to support herself and his dependents without an income. The vast majority of employment law cases is handled on a contingent fee basis. However, the requirements for an attorney to accept a case on this basis are demanding. Since he will not be paid unless he wins, an attorney takes a case on contingency only if the probability of winning is extremely high. In civil rights cases in particular, the amount of time an attorney must invest is substantial. Attorneys who believe prospective clients have a legitimate case, but are not confident they will prevail at trial, will generally be forced to turn down the case.

A high probability of success is not enough. The amount of recovery must be sufficiently large that the attorney's share, which is generally one-third, will adequately compensate him for the substantial amount of time and out-of-pocket expense he will have to invest. Even if the client has clearly been wronged and is virtually certain to prevail in court, the attorney will be forced to turn down the case unless there are substantial damages. A survey of plaintiff employment lawyers found that a prospective plaintiff needed to have a minimum of $60,000 in provable damages — not including pain and suffering or other intangible damages — before an attorney would take the case.

Even this, however, does not exhaust the financial obstacles an employee must overcome to secure representation. In light of their risk of losing such cases, many plaintiffs' attorneys require a prospective client to pay a retainer, typically about $3,000. Others require clients to pay out-of-pocket expenses of the case as they are incurred. Expenses in employment discrimination cases can be substantial. Donohue and Siegelman found that expenses in Title VII cases are at least $10,000 and can reach as high as $25,000. Finally, some plaintiffs' attorneys now require a consultation fee, generally $200–$300, just to discuss their situation with a potential client.

The result of these formidable hurdles is that most people with claims against their employer are unable to obtain counsel, and thus never receive justice. Paul Tobias, founder of the National Employment Lawyer's Association, has testified that ninety-five percent of those who seek help from the private bar with an employment matter do not obtain counsel. Howard's survey of plaintiffs' lawyers produced the same result. A Detroit firm reported that only one of eighty-seven employees who came to them seeking representation was accepted as a client.

* * *

Conclusion

The trend toward arbitration of employment disputes can be either a blessing or a curse for civil rights. At its worst, private arbitration threatens to usher in a dark age in which employers roll back all the gains in equal employment opportunity for which the civil rights movement has fought so long and hard-a nightmare in which employees are forced to take their discrimination complaints into employer-controlled systems that are little better than kangaroo courts.

At its best, however, arbitration holds the potential to make workplace justice truly available to rank-and-file employees for the first time in our history. Our civil justice system has failed at making workplace justice affordable. By reducing the costs, private arbitration holds the potential for bringing justice to many to whom it is currently denied.

This need not be second-class justice. Analysis of the available data shows that employee-plaintiffs generally fare as well in arbitration as they do in court, even though most of the experience it reflects took place before the establishment of the due process standards that currently exist. The quality of justice employees receive in arbitrations under these standards should be even better.

Under these circumstances, it would be a serious mistake for the civil rights community to attempt to stop the trend to employment arbitration. The forces behind this trend may well be irresistible, and trying to stop them may leave us like King Canute, vainly ordering the tide not to come in. More importantly, even if we were to succeed, our "success" would mean leaving rank-and-file employees in a world in which they have little hope of receiving justice.

The better course is to have the wisdom and the courage to recognize that the current system is inadequate, and to seize the opportunity to use arbitration to make it better. This does not mean accepting arbitration as it is unilaterally developed by employers. Arbitration should never be a condition of employment. And even when it is freely chosen, arbitration must provide due process. Instead, our opportunity is to become involved in the development of private arbitration and shape its development so that it becomes a blessing rather than a curse.

Notes and Questions

1.   Mr. Maltby's article was a response to the important research by Professor Lisa Bingham documenting a repeat player effect in arbitration

that Maltby summarizes in his article. For more detailed accounts, see Lisa B. Bingham, *Employment Arbitration: The Repeat Player Effect*, 1 Employee Rights & Emp. Pol'y 189 (1997); Lisa B. Bingham, *On Repeat Players, Adhesive Contracts, and the Use of Statistics in Judicial Review of Employment Arbitration Awards*, 29 McGeorge L. Rev. 223 (1998). For more on repeat players, see Carrie Menkel-Meadow, *Do the "Haves" Come Out Ahead in Alternative Judicial Systems? Repeat Players in ADR*, 15 Ohio St. J. on Disp. Resol. 19 (1999); Marc Galanter, *Why the "Haves" Come Out Ahead: Speculations on the Limits of Legal Change*, 9 L. & Soc'y Rev. 95 (1974).

2.   Professor Ware reviewed the empirical studies relied upon by proponents and opponents of *Gilmer* and concluded that the "studies * * * are at best inconclusive on whether the *Gilmer* rule benefits or harms employees." Stephen J. Ware, *The Effects of Gilmer: Empirical and Other Approaches to the Study of Employment Arbitration*, 16 Ohio St. J. on Disp. Resol. 735, 736 (2001).

Referring to the study by Lewis Maltby and another by William Howard, *Mandatory Arbitration of Employment Discrimination Disputes* (1995) (unpublished Ph.D. dissertation, Arizona State University), Ware asserted that:

> "There is, however, an important reason to be skeptical. * * * Empirical studies can tell us the relative levels of awards and process costs in arbitration and litigation, but that does not mean they can tell us the relative levels of awards and process costs in comparable cases. * * * [I]n reality, nobody knows whether the cases going to arbitration are comparable to the cases going to litigation."

Id. at 755

* * *

> "Empirical studies are vulnerable to the possibility that the studied cases going to arbitration are systematically different from the cases going to litigation."

Id. at 757.

3.   Lewis Maltby discussed the problems created by the high costs of litigation and then asserted that properly structured arbitration, " . . . holds the potential to make workplace justice truly available to rank-and-file employees for the first time in our history." Maltby, *supra*, at page 63. Professor Budnitz, on the other hand, concluded that arbitration's costs " . . . can be so high that they deny consumers access in which to air their disputes." Mark E. Budnitz, *The High Cost of Mandatory Consumer Arbitration*, 67 Law & Contemp. Probs. 133, 161 (2004).

What are we to make of this?

4.   Consumer advocates sometimes assume that juries make better decisions than arbitrators. Professor Christopher Drahozal explored this issue and concluded:

> From a behavioral perspective, arbitral decisionmaking appears to be less subject to cognitive illusions than decisionmaking by juries. This is not an across-the-board conclusion about the superiority of arbitral decisionmaking, but rather a tentative conclusion about the effect of heuristics and cognitive biases on two modes of legal decisionmaking. It

is based largely on experimental studies of decisionmaking by judges, and it recognizes that the comparison between judges and arbitrators is not perfect and that drawing real-world conclusions from experiential results is difficult. If arbitral decisionmaking in fact proves to be less subject to cognitive illusions than jury decisionmaking, it would provide some evidence that arbitrators make "better," or at least no worse, decisions than juries.

The most obvious conclusion to be drawn from this analysis, however, is that more research is needed on how cognitive illusions affect arbitral decisionmaking.

Christopher R. Drahozal, *A Behavioral Analysis of Private Judging,* 67 L. & Contemp. Probs. 105, 131 (Winter/Spring 2004).

5. Do arbitrators favor parties who are more likely to provide future business? Professor Drahozal had this to say about three studies by Professor Lisa Bingham:

Lisa Bingham found a "repeat player effect" in a sample of 270 AAA employment arbitration awards issued in 1993 and 1994. Employees were awarded some recovery in 63% of all awards, but in only 16% of awards against repeat player employers — which Bingham defined as employers who were parties to more than one award in the sample. Employees recovered 48% for their demands against repeat player employers. Bingham made it clear that there were several possible explanations for these results, including that there were "systematic differences in the merits of these cases, in that employees in repeat cases may have weaker legal claims, while employees in the non-repeat cases may have stronger legal claims."

In a follow-up study based on 203 AAA employment arbitration awards from 1993 to 1995, Bingham obtained similar results. She concluded, however, that "these patterns largely correspond with differences in the nature of the basis for arbitration." According to Bingham, "[r]epeat player employers get to arbitration based on an implied contract stemming from a personnel manual or employee handbook," cases in which the employee "may have a substantively weaker legal claim." In short, the repeat player effect Bingham has identified seems to have had more to do with the strength of the repeat player employer's claim (and, perhaps, ability to screen cases) than with the incentives facing the arbitrator. In a subsequent study, Bingham and Simon Sarraf compared outcomes before and after the Employment Due Process Protocol, and found that "employers arbitrating pursuant to an adhesive personnel handbook arbitration clause are less successful in employment arbitration after the Protocol than before." They concluded that "[s]elf-regulation through the Due Process Protocol is making a difference in the outcomes of employment arbitration."

Id. at 127–28.

6. From what you have read so far, would you support a private arbitration system for employees that was structured so as to satisfy Lewis Maltby's fairness concerns?

* * *

7.   More than 500 ABA members responded to a 1985–86 survey of attitudes toward commercial arbitration. The survey concentrated on the arbitration of construction cases pursuant to rules of the American Arbitration Association. In summarizing the results, Professor Stipanowich concluded:

> [M]ost attorneys rated arbitrator qualifications as "good" or "excellent," although more than a third of those responding characterized arbitrator qualifications as no better than "fair."

> * * *

> [A]rbitrators compared favorably with juries and judges in perceived decision-making ability. Almost 40% of those responding rated arbitrators as generally fairer than juries, and another 43% believed they were equally as fair. Twenty-four percent ranked arbitration below bench trial in terms of fairness, but an equal number ranked it higher. The remaining half of the group rated the two equally fair.

> * * *

> On average, the respondents indicated arbitration was a speedier means of dispute resolution than either jury trial or bench trial. The results were clearly more favorable in cases involving smaller amounts of money, particularly during the hearing stage.

> * * *

> On average, the survey group rated arbitration as somewhat less costly than litigation; a number of attorneys, however, indicated that if the questionnaire had permitted it they would have reflected different results depending on the size of the case.

> * * *

> Prominent concerns include attorney caused delays, inadequate arbitrator selection methods and consequent variations in arbitrator quality, the absence of written opinions accompanying arbitral awards, and high administrative costs.

> * * *

> The ABA survey demonstrates that, in general, arbitration is a more than satisfactory alternative to the courts. But the research also indicated that for many, arbitration failed to provide efficient, economical, and expert justice. Having taken its place beside the civil justice system as a primary mechanism for dispute resolution, arbitration must continue to mature and evolve so it can better meet public needs and expectations.

Thomas J. Stipanowich, *Rethinking American Arbitration*, 63 Ind. L.J. 425, 425, 455, 458, 460–62, 477 (1988).

8.   The following survey provides insight into why corporate parties might or might not decide to arbitrate.

Reasons Companies Use Mediation and Arbitration (in percent)

Reasons	Mediation	Arbitration
Saves time	80.1	68.5
Saves money	89.2	68.6
Uses expertise of neutral	53.2	49.9
Preserves good relationships	58.7	41.3
Required by contract	43.4	91.6
Provides more durable resolution	31.7	28.3
Preserves confidentiality	44.9	43.2
Avoids legal precedents	44.4	36.9
More satisfactory settlements	67.1	34.8
More satisfactory process	81.1	60.5
Court mandated	63.1	41.9
Dispute involves international parties	15.3	31.9
Allows parties to resolve disputes themselves	82.9	-
Has limited discovery	-	59.3
Standard industry practice	-	33.7

Barriers to ADR Use (in percent)

Reasons	Mediation	Arbitration
No desire from senior management	28.6	35.0
Too costly	3.9	14.8
Too complicated	4.6	9.9
Non binding	40.9	-
Difficult to appeal	-	54.3
Not confined to legal rules	28.1	48.6
Lack of corporate experience	24.7	25.9
Unwillingness of opposing party	75.7	62.8
Results in compromised outcomes	39.8	49.7
Lack of confidence in neutrals	29.0	48.3
Lack of qualified neutrals	20.2	28.4
Risk of exposing strategy	28.6	-

DAVID B. LIPSKY & RONALD L. SEEBER, THE APPROPRIATE
RESOLUTION OF CORPORATE DISPUTES: A REPORT ON
THE GROWING USE OF ADR BY U.S. CORPORATIONS
17, 26 (1998).

For a comparison of arbitration and litigation, see the Maltby article.

9.   The characteristics identified as advantages of arbitration are sometimes criticized as disadvantages. *See, e.g.*, Richard S. Bayer & Harlan S. Abrahams, *The Trouble With Arbitration*, Litigation, Winter 1985, at 30. For

example, arbitrators' refusal to follow the strict rules of evidence has been praised by some as promoting informality and allowing parties to "get things off their chest;" it has been criticized by others because of the "looseness" it produces in hearings. Dallas L. Jones & Russell A. Smith, *Management and Labor Appraisals and Criticisms of the Arbitration Process: A Report and Comments*, 62 Mich. L. Rev. 1115, 1127–30 (1964). Whether a particular characteristic is an advantage or disadvantage depends upon one's perspective and upon the circumstances. Too many lawyers praise or criticize arbitration in general terms instead of asking whether arbitration is appropriate for particular situations and how arbitration can be tailored to maximize its advantages in specific circumstances.

10.   Parties who agree to arbitrate usually choose an existing system instead of constructing a system tailored to their unique needs. In Stephen D. Houck, *Complex Commercial Arbitration: Designing a Process to Suit the Case,* Arb. J., Sept. 1998, at 3 (1988), the author concludes that, "through a variety of features incorporated into the arbitration agreement, the parties obtained the benefits of full-scale federal litigation while avoiding many of its pitfalls (for example, inordinate expense, long delays, and seemingly anomalous monetary damage awards). * * * "

11.   For each question below, would you recommend use of arbitration in that particular situation? In each instance, give reasons for your recommendation. If you believe you would need additional information before deciding what to recommend, state specifically what you would need and why.

(a) Your contractor client asks whether an arbitration clause should be included in a construction contract covering a $20 million office building project. Your client tells you that, in her experience, such projects generate numerous disputes involving small sums of money and occasional disputes involving large sums.

(b) Your corporate client asks whether you would recommend creation of an arbitration system that permits the company's customers to elect binding arbitration of disputes arising from allegations that the company's products are defective. The company manufactures heating and air conditioning units. Several product liability suits have been filed against the company, some of which have generated unfavorable publicity.

(c) Your homeowner client asks whether he should sue in court or file for arbitration pursuant to the system established by the manufacturer in question (b) above. Your client believes that the air conditioning unit which he purchased is defective and that he has suffered approximately $1,000 in damages. Both the retail dealer and the manufacturer have ignored his complaints about the unit.

(d) The personnel manager of your corporate client asks whether the company should establish a system of binding arbitration to process the complaints of its non-union employees, including allegations of age, race, or sex discrimination. She also asks whether employees should be required to agree to the arbitration process as a condition of obtaining employment with the company.

(e) Your client is the wife in a divorce action. You and her husband's lawyer have been unable to negotiate agreements on property, support, or child custody. The husband's lawyer has proposed binding arbitration of these issues.

12. If you were drafting the arbitration provision in the situation described in note 9(d), what provisions would you include for selection of the arbitrator and payment of the arbitrator? *See* John F. Crawford, Note, Going *'Dutch: Should Employees Have to Split the Costs of Arbitration in Disputes Arising from Mandatory Employment Arbitration Agreements*, 2004 J. Disp. Resol. 278.

Chapter VI

MIXED PROCESSES, ADAPTATIONS, AND OTHER INNOVATIONS

If any one quality characterizes the alternative dispute resolution movement, it may well be innovation. As we have seen, the movement was born out of a felt need by many inside and outside the legal profession to expand beyond traditional public adjudication in the resolution of disputes, and the development of the processes themselves has been a dynamic process of experimentation and adaptation.

In this chapter, we look at this evolution in terms of innovative types of dispute resolution processes, as well as the seemingly inevitable expansion of alternative dispute resolution processes into new contexts. In particular, we look at "mixed" processes, which combine elements of negotiation, mediation, fact finding, or adjudication — the primary dispute resolution processes — as well as three different contexts in which both traditional and mixed processes have been used: public courts, administrative agencies, and the private sector. Each process and context provides different challenges, and opportunities, with regard to many of the questions we have been exploring throughout this book, including the suitability of a dispute resolution process for a particular dispute, and the lawyer's role in helping the client select an appropriate dispute resolution process. You should continue to keep these questions in mind as you read the following materials. Also consider whether and why a mixed process may be more appropriate for a given dispute or dispute resolution system, as well as any arguments against the use of mixed processes, such as confusion, complexity, or cost. Finally, consider how you might combine or adapt the primary processes creatively to address other situations or contexts.

This chapter broadly distinguishes between the public and private spheres, beginning with the public sphere. Section A–1 focuses on the use of primary processes, mixed processes, and other innovations in public courts, and Section B addresses their use in administrative agencies. Section B also looks at their use in the private sphere, including both traditional contexts, such as labor-management relations, as well as such new contexts as online dispute resolution.

A. THE PUBLIC SPHERE

1. THE COURTS

a. The Big Picture

This section includes two readings that provide an overview of the use of alternative dispute resolution in the courts. The first, by federal circuit Judge Dorothy Nelson, addresses ADR in the federal courts, while the second, by Christine Carlson, looks at ADR in the state courts and agencies. As you read these excerpts, note the similar issues that both jurisdictions face in institutionalizing ADR, and think about ways that they might be overcome.

DOROTHY WRIGHT NELSON, ADR IN THE FEDERAL COURTS — ONE JUDGE'S PERSPECTIVE: ISSUES AND CHALLENGES FACING JUDGES, LAWYERS, COURT ADMINISTRATORS, AND THE PUBLIC

17 Ohio St. J. on Disp. Resol. 1, 3–14 (2001).

II. Why Court-Annexed ADR Is Good

There are those who argue that if courts shift their focus to ADR, they will retard the development of the law by removing law-making cases from judicial decision-making. However, even in the absence of alternative procedures, less than five percent of cases go to trial, and in the traditional adjudicatory system, as in alternative procedures, potential law-making cases settle because the parties choose to do so. It is unimaginable that a judge would force parties to trial so that a new legal principle might be set.

Courts have the opportunity to present new models to the community that can help to establish and maintain important norms for behavior of citizens. Alternative models can teach cooperation rather than emphasizing conflict, openness rather than secrecy, and dependence on oneself rather than authorities for the resolution of problems.

Good ADR programs can contribute significantly to the quality of justice by providing better focused, more productive, and more efficient pretrial case development. In good ADR programs, communication across party lines is more direct, less constrained, more flexible, and less stylized than in traditional litigation. Further, they require consideration of facts through a type of exchange that communicates not only empirical information but also interpretive perspective, and they allow for use of norms, which is accommodative rather than binary, pluralist rather than singularist.

In the traditionally litigated case, the litigants themselves seldom participate either in attorney-negotiated settlements or judge-facilitated settlements. Research reveals that litigants express little satisfaction with either, ranking judicial settlement conferences as the least fair method for resolving cases. In addition, because settlement generally focuses on only money, litigants may believe that critical issues of right and wrong have been trivialized.

To those who argue that ADR is unnecessary because most claims settle anyway, the answer is that what litigants want — and what ADR provides — is a forum that they would not otherwise have in which their story may be told.

Frankly, there are times when a sophisticated, knowledgeable neutral can be much better than a judge. Such a neutral in an Early Neutral Evaluation (ENE) proceeding, who has subject matter expertise, can help the parties to understand each other more clearly, as well as the pertinent law and evidence. Most judges are likely to have less time and less subject matter expertise than the evaluator. Further, many judges do not consider it appropriate for them to give an assessment of the case's value. Additionally, the parties may still go to court, so the evaluation may serve as a supplement and not as a substitute for traditional litigation.

An argument can be made that at least some litigants and lawyers have greater confidence in a court ADR process than a private one. A private provider, who may depend on large companies for repeat business, may not engender the same feeling of neutrality, especially if the alternative is a court neutral as is the case in the Ninth Circuit Court of Appeals. In addition, the public may have more confidence in a court-designed process than those developed in the private sector by entities with vested or other economic interests. * * *

Court-annexed ADR in well designed and managed programs can save litigants time and money. An example is the ENE program in the Northern District of California, which brings parties and a volunteer neutral together early in the litigation process to discuss and plan the case. At that time, the neutral addresses one of the major sources of litigation costs — discovery. In an evaluation of the ENE program, one third of the attorneys in the cases reported decreased costs and another third reported no known impact. The median savings by attorneys was $10,000 and $20,000 by the parties.

Last, but certainly not of the least importance, ADR procedures can reduce pretrial demands on judges and allow them to give more time to trials. The purpose of ADR is not to force a reduction in trial rates, but to ensure that trial time is available for cases that need a trial or that will contribute to the development of the law.

III.   BRIEF HISTORY OF ADR IN THE FEDERAL COURTS

The first mediation and arbitration programs began in the 1970s. Summary jury trial and early neutral evaluation were innovations of the 1980s. During that time there were two additional significant developments. The first formal recognition of ADR's role was stated in the 1983 amendment to the *Federal Rule of Civil Procedure 16*. It provided for the use of "extrajudicial procedures to resolve the dispute." The second was an act of Congress passed in 1988, which authorized ten district courts to implement mandatory arbitration programs and an additional ten to establish voluntary arbitration programs. Then, the Civil Justice Reform Act of 1990 (CJRA) gave further impetus to the ADR movement. It required all district courts to develop, with the help of an advisory group of local lawyers, scholars, and other citizens, a district-specific plan to reduce cost and delay in civil litigation. ADR was one of six management principles recommended by the statute. During the early and mid–1990s some federal district courts received modest levels of funding because the CJRA called for a limited number of pilot and demonstration districts. How much money individual courts received depended on the level of initiative and commitment in each court to ADR, and this varied widely from district to district. Indeed, many courts implemented no activity under CJRA and therefore, received no money. * * *

* * * Congress moved in a better direction when it passed the ADR Act of 1998. The Act requires every district court to "devise and implement" an ADR program that compels all civil litigants to consider the use of ADR and which provides them with at least one ADR process. Each court has the discretion (in consultation with the bar and the local U.S. Attorney) to choose which processes it will offer and which categories of cases will be exempt from its ADR program.

The Act provides no money but it does authorize Congress to provide the necessary funding to implement its terms. Thus far, Congress has chosen not to do so. Courts must have the resources to run ADR programs and ensure the quality of ADR services. Despite the lack of current funding, I am optimistic about the positive effects of the Act.* * *

Appellate mediation programs have existed since the late 1970s when the Second Circuit was the first to launch such a program and was followed by the Sixth Circuit in the early 1980s. The Ninth Circuit program, which was launched in the late 1980s, was at first opposed by many members of the bench and bar but is now widely acclaimed throughout our circuit. The court employs eight full-time circuit mediators, including a supervising Chief Circuit Mediator, to facilitate settlement of appeals. * * * Recent statistics show that of 880 cases mediated in 2000, 745 or eighty-five percent were settled. The programs in other circuits vary considerably. Some are very small with only one staff attorney and reach a very small percentage of the civil cases on the docket. Others use some staff professionals, but in most cases the mediators are private lawyers who have been selected and trained by the court. They serve on only a few cases a year, usually on a pro bono basis, while maintaining a full time law practice. * * *

IV. SOME ISSUES AND CONCERNS

A. *What Is the Purpose of ADR in the Federal Court System, and How Do We Evaluate Success?*

There is a real danger that we will expect too much from court-annexed ADR and that we will permit ADR's success to be judged by criteria that fail to reflect the full range of values that ADR can advance. A study of the Demonstration Programs, which were established under the Civil Justice Reform Act, reported that the goals of the courts adopting case management programs varied from court to court. They included a desire to reduce cost and delay, to bring greater uniformity to case management, to establish judicial control of cases, to eliminate unnecessary discovery, and to create a system of accountability for judges and cases. Thus, efficiency and reducing cost and delay appear to be the values that account for much of the interest of the courts in the ADR process. While these values are important, access to ADR, the potential for creative solutions, and the ability of the parties to participate in the outcomes should not be underestimated. Other values include increasing the rationality, the fairness, and the civility of the disputing process; expanding the information base on which parties make key decisions in litigation and settlement; reducing parties' alienation from the justice system; expanding parties' opportunities to act constructively and creatively; helping parties understand and vent emotions; and expanding the parties' tools for dealing with the psychological, social and economic dynamics that always accompany and sometimes drive litigation.

If we measure the success of our programs by the rate or timing of settlements, then court neutrals may permit settlements to dominate their processes. A neutral who feels pressure to "get the case settled" may be tempted to manipulate the parties toward that end. Neutrals will be tempted to be more evaluative than facilitative, which initially at least, should be their primary goal.

Certainly, the purpose of court-annexed ADR should not be defined as permitting courts to unburden themselves of unwanted classes of cases. The purpose of ADR is not to get the case out of the court just to make life easier for judges and administrators. Its purpose is to provide respect for the courts for providing dispute resolution tools that really give the parties an opportunity, successful or not, to try to solve their problems with some help from the neutral provided by the court.

In conclusion, some judges and judicial administrators might be attracted to ADR only or primarily as a docket reduction tool, and this could pose a threat to fairness and other values ADR should be promoting. There is also a risk that some judges and administrators might try to use ADR programs as a dumping ground for categories of cases that are deemed unpopular, unimportant, annoying, or especially difficult. A concern that the limited resources of the court may prompt process design decisions that compromise the quality of the court sponsored programs is also present. Therefore, courts should be very careful to design processes that serve appropriate goals and values.

B. *Should Courts Adopt an "In–House" or an "Out–House" Model of ADR?*

How a court defines the primary purpose of its program and how a court prioritizes the values and interests its program can affect the court's choices for delivering ADR services.

Magistrate Judge Wayne D. Brazil has described five "models" that courts might use for delivering ADR services.

1. Full-time in-house neutrals that the court hires and pays with public funds and who are full-time employees of the court.

2. A court contracts with a non-profit organization that provides the neutrals and administers the program. The parties may or may not pay fees.

3. A court directly pays individuals or firms to serve as neutrals.

4. A court recruits and trains private individuals who serve as neutrals and are available with no charge to the parties.

5. The court refers parties to private neutrals, who charge the parties market rates.

Judge Brazil concludes that no one model is superior to another in all settings but that it depends on a host of assumptions and variables such as purposes of the ADR programs, the kinds of cases and parties to be served, whether the process is mandatory or voluntary, whether the parties are represented by counsel, the volume of cases the system will be asked to accommodate, and the role the court wants the neutral to play.

He suggests that the staff neutral model is the most likely to inspire confidence in the motives that drive the court to establish an ADR process, the least likely to communicate to the public that an ADR process is second rate, and the most likely to communicate that the court defines itself as a service-oriented institution. Also, in this model, the economic and social barriers to participation are likely to be lowest.

On the other hand, staff neutral models that provide for the hiring of only a few neutrals are inferior to those models that use a large and diverse pool of neutrals in inspiring confidence in the political and moral integrity of a program. The models with a larger number of neutrals have a substantially greater capacity to provide parties with neutrals who have subject matter expertise. Further, these models allow courts to offer ADR services to a much larger number of cases than courts that rely on a small cadre of professionals.

The staff neutral model is superior in developing sophisticated neutrals with more refined and sensitive process skills through continuous in-house training. It also provides the most reliable and least expensive performance quality control. However, an important caveat is that there is a greater likelihood that there may be inappropriate communication between the neutral and the judge when the neutral is a full time employee of the courts. Judges are keenly interested in the status of cases assigned to them and may not always be sensitive to confidentiality rules.

Finally, whatever model is used, it is clear that the quality of the neutral is the most important factor in determining the success of the ADR process.

C. *Will Courts Overlegalize ADR, or Will ADR Enhance Court Practices?*

Guarding against the overlegalization of ADR is a real need. In the early 1970s when the University of Southern California Dispute Resolution Center was assisting communities to set up neighborhood courts, some of our faculty were involved in training neighborhood neutrals. One day, two of those neutrals came to my office and suggested that the neutrals be given robes to wear so that they would be given proper respect. At that moment, I realized that our training of neutrals in the art of mediation was not complete! We must keep ADR from being just another arena in which litigation behaviors of some lawyers are played out. These behaviors include pressing specious arguments, concealing significant information or delaying its disclosure, obscuring weaknesses, misleading parties about projected evidence from percipient or expert witnesses, resisting well-made suggestions, intentionally injecting hostility into the process, remaining rigidly attached to positions not sincerely held, or needlessly protracting the proceedings to wear down the other parties or to increase their cost burdens. If you look at the titles of some continuing education course with themes such as "How to Win in ADR" or "Successful Advocacy Strategies for Mediations" it appears that some of these behaviors may be encouraged.

As Professor Carrie Menkel–Meadow suggests, the term "mediation advocate" is an oxymoron. Adversarial behaviors may make mediation, which is the most "alternative" to traditional adversary practice, into an adversarial proceeding, where lawyers on opposite sides prepare briefs or mediation submissions, plan opening statements and case narratives, ask for third party neutral evaluations, and direct their attention to the mediator, when they should be planning with their clients how to negotiate and problem-solve with the other side. Mediation should be a facilitated negotiation seeking agreement and settlement and not a "decision-seeking" process. Ideally, lawyers should be looking for solutions that maximize gain or minimize harm to all those involved in a legal problem. They should be candid with their clients, mediators, arbitrators, judges, and opponents and should refuse to insist on an agreement or outcome that causes injustice or is worse than the outcome the parties could achieve in some other way such as litigation. This is why it is important that all law schools ... teach problem-solving skills. The curriculum should not end with doctrinal analysis, but should include other skills such as counseling, planning, negotiation, decision analysis, and applied psychology. * * *

Equally important is that the popularity of certain features of ADR is beginning to affect court rules and procedures. For instance, mediation and arbitration both permit greater direct participation by parties in the process, and both provide a less adversarial forum. Adoption of new rules for settlement conferences, including encouraging the parties themselves to attend and participate directly in settlement discussions, has already brought ADR features into the court. Thus, the character of our formal legal procedure is changing in response to the demonstrated appeal of process features used by ADR.

* * *

CHRISTINE N. CARLSON, ADR IN THE STATES: GREAT PROGRESS HAS BEEN MADE, BUT THERE IS STILL MUCH TO DO

Disp. Resol. Mag., Summer 2001, at 4, 4–5.

Assessing our progress

In the early 1980s, three state courts created the first state dispute resolution offices. Shortly after those programs got underway, other state government leaders recognized the utility of ADR methods for dealing with environmental, public policy and other kinds of disputes. The National Institute for Dispute Resolution (NIDR) stepped forward and offered seed grants that helped 11 more states get public-policy dispute resolution programs started in the administrative branch or in state universities. By 1990 there were 16 state ADR programs.

A pair of studies by the Policy Consensus Initiative (PCI) indicated that the use of ADR in the states was growing, and at an accelerated rate. A 1998 study attempted to identify which states had comprehensive ADR offices that provided resources and services to government agencies, courts, communities or schools on a statewide basis. It found 30 offices located in 27 states. About half of the centers were located in courts, and the other half in the administrative branch or in state universities. Florida, Ohio and North Carolina each had two programs — one serving state courts and one serving the administrative branch, state and local government, communities, or schools.

In just three years, that landscape changed dramatically, as a second PCI study found more than 175 ADR programs — and undoubtedly some were overlooked. These include the following:

- 39 state-court ADR centers,
- 6 centers housed in the administrative branch,
- 3 statewide cabinet-level ADR coordinating bodies,
- 53 individual agency programs, not including special education, workers compensation or agricultural mediation programs,
- 32 offices of attorneys general that list an ADR contact
- 15 states in which administrative law judges have mediation programs, and
- 34 university-based programs serving state government.

While this growth in the number of state programs is encouraging, real growth in ADR use in state government is still slow. Because the current trend is to cut back government, finding support and resources to initiate new state ADR offices has not been easy. In recent years, the only new comprehensive ADR resource/service centers have been created in state courts. State policy leaders seem to understand and accept new ADR programs in courts more readily than in the policy and administrative branches of government.

* * *

The research also indicates considerable growth in individual agencies with ADR programs. However, numbers may belie the capacity and strength of these programs. Many are one-person operations, directed by someone who has been designated an ADR coordinator (with ADR responsibilities added to existing duties). Frequently, this ADR coordinator has no special knowledge or background and receives no funds for program activities. In states without comprehensive ADR resource/service centers, individual agencies may not have access to necessary resources and expertise to assist in developing their capacity to deliver quality programs and services.

Barriers in states

Further research has identified specific and common barriers to greater use of ADR processes in states:

(1) lack of information and negative perceptions about ADR,

(2) lack of money,

(3) organizational and bureaucratic resistance to change,

(4) uncertainty about authority to use ADR and other legal issues, and

(5) lack of leadership and support from state leaders and the legal community.

It also found that leaders who support the use of ADR processes can overcome these barriers. In addition, developing and disseminating information and materials can help leaders implement ADR policies and programs.

Overcoming institutional resistance to change requires support from top leaders. Leadership from a governor or supreme court justice plays a critical role in successfully introducing dispute resolution and consensus building practices in state government.

Clear legal authority promoting the use of dispute resolution also increases use. This is true not only for the judiciary, but also for administrative agencies. In particular, executive orders are emerging as one of the most effective mechanisms governors can employ to encourage, or direct, administrative agencies to use these practices.

In the past year, four executive orders have been enacted — in Massachusetts, Minnesota, New Mexico and Oregon — to integrate dispute resolution in state government. Three of these states have had long-standing state ADR centers, yet they decided an executive order would help to further enlist state agencies in implementing dispute resolution activities. Executive orders typically require agencies to appoint ADR coordinators, provide training for agency staff, develop plans, and report on how they are using ADR.

Initiating and sustaining state ADR programs requires securing leadership not only from public officials, but also from the bar and from other ADR practitioner organizations. In addition, the private sector is playing an increasingly important role in setting state ADR policies and building support for ADR programs.

The California Dispute Resolution Council is one example of the important role private-sector leadership can play. The Council was organized in 1994 to provide a unified voice for dispute resolution with the state legislature and in other state policy-making arenas. In other states, the bar and other professional organizations are beginning to form committees and councils to gain a say in the policies and programs being developed in their states.

Turf wars

A growing barrier to establishing comprehensive, high-quality ADR programs is the turf battle between the public and private sectors. This issue, which centers on service provision and quality assurance, is both subtle and profound. Some state centers have found ways to address these conflicts productively and to establish an ongoing dialogue with the private sector. Establishing communication, gaining cooperation and building relationships between public and private dispute resolution leaders have proven critical to their success.

* * *

Notes and Questions

1. Judge Nelson's speech mentioned several different and sometimes conflicting purposes for supporting court-annexed ADR programs. These include reducing court loads, saving litigants time and money, and providing a dispute resolution process that is more satisfying than litigation and that produces better outcomes for parties. Which of these do you view as more legitimate for a court-annexed program? Less legitimate? How would you prioritize them?

2. While certainly not unanimous, federal and state judges have generally been supportive of ADR. As long ago as 1992, a survey of federal judges by the Federal Judicial Center found that

• 66% of district court judges disagreed with the proposition that courts should resolve litigation through traditional procedures only;

- 86% disagreed with the proposition that ADR should never be used in the federal courts;

- 56% thought that ADR should be used in the courts because it produces fairer outcomes than traditional litigation in some cases; and

- 86% thought that the role of the federal courts should be to assist parties in resolving their dispute through whatever procedure is best suited to the case.

WILLIAM W. SCHWARZER, ADR AND THE FEDERAL COURTS: QUESTIONS AND DECISIONS FOR THE FUTURE, 7 FJC DIRECTIONS 2 (1994).

Why might some judges be resistant to ADR?

3. Carlson refers to several barriers to institutionalizing ADR in the states, including lack of information and negative perceptions about ADR, lack of money, bureaucratic resistance to change, uncertainty about authority to use ADR and other legal issues, as well as the lack of leadership and support from state leaders and the legal community. Why might these issues be more significant barriers at the state level than at the federal level? State court annexation of ADR processes is discussed in Edward F. Sherman, *A Process Model and Agenda for Civil Justice Reform in the States*, 46 Stan. L. Rev. 1553, 1570–83 (1994).

4. Judge Nelson refers to five different models for the delivery of ADR services that had been identified by U.S. Magistrate Judge Wayne Brazil. These include full-time in-house neutrals who are full-time employees of the court, neutrals who work with non-profit organizations under a contract with the court, private neutrals paid by the court or who perform services for free, as well as private neutrals who charge the parties market rates. Which of these models do you think is most likely to provide the highest quality of neutrals? Which is most likely to inspire confidence and trust in the courts and the rule of law? Which is most likely to be perceived as fair? *See* Wayne D. Brazil, *Comparing Structures for the Delivery of ADR Services by Courts: Critical Values and Concerns*, 14 Ohio St. J. on Disp. Resol. 715 (1999).

5. Carlson notes how quickly ADR programs sprouted up in many states, and that most if not all states have at least some courts with ADR programs. As the preceding question suggests, staffing these programs takes careful consideration, just as it does for federal programs. State and federal court program managers typically develop rosters that include mediators from the local communities, often requiring them to be lawyers, and sometimes requiring them to go through specific training provided or approved by the court. For attorneys interested in mediation practices, positions on these rosters are coveted sources of cases and prestige. Charles Pou Jr. describes the tension this can create with respect to both quality assurance and ethics:

> Decisions over roster admissions and referrals can occasion strong feelings, given the potential to affect egos and livelihoods. There have even been a few bouts of litigation in the arbitration context, where panel composition can be critical.

> In all settings, there is inherently some tension between providers, users and administrators. Providers may seek workloads, opportunities and rewards comparable to their peers, and are not always objective

about their own strengths and weakness. Meanwhile, many users may just want some assurance that they are getting a neutral for their dispute who possesses appropriate ability and style, with minimal transaction and economic costs.

* * *

Roster managers tend to agree with the general consensus that it is difficult to define objectively what constitutes a "qualified" mediator or other neutral. Lacking broadly agreed on standards or certification procedures — and given the controversy that many efforts to address these issues have raised — some entities have "ducked" the issue, and have made no effort to limit or prequalify their rosters. * * *

Most programs ... have established some admission standards in an effort to provide some assurance that listed practitioners possess the necessary competence. As one administrator puts it, "I'd rather risk a few disgruntled neutrals than disgruntled agencies."

Criteria tend to vary depending upon program goals, which in turn affects decisions as to what constitutes "quality practice." Most rosters place relatively low hurdles before neutrals wishing to be listed, except for a few "elite" programs. Roster managers typically focus on standbys like ADR experience, training, mentoring, reputation, recommendations by peers and/or parties, and substantive knowledge in some situations.

* * *

Most roster programs have been considerably less formal, and more subjective, in selection. A few programs have generated comment over "old boy" lists allegedly compiled on a basis of friendship or worse. An extreme case involved a former head of the Wisconsin Employment Relations Commission, who aroused great unhappiness during the 1980s by allegedly exercising his discretion over panel selections so as to eliminate systematically certain experienced arbitrators from all panels. The ensuing scandal, fueled by the agency head's destruction of pertinent public documents, led to a criminal investigation and his resignation.

Charles Pou Jr., *'Wheel of Fortune' or 'Singled Out?': How Rosters 'Matchmake' Mediators*, Disp. Resol. Mag, Spring 1997, at 10, 12.

What factors should be considered in establishing a roster and eligibility for inclusion? What controls should be in place to guard against cronyism? How frequently should a roster be updated? How much information should be made available to parties about roster composition?

6. Although some courts provide mediation or early neutral evaluation through judges or magistrate judges, most court ADR programs rely on nonjudicial neutrals. Most of the mediators, arbitrators, and other neutrals used by the courts are attorneys, with other professionals occasionally authorized to serve in that role.

Not only are attorneys the mainstay of most ADR programs, but in nearly every district the court has created its own roster rather than relying on an already-established list of neutrals or turning to private-sector ADR providers for these services. For example, of the forty-three mediation programs that use nonjudge neutrals, only three rely on an outside organization, such as a bar association or state mediation program, to provide the ADR services. * * *

ELIZABETH PLAPINGER & DONNA STIENSTRA, ADR AND SETTLEMENT IN THE FEDERAL DISTRICT COURTS: A SOURCEBOOK FOR JUDGES AND LAWYERS 7, 8 (1996).

7.   The rise of court-annexed ADR has meant a shift in the nature of what judges do. The "managerial judge" model assumes that judges are expert dispute resolvers, and, "can analyze each dispute, suggest the appropriate methodology for achieving an efficient and fair resolution, and monitor the progress of conflicts to ensure that additional intervention is not necessary." Francis E. McGovern, *Toward a Functional Approach for Managing Complex Litigation*, 53 U. Chi. L. Rev. 440, 442–43 (1986). Professor Judith Resnik has expressed doubts:

> I am deeply skeptical of the capacity of individual judges to craft rules on a case-by-case basis. * * * I do not believe that * * * judges can perform their adjudicatory tasks and still have sufficient time to ascertain which mode of procedure is best suited to each individual case. Moreover, * * * [d]eciding how to mold procedures to a given case may well involve a judge so deeply in managerial and adversarial events that it undermines the ability of the judge to adjudicate — should that become necessary.

Judith Resnik, *Failing Faith: Adjudicatory Procedure in Decline*, 53 U. Chi. L. Rev. 494, 548 (1986). What do you think? Can judges both craft rules and assess cases for the appropriate procedure for dispute resolution? Should they?

8.   Along with the increased ADR responsibility that rests with the judge, a similar responsibility now falls on attorneys and parties. As Stienstra and Plapinger discovered:

> Courts expect attorneys to be knowledgeable about ADR in general and about the court's ADR programs in particular. Many courts' local rules now require attorneys to discuss ADR with their clients and opponents, to address in their case management plan the appropriateness of ADR for the case, and to be prepared to discuss ADR with the judge at the initial Rule 16 scheduling conference.

> These rules indicate the extent to which the courts now expect attorneys to work with the judge to determine whether ADR should be used in a case and, if so, what kind of ADR should be used. The attorneys' and judge's responsibilities merge at the initial case management conference, which in many courts has become the critical event — or the first of several — in determining how and when ADR will be used in the case.

> In the ADR event itself — that is, the mediation session, the ENE conference, or the summary jury trial — clients are generally required to attend. Most courts have not, however, defined the level or kind of participation required by parties and their counsel.

* * *

With the emphasis on case-by-case screening for ADR and the importance of the Rule 16 conference has come a shift in the timing of ADR — or perhaps a recognition that ADR can be used earlier in the case has prompted the emphasis on the Rule 16 conference. In any event, whereas in the past many considered ADR appropriate only for trial-ready cases, now ADR is more often integrated into a court or judge's overall case management practices and is considered much earlier in the case.

ELIZABETH PLAPINGER & DONNA STIENSTRA, ADR AND SETTLEMENT IN THE FEDERAL DISTRICT COURTS: A SOURCEBOOK FOR JUDGES AND LAWYERS 7, 8 (1996).

9. ADR proponents have often sold ADR on efficiency grounds — i.e., that it is faster and less expensive than traditional litigation. However, the many studies of court-annexed ADR have not produced a consensus among scholars. Among the critical studies are JAMES S. KAKALIK, TERENCE DUNWORTH, LAURAL A. HILL, DANIEL MCCAFFREY, MARIAN OSHIRO, NICHOLAS M. PACE & MARY E. VAIANA, AN EVALUATION OF JUDICIAL CASE MANAGEMENT UNDER THE CIVIL JUSTICE REFORM ACT (1996) ("The CJRA pilot program, as the package was implemented, had little effect on time to disposition, litigation costs, and attorneys' satisfaction and views of the fairness of case management"); Lisa Bernstein, *Understanding The Limits of Court–Connected ADR: A Critique of Federal Court–Annexed Arbitration Programs*, 141 U. Pa. L. Rev. 2169, 2176 (1993) (mandatory court-connected arbitration "will tend to systematically disadvantage poorer and more risk-averse litigants"); Kim Dayton, *The Myth of Alternative Dispute Resolution In The Federal Courts*, 76 Iowa L. Rev. 889, 915 (1991) ("[C]laims concerning ADR's potential to reduce costs and delays are exaggerated"); Neil Vidmar & Jeffrey Rice, *Observations About Alternative Dispute Resolution In An Adversary Culture*, 19 Fla. St. U. L. Rev. 89, 97 (1991) (the summary jury trial "largely fails").

For a sample of studies supporting court-annexed ADR, see STEVENS H. CLARKE, LAURA F. DONNELLY & SARA GROVE, COURT-ORDERED ARBITRATION IN NORTH CAROLINA: AN EVALUATION OF ITS EFFECTS (1989) (the program reduced the trial rate in contested cases and lawyers charged less in court-ordered arbitration proceedings); John Barkai & Gene Kassebaum, *Using Court–Annexed Arbitration to Reduce Litigant Costs and to Increase the Pace of Litigation*, 16 Pepp. L. Rev. 543 (1989) (a Hawaii program reduced litigants' costs and the time it takes to terminate cases); Wayne D. Brazil, *A Close Look at Three Court–Sponsored ADR Programs: Why They Exist, How They Operate, What They Deliver and Whether They Threaten Important Values*, 1990 U. Chi. Legal F. 303, 397 ("[E]ach of these programs offers significant benefits to litigants without causing serious harm to competing interests"). Summaries of other studies are included in Lisa Bernstein, *Understanding The Limits of Court–Connected ADR: A Critique of Federal Court–Annexed Arbitration Programs*, 141 U. Pa. L. Rev. 2169, 2174 n.16 (1993).

Studies have consistently found a high degree of satisfaction with court-annexed processes. However, Judge Eisele challenged these findings. G. Thomas Eisele, *Differing Visions — Differing Values: A Comment on Judge Parker's Reformation Model for Federal District Courts*, 46 SMU L. Rev. 1935, 1967–69 (1993).

Deborah Hensler suggests that the reason parties may find greater satisfaction in ADR proceedings has less to do with the efficiency interests that have captivated the courts, and more to do with the process-control issues that have made ADR attractive to businesses and those interested in community justice.

> Interestingly, empirical research on the outcomes of court-annexed ADR procedures suggests a rather different picture of the costs and benefits of these procedures than either ADR proponents or opponents have anticipated. The efficiency gains from court-annexed arbitration and court-mandated family mediation in custody suits appear mixed: The fiscal savings to courts from diverting cases from trial may be outweighed by the costs of running an efficient ADR program, and savings in lawyer time are often modest and not necessarily passed on to litigants through lower legal fees. But the gains in quality of process, at least as assessed by the disputants, appear significant: Because ADR procedures frequently offer litigants with small value cases and modest resources their only practical opportunity for a day in court, parties whose cases are diverted from the traditional negotiation-settlement-trial track to an ADR track are more likely to feel that they have been treated fairly by the justice system and more likely to be satisfied with the process and outcomes than parties whose cases are negotiated to a conclusion, with or without judicial intervention, in the form of a settlement conference. In sum, while the main impetus for ADR in the court context appears to be a desire for efficiency — that is, reductions in cost and delay — the parties' reactions to ADR speak more to the objectives of gaining control over the litigation process that have been associated with the enthusiasm for ADR expressed by the community justice movement and the corporate community.

Deborah R. Hensler, *A Glass Half Full, A Glass Half Empty: The Use of Alternative Dispute Resolution In Mass Personal Injury Litigation*, 73 Tex. L. Rev. 1587, 1593–94 (1995).

10. Attempts to gain public access to court-annexed ADR processes continue to increase. In *Cincinnati Gas and Electric Co. v. General Electric Co.*, 854 F.2d 900 (6th Cir. 1988), the Sixth Circuit rejected an argument by the Cincinnati Post that the First Amendment required the court to permit the newspaper to attend a summary jury trial. The court stressed that the summary jury proceeding would not result in a binding determination. The court reaffirmed its holding that a summary jury trial could be closed to the public in *In re Cincinnati Enquirer, a Division of Gannett Satellite Information, Inc.*, 94 F.3d 198 (6th Cir. 1996).

On the other hand, in *Bank of America National Trust & Savings Association v. Hotel Rittenhouse Associates*, 800 F.2d 339 (3d Cir. 1986), the Third Circuit afforded access to a settlement agreement in spite of the fact that the agreement had been filed under seal at the parties' request. The court asserted that "[e]ven if we were to assume that some settlements would not be effectuated if their confidentiality was not assured, the generalized interest in encouraging settlements does not rise to the level of interests that we have recognized may outweigh the public's common law right of access." *Id.* at 346. The dissenting judge said the majority had reached "an illogical and impractical result." *Id.* at 352.

What factors should be considered in deciding whether the public's right to know will prevail over the parties' need for privacy? *See* STEPHEN B. GOLDBERG, FRANK E.A. SANDER, NANCY H. ROGERS & SARAH RUDOLPH COLE, DISPUTE RESOLUTION 451–63 (3d ed. 2003); Edward D. Sherman, *Policy Issues for State Court ADR Reform,* Alternatives to the High Cost of Litig., Nov. 1995, at 142, 142–43. The case for courthouse confidentiality under appropriate circumstances is made in Arthur R. Miller, *Private Lives or Public Access?,* A.B.A. J., Aug. 1991, at 65.

11.   Assume that you are a member of the local advisory committee for the state court of the jurisdiction in which you practice and that the judges of the court are considering the adoption of a local court rule providing for some form of court-annexed ADR. The judges have asked the committee for recommendations on whether there should be such a court rule, and if such a rule is adopted, which processes should be included in the court rule, and whether participation should be mandatory or voluntary. What position will you take on each of these issues? For additional discussion of designing dispute systems, see Chapter VII, beginning at page 790.

12.   Assume that your client has a dispute with a video production company that he hired to tape his lavish wedding. A technician inadvertently destroyed the master tape and no copies are available. Your client had foregone arranging for photographs because of his confidence in the video production company, which has now offered to refund the $5000 fee. Your client is despondent and furious at the production company. He tells you he is not very concerned about the money, but is motivated principally by revenge — he wants to drive the production company out of business. After you file suit, the director of the court's ADR program sends you a letter indicating that you are required to participate in one of the following court-annexed dispute resolution programs: non-binding arbitration, early neutral evaluation, or mediation. How would you go about helping your client choose?

2.   COURT–ANNEXED MEDIATION

Overwhelmingly, mediation has come to be the most popular form of alternative dispute resolution in the state and federal courts. In this Section, we take a more focused look at how mediation is practiced in civil courts, as well as some unique problems associated with it. In the first section, we take a general look at court-annexed mediation, beginning with a reading by Professors McAdoo, Welsh, and Wissler, which synthesizes the vast accumulation of empirical research that has been conducted in the state and federal courts, and provides practical advice for court program administrators. In the second section, we consider whether courts should require participants to mediate disputes, as well as related problems of how to assure quality participation in court-mandated mediations, and the exceptions to mandatory mediation.

a. An Overview

BOBBI McADOO, NANCY A. WELSH & ROSELLE L. WISSLER, INSTITUTIONALIZATION: WHAT DO EMPIRICAL STUDIES TELL US ABOUT COURT MEDIATION?

Disp. Resol. Mag., Winter 2003, at 8, 8–9.

Most court-connected mediation programs seek successful institutionalization, which we define here as regular and significant use of the mediation process to resolve cases. Voluntary mediation programs rarely meet this goal because they suffer from consistently small caseloads. In contrast, programs that make mediation mandatory (at the request of one party or on a judge's own initiative) have dramatically higher rates of utilization.

Significantly, mandatory referral does not appear to adversely affect either litigants' perceptions of procedural justice or, according to most studies, settlement rates. Further, judicial activism in ordering parties into mediation triggers increased voluntary use of the process, as lawyers begin to request it themselves in anticipation of court referral. An additional benefit of exposing lawyers to mediation is that they are more likely to discuss and recommend the process to their clients.

Another program design option involves requiring lawyers to consider mediation as an integral part of their usual litigation planning. For example, some courts require lawyers to discuss the potential use of mediation or other ADR processes and report the results of that discussion to the court early in the life of a case. Other courts require lawyers to discuss ADR with their clients. These court rules face less lawyer opposition than mandatory case referral and can give lawyers more control over the logistics of mediation (e.g., choice of mediator and timing). Adopting these rules (combined with active judicial support and willingness to order mediation when deemed appropriate) tends to increase requests to use mediation.

The local legal and mediation cultures influence how quickly mediation is integrated into the court system, as well as which program design features are more (or less) acceptable. Knowledgeable leadership from the bar and the judiciary contribute to the growth of mediation programs.

* * *

Which Cases Should Mediate

Many courts have adopted civil mediation programs in order to encourage and obtain the settlement of cases. And, importantly, both lawyers and litigants view mediation more favorably and as more procedurally just when settlement is achieved.

Although it has been suggested that certain general categories of civil cases (e.g., employment, contract) are "best" handled by mediation, there is no empirical support for this notion. Neither settlement rates nor litigants' perceptions of the procedural justice provided by mediation vary with case type. (There is some limited evidence, however, that medical malpractice and product liability cases may be somewhat less likely to settle than other types of tort cases.)

Interestingly, the level of acrimony between the litigants in non-family civil cases does not seem to affect the likelihood of settlement in mediation. Not surprisingly, the cases most likely to settle in mediation are those in which the litigants' positions are closer together, the issues are less complex, or the issue of liability is less strongly contested. Litigants' perceptions of procedural justice do not seem to vary with the tenor of the relationship between the litigants or with these other case characteristics.

Thus, because no case characteristics have been identified for which mediation has detrimental effects, mediation programs do not need to exclude certain types of cases. Some programs may be tempted to exclude the cases that seem likely to reach settlement on their own, without the assistance of a mediator. This choice, however, is likely to limit not only the rate of settlement achieved but also the opportunity to improve litigants' perceptions of the procedural justice of the settlement process and to enhance their views of the courts.

When to Mediate

Without a statute or court rule to the contrary, mediation tends to occur late in the life of a case and often after all discovery is completed. Holding mediation sessions sooner after cases are filed, however, yields several benefits. Cases are more likely to settle, fewer motions are filed and decided, and case disposition time is shorter, even for cases that do not settle in mediation.

Local litigation customs and case management practices affect lawyers' comfort with the early use of mediation, and the chance of settlement is reduced somewhat if lawyers lack critical information about their cases. Discovery does not have to be completed, however, for cases to settle. In addition, the status of dispositive and other motions tends to affect the likelihood of settlement in mediation. If motions are pending, settlement is less likely. Litigants' perceptions of the procedural justice provided by mediation, meanwhile, do not seem to vary with the timing of the session.

Thus, program designers should consider scheduling mediation sessions to be held at some reasonable point before discovery is completed but only after dispositive or other critical motions have been decided.

Who the Mediators Should Be

Mediation is most likely to be successfully institutionalized if the mediators are drawn from the pool that is preferred by lawyers: litigators with knowledge in the substantive areas being mediated. But neither mediators' knowledge of the subject matter of the dispute nor the number of years they have practiced has proved to be related to settlement or to litigants' perceptions of procedural justice.

One characteristic of the mediators, namely having more mediation experience, is related to more settlements. However, several aspects of mediator training, such as the number of hours of training or whether it included role play, tend not to affect settlement. None of these mediator characteristics seem to be related to litigants' perceptions of the procedural justice of mediation.

Thus, program design options that maximize each mediator's level of experience, such as the use of in-house mediators or a limited roster, may enhance the success of the program more than a roster with many mediators who get no or few cases to mediate. Matching mediators to cases based on subject matter expertise makes lawyers more comfortable with the process, but not doing so has not been shown to have detrimental effects on settlement or on litigants' perceptions of justice.

What the mediators should do

The approach that mediators ought to use (facilitative, evaluative, transformative) has been the subject of much debate. Both active facilitation and some types of evaluative interventions tend to produce more settlements as well as heighten perceptions of procedural justice.

For example, when mediators disclose their views about the merits or value of a case, cases are more likely to settle and litigants are more likely to assess the mediation process as fair. By contrast, when mediators keep silent about their views of the case, cases are less likely to settle and litigants' views of procedural justice are not enhanced. But when mediators recommend a particular settlement, litigants' ratings of the procedural fairness of the process suffer, notwithstanding an increased rate of settlement.

When litigants or their lawyers participate more during mediation, cases are more likely to settle than when they participate less. Moreover, the litigants evaluate the mediation process as more fair. In addition, when the lawyers behave more cooperatively during mediation sessions, both the likelihood of settlement and litigant perceptions of procedural fairness increase.

Thus, the training, ethical guidelines and monitoring tools applicable to court-connected mediation programs should encourage mediators to facilitate participation by both litigants and their lawyers and to enhance the amount of cooperation during the session. Programs need not discourage all evaluative interventions, but should restrict those, such as recommending particular settlements, that reduce litigants' perceptions of the fairness of the mediation process.

Roles for lawyers

In civil mediation sessions, lawyers generally speak on their clients' behalf and, consequently, do more of the talking. Neither settlement nor litigants' perceptions of procedural justice tend to be harmed by this allocation of responsibility between the lawyer and client. As noted earlier, greater participation by both lawyers and clients is beneficial. Litigants' presence during the session is important for several reasons, most notably because litigants who are not present view the dispute resolution process as less fair. Lawyers also perceive that their clients' presence changes the lawyers' role in settlement, makes the clients' interests more relevant and influences ultimate outcomes.

Preparation for the mediation session also is important. The more lawyers prepare their clients for mediation, the greater the likelihood of settlement in mediation and the greater the litigants' perception of procedural fairness. As noted earlier, greater cooperation among the lawyers during mediation also has these benefits. Interestingly, both greater client preparation and more cooperation among lawyers lead attorneys as well as their clients to view the mediation process as more fair.

Thus, court-connected mediation programs should encourage litigants to attend and participate in mediation sessions. Attorneys should be expected to prepare their clients for mediation, and mediation programs should provide information to assist their preparation. Lawyers should adopt a cooperative rather than a contentious approach during the session.

Advice for program designers

In this article, we have presented empirical data that address the effects that important program design choices have on institutionalization, settlement and perceptions of justice. We assume that court-connected mediation programs are concerned about all three of these issues, although courts' desire to institutionalize mediation or encourage settlement should never overwhelm their commitment to justice. The research suggests that the following program design options can enhance one or more of these three components without diminishing any of the others:

To maximize the use of court-connected civil mediation programs:

- Enlist the bench and bar in developing a program that fits the local legal culture.

- Obtain on-going judicial support for referring cases to the program.

- Make mediation use compulsory if one side requests it, or require attorneys to consider mediation early in the litigation process.

To increase the likelihood of settlement in mediation:

- Schedule sessions fairly early in the life of a case.

- Require that critical motions be decided before the session.

- Adopt a system that ensures that the mediators get enough cases to keep their mediation skills sharp.

To heighten litigants' perceptions that the program provides procedural justice:

- Require litigants to attend the session and invite them, along with their attorneys, to participate.

- Urge lawyers to adopt a cooperative approach and prepare their clients for mediation.

- Restrict more extreme evaluative interventions such as recommending a specific settlement.

* * *

b. Mandatory Mediation

As Welsh, McAdoo, and Wissler note, parties are often required to mediate cases that have been filed in federal and state courts. The excerpt from Trina Grillo's article, *The Mediation Alternative: Process Dangers for Women*, in Chapter IV beginning at page 478, introduced some of the challenges associated with mandatory mediation where the power disparities between the parties is great, such as may be the case with women in domestic violence situations.

In this subsection, we look at other issues that arise from mandatory mediation. After briefly describing the situation in the federal courts, at least as of the time of the last comprehensive survey of the use of ADR in the federal courts, we focus on two problems. First, we look at the issue of what exceptions may be appropriate to a court-annexed mandatory mediation program, returning to the domestic violence context to explore the issues. We then examine the problem of good faith participation in court-annexed mandatory mediation programs.

ELIZABETH PLAPINGER & DONNA STIENSTRA, ADR
AND SETTLEMENT IN THE FEDERAL DISTRICT
COURTS: A SOURCEBOOK FOR JUDGES
AND LAWYERS 7

(1996).

During the past several years, there has been substantial attention in the federal courts to the issue of *how* cases are referred to ADR, a debate centered largely on the pros and cons of mandatory versus voluntary referral to arbitration. With the emergence of mediation as the primary ADR process, however, and the abandonment of several mandatory arbitration programs, the principal referral mechanisms used today are notably different from those used a few years ago.

Few of the mediation programs refer cases mandatorily and automatically by case type. Most leave to the judge and/or parties the identification of cases suitable for ADR.

Whether the referral is made sua sponte or at the request of one or more parties (both of which are authorized in most programs), the judge has become the focal point for identifying cases appropriate for ADR and for educating attorneys and parties about it. Rather than remaining in the background, as in the mandatory arbitration programs, the newer forms of ADR expect the judge to be very much at the center of ADR use.

Even within the arbitration programs, the picture is much more nuanced than the terminology suggests. In the so-called mandatory programs, for example, the referral is only presumptively mandatory. Courts with these programs provide mechanisms for seeking removal from arbitration, and some courts readily grant such removal. Variation is also found in the voluntary programs, with several courts adhering to the textbook model of participation only if the parties voluntarily come forward, but with several others automatically referring cases on the basis of objective criteria and then permitting unquestioned opt-out by the parties.

Note and Questions

1. As Plapinger and Stienstra observe, federal court ADR programs typically let individual judges decide which cases to refer to mediation instead of mandating mediation by the nature of the claim. Many state court systems, however, do mandate that some classes of cases be mediated, often as a condition for proceeding to trial. For example, California requires mediation for all civil cases valued at $50,000 or less before they may be heard at law. Cal. Civ. Proc. Code § 1141.11(a) (Deering Supp. 1995). Florida and Texas also permit courts to require mediation for all civil cases. *See* Fla. Stat. ch. 44.302 (2003); Tex. Civ. Prac. & Rem. Code Ann. §§ 154.021–023 (West 1997).

2. Would you support a mandatory mediation program for your local court? Would you limit it to certain claims? Would you prefer a local rule that would authorize the court's judges to refer a case to mediation?

i. Exceptions to Compelled Participation in Mediation

Most if not all mandatory mediation programs have at least some exceptions to compelled participation. Trina Grillo's *The Mediation Alternative: Process Dangers for Women* was an early call for an exception for cases involving domestic violence. The following reading discusses how states have responded.

LAUREL WHEELER, COMMENT, MANDATORY FAMILY MEDIATION AND DOMESTIC VIOLENCE
26 S. Ill. U. L.J. 559, 563–70 (2002).

* * *

III. Analysis of the Problem

A. *Domestic Violence Exceptions to Mandatory Mediation*

Most states have developed mandatory family mediation programs, and many of them have addressed the domestic violence problem, although the approaches differ. "Currently, court-connected mediation plans vary widely from state to state, with no consensus among jurisdictions on the role mediation should play when domestic violence somehow taints the process."[30] To deal with cases involving domestic violence, many states force courts to exempt a couple from mediation because of a domestic violence history. The four states that will serve as examples of the various approaches are: Colorado, Ohio, Illinois, and California.

Colorado provides a domestic violence exemption for situations where one party alleges abuse and states that he or she is unwilling to mediate. In *Pearson v. District Court*, one of the few examples of case law on the subject, the Colorado Supreme Court held that a trial court is precluded from ordering a spouse who claims to be victim of domestic violence to participate in mediation with the other spouse, regardless of when the declaration of abuse was filed. The trial court had ordered Karen Sanders to mediate disputes with her former husband in post-dissolution of marriage proceedings. She immediately appealed this order and alleged that "during the course of the marriage [her former husband] was physically and emotionally abusive, and that she 'suffer[ed] severe anxiety episodes when interacting' with her former husband and 'sh[ook] uncontrollably' when in his presence." The court found that "[t]he plain and obvious statutory language forbids a court from ordering mediation where a party claims physical and psychological abuse."

The Colorado rule removes the discretion of the court in all cases where domestic abuse is alleged. Whether or not those charges are substantiated is irrelevant. This ruling creates a system open for manipulation. Parties wishing to avoid mediation could make false allegations of domestic violence. However, mediation has been widely praised in the area of family law because of the need for a "non-adversarial environment in which to decide family law issues." Therefore, it is unlikely that this exception would harm mandatory family mediation programs as a whole.

Ohio law does not offer as complete an exception to parties claiming domestic abuse. Where there is evidence of domestic violence, "Ohio courts must determine that [mediation] is in the best interest of the parties and make specific written findings of fact to support their determinations." The court is able to order mediation even if one parent has been convicted of domestic violence, as long as mediation is still in the parties' "best interest."

California allows local courts to establish their own rules for family mediation programs. Until recently, San Luis Obispo County required only that cases involving allegations of domestic violence "with current restraining orders . . . be screened by a mediator for determining the

---

30. Holly Joyce, Comment, *Mediation and Domestic Violence: Legislative Responses,* 14 J. Am. Acad. Matrim. L. 447, 448 (1997).

necessity of the presence of a support person during mediation, separate waiting areas for the parties, and separate mediation to insure safety and facilitate mediation." Therefore, not only were domestic violence situations not exempt from mandatory mediation, but even where there was a current restraining order in place, the mediation continued with only minimal safety precautions.

Illinois does not go to the extreme to which certain counties in California have gone. For example, the Thirteenth Judicial Circuit, which includes Bureau, Grundy, and LaSalle Counties, allows courts to waive mandatory mediation "for good cause." This gives judges very broad discretion. Domestic violence cases would fall under this exception because the rules also state that every case filed will be ordered to mediation where "there is a reasonable likelihood that mediation can aid the parties in resolution of the dispute." If there is unequal bargaining power, and one party is unwilling to participate because of past domestic violence, this would obviously decrease the likelihood that mediation would be successful in moving these parties towards a resolution.* * *

Whether a jurisdiction chooses to completely exempt domestic violence cases from mediation, as in Colorado, leaves the decision to the court, or leaves cases to be screened by the mediator, it is clear that all programs realize that mandatory mediation poses very real threats to the victim where there is a history of domestic abuse. Domestic violence advocates argue that mediation in these cases is never safe, and could never be in the best interest of the abused. When there is unequal bargaining power, it becomes difficult for even the most talented mediator to reduce differences in power, and the ability of the parties' to effectively engage in mediation is reduced. Advocates for mediation believe that where there is truly unequal bargaining power, the courts would recognize the problem and would not send the couple to mediation in the first place. However, those cases that are not excused by the court are left to the mediator to screen for domestic violence issues. States differ on screening requirements and mediator training in the area of domestic violence, as much as they differ on domestic violence exceptions.

B.   *The Impossible Job of Mediators: How do You Train Mediators to be Investigators?*

Unlike attorney regulation, there are no national requirements or professional standards regarding mediator training. In all jurisdictions, the role of the mediator during the mediation is multifaceted. In a normal mediation, mediators are required to manage the mediation, open communication, keep negotiations moving forward, probe for facts, help parties understand ramifications of agreements reached, and remain neutral. Mediators in the family law arena must not only be trained in the profession of mediation, but must also be knowledgeable about other areas, such as legal, sociological, and psychological issues.

"Mediators should receive sufficient training in the preparation process to enable them to encounter these dynamics and seek appropriate information from the parties when considering the family violence quotient."[52] The courts have established mandatory family mediation programs, and many have determined that mediators may still mediate such difficult cases as those involving domestic violence. Being forced to mediate such cases puts a huge burden on mediators, requiring them to act neutral, while simultaneously searching for psychological clues that one party is a victim of violence.

It is crucial that family mediators be trained, especially in jurisdictions where deciding whether mediation is in the best interests of parties is left to the mediator. "[T]he mediator is often untrained to deal with the psychological complexities of a domestic violence relationship."

Training and educational requirements vary from jurisdiction to jurisdiction. [The Model Standards of Practice for Divorce and Family Mediators require] ... that family mediators be educated so that they would be knowledgeable in family law, and "aware" of the impact family conflict has on "parents, children, and other family members." This would include "education and training in domestic violence and child abuse and neglect."

To provide some guidance as to exactly what level of education and training should be required, the Association of Family and Conciliation Courts adopted the "Model Standards of Practice for Divorce and Family Mediators." The very first standard, which establishes the ultimate goal of mediation, states that "[m]ediation is based on the principle of self-determination by the parties." The mediator's job is to facilitate the parties' assessment of their ability to mediate, their goals, and possible agreements. Self-determination depends on whether the parties have the ability to mediate fairly and on equal footing. In order for both parties to have their needs met, they must have the ability to be advocates for their own needs.

The second standard set out by the Model Standards of Practice is that "[a] family mediator should be qualified by education and training to undertake the mediation." There are no specific training programs outlined, but the Model Standards specify that mediators must be knowledgeable about family law, the psychological impact of family conflict on parents and children, education and training in domestic violence, child abuse and neglect, and special education and training in the process of mediation.

Standard X and XI state that a family mediator "should recognize" family situations which involve child abuse or domestic violence. In the case of child abuse or neglect, Standard X requires the mediator to report abuse to the proper authorities. In cases of domestic violence, however, the mediator is only required to "shape the mediation process accordingly." Neither situation absolutely requires the mediation to end; notwithstanding, some jurisdictions do require the mediation to termi-

52. Douglas D. Knowlton & Tara Lea Muhlauser, *Mediation in the Presence of Domestic Violence: Is it the Light at the End* *of the Tunnel or is a Train on the Track?,* 70 N.D. L Rev. 255, 264 (1994).

nate as soon as this information is learned by the mediator, regardless of whether the parties were willing to mediate. Both Standards X and XI require the mediator to be knowledgeable about the "symptoms and dynamics" of both forms of abuse, and they should not undertake the mediation unless they have "adequate training." The Model Standards are intentionally vague as to what level of training would be considered "adequate" in order to permit individual jurisdictions to draft more specific standards for its mediators. However, this has proven to be a difficult task.

The only time the Model Standards require a mediator to withdraw from mediation is in Standard XII, which states that "[a] family mediator should withdraw from further participation in the mediation process when the mediator reasonably believes that further participation will not further the parties' self-determination." Many argue that if there is a history of violence and abuse between the couple, there are doubts as to the ability of the abused to make decisions free of coercion.

The Model Standards recommended extensive training so that mediators will be able to "recognize a family situation involving child abuse or neglect, report it to the proper authorities, and shape the mediation process accordingly." Critics argue that no amount of training can make a mediator able to discern all signs of domination and abuse in a relationship. More importantly, no person would ever be skilled enough to put a victim on the same power level as her abuser, no matter how "in tune" the mediator is to the dynamics of the relationship. This argument would call for a complete exclusion of all cases where domestic violence has been alleged.

Even if mediators could be trained to put the parties on equal levels and help them reach a voluntary, uncoerced agreement that is in both parties' best interests, the biggest problem is discerning which cases this "screening" is needed. Even experts on domestic violence disagree as to the signs of domestic violence, how the victim will react during a mediation, and even what should be considered "domestic violence." Every victim reacts differently, and every mediator will react differently to those situations.

Until mediators begin to understand, and are properly trained, skilled, and educated to recognize the velocity, force, and coercive power of even a simple involuntary movement (a hand gesture, a blink) and the effect it can have on a victim of intimate violence, they will never understand how the balance of power is inextricably changed with an episode of violence.

It would be next to impossible, no matter how extensively trained the mediator is, to be able to understand that a slight hand movement or word has created a serious level of fear in the victim, and will ultimately impact the outcome of the mediation.

Also, a common tactic used by abusers is reduction of their victim's self-esteem. One of the reasons abused individuals have such a difficult time leaving their abusive spouses is that they have become convinced that they "deserve" the abuse, or that no one will care or help them if they try to leave. Once victims are able to muster the courage to file for divorce, the most dangerous thing for their self-esteem is to carry on a face-to-face conversation with their abuser, especially when the third-party in the room is constrained to complete neutrality. In that situation, abused parties have no advocate, and abusers constantly search for ways to regain control over victims and the outcome of the mediation.

In the worst cases, the batterer also is able to gain control over the mediator. In cases where domestic violence is known by the mediator, the mediator cannot condemn the violent behavior, or the mediator's neutrality will be compromised. Yet, "if the mediator does not condemn the abuse, the batterer's belief that his behavior is acceptable is maintained and the battered woman is disempowered." One mediation participant reported that she "was forced to sit down with the man who for the past twelve years [had] abused me, intimidated me, controlled me by threats and scare tactics, emotionally torn me down and whom I truly fear." She felt the mediator became his advocate because the mediator's reported (sic) to the court that "there had been no physical violence since [he] stopped drinking in 1982, yet hours earlier [her] husband had described in detail to [the mediator] how he had broken into [the] home [about two weeks prior to the mediation session]."

The victim attributed the mediator's lack of neutrality to the fact that her husband had no attorney and was a wonderful "con-artist." These issues arise repeatedly because the abuse almost always stems from a need to control the victim which leads to a need to control the mediator and the process itself. One way the abuser is able to "con" the mediator is that abusers are usually the best mediation participants. The victim will often be unwilling to talk openly, to share the children, and to make any concessions as to visitations or giving up any information. The abuser on the other hand is willing to share the children and discuss multiple options because this "assures his ongoing access to his partner and allows him to continue to manipulate and intimidate her," while at the same time making "him appear the more attractive candidate for custody" and mediation.

Mediators are human. To expect them to be aware of all the dynamics unfolding before them is simply too great a burden on the system. Family mediation does a great deal of good, but by leaving cases with violent pasts in the framework, the workability of the entire system is jeopardized. Looking at all these human complications, it becomes clear that the Colorado approach might be the safest for all involved.

Notes and Questions

1. As Wheeler states, exceptions are common for situations involving domestic violence. Taking a contrary view, Professor Andrew Schepard has argued that mediation programs should not have exceptions for domestic violence, but rather should screen cases for domestic violence, and then permit parties to opt out after hearing about the pros and cons of mediation.

Schepard's concern is that if mediation isn't mandated, parties won't know they have the opportunity to opt out of the adversarial process of litigation. Moreover, he says, mediation may be more helpful than litigation in actually reaching and addressing the problems that lie beneath the dispute, but that parties will not have that opportunity under a rule of automatic exclusion of such cases. *See* ANDREW I. SCHEPARD, CHILDREN, COURTS, AND CUSTODY 105 (2004). Is this a better approach?

2. Because of the prevalence of domestic violence, mediation professional standards generally call for the screening of such cases. As the Wheeler excerpt notes, mediation programs often leave this function to mediators. But is this realistic? Wheeler thinks not, that it is beyond the capacity of mediators to adequately screen for domestic violence, or to manage the problem once it is identified. Do you agree?

3. The scant empirical research on screening does not provide much comfort. In one study, Jessica Pearson found that as few as 30% of mediators actually receive training in domestic violence, and that 20% do not actually do such screening. Jessica Pearson, *Mediating When Domestic Violence Is A Factor: Policies and Practices in Court–Based Divorce Mediation Programs*, 14 Mediation Q. 319, 322–25 (1997). Moreover, as few as 80% of mediation programs even require formal screening, and half of those programs supplement screening instruments with private interviews. *Id.* at 325. *See also* Nancy Thoennes & Jessica Pearson, *Mediation and Domestic Violence Current Policies and Practices*, 33 Fam. & Conciliation Cts. Rev. 6, 11–12 (1995). Would more uniform training requirements and performance standards resolve Wheeler's concerns?

4. For further reading on the issue of domestic violence mediations, see Nancy Ver Steegh, *Yes, No, and Maybe: Informed Decision Making About Divorce Mediation in the Presence of Domestic Violence*, 9 Wm. & Mary J. Women & L. 145 (2003). For more on screening in particular, see Linda K. Girdner, *Mediation Triage: Screening for Spouse Abuse in Divorce Mediation*, 7 Mediation Q. 365 (1990).

5. What other types of mandatory mediation exceptions might be appropriate? How liberally should they be construed as a general matter?

6. In addition to exceptions, some mediation programs permit parties to opt out of a mandatory referral to mediation. However opt-out provisions vary widely in their permissiveness and breadth of coverage. For example, rules for courts in the city of St. Louis permit parties to opt out of mediation simply by advising the court and providing an explanation. In such cases, the rule states "The matter shall not thereafter be referred by the court to alternative dispute resolution absent compelling circumstances, which shall be set out by the court in any order referring the matter to alternative dispute resolution." Mo. 22d Cir. R. 38.5(1). Similarly, an Oregon mandatory mediation program permits parties to opt out if they are represented by counsel and counsel recommends against mediation. *See* Multnomah County Local R. 18.035. By contrast, however, the mandatory mediation rule for the U.S. District Court for the Western District of Missouri provides that "Cases will not normally be allowed to opt out of the program. However, there may be cases where good cause can be demonstrated for opting out." *See* W.D. Mo., Early Assessment Program, § II(C).

ii. The Problem of Good Faith Participation in Mediation

One problem that flows from the mandatory mediation of disputes is the assurance that parties in fact will use the mediation process to attempt to resolve their disputes in good faith. Good faith participation can be an issue in voluntary mediation, but the agreement by the parties to use the process helps assuage concerns about potential abuse. When compelled into mediation by court programs, however, it may well be that neither party really wants to be at the mediation, or may want to use the mediation for exploitation rather than settlement.

One way that some states have addressed this problem, either by statute or court rule, is by requiring the parties to mediate in good faith. In an important article, Professor Kimberlee Kovach argued that states should impose good faith requirements, either through statutes or court rules, to preserve the integrity of the mediation process as a vehicle for resolving disputes according to the underlying interests of the parties. *See* Kimberlee K. Kovach, *Good Faith in Mediation — Requested, Recommended, or Required? A New Ethic*, 38 S. Tex. L. Rev. 575, 580–96 (1997).

Kovach contends such a requirement is necessary to promote reciprocal good faith participation, which is especially important since many mediation participants come to the process from an adversarial mindset. She writes: "[I]f during a mediation, one party fails to cooperate, perhaps by withholding information, how can other parties be expected to cooperate? When participants come to mediation from an adversarial context, often tactics which emphasize and continue adversarial behavior are employed; if good faith participation is not required, the entire procedure will be frustrated." *Id.* at 575. She contends the presence of lawyers in the mediation only worsens the problem, as many may be tempted to abuse the mediation process for as a vehicle for discovery or as a forum for intimidation or other dilatory tactics. Says Kovach: "If good faith is not present, all we will be left with is a pro forma mediation, one more procedural task to be checked off of the long list of items to be covered in order to get to the trial." *Id.*

Kovach's proposal drew strong reactions from supporters and critics, but the idea of a good faith requirement has had legislative appeal. More than 20 states have enacted some form of good faith requirement for court-annexed mediations. At least twenty-one federal district courts and seventeen state courts also have local rules requiring good-faith participation. Several federal district courts have relied on Rule 16 of the Federal Rules of Civil Procedure as the basis for a good-faith requirement in mediation.

In the following excerpt, Professor Lande examines some of the problems with such requirements.

JOHN LANDE, USING DISPUTE SYSTEM DESIGN METHODS TO PROMOTE GOOD–FAITH PARTICIPATION IN COURT–CONNECTED MEDIATION PROGRAMS

50 UCLA L. Rev. 69, 70, 86–89, 93–95, 98–99, 102–04, 106–08 (2002).

What can be done to prevent people from behaving badly in mediation? One litigator described his approach to mediation this way:

"If . . . I act for the Big Bad Wolf against Little Red Riding Hood and I don't want this dispute resolved, I want to tie it up as long as I possibly can, and mandatory mediation is custom made. I can waste more time, I can string it along, I can make sure this thing never gets resolved because . . . I know the language. I know how to make it look like I'm heading in that direction. I make it look like I can make all the right noises in the world, like this is the most wonderful thing to be involved in when I have no intention of ever resolving this. I have the intention of making this the most expensive, longest process but is it going to feel good. It's going to feel so nice, we're going to be here and we're going to talk the talk but we're not going to walk the walk."[2]

Legislatures and courts have adopted rules requiring good faith in mediation, and courts have sanctioned violators. * * *

* * *

C.   Problems with Good–Faith Requirements

1.   *Problems Defining and Proving Good Faith*

The definition of good faith in mediation is one of the most controversial issues about good-faith requirements. Legal authorities establishing good-faith requirements and commentators' proposals do not give clear guidance about what conduct is prohibited. As a result, mediation participants may feel uncertain about what actions mediators and judges would consider bad faith. This uncertainty could result in inappropriate bad-faith charges as well as a chilling of legitimate mediation conduct.

In practice, the courts have limited their interpretation of good faith in mediation to attendance, submission of pre-mediation memoranda, and, in some cases, attendance of organizational representatives with adequate settlement authority. Despite the narrow scope of courts' actual application of good-faith requirements, good-faith language in the legal authorities and commentators' proposals go far beyond these specific matters.

Commentators agree that the definition of good faith needs to be clearly and objectively determinable so that everyone can know what

---

2. Julie Macfarlane, *Culture Change? Commercial Litigators and the Ontario Mandatory Mediation Program,* 2002 J. Disp. Resol 241, 267 (quoting a Toronto litigator) (first alteration in original). * * *

conduct is considered bad faith. Commentators disagree, however, about whether the definition of good faith can be clear, objectively determinable, and predictable, and whether good faith is a function of the reasonableness of participants' offers or their state of mind.

[Professor Kimberlee] Kovach argues that "without an explanation or definition of just what is meant by the term good faith, each party may have in mind something different. It is important that the parties are clear about the term." She maintains that "judging a party's state of mind is too complex and subjective" to be appropriate in determining good faith in mediation. She also contends that bad faith does not include failure to make an offer or "come down enough," stating that "the economic aspects of the negotiations — the offers and responses, in and of themselves — may not create a bad faith claim."

Most of the elements of good-faith definitions do not satisfy Kovach's criteria. Virtually all good-faith elements depend on an assessment of a person's state of mind, which is, by definition, subjective. Consider the following definition from *Hunt v. Woods*:

> A party has not "failed to make a good faith effort to settle" under [the statute] if he has (1) fully cooperated in discovery proceedings, (2) rationally evaluated his risks and potential liability, (3) not attempted to unnecessarily delay any of the proceedings, and (4) made a good faith monetary settlement offer or responded in good faith to an offer from the other party. If a party has a good faith, objectively reasonable belief that he has no liability, he need not make a monetary settlement offer.[87]

Good faith under this definition is not objectively determinable, readily predictable, or independent of parties' states of mind or their bargaining positions. To assess their risk evaluations, courts must determine the merits of the case, whether parties' evaluations are objectively reasonable, and whether their negotiation strategies are deemed acceptable by the courts. Courts make these assessments at subsequent hearings in which there is a great temptation to take advantage of hindsight. Obviously parties' understandings of the law and the facts evolve during the course of litigation so that some things do not become clear for a period of time, perhaps not until trial or even later. To make fair decisions, courts would need to reconstruct the information available to the parties at the time of the mediation. Courts also would need to consider the negotiation history up to the point of the alleged bad faith. Given the norms of negotiation in litigated cases, parties rarely begin negotiations by offering the amount that they believe "the case is worth." The timing and amount of offers often depend on the context of prior offers and the conduct of the litigation more generally. Parties vary

---

87. Id. at 3 (quoting Kalain v. Smith, 495 N.E.2d 572, 574 (Ohio 1986)). Cf. Black's Law Dictionary 701 (7th ed. 1999) (defining good faith as a "state of mind consisting in (1) honesty in belief or purpose, (2) faithfulness to one's duty or obligation, (3) observance of reasonable commercial standards of fair dealing in a given trade or business, or (4) absence of intent to defraud or to seek unconscionable advantage") * * *.

in negotiation philosophy; some prefer to negotiate early and make apparently reasonable offers whereas others prefer to engage in hard bargaining, taking extreme positions and deferring concessions as long as possible. Although Kovach argues that hard bargaining should not be considered bad faith, courts applying the *Hunt* definition could easily interpret it as bad faith. In any event, to determine parties' good faith fairly, courts would need to assess and second-guess the parties' offers and their states of mind. * * *

2. *Overbreadth of Bad–Faith Concept*

Kovach's and [Professor Maureen] Weston's proposed good-faith requirements are so broad that they effectively would prohibit defensible behaviors in mediation. Under Kovach's proposed statute, if one side claims that the other participated in bad faith, the moving party could use the legal process to investigate whether all participants adequately prepared for the mediation, "followed the rules set out by the mediator," engaged in "direct communication" with the other parties, "participated in meaningful discussions with the mediator and all other participants during the mediation," and "remained at the mediation until the mediator determined that the process is at an end or excused the parties." Under Weston's proposed "totality of the circumstances" test, this wide-ranging inquiry would be limited only by the court's discretion.

Both proposals raise many problems. Mediators typically establish "ground rules" at the outset of a mediation, such as a requirement that the participants treat each other with respect and not interrupt each other. Under Kovach's proposed statute, courts could be required to adjudicate whether someone disobeyed the mediator's rules by being disrespectful or interrupting others during the mediation.

Kovach states that "if the parties refuse to share particular knowledge, they should not be compelled to do so. However, it is important that some information be exchanged which would provide an explanation for, or the basis of, the proposed settlement or lack thereof." Under a duty to engage in direct communication and meaningful discussions, parties could be confused about what information they would be compelled to disclose to the mediator and opposing parties. In sensitive mediations, parties often want to withhold information justifying their bargaining strategies. Although exchanging such information in mediation can be helpful and appropriate, court-connected mediation should not be a substitute for formal discovery. Kovach presumably does not intend her proposed statute to be interpreted as such, but that could be the result. * * *

3. *Inclusion of Settlement–Authority Requirement*

Although mediations generally work better when organizational parties send representatives with a reasonable measure of settlement authority, courts have difficulty strictly enforcing such a requirement — and regularly doing so can stimulate counterproductive mediation tactics. Slightly more than half of the courts have found bad faith when

entities fail to send representatives with sufficient settlement authority.
* * *

When courts focus heavily on settlement authority, participants may be distracted from various ways that mediation can help litigants achieve goals other than reaching final monetary settlements. Settlement-authority requirements typically focus only on monetary resolutions; mediation can be useful to explore nonmonetary aspects of disputes. These requirements also assume that cases should be settled at a single meeting; in some cases it may be appropriate to meet several times, especially when organizational representatives need to consult officials within the organization based on information learned at mediation. Moreover, settlement-authority requirements do not recognize benefits of exchanging information, identifying issues, and making partial or procedural agreements in mediation. * * *

4. *Questionable Deterrent Effect and Potential Abuse of Bad–Faith Sanctions*

Sanctioning bad faith in mediation actually may stimulate adversarial and dishonest conduct, contrary to the intent of proponents of a good-faith requirement. Proponents argue that a good-faith requirement would cause people to negotiate sincerely, would deter bad-faith behavior, and, when people violate the requirement, would provide appropriate remedies.

Although a good-faith requirement presumably would deter and punish some inappropriate conduct, it might also encourage surface bargaining, as well as frivolous claims of bad faith or threats to make such claims. Proponents seem to assume that participants who might act in bad faith but for the requirement would behave properly in fear of legal sanctions. It seems at least as likely that savvy participants who want to take inappropriate advantage of mediation would use surface bargaining techniques so that they can pursue their strategies with little risk of sanction. This would be fairly easy given the vagueness of a good-faith requirement. Participants can readily make "lowball" offers that they know the other side will reject and generally go through the motions of listening to the other side and explaining the rationale for their positions. Although attorneys often are quite sincere, making arguments with feigned sincerity is a skill taught in law school and honed in practice. Because mediators are not supposed to force people to settle, participants who are determined not to settle can wait until the mediator gives up. This scenario illustrates how a good-faith requirement could ironically induce dishonesty, when providing more honest responses might put participants in jeopardy of being sanctioned.

Similarly, tough mediation participants could use good-faith requirements offensively to intimidate opposing parties and interfere with lawyers' abilities to represent their clients' legitimate interests. Given the vagueness and overbreadth of the concept of bad faith, innocent participants may have legitimate fears about risking sanctions when they face an aggressive opponent and do not know what a mediator would say if called to testify. In the typical conventions of positional negotiation in which each side starts by making an extreme offer, each side may accuse the other of bad faith. Without the threat of bad-faith sanctions, these moves are merely part of the kabuki dance of negotiation. With the prospect of such sanctions, bad-faith claims take on legal significance that can spawn not only satellite litigation, but satellite mediation as well. After a volley of bad-faith charges in a mediation, mediators may need to focus on bad faith as a real issue rather than simply a negotiation gambit. Moreover, the mediator could be a potential witness in court about the purity of each side's faith in the mediation, further warping the mediator's role. * * *

5. *Weakened Confidentiality of Mediation Communications*

Establishing a good-faith requirement undermines the confidentiality of mediation. The mere prospect of adjudicating bad-faith claims by using mediator testimony can distort the mediation process by damaging participants' faith in the confidentiality of mediation communications and the mediators' impartiality.

Proponents of a good-faith requirement cite the need for an exception to rules providing for confidentiality of communications in mediation. Weston contends that a good-faith requirement is "essentially meaningless if confidentiality privileges restrict the ability to report violations." Noting the existence of some exceptions to confidentiality in mediation, she argues that reports of bad faith should be added to the list of exceptions. Weston and Kovach assert that an exception for bad-faith participation can be clearly and narrowly limited, and that the need for an exception outweighs the general need to encourage open discussion in mediation through confidentiality protections.

Weston recognizes that creating a bad-faith exception to the confidentiality rules is risky. "After-the-fact allegations of ADR [alternative dispute resolution] bad-faith conduct can undermine participants' trust in the confidentiality of ADR, create uncertainty, and potentially impair full use of the process." In addition, "recognizing a privilege exception to report good-faith violations carries the risk that the exception would be misused by disgruntled parties and simply swallow the confidentiality rule." Requiring testimony from a mediator in bad-faith hearings creates related problems. Kovach suggests solving this problem by having mediators file affidavits or testify about the conduct in question without making determinations whether the conduct constitutes bad faith. As Weston notes, however, "permitting disclosures for good-faith-violation claims also raises the concern that the role of the third-party neutral is compromised where the neutral is a witness to the alleged bad-faith ADR conduct."

To solve these problems, Weston recommends that evidence of bad faith be heard by a court in camera to determine whether a confidentiality privilege exception is warranted, preferably by a judge who would not determine the underlying merits of the case. She argues that this approach, "combined with sanctions for asserting frivolous claims of bad-faith participation, balances the concerns for ensuring good-faith participation and justified confidentiality in ADR.''

The proponents have identified correctly concerns that a good-faith requirement could undermine participants' trust in the confidentiality of mediation because of uncertainty about what might later be used in court. An exception for bad faith does not seem as narrow and definite as the proponents suggest, however. The vagueness and overbreadth of the concept contribute to participants' uncertainty about whether their statements in mediation would be used against them.

Proposals for admitting mediators' testimony presume that courts need such testimony to pursue their mission of seeking truth and justice and that mediators' testimony is highly probative and reliable because mediators are the only source of disinterested, neutral evidence about conduct in mediation. Certainly mediators' testimony can be helpful, but one can overstate its value. Much discussion in mediation does not focus on facts strictly relevant to legal issues and often involves feelings, interests, expected consequences of various options, negotiation strategy, and even analysis of hypothetical situations. Moreover, if called to testify at such hearings, mediators may have significant biases even if the mediators have the highest integrity. Mediators would be interested in presenting themselves and their actions in mediation in a favorable light. If a mediator reports that a participant has not participated in good faith, courts should expect that the mediator might emphasize facts consistent with that conclusion and downplay inconsistent facts. Thus, one should not simply assume that mediator testimony is necessarily neutral, probative, and reliable.* * *

6. *Encouragement of Inappropriate Mediator Conduct*

A good-faith requirement gives mediators too much authority over participants to direct the outcome in mediation and creates the risk that some mediators would coerce participants by threatening to report alleged bad-faith conduct. Courts can predict abuse of that authority given the settlement-driven culture in court-connected mediation. The mere potential for courts to require mediators' reports can corrupt the mediation process by instilling fear and doubt in the participants.

Proponents of a good-faith requirement apparently assume that mediators will not abuse any good-faith reporting authority to coerce parties into accepting mediators' opinions about appropriate resolutions. The proponents also seem to assume that even if mediators do not abuse their good-faith reporting authority, participants will not fear taking positions at odds with the mediators' apparent views and will not perceive mediators as biased.

These assumptions are troubling. Kovach warns of the dangers of evaluative mediation, in which mediators express opinions about the merits of the issues. Weston cites risks when the parties have unequal bargaining power and mediators pressure the weaker parties. These risks are very real. When mediators express opinions about specific aspects of a case or its ultimate merits, they risk creating injustice through heavy-handed pressure tactics. Even without the prospect of a later court hearing about good-faith participation, mediation participants sometimes feel pressured to change their positions in response to mediator evaluations and "reality-testing" questions. Under a bad-faith sanctions regime, mediators might apply pressure arising from their authority to testify about bad faith. If local courts hold a sufficient number of bad-faith hearings, participants may reasonably fear the effect of mediators' reports, even if mediators do not threaten to report bad faith. * * *

Notes and Questions

1. Professor Lande notes that only one of the 22 states that have enacted good faith statutory requirements has included a definition of "good faith." *Id.* at 77. He further points out that, at the time his article was written, there were 27 reported cases dealing with bad faith in mediation, and most of them arose out of court-connected mediation programs. The number of reported cases increased in the 1990s, and it can be speculated that the increase was caused by the expanding use of court-mandated mediation and an accompanying legalization of the process. The behaviors alleged to constitute bad faith in the 27 cases fell into 5 categories: (1) failure to attend; (2) failure of an organizational party to send a representative with sufficient settlement authority; (3) inadequate preparation for a mediation —including failure to submit a pre-mediation memorandum or to bring experts to a mediation; (4) insincerity of efforts to resolve the dispute — including claims that a party had not made any offer or any suitable offer, had made inconsistent legal arguments, or had not provided requested documents; and (5) miscellaneous allegations, including failure to sign a mediated agreement and failure to release living expenses pending farmer-lender mediation. *Id.* at 82–83. Professor Lande describes the final outcomes in these cases as follows:

> The final court decisions in these cases generally have been quite consistent in each category. The courts have found bad faith in all the cases in which a party has failed to attend the mediation or has failed to provide a required pre-mediation memorandum. In cases involving allegations that organizational parties have provided representatives without sufficient settlement authority, the courts have split almost evenly. In virtually all of the other cases in which the courts ruled on the merits of the case, they rejected claims of bad faith. In effect, the courts have interpreted good faith narrowly to require compliance with orders to attend mediation, provide pre-mediation memoranda, and, in some cases, produce organizational representatives with sufficient settlement authority.

Id. at 82

2. Professor Kovach suggests the following court rule as an example of what a good faith requirement might look like. Would you support it if it were under consideration by your court?

Rule 1.7 Good Faith in Mediation

A lawyer representing a client in mediation shall participate in good faith.

(a) Prior to the mediation, the lawyer shall prepare by familiarizing herself with the matter, and discussing it with her client.

(b) At the mediation, the lawyer shall comply with all rules of court or statutes governing the mediation process, and counsel her client to do likewise.

(c) During the mediation, the lawyer shall not convey information that is intentionally misleading or false to the mediator or other participants.

3. Would you add a requirement that the participants have settlement authority to Kovach's good faith requirement? How much authority would you require the participant to have?

4. Professor Lande suggests that the concerns raised by Kovach and other supporters of good faith requirements can better be addressed through better design of court-annexed mediation programs. In particular, Lande suggests key stakeholder groups — including litigants, attorneys, courts, and mediators — work together to develop policies that address the problem, including collaborative education about good mediation practice, pre-mediation consultations and submission of documents, a limited and specific attendance requirement, and protections against misrepresentation. If faithfully implemented, he suggests, these policies will enhance the integrity of mediation programs and satisfy the interests of the stakeholder groups without the problems caused by good-faith requirements. *See* John Lande, *Using Dispute System Design to Promote Good–Faith Participation in Court–Connected Mediation Programs*, 50 UCLA L. Rev. 69, 108–39 (2002). What benefits would you see with this approach? What problems would you see?

5. In place of a good-faith requirement, Professor Edward Sherman proposes a "minimal meaningful participation" requirement. This requirement would include requiring the parties to provide each other and the third-party neutral with position papers and other relevant information that lays a basis for meaningful consideration of the case without mandating specific forms of presentation or interaction with the other party. For example, Sherman says "a reasonable order would be that the parties provide a position paper in advance of the ADR proceeding which would include a plain and concise statement of: (1) the legal and factual issues in dispute; (2) the party's position on those issues; (3) the relief sought (including a particularized itemization of all elements of damage claimed); and (4) any offers and counter-offers previously made." On the other hand, Sherman argues program designers should take care not to impose requirements that interfere with trial strategy, such as one that would require the disclosure of privileged attorney work product. *See* Edward F. Sherman, *Court-Mandated Alternative Dispute Resolution: What Form Of Participation Should Be Required?*, 46 SMU L. Rev. 2079, 2101–03 (1993). Does this approach do a better job of getting at the underlying problem? What benefits and problems do you see?

6. The ABA Section of Dispute Resolution in 2004 adopted a policy on good faith participation that responds to many of the concerns described above. It provides that "sanctions are appropriate for violation of rules specifying objectively-determinable conduct. Such rule-proscribed conduct would include but is not limited to: failure of a party, attorney, or insurance

representative to attend a court-mandated mediation for a limited and specified period or to provide written memoranda prior to the mediations. These rules should not be labeled as good faith requirements, however, because of the widespread confusion about the meaning of that term." It also calls for limits on mediator reports to courts about good faith participation, and cites the Uniform Mediation Act with approval. Finally, it calls for greater collaborative planning of court-mandated mediation programs, such as that suggested by Professor Lande. The policy may be found on the ABA Section of Dispute Resolution's web site at http://www.abanet.org/dispute/webpolicy.html#9 (last visited Apr. 2, 2005).

3.   COURT-ANNEXED "MIXED PROCESSES"

As we indicated in Chapter I, "mixed" dispute resolution processes are those that include elements of more than one of the basic processes. This section presents several mixed processes that combine elements of adjudication and negotiation, sometimes in order to foster negotiated settlement.

a.   Court-Annexed Non-Binding Arbitration

Arbitration is relatively rare in the courts, in part out of constitutional concerns. In the most comprehensive study to date, Elizabeth Plapinger and Donna Stienstra found only twenty federal districts with court-annexed arbitration programs and suggested that this "may be in part the result of uncertainty over whether courts other than those authorized by statute may establish arbitration programs." ELIZABETH PLAPINGER & DONNA STIENSTRA, A.D.R. AND SETTLEMENT IN THE FEDERAL DISTRICT COURTS: A SOURCEBOOK FOR JUDGES AND LAWYERS 4–5 (1996). The Civil Justice Reform Act of 1990 did not include arbitration among the listed ADR methods recommended for consideration by district courts. This omission led the General Counsel of the Administrative Office of the U.S. Courts to conclude that "the CJRA does not appear to authorize arbitration in other courts." *Id.* at 5 n.2.

Unlike private arbitrations discussed in Chapter V, which sometimes are unilaterally imposed on parties, court-annexed arbitrations are often voluntary and almost always non-binding. For these reasons, federal and state courts have routinely rejected constitutional challenges to court-annexed ADR programs based on the Seventh Amendment right to a jury trial in civil cases and on the Fourteenth Amendment Due Process Clause. *See, e.g., Riggs v. Scrivner, Inc.*, 927 F.2d 1146 (10th Cir. 1991); *Kimbrough v. Holiday Inn*, 478 F.Supp. 566 (E.D. Pa. 1979); *Firelock Inc. v. District Court*, 776 P.2d 1090 (Colo. 1989); *American Universal Ins. Co. v. DelGreco*, 205 Conn. 178, 530 A.2d 171 (1987). In *New England Merchants Nat'l Bank v. Hughes*, 556 F.Supp. 712 (E.D. Pa. 1983), the defendant failed to appear at a mandatory court-annexed arbitration hearing and offered no explanation. The District Court granted the plaintiff's request for a summary judgment and held that failure to comply with the local arbitration rule precluded the defendant from demanding a trial *de novo. Id.* at 716.

In *Making Alternative Dispute Resolution Mandatory: The Constitutional Issues,* 68 Or. L. Rev. 487 (1989), Professor Dwight Golann concluded that "[s]ubject to specific comments articulated in this article" mandatory, non-binding ADR "may be applied to almost any kind of civil dispute without violating the provisions of the federal constitution or most of its state counterparts." *Id.* at 568. *See also* Lucy V. Katz, *Compulsory Alternative Dispute Resolution and Voluntarism: Two–Headed Monster or Two Sides of the Coin?,* 1993 J. Disp. Resol. 1, 22–31.

Notes

1. During the early 1980s, court-annexed arbitration programs were fairly popular among courts adopting ADR programs. However their popularity has waned considerably since then. Indeed, in the federal courts most court-annexed programs have been dismantled or left to expire at the conclusion of experimental periods. *See* DONNA STIENSTRA & ELIZABETH PLAPINGER, ADR AND SETTLEMENT IN THE FEDERAL DISTRICT COURTS: A SOURCEBOOK FOR JUDGES AND LAWYERS 4–5, 7 (1996); Richard C. Reuben, *The Lawyer Turns Peacemaker*, A.B.A. J., Aug. 1996, at 54, 57–58.

2. Professor Richard Reuben has argued that court-related ADR programs operate under the aegis of state action, and therefore still require programs to provide participants with "minimal but meaningful" due process protections, which vary depending upon the nature of the process. For court-related arbitration, these minimal but meaningful due process standards include the right to a neutral forum, the right to present and confront evidence, and a qualified right to counsel. *See* Richard C. Reuben, *Constitutional Gravity: A Unitary Theory of Alternative Dispute Resolution and Public Civil Justice,* 47 UCLA L. Rev. 949, 952–60 (2000).

b. Summary Jury Trial

THOMAS LAMBROS, THE SUMMARY JURY TRIAL AND OTHER ALTERNATIVE METHODS OF DISPUTE RESOLUTION*
103 F.R.D. 461, 468–69 (1984).

* * *

It is clear that settlement of cases prior to trial provides a cost savings in terms of litigation. One aspect of this savings is the elimination of the need to empanel a jury. Some cases, however, are not amenable to settlement through the usual pretrial methods of dispute resolution, or the alternative methods mentioned above. There may be a variety of reasons for this inability to settle. Litigants may refuse to accept a compromise because emotionally they need a "day in court" to tell their story. Absent the opportunity to hear both sides of the case presented to the finders of fact, a lawyer and his client may be unable to objectively recognize the weaknesses in their position. The lawyer and

---

* Reprinted from 103 F.R.D. 461 with permission of West Publishing Company.

his client may believe they can "pull off" a weak case if only they can get it in front of a jury. These reasons, among others, act as barriers to settlement; barriers which often result in protracted litigation and expense.

The Summary Jury Trial (SJT) provides a means by which to decimate these barriers to settlement. Alternatively, SJT can aid in streamlining jury trials so that the trial process undergoes a more efficient use of time. * * * SJT is the only alternative dispute resolution technique which utilizes the age old jurisprudential concept of trial by jury. It is this concept, the expression of opinion by a jury of peers, which has molded our judicial system and which permits the parties to believe that their story has been told, and a decision reached. No other alternative allows for the use of this basic foundation of our present system.

Initiated in 1980, SJT is counsels' presentation to a jury of their respective views of the case and the jury's advisory decision based on such presentations. It is a flexible pretrial procedure that aids appreciably in the settlement of trial-bound cases.

The SJT can be an effective predictive process for ascertaining probability of results. It is my perception that the sole bar to settlement in many cases is the uncertainty of how a jury might perceive liability and damages. Such uncertainty often arises, for example, in cases involving a "reasonableness" standard of liability, such as in negligence litigation. No amount of jurisprudential refinement of the standard of liability can aid the resolution of such cases. Parties' positions during settlement negotiations in cases of this type are based on an analysis of similar cases within the experience of counsel as to juries' determinations of liability and findings of damages. Such comparison is usually of little value, however, as parties tend to aimlessly grope toward some notion of a likely damages award figure upon which to base their negotiating positions. The parties and the court may become frustrated in cases, especially where neither party wants to fully try the case on the merits and the only roadblock to a meaningful settlement is the uncertainty of how a jury might perceive liability and damages.

The half-day proceeding is designed to provide a "no-risk" method by which the parties may obtain the perception of six jurors on the merits of their case without a large investment of time or money. The proceeding is not binding and in no way affects the parties' rights to a full trial on the merits. SJT is a predictive tool that counsel may use to achieve a just result for their clients at minimum expense.

After preparation and presentation of the case at an SJT, the possibility of a settlement becomes much more real to both sides. Unreasonable demands and offers are reevaluated, and mutually agreeable compromises are worked out in light of the jury's findings.

Notes and Questions

1. One advantage to summary jury trials is that lawyers are typically permitted to question or talk with jurors after they issue their verdict. What

other advantages do you see to the summary jury trial? What disadvantages do you see?

2. The power of a federal district court to order a party to participate in a summary jury trial at one time was open to question. Prior to the 1993 Amendments to Rule 16 of the Federal Rules of Civil Procedure, the Sixth and Seventh Circuits held that federal courts do not have the power to require participation in a summary jury trial. *In re NLO, Inc.*, 5 F.3d 154 (6th Cir. 1993); *Strandell v. Jackson County*, 838 F.2d 884 (7th Cir. 1987). However, the 1993 Amendment made clear that district courts have the power to require parties and their attorneys to attend pre-trial conferences for purposes of "facilitating the settlement of the case." Fed. R. Civ. Proc. 16(a)(5). Since then, courts have consistently held that courts may order parties to a summary jury trial when there is a court rule authorizing the reference. *Ohio ex rel. Montgomery v. Louis Trauth Dairy, Inc.*, 164 F.R.D. 469, 471 (S.D. Ohio 1996) (ruling that *In re NLO, Inc.*, had been "effectively overruled" by the 1993 amendment). *See generally* Amy M. Pugh & Richard A. Bales, *The Inherent Power of Federal Courts to Compel Participation in Nonbinding Forms of Alternative Dispute Resolution*, 42 Duq. L. Rev. 1 (2003).

3. Should the jury in a summary jury trial be told that its verdict will be advisory only? If so, should the jurors be told at the outset or after the jury has recorded its verdict? *See* Avern Cohn, *Summary Jury Trial — A Caution*, 1995 J. Disp. Resol. 299, 300.

4. If you were a U.S. district judge, would you support the adoption of a local court rule giving judges the discretion to "set any appropriate civil case for summary jury trial"? Would you have a different view if you were a lawyer representing clients before the court?

5. Professor Thomas Metzloff has proposed a stronger version of the summary jury trial, one that is binding.

The theory of the binding SJT rejects the common assumption that the process is intended for cases in which conventional negotiations have failed. Instead, it seeks a broader role by providing an ADR option for litigants presently forced to settle, but who would prefer a binding adjudication if the process could be made less expensive and more predictable. The process allows litigants to obtain a binding adjudication of their dispute at a reasonable cost without the risks inherent in the current jury system. * * *

A binding SJT approach offers the potential for significant cost savings to the litigants. Unlike a court's decision to mandate a traditional SJT on the eve of trial, the parties' decision to employ a binding SJT could be made early in the litigation process (perhaps even before suit is filed). After limited discovery, the case could be tried in an abbreviated fashion in which various procedural shortcuts — many borrowed from the typical SJT format, such as the use of summarized evidence — could be employed. The litigants' goal in formatting the process would be more broadly defined than in the classic SJT context, where the court-initiated process is largely driven by an interest in shortening trial lengths. For example, because the parties have committed the resolution of their dispute to the process, they may often be interested in providing more information to the summary jury than would be the case with the traditional SJT. Serving this interest would usually entail the limited use of live or video-taped testimony on critical issues.

* * *

Because the format is not imposed by the court (as is the case with most traditional SJTs), the parties will incur higher transaction costs in terms of establishing ground rules. Over time, however, it is expected that a number of established formats will be developed either by private ADR providers or by the courts themselves. Variables that the parties could consider include: (1) limiting time for argument and presentation of evidence; (2) agreeing upon reductions in the number of witnesses; (3) using affidavits, factual summaries, or videotaped evidence; (4) permitting the jurors to take notes or ask questions; (5) abbreviating jury selection procedures; (6) shortening jury instructions; and (7) agreeing upon a procedure for resolving the case in the event of a hung jury. This approach places a premium value on encouraging creativity by the litigants in terms of SJT design — an important departure from the approach followed by most other courts that have detailed a paradigm SJT model.

Thomas B. Metzloff, *Improving the Summary Jury Trial*, 77 Judicature 9, 11–12 (1993).

6. Describe a situation in which you would recommend that a client participate in a non-binding summary jury trial. A binding summary jury trial.

7. The summary jury trial enjoyed significant popularity in some federal district courts in the years following the publication of Judge Lambros' article. A joint study by the Federal Judicial Center and the CPR Institute for Dispute Resolution found that, "[j]ust over half the [federal district] courts report authorization or use of the summary jury trial.... The level of usage reported by most courts is, however, very low — generally around one or two cases a year." DONNA STIENSTRA & ELIZABETH PLAPINGER, ADR AND SETTLEMENT IN THE FEDERAL DISTRICT COURTS: A SOURCEBOOK FOR JUDGES AND LAWYERS 5 (1996).

c. Early Neutral Evaluation

JOSHUA D. ROSENBERG & H. JAY FOLBERG,
ALTERNATIVE DISPUTE RESOLUTION:
AN EMPIRICAL ANALYSIS*
46 Stan. L. Rev. 1487, 1488, 1489–92, 1493 (1994).

INTRODUCTION

* * *

This article adds to the empirical research by reporting on a quantitative and qualitative study of the ADR program of the United States

District Court for the Northern District of California. The Northern District is one of six courts designated as demonstration districts in the Civil Justice Reform Act of 1990 (CJRA). Prior to the enactment of the CJRA, the Northern District had generated significant national interest in its design and use of an ADR procedure known as early neutral evaluation (ENE). Pursuant to the CJRA, the court retained the authors to evaluate its mandatory ENE program and suggest improvements.

Our most important findings include the following: (1) Approximately two-thirds of those who participated in the mandatory ADR program felt satisfied with the process and believed it worthy of the resources devoted to it (dissatisfaction with the program resulted primarily from dissatisfaction with the particular neutral assigned to the case); (2) while the percentage of parties who reported saving money approximately equaled the percentage who reported that the process resulted in a net financial cost, the net savings were, on average, more than ten times larger than the cost of an ENE session; (3) approximately half the participants in the program reported that participation decreased the pendency time of their cases; (4) the majority of parties and attorneys reported learning information in the ENE session that led to a fairer resolution of their case; and (5) the ENE process varied significantly from case to case and from neutral to neutral, and the most important factor in determining the success of the process in any one case was the individual neutral involved. Consequently, we focused many of our suggestions for improvement on ensuring the quality of the neutrals. While these findings and suggestions are based on the Northern District's ENE program, we believe that they are likely to be relevant for other court-based ADR.

* * *

I. History and Operation of Early Neutral Evaluation

A. *History of the Program*

* * *

The court established a pilot ENE program in 1985. It handled about a dozen cases assigned by Wayne Brazil, the magistrate who administered the program at that time. An early study of the pilot program revealed promising results. In the second phase of the ENE experiment, the court assigned 150 cases in specified subject areas to the program, with sixty-seven actually proceeding through the ENE process. A study of these cases concluded that most ENE participants strongly believed ENE was worthwhile. Based on the apparent success of the experimental program, the court further expanded and refined the ENE program in 1988 and again in 1989.

B. *Design of the ENE Session*

Absent a waiver granted by the court, every party in a case assigned to ENE must attend the ENE session, together with the attorney who will be lead counsel should the case go to trial. If a party is a corporation, it must be represented at the session by a person (other than outside counsel) who has authority both to enter stipulations and to bind the party to the terms of a settlement. Prior to the ENE session, each side must submit to the neutral a statement identifying session participants, major disputed issues, and any discovery that would be a necessary prelude to meaningful settlement discussions. The session is expected to last approximately two hours, during which the following events are expected to take place:

1. The evaluator explains the purposes of the program and outlines the procedures.

2. Each side in turn presents a 15–minute opening statement, either by counsel, client, or both, without interruption from the evaluator or the other party. The statement presents the side's case and legal theories and describes the supporting evidence.

3. The evaluator may then ask questions of both sides to clarify issues, arguments, and evidence, to fill in evidentiary gaps, and to probe for strengths and weaknesses.

4. The evaluator identifies the issues on which the parties agree (and encourages them to enter stipulations where appropriate) and also identifies the important issues in dispute.

5. The evaluator adjourns to another room to prepare a written case evaluation. The evaluation assesses the strengths and weaknesses of each side's case, determines which side is likely to prevail, and establishes the probable range of damages in the event the plaintiff wins.

6. The evaluator returns to the ENE conference room, announces that she has prepared an informal evaluation of the case, and asks the parties if they would like to explore settlement possibilities before she discloses the evaluation to them. If either party declines the offer to begin settlement discussions, the evaluator promptly discloses her written assessment. If, on the other hand, both sides are interested in working on settlement, the evaluator facilitates these discussions.

7. If the parties do not hold settlement discussions or if discussions do not produce a settlement, the evaluator helps the parties develop a plan for efficient case management. This aid may include scheduling motions or discovery that would put the case in a position for rapid settlement or disposition.

8. After the ENE session, the parties may agree to a follow-up session or other activity. With the consent of the court, the parties may engage the evaluator for additional sessions on a compensated basis.

C. *Administration of the Program*

1. *Selection of cases.*

Most ENE cases enter the program pursuant to an automatic assignment system set forth in the court's General Order 26. Subject to certain specific exceptions, the order assigns to the ENE program every even-numbered case in eighteen "nature of suit" categories, as identified by counsel on the cover sheet that must be filed with every complaint. Attorneys whose cases are administratively assigned to ENE may petition the court to have their cases removed from the ENE program. Written petitions are submitted to Magistrate Judge Wayne Brazil, who will grant such petitions upon a showing of good cause. Cases not automatically assigned to ENE may enter the program by stipulation among the parties with approval of a judge, or by referral from the judge assigned to the case, either at a party's request or *sua sponte*.

In cases automatically assigned to ENE, the plaintiff must serve on all defendants a copy of General Order 26 and other papers describing ENE. Once an evaluator has been appointed, the court notifies the parties of the appointment, and the evaluator then schedules the ENE session and notifies the parties. Absent an order from the ENE magistrate or the judge to whom the case is assigned, General Order 26 mandates that ENE sessions be held within forty-five days from the notice of the evaluator's appointment and within 150 days from the filing of the complaint.

2. *Selection and training of evaluators.*

Judges, magistrates, and members of the ADR task force initially recommended evaluators for the ENE program based on their temperament, judgment, intelligence, and subject matter expertise. Later, the ADR task force selected additional attorneys, many of whom were recommended by judges or by respected peers. Some of these attorneys initially volunteered and were later recommended by judges or attorneys already involved with the program.

Early in the life of the ENE program, the ADR task force required all evaluators to attend a training session lasting approximately two and one-half hours. After the first experimental stage of ENE, program organizers videotaped the training session so that evaluators who were unable to attend could watch the tape. Evaluators also received written materials describing the program generally and suggesting how they could best perform their roles.

II.   METHODOLOGY

This study is based on a review of all cases filed from April 1988 through March 1992 that met the subject matter criteria for automatic referral to ENE.

* * *

We received questionnaire responses from 377 (52.4 percent) of the 720 lead attorneys who had attended an ENE session. Of these, 191 had represented plaintiffs and 186 had represented defendants. We received responses from attorneys for all parties in 115 of the 326 cases (35 percent) in which an ENE session was held, and we received responses from a single attorney (either plaintiff's or defendant's) in another 147 cases (45 percent). Overall, we received a reply from at least one side in 262 cases (80 percent).

* * *

Notes and Questions

1.   Rosenberg and Folberg found significant variation in the conduct of the neutral evaluators. They also concluded that levels of attorney satisfaction with ENE depended substantially on the identity of the evaluator. Why might this be the case? Assume you are an attorney whose case has been assigned to ENE and that a specific attorney has been designated the evaluator. Would you be concerned about what to expect in the hearing and how to prepare for it? How might you determine, or take part in the decision to determine, the kind of process the evaluator would conduct? Do you suppose it would be appropriate for you to call the evaluator and inquire about her or his approach? Note that it is generally acceptable for parties or lawyers to have private contact with mediators but not arbitrators.

2.   Is it troublesome to you that different neutral evaluators might evaluate the same case differently? Is such a result consistent with our notions of justice? Should ENE program designers try to standardize the approaches of neutral evaluators? Would such an effort produce a kind of rigidity that would be counterproductive to settlement?

Assuming it would be desirable to standardize the approaches of neutral evaluators, how could this be done? Would more extensive training help? Most mediation training programs are longer than the ENE training program described by Rosenberg and Folberg. Would it be possible to identify persons to serve as neutral evaluators who are likely, by virtue of their backgrounds or personalities, to take an evaluative rather than facilitative approach?

3.   Some mediation scholars have argued that "evaluative mediation" is not really mediation but more closely resembles neutral evaluation. Kimberly K. Kovach & Lela P. Love, *Evaluative Mediation is an Oxymoron*, Alternatives to the High Cost of Litig., Mar. 1996, at 30, 30–31. What might Professors Kovach and Love say about "non-evaluative early neutral evaluation"?

4.   Remember the term "evaluation" can cover a range of activities. In a portion of the article not reprinted here, Rosenberg and Folberg indicate that lawyers felt more satisfied with the ENE process when the mediators "[g]ave views on the merits" than when they "[p]redicted a specific dollar amount for a verdict" or "[s]uggested a specific dollar figure for settlement." Joshua D. Rosenberg & H. Jay Folberg, *Alternative Dispute Resolution: An Empirical Analysis*, 46 Stan. L. Rev. 1487, 1529 (1994). What are likely explanations for this finding?

5.   Does anything in the excerpt from Rosenberg and Folberg suggest that evaluators helped the parties broaden the scope of the problem to be addressed in the session? Is this desirable in the ENE process?

6. ENE has not proven nearly as popular as mediation in court-annexed programs. Why might this be the case? Should ADR program administrators give greater emphasis to ENE?

d. Innovative Processes for Mass Personal Injury Litigation

Massive tort claims raise special management problems for courts. In the following excerpt, Professor Deborah Hensler discusses several innovative approaches that courts have used to manage these cases, and raises the question of whether ADR techniques may also be of further assistance.

DEBORAH R. HENSLER, A GLASS HALF FULL, A GLASS HALF EMPTY: THE USE OF ALTERNATIVE DISPUTE RESOLUTION IN MASS PERSONAL INJURY LITIGATION

73 Tex. L. Rev. 1587, 1606–19, 1623–24 (1995).

IV. How Courts Have Responded to the Challenge

Courts have responded to the challenges posed by mass personal injury litigation by devising streamlined procedures to resolve individual cases, informally aggregating and formally consolidating cases for settlement or trial, facilitating global settlements, and facilitating the design and implementation of administrative processes for delivering compensation to individual claimants. These approaches have been used alone in some litigation, but many mass tort cases have involved the use of two or more of these approaches concurrently or sequentially. These techniques have resolved litigation in trial courts, bankruptcy courts, and private fora. Over time, courts, and some attorneys, appear to have developed a preference for collective mechanisms, such as consolidation and aggregate settlements, over streamlining individual case disposition, and for global settlements resolving all current and future cases.

A. Individual Case Disposition

In the early phases of the asbestos worker injury litigation, many courts experimented with streamlined procedures for resolving individual cases. For example, the Philadelphia Court of Common Pleas adopted a mandatory nonbinding arbitration program for its asbestos cases in the early 1980s. Judges from the court's civil division were assigned to hear cases from a special "asbestos calendar." The hearings were brief (several hours to a couple of days), the rules of evidence were relaxed, and plaintiffs testified and could attend throughout. As in all other court-annexed arbitration programs, the judges' verdicts were advisory only and were intended to facilitate settlement: Any party could reject the judge's verdict and request a de novo trial. Although initial reports on the program claimed some success, it seems to have foundered when the court was unable to schedule de novo trials soon enough after the arbitration hearings to provide parties with an incentive to negotiate settlements based on the arbitration outcome. Ultimately, the court could not keep up with the flood of asbestos case filings even by using this streamlined process in lieu of trial.

A second example of innovation intended to facilitate individual case resolution was the Ohio Asbestos Litigation Plan. Special Masters Francis McGovern and Eric Green, whom Judge Tom Lambros appointed to help resolve his asbestos caseload, devised the plan. The Ohio Plan was a computer-driven model that provided the judge and the parties' attorneys with a historically based case value for each case scheduled for a settlement conference based on selected information about the new case. By providing a historical value for the case, the system's designers hoped to narrow the negotiation space and expedite settlement of individual cases. The Ohio Plan was credited with helping Judge Lambros to clear his asbestos caseload when many other courts had great difficulty disposing of asbestos worker injury suits.

Each of these experiments extended and elaborated upon more traditional judicial settlement processes: In Philadelphia, the court hoped that nonbinding bench verdicts would provide a basis for lawyer negotiations, and some of the judges who heard cases in the special program also held settlement conferences before or after the hearings. In Ohio, the computer-assisted negotiation process was a component of a broader case management plan, in which judicial settlement conferences played a key role.* * *

B.   Informal Grouping and Formal Consolidation of Cases

Because of the scale of the asbestos caseload, some courts have substituted group settlements of large blocks of cases for the more traditional case-at-a-time settlement. For example, in the Los Angeles Superior Court, judges assigned to the special asbestos calendar organized their caseload by date of filing and plaintiff's law firm. Judicial settlement conferences were scheduled to negotiate the disposition of all of a particular law firm's cases from a specified period. The Los Angeles approach to asbestos case disposition built on a long tradition of judicial settlement conferences in that court, as well as on asbestos lawyers' practice of settling large blocks of cases in mass disposition sessions outside the court.

As some judges experimented with mass settlement strategies, others experimented with consolidating cases for trial under Federal Rule of Civil Procedure 42 or state court equivalents. In asbestos litigation, the first attempts at consolidation were modest. In the early 1980s, judges in the Philadelphia Court of Common Pleas and in the federal court in the Eastern District of Texas consolidated a few cases and assigned them to several juries. The juries heard the liability evidence while sitting together, but heard specific causation and damages evidence and deliberated separately. When the juries reached different verdicts on the same liability evidence, the experiments were abandoned.

By the mid–1980s, both the judiciary and the trial bar had grown more assertive about aggregating mass personal injury suits for disposition. During the 1980s, class actions were certified for some or all claims in the Hyatt Skywalk, Bendectin, DES, Dalkon Shield, Shiley heart valve, salmonella (Jewel Foods), Agent Orange, and asbestos litigations. In the early 1980s, appellate courts generally refused to uphold these class action certifications, but by the late 1980s, the appellate response was more mixed and many class actions moved forward. Several of the mass torts that have emerged in this decade, including silicone breast implant cases and tobacco litigation have been certified as class actions.

In the federal courts, multidistricting provided another mechanism for collecting cases. While the Judicial Panel on Multidistricting was slow to assign asbestos worker injury suits to a single judge, the MGM Grand Hotel Fire, DuPont Plaza Hotel Fire, Bendectin, Dalkon Shield, L-tryptophan, DDT, and Agent Orange cases were all multidistricted early in the litigation. In the state courts, cases within a single state have sometimes been transferred to a single jurisdiction, and cases filed within a jurisdiction have often been assigned to a single judge. For example, during the 1980s, all asbestos cases filed in the New Jersey state courts were transferred to Middlesex County. Hyatt Skywalk state cases were assigned to Judge Timothy O'Leary in Kansas City, Jewel Foods salmonella cases were consolidated before a single judge in Cook County, Illinois, and in many state courts, asbestos cases have been assigned to a special asbestos calendar supervised by one judge. To date, the only mechanism for collecting both federal and state cases has been through the bankruptcy courts. Asbestos litigation has led to multiple bankruptcy proceedings involving large groups of cases against certain manufacturers, and the Dalkon Shield litigation ended in bankruptcy court. * * *

C. Devising Global Settlements

1. Settlement Strategies. — Many judges have tried to settle, rather than adjudicate, the cases that have been consolidated before them. In some instances, judges have played a strong role in developing the settlement plan; in others, judges have relied heavily on a special master appointed to help the attorneys shape the plan. The attorneys in turn are usually organized into committees either appointed by the judge or formed voluntarily.

Because asbestos litigation was not multidistricted earlier and initial efforts to certify class actions failed, group settlements of asbestos personal injury claims have involved sets of cases — for example, all cases pending during a particular period in a particular jurisdiction or all claims against a bankrupt defendant — rather than the entire caseload. In contrast, class actions in Agent Orange and the Dalkon Shield bankruptcy proceedings, both of which established bars against future litigation, set the stage for global settlements — settlements that resolve all current and future litigation involving a particular product. Currently, at least three global class settlements have been conditionally certified: *Georgine* (the future claims class settlement of asbestos-related claims against CCR); *Ahearn v. Fibreboard Corp.* (a limited fund mandatory class of all current and future asbestos claims against Fibreboard);

and *Lindsey v. Dow Corning* (an opt-out class settlement of all current and future breast implant product liability claims).

In certain respects, judges' settlement strategies in mass torts have not been very different from the strategy used to settle ordinary tort cases. The judge confers separately with the attorneys for each side, emphasizing the weaknesses in their case and the risks they face if they go to trial. The judge then attempts to move the attorneys' monetary demands and offers toward a middle range within which they can agree upon an amount to settle the litigation. The judge may increase the pressure to settle by requiring attorneys to participate in marathon sessions or threatening to move quickly to trial if the attorneys cannot agree. Judge Jack Weinstein ultimately settled the Agent Orange case (after previous settlement attempts had failed) during marathon sessions the weekend before jury selection was to begin. However, unlike settlements of ordinary tort litigation — or even mass tort settlements involving mass catastrophe, such as hotel fires, or subsets of mass latent injury torts, such as some asbestos settlements — global settlements must create a monetary pool that will cover tens of thousands or hundreds of thousands of claims and that almost certainly will be funded by multiple defendants. Formulas must be devised for allocating the monetary payment among multiple defendants and distributing the settlement fund among claimants. Those attempting to fashion such settlements must grapple with the problems of scientific controversy over causation, uncertainty about the number of current and future claimants, and conflicts among parties, among attorneys, and between parties and attorneys.

2. Elements of Global Settlement Plans. — Judges, special masters, and attorneys have fashioned settlement strategies that have three central components.

a. Aggregate settlement amounts that cap defendants' damages exposure. — The aggregate value of the settlement fund (and the allocation of shares among defendants) is a negotiated amount, which is sometimes determined more by what defendants are willing to pay and plaintiffs' attorneys are willing to accept than by any systematic data on the total size of the claimant population and the severity of their injuries.

* * *

b. Rules for allocating the settlement fund among claimants. — The allocation of dollars from a fund is determined by a grid or matrix — also arrived at through negotiation — that assigns potential claimants to categories with different cash values on the basis of evidence of causation, disease, or injury severity. The development of compensation grids is closely linked to the concept of a limited fund, which seems to lend itself to a rule-based system for allocating compensation. The criteria that underlie compensation grids or matrices are derived from an amalgam of scientific or medical information about the nature of injuries and their appropriate treatment, information about the factors that have determined settlement or trial value before the aggregate settlement, and the amount for which negotiators will settle.

* * *

   c.   *Procedures for distributing compensation.* — Once global settlements are finalized, the daunting task of distributing funds to claimants begins. Most global settlement plans have established a claimants' trust facility to manage the corpus of funds and a claims resolution facility to distribute compensation to claimants. These facilities differ from case to case in many respects, including the options they offer for dispute resolution. Some payment schemes, such as those devised by the DDT settlement and the Agent Orange settlement, are wholly administrative. Recognizing the essentially administrative task of claims payment under the Agent Orange scheme, Judge Weinstein contracted with the Aetna insurance company to distribute compensation. At the other extreme, the first Manville Trust, although intended to rely primarily on negotiation, mediation, and arbitration to decide payment amounts, found itself embroiled in litigation and sank under the pressure of an unanticipated number of filings and size of damage awards. Four claims facilities illustrate the different balances that have been struck between administrative processes and individualized dispute resolution procedures.

   (1) Dalkon Shield. — In an effort to balance efficiency and equity concerns, the Dalkon Shield Claims Facility offered claimants a combination of administrative processes, for no injury and minor injury claims, and ADR processes, for more serious claims, with trial available for those who rejected other options. Under Option 1 of the bankruptcy plan, claimants could receive a flat amount of $725 simply for filing an affidavit that they were Shield users and had sustained injury. More than half of the claimants availed themselves of this option. Under Option 2 of the plan, claimants who presented minimal medical evidence of use and injury could receive scheduled damages ranging from $850 to $5500, depending on the nature of the injury. Under Option 3, claimants who thought they had stronger evidence of causation and damages above the Option 2 cap could enter into more traditional negotiations, including a settlement conference, with the Trust. Plaintiffs' lawyers expected that Option 3 offers would be in line with historical settlement values of Dalkon Shield legal claims. Finally, under Option 4, claimants could elect binding arbitration or trial. To implement the Option 4 portion of the plan, the Trust contracted with the Duke University Private Adjudication Center.

   The implementation of the Dalkon Shield plan seems to have fallen considerably short of what was promised to claimants. The Trust adopted a hard-nosed settlement approach, under which Option 3 claimants were given a "best and final offer," and the settlement conference was used for explaining that offer to the claimant, rather than for negotiating a better offer. Moreover, under one form of arbitration — "fast track" — the amount that arbitrators could award was capped at $10,000 (recently raised to $20,000), and while the arbitrator can award more under the second form, the claimant cannot receive any more than the original settlement offer or the cap — whichever is higher — until all Dalkon Shield claims have been resolved. The Trust justified its approach to claims resolution on the grounds that it needed to conserve funds to assure payment to all eligible claimants. Its policies also seem to have been driven by an anti-lawyer, pro-unrepresented-claimant orientation.* * *

(2) Fibreboard (asbestos). — The *Ahearn* settlement of all future asbestos personal injury claims against Fibreboard contemplates a more complicated seven-step claims disposition process that offers claimants more options. The first three steps mirror the traditional tort process: The claimant submits a claim; the Trust makes an offer; and the two parties negotiate. During this negotiation, the claimant is free to offer additional information (a right that the Dalkon Shield Trust severely circumscribed). If the claim does not settle at step three, the claimant proceeds to mediation. At mediation, the claimant will be present, the claimant's counsel may or may not be present, at the claimant's option. The mediation may be conducted in person or by phone. If the claim is not resolved through mediation, the claimant may then proceed to either binding or nonbinding arbitration. There will be one arbitrator; if the arbitration is nonbinding, the claimant must be present, but if the arbitration is binding, the claimant may choose to be present. Claims will be processed through steps one through five in order of filing, and settlements and awards will be paid over a three-year schedule. Lawyer fees will be capped at twenty-five percent of net recovery after costs. If the claimant is not satisfied with compensation obtainable through the various nonbinding options detailed above, he or she may proceed to trial. At trial, however, the claim is subject to significant constraints, including a prohibition on claiming punitive damages. Trial awards are also subject to longer payment schedules, with annual and lifetime caps.

(3) Lindsey (silicone breast implants). — In contrast to *Ahearn* and to the Dalkon Shield settlements, the *Lindsey* breast implant settlement contemplates a wholly administrative process with no ADR. But *Lindsey* offers claimants three chances to opt out: first, at the time of initial notice, which is now passed; second, when the dollar payments for each cell in the grid are finally set, that is, after any necessary ratcheting down of grid values; and third, in the case of ongoing claimants — those who do not qualify as current disease claimants — if they are offered a payment that is less than the amount paid to the previously paid current disease claimants. As in *Ahearn*, these opt-outs are subject to certain restrictions on their legal claims.

(4) Georgine (CCR asbestos future claims). — Finally, the *Georgine* futures class settlement specifies a dispute resolution process

somewhere between the wholly administrative scheme of *Lindsey* and the more nuanced disposition process proposed for *Ahearn*.

* * *

In sum, how one assesses the contributions of ADR to mass torts depends on how one measures the proverbial water in the glass. Is it half full or half empty? From the perspective of the defendants' and plaintiffs' attorneys who have used negotiation and mediation to create imaginative resolutions of their cases, the glass may well look half full. From the perspective of lay plaintiffs who were not at the table when these agreements were negotiated, who often were not fully informed of the real options that they would have when the agreements were implemented, and whose voices were not heard in the courtrooms when these agreements were debated, the glass may look half empty.

VI. IS THERE A GREATER ROLE FOR ADR?

Devising methods for enhancing parties' control over mass personal injury litigation — taking the promise of ADR seriously — is a tall order. At first blush, it is not clear how courts that are faced with thousands of claims arising in or transferred to a single jurisdiction, can provide litigants more control over and participation in the process without returning to individual case-at-a-time disposition. And, indeed, some have called for such a return. But those who favor individualized case disposition as a viable option should review the early history of asbestos litigation. In that era, when trial judges were more reluctant to innovate and appellate courts were more prone to reject formal aggregative methods for resolving personal injury torts, judges and lawyers used informal ad hoc procedures to achieve collective resolutions. Whereas, today, scholars and practitioners can scrutinize the *Georgine* future-claimant class settlement agreement, in that earlier period few people — including claimants — knew what deals were being struck, who benefited, and who lost as a result. Moreover, the increased availability of aggregation has empowered plaintiffs injured by corporate misbehavior to secure damages for their losses, when that might have been impossible had plaintiffs' attorneys been required to litigate their suits one by one. The history of tobacco litigation in the United States might be different had aggregative procedures — and the plaintiffs' attorneys investment in mass personal injury litigation that they have encouraged — been available two decades ago.

The challenge, then, is to shape aggregative procedures to enhance litigant control and participation within the bounds of what is financially and logistically possible. Clearly, tens of thousands of claimants cannot attend a single hearing; nor is it obvious that all claimants crave such participation. But just as judges have devised strategies for representing diverse plaintiff (and plaintiffs' attorneys) interests on Plaintiff Steering Committees, judges should strive to bring diverse representative plaintiffs into the hearing rooms *before* the final deal is struck rather than after.

* * *

Notes and Questions

1. Would it be better "to coordinate and consolidate pretrial discovery and motions practice but then individually try the tort cases in an appropriate venue"? *See* Roger H. Traugsrud, *Mass Trials in Mass Tort Cases: A Dissent,* 1989 U. Ill. L. Rev. 69, 69.

2. The September 11th Victim Compensation Fund provides another interesting structural model for the processing of mass claims. Enacted by Congress in the immediate aftermath of the September 11th terrorist attacks in New York and Washington, D.C., the fund was designed to provide fast government compensation to the families of the victims for economic and non-economic losses in exchange for their agreement not to sue the airlines, airports, governments, or other possible defendants for damages arising out of the terrorist attacks.

The fund used a no-fault approach in the sense that claimants were entitled to recovery under the fund once they established their relationship to a 9–11 victim; the only question would be how much they would be entitled to recover. In this regard, Congress gave the fund administrator, Professor Kenneth Feinberg of the Georgetown University Law Center, broad authority to determine the "amount of compensation to which the claimant is entitled" taking into account "the harm to the claimant, the facts of the claim, and the individual circumstances of the claimant." Air Transportation Safety and System Stabilization Act, Pub. Law 107–42, § 405(b)(1)(B)(ii), 115 Stat. 238 (2001). Significantly, Congress did not place any limits on overall disbursements from the fund. Feinberg measured economic losses by determining each victim's lost income from September 11, 2001 (the date of death) through his or her retirement, based on the victim's previous three years' income, with reductions for payments from life insurance, pension funds, death benefits programs and other such collateral sources of compensation. He also fixed noneconomic damages for all victims at $250,000 per victim plus $100,000 for each of the victims' surviving children and spouses.

Neither Feinberg's regulations nor his awards in individual cases were subject to appeal. After a slow start, 97% of the persons eligible for recovery ultimately chose to file claims with the fund rather than pursue remedies in court. The structure of the fund has been widely criticized by families of the victims and observers. *See, e.g.,* Robert M. Ackerman, *The September 11th Victim Compensation Fund: An Administrative Response to a National Tragedy,* 10 Harv. Negot. L. Rev. 135 (2005); Janet Cooper Alexander, *Procedural Design and Terror Victim Compensation,* 53 DePaul L. Rev. 627 (2003); George L. Priest, *The Problematic Structure of the September 11th Victim Compensation Fund,* 53 DePaul L. Rev. 527 (2003). What problems do you see? How would you describe Feinberg's role as a dispute resolution professional? What changes to this structure would you recommend?

4. ADMINISTRATIVE AGENCIES

ADR has seen explosive growth in administrative agencies. Former U.S. Attorney General Janet Reno was a strong supporter of ADR during her tenure in the Clinton Administration, and ADR has enjoyed bipartisan support since then. One reason might be the extraordinary number and range of disputes with which administrative agencies get involved. One class of disputes includes those that arise during the course of the fulfillment of their statutory regulatory obligations. For example, the Internal Revenue Service administers the federal tax laws, and now uses mediation to help settle disputes with taxpayers. However, agencies are also involved in disputes in their capacity as employers, and most federal agencies now have alternative dispute resolution programs for the handling of such claims. Finally, administrative agencies are involved in disputes in their capacity as consumers of good and services, and have made extensive use of ADR to resolve public contract disputes.

ADR is also used in other types of disputes, from inter-agency disputes to military combat operations, but the materials that follow address the primary governmental contexts. The first reading, a 2004 federal government-wide report on the use of ADR by government agencies — excluding the courts — demonstrates the remarkable breadth and depth of the institutionalization of ADR within the administrative state. The second reading elaborates upon a topic touched on in Chapter IV, beginning at page 319, the use of dispute resolution during the public rulemaking process of administrative agencies, so-called "reg negs." The third reading is an analysis of one of the government's largest, and most ambitious, employment dispute resolution programs, the U.S. Postal Service's REDRESS program.

a. An Overview

OFFICE OF THE ASSOCIATE ATTORNEY GENERAL,
REPORT TO THE STEERING COMMITTEE
INTERAGENCY ALTERNATIVE DISPUTE
RESOLUTION WORKING GROUP

(March 17, 2004).

The Office of the Associate Attorney General is pleased to present this report on the status of federal alternative dispute resolution ("ADR") to the Steering Committee of the Interagency Alternative Dispute Resolution Working Group. The Attorney General is the Presidentially-appointed leader of federal ADR, and the Steering Committee representatives are experts in that field. * * *

These are challenging times. Terrorism has added a compelling new dimension to the administration of law and justice. In this new world, the emphasis falls — as it must — on counter-terrorism. Yet, at the same time, the United States Government must discharge many other significant mandates. Our federal agencies have many other responsibilities and program areas that are essential to the well-being of the United States and its citizens.

Those who are working for the federal government in those other areas may feel overlooked these days because so much of the spotlight is focused on terrorism-related issues. But they should not feel that way. Their work — and the benefits of ADR — are more important, not less important, in the face of the new national priorities. There is a reason the Secretary of Defense has made the adoption of better business practices one of his top priorities. Good use of ADR at his agency has saved the Department of Defense money and it has avoided litigation. Perhaps even more importantly, ADR enables the leadership at the Department of Defense to eliminate distractions and focus on the war against terrorism.

The Steering Committee is an impressive group of federal officials with an important mission. Its members are the senior ADR professionals appointed pursuant to the Administrative Dispute Resolution Act of 1996. They represent all of the Cabinet departments and many of the independent agencies. They are responsible for facilitating and encouraging agency use of ADR in their respective jurisdictions. Their accomplishments in doing so contribute to the goals, efficiency, and productivity of the federal government and its agencies. A review of their contributions and how they fit into the policy direction of the federal government is enlightening.

The President has given very clear direction for how the government should be guided. First, the government should be results-oriented. Second, the government should be citizen-centered. Third, wherever possible, the government should be market-based.

ADR is transforming the way that the government resolves disputes. In doing so, the federal agencies' ADR programs have implemented the President's policies in many areas. Of course, it is always risky to mention specifics, because those omitted may fear they somehow did not "make the grade." But that is not the case. Practical limitations force a selective listing of just some examples of the many federal successes to illustrate the breadth and scope of their significant contributions to good government.

First, federal ADR programs are implementing the President's directive to make government results-oriented. What matters here is completion, performance, and results. ADR does a better, quicker, and more cost effective job than traditional adversarial processes in resolving disputes that involve the public. Here are some examples:

- At the Federal Energy Regulatory Commission, the use of mediation by its Dispute Resolution Service saves parties, on average, $100,000 in avoided costs by resolving disputes concerning electricity and natural gas. These savings lower energy costs, which can only benefit consumers.

- At the Department of Health and Human Services, the Provider Reimbursement Review Board uses ADR to settle about 150 health care provider disputes each year. It costs $11,000 to hear one of those cases, but only $750 to mediate it, so the cost savings is over $10,000 per case. As an added benefit, while they are at the table, the parties often resolve issues for future cost years, and thereby avert future disputes they would have otherwise faced.

- At the Federal Aviation Administration, the Office of Dispute Resolution for Acquisition has resolved 89% of all contract disputes, ranging from small claims under $100,000 to large, multi-million dollar claims. It has also resolved 67% of all bid protests, ranging from small contract values to large acquisitions valued over one billion dollars. The savings to corporations, in time and money, from avoiding protracted, non-productive litigation, contributes to a better overall business and economic climate.

- The Department of Energy's technology transfer ombuds program deals with issues of licenses, patents, and the Cooperative Research and Development Agreements with non-federal partners. The program has had an 85% success rate and has enabled technological innovation to proceed at a faster rate. Thus, small businesses and entrepreneurs can utilize their limited funds to further their business objectives, rather than engage in litigation.

- At the Environmental Protection Agency, the use of ADR to reach agreement for the cleanup of contaminated Superfund sites has saved private corporations and the government millions of dollars in litigation and transaction costs.

ADR also is demonstrating results in dealing with internal disputes. Unlike traditional adversarial processes, ADR is reducing costs, improving workforce morale, and increasing productivity. For example:

- At the U.S. Air Force, over 2700 workplace disputes were mediated last year. Seventy-five percent (75%) of them were successful. The average cost savings was $14,000 per case. The average time savings was 410 days per case. The number of informal workplace complaints has dropped by 70% and formal complaints have dropped by 56%.

- The Department of Energy saved about $1.3 million dollars over the last three years by mediating longstanding workplace problems.

- The U.S. Postal Service mediates 10,000 workplace disputes every year. Its exit surveys show that 90% of both managers and employees are satisfied with the mediation process. There has been a 40% decline in the percentage of postal service employees who initiate a new EEO complaint.

The program evaluations that enable agencies to demonstrate these results of ADR are equally impressive:

- The Department of Veterans Affairs has created a web-based tracking system for 250 facility locations throughout the country, with data query capabilities, that will enable it to identify best practices as well as areas where improvement is needed.

- At the Environmental Protection Agency, the Conflict Prevention and Resolution Center has created a performance evaluation system that gives continuous feedback for the enhancement of environmental ADR services.

All agencies should strive to use effective tools like these to evaluate their programs, measure their results, and improve their services. That is the best way for an agency to determine whether it has achieved its purpose, and how it can continue improving.

Federal ADR programs are also implementing the President's second directive, which is to make government citizen-centered. What matters here is fostering a good relationship between citizens and their government, and making the government responsive to those citizens. ADR is a tool for the government to do exactly that. Instead of telling citizens what is in their best interest, the government is using ADR to obtain citizen input in a collaborative process that achieves a satisfactory result for everyone. For example:

- The U.S. Institute for Environmental Conflict Resolution provided expertise and resources for 50 site-specific projects in the past year, including the Grand Canyon overflight noise controversy in Arizona, and collaborative water management planning for the Florida Everglades.

- In the past year, the Department of the Interior successfully completed two negotiated rule makings with all interested parties. It used that collaborative process to develop new regulations covering Indian education under the No Child Left Behind Act, and off-road driving on the Fire Island National Seashore in New York.

- The Federal Mediation and Conciliation Service worked with the National Institute of Standards and Technology to obtain public input for the design of new buildings in the wake of post–9/11 structural concerns.

The government is also demonstrating a focus on citizens by using ADR to avert citizen disputes before they arise or to deal with them quickly when they do arise. For example:

- The Department of Education's ombudsman deals with hundreds of federal student loan problems weekly. The program has been successful in resolving long-standing issues, identifying problem trends, and recommending improvements.

- The Federal Energy Regulatory Commission has a policy of encouraging parties to contact its Enforcement Hotline or its Dispute Resolution Service — and consider the use of ADR-before a formal complaint is filed. The successful use of this proactive approach avoids the cost of formal adjudicatory processes for both the Commission and the parties.

In another citizen-centered approach, the government is partnering with citizens to make sure ADR services are available. For example:

- The Federal Mediation and Conciliation Service has a roster of 1,000 private citizens who serve as private judges to settle contract disputes.

- The Environmental Protection Agency, in conjunction with the U.S. Institute for Environmental Conflict Resolution, designed and maintains an extensive roster of private neutral professionals who are experienced in managing environmental disputes. The EPA has also awarded a five-year, $61 million contract for private professional services as needed in any area of environmental ADR, ranging from training and systems design to consensus building and case mediation.

The President's third directive, which is to make government market-based wherever possible, is also supported by federal ADR initiatives. What matters here is enabling businesses to run effectively so that they can foster innovation and competition. Businesses can concentrate on running their business if they can avoid time-consuming and often unnecessary litigation. ADR helps them do just that. Some examples are:

- The Department of Energy used preventive dispute resolution to minimize problems with a multi-billion dollar contract for the cleanup of a former nuclear weapons production facility. That partnering approach contributed to an on-time, on-budget, and safe execution of the contract.

- At the National Mediation Board, more than 600 labor-management cases in the railroad and airline industries have been mediated with only three work stoppages (one of which lasted for less than 90 minutes).

The government is also demonstrating a market approach when it uses ADR to give businesses more choices. For example:

- The Federal Aviation Administration's Office of Dispute Resolution for Acquisition has developed a user-friendly website that provides a plain language guide to practice and procedures. It includes descriptions of past adjudicated cases that allow businesses to assess litigation risks and establish reasonable parameters for ADR settlement.

- In our global economy, the Federal Mediation and Conciliation Service has entered partnerships to build the infrastructure for conflict resolution and prevention in Argentina, Bulgaria, Canada, Colombia, Croatia, Indonesia, Latvia, Mozambique, Peru, Serbia, Thailand, and Uganda.

The government is employing a business approach for its own internal conflict management so that it can save time and money better spent on more critical issues. For example:

- The National Institutes of Health is using ADR to promote scientific innovation by addressing conflicts in authorship, sharing of biological materials, and collaboration among scientists.

- The National Archives and Records Administration created a nationwide integrated conflict management system with preventive services to improve workplace relationships and avert disputes.

There are many more illustrations of ADR success stories. The federal agencies have made those success stories happen, and the ADR experts within the agencies have helped their agencies play a critical role in the President's quest for good government.

* * *

Notes and Questions

1. Are there any agency uses of ADR that you found surprising?

2. As with courts, mediation is overwhelmingly the dispute resolution method of choice among the federal administrative agencies. Indeed, there are significant constraints on the federal government's ability to use arbitration.

Until relatively recently, the federal government was generally prohibited from participating in arbitration because the U.S. Comptroller General took the position that the government had no legal authority to let a private party decide the outcome of a case involving the government. The Administrative Dispute Resolution Act of 1990 explicitly authorized arbitration for federal agencies, but only if it is clearly voluntary. Moreover, agencies cannot require a commitment to arbitration as a condition of entering into a government contract or obtaining a benefit. Finally, unless an agency has explicit statutory authority, it may not use arbitration until it has promulgated official rules prescribing the cases that may be arbitrated and the procedures the agency will follow. *See generally* JEFFREY M. SENGER, FEDERAL DISPUTE RESOLUTION 41–45 (2004). Why might the federal government be stricter about the use of arbitration than mediation?

b.   Setting Agency Policy: 'Reg negs'

Administrative agencies sometimes use ADR in the fulfillment of their statutory missions. For example, the Equal Employment Opportunity Commission frequently mediates employee complaints against employers. In such a context, the alternative dispute resolution process is typically substantially the same as is found in other areas, although some context-specific adaptations are sometimes appropriate.

Administrative agencies also use ADR in their policymaking processes, the most significant of which is known as rulemaking. It is through rulemaking that administrative agencies implement the authority that has been vested in the agency by the legislature to carry out a particular policy objective. For example, the Occupational Safety and Health Administration will use a rulemaking process to promulgate workplace safety standards, and the Environmental Protection Agency will use rulemaking to develop air or water pollution standards. The use of ADR principles has helped revolutionize this process.

Traditional agency rulemaking is a three-part process, in which the agency sends out a notice of proposed rulemaking describing the subject matter of the rulemaking and any preliminary proposals it is considering. In the second stage, the agency conducts a hearing process by which affected parties may make comments to the agencies on its proposals. Finally, once the agency decides the rule it wants to promulgate, it sets forth a clear and concise statement of the rule, along with an explanation of the basis upon which the agency made a decision. This process, which can take years and include many different iterations of the first two stages, is often called "notice and comment rulemaking." See generally PETER L. STRAUSS, TODD D. RAKOFF & CYNTHIA FARINA, GELLHORN AND BYSE'S ADMINISTRATIVE LAW 483–732 (Rev. 10th ed. 2003).

Regulatory negotiations, or "reg negs," change that process by engrafting a dispute resolution process, such as negotiation or mediation, into the notice and comment rulemaking process. As Professor Harter describes below, rather than simply using the notice and comment process to decide unilaterally what the agency's policy will be, an agency using a reg neg facilitates a policy discussion among interested stakeholders about what the rule should be, and if the group achieves consensus, the agency agrees to use the group's proposal as the basis for its rule.

PHILIP J. HARTER, NEGOTIATING REGULATIONS: A CURE FOR THE MALAISE

71 Geo. L.J. 1, 28–31 (1982).

III. THE ADVANTAGES OF RULEMAKING BY NEGOTIATION

The idea of developing rules through negotiation among interested parties received brief attention when John Dunlop proposed it during his tenure as Secretary of Labor. Interest in the idea largely died before being translated into legal requirements or practice. * * *

Negotiating has many advantages over the adversarial process. The parties participate directly and immediately in the decision. They share in its development and concur with it, rather than "participate" by submitting information that the decisionmaker considers in reaching the decision. Frequently, those who participate in the negotiation are closer to the ultimate decisionmaking authority of the interest they represent than traditional intermediaries that represent the interests in an adversarial proceeding. Thus, participants in negotiations can make substantive decisions, rather than acting as experts in the decisionmaking process. In addition, negotiation can be a less expensive means of decisionmaking because it reduces the need to engage in defensive research in anticipation of arguments made by adversaries.

Undoubtedly the prime benefit of direct negotiations is that it enables the participants to focus squarely on their respective interests. They need not advocate and maintain extreme positions before a decisionmaker. Therefore, the parties can develop a feel for the true issues that lie within the advocated extremes and attempt to accommodate fully the competing interests. An example of this benefit occurred when a group of environmentalists opposed the construction of a dam because they feared it would lead to the development of a nearby valley. The proponents of the dam were farmers in the valley who were adversely affected by periodic floods. Negotiations between the two groups, which were begun at the behest of the governor, revealed a common interest in preserving the valley. Without the negotiations the environmentalists would have undoubtedly sued to block construction, and necessarily would have employed adversarial tactics. Negotiations, however, demonstrated the true interests of the parties and permitted them to work toward accommodation.

In another example, an environmental group sued a government agency that granted a permit for a uranium mine, alleging that the environmental impact statement (EIS) was defective. The mine, confronted with protracted litigation and the consequent delay, agreed to negotiations. The attorney for the environmental group queried rhetorically what would have happened if the case had been successful? He thought that the mining company would simply beef up the EIS and continue to build the mine. Negotiations enabled the parties to focus on the issues separating them instead of fighting the legal strawman of a defective EIS. A general agreement resulted from the negotiations. More important, both sides were enthusiastic about the process.

Negotiation enables the parties to rank their concerns and to make trades to maximize their respective interests. In a traditional proceeding an agency may be unable to anticipate the intensity with which the respective parties may view the various provisions of a proposed rule. The agency may focus on an aspect of a rule that is critical to one party, but not of particular interest to other parties. An agency simply would have to guess how to reconcile such an issue because it would not know how to rank the parties' concerns. An interested party, however, could easily decide to accommodate another party in return for concession on a critical point. An example of such a trade off process would be when a beneficiary of a proposed regulation argues that the standard should be stringent with early compliance by the regulated company. A company that must comply with the regulation might counter that the standard should be more lenient with a long lead time for compliance. An agency faced with this situation might decide to require a lax standard in response to the company's claims of excessive burdens and require a short deadline in response to the need for immediate protection. Everyone involved, however, may be more content with precisely the opposite result. A rule allowing a longer time to implement a more stringent standard might benefit both parties because the shorter time for implementation might cause disruption that would offset any savings resulting from the reduced level of regulation.

Rulemaking by negotiation can reduce the time and cost of developing regulations by emphasizing practical and empirical concerns rather than theoretical predictions. In developing a regulation under the current system, an agency must prove a factual case, at least preliminarily, and anticipate the factual information that will be submitted in the record. Because the agency lacks direct access to empirical data, the information used is often of a theoretical nature derived from models. In negotiations, the parties in interest decide together what information is necessary to make a reasonably informed decision. Therefore, the data used in negotiations may not have to be as theoretical or as extensive as it is in an adversary process. For example, one agency proposed a regulation based on highly technical, theoretical data. The parties argued that the theoretical data was unnecessary because it simply did not reflect the practical experiences of the parties and of another agency. The agency determined the validity of the assertion and modified its regulation accordingly. The lesson of this example is that the data can emphasize practical and empirical concerns rather than theoretical predictions. In turn, this emphasis on practical experience can reduce the time and cost of developing regulations by reducing the need for developing extensive theoretical data.

Negotiation also can enable the participants to focus on the details of a regulation. In the adversary process, the big points must be hit and hit hard, while the subtleties and details frequently are overlooked. Or, even if the details are not overlooked, the decisionmaker may not appreciate their consequences. In negotiations, however, interested parties can directly address all aspects of a problem in attempting to formulate workable solutions.

Overarching all the other benefits of negotiations is the added legitimacy a rule would acquire if all parties viewed the rule as reasonable and endorsed it without a fight. Affected parties would participate in the development of a rule by sharing in the decisions, ranking their own concerns and needs, and trading them with other parties. Regardless of whether the horse under design turns out to be a five-legged camel or a Kentucky Derby winner, the resulting rule would have a validity beyond those developed under the current procedures. Moreover, nothing indicates that the results would be of any lesser quality than those developed currently. Surely the *Code of Federal Regulations* stable has as many camels as derby winners.

Negotiation clearly has distinct advantages. It is therefore easy to fall into a "hot tub" view of negotiation as a method of settling disputes and establishing public policy: if only we strip off the armor of an adversarial hearing, everyone will jump into negotiations with beguiling honesty and openness to reach the optimum solution to the problem at hand. In fact, the process is far more complex than that. Negotiation must be carefully analyzed to determine not only whether it can work at all in the regulatory context, but also to identify those situations in which it is appropriate. Moreover, if a form of negotiation is to be used to develop rules issued by a government agency that determines the rights and obligations of the population at large, the process must be sensitive to methods of conducting negotiations and translating any result into a binding rule. Thus, the complex legal issues of how negotiations would relate to the APA and to the traditional political theories and values underlying rulemaking procedures must be examined. * * *

* * *

Notes and Questions

1. Getting the right participants to the bargaining table, or convening, is an important part of the reg neg process. Assume the state Department of Natural Resources needs to resolve a longstanding dispute over river flow problems that implicate environmental aesthetics in a state park, certain endangered species, and tourism in a nearby resort area. Why might the agency want to use a reg neg? Who would it want to have at the bargaining table?

2. How much consensus among stakeholders and interested parties should such a reg neg process require? Absolute? Supermajority? Majority? Should the relative weight of the stakeholders' interests make any difference?

3. In this excerpt, Professor Harter lists several advantages of the reg neg process. What might be some disadvantages? Under what circumstances would they outweigh the advantages of using the reg neg process for the agency?

4. Is a reg neg more suitable for some types of issues than others? *See* Gary E. Marchant & Andrew Askland, *GM Foods: Potential Public Consultation and Participation Mechanisms*, 44 Jurimetrics J. 99, 118–19 (2003).

5. For a case study on reg negs, see Alana S. Knaster & Philip J. Harter, *The Clean Fuels Regulatory Negotiation*, Intergovernmental Perspective, Summer 1992, at 20 (excerpted in Chapter IV, beginning at page 319).

6. For criticisms of reg negs, see Cary Coglianese, *Assessing Consensus: The Promise and Performance of Negotiated Rulemaking*, 46 Duke L.J. 1255 (1997) (they fail to achieve instrumental goals of saving time and reducing litigation); William Funk, *Bargaining Toward The New Millennium: Regulatory Negotiation and the Subversion of the Public Interest*, 46 Duke L.J. 1351 (1997) (they fail to assure adequate role of public interests); Jim Rossi, *Participation Run Amok: The Costs of Mass Participation for Deliberative Agency Decisionmaking*, 92 Nw. U. L. Rev. 173, 217–36 (1997) (they interfere with agency's larger agenda-setting efforts). For responses, see Jody Freedman & Laura I. Langbein, *Regulatory Negotiations and the Legitimacy Benefit*, 9 NYU Envtl. L.J. 60 (2000); Philip J. Harter, *Assessing the*

Assessors: The Actual Performance of Negotiated Rulemaking, 9 NYU Envtl. L.J. 32 (2000). For a repost, see Cary Coglianese, *Assessing the Advocacy of Negotiated Rulemaking: A Response to Philip Harter,* 9 NYU Envtl. L.J. 386 (2001).

c. ADR in the Federal Workplace

As in the private sector, ADR has been particularly popular in the government workplace. Many federal entities, ranging from the Center for Disease Control to the U.S. Air Force, have workplace ADR programs, most of which emphasize mediation. The following reading looks at one such program, offered by the U.S. Postal Service.

LISA BINGHAM, MEDIATION AT WORK: TRANS-FORMING WORKPLACE CONFLICT AT THE UNITED STATES POSTAL SERVICE

IBM Center for the Business of Government
5, 12–23 (2003).

Introduction

Over the past decade, the United States Postal Service (USPS) has emerged as a national leader in the use of appropriate or alternative dispute resolution in employment disputes. Employment disputes include but are not limited to conflict over supervisory decisions (criticism, demeaning or improper treatment), management policies (for example, opportunities for detail into supervisory positions or changing crafts), working conditions, pay and benefits (overtime, leaves of absence, absence for illness, for example), and discipline. The USPS's innovative program for employment disputes is named REDRESS (<u>R</u>esolve <u>E</u>mployment <u>D</u>isputes <u>R</u>each <u>E</u>quitable <u>S</u>olutions <u>S</u>wiftly). * * *

The EEO Complaint Process

The United States Postal Service REDRESS program provides mediation for equal employment opportunity (EEO) disputes, specifically those arising out of a claim of discrimination under federal law. Federal law prohibits discrimination based on race, sex, color, national origin, religion, age, and disability, and also prohibits sexual or racial harassment or retaliation for raising a claim of prohibited discrimination or harassment.

The traditional dispute system design established by the Equal Employment Opportunity Commission for federal discrimination claims is primarily rights-based. An employee may contact an EEO counselor regarding a potential claim. This is called the informal complaint or counseling stage of the process. In USPS and federal agencies, this EEO counselor is a federal employee who will conduct an informal inquiry into the dispute and attempt to resolve it, sometimes in face-to-face meetings between the disputants, but more often through telephone diplomacy. If counseling fails, the employee may file a formal EEO complaint. This triggers a formal investigation into the dispute and may include the taking of sworn statements and depositions. If the complaint is not abandoned or resolved, it may proceed to a formal adjudicatory hearing before an administrative judge. The judge's decision is submitted to the agency for final agency decision. If the employee is dissatisfied with the result, federal court litigation may ensue. This traditional regulatory process is largely rights-based, focusing on legal or contractual rights, obligations, and remedies, although it does provide for conciliation efforts.

This report examines the development and evaluation of REDRESS I, which involves the use of mediation at the informal complaint stage of the EEO process. REDRESS I was designed, pilot-tested, and rolled out nationwide between 1994 and 1999. In November 1999, after the national rollout was complete, the EEOC adopted regulations on standards for federal ADR programs. REDRESS meets, or exceeds, those standards. USPS recently expanded the program to encompass mediation at the formal complaint stage, REDRESS II. * * *

* * *

The Mediation Experiments

* * * The key system design features that continue to be part of the program are that mediation is voluntary for the EEO complainant, but mandatory for the supervisor respondent, who represents USPS as an organizational entity. As required by EEOC regulations, complainants are entitled to bring any representative that they choose to the table. These can include lawyers, union representatives, professional association representatives, family members, co-workers, or friends. USPS, as a party, may also designate a representative. The supervisor respondent must have settlement authority, or be in immediate telephone contact during the process with someone else in the organization authorized to approve the settlement. Mediation occurs during work hours, is private, and generally occurs within two to three weeks of a request.

* * *

The USPS pilot program initially used a facilitative model of practice. After a period of experimentation, USPS chose transformative mediation for the national model. Unlike other models, the USPS model does not permit the mediator to evaluate the case's merits, even if the participants request it. The mediator may not give a personal opinion regarding the merits, any assessment of the likely outcome in court, or specific proposals for settlement. All choices regarding the process, ideas for settlement, and the outcome of mediation are placed in the hands of the parties. This model differs from facilitative mediation in that the parties themselves design the mediation process; the mediator does not structure it for them, but instead asks them a series of questions about how they would like the process to proceed. This model of mediation is essentially participant-designed mediation.

* * *

The National Rollout

* * * The [REDRESS] Task Force created a national roster of experienced mediators. The initial roster of about 3,000 mediators nationwide was the product of a massive outreach effort. USPS REDRESS program staff attended mediator conferences and bar association meetings in an effort to deliver roster application forms (called the ADR Provider Survey) to the most experienced mediators in each geographic area. Minimum qualifications for consideration included at least 24 hours approved mediator training and experience as the lead mediator in at least ten cases. In addition, mediators had to agree to attend at least two additional days (20 hours) of transformative mediation training sponsored by the USPS. Finally, successful applicants had to agree to mediate one case pro bono to afford an opportunity for USPS staff to observe their effectiveness in the transformative framework. Persons who serve as arbitrators for disputes involving USPS or who have brought litigation against USPS within two years prior to application were not eligible for inclusion on the roster. No current or former employees are eligible for inclusion on the roster. This exclusion of current and former employees is intended to maintain the perception of fairness among employees.

In keeping with the transformative model, USPS did not limit the roster to mediators with employment law expertise, because mediators were not expected to evaluate the merits of the cases. Instead, USPS opened the roster to mediators from varied professional backgrounds, including psychology, counseling, and social work. The roster included teachers, academics, human resource professionals, and retirees from these professions. Many of the mediators had extensive experience in family and domestic relations practice. This outreach produced the most diverse roster then available, comprised of 44 percent women and 17 percent minorities.

USPS pays for all program costs, including mediator fees, administration, and training of mediators and participants from the Labor Relations budget at Headquarters. Mediator fees are negotiated locally on an individual basis. The policy is to pay mediators per session — not per case or hour — and also to cover travel expenses. In general, the USPS has recouped its investment in mediator training through the requirement that each mediator do one case *pro bono*.

The USPS took steps to institutionalize quality control. In collaboration with Professors Bush and [Joseph] Folger, it developed specialized advanced 20–hour transformative mediation training for experienced mediators from a variety of different practice models. The USPS identified a cadre of experienced mediation trainers and convened a Train-the-Trainers retreat in March 1998 at which they were taught the REDRESS model. The trainers' job was to fan out across the country to train mediators. * * *

To ensure that mediators did in fact practice the model in which they had been trained, USPS/EEO ADR Specialists observed at least one mediation session for each mediator used from the roster, and often they observed multiple mediation sessions. Surveys of these specialists about what they observed mediators do or say during these sessions indicated both that the specialists understood the model and that they were screening mediators based on implementation of this form of practice. After two years of this screening, the national roster ultimately stabilized at about 1,500 active mediators.

As the trainers fanned out across the country to train mediators, USPS Task Force staff trained key stakeholders and participants. The EEO/ADR coordinators all received 40–hour mediation training and attended the advanced mediator training for potential roster members in their region. Other key stakeholders — including union leadership and shop stewards, plant managers and supervisors, and local postmasters — received four-hour training about mediation and the program. A brochure was mailed to each employee's home. Lastly, supervisors conducted 'stand-ups', brief workplace meetings at which they explained the program to craft employees. Information was also provided through the internal USPS video network and through literature in EEO counseling offices.

Institutionalization

A key step in institutionalization was to build an esprit de corps among the EEO/ADR specialists and coordinators, while at the same time fostering cooperation between the REDRESS program staff and EEO Counselors. One source of possible resistance to any new program is a group that feels its job security is threatened by the program. From the outset, the Task Force was identified as a temporary organization and the EEO/ADR positions as temporary assignments. * * *

* * *

A last element of institutionalization was to set an appropriate goal by which to measure the program's success. Typically, programs before REDRESS used *settlement rate* — the percentage of all cases submitted to mediation that resulted in a settlement — as their barometer. However, settlement is explicitly *not* a goal of transformative mediation. Instead, the goal is to provide the participants with opportunities to take control of their own conflict (empowerment) and reach a better understanding of the other participant's perspective (recognition). It is hoped that the process may provide an opportunity for participants to resolve their conflict, but that is not the mediator's objective. Thus, USPS set *participation rate* — the percentage of all employees offered mediation who agreed to participate in the process — as the key indicator of each district's and area's success. The reasoning was that the program could only affect workplace conflict management if people used it: "We knew that to really have an impact, we needed as many people as possible to accept mediation."

In order for people to use it, someone had to have an incentive to encourage them. Participation rate gave everyone associated with the program that incentive. In contrast, had the program used settlement rate as the measure, there would have been a counterincentive; program staff might have counseled what they perceived as hard-to-settle or intractable cases out of the program. With participation rate as the target, it did not matter whether anyone believed mediation had any likelihood of success. The goal was simply to get people to talk to each other in a safe, private environment. If they resolved their conflict, that was a good thing, but if they failed to do so, it did not reflect adversely on the program staff. Initially, USPS set a goal of 70 percent. Subsequently, it raised the bar to 75%. Each time, the program met this national goal. Headquarters staff eventually developed a one-page bar chart showing participation rate graphically for each of the 85 geographic districts, with recognition and awards for those with the highest participation, to create an incentive structure for EEO staff to support the program, market it, and work to maintain its reputation among employees.

The USPS does maintain records on case closure rate, as distinguished from settlement rate. Case closure includes not only cases where the parties reached a resolution in mediation, but also cases where the parties conclude a formal settlement within 30 days thereafter, or where the complaining party drops, withdraws, or fails to pursue the case to the formal EEO complaint stage. The case closure rate varies from 70 percent to 80 percent.

National REDRESS Evaluation Project

* * *

Results after the National Rollout

* * * Overall, formal EEO complaints have declined by over 25 percent since their peak in 1998 at 14,000 formal complaints.

Researchers also examined various aspects of the program design. One study looked at the role that various kinds of representatives play. The program differs from some private sector Dispute System Designs in that it allows employees to bring any representative they choose to the mediation session, including lawyers, union representatives, professional association representatives, and friends or family. Some employees chose not to bring a representative. * * *

Researchers found that representation in some form had a positive impact on settlement. The settlement rate for mediations where neither party was represented was 55 percent, whereas the settlement rate for mediations where both parties were represented was 61 percent, a statistically significant difference of 6 percent. Representation was also associated with longer mediation sessions. The mean duration for mediations where neither party was represented was 152 minutes, but that number rose to 184 minutes for mediations where both parties were represented.

* * *

A second key result from the exit surveys related to participant satisfaction with mediation fairness. Among complainants who were represented by union or professional association representatives, 91 percent reported being very or somewhat satisfied with the fairness of the mediation. Eighty-eight percent of those represented by fellow employees agreed, while only 76 percent of attorneys were satisfied with the fairness of the proceedings. This is not surprising, given that cases with attorney representatives had the lowest rate of partial or complete resolution of the three types of representatives, and resolution correlates with perceptions of fairness. However, complainants with no representation reported a 91 percent rate of satisfaction, with the highest percentage (67 percent) reporting that they were "very satisfied." (Had they been prohibited from bringing a representative, the result would undoubtedly have been different.)

* * *

Before researchers can assess the impact of a program on agency goals, they must verify that the program has in fact been implemented in accord with its design and that it is functioning; this is called a process evaluation. Researchers looked at implementation of the transformative model through a process evaluation using surveys of USPS program. EEO/ADR specialists and coordinators were asked to describe what they had seen or heard mediators do or say that fostered or interfered with party empowerment or recognition between the parties. This provided a rich collection of descriptions and anecdotes about what was happening in mediation, from the perspective of an outside, dispassionate observer. An analysis revealed that the USPS program staff had correctly categorized mediator moves as fostering or hindering empowerment and recognition, in that their descriptions corresponded with the hallmarks of transformative mediation practice described by Folger and Bush (1995).

Notes and Questions

1. Recall the discussion of the different models of mediation in Chapter IV, beginning at page 288. The use of transformative mediation is unusual in federal agencies. Why do you think the REDRESS program designers chose the transformative model? Critics of the transformative model suggest it is not appropriate for many common disputes. Would the results of the REDRESS program give you more confidence in selecting this model for a workplace dispute resolution program?

2. Professor Bingham stresses the importance of the voluntary character of the REDRESS program for the employees (it was mandatory for the employer). How might the program's implementation and results have been different if the designers had used a mandatory model?

3. The program's designers also made a deliberate decision to schedule the mediations during the normal workday. What are the arguments for and against taking this approach?

4. In constructing their rosters, the program's designers elected not to have current or former USPS employees serve as mediators. In other federal

agencies, departmental employees are commonly used as mediators. Sometimes these positions are as full-time mediators, but more often mediation is a "collateral duty" appended to other responsibilities. What are the advantages and disadvantages of the REDRESS approach? What are the advantages of the "collateral duty" approach?

5.   The REDRESS program did not require the mediators on its roster to have any special background or expertise, including USPS experience. Yet as noted at the outset of the article, the disputes being mediated often were covered by substantive employment statutes and case law, such as Title VII of the Civil Rights Act of 1964. Do you think the program would be more effective if it required mediators to have more of a substantive background in employment issues, or perhaps even to be lawyers? How might such a design choice have affected the implementation and results of the REDRESS program? What kind of background should the REDRESS program managers have?

6.   Professor Bingham notes that the program designers used participation rates rather than settlement rates as a barometer of success. Do you agree with this choice? What are the advantages and disadvantages of this approach?

7.   Professor Bingham states that "... [S]ettlement is explicitly not a goal of the transformative mediation process. Instead, the goal is to provide participants with opportunities to take control of their own conflict (empowerment) and reach a better understanding of the other participant's perspective (recognition). It is hoped that the process may provide an opportunity for participants to resolve their conflict, but that is not the mediator's objective."

In a recently published second edition of their book, On Transformative Mediation (an excerpt of which appears in Chapter IV beginning at page 301), Bush and Folger provide a reformulation of their view on this issue:

> ... [E]ven though the mediator's job is to support empowerment and recognition shifts, the transformative model does not ignore the significance of resolving specific issues. Rather, it assumes that, if the mediators do the job just described, the parties themselves will very likely make positive changes in their interaction and find acceptable terms of resolution for themselves where such terms genuinely exist. * * *

ROBERT A. BARUCH BUSH & JOSEPH FOLGER, THE PROMISE OF MEDIATION: THE TRANSFORMATIVE APPROACH TO CONFLICT (rev. ed. 2005). For additional discussion of evaluating dispute systems, see Chapter VII, beginning at page 790.

8.   The REDRESS model permitted employees to bring in any representative to assist them, if they so chose. Professor Bingham's evaluation found that settlement rates were actually higher in mediations in which both parties were represented than when neither party was represented (61 percent in represented cases versus 55 percent in non-represented cases). Is this result surprising to you? What might explain it?

5. DISPUTE   RESOLUTION   AND   DEMOCRATIC   GOVERNANCE

The foregoing discussion of dispute resolution in the government context has demonstrated the extraordinary breadth and depth that

ADR has become institutionalized in the nation's courts and administrative agencies. Does the fact that the government is involved in all of these cases, as opposed to a private party, have any special implications for the process? In the following excerpt, Professor Reuben contends it does. He argues that when dispute resolution is provided by, administered by, or enforced by a democratic government, it should at least have the benefit of furthering rather than undermining democratic governance.

RICHARD C. REUBEN, DEMOCRACY AND DISPUTE RESOLUTION: THE PROBLEM OF ARBITRATION

67 Law & Contemp. Probs., Winter/Spring 2004, at 279, 279–82, 285–95.

Scholars have approached arbitration, especially under the Federal Arbitration Act, from a variety of perspectives, including doctrinal, historical, empirical, and practical. One aspect that has not yet been fully considered, however, is the relationship between arbitration and constitutional democracy. Yet, as a dispute-resolution process that is often sanctioned by the government, that sometimes inextricably intertwines governmental and private conduct, and that derives its legitimacy from the government, it is appropriate — indeed, our responsibility — to ask whether arbitration furthers the goals of democratic governance. It is only sensible that state-supported dispute resolution in a democracy should strengthen, rather than diminish, democratic governance and the civil society that supports it.

* * *

[This article] establishes an operative understanding of what democracy is, explores the role of dispute resolution in a democracy, and identifies certain core substantive values of democratic governance that may be used to assess the democratic character of a dispute-resolution method, process, or system, namely: personal autonomy, participation, accountability, transparency, rationality, equality, due process, and the promotion of a strong civil society. [It] suggests that public adjudication represents a high embodiment of these values and that, under U.S. democracy, it constitutes democracy's endowment for dispute resolution.

* * *

II.

THE FRAMEWORK FOR A DEMOCRATIC ANALYSIS OF ARBITRATION

* * *

B. *Democracy's Substantive Values and the Centrality of Personal Autonomy and Dignity*

Once one acknowledges dispute resolution as a necessary function of democratic governance, the question becomes how to understand, assess, and constructively cultivate the democratic character of a dispute-resolution method, process, or system. The democracy literature is helpful in this regard. While particular formulations and articulations may vary, most scholars who embrace a broader definition of democracy tend to agree upon its core values. Those values are briefly discussed here to provide a common language and context. To move beyond the intellectual seductions of the counter-majoritarian difficulty, it is helpful to cluster them into three categories: political values, legal values, and social capital values. In brief, the political values are participation, accountability and transparency, and rationality. The legal values are due process and equality. And the social capital values are public trust, social connection and cooperation, and reciprocity.

Before describing these values in more detail, two observations are appropriate. First, these values will be treated separately below for purposes of theoretical analysis, but should be understood as much more integrated in practice, often overlapping and mutually reinforcing, and sometimes barely distinguishable. Second, and more substantively, they should be understood as operating to fulfill democracy's ultimate aspiration of enhancing the capacity and competence of personal autonomy and dignity within a system of collective self-government and social responsibility. This is a primary lesson from the birth of modern Western democracy and from the Enlightenment's repudiation of a divinely ordained socio-political hierarchy, its embrace of individual worth and self-actualization, and its deliberate expression in the grand experiment of U.S. democracy.

The Founders viewed their new nation as a laboratory for the potential of human achievement and constructed a government through a written constitution that would limit the worst instincts of man in his state of nature, while at the same time maximizing the potential for personal autonomy and self-actualization. They accomplished this by a structure that promoted individual and collective choice through elected legislative and executive branches, and through the rights to vote, to hold office, and to engage in political expression. They hoped to create a government and, equally important, a society burgeoning with the vibrancy and creativity that ambition and choice could inspire in political, economic, and social structuring. For these reasons, personal autonomy should be seen as a unifying and synthesizing value that can have a dominating or trumping effect when other supporting democratic values are in tension.

1. *Political Values*

The first, and largest, set of core democratic values may be understood as those primarily intended to foster collective self-governance by enhancing the capacity of individuals to participate in that governance effectively. These include participation, accountability, transparency, and rationality.

   a. Participation. Democracy's essential theory is the consent of the governed, a concept that is implemented through the democratic value of participation. Under this social contract theory, the exercise of coercive government power is seen as legitimate because laws are enacted with the consent of those who will be bound by them. In most democracies, this consent is achieved through representation rather than direct participation.

This individual citizen participation in governance is one of the principle factors distinguishing democratic from authoritarian or totalitarian forms of government, under which the exercise of coercive force is justified through the authority of familial descent, military might, or the raw power of an individual. In the United States, participation in democratic governance is secured through the Constitution's electoral structure for the legislative and executive branches, the decentralization of government through state and local governments, and the rights to vote, to hold office, and to engage in political expression, even if critical of the government or otherwise unpopular.

Majoritarian theorists would generally limit the notion of public participation to the electoral process and the exercise of the franchise. However, a broader understanding of democracy recognizes, fosters, and integrates other aspects of public participation in democratic governance. Jury service is perhaps the most common example of public participation, accepted even by majoritarians, but participation values are also promoted in other areas of the law, such as the notice-and-comment processes in administrative rulemakings.

Deliberative democratists and communitarians would likely go further, considering the public debate on political issues that takes place between and among people, and between and among institutions, as democratic participation.

b. Accountability and transparency. The accountability of elected officials to the general public interrelates with participation, in that government accountability makes individual and public participation meaningful. In this sense, accountability refers to the degree to which the government can be held responsible to the citizenry for its policies, words, and actions.

In U.S. democracy, accountability is constitutionally assured in part through the vesting of the legislative and executive powers in elective offices, thus conditioning the exercise of these powers on voter approval. Significantly, accountability is also fostered constitutionally through the First Amendment rights of speech, press, and petition, and the availability of legal actions to vindicate these rights in the courts.

Accountability is also furthered by a closely related democratic value: transparency. This generally refers to the openness of government decisionmaking, and in the United States is frequently associated with press freedoms secured by the First Amendment, as well as federal and state open records and open meetings laws. Transparency is closely aligned with accountability as a democratic value because it is transparency that makes accountability possible by permitting witness to government actions.

c. Rationality. Rationality, in the democratic sense, refers to the consistency of governmental decisions with the law, social norms, or public expectations. It correlates with notions of equal protection and due process, and in the United States is secured by the Bill of Rights and the Fourteenth Amendment, as well as by statutory protections against arbitrary and capricious decisionmaking by government agencies. Rationality also interrelates with transparency and accountability: To the extent that eligible voters view legislative, executive, or judicial decisions as inconsistent with their expectations, values, or other nonbinding social norms, their votes provide a vehicle through which officials may be held accountable.

2. *Legal Values*

The foregoing political values are complemented by at least two values that pertain to the application of substantive law: equality and due process. Significantly, these legal values also further the central value of personal autonomy by recognizing and protecting the inherent worth and dignity of the individual through fair and equal treatment under the law.

Democracies generally at least aspire to provide equal treatment under the law. This equality, or neutrality, speaks to the notion of the same law being applied in the same manner to all persons, without regard to governmental position, wealth, or social status. Equality in democracy serves to check the influence and power of elites (both governmental and nongovernmental), which in turn helps to assure the stability of the political, social, and economic orders.

In the United States, equality is most prominently enshrined in the Equal Protection Clause of the Fourteenth Amendment. It is also, however, assured through the neutrality and independence of the judiciary, through such means as due process and professional proscriptions against judges receiving compensation from parties. Such protections provide a hedge against factions and capture and rent-seeking in the administration of the rule of law. Due process is closely aligned with equal protection in its operation as a constraint upon arbitrary government action, and is essentially the promise of fair treatment at the hands of the government. While there is considerable debate over the meaning of the term, there seems little question that at least some kind of due process value is embedded deeply in democratic governance.

Due process is enshrined in the Fifth and Fourteenth Amendments to the Constitution. In interpreting those provisions, the Supreme Court has come to distinguish two types of due process: procedural due process (focusing on the procedures required before the government may take one's life, liberty, or property), and the more controversial substantive due process (focusing on the substantive fairness of legislation). Language may vary, but the concepts in these separate strands represent internationally recognized standards.

3. *Social Capital Values*

The final category of core democratic values relates to social capital, in particular the promotion of civil society, a concept that embraces public trust, social connection and cooperation, and reciprocity. While social capital values are familiar to political scientists and organizational behaviorists, their discussion expands democratic theory beyond its traditional governmental moorings in the constitutional law literature.

Civil society is generally recognized as the conceptual space between purely governmental and purely private affairs, where much of our collective societal interaction takes place — "including churches, schools, places of employment, clubs, and other group affiliations." Researchers, led by Harvard political scientist Robert Putnam, have come to recognize that this civil society, spawned by and supporting the structure of democratic governance, is just as important to the consolidation of a healthy democracy as properly functioning political institutions.

In his seminal work, Putnam compared the effectiveness of democracy in the autonomous regions of Italy and found that, measured in terms of institutional efficiency and citizen responsiveness, democracy in some regions was more effective than in others. Putnam found that effective democracies were marked by a civil society that broadly encouraged cooperation, reciprocation, and a sense of common good among citizens at all levels of national life, from social, to political, to economic, and beyond. Such cooperation led to an ever-deepening sense of social trust and order, both horizontally among the citizenry and vertically between the citizenry and its regional and national governmental institutions. In contrast, the less effective democracies were marked by civic traditions of distrust and competition, and a sense of isolation and detachment between and among citizens and their governmental institutions.

The work of Putnam and other social capital theorists strongly suggests that it takes far more than governmental institutions operating according to the substantive political and legal values identified above for a democracy to reach its maximum potential; it also requires the support of a strong civil society, steeped in public trust of governmental institutions, with a sense of social connection and cooperation among citizens and between citizens and their national institutions, as well as a spirit of goodwill, reciprocity, and civic virtue that reinforces this sense of trust and connection. Indeed, it is these seeming intangibles that constitute the foundation upon which a democracy must rest if it is to be sustained, consolidated, and effective.

C. *Democracy's Endowment for Dispute Resolution in the United States*

The core democratic values identified above provide criteria for assessing the democratic character of a method of dispute resolution. When applied to public adjudication in the United States, one sees a very high capacity for democratic dispute resolution. Indeed, public adjudication can be considered a functional baseline endowment for dispute resolution that shapes obligations and expectations regarding the democratic character of other dispute-resolution technologies, such as arbitration.

Courts promote public participation in the development and administration of the rule of law by allowing parties to bring actions to enforce legal rights, as well as by allowing, or requiring, the citizenry to administer the law through jury service. As noted by Justice Anthony Kennedy, jury service is particularly important because "with the exception of voting, for most citizens the honor and privilege of jury duty is their most significant opportunity to participate in the democratic process." This participation fosters social and political stability by permitting individuals to turn to the law for the resolution of disputes rather than resorting to violence or other such means of destructive self-help, as well as by inspiring trust in the rule of law itself.

Similarly, courts promote equality, due process, and rationality by operating according to specific rules of procedure, evidence, and substantive law that have been enacted pursuant to statutory or administrative prescription, or which have evolved over time at common law. Regardless of whether a trial is held before a judge or jury, public adjudication requires legal standards to be used as the basis and process for decisions, with the principle of stare decisis providing an important constraining mechanism on judicial rulings. In this way, judicial proceedings operate at the highest level of formality, with the greatest level of procedural due process protection available at law. This is particularly significant because empirical research repeatedly confirms that participant perceptions of procedural fairness are crucial to the participant's acceptance of the decisional outcome as substantively fair.

There is also significant accountability and transparency in trial-court decisionmaking. The availability of appellate review helps to assure that legal rules are accurately applied and permits the evolution of legal standards as legal principles are tested in new situations. Similarly, while it is rare, jury decisions that stray too far from legal standards may be set aside by a trial-court judge or reversed on appeal. Both judicial and jury trials are open and accountable to the public (a right often exercised through the proxy of the press), as well as to the other branches of government, most notably the legislature, which has the capacity to reverse most judicial decisions through legislation.

Finally, as instruments of the rule of law, courts help generate a rich reserve of social capital that generally revolves around common compliance with law. Public adjudication constrains the arbitrary exercise of power by elites, the powerful, and other governmental or nongovernmental factions, which in turn promotes a sense of fairness and equality that inspires reciprocal mutual compliance with the law — the belief that we should follow the law because we know that the same rules will apply to all people and because we expect others to follow the law as well. From Nixon to Enron, the court of law is the great equalizer in a democracy. This also promotes both public and private stability — private stability by providing public standards by which citizens can order their private affairs, and public stability by assuring the peaceful use and transition of political power. Finally, courts and the law provide for the legitimacy of the political, economic, and social order by assuring legal constraints, compliance, and stability. This social capital is substantial, but is still capable of diminishment, as we see later in Part IV.

* * *

Notes and Questions

1.   Professor Reuben contends that judicial and alternative dispute resolution processes are material factors in democratic governance. For much of the last 50 years, however, legal scholarship has tended toward a narrower view of the role of courts in democratic governance: that of policing access to, and the operation of, the elective branches. The seminal elaboration of this view is JOHN HART ELY, DEMOCRACY AND DISTRUST 87–88, 101–04 (1980) (articulating "representation-reinforcing" theory of American democracy). *See also* JESSE H. CHOPER, JUDICIAL REVIEW AND THE NATIONAL POLITICAL PROCESS: A FUNCTIONAL RECONSIDERATION OF THE ROLE OF THE SUPREME COURT 4–6 (1980) (review appropriate when necessary to vindicate certain individual rights). Which side has the better view?

2.   Professor Reuben identifies several criteria for determining the "democratic character" of dispute resolution, grouped into three sets of values. The first set, political values, includes participation, accountability, transparency, and rationality. The second, legal values, includes equality and due process. The third, social capital values, includes trust in government and a strong civil society. Using these criteria, would arbitration have a more democratic or less democratic character than public adjudication? How about mediation? Early neutral evaluation? Other processes? What are the implications for the use of these methods in court-related or administrative programs? For an analysis of the democratic character of arbitration, see Richard C. Reuben, *Democracy and Dispute Resolution: The Problem of Arbitration,* 67 Law & Contemp. Probs., Winter/Spring 2004, at 279, 298–310. For an analysis of the democratic character of mediation, see Richard C. Reuben, *Democracy and Dispute Resolution: Systems Design and the New Workplace,* 10 Harv. Negot. L. Rev. 11 (2005).

3.   A key question for the courts concerns the standard for determining whether an arbitration provision constitutes a valid waiver of trial and related rights. Some scholars, such as Professor Jean Sternlight, have argued in favor of a higher constitutional standard, at least when Seventh Amendment rights to a civil jury trial are at stake. *See* Jean R. Sternlight, *Mandatory Binding Arbitration and the Demise of the Seventh Amendment Right to a Jury Trial,* 16 Ohio St. J. on Disp. Resol. 669 (2001); *see also* Richard C. Reuben, *Constitutional Gravity: A Unitary Theory of Alternative Dispute Resolution and Public Civil Justice,* 47 UCLA L. Rev. 949, 1017–28 (2000). Others, such as Professor Stephen Ware, have argued for a much lower contract standard. *See* Stephen J. Ware, *Arbitration Clauses, Jury–Waiver Clauses, and Other Contractual Waivers of Constitutional Rights,* Law & Contemp. Probs., Winter/Spring 2004, at 167. Does the democratic character of arbitration auger in favor of a higher or lower standard?

4.   Scholars have identified a relationship between trust in the courts and the willingness to comply with law. Several empirical studies by Profes-

sor Tom Tyler have consistently found that trust in legal institutions far exceeds other factors — including agreement in the substantive correctness of the law — as the primary determinant of the willingness to comply with legal rules. Tyler's research further suggests that people begin with a trusting posture, or "illusion of benevolence" toward legal institutions, and then test that trust with each interaction with the institution. Tom R. Tyler, *Public Mistrust of the Law: A Political Perspective*, 66 U. Cin. L. Rev. 847, 868 (1998). What might this research suggest for the implications for the design of governmental dispute resolution programs? *See generally* Wayne D. Brazil, *Structures for the Delivery of ADR Services by Courts: Critical Values and Concerns,* 14 Ohio St. J. on Disp. Resol. 715 (1999).

5. Political scientist Robert Putnam has pioneered so-called "social capital" theory, which generally contends that the relationship between and among the citizenry of a democracy, and between the citizenry and its government institutions is as important to the effectiveness of a democracy as its electoral institutions. *See generally* ROBERT D. PUTNAM, MAKING DEMOCRACY WORK: CIVIC TRADITIONS IN MODERN ITALY (1993). What might be the relationship between Tyler's research on trust and the rule of law, and Putnam's social capital theory? *See* Richard C. Reuben, *Democracy and Dispute Resolution: The Problem of Arbitration*, 67 Law & Contemp. Probs., Winter/Spring 2004, at 279, 309–18.

B. THE PRIVATE SPHERE

As we have seen, the government has provided an important place for expansion and innovation in dispute resolution. The private sector has also seen this growth as well, and in this section, we lay out several of the different ADR techniques that have been used successfully in the private sector.

In Subsection 1, we examine a wide variety of traditional dispute resolution mechanisms that build on the methods discussed in earlier chapters. In this regard, we look first at two different methods of adjudication: the mini-trial (which roughly parallels the summary jury trial) and private judging, which is similar to arbitration except private judges are bound to apply the law, and their decisions are fully appealable as court judgments. We then consider med-arb, a two-step process in which the parties attempt to mediate their dispute, and if they are not successful, move on to arbitration. Finally, Subsection 1 closes with a reading on the ombuds, a unique vehicle for dispute resolution that originated in the public sector but which has seen considerable growth in the private sector in recent years.

In Subsection 2, we look at two more novel forms of dispute resolution processes. The first is collaborative law, a way of altering the structure of negotiation to enhance the possibility of an interest-based outcome. Collaborative lawyering has been popular in recent years in the family law area, and may expand to other areas. But it raises important questions about the roles and obligations of lawyers in the process. We then consider partnering, which is a vehicle for the preventive management of disputes that has been pioneered in the construction industry, but which may have further applications.

Finally, in Subsection 3, we close out this chapter with a look at the application of dispute resolution methods and principles in an entirely different context, online dispute resolution.

1. EARLY PROCESS VARIATIONS

a. The Mini-Trial

ERIC D. GREEN, CORPORATE ALTERNATIVE DISPUTE RESOLUTION

1 Ohio St. J. on Disp. Resol. 203, 238–42 (1986).

The mini-trial is the leading example of the new hybrid corporate private dispute resolution processes. It essentially structures private negotiation by combining elements of negotiation, mediation, and adjudication in a new way. The mini-trial is used most often in business disputes when the parties are at an impasse because of a good faith disagreement about the likely outcome if the dispute is litigated, the existence of emotional barriers to resolution caused by the parties' (or, sometimes, the lawyers') personal antagonism, or the parties' inability to fashion a settlement that is responsive to all of their needs and rights.

A mini-trial can overcome a negotiation impasse by doing the following:

(a) Focusing the negotiation on the legal merits at the heart of the dispute, thus overcoming the barrier to resolution caused by the parties' differing assessments of the likely outcome of the case in court; and

(b) Reconverting into a business problem what has often been transformed by the litigation process into a technical, lawyers' fight. This reconversion is achieved by bringing in new negotiators — usually high level, nonlegal managers who are not emotionally involved in the dispute, but who have authority to settle the case and who can view the dispute in a broader context in which imaginative, integrative solutions are more likely to be found. The presence of these nonlegal representatives of the clients also brings together the true parties in interest, who often are better able than the legal representatives to assess the strategic risks and overall importance of the case to the client.

Although the specific procedures of a mini-trial may vary depending on the case and the parties' desires, most mini-trials contain these key elements:

(1) The parties *voluntarily agree* to conduct a mini-trial. There is no statutory, regulatory, or (usually) contractual obligation to participate in a mini-trial. Parties may terminate the mini-trial at any time.

(2) The parties negotiate and sign a "protocol" or *procedural agreement* that spells out the steps and timing of the mini-trial process. This agreement usually specifies the parties' obligations and responsibilities

in the mini-trial process, their right to terminate the process, and certain legal matters such as confidentiality of the proceedings and the effect of the process on any pending or future litigation. This agreement may be quite short and simple or it may resemble ad hoc, private rules of civil procedure.

(3) Prior to the mini-trial, the parties *informally exchange key documents,* exhibits, summaries of witnesses' testimony, and short introductory statements in the nature of briefs. If necessary, the parties may engage in shortened, expedited depositions and other discovery without prejudice to their right to take full discovery later if the mini-trial does not settle the case.

(4) The *parties select a mutually acceptable neutral advisor to preside* over the mini-trial. Unlike an arbitrator or judge, the neutral advisor has no authority to make a binding decision, but at the mini-trial, the neutral advisor may ask questions that probe the strengths and weaknesses of each party's case. Also, after the mini-trial the neutral advisor may be asked by the parties' representatives to advise them on what the likely outcome would be if the case went to trial. Selection of a respected neutral advisor with credibility is very important for each side. One of the principal goals of the participants if they cannot obtain a favorable settlement in direct negotiations is to persuade the neutral advisor to advise the opponent that it would be better off settling than taking the case to trial.

In most mini-trials, the parties select a former judge as the neutral advisor because they believe that a person with prior judicial experience is best able to give them sound advice on likely trial outcomes. But parties generally try to select a former judge who recognizes the difference between the adjudicative function and the advisory role the neutral advisor plays at a mini-trial. In some mini-trials, especially those that turn on the resolution of a technical or economic issue, the parties may select a nonjudicial expert in the subject matter as the neutral advisor. In other mini-trials, the parties dispense with the neutral advisor altogether and rely solely on their business representatives to preside over the mini-trial and to conduct the negotiations privately. Another approach used at some mini-trials is to have a less active facilitator set up the mini-trial and chair it, but not advise the parties as to likely trial outcomes. In still other cases, the parties want the neutral advisor to attempt to mediate a resolution of the dispute. The function the neutral advisor is expected to perform will determine the kind of person best suited for the role. As a practical matter, however, it may be difficult to know in advance what will be required of the neutral advisor. Thus, the most successful neutral advisors have been those who are capable of playing the roles of advisor, mediator, and facilitator as the situation dictates and the parties ultimately determine.

(5) At the mini-trial itself, the parties' *lawyers make concise, summary presentations of their best case.* Mini-trials may last from half a day to three or four days (two days is average). Thus, presentations are

usually limited to from one to six hours for each side, depending on the complexity of the issues. Generally, each party retains complete discretion over how it will use its allotted time. In some cases, the entire presentation is made by the lawyers, similar to an appellate or closing argument. In others, the lawyers call key witnesses to explain parts of the case. Often, key documents are used to explain the case. Quite often, the parties' experts testify on technical issues. At other mini-trials, parties have used movies, views of the scene, and other imaginative devices to communicate the essence of a case in the short time allotted.

At the mini-trial, rules of evidence do not apply. Thus, if there is testimony by witnesses, it tends to be in a narrative form under informal questioning by counsel rather than in the precise question and answer form of trial examination. In most mini-trials, time is set aside for rebuttal. This may include an opportunity for questions to opposing counsel, witnesses, and experts, again in an informal, modified cross-examination format. It may also include an open question and answer session in which expert may question expert, lawyer may question lawyer, and client may question client, or any variation of these combinations.

Although mini-trial formats may vary considerably, the common goal is to employ a procedure that effectively draws out the strengths and weaknesses of each side, including the persuasiveness of counsel and witnesses, in a short time.

(6) Mini-trial *presentations are made to high-level representatives of the parties* who have clear settlement authority. In most cases, the representatives are nonlawyers who have not been involved in creating or trying to resolve the underlying dispute, but who have authority or at least persuasive power over the decision of whether to settle. In cases involving businesses, the party representatives are generally at least one level higher in the corporate hierarchy than the business people who have been involved in the case prior to the mini-trial.

At the mini-trial, the nonlegal party representatives listen, observe, and ask questions to clarify points, much like a judge or arbitrator would, but they do not sit with or assist the advocates. Immediately after the parties' adversarial presentations on the merits of the case, the nonlegal representatives meet privately and attempt to negotiate a resolution. The theory behind the mini-trial is that the party representatives, armed with a crash course on the merits of the dispute (but without any emotional or face-saving motivations) and aware of the larger interests of their side, will be better able than the advocates or lower-level party representatives to appraise their positions and negotiate a mutually beneficial settlement.

(7) If the nonlegal representatives are unable to negotiate a settlement immediately after the mini-trial, they may schedule further talks or presentations. They may also call in the neutral advisor and ask for the advisor's views on likely trial outcomes. In the negotiation terminology of Fisher and Ury, the neutral advisor's opinion gives both sides an

expert's view of its BATNA — "best alternative to a negotiated agreement." Armed with this data, the nonlegal representatives may negotiate further. If a settlement is reached, the dispute is over, as with any negotiated settlement, and any pending litigation is dismissed. If the case is not settled, the parties are free to resume any other dispute resolution process including adjudication. Most mini-trial agreements specify, however, that the entire process, including the opinion of the neutral advisor and any statements made in the course of the mini-trial, is confidential and inadmissible in any subsequent proceeding. The parties also agree that the neutral advisor may not testify or consult with any party in that case.

The hybrid nature of the mini-trial should be apparent from this description. For example, the mini-trial provides the parties the opportunity to present proofs and arguments on the merits of the case — Fuller's classic definition of adjudication — but in a process that has greater capacity to arrive at "win/win" results (negotiation) because the business representatives can work out their own integrative solution. The parties set their own rules of procedure and select a third party to help them resolve the dispute by considering the proper outcome (arbitration). But the third party has no binding decision-making capacity (mediation). The procedure is private (arbitration, mediation, negotiation), but is usually carried on within the structure of an on-going adjudication, and the goal is agreement rather than consistency with substantive law (negotiation and mediation).

The first mini-trial was held in 1977 to resolve a legally and technically complex patent infringement case. Since then it has been used to settle product liability, commercial, contract, distributor termination, insurance, construction, employee grievance, toxic tort, antitrust, and trade secret cases. Most of the mini-trials have involved multiparty disputes and some have involved cases between individual plaintiffs and businesses. Others have involved governmental entities. While most mini-trials have been conducted under custom-structured ad hoc procedures, there is a growing tendency to attempt to codify the minitrial. In 1984, the Zurich, Switzerland Chamber of Commerce established the first public mini-trial forum and panel complete with rules. Shortly thereafter, the Center for Public Resources announced that it would act as an administrator for mini-trials under rules it would promulgate.

The following factors should be considered to determine whether a mini-trial might be employed, and the exact form it might take:

— Stages of the dispute

— Types of issues at the heart of the dispute

— Motivations and relationship of the parties

* * *

Notes and Questions

1.   What kinds of disputes are most appropriate for mini-trials? Professor Green suggests that the best results are obtained when complex questions of mixed law and fact exist and when litigation is apt to be long and costly. Examples are patent, products liability, contract, antitrust, and unfair competition cases.

When are other processes preferable to mini-trials? Green suggests that other processes should be considered when a case turns solely on legal issues or factual disputes involving credibility, when litigation is used for tactical reasons, and when delay gives one side a substantial advantage over the other.

2.   Consider the advantages and disadvantages of mini-trials, binding arbitration, and litigation in disputes between corporations and former executives who allege they were discharged for an improper reason. If you represented the former executive, would you recommend litigation, arbitration, or a mini-trial? If you represented the corporation, would you recommend litigation, arbitration, or a mini-trial? In each instance, if you believe you would need additional information before deciding what to recommend, what would you need to know, and why?

b.   Private Judging

BARLOW F. CHRISTENSEN, PRIVATE JUSTICE: CALIFORNIA'S GENERAL REFERENCE PROCEDURE

1982 Am. B. Found. Res. J. 79, 79–82.

Delay in the courts is probably the most serious, the most pressing, and the most persistent of the problems of judicial administration. It is a problem which absorbs the major portion of judicial reform effort. It is also a problem to which a complete and final solution has not yet been found.

A recent response to the problem of court delay has generated some interest and discussion. This innovation is the trial of cases by retired judges under the California general reference statute, a practice which has come to be called "rent-a-judge" by the popular press. The procedure appears to be a useful device, but it raises some questions that perhaps deserve discussion. * * *

In California, as in other states with similar statutes, use of the reference procedure seems generally in the past to have been limited to the circumstances specified in the nonconsensual portion of the statute — that is, to the hearing and determining of specific issues or questions of fact, especially in cases involving "examination of a long account." In 1976, however, some enterprising Los Angeles County lawyers, representing opposing parties in a case in which some issues appeared appropriate for reference to a referee, noted that the consensual section of the statute was not limited just to specific issues or questions or to particular kinds of cases. Rather, it seemed very broad; with the consent of the parties, a reference might be made to a referee "to try any *or all* of the issues in an action or proceeding."

* * *

II.   THE ELEMENTS OF THE PROCEDURE

The general reference procedure, as it is presently being used in California, includes a number of elements, not all of which derive directly from the statute. One element that does flow from the statute is the need for the consent of the parties. It appears that an entire case can be sent to a referee for trial only when both parties to the case agree to the reference. While the statute empowers the court to select a referee if the parties do not agree, in practice the parties themselves usually choose the referee.

* * *

Trials by referees are conducted as proper judicial trials, following the traditional rules of procedure and evidence. Transcripts are made of the proceedings, and the judgment of the referee becomes the judgment of the court. It is thus enforceable and appealable, as any other judgment would be. One lawyer who uses the reference procedure suggests that parties might agree to submit disputes to retired judges for decision independently, without any court order, but that they use the statutory procedure to preserve their rights of enforcement and appeal. Unlike trials in courts, however, trials by referees are conducted privately, without the presence of either the public or the press. Again, there appears to be no statutory requirement that this be so.

In theory, almost any kind of case might be referred to a referee for trial. The consensual portion of the statute imposes no restrictions. In practice, however, the procedure has been used primarily in technical and complex business litigation involving substantial amounts of money. The case in which the procedure was first used, for instance, was a complicated dispute between a medical billing company and two attorneys who had acquired interests in the company. Other examples have been a suit by major oil companies against a California governmental agency over air pollution control standards, a contract dispute between a nationally known television entertainer and his broadcasting company employer, and an action between a giant motor vehicle manufacturer and one of its suppliers over the quality of parts supplied.

* * *

Notes and Questions

1.   What advantages do you see to the use of this private judging process for the parties and their lawyers? For the courts? For society at large?

2.   Recall the critique of settlement by Owen Fiss in Chapter I, beginning at page 21. Do any of the concerns he raised about settlement apply to this essentially adjudicatory process?

3.   California's chief justice appointed an advisory committee to study policy issues raised by private judging. The 1990 report of the advisory committee concluded that private judging benefits those who use the procedure and that the various concerns expressed did not warrant its elimination. JUDICIAL COUNCIL OF CAL., THE REPORT AND RECOMMENDATIONS OF THE JUDICIAL COUNCIL ADVISORY COMMITTEE ON PRIVATE JUDGES (1990). The report states:

> [o]n the present state of the evidence, we cannot conclude that the fears about private judging creating a two-tier system of justice, "one for the wealthy and one for the poor," are warranted. Even if they were, the committee is dubious about whether that would justify elimination of the private judging alternative. We believe that private judging is attractive in large measure because the public system is not able to resolve all civil disputes in a timely fashion. Improving the public system, not eliminating the private alternative, is the appropriate response.

Id. at 22–23

4.   If you were a member of the California legislature, would you support legislation prohibiting the referral of cases to private judges? Would you support an amendment requiring trials under the reference procedure to be open to the public? For an analysis of the arguments for and against private judging, see David J. Shapiro, *Private Judging in the State of New York: A Critical Introduction*, 23 Colum. J.L. & Soc. Probs. 275, 310–14 (1990). For a helpful study of the major private ADR firms in Los Angeles, see ELIZABETH RALPH, ERIK MOLLER & LAURA PETERSEN, ESCAPING THE COURTHOUSE: PRIVATE DISPUTE RESOLUTION IN LOS ANGELES (1994).

5.   If you were an attorney advising a client on whether to use a private judge pursuant to the California reference procedure, what factors would you consider? *See* Winslow Christian, *Private Judging* §§ 40.4, 40.5, in THE ALTERNATIVE DISPUTE RESOLUTION PRACTICE GUIDE (Bette J. Roth, Randall W. Wulff & Charles A. Cooper eds. 1993).

c. Med-arb

STEPHEN GOLDBERG, THE MEDIATION OF GRIEVANCES UNDER A COLLECTIVE BARGAINING CONTRACT: AN ALTERNATIVE TO ARBITRATION

77 Nw. U. L. Rev. 270, 281–84 (1982).

MEDIATION AS AN ALTERNATIVE TO ARBITRATION

The Mediation Process

In order to enable employers and unions to accomplish more satisfactorily the goal of resolving disputes in a speedy, inexpensive, and informal fashion which also holds promise of improving those unsatisfactory relationships that contribute to frequent resort to arbitration, I propose that the resolution of grievances through arbitration be substantially replaced by the resolution of grievances through a particular type of mediation.

The Proposal. Under the method here proposed, the parties would have the option of resorting to mediation rather than going directly to arbitration after the final step of the internal grievance procedure. The mediation procedure would be entirely informal in nature. The relevant facts would be elicited in a narrative fashion to the extent possible, rather than through examination and cross-examination of witnesses. The rules of evidence would not apply, and no record of the proceedings would be made. All persons involved in the events giving rise to the grievance would be encouraged to participate fully in the proceedings, both by stating their views and by asking questions of the other participants in the hearing.

The primary effort of the mediator would be to assist the parties in settling the grievance in a mutually satisfactory fashion. In attempting to achieve a settlement, the mediator would be free to use all the techniques customarily associated with mediation, including private conferences with only one party. If settlement is not possible, the mediator would provide the parties with an immediate opinion, based on their collective bargaining agreement, as to how the grievance would be decided if it went to arbitration. That opinion would not be final and binding but would be advisory. It would be delivered orally and would be accompanied by a statement of the reasons for the mediator's opinion. The advisory opinion could be used as the basis for further settlement discussions or for withdrawal or granting of the grievance. If the grievance is not settled, granted, or withdrawn, the parties would be free to arbitrate. If they do, the mediator could not serve as arbitrator, and nothing said or done by the parties or the mediator during mediation could be used against a party during arbitration.

The Proposal's Advantages. If grievances can be resolved through mediation, the advantages to the parties would be significant. First, mediation would be substantially quicker and less expensive than arbitration because the mediator would settle or give an advisory decision on the same day that the grievance is considered. This would eliminate the cost and delay associated with obtaining a transcript, filing briefs, and writing a decision. Furthermore, since the proceedings would be informal, the parties may choose to proceed without attorneys, resulting in still further savings of time and money.

Those parties with a substantial number of grievances could obtain still further savings in time and money by arranging for the mediator to consider more than one grievance per day. In addition, the parties could schedule mediation on a regular basis, with a mediator selected in advance. This would eliminate the wait for a free day in a busy mediator's schedule, and could result in the final resolution of grievances in 15–30 days from the completion of the internal steps of the grievance procedure.

Employees would benefit not only from the promptness with which their grievances would be resolved, they would also benefit from the process itself. Free of the constraints imposed by the quasi-judicial procedure of eliciting facts by direct and cross-examination, employees would have the opportunity to tell their stories as they wished. Furthermore, everyone at the mediation conference, including management personnel, would have the opportunity to talk to each other, not just to an examiner, cross-examiner, or arbitrator. Under this procedure, all the participants should feel that they have been heard fully and dealt with fairly, regardless of the outcome. Mediation thus may achieve more satisfactorily than does arbitration the catharsis and employee acceptability sought by arbitration.

The mediation process also offers hope of alleviating some of the situational characteristics which contribute to a large volume of arbitration. Frequently, such a volume of arbitration results from a combative relationship in which the parties approach grievances in a highly adversarial fashion. The arbitration process is unlikely to alter this attitude because of its adjudicative mode. The mediation process, however, compels a different approach. It eliminates the concept of "winning" a grievance, substituting the concept of negotiations leading to a mutually satisfactory resolution. To the extent that the parties focus on seeking a mutually satisfactory outcome through negotiations, they should develop a mutual understanding of each other's concerns. This mutual understanding, in turn, should lead not only to the resolution of more grievances without resort to mediation or arbitration, but also to the improvement of their entire relationship.

* * *

In addition to potentially improving the relationship of the parties, mediation also offers the prospect of a more satisfactory substantive resolution of contractual disputes than does arbitration. It is a truism of industrial relations that the negotiators of a collective bargaining contract can never anticipate and deal with all the issues which are likely to arise during its term. Hence, some issues inevitably arise which the contract does not clearly address. An arbitrator called upon to determine the "correct" interpretation of the contract in a grievance presenting such an issue will examine the language of the contract, its bargaining history, prior practice, and various canons of construction, and conclude that, if the negotiators had foreseen the particular problem and been able to resolve it, it is more likely that they would have resolved it in one way rather than another.

A resolution of the disputed issue through negotiation at the time the dispute arises is more likely to satisfy the parties, in light of their current interests and concerns, however, than is an arbitrator's probabilistic estimate as to how they would have resolved the dispute had they been able to do so at the time of the contract negotiations. While mediation does not guarantee that the parties will achieve a current solution to a current problem, the likelihood of attaining such a result is one of the strengths of the mediatory approach to dispute resolution.

Finally, the mediation process described here, in which the mediation step is entirely separate from the final and binding arbitration step, offers substantial advantages over the impartial chairman approach, in which the roles of mediator and adjudicator are combined. The fact that the "pure" mediator has no power to issue a binding award means that the parties need not fear that their contractual rights will be overridden to serve the mediator's interest in obtaining a settlement or in furthering their relationship. The separation of the mediatory function from the power to issue a final and binding decision also means that the parties need not fear that facts disclosed to the mediator in an effort to obtain a settlement will be used against them in the event no settlement is reached. This should increase their willingness to be candid with the mediator and so increase the prospects for settlement.

* * *

Notes and Questions

1. Professor Goldberg's proposal, which was implemented in 1980 in the bituminous coal industry, includes the issuance of a non-binding opinion indicating how the mediator believes the grievance would be decided if it went to arbitration. As an alternative, the mediator could serve as an arbitrator if the mediation fails, with power to issue a binding decision. The position of the mediator-arbitrator in such a process would resemble that of a judge who works to bring about settlement and then presides over the trial. The parties may take the mediator's recommendations more seriously because they know he will have the power of decision if negotiations fail. Moreover, it may save hearing time because the arbitrator becomes familiar with the case while serving as mediator.

2. Professor Lon Fuller has articulated several reasons why the same person should not serve as both mediator and arbitrator. He asserted that the essence of an adjudicative process such as arbitration is a guarantee of opportunity to present proofs and argument. He also maintained that private conferences with parties are incompatible with such a guarantee because the party who did not participate in the private conference cannot know toward what she should direct her presentation. In mediation, on the other hand, Fuller thought private conferences usually are essential to success. He also argued that the types of facts that are relevant differ in arbitration and mediation. The differences arise, he thought, because the objective of mediation is a settlement most nearly meeting the interests of both parties while the objective of arbitration is a decision based on the contract. To Fuller, such different objectives call for different facts. Further, Fuller noted that a mediator learns things that should have no bearing on his decision as an arbitrator. For a further discussion, see LON FULLER, COLLECTIVE BARGAINING AND THE ARBITRATOR, PROCEEDINGS, FIFTEENTH ANNUAL MEETING, NATIONAL ACADEMY OF ARBITRATORS 8, 8–9, 24–25, 29–33 (1962).

In *Township of Aberdeen v. Patrolmen's Benevolent Ass'n, Local* 163, 286 N.J.Super. 372, 669 A.2d 291 (App. Div. 1996), the same person served first as mediator and then as arbitrator in a dispute between a local government and a union representing police officers over the terms of a collective bargaining agreement. The trial and appellate courts held that information learned during the mediation process could not be considered during the arbitration process.

If you were representing a client in a mediation, and the mediator offered to change the process to arbitration, would you advise your client to accept the offer?

3.   Professor Goldberg believes that med-arb usually will be faster and cheaper than arbitration. If these goals are important to the parties, can they be achieved just as well by modifying the arbitration process? For example, some contracts provide for expedited arbitration in which the arbitrator issues an oral decision at the conclusion of the parties' presentations and some contracts prohibit the use of lawyers in arbitration hearings.

4.   For a case study of a med-arb with an analysis that responds to critiques of the process, see Stephen B. Goldberg, *The Case of the Squabbling Authors: A "Med–Arb" Response*, 6 Negotiation J. 391 (1990).

5.   "Arb-med" is similar to med-arb, except that it begins as an arbitration, but converts to a mediation after the presentation of evidence to the arbitrator. The arbitrator makes and records a decision, which is withheld from the parties while they attempt to mediate the dispute. If the parties settle, that ends the matter and the arbitrator's decision is never disclosed to the parties. If the parties do not settle, then the arbitrator's award is disclosed to the parties and is binding upon them. Writing in the context of airline industry strikes, arbitrator Arnold Zack describes the benefits of arb-med:

[An] advantage of arb-med is that it will encourage greater openness. Because the arbitrator's decision may ultimately decide the merits of the dispute, the parties will have good reason to disclose all pertinent information to the arbitrator. That is not the case under the present system. At this time there is no incentive for the parties to reveal to the mediator potentially damaging information that would encourage settlement. * * * Thus, mediation under the present system places a premium on evasiveness.* * *

[Moreover, the] arbitration format ... forces the disclosure that having the mediation first tends to discourage. * * *

I espouse arb-med for the airline industry because it provides finality while offering the parties the greatest number of options to reach their own agreement. They can ... reach agreement in direct negotiations to avoid entering the spillway to arbitration. They can agree to settle during arbitration, as they perceive the evidence from the other side winning over the arbitrator. They can also settle during the mediation phase, as they weigh the likelihood of their having done better or worse than the outcome inscribed in that secured envelope. Even if they do not settle during the mediation, they can use the arbitrator's announced award to work out an agreement that better satisfies them both. The parties can even ask the arbitrator to recast the decision to reflect that final agreement. The goal of the arb-med process is settlement, which can be better achieved by the availability of conducting the arbitration hearing first.

Arnold Zack, The *Quest for Finality in Airline Disputes: A Case for Arb–Med*, Disp. Resol. J., Jan. 2004, at 34, 36–38.

Would you consider using arb-med? In what kinds of cases? What kinds of cases might be inappropriate for arb-med?

d. Ombuds

PHILIP J. HARTER, OMBUDS — A VOICE FOR THE PEOPLE
Disp. Resol. Mag., Winter 2005, at 5, 5–6.

While the process of oversight and accountability can be traced to antiquity, the modern version of ombuds starts two hundred years ago in Sweden when the Parliament appointed an overseer — the "Justitieombudsman" — to ensure that the royal officers obeyed the law; interestingly, that action followed by a century the King himself appointing someone for the same purpose.

The proliferation of ombuds

Since then, ombuds have sprouted in all sorts of institutions, and they are now a varied lot. A number of them, especially in emerging democracies, are designed to protect civil rights and human dignity.

The Comptroller General of the United States — a de facto ombuds if not one in name — investigates on behalf of Congress to ensure the executive branch performs adequately. Government agencies themselves have established similar offices to investigate allegations of wrong doing or to receive and process complaints over maladministration.

Companies likewise have created ombuds to field complaints, to work out difficult issues in the workplace, and in this era of corporate scandals, to provide a means by which insiders can call potentially difficult issues to the attention of senior management. Newspapers have them to serve as a "watchdog" on behalf of the public. Others investigate complaints filed on behalf of vulnerable people and, if the facts merit, they become advocates for redressing wrongs and securing change.

To demonstrate the full breadth of movement, one newly established office is "to make sure hundreds of homeowners get speedy relief from overflows of raw sewage in their basements." Ombuds are, therefore, a voice for the many: taxpayers, citizens, employees, customers, and vulnerable populations; they exist and are needed in both public and private settings.

This proliferation, at least in the United States, undoubtedly reflects a number of forces coming together. Probably one is that for many the term "ombuds" is not fully understood but connotes someone who protects the people against overreaching or incompetence.

Surely such a person would be welcome in the current environment: We have witnessed scandals of all sorts, and there is an extensive distrust of the Establishment. This leads to a feeling that things are out of control and that someone needs to help "get it right." That is, the system needs to be designed to provide accountability. For example, over the strong dissent of the Bush Administration, Congress is seeking to protect whistleblowers who expose official wrongdoing. An ombuds would be a suitable response that would meet many of the currently politicized issues.

Part of this accountability is to ensure that important issues are not decided behind closed doors but rather the reasons for doing something are transparent and responsive. Part of it is to ensure that people get what they are promised and official duties met. This is all the more important currently since the courts have cut back on standing to challenge general actions of the government and mounting a complaint can be ferociously expensive for an average citizen so that reliance on private vindication is becoming more difficult.

Further, so much of the recent public emphasis has been on efficiency and the market as opposed to non-monetary values, and part of the movement is likely based on a desire to make sure that basic fairness and the protection of rights are recognized as well. An ombuds is often seen as a means of holding the powerful accountable; for raising an issue to a level where it can be addressed; and for working out clashes within an organization shy of litigation or tearing an office apart with controversy. Indeed, senior management of an entity may well wish to establish an ombuds office to help resolve controversies internally, without forcing recourse to the courts, and to provide a means for raising managerial issues so they can be confronted responsibly.

Essential characteristics and functions

Given the extraordinary variety of issues ombuds address, the logical question arises as to just what do these people called ombuds have in common and how do they function.

At bottom, an ombuds is authorized to receive complaints and questions from a defined constituency about issues within the ombuds' jurisdiction.

To a very real extent, the foundation of the process is the ombuds' charter that defines the nature of the duties and to whom the office responds. For example, the traditional ombuds that is created by a legislature hears complaints from the citizens about the activities of the executive, whereas in a company it may be that an ombuds would hear only complaints from employees about designated issues or from customers. It is necessary to define this jurisdiction — who complains and what is complained about — in advance and in a publicly available document.

Importantly, the charter should specify whether an ombuds who helps resolve workplace issues can — or cannot — get involved in potentially explosive issues like sexual harassment or racial discrimination. Unlike a court, the ombuds customarily has discretion as to whether or not to accept the complaint and may also act on its own initiative.

The ombuds then develops sufficient information and takes appropriate action, such as issuing a report (which may or may not be public depending on the circumstances) with recommendations; raising the issue to an appropriate level within the organization; working out an agreement addressing the issue; or providing information so that the complainant can take individual action. An ombuds is not limited to addressing just individual complaints, however, but also is in a position to see trends or patterns so the ombuds frequently will point out systemic or general problems or issues. Importantly, an ombuds does not have authority to compel action of any sort.

An ombuds office must possess three essential characteristics to function effectively and with integrity: (1) It must be independent from control of anyone who may be the subject of a complaint or inquiry; were it otherwise, the ombuds is not likely to take strong, appropriate action. (2) The ombuds must conduct investigations or inquiries in an impartial manner, without bias or preconceived orientations; once the facts are determined, however, the ombuds may become an advocate for securing appropriate change. (3) The ombuds must not voluntarily disclose matters provided in confidence, and the establishing institution needs to assure the ombuds and those using the office that it will not seek anything provided confidentially; were it otherwise, those who come to the office could be badly hurt. These are characteristics that all ombuds should share, regardless of where they are located, how they function, or subjects addressed.

Four types of ombuds

In addition, it is helpful to differentiate among several types of ombuds, since as a practical matter how they operate differs slightly by category and to a certain degree they are conceptually distinct. The four types are:

• **Legislative.** A legislative ombuds is created by and is regarded as part of the legislature and the office is designed to hold the executive accountable; it reports to the legislature.

• **Executive.** An executive ombuds may be located in either public or private sector and receives complaints concerning the actions and failures to act of an agency, company, division, or some specified group, including its personnel and contractors. It may work to hold the agency, company, or NGO accountable, or the executive ombuds may work with officials to improve performance.

• **Organizational.** An organizational ombuds works to facilitate the fair and equitable resolution of issues that arise in the workplace. Thus, an organizational ombuds receives complaints and concerns from employees of the institution that employs the ombuds.

• **Advocate.** An advocate ombuds serves as an advocate on behalf of a group that is designated in the charter, usually for a specified vulnerable population. What differentiates an advocate ombuds from simply an advocate on behalf of that population is that an advocate ombuds, unlike a traditional advocate, conducts the investigation into a complaint in an objective, impartial manner and only becomes an advocate for the complainant if the facts support the claim.

An ombuds obviously has a complex relationship with the institution in which it works. Often it is an in-house goad whose job is to make sure those in authority abide by the rules. In the words of one charter, the ombuds is to investigate "abuse or unjustifiable exercise of power or unfair, capricious, discourteous or other improper conduct or undue delay" and "to rectify any act or omission by ... any ... means that may be expedient in the circumstances."

In other instances the ombuds serves as a mediator who attempts to work out agreements that would rectify the situation. But for this to work, the ombuds must be seen as impartial and effective. That in turn means that the ombuds must be fairly autonomous within the institution and able to function independently and without interference. In many ways, the same notion applies to an ombuds as underlies the separation of functions that protects the integrity of administrative law judges in government hearings.

* * *

Notes and Questions

1. Ombuds have been around for generations. But a relatively new, and vibrant, area of growth has been in the organizational context. As Mary Rowe explains:

Corporate ombudsmen handle a wide variety of problems:

Many ombuds offices now keep careful statistics. Pilot surveys indicate that once an office is up and running, it appears to get calls from two to eight percent of the constituent community each year. Practitioners commonly report a considerable fraction of very brief contacts to the office (which may or may not be serious problems).

One practitioner estimates about one-tenth of the contacts to the office concern rather serious problems in terms of (potential) disruption to the individual and/or the company. Another practitioner estimates that, at any given time, the "open" office case load runs at about 12–15 percent of the yearly caseload, indicating that many problems can be resolved rather promptly.

Common topics include salary and benefits; promotion and demotion; performance appraisals; job security and retirement issues; company policies; discipline/termination; discrimination and harassment; safety, ethics and whistle-blowing; transfers; personality conflicts/meanness; information/referral; suggestions; working conditions; personal health, mentoring, and counseling issues; management practices; bizarre behavior and problems. Established offices that are reasonably well-known in a sizable company will see all these kinds of contacts each year. The profile of concerns, however, varies somewhat, company to company.

A majority of ombuds practitioners in companies where at least some employees are unionized, do see bargaining unit employees. Union employees are, however, appropriately referred elsewhere if they bring up concerns that are covered by the union contract. Ombuds offices are typically very respectful of their local unions and practitioners commonly report good relations with bargaining unit officers. In fact many an ombudsman has had union officers as clients in the office.

Mary B. Rowe, *The Corporate Ombudsman: An Overview and Analysis*, 3 Negotiation. J. 127, Apr. 1987, at 135.

For more on the role of ombuds, *see Howard Gadlin & Ellen J. Waxman, An Ombudsman Serves as a Buffer Between and Among Individuals and Large Institutions,* Disp. Resol. Mag, Summer 1998, at 21; Mary B. Rowe, *Options, Functions, and Skills: What an Organizational Ombudsman Might Want to Know*, 11 Negotiation. J. 103 (1995); Merle Waxman, *A Nonlitigational Approach to Conflict Resolution: The Medical Center as a Model*, Arb. J., Mar. 1987, at 25 (describing use of ombuds in a large medical center).

2. Should communications to an ombuds be confidential? For most ombuds, confidentiality is an article of faith, enshrined in their most significant profession standards. *See* A.B.A. Standards for the Establishment and Operation of Ombuds Offices (2001). However, the courts have been less sympathetic. In the most significant opinion to date, *Carman v. McDonnell Douglas Corp.*, 114 F.3d 790 (8th Cir. 1997), the Eighth Circuit ruled that communications to an ombuds are not privileged from discovery. The court said:

> We are especially unconvinced that "no present or future [McDonnell Douglas] employee could feel comfortable airing his or her disputes with the Ombudsman because of the specter of discovery." See Appellee's Br. 45. An employee either will or will not have a meritorious complaint. If he does not and is aware that he does not, he is no more likely to share the frivolousness of his complaint with a company ombudsman than he is with a court. If he has a meritorious complaint that he would prefer not to litigate, then he will generally feel that he has nothing to hide and will be undeterred by the prospect of civil discovery from sharing the nature of his complaint with the ombudsman. The dim prospect that the employee's complaint might someday surface in an unrelated case strikes us as an unlikely deterrent. Again, it is the perception that the ombudsman is the company's investigator, a fear that does not depend upon the prospect of civil discovery, that is most likely to keep such an employee from speaking openly.

> McDonnell Douglas also argues that failure to recognize an ombudsman privilege will disrupt the relationship between management and

the ombudsman's office. In cases where management has nothing to hide, this is unlikely. It is probably true that management will be less likely to share damaging information with an ombudsman if there is no privilege. Nonetheless, McDonnell Douglas has provided no reason to believe that management is especially eager to confess wrongdoing to ombudsmen when a privilege exists, or that ombudsmen are helpful at resolving disputes that involve violations of the law by management or supervisors. If the chilling of management-ombudsman communications occurs only in cases that would not have been resolved at the ombudsman stage anyway, then there is no reason to recognize an ombudsman privilege.

Id. at 794.

Do you agree with the Eighth Circuit? Recall from Chapter IV that the Uniform Mediation Act, echoing the laws of most states, provides a privilege for mediation communications. How are ombuds different than mediators in this regard? Why should the law treat them differently?

3.   The problem of when a communication to an ombuds may constitute notice to the entity for purposes of triggering federal anti-discrimination laws was a difficult issue for the drafters of the ABA Ombuds Standards, promulgated in 2001 and amended in 2004. On one hand, confidentiality is an important part of the ombuds process, which led many professional ombuds to assume that communications to an ombuds could never be notice to the company. On the other hand, attorneys concerned with the rights of workers believed that any communication to the ombuds should constitute notice to the entity because the ombuds works for the entity. How would you resolve this tension? To see how the drafters addressed it, see A.B.A. STANDARDS FOR THE ESTABLISHMENT AND OPERATIONS OF OMBUDS OFFICES § F (2001).

4.   If you were a union secretary, electrician, or lab assistant employed by a company with an ombuds office, would you prefer to go to the ombuds or the union for help with your dispute? Would your answer depend on the nature of your complaint? The nature of your job? Your relationship with your supervisors? Political considerations?

5.   Some ombuds have suggested that the most important personal characteristic of a mediator or neutral, is an interest in fostering the growth of others. Where does this approach to mediation fit on the grid described in Leonard Riskin, *Mediation Orientation, Strategies, and Techniques: A Grid for the Perplexed*, 1 Harv. Negot. L. Rev. 7 (1996) (excerpted in Chapter IV, beginning at page 288). Does this approach seem similar to the "transformative" orientation to mediation described by Robert A. Baruch Bush and Joseph Folger, *The Promise of Mediation: Responding to Conflict Through Empowerment and Recognition* (1994) (an excerpt from which appears in Chapter IV, beginning at page 301)?

2.   RECENT INNOVATIONS AND ADAPTATIONS

Different contexts bring different challenges to dispute resolution, and help spur the innovative path of the ADR movement. In this section, we take a brief look at three permutations on the cutting edge. The first explores collaborative lawyering, a way of changing the structure of legal negotiations to maximize the potential for interest-based solutions. The second looks at partnering, a way of restructuring business relationships with respect to disputes on large projects that involve many different parties, such as in the construction industry. The third section provides an overview of the new field of online dispute resolution, in which the traditional methods are applied to a very different context.

a. Collaborative Lawyering

JOHN LANDE, POSSIBILITIES FOR COLLABORATIVE LAW: ETHICS AND PRACTICE OF LAWYER DISQUALIFICATION AND PROCESS CONTROL IN A NEW MODEL OF LAWYERING

64 Ohio St. L.J. 1315, 1315–30 (2003).

Is collaborative law (CL) a revolutionary idea whose time has come? CL proponents say that it constitutes a "paradigm shift" in dealing with legal cases and that it is the "next generation" of family dispute resolution. CL practitioners seek to provide a more civilized process than in traditional litigation, produce outcomes meeting the needs of both parties, minimize costs, and increase clients' control, privacy and compliance with agreements. CL encourages spouses to honor the positive connections between them so that they can divorce respectfully and maintain good relationships with children and other relatives.

In CL, the lawyers and clients agree to negotiate from the outset of the case using a problem-solving approach in negotiation. Despite widespread interest in problem-solving by academics and professional leaders and rhetorical support by practitioners, in practice, much legal negotiation and mediation apparently relies on traditional positional negotiation processes.

CL lawyers and parties negotiate primarily in "four-way" meetings in which all are expected to participate actively. Lawyers are committed to "keep the process honest, respectful, and productive on both sides." The parties are expected to be respectful, provide full disclosure of all relevant information, and address each other's legitimate needs. Under CL theory, parties have "shadow" feelings (such as anger, fear, and grief), which are "expected and accepted, but not permitted to direct the dispute-resolution process." CL theory provides that each lawyer is responsible for moving parties away from artificial bargaining positions to focus on their real needs and interests to seek "win-win" solutions. Some theorists suggest that the CL agreement effectively "amounts to a 'durable power of attorney,' directing the lawyers to take instructions from the client's higher-functioning self, and to politely disregard the instructions that may emerge from time to time during the divorce process when a less high-functioning self takes charge of the client." If a lawyer determines that his or her client is participating in bad faith, the lawyer must withdraw. As a result, the lawyer's continued participation effectively vouches for the client's good faith.

Under CL theory, CL creates a metaphorical "container" around the lawyers and clients to help focus on negotiation. CL creates this container through a mutual withdrawal agreement that disqualifies both lawyers from continuing to represent their clients if either party chooses to discontinue with CL and proceed in litigation. This agreement is intended to align parties' and lawyers' incentives to promote settlement. Virtually all CL practitioners believe that this agreement is the "irreducible minimum condition" for calling a practice collaborative law.

CL proponents contend that CL can avoid structural flaws in mediation. Mediation is often inadequate, they argue, due to mediators' difficulties in managing power imbalances and emotional dynamics of the parties. Parties presumably receive limited legal input from the mediators, who are supposed to be neutral and are not supposed to provide legal advice. Some parties in mediation do not have consulting lawyers. Even when parties do have such lawyers, the lawyers often do not participate, are limited to advising "from the sidelines," and may undo mediated agreements. As a result, Pauline Tesler argues that mediation is appropriate only for a relatively small group of "high-functioning, low-conflict" spouses whereas CL is appropriate for the vast majority of divorcing couples, excluding only a relatively small proportion of couples who are so low-functioning or have so much conflict that they require traditional adversarial lawyers to litigate and judges to make decisions.

The CL movement has grown rapidly and legal authorities have embraced it with remarkable speed. Professional leaders recognize CL as a major innovation in dispute resolution practice barely a decade after it was first developed in 1990. In the 1990s, CL practitioners developed practice groups in many localities to train and socialize CL practitioners, publicly identify CL lawyers, develop local CL practice protocols, build demand for CL, and form referral networks for CL cases. During this period, CL proponents wrote articles in professional journals to describe CL and advocate its use. In 1999, the American Institute of Collaborative Professionals began publishing a journal, The Collaborative Quarterly. In 2000, Harvard Law Professor Robert H. Mnookin and his co-authors recommended that lawyers use CL to create incentives for problem-solving. In 2000, a California court established a "Collaborative Law Department." In 2001, the American Bar Association Section of Family Law published a CL manual with practice forms. In 2001, Texas enacted the first statute authorizing CL. In 2002, the American Bar Association Section of Dispute Resolution bestowed its first "Lawyer as Problem Solver" Award, to honor two CL founders-Stuart Webb, a Minneapolis family lawyer, and Pauline Tesler, a Northern California family lawyer and the author of the ABA CL manual. In 2003, several law schools started offering courses on CL including Hamline University, Santa Clara University, and the University of British Columbia. Major dispute resolution organizations have featured sessions about CL at their annual conferences.

Much CL theory and practice clearly is valuable. CL leaders and practitioners deserve great credit for promoting protocols of early commitment to negotiation, interest-based joint problem-solving, collaboration with professionals in other disciplines, and intentional development of a new legal culture through activities of local practice groups. If CL practice becomes firmly institutionalized, it could influence traditional legal practice, which might be its most significant impact.

Although CL promises to provide significant benefits, some aspects of CL theory and practice may be quite problematic. This Article focuses particularly on the disqualification agreement, which CL practitioners argue is essential to create a positive negotiation environment and encourage parties to settle. Though this encouragement is undoubtedly helpful in many cases, it also can invite abuse. This agreement creates incentives for lawyers to pressure their clients to settle inappropriately and leave clients without an effective advocate to promote their interests and protect them from settlement pressure. Indeed, the disqualification agreement may violate ethical rules designed to protect clients from being pressured by their lawyers. Thus this Article identifies a major paradox of CL: the feature that CL practitioners believe to be indispensable may actually conflict with ethical norms and harm some clients. In particular, this Article analyzes how the disqualification agreement may effectively increase lawyers' control of negotiation and decrease clients' control. Even if courts and ethics committees do not determine that the disqualification agreement violates ethical rules, its operation raises serious concerns about the nature and effects of CL practice. Moreover, although CL practitioners would dearly love to extend CL practice to general civil and business disputes, the disqualification agreement is a major barrier to acceptance by major businesses and law firms.

This Article offers only conditional conclusions about the merits of the disqualification agreement and CL practice generally because most courts and bar association ethics committees have not yet grappled with difficult cases involving CL and there is virtually no empirical research analyzing how people have used it and what the results have been. [T]raditional rules of legal ethics do not clearly answer questions about the propriety of disqualification agreements and thus recommends that courts and ethics committees should approve them if they find that these agreements do not produce a significant risk of serious harm to clients. This Article urges CL groups to experiment by offering clients similar processes with and without disqualification agreements to provide clients greater choice and to test the effects of the disqualification agreements.

Questions

1. Would you feel your obligation to represent your clients zealously would be compromised, or enhanced, by a collaborative law agreement?

2. Recall the different models for the attorney-client relationship discussed in Chapter II (traditional, client-centered, and collaborative). Which of the three might lend itself to collaborative lawyering? How would a

collaborative law arrangement affect negotiations between the attorney and the client? Would the lawyer have more or less control?

3. Would you advise your client to be forthright with respect to sensitive information during a collaborative law negotiation?

4. Collaborative lawyering was largely pioneered in the family law area. What other types of disputes might lend themselves to a collaborative law arrangement? What types would not?

5. What barriers might there be to establishing a collaborative law group in your community?

b. Partnering

JOHN G. BICKERMAN, PARTNERING IN THE CONSTRUCTION INDUSTRY: TEAMING UP TO PREVENT DISPUTES

Prob. & Prop. Mar./Apr. 1995, at 61, 61, 61–63, 64.

Construction projects involve a complex web of relationships among owners, developers, general and subcontractors, architects, suppliers and future users such as tenants or purchasers. Success of a project often requires close teamwork, cooperation and flexibility to adapt to constantly changing circumstances. Not long ago, projects involved local participants who knew each other and had long-term relationships. They shared a certain level of trust and interdependence. The economic well-being of one depended on the profitability and success of its contracting partners.

Today, relationships among construction parties have broken down. Technological improvements make building projects more complicated and mandate greater sophistication and expertise. Because projects are less likely to be local or even regional, parties frequently do not know each other and are unlikely to maintain continuing working relationships.

* * *

Partnering can realign relationships in a cooperative and economically beneficial manner. Lawyers also can thrive by advising clients on maximizing the benefits of these new relationships instead of protecting clients against all real or imagined risks.

Preventing Disputes Through Partnering

The success of ADR techniques depends on identifying the needs and interests of parties and maximizing solutions that recognize those needs and interests — in other words, finding "win-win" outcomes. Partnering applies the "win-win" philosophy to construction projects by reforming the working relationships of the complex network of project participants. Rather than promoting competition for the moment, value is placed on long-term relationships that extend beyond a single project.

Long-term profitability is prized above the profit of a single job. Instead of responding to the four corners of the specifications in a bid proposal, parties learn the needs and advance the objectives of one another. Innovation and deviation from specifications are encouraged. Thus, the concept of partnering can be summarized in three dimensions: trust, shared vision and longterm commitment. All parties hold stakes in the successful outcome of the project and share risks and rewards.

Reversing 100 Years of Learned Behavior

Partnering is not pie in the sky. Fortune 500 companies — including Bechtel, Shell Oil, Union Carbide, DuPont, Procter & Gamble and IBM — have been entering into partnering relationships for the last decade. The United States Army Corps of Engineers uses partnering frequently and credits partnering with the success of such large projects as the $70 million Tombigbee Waterway, the multimillion dollar Bonneville Navigation Lock renovation and the construction of the Cape Canaveral Test Operation Control Center project. The Corps has used partnering at least 18 other times. The United States Air Force salvaged a multimillion dollar construction project at Patrick Air Force Base through partnering.

The mechanics of partnering are surprisingly simple. First and most critically, the parties must agree to adopt the process. Senior management must understand the concept and commit the company. Managers must comprehend the implications of the partnering arrangement positively, judge partnering's value to the organization and make an endorsement to proceed.

Second, the intent to use partnering must be communicated to prospective bidders as early as possible — ideally, in the request for proposals or the bid invitation. As finalists are identified through the bidding process, the partnering arrangement must be explained to senior management of potential contractors. Final awards should be based, in part, on the commitment of bidders to embrace a partnering arrangement.

Third, senior management of all organizations that have agreed to partnering must communicate their commitment to staff who will be responsible for performing the design and construction tasks. Partnering starts at the top and must emanate through the organization to reach the multitude of significant individuals who, because of their constant interaction, make or break the partnering arrangement.

Fourth, the parties should select a neutral facilitator to assist the partnering process. Partnering depends on trust and open communication. Particularly at the outset, when participants' needs and objectives must be articulated clearly to other organizations, a neutral's participation could be essential to the success of the partnering arrangement.

Fifth, shortly after contract award and before start-up, all parties should meet to develop a charter. The charter is a noncontractual statement embodying the objectives and expectations of the parties and setting forth principles by which all signatories agree to conduct themselves. The process of creating a partnering charter is intended to fuse members of different organizations into a cohesive unit that shares common goals.

Partnering Differences

The partnering charter that expresses the parties' joint expectations and shared vision can change the behavior and accepted practices of the parties. For example, partnering can alter the way participants allocate risk, share rewards and resolve disputes.

Over time, risk allocation has shifted steadily downstream to smaller and smaller parties that frequently are least able to absorb the risk and most often have inferior bargaining power to negotiate otherwise. Owners, particularly public owners, have become more averse to risk in recent years. Owners have sought to "fix" the costs of a project at the outset and thus have shifted the risk of surprises to other parties.

Typically, owners can shift risk in three ways. First, they may use contractual provisions that deny contractors damages for delay. Under normal conditions, contractors base their bids on being able to perform according to a pre-ordained work schedule. Although some contingencies may be built into the bids, if an owner substantially interferes with a contractor's start-up or access, the unintended delays increase the contractor's cost. Contractors who are unable to recoup increased expenses due to delay through no fault of their own may be resentful and seek other ways to recover lost profit.

Second, owners may seek to avoid responsibility for differing conditions. If actual conditions are different from those a contractor in good faith expected (and based its bid on), then a contractor may reasonably expect additional compensation for additional work. A provision that requires a contractor to assume the risk of differing conditions asks that contractor to pay for circumstances over which it has no control.

Third, owners desire global indemnification against all potential claims. Owner indemnification clauses are primarily intended to protect owners against claims from workplace injuries by the contractor's employees. Other claims appear to be relatively insignificant. Although owners may reasonably require contractors to indemnify them against claims for job site injuries to third parties, many clauses now require complete owner indemnification, even for claims caused by owner negligence over which the contractor has no control.

A more sensible allocation of risks achieved through partnering might lessen conflict among construction participants during a project. Satisfied participants are those that can earn a reasonable profit for work performed. The seeds of discord are sown when a participant does not realize a profit because it shouldered an unreasonable share of the risks. A partnering arrangement that acknowledges the rights of all parties to earn a reasonable profit for work performed is more likely to result in a sensible and manageable allocation of risks that, in turn, avoids disputes. Thus, the product of a partnering agreement might be allocation of the risk of unknown events to all parties. Similarly, a partnering arrangement could include a compensation mechanism for delay that increases contractor expenses.

A partnering arrangement might lead to an agreement by the contractors to carry insurance for owner liability for workplace injuries. This coverage is relatively affordable and would limit the scope of indemnification clauses to the most likely risks. Contractors also could insure architects and other design professionals, thereby effectively indemnifying these parties against claims for workplace injuries. Owners, in turn, might agree to limit the liability of contractors and design professionals and carry insurance for excess risks. The potential solutions to the problems of risk are limited only by the ingenuity of the partnering participants.

Just as risks can be shared in a partnering arrangement, so too can the parties share rewards when goals are met. A partnering arrangement can set out positive incentives that reinforce cooperative relationships. All parties may realize benefits if the project is a success.

For example, increases in revenues or cost savings from early completion or efficient construction could be shared according to a pre-negotiated formula for the parties. Alternatively, an owner could regularly evaluate performance. The contractor's performance could be graded based on objective, predetermined criteria that extend beyond timeliness of completion and include quality criteria. Based on the grades received, the contractor would be entitled to additional payments.

Under a third scheme, in lieu of rewarding individual contractors, incentives could be tied to the work of several different participants. Parties whose joint gain depends on collectively reaching certain goals may work together more cooperatively and effectively.

Finally, rewards can be extended to individual employees. Rewarding key personnel with performance bonuses may encourage success. A partnering arrangement recognizes the desire of all individuals and parties to share in the rewards of a job well done. An incentive scheme is a likely manifestation of a partnering arrangement.

Resolving Disputes as They Occur

By opening communication lines, partnering should reduce conflict, but disagreements during construction are inevitable. No matter how well one plans, disputes occur. Resolving disputes when they arise in the course of construction is cost-effective and, more important, instrumental in maintaining positive working relationships among construction parties. If disputes fester and await resolution until project completion, positions harden. Less expensive solutions that could have been implemented during the course of construction are lost. Informal dispute resolution techniques yield to more expensive formalized procedures such as arbitration or litigation.

Although partnering may not eliminate all arguments, the arrangement provides the foundation for prompt dispute resolutions. For example, "step negotiations" provide for the measured escalation of a dispute to ascending orders of management. If a dispute cannot be resolved by the line staff, the immediate supervisors (who may not be as intimately invested in the decision) are asked to confer and seek a solution. Junior management has a powerful incentive to demonstrate to their superiors their problem-solving abilities and to keep messy problems from moving up the hierarchy. If the immediate supervisors fail, their superiors step in. In that way, more senior management is "on call" to resolve problems before they get out of hand. Under a partnering arrangement, step negotiations are more likely to succeed because senior management has committed itself to cooperate and make conflict settlement a priority.

* * *

The Lawyer's Role

Under the adversarial model of construction contracting, lawyers draft and implement contractual provisions that protect their clients from such uncertainties as the untoward behavior of other parties and shift the consequences of the unknown to others. The goal, of course, is to maximize the client's profit on each project. When contract language is not followed, lawyers attempt to vindicate their client's rights through lawsuits, arbitration or ADR.

The same skills that make lawyers so good in the adversarial model have application to the cooperative model associated with partnering. Lawyers are trained to identify client needs and interests. They can be skilled communicators through the written and spoken word. Lawyers may also be able to lend a more objective eye to critical issues than a client blinded by its partisan perspective. In a partnering arrangement, lawyers can be valuable resources to clients, using these skills to develop the partnering charter. When disputes arise, lawyers may be more likely to understand the needs of other parties and craft solutions that address those needs while meeting the client's interests as well. In addition, experienced lawyers could make excellent facilitators or job site neutrals.

c. Online Dispute Resolution

ETHAN KATSH, *ONLINE DISPUTE RESOLUTION* IN THE HANDBOOK OF DISPUTE RESOLUTION

(Robert Bordone & Michael Moffitt Eds.)
425–437 (2005).

Online dispute resolution (ODR) applies the tools and resources of cyberspace to the goals and processes of dispute resolution. ODR uses high-speed computer networks and powerful information-processing machines to deliver both expertise and information from afar. ODR's initial efforts were focused on disputes arising out of online activities. The lessons learned in that environment are now being applied to enhance dispute resolution efforts that involve face-to-face interactions and off-line disputes.

ODR is based on the premise that every model of dispute resolution — from the simplest to the most complex, both in and out of court — involves generating, communicating, evaluating, processing, and managing information. * * *

ODR draws many themes and concepts from dispute resolution processes such as negotiation, mediation, and arbitration. ODR gives the parties a medium for communicating when they have not planned to meet face-to-face, or cannot do so. As software is added to communication, even software as simple as a Website, capabilities for managing and shaping information are added to the capabilities for communicating information. Such software adds to the array of resources and tools that a third party or the disputants themselves can employ.

In describing ODR, some commentators have begun to describe the role of technology as that of a "fourth party." This concept recognizes the role and value of software as the network is used as more than a simple conduit. The fourth-party concept suggests that software aids or collaborates with a third party, but does not generally replace it. A fourth-party tool, for example, might allow parties to clarify issues before a face-to-face session or help to identify party priorities during a meeting. In essence, software and mediators are involved in a similar task, namely the management of information and communication. The third party has skills and capabilities that may be more useful than what a fourth party can provide, but some tools embedded in software can be more powerful or more efficiently applied by machine than by a person. Traditionally, third parties have used a variety of communication tools, such as colored markers and charts, but the fourth party concept suggests the emergence of an online resource that collaborates with third parties and that is different from those traditional tools. * * *

A BRIEF HISTORY OF ODR

Although the Internet began in 1969, a need for ODR did not emerge until the early 1990s. For its first two decades, the Internet was used by a limited number of people in a limited number of ways. Those with Internet access were associated either with the military or with academic institutions, and even in those environments, relatively few computers had Internet access. While screens with images and e-mail with advertisements are commonplace today, they were unknown at that time. The World Wide Web was not invented until 1989, and, perhaps even more significantly, the National Science Foundation banned commercial activity from the Internet until 1992.

In the early 1990s, groups used listserves to communicate, and this form of online discussion soon generated "flaming" and violations of "netiquette," personal attacks that violated generally accepted norms for online discussions. Disputes also arose involving participants in role-playing games that allowed one to create an online identity and interact with others in a virtual "space." Various online mechanisms were employed to deal with these conflicts, but there were no organized dispute resolution institutions devoted specifically to ODR. Indeed, the acronym *ODR* had not yet been invented.

The decision by the National Science Foundation in 1992 to lift its ban on Internet-based commercial activity was highly controversial and enormously significant. After the ban's removal, disputes related to online commerce began to surface. In 1994, for example, the first commercial spam occurred when two lawyers tried to recruit clients to participate in an immigration scam. A few months later, the U.S. Federal Trade Commission filed its first case alleging online fraud.[7] The case involved an AmericaOnline subscriber who advertised the following: "FOR JUST $99.00 WE WILL SHOW YOU HOW TO CREATE A BRAND NEW CREDIT FILE AT ALL 3 OF THE MAJOR CREDIT BUREAUS ... 100% LEGAL AND 200% GUARANTEED." The FTC did not consider the process to be legal or guaranteed. As a result of the FTC action, the subscriber agreed to stop advertising credit repair programs and to provide compensation to consumers.

The idea for online dispute resolution emerged from the recognition that the number of disputes would grow as the range of online activities grew. The origins of ODR, therefore, are traceable to a simple insight: the more transactions and interactions there are online, the more disputes there will be. In addition, people understood that the Internet was an information resource that should be able to support information-dependent activities such as dispute resolution. In other words, the Internet was part of the problem because it generated disputes, but it was also part of the solution because it might have resources to respond to disputes.

The National Center for Automated Information Research (NCAIR) sponsored a conference on online dispute resolution in 1996. The conference was the most significant ODR development during the mid–1990s, as it led to the funding of three experimental ODR projects. The Virtual Magistrate project aimed at resolving disputes between Internet service providers and users. The University of Massachusetts Online Ombuds Office hoped to facilitate dispute resolution on the Internet generally. Finally, the University of Maryland wanted to see if ODR could be employed in family disputes in which parents were located at a distance.

The years from 1996 on have been a period of significant activity and notable achievement for ODR. The United Nations now holds an annual ODR conference and has formed an Expert Group on ODR. ODR has become accepted as a necessary process, one that can even be used to resolve traditional disputes originating offline. The key questions con-

---

7. See Federal Trade Commission. "FTC Targets Advertising on 'Information Superhighway': Credit Repair Co. Urged Consumers to Falsify Data, FTC Charged." [http://www.ftc.gov/opa/predawn/F95/chase-consultin.htm]. September 1994.

cerning ODR now involve the design, testing, and adoption of new tools and systems, not viability or value.

TWO EXAMPLES OF ODR

The two most widely known and used ODR venues in cyberspace-related disputes are the online auction site eBay and the domain name dispute resolution process designed by the Internet Corporation for Assigned Names and Numbers (ICANN). Since March 2000, an Internet start-up, SquareTrade.com, has handled over one and a half million disputes, mostly related to eBay transactions, wholly through online processes of negotiation and mediation. SquareTrade is probably the largest private dispute resolution provider in the world. Approximately eight thousand domain name disputes between trademark owners and domain name holders have been resolved through ICANN's Uniform Dispute Resolution Policy, a nonbinding arbitration process.

EBay: Assisted Negotiation, Then Mediation

EBay is an online auction site that makes it possible for sellers and buyers located anywhere to deal with one another. The service has over ninety-two million registered users and lists over fourteen million items for sale each day. EBay itself is not a party to any transaction and, in general, assumes no responsibility for problems that arise between buyers and sellers. In 1999, eBay decided that having a dispute resolution process might strengthen trust between buyers and sellers. After a pilot project conducted by the Center for Information Technology and Dispute Resolution mediated over two hundred disputes, eBay selected an Internet start-up, SquareTrade, to be its dispute resolution provider. Before providing a human mediator, SquareTrade uses a technology-supported negotiation process in which parties try to resolve the dispute themselves before requesting a mediator. SquareTrade also uses the Web, rather than e-mail, as the means for communicating and working with disputants.

SquareTrade's use of the Web illustrates how relatively small changes in communication can have large consequences. Most who file complaints with SquareTrade have already tried to negotiate via e-mail and have reached an impasse. Not only do parties seem more willing to negotiate via the Web than through e-mail, but the negotiations are more frequently successful. SquareTrade's Website provides a more structured set of exchanges than does e-mail. SquareTrade recognized that almost all eBay disputes fall into eight to ten categories, allowing it to create forms that clarify and highlight both the parties' disagreements and their desired solutions. While parties have an opportunity to describe concerns in their own words, the forms and the form summaries they receive reduce the amount of free text complaining and demanding, and thus lower the amount of anger and hostility between them.

Negotiation, as classically defined, takes place between the disputants, without the presence of third parties. SquareTrade's use of the Web in negotiations adds a novel element to traditional negotiation, a kind of "virtual presence." The Website frames the parties' communication and provides some of the value traditionally provided by a mediator. Perhaps as parties increase their use of technology in negotiation, the distinction between negotiation and mediation will become less stark.

When Web-based negotiation fails, SquareTrade provides a human mediator for a modest fee. The conversation is facilitated by a third-party neutral using the Web interface. Because the parties are using the Web, they do not all need to participate at the same time.

ODR and Arbitration: ICANN and Domain Name Disputes

The demand for domain names grew as commercial activity on the Internet grew and as businesses wanted potential customers to have an easy way to find them. The domain name system had been designed before commercial activity was permitted on the Internet. No one had anticipated that many businesses with similar names might want the same domain name, or that owners of trademarks would be upset if someone registered a domain name that was similar to a trademark. The combination of domain name scarcity and the concerns of trademark holders led to disputes over domain names.

In 1998, the U.S. government agreed to allow a new organization, ICANN, manage the domain name system. One of the first things ICANN did was enact the Uniform Dispute Resolution Policy (UDRP), establishing both a process and a set of rules for deciding domain name disputes. Both the modified arbitration process ICANN chose and the systems which have implemented this approach represent another step in moving dispute resolution online.

UDRP dispute resolution occurs without face-to-face meetings and, except in rare instances, without telephone communication. The process employed by the two most active current dispute resolution providers, the National Arbitration Forum (NAF) and the World Intellectual Property Organization (WIPO), is dispute resolution at a distance but involves only limited use of the Internet. Both current providers have online systems that could be used, and probably will be in the future. Parties submit online filings with increasing frequency, and sometimes parties use e-mail. Unlike the eBay mediations, however, NAF and WIPO do not use the Web for their dispute resolution sessions.

The UDRP is not classic arbitration because the decisions are not binding or enforceable in court. UDRP arbitrators are called "panelists," since the word "arbitrator" denotes someone who can make a decision enforceable in court. When parties register for a domain name, they agree to terms in a contract that empower UDRP panelists to make decisions. The panelists' decisions are enforced by changes entered in the domain name registry. The UDRP created an efficient, unorthodox, yet controversial, process.

ODR FOR OFFLINE DISPUTES: ENHANCING ADR AND UNBUNDLING ODR

The SquareTrade and ICANN processes involve no face-to-face meetings. They are conducted wholly at a distance. The need for ODR with no physical meetings is most obvious in cases that arise online and when, because of distance, it is not feasible to meet face-to-face or go to court. It is not surprising that ODR was first directed at such disputes as well. ODR has grown in part because it is valuable for resolving traditional offline disputes. SquareTrade, for example, now resolves real estate disputes between home buyers and sellers. When the power of the computer to process information is added to the power of the network to transmit information the result is an array of dispute resolution processes that can be employed in any dispute, whether it arises, or is handled, online or offline.

A Simple Example: Automated Blind Bidding Processes

Blind bidding systems allow disputing parties to submit settlement offers to a computer and, if the offers are within a certain range, often thirty percent of each other, to split the difference. Blind bidding is attractive because if the parties do not reach settlement, the offers are never revealed. This practice encourages parties to be more truthful about their "bottom line."

Blind bidding is a negotiation tool, a technique that, if done offline and without a computer, would be cumbersome. The efficiency of blind bidding is that the computer transmits and receives information, processes it, and makes distinctions between what is private and public. If the offers are within the thirty percent range, for example, the parties are informed that there is a settlement. If not, no information about the offer is revealed to the parties.

Thus far, blind bidding has been employed mainly in claims against insurance companies. These are claims that are generally settled at some point through negotiation. The traditional process of resolution in such cases, involving personal injury lawyers and insurance claim adjusters, is often lengthy and inefficient. There are problems with the parties and their representatives playing phone tag and posturing in ways that often take up time. A human third party could accept offers in a manner similar to the way a computer accepts offers in a blind bidding system, but could never do so as efficiently.

Blind bidding systems are both efficient and simple to use. They are also extremely limited, since they work only with disputes in which a single variable is contested. This variable must involve numbers so that the machine can make the necessary calculations. The insurance context is a fitting first arena for blind bidding because such differences often focus exclusively on money and the existing dispute resolution system is both expensive and inefficient.

The future of blind bidding will inevitably broaden beyond insurance company disputes. In many mediations or arbitrations, there are initially numerous differences, but ultimately only a monetary issue. Blind bidding technology could be helpful in such situations. In other situations, blind bidding might be an option before beginning a lengthier process. Blind bidding is a tool that can be added at any phase of a dispute resolution process.

Blind bidding also raises the question of what else a network-connected computer can do to assist parties involved in a dispute. Blind bidding is such a simple tool that it could easily be taken for granted if viewed only as a merging of a calculator with the network. Computers, however, are much more than calculators, and systems can be built to process and evaluate qualitative information.

A More Complex Example: SmartSettle

SmartSettle is much more sophisticated negotiation software than the blind bidding systems. It is intended for use in a range of disputes — simple or complex, single-issue or multi-issue, two-party or multiparty, comprising quantitative or qualitative issues, of short or long duration, or involving interdependent factors and issues. SmartSettle will never be as easy to use as blind bidding, and may not be needed for common and relatively simple disputes. However, experience with the software has demonstrated that network-connected computers can bring solutions that may not have been apparent to disputing parties.

SmartSettle moves disputants through several stages that clarify the issues in dispute, how strongly the parties feel about these issues, and the range of acceptable outcomes. In the early phases, SmartSettle provides a structure to clarify and assess issues that, by itself, can help parties reach consensus. What is most novel about SmartSettle, however, is that it can take a tentative agreement and suggest alternative approaches that may give each party a more favorable outcome.

While blind bidding involves only one quantifiable issue, SmartSettle may involve many issues. At the beginning of negotiations, parties are asked to place values on their different interests and demands. A family dispute, for example, may include issues of child support, the division of assets, care and custody schedules, and other relationship issues. A successful end result will involve trade-offs by each party. SmartSettle works to combine interests and issues into packages or groups so that the parties can see the impact of various decisions, enabling them to reach an end result that meets their needs. With SmartSettle, the computer not only stores the users' information and transmits it electronically, but also makes suggestions that will provide the parties with an attractive combination of settlement options.

THE "FOURTH" PARTY

E-mail negotiations simply have people at two ends of a network, thus allowing quick communication among parties who might not have been able otherwise to communicate. Negotiation with almost no over-head may be the most common method for attempting or beginning online negotiation. What the Web permits, and what blind bidding, SmartSettle, and SquareTrade demonstrate, is that there can be value in adding computer-processing capabilities to the people at the ends of the network.

The fourth-party metaphor alludes more to software such as Smart-Settle than to blind bidding, more to something that is an influence on the process of negotiation and something that adds value to the third-party roles of mediator or arbitrator. This fourth party can alter the role(s) of a third party, since the third party will increasingly be working with an electronic ally.

The fourth party enhances the process and does more than simply deliver information across the network. For example, blind bidding is a system that involves communicating, calculating, evaluating, and apply-ing a set of rules to the results of the calculation. Similarly, SmartSettle takes data that has been entered and, using more sophisticated algor-ithms, evaluates and then responds to offers. The fourth-party approach assumes that although face-to-face encounters provide a rich and flexible opportunity for communication, they are neither perfect nor complete. The fourth party will grow more useful and the network more valuable in dispute resolution as we gain experience using information manage-ment and processing tools.

Efficient information management and organization, including effec-tive displays of information for disputants, allows SquareTrade to pro-cess a large number of disputes. Thus an important difference between e-mail negotiation and SquareTrade's Web-based negotiation is that SquareTrade provides a much higher level of information management. SquareTrade does not evaluate positions and recommend solutions but instead clarifies issues and presents information onscreen that highlights areas of agreement and difference. Like a mediator, the software main-tains a respectful discourse between the parties until the contours of a solution appear.

The challenge for ODR is to facilitate information processing along with efficiencies in transmission. In the past, many inefficiencies arising from the distance between the parties were considered "tolerated ineffi-ciencies" in that nothing could be done to bridge distance and time constraints. The network, however, significantly changes disputants' ability to overcome these tolerated inefficiencies. As we grow more comfortable with the network, we realize that certain parts of how third parties handle disputes need to be reevaluated. For example, we have new tools for communicating with parties in between face-to-face ses-sions. Should we do so? For this and other instances of tolerated inefficiencies, we need to decide whether what we are accustomed to is still appropriate given the new tools we are acquiring that allow us to change how and where interactions with parties might take place.

Notes and Questions

1.   Confidentiality is a concern with online dispute resolution. There are at least four sources of confidentiality in online dispute resolution: encryption, which prevents the interception of data or renders intercepted data meaningless; laws that preclude the interception of electronic communications; private confidentiality agreements, which bar the disclosure of dispute resolution communications; and professional industry standards. For example, SquareTrade lists "confidentiality, privacy and security" among its standards of dispute resolution practice. *See* www.square-trade.com/cnt/jsp/lgl/standards_med.jsp (last visited Apr. 2, 2005). For a general discussion, see Llewellyn Joseph Gibbons, *Private Law, Public "Justice": Another Look At Privacy, Arbitration, and Global E–Commerce*, 15 Ohio St. J. on Disp. Resol. 769, 773–78 (2000).

2.   Many mediators believe that there is an intangible quality or dynamic that arises "in the room" of a traditional "face-to-face" mediation session, where the parties (and the mediator), are able to evaluate the credibility of statements and to assess options that emerge during the meeting. Under this view, non-verbal communication can often be as important as verbal communication. *See generally* Barbara Madonik, I Hear What You Say, But What Are You Telling Me? The Strategic Use of Nonverbal Communication In Mediation (2001). Online mediation is only textual, however, meaning that parties do not have the opportunity to assess, for example, tone of voice, or body language, or reactions to statements. How would the absence of this information affect a mediation? Would your answer depend upon the subject matter of the mediation?

3.   As Professor Katsh describes, ODR has been effective in handling disputes involving online providers such as EBay. Are there other types of disputes that ODR might be less suited for? Would it be helpful to integrate online technology into a broader dispute resolution effort? For example, in a public policy mediation, might it be helpful to use web-based preference polling to assess the relative strengths and weaknesses of specific proposals? How about using email to facilitate a dispute between business partners?

4.   What are the implications of online mediation for mediator style? Would an online format necessarily lend itself to a more elicitive or directive style? According to Katsh, SquareTrade mediators may not evaluate. Is there something about the online environment that might have led the program designers to include this prohibition?

5.   Time and geography appear to be two dimensions in which online dispute resolution adds potential value. There is no need for simultaneous convening of the parties, since the parties can respond to mediation communications from their homes, offices, even internet cafes. That means ODR can be used by people in different parts of the country, and indeed the world. Similarly, parties might have greater choice with respect to mediators because the mediators need not come from the same community (assuming the ODR provider permits consumers to know the identity of the neutral). Moreover, the fact that the online mediation may not be conducted in "real" time might give parties more time to reflect on statements made during the mediation. What disadvantages might this flexibility create? For a nice

summary of the pros and cons of using online dispute resolution, see Orna Rabinovich, *Going Public: Diminishing Privacy in Dispute Resolution in the Internet Age,* 7 Va. J.L. & Tech. 4, 89–109 (2002).

6.   How might online mediation affect power disparities between the parties? *See* Robert C. Bordone, Note, *Electronic Online Dispute Resolution: A Systems Approach — Potential, Problems, and a Proposal,* 3 Harv. Negot. L. Rev. 175, 185–93 (1998).

7.   Would you expect online mediation to improve or exacerbate cultural barriers to dispute resolution? *See* Orna Rabinovich, *Going Public: Diminishing Privacy in Dispute Resolution in the Internet Age,* 7 Va. J.L. & Tech. 4, 107 (2002).

8.   As we saw in Chapter III, the establishment of rapport between negotiators can be helpful in overcoming interpersonal friction and finding cooperative agreements. Social scientists have found that rapport-building also facilitates negotiations conducted by email. *See* Michael Morris, Janice Nadler, Terri Kurtzberg & Leigh Thompson, *Schmooze or Lose: Social Friction and Lubrication in E–Mail Negotiations,* 6 Group Dynamics 89 (2002). However, empirical research has also demonstrated that email negotiators also suffer from various psychological biases, including the "burned bridge" bias (tendency to engage in some riskier interpersonal behaviors they would when negotiating face to face), the "squeaky wheel" bias (tendency to adopt more aversive emotional style when negotiating by email than might be used during face-to-face negotiations), and the "sinister attribution" bias (tendency to attribute diabolical motivations to the other persons behavior). *See* Leigh Thompson & Janice Nadler*, Negotiating Via Information Technology,* 58 J. Soc. Issues 109 (2002).

9.   The American Bar Association Task Force on Electronic Commerce and Alternative Dispute Resolution in 2002 issued a report making several recommendations for the future of "business-to-business" and "business-to-consumer disputes." The task force recommended that the e-commerce industry place greater emphasis on prevention of e-commerce disputes, urged it to continue to develop codes of conduct and trustmarks with respect to dispute resolution programs, and called on it to make efforts to educate consumers about them. It also encouraged consumers to use alternative methods of resolving e-commerce disputes, such as following the dispute handling systems at companies with whom they are transacting business, as well as alternative forums such as escrow services and credit card charge-back mechanisms when engaged in online transactions. A copy of the report may be obtained from the ABA Section of Dispute Resolution's web site at http://www.abanet.org/dispute/finaldraft.doc (last visited Apr. 2, 2005).

Chapter VII

DESIGNING AND SELECTING DISPUTE RESOLUTION PROCESSES

Lawyers design and select dispute resolution processes at a variety of levels. At the most general level, lawyers are involved in developing broad systems for resolving a range of disputes. For example, lawyers may participate in the creation or reform of the processes by which disputes are resolved through a court system. Lawyers also help individual clients to devise broad systems for resolving the types of disputes in which they are involved. For instance, a corporate client may need assistance developing a structure within which the client can resolve broad classes of consumer complaints, employee conflicts, and disputes with suppliers. In addition, lawyers are involved in helping individual clients select mechanisms for resolving individual disputes either before — e.g., helping a client draft a dispute resolution clause in a contractual agreement — or after the dispute arises — e.g., advising a client about the mechanisms available to help resolve a divorce. As we have seen in previous chapters, the selection of a dispute resolution process and decisions about how that process is to be organized and conducted are inextricably connected. Decisions about how the process is to be carried out may take place before the process begins, as the process unfolds, or both.

The interests and values one wishes to foster have a substantial influence on how one constructs or selects a dispute resolution process. These interests and values are likely to vary with one's circumstances and role. Thus, a proposal to establish a mandatory court-annexed mediation program might be seen quite differently by the Governor, by judges at various levels, by court staff, by lawyers concerned about their profession, by lawyers representing particular clients or classes of clients, by the litigants themselves, and so on. And, of course, perspectives will differ among individuals in each of these categories. If a system or process for resolving disputes is to function appropriately, it is important to consider each of these interests. As you work through this chapter, keep in mind the perspectives of these important constituents.

Building and choosing dispute resolution processes have been implicit issues in each of the preceding chapters. Chapter I introduced the issues in broad terms. Chapter II considered the interviewing and counseling processes that an attorney can use to assist a client in selecting a method for resolving a particular dispute. In Chapters III through VI, we persistently inquired into the circumstances under which a particular dispute resolution method — or one of its many possible variants — was preferable to other methods. This chapter draws on these previous discussions, concentrating both on how to create a system for resolving disputes generally and on how to choose a dispute resolution mechanism for an individual dispute. Examining these topics builds on the reader's accumulated knowledge of particular processes and their comparative strengths and weaknesses.

In Section A, we reflect on several overarching considerations that come into play when designing and selecting dispute resolution processes. In Section B, we explore the processes by which systems for resolving disputes are designed and evaluated. In Section C, we examine the issues surrounding how to advise individual clients about dispute resolution processes. Finally, in section D, the chapter ends, fittingly, with an exercise that requires the student to advise a client about dispute resolution options.

A.   OVERARCHING CONSIDERATIONS

1. IN GENERAL

Whether one is thinking about designing a system for resolving many disputes over time or attempting to select a dispute resolution process to resolve a particular dispute, many common issues arise. First, the building blocks of a dispute resolution system and the options available to select from are the mechanisms that you have learned about in the previous chapters of this book. Whether designing a comprehensive system to resolve disputes or selecting a mechanism to resolve a particular dispute, the relative advantages and disadvantages of the various mechanisms are important factors to consider. System designers or attorneys advising clients about dispute resolution processes must also consider the appropriateness of a particular dispute resolution process given the circumstances of the system or case. The first excerpt in this section, the Report of the Ad Hoc Panel on Dispute Resolution and Public Policy that was convened in 1983 by the National Institute for Dispute Resolution, provides a comparative analysis of various dispute resolution processes.

Second, when designing a system or selecting a process, attention must be paid to how the process will be perceived by the participants. Research on how disputants assess the procedural fairness of a dispute resolution process demonstrates that judgments of procedural justice have a strong influence on disputants' willingness to use the process, their satisfaction with the process, and their willingness to comply with the outcome of the process. In the second excerpt in this section, Professor Nancy Welsh summarizes the findings of research on procedural justice and points to its importance for dispute resolution.

Third, important issues of public policy arise when designing dispute resolution systems or selecting dispute resolution processes for particular disputes. In thinking about appropriate mechanisms for resolving particular kinds of disputes, attention should be paid to concerns that have been raised over, for example, the need for precedent, the need to protect the rights of those who are disadvantaged, or the need to protect the public interest. The final two excerpts in this section, one by Judge Harry Edwards and one by Professors Frank Sander and Stephen Goldberg, address these public policy questions.

As you read these excerpts consider the following questions: What are the advantages and disadvantages of different dispute resolution mechanisms? Under what circumstances is one or another dispute resolution process more or less appropriate? How should choices among alternatives be made? What problems might be solved or created by increased resort to the different dispute resolution processes? Consider these questions, but do not expect clear or final answers to all of them.

NAT'L INST. FOR DISPUTE RESOLUTION, PATHS TO JUSTICE: MAJOR PUBLIC POLICY ISSUES OF DISPUTE RESOLUTION

3–4, 8–18, 30, 34–35 (1983).

CHOOSING AMONG DISPUTE RESOLUTION OPTIONS

No one approach is best for resolving all disputes. The nature of the dispute and the disputants will, in large measure, determine which dispute resolution method is most appropriate. Among the characteristics that might suggest one approach over another are whether the relationship among disputants is of a continuing nature, the disputants' financial circumstances, their desire for privacy and control of the dispute resolution process, and the urgency of resolving the dispute.

One must be wary of ascribing particular attributes to one or another methods of dispute resolution, however. Litigation is not always final, although that is a commonly perceived benefit; mediation may not enable parties to work together in the future, as is often suggested; arbitration may not always be less expensive than pursuing a case in court. And all dispute resolution methods may have unanticipated consequences that make them more or less desirable in particular instances.

With that caveat, the Panel reviewed the advantages and disadvantages of three major kinds of dispute resolution methods: litigation, arbitration, and mediation.

ADVANTAGES AND DISADVANTAGES OF THE COURTS

The concern expressed repeatedly by the Panel is that courts are simply too expensive and too time consuming. Although the government subsidizes a great deal of the cost of running the courts, their full use requires expensive lawyers and the time of the disputants. These costs mean that courts are generally inaccessible to all but the most wealthy parties. Hence, the courts tend to be the province of large organizations and concomitantly the ten-year anti-trust case consumes a disproportionate share of judicial resources. Thus, although courts are vitally important for protecting private rights and concerns, the delay and costs may render them ineffective in discharging this critical duty.

— Because of the relatively structured approach courts use, the range of remedies available to the court may be quite limited. Indeed, lawyers may have to reframe the issues separating the parties to fit a particular legal doctrine and, thus, may change the nature of the dispute. As a result, the court is often not able to address the real issues and tailor an appropriate remedy.

— Courts largely rely on a formal adversarial process that may further antagonize the disputing parties. Thus, a judicial approach may not be the preferred forum for settling disputes in which the parties will continue to have a close working or living relationship. Further, because the process is also somewhat mystifying to many laymen, they may become estranged from the court.

— Some disputes require a technical expertise for their resolution and, since judges are necessarily generalists, courts may be inappropriate for some controversies. In others, even though courts could be educated sufficiently to make the decision, that may not be an efficient use of resources. Moreover, the existing expertise of the parties is generally not tapped in shaping a resolution because of the way roles are defined. . . .

These concerns notwithstanding, courts continue to provide indispensable services to society. They are the appropriate forum when the purpose is to establish a societal norm or legal precedent. Thus, for example, if the underlying cause of a dispute is not a disagreement over how to apply an accepted norm but rather a need to create such a principle, then courts — or the legislature — are the appropriate forum. Groups and individuals who lack economic power or social status are likely to need the courts to protect their rights and preserve their leverage in dealing with others.

Courts are also the preferred method of establishing a record of something that happened in the past. If the resolution of a dispute turns on reconstructing the facts — or at least on developing an authoritative version of the facts — then courts best serve that function. They also provide the official recognition and basis for enforcement which society demands in the resolution of some disputes, such as divorce and bankruptcy, for example.

Some cases get to court not because they have these characteristics that commend them for judicial resolution, but because of the exigencies of the situation. Some issues are sufficiently controversial that at least one of the disputants does not want to take the responsibility for voluntarily participating in its resolution. Instead, the dispute will be submitted to adjudication to deflect responsibility for the eventual, possibly unpopular, decision. School desegregation and other sensitive cases involving elected officials often fall into this category. Another example is the corporate dispute where the stakes are too high for a middle level officer to take responsibility for losing and, hence, the matter is submitted to a court to neutralize responsibility. Courts are also used sometimes when one party wants to delay a decision for as long as possible.

Most cases that are filed do not go all the way to judicial resolution. Nevertheless, filing a lawsuit may serve important functions and be a necessary prelude to using other methods for resolving disputes. It crystallizes the issues and provides the disputants with ways of compelling participation, procedures for sharing information, motivation for taking action, and deadlines for doing so. Thus, many cases are resolved through "bargaining in the shadow of the law."

* * *

ADVANTAGES AND DISADVANTAGES OF OTHER FORMS OF DISPUTE RESOLUTION

Arbitration and mediation are the two most widely known nonlitigative methods of dispute resolution. Arbitration, widely accepted and used in labor and management grievances and in some commercial settings, has special advantages over the courts, among them:

— It can be initiated without long delays; the procedure is relatively short; and a decision can be reached promptly.

— Relaxed rules of evidence enhance flexibility and the process is more streamlined than a judicial proceeding.

— The parties may select the applicable norms — that is, they can specify a particular body of law as a basis for a decision that might not be relevant in a court setting.

— The parties are able to choose the arbitrator.

— The arbitrator can be required to have expertise in the subject matter of the dispute.

— The resolution can be tailored to the circumstances.

— The dispute can be kept private since the decision is not necessarily a public document, as it would be in a court proceeding.

— Arbitration may be less expensive than going to trial.

— An arbitrator's decision is final and may be binding on the parties.

— The award in binding arbitration usually is enforceable by a court with little or no review.

In sum, with arbitration, decisions can be reached with relative speed and finality. Arbitration has proved especially valuable to parties that have a large number of disputes which must be resolved during the course of a contractual relationship. Labor-management and contractor-subcontractor relationships are examples.

But the efficiency of arbitration sometimes may be achieved at the expense of the "quality of justice" in an individual decision. In commercial and labor cases, where there is a high volume of cases with fairly low stakes, trade-offs between an expeditious, inexpensive arbitration process and the assurance of a more studied decision in each case may be acceptable. In other types of disputes, parties may not agree to arbitration because they want the protection offered by the courts, or they want to maintain control over a settlement through a process of negotiation. Thus, for example, a party may be more willing to use arbitration to determine the amount in controversy than initially to establish liability.

Further, arbitration has become so formalized in labor relations that it has developed some of the problems of procedure and delay present in judicial process. It should be noted, too, that an arbitration hearing may be more expensive and time consuming than the negotiated settlement which might otherwise have occurred.

Mediation is a valuable approach to the many disputes that are better settled through negotiation than adjudication. Among the benefits of mediation:

— It may provide an opportunity to deal with underlying issues in a dispute.

— It may build among disputants a sense of accepting and owning their eventual settlement.

— It has a tendency to mitigate tensions and build understanding and trust among disputants, thereby avoiding the bitterness which may follow adjudication.

— It may provide a basis by which parties negotiate their own dispute settlements in the future.

— It is usually less expensive than other processes.

But mediation, too, has potential shortcomings. It can be time consuming, lack an enforcement mechanism when done outside the courts (although agreements may be enforceable as contracts), and depends on the voluntary participation of all parties to a dispute and their willingness to negotiate in good faith. It does not always result in an agreement and, therefore, the resolution of a dispute.

It also raises a series of considerations related to the role of the mediator. In general, mediation works best when the parties have a rough parity of power, resources, and information. But, what is the responsibility of the mediator if there is a significant power imbalance among parties or if one party is uninformed or misinformed about the law or facts needed to make a sound decision? Should the mediator, or anyone else, have the responsibility to make certain an agreement has a principled basis and is not reached out of ignorance or fear? Should a mediator refuse to take part in resolving a dispute if one or another party may be hurt in the process or have their confidences disclosed? What are the consequences if the mediator becomes interventionist and is not perceived as impartial? In sum, assuming they can be defined, how are the ethics of the mediator assured? And, what is the appropriate role for the lawyer when a client is attempting to reach a mediated settlement?

Beyond the specifics of arbitration and mediation, there are general concerns about nonjudicial methods of dispute resolution. These methods, which might reach settlements without the use of lawyers or counselors, may lead disputants to make choices they would avoid if they were better informed. This is an area of particular concern related to women, the poor, the elderly, persons for whom English is a second language, and other classes of disputants who are traditionally less powerful or less skilled at negotiation than their opponents. Further, nonlitigative methods may merely give the appearance of resolving some disputes while avoiding a finding of more extensive liability or leaving fundamental issues unsettled (e.g., an individual settlement in a products liability case while the company keeps manufacturing the defective part or an individual settlement of a discrimination complaint while the organization continues the prohibited practice).

* * *

It should also be noted that efforts to settle disputes may not be productive if the parties have not sufficiently narrowed the issues, developed the facts, and concluded that compromise is in their best interests. Disputes somehow must be ripe for resolution before they can be settled satisfactorily . . . . .

DISPUTE RESOLUTION PRINCIPLES

Comparison of various methods of dispute resolution raises complex issues. More empirical information is needed before any definite statements can be made about the appropriateness of one method over another in a particular kind of dispute. The Panel was able to conclude, however, that there are a number of major criteria by which a dispute resolution mechanism can be judged:

1.   It must be accessible to disputants. This means that the forum for resolution should be affordable to disputants as well as accessible in terms of physical location and hours of operation. Parties should be comfortable in the forum and feel that it is responsive to their interests.

2.   It must protect the rights of disputants. In cases where there is a parity of resources, influence, and knowledge, this may not be a concern. But where one party is at a disadvantage, his or her rights may be jeopardized by choice of the forum. For instance, the poorer

litigant may not be able to afford full discovery, expert witnesses, etc. Similarly, a party may unnecessarily forfeit rights in mediation if without counsel.

3. It should be efficient in terms of cost and time and, so, may have to be tailored to the nature of the dispute. Time is very important in many instances, and the forum for settlement should respond to this imperative. For example, it is obviously vital to the elderly that their disputes be settled quickly. Some disputes, especially those involving highly charged emotional issues, may take some time to settle; factual disputes may be more amenable to expeditious handling.

4. It must be fair and just to the parties to the dispute, to the nature of the dispute, and when measured against society's expectations of justice.

5. It should assure finality and enforceability of decision. Although the mechanism itself can discourage appeals, it may be that disputants' belief that the process was fair that will be the principal component of finality. In coercive situations, due process concerns will require that there are proceedings for review of decisions.

6. It must be credible. The parties, their lawyers, and other representatives must recognize the forum as part of a legitimate system of justice. People who practice the alternatives, especially as judicial adjuncts, must be competent, well-trained, and responsible. Society, too, must have faith in the alternative and recognize its legitimacy.

7. It should give expression to the community's sense of justice through the creation and dissemination of norms and guidelines so that other disputes are prevented, violators deterred, and disputants encouraged to reach resolution on their own.

The Panel recognized that it is unlikely that any dispute resolution mechanism will be equally strong in all of the seven criteria. Rather, choices will have to be made concerning which qualities are the most essential with respect to particular kinds of disputes. It is through this process of decisionmaking and monitoring outcomes that some assessment can be made of the real implications of various forms of dispute resolution. For instance, one could argue that mediation is a better approach to resolving property and custody issues in a divorce because of the interest in facilitating a workable long-term relationship; however, some fear that without counsel present during negotiation, a woman, unused to asserting herself, will settle for less than she would be awarded through judicial proceedings; others observe that courts are generally biased against awarding custody to men. These differences in perspective demonstrate that there is much information needed before dispute resolution methods for particular kinds of disputes can be described.

* * *

APPENDICES

APPENDIX 1: TABLES

General Observations on the Comparison and Evaluation of the Various Dispute Resolution Mechanisms

- Dispute mechanisms do not exist in isolation, but in close proximity to one another. They interact with and influence one another. Thus, for example, many mechanisms that work by agreement depend on the threat of resort to institutions with coercive powers. And much of what coercive institutions do, in fact, is to induce and ratify agreements between disputants.

- We usefully distinguish pure types like adjudication and mediation, but institutions usually do not operate in accordance with a single prototype. In practice, these types are combined, and much dispute processing deviates from the avowed prototype. This is particularly true of courts, where what starts as adjudication may end up as a form of mediation. And, generally, the mechanisms employing third parties with the power to make binding decisions often create a setting for negotiations between the disputants.

- Each of the types listed on the tables that follow is a composite, spanning a wide range of actual instances. For example, arbitration includes court-annexed arbitration, arbitration by standing bodies of experts within trade associations, commercial arbitration by ad hoc arbitrators supplied by the American Arbitration Association, etc. Hence the list of qualities associated with a particular mechanism can only be general and suggested and must be reassessed in relation to any specific stance of the type.

- In accounting features as strengths (advantages) or weaknesses (disadvantages), we should recall that this depends on what we want to achieve. For example, absence of a constraint to decide according to pre-existing rules may be accounted an advantage if we seek primarily resolution of the dispute at hand but may be a disadvantage if we seek to set a precedent for resolution of large numbers of claims or to forward public policy embodied in a rule.

- We must examine the advantages and disadvantages of the alternative mechanisms in both the public and private sectors. In seeking such comparisons, we must avoid false comparison between the ideal functioning of one institution and the actual functioning of another.

* * *

Table 4: Advantages/Disadvantages Associated With Dispute Resolution Mechanisms Court Adjudication

Table 4: Advantages/Disadvantages Associated With Dispute Resolution Mechanisms

1. Court Adjudication	2. Arbitration	3. Mediation/Negotiation	4. Administrative Decision-Making	5. Ombudsman	6. Internal Tribunal
– announces and applies public norms	– privacy	– privacy	– defines problem systematically	– not disruptive to ongoing relations	– privacy
– precedent	– parties control forum	– parties control process	– devises aggregate solution	– flexible	– responsive to concerns of disputants
– deterrence	– enforceability	– reflects concerns and priorities of disputants	– flexibility in obtaining relevant information	– self-starting	– enforceability
– uniformity	– expeditious	– flexible	– can accommodate multiple criteria	– easy access	
– independence	– expertise	– finds integrative solutions			
– binding/closure	– tailors remedy to solution	– addresses underlying problem			
– enforceability	– choice of applicable norms	– process educates disputants			
– already institutionalized		– high rate of compliance			
– publicly funded					
(disadvantages)					
– expensive	– no public norms	– lacks ability to compel participation	– no control by parties	– not enforceable	– not independent
– requires lawyers and relinquishes control to them	– no precedent	– not binding	– not independent	– no control by parties	– no due process safeguards
– mystifying	– no uniformity	– weak closure	– not individualized		– not based on public norms
– lack of special substantive experience	– lack of quality	– no power to induce settlements			– may reflect imbalance within organization
– delay	– becoming encumbered by increasing "legalization"	– no due process safeguards			
– time-consuming		– reflects imbalance in skills (negotiation)			
– issues redefined or narrowed		– lacks enforceability			
– limited range of remedies		– outcome need not be principled			
– no compromise		– no application/development of public standards			
– polarizes, disruptive					

TABLE 5: Partial Listing of Characteristics That May Argue for One or Another Type of Mechanism as Appropriate

	Adjudication	Arbitration	Mediation/Negotiation
ARGUES FOR	- need to create a public norm - need to offset power imbalance - need for decision on past events - need to compel participation	- high volume - premium on speed, privacy, closure	- desire to preserve continuing relations - emphasis on future dealings - need to avoid win-lose decision - premium on control by disputants - multiple parties and issues - absence of clear legal entitlement
ARGUES AGAINST	- high volume, low stakes - continuing relations - need for speedy resolution	- need for precedent	- need to compel participation - need to enforce agreements - need to create a public norm

Notes and Questions

1.   What factors characterize disputes that are best suited for mediation? For arbitration? For litigation? Despite the apparent simplicity of Table 5 in the preceding reading, such questions are difficult to answer in the abstract. As we have seen in previous chapters, goals, styles, and practices will vary among creators of and participants in dispute resolution processes. In addition, within each broad category of dispute resolution method, we find many quite different processes. For example, in some negotiations and mediations, parties have no opportunity to participate directly and no one makes an effort to address underlying interests. In some courts — such as small claims courts — it is common for lawyers not to appear. Mediation can be voluntary or mandated by a court, mediation may come at different stages of the process, mediators may be selected and paid differently, and mediators and other participants may exercise differing degrees of influence. Arbitration can involve one or three arbitrators, pre- or post-hearing briefs or no briefs. Ask yourself how these differences in form might influence the dispute resolution process and decisions about what dispute resolution processes to offer or select.

2.   In an excerpt in Chapter I, beginning at page 6, Bernard Mayer, a well-known mediator, suggests that it is valuable to consider conflict along three dimensions — cognitive, emotional, and behavioral — and that true resolution occurs only if there is resolution in all three dimensions. To what extent do the various dispute resolution processes have the potential to address each dimension? For a given case or category of cases, who should decide which dimensions should be addressed or how they might be prioritized? Should such decisions be made by program designers or by participants in the processes?

3.   Note also that the processes described here are not mutually exclusive. A system for resolving disputes may incorporate several of these

processes under the appropriate circumstances. *See infra* at pages 818–839. Similarly, the parties to an individual dispute may utilize several different processes before it is ultimately resolved. See pages 862–879 below. As Professor Jean Sternlight notes:

> I see that an intertwining between litigation and other forms of dispute resolution is inevitable. Some disputants will always choose to settle their disputes, and there seems to be no way that a society could force them to resolve the dispute through litigation rather than through settlement. Just as settlements occur in the "shadow of the law," that is, that the possibility of a litigated solution is often what drives disputants to resolve the dispute through mediation or negotiation, so too does litigation take place in the shadow of settlement. As lawyers and disputants litigate cases they do, or at least should, always keep in mind the possibility of negotiation or mediation. Thus, it is generally a mistake to consider that one form of dispute resolution is entirely a substitute for others.

Jean R. Sternlight, *ADR is Here: Preliminary Reflections on Where it Fits in a System of Justice*, 3 Nev. L.J. 289, 295–96 (2002/2003).

2. PROCEDURAL JUSTICE

Several of the criteria the Panel gives for judging a dispute resolution mechanism relate to the fairness, justice, and legitimacy of the process. To be viewed as legitimate, a process for resolving disputes must not only result in just substantive outcomes (i.e., distributive justice), but must also consist of procedures that are perceived to be fair (i.e., procedural justice). In designing and choosing processes for resolving disputes, it is important to consider the experiences and reactions of the individuals who participate in the procedure. Below, Professor Nancy Welsh discusses the role of procedural justice in dispute resolution.

NANCY A. WELSH, MAKING DEALS IN COURT–CONNECTED MEDIATION: WHAT'S JUSTICE GOT TO DO WITH IT?

79 Wash. U. L.Q. 787, 817–26 (2001).

II. UNDERSTANDING PROCEDURAL JUSTICE

What does "justice" mean? What types of justice must or should the courts provide? This Article focuses primarily upon one type of justice — procedural justice. Procedural justice is concerned with the fairness of the procedures or processes that are used to arrive at outcomes. Distributive justice, in contrast, focuses on perceptions of and criteria to determine the substantive fairness of the outcomes themselves.

* * *

A. The Effects of Procedural Justice

Although issues of procedural justice often do not attract as much public attention as concerns about distributive justice, research has shown that when people experience dispute resolution and decisionmaking procedures, they "pay a great deal of attention to the way things are done [i.e., how decisions are made] and the nuances of their treatment by others." As a result, perceptions of procedural justice profoundly affect people's perceptions of distributive justice, their compliance with the outcomes of decision-making procedures and processes, and their perceptions of the legitimacy of the authorities that determine such outcomes. Perhaps surprisingly, perceptions of distributive justice generally have a much more modest impact than perceptions of procedural justice.

Research has repeatedly confirmed that people's perceptions of procedural justice mediate or influence their perceptions of distributive justice. Disputants who believe that they have been treated in a procedurally fair manner are more likely to conclude that the resulting outcome is substantively fair. In effect, a disputant's perception of procedural justice anchors general fairness impressions or serves as a fairness heuristic. Further, research has indicated that disputants who have participated in a procedure that they evaluated as fair do not change their evaluation even if the procedure produces a poor or unfair outcome.

The perception of procedural justice also serves as a shortcut means of determining whether to accept or reject a legal decision or procedure. Disputants who believe that they were treated fairly in a dispute resolution procedure are more likely to comply with the outcome of that procedure. This effect will occur even if outcomes do not favor the disputants or they are actually unhappy with the outcomes.

Disputants' perceptions of the procedural justice provided by a decision-making authority also affect the respect and loyalty accorded to the authority. This effect is particularly strong for the courts. Thus, litigants' reactions to the institution of the judiciary and their compliance with decisions arising out of court-mandated procedures do not depend simply (or even primarily) upon whether they feel that they won or lost their cases. Rather, litigants' reactions depend largely upon their "experience of legal procedures."

B. Process Characteristics That Enhance Perceptions of Procedural Justice

Several rather specific process characteristics enhance perceptions of procedural justice. First, perceptions of procedural justice are enhanced to the extent that disputants perceive that they had the opportunity to present their views, concerns, and evidence to a third party and had control over this presentation ("opportunity for voice"). Second, disputants are more likely to perceive procedural justice if they perceive that the third party considered their views, concerns, and evidence. Third, disputants' judgments about procedural justice are affected by the perception that the third party treated them in a dignified, respectful manner and that the procedure itself was dignified. Although it seems that a disputants' perceptions regarding a fourth factor — the impartiality of the third party decision maker — also ought to affect procedural justice judgments, it appears that disputants are influenced more strongly by their observations regarding the third party's even-handedness and attempts at fairness.

Through a long series of experiments involving many different settings and situations, disputants' opportunity for voice has been found to "reliably affect" perceptions of procedural justice. "[W]hen disputants [feel] that they [have] been allowed a full opportunity to voice their views, concerns, and evidence, the disputing process [is] seen as fairer and the outcome [is] more likely to be accepted." Concerns regarding the opportunity for voice apply in a variety of settings, including the courtroom, arbitration proceedings, contacts with the police, political decision making, and decision making in work organizations. Even in countries where the judicial systems typically use nonadversarial procedures, citizens often prefer procedures that allow a full opportunity for voice. Perhaps most surprisingly, both field and laboratory studies have demonstrated that the opportunity for voice heightens disputants' judgments of procedural justice even when they know that their voice will not and cannot influence the final outcome.

These research results are helpful as we consider the application of procedural justice to court-connected mediation, but they raise several important questions: What counts as a full opportunity for voice? How much freedom and time must disputants be given? What represents sufficient control by disputants over the presentation of their views, concerns, and evidence? Can an agent's presentation fulfill the disputants' opportunity for voice? Many of the procedural justice studies deal with these questions, directly or indirectly. * * *

The other three process characteristics that influence procedural justice judgments center upon the behavior of the third party. In particular, disputants assess the extent to which the third party hears and considers their presentations, treats them with dignity and respect, and tries to be fair and even-handed. Disputants seek assurance that the decision maker has given adequate consideration to their presentations. Apparently, while disputants care very much about having the opportunity for voice, they also wish to know that they have been heard. In one study examining citizens' interactions with police and judges, researchers found that the effect of providing an opportunity for voice was significantly enhanced if citizens also believed that the police and judges considered their views before they made decisions. Indeed, a third party's behavior, including the third party's consideration of the disputants' views, independently affects perceptions of procedural justice and "acts as a filter for ... and an amplifier of" the disputants' subjective assessments of their control over both the outcome and the process within a particular procedure.

Disputants' perceptions of procedural justice also are influenced by how the third party interacts with them on an interpersonal level. In particular, disputants assess the degree to which the third party treats them in a polite and dignified fashion and tries to be fair and evenhanded. Research has shown that disputants' procedural justice judgments are strongly influenced by the dignity or lack of dignity in decision-making proceedings. For example, in one study comparing litigants' reactions to the third-party processes of trial, arbitration, and judicial settlement conferences, the litigants gave much higher procedural justice rankings to trial and arbitration, even though these proceedings required the litigants to surrender decision-making control. Most litigants perceived trial and arbitration as dignified and careful. In contrast, settlement conferences were more likely to strike litigants as undignified and contrary to the litigants' sense of procedural fairness. Dignified and respectful treatment demonstrates to citizens that authorities recognize their own role as that of "public servants and [recognize] ... the role of citizens as clients who have a legitimate right to certain services." Interestingly, while authorities' politeness and respect for citizens' rights have been found to influence all citizens' perceptions of procedural justice, some research suggests that minority group members particularly value the existence of these qualities in their interactions with authorities.

Significantly, several studies have shown that disputants value these process characteristics as much as, or even more than, control over the final decision (also termed "decision control"). Disputants particularly have identified the opportunity for voice as just as valuable as decision control. Other studies have demonstrated that disputants actually prefer processes in which they surrender decision control (e.g., trial and arbitration) if they perceive that these processes provide more opportunity for voice and more dignified treatment than the available consensual processes. This finding is consistent with other studies that have found that disputants' procedural justice judgments are affected much more strongly by variations in process control than by variations in decision control.

Notes and Questions

1. Procedural justice research such as that described by Professor Welsh has demonstrated that perceptions of procedural justice play a significant role in disputants' willingness to use dispute resolution processes, their satisfaction with such processes, and their willingness to comply with the outcomes of such processes. For example, in a study of 411 felony defendants, Professor Tom Tyler and his colleagues found that defendants' assessments of the procedural fairness of their experience more strongly influenced their views of legal authorities than did the length of their sentences. Tom R. Tyler, Jonathan D. Casper, & Bonnie Fisher, *Maintaining Allegiance Toward Political Authorities: The Role of Prior Attitudes and the Use of Fair Procedures*, 33 Am. J. Pol. Sci. 629 (1989). In another study, Professor E. Allan Lind and his colleagues studied individual and corporate civil disputants who were required to participate in court-annexed nonbinding arbitration programs. Disputants could either accept the arbitration award or could reject it and proceed to a trial. The researchers found that the disputants' decisions were more strongly influenced by their perceptions

of the procedural justice of the arbitration proceeding, than by the size of the arbitration award. E. Allan Lind, Tom R. Tyler, Carol T. Kulik, Maureen Ambrose, & Maria V. de Vera Park, *Individual and Corporate Dispute Resolution: Using Procedural Fairness as a Decision Heuristic*, 38 Admin. Sci. Q. 224 (1993). For further reading on procedural justice, see E. ALLAN LIND & TOM R. TYLER, THE SOCIAL PSYCHOLOGY OF PROCEDURAL JUSTICE (1988); Tom R. Tyler & E. Allan Lind, *Procedural Justice*, in HANDBOOK OF JUSTICE RESEARCH IN LAW 65 (Joseph Sanders & V. Lee Hamilton eds., 2001).

2.   How would you assess each of the various dispute resolution processes you have studied for their potential effects on procedural justice? Within each broad category of disputes resolution process, how might these effects change with variations in procedures?

3.   Psychological research indicates that the effects of procedural justice occur in two different ways. As Professor Welsh explains:

> Two theories — the "social exchange" theory and the "group value" theory — together explain the importance of procedural justice. According to the social exchange theory, disputants value the opportunity for voice because this provides them with the opportunity to influence the decision maker and indirectly influence the final outcome. Disputants "evaluate procedures in terms of the immediate financial and social benefits they receive from the procedure." Thus, procedure is important because it serves the disputants' goals of achieving favorable outcomes. As previously noted, however, research has shown that disputants value voice even when they know they cannot influence outcomes. This suggests that voice has a significance that is independent of its effect upon the outcome.

> A second theory, the "group value" theory, supplements the social exchange theory and helps to explain the inherent value of voice. The group value theory views procedures as something more than a means to achieve outcomes. The theory "emphasize[s] the symbolic and psychological implications of procedures for feelings of inclusion in society and for the belief that the institution using the procedure holds the person in high regard." By focusing on the symbolism and psychological implications of procedures, the group value theory explains the overwhelming importance of voice in affecting perceptions of procedural justice, even when such voice will not affect the outcome of a decision-making forum. The theory also provides a means for understanding the importance of dignified treatment and consideration of the views expressed by the disputants. All of these cues send powerful messages to disputants regarding their status in society, which then "validates their self-identity, self-esteem, and self-respect."

Nancy A. Welsh, *Making Deals in Court–Connected Mediation: What's Justice Got to Do With It?* 79 Wash. U. L.Q. 787, 826–27 (2001).

4.   The factors identified by research on the determinants of procedural justice can be used to design and select systems for resolving disputes that maximize or enhance participants' views of procedural justice. How would you structure a mediation process to best provide disputants with a sense of procedural justice?

5. In a RAND Corporation study of tort litigants' views of traditional trials, court-annexed arbitration, and judicial settlement conferences, the researchers concluded that litigants viewed trials and court-annexed arbitration as more fair and dignified than bilateral settlement negotiations. Judicial settlement conferences, in contrast, were viewed with more discomfort than the process of bilateral settlement negotiation, possibly because the litigants were often excluded from the conferences. E. Allen Lind, Robert MacCoun, Patricia Ebener, William L.F. Felstiner, Deborah R. Hensler, Judith Resnik & Tom R. Tyler, *In the Eye of the Beholder: Tort Litigants' Evaluations of their Experiences in the Civil Justice System*, 24 Law & Soc'y Rev. 953 (1990).

6. Consider the desires of disputants as articulated by Professor Jean Sternlight:

> Unfortunately, some people who opine on dispute resolution issues have a tendency to say that they or we know what disputants really want, when in fact the evidence is quite sparse. Thus, some mediation advocates overstate their case, suggesting that most everyone would prefer a conciliated, non-legal solution to a trial. Along somewhat the same lines, an increasing number of judges and lawyers tend to say that trials are terrible, and too much of an uncontrollable gamble for disputants, although it is not clear disputants actually share this view. Some lawyers feel it is their responsibility to educate disputants as to the failings of our litigation system. At the same time, some trial advocates also overstate their case, suggesting that most, or all, litigants would prefer to resolve their disputes in the public and adversarial courtroom.

> * * *

> I believe [research] will ultimately show that disputants are generally looking for three benefits from a dispute resolution system: (1) a system that provides them with a substantively fair/just result; (2) a system that meets the procedural justice criteria of voice, participation, and dignity as set out above; and (3) a system that helps them to achieve other personal and emotional goals, such as reconciliation, or that at least does not leave them feeling worse, emotionally and psychologically. The first two points seem fairly obvious. It is hard to imagine that any system can be tolerated as fair and just in the long term if it in fact consistently yields unfair results. In addition, although the social science literature on procedural justice needs to be developed further, and while its applicability to other kinds of societies needs to be verified, as a preliminary matter, it seems clear that the perception of justice is quite important to disputants.

> The third goal is the least obvious, at least to those of us who are used to Western conceptions of justice. We recognize that disputants have emotional needs and desires. They may seek revenge, forgiveness, or reconciliation, among other things. However, we in the West have been trained to think that these emotional needs should not necessarily be served by a system of justice, or at least by a system of law. Instead, since the Enlightenment, we have become accustomed to thinking of a justice system in an almost mechanical fashion, as an institution designed to resolve disputes fairly, effectively, and according to neutral

legal principles. Yet, not all societies share this limited vision as to the goals of a system of justice. Instead, many see the purposes of justice more broadly, as bringing the members of society back into balance or harmony. I believe there is no reason why we should not continue to have our system of justice serve these emotional needs, as well as the other goals set out above. Why should we not take into account psychological and emotional factors, as well as other social policies, when we set up our legal system? Surely these factors can be considered in drafting our legal procedures, just as they are considered when we adopt substantive laws. Indeed, given the inevitability that the manner in which we structure a system of procedure will impact disputants, psychologically and emotionally, do we not have an obligation to try to make this impact positive rather than negative?

Jean R. Sternlight, *ADR is Here: Preliminary Reflections on Where it Fits in a System of Justice*, 3 Nev. L.J. 289, 297–300 (2002/2003).

7. Consider the September 11th Victim Compensation Fund of 2001, Pub. L. No. 107–42, § 401 (codified at 28 C.F.R. § 104 (2003)), as a process for resolving disputes in an alternative forum. The Fund was created in the aftermath of the September 11, 2001 terrorist attacks on the World Trade Center and the Pentagon to provide compensation to injured victims and the families of deceased victims. In exchange for waiving their right to sue for damages, eligible persons were entitled to compensation for economic and non-economic losses as determined by a schedule based on factors such as age, income, and number of dependents and reduced by collateral sources of funds such as life insurance. Tom Tyler and Hulda Thorisdottir argue that both the process of designing the Fund and the dispute resolution mechanisms initially employed by the Fund were not consistent with principles of procedural justice:

> The Fund lacks many of the procedural features that have been shown to facilitate the willingness to accept decisions made by third-party authorities:
>
> > (1) The manner in which the Fund was initially created lacked these features, because there were no hearings or other forums in which people could articulate their views about what type and level of compensation was appropriate. People did not have the opportunity to have input into creating the Fund and establishing its operating principles. Instead, Congress established the Fund in a short period of time without public hearings, and the initial design of the plan did not call for hearings involving the families of victims to discuss how compensation should be determined.
>
> > (2) The manner in which the Fund was to be implemented also lacked features such as participation, transparency, and accountability, that are typically viewed as part of fair procedures. Victims' families were not entitled to hearings, nor were the rules of allocation clearly stated. Further, there were no appeal mechanisms. Placing most of the authority for implementation in the judgments of one person, no matter how competent or well motivated, does not reflect procedural justice.

Tom R. Tyler & Hulda Thorisdottir, *A Psychological Perspective on Compensation for Harm: Examining the September 11th Victim Compensation Fund*, 53 DePaul L. Rev. 355, 375–76 (2003).

For more on the design of the Victim Compensation Fund, see Janet Cooper Alexander, *Procedural Design and Terror Victim Compensation*, 53 DePaul L. Rev. 627 (2003); Stephan Landsman, *A Chance to be Heard: Thoughts About Schedules, Caps, and Collateral Source Deductions in the September 11th Victim Compensation Fund*, 53 DePaul L. Rev. 393 (2003). Distribution of payments from the Fund was completed in June 2004 with approximately $7 billion having been paid to more than 5000 families. David W. Chen, *After Weighing Value of Lives, 9/11 Fund Completes Its Task*, N.Y. Times, June 16, 2004, at A1. How might the Fund have been designed differently to take into account the findings of procedural justice research and principles of dispute systems design?

8.   Procedural justice researchers have also studied the effects of assessments of procedural justice on compliance with the law. Interestingly, these studies have consistently shown that trust in legal institutions far exceeds other factors — including agreement in the substantive correctness of the law — as the primary determinant of compliance with law. Tom R. Tyler, *Public Mistrust of the Law: A Political Perspective*, 66 U. Cin. L. Rev. 847, 856–58 (1998). More specifically, the research suggests that people are most willing to comply with the law when it is perceived to be legitimate, in the sense that it is entitled to or deserving of compliance, and the primary determinants of this entitlement or legitimacy are perceived procedural fairness and trust in the motives of legal authorities. *Id.* at 859–66. Is this consistent with your experience? Why might the core values of procedural justice resonate so deeply? Professor Reuben suggests one reason might be their consistency with fundamental democratic values, including personal autonomy, participation, transparency, equality, and due process. Richard C. Reuben, *Democracy and Dispute Resolution: The Problem with Arbitration*, 67 Law & Contemp. Probs., Winter/Spring 2004, at 79.

9.   The influence of procedural justice on disputant decision making also raises the possibility that disputants will be manipulated or misled by procedures with which they are satisfied, but that lead to arguably unjust or objectively disadvantageous results — sometimes referred to as "false consciousness." What ethical issues might be raised about the use of procedural justice as a technique for social influence? *See* Tom R. Tyler, *Procedural Strategies for Gaining Deference: Increasing Social Harmony or Creating False Consciousness?* in Social Influences on Ethical Behavior in Organizations (John M. Darley, David M. Messick, & Tom R. Tyler eds., 2001).

3. PUBLIC POLICY IMPLICATIONS

In addition to the procedural justice implications of a method of dispute resolution, it is also important to consider public policy implications when using alternative dispute resolution mechanisms. The final two excerpts in this section address important public policy issues that are raised by the growing interest in and use of alternatives to traditional litigation. First, U.S. Court of Appeals Judge Harry T. Edwards, a prominent labor arbitrator and law professor before his appointment to the bench, asserts that society's approach to ADR should vary depending on whether ADR is being proposed as an adjunct to or separate from the courts, and whether the disputes submitted to an ADR system involve significant public rights and duties. He is least concerned when private disputes are resolved in ADR systems annexed to courts and most concerned when public law issues are resolved in ADR systems that are independent of the courts. Second, Professors Frank Sander and Stephen Goldberg discuss considerations that are relevant when process selection is viewed from a public perspective.

HARRY EDWARDS, ALTERNATIVE DISPUTE RESOLUTION: PANACEA OR ANATHEMA?

99 Harv. L. Rev. 668, 671–72, 675–82 (1986).

Given the inadequacy of traditional responses to the manifold problems with our court systems, it is not surprising that many commentators believe that we must develop new approaches for dispute resolution in lieu of litigation. Generally, I concur, but I think that there are two critical threshold inquiries that we must make before we leap to embrace any system of ADR. First, we should consider whether an ADR mechanism is being proposed to facilitate existing court procedures, or as an alternative wholly separate from the established system. Second, we must consider whether the disputes that will be resolved pursuant to an ADR system will involve significant public rights and duties. In other words, we must determine whether ADR will result in an abandonment of our constitutional system in which the "rule of law" is created and principally enforced by legitimate branches of government and whether rights and duties will be delimited by those the law seeks to regulate. Perhaps the best way to conceptualize these critical issues is by reference to a simple matrix:

	Private Disputes	Public Disputes
ADR in Court	Private Disputes Resolved by Adjuncts to Courts	Public Law Issues Resolved by Adjuncts to Courts
ADR Outside Court	Private Disputes Resolved by Independent Mechanisms	Public Law Issues Resolved by Independent Mechanisms

Obviously, many disputes cannot be easily classified as solely *private* disputes that implicate no constitutional or public law. Many commentators have tried to distinguish "public" and "private" disputes; but, in my view, no one has been fully successful in this effort. The problem is that hidden in many seemingly private disputes are often difficult issues of public law. In this Commentary, I offer no easy solution to the definitional problem of public/private disputes. I do suggest, however, that there are a number of public law cases that are easily identifiable as such. These include constitutional issues, issues surrounding existing government regulation, and issues of great public concern. The latter category might include, for example, the development of a legal standard of strict liability in products liability cases. Although less easily identifiable than constitutional and regulatory issues, such issues of great public concern can be accommodated so long as ADR mechanisms are created as adjuncts to existing judicial or regulatory systems, or if these issues can be relitigated in court after initial resolution pursuant to ADR.

My purpose in creating a public/private law matrix is not to give court administrators a fool-proof method of assigning cases to appropriate dispute resolution systems. Instead, the matrix helps to illuminate those aspects of ADR that should give rise to the greatest concern. In particular, we must focus on the quadrant of the matrix that would allow for the resolution of public law disputes in ADR systems that are totally divorced from courts. ADR mechanisms falling within this quadrant, I believe, are wholly inappropriate.

In the remainder of this Commentary I will explore the hazards and possibilities presented by each quadrant in the matrix, beginning with two quadrants that involve the use of ADR as an adjunct to our traditional court system.

* * *

III.   The Role of ADR as an "Alternative" System

It is clear, however, that a number of ADR proponents have a far more ambitious vision of ADR than that set forth so far. Some, such as Jerold Auerbach, seem to favor community resolution of disputes using community values instead of the rule of law. Others, such as the Chief Justice, complain that "there is some form of mass neurosis that leads many people to think courts were created to solve all the problems of mankind," and believe that ADR must be used to curb the "flood" of "new kinds of conflicts" (such as "welfare * * * claims under the Equal Protection Clause") that have purportedly overwhelmed the judicial system. In either case, these ADR advocates propose a truly revolutionary step — the resolution of cases through ADR mechanisms free from any judicial monitoring or control.

If we can assume that it is possible to finance and administer truly efficient *systems* of dispute resolution, then there would appear to be no significant objections to the use of even wholly independent ADR mechanisms to resolve private disputes that do not implicate important public values. For instance, settling minor grievances between neighbors according to local mores or resolving simple contract disputes by commercial norms may lead to the disposition of more disputes and the greater satisfaction of the participants. In strictly private disputes, ADR mechanisms such as arbitration often are superior to adjudication. Disputes can be resolved by neutrals with substantive expertise, preferably chosen by the parties, and the substance of disputes can be examined without issue-obscuring procedural rules. Tens of thousands of cases are resolved this way each year by labor and commercial arbitration, and even more private disputes undoubtedly could be better resolved through ADR than by adjudication.

However, if ADR is extended to resolve difficult issues of constitutional or public law — making use of nonlegal values to resolve important social issues or allowing those the law seeks to regulate to delimit public rights and duties — there is real reason for concern. An oft-forgotten virtue of adjudication is that it ensures the proper resolution and application of public values. In our rush to embrace alternatives to litigation, we must be careful not to endanger what law has accomplished or to destroy this important function of formal adjudication. As Professor Fiss notes:

> Adjudication uses public resources, and employs not strangers chosen by the parties but public officials chosen by a process in which the public participates. These officials, like members of the legislative and executive branches, possess a power that has been defined and conferred by public law, not by private agreement. Their job is not to maximize the ends of private parties, not simply to secure the peace, but to explicate and give force to the values embodied in authoritative texts such as the Constitution and statutes: to interpret those values and to bring reality in accord with them.

The concern here is that ADR will replace the rule of law with nonlegal values. J. Anthony Lucas' masterful study of Boston during the busing crisis highlights the critical point that often our nation's most basic values — such as equal justice under the law — conflict with local nonlegal mores. This was true in Boston during the school desegregation battle, and it was true in the South during the civil rights battles of the sixties. This conflict, however, between national public values reflected in rules of law and nonlegal values that might be embraced in alternative dispute resolution, exists in even more mundane public issues.

For example, many environmental disputes are now settled by negotiation and mediation instead of adjudication. Indeed, as my colleague Judge Wald recently observed, there is little hope that Superfund legislation can solve our nation's toxic waste problem unless the vast bulk of toxic waste disputes are resolved through negotiation, rather than litigation. Yet, as necessary as environmental negotiation may be, it is still troubling. When Congress or a government agency has enacted strict environmental protection standards, negotiations that compromise these strict standards with weaker standards result in the application of values that are simply inconsistent with the rule of law. Furthermore, environmental mediation and negotiation present the danger that environmental standards will be set by private groups without the democratic checks of governmental institutions. Professor Schoenbrod recently has written of an impressive environmental mediation involving the settlement of disputes concerning the Hudson River. According to Schoenbrod, in that case private parties bypassed federal and state agencies, reached an accommodation on environmental issues, and then presented the settlement to government regulators. The alternative to approval of the settlement was continued litigation, which was already in its seventeenth year, with no end in sight.

The resulting agreement may have been laudable in bringing an end to protracted litigation. But surely the mere resolution of a dispute is not proof that the public interest has been served. This is not to say that private settlements can never produce results that are consistent with the public interest; rather, it is to say that private settlements are troubling when we have no assurance that the legislative- or agency-mandated standards have been followed, and when we have no satisfactory explanation as to why there may have been a variance from the rule of law.

In the Hudson River example, we should be concerned if private negotiators settled the environmental dispute without any meaningful input or participation from government regulators, or if the private parties negotiated a settlement at variance with the environmental standard that had been established by government agencies. If, however, government agencies promulgated the governing environmental standards pursuant to legislatively established rulemaking procedures (which, of course, involve public participation), and if the private parties negotiated a settlement in accordance with these agency standards and subject to agency approval, then the ADR process may be seen to have worked well in conjunction with the rule of law. Indeed, the environmental negotiators may have facilitated the implementation of the rule of law by doing what agency regulators had been unable to achieve for seventeen years.

A subtle variation on this problem of private application of public standards is the acceptance by many ADR advocates of the "broken-telephone" theory of dispute resolution that suggests that disputes are simply "failures to communicate" and will therefore yield to "repair service by the expert 'facilitator.' " This broken-telephone theory was implicitly illustrated in a speech by Rosalynn Carter describing the admittedly important work of the Carter Center at Emory University in Atlanta. The Carter Center recently conducted a seminar that brought together people on both sides of the tobacco controversy. According to Rosalynn Carter, "when those people got together, I won't say they hated each other, but they were enemies. But in the end, they were bringing up ideas about how they could work together."

This result is praiseworthy — mutual understanding and good feeling among disputants obviously facilitates intelligent dispute resolution — but there are some disputes that cannot be resolved simply by mutual agreement and good faith. It is a fact of political life that many disputes reflect sharply contrasting views about fundamental public values that can never be eliminated by techniques that encourage disputants to "understand" each other. Indeed, many disputants understand their opponents all too well. Those who view tobacco as an unacceptable health risk, for example, can never fully reconcile their differences with the tobacco industry, and we should not assume otherwise. One essential function of law is to reflect the public resolution of such irreconcilable differences; lawmakers are forced to choose among these differing visions of the public good. A potential danger of ADR is that disputants who seek only understanding and reconciliation may treat as irrelevant the choices made by our lawmakers and may, as a result, ignore public values reflected in rules of law.

We must also be concerned lest ADR becomes a tool for diminishing the judicial development of legal rights for the disadvantaged. Professor Tony Amsterdam has aptly observed that ADR may result in the reduction of possibilities for legal redress of wrongs suffered by the poor and underprivileged, "in the name of increased access to justice and judicial efficiency." Inexpensive, expeditious, and informal adjudication is not always synonymous with *fair* and *just* adjudication. The decision-makers may not understand the values at stake and parties to disputes do not always possess equal power and resources. Sometimes because of this inequality and sometimes because of deficiencies in informal processes lacking procedural protections, the use of alternative mechanisms will produce nothing more than inexpensive and ill-informed decisions. And these decisions may merely legitimate decisions made by the existing power structure within society. Additionally, by diverting particular types of cases away from adjudication, we may stifle the development of law in certain disfavored areas of law. Imagine, for example, the impoverished nature of civil rights law that would have resulted had all race discrimination cases in the sixties and seventies been mediated rather than adjudicated. The wholesale diversion of cases involving the legal rights of the poor may result in the definition of these rights by the powerful in our society rather than by the application of fundamental societal values reflected in the rule of law.

Family law offers one example of this concern that ADR will lead to "second-class justice." In the last ten years, women have belatedly gained many new rights, including new laws to protect battered women and new mechanisms to ensure the enforcement of child-support awards. There is a real danger, however, that these new rights will become simply a mirage if all "family law" disputes are blindly pushed into mediation. The issues presented extend beyond questions of unequal bargaining power. For example, battered women often need the batterer ordered out of the home or arrested — goals fundamentally inconsistent with mediation.

Some forms of mediation, however, would protect the public values at stake. Professors Mnookin and Kornhauser suggest, for example, that divorce settlements can be mediated successfully despite disparities in bargaining power by requiring court review of settlements that deviate from a predefined norm. Additionally, some disputes that are not otherwise subject to court review also might be well suited for mediation. Many cases, however, may require nothing less than judicial resolution. At the very least we must carefully evaluate the appropriateness of ADR in the resolution of particular disputes.

Even with these concerns, however, there are a number of promising areas in which we might employ ADR in lieu of traditional litigation. Once a body of law is well developed, arbitration and other ADR mechanisms can be structured in such a way that public rights and duties would not be defined and delimited by private groups. The recent experience of labor arbitrators in the federal sector, who are required to police compliance with laws, rules, and regulations, suggests that the interpretation and application of law may not lie outside the competence of arbitrators. So long as we restrict arbitrators to the application of clearly defined rules of law, and strictly confine the articulation of public law to our courts, ADR can be an effective means of reducing mushrooming caseloads. Employment discrimination cases offer a promising example. Many employment discrimination cases are highly fact-bound and can be resolved by applying established principles of law. Others, however, present novel questions that should be resolved by a court. If the more routine cases could be certified to an effective alternative dispute resolution system that would have the authority to make some final determinations, the courts could devote greater attention to novel legal questions, and the overall efficiency of an anti-discrimination law might be enhanced.

* * *

Finally, there are some disputes in which community values — coupled with the rule of law — may be a rich source of justice. Mediation of disputes between parents and schools about special education programs for handicapped children has been very successful. A majority of disputes have been settled by mediation, and parents are generally positive about both the outcome and the process. At issue in these mediations is the appropriate education for a child, a matter best resolved by parents and educators — not courts. Similarly, many landlord-tenant disputes can ultimately be resolved only by negotiation. Most tenant "rights" are merely procedural rather than substantive. Yet tenants desire *substantive* improvement in housing conditions or assurances that they will not be evicted. Mediation of landlord-tenant disputes, therefore, can be very successful — often more successful than adjudication — because both parties have much to gain by agreement.

In both of these examples, however, the option of *ultimate* resort to adjudication is essential. It is only because handicapped children have a statutory right to education that parent-school mediation is successful. It is only because tenants have procedural rights that landlords will bargain at all.

ADR can thus play a vital role in constructing a judicial system that is both more manageable and more responsive to the needs of our citizens. It is essential — as the foregoing examples illustrate — that this role of ADR be strictly limited to prevent the resolution of important constitutional and public law issues by ADR mechanisms that are independent of our courts. Fortunately, few ADR programs have attempted to remove public law issues from the courts. Although this may merely reflect the relative youth of the ADR movement, it may also manifest an awareness of the danger of public law resolution in nonjudicial fora.

FRANK E.A. SANDER & STEPHEN B. GOLDBERG, FITTING THE FORUM TO THE FUSS: A USER–FRIENDLY GUIDE TO SELECTING AN ADR PROCEDURE

10 Negotiation J. 49, 60–61 (1994).

When a process selection is made from a public perspective, the public interest must also be considered. If the dispute is one in which a trial is likely to be lengthy, and so consume precious court time, there may be a public interest in referring the dispute to *some* form of ADR. Beyond that, one must ask if there is a public interest in having the dispute resolved pursuant to a *particular* procedure. For example, the referral of child custody disputes to mediation is required by law in several jurisdictions. The disputing parents may believe that they have no interest in a better relationship, but only in vindication, and hence prefer court to mediation. However, many states believe that a better relationship between the parents serves the public interest by improving the life of the child, and so mandate that child custody disputes go first to mediation.

The final question that must be asked in the public context is whether the public interest will be better served by a court decision than by a private settlement. If, for example, the dispute raises a significant question of statutory or constitutional interpretation, a court resolution might be preferable to a private settlement. While a court normally has no power to prevent parties from settling their own dispute, it does not follow that the court, as a public agency, should encourage or assist settlement in such a case.

Litigation may also serve the public interest better than mediation in cases of consumer fraud, which are often handled by the consumer protection division of an attorney general's office. Here not only the issue of *precedent,* but also the related issue of *recurring violations,* is key. The establishment of a general principle or a class remedy, by means of a class action, is clearly preferable to a series of repetitive and inconsistent mediations.

Another situation in which public adjudication is called for is when there is a *need for sanctioning.* If the defendant's conduct constitutes a public danger (assault with a deadly weapon, say, or maintaining a building in a grossly unsafe condition), ADR is inappropriate.

Finally, two more situations may militate against any use of ADR. First, *one or more of the parties may be incapable of negotiating effectively.* An unsophisticated pro se litigant, for example, may be vulnerable to exploitation in an ADR process. (On the other hand, such an individual, if not represented by a lawyer, may not fare better in court.) Second, court process may be required for some other reason: for example, *when serious issues of compliance or discovery are anticipated.*

* * *

Notes and Questions

1. From a public policy perspective, how would you react to proposals for mandatory mediation of all civil actions or all personal injury claims? What would be the costs and benefits? Would your answers be affected by what you assume about the approaches to mediation that would be employed or available?

2. Judge Edwards' principal concern about the use of ADR is that public disputes will be resolved through private means. He cites the controversy over the regulation of tobacco as an example of the kind of disagreement that "cannot be resolved simply by mutual agreement and good faith." Consider the similar controversy over the regulation of firearms. Assume that Congress authorized the Bureau of Alcohol, Tobacco, Firearms, and Explosives (ATF) to set up a negotiated rulemaking process (discussed in Chapter VI, beginning at page 737) to develop rules for the regulation of firearms. The agency will hire an outside mediator to conduct the proceedings and to determine that all appropriate interests are represented. The ATF, which will be represented in the proceedings, will agree to base its regulations on the proposal produced by this process. As a citizen, how would you react to such an announcement? What concerns might you have? As a citizen, again, how would you react if the terms of settlement of a products liability case against a gun manufacturer were filed under seal at the parties' request?

3. Professor Richard Delgado and his co-authors argue that informal processes may foster racial and ethnic prejudice, since studies show that people are more apt to act on prejudicial attitudes in informal than in formal settings. They believe that ADR should be reserved for disputes between parties with comparable status and power and that steps should be taken to reduce bias when the issue to be adjudicated touches a sensitive or intimate area of life. Richard Delgado, Chris Dunn, Pamela Brown, Helena Lee, & David Hubbert, *Fairness and Informality: Minimizing the Risk of Prejudice in Alternative Dispute Resolution*, 1985 Wis. L. Rev. 1359, 1402–1403. Recall also the findings of the Metrocourt study excerpted in Chapter IV, at page 475.

4. The Administrative Dispute Resolution Act of 1990 included a provision stating that "An agency shall consider not using a dispute resolution proceeding if —

(1) a definitive or authoritative resolution of the matter is required for precedential value, and such a proceeding is not likely to be accepted generally as an authoritative precedent;

(2) the matter involves or may bear upon significant questions of Government policy that require additional procedures before a final resolution may be made, and such a proceeding would not likely serve to develop a recommended policy for the agency;

(3) maintaining established policies is of special importance, so that variations among individual decisions are not increased and such a proceeding would not likely reach consistent results among individual decisions;

(4) the matter significantly affects persons or organizations who are not parties to the proceeding;

(5) a full public record of the proceeding is important, and a dispute resolution proceeding cannot provide such a record; and

(6) the agency must maintain continuing jurisdiction over the matter with authority to alter the disposition of the matter in the light of changed circumstances, and a dispute resolution proceeding would interfere with the agency's fulfilling that requirement.''

5 U.S.C. § 582(b) (1994) (*repealed by* Administrative Dispute Resolution Act of 1996, Pub. L. No. 104–320, § 4). Although § 582 was repealed, the Act added 5 U.S.C. § 572(b) (2000), which contains the same language.

What do these recommendations for situations in which it may be best not to use ADR suggest about the relationship between alternative dispute resolution and the law? Under what circumstances are rule of law values more desirable than dispute settlement values?

5.　The articles by Judge Edwards and by Professors Goldberg and Sander raise the notion that litigation consumes public resources (e.g., courts, judicial resources) and produces public benefits (e.g., precedent, application of public values). Making a comparison to public roads and the phenomenon of "induced traffic," Professors Tracey George and Chris Guthrie argue that courts are impure public goods:

Courts and roadways might appear to be pure public goods because each has an aspect (or output) that is enjoyed by the whole community equally. The highway system appears to be a pure public good in that the availability of roadways allows for the economic growth and development of a city, state, and nation. Likewise, the justice system appears to be a pure public good because the courts resolve disputes peacefully and articulate legal rules that enable people to order their lives. Those benefits (or outputs) are nonexcludable and nonrival.

Both courts and roadways, however, have aspects (or outputs) that are not purely public. The individualized use of either good (i.e., the resolution of one person's complaint or one commuter's use of the road) is inherently divisible and rival, as one person's presence precludes others from using the same part of the good during that period. The larger the number of person using courts or roads, the greater the effect on the use by others due to congestion and crowding. Thus, the judicial and highway systems are more appropriately categorized as impure public goods, comprised of both pure and impure aspects.

* * *

Court reformers may face an unwelcome surprise if they allocate additional resources to courts. Rather than facilitating the efficient resolution of existing cases, they might actually induce litigation. More courthouses, more courtrooms, and more judges may simply mean that more litigants bring their disputes to court.

* * *

Thus, we believe that society should think about courts not in isolation but rather as one of many dispute resolution processes that claimants can use to seek redress for harms allegedly suffered. We support, in other words, the erection of literal or figurative "multi-door courthouses" containing "a flexible and diverse panoply of dispute resolution processes (or combination of processes)" for disputants.

Tracey E. George & Chris Guthrie, *Induced Litigation*, 98 Nw. U. L. Rev. 545, 555–56 (2004).

6. Consider several other important public policy issues: How should we fund the study and implementation of alternatives to traditional litigation? What incentives do you imagine could be provided to encourage the use of alternative dispute resolution processes?

B. DESIGNING AND EVALUATING DISPUTE SYSTEMS

In this section we move from the general considerations important to both designing and selecting dispute resolution processes to explicit consideration of the techniques used in designing and evaluating dispute resolution systems.

1. DISPUTE SYSTEMS DESIGN

The field of dispute systems design explores how processes or programs for resolving conflict are created and developed. This section will explore how many different types of dispute resolution systems may be designed for a variety of settings — e.g., systems for resolving disputes under the auspices of a court, systems within organizations for resolving internal disputes, systems created by an organization for dealing with disputes with outside parties such as customers or suppliers, or systems created to deal with disputes that arise during the operation of a contract. Dispute systems designers consider questions such as: What types of disputes occur in the organization? How does the organization handle conflict? How can the system be designed to prevent the unnecessary escalation of conflict? What dispute resolution processes should be used and how will these processes interrelate? How will the system be structured? How will the system be funded? Under what conditions will people access and use the system? How will the system be evaluated?

a. Basic Concepts

The first two excerpts in this subsection offer two approaches to dispute systems design.

In the first excerpt, the pioneers of the field, Professors Jeanne Brett, Stephen Goldberg, and William Ury describe their principles for designing systems to resolve disputes. In the second, Cathy Costantino advocates what she and a co-author, Christina Sickles Merchant, call "interest-based conflict management systems design," which emphasizes involving stakeholders (end-users, customers, labor unions, and others) in the creation of conflict management systems.

JEANNE M. BRETT, STEPHEN B. GOLDBERG & WILLIAM L. URY, DESIGNING SYSTEMS FOR RESOLVING DISPUTES IN ORGANIZATIONS

45 Am. Psychologist 162, 162–63, 165–69 (1990).

Two oil companies, about to engage in a joint venture, agree in advance to try to resolve all disputes in a partnership committee. If direct negotiations fail, senior executives from each company who are otherwise uninvolved in the joint venture will try to resolve the dispute by using a mix of mediation and negotiation procedures. If they cannot, the dispute will be sent to arbitration.

At the Catholic Archdiocese of Chicago, school administrators, looking for a better way to resolve disputes about teacher dismissals and student suspensions, designed a multistep dispute resolution system that requires negotiation between disputing parties, provides advice from a school conflict-management board, and offers the services of a trained mediator.

IBM and Fujitsu, after disputing for years over hundreds of charges that Fujitsu had wrongfully used IBM software, negotiated a system that allowed Fujitsu to examine and use IBM software in exchange for adequate compensation. Future disputes about use will be resolved by a neutral technical expert; future disputes about compensation will be resolved by arbitration.

In these situations managers and the consultants who worked with them designed multiprocedure systems for resolving disputes without resort to litigation. Their dispute systems designs were intuitive, based on their recognition that an ongoing series of disputes was inevitable and that currently available procedures were costly.

In 1980 we found ourselves in a similar situation. We had been asked to consult at Caney Creek (a pseudonym), a coal mine in eastern Kentucky, where conflict had reached monumental proportions. In the prior two years there had been 27 wildcat strikes, management had regularly taken the union to court for breach of the no-strike clause in the contract, and 115 miners had been jailed overnight. There had been bomb threats, sabotage, and theft. Productivity was so low that management was considering closing the mine.

The Union contract provided for a four-step procedure for the resolution of grievances: (a) negotiation between miner and supervisor; (b) negotiation between local mine management and a committee that represented the miners; (c) negotiation between a representative of the company and a district-level representative of the union; and (d) binding arbitration. At Caney Creek, as at other high strike mines, little serious negotiation occurred at the local level, and miners had little confidence that arbitration would resolve disputes satisfactorily. Working with union and management officials, we designed a program of changes intended to encourage miners and managers to resolve their disputes by negotiating the interests underlying their positions rather than focusing on intractable positional differences and then helped them put the program into practice. Afterward, bomb threats ceased, sabotage and theft decreased, and productivity improved. There were no wildcat strikes until the national contract expired, nearly a year later.

At the same time we were working at Caney Creek, we began an experiment in mediating grievances in the coal industry. On the basis of our prior research and Stephen B. Goldberg's own experience as an arbitrator in the industry, Goldberg thought that mediation inserted between the negotiation (third) and arbitration (fourth) steps of the coal industry grievance procedure would be able to uncover and resolve the problems underlying a grievance, problems that seldom surfaced at arbitration where grievances were typically dealt with exclusively on contractual terms. One of Goldberg's arbitration cases illustrates this point. A miner filed a series of grievances claiming that his foreman was doing work that should have been done by union members. Goldberg denied the miner's grievances and only learned later that the miner believed that his frequent assignments to shovel muck from the mine's sump hole were unfair, but because he had no grounds to file a grievance on the job assignment, he sought other contractual grounds on which to file a grievance against his foreman. Arbitration neither resolved the real problem, the miner's job assignments, nor did anything to improve the relationship between the miner and his foreman.

The mediation of grievances experiment, too, was successful and led us to reflect on just what it was from the perspective of the theory of dispute resolution that we and others were trying to do. We were not mediators — that is, we were not helping to settle specific disputes. Rather we were dispute systems designers — helping disputants change the way they handled disputes. Our interventions were not limited to suggesting new procedures, but extended to organizing procedures into a sequence and working with the parties to help them acquire the motivation, negotiation skills, and resources to use their new system successfully.

* * *

Cutting the Costs and Reaping the Benefits of Conflict: Principles of Dispute Systems Design

* * *

Our six principles of dispute system design are guidelines for cutting the costs of conflict and realizing the benefits and are applicable to disputes within and between organizations.

Principle 1: Consultation Before Disputing, Feedback After

Our assumptions that conflict is inevitable in organizations and is often an early warning of need for change imply that organizations should make a significant effort to discuss issues that may cause disputes and to learn from those disputes that do occur. Consultation before disputes erupt can minimize the occurrence of unnecessary disputes. Feedback after a dispute has occurred helps managers take action to prevent reoccurrence. Two examples illustrate these points.

Consultation. When Pacific Bell went through the transition of deregulation, the company and the union formed Common Interest Forums to discuss ways to work together and prevent unnecessary disputes. These forums provided opportunities for management to consult with the union before initiating action. Management was not committed to negotiate over such intended actions but could do so if the union raised unexpected oppositions.

Feedback. Managers and lawyers at some consumer-product companies regularly analyze consumer complaints to determine what changes in product design might reduce the likelihood of similar disputes in the future. In some states consumer mediation agencies keep records of complaints against each merchant. The agency alerts the proper state authorities when repeated complaints are lodged against the same merchant. In this way state action to prevent the merchant from continued unlawful practices can be instituted.

Principle 2: Put the Focus on Interests

Negotiation is almost always available to disputants. The challenge lies in using negotiation to reconcile interests. Framing negotiations as a cooperative rather than competitive exercise facilitates interests-based resolutions, as does an exchange of information about interests, either directly by sharing information or indirectly through the exchange of proposals. Providing negotiation skills training that focuses on techniques for reconciling interests may not only increase skills but may also establish norms about how disputes are to be handled within an organization. Additionally, successful resolution of disputes in simulated negotiations training may generate expectations that interests-based negotiations can be successful and may thus motivate disputants to use interest-based procedures.

* * *

Principle 3: Build in "Loop–Backs" to Negotiations

Sometimes negotiations fail because the parties' perceptions of who is right or who is more powerful are so different that they cannot establish a range in which to negotiate. Information about how rights standards have been applied in other disputes can serve to narrow the gap between the parties' expectations of the outcome of a rights contest and thus make agreement possible.

For interorganizational disputes advisory arbitration (in which a third party provides a nonbinding decision concerning how a case would be resolved in court) may be the simplest procedures for acquiring rights information. Disputants within organizations may use information about corporate norms to help them establish a bargaining range. An example illustrates this point.

Two strategic business units of an organization were negotiating over what one would pay the other in return for the transfer of some magnet technology. When negotiations broke down, the directors of the two units could have turned the dispute over to the corporation's president, but this was risky in absence of information about what the president might do. Instead, they went to the director of another unit, whom they asked about previous transfers of technology between units, in particular, how profits had been shared. Precedent provided a norm to help them define the bargaining range and negotiate a resolution.

There are also loop-back procedures that help avoid power contests. Rarely does a negotiated agreement look so attractive as when the parties are on the verge of a costly power contest. For this reason a cooling-off period, a specified time during which the disputants refrain from a power contest, can be effective. Such periods are mandated by the Taft–Hartley Act and the Railway Labor Act before strikes that threaten to cause a national emergency, but they are just as applicable to small-scale conflict. For example, "sleeping on" a decision or talking it over with an uninvolved third party before taking action are practical rules of thumb that let emotions cool and rationality reassert itself.

* * *

Principle 4: Provide Low–Cost Rights and Power Procedures

In some disputes interests are so opposed that agreement is not possible. Thus, effective dispute resolution systems have low-cost procedures for providing final resolution of disputes on the basis of rights or power. Joint-venture agreements ... often provide for arbitration. Management hierarchy provides the same mechanism for final resolution of disputes within organizations. Voting resolves proxy battles like the one between Texaco and Carl Icahn, the corporate raider.

Principle 5: Arrange Procedures in a Low-to-High Cost Sequence

Our designing principles — consultation before disputing, feedback after — put the focus on interests, provide procedures that loop back to negotiations, and provide low cost rights and power procedures; the principles suggest creating dispute resolution systems in which procedures are arranged in a low-to-high cost sequence. These principles are the building blocks of a dispute resolution system. Table 1 shows a menu of procedures to draw on in designing such a sequence.

Table 1. Menu of Procedures Least Costly to Most Costly

Procedure	Example
Prevention procedures	Consultation
	Feedback
Interest-based procedures	Negotiation
	Mediation

Procedure	Example
"Loop-back" procedures	Rights
	Information procedures
	Advisory arbitration
	Power
	Cooling-off periods
	Third-party intervention
Low-cost rights and power procedures	Rights—arbitration
	Power—voting

Depending on the characteristics of the organization or interorganizational relationship in which the new dispute resolution system is to be embedded, the designer may wish to select more than one procedure from a category. For example, in our grievance-mediation experiment in the coal industry, we added interests-based mediation to a system that already provided for negotiation. Our decision about where to place the mediation in the coal industry's sequence of procedures for resolving grievances was based both on considerations of costs and the effect of the new procedure on the old ones. Mediation at the mine site would not only be prohibitively expensive but also would likely encourage disputants to treat negotiation as pro forma and become dependent on the mediator instead of themselves for resolving disputes. Thus, a sequence of procedures, each only slightly more costly than the previous one, may have the paradoxical effect of encouraging use of higher procedures. The best means to guard against this is to space procedures sufficiently far apart that increased transaction costs are noticeable.

Principle 6: Provide Disputants with the Necessary Negotiation Skills, Resources, and Motivation

Designing procedures according to these principles is not sufficient to reduce the costs of dispute resolution and to realize its benefits. Disputants must have the negotiation skills, the resources, and the motivation to use the system.

Issues in training negotiation skills. A dispute resolution system that meets our costs criteria is one in which a relatively high proportion of disputes are resolved through interest-based procedures. The Achilles heel of our system may be negotiation skills. Negotiators seem to be better at maximizing their own gains (distributive bargaining) than they are at maximizing joint gains (integrative bargaining). It is intuitive to many that when negotiating over a single issue, say the purchase price of a company, the buyer makes a low initial offer, the seller makes high initial demand, and the two make concessions in a reciprocal fashion until they reach agreement or impasse. Negotiators also seem to know intuitively how to compromise by splitting the difference between their positions. What they do not do very well is to find agreements that integrate interests, agreements by which they receive more than they would have had they simply compromised on each issue.

* * *

Overcoming cognitive biases that limit effectiveness of interests-based negotiations may take rather sophisticated negotiation training. Does this mean that dispute systems design is limited to situations in which such training is possible or to people whose attitudes or abilities indicate that they would benefit from training? We do not think so. In many seriously distressed dispute resolution situations, like Caney Creek mine, schools, or even penitentiaries, disputes are normally resolved by power contests, such as strikes or fights. Dispute systems design coupled with training that does little more than expose disputants to interest-based negotiations has been successful in getting disputants to talk their disputes through to resolution instead of fighting them out. Although these resolutions may show signs of cognitive biases, transaction and other costs of disputing have been reduced.

* * *

Motivating disputants to use new low-cost procedures. One of the most difficult issues in dispute system design is motivating the parties to use interests-based procedures, procedures that loop back to negotiations, and low-cost rights or power procedures. Parties often engage in procedures that generate high costs and fail to use procedures that would seem to be less costly and potentially more beneficial. Why? Sometimes interests-based procedures are not available, parties lack negotiation skills to use them successfully, or they do not have the necessary resources. Often, however, the problem is one of motivation.

At Caney Creek mine we were faced with frequent wildcat strikes despite the availability of a contractual grievance procedure that provided for three stages of negotiation and binding arbitration. We found some miners were reluctant to raise grievances with their foreman because of fear of retaliation. Others felt that the grievance procedure deprived them of a voice. Union and company representatives would argue about contractual technicalities far removed from the actual problem as the miner perceived it. Miners were passive observers at arbitration and often would have to wait months for the arbitrator's decision. Any miner, in contrast, could instigate a wildcat strike and receive immediate attention. Even if the strike failed to get the miners what they wanted, their voice would be heard, and they would receive the emotional satisfaction of revenge. In many instances the motivation to strike outweighed the motivation to use the contractual grievance procedures.

We are doubtful that a Caney Creek miner with a grievance weighed the pros and cons of alternative courses of action before striking. However, for a dispute systems designer who is trying to understand why parties are using what seems to be high cost procedures, it is useful to analyze the incentives associated with the use of alternative procedures. Some incentives have to do with expected outcomes, others with characteristics of the procedures themselves.

Incentives associated with outcomes. Disputants prefer procedures that generate outcomes that meet their interests and avoid those in which they believe outcomes are risky. As a result, powerful parties who believe they have been winning with old procedures may be extremely reluctant to cooperate with dispute systems design. It may be that the weaker party will have to champion the dispute system design and the focus on interests. In the long run, however, the stronger party should also prefer a system that preserves its strength but reduces transaction costs and increases satisfaction with outcomes. The costs of imposing one's will can be high. Threats must be backed up by actions from time to time. The weaker party may fail to comply fully with the settlement imposed by power and thereby force the more powerful party to engage in expensive policing. Thus, even for a party who has been winning, a focus on interests, within the bounds set by power, may be more desirable than would appear at first glance.

Incentives associated with process. Empirical research has identified several procedural characteristics that affect parties' procedural preferences. Two of these are outcome control and voice. Evidence from a wide variety of contexts indicates that disputants prefer procedures in which they retain outcome control or final authority over the resolution of the dispute. Furthermore, despite laboratory evidence to the contrary, mediation, an interest-based procedure in which disputants retain outcome control, appears to be quite effective in resolving disputes when parties have an ongoing relationship and even when they do not. Other research suggests that procedures in which disputants simply have a veto, for example, advisory arbitration in which the third party makes recommendation after hearing evidence presented in an adjudicative format, are not particularly successful in resolving disputes, possibly because the parties do not participate in formulating the resolution and, therefore, feel little ownership of it.

Parties also prefer procedures that give them voice, the opportunity to present their side of the dispute or to frame the dispute from their own perspective. However, it is not entirely clear whether it is voice qua voice that is important or whether having voice results in perceptions of greater influence over ultimate decision.

Another aspect of voice that has not received empirical attention is the opportunity to express emotions. It may be that in emotionally charged disputes parties prefer procedures that provide for the controlled expression of emotion and the acknowledgment by the blamed party of the validity of such emotions. An apology, for instance, can often defuse emotion and make problem solving negotiation possible.

* * *

Notes and Questions

1. In their book, GETTING DISPUTES RESOLVED: DESIGNING SYSTEMS TO CUT THE COSTS OF CONFLICT (1988), Professors Ury, Brett, and Goldberg shifted the focus from the resolution of individual disputes to consideration of resolving streams of disputes that arise over time. *See also* ASS'N FOR CONFLICT

RESOLUTION, DESIGNING INTEGRATED CONFLICT MANAGEMENT SYSTEMS; CATHERINE CRONIN-HARRIS, BUILDING ADR INTO THE CORPORATE LAW DEPARTMENT: ADR SYSTEMS DESIGN (1997); DAVID B. LIPSKY, RONALD L. SEEBER & RICHARD D. FINCHER, EMERGING SYSTEMS FOR MANAGING WORKPLACE CONFLICT (2003); KARL A SLAIKEU & RALPH H. HASSON, CONTROLLING THE COSTS OF CONFLICT: HOW TO DESIGN A SYSTEM FOR YOUR ORGANIZATION (1998); FEDERAL ADR PROGRAM MANAGER'S RESOURCE MANUAL, *available at* http://www.usdoj.adr.gov/ manual/ (last visited Feb. 27, 2005).

2. Some court-annexed dispute resolution programs effectively have "loop-backs" to negotiation. Moreover, it is common in litigated cases to "loop-back" to negotiation between (and especially right before) formal legal proceedings. *See* Thomas B. Metzloff, *Resolving Malpractice Disputes: Imaging the Jury's Shadow*, Law & Contemp. Probs., Winter/Spring 1991, at 43, 59 n.54 (finding that many cases settle right before trial).

3. See David O'Connor, *The Design of Self–Supporting Dispute Resolution Programs*, 8 Negotiation J. 85 (1992), for a discussion of the Massachusetts Office of Dispute Resolution's design and development of programs that connect disputing parties with dispute resolvers. At the time the article was written, the Massachusetts Office had developed a dozen such programs. The costs of such programs are covered by fees paid by disputants. For descriptions of the design of several other programs, see *Dispute Systems Design: A Special Section*, 5 Negotiation J. 355 (Stephen B. Goldberg, Jeanne M. Brett & William L. Ury eds., 1989).

4. Cathy A. Costantino and Christina Sickles Merchant advanced the growing field of dispute systems design in their book, DESIGNING CONFLICT MANAGEMENT SYSTEMS (1996). They suggest that an emphasis on the expertise of the outside dispute system designer can result in a failure of the organization itself to study what is wrong with the existing way of processing disputes. *Id.* at 47. They advocate what they call "interest-based conflict management systems design," which emphasizes involving stakeholders (end-users, customers, labor unions, and others) in the creation of conflict management systems. *Id.* at 48, 78. Consider the following description of their comprehensive approach to dispute systems design.

CATHY COSTANTINO, USING INTEREST–BASED TECHNIQUES TO DESIGN CONFLICT MANAGEMENT SYSTEMS
12 Negotiation J. 207, 207–14 (1996).

As practitioners and dispute systems designers, how often have we used our expertise to create a dispute resolution program that we think is effective, accessible, even elegant — only to discover that no one uses it? Our wonderful design for resolving disputes quicker, cheaper, and more amicably may look great on paper, in a sheaf of corporate policies and procedures or in a box on some organizational chart; but unfortunately, it never sees the light of day. It is a field of dreams that becomes a field of despair.

In working with organizations and doing large-scale dispute systems design projects, many of us have discovered that one of the keys to creating "successful" conflict management systems (not merely dispute resolution programs) that are actually *used* by disputants (and that continue to be used) is to involve *all* the stakeholders in the design process. That is, the designer works with both organizational and individual stakeholders to gather information, identify interests, develop options, and build together to create a design that satisfies everyone's needs for fairness, participation, and resolution.

In effect, a conflict management systems designer is really the mediator of a system: facilitating the creation of a conflict management system *with* the stakeholders, not *for* them, and ensuring that the necessary parties are at the design table. By doing so, the designer not only assures that alternative dispute resolution (ADR) methods are made available to disputants, but also that the design process itself is interest-based.

In our recent book (Costantino and Merchant 1996), we argue that if there is an incongruity or dissonance between the dispute resolution method and the design method (that is, when an interest-based method such as mediation is imposed on disputants through a rights-based design such as mandatory mediation), there is greater likelihood that the disputants will resist using the system or may even sabotage it. Based on our works over the years with large-scale organizational designs in both the public and private sector, we have come to the conclusion that integrated, interest-based conflict management systems created through participative, interest-based design processes hold the greatest potential for durable, usable, and effective methods to resolve disputes on a systematic, rather than a case-by-case basis.

This interest-based design model uses principles from organization development, dispute systems design, and ADR, and builds on the work of Ury, Brett, and Goldberg (1988) and their paradigm of interests, rights, and power as methods to resolve disputes. Our "next generation" model of "interest-based conflict management systems design" urges maximum participation by stakeholders in the design process.

But how does a practitioner actually "do" an interest-based design? How does one translate these lofty principles into practice? Unlike the slogan used by Nike in its ubiquitous advertising campaign, we cannot urge practitioners to "just do it." There's far more to it than that.

At least six tasks (not necessarily linear) are necessary to facilitate an effective, interest-based conflict management system: entry and contracting, organizational assessment, design architecture, training and education, implementation and evaluation.

Entry and Contracting

How one enters the system — whether as an internal design specialist or an external consultant — affects the system. Even if the organization chooses not to change its conflict management system as a result of the designer's intervention, the designer's entry into the system has an impact.

For the system to choose to initiate change, there must be both a presenting problem and a perceived opportunity. The presenting problem might include a backlog of cases, negative publicity, or the increased cost of disputes. Perceived opportunities might include reduction of financial exposure, improving public perceptions of the organization, or improving relations with customers, employees or the community.

Once the designer enters the system, the contracting process begins among the designer, leadership, and key stakeholders. Among the questions to be considered are: Which key stakeholders need to be involved in the design process (end-users, customers, unions)? Is there a commitment that leadership will allow these stakeholders to participate in the process? Do the stakeholders understand the basic change principles, including the possibility that there may be no need for change? Will the parties accept evaluation and feedback throughout the design process? Are they willing to serve as partners with one another in collaborative problem identification and resolution? Is there agreement as to who (leadership, committee, collective consensus) will make the final decision about revising the conflict management system?

During the entry/contracting process, the designer serves several roles: *catalyst* for triggering change within the system without becoming part of the reaction; educator to teach the organization and its stakeholders about conflict and change; *facilitator* in assisting the system to work together to identify interests and create options; *translator* to interpret various interests and options to other parts of the system; and *agent of reality*, to identify those areas where change may be difficult, where resistance can be expected, or where there may be constraints which inhibit change.

At this stage of the process, several traps and pitfalls may ensnare the designer. These dangers include: *enabling*, which involves the organization and its stakeholders becoming dependent upon the designer for approval, feedback and options rather than relying on themselves; *being the bad guy*, or management using the designer as the messenger to deliver "bad news" and-or to tell the other stakeholders what is not possible and what is not negotiable; *playing the savior*, a situation where the designer believes he or she is indispensable and can control the ultimate success or failure of the design; and *letting it fail*, where the designer resists the temptation to "fix" the system or to force it to change.

Organizational Assessment

This stage is often skipped over by designers who imprudently want to jump right into the "fun" part of the process — inventing options and solutions. However, organizational assessment, similar to gathering information in a mediation, is critical not only because it helps determine what is necessary for the intervention, but also because it establishes the goals of any new or revised system so they can be evaluated.

The designer needs to assess the *organization* (its culture, customers and attitude towards conflict); the *disputes* (types, numbers, nature and cost); the *resolution methods* (prevention, use of formal or informal techniques, and who decides which method to use); and the *results* (cost, durability, satisfaction and effect on the organization and its stakeholders). A solid organizational assessment is accomplished through the use of such techniques as surveys, interviews and focus groups (the designer must be able to guarantee a safe environment for stakeholders to disclose information, without fear of reprisal). The information gathered from the assessment is then collated and presented to the responsible decision maker(s), who can either choose to revise the system or maintain the status quo.

Design Architecture

Once a decision has been made to revise the conflict management system, design architecture looks at the *whether*, *when* and *how* of the new system. Whereas entry and contracting and organizational assessment involve the big picture, or "macro" aspects of the design, design architecture focuses on the disputes themselves and methods of resolution — the "micro" aspects of managing conflict. In general, system designers should follow six principles of design architecture:

Whether to Use ADR:

- Principle 1: *Develop guidelines for whether ADR is appropriate.* Although ADR is an acronym for alternative dispute resolution, we prefer to think of it as "appropriate dispute resolution." Is ADR appropriate for this type of conflict, and if so, what type of ADR? The method must be congruent with the culture of the organization, further the organizational goals and mission, and have some benefit for the disputants.

- Principle 2: *Tailor the ADR process to the particular problem.* Aside from the organizational fit, there must also be a process fit: The ADR method should meet the interests of the particular dispute and the particular disputants. For example, choosing mediation when, in fact, the nuances of the particular case and the interests of the disputants indicate that neutral fact-finding would be more appropriate can lead to a conclusion that ADR is not effective when the mediation is not effective. In actuality, it may be that ADR was appropriate, but mediation was not. The appropriate process will depends on a variety of factors, including the goals of the disputants, their tolerance for risk and the relationship of the parties.

When to Use ADR:

- Principle 3: *Build in preventative methods of ADR.* As practitioners, we often forget that preventive ADR methods such as partnering, joint problem solving, and negotiated rulemaking can be effective. It may be useful for the designer to think of developing a range of preventative methods in a variety of contexts, such as the individual, the group, the organization, and the community, and within the global environment. As organizations continue to adopt "best practices" in their day-to-day operations and relationships — to compete, to control costs and to maximize resources — dispute prevention becomes increasingly important.

- Principle 4: *Make sure that disputants have the necessary knowledge and skills to choose and use ADR.* For example, labor and management need to know how to engage in interest-identification processes, brainstorming and consensus decision making in order to use interest-based negotiation. A dissatisfied customer needs to know what mediation is (and what it is not) before deciding to choose it. Disputants need to know not only what the process is, but also how to participate in it effectively. Much of this can be taught and modeled in appropriate training and educational sessions.

How to Use ADR:

- Principle 5: *Create ADR systems that are simple to use and easy to access, and that resolve disputes early, at the lowest organizational level, with the least bureaucracy.* For disputants to choose ADR, it must be easier to use, faster, and more effective than the current dispute resolution method. As practitioners know, the introduction of new processes in organizations tends to generate an almost irresistible tendency to over-control. To make ADR difficult to use and impossible to access, a design architect should follow this recipe: Require multiple levels of approval, increase the bureaucratic paperwork requirements as the process proceeds, make it difficult to get approval to use ADR by having only one or two people who can make the decision, do not give line or staff personnel the authority to commit to use ADR or to a settlement, send messages that the organization does not support ADR, that it is "risky" behavior. Voila — you have created a system that is ready to boil over!

- Principle 6: *Allow disputants to retain maximum control over choice of ADR method and selection of neutral whenever possible.* Not surprisingly, practitioners have found that disputants are likely to be more resistant to an ADR process if they are not involved in selecting it, and even more resistant if they have little or no voice in determining who the neutral will be. When an organization imposes a certain resolution method on disputants, practitioners have discovered that disputants are somewhat less resistant as long as they retain a degree of control over the selection of the neutral. *   *   *

Training and Education

Although the terms are used interchangeably, training and education are not the same. ADR education is a dynamic, ongoing process of increasing awareness about conflict, responses to it, and choices about conflict management. ADR training is more skills-based and competency-based. Several myths about ADR training and education are rife in organizations today, including the following.

All stakeholders need identical ADR training and education. There is a misrepresentation that all stakeholders (including senior and midlevel management) need to be skills-trained as mediators or neutrals of some type. The result is that organizations are often spending exorbitant amounts of money training personnel as mediators, when these people will be overseeing ADR programs, selecting cases for ADR or sitting at the table during ADR proceedings as a user/consumer. Our experience has shown that, if people are trained in skills that they have little chance to use, they become frustrated and reluctant to use the system at all.

ADR training and education is best conducted by outside ADR experts and consultants. Not only is this myth expensive, it can also be a form of rights-based design. That is, the outside vendors decide what kind of training and education is best for the organization, and decide what types of "problems" or "role plays" will be used. As a result, the training strategy is often inappropriate or irrelevant for the particular organization. This is particularly true where vendors are using "off-the-shelf" training modules. We have found it helpful to use team teaching and partnering arrangements that pair an outside consultant with a stakeholder or organizational representative, not just to design the training, but to actually teach it. The consultant provides the architectural and technical part of the training (subject matter and technique) and the stakeholder adds the organizational and cultural components (process and context). It is also useful to design organization-specific training problems similar to the types that participants will actually face.

Only organizational stakeholders should be trained and educated. Those who are designing ADR training and education often forget that organizational stakeholders are only half the equation: To engage in ADR approaches, one needs *all* the disputants engaged, educated and in some cases trained. Many will raise their eyebrows at this suggestion: Why train and educate one's "opponents"? The answer is simple: Without bilateral (and ideally joint) training and education, the program's projected timed efficiencies, cost savings, enhancement of satisfaction levels, and durability of results are unlikely to become reality.

Once they are trained and educated, stakeholders will use ADR. Just because they have the skill and knowledge to use the system does not mean that stakeholders will do so. If you build it, it is not necessarily true that they will come; they must have a reason to come. We are constantly amazed at the number of organizations that assume that once they provide ADR training and education, people will somehow magically begin to use ADR. In addition, disputants must be able to figure out that use of the system offers rewards and incentives to them — they must know the answers to the "What's–In–It–For–Me?" questions.

Once these myths are dispelled, designers can recommend one or more of five types of ADR training and education:

Marketing Efforts. The purpose here is to get "buy-in" for ADR from stakeholders and managers. Typically, this education is limited to one or two hours, and includes examples and "success" stories.

Awareness education. Here, the purpose is to educate stakeholders about what ADR is, how it is used in the particular organizational setting, and guidelines for using ADR. We have found that half-day sessions with an interactive component work well.

Conflict management and communication training. This type of training is generic and not geared towards a particular form of ADR. The purpose is to introduce skills that can be used in day-to-day life, or serve as the foundation for additional ADR training. We believe such training is most effective if it is no more than one day in length and interactive.

Consumer/User training. Aimed at the stakeholders who will actually be using ADR procedures, this training targets those who will be sitting at the table negotiating or participating in an ADR proceeding. It offers practical guidance on such areas as: how to select a neutral, how to identify interests, and how to develop strategies and options. We believe that it is critical for students to participate in a mock ADR proceeding; such training typically involves a full day, and no more than two.

Training of third-party neutrals. This intensive skills training is targeted only for those who will actually serve as neutrals: mediators, arbitrator, evaluators. It is usually of longer duration (no less than three days), more intensive and more interactive, and limited in size (ideally no more than 12 students per instructor).

Implementation

Starting small and thinking big can be useful at this stage of the design process. Starting with a small, time-limited, clearly defined pilot project helps to determine the willingness of stakeholders to change, makes it safer for individuals in the old system to experiment with new behaviors and rewards, and tests the suitability of the design to see whether it fits the organization. In addition, a pilot effort can uncover unknown costs, expectations, and attitudes that may impede adoption of the new system. In setting up this kind of small-scale experiment, it is useful to:

- select individuals to be responsible for the administration of the pilot;

- look to other sources for experience, expertise, and success stories;

- identify stakeholders who will be affected by the pilot;

- choose a pilot linked to organizational goals; and

- select the site of the pilot project with success in mind.

Once the experimental effort has been completed and evaluated, we recommend the "4–T Approach" to expand the pilot to the full organization: Tout the Pilot (promote publicity and results); Test the Pilot (do not assume that because it worked in one part of the organization it will necessarily work in another setting); Tailor the Pilot (reassess and make sure that the disputes in the expanded arena are appropriate for ADR, and that the appropriate method of ADR is chosen); and Team the Effort (use an ADR team, task force, or steering committee).

Evaluation

A common belief these days is that ADR is "better." The obvious questions are: Better at what, and if it is better how do you know? There are several components to evaluating a conflict management system, a task that should take place throughout the life of the design process, rather than being just tacked on at the end. These include: clarify goals, determine evaluation baseline data, chart progress towards goals, modify the system in response to feedback, measure the results, reclarify the goals, and start the evaluation cycle again. Two distinct measurements can be the focus of ADR evaluation:

ADR's effectiveness and impact. In this case, the evaluation deals with the success or failure of the ADR process: its efficiency (change in costs and time); effectiveness (nature of outcomes, durability of resolutions; effect on organizational environment); and satisfaction levels of the system's users (with process, relationships and outcomes).

ADR program administration and operation. This kind of evaluation gauges the merits of the particular ADR programs: its administration/operation (structures and procedures, guidelines and standards, lines of responsibility, sufficiency of resources and coordination of relationships); service delivery (access to system, procedures in use, and selection of cases); and program quality (training and education, selection of neutrals, and competence of neutrals).

In Conclusion

When these six tasks are combined with an interest-based design process that actively involves stakeholders through openness, participation and feedback, the likelihood of a durable, effective conflict management system increases.

Perhaps as designers we *can* plant a field of dreams and not a field of despair in our work and in the processes we help to create, if we apply the very interest-based principles that we have been espousing for so long. Perhaps it is time that as designers we become personally congruent and "walk-the-walk" of interest-based processes in our design work.

Notes and Questions

1. Importantly, the sequence that Costantino describes includes more than just the "off-the shelf" design of a dispute resolution system that is provided by a consultant. Instead, she describes a process that is attuned to the differences among organizations, that involves the participants in creating the new system, that recognizes and addresses barriers to the adoption of a new system, and that highlights the need for on-going assessment and evaluation. Recall the distinction between client bias (emphasizing a concern for the client's idiosyncratic situation) and process bias (emphasizing a preference for a particular method of dispute resolution) described in Chapter I, beginning at page 61. How do the interest-based dispute system design processes that Costantino advocates seem to resolve this distinction? *See* James E. Westbrook, *The Problems with Process Bias*, 1989 J. Disp. Resol. 309.

2. In practice, the design processes that Costantino describes — entry and contracting, organizational assessment, design architecture, training and education, implementation, and evaluation — may unfold in a non-linear or recursive fashion. For example, participants may need to be informed about the design method early in the process, may need to be educated about conflict and dispute resolution on an on-going basis, and may need to be trained to use the system once it is developed. Similarly, consideration of how the new system will be evaluated should start at the beginning of the process as the old system is assessed, processes for data collection are incorporated in the design of the system, and baseline data is collected.

3. How do the principles of design architecture described by Costantino compare to the principles of dispute systems design articulated in the excerpt by Brett, Goldberg, and Ury? How might the differences in their approaches to dispute systems design influence their views of the role of the dispute systems designer? Which approach would you be more likely to use?

4. When designing a system for resolving disputes, the designer and the stakeholders should consider all aspects of the system including:

- the type(s) of dispute resolution processes that are appropriate for the organization

- the progression of dispute resolution processes that will be employed

- the types of cases that will be eligible and how they will be selected

- how the neutrals will be selected, trained, and paid

- what parties will have a role and what those roles will be

- what resources are available

- how participants will be informed about and trained to use the system

- whether the program will be voluntary or mandatory

- how the system will be evaluated.

These factors can be used both for assessing the current system for resolving disputes and for designing and evaluating any new system that is implemented. In considering these design elements, the designers and stakeholders ought to consider how the system is likely to affect the cognitive, emotional, and behavioral aspects of conflict and its resolution as described in Chapter I, beginning at page 54.

5.   Management guru Peter F. Drucker and others have argued that the fundamental nature of the American workplace has changed in the last quarter of a century, and in a way that has important implications for dispute resolution systems within these organizations. *See* Peter Drucker, *The New Society of Organizations*, Harv. Bus. Rev., Sept./Oct. 1992, at 95, 100; Katherine Van Wezel Stone, *Dispute Resolution in the Boundaryless Workplace*, 16 Ohio St. J. on Disp. Resol. 467, 471–79 (2001). In this view, the "old" workplace could be characterized by fixed, clearly defined jobs and career paths, job security in exchange for corporate loyalty, and hierarchical command. Katherine Van Wezel Stone, *The New Psychological Contract: Implications for the Changing Workplace for Labor and Employment Law*, 48 UCLA L. Rev. 519, 534 (2001). The "new" workplace, however, is more of a partnership, with employers and employees seen as stakeholders sharing opportunities for the satisfaction of mutual interests, employees enjoying much greater mobility outside of the firm, and no expectation of long-term employment by either labor or management. *Id.* at 568–72. Professor Reuben argues that the values that support the new workplace are consistent with many deeply rooted democratic values, including self-determination, participation in governance, and equality and due process in treatment. Richard C. Reuben, *Democracy and Dispute Resolution: Systems Design and the New Workplace,* 10 Harv. Negot. L. Rev. 11 (Spring 2005). Reuben contends that mediation, nonbinding arbitration, and other ADR methods further these principles by expanding the range of options available for dispute resolution, by allowing for integrative results, and by contributing to the creation of more productive, more effective, and more stable workplace environments. Id at 39–66. Do you agree? Think of your own work history.

6.   Both the excerpt by Brett, Goldberg, and Ury and the excerpt by Costantino note the importance of providing incentives to encourage people to use the system. Social psychologist Kurt Lewin has described individuals as existing within a force field, subject to a variety of pressures on their behavior. He argues that behavioral change should be considered in this context. As Costantino and Merchant explain:

> As most practitioners have frequently witnessed, the status quo of any system is the result of forces driving change in opposition to forces restraining change. This balanced driving/restraining equation describes a system in its steady state at any point in time. Lewin suggested that the system's status quo can be changed by one of three methods: (1) increasing the forces driving change, (2) reducing the forces restraining change, or (3) converting restraining forces into driving forces. Common use of force field analysis in [organizational development] change efforts has revealed that focusing on the second method — reducing the forces that restrain change — often yields faster and more effective results than any other. Force field analysis is particularly useful in designing conflict management systems because it is often a series of specific restraints that operate to prevent or inhibit those with a dispute from using dispute resolution procedures. For example, in an organization where the chief dispute resolution mechanism is litigation, a manager's decision to pursue something other than litigation, perhaps some form

of alternative dispute resolution (ADR), may be most strongly influenced by the number of additional "permission memos" that have to be written to justify ADR use (a restraining force). This restraining force may have a greater impact on an employee deciding whether to recommend ADR than possible recognition in the company newsletter for saving litigation costs (a driving force).

CATHY A. CONSTANTINO & CHRISTINA SICKLES MERCHANT, DESIGNING CONFLICT MANAGEMENT SYSTEMS 28–29 (1996). *See also* KURT LEWIN, FIELD THEORY IN SOCIAL SCIENCE (1951).

7. In the same spirit as Costantino and Merchant, Professor John Lande has recommended that courts use principles of dispute resolution systems design to develop rules and procedures to address the problem of bad faith in mediation. John Lande, *Using Dispute Systems Design Methods to Promote Good–Faith Participation in Court–Connected Mediation Programs*, 50 UCLA L. Rev. 69 (2002).

b. Self-Determination in Systems Design

Central to Costantino and Merchant's approach to dispute systems design is the notion of disputant self-determination. Chapter IV described the importance of disputant self-determination in mediation. Self-determination at the level of designing the system for resolving disputes is similar but distinct, as Professor Lisa Bingham explains below.

LISA B. BINGHAM, SELF–DETERMINATION IN DISPUTE SYSTEM DESIGN AND EMPLOYMENT ARBITRATION

56 U. Miami L. Rev. 873, 879–80, 881–86 (2002).

There is an issue underlying these efforts, a current of tension in the discussions, that concerns one of the core values underlying ADR: disputant self-determination. Proponents of alternative or appropriate dispute resolution often argue its chief value is disputant control over the process. This notion of disputant control or self-determination is distinct from legal consent. It is not the same concept as voluntary consent for purposes of imputing agreement to an adhesive arbitration clause. Instead, self-determination includes procedural justice notions of a disputant's perceptions of control and fairness. I argue here that dispute systems vary across two separate dimensions of disputant self-determination. Those dimensions are disputant self-determination in the design of the system as a whole, and disputant self-determination within a given case using a specific dispute resolution process provided by the overall system design. Self-determination in dispute system design includes making choices regarding what cases are subject to the process, which process or processes in sequence are available (mediation, early neutral evaluation, and binding arbitration, for example), what due process rules apply, and other structural choices for setting up a private justice system. Self-determination at the case level includes whether the process results in a voluntary, negotiated settlement agreement or an imposed binding third party decision. It includes self-determination as to process and outcome within a given dispute involving a single set of parties. Most discussions of self-determination in dispute resolution tend to ignore the system design level, or assume that self-determination is present, or conflate the two levels.

* * *

I. SELF-DETERMINATION WITHIN A SINGLE CASE CONTRASTED WITH SELF-DETERMINATION IN DISPUTE SYSTEM DESIGN

The Model Standards of Conduct for Mediators provide in several sections for party "self-determination." They suggest that mediation is based on the principle of self-determination, that mediators must have qualifications necessary to satisfy the reasonable expectations of the parties, that mediators must conduct the process in a manner consistent with party self-determination, and that they have a duty to improve the practice of mediation. These standards do not define self-determination, nor do they distinguish between self-determination at the case level and self-determination in system design. I use self-determination at the case level to refer to a single set of disputing parties in conflict within a given dispute resolution process, for example, a single mediation case or a single arbitration case. Self-determination at this level refers to the parties' experience of control over both process and outcome in a single dispute.

Self-determination in dispute system design refers to control over the structure of a process or set of processes to handle a series of disputes. There is an established and growing body of literature on dispute system design that focuses primarily on a dispute resolution program within an organization, not the courts. Most of these discussions assume that the sponsoring company, organization, or agency will make the ultimate choices about the final dispute system design. Since the leading professional organizations approved Model Ethical Standards at a time when courts had already implemented mandatory mediation programs, it is reasonable to conclude that its drafters contemplated self-determination as to outcome at the individual case level. In mandatory court-annexed programs, legislatures and courts effectively make dispute system design choices for the parties before the parties use mediation for a given case. The legislatures authorized courts to mandate mediation and the courts are exercising that power.

* * *

Relatively little commentary discusses self-determination in the area of dispute system design. Increasingly, commentators advocate requiring that counsel inform clients of alternative or appropriate dispute resolution generally, and the different kinds of processes in particular. This provides an opportunity for party self-determination in dispute system design, if only the design of a process for a single case. Scholars advocate fully informed consent by clients; this requires that lawyers and their clients understand the difference between mediation and arbitration, and the differences among various models of mediation. However, there is often an unstated assumption that the client is represented by counsel and has a choice in how to design an ADR process for the case. Many disputants act pro se. The most controversial new systems give employee or consumer disputants no choices in ADR system design and may even prohibit representation by counsel.

Table 1. Self–Determination at the Case Level
and in Dispute System Design.

Self–Determination in System Design	Self–Determination in Individual Case	
	Parties Control Outcome	Third Party Controls Outcome
Both/All Parties	A. Ad hoc mediation Ad hoc non-binding evaluative processes	D. Ad hoc arbitration Labor arbitration Negotiated binding processes
One Party	B. Mandatory or voluntary mediation Mandatory or voluntary non-binding processes	E. Adhesive binding arbitration
Third Party	C. Court-annexed mediation or non-binding processes (mandatory or voluntary) Public sector labor mediation	F. Court or administrative adjudication Legislated binding arbitration

In parallel to this commentary is the increasingly heated discussion among arbitration scholars regarding the legitimacy of adhesive arbitration clauses, or "mandatory arbitration." The current state of the law is that the stronger contracting party may require the weaker contracting party to participate in arbitration of any disputes arising out of the contract through an adhesive clause, provided that clause meets the standards for enforcing a contract in that jurisdiction. These standards include defenses such as duress, unconscionability, fraud, and, to a limited extent, public policy. In this context, if the weaker party proceeds with the economic relationship (employment, health care treatment, purchase of consumer goods and services), the weaker party is deemed to have consented to the clause. The entire economic relationship is presented as a take it or leave it offer; dispute system design is part of this larger whole. This is consent as a legal concept. A variety of disgruntled would-be litigants would assert forcefully that it is not voluntary consent or self-determination as a subjective, psychological concept. In this context, it is clear that the weaker party and its counsel have no control over dispute system design — at least that is the case after the parties have entered into the economic relationship. The economically more powerful party has already made all the design choices in adopting the arbitration plan. Some scholars argue that arbitration in these contexts should not be called appropriate or alternative dispute resolution at all. Professor Fiss's argument against settlement is most forceful here because the disputants who might be motivated to make new law or set precedent are contractually disabled from doing so.

This debate illustrates the tension between self-determination as an underlying core value of ADR and the notion of legal consent as a historical reality. Distinguishing between self-determination at the case level and self-determination in system design can foster a more productive discussion of this tension. Table 1 is an effort to illustrate the different dimensions of self-determination in ADR.

* * *

Notes and Questions

1. Professor Bingham distinguishes between self-determination at the system design level and at the case level. At the case level, she combines self-determination as to process and outcome. In an article excerpted in Chapter IV at page 423, Professor Leonard Riskin proposed grids to address three categories of decision making in mediation: substantive, procedural, and meta-procedural. Leonard L. Riskin, *Decisionmaking in Mediation: The New Old Grid and the New New Grid System*, 79 Notre Dame L. Rev. 1 (2003). His "new new grid system" emphasizes that a mediation participant can exercise quite different degrees of influence in each category of decision making. That system also makes it clear that many procedural decisions — which could be called dispute resolution design decisions — can be made moment to moment during a mediation.

2. Dispute systems can be designed for individual organizations, courts, agencies, or even countries. Consider the following: "Imagine a society emerging from some sort of armed conflict. Though a peace agreement has been negotiated to halt the violence, the more significant challenge is to design a set of institutions that will allow this society to manage peacefully the ongoing conflicts about the shape of political, economic, and social life into the future. The commission charged with designing this set of political institutions quickly realizes that although these institutions must achieve several goals, their principal purpose is to create a permanent institutional capacity for collective problem solving. They turn to the dispute resolution literature to seek advice on the details of institutional design: how should the institutions be structured, who should the members be, what processes should be centralized, how should decisions be made, how should issue areas be disaggregated and assigned? Can they use the fruits of dispute resolution literature to 'hardwire' the institution in ways that will maximize its chances for peacefully resolving disputes?" Khalil Z. Shariff, *Designing Institutions to Manage Conflict: Principles for the Problem Solving Organization*, 8 Harv. Negot. L. Rev. 133 (2003).

2. EVALUATING DISPUTE RESOLUTION SYSTEMS

Essential to any evolving system is a process of evaluation to determine how the system is functioning. Questions that might be addressed by evaluation include:

- How is the system functioning?
- What needs is it meeting?
- What needs is it failing to meet?
- Has the program been implemented as intended?
- How is the program operating?
- What effects is the program having?
- Under what circumstances and for which types of cases, does the program have these effects?
- What unintended effects are occurring?
- How satisfied are participants?
- Is the program operating efficiently?

Deborah Hensler has noted: "As legislatures and courts continue to expand mandates for ADR in federal and state courts, the need to know what in fact the ADR revolution has wrought for good or ill becomes more pressing. The urge to protect the infant innovation from too careful scrutiny needs to give way to hard assessment of potential gains and losses from the new vision of legal dispute resolution." Deborah Hensler, *A Research Agenda: What We Need to Know about Court–Connected ADR*, Disp. Resol. Mag., Fall 1999, at 15.

a.   The Process of Evaluation

In the following excerpt, Donna Stienstra, a senior analyst for the Federal Judicial Center, the research arm of the federal judiciary, describes the process of evaluation. The following notes and questions explore the importance of the evaluation function.

DONNA STIENSTRA, EVALUATING AND MONITORING ADR PROCEDURES
FJC Directions, Dec. 1994, at 24, 24–25.

Courts considering for the first time whether to adopt an alternative dispute resolution procedure are often frustrated by a lack of good information about whether ADR "works." Courts that already have ADR programs in place often face a different frustration — lack of information about whether their particular ADR procedure is working. In addition, policy makers who wish to consider broad policy questions related to ADR often lack adequate empirical information to assist their deliberations. In response to these problems, individual courts and others have begun to consider how to collect more and better information about how ADR works and what its effects are.

Recognizing the need for good information is, of course, far easier than collecting it. To carry out a sound and reliable data-collection project requires careful planning at the outset and close attention throughout. This may seem a daunting task to courts whose resources are already taxed. Yet the reward for carefully planned evaluations can be a wealth of information useful not only to the individual court undertaking the evaluation but also to others who need to know more about the effects of ADR.

How, then, can a court collect useful information about its ADR procedures? It may be helpful to think about this process as having three principal tasks: identifying the appropriate data, preparing the data collection methods, such as questionnaires, and establishing the evaluation design, or the road map for collecting the data.

Identifying the appropriate data

While it is tempting, when conducting an evaluation, to ask for information on many aspects of the litigation process, an evaluation can quickly go off track if a court does not have a good idea of what it needs to know. To narrow the possible choices — and to make certain that all necessary information is obtained — a court should look to the nature and purpose of its ADR program. What is it supposed to accomplish for the court? What is it supposed to do for the litigants? For example, if the purpose of a court's mediation program is to save litigant costs, time to disposition — though interesting — is the wrong information to use when assessing the program's impact. The more explicit a court has been at the outset in defining the purpose of its ADR program, the more guidance it will provide to those who have to determine whether the program is working.

Equally important, a court should consider very carefully the different dimensions of the effects it wants to measure. Litigant costs, for instance, may be thought of solely as the number of dollars spent on fees and other legal expenses, but this narrow focus excludes other costs, such as absence from work or emotional toll of the litigation process, that may [be] of equal significance to litigants. Similarly, in programs that seek to reduce litigation delay, a court must determine whether it needs to measure the actual number of hours spent (by judges, attorneys, or whomever) or the time that elapses between stages of a case (e.g., from filing to disposition).

Preparing the data collection methods

Once a court has determined what to measure, it may find that several different types of data collection methods are needed. Some ADR effects, such as time to disposition, can be evaluated though routinely collected caseload statistics, but others may best be evaluated by questionnaires or interviews that ask those involved in the ADR procedure how they think it's working. Still other effects, such as delay, may best be measured through both methods. Some concepts — quality of justice, for instance — simply may not be measurable at all, at least not by standard data collection methods.

Designing the data collection instruments themselves is another important aspect of an evaluation. Questionnaires are one of the most frequently used methods because they are inexpensive relative to the amount of information obtained, but they present many pitfalls and should be used carefully. They are generally used when one wants to generalize about a population — for example, attorneys who litigate in the district — and such generalization is risky if response rates are low or questions are imprecise. (To feel more confident of questionnaire results, courts should consider working with someone trained in designing questionnaires who can help craft questions.)

Courts should not overlook the usefulness of other methods, such as focus groups, which are helpful when generalization is not needed, or collecting information from dockets. Finally, it is very important to decide on data collection methods early, even as the ADR procedure is designed, so that important information is not lost. Some evaluations may require information that is not routinely collected, such as the identity of the mediator or arbitrator or the names and addresses of litigants with cases in mediation, and new docketing procedures may have to be developed to record such data.

Establishing the evaluation design

Although data collection tools are important, they are more useful if guided by an overall evaluation design that tells court personnel when and how to use them. Evaluations of new programs are generally of two types: evaluation of program *implementation* and evaluation of program *effects*. To evaluate implementation, a court would look at how its program is used. Do judges and parties submit cases to the procedure, or is it ignored? If other litigation activities are to be tolled, does this in fact happen? For this type of evaluation, the court might examine the dockets in a sample of cases to identify just what happens in these cases.

If a court can assume that successful implementation — that is, faithful use — necessarily leads to the desired effects, evaluation of program implementation may be sufficient. But if this assumption cannot be made, or if the court wants to understand whether the program has other unanticipated effects, it will need to conduct an evaluation of effects as well. Ascertaining what effects were caused by the program or procedure necessarily requires a basis for comparison. For instance, data showing that cases in the program take an average of nine months from filing to disposition do not reveal whether the program has increased or decreased the disposition time — or had an effect on it at all. What is needed is some idea of what these cases' average time to disposition would have been absent the program.

The best design for making such a determination is to compare a group of cases not subject to the program, a "comparison" or "control" group, with a group of cases subject to the program, an "experimental" group. In this design, every case eligible for the ADR program is randomly assigned to one or the other of these two groups. This means all cases are exposed to the same conditions *except for* the ADR program, which is applied only to the experimental cases. If after following this procedure the court finds a difference between the two groups on some measure — average disposition time, for example — it can infer the program had an effect. (For guidance on the ethical considerations of using experimental designs in court settings, *see Experimentation in the Law: Report of the Federal Judicial Center Advisory Committee on Experimentation in the Law* (1981), available on WESTLAW as well as from the Center.)

A number of courts have used random assignment to determine the effectiveness of their ADR procedures, and any court planning an evaluation should at least consider using this design. An assessment that relies on some other kind of comparison group — say, a comparison of cases terminated before the programs began with cases terminated after going through the program — may reflect influences other than those of the program. For instance, there might be a change over time in the type of case filed or a difference in the economic conditions in which they were litigated. Random assignment accounts for those influences and therefore permits more powerful conclusions about the causal effect of an ADR program.

While comparisons are critical for making causal inferences, they are reliable only if apples are compared with apples. A common error is to compare cases selected for a program to cases not selected, where the selection relied on judicial or staff discretion rather than random assignment. For example, when judges are called on to select suitable cases for an arbitration program, they will chose cases they believe are amenable to arbitration and leave cases they consider less suitable to be resolved by other means. Comparing these two groups of cases, which are clearly different, will not give reliable conclusions about the effect of arbitration.

One final point: Decisions about overall evaluation design and data collection methods are linked, and neither should be made without considering the other. For example, asking attorneys for their subjective assessments of cost savings is an unreliable measure of impact of an ADR program on litigation costs. The quality of these subjective evaluations can be enhanced, however, by combining random assignments of cases with an objective question to all attorneys about litigation costs: "What were the fees and costs for this case?" By comparing the answers of attorneys whose cases were and were not subject to the ADR program, the court would obtain a far better measure of the program's impact on costs than by addressing subjective questions only to the attorneys subject to the program.

In undertaking evaluations of their ADR programs, courts should keep in mind that just as these programs have their own unique context and purposes, so may their evaluation approaches differ from others. Further, courts may find it helpful to use experts from sources like the [Federal Judicial] Center's Research Division or local colleges and universities. Whatever the approach used, ensuring quality dispute resolution services requires that those adopting ADR understand the effects of their programs. This information, when shared with others, will also help build a body of knowledge that will enable us all to assess the costs and benefits of ADR for the courts and litigants.

Notes and Questions

1.   Evaluative research is useful in order to find out what is actually going on in a program, how the parties understand and experience the processes, what the effects of a process are, which processes participants prefer, and so on. *See* EMIL J. POSAVAC & RAYMOND G. CAREY, PROGRAM EVALUATION: METHODS AND CASE STUDIES (6th ed. 2002).

2.   Systematic evaluation is particularly important given the limits of our casual observation of the world. Much of human intuition and perception is unconscious, unsystematic, and limited by our capacities to perceive, pay attention to, and remember what happened. This can, on occasion, lead us to reach incorrect conclusions. Thus, if we think that a dispute resolution process is effective, it is likely that our casual observation of the process will confirm our belief. Systematic evaluation allows us to attempt to more objectively explore those beliefs. *See generally* THOMAS GILOVICH, HOW WE KNOW WHAT ISN'T SO (1991); HEURISTICS AND BIASES: THE PSYCHOLOGY OF INTUITIVE JUDGMENT (Thomas Gilovich, Dale Griffin & Daniel Kahneman eds., 2002).

3.   Importantly, psychological research suggests that we are prone to perceiving relationships where none exist, a phenomenon referred to as illusory correlation:

> Imagine yourself participating in a pioneering study of how people associate events. Psychologists William Ward and Herbert Jenkins show you the results of a hypothetical fifty-day cloud seeding experiment. They tell you for each day whether clouds were seeded and whether it rained. The information is a random mix: sometimes it rained after seeding, sometimes not. If you *believe* that cloud seeding works, might you be more likely to notice and recall days with both seeding and rain? In Ward and Jenkins' experiment, and in many others since, people have become convinced that they really see precisely what they expected. An overstated Chinese proverb has the idea: "Two-thirds of what we see is behind our eyes."

> "Illusory correlations" — perceiving relationships where none exist — help explain many a superstition, such as the presumption that more babies are born when the moon is full or that infertile couples who adopt are more likely to conceive. Salient coincidences, such as those who conceive after adopting, capture our attention. We focus on them and are less likely to notice what's equally relevant to assessing correlations — those who adopt and never conceive, those who conceive without adopting, and those who neither adopt nor conceive. Only when given all this information can we discern whether parents who adopt have elevated conception rates.

> Such illusory intuitions help explain why for so many years people believed (as many still do) that sugar made children hyperactive, that cell phones caused brain cancer, that getting cold and wet caused colds

and that weather changes trigger arthritis pain. Physician Donald Redelmeier, working with Amos Tversky, followed eighteen arthritis patients for fifteen months. The research recorded their subjects' pain reports, as well as each day's temperature, humidity, and barometric pressure. Despite the patients' beliefs, the weather was uncorrelated with their discomfort, either on the same day or up to two days earlier or later. Shown columns of random numbers labeled "arthritis pain" and "barometric pressure," even college students saw an illusory correlation. We are, it seems, eager to detect patterns, even when they're not there.

* * *

Shortly after I wrote this, a journalist called, seeking help with a story on why so many famous people (Bill Clinton, Hillary Clinton, Jimmy Carter) have embarrassing brothers. Do they? I responded. Or is it our attention is just drawn to salient conjunctions of famous people and boorish brothers? Is boorishness less frequent among men with unfamous siblings, or just less memorable? If we easily deceive ourselves by intuitively seeing what is not there, the remedy is simple: Show me the evidence. Gather and present the comparison data.

DAVID G. MEYERS, INTUITION: ITS POWERS AND PERILS 113–14 (2002). How might "illusory correlation" interfere with an intuitive assessment of the effectiveness of a dispute resolution process or system?

4. In addition, psychological research suggests that we intuitively tend to seek out information that confirms our theories, rather than systematically attempting to gather accurate information:

We also actively seek information that confirms our ideas, a phenomenon known as "confrontation bias." Peter Wason demonstrated our preference for confirmation bias in a famous experiment with British university students. He gave students the three-number sequence 2–4–6 and asked them to guess the rule he used to devise the series. First, however, he invited them to test their hunches by generating their own three-number sequences. Each time Wason told them whether their sets conformed to his rule. (Stop: If Wason walked in on you right now, what three numbers might you try out on him? If he answered "yes," what additional three numbers might you put to him?) Once they had tested enough to feel certain they understood the rule, they were to announce it.

The result? Often wrong but seldom in doubt. Only one in five of these confident people correctly discerned the rule, which was simply any three ascending numbers. Typically, Wason's students formed a wrong idea ("counting by two's?") and then searched only for confirming evidence, for example by testing 6–8–10, 31–33–35, and so forth. (Perhaps you, too, would have tested your hunch by seeking to confirm rather than disconfirm it?) Experiments on our preferences for belief-confirming evidence would not have surprised Francis Bacon, whose 1620 *Novum Organum* anticipated our modern understanding of the limits of intuition: "The human understanding, when a proposition has been once laid down ... forces everything else to add fresh support and confirmation.''

Try another of Wason's classical little problems, one that has been the subject of much research and debate: Which cards must you turn over to determine whether this rule is true or false: ''If there is a vowel on one side, then there is an even number on the other side.''

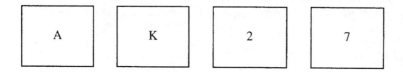

Like everyone else responding to this problem, you probably first wanted to turn over the A. So far, so good. Some stop there, but we need to turn over one more card. Most folks, seeking to confirm the rule, want to turn over the 2. But if there's a consonant on the other side, this card would be irrelevant to the rule (''If there is a *vowel* on the other side ...''). Only 4 percent of people correctly turned over the 7. (If there's a vowel on the other side, the rule is false; if not, it's irrelevant.) Our confirmation bias on these tasks suggests that natural human reasoning is flawed, or at least better suited to assessing probabilities than executing logic.

DAVID G. MEYERS, INTUITION: ITS POWERS AND PERILS 116–17 (2002). How might you explain how ''confirmation bias'' compounds the need for systematic research into the effects of dispute resolution procedures?

5. When conducting evaluation research it is important to consider data obtained from a variety of sources using a variety of methods:

Each technique for gathering information has its shortcomings. Experimentation is limited by artificiality, observation by unreliability, interviews by interviewer bias, and so on. There is no ideal research technique in the behavioral sciences. The advantages may lie along one dimension, such as economy; the disadvantages along another, such as objectivity. The goal of the researcher is not to find the single best method.

For most problems, several procedures will be better than one. Even though each has its limitations, these tend not to be the same limitations. The artificiality of the laboratory can be supplemented by observation, which is high on naturalness but low on reliability; the questionnaire, which can be given to many people quickly, can be supplemented by detailed interviews with a few people to probe more deeply into significant issues. This has been described as the methods of converging operations. A number of different research techniques are applied, each with somewhat different limitations and yielding somewhat different data.

ROBERT SOMMER & BARBARA SOMMER, A PRACTICAL GUIDE OF BEHAVIORAL RESEARCH: TOOLS AND TECHNIQUES 6–7 (5th ed. 2002).

6.   What variables might it be useful to measure in evaluating an ADR program? What are the strengths and weaknesses of each variable? How would you measure each variable and where would you obtain the data? Be specific. Consider the utility and difficulty of measuring the following:

- time savings

- cost savings

- parties' satisfaction (with the process? with the outcome? with the mediator?)

- attorneys' satisfaction (with the process? with the outcome? with the mediator?)

- settlement rates

- parties' compliance with the settlements reached

- perceived fairness (according to whom? parties? outside expert?) (of process? of outcome?)

- effects on relationships

- changes in social values about disputing

- changes in the role or behavior of lawyers.

7.   Ideally, researchers would conduct field experiments in which cases are randomly assigned to either the dispute resolution program or a control group of cases that do not participate in the program. Such field experiments are infrequent. One notable exception is the Early Assessment Program in the U.S. District Court for the Western District of Missouri, a demonstration program that was established under the Civil Justice Reform Act. The court permitted cases to be randomly assigned to three different groups: 1. cases that were required to use the Early Assessment Program; 2. cases in which the parties were allowed to voluntarily choose whether to use the Early Assessment Program; and 3. cases that were not allowed to use the program. *See* DONNA STIENSTRA, MOLLY JOHNSON & PATRICIA LOMBARD, A STUDY OF THE FIVE DEMONSTRATION PROGRAMS ESTABLISHED UNDER THE CIVIL JUSTICE REFORM ACT OF 1990, FEDERAL JUDICIAL CENTER 215–53 (1997). As Stienstra notes, using this type of experimental design allows the researcher to attribute different outcomes among the groups to the functioning of the program.

8.   Professor Deborah Hensler draws an analogy between the type of empirical research that is needed in the field of ADR and the research that has become commonplace in the field of medicine:

As I consider the state of ADR research today, I often think of the evolution of modern medicine. Over the last century, much has been learned about the nature of disease and antidotes for illness. This progress was a result of applying rigorous and objective investigative techniques (in particular, randomized clinical trials), reporting research results accurately and completely, and engaging in free wheeling debate about the meaning of the findings. Of course, not all health care providers nor all manufacturers of drugs and devices have applauded these investigations or their results; some of modern medicine's failures are traceable to inadequate research, flawed reporting, or unwillingness to heed research results. But over time, the patent medicines and folk therapies of yesterday have been replaced by products and therapies whose claimed benefits and side-effects have an evidentiary basis. Some of these products and therapies will be set aside, as new empirical research reveals their shortcomings, or produces better alternatives. As a result, some practitioners and manufacturers will suffer a temporary loss of revenue, while they adjust their practices to newly available evidence. Some of them may wish that the research had turned out differently. Others may long for the days when a single bottle held the promise of curing-all. But most of us would agree that we are better served by knowing more about the complexities of disease and health, and about the benefits and limitations of alternative health care regimes. I think it would be good for all of us if we could adopt this model of knowledge-building for the ADR field as well.

Deborah R. Hensler, *ADR Research at the Crossroads*, 2000 J. Disp. Resol. 71, 77–78 (2000). Consider our experience with this model in medicine — what do you see as the advantages and disadvantages of this approach? What are the implications for designing systems for dispute resolution?

b.   The Value of Evaluation Research

As you can see, the process of evaluating dispute resolution systems can be demanding. In the following excerpt, Professor Robert MacCoun and his colleagues demonstrate why such work is worth the effort — that is, the value of evaluation research.

ROBERT J. MACCOUN, E. ALLAN LIND, DEBORAH R. HENSLER, DAVID L. BRYANT & PATRICIA A. EBENER, ALTERNATIVE ADJUDICATION: AN EVALUATION OF THE NEW JERSEY AUTOMOBILE ARBITRATION PROGRAM

v-xi (1988).

Executive Summary

BACKGROUND

In recent years, legislators and court officials have become increasingly interested in the use of alternative dispute resolution (ADR) procedures to dispose of civil lawsuits. ADR programs divert certain cases from the regular trial court calendar to some form of arbitration or mediation process. The goals of these procedures are to reduce congestion on trial calendars, to diminish court costs, to speed case disposition, and to reduce costs and time for litigants.

In court-based ADR programs, the courts retain administrative control of the cases. One court-based ADR procedure that has been particularly popular with legislators and court officials is *court-annexed arbitration*. These programs divert certain classes of cases to a relatively informal hearing before one or more experienced attorneys, who provide a decision on liability and damages. Typically, the parties to the case may then either accept the award or reject it and demand trial *de novo*. If they choose the latter, the case returns to the court's calendar and moves along to trial.

In 1983, New Jersey introduced mandatory arbitration of automobile injury lawsuits in Burlington and Union counties as an experimental procedure. The Institute for Civil Justice was asked to help design the experiment and evaluated the pilot program in 1984. The program was adopted statewide in 1985. The New Jersey Administrative Office of the Courts asked ICJ to evaluate the program's effectiveness, and evaluation began in 1986.

RESEARCH APPROACH

The ICJ's evaluation posed five basic questions:

- How was the program working?
- Did it change disposition patterns?
- Did it speed disposition?
- Did it reduce litigant's costs?
- Do participants like it?

To address these questions, we needed to:

1. Examine lawsuits representing the entire range of auto negligence cases filed in New Jersey;

2. Include cases from multiple courts, reflecting the diversity of caseload composition, resource constraints, local legal culture, and arbitration program implementation statewide;

3. Compare auto cases filed before the program was implemented with those filed after its implementation to ascertain whether the total system of auto negligence litigation had changed during that period;

4. Investigate differences in the postarbitration period between cases assigned to arbitration and those unassigned (presumably because of ineligibility); and

5. Collect data from multiple sources to measure the key program outcome variables.

To implement this evaluation scheme, we randomly sampled more than 1,000 auto negligence cases filed in eight New Jersey courts in the second half of 1983 (before the program's inception) and the second half of 1985. The latter included cases assigned to arbitration as well as cases that were not. We sampled cases by the date at which they were filed (rather than the date at which they were arbitrated or terminated) because this strategy allowed us to examine whether a change in the litigation environment provided by the courts — the arbitration program — influenced the manner in which cases were litigated from the day they were filed. For each case sampled, we collected two kinds of data: (1) we abstracted data from court records, and (2) we surveyed attorneys to obtain data from their records.

To obtain data about how participants evaluated the arbitration program in which they were involved, we conducted a survey of approximately 300 litigants and 400 attorneys immediately after their arbitration hearings. The sample for this survey was drawn from all eight courts.

CONCLUSIONS

Effects on Program Functioning

* * * The following conclusions can be drawn from these data:

The program captures a significant fraction of auto negligence cases, but relatively few are disposed of by an arbitration judgment. In our sample, about 68 percent of the cases were assigned to the program, but many of them settled before they reached an arbitration hearing. Just over half of the assigned cases (about 55 percent) were actually arbitrated, and about 40 percent of those were terminated by the arbitration judgment.

More than half of the arbitrated cases are appealed, but trials de novo *are rare.* Only 10 percent of the arbitrated cases actually went to a trial *de novo*; this is only 3 percent of all the cases that were assigned to the program, or 2 percent of all the auto negligence filings. Disputants may file an appeal primarily as a bargaining tactic; we found that over 80 percent of appealed cases settled before a trial took place.

Effects on Litigation and Disposition Patterns

We were unable to detect a significant effect of the program on the trial rate. However, trial rates were initially quite low (less than 5 percent), making it difficult to measure any further reduction. We estimate that our sample size was large enough to allow us to detect a fairly modest effect on the trial rate, but we would have needed a considerably larger sample to detect a reduction of 1 or 2 percent. It should be noted that a small reduction in the trial rate might be sufficient to bring about meaningful reduction in judicial workload.

Cases that are assigned to the program are more likely to be adjudicated. Before the program was introduced, most answered cases settled or were dismissed without an adjudicatory hearing — that is, without a trial. The arbitration program has provided disputants with an alternative adjudicatory option: an arbitration hearing.

Assigned cases terminate at a slower rate; the delay appears to be linked to the scheduling of arbitration hearings. Cases assigned to the arbitration program in 1985 terminated at a significantly slower rate than either the unassigned cases or the cases filed in 1983. This effect was especially pronounced in the first 12 months after filing. However, the assigned cases began terminating more rapidly after this point, and the assigned cases had almost closed the gap 18 months after filing. We believe that this later acceleration may have occurred because many disputants postponed settlement negotiations while waiting for an arbitration hearing.

Effects on Case Activity and Private Costs

The program appears to have slightly increased case activity by attorneys and court staff. We believe that this increase reflects a new set of litigation activities brought about by the introduction of the arbitration program: scheduling, preparing for, and participating in an arbitration hearing.

The program has not had a measurable effect on attorney hours and fees.

Litigant and Attorney Evaluations

Disputants were generally quite favorable in their evaluation of arbitration. Both litigants and attorneys viewed arbitration hearings as fair procedures and felt that their cases had received high-quality treatment by the arbitrators. Disputants rarely reported that the arbitrators had been unprepared, had shown favoritism, or had simply "split the difference" instead of reaching a principled judgment on the merits of the case. Moreover, the majority of litigants and attorneys rated arbitration as a more efficient procedure than either trial by jury or trial by judge.

On average, plaintiffs and their attorneys were more favorable in their evaluation of arbitration than defendants and defense attorneys; this discrepancy appeared to reflect the fact that the arbitrators usually awarded at least some money to the plaintiffs. Also, attorneys were more favorable than litigants in their evaluation of arbitration. Nevertheless, although most attorneys viewed arbitration as a fair procedure, about half of them felt that a jury trial was even fairer.

IMPLICATIONS FOR COURT POLICY

Efficiency and Expediency Claims Reconsidered

Our findings illustrate the importance of systematic empirical evaluation of ADR programs. The claim that arbitration is a mechanism for expediting tort litigation is intuitively plausible and is often viewed as self-evident; however, our data suggest a more complicated story. While we found no evidence to dispute the claim that arbitration is a more efficient form of adjudication than trial, this ignores the fact that *very few cases ever go to trial.* If an ADR program diverts a significant number of cases from trial, then it is likely to reduce public and private litigation costs as well as court congestion and delay. However, if the perception that trial is prohibitively time-consuming and expensive is motivating litigants to settle cases privately, then a program that offers an informal alternative might induce many of them to change their minds and wait for a hearing. As a result, the program will divert cases from private settlement. Since more cases were settled privately than were tried, the net result may be an increase in the proportion of cases that are disposed of through court involvement. We suspect that this scenario characterizes the introduction of court-annexed arbitration in New Jersey.

Lessons for Implementation

Without a controlled experiment, we cannot be certain about our suggestions for improving implementation; however, the following conclusions appear plausible:

Prescreening appears to reduce trial de novo *requests*. Administrators in courts that are not currently prescreening cases might consider whether the potential decrease in trial *de novo* requests justifies the additional effort.

Early hearings can expedite the termination of cases. We found a significant relationship between the time a case took to reach an arbitration hearing and the amount of time a case took to terminate. We believe that assigned cases might terminate more quickly if the litigants, attorneys, and court personnel cooperate to bring about earlier hearings.

The size of the arbitration panel and the method of rescheduling cases for trial had minimal effects. We found little evidence to justify strong policy recommendations regarding either the size of the arbitration panel or the manner in which arbitrated cases are scheduled for trial.

Arbitration Meets a Demand for Informal Adjudication

It appears that the New Jersey arbitration program is providing a service to disputants involved in auto negligence suits, albeit a service somewhat different from what the designers might have envisioned. The program appears to be meeting a demand for informal adjudication. Disputants want a hearing — an opportunity to present their case before an impartial third party and to receive a judgment based on the merits of the case. Moreover, they want a hearing to be dignified, respectful, and impartial, and they feel that arbitration hearings in New Jersey meet these criteria. Attorneys do not appear to mind the fact that arbitration hearings are informal, and litigants actually see this informality as a plus. In fact, it appears that disputants who might otherwise settle privately are willing to wait a year or more to take their case to arbitration. Thus, the arbitration program is providing an opportunity for more cases to be adjudicated, and it appears to be doing so without adding to private litigation costs.

Notes and Questions

1.   How would you interpret the findings of the New Jersey arbitration study? Was the program "successful"? Note that how you answer this question may depend on what you see as the goals of the program — for

example, was the program intended to save time and money, to provide "access to justice," or to satisfy some other interest?

2.   The importance of a study such as the New Jersey arbitration evaluation is not to answer a simple question about whether or not court-annexed arbitration "works." Instead, the significance of evaluation studies such as the one described here is to help illuminate the circumstances under which a process has particular effects. Accordingly, the study sheds lights on design issues such as the role of pre-screening and early hearings. In 1996, the RAND Corporation released the results of an evaluation of ADR in six federal courts under the Civil Justice Reform Act. The study concluded that there was "no strong statistical evidence that the mediation or neutral evaluation programs, as implemented in the six districts studied, significantly affected time to disposition, litigation costs, or attorney views of fairness or satisfaction with case management." JAMES S. KAKALIK, TERENCE DUNWORTH, LAURAL A. HILL, DANIEL MCCAFFREY, MARIAN OSHIRO, NICHOLAS M. PACE & MARY E. VAIANA, AN EVALUATION OF MEDIATION AND EARLY NEUTRAL EVALUATION UNDER THE CIVIL JUSTICE REFORM ACT, xxxiv (1996). Professor Craig McEwen proposes reframing these findings as follows: "Lawyers and parties in federal courts fail to make effective use of mediation and early neutral evaluation to speed resolution and reduce costs." Craig McEwen, *Managing Corporate Disputing: Overcoming Barriers to the Effective Use of Mediation for Reducing the Cost and Time of Litigation*, 14 Ohio St. J. on Disp. Resol. 1, 3 (1998). How might this reframing change the nature of the response to the report's findings? Compare these findings to those from the study of the Early Assessment Program in the U.S. District Court for the Western District of Missouri. DONNA STIENSTRA, MOLLY JOHNSON & PATRICIA LOMBARD, A STUDY OF THE FIVE DEMONSTRATION PROGRAMS ESTABLISHED UNDER THE CIVIL JUSTICE REFORM ACT OF 1990, FEDERAL JUDICIAL CENTER 215–53 (1997) (finding savings in time and money).

3.   The results of the MacCoun et al research in New Jersey highlight the importance of defining a comparison group with which to compare cases resolved through a dispute resolution process. Professor Chris Guthrie notes: "In a system where a tiny fraction of cases is actually tried, what matters most is not how litigants rate mediation relative to *trial* but how they rate mediation relative to the *litigation processes that are actually likely to lead to the resolution of the dispute.* Data from federal and state courts show that litigants are likely to resolve their disputes not through trials on the merits but rather through pre-trial motions or settlement. In fiscal year 2000, for example, the federal district courts 'terminated' 259,637 civil cases. Only 3,131 (or 1.2%) of these culminated in a jury verdict and 1,532 or (.6%) in a bench verdict. Of the 98.2% of cases that did not culminate in a trial verdict, most were resolved through: 1. dismissals for lack of jurisdiction, voluntary dismissals, settlements, or other dismissals (53.3%); 2. transfers to other courts, remands to state court, judgments on award of arbitrators, trials de novo following arbitration judgments, or other judgments (18.5%); 3. pretrial motions (12.8%); or 4. default judgments (8.2%). These fiscal year 2000 data are consistent with federal court data from prior years as well as available state court data." Chris Guthrie, *Procedural Justice Research and the Paucity of Trials*, 2002 J. Disp. Resol. 127, 128–29 (2002).

4.   For other research evaluating dispute resolution processes, see, for example, E. Allen Lind, Robert MacCoun, Patricia Ebener, William L.F. Felstiner, Deborah R. Hensler, Judith Resnik & Tom R. Tyler, *In the Eye of the Beholder: Tort Litigants' Evaluations of Their Experiences in the Civil Justice System*, 24 Law & Soc'y Rev. 953 (1990); Bobbi McAdoo, *A Report to the Minnesota Supreme Court: The Impact of Rule 114 on Civil Litigation Practice in Minnesota*, 25 Hamline L. Rev. 401 (2002); Joshua D. Rosenberg & H. Jay Folberg, *Alternative Dispute Resolution: An Empirical Analysis*, 46 Stan. L. Rev. 1487 (1994) (excerpted in Chapter VI, beginning at page 718); Roselle Wissler, *The Effects of Mandatory Mediation: Empirical Research on the Experience of Small Claims and Common Pleas Courts*, 33 Willamette L. Rev. 565 (1997). For a review of empirical research assessing mediation and neutral evaluation, see Roselle L. Wissler, *The Effectiveness of Court Connected Dispute Resolution in Civil Cases*, 22 Conflict Resol. Q. 55 (2004).

5.   For additional information about how to do evaluation research, see for example, DAVID L. FAIGMAN, DAVID H. KAYE, MICHAEL J. SAKS, & JOSEPH SANDERS, SCIENCE IN THE LAW: STANDARDS, STATISTICS, AND RESEARCH ISSUES (2002); JEFFREY KATZER, KENNETH H. COOK, & WAYNE W. CROUCH, EVALUATING INFORMATION: A GUIDE FOR USERS OF SOCIAL SCIENCE RESEARCH (4th ed. 1998); MELINDA OSTERMEYER & SUSAN L. KEILITZ, MONITORING AND EVALUATING COURT-BASED DISPUTE RESOLUTION PROGRAMS: A GUIDE FOR JUDGES AND COURT MANAGERS (1997); ELIZABETH ROLPH & ERIK MOLLER, EVALUATING AGENCY ALTERNATIVE DISPUTE RESOLUTION PROGRAMS: A USER'S GUIDE TO DATA COLLECTION AND USE (1995); BARBARA SOMMER & ROBERT SOMMER, A PRACTICAL GUIDE TO BEHAVIORAL RESEARCH: TOOLS AND TECHNIQUES (5th ed. 1997); ADR Program Evaluation Recommendations, 65 Fed. Reg. 59,200 (Oct. 4, 2000), *available at* http://www.adr.gov/pdf/evalu.pdf (last visited Feb. 25, 2005).

C. ADVISING CLIENTS IN SELECTING A DISPUTE RESOLUTION PROCESS

Next we turn to the process of advising an individual client about the dispute resolution processes available to her. Specifically, we examine how a lawyer can gain a deeper understanding of the client's situation and needs in order to advise the client about what would likely happen in court and about the potential advantages and disadvantages of various methods of dispute resolution. Both the attorney and the client must have an expanded understanding of the interests involved and the likely outcomes in order for the client to effectively reach a decision about which course to pursue.

In the first excerpt, Professor Roselle Wissler describes some potential barriers to attorneys' discussion of ADR with clients, and presents empirical research describing the role of these barriers in practice. In the second and third excerpts, we examine the nature of the discussion of dispute resolution processes with clients. The factors identified by Professors Frank Sander and Stephen Goldberg and the questionnaire prepared by CPR can be used in assisting such clients in choosing an appropriate process for resolving a particular dispute. The final excerpt discusses the use of dispute resolution clauses in business agreements.

1.   BARRIERS TO DISCUSSION, USE OF ADR

ROSELLE L. WISSLER, BARRIERS TO ATTORNEYS' DISCUSSION AND USE OF ADR

19 Ohio St. J. on Disp. Resol. 459, 462–68, 470–72, 493–97, 500 (2004).

Various methods to increase voluntary ADR use have been proposed and adopted, including providing ADR information or education to attorneys, encouraging or requiring attorneys to discuss ADR options with clients, and requiring attorneys to discuss possible ADR use with opposing counsel. Underlying these approaches is the assumption that certain factors operate as barriers that constrain attorneys from regularly considering and using ADR processes. Commonly cited impediments include attorneys' lack of knowledge about ADR processes, attorneys' unfavorable views of ADR, attorneys' concerns that proposing ADR will be seen as a "sign of weakness," the routines and economics of law practice, and the lack of judicial involvement.

* * *

II.   A REVIEW OF POTENTIAL BARRIERS TO ATTORNEYS' DISCUSSION AND USE OF ADR

A.   *Attorneys' Knowledge of ADR Processes*

Commentators maintain that attorneys should be informed about ADR in order to be able to counsel clients about litigation and ADR options and to participate effectively in a range of dispute resolution processes. Attorneys who do not feel sufficiently familiar with ADR processes to discuss them with clients and opposing counsel and to participate in them might be reluctant to discuss or use ADR.

* * *

B.   *Attorneys' Views of ADR*

Attorneys' views of ADR, negotiation, and litigation are thought to play a role in their willingness to discuss and use ADR. Attorneys who view ADR as offering few advantages, while creating disadvantages relative to negotiation and trial, might be hesitant to consider ADR.

Attorneys' concerns about ADR could reflect misperceptions as a result of unfamiliarity with ADR. In addition, attorneys might not see the appropriateness or value of ADR because their training, "philosophical map," and practice emphasize an adversarial rather than a problem-solving perspective. And for some attorneys, negative perceptions of ADR could be the direct result of experience with a poor quality ADR session.

Several cognitive barriers that hinder negotiation and settlement also might affect attorneys' views and impede their use of ADR. For instance, if "optimistic overconfidence" leads to overestimates of the likelihood of favorable case outcomes, attorneys will be less likely to see a need to use ADR to facilitate settlement. If their consideration of ADR is "framed" in terms of what will be lost relative to litigation rather than what will be gained, attorneys will be less likely to use ADR. And if their opponent proposes ADR, "reactive devaluation" will lead attorneys to suspect that using ADR will be to their disadvantage and to view it less positively.

In addition, attorneys' economic interests could color their views of the relative benefits of ADR and litigation. Attorneys who are paid on a contingent-fee basis might give insufficient weight to the importance of their client's non-monetary goals and, thus, attach less importance to ADR's potential for addressing those interests. And because contingent-fee lawyers have an interest in resolving modest cases quickly, they might view ADR as producing a more expensive and slower resolution than a negotiated settlement. By contrast, attorneys paid on an hourly fee basis might attach extra weight to full, formal discovery and to the benefits their clients can derive by delaying settlement or threatening to go to trial. And attorneys' estimates of whether their long-term compensation, advancement, and prestige would benefit more from clients' increased use of ADR or of litigation also could affect their views of these options.

The structural and strategic aspects of litigation that are thought to impede early settlement are also likely to affect attorneys' views of when or whether to discuss ADR. The demands of numerous other active cases and the lack of early court deadlines contribute to not assessing cases early for their ADR or settlement potential. The virtually automatic progression of litigation and the inertia of following the usual process, combined with the escalation of commitment and strategic moves in negotiation, make it difficult to stop the process and propose ADR.

One specific view of ADR that is frequently mentioned as a barrier is the concern that proposing ADR is viewed as a sign of weakness. Attorneys might be reluctant to discuss ADR if they think it will be interpreted by clients as a lack of commitment to their case or by opposing counsel as a lack of confidence or resolve. In addition to strategic considerations in the instant case, some attorneys might have a more general interest in establishing a reputation for being a fierce litigator and, thus, might not propose ADR if they think doing so will make them look weak.

* * *

C. *Judicial Involvement*

Given the many impediments to ADR use discussed above, judicial involvement in the consideration of ADR processes might be needed to overcome them. Judges' support for the use of ADR can enhance attorneys' views of the value and appropriateness of ADR. Of course, some of the same factors that are thought to keep attorneys from discussing ADR might also act as barriers to greater judicial encouragement of ADR. For instance, judges might be reluctant to suggest ADR if they themselves are not knowledgeable about or supportive of ADR. In addition, judges are likely to be hesitant to discuss ADR with litigants due to concerns about interfering with the attorney-client relationship. And unless the discussion of ADR options is integrated into an existing case management system, caseload and scheduling pressures are likely to prevent judicial involvement.

* * *

III.   THE PRESENT STUDY: SURVEY PROCEDURE AND RESPONDENT CHARACTERISTICS

Questionnaires were mailed to all members of the Trial Practice Section of the State Bar of Arizona in June 2001. At that time, Arizona attorneys had no explicit obligation to consider ADR. The questionnaire asked the attorneys about their discussions and use of ADR in the context of their Arizona state court civil practice during the preceding two years. The attorneys also were asked about their knowledge of different ADR processes, potential benefits of and barriers to using ADR, and the nature of their law practice.

Four hundred forty-six completed questionnaires were received, for a response rate of 45%. * * * Because we assumed that attorneys whose practice involved a greater proportion of civil litigation would provide more informed judgments, we limited the analyses reported in this Article to those attorneys who devoted half or more of their practice to civil litigation. This excluded 17 (4%) of the respondents. Thus, the findings reported in this article are based on the 426 Trial Practice Section members who devoted at least half of their practice to civil litigation. On average, these attorneys devoted 94% of their practice to civil litigation.

* * *

VI.   SUMMARY AND IMPLICATIONS OF THE RESEARCH FINDINGS FOR ADR POLICY

A.   *Summary*

Discussing ADR processes has become a common practice for Arizona civil litigation attorneys, although not in all of their cases. Three-fourths of attorneys discussed ADR with their clients in three-fourths or more of their cases. Attorneys discussed ADR with opposing counsel less frequently, with nearly half of the attorneys doing so in three-fourths or more of their cases. These ADR discussions generally did not take place early in the life of a case. Nor did ADR discussions automatically translate into ADR use: one-fifth of attorneys used voluntary ADR processes in three-fourths or more of their cases. Although attorneys who more frequently discussed ADR with clients and opposing counsel used voluntary ADR processes more often, those who tended to discuss ADR early were not more likely to use ADR.

The findings are consistent with assumptions that certain ADR-specific factors constrain attorneys' voluntary discussion and use of ADR. Attorneys who reported less judicial encouragement of ADR, a lower rate of settlement in ADR cases, less familiarity with ADR, less favorable views of ADR, and less support for mandatory ADR policies tended to discuss and use ADR in a smaller proportion of their cases. Taken together, these factors were strongly related to how often attorneys voluntarily discussed and used ADR. Attorneys' views regarding whether ADR provided free discovery or whether the supply of qualified neutrals was sufficient were not related to how often they discussed or used ADR.

Only a subset of these factors — attorneys' views regarding ADR's benefits, their familiarity with the processes, and the degree of judicial encouragement of ADR use — were related to how often attorneys first discussed ADR early in a case, and their combined impact was small. These ADR-specific factors apparently play less of a role in the timing of ADR discussions than do other factors, such as those that affect the timing of the negotiation process more generally.

Despite the strong relationship between these factors and attorneys' discussion and use of ADR, most of the barriers were not widespread. That is, fewer than one-fifth of the attorneys were unfamiliar with the various ADR processes, thought others viewed proposing ADR as a sign of weakness, reported that fewer than half of their ADR cases had settled, or thought ADR did not offer substantial benefits, greater client satisfaction, and earlier settlements. A larger proportion of attorneys, however, reported a low rate of judicial encouragement of ADR and were opposed to mandates requiring the discussion and use of ADR.

B.   Implications for Policies to Increase Voluntary ADR Use

In this section, we discuss what the findings of the present study and other empirical studies suggest about the potential effectiveness of two approaches for increasing voluntary ADR use, namely expanded ADR education and mandated ADR consideration. First, however, we must note a caution in extrapolating from the findings of the present study, based on data regarding voluntary discussions, to situations that involve mandatory consideration of ADR. Once the voluntary aspect of ADR discussions is removed, the comparative and the combined impacts of the various factors on ADR use could be dramatically different.

1.   Expanding ADR Education and Information

One set of proposals to increase voluntary ADR use focuses on increasing attorneys' familiarity with ADR, either through the expansion of law school or continuing education course offerings or through ADR information provided by the court at the time of filing. The present study found that attorneys who were less familiar with ADR were less likely to discuss and use ADR. In addition, attorneys who were less knowledgeable about ADR were less likely to think ADR offered benefits and were more likely to think proposing ADR signaled weakness, and attorneys who held these views discussed and used ADR less often.

Thus, these findings suggest that efforts to increase attorneys' familiarity with ADR processes might increase how often they discuss and use ADR. And, presumably, educational efforts also would enhance the effective use of ADR by giving attorneys a better understanding of which processes address which sources of impasse or client goals and how the different processes could be structured or combined to address case-specific needs. The findings of other studies, however, suggest that the impact of increased ADR education on ADR use might be small, and smaller than if the increased familiarity had been acquired instead through direct experience with ADR processes.

The impact of ADR information, education, and training might be enhanced if it is targeted not only at attorneys but also at judges and regular users of legal services. In the present study, judicial encouragement of ADR use was the factor that had the strongest impact on the frequency of attorneys' discussion and use of ADR. Judges' greater familiarity with the various ADR processes might enhance their ability to discuss ADR with attorneys and their willingness to suggest the use of ADR. Efforts to inform "repeat player" litigants about ADR processes might lead them to be more receptive to their attorneys' presentation of those options, although direct experience with ADR is likely to have an even greater effect. Educational efforts alone, however, are likely to have a limited impact on ADR use because they address only a subset of the barriers to considering ADR.

2. *Mandating ADR Discussions with Clients or Opposing Counsel*

Other proposed approaches to increase voluntary ADR use are to encourage or require attorneys to discuss the possible use of ADR with their clients, with opposing counsel, or with both. These duties have been incorporated in aspirational creeds, professional responsibility or ethics codes, and statutes or court rules. The nature of the obligation to consult with clients about ADR ranges from simply advising clients of the availability of ADR processes or giving them the court's ADR brochure, to providing an assessment of the advantages and disadvantages of available ADR options and assistance in selecting the most appropriate process.

Will these suggestions or requirements increase the frequency of attorneys' ADR discussions and, if so, will that result in increased voluntary ADR use?

* * *

Overall, the findings [of existing research] seem to suggest that the components of a mandatory discussion rule that would enhance its effectiveness include: a requirement that attorneys provide their clients ADR information and discuss ADR with opposing counsel; a deadline by which the discussions must take place, a reporting requirement, and enforcement; a court conference to assist attorneys in choosing an ADR process; and active judicial involvement. The findings of the present study shed further light on why these components seem likely to enhance the effectiveness of mandatory ADR discussion requirements in increasing voluntary ADR use, and on what other components might be helpful.

Notes and Questions

1. What other barriers to discussing ADR with clients or using ADR can you think of? Make a list of these barriers. Think about how each barrier might be addressed in the design of a dispute resolution system. Do the barriers vary when considered at the client, firm, and professional levels?

2. A study of the use of ADR in Missouri explored the reasons that some attorneys had not used ADR. The most common reasons cited were that their cases were "not appropriate" for ADR, that the court did not actively encourage or order ADR, that they preferred trial, that they settle cases as well or better without ADR, and that ADR would impose an unnecessary expense. Bobbi McAdoo & Art Hinshaw, *The Challenge of Institutionalizing Alternative Dispute Resolution: Attorney Perspectives on the Effect of Rule 17 on Civil Litigation in Missouri*, 67 Mo. L. Rev. 473, 489 (2002).

3. Many commentators have argued that attorneys should have the ethical responsibility to discuss with clients the differing methods by which they can resolve their disputes. *See e.g.*, Carrie Menkel–Meadow, *Ethics in ADR: The Many "Cs" of Professional Responsibility and Dispute Resolution*, 28 Fordham Urb. L.J. 979, 981 (2001) (arguing for "an ethical obligation to counsel clients about the multiple ways to resolving problems and planning transactions"). The Model Rules of Professional Conduct provide:

> Rule 1.2 Scope of Representation and Allocation of Authority Between Client and Lawyer
>
> > (a) .. a lawyer shall abide by a client's decisions concerning the objectives of representation and, as required by Rule 1.4, shall consult with the client as to the means by which they are to be pursued ...
>
> Rule 1.4 Communication
>
> > (a) A lawyer shall ... reasonably consult with the client about the means by which the client's objectives are to be accomplished ...
>
> Rule 2.1 Advisor
>
> Comment
>
> > (5) .. Similarly, when a matter is likely to involve litigation, it may be necessary under Rule 1.4 to inform the client of forms of dispute resolution that might constitute reasonable alternatives to litigation
> >
> > ...

Many jurisdictions *require* lawyers to counsel their clients about the availability and appropriateness of alternative methods of resolving disputes. *See, e.g.*, Ga. Code of Prof'l. Responsibility, EC 7–5 (amended April 15, 1993) ("A lawyer as advisor has a duty to advise the client as to various forms of dispute resolution. When a matter is likely to involve litigation, a lawyer has a duty to inform the client of forms of dispute resolution which might constitute reasonable alternatives to litigation."); Minn. Gen. Prac. Rule 114.03(b) (1996) (requiring attorneys to "provide clients with ADR information"); N.D. Rules of Court 8.8(a) (2001) (requiring the filing of a statement certifying "that the parties have discussed ADR participation with each other and that the parties' lawyers have discussed ADR with their clients"). Professor Robert Cochran has argued for "the extension of malpractice liability to attorneys who fail to allow clients the choice of whether to pursue mediation or arbitration." Robert F. Cochran, Jr., *Legal Representation and the Next Steps Toward Client Control: Attorney Malpractice for the Failure to Allow the Client to Control Negotiation and Pursue Alternatives to Litigation*, 47 Wash. & Lee. L. Rev. 819, 869 (1990).

4. Some law firms have not only overcome the barriers described above, but have specifically decided to provide ADR services. *See* CATHERINE CRONIN-HARRIS, BUILDING ADR INTO THE LAW FIRM: ADR SYSTEMS DESIGN (1997); *Private Firm Will Open ADR Center*, 16 Alternatives 42 (1998). In addition, it is the practice of some law firms to appoint "settlement counsel" for a particular case. This involves appointing an attorney, separate from the trial counsel, whose role is to focus on the settlement discussions. William F. Coyne, *The Case for Settlement Counsel*, 14 Ohio St. J. on Disp. Resol. 367 (1999); James E. McGuire, *Why Litigators Should Use Settlement Counsel*, 18 Alternatives 107 (2000). As we saw in Chapter VI, some attorneys now practice "collaborative law" in which the attorneys for both sides agree to work with the parties to resolve the dispute. The attorneys agree, however, that they will not represent the clients in court and will withdraw if the case is litigated. Pauline H. Tesler, *Collaborative Law Neutrals Produce Better Resolutions*, 21 Alternatives 1 (2003). *See also* John Lande, *Possibilities for Collaborative Law: Ethics and Practice of Lawyer Disqualification and Process Control in a New Model of Lawyering*, 64 Ohio St. L.J. 1315 (2003) (raising ethical and other questions about collaborative lawyering) an excerpt of which appears in Chapter VI at page 771.

5. If you were a member of the management committee of a large law firm, would you support any or all of the following steps:

- establishing an ADR practice group to act as advocates for clients in ADR proceedings and assist clients in building and choosing dispute resolution processes;

- establishing an ADR practice group that would provide neutrals for mediation, arbitration, and various mixed processes;

- hiring an ADR specialist to advise and assist the lawyers in the firm?

Might some law firms shun ADR procedures because they produce fewer billable hours than litigation? Eric Green, who was a mediator in the antitrust case brought by the U.S. Justice Department against Microsoft Corp., has a response to such concerns: " 'Don, baby, if you don't do it, Jack will do it, and your client will end up going to him.' You have to get across that the long-term interests of all lawyers are to serve the needs of their clients." David Berreby, *Thoughts on ADR: An Interview with a Veteran Neutral*, Alternatives to High Cost Litig., May 1986, at 3, 14.

2. SELECTING A PROCESS

The next two excerpts offer different approaches for assessing the suitability of a case for ADR. The first, by Professors Sander and Goldberg, proposes a simple preference-weighting system. The second, by the CPR Institute for Dispute Resolution, is structured as a questionnaire.

FRANK E.A. SANDER & STEPHEN B. GOLDBERG, MAKING THE RIGHT CHOICE

A.B.A. J., Nov. 1993, at 66, 66–68.

There are a number of reasons for discussing alternative dispute resolution with your clients when they come to you with a problem. Foremost is the possibility that ADR — a collection of techniques designed to take disputes out of court and settle them more quickly and economically — will satisfy clients' dispute resolution goals better than litigation and at lower cost.

Furthermore, your business clients expect you to do so. If you don't, they're likely to bring it up themselves, or opposing counsel will do so, or the dispute will end up in one of a growing number of courts with ADR programs. Finally, you may be under an ethical obligation to advise clients of potential ADR options.

The difficult question, then, is not whether to discuss ADR with your clients but which procedure, if any, to recommend. This article is intended to assist you in making those critical decisions.

Before you pick an ADR technique, ask yourself two basic questions: First, what are the client's *goals* in choosing a dispute resolution procedure? Second, if the client is amenable to settlement, what are the *obstacles*?

Next, by using the tables that accompany this article (which have been compiled from the experiences of ADR professionals), determine which ADR procedures are most likely to satisfy the client's goals and, if settlement is sought, which procedures are most likely to overcome settlement obstacles.

Here's a hypothetical to show how the tables work. Your client is Mary Stone, the president of Hal Corp., a computer manufacturer. The Leasco Corp. purchased 100 computers for $5 million, but has since defaulted on the contract, claiming that Stone's sales personnel misrepresented the computers' capabilities. [Text continues on page 863.]

Rating ways to achieve clients' goals

How to apply this table: Select from the first column all of the objectives that are important to a client. Then consider the extent to which each alternative dispute resolution technique satisfies those objectives, using the ratings of 0 for unlikely, 1 for somewhat, 2 for substantially and 3 for very substantially.

Objectives	Nonbinding procedures				Binding procedures	
	Mediation	Minitrial	Summary jury trial	Early neutral evaluation	Arbitration	Court
Minimize Costs	3	2	2	3	1	0
Speed	3	2	2	3	1	0
Privacy*	3	3	2	2	3	0
Maintain or improve relationship**	3	2	2	1	1	0
Vindication	0	1	1	1	2	3
Neutral Opinion***	0	3	3	3	3	3
Precedent****	0	0	0	0	2	3
Maximizing or minimizing recovery	0	1	1	1	2	3

*If the neutral evaluator is selected by the parties, neutral evaluation offers as much privacy as other processes. If a mediator, minitrial neutral or arbitrator is imposed by a court, that procedure would have a lower privacy rating.

** If an early neutral evaluator were to use negotiation between the principals, the process would receive the same rating as a summary jury trial or minitrial.

*** A neutral evaluation that follows a full presentation of evidence and argument is likely to be given greater weight by the parties than is a neutral opinion based upon a more truncated presentation.

****Although mediation normally seeks to provide a solution to the specific dispute, the parties could agree on a new rule for future cases and eliminate the need for a formal precedent.

CHARTS BY JEFF DIONISE

The purchase was made on a standard installment sales contract having a payment schedule of $100,000 per month, covering principal and interest. Leasco stopped paying just as the warranty period ended.

Stone emphatically denies Leasco's claims that Hal Corp. misrepresented the abilities of its computers. She says that Leasco owes Hal Corp. $300,000 in overdue installments, plus $4,880,000 under an acceleration clause, a total of $5,180,000. Should she file suit or use ADR?

The answer depends on what Ms. Stone hopes to accomplish. If Hal Corp. is primarily interested in a speedy and inexpensive resolution of the dispute that also will re-establish the parties' existing relationship — which is true of most clients in most business disputes — then mediation will be the preferred procedure.

Mediation receives top scores on the goals table for achieving the goals of low cost, high speed, maintaining or improving the relationship, and assuring privacy — an interest that is present in many business disputes.

Procedures other than mediation are preferable only when the client's primary interests are in establishing a precedent, being vindicated, or maximizing (or minimizing) recovery.

Suppose, however, it is more important for the Hal Corp. to demonstrate that it will not tolerate frivolous breach of valid contracts than it is for it to maintain a working relationship with Leasco.

If Ms. Stone wants vindication, the goals table shows that any of the evaluative procedures — minitrial (a summary presentation to settlement representatives of the parties), summary jury trial, early neutral evaluation, arbitration or court — will be useful, but that arbitration or litigation, in particular, is the most satisfactory.

If the goal is to establish precedent and be publicly vindicated, then only litigation will do.

Litigation, however, is not the best method to choose if Ms. Stone's primary concern is prompt financial recovery — perhaps because Hal Corp. has financial problems. While litigation is most likely to maximize recovery, the process is a protracted one.

In using the goals table, it's necessary to balance the importance of a goal against the total score.

Let's say that a client's goals are to maintain the relationship, receive a neutral opinion, and maximize privacy. The top scoring method is the minitrial, which receives a score of eight points.

That, however, doesn't mean it's the most suitable method. If the most important goal is that of re-establishing the working relationship, mediation becomes the most attractive choice. In short, a lawyer using the goals table must not only determine the client's objectives, but also must *prioritize* them.

Furthermore, it is often possible to blend or link different processes (such as mediation and neutral evaluation) to develop a hybrid process.

One final point concerning client goals: Some contend that ADR should be avoided altogether when one party will be sure to win if the matter is litigated. We disagree.

First, ADR can be useful in convincing the likely loser to concede and spare the parties the cost of litigation. Also, the "loser" is more likely to comply fully with an agreed-upon outcome than with a court order.

What's more, ADR is far more likely to preserve the parties' relationship. Thus, the prospect of a victory in litigation is not a sufficient reason to avoid ADR.

There are some circumstances in which settlement will not be in the client's interest. The client may want a binding precedent or may want to impress other potential litigants with its position and the costs of asserting claims against it.

Or the client may be in a situation in which there are no relational concerns. The only issue is whether it must pay money; there is no prejudgment interest, and the cost of contesting the claim is less than the interest earned on the money. In these and a small number of other situations, settlement is not the recommended choice.

Most of the time, however, settlement is the best option for clients. In fact, the very reason clients may seek a lawyer is that they cannot obtain settlement on their own. The lawyer's task is to not only consider what the client wants but also the barriers to settlement. The second table matches techniques to particular obstacles.

The most common obstacles are an inability to communicate clearly different views of the facts or the legal outcome if settlement is not reached. Resolution also will be difficult if each of the disputing parties is deeply attached to some principle that must be abandoned or compromised to resolve the dispute.

If one or more of the negotiators represents an institution or group, constituency pressures may impede agreement. Different elements within the institution or group may have different interests in the dispute, or the negotiator may have staked a political or job future on attaining a certain result. Alternatively, the resolution of one dispute may have an effect on other disputes involving one or both parties. [Text continues on page 866.]

Assessing the likelihood of overcoming impediments to settlement

How to apply this table: Identify from the first column each impediment to settlement. Then consider the likelihood of each procedure to overcome the impediment, using the ratings of 0 for unlikely, 1 for sometimes useful, 2 for often useful and 3 for most likely to be useful.

	Procedures			
Impediments	Mediation	Minitrial	Summary jury trial	Early neutral evaluation
Poor communication	3	1	1	1
Need to express emotions	3	1	1	1
Different view of facts	2	2	2	2
Different view of law	2	3	3	3
Important principle	1	0	0	0
Constituent pressure*	3	2	2	2
Linkage to other issues	2	1	1	1
Multiple parties	2	1	1	1
Different lawyer-client interests	2	1	1	1
Expectation of large judgment or sense it's unlikely	0	1	1	1

*All procedures would have the same value as mediation if they include mediation authority.

Lawyers and clients often have divergent attitudes and interests concerning settlement. This may be a matter of personality (one may be a fighter, the other a problem-solver) or of money. A lawyer who is paid on an hourly basis stands to profit handsomely from a trial, and may be less interested in settlement than is the client.

Another substantial barrier is the "jackpot syndrome" — where the plaintiff is confident of obtaining in court a financial recovery far exceeding its damages, either treble or punitive damages, and the defendant thinks such an award is highly unlikely.

Mediation scores higher on the impediments table than any other procedure for overcoming impediments to settlement. If, for example, an inability to communicate clearly is due to the emotional spillover of a bad relationship between the parties, the mediator can physically separate them and intervene to pass along all communications.

If the divergent interests of different groups within an institution impede settlement, the mediator can mediate among those groups. If linkage to other disputes is a problem, the mediator can make that linkage explicit, which the parties often fail to do, and encourage exploration of that linkage. Enlarging the topics for discussion may, paradoxically, make settlement easier by creating more opportunity for tradeoffs.

If different views of the facts or the legal outcome are barriers to settlement, mediation is often successful if the mediator can persuade the parties to search for mutually acceptable outcomes without determining which of their views is "right." (If not, a non-binding appraisal of the likely outcome of a trial, using a minitrial, summary jury trial or early neutral evaluation may be helpful.)

When issues of principle are at stake, techniques that seek to evaluate or judge the competing principles are unlikely to be successful. A skilled mediator, however, often can find a creative way of reconciling competing principles through a mutually satisfactory compromise.

Because mediation is so often the preferred procedure for overcoming the impediments to settlement, we suggest a rule of "presumptive mediation" — that mediation, if it is capable of satisfying the client's goals, and is not clearly incapable of overcoming the barriers to settlement, should be the first procedure used.

If mediation is not successful, the mediator can then recommend a different procedure. If, for example, the parties are so far apart in their views of the facts or law that meaningful settlement negotiations cannot take place, the mediator can recommend a referral to one of the evaluative procedures to move the parties closer together. Once that has been accomplished, mediated settlement negotiations can continue.

A strength of this approach is that the parties will be more amenable to taking advice when it comes from a mediator. Thus, the approach of presumptive mediation seems promising, particularly when the parties are having difficulty in agreeing on an ADR procedure.

The same principles apply where a judge, rather than a litigant, is searching for an appropriate ADR process. Only then, account also must be taken of public goals as well as those of the disputants.

Notes and Questions

1.   When using the system that Professors Goldberg and Sander recommend, remember that variations in procedures within the broad categories of dispute resolution can influence the utility of this methodology. Keep in mind also that more than one process may be used at different stages of a dispute.

2.   What problems might arise as you try to use the Sander–Goldberg model?

CPR INST. FOR DISPUTE RESOLUTION, ADR SUITABILITY GUIDE 22–25 (2001)

CPR Mediation Screen Questions Worksheet[1]

Beginning with the Benchmark Question, answer each question by indicating the choice that describes most accurately the dispute you are considering.

BENCHMARK QUESTION

Before you begin, in order to provide a benchmark against which to compare your analysis, indicate here whether your instinct, unaided by analysis, tells you that settlement of this dispute:

___ (a) Is not foreseeable at any stage.

___ (b) Is highly likely, even if only on the courthouse steps.

FACTOR ONE: The Parties' Goals for Managing the Dispute

A.   Overarching Goals

1.   **How important to the parties is maintaining a relationship with each other?**

___ (a) One or both sides cares only about the substantive outcome; the impact on the relationship with the other side is irrelevant.

___ (b) Although the substantive outcome is important, both sides would benefit to some degree from preserving or enhancing their relationship.

___ (c) Preservation or even improvement of the relationship is of considerable importance to both sides.

2. **How important to the parties is maintaining control over the *outcome* of the dispute?**

___ (a) Both sides prefer to have a judge [or arbitrator] decide the outcome.

___ (b) Maintaining control over the outcome is moderately important to at least one of the parties.

___ (c) Controlling the outcome is important to both parties.

3. **How important to the parties is maintaining control over the *process* by which the dispute is resolved?**

___ (a) Neither side cares at all about maintaining control over the process used to resolve the dispute.

___ (b) Maintaining control over the process is moderately important to at least one of the parties.

___ (c) Controlling the process is an important desire of both sides.

B. **Legal Goals**

4. **What is the likelihood that this case can be disposed of by a prompt, dispositive motion?**

___ (a) Very likely.

___ (b) A possibility.

___ (c) Very unlikely.

5. **Is injunctive relief, a legal precedent from a court or other relief only available from a adjudicative body needed by a party?**

___ (a) Very likely.

___ (b) A possibility.

___ (c) Very unlikely.

6. **How certain is the need to engage in formal discovery?**

___ (a) Totally certain; only formal and extensive discovery is likely to surface crucial information.

___ (b) Uncertain; it may be possible to acquire the relevant information in other ways.

___ (c) Unnecessary; both sides would be better served by avoiding burdensome or intrusive formal discovery.

7. **Do the parties only seek a neutral evaluation on the extent of damages or other specific issue?**

___ (a) Very likely.

___ (b) A possibility.

___ (c) Very unlikely.

C. Pragmatic Goals (Costs and Risks)

8. **What are the estimated monetary costs of pursuing litigation [arbitration] relative to what either side can realistically expect to recover by a decision in its favor?**

    ___ (a) Small, relative to the potential gain.

    ___ (b) The monetary costs are by no means negligible, but may be worth expending.

    ___ (c) High, given what is at stake.

9. **How important is a speedy resolution of the dispute?**

    ___ (a) Either unimportant to both parties or one party is best served by delaying resolution.

    ___ (b) Moderately important to both sides.

    ___ (c) Very important to both sides.

10. **Is there a need for privacy in the resolution process?**

    ___ (a) No, this is not a need of either side.

    ___ (b) Yes, this is a likely need, but only for one side.

    ___ (c) Yes, this is a likely need of both sides.

11. **How likely is it that a party will gain a financial bonanza by going to court [or arbitration]?**

    ___ (a) Very likely.

    ___ (b) The possibility is there, but with low probability.

    ___ (c) Virtually nonexistent.

FACTOR TWO: The Suitability of the Dispute for a Problem Solving Process

A. The Parties' Capacity for Problem Solving

12. **To what extent are matters of fundamental principle at stake?**

    ___ (a) Clearly at stake for at least one of the parties.

    ___ (b) Hard to judge with accuracy.

    ___ (c) Not a factor for either side.

13. **How important to the parties is the securing of public vindication?**

    ___ (a) An important objective for at least one side.

    ___ (b) Moderately important or hard to judge.

    ___ (c) Of no interest to either side.

14. **How certain are the parties that they will prevail in court [or arbitration]?**

    ___ (a) At least one side is confident it will prevail.

___ (b) Hard to judge with accuracy.

___ (c) Neither side is certain it will prevail.

15. **How receptive is the leadership on each side to the general idea of mediation?**

___ (a) Unsupportive or uninterested.

___ (b) Moderately receptive but with little or no experience with mediation.

___ (c) Very receptive.

B. **The Quality of the Parties' Relationship**

16. **What is the emotional climate between the parties?**

___ (a) One of deep-seated hostility, contempt, and distrust.

___ (b) Moderately antagonistic and distrustful.

___ (c) Relatively objective.

17. **What is the relative "power" of the parties as to their financial resources and business sophistication?**

___ (a) So disparate that one side may gain advantage over the other outside the civil justice system.

___ (b) There is a moderate disparity of power.

___ (c) Substantially comparable.

18. **How compatible are the styles of opposing counsel (as distinct from the parties themselves)?**

___ (a) It would be hard to imagine more contrasting legal styles and frameworks for dealing with conflict.

___ (b) Moderate differences exist.

___ (c) The attorneys' styles and frameworks for dealing with conflict are highly compatible.

C. **Practical Realities**

19. **Do the parties have the necessary resources to negotiate worthwhile trade-offs or to create new options?**

___ (a) A major problem is the lack of resources of any kind.

___ (b) Resources exist, but are not abundant.

___ (c) Reasonably good resources are available.

20. **Is this a dispute that involves critical areas of managerial responsibility (e.g., matters of corporate finance or corporate reorganization)?**

___ (a) Yes, and in very significant ways.

___ (b) Perhaps.

___ (c) No.

21. **What is the stance toward mediation of the jurisdiction in which the dispute is pending?**

____ (a) The court has little or no interest in mediation and/or has taken no steps to encourage mediation.

____ (b) Ambivalent, unclear, or modest.

____ (c) Very positive and encouraging and/or mediation is required for this kind of dispute.

FACTOR THREE: The Potential Benefits of Mediation for the Dispute in Question

Would mediation benefit the parties by:

22. **helping them clarify the issues in dispute?**

____ (a) No.

____ (b) Perhaps.

____ (c) Yes.

23. **helping them to channel or control anger or other negative emotions?**

____ (a) No.

____ (b) Perhaps.

____ (c) Yes.

24. **giving one or both parties an opportunity to tell their stories and to be fully heard by the other side?**

____ (a) No.

____ (b) Perhaps.

____ (c) Yes.

25. **providing an opportunity for an apology?**

____ (a) No, an apology would not be relevant or helpful.

____ (b) Perhaps.

____ (c) Yes, an apology would be very useful.

26. **providing them with a "reality check" from a knowledgeable intermediary on their positions or expectations?**

____ (a) No.

____ (b) Perhaps.

____ (c) Yes.

27. **providing a confidential setting in which to explore each other's interests and needs?**

____ (a) No.

____ (b) Perhaps.

____ (c) Yes.

28. **helping them to explore the possibility for trade-offs or creative solutions?**

____ (a) No.

____ (b) Perhaps.

____ (c) Yes.

29. **helping to educate the decision-makers on either side?**

____ (a) No.

____ (b) Perhaps.

____ (c) Yes.

30. **providing an intermediary who could make offers and counteroffers more acceptable by presenting them as his or her own ideas?**

____ (a) No.

____ (b) Perhaps.

____ (c) Yes.

31. **providing an intermediary who can reframe proposals?**

____ (a) No.

____ (b) Perhaps.

____ (c) Yes.

Interpreting Screen Responses and Practice Tips

Once you have answered all the questions, add up and record the number of (a), (b), and (c) responses in each of the three diagnostic categories.

* * *

Interpreting the Scores

The Screen is intended as a stimulus to analytic thinking and decision-making, not as a definitive measure of which cases should and should not be mediated. A response pattern in which (c) responses are significantly more frequent than (a) or (b) responses for all three factors suggests a dispute that is an excellent candidate for mediation. A preponderance of (b) responses for all factors suggests a dispute for which mediation may have value, despite some inauspicious signs. Alternatively, this may be a sign that the dispute is better suited for another type of nonbinding process, and a review of those processes should be made before deciding upon mediation.... A significant number of (a) responses across all three factors suggests that arbitration or litigation may be more appropriate....

Notes and Questions

1. If the patterns of responses are inconsistent, the authors of the Screen suggest that the attorney consider whether there are other factors at

play that are not covered by the screening questions. They also suggest that consideration be given to how the factors weigh against each other: "the weight to be given to each of these factors and their component elements must be assessed individually in light of experience and good judgment. In some cases, a single item or factor may provide such a compelling reason for mediation, or such an overwhelming obstacle to it, as to outweigh several counter-indicative answers." CPR INST. FOR DISPUTE RESOLUTION, ADR SUITABILITY GUIDE 26 (2001). For example, preserving the relationship between the parties may be of such importance as to outweigh other factors. In contrast, the potential for violence or a significant power imbalance may in some instances be enough to offset other potential benefits of mediation. In this regard, recall the excerpt from Trina Grillo, *The Mediation Alternative: Process Dangers for Women*, 100 Yale L.J. 1545 (1991), in Chapter IV, at page 477.

2. In addition to the questions posed by Goldberg and Sander and by the CPR Screen, consider whether, and how, you might discuss with clients the cognitive, emotional, and behavioral dimensions of their conflict and its resolution as described in Chapter I, beginning at page 6. What kind of discussion might you have with a client to explore these three dimensions? How might you discuss the ways in which a particular conflict is discernable in each of these dimensions and how the conflict might be resolved along each dimension? What implications might that discussion have for the selection of a dispute resolution process or for decisions about how the process is to be carried out?

3. It is not always easy to select a dispute resolution procedure through asking the kinds of questions suggested by Goldberg and Sander or those in the CPR Screen. As Goldberg and Sander indicate, one goal may be so important that it virtually dictates which process is most desirable. In addition, the clients or lawyers may not know, before a dispute resolution process begins, exactly what their goals are, what sorts of outcomes (problem-solving as opposed to adversarial) are possible or desirable, or what obstacles are likely to impede a consensual resolution. Do these factors raise any doubts in your mind about the value of the processes proposed by Goldberg and Sander or CPR? Do they — combined with the "participatory" model of professional-client relations advocated in Chapter II — suggest that a dialogue between lawyer and client would lead to the best decision by the client? Consider how you might apply the client counseling and interviewing techniques that you learned about in Chapter II to help you gather the information covered by the screening tool and to counsel your client about the appropriate dispute resolution options.

4. If, in a given case, parties and lawyers are having difficulty knowing the parties' precise goals and obstacles, how should they proceed? Will they be best off beginning with a mediation — because it offers more potential for fulfilling goals and overcoming obstacles than do the other processes? If so, who should influence procedural decisions, such as whether the mediator should evaluate, and who should influence substantive decisions, such as the definition of the problem? *See* Leonard L. Riskin, *Decisionmaking in Mediation: The New Old Grid and the New New Grid System*, 79 Notre Dame L. Rev. 1 (2003), excerpted in Chapter IV, beginning at page 423.

5. Just as with the evaluation of ADR programs, see *supra*, beginning on page 839, when choosing among processes it is important to define the appropriate comparison:

> Because civil case mediation occurs in the midst of a "litigotiation" process that seldom ends in trial, its most likely role is to facilitate settlements that would otherwise have occurred rather than to substitute for trial. Therefore, we should be skeptical of focusing our comparisons of 'what parties want' on their choice or assessments of mediation and trial. In this context, the significant research and policy questions turn on comparisons between lawyer-assisted mediation and lawyer-driven negotiation.

Craig A. McEwen & Roselle L. Wissler, *Finding Out If it is True: Comparing Mediation and Negotiation through Research*, 2002 J. Disp. Resol. 131, 133–34 (2002).

6. Eric Green, in an interview, made the following comments on analyzing cases for ADR potential:

> [T]he first thing to do, Professor Green says, "is to begin with the question, 'Why is this situation at an impasse?' In other words, identify the impediment."

> One of the most common hurdles is "an honest-to-God difference of opinion about who's going to win. It's kind of shocking that there is one, when you consider that each side has formed its opinion after getting the advice of some of the best legal counsel in the country, but often the impediment is that both sides have completely different views of the case. If each thinks that they have a 75 percent chance of winning, there's no zone of agreement on which to make a settlement."

> This is the kind of impasse against which the mini-trial is very effective, Professor Green says. "You have to add to the information available to both sides, to give them more compatible assessments of the case," he says, "and trying the case before a neutral party is a very good way to do that."

> Another common reason for impasse is the parties' linking the matter to other disputes. "Then you have to expand the task to settling all the related disputes," Green advises. "You've got to attack them all."

* * *

> This is one of the reasons why it is important to become acquainted with the parties beyond their particular claims in the case at hand, Green says. The consultant trying to settle a dispute needs to know if other disputes are involved, or if there are "constituent pressures" on the negotiators for either side. If someone's stuck in their position because of decisions elsewhere on their side, he says, "it's like two dynamite trucks heading for each other on a narrow road, after one of the drivers has thrown his steering wheel out the window."

> Getting the steering wheel back requires finding out who ordered it tossed out the window.

"One of your first tasks is to find out who's really calling the shots in the case," Professor Green says. That is the person the neutral must deal with, whatever his or her official relationship to the dispute.

No one particular type of lawyer or executive is more prone to be interested in a settlement, he says. "I've seen cases where the senior partner of the outside counsel is calling the shots, and thank God he is. Other times, maybe a strong inside counsel is in charge. On the other hand, sometimes you're glad to hear it's the executive of the company."

"The danger is not that someone in charge is hostile to dispute resolution, but rather that there may be no one in charge at all," he says. "Especially if there's a lot of insurance and reinsurance involved in the case, you often can't find anyone with authority who cares. Then, my role can be to help focus the problem — just by bringing it to someone's attention."

David Berreby, *Thoughts on ADR: An Interview with a Veteran Neutral*, 4 Alternatives to High Cost Litig., May 1986, at 14, 14–15.

7.   Client counseling about alternative methods of resolving disputes may also take place prior to the time at which a specific dispute arises. Transactional attorneys in particular are often involved in helping clients to plan ahead in selecting mechanisms by which to resolve their disputes. Consider the following excerpt:

KATHLEEN M. SCANLON & HARPREET K. MANN, A GUIDE TO MULTI–STEP DISPUTE RESOLUTION CLAUSES

ADR Counsel In–Box, No. 8, 20 Alternatives (centerfold pullout September 2002).

Dispute resolution planning is becoming a critical function of corporate law departments, law firms, and public sector legal departments. Powerful economic incentives, increased emphasis on risk management, and the growing complexity of dispute resolution options are among the reasons that compel private and public sector lawyers to engage in dispute resolution planning.

Predispute resolution clauses are an important component in dispute resolution planning for business-to-business transactions. Agreeing upon a process to manage disputes before they arise yields multiple benefits, including efficiency, predictability, and controlled risks . . . . .

OVERVIEW

For many decades, simple, stand-alone, standardized arbitration clauses had been the extent of ADR clause drafting in many business-to-business agreements. If litigation, rather than arbitration, was contemplated to resolve future disputes, provisions relating to forum selection, choice-of-law, and a few other select items may have been addressed in the contract. Presently, much more sophisticated drafting techniques exist. Most notable is the use of the multi-step, or multi-tiered, dispute resolution clause.

A multi-step clause provides for sequential stages of dispute resolution. Negotiation and mediation are commonly used prior to the parties resorting to arbitration or litigation. The rationale underlying this sequential use of negotiation and/or mediation in the first instance is that it provides the parties with an opportunity to develop creative, business-oriented solutions before investing time and money in an adversarial process, such as arbitration or litigation. The use of multi-step clauses to manage disputes effectively and efficiently reflects sound legal and business judgment in many circumstances. Companies across a cross-section of industries are using some form of multi-step dispute resolution clause in their agreements when appropriate.

CPR MODEL MULTI–STEP CLAUSE (Negotiation–Mediation–Arbitration)

(A) The parties shall attempt in good faith to resolve any dispute arising out of or relating to this [Agreement] [Contract] promptly by negotiation between executives who have authority to settle the controversy and who are at a higher level of management than the persons with direct responsibility for administration of this contract. Any person may give the other party written notice of any dispute not resolved in the normal course of business. Within [15] days after delivery of the notice, the receiving party shall submit to the other a written response. The notice and response shall include (a) a statement of that party's position and a summary of arguments supporting that position, and (b) the name and title of the executive who will represent that party and of any other person who will accompany the executive. Within [30] days after delivery of the initial notice, the executives of both parties shall meet at a mutually acceptable time and place, and thereafter as often as they reasonably deem necessary, to attempt to resolve the dispute. All reasonable requests for information made by one party to the other will be honored.

All negotiations pursuant to this clause are confidential and shall be treated as compromise and settlement negotiations for purposes of applicable rules of evidence.

(B) If the dispute has not been resolved by negotiation as provided herein within [45] days after delivery of the initial notice of negotiation, [or if the parties failed to meet within [20] days,] the parties shall endeavor to settle the dispute by mediation under the CPR Mediation Procedure [then currently in effect OR in effect on the date of this Agreement], [provided, however, that if one party fails to participate in the negotiation as provided herein, the other party can initiate mediation prior to the expiration of the [45] days]. Unless otherwise agreed, the parties will select a mediator from the CPR Panels of Distinguished Neutrals.

(C) Any dispute arising out of or relating to this [Agreement] [Contract], including the breach, termination or validity thereof, which has not been resolved by mediation as provided herein [within [45] days after initiation of the mediation procedure] [within [30] days after the appointment of a mediator], shall be finally resolved by arbitration in accordance with the CPR Rules for Non–Administered Arbitration [then currently in effect OR

in effect on the date of this Agreement], by [a sole arbitrator] [three independent and impartial arbitrators, of whom each party shall designate one] [three arbitrators of whom each party shall appoint one in accordance with the 'screened' appointment procedure provided in Rule 5.4] [three independent and impartial arbitrators, none of whom shall be appointed by either party]; [provided, however, that if one party fails to participate in either the negotiation or mediation as agreed herein, the other party can commence arbitration prior to the expiration of the time periods set forth above.]

The arbitration shall be governed by the Federal Arbitration Act, 9 U.S.C. §§ 1–16, and judgment upon the award rendered by the arbitrator(s) may be entered by any court having jurisdiction thereof. The place of arbitration shall be (city, state).

For additional model CPR multistep clauses and corporate examples, see CPR Drafter's Deskbook (CPR, 2002) (Appendix A & Section 3).

WHEN TO CONSIDER USING MULTI–STEP CLAUSES

When to consider using a multistep clause requires an assessment of the potential benefits and concerns:* * *

AT A GLANCE

Advantages...	Concerns...
Providing for a negotiation or mediation period is highly desirable because there is a process in place to keep everyone talking early in a dispute.	Prevents a case-by-case determination of an appropriate ADR process and conceivably a dispute that may not be amenable to negotiation or mediation, for example, may end up in such a process. Such an outcome could result in delay and needless costs. But the parties can always jointly agree to forgo or limit participation under such circumstances.
Although the people involved in a deal today may have an excellent relationship, they may not be at the company in the future when a dispute arises. Offering any of the new people a means to resolve a dispute other than litigation may enable them to constructively resolve a dispute which otherwise could deteriorate into adversarial litigation. Avoids the situation of "What do we do now?" when a dispute arises.	Can raise the possibility of strategic participation (e.g., only to obtain free discovery) and tangential enforcement litigation. Parameters of good-faith participation are evolving. Moreover, examples exist of parties seeking to stay arbitration or litigation until negotiation or mediation is held pursuant to a multi-step clause. While the case law is not extensive, there is authority that agreements to engage in consensual processes can be enforceable. Also can raise the possibility of precluding enforcement of an arbitration clause when both parties fail to request mediation.
Multi-step approach gives the parties a concrete reason to fully explore whether a consensual, potentially more satisfactory resolution is possible before investing the significant resources typically required by arbitration or litigation.	

Notes and Questions

1. Additional issues that might be addressed in the contract include procedures for the selection of a neutral, confidentiality, discovery, statutes

of limitation, which disputes are subject to the clause, and other variations in the procedures desired. For sample dispute resolution provisions, drafting checklists, and discussion of the various alternatives, see CORINNE COOPER & BRUCE E. MEYERSON, A DRAFTER'S GUIDE TO ALTERNATIVE DISPUTE RESOLUTION (1991); KATHLEEN M. SCANLON, DRAFTER'S DESKBOOK FOR DISPUTE RESOLUTION CLAUSES (2002). *See also* JAY E. GRENIG, ALTERNATIVE DISPUTE RESOLUTION WITH FORMS (2d ed. 1997). You should note that to the extent parties to a contract craft a set of procedures for resolving disputes under the contract, they have engaged in a form of dispute systems design. How might you apply the dispute systems design principles detailed in the previous section in this context?

2. It is becoming increasingly necessary for transactional lawyers and litigators to work together to provide appropriate dispute resolution to clients. Consider the following:

> [T]ransaction lawyers and trial lawyers can provide the best client service to business entities by working together, from the drafting state through to advising the client how to conduct the mediation.

> The transaction lawyer needs to know much more today then years ago to draft an ADR clause that will satisfy client goals, needs and interests. Consultation with ADR-knowledgeable trial counsel at the drafting stage is essential on matters such as the parameters for enforceable confidentiality and many outcome-influencing clause provisions. Such consultation at the mediation stage also is important to the client and trial counsel because the transaction lawyer knows the deal, the client and probably the other parties. It makes sense.

Donald Lee Rome, *Business Mediation's Orientation Focuses Detail on Printed Words*, 21 Alternatives 21, 21 (2003).

3. In the mid–1990s, Professor John Lande surveyed 178 business executives and corporate counsel in four states about their opinions and experiences with litigation and ADR. Approximately one-quarter (24%) of respondents indicated that their firms had "unofficial policies favoring the use of ADR contract clauses" and that an additional 10% worked at firms that had "adopted official policies directing ... use of ADR clauses." John Lande, *Getting the Faith: Why Business Lawyers and Executives Believe in Mediation*, 5 Harv. Negot. L. Rev. 137, 196 (2000).

4. Professor Amy Schmitz explores the tension between statutory and common law approaches to the enforcement of ADR clauses. She argues that ADR clauses providing for non-binding processes ought to be clearly distinguished from clauses providing for binding arbitration (the enforcement of which is governed by the Federal Arbitration Act and the Uniform Arbitration Act) and makes the case that "[c]ontract and remedy law provide courts with the tools to develop a coherent and refreshed approach for determining proper enforcement of these [non-binding] ADR agreements." Amy J. Schmitz, *Refreshing Contractual Analysis of ADR Agreements by Curing Bipolar Avoidance of Modern Common Law*, 9 Harv. Negot. L. Rev. 1, 74 (2004).

5. Recall the discussion in Chapter V over the use of mandatory and binding arbitration provisions, beginning at page 554. Would you include a

mandatory arbitration provision as part of a multi-step dispute resolution provision? Why? Why not?

6.   You have been asked to draft a proposed dispute resolution clause for the three clients of your law firm described below. Summarize the principal features of the clauses you will recommend for each.

a.   A client has been selected as the general contractor for a multi-million dollar office building that will serve as the home-office for an insurance company. The client is likely to do other construction work for this company in the future. The construction contract will contain a provision for dealing with disputes that arise.

b.   Susan, your client, and John, her husband of five years, are divorcing. They have agreed that the two children will remain with Susan during the school year but will spend their Christmas and summer vacations with John.

Susan is concerned about the environment in which her children will live while with John, especially if he remarries, and where John will take them on trips. Living with John has convinced her that he may take the children to places where they might not be safe. John has agreed to "consult" with Susan on proposed trips with the children, to have the children call Susan at least once a week while they are with him, and to allow Susan to visit his home once each summer vacation and make "suggestions" regarding the children's safety and needs. Susan is concerned that disputes will arise in the implementation of these arrangements. John has agreed to consider including in the separation agreement a dispute resolution clause covering such disputes.

c.   An insurance company client is reviewing the language of its policies covering products liability of large manufacturers. It is considering adding a dispute resolution clause to deal with disagreements involving issues such as coverage and duty to defend.

D.   CHOOSING AND BUILDING DISPUTE RESOLUTION PROCESSES

The Daily Bugle*

GENERAL INFORMATION FOR BOTH PARTICIPANTS

Two weeks ago, the *Daily Bugle,* its editor, and one of its reporters, Terry Ives, were sued for defamation by John Roark, M.D. The article that was the basis of the suit described the latest in a series of fires in slum housing, pointing out that the building in which the fire took place was so poorly managed that some tenants lacked heat. It contained the following language, which includes statements that Roark alleges to be false and defamatory:

---

* The role-play instructions were prepared by Professor Nancy Rogers, based upon *Tape IV: The Roark v. Daily Bugle Libel Claim,* Dispute Resolution and Lawyers Video Tape Series (Distributed by West Publishing Co. (1991)), which was based upon Nanette Laughrey and Sandra David- son Scott, "The Doctor and the Daily Bugle: A Process Selection Exercise," in the Instructor's Manual for Tape IV. Confidential Instructions for both participants appear in the Instructor's Manual for Tape IV, and on the casebook's TWEN web site at www.lawschool.westlaw.com.

The destroyed building is owned by slum landlord Dr. John Roark, county property records reveal. Dr. Roark is a prominent orthopedic surgeon.... A source in the Fire Marshall's office indicated that the office is not ruling out the possibility of arson because it is not uncommon for owners of tenements to intentionally burn them to collect insurance.

Roark alleges that the reporter was negligent — property records show that he was only a limited partner in the group owning the property — and that the reporter acted with malice. He states that the newspaper refused his request for a retraction. He seeks $250,000 in actual damages for harm to his reputation, lost income in his medical practice, aggravation of a serious health problem, and mental anguish. He also seeks $1 million in punitive damages.

Defamation is a communication of an untruth to a third person that harms a person's reputation or causes harm in that person's business. Truth is a defense. Public figures must show that the defendant acted with actual malice in order to recover. In this jurisdiction, private individuals need only show negligence in order to recover actual damages. Actual malice must be shown in order to recover punitive damages.

In this jurisdiction, the reporter has a privilege to refuse disclosure of a source who has been promised confidentiality. However, under the privilege statute, the judge decides in each instance whether the need for disclosure outweighs the harm caused by disclosure, specifically the harm to the public interest in promoting dissemination of news by assuring the anonymity of sources.

Exercise 1: Counsel for Dr. Roark is to meet with Dr. Roark, explain the options for resolving the dispute, and help the client decide which option(s) the lawyer should promote in a forthcoming meeting with counsel for the *Daily Bugle*.

Exercise 2: Like any newspaper, the *Daily Bugle* must deal with defamation claims as an on-going part of its business. Work in teams to design a system that the *Daily Bugle* can use to address these conflicts in the future.

Chapter VIII

LOOKING AHEAD

In the preceding chapters, we have covered a lot of ground about the nature of the various methods of dispute resolution, their potential advantages and disadvantages, and the challenges of integrating them into our roles as lawyers. But as we have seen, the field of dispute resolution is dynamic, not static, and is constantly evolving with new applications, insights, and skills. We covered some of this innovation in Chapter VI, in our discussion of such recent adaptations as collaborative lawyering, partnering, and online dispute resolution. In this short, concluding chapter, we continue taking a brief look at the road ahead. We first will look at new connections for the field, in particular exploring how the modern ADR movement fits within other movements in the law to humanize the process of conflict resolution. We then turn to new skills that ADR professionals are coming to use to improve their practices and quality of life, focusing on the use of mindfulness mediation as a vehicle for expanding self-awareness and fostering other virtues of so-called emotional intelligence. Finally we explore how interested students may get started in the field, beginning with a general discussion of the professional organizations that can provide for initial entrée, and then providing several personal stories of current practitioners.

A. NEW CONNECTIONS

As we saw in Chapter I, the modern ADR movement was born of many forces, including the recognition by leaders and pioneers within the legal profession that traditional litigation may not be the best vehicle for the resolution of some problems. This casebook has focused primarily on the resolution of formal legal disputes, and the degree to which the methods we have discussed are capable of resolving the behavioral, cognitive, and emotional dimensions of conflict. Yet, the development of the dispute resolution field is only part of a larger tapestry of efforts to make conflict resolution more responsive to human needs. In the following excerpt, Professor Susan Daicoff provides a sense of this terrain, discussing several "vectors" of what she calls "the comprehensive law movement."

SUSAN DAICOFF, THE ROLE OF THERAPEUTIC JURISPRUDENCE WITHIN THE COMPREHENSIVE LAW MOVEMENT *IN* DENNIS STOLLE, DAVID B. WEXLER, AND BRUCE J. WINICK, PRACTICING THERAPEUTIC JURISPRUDENCE

471–482 (2000).

The Vectors of the Comprehensive Law Movement

There are about ten or eleven vectors of the comprehensive law movement. Preventive law, which developed in the 1930s to 1950s, may be the oldest vector; many of the others emerged in the late 1980s or early 1990s, such as therapeutic jurisprudence and holistic law. Several are even newer, such as transformative mediation and creative problem solving. Others are likely to continue to emerge. Some are more concrete, practical, and tangible while others are more theoretical and academic. Some focus on dispute resolution while others encompass nonconflictual legal matters such as estate planning. Some focus on criminal law, some on civil law, some on law in the courts, and others on law outside the courts, yet all share the two common features outlined above. * * *

Therapeutic jurisprudence

Therapeutic jurisprudence ("Tj") focuses on the therapeutic or countertherapeutic consequences of the law and legal procedures on people. Specifically, it focuses on the effect on the individuals or groups of people involved, including the clients and their families, friends, lawyers, judges, and communities. It attempts to reform law and legal processes in order to promote the psychological wellbeing of the people they affect.* * *

Although Tj was originally applied mainly in the area of mental health law, it has been widely applied to a number of substantive law areas as well as to legal processes. Its popularity and applications have quickly grown since its emergence around 1990. Its scope has broadened from proposing law reform to asking how existing law can be applied more therapeutically. For example, Tj proposes that the practicing lawyer identify, consider, and seek to improve the psychological effects any proposed legal action or process may have on the individuals and groups involved. More recently, Tj has been utilized in police work, judging, specialized courts, and the appellate opinion process.

Recent applications of Tj illustrate the optimal effect it can have on individuals' mental health. For example, drug treatment courts explicitly provide defendants with an option to convert a legal crisis into an opportunity for recovery from drug and alcohol addiction and for sustained life change. They do this by utilizing the substance abuse treatment knowledge about what works, about the need for continued support from the court, and about relapse, etc. Domestic violence courts similarly provide an opportunity for offenders not simply to experience short-term punishment but actually to move into a transformational process encouraging positive and long-term change. Even the words used in a judge's opinion or interaction with the litigants can be nontherapeutic or therapeutic, if chosen with an appreciation for the psychology underlying the case. In some cases, the judge may be the only person with sufficient power, authority, or opportunity to persuade or support a troubled, defensive, or isolated individual to change.* * *

Preventive Law

Preventive law is a long-standing, harm-averse movement within the legal profession that explicitly seeks to intervene in legal matters before disputes arise. It advocates proactive intervention to avoid litigation and other conflicts. It emphasizes the lawyer-client relationship, clients' relationships with others in general, and planning. While not explicitly therapeutic, preventive law certainly recognizes the enormous psychological and financial costs involved in litigation and seeks to avoid those negative outcomes. In many cases, its application would preserve ongoing relationships by intervening in potentially troublesome situations before they erupt into litigations.

Employment law is particularly appropriate for the practice of preventive law. There are often situations in which an employer knows that an employee is disgruntled and not performing optimally, but hesitates to deal effectively with the situation. The employee's performance continues to decline, the situation becomes embittered, the employer fires the employee for nonperformance, and the employee sues the employer with possibly a real grievance. The entire situation could have been prevented and the employment relationship salvaged, if the lawyer had practiced effective preventive law. However, resolution of the difficulty between the employer and employee may require that the lawyer be sensitive to and proficient with interpersonal dynamics, again emphasizing the potentially psychological aspects of this type of practice.

Therapeutic jurisprudence/Preventive Law

Perhaps due to this need in preventive law sometimes for sensitivity to the psychological aspects of legal matters, it became clear that Tj and preventive law could benefit from each other. Therapeutic jurisprudence originated primarily as an academic discipline focused on theory, while preventive law focused on ways of practicing law. Preventive law therefore offered Tj a practical framework and a set of procedures that helped Tj lawyers actually apply the law therapeutically. Preventive law benefitted from Tj's explicit focus on the psychology of law. Thus, in a series of articles, the two vectors were, for many purposes, joined as an integrated approach to law and lawyering.

For example, an integrated, Tj/PL approach asks the lawyer to identify "psycholegal soft spots," or areas of psychological effect that a strict legal analysis would overlook or ignore. It then proposes that the lawyer raise these concerns with the client and, through the resulting dialogue, seek a course of action that takes these concerns into account. For example, an estate planner will discuss with the client the psychological effects a bequest will have on the testator's children. If the will leaves a bequest outright to one child and in trust for the other because the testator trusts the judgment of one child and not the other, then certain psychological consequences may result. The less trustworthy child may feel that his or her parent did not love him or her as much as he or she loved the other child, even though the lack of the parent's trust was justified. Or, the estate planner or divorce lawyer will be sensitive to the psychological dynamics of the grief process, when dealing with a client diagnosed with AIDS or one undergo a divorce, respectively. The lawyer in these cases will be prepared for dealing with the client's resistance to cooperation with the lawyer, if the client is in denial about his or her medical or marital condition.

The lawyer also will need to be patient with the client and may need to assist the client in moving through denial into the next phase of the grief process.

Restorative justice

Restorative justice refers to a movement in criminal law in which criminal justice and criminal sentencing are carried out by the community, the victim, and the offender in a collaborative process. In this process, all players are present and the process focuses on the relationships between the offender, the victim, and the community. It is the antithesis of a topdown, hierarchical system where the judge, who is on top, imposes a sentence on the defendant, who is below the judge in the hierarchy. * * *

It appears to have been most enthusiastically employed in Australia, Canada, and the United Kingdom, although it is being used in a number of American jurisdictions. It bears a resemblance to traditional Native American and aboriginal justice in its emphasis on the community and on the therapeutic value of "normal, reintegrative shame" (which is acknowledged by the offender), rather than on privately imposed punishment.

Procedural Justice

Procedural justice refers to empirical studies finding that, in judicial procedures, litigants' satisfaction sometimes depends nearly as much upon certain psychological factors as upon the actual outcome of the legal matter (e.g., winning vs. losing). These factors are: being treated with respect and dignity, being heard, having an opportunity to speak and participate, and how trustworthy the authorities appear and behave. It does not advocate any particular way of administering the law other than recommending that, for optimal participant satisfaction and thus optimal dispute resolution, judges and attorneys must treat litigants and other individuals with respect and dignity, they must be authentic, honest, and trustworthy, and legal processes must provide participants with an opportunity to speak freely. * * *

Facilitative Mediation

As mediation developed within the ADR movement, it began to split into two forms, evaluative and facilitative. In evaluative mediation, the mediator functions as a third-party evaluator of the parties' cases and can adopt an authoritative, adjudicatory posture. The evaluative mediator is likely to evaluate the merits of the parties' legal positions, discuss what they would probably obtain if they litigated the case, and use that information to move the parties towards agreements. In contrast, facilitative mediation is a three-party process in which the mediator seeks to assist each party to express their needs and reach a solution acceptable to both parties. The therapeutic aspects of facilitative mediation have been noted. It can empower the parties, give them a feeling of control and ownership over the process and its outcome, and lead to a greater sense of agreement and resolution between the parties. However, it is worth noting that there are times when evaluative mediation, albeit possibly less collaborative and party-centered, may actually be more therapeutic than facilitative mediation. For example, evaluative mediation might be therapeutic where there is a great power imbalance between the parties or where one party is unaware of what he or she might be entitled to in a litigated outcome and could subjugate himself or herself unnecessarily without such information.

Transformative Mediation

Transformative mediation is a newer form of mediation that emerged around 1994. It sees mediation as an opportunity for the parties to learn how to resolve disputes more effectively. It explicitly seeks to change the parties in the mediation process to improve their conflict resolution abilities so that they can resolve future disputes themselves, without help. In this process, the procedure and the players are dynamic. The process is not viewed as a one-shot, static event accomplishing the resolution of simply one dispute. Instead, the parties are moved towards effective, continuing relationships with each other. It is obviously particularly appropriate in family law and employment law settings.* * *

Collaborative Law

Collaborative law is a nonlitigative, collaborative process employed mainly in divorce law, where the spouses and their respective attorneys resolve the issues outside of court in a four-party process. It differs from mediation in that no third party is involved; it is a four-way process rather than a three-party process and it involves six ongoing relationships between the four individuals involved (i.e., lawyer-client, client-client, and lawyer-lawyer). It differs from traditional settlement negotiations in that: (1) no formal court proceedings are usually instituted until settlement is reached; and (2) the attorneys are contractually forbidden from representing their clients in court should the agreement process break down. It accomplishes resolution of the parties' dispute by engaging the divorcing spouses and their respective attorneys in a series of collaborative, four-way discussions designed to reach settlement outside of litigation. Because the attorneys must withdraw if the process breaks down, the attorneys' financial interests are aligned with the clients' —

all four people want to reach settlement. This contrasts with the usual process, in which the lawyers "win" whether the clients settle or not, since they simply litigate the case if settlement negotiations break down. This aspect is said to have a definite salutary effect on the lawyers' motivation to achieve resolution. Because of the personal investment of all four parties in achieving resolution, proponents maintain that more creative, altruistic, and harmonious solutions are proposed and implemented in collaborative law. * * * Although currently being used only in the domestic area, collaborative law is appropriate for a number of other areas, such as employment law and probate law.

Holistic Law

Holistic law or holistic justice is a movement that arose among practicing lawyers around 1990. The web site for the International Alliance of Holistic Lawyers explains that holistic law:

> acknowledges the need for a humane legal process with the highest level of satisfaction for all participants; honor[s] and respect[s] the dignity and integrity of each individual; promote[s] peaceful advocacy and holistic legal principles; value[s] responsibility, connection and inclusion; encourages compassion, reconciliation, forgiveness and healing; practices deep listening, understands and recognizes the importance of voice; contribute[s] to peace building at all levels of society; recognize[s] the opportunity in conflict; draw[s] upon ancient intuitive wisdom of diverse cultures and traditions; and [encourages the lawyer to] enjoy the practice of law.

It is explicitly interdisciplinary, allows the lawyer to incorporate his or her own morals and values into client representation, and seeks to "do the right thing" for the lawyer, clients, and others involved. Like holistic medicine, it uses a broad, holistic approach to solve legal problems and it deals with legal matters in a humane, often collaborative, and frequently healing fashion.* * * Some of the philosophies of the individual lawyers involved may be rooted in humanistic principles, some in New Age principles, some in psychology, some in religion or spirituality, and others in universal moral principles. * * *

Creative Problem Solving

Creative problem solving ("CPS") is a very broad discipline that is explicitly humanistic, interdisciplinary, creative, and preventive in its approach to legal problems. It seeks to find solutions to legal problems using a broader approach than is traditionally associated with legal work. It has been described as:

> ... an evolving approach to law. It combines law, sociology, social anthropology, and the behavioral sciences (particularly cognitive psychology, group dynamics, and decision-making) in a holistic fashion. It also includes the assessment of the impact of business theory and economics [and] sciences and applied sciences['] ... diagnostic and planning skills. In Creative Problem Solving, problems are thought of as multidimensional, often requiring non-legal

or multidisciplinary solutions. Most conflicts have interconnected causes and their effects often impinge on competing jurisdictions and disciplines. In short, entrenchment of law and legal precepts can sometimes work against the solving of problems. In fact, Creative Problem Solving requires the parties to part with the linear understanding of history of the situation.[1] * * *

The American Bar Association has been active in sponsoring discussion about the scope and efficacy of creative problem solving. Some of its proponents view CPS as an "umbrella" discipline incorporating all of the other vectors under its aegis. It has recently been associated in some ways with preventive law, illustrating yet another bridge between vectors.

Specialized Courts

Specialized courts, such as drug treatment courts, mental health courts, and domestic violence courts, take an explicitly therapeutic approach to their treatment of alcohol- and drug-addicted individuals, those with mental disabilities, and those involved in domestic violence. They use psychological insights about human nature and the nature of the mental problems involved to achieve optimal results of the judicial interface with people's lives. In some cases, these courts' approach has dramatically reduced recidivism rates among offenders. Their popularity in recent years and efficacy demands that they be included as a vector of this movement, albeit in the area of judging rather than in the area of lawyering. Not only have they had a salutary effect upon the troubled individuals brought to court, but the effects of their work have also rejuvenated the spirits of the lawyers and judges involved.

Notes and Questions

1. The aim of the comprehensive law movement is to "optimize human well-being and focus on extra-legal concerns, including the emotions of those involved and relationships." *See* Carolyn Copps Hartley & Carrie J. Petrucci, *Justice, Ethics, and Interdisciplinary Teaching and Practice: Practicing Culturally Competent Therapeutic Jurisprudence: A Collaboration between Social Work and Law*, 14 Wash. U. J.L. & Pol'y 133, 171–73 (2004). Professor Daicoff has expanded her exploration of this movement in SUSAN S. DAICOFF, LAWYER, KNOW THYSELF: A PSYCHOLOGICAL ANALYSIS OF PERSONALITY STRENGTHS AND WEAKNESSES (2004).

2. As you recall from Chapter I, Professor Frank E.A. Sander is widely credited with heralding the dawn of the modern ADR movement with his speech calling for what has been come to be known as the "multi-door courthouse." Is the comprehensive law movement an extension of that concept?

---

1. James M. Cooper, *Towards a New Architecture: Creative Problem Solving and the Evolution of Law*, 34 Calif. West. L. Rev. 297, 312–13 (1998) (citations omitted). *See* Linda Morton, *Teaching Creative Problem Solving: A Paradigmatic Approach*, 34 Calif. West. L. Rev. 374, 376–78 (1998) (further describing creative problem solving and its use in legal education). The web site for the McGill Center for Creative Problem Solving at California Western School of Law is found at http://www.cps.cwsl.edu.

3. Which, if any, of the vectors are likely to become part of the mainstream of American law? What barriers do you see to this progression?

4. As we saw with the "brief take" on victim-offender mediation in Chapter IV, beginning at page 326, restorative justice has been a particularly active vector within the comprehensive law movement. For other applications, see, e.g., Ann Skelton, *Restorative Justice as a Framework for Juvenile Justice*, 42 Brit. J. Criminology 496 (2002); Carrie J. Niebur Eisnaugle, *International Truth Commission: Utilizing Restorative Justice as an Alternative to Retribution*, 36 Vand. J. Transnat'l L. 209 (2003); Kristen F. Grunewald & Priya Nath, *Defense-Based Victim Outreach: Restorative Justice in Capital Cases*, 15 Cap. Def. J. 315 (2003). For a thorough treatment, see Symposium, *The Restorative Justice Conference*, 2003 Utah L. Rev. 1.

5. There has been considerable experimentation with specialized courts to deal with drug offenses. For a discussion of so-called "drug courts," see John S. Goldkamp, *The Drug Court Response: Issues and Implications for Justice Change*, 63 Alb. L. Rev. 923 (2000); James L. Nolan Jr., Reinventing Justice: The American Drug Court Movement (2001). For a critique, see Martin B. Hoffman, *The Drug Court Scandal*, 78 N.C. L. Rev. 1437 (2000).

6. The restorative justice concept has also been adapted to the administrative context. For example, some agencies have experimented with a New Zealand innovation called the Family Group Conference, in which a social worker for an agency investigating juvenile delinquency or child abuse, for example, convenes a meeting of all immediate family members and relevant professionals to address the presenting problem. For a discussion, see Susan M. Chandler & Marilou Giovannucci, *Family Group Conferences: Transforming Traditional Child Welfare Policy and Practice*, 42 Fam. Ct. Rev. 216 (2004); Allison Morris, *Youth Justice in New Zealand*, 31 Crime & Just. 243 (2004).

B. NEW SKILLS

Much of our aim in this book has been to raise your awareness of the various issues that need to be taken into account when considering a dispute resolution option, such as the different approaches to negotiation and mediation and their implications, doctrinal issues in arbitration, and empirical questions in evaluation. Such awareness elevates our capacity to use the dispute resolution methods appropriately, effectively and wisely, whether we are negotiating a matter on behalf of a client, representing a client in a mediation, serving as an arbitrator, designing a dispute resolution program for a court, or engaging in another form of dispute resolution or conflict management.

We have also sought to provide the skills with which to practice dispute resolution, skills such as listening, inquiry, analysis of interests and other issues, and the management of power imbalances. These are foundational skills that in some respects are easily taught, but take a lifetime to master.

As the excerpt on the mediator's "presence" by David Hoffman and Daniel Bowling in Chapter IV indicates, beginning at page 405, dispute resolution professionals are joining business, education, and other professionals in recognizing the importance of self-awareness, and other aspects of "emotional intelligence."

A concept pioneered by Daniel Goleman, emotional intelligence may be understood as the set of competencies that arise from our understanding of our emotions, our physiological systems, and the interactions we have with other people, situations, events, etc. *See* DANIEL GOLEMAN, EMOTIONAL INTELLIGENCE: WHY IT CAN MATTER MORE THAN I.Q. (1995). These competencies lie in essentially two domains. The first is our personal competencies, which include not only self-awareness, but also self-management, how we conduct ourselves in light of the qualities and characteristics about ourselves about which we have become self aware. The second set of competencies deal with how we manage our interactions with others, including our basic awareness of social relationships and our capacity to manage those relationships. *See* HENDRIE WEISENGER, EMOTIONAL INTELLIGENCE AT WORK XVI-XXII (1998). The general idea in the dispute resolution context is that the better we understand ourselves, our emotions, our relationships with others, etc., the better we will be able to handle ourselves when we are involved in conflict or engaged in a process of dispute resolution.

There are a variety of emotional intelligence skills, such as empathy, communication, and leadership, many of which can be cultivated with practice and training. Self-awareness is a foundational part of this skill set, and in the following excerpt, Professor Riskin discusses the use of mindfulness meditation as a technique for fostering such awareness, as well as empathy, presence of mind, and the capacity for connecting with others effectively as lawyers, dispute resolution professionals, and people.

LEONARD L. RISKIN, MINDFULNESS: FOUNDATIONAL TRAINING FOR DISPUTE RESOLUTION

54 J. Leg. Educ. 79 (2004).

I want to begin with a profound problem that afflicts all of us as teachers, students, and practitioners of dispute resolution. It was brought home to me about two weeks after the attacks of September 11, 2001, in an e-mail message I received from a friend who lives in Washington, D.C., not far from the Pentagon. My friend told me that he had been abroad on September 11, and on his return he found an e-mail message that included the following reading:

> If you can start the day without caffeine or pep pills,
> If you can be cheerful, ignoring aches and pains,
> If you can resist complaining and boring people with your troubles,
> If you can eat the same food every day and be grateful for it,
> If you can understand when loved ones are too busy to give you time,
> If you can overlook when people take things out on you when, through no fault of yours, something goes wrong,

If you can take criticism and blame without resentment,
If you can face the world without lies and deceit,
If you can conquer tension without medical help,
If you can relax without liquor,
If you can sleep without the aid of drugs,
Then you are probably a dog.

[Robert D. Hutchison, Untitled]

A Problem: Mindlessness in Counseling, Negotiating, and Mediating

It is a fact of the human condition that we are suffused with fears, insecurities, passions, impulses, judgments, rationalizations, assumptions, biases, and the mental shortcuts that some academics call "heuristics." These can be more or less available to our conscious awareness, and we can be more or less able to resist them.

Such mental and emotional influences, of course, help guide us through life and through professional activities, including teaching, resolving disputes, and lawyering. The problem is that they also can interfere with our ability to do these activities well. They can, for instance, draw our attention away from where we want it to be. When we want to listen to a client or read a document, we may be distracted by worries about whether the client likes us, or by thoughts (or chains of thoughts) about almost anything: the laundry, whether we made the right career choice, or why we didn't schedule that trip to Hawaii. The less conscious awareness we have of these impulses, fears, passions, thoughts, and habitual assumptions and behaviors, the more likely we are to succumb to them.

The mind tends to wander, and very often we do not realize where it has gone. Usually it is dwelling in the past or future, keeping us from paying attention to the present moment. Understood in this way, intermittent mindlessness can affect and afflict just about everyone in conducting virtually any activity.

Mindlessness impairs our work as practitioners of dispute resolution in several ways. For example, it could mean that a mediator or negotiator is not very "present" with the other participants or with himself, i.e., not fully aware of what is going on. This diminishes the professional's ability to gather information and to listen to, and understand, others and himself, and even to achieve satisfaction from his work. The second problem is that, in the grip of mindlessness, we sometimes rely on old habits and assumptions, rather than deciding what behavior is most suitable in the precise circumstances we are encountering. To Harvard psychology professor Ellen Langer, mindlessness means "the light's on but nobody's at home." Manifestations include being "trapped by categories," "automatic behavior," and "acting from a single perspective." As mediators, for instance, we might routinely impose the same rules of procedure (e.g., that we caucus immediately after the first joint session, or that we never caucus), case after case, irrespective of the differences in issues and parties.

* * *

A Potential Solution: Mindfulness in Practice and Mindfulness Meditation

Mindfulness, as I use the term, means being aware, moment to moment, without judgment, of one's bodily sensations, thoughts, emotions, and consciousness. It is a systematic strategy for paying attention and for investigating one's own mind that one cultivates through meditation and then deploys in daily life. The meditation practice begins with developing concentration, usually by focusing on the breath. Next the meditator directs his attention to bodily sensations, emotions, and thoughts, then works toward "bare attention," a nonjudgmental moment-to-moment awareness of bodily sensations, sounds, thoughts, and emotions as they arise and fall out of consciousness. Mindfulness meditation (also known as insight meditation and vipassana meditation) both requires and produces a measure of equanimity, which reinforces the ability to fix attention where we want it to be.

The practice has a number of other potential benefits that motivate people to participate. It commonly helps people deal better with stress, improve concentration, develop self-understanding (which helps them clarify their own goals and motivations) and understanding of others, and feel compassion and empathy. Recently scientists have documented that mindfulness meditation also improves the functioning of the meditator's immune system and even produces "happiness," as measured by brainwave activity, actually shifting a person's disposition, not just her mood. In Buddhist philosophy, meditation is an important part of the quest for freedom from the suffering caused by craving and aversion.

It also seems likely to improve performance in virtually any kind of activity. The kinds of outcomes it fosters correlate with success in a variety of fields. Daniel Goleman — a psychologist, journalist, and authority on meditation — has articulated the concept of emotional intelligence, which he distinguishes from academic intelligence, the basis for the IQ and most other intelligence tests. This idea of emotional intelligence entails five "basic emotional and social competencies": self-awareness, self-regulation, motivation, empathy, and social skills. Goleman argues, marshaling a great deal of empirical evidence, that emotional intelligence is much more important than academic intelligence in predicting success at virtually any occupation or profession — assuming, of course, an adequate level of academic intelligence.

As I have shown above, mindfulness meditation can help develop the first four of these emotional intelligence competencies: self-awareness, self-regulation, motivation, and empathy. These, in turn, are likely to help produce the fifth emotional intelligence competency: social skills.

Although mindfulness meditation derives from ancient practices taught by the Buddha, in recent years it has found employment in a variety of secular settings. In the U.S., for instance, specialized programs have appeared for medical patients in chronic pain; professional basketball players; journalists; undergraduate, nursing, and medical students; corporate and foundation executives; and Green Berets. Most important for our purposes, extensive meditation instruction has been offered to lawyers in at least three large law firms (the Boston offices of Hale and Dorr and Nutter, McClennan & Fish and the Minneapolis office of Leonard, Street & Deinard) and to persons who work in the criminal justice system. A variety of programs, ranging widely in length, intensity, and scope, have been offered to law students at Cardozo, Columbia, Denver, Hamline, Harvard, Hastings, Miami, Missouri–Columbia, North Carolina, Stanford, Suffolk, and Yale. Mindfulness meditation also has been a central focus of many programs for lawyers across the U.S., ranging from five-day retreats to brief introductory sessions, some of which have carried CLE credit. Some of the law school and post-law school efforts have had a range of focuses, including managing stress, developing spiritually, clarifying motivations, or enhancing skills in law school, law practice, or law teaching.

In recent years mindfulness meditation has appeared in a variety of programs in connection with teaching negotiation or mediation. Mindfulness can help negotiators and mediators in several ways. It provides methods for calming the mind, concentrating, experiencing compassion and empathy, and achieving an awareness of, and "distance" from, thoughts, emotions, and habitual impulses that can interfere with making good judgments and with building rapport and motivating others. Thus, it can help us make appropriate strategic decisions, moment to moment. In a negotiation, for instance, when our counterpart issues a threat and we feel an impulse to retaliate, mindfulness helps us to "insert a wedge of awareness" and to examine that impulse and decide whether retaliation is more appropriate than another move that would more likely foster value creating, understanding, or healing. In addition, there is evidence that a positive mood enhances performance in problem-solving negotiation. And it seems reasonable to suspect that mindfulness could help negotiators be more aware of certain deep assumptions, including those based on ethnicity or culture, and of psychological processes that can interfere with wise decision making, such as reactive devaluation, optimistic overconfidence, risk aversion, and anchoring.

Mindfulness allows mediators to make better judgments about how the mediation process should work because it enables them to keep a focus on goals and to maintain a moment-to-moment awareness (to be "present" with themselves and others). In addition, a mediator's presence, especially her degree of calm, can dramatically affect the participants' moods and conduct.

* * *

The education and training programs that deal with mindfulness and negotiation or mediation include mindfulness meditation instruction and practice as well as exercises and discussions on how to bring mindful awareness into professional practice and other aspects of daily life. They generally begin with the basics: meditating on the breath (in part to enhance the ability to concentrate) and on sound, bodily sensations, emotions, and thoughts. All of this helps prepare the student for what is called "bare attention," an awareness of whatever passes through one's consciousness. Most of these programs present a very brief introduction to a small range of meditative practices, sometimes including yoga. Although students typically learn some techniques they can employ immediately, the leaders of such programs also hope the students will be inspired to develop their mindfulness through continued meditation and study, alone and with groups.

Exercises on listening (active or not) often form important parts of such programs. Students, already in a reasonably mindful state, are asked to engage in activities in which their ability to listen is challenged by emotional or other distractions, and they are asked to be aware of these distractions. The programs also include exercises on negotiation that encourage the students to notice and examine the assumptions about negotiation that they hold and implement. Similarly, in mediation training, exercises are intended to examine assumptions, strategies, and techniques, at many levels of the decision-making process. In addition, students notice the related bodily sensations and emotions.

* * *

In this brief essay I meant to demonstrate the potential value of mindfulness meditation and to suggest questions to address as we move forward. The future of this work is not clear to me. It seems counter to many established practices and perspectives in our field. But there is reason for optimism. The use of mindfulness and other contemplative practices is growing rapidly in society and in the legal profession. Numerous organizations have supported programs in mindfulness for lawyers or mediators. These include established entities, such as the AALS Section on Dispute Resolution, the ABA Section of Dispute Resolution, the CPR Institute for Dispute Resolution, the Association for Conflict Resolution, and prominent law firms and law schools. In addition, many established meditation organizations and teachers are available to provide training and practice opportunities. Some of these — such as the Center for Mindfulness in Medicine, Health Care and Society; the Center for Contemplative Mind in Society; and the Spirit Rock Meditation Center — already provide meditation instruction to lawyers. And two newly created programs — the Harvard Negotiation Insight Initiative and the Initiative on Mindfulness in Law and Dispute Resolution at the University of Missouri–Columbia School of Law — will bring additional energy and people into this work.

In order to plan and implement programs in mindfulness and dispute resolution — or to decide not to do so — we must be clear about our intentions. Mindfulness meditation can serve a range of goals, from lightening up, to improving our professional practices and our lives, to a kind of spiritual freedom. And, of course, nothing is more helpful in understanding our goals and the mental and emotional obstacles to achieving them than the nonjudgmental awareness that is the essence of mindfulness.

Notes and Questions

1. Can you remember a time when you read a few pages of a book — perhaps even this book — and then realized that you had no idea was those pages said? Your eyes covered the words, but where was your mind? This is the experience of what Professor Riskin refers to as mindlessness.

To get a sense of mindfulness, try this exercise: Close your eyes and focus on the sensation of the breath as it enters and leaves the nostrils. To help yourself stay focused, count each exhalation up to ten. When you reach ten, or when you realize you have lost track, begin again at one. All the while, notice, as best you can — without judging — whatever pulls your attention away breath, including thoughts, sounds, smells, emotions, and sensations in the body. This sense of observing the mind may be considered mindfulness, and as Professor Riskin's article suggests, may be cultivated through a meditation practice. This kind of non-judgmental awareness is the essence of mindfulness. It's very simple, but not easy.

2. Mindfulness and other forms of meditation are the subject of active research by psychologists, neurologists, and other scientists. For example, psychologist Paul Eckman, one of the world's pre-eminent experts on the science of emotion, conducted a set of experiments on a European-born Tibetan monk by the name of Lama Öser at the Human Interaction Laboratory at the University of California at San Francisco. Two of these experiments are particularly relevant to dispute resolution and conflict management.

In one experiment, Eckman asked Öser to identify such facial microexpressions as anger, contempt, and fear after seeing pictures of faces for just an instant (either one-fifth of a second or one-thirtieth of a second). These are the kinds of instinctive facial expressions that occur unwittingly and reveal true emotion, even before culturally learned emotional responses take effect. Remarkably, Öser and another advanced Western meditator tested two standard deviations above the norm in recognizing these superquick facial signs of emotions — far better than any of the other 5,000 people Eckman had tested. "They do better than policemen, lawyers, psychiatrists, customs officials, judges, even secret service agents," the group that had previously been the most accurate, Eckman later marveled. He noted that the capacity to excel on this test suggested a heightened ability to respond more accurately to the emotions of others with empathy. DANIEL GOLEMAN, DESTRUCTIVE EMOTIONS: HOW CAN WE OVERCOME THEM? 13–14 (2003).

In a second test, Eckman evaluated Öser's ability to suppress his so-called startle reflex, a common, primitive muscular response to a loud, surprising sound or sudden jarring sight. Ordinarily, the reflex starts about two-tenths of a second after hearing a sound and ends around a half second after the sound. A classic study in the 1940s, replicated many times since then, demonstrated that it is impossible to prevent the startle response. Yet, Öser did not startle when presented with a stimulus while meditating.

"When Öser tries to suppress the startle, it almost disappears," Eckman later said. "We've never found anyone who can do that. Nor have any other researchers. This is a spectacular accomplishment. We don't have any idea of the anatomy that would allow him to suppress the startle reflex." From a dispute resolution perspective, experiments suggest that meditation might enhance one's ability to respond to a conflict stimulus less reflexively and more constructively, which is important regardless of whether one is intervening in a conflict as a lawyer, mediator, arbitrator, or judge, or dealing with one's own conflict.

3.   University of Wisconsin neuroscientist Richard Davidson has spent years studying the neurology of constructive and destructive emotions. This research has narrowed in on the prefrontal cortex as the region of the brain in which emotions are processed. More specifically, his research has found that when people have high levels of brain activity in the left prefrontal cortex, they simultaneously report positive feelings such as happiness, enthusiasm, joy, high energy, and alertness. By contrast, people with a higher level of activity in the right prefrontal cortex tend to report more distressing emotions, such as sadness, anxiety, and worry. Through such experiments, Davidson concludes that each of us has an emotional set-point that is based on the ratio between left and right prefrontal cortex activity, and that this set point provides something of a barometer of the daily moods we are likely to experience.

Davidson also conducted a series of functional MRI (fMRI) tests on Lama Öser to determine the degree to which Öser's meditation affected the activity of his left and right prefrontal cortex. Öser used six different forms of meditation, including clear mind meditation, visualizations, and loving-kindness meditation, in which the meditator seeks to generate compassionate or well-wishing thoughts toward himself or herself, or toward others. The fMRI data clearly indicated that large networks in Öser's brain changed with each mental state he generated. Such shifts in brain activity between mind states are unusual, except for significant shifts in consciousness, such as between sleeping and wakefulness. Davidson takes this evidence to support his thesis that with significant practice, meditation techniques can allow people to push their emotional set-points in more constructive directions. Id. at 11–13. From a dispute resolution perspective, such an effort would contribute to personal conflict management, as well as the capacity of a dispute resolution professional to work effectively with disputing parties.

4.   Davidson and his colleagues also did research on high tech executives in Madison, Wisconsin, who meditated a fraction as much as the Tibetan Lama. They found that during the course of their eight-meditation practice, these executives increased they level of brainwave activity in the left prefrontal cortex — and also improved their immune functions. Richard J. Davidson, et al., *Alterations in Brain and Immune Function Produced by Mindfulness Meditation*, 65 Psychosomatic Med. 564 (2003).

5.   Mindfulness can help students transfer skills from the classroom simulations into actual practice.

> Students learn from each of these [classroom] activities, of course. They do so partly in the same way that football players learn from practice drills in blocking and tackling, followed by critiques of their performance. But football players cannot execute blocks and tackles well

unless ... they have a certain minimal amount of strength. For that reason, football training routinely includes weightlifting and other methods of building muscles.

Similarly, for a person to appropriately implement the strategies associated with the new approaches to mediation and negotiation and lawyering, she must have a set of foundational capacities, including awareness, emotional sophistication, and understanding. * * *

Leonard L. Riskin, *Mindfulness: Foundational Training for Dispute Resolution,* 54 J. Leg. Educ. 79 (2004).

6. In recent years, programs on mindfulness meditation have been offered for students at nine U.S. law schools. *See* Leonard L. Riskin, *The Contemplative Lawyer: On the Potential Benefits of Mindfulness Meditation to Law Students, Lawyers, and their Clients,* 7 Harv. Negot. L. Rev. 1 (2002). For further information about such programs, as well as other mindfulness programs for lawyers — sponsored by law firms, bar associations, corporations, government agencies and non-profit organizations — see the web sites of The Center for Contemplative Mind in Society, www.contemplative-mind.org; the Harvard Negotiation Insight Initiative, which is dedicated to the study of wisdom traditions and their potential impact on dispute resolution, http://www.pon.harvard.edu/hnii and the Initiative on Mindfulness in Law and Dispute Resolution, http://www.law.missouri.edu/csdr/mindfulness/programs/

C. NEW OPPORTUNITIES

For many students, the study of ADR presents an unfamiliar picture of what life as a lawyer might be like. A common question is what ADR practice is like in "the real world," and how can I get started? In this section, we try to answer those questions by referring readers to the experiences of others who have asked those same questions. We begin with brief overview of the professional organizations that support dispute resolution practitioners, attorneys, and others interested in the field. We then conclude this chapter, and the book, with excerpts from a collection of personal stories telling how some dispute resolution professionals came to work in the field, with several writers addressing particular aspects of the question.

1. ENTERING THE STREAM: PROFESSIONAL ORGANIZATIONS

Like many other endeavors, a dispute resolution practice can be difficult when going alone. Many dispute resolution practitioners connect with the field through state and national dispute resolution professional organizations.

Through these organizations many working in dispute resolution share their professional experiences, learn new skills, and develop professional networks for support and advancement that may assist in a wide variety of ways. These organizations also often help define professional standards on pressing issues by studying and/or drafting professional guidance standards themselves, or by participating in the research and drafting of such standards by others.

As of this writing, there are two major national organizations — the American Bar Association Section of Dispute Resolution and the Association for Conflict Resolution (ACR) — which seek to serve a broad array of areas within the profession. There are several other smaller but important organizations that are more focused on a particular area or type of practice, such as the National Association of Family and Community Mediators and the Victim Offender Mediation Association.

Both the ABA SDR and ACR have student divisions, and encourage the creation and growth of chapters at individual law schools. The ABA Section of Dispute Resolution is the larger of the two, with approximately 10,000 members as compared to about 6,000 members of ACR. Both organizations welcome lawyers and non-lawyers, but, not surprisingly, the ABA tends to attract those with law backgrounds while ACR tends to attract those with non-law backgrounds. Despite these differences, many ADR professionals belong to both organizations, so each includes members from across the field, including: full and part-time practitioners and trainers, educators, judges, and public and private program managers, among others. Both have large and informative annual meetings, with the ABA's typically in the Spring and ACR's in the Fall. Both the ABA SDR and ACR have multiple standing committees (such as committees on mediation, arbitration, and legislation) as well as special committees and task forces to focus on particular problems (such as professional training and certification), and sometimes participate jointly on policy-setting committees for the field, such as with the drafting of the Model Standards of Conduct for Mediators. ACR has regional organizations and chapters in many states chapters, including: Arizona, California, Florida, Georgia, Delaware, Georgia, Hawaii, Illinois, Maryland, Michigan, Minnesota, New England, New Jersey, New York, North Carolina, Pennsylvania, Texas, Virginia, and Washington, D.C. More about these two organizations can be found on their web sites. The ABA's web address is www.abanet.org/dispute. ACR's web address is www.acrnet.org. State and local bar associations also tend to have committees or sections on dispute resolution, which work with courts and present programs on ADR topics.

Other professional organizations of note include:

  • **National Association for Community Mediation**. NAFCM supports the maintenance and growth of community-based mediation programs and processes, participates in policy making, and encourages the development and sharing of resources for these efforts.

  • **Victim Offender Mediation Association.** VOMA is an international membership association that supports and assists people and communities working at restorative models of justice. VOMA provides resources, training, and technical assistance in victim-offender mediation, conferencing, circles, and related restorative justice practices.

● **Academy of Family Mediators.** AFM members provide mediation services to families facing decisions involving separation, divorce, child custody, parenting, visitation, property division, wills and estates, elder care, spouse support or alimony, child support, family business, pre-nuptial agreements, and many other disputes, conflicts, or issues involving the family.

● **Association of Family and Conciliation Courts.** AFCC is an association of family, court, and community professionals.

● **Chartered Institute of Arbitrators.** The Institute is an international organization dedicated to the advancement of international commercial arbitration.

2. PERSONAL STORIES

The following excerpts, drawn from *ADR Personalities and Practice Tips*, by James Alfini and Eric Galton, give a sense of how others have traveled the path into dispute resolution, and include many practical suggestions for getting started.

JAMES J. ALFINI & ERIC GALTON, ADR PERSONALITIES AND PRACTICE TIPS

6–8, 13–14, 50–53, 104–07, 136–39 (1998).

Dana L. Curtis

Ms. Curtis tells the story of how interest in dispute resolution sparked during law school turned into a career, thanks to some mentoring by an accomplished practitioner.

I knew I wanted to be a mediator when I was introduced to mediation in a second-year law school course. My other courses, though interesting intellectually, minimized the role of the human being behind the legal claims. Mediation focused on the individuals involved and on the meaning they attached to the dispute. The parties' priorities could be the most important reference point for resolution. In addition to, or instead of, the rule of law, their concerns, needs, fears, hopes and desires all mattered. As well as seeing how mediation could better meet the needs of the parties than a litigated resolution, I realized that mediation better utilized my strengths. As a mediator, I could use relationship and communication skills I had developed in my first career as a teacher.

Full of enthusiasm for mediation, I asked my professor where to learn about mediating as a career. He referred me to Gary Friedman, a pioneer lawyer mediator and Director of the Center for Mediation in Law in Mill Valley, California. I sought Gary's advice about mediating employment and other commercial disputes. He encouraged me, but warned that such a career would be difficult to forge, as the application of mediation in civil disputes was uncommon at that time. He also noted that I seemed to have what it would take — the commitment to mediation and an entrepreneurial spirit, evidenced by the fact that I had entered law school as a single mother after moving to California from Idaho with my three children.

Gary advised me to remain committed, to be patient and to get litigation experience to enhance my credibility with lawyers and my understanding of the legal process. Following his advice, after law school I clerked for a California Supreme Court associate justice and thereafter joined a large San Francisco law firm, practicing commercial and employment litigation in San Jose and San Francisco. I began as an enthusiastic associate and during much of my first year of practice seriously considered a long-term litigation career. Before long, my enthusiasm abated. The enormity of financial and human resources spent on litigation astounded me. The inefficiency of the discovery process (where the object, it seemed to me, was to provide the other side with as little information as possible), the lack of predictability and fairness of jury trials, and the failure of litigation to address the clients' true needs all left me disaffected.

In addition, the demands of big firm practice, the often sixty and sometimes eighty hour work weeks, and the isolation I experienced among 200 other big firm lawyers convinced me that I was not willing to sacrifice more years of "being" for "becoming." The idea of partnership became unthinkable. As one of my law school friends put it, partnership is like a pie eating contest where the prize is more pie.

I dreamed of mediating. Although I had trained as a mediator and had been teaching mediation for several years, I was unable to see a way to make the transition. During this time of profound dissatisfaction with my career, I spent an evening with four dear women friends, as I had been doing on a bimonthly basis for several years. That night I spoke of my life consumed with work, of the months without a day off, of the weeks in a hotel room, of the frustrations of a difficult trial and of the day-to-day failure of my career to provide deep, personal meaning for me. What followed caused me finally to initiate change in my life. One of my friends looked me in the eye and said, "Dana, you will die if you don't leave your job." I knew she was right. If not physically, I was dying spiritually. The next day, without knowing what else I would do, I gave notice that I would be leaving the firm.

A few days later, I ran into Gary Friedman on the street in San Francisco. When he discovered I was leaving my law practice, he invited me to meet with him. Over a series of meetings, I learned that he was becoming increasingly interested in mediation of civil disputes and would like to work closely with lawyers who were pursuing commercial mediation. Within a few months, I hung out my mediation shingle (literally!) at Gary's office in Mill Valley. There, I practiced mediation for two years with Laura Farrow, another lawyer who left the firm at the same time I did. It was an exciting time — the invigoration of moving from a high-rise Financial District office to a renovated house with rose bushes, even an apple tree, in the yard, where at last my whole heart was in my work, as well as the uncertainty of whether a mediation practice could actually support my family.

The years I spent at Mediation Law Offices enabled me to develop a successful practice and to build a foundation that has been important in my practice and in my teaching. By working closely with Gary, I became more effective and more reflective. Following most mediations, I would write a critique of the process and meet with Gary to reflect on the dynamic between the parties and within myself. I was also able to consult with Gary on the spot. At the outset of one early divorce mediation, for example, a couple told me they had come to ask me to write up an agreement they had already reached. Essentially, the agreement provided the husband would have custody of the children and all but $10,000 of their community property assets, which totaled about $300,000. I had been ready to launch into the first phase of mediation, discussing the process and helping the parties to decide if they wanted to go forward, but I was thrown by this request. Excusing myself to get some papers, I ducked into Gary's office and in three minutes worked out an approach that engaged the parties in discussion about the efficacy of their agreement without compromising my neutrality.

After two years at Mediation Law Offices, I had the opportunity to become a Circuit Court Mediator for the U. S. Court of Appeals for the Ninth Circuit in San Francisco. I was persuaded to leave private practice by the promise of an endless array of Federal cases to mediate and steady paycheck. In the Ninth Circuit Mediation Program, I worked with five other full-time mediators to resolve cases on appeal. It was a mediator's dream come true. We selected our caseload from hundreds of diverse civil appeals. On any day, we might conduct a telephone mediation in a securities case, an employment discrimination dispute, a products liability matter, an IRS appeal, a bankruptcy case or an insurance coverage dispute. Several times a month, I would mediate in person, often in complex multi-party disputes. It was a time of applying my experience and knowledge of a face-to-face mediation model, where the parties could reach understanding in order to craft a resolution that addressed their priorities, not just their assessment of their legal positions. I sought to provide more than a settlement conference. In fact, when I began to speak of legal argument in mediation as an *option*, not a *given*, I was surprised by how frequently the parties, and even their lawyers, agreed that discussing the law would not be productive. The first time I suggested that we may not want to discuss the law, the plaintiff (in an employment discrimination case) said, "Thank God! If I had to listen for five more minutes to the company's lawyer telling me what a rotten case I have, I'd leave!"

During the three years I worked at the Ninth Circuit, I mediated hundreds of appeals. I learned that it is never too late for mediation. It was not unusual for a case to have been in litigation for ten years or more — and still settle! I also learned the approach required of an appellate mediator: how to unravel a long history of misunderstanding; how to address the harm the parties inflict upon one another in litigation, which often eclipses the original grievance; how to use the parties' experience with numerous failed negotiations, settlement conferences and mediations to structure a mediation process that avoids repeating their failures. On a more practical note, I learned how to discuss the law, and especially legal issues unique to appeals, without crowding out other reference points for decision; I learned about effective facilitation of both distributional and interest-based negotiations; and I learned how to turn mandatory mediation into a voluntary process — and to believe in it!

Eric R. Galton

It is common for dispute resolution professionals to begin by "hanging out a shingle." Mr. Galton provides some suggestions for getting started.

Mediation Markets

Basically, you will enter one of three distinct ADR markets: first, a "no market situation" in which no one makes a living "doing ADR"; second, a developing ADR market; or, third, an oversaturated ADR market (yes, they really do exist). The realities of developing an ADR practice depend upon which sort of market you are entering.

On the other hand, regardless of which market you are confronting, you should not make an ADR practice commitment until you first do the following things:

- Visit with at least three neutrals who are in fact engaged in a full time ADR practice. . . .
- Take the required mediation training.
- Observe three live mediations conducted by experienced neutrals.
- Conduct five pro bono mediations.

While these steps will not guarantee whether you will make it or succeed as a neutral, you will undoubtedly develop a strong feeling whether this kind of work is or is not for you. If you remain convinced this work is something you wish to do, your practice development steps will vary depending upon the type of market.

Oversaturated Market.

An oversaturated market is one in which several generations of mediators have entrenched themselves. This market has already ferreted out mediators who are deemed "unsuccessful." The remaining mediators have identifiable sectors of loyal clients. This market may have even, perhaps not expressly, identified mediators by style and the grade of complexity of a case (routine, complex, impossible). Mediators may be perceived as interchangeable within these subgroups or stratas. I am also assuming that in such a market and in court annexed cases the *lawyers* select the mediator (in some venues, this is not the case).

In such markets, I see two wildly different approaches. They are as follows:

Develop a Niche. Certain types of disputes require a neutral with specific skills or expertise; i.e. family law, intellectual property, tax etc. Or, certain services, even in an oversaturated market, may not be available.

Permit me to provide an illustration of the latter. Jane Meddler, a budding and hopeful neutral, determines she has three hundred competitors with established practices. Jane also notices that these mediators offer full-day or half-day rates. Jane further realizes that certain cases do not require that time commitment, need a lower rate, and also need a more evaluative approach. Jane offers two hours [of] assisted settlement conferences, charging $400.00 per party. She provides a case evaluation, and a service at a cost which is substantially less than a full day rate with an experienced mediator.

Patience: Cream Rises to the Top. Alternatively, you do not want to be identified in a niche and you believe that you can compete heads up with the local talent. I would suggest the following plan:

- Be patient. Do not quit your day job.
- Contact lawyers you really know well, advise them of your training and commitment, and ask for a tryout. Inevitably, their preferred neutrals will have scheduling conflicts.
- When you finally get the call, excel and resolve the dispute. As a general rule, each successful mediation creates four new ones. I know ... success, from the mediation perspective, does not always mean or require the matter to settle. Success in the marketplace is defined as the consistent ability to resolve disputes. More blatantly stated, if you obtain and resolve four cases in your first month, you should be seeing eight to nine referrals per month by your twelfth month.

Developing Market

In a developing market, others have gone before you, created the potential for the market, and have developed something of a following.

Assuming you have received your training and made an informed decision that mediation is for you, I would suggest the following approach:

- Keep your day job. You do not know how the market will respond to your efforts nor do you know whether you will succeed as a mediator or enjoy the practice.
- Do a direct mail piece to those colleagues you really know. Outline your training, your commitment, and specify your fee structure.
- Follow-up the direct mail with telephone calls and office visits. Letters may be easily dismissed or forgotten.
- Contact practicing mediators you know and make them aware that you are prepared to accept their conflicts or cases they do not have the time to handle. Most mediators enter into informal cross-referral pacts, usually without a referral fee being paid.

- Should the courts in your jurisdiction maintain a list of qualified mediators, do what is necessary to get on such a list.

- Consider developing an identity as a "specialist" in a particular area.

No Market

If you think about it, the maximum opportunity and greatest difficulty in creating a mediation practice exists in a venue in which no one has established a viable mediation practice.

In these venues, most people will advise you that you cannot succeed. Depending upon your personality, such naysaying may be music to your ears. But, you need to exercise your communication skills and find out why people believe you will not succeed.

Again, my frame of reference is court-annexed mediation, so the questions I would ask are in that context and are as follows:

- Are the local judges opposed to mediation and why? If judges, are opposed, you need to educate the judges about the value of the mediation process.

- Are local lawyers opposed to mediation and why? Most lawyers oppose what they do not understand. Again, your mission is to educate lawyers and explain that mediation is good for both their clients and them.

- Have others before you attempted to develop a mediation practice and failed? If so, why?

Your primary job will be to educate those who are in a position to refer cases. Anticipate skepticism, distrust, and ignorance. But, as a bright beacon in the fog, keep this one unmistakable truth in mind — most of the greatest skeptics and naysayers about the process become the most outspoken proponents of the process after a successful mediation. These people will tell countless friends, "I did not believe in mediation, I never thought this case would settle, and it did." The only thing you need are a few opportunities to prove the process works to these skeptics. If you are able to be given a few chances, your work will market itself.

Public Service and Professional Development Considerations

Regardless of which of the three markets you enter, you will underscore your commitment to the practice by devoting some time to public service ADR projects and professional development matters. Such activities will enrich your new life as a mediator and allow you to give something back to the community. You might consider any of the following:

- Make a point of handling at least four cases per year on a pro bono basis. Many cases are appropriate candidates for mediation, but the parties may not be able to afford the services of a mediator.

- Volunteer to create a peer mediation program in a local elementary, junior high, or high school. If such programs already exist, adopt a school and train a class of students.

- Certain community, public policy matters may need the volunteer services of a qualified mediator.

- If your local courts have a Settlement Week program or are initiating one, volunteer.

- Join any local ADR groups or sections. Cross-talk with your colleagues is both necessary and helpful.

- Join national ADR groups or associations (e.g., the ABA Section of Dispute Resolution or Society of Professionals in Dispute Resolution [SPIDR]). In addition to providing necessary collegiality and insight into the experiences of other neutrals from a nationwide perspective, these groups, among others, are leaders in the development of ADR!

- Make a commitment, whether required or not, to at least twenty hours per year of continuing education in mediation. One never stops learning and it is beneficial to learn the perspectives and techniques of others.

Kathy Fragnoli

Ms. Fragnoli provides more tips for getting started in mediation and arbitration, including the incorporation of training into one's dispute resolution practice.

Mediation

Volunteer until you are really good. In my opinion, it usually takes about 30 mediations to even approach a point where you are ready to charge for your services. When you are there, you will know it. Only then should you start introducing yourself as a mediator for hire. Attorneys who use you in a volunteer setting will recommend you to others. Most attorney mediators charge $1,500 per day in Texas. As with any business, word of mouth takes time. Plan to eat macaroni and cheese for two years. If you do not use professional mediation rooms, nice stationery and a good voice mail system, plan to eat macaroni and cheese for six years.

For local court ordered disputes, I have become associated with a local mediation firm called Burdin Mediations. Burdin markets six mediators and is a full service mediation company with two locations, very upscale space and three full time administrators. They schedule my local mediation cases (around my obligations to other clients), and handle all billing. In exchange, I pay them a portion of my fee from each case.

It is difficult to become associated with most services like Burdin unless you already have a following or a niche market. New mediators may want to join together to share space and administrative help if they are unable to become a member of an established mediation firm.

Another option for mediators is to look for opportunities with state and federal agencies who contract for mediation services. Ask your local Small Business Administration Office to help you search for such opportunities.

Arbitration

Without substantive experience in a particular field, it is difficult to get started as an arbitrator. However, many labor arbitrators are willing to let those who are interested in entering the field serve as interns and observe hearings. After interning, the American Arbitration Association in New York will list you as a labor arbitrator if you provide letters of recommendation from four different management representatives and four unions. Labor arbitrators typically bill about $1,600 per case which includes travel, hearing and writing time.

The National Association of Securities Dealers will list you as an arbitrator even if you have very limited experience. They pay only $200 per day, but you sit on a panel with two other arbitrators and do not have to write a lengthy decision — only a few sentence award. Serving on one of these panels is a good way to see if you enjoy the process. Without a listing on panels such as the one AAA maintains, it is nearly impossible to serve as a private arbitrator.

ADR Training

Training is, by far, the most rewarding segment of my practice. Besides being financially profitable, it is extremely satisfying to "create" new mediators or to teach organizations conflict resolution skills. In addition to mediator training, I provide seminars on interest based negotiation skills designed especially for women in law or business.

ADR practitioners who think they would enjoy the platform should start developing their public speaking skills by volunteering at a local dispute resolution center. Another way to get started is to call local business clubs about volunteering to give an after dinner speech on ADR. Soon you may find, as I did, that businesses will be interested in paying you to teach a full day (or week long!) seminar.

Jeffrey G. Kichaven

Mr. Kichaven describes the transition to commercial mediation from a traditional business litigation practice.

An ADR practice — as a professional mediator — is not for the faint of heart. Too often, when I ask aspiring mediators what attracts them to the field, they tell me that they are, in some way or to some degree, averse to the "conflict" inherent in litigation and other aspects of law practice, and want to get away from that. These people are not likely to make it as mediators.

First, there is no career, as a mediator or anything else, that will provide satisfaction if it is an "escape" from something else rather than something to which you are drawn in its own right. Relationships "on the rebound," whether in romance or career, rarely succeed over the long haul. If one seeks a career as mediator just to escape from the conflict inherent in litigation, without a passion for what mediation has to offer, the likelihood of enhanced career satisfaction, to me, is small.

Second, though, and perhaps more importantly, mediation is not an alternative to "conflict" at all. It is the essence of conflict. In mediation, the parties can bare their souls; there are no rules of evidence or civil procedure, no concept of courtroom decorum, no transcription of the record, to keep the discussion tightly and unemotionally focused on the legal claims and defenses set forth in the pleadings. The parties can plumb the depths of their business and personal relationships. And, if the mediator is any good, that discussion is not only tolerated, it is encouraged. The deeper the parties' relationship is explored, the more likely the parties will achieve a high degree of clarity, and a durable, comprehensive, mutually-satisfying resolution. The road to this kind of resolution is generally not easy to tread. The effective mediator must model, among other things, the courage to look the conflict square in the eye, and say the things which have for too long gone unsaid. A mediator whose goal is to "smooth over" the conflict, and require "nice-nice" behavior all around, is unlikely to give the parties or the process what they all deserve.

When I graduated from Harvard Law School in 1980, I joined a rough, tough, take-no-prisoners business litigation firm in my home city, Los Angeles. I was one of the youngest members of my graduating class; I received my J.D. about two weeks before my 24th birthday.

In my mid–20s, the scorched-earth style of litigation was great fun. I fashioned myself as a kind of "Errol Flynn of litigation," swashbuckling my way through conflicts, heroically swinging in on the chandelier, sword drawn, thrusting it through the chest of the "bad guy" as I pounced. This almost always provoked retaliation from the other side, and hence became very expensive for the clients; it was also consuming of my time and psyche. In the highly adversarial mode, nobody cuts anybody else any slack. This razor's edge between "perfection" and "disaster" produced a high degree of anxiety.

In addition, I found it hard to "turn it on" at the office and "turn it off" at home. In part, that is because there was relatively little time at home. Before I was married, and then before we had children, it was no big deal to work around the clock as needed, which seemed to be almost all the time.

As I got older (and, if I dare say so, more mature), my thoughts changed. Time with my family became a higher priority as my family expanded (we have 3 kids) and grew. But at least as important was the perspective I began to develop on the litigation process itself. Yes, there ARE some cases in which the take-no-prisoners approach is required.

And, if you are involved in one of those cases, you must fight fire with fire. But not every case calls for that approach. Indeed, the number of such cases on any given lawyer's desk is likely smaller than that lawyer might at first perceive. When you are in the middle of the war, however, it is difficult to see that there might be another way, which might serve the client's interests even better.

Many times, I would question my partners as to whether there was another way. "This litigation is awfully expensive and time consuming for the client," I often thought, "and the parties to this lawsuit, who once had a solid business relationship, will probably never do business with each other again once we are done with the hostility this litigation is engendering." It just seemed to me that there must be a better way to serve the client's interests; the client, after all, was not in the business of prosecuting or defending lawsuits; the client was in one type or another of widget business, and we rarely looked at how the litigation would affect the client's long- and short-term interests in the overall health and prosperity of its business.

These questions did not particularly endear me to my partners, some of whom perceived mediation as little more than a foolish means of resolving cases less remuneratively. The rainmakers stopped asking for me to work on their cases, since I persisted in asking whether "another way" might better serve the client's interest, and, incidentally, reduce the amount of rainfall per cloud. Eventually, my partners and I came to realize that the situation, which had worked so well for all of us in previous years, was no longer working, and so, amicably, I left to make my way in the world.

I joined three friends, also big-firm veterans, in a small-firm practice. At first, I tried to pursue big-ticket business litigation cases, but with an ADR-oriented twist — in essence, taking my old practice as a base, and "fixing" what I didn't like about it. At the same time, I started to take on cases as a mediator, through court panels on which I had volunteered. It soon became apparent to me — and even more apparent to my wife — which type of work I preferred. My wife commented that, when I came home at night, she could tell which days I had been mediating and which days I had been litigating. When I had been mediating, I was happier and more relaxed. In one stretch, in the spring of 1996, she said to me that it had become obvious which type of work I preferred; that, for months, I had been "flirting" with the idea of becoming a full-time neutral; and that I should stop trying to "fix" my old practice, and have the courage to create something totally new, a mediation practice. With her encouragement, I took that plunge in mid–1996, and have not looked back.

There are plenty of pressures on a mediator, just as there are plenty of pressures on a litigator. But they are different pressures, and I greatly prefer the one over the other.

As a litigator, I always found it difficult to leave my work at the office, to put it down and relax, when it was time to spend time with my family or pursue other activities. When cases take years to resolve, they consume a prominent part of the litigator's (or at least THIS litigator's) mind-space. I was always concerned that some tyro on the umpteenth floor of some big office building was staying up late working on ways to outsmart me. Many times, I was right! So I felt I had to spend my time fighting back — generally, ALL of my time! I felt that I was always "on."

As a mediator, that pressure is gone. My involvement with most cases is relatively brief — a few days, a week at most. When one case is done (whether settled or brought to impasse), I am done, too, until the next case starts. This makes for infinitely better evenings, weekends and vacations.

The other pressure, though, also arises from the fact that my involvement with cases is relatively brief. That is the pressure to keep new cases coming in all the time. As in the semiconductor industry, my "book to bill" ratio is critical. New cases must be brought in as rapidly as current cases are handled, if the business is to prosper. So, I spend a huge amount of time marketing. Fortunately, most of the marketing activities are things I enjoy — meeting people and talking to them about how ADR can help them, whether as transactional lawyer, litigator or client; writing and speaking; and bar activities. As my "computer guy," Dan Turner, said when we were discussing our respective passions, for computer technology and dispute resolution, "find something you love to do, and never work another day in your life!"

Ironically, I think that my 15 years in rough-and-ready business litigation uniquely prepared me for service as a mediator, and is my biggest marketing plus. The reason is that ADR professionals are changing their perception about their "clients." We now understand that, in a very significant sense, *other lawyers ARE our clients*, no less than the underlying business clients who are parties to the dispute.

In my experience (and I think this fairly mirrors the experiences of others), it is other lawyers who make our phones ring with new business. The underlying business clients may have an inchoate sense that the processes of traditional litigation are not getting them where they want to be going with their dispute (or at least not getting them there as quickly, affordably or smoothly as they want), but likely do not have the knowledge that mediation may be the way out of their box. It is other lawyers — in-house counsel as well as law firm partners — who are aware of the specific alternatives, and who know that we mediators are the people to call.

But other lawyers will not call us if they perceive that we do not appreciate them, their situations, and their problems. And to be sure, lawyers often have just as many "problems" as the underlying business clients. The client-with-unrealistic-expectations and the hard-to-collect-receivable are just two on a much longer list. So, from a business sense and a professional sense as well, we must acknowledge that the lawyers are stake-holders in the dispute, too, and we have to deal with them and their interests straight-up.

In marketing my mediation practice, I have found that my past experience gives other lawyers confidence that I will do the job for them as well as for their clients; that I can and will understand and deal with their concerns, interests and problems. Other lawyers know that I have walked miles in their shoes. They are comfortable that I am "like them" in material ways.

Questions

If you hope to incorporate work as an ADR neutral into your professional practice, which of these stories seems most helpful to you? What else would you like to know about developing a neutral practice? For more, see FOREST S. MOSTEN, MEDIATION CAREER GUIDE: A STRATEGIC APPROACH FOR BUILDING A SUCCESSFUL PRACTICE (2001).

Appendix A

FEDERAL RULES OF
CIVIL PROCEDURE
RULE 16

Rule 16. Pretrial Conferences; Scheduling; Management

(a) **Pretrial Conferences; Objectives.** In any action, the court may in its discretion direct the attorneys for the parties and any unrepresented parties to appear before it for a conference or conferences before trial for such purposes as

(1) expediting the disposition of the action;

(2) establishing early and continuing control so that the case will not be protracted because of lack of management;

(3) discouraging wasteful pretrial activities;

(4) improving the quality of the trial through more thorough preparation; and

(5) facilitating the settlement of the case.

(b) **Scheduling and Planning.** Except in categories of actions exempted by district court rule as inappropriate, the district judge, or a magistrate judge when authorized by district court rule, shall, after receiving the report from the parties under Rule 26(f) or after consulting with the attorneys for the parties and any unrepresented parties by a scheduling conference, telephone, mail, or other suitable means, enter a scheduling order that limits the time

(1) to join other parties and to amend the pleadings;

(2) to file motions; and

(3) to complete discovery.

The scheduling order may also include

(4) modifications of the times for disclosures under Rules 26(a) and 26(e)(1) and of the extent of discovery to be permitted;

(5) the date or dates for conferences before trial, a final pretrial conference, and trial; and

    (6) any other matters appropriate in the circumstances of the case.

The order shall issue as soon as practicable but in any event within 90 days after the appearance of a defendant and within 120 days after the complaint has been served on a defendant. A schedule shall not be modified except upon a showing of good cause and by leave of the district judge or, when authorized by local rule, by a magistrate judge.

    (c) Subjects for Consideration at Pretrial Conferences. At any conference under this rule consideration may be given, and the court may take appropriate action, with respect to

    (1) the formulation and simplification of the issues, including the limitation of frivolous claims or defenses;

    (2) the necessity or desirability of amendments to the pleadings;

    (3) the possibility of obtaining admissions of fact and of documents which will avoid unnecessary proof, stipulations regarding the authenticity of documents, and advance rulings from the court on the admissibility of evidence;

    (4) the avoidance of unnecessary proof and of cumulative evidence, and limitations or restrictions on the use of testimony under Rule 702 of the Federal Rules of Evidence;

    (5) the appropriateness and timing of summary adjudication under Rule 56;

    (6) the control and scheduling of discovery, including orders affecting disclosures and discovery pursuant to Rule 26 and Rules 29 through 37;

    (7) the identification of witnesses and documents, the need and schedule for filing and exchanging pretrial briefs, and the date or dates for further conferences and for trial;

    (8) the advisability of referring matters to a magistrate judge or master;

    (9) settlement and the use of special procedures to assist in resolving the dispute when authorized by statute or local rule;

    (10) the form and substance of the pretrial order;

    (11) the disposition of pending motions;

    (12) the need for adopting special procedures for managing potentially difficult or protracted actions that may involve complex issues, multiple parties, difficult legal questions, or unusual proof problems;

    (13) an order for a separate trial pursuant to Rule 42(b) with respect to a claim, counterclaim, cross-claim, or third-party claim, or with respect to any particular issue in the case;

(14) an order directing a party or parties to present evidence early in the trial with respect to a manageable issue that could, on the evidence, be the basis for a judgment as a matter of law under Rule 50(a) or a judgment on partial findings under Rule 52(c);

(15) an order establishing a reasonable limit on the time allowed for presenting evidence; and

(16) such other matters as may facilitate the just, speedy, and inexpensive disposition of the action.

At least one of the attorneys for each party participating in any conference before trial shall have authority to enter into stipulations and to make admissions regarding all matters that the participants may reasonably anticipate may be discussed. If appropriate, the court may require that a party or its representative be present or reasonably available by telephone in order to consider possible settlement of the dispute.

(d) **Final Pretrial Conference.** Any final pretrial conference shall be held as close to the time of trial as reasonable under the circumstances. The participants at any such conference shall formulate a plan for trial, including a program for facilitating the admission of evidence. The conference shall be attended by at least one of the attorneys who will conduct the trial for each of the parties and by any unrepresented parties.

(e) **Pretrial Orders.** After any conference held pursuant to this rule, an order shall be entered reciting the action taken. This order shall control the subsequent course of the action unless modified by a subsequent order. The order following a final pretrial conference shall be modified only to prevent manifest injustice.

(f) **Sanctions.** If a party or party's attorney fails to obey a scheduling or pretrial order, or if no appearance is made on behalf of a party at a scheduling or pretrial conference, or if a party or party's attorney is substantially unprepared to participate in the conference, or if a party or party's attorney fails to participate in good faith, the judge, upon motion or the judge's own initiative, may make such orders with regard thereto as are just, and among others any of the orders provided in Rule 37(b)(2)(B), (C), (D). In lieu of or in addition to any other sanction, the judge shall require the party or the attorney representing the party or both to pay the reasonable expenses incurred because of any noncompliance with this rule, including attorney's fees, unless the judge finds that the noncompliance was substantially justified or that other circumstances make an award of expenses unjust.

(As amended Apr. 28, 1983, eff. Aug. 1, 1983; Mar. 2, 1987, eff. Aug. 1, 1987; Apr. 22, 1993, eff. Dec. 1, 1993.)

Appendix B

UNIFORM MEDIATION ACT (2003)

SECTION 1. TITLE. This [Act] may be cited as the Uniform Mediation Act.

SECTION 2. DEFINITIONS. In this [Act]:

(1) "Mediation" means a process in which a mediator facilitates communication and negotiation between parties to assist them in reaching a voluntary agreement regarding their dispute.

(2) "Mediation communication" means a statement, whether oral or in a record or verbal or nonverbal, that occurs during a mediation or is made for purposes of considering, conducting, participating in, initiating, continuing, or reconvening a mediation or retaining a mediator.

(3) "Mediator" means an individual who conducts a mediation.

(4) "Nonparty participant" means a person, other than a party or mediator, that participates in a mediation.

(5) "Mediation party" means a person that participates in a mediation and whose agreement is necessary to resolve the dispute.

(6) "Person" means an individual, corporation, business trust, estate, trust, partnership, limited liability company, association, joint venture, government; governmental subdivision, agency, or instrumentality; public corporation, or any other legal or commercial entity.

(7) "Proceeding" means:

    (A) a judicial, administrative, arbitral, or other adjudicative process, including related pre-hearing and post-hearing motions, conferences, and discovery; or

    (B) a legislative hearing or similar process.

(8) "Record" means information that is inscribed on a tangible medium or that is stored in an electronic or other medium and is retrievable in perceivable for

(9) "Sign" means:

(A) to execute or adopt a tangible symbol with the present intent to authenticate a record; or

(B) to attach or logically associate an electronic symbol, sound, or process to or with a record with the present intent to authenticate a record.

SECTION 3. SCOPE.

(a) Except as otherwise provided in subsection (b) or (c), this [Act] applies to a mediation in which:

(1) the mediation parties are required to mediate by statute or court or administrative agency rule or referred to mediation by a court, administrative agency, or arbitrator;

(2) the mediation parties and the mediator agree to mediate in a record that demonstrates an expectation that mediation communications will be privileged against disclosure; or

(3) the mediation parties use as a mediator an individual who holds himself or herself out as a mediator or the mediation is provided by a person that holds itself out as providing mediation.

(b) The [Act] does not apply to a mediation:

(1) relating to the establishment, negotiation, administration, or termination of a collective bargaining relationship;

(2) relating to a dispute that is pending under or is part of the processes established by a collective bargaining agreement, except that the [Act] applies to a mediation arising out of a dispute that has been filed with an administrative agency or court;

(3) conducted by a judge who might make a ruling on the case; or

(4) conducted under the auspices of:

(A) a primary or secondary school if all the parties are students or

(B) a correctional institution for youths if all the parties are residents of that institution.

(c) If the parties agree in advance in a signed record, or a record of proceeding reflects agreement by the parties, that all or part of a mediation is not privileged, the privileges under Sections 4 through 6 do not apply to the mediation or part agreed upon. However, Sections 4 through 6 apply to a mediation communication made by a person that has not received actual notice of the agreement before the communication is made.

Legislative Note: To the extent that the Act applies to mediations conducted under the authority of a State's courts, State judiciaries should consider enacting conforming court rules.

SECTION 4. PRIVILEGE AGAINST DISCLOSURE; ADMISSIBILITY; DISCOVERY.

(a) Except as otherwise provided in Section 6, a mediation communication is privileged as provided in subsection (b) and is not subject to discovery or admissible in evidence in a proceeding unless waived or precluded as provided by Section 5.

(b) In a proceeding, the following privileges apply:

(1) A mediation party may refuse to disclose, and may prevent any other person from disclosing, a mediation communication.

(2) A mediator may refuse to disclose a mediation communication, and may prevent any other person from disclosing a mediation communication of the mediator.

(3) A nonparty participant may refuse to disclose, and may prevent any other person from disclosing, a mediation communication of the nonparty participant.

(c) Evidence or information that is otherwise admissible or subject to discovery does not become inadmissible or protected from discovery solely by reason of its disclosure or use in a mediation.

Legislative Note: The Act does not supersede existing state statutes that make mediators incompetent to testify, or that provide for costs and attorney fees to mediators who are wrongfully subpoenaed. See, e.g., Cal. Evid. Code Section 703.5 (West 1994).

SECTION 5. WAIVER AND PRECLUSION OF PRIVILEGE.

(a) A privilege under Section 4 may be waived in a record or orally during a proceeding if it is expressly waived by all parties to the mediation and:

(1) in the case of the privilege of a mediator, it is expressly waived by the mediator; and

(2) in the case of the privilege of a nonparty participant, it is expressly waived by the nonparty participant.

(b) A person that discloses or makes a representation about a mediation communication which prejudices another person in a proceeding is precluded from asserting a privilege under Section 4, but only to the extent necessary for the person prejudiced to respond to the representation or disclosure.

(c) A person that intentionally uses a mediation to plan, attempt to commit or commit a crime, or to conceal an ongoing crime or ongoing criminal activity is precluded from asserting a privilege under Section 4.

SECTION 6. EXCEPTIONS TO PRIVILEGE.

(a) There is no privilege under Section 4 for a mediation communication that is:

(1) in an agreement evidenced by a record signed by all parties to the agreement;

(2) available to the public under [insert statutory reference to open records act] or made during a session of a mediation which is open, or is required by law to be open, to the public;

(3) a threat or statement of a plan to inflict bodily injury or commit a crime of violence;

(4) intentionally used to plan a crime, attempt to commit or commit a crime, or to conceal an ongoing crime or ongoing criminal activity;

(5) sought or offered to prove or disprove a claim or complaint of professional misconduct or malpractice filed against a mediator;

(6) except as otherwise provided in subsection (c), sought or offered to prove or disprove a claim or complaint of professional misconduct or malpractice filed against a mediation party, nonparty participant, or representative of a party based on conduct occurring during a mediation; or

(7) sought or offered to prove or disprove abuse, neglect, abandonment, or exploitation in a proceeding in which a child or adult protective services agency is a party, unless the

[Alternative A: [State to insert, for example, child or adult protection] case is referred by a court to mediation and a public agency participates.]

[Alternative B: public agency participates in the [State to insert, for example, child or adult protection] mediation].

(b) There is no privilege under Section 4 if a court, administrative agency, or arbitrator finds, after a hearing in camera, that the party seeking discovery or the proponent of the evidence has shown that the evidence is not otherwise available, that there is a need for the evidence that substantially outweighs the interest in protecting confidentiality, and that the mediation communication is sought or offered in:

(1) a court proceeding involving a felony [or misdemeanor]; or

(2) except as otherwise provided in subsection (c), a proceeding to prove a claim to rescind or reform or a defense to avoid liability on a contract arising out of the mediation.

(c) A mediator may not be compelled to provide evidence of a mediation communication referred to in subsection (a)(6) or (b)(2).

(d) If a mediation communication is not privileged under subsection (a) or (b), only the portion of the communication necessary for the application of the exception from nondisclosure may be admitted. Admission of evidence under subsection (a) or (b) does not render the evidence, or any other mediation communication, discoverable or admissible for any other purpose.

Legislative Note: If the enacting state does not have an open records act, the following language in paragraph (2) of subsection (a) needs to be deleted: "available to the public under [insert statutory reference to open records act] or".

SECTION 7. PROHIBITED MEDIATOR REPORTS.

(a) Except as required in subsection (b), a mediator may not make a report, assessment, evaluation, recommendation, finding, or other communication regarding a mediation to a court, administrative agency, or other authority that may make a ruling on the dispute that is the subject of the mediation.

(b) A mediator may disclose:

(1) whether the mediation occurred or has terminated, whether a settlement was reached, and attendance;

(2) a mediation communication as permitted under Section 6; or

(3) a mediation communication evidencing abuse, neglect, abandonment, or exploitation of an individual to a public agency responsible for protecting individuals against such mistreatment.

(c) A communication made in violation of subsection (a) may not be considered by a court, administrative agency, or arbitrator.

SECTION 8. CONFIDENTIALITY. Unless subject to the [insert statutory references to open meetings act and open records act], mediation communications are confidential to the extent agreed by the parties or provided by other law or rule of this State.

SECTION 9. MEDIATOR'S DISCLOSURE OF CONFLICTS OF INTEREST; BACKGROUND.

(a) Before accepting a mediation, an individual who is requested to serve as a mediator shall:

(1) make an inquiry that is reasonable under the circumstances to determine whether there are any known facts that a reasonable individual would consider likely to affect the impartiality of the mediator, including a financial or personal interest in the outcome of the mediation and an existing or past relationship with a mediation party or foreseeable participant in the mediation; and

(2) disclose any such known fact to the mediation parties as soon as is practical before accepting a mediation.

(b) If a mediator learns any fact described in subsection (a)(1) after accepting a mediation, the mediator shall disclose it as soon as is practicable.

(c) At the request of a mediation party, an individual who is requested to serve as a mediator shall disclose the mediator's qualifications to mediate a dispute.

(d) A person that violates subsection [(a) or (b)] [(a), (b), or (g)] is precluded by the violation from asserting a privilege under Section 4.

(e) Subsections (a), (b), [and] (c), [and] [(g)] do not apply to an individual acting as a judge.

(f) This [Act] does not require that a mediator have a special qualification by background or profession.

[(g) A mediator must be impartial, unless after disclosure of the facts required in subsections (a) and (b) to be disclosed, the parties agree otherwise.]

SECTION 10. PARTICIPATION IN MEDIATION. An attorney or other individual designated by a party may accompany the party to and participate in a mediation. A waiver of participation given before the mediation may be rescinded.

SECTION 11. INTERNATIONAL COMMERCIAL MEDIATION

(a) In this section, "Model Law" means the Model Law on International Commercial Conciliation adopted by the United Nations Commission on International Trade Law on 28 June 2002 and recommended by the United Nations General Assembly in a resolution (A/RES/57/18) dated 19 November 2002, and "international commercial mediation" means an international commercial conciliation as defined in Article 1 of the Model Law.

(b) Except as otherwise provided in subsections (c) and (d), if a mediation is an international commercial mediation, the mediation is governed by the Model Law.

(c) Unless the parties agree in accordance with Section 3(c) of this [Act] that all or part of an international commercial mediation is not privileged, Sections 4, 5, and 6 and any applicable definitions in Section 2 of this [Act] also apply to the mediation and nothing in Article 10 of the Model Law derogates from Sections 4, 5, and 6.

(d) If the parties to an international commercial mediation agree under Article 1, subsection (7), of the Model Law that the Model Law does not apply, this [Act] applies.

Legislative Note. The UNCITRAL Model Law on International Commercial Conciliation may be found at www.uncitral.org/en-index.htm. Important comments on interpretation are included in the Draft Guide to Enactment and Use of UNCITRAL Model Law on International Commercial Conciliation. The States should note the Draft Guide in a Legislative Note to the Act. This is especially important with respect to interpretation of Article 9 of the Model Law.

SECTION 12. RELATION TO ELECTRONIC SIGNATURES IN GLOBAL AND NATIONAL COMMERCE ACT. This [Act] modifies, limits, or supersedes the federal Electronic Signatures in Global and National Commerce Act, 15 U.S.C. Section 7001 et seq., but this [Act] does not modify, limit, or supersede Section 101(c) of that Act or authorize electronic delivery of any of the notices described in Section 103(b) of that Act.

SECTION 13. UNIFORMITY OF APPLICATION AND CON-STRUCTION. In applying and construing this [Act], consideration should be given to the need to promote uniformity of the law with respect to its subject matter among States that enact it.

SECTION 14. SEVERABILITY CLAUSE. If any provision of this [Act] or its application to any person or circumstance is held invalid, the invalidity does not affect other provisions or applications of this [Act] which can be given effect without the invalid provision or application, and to this end the provisions of this [Act] are severable.

SECTION 15. EFFECTIVE DATE. This [Act] takes effect
. . . .

SECTION 16. REPEALS. The following acts and parts of acts are hereby repealed:

(1)

(2)

(3)

SECTION 17. APPLICATION TO EXISTING AGREEMENTS OR REFERRALS.

(a) This [Act] governs a mediation pursuant to a referral or an agreement to mediate made on or after [the effective date of this [Act]].

(b) On or after [a delayed date], this [Act] governs an agreement to mediate whenever made.

Appendix C

THE MODEL STANDARDS OF CONDUCT FOR MEDIATORS (1994)

[*Editor's Note:* These standards were approved in 1994 by the American Arbitration Association, the American Bar Association Section of Dispute Resolution, and the Society of Professionals in Dispute Resolution (in principle). For a critique, see Jamie Henikoff and Michael Moffitt, *Remodeling the Model Standards of Conduct for Mediators,* 2 Harv. Negot. L. Rev. 87 (1997). A task force of the American Arbitration Association, American Bar Association, and the Association for Conflict Resolution was revising these standards as this edition went to press.]

INTRODUCTORY NOTE

The initiative for these standards came from three professional groups: the American Arbitration Association, the American Bar Association, and the Society of Professionals in Dispute Resolution.

The purpose of this initiative was to develop a set of standards to serve as a general framework for the practice of mediation. The effort is a step in the development of the field and a tool to assist practitioners in it — a beginning, not an end. The standards are intended to apply to all types of mediation. It is recognized, however, that in some cases the application of these standards may be affected by laws or contractual agreements.

PREFACE

The standards of conduct for mediators are intended to perform three major functions: to serve as a guide for the conduct of mediators; to inform the mediating parties; and to promote public confidence in mediation as a process for resolving disputes. The standards draw on existing codes of conduct for mediators and take into account issues and problems that have surfaced in mediation practice. They are offered in the hope that they will serve an educational function and to provide assistance to individuals, organizations, and institutions involved in mediation.

Mediation is a process in which an impartial third party — a mediator facilitates the resolution of a dispute by promoting voluntary agreement (or "self-determination") by the parties to a dispute. A mediator facilitates communications, promotes understanding, focuses the parties on their interests, and seeks creative problem solving to enable the parties to reach their owl, agreement. These standards give meaning to this definition of mediation.

I. SELF–DETERMINATION

A MEDIATOR SHALL RECOGNIZE THAT MEDIATION IS BASED ON THE PRINCIPLE OF SELF–DETERMINATION BY THE PARTIES

Self-determination is the fundamental principle of mediation. It requires that the mediation process rely upon the ability of the parties to reach a voluntary, uncoerced agreement. Any party may withdraw from mediation at any time.

Comments

The mediator may provide information about the process, raise issues, and help parties explore options. The primary role of the mediator is to facilitate a voluntary resolution of a dispute. Parties shall be given the opportunity to consider all proposed options.

A mediator cannot personally ensure that each party has made a fully informed choice to reach a particular agreement, but it is a good practice for the mediator to make the parties aware of the importance of consulting other professionals, where appropriate, to help them make informed decisions.

II. IMPARTIALITY

A MEDIATOR SHALL CONDUCT THE MEDIATION IN AN IMPARTIAL MANNER

The concept of mediator impartiality is central to the mediation process. A mediator shall mediate only those matters in which she or he remains impartial and evenhanded. If at any time the mediator is unable to conduct the process in an impartial manner, the mediator is obligated to withdraw.

Comments

A mediator shall avoid conduct that gives the appearance of partiality toward one of the parties. The quality of the mediation process is enhanced when the parties have confidence in the impartiality of the mediator.

When mediators are appointed by a court or institution, the appointing agency shall make reasonable efforts to ensure that mediators serve impartiality.

A mediator should guard against partiality or prejudice based on the parties' personal characteristics, background or performance at the mediation.

III. CONFLICTS OF INTEREST

A MEDIATOR SHALL DISCLOSE ALL ACTUAL AND POTENTIAL CONFLICTS OF INTEREST REASONABLY KNOWN TO THE MEDIATOR

AFTER DISCLOSURE, THE MEDIATOR SHALL DECLINE TO MEDIATE UNLESS ALL PARTIES CHOOSE TO RETAIN THE MEDIATOR

THE NEED TO PROTECT AGAINST CONFLICTS OF INTEREST ALSO GOVERNS CONDUCT THAT OCCURS DURING AND AFTER THE MEDIATION

A conflict of interest is a dealing or a relationship that might create an impression of possible bias. The basic approach to questions of conflict of interest is consistent with the concept of self-determination. The mediator has a responsibility to disclose all actual and potential conflicts that are reasonably known to the mediator and could reasonably be seen as raising a question about impartiality. If all parties agree to mediate after being informed of conflicts, the mediator may proceed with the mediation. If, however, the conflict of interest casts serious doubt on the integrity of the process, the mediator shall decline to proceed.

A mediator must avoid the appearance of conflict of interest both during and after the mediation. Without the consent of all parties, a mediator shall not subsequently establish a professional relationship with one of the parties in a related matter, or in an unrelated matter under circumstances which would raise legitimate questions about the integrity of the mediation process.

Comments

A mediator shall avoid conflicts of interests in recommending the services of other professionals. A mediator may make reference to professional referral services of associations which maintain rosters of qualified professionals.

Potential conflicts of interest may arise between administrators of mediation programs and mediators and there may be strong pressures on the mediator to settle a particular case or cases. The mediator's commitment must be to the parties and the process. Pressure from outside of the mediation process should never influence the mediator to coerce parties to settle.

IV. COMPETENCE

A MEDIATOR SHALL MEDIATE ONLY WHEN THE MEDIATOR HAS THE NECESSARY QUALIFICATIONS TO SATISFY THE REASONABLE EXPECTATIONS OF THE PARTIES

Any person may be selected as a mediator, provided that the parties are satisfied with the mediator's qualifications. Training and experience in mediation, however, are often necessary for effective mediation. A person who offers herself or himself as available to serve as a mediator gives parties and the public the expectation that she or he has the competency to mediate effectively. In court-connected or other forms of mandated mediation, it is essential that mediators assigned to the parties have the requisite training and experience.

Comments

Mediators should have available for the parties information regarding their relevant training, education and experience.

The requirements of appearing on a list of mediators must be made public and available to interested persons.

When mediators are appointed by a court or institution, the appointing agency shall make reasonable efforts to ensure that each mediator is qualified for the particular mediation.

V. CONFIDENTIALITY

A MEDIATOR SHALL MAINTAIN THE REASONABLE EXPECTATIONS OF THE PARTIES WITH REGARD TO CONFIDENTIALITY

The reasonable expectations of the parties with regard to confidentiality shall be met by the mediator. The parties' expectations of confidentiality depend on the circumstances of the mediation and any agreements they may make. A mediator shall not disclose any matter that a party expects to be confidential unless given permission by all parties or unless required by law or other public policy.

Comments

The parties may make their own rules with respect to confidentiality, or accepted practice of an individual mediator or institution may dictate a particular set of expectations. Since the parties expectations' regarding confidentiality are important, the mediator should discuss these expectations with the parties.

If the mediator holds private sessions with a party, the nature of these sessions with regard to confidentiality should be discussed prior to undertaking such sessions.

In order to protect the integrity of the mediation, a mediator should avoid communicating information about how the parties acted in the mediation process, the merits of the case, or settlement offers. The mediator may report, if required, whether parties appeared at a scheduled mediation.

Where the parties have agreed that all or a portion of the information disclosed during a mediation is confidential, the parties' agreement should be respected by the mediator.

Confidentiality should not be construed to limit or prohibit the effective monitoring, research, or evaluation of mediation programs by responsible persons. Under appropriate circumstances, researchers may be permitted to obtain access to statistical data and, with the permission of the parties, to individual case files, observations of live mediations, and interviews with participants.

VI. QUALITY OF THE PROCESS

A MEDIATOR SHALL CONDUCT THE MEDIATION FAIRLY, DILIGENTLY, AND IN A MANNER CONSISTENT WITH THE PRINCIPLE OF SELF DETERMINATION BY THE PARTIES

A mediator shall work to ensure a quality process and to encourage mutual respect among the parties. A quality process requires a commitment by the mediator to diligence and procedural fairness. There should be adequate opportunity for each party in mediation to participate in the discussions. The parties decide when and under what conditions they will reach an agreement or terminate a mediation.

Comments

A mediator may agree to mediate only when he or she is prepared to commit the attention essential to an effective mediation.

Mediators should only accept cases when they can satisfy the reasonable expectations of the parties concerning the timing of the process. A mediator should not allow a mediation to be unduly delayed by the parties or their representatives.

The presence or absence of persons at a mediation depends on the agreement of the parties and mediator. The parties and mediator may agree that others may be excluded from particular sessions or from the entire mediation process.

The primary purpose of a mediator is to facilitate the parties' voluntary agreement. This role differs substantially from other professional-client relationships. Mixing the role of mediator and the role of a professional advising a client is problematic, and mediators must strive to distinguish between the roles. A mediator should therefore refrain from providing professional advice. Where appropriate, a mediator should recommend that parties seek outside professional advice, or consider resolving their dispute through arbitration, counselling, neutral evaluation, or other processes. A mediator who undertakes, at the request of the parties, an additional dispute resolution role in the same matter assumes increased responsibilities and obligations that may be governed by the standards of the other professions.

A mediator shall withdraw from a mediation when incapable of serving or when unable to remain impartial.

A mediator shall withdraw from the mediation or postpone a session if the mediation is being used to further illegal conduct, or if a party is unable to participate due to drug, alcohol, or other physical or mental incapacity. Mediators should not permit their behavior in the mediation process to be guided by a desire for a high settlement rate.

VII.   ADVERTISING AND SOLICITATION

A MEDIATOR SHALL BE TRUTHFUL IN ADVERTISING AND SOLICITATION FOR MEDIATION

Advertising or any other communication with the public concerning services offered or regarding the education, training, and expertise of a mediator should be truthful. Mediators shall refrain from promises and guarantees of results.

Comments

It is imperative that communication with the public educate and instill confidence in the process.

In an advertisement or other communication to the public, a mediator may make reference to meeting state, national, or private organization qualifications only if the entity referred to has a procedure for qualifying mediators and the mediator has been duly granted the requisite status.

VIII.   FEES

A MEDIATOR SHALL FULLY DISCLOSE AND EXPLAIN THE BASIS OF COMPENSATION, FEES AND CHARGES TO THE PARTIES

The parties should be provided sufficient information about fees at the outset of a mediation to determine if they wish to retain the services of a mediator. If a mediator charges fees, the fees shall be reasonable considering, among other things, the mediation service, the type and complexity of the matter, the expertise of the mediator, the time required, and the rates customary in the community. The better practice in reaching an understanding about fees is to set down the arrangements in a written agreement.

Comments

A mediator who withdraws from a mediation should return any unearned fee to the parties.

A mediator should not enter into a fees agreement which is contingent upon the result of the mediation or amount of the settlement.

Co-mediators who share a fee should hold to standards of reasonableness in determining the allocation of fees.

A mediator should not accept a fee for referral of a matter to another mediator or to any other person.

IX.   OBLIGATIONS TO MEDIATION PROCESS

Mediators have a duty to improve the practice of mediation.

Comments

Mediators are regarded as knowledgeable in the process of mediation. They have an obligation to use their knowledge to help educate the public about mediation; to make mediation accessible to those who would like to use it; to correct abuses; and to improve their professional skills and abilities.

Appendix D

FEDERAL ARBITRATION ACT

9 U.S.C. § 1 et seq. (1994).

CHAPTER 1 — GENERAL PROVISIONS

§ 1. "Maritime Transactions" and "Commerce" Defined; Exceptions to
Operation of Title

"Maritime transactions", as herein defined, means charter parties,
bills of lading of water carriers, agreements relating to wharfage, supplies furnished vessels or repairs to vessels, collisions, or any other
matters in foreign commerce which, if the subject of controversy, would
be embraced within admiralty jurisdiction; "commerce", as herein defined, means commerce among the several States or with foreign nations,
or in any Territory of the United States or in the District of Columbia, or
between any such Territory and another, or between any such Territory
and any State or foreign nation, or between the District of Columbia and
any State or Territory or foreign nation, but nothing herein contained
shall apply to contracts of employment of seamen, railroad employees, or
any other class of workers engaged in foreign or interstate commerce.

§ 2. Validity, Irrevocability and Enforcement of Agreements to Arbitrate

A written provision in any maritime transaction or a contract
evidencing a transaction involving commerce to settle by arbitration a
controversy thereafter arising out of such contract or transaction, or the
refusal to perform the whole or any part thereof, or an agreement in
writing to submit to arbitration an existing controversy arising out of
such a contract, transaction, or refusal, shall be valid, irrevocable, and
enforceable, save upon such grounds as exist at law or in equity for the
revocation of any contract.

§ 3. Stay of Proceedings Where Issue Therein Referable to Arbitration

If any suit or proceeding be brought in any of the courts of the
United States upon any issue referable to arbitration under an agreement in writing for such arbitration, the court in which such suit is

pending, upon being satisfied that the issue involved in such suit or proceeding is referable to arbitration under such an agreement, shall on application of one of the parties stay the trial of the action until such arbitration has been had in accordance with the terms of the agreement, providing the applicant for the stay is not in default in proceeding with such arbitration.

§ 4.   Failure to Arbitrate Under Agreement; Petition to United States Court Having Jurisdiction for Order to Compel Arbitration; Notice and Service Thereof; Hearing and Determination

A party aggrieved by the alleged failure, neglect, or refusal of another to arbitrate under a written agreement for arbitration may petition any United States district court which, save for such agreement, would have jurisdiction under Title 28, in a civil action or in admiralty of the subject matter of a suit arising out of the controversy between the parties, for an order directing that such arbitration proceed in the manner provided for in such agreement. Five days' notice in writing of such application shall be served upon the party in default. Service thereof shall be made in the manner provided by the Federal Rules of Civil Procedure. The court shall hear the parties, and upon being satisfied that the making of the agreement for arbitration or the failure to comply therewith is not in issue, the court shall make an order directing the parties to proceed to arbitration in accordance with the terms of the agreement. The hearing and proceedings, under such agreement, shall be within the district in which the petition for an order directing such arbitration is filed. If the making of the arbitration agreement or the failure, neglect, or refusal to perform the same be in issue, the court shall proceed summarily to the trial thereof. If no jury trial be demanded by the party alleged to be in default, or if the matter in dispute is within admiralty jurisdiction, the court shall hear and determine such issue. Where such an issue is raised, the party alleged to be in default may, except in cases of admiralty, on or before the return day of the notice of application, demand a jury trial of such issue, and upon such demand the court shall make an order referring the issue or issues to a jury in the manner provided by the Federal Rules of Civil Procedure, or may specially call a jury for that purpose. If the jury find that no agreement in writing for arbitration was made or that there is no default in proceeding thereunder, the proceeding shall be dismissed. If the jury find that an agreement for arbitration was made in writing and that there is a default in proceeding thereunder, the court shall make an order summarily directing the parties to proceed with the arbitration in accordance with the terms thereof.

§ 5.   Appointment of Arbitrators or Umpire

If in the agreement provision be made for a method of naming or appointing an arbitrator or arbitrators or an umpire, such method shall be followed; but if no method be provided therein, or if a method be provided and any party thereto shall fail to avail himself of such method, or if for any other reason there shall be a lapse in the naming of an arbitrator or arbitrators or umpire, or in filling a vacancy, then upon the application of either party to the controversy the court shall designate and appoint an arbitrator or arbitrators or umpire, as the case may require, who shall act under the said agreement with the same force and effect as if he or they had been specifically named therein; and unless otherwise provided in the agreement the arbitration shall be by a single arbitrator.

§ 6. Application Heard as Motion

Any application to the court hereunder shall be made and heard in the manner provided by law for the making and hearing of motions, except as otherwise herein expressly provided.

§ 7. Witnesses Before Arbitrators; Fees; Compelling Attendance

The arbitrators selected either as prescribed in this title or otherwise, or a majority of them, may summon in writing any person to attend before them or any of them as a witness and in a proper case to bring with him or them any book, record, document, or paper which may be deemed material as evidence in the case. The fees for such attendance shall be the same as the fees of witnesses before masters of the United States courts. Said summons shall issue in the name of the arbitrator or arbitrators, or a majority of them, and shall be signed by the arbitrators, or a majority of them, and shall be directed to the said person and shall be served in the same manner as subpoenas to appear and testify before the court; if any person or persons so summoned to testify shall refuse or neglect to obey said summons, upon petition the United States district court for the district in which such arbitrators, or a majority of them, are sitting may compel the attendance of such person or persons before said arbitrator or arbitrators, or punish said person or persons for contempt in the same manner provided by law for securing the attendance of witnesses or their punishment for neglect or refusal to attend in the courts of the United States.

§ 8. Proceedings Begun by Libel in Admiralty and Seizure of Vessel or Property

If the basis of jurisdiction be a cause of action otherwise justiciable in admiralty, then, notwithstanding anything herein to the contrary, the party claiming to be aggrieved may begin his proceeding hereunder by libel and seizure of the vessel or other property of the other party according to the usual course of admiralty proceedings, and the court shall then have jurisdiction to direct the parties to proceed with the arbitration and shall retain jurisdiction to enter its decree upon the award.

§ 9. Award of Arbitrators; Confirmation; Jurisdiction; Procedure

If the parties in their agreement have agreed that a judgment of the court shall be entered upon the award made pursuant to the arbitration, and shall specify the court, then at any time within one year after the award is made any party to the arbitration may apply to the court so specified for an order confirming the award, and thereupon the court must grant such an order unless the award is vacated, modified, or corrected as prescribed in sections 10 and 11 of this title. If no court is specified in the agreement of the parties, then such application may be made to the United States court in and for the district within which such award was made. Notice of the application shall be served upon the adverse party, and thereupon the court shall have jurisdiction of such party as though he had appeared generally in the proceeding. If the adverse party is a resident of the district within which the award was made, such service shall be made upon the adverse party or his attorney as prescribed by law for service of notice of motion in an action in the same court. If the adverse party shall be a nonresident, then the notice of the application shall be served by the marshal of any district within which the adverse party may be found in like manner as other process of the court.

§ 10. Same; Vacation; Grounds; Rehearing

(a) In any of the following cases the United States court in and for the district wherein the award was made may make an order vacating the award upon the application of any party to the arbitration—

(1) Where the award was procured by corruption, fraud, or undue means.

(2) Where there was evident partiality or corruption in the arbitrators, or either of them.

(3) Where the arbitrators were guilty of misconduct in refusing to postpone the hearing, upon sufficient cause shown, or in refusing to hear evidence pertinent and material to the controversy; or of any other misbehavior by which the rights of any party have been prejudiced.

(4) Where the arbitrators exceeded their powers, or so imperfectly executed them that a mutual, final, and definite award upon the subject matter submitted was not made.

(5) Where an award is vacated and the time within which the agreement required the award to be made has not expired the court may, in its discretion, direct a rehearing by the arbitrators.

(b) The United States district court for the district wherein an award was made that was issued pursuant to section 580 of title 5 may make an order vacating the award upon the application of a person, other than a party to the arbitration, who is adversely affected or aggrieved by the award, if the use of arbitration or the award is clearly inconsistent with the factors set forth in section 572 of title 5.

§ 11. Same; Modification or Correction; Grounds; Order

In either of the following cases the United States court in and for the district wherein the award was made may make an order modifying or correcting the award upon the application of any party to the arbitration—

(a) Where there was an evident material miscalculation of figures or an evident material mistake in the description of any person, thing, or property referred to in the award.

(b) Where the arbitrators have awarded upon a matter not submitted to them, unless it is a matter not affecting the merits of the decision upon the matter submitted.

(c) Where the award is imperfect in matter of form not affecting the merits of the controversy.

The order may modify and correct the award, so as to effect the intent thereof and promote justice between the parties.

§ 12.   Notice of Motions to Vacate or Modify; Service; Stay of Proceedings

Notice of a motion to vacate, modify, or correct an award must be served upon the adverse party or his attorney within three months after the award is filed or delivered. If the adverse party is a resident of the district within which the award was made, such service shall be made upon the adverse party or his attorney as prescribed by law for service of notice of motion in an action in the same court. If the adverse party shall be a nonresident then the notice of the application shall be served by the marshal of any district within which the adverse party may be found in like manner as other process of the court. For the purposes of the motion any judge who might make an order to stay the proceedings in an action brought in the same court may make an order, to be served with the notice of motion, staying the proceedings of the adverse party to enforce the award.

§ 13.   Papers Filed With Order on Motions; Judgment; Docketing; Force and Effect; Enforcement

The party moving for an order confirming, modifying, or correcting an award shall, at the time such order is filed with the clerk for the entry of judgment thereon, also file the following papers with the clerk:

(a) The agreement; the selection or appointment, if any, of an additional arbitrator or umpire; and each written extension of the time, if any, within which to make the award.

(b) The award.

(c) Each notice, affidavit, or other paper used upon an application to confirm, modify, or correct the award, and a copy of each order of the court upon such an application.

The judgment shall be docketed as if it was rendered in an action.

The judgment so entered shall have the same force and effect, in all respects, as, and be subject to all the provisions of law relating to, a judgment in an action; and it may be enforced as if it had been rendered in an action in the court in which it is entered.

§ 14. Contracts Not Affected

This title shall not apply to contracts made prior to January 1, 1926.

§ 15. Inapplicability of the Act of State Doctrine

Enforcement of arbitral agreements, confirmation of arbitral awards, and execution upon judgments based on orders confirming such awards shall not be refused on the basis of the Act of State doctrine.

§ 16. Appeals

(a) An appeal may be taken from—

(1) an order—

(A) refusing a stay of any action under section 3 of this title,

(B) denying a petition under section 4 of this title to order arbitration to proceed,

(C) denying an application under section 206 of this title to compel arbitration,

(D) confirming or denying confirmation of an award or partial award, or

(E) modifying, correcting, or vacating an award;

(2) an interlocutory order granting, continuing, or modifying an injunction against an arbitration that is subject to this title; or

(3) a final decision with respect to an arbitration that is subject to this title.

(b) Except as otherwise provided in section 1292(b) of title 28, an appeal may not be taken from an interlocutory order—

(1) granting a stay of any action under section 3 of this title;

(2) directing arbitration to proceed under section 4 of this title;

(3) compelling arbitration under section 206 of this title; or

(4) refusing to enjoin an arbitration that is subject to this title.

CHAPTER 2 — CONVENTION ON THE RECOGNITION AND ENFORCEMENT OF FOREIGN ARBITRAL AWARDS [omitted]

CHAPTER 3 — INTER–AMERICAN CONVENTION ON INTERNATIONAL COMMERCIAL ARBITRATION [omitted]

Appendix E

UNIFORM ARBITRATION ACT

7 U.L.A. 1 (1997).

§ 1. Validity of Arbitration Agreement.

A written agreement to submit any existing controversy to arbitration or a provision in a written contract to submit to arbitration any controversy thereafter arising between the parties is valid, enforceable and irrevocable, save upon such grounds as exist at law or in equity for the revocation of any contract. This act also applies to arbitration agreements between employers and employees or between their respective representatives [unless otherwise provided in the agreement].

§ 2. Proceedings to Compel or Stay Arbitration.

(a) On application of a party showing an agreement described in Section 1, and the opposing party's refusal to arbitrate, the Court shall order the parties to proceed with arbitration, but if the opposing party denies the existence of the agreement to arbitrate, the Court shall proceed summarily to the determination of the issue so raised and shall order arbitration if found for the moving party, otherwise, the application shall be denied.

(b) On application, the court may stay an arbitration proceeding commenced or threatened on a showing that there is no agreement to arbitrate. Such an issue, when in substantial and bona fide dispute, shall be forthwith and summarily tried and the stay ordered if found for the moving party. If found for the opposing party, the court shall order the parties to proceed to arbitration.

(c) If an issue referable to arbitration under the alleged agreement is involved in an action or proceeding pending in a court having jurisdiction to hear applications under subdivision (a) of this Section, the application shall be made therein. Otherwise and subject to Section 18, the application may be made in any court of competent jurisdiction.

(d) Any action or proceeding involving an issue subject to arbitration shall be stayed if an order for arbitration or an application therefor has been made under this section or, if the issue is severable, the stay may be with respect thereto only. When the application is made in such action or proceeding, the order for arbitration shall include such stay.

(e) An order for arbitration shall not be refused on the ground that the claim in issue lacks merit or bona fides or because any fault or grounds for the claim sought to be arbitrated have not been shown. Unif.Arbitration Act § 2

§ 3. Appointment of Arbitrators by Court.

If the arbitration agreement provides a method of appointment of arbitrators, this method shall be followed. In the absence thereof, or if the agreed method fails or for any reason cannot be followed, or when an arbitrator appointed fails or is unable to act and his successor has not been duly appointed, the court on application of a party shall appoint one or more arbitrators. An arbitrator so appointed has all the powers of one specifically named in the agreement.

§ 4. Majority Action by Arbitrators.

The powers of the arbitrators may be exercised by a majority unless otherwise provided by the agreement or by this act.

§ 5. Hearing.

Unless otherwise provided by the agreement:

(a) The arbitrators shall appoint a time and place for the hearing and cause notification to the parties to be served personally or by registered mail not less than five days before the hearing. Appearance at the hearing waives such notice. The arbitrators may adjourn the hearing from time to time as necessary and, on request of a party and for good cause, or upon their own motion may postpone the hearing to a time not later than the date fixed by the agreement for making the award unless the parties consent to a later date. The arbitrators may hear and determine the controversy upon the evidence produced notwithstanding the failure of a party duly notified to appear. The court on application may direct the arbitrators to proceed promptly with the hearing and determination of the controversy.

(b) The parties are entitled to be heard, to present evidence material to the controversy and to cross-examine witnesses appearing at the hearing.

(c) The hearing shall be conducted by all the arbitrators but a majority may determine any question and render a final award. If, during the course of the hearing, an arbitrator for any reason ceases to act, the remaining arbitrator or arbitrators appointed to act as neutrals may continue with the hearing and determination of the controversy.

§ 6. Representation by Attorney.

A party has the right to be represented by an attorney at any proceeding or hearing under this act. A waiver thereof prior to the proceeding or hearing is ineffective.

§ 7. Witnesses, Subpoenas, Depositions.

(a) The arbitrators may issue (cause to be issued) subpoenas for the attendance of witnesses and for the production of books, records, documents and other evidence, and shall have the power to administer oaths. Subpoenas so issued shall be served, and upon application to the Court by a party or the arbitrators, enforced, in the manner provided by law for the service and enforcement of subpoenas in a civil action.

(b) On application of a party and for use as evidence, the arbitrators may permit a deposition to be taken, in the manner and upon the terms designated by the arbitrators, of a witness who cannot be subpoenaed or is unable to attend the hearing.

(c) All provisions of law compelling a person under subpoena to testify are applicable.

(d) Fees for attendance as a witness shall be the same as for a witness in the . . . Court.

§ 8. Award.

(a) The award shall be in writing and signed by the arbitrators joining in the award. The arbitrators shall deliver a copy to each party personally or by registered mail, or as provided in the agreement.

(b) An award shall be made within the time fixed therefor by the agreement or, if not so fixed, within such time as the court orders on application of a party. The parties may extend the time in writing either before or after the expiration thereof. A party waives the objection that an award was not made within the time required unless he notifies the arbitrators of his objection prior to the delivery of the award to him.

§ 9. Change of Award by Arbitrators.

On application of a party or, if an application to the court is pending under Sections 11, 12 or 13, on submission to the arbitrators by the court under such conditions as the court may order, the arbitrators may modify or correct the award upon the grounds stated in paragraphs (1) and (3) of subdivision (a) of Section 13, or for the purpose of clarifying the award. The application shall be made within twenty days after delivery of the award to the applicant. Written notice thereof shall be made within twenty days after delivery of the award to the appellant. Written notice thereof shall be given forthwith to the opposing party, stating he must serve his objections thereto, if any, within ten days from the notice. The award so modified or corrected is subject to the provisions of Sections 11, 12 and 13.

§ 10. Fees and Expenses of Arbitration.

Unless otherwise provided in the agreement to arbitrate, the arbitrators' expenses and fees, together with other expenses, not including counsel fees, incurred in the conduct of the arbitration, shall be paid as provided in the award.

§ 11. Confirmation of an Award.

Upon application of a party, the Court shall confirm an award, unless within the time limits hereinafter imposed grounds are urged for vacating or modifying or correcting the award, in which case the court shall proceed as provided in Sections 12 and 13.

§ 12. Vacating an Award.

(a) Upon application of a party, the court shall vacate an award where:

(1) The award was procured by corruption, fraud or other undue means;

(2) There was evident partiality by an arbitrator appointed as a neutral or corruption in any of the arbitrators or misconduct prejudicing the rights of any party;

(3) The arbitrators exceeded their powers;

(4) The arbitrators refused to postpone the hearing upon sufficient cause being shown therefor or refused to hear evidence material to the controversy or otherwise so conducted the hearing, contrary to the provisions of Section 5, as to prejudice substantially the rights of a party; or

(5) There was no arbitration agreement and the issue was not adversely determined in proceedings under Section 2 and the party did not participate in the arbitration hearing without raising the objection; but the fact that the relief was such that it could not or would not be granted by a court of law or equity is not ground for vacating or refusing to confirm the award.

(b) An application under this Section shall be made within ninety days after delivery of a copy of the award to the applicant, except that, if predicated upon corruption, fraud or other undue means, it shall be made within ninety days after such grounds are known or should have been known.

(c) In vacating the award on grounds other than stated in clause (5) of Subsection (a) the court may order a rehearing before new arbitrators chosen as provided in the agreement, or in the absence thereof, by the court in accordance with Section 3, or if the award is vacated on grounds set forth in clauses (3) and (4) of Subsection (a) the court may order a rehearing before the arbitrators who made the award or their successors appointed in accordance with Section 3. The time within which the agreement requires the award to be made is applicable to the rehearing and commences from the date of the order.

(d) If the application to vacate is denied and no motion to modify or correct the award is pending, the court shall confirm the award. As amended Aug. 1956.

§ 13. Modification or Correction of Award.

(a) Upon application made within ninety days after delivery of a copy of the award to the applicant, the court shall modify or correct the award where:

(1) There was an evident miscalculation of figures or an evident mistake in the description of any person, thing or property referred to in the award;

(2) The arbitrators have awarded upon a matter not submitted to them and the award may be corrected without affecting the merits of the decision upon the issues submitted; or

(3) The award is imperfect in a matter of form, not affecting the merits of the controversy.

(b) If the application is granted, the court shall modify and correct the award so as to effect its intent and shall confirm the award as so modified and corrected. Otherwise, the court shall confirm the award as made.

(c) An application to modify or correct an award may be joined in the alternative with an application to vacate the award.

§ 14. Judgment or Decree on Award.

Upon the granting of an order confirming, modifying or correcting an award, judgment or decree shall be entered in conformity therewith and be enforced as any other judgment or decree. Costs of the application and of the proceedings subsequent thereto, and disbursements may be awarded by the court.

§ 15. Judgment Roll, Docketing.

(a) On entry of judgment or decree, the clerk shall prepare the judgment roll consisting, to the extent filed, of the following:

(1) The agreement and each written extension of the time within which to make the award;

(2) The award;

(3) A copy of the order confirming, modifying or correcting the award; and

(4) A copy of the judgment or decree.

(b) The judgment or decree may be docketed as if rendered in an action.

§ 16. Applications to Court.

Except as otherwise provided, an application to the court under this act shall be by motion and shall be heard in the manner and upon the notice provided by law or rule of court for the making and hearing of motions. Unless the parties have agreed otherwise, notice of an initial application for an order shall be served in the manner provided by law for the service of a summons in an action.

§ 17. Court, Jurisdiction.

The term "court" means any court of competent jurisdiction of this State. The making of an agreement described in Section 1 providing for arbitration in this State confers jurisdiction on the court to enforce the agreement under this Act and to enter judgment on an award thereunder.

§ 18. Venue.

An initial application shall be made to the court of the [county] in which the agreement provides the arbitration hearing shall be held or, if the hearing has been held, in the county in which it was held. Otherwise the application shall be made in the [county] where the adverse party resides or has a place of business or, if he has no residence or place of business in this State, to the court of any [county]. All subsequent applications shall be made to the court hearing the initial application unless the court otherwise directs.

§ 19. Appeals.

(a) An appeal may be taken from:

(1) An order denying an application to compel arbitration made under Section 2;

(2) An order granting an application to stay arbitration made under Section 2(b);

(3) An order confirming or denying confirmation of an award;

(4) An order modifying or correcting an award;

(5) An order vacating an award without directing a rehearing; or

(6) A judgment or decree entered pursuant to the provisions of this act.

(b) The appeal shall be taken in the manner and to the same extent as from orders or judgments in a civil action.

§ 20. Act Not Retroactive.

This act applies only to agreements made subsequent to the taking effect of this act.

§ 21. Uniformity of Interpretation.

This act shall be so construed as to effectuate its general purpose to make uniform the law of those states which enact it.

§ 22. Constitutionality.

If any provision of this act or the application thereof to any person or circumstance is held invalid, the invalidity shall not affect other provisions or applications of the act which can be given effect without the invalid provision or application, and to this end the provisions of this act are severable.

§ 23. Short Title.

This act may be cited as the Uniform Arbitration Act.

§ 24. Repeal.

All acts or parts of acts which are inconsistent with the provisions of this act are hereby repealed.

§ 25. Time of Taking Effect.

This act shall take effect....

Appendix F

AMERICAN ARBITRATION ASSOCIATION

Commercial Arbitration Rules and Mediation Procedures (Including Procedures for Large, Complex Commercial Disputes) (2003)

Administrative Fees

The AAA charges a filing fee based on the amount of the claim or counterclaim. This fee information, which is included with these rules, allows the parties to exercise control over their administrative fees.

The fees cover AAA administrative services; they do not cover arbitrator compensation or expenses, if any, reporting services, or any post-award charges incurred by the parties in enforcing the award.

* * *

(Commercial Arbitration Rules Only)

R–1. Agreement of Parties[1][2]

(a) The parties shall be deemed to have made these rules a part of their arbitration agreement whenever they have provided for arbitration by the American Arbitration Association (hereinafter AAA) under its Commercial Arbitration Rules or for arbitration by the AAA of a domestic commercial dispute without specifying particular rules.

---

1. The AAA applies the *Supplementary Procedures for Consumer–Related Disputes* to arbitration clauses in agreements between individual consumers and businesses where the business has a standardized, systematic application of arbitration clauses with customers and where the terms and conditions of the purchase of standardized, consumable goods or services are nonnegotiable or primarily non-negotiable in most or all of its terms, conditions, features, or choices. The product or service must be for personal or household use. The AAA will have the discretion to apply or not to apply the Supplementary Procedures and the parties will be able to bring any disputes concerning the application or non-application to the attention of the arbitrator. Consumers are not prohibited from seeking relief in a small claims court for disputes or claims within the scope of its jurisdiction, even in consumer arbitration cases filed by the business.

2. A dispute arising out of an employer promulgated plan will be administered under the AAA's National Rules for the Resolution of Employment Disputes.

These rules and any amendment of them shall apply in the form in effect at the time the administrative requirements are met for a demand for arbitration or submission agreement received by the AAA. The parties, by written agreement, may vary the procedures set forth in these rules. After appointment of the arbitrator, such modifications may be made only with the consent of the arbitrator.

(b) Unless the parties or the AAA determines otherwise, the Expedited Procedures shall apply in any case in which no disclosed claim or counterclaim exceeds $75,000, exclusive of interest and arbitration fees and costs. Parties may also agree to use these procedures in larger cases. Unless the parties agree otherwise, these procedures will not apply in cases involving more than two parties. The Expedited Procedures shall be applied as described in Sections E–1 through E–10 of these rules, in addition to any other portion of these rules that is not in conflict with the Expedited Procedures.

(c) Unless the parties agree otherwise, the Procedures for Large, Complex Commercial Disputes shall apply to all cases in which the disclosed claim or counterclaim of any party is at least $500,000, exclusive of claimed interest, arbitration fees and costs. Parties may also agree to use the Procedures in cases involving claims or counterclaims under $500,000, or in nonmonetary cases. The Procedures for Large, Complex Commercial Disputes shall be applied as described in Sections L-I through L–4 of these rules, in addition to any other portion of these rules that is not in conflict with the Procedures for Large, Complex Commercial Disputes.

(d) All other cases shall be administered in accordance with Sections R–1 through R–54 of these rules.

The AAA applies the Supplementary Procedures for Consumer–Related Related Disputes to arbitration clauses in agreements between individual consumers and businesses where the business has a standardized, systematic application of arbitration clauses with customers and where the terms and conditions of the purchase of standardized, consumable goods or services are nonnegotiable or primarily non-negotiable in most or all of its terms, conditions, features, or choices. The product or service must be for personal or household use. The AAA will have the discretion to apply or not to apply the Supplementary Procedures and the parties will be able to bring any disputes concerning the application or non-application to the attention of the arbitrator. Consumers are not prohibited from seeking relief in a small claims court for disputes or claims within the scope of its jurisdiction, even in consumer arbitration cases filed by the business.

+ A dispute arising out of an employer promulgated plan will be administered under the AAA's National Rules for the Resolution of Employment Disputes.

R–2. AAA and Delegation of Duties

When parties agree to arbitrate under these rules, or when they provide for arbitration by the AAA and an arbitration is initiated under these rules, they thereby authorize the AAA to administer the arbitration. The authority and duties of the AAA are prescribed in the agreement of the parties and in these rules, and may be carried out through such of the AAA's representatives as it may direct. The AAA may, in its discretion, assign the administration of an arbitration to any of its offices.

R–3. National Roster of Arbitrators

The AAA shall establish and maintain a National Roster of Commercial Arbitrators ("National Roster") and shall appoint arbitrators as provided in these rules. The term "arbitrator" in these rules refers to the arbitration panel, constituted for a particular case, whether composed of one or more arbitrators, or to an individual arbitrator, as the context requires.

R–4. Initiation under an Arbitration Provision in a Contract

(a) Arbitration under an arbitration provision in a contract shall be initiated in the following manner:

  (i) The initiating party (the "claimant") shall, within the time period, if any, specified in the contract(s), give to the other party (the "respondent") written notice of its intention to arbitrate (the "demand"), which demand shall contain a statement setting forth the nature of the dispute, the names and addresses of all other parties, the amount involved, if any, the remedy sought, and the hearing locale requested.

  (ii) The claimant shall file at any office of the AAA two copies of the demand and two copies of the arbitration provisions of the contract, together with the appropriate filing fee as provided in the schedule included with these rules.

  (iii) The AAA shall confirm notice of such filing to the parties.

(b) A respondent may file an answering statement in duplicate with the AAA within 15 days after confirmation of notice of filing of the demand is sent by the AAA. The respondent shall, at the time of any such filing, send a copy of the answering statement to the claimant. If a counterclaim is asserted, it shall contain a statement setting forth the nature of the counterclaim, the amount involved, if any, and the remedy sought. If a counterclaim is made, the party making the counterclaim shall forward to the AAA with the answering statement the appropriate fee provided in fee schedule included with these rules.

(c) If no answering statement is filed within the stated time, respondent will be deemed to deny the claim. Failure to file an answering statement shall not operate to delay the arbitration.

(d) When filing any statement pursuant to this section, the parties are encouraged to provide descriptions of their claims in sufficient detail to make the circumstances of the dispute clear to the arbitrator.

R–5. Initiation under a Submission

Parties to any existing dispute may commence an arbitration under these rules by filing at any office of the AAA two copies of a written submission to arbitrate under these rules, signed by the parties. It shall contain a statement of the nature of the dispute, the names and addresses of all parties, any claims and counterclaims, the amount involved, if any, the remedy sought, and the hearing locale requested, together with the appropriate filing fee as provided in the schedule included with these rules. Unless the parties state otherwise in the submission, all claims and counterclaims will be deemed to be denied by the other party.

R–6. Changes of Claim

After filing of a claim, if either party desires to make any new or different claim or counterclaim, it shall be made in writing and filed with the AAA. The party asserting such a claim or counterclaim shall provide a copy to the other party, who shall have 15 days from the date of such transmission within which to file an answering statement with the AAA. After the arbitrator is appointed, however, no new or different claim may be submitted except with the arbitrator's consent.

R–7. Jurisdiction

(a) The arbitrator shall have the power to rule on his or her own jurisdiction, including any objections with respect to the existence, scope or validity of the arbitration agreement.

(b) The arbitrator shall have the power to determine the existence or validity of a contract of which an arbitration clause forms a part. Such an arbitration clause shall be treated as an agreement independent of the other terms of the contract. A decision by the arbitrator that the contract is null and void shall not for that reason alone render invalid the arbitration clause.

(c) A party must object to the jurisdiction of the arbitrator or to the arbitrability of a claim or counterclaim no later than the filing of the answering statement to the claim or counterclaim that gives rise to the objection. The arbitrator may rule on such objections as a preliminary matter or as part of the final award.

R–8. Mediation

At any stage of the proceedings, the parties may agree to conduct a mediation conference under the Commercial Mediation Procedures in order to facilitate settlement. The mediator shall not be an arbitrator appointed to the case. Where the parties to a pending arbitration agree to mediate under the AAA's rules, no additional administrative fee is required to initiate the mediation.

R–9. Administrative Conference

At the request of any party or upon the AAA's own initiative, the AAA may conduct an administrative conference, in person or by telephone, with the parties and/or their representatives. The conference may address such issues as arbitrator selection, potential mediation of the dispute, potential exchange of information, a timetable for hearings and any other administrative matters.

R–10. Fixing of Locale

The parties may mutually agree on the locale where the arbitration is to be held. If any party requests that the hearing be held in a specific locale and the other party files no objection thereto within 15 days after notice of the request has been sent to it by the AAA, the locale shall be the one requested. If a party objects to the locale requested by the other party, the AAA shall have the power to determine the locale, and its decision shall be final and binding.

R–11. Appointment from National Roster

If the parties have not appointed an arbitrator and have not provided any other method of appointment, the arbitrator shall be appointed in the following manner:

(a) Immediately after the filing of the submission or the answering statement or the expiration of the time within which the answering statement is to be filed, the AAA shall send simultaneously to each party to the dispute an identical list of 10 (unless the AAA decides that a different number is appropriate) names of persons chosen from the National Roster. The parties are encouraged to agree to an arbitrator from the submitted list and to advise the AAA of their agreement.

(b) If the parties are unable to agree upon an arbitrator, each party to the dispute shall have 15 days from the transmittal date in which to strike names objected to, number the remaining names in order of preference, and return the list to the AAA. If a party does not return the list within the time specified, all persons named therein shall be deemed acceptable. From among the persons who have been approved on both lists, and in accordance with the designated order of mutual preference, the AAA shall invite the acceptance of an arbitrator to serve. If the parties fail to agree on any of the persons named, or if acceptable arbitrators are unable to act, or if for any other reason the appointment cannot be made from the submitted lists, the AAA shall have the power to make the appointment from among other members of the National Roster without the submission of additional lists.

(c) Unless the parties agree otherwise when there are two or more claimants or two or more respondents, the AAA may appoint all the arbitrators.

R–12. Direct Appointment by a Party

(a) If the agreement of the parties names an arbitrator or specifies a method of appointing an arbitrator, that designation or method shall be followed. The notice of appointment, with the name and address of the arbitrator, shall be filed with the AAA by the appointing party. Upon the request of any appointing party, the AAA shall submit a list of members of the National Roster from which the party may, if it so desires, make the appointment.

(b) Where the parties have agreed that each party is to name one arbitrator, the arbitrators so named must meet the standards of Section R-17 with respect to impartiality and independence unless the parties have specifically agreed pursuant to Section R–17(a) that the party-appointed arbitrators are to be non-neutral and need not meet those standards.

(c) If the agreement specifies a period of time within which an arbitrator shall be appointed and any party fails to make the appointment within that period, the AAA shall make the appointment.

(d) If no period of time is specified in the agreement, the AAA shall notify the party to make the appointment. If within 15 days after such notice has been sent, an arbitrator has not been appointed by a party, the AAA shall make the appointment.

R–13. Appointment of Chairperson by Party–Appointed Arbitrators or Parties

(a) If, pursuant to Section R-1 2, either the parties have directly appointed arbitrators, or the arbitrators have been appointed by the AAA, and the parties have authorized them to appoint a chairperson within a specified time and no appointment is made within that time or any agreed extension, the AAA may appoint the chairperson.

(b) If no period of time is specified for appointment of the chairperson and the party appointed arbitrators or the parties do not make the appointment within 15 days from the date of the appointment of the last party-appointed arbitrator, the AAA may appoint the chairperson.

(c) If the parties have agreed that their party-appointed arbitrators shall appoint the chairperson from the National Roster, the AAA shall furnish to the party-appointed arbitrators, in the manner provided in Section R–11, a list selected from the National Roster, and the appointment of the chairperson shall be made as provided in that Section.

R–14. Nationality of Arbitrator

Where the parties are nationals of different countries, the AAA, at the request of any party or on its own initiative, may appoint as arbitrator a national of a country other than that of any of the parties. The request must be made before the time set for the appointment of the arbitrator as agreed by the parties or set by these rules.

R–15. Number of Arbitrators

If the arbitration agreement does not specify the number of arbitrators, the dispute shall be heard and determined by one arbitrator, unless the AAA, in its discretion, directs that three arbitrators be appointed. A party may request three arbitrators in the demand or answer, which request the AAA will consider in exercising its discretion regarding the number of arbitrators appointed to the dispute.

R–16. Disclosure

(a) Any person appointed or to be appointed as an arbitrator shall disclose to the AAA any circumstance likely to give rise to justifiable doubt as to the arbitrator's impartiality or independence, including any bias or any financial or personal interest in the result of the arbitration or any past or present relationship with the parties or their representatives. Such obligation shall remain in effect throughout the arbitration.

(b) Upon receipt of such information from the arbitrator or another source, the AAA shall communicate the information to the parties and, if it deems it appropriate to do so, to the arbitrator and others.

(c) In order to encourage disclosure by arbitrators, disclosure of information pursuant to this Section R–16 is not to be construed as an indication that the arbitrator considers that the disclosed circumstance is likely to affect impartiality or independence.

R–17. Disqualification of Arbitrator

(a) Any arbitrator shall be impartial and independent and shall perform his or her duties with diligence and in good faith, and shall be subject to disqualification for

(i) partiality or lack of independence,

(ii) inability or refusal to perform his or her duties with diligence and in good faith, and

(iii) any grounds for disqualification provided by applicable law. The parties may agree in writing, however, that arbitrators directly appointed by a party pursuant to Section R-12 shall be nonneutral, in which case such arbitrators need not be impartial or independent and shall not be subject to disqualification for partiality or lack of independence.

(b) Upon objection of a party to the continued service of an arbitrator, or on its own initiative, the AAA shall determine whether the arbitrator should be disqualified under the grounds set out above, and shall inform the parties of its decision, which decision shall be conclusive.

R–18. Communication with Arbitrator

(a) No party and no one acting on behalf of any party shall communicate ex parte with an arbitrator or a candidate for arbitrator concerning the arbitration, except that a party, or someone acting on behalf of a party, may communicate ex parte with a candidate for direct appointment pursuant to Section R-12 in order to advise the candidate of the general nature of the controversy and of the anticipated proceedings and to discuss the candidate's qualifications, availability, or independence in relation to the parties or to discuss the suitability of candidates for selection as a third arbitrator where the parties or party designated arbitrators are to participate in that selection.

(b) Section R-18(a) does not apply to arbitrators directly appointed by the parties who, pursuant to Section R-17(a), the parties have agreed in writing are non-neutral. Where the parties have so agreed under Section R-17(a), the AAA shall as an administrative practice suggest to the parties that they agree further that Section R-18(a) should nonetheless apply prospectively.

R-19. Vacancies

(a) If for any reason an arbitrator is unable to perform the duties of the office, the AAA may, on proof satisfactory to it, declare the office vacant. Vacancies shall be filled in accordance with the applicable provisions of these rules.

(b) In the event of a vacancy in a panel of neutral arbitrators after the hearings have commenced, the remaining arbitrator or arbitrators may continue with the hearing and determination of the controversy, unless the parties agree otherwise.

(c) In the event of the appointment of a substitute arbitrator, the panel of arbitrators shall determine in its sole discretion whether it is necessary to repeat all or part of any prior hearings.

R-20. Preliminary Hearing

(a) At the request of any party or at the discretion of the arbitrator or the AAA, the arbitrator may schedule as soon as practicable a preliminary hearing with the parties and/or their representatives. The preliminary hearing may be conducted by telephone at the arbitrator's discretion.

(b) During the preliminary hearing, the parties and the arbitrator should discuss the future conduct of the case, including clarification of the issues and claims, a schedule for the hearings and any other preliminary matters.

R-21. Exchange of Information

(a) At the request of any party or at the discretion of the arbitrator, consistent with the expedited nature of arbitration, the arbitrator may direct

  (i) the production of documents and other information, and

  (ii) the identification of any witnesses to be called.

(b) At least five business days prior to the hearing, the parties shall exchange copies of all exhibits they intend to submit at the hearing.

(c) The arbitrator is authorized to resolve any disputes concerning the exchange of information.

R-22. Date, Time, and Place of Hearing

The arbitrator shall set the date, time, and place for each hearing. The parties shall respond to requests for hearing dates in a timely manner, be cooperative in scheduling the earliest practicable date, and adhere to the established hearing schedule. The AAA shall send a notice of hearing to the parties at least 10 days in advance of the hearing date, unless otherwise agreed by the parties.

R–23. Attendance at Hearings

The arbitrator and the AAA shall maintain the privacy of the hearings unless the law provides to the contrary. Any person having a direct interest in the arbitration is entitled to attend hearings. The arbitrator shall otherwise have the power to require the exclusion of any witness, other than a party or other essential person, during the testimony of any other witness. It shall be discretionary with the arbitrator to determine the propriety of the attendance of any other person other than a party and its representatives.

R–24. Representation

Any party may be represented by counsel or other authorized representative. A party intending to be so represented shall notify the other party and the AAA of the name and address of the representative at least three days prior to the date set for the hearing at which that person is first to appear. When such a representative initiates an arbitration or responds for a party, notice is deemed to have been given.

R–25. Oaths

Before proceeding with the first hearing, each arbitrator may take an oath of office and, if required by law, shall do so. The arbitrator may require witnesses to testify under oath administered by any duly qualified person and, if it is required by law or requested by any party, shall do so.

R–26. Stenographic Record

Any party desiring a stenographic record shall make arrangements directly with a stenographer and shall notify the other parties of these arrangements at least three days in advance of the hearing. The requesting party or parties shall pay the cost of the record. If the transcript is agreed by the parties, or determined by the arbitrator to be the official record of the proceeding, it must be provided to the arbitrator and made available to the other parties for inspection, at a date, time, and place determined by the arbitrator.

R–27. Interpreters

Any party wishing an interpreter shall make all arrangements directly with the interpreter and shall assume the costs of the service.

R–28. Postponements

The arbitrator may postpone any hearing upon agreement of the parties, upon request of a party for good cause shown, or upon the arbitrator's own initiative.

R–29. Arbitration in the Absence of a Party or Representative

Unless the law provides to the contrary, the arbitration may proceed in the absence of any party or representative who, after due notice, fails to be present or fails to obtain a postponement. An award shall not be made solely on the default of a party. The arbitrator shall require the party who is present to submit such evidence as the arbitrator may require for the making of an award.

R–30. Conduct of Proceedings

(a) The claimant shall present evidence to support its claim. The respondent shall then present evidence to support its defense. Witnesses for each party shall also submit to questions from the arbitrator and the adverse party. The arbitrator has the discretion to vary this procedure, provided that the parties are treated with equality and that each party has the right to be heard and is given a fair opportunity to present its case.

(b) The arbitrator, exercising his or her discretion, shall conduct the proceedings with a view to expediting the resolution of the dispute and may direct the order of proof, bifurcate proceedings and direct the parties to focus their presentations on issues the decision of which could dispose of all or part of the case.

(c) The parties may agree to waive oral hearings in any case.

R–31. Evidence

(a) The parties may offer such evidence as is relevant and material to the dispute and shall produce such evidence as the arbitrator may deem necessary to an understanding and determination of the dispute. Conformity to legal rules of evidence shall not be necessary. All evidence shall be taken in the presence of all of the arbitrators and all of the parties, except where any of the parties is absent, in default or has waived the right to be present.

(b) The arbitrator shall determine the admissibility, relevance, and materiality of the evidence offered and may exclude evidence deemed by the arbitrator to be cumulative or irrelevant.

(c) The arbitrator shall take into account applicable principles of legal privilege, such as those involving the confidentiality of communications between a lawyer and client.

(d) An arbitrator or other person authorized by law to subpoena witnesses or documents may do so upon the request of any party or independently.

R–32. Evidence by Affidavit and Post-hearing Filing of Documents or Other Evidence

(a) The arbitrator may receive and consider the evidence of witnesses by declaration or affidavit, but shall give it only such weight as the arbitrator deems it entitled to after consideration of any objection made to its admission.

(b) If the parties agree or the arbitrator directs that documents or other evidence be submitted to the arbitrator after the hearing, the documents or other evidence shall be filed with the AAA for transmission to the arbitrator. All parties shall be afforded an opportunity to examine and respond to such documents or other evidence.

R–33. Inspection or Investigation

An arbitrator finding it necessary to make an inspection or investigation in connection with the arbitration shall direct the AAA to so advise the parties. The arbitrator shall set the date and time and the AAA shall notify the parties. Any party who so desires may be present at such an inspection or investigation. In the event that one or all parties are not present at the inspection or investigation, the arbitrator shall make an oral or written report to the parties and afford them an opportunity to comment.

R–34. Interim Measures**

(a) The arbitrator may take whatever interim measures he or she deems necessary, including injunctive relief and measures for the protection or conservation of property and disposition of perishable goods.

(b) Such interim measures may take the form of an interim award, and the arbitrator may require security for the costs of such measures.

(c) A request for interim measures addressed by a party to a judicial authority shall not be deemed incompatible with the agreement to arbitrate or a waiver of the right to arbitrate.

** The Optional Rules may be found below.

R–35. Closing of Hearing

The arbitrator shall specifically inquire of all parties whether they have any further proofs to offer or witnesses to be heard. Upon receiving negative replies or if satisfied that the record is complete, the arbitrator shall declare the hearing closed. If briefs are to be filed, the hearing shall b e declared closed as of the final date set by the arbitrator for the receipt of briefs. If documents are to be filed as provided in Section R–32 and the date set for their receipt is later than that set for the receipt of briefs, the later date shall be the closing date of the hearing. The time limit within which the arbitrator is required to make the award shall commence, in the absence of other agreements by the parties, upon the closing of the hearing.

R–36. Reopening of Hearing

The hearing may be reopened on the arbitrator's initiative, or upon application of a party, at any time before the award is made. If reopening the hearing would prevent the making of the award within the specific time agreed on by the parties in the contract(s) out of which the controversy has arisen, the matter may not be reopened unless the parties agree on an extension of time. When no specific date is fixed in the contract, the arbitrator may reopen the hearing and shall have 30 days from the closing of the reopened hearing within which to make an award.

R–37. Waiver of Rules

Any party who proceeds with the arbitration after knowledge that any provision or requirement of these rules has not been complied with and who fails to state an objection in writing shall be deemed to have waived the right to object.

R–38. Extensions of Time

The parties may modify any period of time by mutual agreement. The AAA or the arbitrator may for good cause extend any period of time established by these rules, except the time for making the award. The AAA shall notify the parties of any extension.

R–39. Serving of Notice

(a) Any papers, notices, or process necessary or proper for the initiation or continuation of an arbitration under these rules, for any court action in connection therewith, or for the entry of judgment on any award made under these rules may be served on a party by mail addressed to the party, or its representative at the last known address or by personal service, in or outside the state where the arbitration is to be held, provided that reasonable opportunity to be heard with regard to the dispute is or has been granted to the party.

(b) The AAA, the arbitrator and the parties may also use overnight delivery or electronic facsimile transmission (fax), to give the notices required by these rules. Where all parties and the arbitrator agree, notices may be transmitted by electronic mail (E-mail), or other methods of communication.

(c) Unless otherwise instructed by the AAA or by the arbitrator, any documents submitted by any party to the AAA or to the arbitrator shall simultaneously be provided to the other party or parties to the arbitration.

R–40. Majority Decision

When the panel consists of more than one arbitrator, unless required by law or by the arbitration agreement, a majority of the arbitrators must make all decisions.

R–41. Time of Award

The award shall be made promptly by the arbitrator and, unless otherwise agreed by the parties or specified by law, no later than 30 days from the date of closing the hearing, or, if oral hearings have been waived, from the date of the AAA's transmittal of the final statements and proofs to the arbitrator.

R–42. Form of Award

(a) Any award shall be in writing and signed by a majority of the arbitrators. It shall be executed in the manner required by law.

(b) The arbitrator need not render a reasoned award unless the parties request such an award in writing prior to appointment of the arbitrator or unless the arbitrator determines that a reasoned award is appropriate.

R–43. Scope of Award

(a) The arbitrator may grant any remedy or relief that the arbitrator deems just and equitable and within the scope of the agreement of the parties, including, but not limited to, specific performance of a contract.

(b) In addition to a final award, the arbitrator may make other decisions, including interim, interlocutory, or partial rulings, orders, and awards. In any interim, interlocutory, or partial award, the arbitrator may assess and apportion the fees, expenses, and compensation related to such award as the arbitrator determines is appropriate.

(c) In the final award, the arbitrator shall assess the fees, expenses, and compensation provided in Sections R–49, R–50, and R–5 1. The arbitrator may apportion such fees, expenses, and compensation among the parties in such amounts as the arbitrator determines is appropriate.

(d) The award of the arbitrators may include:

    (i) interest at such rate and from such date as the arbitrators may deem appropriate; and

    (ii) an award of attorneys' fees if all parties have requested such an award or it is authorized by law or their arbitration agreement.

R–44. Award upon Settlement

If the parties settle their dispute during the course of the arbitration and if the parties so request, the arbitrator may set forth the terms of the settlement in a "consent award." A consent award must include an allocation of arbitration costs, including administrative fees and expenses as well as arbitrator fees and expenses.

R–45. Delivery of Award to Parties

Parties shall accept as notice and delivery of the award the placing of the award or a true copy thereof in the mail addressed to the parties or their representatives at the last known addresses, personal or electronic service of the award, or the filing of the award in any other manner that is permitted by law.

R–46. Modification of Award

Within 20 days after the transmittal of an award, any party, upon notice to the other parties, may request the arbitrator, through the AAA, to correct any clerical, typographical, or computational errors in the award. The arbitrator is not empowered to redetermine the merits of any claim already decided. The other parties shall be given 10 days to respond to the request. The arbitrator shall dispose of the request within 20 days after transmittal by the AAA to the arbitrator of the request and any response thereto.

R–47. Release of Documents for judicial Proceedings

The AAA shall, upon die written request of a party, furnish to the party, at the party's expense, certified copies of any papers in the AAA's possession that may be required in judicial proceedings relating to the arbitration.

R–48. Applications to Court and Exclusion of Liability

(a) No judicial proceeding by a party relating to the subject matter of the arbitration shall be deemed a waiver of the party's right to arbitrate.

(b) Neither the AAA nor any arbitrator in a proceeding under these rules is a necessary or proper party in judicial proceedings relating to the arbitration.

(c) Parties to an arbitration under these rules shall be deemed to have consented that judgment upon the arbitration award may be entered in any federal or state court having jurisdiction thereof.

(d) Parties to an arbitration under these rules shall be deemed to have consented that neither the AAA nor any arbitrator shall be liable to any party in any action for damages or injunctive relief for any act or omission in connection with any arbitration under these rules.

R–49. Administrative Fees

As a not-for-profit organization, the AAA shall prescribe an initial filing fee and a case service fee to compensate it for the cost of providing administrative services. The fees in effect when the fee or charge is incurred shall be applicable. The filing fee shall be advanced by the party or parties making a claim or counterclaim, subject to final apportionment by the arbitrator in the award. The AAA may, in the event of extreme hardship on the part of any party, defer or reduce the administrative fees.

R–50. Expenses

The expenses of witnesses for either side shall be paid by the party producing such witnesses. All other expenses of the arbitration, including required travel and other expenses of the arbitrator, AAA representatives, and any witness and the cost of any proof produced at the direct request of the arbitrator, shall be borne equally by the parties, unless they agree otherwise or unless the arbitrator in the award assesses such expenses or any part thereof against any specified party or parties.

R–51. Neutral Arbitrator's Compensation

(a) Arbitrators shall be compensated at a rate consistent with the arbitrator's stated rate of compensation.

(b) If there is disagreement concerning the terms of compensation, an appropriate rate shall be established with the arbitrator by the AAA and confirmed to the parties.

(c) Any arrangement for the compensation of a neutral arbitrator shall be made through the AAA and not directly between the parties and the arbitrator.

R–52. Deposits

The AAA may require the parties to deposit in advance of any hearings such sums of money as it deems necessary to cover the expense of the arbitration, including the arbitrator's fee, if any, and shall render an accounting to the parties and return any unexpended balance at the conclusion of the case.

R–53. Interpretation and Application of Rules

The arbitrator shall interpret and apply these rules insofar as they relate to the arbitrator's powers and duties. When there is more than one arbitrator and a difference arises among them concerning the meaning or application of these rules, it shall be decided by a majority vote. If that is not possible, either an arbitrator or a party may refer the question to the AAA for final decision. All other rules shall be interpreted and applied by the AAA.

R–54. Suspension for Nonpayment

If arbitrator compensation or administrative charges have not been paid in full, the AAA may so inform the parties in order that one of them may advance the required payment. If such payments are not made, the arbitrator may order the suspension or termination of the proceedings. If no arbitrator has yet been appointed, the AAA may suspend the proceedings.

EXPEDITED PROCEDURES

E–1. Limitation on Extensions

Except in extraordinary circumstances, the AAA or the arbitrator may grant a party no more than one seven-day extension of time to respond to the demand for arbitration or counterclaim as provided in Section R–4.

E–2. Changes of Claim or Counterclaim

A claim or counterclaim may be increased in amount, or a new or different claim or counterclaim added, upon the agreement of the other party, or the consent of the arbitrator. After the arbitrator is appointed, however, no new or different claim or counterclaim may be submitted except with the arbitrator's consent. If an increased claim or counterclaim exceeds $75,000, the case will be administered under the regular procedures unless all parties and the arbitrator agree that the case may continue to be processed under the Expedited Procedures.

E–3. Serving of Notices

In addition to notice provided by Section R–39(b), the parties shall also accept notice by telephone. Telephonic notices by the AAA shall subsequently be confirmed in writing to the parties. Should there be a failure to confirm in writing any such oral notice, the proceeding shall nevertheless be valid if notice has, in fact, been given by telephone.

E–4. Appointment and Qualifications of Arbitrator

(a) The AAA shall simultaneously submit to each party an identical list of five proposed arbitrators drawn from its National Roster from which one arbitrator shall be appointed.

(b) The parties are encouraged to agree to an arbitrator from this list and to advise the AAA of their agreement. If the parties are unable to agree upon an arbitrator, each party may strike two names from the list and return it to the AAA within seven days from the date of the AAA's mailing to the parties. If for any reason the appointment of an arbitrator cannot be made from the list, the AAA may make the appointment from other members of the panel without the submission of additional lists.

(c) The parties will be given notice by the AAA of the appointment of the arbitrator, who shall be subject to disqualification for the reasons specified in Section R-1 7. The parties shall notify the AAA within seven days of any objection to the arbitrator appointed. Any such objection shall be for cause and shall be confirmed in writing to the AAA with a copy to the other party or parties.

E–5.   Exchange of Exhibits

At least two business days prior to the hearing, the parties shall exchange copies of all exhibits they intend to submit at the hearing. The arbitrator shall resolve disputes concerning the exchange of exhibits.

E–6.   Proceedings on Documents

Where no party's claim exceeds $10,000, exclusive of interest and arbitration costs, and other cases in which the parties agree, the dispute shall be resolved by submission of documents, unless any party requests an oral hearing, or the arbitrator determines that an oral hearing is necessary. The arbitrator shall establish a fair and equitable procedure for the submission of documents.

E–7.   Date, Time, and Place of Hearing

In cases in which a hearing is to be held, the arbitrator shall set the date, time, and place of the hearing, to be scheduled to take place within 30 days of confirmation of the arbitrator's appointment. The AAA will notify the parties in advance of the hearing date.

E–8.   The Hearing

(a) Generally, the hearing shall not exceed one day. Each party shall have equal opportunity to submit its proofs and complete its case. The arbitrator shall determine the order of the hearing, and may require further submission of documents within two days after the hearing. For good cause shown, the arbitrator may schedule additional hearings within seven business days after the initial day of hearings.

(b) Generally, there will be no stenographic record. Any party desiring a stenographic record may arrange for one pursuant to the provisions of Section R–26.

E–9.   Time of Award

Unless otherwise agreed by the parties, the award shall be rendered not later than 14 days from the date of the closing of the hearing or, if oral hearings have been waived, from the date of the AAXs transmittal of the final statements and proofs to the arbitrator.

E–10. Arbitrator's Compensation

Arbitrators will receive compensation at a rate to be suggested by the AAA regional office.

PROCEDURES FOR LARGE, COMPLEX COMMERCIAL DISPUTES

L–1. Administrative Conference

Prior to the dissemination of a list of potential arbitrators, the AAA shall, unless the parties agree otherwise, conduct an administrative conference with the parties and/or their attorneys or other representatives by conference call. The conference will take place within 14 days after the commencement of the arbitration. In the event the parties are unable to agree on a mutually acceptable time for the conference, the AAA may contact the parties individually to discuss the issues contemplated herein. Such administrative conference shall be conducted for the following purposes and for such additional purposes as the parties or the AAA may deem appropriate:

(a) to obtain additional information about the nature and magnitude of the dispute and the anticipated length of hearing and scheduling;

(b) to discuss the views of the parties about the technical and other qualifications of the arbitrators;

(c) to obtain conflicts statements from the parties; and

(d) to consider, with the parties, whether mediation or other non-adjudicative methods of dispute resolution might be appropriate.

L–2. Arbitrators

(a) Large, Complex Commercial Cases shall be heard and determined by either one or three arbitrators, as may be agreed upon by the parties. If the parties are unable to agree upon the number of arbitrators and a claim or counterclaim involves at least $1,000,000, then three arbitrators shall hear and determine the case. If the parties are unable to agree on the number of arbitrators and each claim and counterclaim is less than $1,000,000, then one arbitrator shall hear and determine the case.

(b) The AAA shall appoint arbitrators as agreed by the parties. If they are unable to agree on a method of appointment, the AAA shall appoint arbitrators from the Large, Complex Commercial Case Panel, in the manner provided in the Regular Commercial Arbitration Rules. Absent agreement of the parties, the arbitrators shall not have served as the mediator in the mediation phase of the instant proceeding.

L–3. Preliminary Hearing

As promptly as practicable after the selection of the arbitrators, a preliminary hearing shall be held among the parties and/or their attorneys or other representatives and the arbitrators. Unless the parties agree otherwise, the preliminary hearing will be conducted by telephone conference call rather than in person. At the preliminary hearing the matters to be considered shall include, without limitation:

  (a) service of a detailed statement of claims, damages and defenses, a statement of the issues asserted by each party and positions with respect thereto, and any legal authorities the parties may wish to bring to the attention of the arbitrators;

  (b) stipulations to uncontested facts;

  (c) the extent to which discovery shall be conducted;

  (d) exchange and premarking of those documents which each party believes may be offered at the hearing;

  (e) the identification and availability of witnesses, including experts, and such matters with respect to witnesses including their biographies and expected testimony as may be appropriate;

  (f) whether, and the extent to which, any sworn statements and/or depositions may be introduced;

  (g) the extent to which hearings will proceed on consecutive days;

  (h) whether a stenographic or other official record of the proceedings shall be maintained;

  (i) the possibility of utilizing mediation or other non-adjudicative methods of dispute resolution; and the procedure for the issuance of subpoenas.

By agreement of the parties and/or order of the arbitrators, the pre-hearing activities and the hearing procedures that will govern the arbitration will be memorialized in a Scheduling and Procedure Order.

L–4. Management of Proceedings

  (a) Arbitrator(s) shall take such steps as they may deem necessary or desirable to avoid delay and to achieve a just, speedy and cost-effective resolution of Large, Complex Commercial Cases.

  (b) Parties shall cooperate in the exchange of documents, exhibits and information within such party's control if the arbitrators consider such production to be consistent with the goal of achieving a just, speedy and cost-effective resolution of a Large, Complex Commercial Case.

  (c) The parties may conduct such discovery as may be agreed to by all the parties provided, however, that the arbitrators may place such limitations on the conduct of such discovery as the arbitrators shall deem appropriate. If the parties cannot agree on production of documents and other information, the arbitrators, consistent with the expedited nature of arbitration, may establish the extent of the discovery.

(d) At the discretion of the arbitrators, upon good cause shown and consistent with the expedited nature of arbitration, the arbitrators may order depositions of, or the propounding of interrogatories to, such persons who may possess information determined by the arbitrators to be necessary to determination of the matter.

(e) The parties shall exchange copies of all exhibits they intend to submit at the hearing 10 business days prior to the hearing unless the arbitrators determine other-wise.

(f) The exchange of information pursuant to this rule, as agreed by the parties and/or directed by the arbitrators, shall be included within the Scheduling and Procedure Order.

(g) The arbitrator is authorized to resolve any disputes concerning the exchange of information.

(h) Generally hearings will be scheduled on consecutive days or in blocks of consecutive days in order to maximize efficiency and minimize costs.

Fees

An initial filing fee is payable in full by a filing party when a claim, counterclaim or additional claim is filed. A case service fee will be incurred for all cases that proceed to their first hearing. This fee will be payable in advance at the time that the first hearing is scheduled. This fee will be refunded at the conclusion of the case if no hearings have occurred. However, if the Association is not notified at least 24 hours before the time of the scheduled hearing, the case service fee will remain due and will not be refunded.

These fees will be billed in accordance with the following schedule:

Amount of Claim—Initial Filing Fee	Case Service Fee
Above $0 to $10,000—$500	$200
Above $10,000 to $75,000—$750	$300
Above $75,000 to $150,000—$1,500	$750
Above $150,000 to $300,000—$2,750	$1,250
Above $300,000 to $500,000—$4,250	$1,750
Above $500,000 to $1,000,000—$6,000	$2,500
Above $1,000,000 to $5,000,000—$8,000	$3,250
Above $5,000,000 to $10,000,000—$10,000	$4,000
Above $10,000,000—*	*
Nonmonetary Claims**1 $3,250	$1,250

Refund Schedule

The AAA offers a refund schedule on filing fees. For cases with claims up to $75,000, a minimum filing fee of $300 will not be refunded. For all other cases, a minimum fee of $500 will not be refunded. Subject to the minimum fee requirements, refunds will be calculated as follows:

100% of the filing fee, above the minimum fee, will be refunded if the case is settled or withdrawn within five calendar days of filing.

50% of the filing fee, in any case with filing fees in excess of $500, will be refunded if the case is settled or withdrawn between six and 30 calendar days of filing. Where the filing fee is $500, the refund will be $200.

25% of the filing fee will be refunded if the case is settled or withdrawn between 31 and 60 calendar days of filing.

No refund will be made once an arbitrator has been appointed (this includes one arbitrator on a three-arbitrator panel). No refunds will be granted on awarded cases.

Note: the date of receipt of the demand for arbitration with the AAA will be used to calculate refunds of filing fees for both claims and counter-claims.

Hearing Room Rental

The fees described above do not cover the rental of hearing rooms, which are available on a rental basis. Check with the AAA for availability and rates.

Appendix G

AMERICAN ARBITRATION ASSOCIATION, SAMPLE ADR CLAUSES

Here are some sample ADR clauses that address a variety of processes and in some cases, issues within those processes. They are drawn from clauses found in American Arbitration Association, *Drafting Dispute Resolution Clauses — A Practical Guide* (Amended Jan. 1, 2004). As you read them, think about what additional issues you may want to address as you draft a dispute resolution clause for a particular context. What do these clauses cover? What do they not cover?

1. Negotiation

In the event of any dispute, claim, question, or disagreement arising from or relating to this agreement or the breach thereof, the parties hereto shall use their best efforts to settle the dispute, claim, question, or disagreement. To this effect, they shall consult and negotiate with each other in good faith and, recognizing their mutual interests, attempt to reach a just and equitable solution satisfactory to both parties. If they do not reach such solution within a period of 60 days, then, upon notice by either party to the other, all disputes, claims, questions, or differences shall be finally settled by arbitration administered by the American Arbitration Association in accordance with the provisions of its Commercial Arbitration Rules.

2. Mediation

If a dispute arises out of or relates to this contract, or the breach thereof, and if the dispute cannot be settled through negotiation, the parties agree first to try in good faith to settle the dispute by mediation administered by the American Arbitration Association under its Commercial Mediation Rules before resorting to arbitration, litigation, or some other dispute resolution procedure.

3. Arbitration

a. Submission to arbitration

Any controversy or claim arising out of or relating to this contract, or the breach thereof, shall be settled by arbitration administered by the American Arbitration Association in accordance with its Commercial [or other] Arbitration Rules [including the Optional Rules for Emergency Measures of Protection], and judgment on the award rendered by the arbitrator(s) may be entered in any court having jurisdiction thereof.

b. Selection of the arbitrator

The arbitrator selected by the claimant and the arbitrator selected by respondent shall, within 10 days of their appointment, select a third neutral arbitrator. In the event that they are unable to do so, the parties or their attorneys may request the American Arbitration Association to appoint the third neutral arbitrator. Prior to the commencement of hearings, each of the arbitrators appointed shall provide an oath or undertaking of impartiality.

c. Baseball arbitration

Each party shall submit to the arbitrator and exchange with each other in advance of the hearing their last, best offers. The arbitrator shall be limited to awarding only one or the other of the two figures submitted.

d. Discovery

Consistent with the expedited nature of arbitration, each party will, upon the written request of the other party, promptly provide the other with copies of documents [relevant to the issues raised by any claim or counterclaim] [on which the producing party may rely in support of or in opposition to any claim or defense]. Any dispute regarding discovery, or the relevance or

e. Depositions

At the request of a party, the arbitrator(s) shall have the discretion to order examination by deposition of witnesses to the extent the arbitrator deems such additional discovery relevant and appropriate. Depositions shall be limited to a maximum of [three] [insert number] per party and shall be held within 30 days of the making of a request. Additional depositions may be scheduled only with the permission of the [arbitrator(s)] [chair of the arbitration panel], and for good cause shown. Each deposition shall be limited to a maximum of [three hours] [six hours] [one day's] duration. All objections are reserved for the arbitration hearing except for objections based on privilege and proprietary or confidential information.

f. Remedies

Example 1. The arbitrators will have no authority to award punitive or other damages not measured by the prevailing party's actual damages, except as may be required by statute.

Example 2. In no event shall an award in an arbitration initiate under this clause exceed ____.

Example 3. If the arbitrator(s) find liability in any arbitration initiated under this clause, they shall award liquidated damages in the amount of $_____.

g. Reasoned Opinions

The award of the arbitrators shall include findings of fact [and conclusions of law].

4. Med–Arb

If a dispute arises from or relates to this contract or the breach thereof, and if the dispute cannot be settled through direct discussions, the parties agree to endeavor first to settle the dispute by mediation administered by the American Arbitration Association under its Commercial Mediation Rules before resorting to arbitration. Any unresolved controversy or claim arising from or relating to this contract or breach thereof shall be settled by arbitration administered by the American Arbitration Association in accordance with its Commercial Arbitration Rules, and judgment on the award rendered by the arbitrator may be entered in any court having jurisdiction thereof. If the parties agree, a mediator involved in the parties' mediation may be asked to serve as the arbitrator.

5. Judicial Reference

It is hereby stipulated by the parties hereto, through their respective undersigned counsel, that trial by jury is waived as to [specify] herein; that [the issue or cause] be referred to [name] as referee to hear and determine [the issue or all issues in this case whether of fact or law] and to report his or her statement of decision to the [court] within 20 days after testimony and argument are concluded and that judgment may be entered thereon as if the action had been tried by the court; that the costs of the referee be home [as the parties agree or the court determines at time of appointment]; and that an order to this effect may be entered accordingly without further notice. This general reference shall be administered by the American Arbitration Association under its Judicial Reference Procedures.

6. Confidentiality.

Except as may be required by law, neither a party nor an arbitrator may disclose the existence, content, or results of any arbitration hereunder without the prior written consent of both parties.

7. Some special contexts

a. Employment

If a dispute arises out of or relates to this [employment application; employment ADR program; employment contract] or the breach thereof, and if the dispute cannot be settled through negotiation, the parties agree first to try in good faith to settle the dispute by mediation administered by the American Arbitration Association under its National Rules for the Resolution of Employment Disputes, before resorting to arbitration, litigation or some other dispute resolution procedure.

b. Intellectual Property

1. Submission to arbitration

We, the undersigned parties, hereby agree to submit to arbitration administered by the American Arbitration Association under its Patent Arbitration Rules the following controversy: (describe briefly). We further agree that the above controversy be submitted to (one) (three) arbitrator(s), and that a judgment of any court having jurisdiction may be entered on the award.

2. Selection of the arbitrator

The arbitrators will be selected from a panel of persons having experience with and knowledge of electronic computers and the computer business, and at least one of the arbitrators selected will be an attorney.

c. International

Any dispute, controversy, or claim arising out of or relating to this contract, or the breach, termination, or invalidity thereof, shall be settled by arbitration under the UNCITRAL Arbitration Rules in effect on the date of this contract. The appointing authority shall be the International Centre for Dispute Resolution. The case shall be administered by the International Centre for Dispute Resolution under its Procedures for Cases under the UNCITRAL Arbitration Rules.

8. Consolidating disputes

The owner, the contractor, and all subcontractors, specialty contractors, material suppliers, engineers, designers, architects, construction lenders, bonding companies, and other parties concerned with the construction of the structure are bound, each to each other, by this arbitration clause, provided that they have signed this contract or a contract that incorporates this contract by reference or signed any other agreement to be bound by this arbitration clause. Each such party agrees that it may be joined as an additional party to an arbitration involving other parties under any such agreement. If more than one arbitration is begun under any such agreement and any party contends that two or more arbitrations are substantially related and that the issues should be heard in one proceeding, the arbitrator(s) selected in the first-filed of such proceedings shall determine whether, in the interests of justice and efficiency, the proceedings should be consolidated before that (those) arbitrator(s).

* * *

Index

References are to Pages

†